PHP5 and
MySQL® Bible

PHP5 and MySQL® Bible

**Tim Converse and Joyce Park
with Clark Morgan**

Wiley Publishing, Inc.

PHP5 and MySQL® Bible

Published by
Wiley Publishing, Inc.
10475 Crosspoint Boulevard
Indianapolis, IN 46256
www.wiley.com

Copyright © 2004 by Wiley Publishing, Inc., Indianapolis, Indiana

Published simultaneously in Canada

ISBN: 0-7645-5746-7

Manufactured in the United States of America

10 9 8 7 6 5

1B/SR/QU/QU/IN

No part of this publication may be reproduced, stored in a retrieval system or transmitted in any form or by any means, electronic, mechanical, photocopying, recording, scanning or otherwise, except as permitted under Sections 107 or 108 of the 1976 United States Copyright Act, without either the prior written permission of the Publisher, or authorization through payment of the appropriate per-copy fee to the Copyright Clearance Center, 222 Rosewood Drive, Danvers, MA 01923, (978) 750-8400, fax (978) 646-8600. Requests to the Publisher for permission should be addressed to the Legal Department, Wiley Publishing, Inc., 10475 Crosspoint Blvd., Indianapolis, IN 46256, (317) 572-3447, fax (317) 572-4447, E-Mail: permcoordinator@wiley.com.

For general information on our other products and services or to obtain technical support, please contact our Customer Care Department within the U.S. at (800) 762-2974, outside the U.S. at (317) 572-3993 or fax (317) 572-4002.

Wiley also publishes its books in a variety of electronic formats. Some content that appears in print may not be available in electronic books.

Library of Congress Control Number: 2004103176

About the Authors

Tim Converse has written software to recommend neckties, answer questions about space stations, pick value stocks, and make simulated breakfast. He has an M.S. in Computer Science from the University of Chicago, where he taught several programming classes. He is now an engineering manager in the Web search group at Yahoo!.

Joyce Park has an M.A. in history from the University of Chicago, and has worked for several Silicon Valley startups including Epinions, KnowNow, and Friendster. She is a co-lead of the Mod-pubsub Open Source project.

Clark Morgan is a Web application and educational software developer with more than five years' experience writing PHP. He works primarily with medical clients and related businesses. Originally from Boston, he now lives and works in Jacksonville, Florida, with his wife and two children. Clark spends entirely too much of his free time reading other people's computer books.

Credits

Acquisitions Editor
Debra Williams Cauley

Development Editor
Sara Shlaer

Production Editor
Eric Newman

Technical Editors
Chris Cornell
David Wall

Copy Editor
C. M. Jones

Editorial Manager
Mary Beth Wakefield

Vice President & Executive Group Publisher
Richard Swadley

Vice President and Executive Publisher
Bob Ipsen

Vice President and Publisher
Joseph B. Wikert

Executive Editorial Director
Mary Bednarek

Project Coordinator
April Farling

Graphics and Production Specialists
Beth Brooks
Sean Decker
Carrie Foster
Lauren Goddard

Quality Control Technician
Laura Albert
Carl William Pierce

Permissions Editor
Carmen Krikorian

Media Development Specialist
Angela Denny

Proofreading and Indexing
TECHBOOKS Production Services

Preface

Welcome to *PHP5 and MySQL Bible*!

Although we're biased, we believe that the PHP Web-scripting language is the hands-down winner in its niche — by far the easiest and most flexible server-side tool for getting great Web sites up and running in a hurry. Although millions of Web programmers worldwide *could* be wrong, in this particular case, they're not. MySQL is the most popular open-source database platform, and it is the first choice of many for creating database-backed PHP-driven Web sites

As we write this, PHP5 is in its third beta version, and PHP has continued to grow in reach, adoption, and features since we wrote the first two versions of this book.

What Is PHP?

PHP is an open-source, server-side, HTML-embedded Web-scripting language that is compatible with all the major Web servers (most notably Apache). PHP enables you to embed code fragments in normal HTML pages — code that is interpreted as your pages are served up to users. PHP also serves as a "glue" language, making it easy to connect your Web pages to server-side databases.

Why PHP?

We devote nearly all of Chapter 1 to this question. The short answer is that it's free, it's open source, it's full featured, it's cross-platform, it's stable, it's fast, it's clearly designed, it's easy to learn, and it plays well with others.

What's New in This Edition?

Although this book has a new title, it is in some sense a third edition. Previous versions were:

+ *PHP 4 Bible*. Published in August 2000, covering PHP through version 4.0.

+ *PHP Bible, Second Edition*. Published in September 2002, a significantly expanded version of the first edition, current through PHP 4.2.

Our initial plan for this book was to simply reorganize the second edition and bring it up to date with PHP5. We realized, however, that although the previous editions covered PHP/MySQL interaction, we had left readers in the dark about how to create and administer MySQL databases in the first place, and this led to many reader questions. As a result, we decided to beef up the coverage of MySQL and change the title.

New PHP5 features

Although much of PHP4's functionality survives unchanged in PHP5, there have been some deep changes. Among the ones we cover are:

✦ Zend Engine 2 and the new object model, with support for private/protected members, abstract classes, and interfaces

✦ PHP5's completely reworked XML support, built around libmxl2

✦ Exceptions and exception handling

MySQL coverage

We now cover MySQL 4.0 installation, database design, and administration, including backups, replication, and recovery. As with previous editions, we devote much of the book to techniques for writing MySQL-backed PHP applications.

Other new material

In addition to MySQL- and PHP5-specific features, we've added:

✦ Improved coverage of databases other than MySQL (Oracle, PostgreSQL, and the PEAR database interaction layer)

✦ The PEAR code repository

✦ A chapter on integrating PHP and Java

✦ Separate chapters on error-handling and debugging techniques

Finally, we reorganized the entire book, pushing more advanced topics toward the end, to give beginners an easier ramp up.

Who wrote the book?

The first two editions were by Converse and Park, with a guest chapter by Dustin Mitchell and tech editing by Richard Lynch. For this version, Clark Morgan took on much of the revision work, with help by Converse and Park as well as by David Wall and Chris Cornell, who also contributed chapters and did technical editing.

Whom This Book Is For

This book is for anyone who wants to build Web sites that exhibit more complex behavior than is possible with static HTML pages. Within that population, we had the following three particular audiences in mind:

✦ Web site designers who know HTML and want to move into creating dynamic Web sites

✦ Experienced programmers (in C, Java, Perl, and so on) without Web experience who want to quickly get up to speed in server-side Web programming

✦ Web programmers who have used other server-side technologies (Active Server Pages, Java Server Pages, or ColdFusion, for example) and want to upgrade or simply add another tool to their kit.

We assume that the reader is familiar with HTML and has a basic knowledge of the workings of the Web, but we do not assume any programming experience beyond that. To help save time for more experienced programmers, we include a number of notes and asides that compare PHP with other languages and indicate which chapters and sections may be safely skipped. Finally, see our appendixes, which offer specific advice for C programmers, ASP coders, and pure-HTML designers.

This Book Is Not the Manual

The PHP Documentation Group has assembled a great online manual, located at www.php.net and served up (of course) by PHP. This book is not that manual or even a substitute for it. We see the book as complementary to the manual and expect that you will want to go back and forth between them to some extent.

In general, you'll find the online manual to be very comprehensive, covering all aspects and functions of the language, but inevitably without a great amount of depth in any one topic. By contrast, we have the leisure of zeroing in on aspects that are most used or least understood and give background, explanations, and lengthy examples.

How the Book Is Organized

This book is divided into five parts, as the following sections describe.

Part I: PHP: The Basics

This part is intended to bring the reader up to speed on the most essential aspects of PHP, with complexities and abstruse features deferred to later Parts.

- ✦ Chapters 1 through 4 provide an introduction to PHP and tell you what you need to know to get started.
- ✦ Chapters 5 through 10 are a guide to the most central facets of PHP (with the exception of database interaction): the syntax, the datatypes, and the most basic built-in functions.
- ✦ Chapter 11 is a guide to the most common pitfalls of PHP programming.

Part II: PHP and MySQL

Part II is devoted both to MySQL and to PHP's interaction with MySQL.

- ✦ Chapters 12 and 13 provide a general orientation to Web programming with SQL databases, including advice on how to choose the database system that is right for you.
- ✦ Chapter 14 covers installation and administration of MySQL databases, and Chapter 15 is devoted to PHP functions for MySQL.
- ✦ Chapters 16 and 17 are detailed, code-rich case studies of PHP/MySQL interactions.
- ✦ Chapters 18 and 19 provide tips and gotchas specific to PHP/MySQL work.

Part III: Advanced Features and Techniques

In this part we cover more advanced and abstruse features of PHP, usually as self-contained chapters, including object-oriented programming, session handling, exception handling, using cookies, and regular expressions. Chapter 32 is a tour of debugging techniques, and Chapter 33 discusses programming style.

Part IV: Connections

In this part we cover advanced techniques and features that involve PHP talking to other services, technologies, or large bodies of code.

✦ Chapters 34 through 36 cover PHP's interaction with other database technologies (PostgreSQL, Oracle, and the PEAR database abstraction layer).

✦ Chapters 37 through 42 cover self-contained topics: PHP and e-mail programs, combining PHP with JavaScript, integrating PHP and Java, PHP and XML, PHP-based Web services, and creating graphics with the gd image library.

Part V: Case Studies

Here we present six extended case studies that wrap together techniques from various early chapters.

✦ Chapter 43 takes you through the design and implementation of a weblog.

✦ Chapter 44 presents a user authentication system in detail.

✦ Chapter 45 shows how to build a rating system that lets users vote on content.

✦ Chapter 46 discusses a soup-to-nuts implementation of a novel trivia quiz game.

✦ Chapter 47 is a study of the process of converting a static HTML site to dynamic PHP.

✦ Chapter 48 uses the gd image library to visualize data from a MySQL database.

Appendixes

At the end, we offer three "quick-start" appendixes, for use by people new to PHP but very familiar with either C (Appendix A), Perl (Appendix B), or pure HTML (Appendix C). If you are in any of these three situations, start with the appropriate appendix for an orientation to important differences and a guide to the book. The final appendix (D) is a guide to important resources, Web sites, and mailing lists for the PHP community.

Conventions Used in This Book

We use a monospaced font to indicate literal PHP code. Pieces of code embedded in lines of text look like this, while full code listing lines look as follows:

```
print("this");
```

If the appearance of a PHP-created Web page is crucial, we include a screenshot. If it is not, we show textual output of PHP in monospaced font. If we want to distinguish the PHP output as seen in your browser from the actual output of PHP (which your browser renders), we call the former *browser output*.

If included in a code context, *italics* indicate portions that should be filled in appropriately, as opposed to being taken literally. In normal text, an *italicized* term means a possibly unfamiliar word or phrase.

What the Icons Mean

Icons similar to the following example are sprinkled liberally throughout the book. Their purpose is to visually set off certain important kinds of information.

 Tip — Tip icons indicate PHP tricks or techniques that may not be obvious and that enable you to accomplish something more easily or efficiently.

 Note — Note icons usually provide additional information or clarification but can be safely ignored if you are not already interested. Notes in this book are often audience-specific, targeted to people who already know a particular programming language or technology.

 Caution — Caution icons indicate something that does not work as advertised, something that is easily misunderstood or misused, or anything else that can get programmers into trouble.

 Cross-Reference — We use this icon whenever related information is in a different chapter or section.

The Web Site and Sample Code

All the sample code from the book, as well as supplementary material we develop after press time, can be found at our Web site at www.troutworks.com/phpbook. You can also find the sample code at www.wiley.com/compbooks/converse.

We want to hear from you! Please send us e-mail at phpbook@troutworks.com with comments, errata, kudos, flames, or any other communication that you care to send our way.

Acknowledgments

This project began out of a conversation with Debra Williams Cauley, our acquisitions editor at Wiley. She managed the project, found additional contributors, and maintained a sense of humor as she insulated naive first-time authors from the harsh realities of the publishing business. (For the next two editions, she insulated naive second-time and third-time authors, respectively.)

Sara Shlaer was the development editor who coordinated everything among the contributors, stayed on us to make the project not quite as late as it would otherwise have been, and critiqued our drafts in detail, making some great saves along the way. Clark Morgan did the majority of the revision of previous material. David Wall and Chris Cornell each wrote novel chapters, revised previous chapters, and served as technical reviewers.

Thanks to the Webmasters of the PHP team for permission to reproduce a graph of PHP usage; the folks at Zend for permission to use screenshots of their Zend Studio product; Amazon.com for data in the Web services chapter; KnowNow, Inc., for permission to excerpt code originally owned by them; Mimi Yin for her fabo design work; Alex Selkirk for permission to reproduce material from Opencortex.org; Tim Perdue for inspiration; Hoang Nguyen for debugging help; and Jeff Barr of Syndic8.com for timely aid.

Our obvious thanks go to everyone who created PHP itself (Rasmus Lerdorf, Zeev Suraski, Andi Gutmans, Thies Arntzen, Stig Bakken, Sascha Schumann, Andrei Zmievski, Sterling Hughes, Wez Furlong, George Schlossnagle, Dan Libby, Sam Ruby, and a host of other contributors), the people who have documented PHP (Stig Bakken, Alexander Aulbach, Egon Schmid, Lars Torben Wilson, Jim Winstead, and others), and everyone on the PHP mailing list. Special thanks to Rasmus, Sascha, and Richard Lynch for mailing-list answers to our own questions. Finally, both Converse and Park would like thank their spouses for their support while this book was being written and revised. In a very literal sense, we couldn't have done it without them.

Contents at a Glance

Contents

PHP: The Basics

◆　　◆　　◆　　◆

◆　　◆　　◆　　◆

Why PHP and MySQL?

This first chapter is an introduction to PHP, MySQL, and the inter-action of the two. In it, we'll try to address some of the most common questions about these tools, such as "What are they?" and "How do they compare to similar technologies?" Most of the chapter is taken up with an enumeration of the many, many reasons to choose PHP, MySQL, or the two in tandem. If you're a techie looking for some ammunition to lob at your PHB ("Pointy-Haired Boss" for those who don't know the Dilbert cartoons) or a manager asking yourself what is this P-whatever thing your geeks keep whining to get, this chapter will provide some preliminary answers.

What Is PHP?

PHP is the Web development language written by and for Web developers. PHP stands for *PHP: Hypertext Preprocessor.* The product was originally named *Personal Home Page Tools,* and many people still think that's what the acronym stands for. But as it expanded in scope, a new and more appropriate (albeit GNU-ishly recursive) name was selected by community vote. PHP is currently in its fifth major rewrite, called PHP5 or just plain PHP.

PHP is a server-side scripting language, which can be embedded in HTML or used as a standalone binary (although the former use is much more common). Proprietary products in this niche are Microsoft's Active Server Pages, Macromedia's ColdFusion, and Sun's Java Server Pages. Some tech journalists used to call PHP "the open source ASP" because its functionality is similar to that of the Microsoft product — although this formulation was misleading, as PHP was developed before ASP. Over the past few years, however, PHP and server-side Java have gained momentum, while ASP has lost mindshare, so this comparison no longer seems appropriate.

We'll explore server-side scripting more thoroughly in Chapter 2, but for the moment you can think of it as a collection of super-HTML tags or small programs that run inside your Web pages — except on the server side, before they get sent to the browser. For example, you can use PHP to add common headers and footers to all the pages on a site or to store form-submitted data in a database.

Strictly speaking, PHP has little to do with layout, events, on the fly DOM manipulation, or really anything about what a Web page looks and sounds like. In fact, most of what PHP does is invisible to the end user. Someone looking at a PHP page will not necessarily be able to tell that it was not written purely in HTML, because usually the result of PHP *is* HTML.

PHP is an official module of Apache HTTP Server, the market-leading free Web server that runs about 67 percent of the World Wide Web (according to the widely quoted Netcraft Web server survey). This means that the PHP scripting engine can be built into the Web server itself, leading to faster processing, more efficient memory allocation, and greatly simplified maintenance. Like Apache Server, PHP is fully cross-platform, meaning it runs native on several flavors of Unix, as well as on Windows and now on Mac OS X. All projects under the aegis of the Apache Software Foundation — including PHP — are open source software.

What Is MySQL?

MySQL (pronounced My Ess Q El) is an open source, SQL Relational Database Management System (RDBMS) that is free for many uses (more detail on that later). Early in its history, MySQL occasionally faced opposition due to its lack of support for some core SQL constructs such as subselects and foreign keys. Ultimately, however, MySQL found a broad, enthusiastic user base for its liberal licensing terms, perky performance, and ease of use. Its acceptance was aided in part by the wide variety of other technologies such as PHP, Java, Perl, Python, and the like that have encouraged its use through stable, well-documented modules and extensions. MySQL has not failed to reward the loyalty of these users with the addition of both subselects and foreign keys as of the 4.1 series.

Databases in general are useful, arguably the most consistently useful family of software products — the "killer product" of modern computing. Like many competing products, both free and commercial, MySQL isn't a database until you give it some structure and form. You might think of this as the difference between a database and an RDBMS (that is, RDBMS plus user requirements equals a database).

There's lots more to say about MySQL, but then again, there's lots more space in which to say it.

The History of PHP

Rasmus Lerdorf — software engineer, Apache team member, and international man of mystery — is the creator and original driving force behind PHP. The first part of PHP was developed for his personal use in late 1994. This was a CGI wrapper that helped him keep track of people who looked at his personal site. The next year, he put together a package called the *Personal Home Page Tools* (a.k.a. the *PHP Construction Kit*) in response to demand from users who had stumbled into his work by chance or word of mouth. Version 2 was soon released under the title PHP/FI and included the *Form Interpreter*, a tool for parsing SQL queries.

By the middle of 1997, PHP was being used on approximately 50,000 sites worldwide. It was clearly becoming too big for any single person to handle, even someone as focused and energetic as Rasmus. A small core development team now runs the project on the open source "benevolent junta" model, with contributions from developers and users around the world. Zeev Suraski and Andi Gutmans, the two Israeli programmers who developed the PHP3 and PHP4 parsers, have also generalized and extended their work under the rubric of Zend.com (*Zeev, Andi, Zend,* get it?).

The fourth quarter of 1998 initiated a period of explosive growth for PHP, as all open source technologies enjoyed massive publicity. In October 1998, according to the best guess, just over 100,000 unique domains used PHP in some way. Just over a year later, PHP broke the one-million domain mark. When we wrote the first edition of this book in the first half of 2000, the number had increased to about two million domains. As we write this, approximately 15 million public Web servers (in the software sense, not the hardware sense) have PHP installed on them.

Public PHP deployments run the gamut from mass-market sites such as Excite Webmail and the Indianapolis 500 Web site, which serve up millions of pageviews per day, through "mass-niche" sites such as Sourceforge.net and Epinions.com, which tend to have higher functionality needs and hundreds of thousands of users, to e-commerce and brochureware sites such as The Bookstore at Harvard.com and Sade.com (Web home of the British singer), which must be visually attractive and easy to update. There are also PHP-enabled parts of sites, such as the forums on the Internet Movie Database (imdb.com); and a large installed base of nonpublic PHP deployments, such as LDAP directories (MCI WorldCom built one with over 100,000 entries) and trouble-ticket tracking systems.

In its newest incarnation, PHP5 strives to deliver something many users have been clamoring for over the past few years: much improved object-oriented programming (OOP) functionality. PHP has long nodded to the object programming model with functions that allow object programmers to pull out results and information in a way familiar to them. These efforts still fell short of the ideal for many programmers, however, and efforts to force PHP to build in fully object-oriented systems often yielded unintended results and hurt performance. PHP5's newly rebuilt object model brings PHP more in line with other object-oriented languages such as Java and C++, offering support for features such as overloading, interfaces, private member variables and methods, and other standard OOP constructions.

With the crash of the dot-com bubble, PHP is poised to be used on more sites than ever. Demand for Web-delivered functionality has decreased very little, and emerging technological standards continue to pop up all the time, but available funding for hardware, licenses, and especially headcount has drastically decreased. In the post-crash Web world, PHP's shallow learning curve, quick implementation of new functionality, and low cost of deployment are hard arguments to beat.

The History of MySQL

Depending on how much detail you want, the history of MySQL can be traced as far back as 1979, when MySQL's creator, Monty Widenius, worked for a Swedish IT and data consulting firm, TcX. While at TcX, Monty authored UNIREG, a terminal interface builder that connected to raw ISAM data stores. In the intervening 15 years, UNIREG served its makers rather well through a series of translations and extensions to accommodate increasingly large data sets.

In 1994, when TcX began working on Web data applications, chinks in the UNIREG armor, primarily having to do with application overhead, began to appear. This sent Monty and his colleagues off to look for other tools. One they inspected rather closely was Hughes mSQL, a light and zippy database application developed by David Hughes. mSQL possessed the distinct advantages of being inexpensive and somewhat entrenched in the market, as well as featuring a fairly well-developed client API. The 1.0 series of mSQL release lacked indexing, however, a feature crucial to performance with large data stores. Although the 2.0 series of mSQL would see the addition of this feature, the particular implementation used was not compatible with UNIREG's B+-based features. At this point, MySQL, at least conceptually, was born.

Monty and TcX decided to start with the substantial work already done on UNIREG while developing a new API that was substantially similar to that used by mSQL, with the exception of the more effective UNIREG indexing scheme. By early 1995, TcX had a 1.0 version of this new product ready. They gave it the moniker MySQL and later that year released it under a combination open source and commercial licensing scheme that allowed continued development of the product while providing a revenue stream for MySQL AB, the company that evolved from TcX.

Over the past ten years, MySQL has truly developed into a world class product. MySQL now competes with even the most feature-rich commercial database applications such as Oracle and Informix. Additions in the 4.x series have included much-requested features such as transactions and foreign key support. All this has made MySQL the world's most used open source database.

Reasons to Love PHP and MySQL

There are ever so many reasons to love PHP and MySQL. Let us count a few.

Cost

PHP costs you nothing. Zip, zilch, nada, not one red cent. Nothing up front, nothing over the lifetime of the application, nothing when it's over. Did we mention that the Apache/PHP/MySQL combo runs great on cheap, low-end hardware that you couldn't even *think* about for IIS/ASP/SQL Server?

MySQL is a slightly different animal in its licensing terms. Before you groan at the concept of actually using commercial software, consider that although MySQL is open-source licensed for many uses, it is not and has never been primarily community-developed software. MySQL AB is a commercial entity with necessarily commercial interests. Unlike typical open source projects, where developers often have regular full-time (and paying) day jobs in addition to their freely given open source efforts, the MySQL developers derive their primary income from the project. There are still many circumstances in which MySQL can be used for free (basically anything nonredistributive, which covers most PHP-based projects), but if you make money developing solutions that use MySQL, consider buying a license or a support contract. It's still infinitely more reasonable than just about any software license you will ever pay for.

For purposes of comparison, Table 1-1 shows some current retail figures for similar products in the United States. All prices quoted are for a single-processor public Web server with the most common matching database and development tool; *$0* means a no-cost alternative is a common real-world choice.

Table 1-1: Comparative Out-of-Pocket Costs

Item	ASP/SQL Server	ColdFusion MX/SQL Server	JSP/Oracle	PHP/MySQL
Development tool	$0–2499	$599	$0–~2000	$0–249
Server	$999	$2298	$0–~35,000	$0
RDBMS	$4999	$4999	$15,000	$0–220

Open source software: don't fear the cheaper

But as the bard so pithily observed, we are living in a material world — where we've internalized maxims such as, "You get what you pay for," "There's no such thing as a free lunch," and "Things that sound too good to be true usually are." You (or your boss) may, therefore, have some lingering doubts about the quality and viability of no-cost software. It probably doesn't help that until recently software that didn't cost money — formerly called *freeware*, *shareware*, or *free software* — was generally thought to fall into one of three categories:

✦ Programs filling small, uncommercial niches

✦ Programs performing grungy, low-level jobs

✦ Programs for people with bizarre socio-political issues

It's time to update some stereotypes once and for all. We are clearly in the middle of a sea change in the business of software. Much (if not most) major consumer software is distributed without cost today; e-mail clients, Web browsers, games, and even full-service office suites are all being given away as fast as their makers can whip up Web versions or set up FTP servers. Consumer software is increasingly seen as a loss-leader, the flower that attracts the pollinating honeybee — in other words, a way to sell more server hardware, operating systems, connectivity, advertising, optional widgets, or stock shares. The full retail price of a piece of software, therefore, is no longer a reliable gauge of its quality or the eccentricity-level of its user.

On the server side, open source products have come on even stronger. Not only do they compete with the best commercial stuff; in many cases there's a feeling that they far exceed the competition. Don't take our word for it! Ask IBM, any hardware manufacturer, NASA, Amazon.com, Rockpointe Broadcasting, Ernie Ball Corporation, the Queen of England, or the Mexican school system. If your boss still needs to be convinced, further ammunition is available at `www.opensource.org` and `www.fsf.org`.

The PHP license

The freeness of open source and Free software is guaranteed by a gaggle of licensing schemes, most famously the *GPL* (*G*nu *G*eneral *P*ublic *L*icense) or *copyleft*. PHP used to be released under both the GPL and its own license, with each user free to choose between them. This has recently changed. The program as a whole is now released under its own extremely laissez-faire PHP license on the model of the BSD license, whereas Zend as a standalone product is released under the *Q Public License* (this clause applies *only* if you unbundle Zend from PHP and try to sell it).

You can read the fine print about the relevant licenses at these Web sites:

✦ `www.php.net/license/`

✦ `www.mysql.com/doc/en/GPL_license.html`

✦ `www.troll.no/qpl/annotated.html`

Most people get PHP or MySQL via download, but you may have paid for it as part of a Linux distribution, a technical book, or some other product. In that case, you may now be silently disputing our assertion that PHP costs nothing. Here's the twist: Although you can't require a fee for most open source software, you *can* charge for delivering that software in a more convenient format — such as by putting it on a disk and shipping the disk to the customer. You can also charge anything the market will bear for being willing to perform certain services or accept certain risks that the development team may not wish to undertake. For instance, you are allowed to charge money for guaranteeing that every copy of the software you distribute will be virus-free or of reasonable quality, taking on the risk of being sued if a bunch of customers get bad CD-ROMs that contain hard-drive-erasing viruses.

Usually, open source software users can freely choose the precisely optimal cost-benefit equation for each particular situation: no cost and no warranties, or expensive but well supported, or something in between. No organized attempt has been made yet to sell service and support for PHP (although presumably that will be one of the value-adds of Zend). MySQL AB does sell support as part some of its licensing packages for the MySQL product. Other open source products, such as Linux, have companies such as Red Hat standing by to answer your questions, but the commercialization process is still in the early stages for PHP.

Ease of Use

PHP is easy to learn, compared to the other ways to achieve similar functionality. Unlike Java Server Pages or C-based CGI, PHP doesn't require you to gain a deep understanding of a major programming language before you can make a trivial database or remote-server call. Unlike Perl, which has been semijokingly called a "write-only language," PHP has a syntax that is quite easy to parse and human-friendly. And unlike ASP.NET, PHP is stable and ready to solve your problems today.

Many of the most useful specific functions (such as those for opening a connection to an Oracle database or fetching e-mail from an IMAP server) are predefined for you. A lot of complete scripts are waiting out there for you to look at as you're learning PHP. In fact, it's entirely possible to use PHP just by modifying freely available scripts rather than starting from scratch — you'll still need to understand the basic principles, but you can avoid many frustrating and time-consuming minor mistakes.

We must mention one caveat: *Easy* means different things to different people, and for some Web developers it has come to connote a graphical, drag-and-drop, What You See Is What You Get development environment. To become truly proficient at PHP, you need to be comfortable editing HTML by hand. You can use WYSIWYG editors to design sites, format pages, and insert client-side features before you add PHP functionality to the source code. There are even ways, which we'll detail in Chapter 3, to add PHP functions to your favorite editing environment. It's not realistic, however, to think you can take full advantage of PHP's capabilities without ever looking at source code.

Most advanced PHP users (including most of the development team members) are diehard hand-coders. They tend to share certain gut-level, subcultural assumptions — for instance, that hand-written code is beautiful and clean and maximally browser-compatible and therefore the only way to go — that they do not hesitate to express in vigorous terms. The PHP community offers help and trades tips mostly by e-mail, and if you want to participate, you have to be able to parse plain-text source code with facility. Some WYSIWYG users occasionally ask list members to diagnose their problems by looking at their Web pages instead of their source code, but this rarely ends well.

That said, let us reiterate that PHP really is easy to learn and write, especially for those with a little bit of experience in a C-syntaxed programming language. It's just a little more involved than HTML but probably simpler than JavaScript and definitely less conceptually complex than JSP or ASP.NET.

If you have no relational database experience or are coming from an environment such as Microsoft Access, MySQL's command line interface and lack of implicit structure may at first seem a little daunting. Again, the word *easy* is relative. However, MySQL's increasingly faithful adherence to the ANSI SQL-92 standard and a comprehensive suite of external client programs, coupled with graphical administration tools such as PHPMyAdmin and the new MySQL Control Center, will get even neophyte users up and running quickly compared to other databases. None of these will substitute for learning a little theory and employing good design practices, but that subject is for another chapter.

HTML-embeddedness

PHP is embedded within HTML. In other words, PHP pages are ordinary HTML pages that escape into PHP mode only when necessary. Here is an example:

```
<HEAD>
<TITLE>Example.com greeting</TITLE>
</HEAD>
<BODY>
<P>Hello,
<?php
// We have now escaped into PHP mode.
// Instead of static variables, the next three lines
// could easily be database calls or even cookies;
// or they could have been passed from a form.
$firstname = 'Joyce';
$lastname = 'Park';
$title = 'Ms.';
echo "$title $lastname";
// OK, we are going back to HTML now.
?>
. We know who you are!  Your first name is <?php echo
$firstname; ?>.</P>

<P>You are visiting our site at <?php echo date('Y-m-d H:--i:s');
?></P>

<P>Here is a link to your account management page:  <A
HREF="http://www.example.com/accounts/<?php echo
"$firstname$lastname"; ?>/"><?php echo $firstname; ?>'s account
management page</A></P>
</BODY>
</HTML>
```

When a client requests this page, the Web server *preprocesses* it. This means it goes through the page from top to bottom, looking for sections of PHP, which it will try to resolve. For one thing, the parser will suck up all assigned variables (marked by dollar signs) and try to plug them into later PHP commands (in this case, the echo function). If everything goes smoothly, the preprocessor will eventually return a normal HTML page to the client's browser, as shown in Figure 1-1.

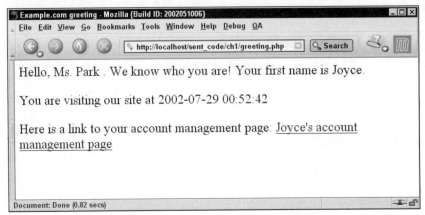

Figure 1-1: A result of preprocessed PHP

If you peek at the source code from the client browser (select Source or Page Source from the View menu, or right-click if you're using the AOL browser), it will look like this:

```
<HEAD>
<TITLE>Example.com greeting</TITLE>
</HEAD>
<BODY>
<P>Hello,
Ms. Park
. We know who you are!  Your first name is Joyce.</P>

<P>You are visiting our site at 2002-04-21 19-34-24</P>

<P>Here is a link to your account management page:  <A
HREF="http://www.example.com/accounts/JoycePark/">Joyce's account
management page</A></P>
</BODY>
</HTML>
```

This code is exactly the same as if you were to write the HTML by hand. So simple!

The HTML-embeddedness of PHP has many helpful consequences:

- ✦ PHP can quickly be added to code produced by WYSIWYG editors.
- ✦ PHP lends itself to a division of labor between designers and scripters.
- ✦ Every line of HTML does not need to be rewritten in a programming language.
- ✦ PHP can reduce labor costs and increase efficiency due to its shallow learning curve and ease of use.

Perhaps the sweetest thing of all about embedded scripting languages is that they don't need to be compiled into binary code before they can be tested or used—just write and run. PHP is interpreted (as are many newish computer languages), although the Zend Engine does some behind-the-scenes precompiling into an intermediate form for greater speed with complex scripts.

But what if you happen to want compilation? This can be desirable if you wish to distribute nonreversible binaries so others can use the code without being able to look at the source. The Zend team now offers a precompiler, *Zend Encoder*, which will deliver the code in a non-reversible intermediate representation, as well as substantially speed up large complex PHP scripts.

Cross-platform compatibility

PHP and MySQL run native on every popular flavor of Unix (including Mac OS X) and Windows. A huge percentage of the world's HTTP servers run on one of these two classes of operating systems.

PHP is compatible with the three leading Web servers: Apache HTTP Server for Unix and Windows, Microsoft Internet Information Server, and Netscape Enterprise Server (a.k.a. iPlanet Server). It also works with several lesser-known servers, including Alex Belits' fhttpd, Microsoft's Personal Web Server, AOLServer, and Omnicentrix's Omniserver application server. Specific Web-server compatibility with MySQL is not required, since PHP will handle all the dirty work for you.

Table 1-2 shows a brief matrix of the possible OS/Web-server combinations.

Table 1-2: Operating Systems and Web Servers for PHP

Variables	*UNIX*	*Windows*
Flavors	AIX, A/UX, BSDI, Digital UNIX/Tru64, FreeBSD, HP-UX, IRIX, Linux, Mac OS X, NetBSD, OpenBSD, SCO UnixWare, Solaris, SunOS, Ultrix, Xenix, and more	Windows 95/98/ME Windows NT/2000/XP/2003
Web servers	Apache, fhttpd, Netscape	IIS, PWS, Netscape, Apache, Omni

Now that PHP runs on Macintosh, PHP is almost totally cross-platform. You can develop on almost any client OS using your favorite tools and then upload your PHP scripts to a server on almost any OS. We'll discuss the development process in more detail in Chapter 3.

Not tag-based

PHP is a real programming language. ColdFusion, by contrast, is a bunch of predefined tags, like HTML. In PHP, you can define functions to your heart's content just by typing a name and a definition. In ColdFusion, you have to use tags developed by other people or go through the Custom Tag Extension development process.

As a witty PHP community member once said, "ColdFusion makes easy things easy, and medium-hard things impossible." And as every programmer will agree, once you experience the power of curly brackets and loops, you never go back to tags.

Stability

The word *stable* means two different things in this context:

✦ The server doesn't need to be rebooted often.

✦ The software doesn't change radically and incompatibly from release to release.

To our advantage, both of these connotations apply to both MySQL and PHP.

Apache Server is generally considered the most stable of major Web servers, with a reputation for enviable uptime percentages. Although it is not the fastest nor the easiest to administer, once you get it set up, Apache HTTP Server seemingly never crashes. It also doesn't require server reboots every time a setting is changed (at least on the Unix side). PHP inherits this reliability; plus, its own implementation is solid yet lightweight. In a two-and-a-half-month head-to-head test conducted by the Network Computing labs in October 1999, Apache Server with PHP handily beat both IIS/Visual Studio and Netscape Enterprise Server/Java for stability of environment.

PHP and MySQL are also both stable in the sense of feature stability. Their respective development teams have thus far enjoyed a clear vision of their project and refused to be distracted by every new fad and ill-thought-out user demand that comes along. Much of the effort goes into incremental performance improvements, communicating with more major databases, or adding better session support. In the case of MySQL, the addition of reasonable and expected new features has hit a rapid clip. For both PHP and MySQL, such improvements have rarely come at the expense of compatibility. Applications written in PHP3 will function with little or no revision for PHP4 and 5. And because of the standards-based SQL support, MySQL 3.x databases are easily moved to more current versions (and most likely always will be).

Speed

PHP is pleasingly zippy in its execution, especially when compiled as an Apache module on the Unix side. The MySQL server, once started, executes even very complex queries with huge result sets in record-setting time.

PHP5 is much faster for almost every use than CGI scripts. There is an unfortunate grain of truth to the joke that CGI stands for "Can't Go Instantly." Although many CGI scripts are written in C, one of the lowest-level and therefore speediest of the major programming languages, they are hindered by the fact that each request must spawn an entirely new process after being handed off from the `http` daemon. The time and resources necessary for this handoff and spawning are considerable, and there can be limits to the number of concurrent processes that can be running at any one time. Other CGI scripting languages such as Perl and Tcl can be quite slow. Most Web sites have moved away from use of CGI for performance and security reasons.

Although it takes a slight performance hit by being interpreted rather than compiled, this is far outweighed by the benefits PHP derives from its status as a Web server module. When compiled this way, PHP becomes part of the `http` daemon itself. Because there is no transfer to and from a separate application server (as there is with ColdFusion, for instance) requests can be filled with maximum efficiency.

Although no extensive formal benchmarks have compared the two, much anecdotal evidence and many small benchmarks suggest that PHP is at least as fast as ASP and readily outperforms ColdFusion or JSP in most applications.

Open source licensing

We've already dealt with the cost advantages of open source software in the "Cost" section of this chapter. The other major consequence of these licenses is that the complete source code for the software must be included in any distribution.

In fact, the Unix version of PHP is released *only* as source code; so far, the development team has staunchly resisted countless pleas to distribute official binaries for any of the Unixes. At first, new users (particularly those also new to Unix) tend to feel that source code is about as useful as a third leg, and most vastly prefer a nice convenient rpm. But there are both pragmatic and idealistic reasons for including folders full of pesky .c and .h files.

The most immediate pragmatic advantage is that you can compile your PHP installation with only the stuff you really need for any given situation. This approach has performance and security advantages. For instance, you can put in hooks to the database(s) of your choice. You can recompile as often as you want: maybe when an Apache security release comes out, or when you wish to support a new database application. By compiling a custom application specifically suited to your system, or any given snapshot of your system, performance and stability are increased over their already respectable baseline.

What sets open source software apart from its competitors is not just price but control. Plenty of consumer software is now given away under various conditions. Careful scrutiny of the relevant licenses, however, will generally reveal limits as to how the software can be used. Maybe you can run it at home but not at the office. Perhaps you can load it on your laptop, but you're in violation if you use it for business purposes. Or, most commonly, you can use it for anything you want but forget about looking at the code — much less changing it. There are even community licenses that force you to donate your improvements to the codebase but charge you for use of the product at the end!

Caution   Don't even *think* about coming back with a riposte that involves violating a software license — we're covering our ears; we're *not* listening! Especially with the explosion in no-cost software, there's just no good reason to break the law. Besides, it's bad karma for software developers. What goes around, comes around, don't ya know?

For all their *openness*, the licenses for MySQL and PHP are quite different. You should not assume that you understand the MySQL terms simply because you have read the PHP license. They have many similarities to be sure but also some radically different provisions, especially when it comes to when you should pay.

Table 1-3 shows examples of the various source and fee positions in today's software marketplace.

Table 1-3: Source/Fee Spectrum

Fee Structure	Closed Source	Controlled Source	Open Source
Fee for all uses	Macromedia ColdFusion	—	—
Fee for some uses	Corel WordPerfect	Sun Java	MySQL
No fee for any use	Microsoft IE	Sun StarOffice	GPLed software

Genuinely open source software like PHP cannot seek to limit the purposes for which it is used, the people allowed to use it, or a host of other factors. The most critical of these rights is the one allowing users to make and distribute any modifications along with the original software. In the most extreme case, where one or more developers decide to release a separate, complete version of a piece of software, this practice is referred to as *code forking*.

If somewhere down the road you develop irreconcilable differences with the PHP development team, you can take every bit of code they've labored over for all these years and use it as the basis of your own product. You couldn't call it PHP, and you'd have to include stuff in your documentation that gave due credit to the authors — the rationale is that source code distributions make it next to impossible for any single person or group to hijack a program to the detriment of the community as a whole, because every user always has the power to take the source and walk.

Users new to the open source model should be aware that this right is also enjoyed by the developers. At any time, Rasmus, Zend, and company can choose to defect from the community and put all their future efforts into a commercial or competing product based on PHP. Of course, the codebase up to this point would still be available to anyone who wanted to pick up the baton, and for a product as large as PHP that could be a considerable number of volunteer developers.

This leads to one other oft-forgotten advantage of open source software: You can be pretty sure the software will be around in a few years, no matter what. In these days of products with the life spans of morning glories, it's hard to pick a tool with staying power. Fans of OS/2, Amiga, NeXT, Newton, Firefly, Netscape, BeOS, Napster, and a host of other once-hot technologies know the pain of abandonment when a company goes belly-up, decides to stop supporting a technology, or is sold to a buyer with a new agenda. The open source model reduces the chances of an ugly emergency port in a couple of years and thus makes long-term planning more realistic.

Many extensions

PHP makes it easy to communicate with other programs and protocols. The PHP development team seems committed to providing maximum flexibility to the largest number of users.

Database connectivity is especially strong, with native-driver support for about 15 of the most popular databases plus ODBC. In addition, PHP supports a large number of major protocols such as POP3, IMAP, and LDAP. PHP4 added support for Java and distributed object architectures (COM and CORBA), making n-tier development a possibility for the first time. PHP5 extends this support even further, offering a fully incorporated GD graphics library and revamped XML support with DOM and simpleXML.

Most things that PHP does not support are ultimately attributable to closed-source shops on the other end. For instance, Microsoft has not thus far been eager to cooperate with open source projects like PHP. Potential users who complain about lack of native Mac OS 9 or .NET support on the PHP mailing list are simply misinformed about where the fault lies.

Fast feature development

Users of proprietary Web development technologies can sometimes be frustrated by the glacial speed at which new features are added to the official product standard to support emerging technologies. With PHP, this is not a problem. All it takes is one developer, a C compiler, and a dream to add important new functionality. This is not to say that the PHP team will accept every random contribution into the official distribution without community buy-in, but independent developers can and do distribute their own extensions which may be later folded into the main PHP package in more or less unitary form. For instance, Dan Libby's elegant xmlrpc-epi extension was adopted as part of the PHP distribution in version 4.1, a few months after it was first released as an independent package.

PHP development is also constant and ongoing. Although there are clearly major inflection points, such as the transition between PHP4 and PHP5, these tend to be most important deep in the guts of the parser — people were actually working on major extensions throughout the transition period without critical problems. Furthermore, the PHP group subscribes to the open source philosophy of "release early, release often," which gives developers many opportunities to follow along with changes and report bugs. Compare this release scheme to the .NET transition, which has left developers with almost a year in which Microsoft is not really improving IIS but has not yet released a prime-time version of .NET server.

It hasn't always been the case that MySQL added new features in a timely fashion. It would probably be fair to say that a significant chunk of PostgreSQL users are former MySQL users frustrated by the lack of transaction support, for example. However, the 4.0 and 4.1 versions have remedied this and other inequities. Transactions are in the software today, while subselects and foreign keys are experimental but coming along nicely.

Popularity

PHP is fast becoming one of the most popular choices for so-called two-tier development (Web plus data). Figure 1-2 charts growth since 1999.

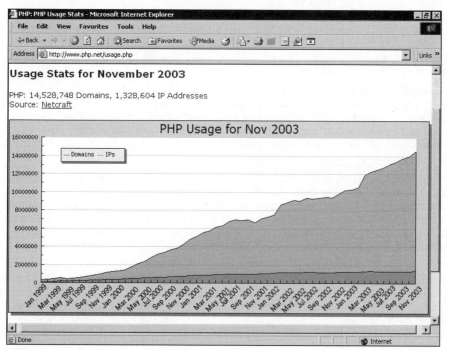

Figure 1-2: Netcraft survey of PHP use

Although it's not evident from this graphic, the period October 1998 through October 1999 showed 800 percent growth in the number of domains. As Web sites become even more ubiquitous, and as more of them go beyond simple static HTML pages, PHP is expected to gain ground quickly in absolute numbers of users.

Although it's somewhat more difficult to get firm figures, it seems that PHP is also in a strong position relative to similar products. According to a 2002 Zend report, Microsoft Active Server Pages technology appears to be utilized on about 24 percent of Web servers, whereas ColdFusion is implemented on approximately 4 percent of surveyed domains. PHP is used on over 24 percent of all Web servers, as measured by a larger and more accurate sample, and is now said to be the most popular server-side scripting language on the Web.

Active Server Pages and ColdFusion used to be highly visible because they tended to be disproportionately selected by large e-commerce sites. However, the realities of the Web finally caught up with us — and it is the flashy e-commerce sites that were disproportionately thinned by the dot-bomb crash. It is now becoming clearer that most Web sites are informational rather than direct revenue centers and, therefore, do not repay high development expenses in an immediate way. PHP enjoys substantial advantages over its competitors in this development category, which has turned out to be the majority of the Internet.

Not proprietary

The history of the personal computer industry to date has largely been a chronicle of proprietary standards: attempts to establish them, clashes between them, their benefits and drawbacks for the consumer, and how they are eventually replaced with new standards.

But in the past few years the Internet has demonstrated the great convenience of voluntary, standards-based, platform-independent compatibility. E-mail, for example, works so well because it enjoys a clear, firm standard to which every program on every platform must conform. New developments that break with the standard (for example, HTML-based e-mail stationery) are generally regarded as deviations, and their users find themselves having to bear the burdens of early adoption.

Furthermore, customers (especially the big-fish businesses with large systems) are fed up with spending vast sums to conform to a proprietary standard — only to have the market uptake not turn out as promised. Much of the current momentum toward XML and Web services is driven by years of customer disappointment with Java RMI, CORBA, COM, and even older proprietary methods and data formats.

Right now, software developers are in a period of experimentation and flux concerning proprietary versus open standards. Companies want to be sure they can maintain profitability while adopting open standards. There have been some major legal conflicts related to proprietary standards, which are still being resolved. These could eventually result in mandated changes to the codebase itself or even affect the futures of the companies involved. In the face of all this uncertainty, a growing number of businesses are attracted to solutions that they know will not have these problems in the foreseeable future.

PHP is in a position of maximum flexibility because it is, so to speak, *antiproprietary*. It is not tied to any one server operating system, unlike Active Server Pages. It is not tied to any proprietary cross-platform standard or middleware, as Java Server Pages or ColdFusion are. It is not tied to any one browser or implementation of a programming language or database. PHP isn't even doctrinaire about working only with other open source software. This independent but cooperative pragmatism should help PHP ride out the stormy seas that seem to lie ahead.

Strong user communities

PHP is developed and supported in a collaborative fashion by a worldwide community of users. Some animals (such as the core developers) are more equal than others—but that's hard to argue with, because they put in the most work, had the best ideas, and have managed to maintain civil relationships with the greatest number of other users.

The main advantage for most new users is technical support without charge, without boundaries, and without the runaround. People on the mailing list are available 24/7/365 to answer your questions, help debug your code, and listen to your gripes. The support is human and real. PHP community members might tell you to read the manual, take your question over to the appropriate database mailing list, or just stop your whining—but they'll never tell you to wipe your C drive and then charge you for the privilege. Often, they'll look at your code and tell you what you're doing wrong or even help you design an application from the ground up.

As you become more comfortable with PHP, you may wish to contribute. Bug tracking, offering advice to others on the mailing lists, posting scripts to public repositories, editing documentation, and, of course, writing C code are all ways you can give back to the community.

MySQL, while open-source licensed for nonredistributive uses, is somewhat less community driven in terms of its development. Nevertheless, it benefits from a growing community of users who are actively listened to by the development team. Rarely has a software project responded so vigorously to community demand. And the community of users can be extremely responsive to other users who need help. It's a point of pride with a lot of SQL gurus that they can write the complicated queries that get you the results you are looking for but had struggled with for days. In many cases, they'll help you for nothing more than the enduring, if small, fame that comes with the archived presence of their name on Google Groups. Try comparing *that* with $100 per incident support.

Summary

PHP and MySQL, individually or together, aren't the panacea for every Web development problem, but they present a lot of advantages. PHP is built by Web developers for Web developers and supported by a large and enthusiastic community. MySQL is a powerful standards-compliant RDBMS that comes in at an extremely competitive price point, even more so if you qualify for free use. Both technologies are clear-cut cases of the community banding together to address its own needs.

✦   ✦   ✦

Server-Side Web Scripting

✦   ✦   ✦   ✦

In This Chapter

Understanding static
and dynamic Web
pages

Client-side versus server-
side scripting

An introduction to
server-side scripting

✦   ✦   ✦   ✦

This chapter is about server-side scripting and its relationship to both static HTML and common client-side technologies. By the end, you can expect to gain a clear understanding of what kinds of things PHP can and cannot do for you, along with a general understanding of how it can interact with client-side code (JavaScript, Java applets, Flash, style sheets, and the like).

Static HTML

The most basic type of Web page is a completely static, text-based one, written entirely in HTML. Take the simple HTML-only page that Figure 2-1 shows as an example.

The following example displays the source code for the Web page shown in Figure 2-1:

```
<HTML>
<HEAD>
<TITLE>Books about Open Source and Free Software</TITLE>
<META NAME=KEYWORDS CONTENT="Open Source, Free Software,
software development, books">
</HEAD>

<BODY>
<CENTER><H3>Books about Open Source and Free
Software</H3></CENTER>

<H5>History and background</H5>
<UL>
<LI><A HREF="bkLevyHackers.html">Hackers:  heroes of the
computer revolution</A> by Levy, Steven (1984)</LI>
<LI><A HREF="bkTorvaldsFun.html">Just for Fun:  the
story of an
accidental revolutionary</A> by Torvalds, Linus and David
Diamond (2001)</LI>
<LI><A HREF="bkWilliamsFreedom.html">Free as in
Freedom:
Richard Stallman's crusade for Free Software</A> by
Williams,
```

```
Sam (2002)</LI>
</UL>

<H5>Philosophy and inspiration</H5>
<UL>
<LI><A HREF="bkRaymondBazaar.html">The Cathedral and the
Bazaar</A> by Raymond, Eric S. (1999)</LI>
<LI><A HREF="bkRosenbergSource.html">Open Source: the
unauthorized white papers</A> by Rosenberg, Donald K.
(2000)</LI>
</UL>


<H5>Technical grounding</H5>
<UL>
<LI><A HREF="bkBachSystem.html">Design of the Unix Operating
System</A> by Bach, Maurice J. (1987)</LI>
<LI><A HREF="bkBarCVS.html">Open Source Development with CVS,
2nd edition</A> by Bar, Moshe and Karl Franz Fogel (2001)</LI>
<LI><A HREF="bkNegusBible.html">Red Hat Linux 7.2 Bible</A> by
Negus, Christopher (2001)</LI>
</UL>


</BODY>
</HTML>
```

Figure 2-1: A static HTML example

After a client computer makes an HTTP request for this page from the server machine across the Web or an intranet, as shown in Figure 2-2, the server simply passes along whatever text it finds in the file.

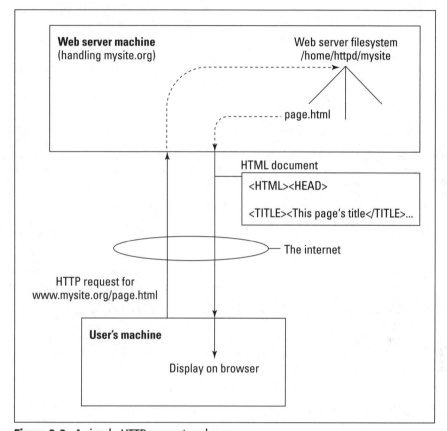

Figure 2-2: A simple HTTP request and response

After this data gets back to the client machine, the browser does its best to render the page according to its understanding of precisely what kind of code it is, user preferences, monitor size, and other factors. The contents of the HTML file on the server are exactly the same as the source code of the page on the client.

Very plain, static HTML, such as the code in this example, offers certain advantages, such as the following:

✦ Any browser can display it adequately.

✦ Many other kinds of devices can display it adequately.

✦ Each request is fulfilled quickly and uses minimal resources.

✦ HTML is easy to learn or produce automatically.

✦ Web developers can make small changes to individual pages quickly.

Of course, static HTML has its downsides, including the following limitations:

✦ It makes control of design and layout difficult.

✦ It doesn't scale up to a large number of pages.

✦ It's not very interactive.

✦ It makes including meaningful metadata about the page difficult.

✦ It can't cope with rapidly changing content or personalization.

For all these reasons, static HTML has become a mark of amateurishness or ideological rigor (as in the home pages of computer science professionals who believe all Web pages should conform to HTML 3.1 and be readable on all devices).

Numerous additional technologies were developed in response to these limitations, including JavaScript, VBScript, Cascading Style Sheets, and Java applets on the client side, and server-side scripting offering features such as database connectivity. Many server-side scripting languages, such as PHP, also come with full support for XML and XSL, both of which appear as part of various other specifications (XHTML, XSLT, XPath, ICE, and so on).

You can save yourself a lot of headaches if you take the time to understand exactly what functionality each of these technologies can and can't be expected to add to your Web site. The basic question to ask yourself about any given Web site task: Where is the computation happening—on the client or on the server?

Note What does *dynamic* mean? A basic and often-repeated distinction exists between *static* and *dynamic* Web pages—but *dynamic* can mean almost anything beyond plain-vanilla HTML. Web developers use the term to describe both client- and server-side functions. On the client, it can mean multimedia presentations, scrolling headlines, pages that update themselves automatically, or elements that appear and disappear. On the server, the term generally denotes content assembled *on the fly*, at the time the page is requested. If you display the current date and time on a page, for example, the content will change from one occasion to another and thus will be dynamic.

Client-Side Technologies

The most common additions to plain HTML are on the client side. These add-ons include formatting extensions such as Cascading Style Sheets and Dynamic HTML; client-side scripting languages such as JavaScript; VBScript; Java applets; and Flash. Support for all these technologies is (or is not, as the case may be) built into the Web browser. They perform the tasks described in Table 2-1, with some overlap.

Table 2-1: Client-Side HTML Extensions

Client-Side Technology	Main Use	Example Effects
Cascading Style Sheets, Dynamic HTML	Formatting pages: controlling size, color, placement, layout, timing of elements	Overlapping, different colored/sized fonts Layers, exact positioning
Client-side scripting (JavaScript, VBScript)	Event handling: controlling consequences of defined events	Link that changes color on mouseover Mortgage calculator

Client-Side Technology	Main Use	Example Effects
Java applets	Delivering small standalone applications	Moving logo Crossword puzzle
Flash animations	Animation	Short cartoon film

The page shown in Figure 2-3 is based on the same content as that in Figure 2-1. As you can see from the following source code, however, this example adds style sheets and client-side scripting as well as somewhat more sophisticated HTML.

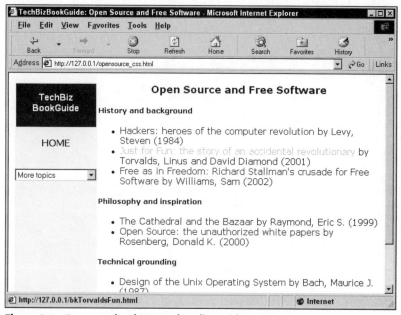

Figure 2-3: An example of HTML plus client-side scripting

```
<HTML>
<HEAD>
<TITLE>TechBizBookGuide: Open Source and Free Software</TITLE>
<META NAME=KEYWORDS CONTENT="Open Source, Free Software,
software development, books">
<STYLE TYPE="text/css">
<!--
BODY, P       {color: black; font-family: verdana; font-size: 10
pt}
H1        {margin-top: 10; color: white; font-family: arial;
font-size: 12 pt}
H2        {margin-bottom: -10; color: black; font-family:
```

```
verdana; font-size: 18 pt}
A:link, A:visited    {color: #000080; text-decoration: none}
.roll      {  }
A.roll:hover  {color: #8FBc8F}
-->
</STYLE>

<SCRIPT LANGUAGE="JavaScript">
<!--
   function ListVisit(form, i) {
      // get the URL from options
      var site = form.elements[i].selectedIndex;
      // if it's not the first (null) option, go there
      if( site >= 1 ) {
          top.location = form.elements[i].options[ site].value;
      }
      // and then reselect the null (it functions as a label)
      form.elements[i].selectedIndex = 0;
    }

//-->
</SCRIPT>
</HEAD>

<BODY>
<TABLE BORDER=0 CELLPADDING=0 WIDTH=100%>
<TR>
<TD BGCOLOR="#F0F8FF" ALIGN=CENTER VALIGN=TOP WIDTH=17%>
   <TABLE CELLPADDING=5 WIDTH=100%>
   <TR ALIGN=CENTER>
   <TD BGCOLOR="#000080">
   <H1>TechBiz<BR>BookGuide</H1>
   </TD></TR></TABLE>
   <BR>
   <A HREF="index.php"><B>HOME</B></A><BR><BR>
   <BR>
   <FORM action="">
   <SELECT NAME="topics" onChange="ListVisit(this.form, 0)">
   <OPTION>More topics
   <OPTION VALUE="commercial.html">Commercial software
   <OPTION VALUE="hardware.html">Hardware
   <OPTION VALUE="telephony.html">Telephony
   </SELECT></FORM><BR>
</TD>
<TD BGCOLOR="#FFFFFF" ALIGN=LEFT VALIGN=TOP WIDTH=83%>
<CENTER><H3>Open Source and Free Software</H3></CENTER>

<H5>History and background</H5>
<UL>
<LI><A HREF="bkLevyHackers.html" class="roll">Hackers:  heroes
of the computer revolution</A> by Levy, Steven (1984)</LI>
```

```
<LI><A HREF="bkTorvaldsFun.html" class="roll">Just for Fun:  the
story of an accidental revolutionary</A> by Torvalds, Linus and
David Diamond (2001)</LI>
<LI><A HREF="bkWilliamsFreedom.html" class="roll">Free as in
Freedom:  Richard Stallman's crusade for Free Software</A>
by Williams, Sam (2002)</LI>
</UL>

<H5>Philosophy and inspiration</H5>
<UL>
<LI><A HREF="bkRaymondBazaar.html" class="roll">The Cathedral
and the Bazaar</A> by Raymond, Eric S. (1999)</LI>
<LI><A HREF="bkRosenbergSource.html" class="roll">Open Source:
the unauthorized white papers</A> by Rosenberg, Donald K.
(2000)</LI>
</UL>


<H5>Technical grounding</H5>
<UL>
<LI><A HREF="bkBachSystem.html" class="roll">Design of the Unix
Operating System</A> by Bach, Maurice J. (1987)</LI>
<LI><A HREF="bkBarCVS.html" class="roll">Open Source Development
with CVS, 2nd edition</A> by Bar, Moshe and Karl Franz Fogel
(2001)</LI>
<LI><A HREF="bkNegusBible.html" class="roll">Red Hat Linux 7.2
Bible</A> by Negus, Christopher (2001)</LI>
</UL>

</TD>
</TR></TABLE>
</BODY>
</HTML>
```

Unfortunately, the best thing about client-side technologies is also the worst thing about them: They depend entirely on the browser. Wide variations exist in the capabilities of each browser and even among versions of the same brand of browser. Individuals can also choose to configure their own browsers in awkward ways: Some people disable JavaScript for security reasons, for example, which makes it impossible for them to view sites that overuse JavaScript for navigation (as we deliberately did in the preceding code sample).

Furthermore, many consumers are very slow to upgrade their browsers for reasons of cost or technical anxiety or both. The savvy Web developer should also consider the implications of device-based browsing, universal accessibility, and a global audience. The fact that the huge mass-market sites trying to reach the widest audiences, such as Yahoo! and Amazon, continue to resist using style sheets and JavaScript more than seven years after these standards were adopted is no accident. Against the urging of the World Wide Web Consortium, many sites continue to stubbornly cling to their FONT tags and BGCOLOR attributes as the only way to survive in the face of customers who insist on using AOL 3.0 on five-year-old Macintoshes with 13-inch monitors. The stubborn unwillingness of the public to upgrade is the bane of client-side developers, causing them to frequently suffer screaming nightmares and/or existential meltdowns in the dark, vulnerable hours before dawn. The bottom-line irony is that, even after almost ten years of explosive Web progress, the only thing that a developer can absolutely, positively know that the client is going to see is plain text-based HTML (or, rather, the subset of HTML that's widely supported and has stood the tests of time and usefulness).

Finally, client-side technologies cannot do anything that requires connecting to a back end server. JavaScript cannot assemble a customized drop-down list on the fly from user preferences stored in a database—if a change is needed in the list, the Web developer must go in and edit the page by hand. (Server-side JavaScript does exist, but no one much uses it.) This gap is filled by server-side scripting.

In summation, anything to do with layout or browser events happens on the client. Generally speaking, anything that looks cool or depends on the movements of the mouse is client-side. The faster you see some event happening, the more likely that the client is handling it, because high speed indicates that no request to and download from the server is necessary.

Note   *Java applets*, also known as *client-side Java*, are considerably less dependent on the browser than are other client-side technologies. As the name suggests, applets are complete little Java applications delivered across the Internet. But instead of interacting directly with the client's operating system as do applications that written in other programming languages, Java applets run on a piece of middleware known as a *Java Virtual Machine*. You can think of the JVM as an operating system living on top of your real operating system, like the aliens taking over human bodies in a gazillion cheesy sci-fi movies. Most recent browsers incorporate a JVM, and you can also download one separately. This division of labor enables applets to use the rendering capabilities of a browser without being limited to the browser's relatively puny functionality.

Applets have suffered under an early reputation for picayune pointlessness because they were initially used for a category of thing that we might term *dancing Chihuahuas*—logos that look as if they're made out of gelatin, scrolling headlines, bouncing links, and other headache-inducing frivolities. Luckily, applets have since been redeemed by useful, humanistic purposes such as crossword puzzles, Tower of Hanoi simulations, and virtual ways to try on ensembles of clothing and accessories.

Server-Side Scripting

Figure 2-4 shows a schematic representation of a server-side scripting data flow.

Client-side scripting is the glamorous, eye-catching part of Web development. In contrast, server-side scripting is invisible to the user. Pity the poor server-side scripters, toiling away in utter obscurity, trapped in the no-man's land between the Web server and the database while their arty brethren brazenly flash their wares before the public gaze.

Server-side Web scripting is mostly about connecting Web sites to back end servers, such as databases. This enables the following types of two-way communication:

✦ **Server to client:** Web pages can be assembled from back end-server output.

✦ **Client to server:** Customer-entered information can be acted upon.

Common examples of client-to-server interaction are online forms with some drop-down lists (usually the ones that require you to click a button) that the script assembles dynamically on the server.

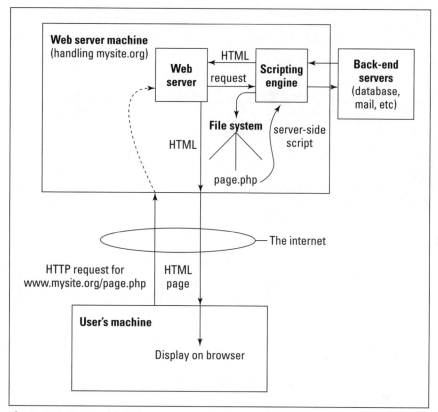

Figure 2-4: Server-side tasks

Server-side scripting products consist of two main parts: the scripting language and the scripting engine (which may or may not be built into the Web server). The engine parses and interprets pages written in the language.

Often, the same company or team develops both parts for use only with each other—PHP3 and ColdFusion are both examples of this practice. However, exceptions to this rule do exist. Java Server Pages (JSP), for example, are written in a standard programming language rather than in a special-purpose scripting language, and third parties (for example, Macromedia JRun, Apache Tomcat) have developed several interchangeable scripting engines that can be used to run JSP code on a Web site.

In theory, Active Server Pages enables you to use almost any scripting language and one of several matching ActiveX scripting engines (although, in practice, using anything but the Windows/IIS/VBScript/JScript combination is highly problematic). Since version 4.0, PHP is also a bikini scripting technology, because the scripting engine (Zend) is theoretically separable from the PHP programming language.

Figure 2-5 shows a simple example of server-side scripting—a page assembled on the fly from a database, followed by the server-side source and the client-side source. We include database calls (which we don't get around to explaining until Part II of this book) and leave out some of the included files, because we intend this example to show the final product of PHP rather than serve as a piece of working code.

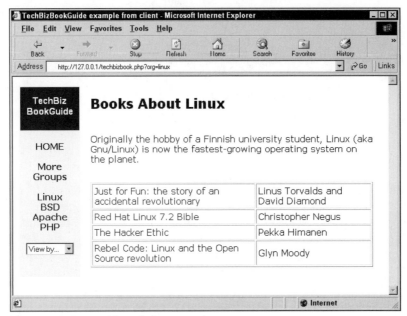

Figure 2-5: Server-side scripting example

The following PHP code shows the source on the server:

```
<HTML>
<HEAD>
<TITLE>TechBizBookGuide example from server</TITLE>
<?php include_once("tbbg-style.css"); ?>
<?php include_once("javascript.inc"); ?>
</HEAD>
<BODY>
<?php
include_once("tbbg-navbar.txt");
$org = $_GET['org'];
?>
<TD BGCOLOR="#FFFFFF" ALIGN=LEFT VALIGN=TOP WIDTH=83%>
    <TABLE CELLPADDING=5 WIDTH=100%><TR><TD ALIGN=LEFT
VALIGN=MIDDLE>
    <H2>Books about <?php echo $org; //passed in from URL
?></H2><BR></TD></TR>
    <TR><TD WIDTH=50% ALIGN=LEFT>
    <?php
    $dbh = mysql_connect('localhost', 'mysqluser') or die("Unable
to open database");
```

```
    mysql_select_db("techbizbookguide") or die("Unable to access
database");
    $query = "SELECT Blurb FROM Org WHERE OrgName = '$org'";
    $qresult = mysql_query($query) or die(mysql_error());
    $blurb = mysql_fetch_array($qresult) or die(mysql_error());
    print("$blurb[0]");
    ?>
    </TD></TR>
    <TR><TD ALIGN=LEFT>
       <TABLE BORDER=1 CELLPADDING=3>
       <?php
       $query2 = "SELECT ID, Title, AuthorFirst, AuthorLast
                  FROM bookinfo
                  WHERE OrgName='$org'
                  ORDER BY AuthorLast";
       $qresult2 = mysql_query($query2) or die(mysql_error());
       while ($titlelist = mysql_fetch_array($qresult2)) {
          $bookID = $titlelist[0];
          $title = $titlelist[1];
          $authorfirst = $titlelist[2];
          $authorlast = $titlelist[3];
          print("<TR><TD><A HREF=\"book.php?bn=$bookID\"
class=\"roll\"> $title</A></TD><TD>$authorfirst
$authorlast</TD>");
       }
       ?>
       </TR></TABLE>
    </TD></TR></TABLE>
</TD></TR></TABLE>
</BODY></HTML>
```

After the preceding PHP source code is parsed by the PHP scripting engine, the following client-side code will be produced by the Web server and sent to the browser.

```
<HTML>
<HEAD>
<TITLE>TechBizBookGuide example from client</TITLE>
<STYLE TYPE="text/css">
<!--
BODY      {color: black; font-family: verdana; font-size: 10 pt}
H1        {margin-top: 10; color: white; font-family: arial;
font-size: 12 pt}
H2        {margin-bottom: -10; color: black; font-family:
verdana; font-size: 18 pt}
A:link, A:visited    {color: #000080; text-decoration: none}
.roll     {   }
A.roll:hover  {color: #008080}
-->
</STYLE>
<SCRIPT LANGUAGE="JavaScript">
<!--
   function ListVisit(form, i) {
      // get the URL from options
      var site = form.elements[i].selectedIndex;
```

```
                // if it's not the first (null) option, go there
                if( site >= 1 ) {
                top.location = form.elements[i].options[site].value;
                }
                // and then reselect the null (it functions as a label)
                form.elements[i].selectedIndex = 0;
            }
        //-->
</SCRIPT>
</HEAD>

<BODY>
<TABLE BORDER=0 CELLPADDING=0 WIDTH=100%>
<TR>
<TD BGCOLOR="#F0F8FF" ALIGN=CENTER VALIGN=TOP WIDTH=17%>
    <TABLE CELLPADDING=5 WIDTH=100%>
    <TR ALIGN=CENTER>
    <TD BGCOLOR="#000080">
    <H1>TechBiz<BR>BookGuide</H1>
    </TD></TR></TABLE>
    <BR>
    <A HREF="index.php"><B>HOME</B></A><BR><BR>
    <B>More</B><BR>
    <B>Groups</B><BR><BR>
    <A HREF="techbizbook.php?org=linux"
class="roll"><B>Linux</B></A>
    <BR>
    <A HREF="techbizbook.php?org=bsd" class="roll"><B>BSD</B></A>
    <BR>
    <A HREF="techbizbook.php?org=apache"
class="roll"><B>Apache</B></A>
    <BR>
    <A HREF="techbizbook.php?org=php" class="roll"><B>PHP</B></A>
    <BR><BR>
    <FORM action="">
    <Select onChange="ListVisit(this.form, 0)">
    <OPTION>View by...
    <OPTION VALUE="author.php">Author
    <OPTION VALUE="people.php">People
    <OPTION VALUE="themes.php">Themes
    <OPTION VALUE="role.php">Roles
    <OPTION VALUE="size.php">Group size
    </SELECT></FORM><BR>
</TD>
<TD BGCOLOR="#FFFFFF" ALIGN=LEFT VALIGN=TOP WIDTH=83%>
    <TABLE WIDTH=100% CELLPADDING=15><TR><TD ALIGN=LEFT
VALIGN=MIDDLE>
    <H2>Books About Linux</H2><BR></TD></TR>
    <TR><TD WIDTH=50% ALIGN=LEFT>Originally the hobby of a
Finnish university student, Linux (aka Gnu/Linux) is now the
fastest-growing operating system on the planet.</TD></TR>
    <TR><TD ALIGN=LEFT>
```

```
      <TABLE BORDER=1 CELLPADDING=3>
      <TR><TD><A HREF="book.php?book=1" class="roll">Just for
Fun:  the story of an accidental
revolutionary</A></TD><TD>Linus Torvalds and David Diamond</TD>
      <TR><TD><A HREF="book.php?book=2" class="roll">Red Hat
Linux 7.2 Bible</A></TD><TD>Christopher Negus</TD>
      <TR><TD><A HREF="book.php?book=3" class="roll">The Hacker
Ethic</A></TD><TD>Pekka Himanen</TD>
      <TR><TD><A HREF="book.php?book=4" class="roll">Rebel Code:
Linux and the Open Source revolution</A></TD><TD>Glyn
Moody</TD>
      </TR></TABLE>
    </TD></TR></TABLE>
</TD></TR></TABLE>
</BODY></HTML>
```

This particular page isn't significantly more impressive to look at than the plain HTML version at the beginning of the chapter. Passing one different variable, however, results in the automatic generation of any number of unique pages — in this case, pages listing the books by criteria other than the author's last name — without any further work. If we add some new books about another company to the database, these lists automatically get updated to reflect the new data on each subsequent page load.

As you can see from these two different source-code listings, you cannot view server-side scripts from the client. All the heavy lifting happens before the code gets shoved down the pipe to the client. After emerging from the Web server, the code appears on the other end as normal HTML and JavaScript, which also means that you can't tell which server-side scripting language was used unless something in the header or URL gives it away (which usually is the case, as the page you are requesting often ends with .jsp or .php). These scripts, incidentally, were written in PHP using the MySQL database as back end; you can learn all about these techniques in Part II of this book.

Server-side or Client-side?

There are client-side methods and server-side methods to accomplish many tasks. When sending e-mail, for example, the client-side way is to open up the mail client software with a pread-dressed blank e-mail message after the user clicks a MAILTO link. The server-side method is to make the user fill out a form, and the contents are formatted as an e-mail that gets sent via an SMTP server (which very well could be the same machine as the server-side script is executing on). You can also choose between client methods and server methods of browser-sniffing, form-validation, drop-down lists, and arithmetic calculation. Sometimes you see subtle but meaningful differences in functionality (server-side drop-downs can be assembled dynamically; client-side cannot) but not always.

How to choose? Know your audience. Server-side methods are generally a bit slower at runtime because of the extra transits they must make, but they don't assume anything about your visitor's browser capabilities and take less developer time to maintain. These qualities make them good for mass-market and educational sites. If you're one of the lucky few developers who's absolutely positive that your visitors all have up-to-date browsers and good throughput, you can feel free to go wild with the scripting and graphics. Finally, remember that you can use PHP to generate both static HTML and JavaScript — thus enjoying the best of both worlds, as we explain in Chapter 38.

Note   Recent developments in programming languages are increasingly blurring the difference between *programming* and *scripting*. PHP, for example, definitely uses most of the same control structures as other programming languages do. Fully interpreted HTML-embedded languages such as ASP, however, are still considered to be on the scripting side of the line, whereas separately compiled binaries are a definite mark of programming. But because PHP since version 4 is dynamically compiled, it's officially a real programming language — and don't let anyone tell you otherwise. This change accounts for much of the screaming speed of PHP nowadays, which moves into the same class as Perl.

What Is Server-Side Scripting Good for?

The client looks good, but the server cooks good. What server-side scripting lacks in eye-candy sex appeal, it more than makes up for in sheer usefulness. Most Web users probably interact with the products of server-side scripting on a daily, if not an hourly, basis.

One category of things that server-side scripting just absolutely can't help you with is real-time, 3-D shoot-'em-ups. The more immediately responsive and graphics-intensive a project needs to be, the less suitable (and capable) PHP is for it. At the moment, the Web is simply too slow a channel for these purposes (although broadband users are changing that).

On the other hand, server-side scripting languages such as PHP perfectly serve most of the truly useful aspects of the Web, as such as the items in this list:

- ✦ Content sites (both production and display)
- ✦ Community features (forums, bulletin boards, and so on)
- ✦ E-mail (Web mail, mail forwarding, and sending mail from a Web application)
- ✦ Customer-support and technical-support systems
- ✦ Advertising networks
- ✦ Web-delivered business applications
- ✦ Directories and membership rolls
- ✦ Surveys, polls, and tests
- ✦ Filling out and submitting forms online
- ✦ Personalization technologies
- ✦ Groupware
- ✦ Catalog, brochure, and informational sites
- ✦ Games (for example, chess) with lots of logic but simple/static graphics
- ✦ Any other application that needs to connect a backend server (database, LDAP, and so on) to a Web server

PHP can handle all these essential tasks — and then some.

But enough rhetoric! Now that you have a firm grasp of the differences between client-side and server-side technologies, you can get on to the practical stuff. In Chapter 3, we show you how to get, install, and configure PHP for yourself (or find someone to do it for you).

Summary

To understand what PHP (or any server-side scripting technology) can do for you, having a firm grasp on the division of labor between client and server is crucial. In this chapter, we work through examples of plain, static HTML; HTML with client-side additions such as JavaScript and Cascading Style Sheets; and PHP-generated Web pages as viewed from both the server and the client.

Client-side scripting can be visually attractive and quickly responsive to user inputs, but anything beyond the most basic HTML is subject to browser variation. Static client-side scripts also require more developer time to maintain and update, because pages cannot be dynamically generated from a constantly changing datastore. Server-side programming and scripting languages, such as PHP, can connect databases and other servers to Web pages.

Since version 4, PHP differs architecturally from some other server-side tools and even from PHP3. PHP is now dynamically compiled, which makes it faster at runtime. Since PHP4, the scripting engine, Zend, has also been separate from the scripting language (PHP).

✦　　✦　　✦

Getting Started with PHP

In this chapter, we'll discuss the pros and cons of the various Web hosting options: outsourcing, self-hosting, and various compromises. Then we'll give detailed directions for installing PHP and finish with a few tips on finding the right development tool. By the end of the chapter, you should be ready to write your first script.

Hosting versus DIY

The first major decision you need to make is: Who will host your PHP-enabled Web site — you or a Web hosting service? Also, will you need a separate development setup; if so, who will host it? If you've already made these decisions (and knew what you were doing), feel free to skip right to the installation section of this chapter, "Installing PHP."

The ISP option

Remote hosting is a very popular option as a large number of companies — probably the vast majority of Webhosts today — offer PHP-enabled Web sites. These are some basic pros and cons to keep in mind.

The good

Outsourced hosting has a lot of advantages. The ISP will (in theory) handle many of the crucial technical and administrative details necessary to keep a site running, such as:

+ Hardware

+ Software upgrades

+ InterNIC registration, IP addressing, DNS

+ Mail servers (POP/IMAP and SMTP)

+ Bandwidth

+ Power supply

+ Backups

+ Security

There's no cozier feeling than the one you get just before you fall asleep, knowing that some poor schmo at your ISP will be getting the pager message in the middle of the night if something goes wrong with your site. Lurking crackers, downed power lines, munged backup tapes — all that is your host's headache now. Especially for developers who have little experience with system-administration issues, outsourcing can be a major time saver.

Web hosting is also extremely cost effective in most situations. PHP on Linux or one of the BSDs is almost ridiculously inexpensive and widely available. Currently, only a few companies offer PHP on an NT server platform, and some of them can be pricey. As the Miracles so eloquently urge, "You better shop around (shop, shop ooh)."

The bad

Of course, there can be some serious disadvantages to Web hosting.

Most of these have to do with control. When you go ISP, you're basically a guest in someone else's house and have to play by his rules. Maybe you're a welcome paying guest, a veritable parlor boarder — but the fact remains that when you live in someone else's establishment, you can't just strip down to your undies and lipsync your way through a high-volume version of "Proud Mary" on the dining-room table whenever you feel like it. People are trying to eat, pal.

A few years ago, the most central issue for PHP was module versus CGI. PHP runs best and fastest as a module (in other words, built into the Web server itself rather than running as a separate process). Almost everyone prefers to use the module version if possible. Some ISPs prefer to run the CGI version of PHP, however, because it's much simpler to administer safely on a shared Web server. Thankfully, as more Web hosting services set up shop, it's much easier to find one that will give you the module.

Currently, the biggest problem with outsourced PHP hosting is the nonavailability of other programs. Obviously, ISPs have a strong incentive to control the programs you are allowed to run on their servers. However, a lot of a PHP's value comes from its job as a glue between various services and protocols. It can be extremely frustrating to be prevented from running a common and useful utility, such as ImageMagick or HTML Tidy, because your Web host won't allow you to run unauthorized binaries or link to libraries outside your home directory.

Also, ISPs generally are not going to give you a choice of which version of PHP to use. Sometimes they can be quite strict in which extensions they'll build for you, and sometimes they can be very slow to upgrade to a new major release. Therefore, some PHP packages — even potentially some of the code in this book, if your host is a late adopter of PHP5 — will not run for you unaltered.

A good rule of thumb is: The more common your needs are, the more possible and appropriate it is to outsource your hosting. The more oddball and/or bleeding-edge your needs are, the more you're going to be pushed to host your own whether you want to or not. Of course the unspoken realpolitik addendum to this is: The bigger you are and the more money you have to spend, the more weight you have available to throw around.

A few factors will make it considerably more difficult for you to find a hosting service:

✦ Generally objectionable content (hate, porn)

✦ Unsolicited mailings (aka spam)

✦ Content that attracts crackers (security info)

✦ Potentially legally actionable content

✦ Need for unusual server-side hardware, OS, or software

✦ Need for super-high bandwidth, especially if unpredictable

If you're in one of these categories, you need to mention it up front — you'll just get the boot anyway once they find out. Chances are good that you won't get to do much shopping around — if you can find any hosting situation, grab it before they change their minds and look for a better deal later.

Finally, we must mention the most important negative factor of all: the frustration and anxiety caused by a bad hosting experience. Words cannot describe the teeth-grinding, stomach-churning, scream-suppressing state of existence caused by your site crashing just when you've been featured on Slashdot, thereby making you look like a total technoposer as well as losing all the good pub you so richly deserve.

That's not even mentioning more common problems such as lost e-mail, disappearing DNS, unexplained site outages, deleted databases (this actually happened to us once), lack of back-ups, suffering through an hour-long telephone wait just to talk to some tech supportie who's never been within ten feet of a server, never getting a response to your polite e-mails, and being overbilled for the privilege (not that we're bitter, and anyway our lawyer says we can't name any names).

Bottom line: If you choose hosting, you do so at your own peril. Always be ready to make a quick getaway, which might entail eschewing the cheapest or most fully featured deal in favor of one without long-term contracts and/or prepayments. Conversely, don't be an utter jerk when you deal with the employees of your hosting company. If you've never outsourced hosting before, take the time to understand the difference between things you can legitimately blame on the Web host (bad tech support) and things that are basically Acts of Fate (Internet traffic in your entire metro area goes out).

The details

If you've decided on the hosting option, you will enjoy a plethora of choices in today's marketplace. Novice shoppers should be aware, however, that the term *ISP* (or even *Web host*) can mean almost anything these days.

Table 3-1 provides a guide to the specializations and their most appropriate uses. (The companies mentioned are intended as examples only; this does not constitute an endorsement or recommendation of their services.)

Table 3-1: Varieties of ISPs

Type of ISP	Keywords	PHP Users
Consumer ISP (Earthlink, RoadRunner)	Home DSL, cable modem	Home self-hosting of small sites
Free Web host	Free Web hosting under certain circumstances	Small sites, often in exchange for showing ads
Commercial Web hosting	Web hosting, virtual hosting, colocation, dedicated server	Most outsourced sites
Site development	Design, promotion, custom development, consulting	Sites that want to outsource Web development as well as hosting
Access provider (UUNet)	T-1, DS-3, commercial DSL	Self-hosters

Although finding a good Web hosting service sometimes seems as difficult as finding a life-long mate, there are now listing resources to make it easier:

✦ www.od-site.com/php

✦ www.webhostingtalk.com/

✦ www.ispcheck.com

Pay special attention to the user comments, good and bad. Ask your friends and colleagues about their experiences. Search the PHP user list archives — people occasionally make recommendations and comment on bad experiences they've had.

Probably the single most contentious post-signup issue is throughput. Be wary of the phrase *unlimited traffic/bandwidth/hits*. Recall the query of the wise middle-aged baseball manager when the elderly team owner offered him the job for life: "Whose life are we talking about?" Analogously, a level of bandwidth that would never be tested by Joe's Epic Poetry Appreciation Site is probably not going to feel quite so roomy to a Web site featuring free streaming video of scantily clad supermodels. Before you sign up for any deal, you need to assess where you're going to fall on this continuum.

Caution   Be extra careful of the amount of disk space that comes with your service plan, especially if you have a large or graphics-heavy site. If you exceed the limit, you will generally be charged exorbitant rates for every fraction of a megabyte of extra space per month. One thing that contributes to this problem is log files; delete them or download them to some cheaper form of storage on a regular basis.

Tip   How to guesstimate your bandwidth needs: 1GB of traffic per month is equal to 100,000 views of files averaging 10K (including graphics, text, ads unless they're third-party served, everything — measuring from a client, not the server). You do the arithmetic.

The self-hosting option: Pros and cons

Self-hosting is becoming a realistic option for more sites as the price of connectivity goes down. It's the ultimate in command and control, and it offers substantial security advantages — if you have the expertise to take advantage of them. Running your own setup means problems get solved faster because you don't have to waste time hanging on a tech support line, and many just feel it's more fun. There's just no substitute for being able to put your hands on the actual server machine whenever you want. Remember that if you have unusual, objectionable, or cutting-edge needs, you may be forced to serve your own site whether you want to or not.

On the flip side, self-hosting requires tons more work and can be quite a bit more expensive, especially for the smallish-to-midsize site. Plus, a self-hosted site is going to be only as good as your available skill set. So if no one on your team knows much about security, you can expect to have security problems (although, at least, you'll be aware of your weaknesses, unlike the false comfort that comes when your hosting service fails to inform you that their security expert quit three months ago).

More existentially, you have no one to blame but yourself if things go wrong. If you can look yourself in the mirror every morning and think "It's all on me and I feel great," you have the necessary self-confidence for self-hosting.

Compromise solutions

Of course, outsourcing and self-hosting are actually poles on a continuum. Several *compromise* solutions exist that attempt to offer the best of both worlds.

Colocation

Colocation means you crate up your server machine and ship it to the hosting company, who will hook up your machine to its network and monitor it for you. You are responsible for purchasing, licensing, insuring, installing, configuring, and maintaining all software and hardware, except the uninterruptible power supply. The host does not mess with your box at all, beyond the occasional reboot — for which it generally charges you extra. If you want any technical support whatsoever, you must either go to the location yourself or pay hundreds of dollars an hour for the staff's gentle ministrations — and if you're in a colocation situation, chances are good that you're using products for which they have no training.

Dedicated server

A *dedicated server* is just what it sounds like: The hosting service will buy a server, fit it out to your tastes (on your dime, of course), and hook it up to its network; then all the processor cycles belong to you. Generally, you get technical support with your service. This is much more secure than a shared server environment and relatively cost-effective for a midsize site. If you have the administrative chops to run your own server remotely, and more than just a handful of clients, this option is extremely cost-effective.

Caution   A lot of the pitfalls of self-hosting still apply, most notably security, which becomes a broader, more difficult discipline every day. A very wise man once said, "If security is important to you, unplug your network cable." Not an encouraging maxim to be sure, but this should be a factor — perhaps even the main factor — in deciding on any option that requires you to administer your own server.

Outsource production, self-host development

This option involves two complete setups: an *outsourced production site* and an identical in-house *development server* or servers. Dividing things up this way can offer the best of both worlds, letting someone else take the emergency pager messages in the middle of the night while still enjoying the intimacy of playing on your very own server. If you're located in an area with limited connectivity choices, this option can be a lifesaver. It is also one of the best choices for larger sites with more developers.

Installing PHP

If you've decided to completely outsource PHP hosting and know a competent sysadmin to perform all workstation installs, feel free to skip the rest of this chapter. We are bound, however, to recommend that you install your own software at first, even if it's only on your personal development machine, so that you have more exposure to and understanding of the development environment, as well as creating a safe place to test your work without jeopardizing the security and functionality of production systems.

Before you can begin

Before you can install PHP on any platform, you need:

- ✦ A server or workstation with enough RAM for your OS.

- ✦ A Unix, Mac OS X, or Windows operating system installed.

- ✦ A working, dedicated Internet connection if you are running a production site; and/or installation on an intranet for a development site; or neither if you are running a totally standalone PHP setup (although without an Internet connection, you must find another source for the necessary software packages).

Help for these prerequisites is beyond the scope of this book. You might want to look at the following sources for networking information:

- ✦ World of Windows Networking (www.wown.com)

- ✦ Linux Documentation Project (www.linuxdoc.org/HOWTO/HOWTO-INDEX/howtos.html)

If you plan to install PHP on Windows, you'll also need:

- ✦ A working PHP-supported Web server. Under previous versions of PHP, IIS/PWS was the easiest choice because a module version of PHP was available for it; but PHP now has added a much wider selection of modules for Windows.

- ✦ A correctly installed PHP-supported database (if you plan to use one)

- ✦ The PHP Windows binary distribution (download it at www.php.net/downloads.php)

- ✦ A utility to unzip files (search http://download.cnet.com for PC file compression utilities)

Apache2 and PHP

Apache is probably the Web server most commonly used with PHP and MySQL — so common that the acronym LAMP has emerged to describe precisely this combo (Linux Apache MySQL PHP). At the moment, both Apache and PHP are in the middle of major releases — and unfortunately there are reasons why the two upgrades may be incompatible.

The main change in the huge architectural update of Apache2 is thread-safety. In Apache1, each server request spawned a separate child process. This has one huge advantage — if one process fails, it will not crash the whole server. However, it also leads to perceived inefficiencies on some operating systems, particularly Windows — although in many cases, particularly Linux, Apache2 is not more efficient than Apache1.

Unfortunately, a lot of PHP extensions cannot easily be made thread-safe and probably never will. The PHP development team, therefore, has gone on record recommending against an upgrade to Apache2 in a production environment. This recommendation will, in turn, slow the adoption of Apache2 by preventing people from finding bugs so they can be fixed. It's unclear if this recommendation will change.

So here's the bottom line: Most PHP users do not need to upgrade to Apache2. Users of high-load production systems may be risking a total httpd crash if one thread goes down. PHP performance is unlikely to be improved on Linux, although it may be on Solaris or Windows. If you do choose to upgrade to Apache2, prefork mode is far safer than multithreaded mode, although it doesn't offer much performance gain over Apache1.

If you plan to install PHP on Unix, you'll also need:

✦ The PHP source distribution (`www.php.net/downloads.php`)

✦ The latest Apache source distribution (`www.apache.org/dist/` — look for the highest odd number that ends with the `.tar.gz` suffix)

✦ A working PHP-supported database, if you plan to use one

✦ Any other supported software to which PHP must connect (mail server, BCMath package, JDK, and so forth)

✦ An ANSI C compiler

✦ Gnu make (starting with PHP4, it can't be any other make version, which is particularly relevant for non-GPLed Unices like Solaris and BSD — you can freely download it at `www.gnu.org/software/make`)

✦ Bison and flex (Enter `find . -name bison -print` and `find . -name flex -print` from the `/usr` directory to check if you have them already, or just let gcc check for them during the make process. If not, you can download Bison from `www.gnu.org/software/bison` and flex from `ftp://ftp.ee.lbl.gov`.)

Tip
Remember that any extra servers or software libraries to which PHP will connect need to be installed *before* you build. A database is the most common type of external server. Other examples are the BCMath package, an IMAP server, the mcrypt library, and the expat XML parser (unless you use Apache, with which it is bundled).

Now you're ready to actually install PHP. The difference between building as an Apache module and building as a CGI executable is very small. In fact, it comes down to leaving off the `--with-apache` or `--with-apxs` flags when configuring. Many users compile both the module and the CGI versions at the same time for convenience.

Tip
In the past, various parties have offered programs (such as PHPTriad, Nusphere MySQL, and Zend Launchpad) that install Apache, PHP, and sometimes MySQL for you in one fell swoop. As a result of licensing issues, most of these seem to have gone away.

Installation procedures

Because of PHP's strong commitment to cross-platform operability, there are far too many specific installation methods to fully list here. We have tried to cover what we believe to be the most popular platforms for PHP, but trying to write the installation instructions for every possible operating system and Web server would have resulted in a prohibitively long chapter.

Furthermore, while PHP installation procedures under Unix have been stable for years, Windows installs have gone through quite a bit of flux since PHP4 was first released. Part of this is due to actions on the part of the PHP team; part of this is due to changes in the Windows product line such as the introduction of Windows XP and planned changes in IIS. PHP now also runs on Macintosh OS X, and that installation has only fairly recently stabilized.

In response to such rapid change, we can only caution you that for the freshest information on installation you should visit the PHP Web site (`www.php.net/docs.php`) on each download. Even if you've installed PHP a gazillion times before, there might be something new and different on the gazillion-and-first occasion.

Unix and Apache

Tip

In the instructions that follow, we assume you are using Apache1. If you wish to use Apache2, simply change all the references to `apache` or `apxs` to `apache2` and `apxs2`, and change the version numbers of the directories from `1.3.x` to `2.0.x`.

The first time you build your own HTTP daemon from source, you might be a little apprehensive. But the process is fairly straightforward, and it's worth the effort to compile your Web server yourself instead of being dependent on other people's packages, which are often weeks or months out of date. And hey, it's a genuine rush when it works! Once you do it a couple of times, it's a breeze — one of us once had a job where we recompiled the Apache server at least weekly if not daily, and after that it was totally routine.

For those who have already successfully built an earlier version of PHP, the procedure is exactly the same — only it takes a lot longer than before.

Caution

Your Red Hat, Mandrake, or SuSE Linux installation may have come with RPM versions of Apache and PHP; or your Debian Linux may have come with an apt package. You *must* remove these packages before compiling your new PHP! In addition, you may have RPM or apt versions of third-party servers, such as MySQL or PostgreSQL, which are generally installed differently from their source counterparts. If you encounter problems, look in the documentation for installation locations, or uninstall the packages and reinstall from scratch.

In the following directions, you will type the code fragments into each shell prompt.

Tip

Remember to log in as the root user first if you are installing in a root-owned directory. Remember to stop and uninstall your previous Apache server if you had one.

To start your build, just follow these steps:

1. If you haven't already done so, unzip and untar your Apache source distribution. Unless you have a reason to do otherwise, `/usr/local` is the standard place.

```
gunzip -c apache_1.3.x.tar.gz
tar -xvf apache_1.3.x.tar
```

2. Build the Apache server: If you are installing somewhere other than `/usr/local`, this is the time to say so with the `--prefix` flag as follows. If you are installing in `/usr/local`, don't worry that the `apache` directory mentioned in a moment doesn't exist — it will by the end of the build process. The `--enable-so` flag will allow Apache to load PHP support (and many other things) as a module called a *Shared Object*. This is how we'll build our PHP module later on. After the configuration finishes, the next two commands will build the binaries and then drop everything in the appropriate place according the target of our `--prefix` flag.

```
cd apache_1.3.x
./configure --prefix=/usr/local/apache --enable-so
make
make install
```

3. Unzip and untar your PHP source distribution. Unless you have a reason to do otherwise, `/usr/local` is the standard place.

```
cd ..
gunzip -c php-5.x.tar.gz
```

```
tar -xvf php-5.x.tar
cd php-5.x
```

4. Configure your PHP build. (Configuring PHP is a topic so large and important that it would not fit into this chapter, so please flip over to Chapter 30 for more information.) The most common are the options to build as an Apache module, which you almost certainly want, and with specific database support. The example build here is an Apache module with MySQL support built using apxs, but your flags may be completely different.

```
./configure
--with-apxs=/usr/local/apache/bin/apxs
--with-mysql=/usr/local/mysql
```

5. Make and install the PHP module.

```
make
make install
```

6. Install the php.ini file. Edit this file to get configuration directives; see the options listed in Chapter 30. At this point, we highly recommend that new users set error reporting to E_ALL on their development machines.

```
cd ../../php-5.x
cp php.ini-dist /usr/local/lib/php.ini
```

7. Tell your Apache server where you want to serve files from, and what extension(s) you want to identify PHP files (.php is the standard, but you can use .html, .phtml, or whatever you want). Go to your HTTP configuration files (/usr/local/apache/conf or whatever your path is), and open httpd.conf with a text editor. Search for the word DocumentRoot (which should appear twice), and change both paths to the directory you want to serve files out of (in our case, /home/httpd). We recommend a home directory rather than the default /usr/local/apache/htdocs because it is more secure, but it doesn't have to be in a home directory. Any reasonably protected location outside of the Apache tree represents an improvement over the default.

Add at least one PHP extension directive, as shown in the first line of code that follows. In the second line, we've also added a second handler to have all HTML files parsed as PHP (which does impose a small performance hit and should not be done if your architecture uses the .html file extension strictly for HTML-only files). This would also be a good time for you to ensure that Apache knows what domain alias or IP address to listen for. (If you have no idea what this means, search httpd.conf for the word ServerName, add the word localhost right after it, and use that as your domain name until you get a better one.)

```
AddType application/x-httpd-php .php
AddType application/x-httpd-php .html
```

8. Restart your server. Every time you change your HTTP configuration or php.ini files, you must stop and start your server again. An HUP signal will not suffice.

```
cd ../bin
./apachectl start
```

9. Set the document root directory permissions to world-executable. The actual PHP files in the directory need only be world-readable (644). If necessary, replace /home/httpd with your document root below.

```
chmod 755 /home/httpd/html/php
```

10. Open a text editor. Type: <?php phpinfo(); ?>. Save this file in your Web server's document root as info.php. Start any Web browser and browse the file—you must always use an HTTP request (http://www.testdomain.com/info.php or http://localhost/info.php or http://127.0.0.1/info.php) rather than a filename (/home/httpd/info.php) for the file to be parsed correctly. You should see a long table of information about your new PHP5 installation. Congratulations!

Cross-Reference   Many Apache production servers do not use a php.ini file; it can be undesirable to have two different configuration files in two different locations. You can replicate many of the configuration directives of php.ini in your Apache httpd.conf file. At a minimum, you probably want to set the include path and error reporting levels, because the default settings for these are often unsatisfactory. See Chapter 30 for more details.

Mac OS X and Apache

One of the most exciting developments in open source recently has been the partial opening of the Macintosh platform. Most observers view OS X as a super-stylish GUI on top of a full BSD implementation—possibly the combination that will put a Unix machine in every home.

In keeping with this dual nature, Mac users have the choice of either a binary or a source installation. In fact, your OS X probably came with Apache and PHP preinstalled. This is likely to be quite an old build, and it probably lacks many of the less common extensions. However, if all you want is a quick and dirty Apache + PHP + MySQL/PostgreSQL setup on your laptop, this is certainly the easiest way to fly. All you need to do is edit your Apache configuration file and turn on the Web server. So just follow these steps (and again, the code following each step is what you enter to actually perform the step):

1. Open the Apache config file in a text editor as root.

```
sudo open -a TextEdit /etc/httpd/httpd.conf
```

2. Edit the file. Uncomment the following lines:

```
Load Module php5_module
AddModule mod_php5.c
AddType application/x-httpd-php .php
```

3. You may also want to uncomment the <Directory /home/*/Sites> block or otherwise tell Apache which directory to serve out of.

4. Restart the Web server.

```
sudo apachectl graceful
```

5. Now open a text editor. Type <?php phpinfo(); ?>. Save this file in your Sites folder as info.php. Start any Web browser and browse the file—you must always use an HTTP request (http://www.testdomain.com/~username/info.php or http://localhost/~username/info.php or http://127.0.0.1/~username/info.php) rather than a filename (/home/username/info.php) for the file to be parsed correctly.

You should see a long table of information about your new PHP5 installation. Congratulations!

If you find you don't have the PHP module, or if you'd like to upgrade your module to a newer version, you can download it from several locations on the Internet. One such source is Marc Liyanage in Switzerland, whose URL we are using here:

```
http://www2.entropy.ch/download/Entropy-PHP-5.0.0.dmg
```

Double-click the resulting disk image and follow the directions.

Source builds on OS X can be tricky. The directory structure and some of the necessary tools are different, and Apple's own included binaries have been nonstandard. At the moment, compilation from source is not recommended for new PHP users without significant Unix experience. If you want to try it anyway, a good article is available at Stepwise.com: www.stepwise.com/Articles/Workbench/2001-10-11.01.html.

The installation situation on OS X is likely to be in flux for the foreseeable future. Always check the OS X installation page at www.php.net/manual/en/install.macosx.php before installation of a fresh version of PHP.

Windows NT/2000/XP and IIS

The Windows server installation of PHP5 running IIS is much simpler than on Unix, since it involves a precompiled binary rather than a source build.

There are currently two choices of binary for Windows: the Installshield self-installer version and the manual zipfile. The self-installer may seem easier, but it has several limitations: It works only with IIS and Xitami Web servers; it provides only the CGI version rather than the module; it lacks automatic setup of extensions; and it is notably insecure. Any serious PHP installation on Windows will choose the manual installation instead.

To start your installation, follow these steps:

1. Extract the binary archive using your unzip utility; C:\PHP is a common location.

2. Copy some .dll files from your PHP directory to your systems directory (usually C:\Winnt\System32). You need php5ts.dll for every case. You will also probably need to copy the file corresponding to your Web server module—C:\PHP\Sapi\php5isapi.dll. It's possible you will also need others from the dlls subfolder—but start with the two mentioned above and add more if you need them.

3. Copy either php.ini-dist or php.ini-recommended (preferably the latter) to your Windows directory (C:\Winnt or C:\Winnt40), and rename it php.ini. Open this file in a text editor (for example, Notepad). Edit this file to get configuration directives; see the options listed in Chapter 30. We highly recommend new users set error reporting to E_ALL on their development machines at this point. For now, the most important thing is the doc_root directive under the Paths and Directories section—make sure this matches your IIS Inetpub folder (or wherever you plan to serve out of).

4. Stop and restart the WWW service. Go to the Start menu ➪ Settings ➪ Control Panel ➪ Services. Scroll down the list to IIS Admin Service. Select it and click Stop. After it stops (the status message will inform you), select World Wide Web Publishing Service and click Start. Stopping and restarting the service from within Internet Service Manager (by right-clicking the globe icon) will not suffice. Since this is Windows, you may also wish to reboot.

5. Open a text editor (for example, Notepad). Type: `<?php phpinfo(); ?>`. Save this file in your Web server's document root as `info.php`. Start any Web browser and browse the file — you must always use an HTTP request (`http://www.testdomain.com/info.php` or `http://localhost/info.php` or `http://127.0.0.1/info.php`) rather than a filename (`C:\inetpub\wwwroot\info.php`) for the file to be parsed correctly. You should see a long table of information about your new PHP5 installation. Congratulations!

Tip   Some Windows users have reported that they must put their `php.ini` files in the same directory as their `php.exe` executables for the CGI version of PHP. This is not ideal for security reasons. It would be better to keep this file out of the Web tree entirely. Now that PHP offers good modules for many common Windows Web servers, use one of these if you can.

Windows and Apache

PHP 4.0 introduced the long-awaited Windows Apache module. Until then, Apache users on Windows could run only the CGI version of PHP, which was slow and less secure. PHP 4.1 brought significant improvements in performance and stability for this module. The Apache developers are also putting a special effort into rapidly improving their Windows HTTP server. For all these reasons, there is really no better time to try Apache — plus it works great even on those aging 98/Me machines.

Caution   As of PHP 4.3, Windows 95 is no longer supported by PHP. Windows 98 and ME will doubtless be dropped fairly soon also.

To install Apache with PHP on Windows:

1. Download Apache server from `www.apache.org/dist/httpd/binaries/win32`. You want the current stable release version with the `no_src.msi` extension (You can try the `.exe` version if there is one, but it doesn't work on all systems and isn't any easier). Double-click the installer file to install; `C:\Program Files` is a common location. The installer will also ask you whether you want to run Apache as a service (takes more cycles, but it's available from the taskbar) or from the command line or DOS prompt. We recommend you do not install as a service, as this may cause problems with startup and shutdown on some computers.

2. Extract the PHP binary archive using your unzip utility; `C:\PHP` is a common location.

3. Copy some `.dll` files from your PHP directory to your system directory (usually `C:\Windows`). You need `php5ts.dll` for every case. You will also probably need to copy the file corresponding to your Web server module — `C:\PHP\Sapi\php5apache.dll` — to your Apache modules directory. It's possible that you will also need others from the `dlls` subfolder — but start with the two mentioned previously and add more if you need them.

4. Copy either `php.ini-dist` or `php.ini-recommended` (preferably the latter) to your Windows directory, and rename it `php.ini`. Open this file in a text editor (for example, Notepad). Edit this file to get configuration directives; see the options listed in Chapter 30. At this point, we highly recommend that new users set error reporting to `E_ALL` on their development machines.

5. Tell your Apache server where you want to serve files from and what extension(s) you want to identify PHP files (`.php` is the standard, but you can use `.html`, `.phtml`, or whatever you want). Go to your HTTP configuration files (`C:\Program Files\Apache Group\Apache\conf` or whatever your path is), and open `httpd.conf` with a text editor. Search for the word `DocumentRoot` (which should appear twice) and change both paths to the directory you want to serve files out of. (The default is `C:\Program Files\Apache Group\Apache\htdocs`.) Add at least one PHP extension directive as shown in the first line of the following code:

```
LoadModule php5_module modules/php5apache.dll
AddType application/x-httpd-php .php .phtml
```

6. You may also need to add the following line:

```
AddModule mod_php5.c
```

7. This would also be a good time for you to ensure that Apache knows what domain alias or IP address to listen for. (If you have no idea what this means, search `httpd.conf` for the word `ServerName`, add the word `localhost` right after it, and use that as your domain name until you get a better one.)

8. Stop and restart the WWW service. Go to the Start menu ➪ Programs ➪ Apache HTTP Server ➪ Control Apache HTTP Server ➪ Stop/Start; or run Apache from the MS-DOS prompt.

9. Open a text editor (for example, Notepad). Type: `<?php phpinfo(); ?>`. Save this file in your Web server's document root as `info.php`. Start any Web browser and browse the file — you must always use an HTTP request (`www.testdomain.com/info.php` or `http://localhost/info.php` or `http://127.0.0.1/info.php`) rather than a filename (`C:\Program Files\Apache Group\Apache\htdocs\info.php`) for the file to be parsed correctly. You should see a long table of information about your new PHP5 installation. Congratulations!

Cross-Reference
If you follow these directions and don't get the results you expected, don't panic! Check out Chapter 11 for common gotchas and quirks. If that doesn't help, check out the comments on the relevant pages in the PHP online manual — users leave specific tips for specific setups they've had problems with.

Other Web servers

PHP has been successfully built and run with many other Web servers, such as Netscape Enterprise Server, Xitami, Zeus, and thttpd. Module support for AOLServer, NSAPI, and fhttpd is available. See the relevant pages on the PHP online manual's installation section.

Development tools

When it comes to development tools, PHP used to fall between the cracks — between tools originally designed for other programming languages and those mainly used to create pretty HTML. It's certainly possible to write a complex 2000-line program that touches several other services and filesystems and outputs the string 1 to the browser on completion. On the other hand, there are many people whose main use of PHP is to slap common headers and footers on what amounts to a bunch of static HTML pages. With such a diversity of usages, it's perhaps not so amazing that the perfect PHP development environment — user-friendly enough for the designers, but light and powerful enough for the geeks — has been elusive.

Those coming to PHP from a strictly client-side perspective probably have the hardest adjustment to make. There's no such thing as a plush development environment with wizards and drag-and-drop icons and built-in graphics manipulation. If that sort of thing is important to you, you can use a WYSIWYG editor to format the page and then add PHP functionality later using a text editor. The downside of this strategy is, of course, that machine-written code is often not very human-readable — but one must suffer to be pretty.

The last year and a half, however, has seen substantial change in the market. Plenty of editors for both Windows and Linux now offer at least syntax highlighting for PHP. Several of these can map drive locations to server names so you can debug in place. Even the WYSIWYG Dreamweaver now claims some degree of PHP support. It still can't write the code for you, and you probably wouldn't want that if it could — but it won't change your code either.

Caution   Be particularly careful with using Microsoft FrontPage as a PHP editor, as it seems to cause problems for many users. At a minimum, you will need to enable (by choosing the option in your `php.ini` file) and use ASP-style tags; or use JavaScript-style `<SCRIPT>` tags consistently, which can be a pain.

Old-school programmers will have less of a learning curve, since they can treat PHP like any other server-side programming language that may or may not happen to output HTML to a browser. Most PHP users in this category seem to prefer simple text editors. Generally, these products will afford you a modest amount of help, such as syntax highlighting, brace matching, or tag closing — most of which is about helping you avoid stupid mistakes rather than actually writing the script for you.

The most exciting development in PHP tools to date has been the release of Zend Studio, which is in 3.0 release as of this writing. This product combines a powerful debugger with an attractive (although still non-WYSIWYG) editing environment. The intelligent product design will clearly help you save time on repetitive tasks such as looking up the exact syntax of PHP functions and zeroing in on bugs faster — and since developer time is money, the modest cost of the product should be quickly recouped in increased productivity. You can really tell that the makers of this IDE know PHP inside and out — Zend Studio is the first development tool for PHP that isn't obviously repurposed from some other use. Figure 3-1 is a screenshot of the main Zend Studio console.

As you can see from Figure 3-1, Zend Studio gives you the ability to "run" a PHP script and view the HTML output in the window on the right — instead of having to View Source on a browser, which can be frustrating due to nonstandard results and funky viewers. The debugging functions give you plenty of power — you can step through a script line by line or step into and out of functions, set breakpoints, perform a stacktrace, track all the global and local variables used by a page or watch a particular variable — in an easy-to-use GUI, as well as alerting you to problematic issues such as undeclared variables. Syntax highlighting and code indentation are lovely and easily customizable — these are notoriously difficult for new users to handle in `emacs` or `vi` — and code completion can save you many, many lookups in the PHP online manual ("Is it `strreplace` or `str_replace`, and what order do the arguments come in?"). You can also get autocomplete help with your HTML, especially handy for remembering the allowable attributes of each tag. You can even register your own user-defined functions on the code completion list, making them easy to use without having to constantly refer to the definition — a godsend if you love to pass tons of variables into your functions. The bigger and more complex and more heavily functionalized your codebase is, the more an IDE like this can help you.

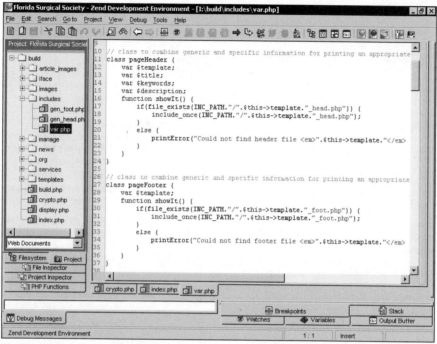

Figure 3-1: Screenshot of Zend Studio IDE

Remember that your development client doesn't necessarily have to be on the same operating system as the server—this is the beauty of truly cross-platform development. This is particularly valuable if you're using a Unix server, where (to paraphrase *The Blues Brothers*) "We have both kinds of editor: emacs and vi." It must be admitted that Macintosh and Windows have a wider selection of slicker, more user-friendly text editors. Unix, on the other hand, makes it easy to support multiple client OSes. Many development shops take advantage of this "best of all worlds" situation. emacs, vi, and Zend Studio are editors that come in all the major client platforms—so if your team standardizes on one of those, you will be able to accommodate all client OS preferences.

Table 3-2 shows a matrix of the most popular programmer's editors, with information on the different operating systems they run on.

Caution

If you're going to have developers using multiple OSes, remember that linebreaks and some other characters are incompatible between Windows and Unix. Unix-style linebreaks show up as black boxes in Notepad, while Windows linebreaks look like ^M in Unix text editors. Your PHP scripts will probably still work fine (although in some version control situations it can break code), but you'll drive each other crazy if you have to edit each other's code. The best way to deal with the incompatible linebreaks issue, and a heck of a good idea for a lot of other reasons, is to use a version control system such as CVS and set it to strip linebreaks.

In addition to these popular choices, Keith Edmunds maintains a longer list of PHP-suitable text editors, many available at no or low cost from `http://phpeditors.linuxbackup.co.uk/`.

Take a deep breath—after all that installing and configuring, you should now be ready to write your first PHP script, which you'll do in Chapter 4.

Table 3-2: Popular PHP Editors by Platform

Platform	Product	Description
Macintosh	BBEdit (`www.barebones.com`)	Many Mac developers can't imagine life without it. Integrated in the Mac version of WYSIWYG package Macromedia Dreamweaver. A no-cost version, BBEdit Lite, is also available.
Unix Windows Macintosh	emacs (`www.gnu.org/software/emacs`) xemacs (`www.xemacs.org`)	Not for the faint of heart. Good PHP syntax highlighting is finally available at `http://sourceforge.net/projects/php-mode/`. Available on every OS imaginable.
Unix Windows Macintosh	vim (`www.vim.org`)	An improved variant of `vi`, now standard on many Unices. This is the kinder, gentler Unix hacker's editor, with a notably friendly community. It was the first major editor to have PHP syntax highlighting. Available on almost every OS.
Linux Windows Macintosh	Zend Studio (`www.zend.com`)	The first development tool specifically designed for PHP. debugger, code completion, and HTML output viewer.
Windows	HomeSite (`www.macromedia.com/software/homesite/`)	Perennially popular Windows commercial text editor. Integrated with the Windows version of WYSIWYG package Macromedia Dreamweaver.
Windows	Notepad (included with all Windows systems)	Believe it or not, many people build fine sites using this crudest of tools.

Summary

Before you can use PHP, you need to decide whether you will self-host, outsource, or adopt a compromise solution, such as colocation. Some important factors in the decision are cost, size and traffic of site, unusual hardware or software needs, type of content, and desire for control. The best candidates for external Web hosting are small sites without unusual requirements or sites large enough to require at least one entire server to themselves.

If you decide to self-host or maintain a development environment, detailed installation instructions are provided in previous sections of this chapter for the most common platforms. PHP5 has SAPI support for many other Web servers, but installation directions for all of them would have made this chapter unreasonably lengthy.

Finally, before you can start developing, you will want to give some thought to which development tools are best adapted to PHP. Although the long-awaited PHP-specific IDE is now available from Zend, most PHP developers still simply use their favorite text editors. It is possible to add PHP to the product of a WYSIWYG editor, but it can be messy.

✦　　✦　　✦

Adding PHP to HTML

After all those preliminary exertions, we finally get to the point of writing our first PHP scripts. Here you'll learn about PHP mode, PHP tags, and how to include other files in your PHP scripts. You'll also write your very first PHP program.

Your HTML Is Already PHP-Compliant!

PHP is already perfectly at home with HTML — in fact, it is generally embedded within HTML. As you'll see in later chapters, PHP rides piggyback on some of the cleverer parts of the HTML standard, such as forms and cookies, to do all kinds of useful things.

Anything compatible with HTML on the client side is also compatible with PHP. PHP could not care less about chunks of JavaScript, calls to music and animation, applets, or anything else on the client side. PHP will simply ignore those parts, and the Web server will happily pass them on to the client.

It should thus be clear that you can use any method of developing Web pages and simply add PHP to that method. If you're comfortable having teams work on each page using huge multimedia graphics suites, you can keep on doing that. The general point is that you don't need to change tools or workflow order — just do what you've been doing and add the server-side functionality at the end.

Escaping from HTML

By now you're probably wondering: How does the PHP parser recognize PHP code inside your HTML document? The answer is that you tell the program when to spring into action by using special PHP tags at the beginning and end of each PHP section. This process is called *escaping from HTML* or *escaping into PHP*.

Caution — Not to confuse you, but *escape* in this sense should not be confused with another common use of the term *escape* in PHP: putting a backslash in front of certain special characters (such as tab and newline) within double-quoted strings. Escaping strings is explained in Chapter 8.

Everything within these tags is understood by the PHP parser to be PHP code. Everything outside of these tags does not concern the server and will simply be passed along and left for the client to sort out whether it's HTML or JavaScript or something else.

There are four styles of PHP tags and different rationales for using them. Part of the decision, however, is simply individual preference: what the individual programmer is comfortable with or what a team has decided upon for reasons of their own.

Canonical PHP tags

The most universally effective PHP tag style is:

```
<?php   ?>
```

If you use this style, you can be positive that your tags will always be correctly interpreted. Unless you have a very, very strong reason to prefer one of the other styles, use this one. Some or all of the other styles of PHP tag may be phased out in the future—only this one is certain to be safe.

Short-open (SGML-style) tags

Short or short-open tags look like this:

```
<?   ?>
```

Short tags are, as one might expect, the shortest option. Those who escape into and out of HTML frequently in each script will be attracted by the prospect of fewer keystrokes; however, the price of shorter tags is pretty high. You must do one of two things to enable PHP to recognize the tags:

✦ Choose the `--enable-short-tags` configuration option when you're building PHP.

✦ Set the `short_open_tag` setting in your `php.ini` file to `on`. This option must be disabled to parse XML with PHP because the same syntax is used for XML tags.

Caution   There used to be a third way to enable short-open tags: the `short_open()` function. This ceased to be supported as of PHP4.

There are several reasons to resist the temptation of the short-open tag. The most compelling reason now is that this syntax is not compatible with XML—and since XHTML is a type of XML, this implies that none of your code will be able to validate as XHTML. PHP code written with short-open tags is less portable because you can't be sure another machine will have enabled them. Short-open tags are also harder to pick out visually on the page, and many syntax-highlighting schemes don't support them. Beginners should be encouraged to start off with the canonical style tag if at all possible.

The short-open tag was one of many hacky ease-of-use ideas that ended up biting the PHP community years later. The PHP development team must now struggle to balance desires for a more standard and consistent syntax with a large installed userbase, which has written a huge pile of code in the old style. As XML becomes more and more central to Web development, and as we move toward XHTML as the standard for Web page development, the short-open tag faces a shaky future. Do yourself a favor and start moving toward the canonical PHP tags now.

Tip If you've made the virtuous decision to eschew the short-open tag, remember to disable it in your `php.ini` file. You want to see an error message when you inadvertently forget to complete your tag correctly.

ASP-style tags

ASP-style tags mimic the tags used by Microsoft Active Server Pages to delineate code blocks. ASP-style tags look like this:

```
<%    %>
```

People who use FrontPage as a development tool often choose this style. To use ASP-style tags, you will need to set the configuration option in your `php.ini` file. Obviously, if you use ASP-style tags and the `.asp` suffix (which you may wish to do if you're converting from an ASP site or spoofing ASP for some reason), you will need to disable ASP on your IIS server. Otherwise, two different scripting engines will be trying to parse the same blocks of code with unpredictable results.

HTML script tags

HTML script tags look like this:

```
<SCRIPT LANGUAGE="PHP">   </SCRIPT>
```

Although this is effective and also gets around the FrontPage problems, it can be cumbersome in certain situations, such as quick pop-in variable replacement. In particular, be careful if you use lots of JavaScript on your site since the close-script tags are fatally ambiguous. The HTML script tag is best used for fairly sizable blocks of PHP code.

Hello World

Now we're ready to write our first PHP program. Open a new file in your preferred editor. Type:

```
<HTML>
<HEAD>
<TITLE>My first PHP program</TITLE>
</HEAD>

<BODY>
<?php
print("Hello, cruel world<BR><BR>\n");
phpinfo();
?>
</BODY>
</HTML>
```

In most browsers, nothing but the PHP section is strictly necessary. However, it's a good idea to get in the habit of always using a well-formed HTML structure in which to embed your PHP.

If you don't see something pretty close to the output shown in Figure 4-1, you have a problem—most likely some kind of installation or configuration glitch. Review Chapter 3, and make doubly sure your installation succeeded.

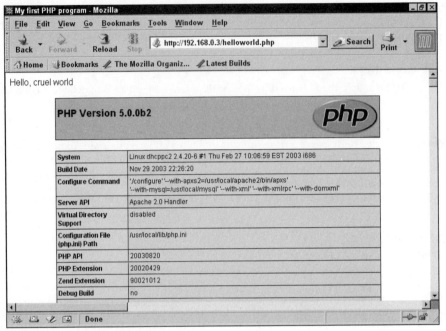

Figure 4-1: Your first PHP script

Refer to Chapter 3 for installation instructions, and forward to Chapter 30 for configuration options. Chapter 11 diagnoses some common early problems and gives debugging hints.

Jumping in and out of PHP mode

At any given moment in a PHP script, you are either in PHP mode or you're out of it in HTML. There's no middle ground. Anything within the PHP tags is PHP; everything outside is plain HTML, as far as the server is concerned.

You can escape into PHP mode with giddy abandon, as often and as briefly or lengthily as necessary. For example:

```
<?php $id = 1; ?>
<FORM METHOD="POST" ACTION="registration.php"">
<P>First name:
<INPUT TYPE="TEXT" NAME="firstname" SIZE="20">
<P>Last name:
<INPUT TYPE="TEXT" NAME="lastname" SIZE="20">
<P>Rank:
<INPUT TYPE="TEXT" NAME="rank" SIZE="10">
<INPUT TYPE="HIDDEN" NAME="serial number" VALUE="<?php
echo $id; ?>">
<INPUT TYPE="submit"SUBMIT" VALUE="INPUT"">
</FORM>
```

Notice that things that happened in the first PHP mode instance — in this case, a variable being assigned — are still valid in the second. In Chapter 5, you'll learn more about what happens to variables when you skip in and out of PHP mode. In Chapter 33, you'll also learn about different styles of using PHP mode.

Including files

Another way you can add PHP to your HTML is by putting it in a separate file and calling it by using PHP's `include` functions. There are four `include` functions:

- ✦ `include('/filepath/filename')`
- ✦ `require('/filepath/filename')`
- ✦ `include_once('/filepath/filename')`
- ✦ `require_once('/filepath/filename')`

In previous versions of PHP, there were significant differences in functionality and speed between the `include` functions and the `require` functions. This is no longer true; the two sets of functions differ only in the kind of error they throw on failure. `Include()` and `include_once()` will merely generate a warning on failure, while `require()` and `require_once()` will cause a fatal error and termination of the script.

As suggested by the names of the functions, `include_once()` and `require_once()` differ from simple `include()` and `require()` in that they will allow a file to be included only once per PHP script. This is extremely helpful when you are including files that contain PHP functions, because redeclaring functions results in an automatic fatal error. In larger PHP systems, it's quite common to include files which include other files which include other files — it can be difficult to remember whether you've included a particular function before, but with `include_once()` or `require_once()` you don't have to.

How do you decide on a preferred `include` function? In essence, you must decide whether you want to force yourself to write good code on pain of fatal error or whether you want it to run regardless of certain common errors on your part. The strictest alternative is `require()`, which will bring everything grinding to a halt if your code isn't perfect; the least strict is `include_once()`, which will good-naturedly hide the consequences of some of your bad coding habits.

The most common use of PHP's `include` capability is to add common headers and footers to all the Web pages on a site. For example, a simple header file (cleverly named `header.inc`) might look like this:

```
<HTML>
<HEAD>
<TITLE>A site title</TITLE>
</HEAD>

<BODY>
```

Similarly, a footer file called `footer.inc` might consist of:

```
<P>Copyright 1995 - 2002</P>
</BODY>
</HTML>
```

They are called from a PHP page this way:

```
<?php
require_once($_SERVER['DOCUMENT_ROOT'].'/header.inc');
?>
<P>This is some body text for this particular page.</P>
<?php
require_once($_SERVER['DOCUMENT_ROOT'].'/footer.inc');
?>
```

Obviously, this single move greatly enhances the maintainability and scalability of an entire site. Now, if you want a different look and feel or if you need to update the copyright notice, you can alter one file instead of identical lines in dozens of HTML pages.

Tip   When including files, remember to set the `include_path` directive correctly in your `php.ini` file. Remember that you can include files from above or entirely outside your Web tree by proper use of this directive. See Chapter 30 for more information.

As you can see from the preceding example, PHP's `include` functions simply pass along the contents of the included file *as text*. Many people think that because an `include` function occurs inside PHP mode, the included file will also be in PHP mode. This is not true! Actually, the server escapes back into HTML mode at the beginning of each included file and silently returns to PHP mode at the end, just in time to catch the semicolon.

As always, you need to say when you intend something to be PHP by using PHP opening and closing tags. Any part of an included file that needs to be executed as PHP should be enclosed in valid PHP tags. If the entire file is PHP (very common in files of functions), the entire file must be enclosed within PHP tags.

Take the following file, `database.inc`:

```
$db = mysql_connect('localhost', 'db_user', 'db_password');
mysql_select_db('my_database');
```

Caution   We can't emphasize this enough: If you're having problems including PHP files, particularly if you're seeing output you don't expect or not seeing output you do expect, be *ABSOLUTELY POSITIVE* that you've put PHP tags at the beginning and end of the included file.

If you were to foolishly include this file from a PHP script, your database variables would be visible to the world in plain text — because you neglected to use PHP tags, the parser assumes this block of code is HTML. A correct version of the `database.inc` file would look like this:

```
<?php
$db = mysql_connect('localhost', 'db_user', 'db_password');
mysql_select_db('my_database');
?>
```

Caution   For all PHP files included from other files, you must ensure that there are no empty new lines at the end of the file. Remember, anything outside a PHP block is considered HTML, even a blank line. Blank lines, or even blank spaces outside a closing PHP tag, will be interpreted as output. If you include the file in a situation where you cannot have output — say before using HTTP headers — your script will fail with a big error message about the output stream having already been started in your included file. See Chapter 11 for an example.

Summary

PHP is easy to embed in HTML. You can use whatever HTML-production method you're already comfortable with and simply add the PHP sections later. PHP additions can range from simply echoing a single-digit integer to writing long chunks of code.

Every PHP block, short or long, is set off by PHP tags. There are several styles of PHP tags, but everyone should be encouraged to use the canonical style. You can also include PHP in files by using the `include` functions — but remember that the contents of the included files will not be recognized as PHP unless surrounded by PHP tags.

✦ ✦ ✦

Syntax and Variables

In this chapter, we cover the basic syntax of PHP — the rules that all well-formed PHP code must follow. We explain how to use variables to store and retrieve information as your PHP code executes and the type system that governs what kinds of values can be stored in the first place. Finally, we look at the simplest ways to display text that will show up in your user's browser window.

PHP Is Forgiving

The first and most important thing to say about the PHP language is that it tries to be as forgiving as possible. Programming languages vary quite a bit in terms of how stringently syntax is enforced. Pickiness can be a *good* thing because it helps make sure that the code you're writing is really what you mean. If you are writing a program to control a nuclear reactor and you forget to assign a variable, it is far better to have the program be rejected than to create behavior different from what you intended. PHP's design philosophy, however, is at the other end of the spectrum. Because PHP started life as a handy utility for making quick-and-dirty Web pages, it emphasizes convenience for the programmer over correctness; rather than have a programmer do the extra work of redundantly specifying what is meant by a piece of code, PHP requires the minimum and then tries its best to figure out what was meant. Among other things, this means that certain syntactical features that show up in other languages, such as variable declarations and function prototypes, are simply not necessary.

With that said, though, PHP can't read your mind; it has a minimum set of syntactical rules that your code must follow. Whenever you see the words `parse error` in your browser window instead of the cool Web page you thought you had just written, it means that you've broken these rules to the point that PHP has given up on your page.

HTML Is Not PHP

The second most important thing to understand about PHP syntax is that it applies only within PHP. Because PHP is embedded in HTML documents, every part of such a document is interpreted as either PHP or HTML, depending on whether that section of the document is enclosed in PHP tags.

PHP syntax is relevant only within PHP, so we assume for the rest of this chapter that PHP mode is in force—that is, most code fragments will be assumed to be embedded in an HTML page and surrounded with the appropriate tags.

PHP's Syntax Is C-Like

The third most important thing to know about PHP syntax is that, broadly speaking, it is like the C programming language. If you happen to be one of the lucky people who already know C, this is very helpful; if you are uncertain about how a statement should be written, try it first the way you would do it in C, and if that doesn't work, look it up in the manual. The rest of this section is for the other people, the ones who don't already know C. (C programmers might want to skim the headers of this section and also see Appendix A, which is specifically for C programmers.)

PHP is whitespace insensitive

Whitespace is the stuff you type that is typically invisible on the screen, including spaces, tabs, and carriage returns (end-of-line characters). PHP's whitespace insensitivity does not mean that spaces and such never matter. (In fact, they are crucial for separating the *words* in the PHP language.) Instead, it means that it almost never matters *how many* whitespace characters you have in a row—one whitespace character is the same as many such characters.

For example, each of the following PHP statements that assigns the sum of 2 + 2 to the variable $four is equivalent:

```
$four = 2 + 2;      // single spaces
$four <tab>=<tab>2<tab>+<tab>2  ;    // spaces and tabs
$four           =
2
+
2;  // multiple lines
```

The fact that end-of-line characters count as whitespace is handy, because it means you never have to strain to make sure that a statement fits on a single line.

PHP is sometimes case sensitive

Having read that PHP isn't picky, you may be surprised to learn that it is sometimes case sensitive (that is, it cares about the distinction between lowercase and capital letters). In particular, all variables are case sensitive. If you embed the following code in an HTML page:

```
<?php
  $capital = 67;
  print("Variable capital is $capital<BR>");
  print("Variable CaPiTaL is $CaPiTaL<BR>");
?>
```

The output you will see is:

```
Variable capital is 67
Variable CaPiTaL is
```

The different capitalization schemes make for different variables. (Surprisingly, under the default settings for error reporting, code like this fragment will not produce a PHP error — see the section "Unassigned variables," later in this chapter.)

On the other hand, unlike in C, function names are *not* case sensitive, and neither are the basic language constructs (if, then, else, while, and the like).

Statements are expressions terminated by semicolons

A *statement* in PHP is any *expression* that is followed by a semicolon (;). If expressions correspond to phrases, statements correspond to entire sentences, and the semicolon is the full stop at the end. Any sequence of valid PHP statements that is enclosed by the PHP tags is a valid PHP program. Here is a typical statement in PHP, which in this case assigns a string of characters to a variable called $greeting:

```
$greeting = "Welcome to PHP!";
```

The rest of this subsection is about how such statements are built from smaller components and how the PHP interpreter handles the evaluation of statements. (If you already feel comfortable with statements and expressions, feel free to skip ahead.)

Expressions are combinations of tokens

The smallest building blocks of PHP are the *indivisible tokens*, such as numbers (3.14159), strings ("two"), variables ($two), constants (TRUE), and the special words that make up the syntax of PHP itself (if, else, and so forth). These are separated from each other by whitespace and by other special characters such as parentheses and braces.

The next most complex building block in PHP is the *expression*, which is any combination of tokens that has a value. A single number is an expression, as is a single variable. Simple expressions can also be combined to make more complicated expressions, usually either by putting an *operator* in between (for example, 2 + (2 + 2)), or by using them as input to a function call (for example, pow(2 * 3, 3 * 2)). Operators that take two inputs go in between their inputs, whereas functions take their inputs in parentheses immediately after their names, with the inputs (known as *arguments*) separated by commas.

Expressions are evaluated

Whenever the PHP interpreter encounters an expression in code, that expression is immediately *evaluated*. This means that PHP calculates values for the smallest elements of the expression and successively combines those values connected by operators or functions, until it has produced an entire value for the expression. For example, successive steps in an imaginary evaluation process might look like:

```
$result = 2 * 2 + 3 * 3 + 5;
        (= 4 + 3 * 3 + 5)   //imaginary evaluation steps
        (= 4 + 9 + 5)
        (= 13 + 5)
        (= 18)
```

with the result that the number 18 is stored in the variable $result.

Precedence, associativity, and evaluation order

There are two kinds of freedom PHP has in expression evaluation: how it groups or associates subexpressions and the order in which it evaluates them. For example, in the evaluation process just shown, multiplications were associated more tightly than additions, which affects the end result.

The particular ways that operators group expressions are called *precedence rules* — operators that have higher precedence win in grabbing the expressions around them. If you want, you can memorize the rules, such as the fact that * always has higher precedence than +. Or you can just use the following cardinal rule: When in doubt, use parentheses to group expressions.

For example:

```
$result1 = 2 + 3 * 4 + 5; // is equal to 19
$result2 = (2 + 3) * (4 + 5); // is equal to 45
```

Operator precedence rules remove much of the ambiguity about how subexpressions are associated. But what about when two operators have the same precedence? Consider this expression:

```
$how_much = 3.0 / 4.0 / 5.0;
```

Whether this is equal to 0.15 or 3.75 depends on which division operator gets to grab the number 4.0 first. There is an exhaustive list of rules of associativity in the online manual, but the rule to remember is that associativity is usually left-before-right — that is, the preceding expression would evaluate to 0.15, because the leftmost of the two division operators wins the dispute over precedence.

The final wrinkle is order of evaluation, which is not quite the same thing as associativity. For example, look at the arithmetic expression:

```
3 * 4 + 5 * 6
```

We know that the multiplications will happen before the additions, but that is not the same as knowing which multiplication PHP will perform first. In general, you need not worry about evaluation order, because in almost all cases it will not affect the result. You can construct weird examples where the result does depend on order of evaluation, usually by making assignments in subexpressions that are used in other parts of the expression. For example:

```
$huh = ($this = $that + 5) + ($that = $this + 3);   // BAD
```

But don't do this, okay? PHP may or may not have a predictable order of evaluation of expressions, but you shouldn't depend on it — so we're not going to tell you! (The one legitimate use of relying on left-to-right evaluation order is in short-circuiting Boolean expressions, which we cover in Chapter 6.)

Expressions and types

Usually, the programmer is careful to match the types of expressions with the operators and functions that combine them. Common expressions are *mathematical* (with mathematical operators combining numbers) or *Boolean* (combining true-or-false statements with *and*s and *or*s) or *string expressions* (with operators and functions constructing strings of characters). As with the rest of PHP, however, the treatment of types is surprisingly forgiving. Consider the following expression, which deliberately mixes the types of subexpressions in an inappropriate way:

```
2 + 2 * "nonsense" + TRUE
```

Rather than produce an error, this evaluates to the number 3. (You can take this as a puzzle for now, but we will explain how such a thing can happen in the "Types in PHP" section of this chapter.)

Assignment expressions

A very common kind of expression is the *assignment*, where a variable is set to equal the result of evaluating some expression. These have the form of a variable name (which always starts with a $), followed by a single equal sign, followed by the expression to be evaluated. For example:

```
$eight = 2 * (2 * 2)
```

assigns the variable $eight the value you would expect.

An important thing to remember is that even assignment expressions are expressions and so have values themselves! The value of an expression that assigns a variable is the same as the value assigned. This means that you can use assignment expressions in the middle of more complicated expressions. If you evaluate the statement:

```
$ten = ($two = 2) + ($eight = 2 * (2 * 2))
```

each variable would be assigned a numerical value equal to its name.

Reasons for expressions and statements

There are usually only two reasons to write an expression in PHP: for its *value* or for a *side effect*. The value of an expression is passed on to any more complicated expression that includes it; side effects are anything else that happens as a result of the evaluation. The most typical side effects involve assigning or changing a variable, printing something to the user's screen, or making some other persistent change to the program's environment (such as interacting with a database).

Although statements are expressions, they are not themselves included in more complicated expressions. This means that the only good reason for a statement is a side effect! It also means that it is possible to write legal (yet totally useless statements) such as the second of these:

```
print("Hello");  // side effect is printing to screen

2 * 3 + 4;  // useless - no side effect

$value_num = 3 * 4 + 5;  // side effect is assignment

store_in_database(49.5);  // side effect to DB
```

Braces make blocks

Although statements cannot be combined like expressions, you can always put a sequence of statements anywhere a statement can go by enclosing them in a set of curly braces.

For example, the if construct in PHP has a test (in parentheses) followed by the statement that should be executed if the test is true. If you want more than one statement to be executed when the test is true, you can use a brace-enclosed sequence instead. The following pieces of code (which simply print a reassuring statement that it is still true that 1 + 2 is equal to 3) are equivalent:

```
if (3 == 2 + 1)
   print("Good - I haven't totally lost my mind.<BR>");

if (3 == 2 + 1)
   {
      print("Good - I haven't totally ");
      print("lost my mind.<BR>");
   }
```

You can put any kind of statement in a brace-enclosed block, including, say, an `if` statement that itself has a brace-enclosed block. This means that `if` statements can have other `if` statements inside them. In fact, this kind of nesting can be done to an arbitrary number of levels.

Comments

A *comment* is the portion of a program that exists only for the human reader. The very first thing that a program executor does with program code is to strip out the comments, so they cannot have any effect on what the program does. Comments are invaluable in helping the next person who reads your code figure out what you were thinking when you wrote it, even when that person is yourself a week from now.

PHP drew its inspiration from several different programming languages, most notably C, Perl, and Unix shell scripts. As a result, PHP supports styles of comments from all those languages, and those styles can be intermixed freely in PHP code.

C-style multiline comments

The *multiline* style of commenting is the same as in C: A comment starts with the character pair `/*` and terminates with the character pair `*/`. For example:

```
/*  This is
    a comment in
    PHP */
```

The most important thing to remember about multiline comments is that they cannot be nested. You cannot put one comment inside another. If you try, the comment will be closed off by the first instance of the `*/` character pair, and the rest of what was intended to be an enclosing comment will instead be interpreted as code, probably failing horribly. For example:

```
/* This comment will /* fail horribly on the
    last word of this */ sentence
*/
```

This is an easy thing to do unintentionally, usually when you try to deactivate a block of commented code by "commenting it out."

Single-line comments: # and //

In addition to the `/* ... */` multiple-line comments, PHP supports two different ways of commenting to the end of a given line: one inherited from C++ and Java and the other from Perl and shell scripts. The shell-script-style comment starts with a pound sign, whereas the C++ style comment starts with two forward slashes. Both of them cause the rest of the current line to be treated as a comment, as in the following:

```
#  This is a comment, and
 #  this is the second line of the comment
 // This is a comment too.  Each style comments only
 // one line so the last word of this sentence will fail
horribly.
```

The very alert reader might argue that single-line comments are incompatible with what we said earlier about whitespace insensitivity. That would be correct — you will get a very different result if you take a single-line comment and replace one of the spaces with an end-of-line character. A more accurate way of putting it is that, after the comments have been stripped out of the code, PHP code is whitespace insensitive.

Variables

The main way to store information in the middle of a PHP program is by using a variable — a way to name and hang on to any value that you want to use later.

Here are the most important things to know about variables in PHP (more detailed explanations will follow):

✦ All variables in PHP are denoted with a leading dollar sign ($).

✦ The value of a variable is the value of its most recent assignment.

✦ Variables are assigned with the = operator, with the variable on the left-hand side and the expression to be evaluated on the right.

✦ Variables can, but do not need, to be declared before assignment.

✦ Variables have no intrinsic type other than the type of their current value.

✦ Variables used before they are assigned have default values.

PHP variables are Perl-like

All variables in PHP start with a leading $ sign just like scalar variables in the Perl scripting language, and in other ways they have similar behavior (need no type declarations, may be referred to before they are assigned, and so on). (Perl hackers may need to do no more than skim the headings of this section, which is really for the rest of us.)

After the initial $, variable names must be composed of letters (uppercase or lowercase), digits (0–9), and underscore characters (_). Furthermore, the first character after the $ may not be a number.

Declaring variables (or not)

This subheading is here simply because programmers from some other languages might be looking for it — in languages such as C, C++, and Java, the programmer must declare the name and type of any variable before making use of it. However in PHP, because types are associated with values rather than variables, no such declaration is necessary — the first step in using a variable is to assign it a value.

Assigning variables

Variable assignment is simple — just write the variable name, and add a single equal sign (=); then add the expression that you want to assign to that variable:

```
$pi = 3 + 0.14159; // approximately
```

Note that what is assigned is the result of evaluating the expression, not the expression itself. After the preceding statement is evaluated, there is no way to tell that the value of $pi was created by adding two numbers together.

It's conceivable that you will want to actually print the preceding math expression rather than evaluate it. You can force PHP to treat a mathematical variable assignment as a string by quoting the expression:

```
$pi = "3 + 0.14159";
```

Reassigning variables

There is no interesting distinction in PHP between assigning a variable for the first time and changing its value later. This is true even if the assigned values are of different types. For example, the following is perfectly legal:

```
$my_num_var = "This should be a number - hope it's reassigned";
$my_num_var = 5;
```

If the second statement immediately follows the first one, the first statement has essentially no effect.

Unassigned variables

Many programming languages will object if you try to use a variable before it is assigned; others will let you use it, but if you do you may find yourself reading the random contents of some area of memory. In PHP, the default error-reporting setting allows you to use unassigned variables without errors, and PHP ensures that they have reasonable default values.

Cross-Reference

If you would like to be warned about variables that have not been assigned, you should change the error-reporting level to E_ALL (the highest level possible) from the default level of error reporting. You can do this either by including the statement error_reporting(E_ALL); at the top of a script or by changing your php.ini file to set the default level (see Chapters 30 and 31).

Default values

Variables in PHP do not have intrinsic types — a variable does not know in advance whether it will be used to store a number or a string of characters. So how does it know what type of default value to have when it hasn't yet been assigned?

The answer is that, just as with assigned variables, the type of a variable is interpreted depending on the context in which it is used. In a situation where a number is expected, a number will be produced, and this works similarly with character strings. In any context that treats a variable as a number, an unassigned variable will be evaluated as 0; in any context that expects a string value, an unassigned variable will be the empty string (the string that is zero characters long).

Checking assignment with IsSet

Because variables do not have to be assigned before use, in some situations you can actually convey information by selectively setting or not setting a variable! PHP provides a function called IsSet that tests a variable to see whether it has been assigned a value.

As the following code illustrates, an unassigned variable is distinguishable even from a variable that has been given the default value:

```
$set_var = 0; //set_var has a value
             //never_set does not
print("set_var print value: $set_var<BR>");
```

```
print("never_set print value: $never_set<BR>");
if ($set_var == $never_set)
  print("set_var is equal to never_set!<BR>");
if (IsSet($set_var))
  print("set_var is set.<BR>");
else
  print("set_var is not set.<BR>");
if (IsSet($never_set))
  print("never_set is set.<BR>");
else
  print("never_set is not set.");
```

Oddly enough, this code will produce the following output:

```
set_var print value: 0
never_set print value:
set_var is equal to never_set!
set_var is set.
never_set is not set.
```

The variable $never_set has never been assigned, so it produces an empty string when a string is expected (as in the print statement) and a zero value when a number is expected (as in the comparison test that concludes that the two variables are the same). Still, IsSet can tell the difference between $set_var and $never_set.

Assigning a variable is not irrevocable — the function unset() will restore a variable to an unassigned state (for example, unset($set_var); will make $set_var into an unbound variable, regardless of its previous assignments).

Variable scope

Scope is the technical term for the rules about when a name (for, say, a variable or function) has the same meaning in two different places and in what situations two names spelled exactly the same way can actually refer to different things.

Any PHP variable not inside a function has *global* scope and extends throughout a given "thread" of execution. In other words, if you assign a variable near the top of a PHP file, the variable name has the same meaning for the rest of the file; and if it is not reassigned, it will have the same value as the rest of your code executes (except inside the body of functions).

The assignment of a variable will not affect the value of variables with the same name in other PHP files or even in repeated uses of the same file. For example, let's say that you have two files, startup.php and next_thing.php, which are typically visited in that order by a user. Let's also say that near the top of startup.php, you have the line:

```
$username = "Jane Q. User";
```

which is executed only in certain situations. Now, you might hope that, after setting that variable in startup.php, it would also be preset automatically when the user visited next_thing.php, but no such luck. Each time a PHP page executes, it assigns and reassigns variables as it goes, and those variables disappear at the end of a page's production. Assignments of variables in one file do not affect variables of the same name in a different file or even in other requests for the same file.

Obviously, there are many situations in which you would like to hold onto information for longer than it takes to generate a particular Web page. There are a variety of ways you can accomplish this, and the different techniques are a lot of what the rest of this book is about. For example, you can pass information from page to page using GET and POST variables (Chapter 7), store information persistently in a database (all of Part II of this book), associate it with a user's session using PHP's session mechanism (Chapter 24), or store it on a user's hard disk via a cookie (Chapter 24).

Functions and variable scope

Except inside the body of a function, variable scope in PHP is quite simple: Within any given execution of a PHP file, just assign a variable, and its value will be there for you later. We haven't yet covered how to define your own functions, but it's worth a look-ahead note: Variables assigned within a function are *local* to that function, and unless you make a special declaration in a function, that function won't have access to the global variables defined outside the function, even when they are defined in the same file. (We will discuss the scope of variables in functions in depth when we cover function definitions in Chapter 6.)

You can switch modes if you want

One scoping question that we had the first time we saw PHP code was: Does variable scope persist across tags? For example, we have a single file that looks like:

```
<HTML>
<HEAD>
<?php
  $username = "Jane Q. User";
?>
</HEAD>
<BODY>
<?php
  print("$username<BR>");
?>
</BODY>
</HTML>
```

Should we expect our assignment to $username to survive through the second of the two PHP-tagged areas? The answer is yes — variables persist throughout a thread of PHP execution (in other words, through the whole process of producing a Web page in response to a user's request). This is a single manifestation of a general PHP rule, which is that the *only* effect of the tags is to let the PHP engine know whether you want your code to be interpreted as PHP or passed through untouched as HTML. You should feel free to use the tags to switch back and forth between modes whenever it is convenient.

Constants

In addition to variables, which may be reassigned, PHP offers constants, which have a single value throughout their lifetime. Constants do not have a $ before their names, and by convention the names of constants usually are in uppercase letters. Constants can contain only scalar values (numbers and string). Constants have global scope, so they are accessible everywhere in your scripts after they have been defined — even inside functions.

For example, the built-in PHP constant E_ALL represents a number that indicates to the error_reporting() function that all errors and warnings should be reported. A call to error_reporting() might look like this:

```
error_reporting(E_ALL);
```

This is identical to calling `error_reporting()` on the integer value of E_ALL, but is better because the actual value of E_ALL may change from one version of PHP to the next.

It's also possible to create your own constants using the `define()` form, although this is more unusual than referring to built-in constants. The code:

```
define(MY_ANSWER, 42);
```

would cause MY_ANSWER to evaluate to 42 everywhere it appears in your code. There is no way to change this assignment after it has been made, and like variables, constants that are not part of PHP itself do not persist across pages unless they are explicitly passed to a new page. Ultimately, you probably will not need to define constants very often, if ever. When created constants are used, they are generally most usefully defined in an external include file and might be used for such information as a sales-tax rate or perhaps an exchange rate.

Types in PHP: Don't Worry, Be Happy

All programming languages have some kind of type system, which specifies the different kinds of values that can appear in programs. These different types often correspond to different bit-level representations in computer memory, although in many cases programmers are insulated from having to think about (or being able to mess with) representations in terms of bits.

PHP's type system is simple, streamlined, and flexible, and it insulates the programmer from low-level details. PHP makes it easy not to worry too much about typing of variables and values, both because it does not require variables to be typed and because it handles a lot of type conversions for you.

No variable type declarations

As you saw in Chapter 4, the type of a variable does not need to be declared in advance. Instead, the programmer can jump right ahead to assignment and let PHP take care of figuring out the type of the expression assigned:

```
$first_number = 55.5;
$second_number = "Not a number at all";
```

Automatic type conversion

PHP does a good job of automatically converting types when necessary. Like most other modern programming languages, PHP will do the right thing when, for example, doing math with mixed numerical types. The result of the expression

```
$pi = 3 + 0.14159
```

is a floating-point (double) number, with the integer 3 implicitly converted into floating point before the addition is performed.

Types assigned by context

PHP goes further than most languages in performing automatic type conversions. Consider:

```
$sub = substr(12345, 2, 2);
print("sub is $sub<BR>");
```

The substr function is designed to take a string of characters as its first input and return a substring of that string, with the start point and length determined by the next two inputs to the function. Instead of handing the function a character string, however, we gave it the integer 12345. What happens? As it turns out, there is no error, and we get the browser output:

```
sub is 34
```

Because substr expects a character string rather than an integer, PHP converts the number 12345 to the character string '12345', which substr then slices and dices.

Because of this automatic type conversion, it is very difficult to persuade PHP to give a type error — in fact, PHP programmers need to exercise a little care sometimes to make sure that type confusions do not lead to error-free but unintended results.

Type Summary

PHP has a total of eight types: integers, doubles, Booleans, strings, arrays, objects, NULL, and resources.

✦ *Integers* are whole numbers, without a decimal point, like 495.

✦ *Doubles* are floating-point numbers, like 3.14159 or 49.0.

✦ *Booleans* have only two possible values: TRUE and FALSE.

✦ *NULL* is a special type that only has one value: NULL.

✦ *Strings* are sequences of characters, like 'PHP 4.0 supports string operations.'

✦ *Arrays* are named and indexed collections of other values.

✦ *Objects* are instances of programmer-defined classes, which can package up both other kinds of values and functions that are specific to the class.

✦ *Resources* are special variables that hold references to resources external to PHP (such as database connections).

Of these, the first five are *simple types*, and the next two (arrays and objects) are *compound* — the compound types can package up other arbitrary values of arbitrary type, whereas the simple types cannot. We treat only the simple types in this chapter, since arrays (Chapter 9) and objects (Chapter 20) need chapters all to themselves. Finally, the thorniest details of the type system, including discussion of the resource type, are deferred to Chapter 25.

The Simple Types

The simple types in PHP (integers, doubles, Booleans, NULL, and strings) should mostly be familiar to those with programming experience (although we will not assume that experience and will explain them in detail). The only thing likely to surprise C programmers is how few types there are in PHP.

Many programming languages have several different sizes of numerical types, with the larger ones allowing a greater range of values, but also taking up more room in memory. For example, the C language has a short type (for relatively small integers), a long type (for possibly larger integers), and an int type (which might be intermediate, but in practice is sometimes identical either to the short or long type). It also has floating-point types, which vary in their precision. This kind of typing choice made sense in an era when tradeoffs between memory use and functionality were often agonizing. The PHP designers made what we think is a good decision to simplify this by having only two numerical types, corresponding to the largest of the integral and floating-point types in C.

Integers

Integers are the simplest type — they correspond to simple whole numbers, both positive and negative. Integers can be assigned to variables, or they can be used in expressions, like so:

```
$int_var = 12345;
$another_int = -12345 + 12345; // will equal zero
```

Read formats

Integers can actually be read in three formats, which correspond to bases: *decimal* (base 10), *octal* (base 8), and *hexadecimal* (base 16). Decimal format is the default, octal integers are specified with a leading 0, and hexadecimals have a leading 0x. Any of the formats can be preceded by a - sign to make the integer negative. For example:

```
$integer_10 = 1000;
$integer_8 = -01000;
$integer_16 = 0x1000;
print("integer_10: $integer_10<BR>");
print("integer_8: $integer_8<BR>");
print("integer_16: $integer_16<BR>");
```

yields the browser output:

```
integer_10: 1000
integer_8: -512
integer_16: 4096
```

Note that the read format affects only how the integer is converted as it is read — the value stored in $integer_8 does not remember that it was originally written in base 8. Internally, of course, these numbers are represented in binary format; we see them in their base 10 conversion in the preceding output because that is the default for printing and incorporating int variables into strings.

Range

How big (or small) can integers get? Because PHP integers correspond to the C long type, which in turn depends on the word-size of your machine, this is difficult to answer definitively. For most common platforms, however, the largest integer is $2^{31} - 1$ (or 2,147,483,647), and the smallest (most negative) integer is $-(2^{31} - 1)$ (or –2,147,483,647).

As far as we know, there is no PHP constant (like MAXINT in C) that will tell you the largest integer on your implementation. If you really need integers even larger or smaller than the preceding, PHP does have some arbitrary-precision functions — see the BC section of the "Mathematics" chapter (Chapter 27).

Doubles

Doubles are floating-point numbers, such as:

```
$first_double = 123.456;
$second_double = 0.456
$even_double = 2.0;
```

Note that the fact that $even_double is a "round" number does not make it an integer. Integers and doubles are stored in different underlying formats, and the result of:

```
$five = $even_double + 3;
```

is a double, not an integer, even if it prints as 5. In almost all situations, however, you should feel free to mix doubles and integers in mathematical expressions, and let PHP sort out the typing.

By default, doubles print with the minimum number of decimal places needed — for example, the code:

```
$many = 2.2888800;
$many_2 = 2.2111200;
$few = $many + $many_2;
print("$many + $many_2 = $few<BR>");
```

produces the browser output:

```
2.28888 + 2.21112 = 4.5
```

Cross-Reference   If you need finer control of printing, see the printf function in Chapter 8.

Read formats

The typical *read format* for doubles is -X.Y, where the - optionally specifies a negative number, and both X and Y are sequences of digits between 0 and 9. The X part may be omitted if the number is between –1.0 and 1.0, and the Y part can also be omitted. Leading or trailing zeros have no effect. All the following are legal doubles:

```
$small_positive = 0.12345;
$small_negative = -.12345;
$even_double = 2.00000;
$still_double = 2.;
```

In addition, doubles can be specified in scientific notation, by adding the letter e and a desired integral power of 10 to the end of the previous format — for example, 2.2e-3 would correspond to 2.2×10^{-3}. The floating-point part of the number need not be restricted to a range between 1.0 and 10.0. All the following are legal:

```
$small_positive = 5.5e-3;
print("small_positive is $small_positive<BR>");
$large_positive = 2.8e+16;
print("large_positive is $large_positive<BR>");
$small_negative = -2222e-10;
print("small_negative is $small_negative<BR>");
$large_negative = -0.00189e6;
print("large_negative is $large_negative<BR>");
```

The preceding code produces the following browser output:

```
small_positive is 0.0055
large_positive is 2.8E+16
small_negative is -2.222E-07
large_negative is -1890
```

Notice that, just as with octal and hexadecimal integers, the read format is irrelevant once PHP has finished reading in the numbers — the preceding variables retain no memory of whether they were originally specified in scientific notation. In printing the values, PHP is making its own decisions to print the more extreme values in scientific notation, but this has nothing to do with the original read format.

Booleans

Booleans are true-or-false values, which are used in control constructs like the testing portion of an if statement. As we will see in Chapter 6, Boolean truth values can be combined using logical operators to make more complicated Boolean expressions.

Boolean constants

PHP provides a couple of constants especially for use as Booleans: TRUE and FALSE, which can be used like so:

```
if (TRUE)
  print("This will always print<BR>");
else
  print("This will never print<BR>");
```

Interpreting other types as Booleans

Here are the rules for determine the "truth" of any value not already of the Boolean type:

✦ If the value is a number, it is false if exactly equal to zero and true otherwise.

✦ If the value is a string, it is false if the string is empty (has zero characters) *or* is the string "0", and is true otherwise.

✦ Values of type NULL are always false.

✦ If the value is a compound type (an array or an object), it is false if it contains no other values, and it is true otherwise. For an object, *containing a value* means having a member variable that has been assigned a value.

✦ Valid resources are true (although some functions that return resources when they are successful will return FALSE when unsuccessful).

Cross-Reference
For a more complete account of converting values across types, see Chapter 25.

Examples

Each of the following variables has the truth value embedded in its name when it is used in a Boolean context.

```
$true_num = 3 + 0.14159;
$true_str = "Tried and true"
$true_array[49] = "An array element"; // see next section
$false_array = array();
$false_null = NULL;
$false_num = 999 - 999;
$false_str = ""; // a string zero characters long
```

Don't use doubles as Booleans

Note that, although Rule 1 implies that the double 0.0 converts to a false Boolean value, it is dangerous to use floating-point expressions as Boolean expressions, due to possible rounding errors. For example:

```
$floatbool = sqrt(2.0) * sqrt(2.0) - 2.0;
if ($floatbool)
    print("Floating-point Booleans are dangerous!<BR>");
else
    print("It worked ... this time.<BR>");
print("The actual value is $floatbool<BR>");
```

The variable $floatbool is set to the result of subtracting two from the square of the square root of two — the result of this calculation should be equal to zero, which means that $floatbool is false. Instead, the browser output we get is:

```
Floating-point Booleans are dangerous!
The actual value is 4.4408920985006E-16
```

The value of $floatbool is very close to 0.0, but it is nonzero and, therefore, unexpectedly true. Integers are much safer in a Boolean role — as long as their arithmetic happens only with other integers and stays within integral sizes, they should not be subject to rounding errors.

NULL

The world of Booleans may seem small, since the Boolean type has only two possible values. The *NULL type*, however, takes this to the logical extreme: The type NULL has only one possible value, which is the value NULL. To give a variable the NULL value, simply assign it like this:

```
$my_var = NULL;
```

The special constant NULL is capitalized by convention, but actually it is case insensitive; you could just as well have typed:

```
$my_var = null;
```

So what is special about NULL? NULL represents the *lack* of a value. (You can think of it as the *nonvalue* or the *unvalue*.) A variable that has been assigned the value NULL is nearly indistinguishable from a variable that has not been set at all. In particular, a variable that has been assigned NULL has the following properties:

✦ It evaluates to FALSE in a Boolean context.

✦ It returns FALSE when tested with IsSet(). (No other type has this property.)

✦ PHP will not print warnings if you pass the variable to functions and back again, whereas passing a variable that has never been set will sometimes produce warnings.

The NULL value is best used for situations where you want a variable not to have a value, intentionally, and you want to make it clear to both a reader of your code and to PHP that this is what you want. The latter point is particularly relevant when passing variables to functions.

For example, the following pseudocode may print a warning (depending on your error-reporting settings) if the variable $authorization has never been assigned before you pass it to your test_authorization() function.

```
if (test_authorization($authorization)) {
    // code that grants a privilege of some sort
}
```

On the other hand, code like this:

```
$authorization = NULL;
// code that might or might not set $authorization
if (test_authorization($authorization)) {
  // code that grants a privilege of some sort
}
```

does not cause an unbound-variable warning, assuming that you have written test_
authorization() to handle arguments that might be NULL. It also makes clear to a reader
of the code that you intend for the variable to lack a value unless there's a case where it is
assigned.

Strings

Strings are character sequences, as in the following:

```
$string_1 = "This is a string in double quotes.";
$string_2 = 'This is a somewhat longer, singly quoted string';
$string_39 = "This string has thirty-nine characters.";
$string_0 = ""; // a string with zero characters
```

Strings can be enclosed in either single or double quotation marks, with different behavior at
read time. Singly quoted strings are treated almost literally, whereas doubly quoted strings
replace variables with their values as well as specially interpreting certain character
sequences.

Singly quoted strings

Except for a couple of specially interpreted character sequences, singly quoted strings read
in and store their characters literally. The following code:

```
$literally = 'My $variable will not print!\\n';
print($literally);
```

produces the browser output:

```
My $variable will not print!\n
```

Singly quoted strings also respect the general rule that quotes of a different type will not
break a quoted string. This is legal:

```
$singly_quoted = 'This quote mark: " is no big deal';
```

To embed a single quote (such as an apostrophe) in a singly quoted string, escape it with a
backslash, as in the following:

```
$singly_quoted = 'This quote mark\'s no big deal either';
```

Although in most contexts backslashes are interpreted literally in singly quoted strings, you
may also use two backslashes (\\) as an escape sequence for a single (nonescaping) backslash. This is useful when you want a backslash as the final character in a string, as in:

```
$win_path = 'C:\\InetPub\\PHP\\';
print("A Windows-style pathname: $win_path<BR>");
```

which displays as

```
A Windows-style pathname: C:\InetPub\PHP\
```

Note   We could have used single backslashes to produce the first two backslashes in the output, but the escaping is necessary at the end of the string so that the closing quote will *not* be escaped.

These two escape sequences (\\ and \') are the *only* exceptions to the literal-mindedness of singly quoted strings.

Doubly quoted strings

Strings that are delimited by double quotes (as in "this") are preprocessed in both the following two ways by PHP:

✦ Certain character sequences beginning with backslash (\) are replaced with special characters.

✦ Variable names (starting with $) are replaced with string representations of their values.

The escape-sequence replacements are:

✦ \n is replaced by the newline character

✦ \r is replaced by the carriage-return character

✦ \t is replaced by the tab character

✦ \$ is replaced by the dollar sign itself ($)

✦ \" is replaced by a single double-quote (")

✦ \\ is replaced by a single backslash (\)

The first three of these replacements make it easy to visibly include certain whitespace characters in your strings. The \$ sequence lets you include the $ symbol when you want it, without it being interpreted as the start of a variable. The \" sequence is there so that you can include a double-quote symbol without terminating your doubly quoted string. Finally, because the \ character starts all these sequences, you need a way to include that character literally, without it starting an escape sequence — to do this, you preface it with itself.

Just as with singly quoted strings, quotes of the opposite type can be freely included without an escape character:

```
$has_apostrophe = "There's no problem here";
```

Single versus double quotation marks

PHP does some preprocessing of doubly quoted strings (strings with quotes like "this") before constructing the string value itself. For one thing, variables are replaced by their values (as in the preceding example). To see that this replacement is really about the quoted string rather than the print construct, consider the following code:

```
$animal = "antelope"; // first assignment
$saved_string = "The animal is $animal<BR>";
$animal = "zebra"; // reassignment
print("The animal is $animal<BR>"); //first display line
print($saved_string); //second display line
```

What output would you expect here? As it turns out, your browser would display:

```
The animal is zebra
The animal is antelope
```

And the browser displays the preceding output in exactly that order. This is because
"antelope" is spliced into the string $saved_string, before the $animal variable is reassigned. In addition to splicing variable values into doubly quoted strings, PHP also replaces
some special multiple-character *escape sequences* with their single-character values. The
most commonly used is the end-of-line sequence ("\n") — in reading a string like:

```
"The first line \n\n\nThe fourth line"
```

Variable interpolation

Whenever an unescaped $ symbol appears in a doubly quoted string, PHP tries to interpret
what follows as a variable name and splices the current value of that variable into the string.
Exactly what kind of substitution occurs depends on how the variable is set:

✦ If the variable is currently set to a string value, that string is interpolated (or spliced)
   into the doubly quoted string.

✦ If the variable is currently set to a nonstring value, the value is converted to a string,
   and then that string value is interpolated.

✦ If the variable is not currently set, PHP interpolates nothing (or, equivalently, PHP
   splices in the empty string).

An example:

```
$this = "this";
$that = "that";
$the_other = 2.2000000000;
print("$this,$not_set,$that+$the_other<BR>");
```

produces the PHP output

```
this,,that+2.2<BR>
```

which in turn, when seen in a browser, looks like:

```
this,,that+2.2
```

If you find any part of this example puzzling, it is worth working through exactly what PHP
does to parse the string in the print statement. First, notice that the string has four $ signs,
each of which is interpreted as starting a variable name. These variable names terminate at
the first occurrence of a character that is not legal in a variable name. Legal characters are
letters, numbers, and underscores; the *illegal* terminating characters in the preceding print
string are (in order) a comma, another comma, the plus symbol (+), and a left angle bracket
(<). The first two variables are bound to strings ('this' and 'that'), so those strings are
spliced in literally. The next variable ($not_set) has never been assigned, so it is omitted
entirely from the string under construction. Finally, the last variable ($the_other) is discov-
ered to be bound to a double — that value is converted to a string ("2.2"), which is then
spliced into our constructed string.

 Cross-Reference   For more about converting numbers to strings, see the "Assignment and Coercion" section in
Chapter 25.

As we said earlier in this chapter, all this interpretation of doubly quoted strings happens
when the string is *read,* not when it is printed. If we saved the example string in a variable
and printed it out later, it would reflect the variable values in the preceding code even if the
variables had been changed in the meantime.

Cross-Reference In addition to single-quotes and double-quotes, there is another way to create strings (called the *heredoc* syntax), which in some ways makes it even easier to splice in the values of variables. We cover it in Chapter 8.

Newlines in strings

Although PHP offers an escape sequence (\n) for newline characters, it is good to know that you can literally include new lines in the middle of strings, which PHP also treats as a newline characters. This capability turns out to be convenient when creating HTML strings, because browsers will ignore the line breaks anyway, so we can format our strings with line breaks to make our PHP code lines short:

```
print("<HTML><HEAD></HEAD><BODY>My HTML page is too big
to fit on a single line, but that doesn't mean that I
need multiple print statements!</BODY></HTML>");
```

We produced this statement in our text editor by literally hitting the Enter key at the end of the first two lines — these newlines are preserved in the string, so the single `print` statement will produce three distinct lines of PHP output. (Your mileage may vary depending on your text editor — if your editor automatically wraps lines in displaying them, you may see three lines of code that are actually one long line.) Of course, the browser program will ignore these newlines and will make its own decisions about whether and where to break the lines in display, but you will see the linebreaks if you use View Source in your browser to see the HTML itself.

Limits

There are no artificial limits on string length — within the bounds of available memory, you ought to be able to make arbitrarily long strings.

Output

Most of the constructs in the PHP language execute *silently* — they don't print anything to output. The only way that your embedded PHP code will display anything in a user's browser program is either by means of statements that print something to output or by calling functions that, in turn, call `print` statements.

Echo and print

The two most basic constructs for printing to output are `echo` and `print`. Their language status is somewhat confusing, because they are basic constructs of the PHP language, rather than being functions. As a result, they can be used either with parentheses or without them. (Function calls always have the name of the function first, followed by a parenthesized list of the arguments to the function.)

Echo

The simplest use of `echo` is to print a string as argument, for example:

```
echo "This will print in the user's browser window.";
```

Or equivalently:

```
echo("This will print in the user's browser window.");
```

Both of these statements will cause the given sentence to be displayed, without displaying the quote signs. (*Note for C programmers:* Think of the HTTP connection to the user as the standard output stream for these functions.)

You can also give multiple arguments to the unparenthesized version of echo, separated by commas, as in:

```
echo "This will print in the ", "user's browser window.";
```

The parenthesized version, however, will not accept multiple arguments:

```
echo ("This will produce a ", "PARSE ERROR!");
```

Print

The command print is very similar to echo, with two important differences:

✦ Unlike echo, print can accept only one argument.

✦ Unlike echo, print returns a value, which represents whether the print statement succeeded.

The value returned by print will be 1 if the printing was successful and 0 if unsuccessful. (It is rare that a syntactically correct print statement will fail, but in theory this return value provides a means to test, for example, if the user's browser has closed the connection.)

Both echo and print are usually used with string arguments, but PHP's type flexibility means that you can throw pretty much any type of argument at them without causing an error. For example, the following two lines will print exactly the same thing:

```
print("3.14159");  // print a string
print(3.14159);    // print a number
```

Technically, what is happening in the second line is that, because print expects a string argument, the floating-point version of the number is converted to a string value before print gets hold of it. However, the effect is that both print and echo will reliably print out numbers as well as string arguments.

For the sake of simplicity and uniformity, we will typically use the parenthesized version of print in our examples, rather than using echo.

Cross-Reference

In addition to the printing functions discussed here, there are two printing functions used mostly for debugging: print_r() and var_dump(). The point of these functions is to help you visualize what's going on with compound data structures like arrays, so we cover them along with the details of arrays in Chapter 9.

Variables and strings

C programmers are accustomed to using a function called printf, which allows you to splice values and expressions into a specially formatted printing string. PHP has analogous functions (which we will cover in Chapter 7), but as it turns out we can get much of the same functionality just by using print (or echo) with quoted strings. For example, the fragment:

```
$animal = "antelope";
$animal_heads = 1;
$animal_legs = 4;
print("The $animal has $animal_heads head(s).<BR>");
print("The $animal has $animal_legs leg(s).<BR>");
```

will produce the following output in the browser:

```
The antelope has 1 head(s).
The antelope has 4 leg(s).
```

The values for the variables we included in the string have been neatly spliced into the printed output. This makes it very easy to quickly produce Web pages with content that varies depending on how variables have been set. It is not the result of any magical properties of print, however — the magic is really happening in the interpretation of the quoted string itself.

HTML and linebreaks

One mistake often made by new PHP programmers (especially those from a C background) is to try to break lines of text in their browsers by putting end-of-line characters ("\n") in the strings they print. To understand why this doesn't work, you have to distinguish the *output* of PHP (which is usually HTML code, ready to be sent over the Internet to a browser program) from the way that output is rendered by the user's browser. Most browser programs will make their own choices about how to split up lines in HTML text, unless you force a line break with the <BR> tag. End-of-line characters in strings will put line breaks in the HTML source that PHP sends to your user's browser (which can still be useful for creating readable HTML source), but they will usually have no effect on the way that text looks in a Web page.

Summary

PHP code follows a basic set of syntactical rules, mostly borrowed from programming languages such as C and Perl. The syntactical requirements of PHP are minimal, and in general PHP tries to display results when it can rather than generating an error.

PHP has eight types: integer, double, Boolean, NULL, string, array, object, and resource. Five of these are simple types: Integers are whole numbers, doubles are floating-point numbers, Booleans are true-or-false values, NULL has just one value (NULL), and strings are sequences of characters. *Arrays* are a compound type that holds other PHP values, indexed either by integers or by strings. *Objects* are instances of programmer-defined classes, which can contain both member variables and member functions, and which can inherit functions and data types from other classes. (We address arrays in Chapter 9 and objects in Chapter 20.) Finally, *resources* are special references to memory allocated from external programs, which memory PHP frees automatically when they are no longer needed (we cover resources in Chapter 25).

Only values are typed in PHP — variables have no inherent type other than the value of their most recent assignment. PHP automatically converts value types as demanded by the context in which the value is used. The programmer can also explicitly control types by means of both conversion functions and type casts.

PHP code is whitespace insensitive, and although variable names are case sensitive, basic language constructs and function names are not. Simple PHP expressions are combined into larger expressions by operators and function calls, and statements are expressions with a terminating semicolon. Variables are denoted by a leading $ character and are assigned using the = operator. They need no type declarations and have reasonable default values if used before they are assigned. Variable scope is global except inside the body of functions, where it is local to the function unless explicitly declared otherwise.

The simplest way to send output to the user is by using either echo or print, which output their string arguments. They are particularly useful in combination with doubly quoted strings, which automatically replace embedded variables with their values.

✦   ✦   ✦

Control and Functions

It's difficult to write interesting programs if you can't make the course of program execution depend on anything. In a weak sense, the behavior of code that prints variables depends on the variable values, but that is as exciting as filling out a template. As programmers, we want programs that react to something (the world, the time of day, user input, or the contents of a database) by doing something different.

This kind of program reaction requires a *control structure,* which indicates how different situations should lead to the execution of different code. In Chapter 5, we informally used the if control structure without really explaining it; in this chapter, we lay out every kind of control structure offered by PHP and study their workings in detail.

Note   Experienced C programmers: Of all the features in PHP, control is probably the most reliably C-like—all the structures you are used to are here, and they work the same way.

The two broad types of control structures we will talk about are *branches* and *loops.* A branch is a fork in the road for a program's execution—depending on some test or other, the program goes either left or right, possibly following a different path for the rest of the program's execution. A loop is a special kind of branch where one of the execution paths jumps back to the beginning of the branch, repeating the test and possibly the body of the loop.

Before we can make interesting use of control structures, however, we have to be able to construct interesting tests. We'll start from the very simplest of tests, working our way up from the constants TRUE and FALSE and then move on to using these tests in more complicated code.

Any real programming language has some kind of capability for *procedural abstraction*—a way to name pieces of code so that you can use them as building blocks in writing other pieces of code. Some scripting languages lack this capability, and we can tell you from our own sorrowful experience that complex server-side code can quickly become unmanageable without it.

PHP's mechanism for this kind of abstraction is the *function.* There are really two kinds of functions in PHP—those that have been built into the language by the PHP developers and those defined by individual PHP programmers.

In this chapter, we also look at how to use the large body of functions already provided in PHP and then, a bit later, how to define your own functions. Luckily, there is no real difference between using a built-in function and using your own functions. But first, let's discuss control.

Boolean Expressions

Every control structure in this chapter has two distinct parts: the *test* (which determines which part of the rest of the structure executes), and the *dependent code* itself (whether separate branches or the body of a loop). Tests work by evaluating a *Boolean expression*, an expression with a result treated as either true or false.

Boolean constants

The simplest kind of expression is a simple value, and the simplest Boolean values are the constants TRUE and FALSE. We can use these constants anywhere we would use a more complicated Boolean expression, and vice versa. For example, we can embed them in the test part of an if-else statement:

```
if (TRUE)
  print("This will always print<BR>");
else
  print("This will never print<BR>");
```

Or equivalently:

```
if (FALSE)
  print("This will never print<BR>");
else
  print("This will always print<BR>");
```

Logical operators

Logical operators combine other logical (aka Boolean) values to produce new Boolean values. The standard logical operations (and, or, not, and exclusive-or) are supported by PHP, which has alternate versions of the first two, as shown in Table 6-1.

Table 6-1: Logical Operators

Operator	Behavior
and	Is true if and only if both of its arguments are true.
or	Is true if either (or both) of its arguments are true.
!	Is true if its single argument (to the right) is false and false if its argument is true.
xor	Is true if either (but not both) of its arguments are true.
&&	Same as and, but binds to its arguments more tightly. (See the discussion of precedence later in the chapter.)
||	Same as or but binds to its arguments more tightly.

The && and || operators will be familiar to C programmers. The ! operator is usually called not, since it negates the argument it operates on.

As an example of using logical operators, consider the following expression:

```
(($statement_1 && $statement_2) ||
 ($statement_1 && !$statement_2) ||
 (!$statement_1 && $statement_2) ||
 (!$statement_1 && !$statement_2))
```

This is a *tautology*, meaning that it is always true regardless of the values of the statement variables. There are four possible combinations of truth values for the two variables, each of which is represented by one of the && expressions. One of these four must be true, and because they are linked by the || operator, the entire expression must be true.

Here's another, slightly trickier tautology using xor:

```
(($statement_1 and $statement_2 and
  $statement_3) xor
 ((!($statement_1 and $statement_2)) or
  (!($statement_1 and $statement_3)) or
  (!($statement_2 and $statement_3))))
```

In English, this expression says, "Given three statements, one and only one of the following two things hold—either 1) all three statements are true, or 2) there are two statements that are not both true."

Precedence of logical operators

Just as with any operators, some logical operators have higher precedence than others, although precedence can always be overridden by grouping subexpressions using parentheses. The logical operators listed in declining order of precedence are: !, &&, ||, and, xor, or. Actually, and, xor, and or have much lower precedence than the others, so that the assignment operator (=) binds more tightly than and, but less tightly than &&.

Cross-Reference   A complete table of operator precedence and associativity can be found in the online manual at www.php.net.

Logical operators short-circuit

One very handy feature of Boolean operators is that they associate left to right, and they *short-circuit*, meaning that they do not even evaluate their second argument if their truth value is unambiguous from their first argument. For example, imagine that you wanted to determine a very approximate ratio of two numbers, but also wanted to avoid a possible division-by-zero error. You can first test to make sure that the denominator is not zero by using the != (not-equal-to) operator:

```
if ($denom != 0 && $numer / $denom > 2)
   print("More than twice as much!");
```

In the case where $denom is zero, the && operator should return false regardless of whether the second expression is true or false. Because of short-circuiting, the second expression is not evaluated, so an error is avoided. In the case where $denom is not zero, the && operator does not have enough information to reach a conclusion about its truth value, so the second expression is evaluated.

So far, all we've formally covered are the TRUE and FALSE constants and how to combine them to make other true-or-false values. Now we'll move on to operators that actually let you make meaningful Boolean tests.

Comparison operators

Table 6-2 shows the comparison operators, which can be used for either numbers or strings (although you should see the cautionary sidebar entitled "Comparing Things That Are Not Integers").

Table 6-2: Comparison Operators

Operator	Name	Behavior
==	Equal	True if its arguments are equal to each other, false otherwise
!=	Not equal	False if its arguments are equal to each other, true otherwise
<	Less than	True if the left-hand argument is less than its right-hand argument, but false otherwise
>	Greater than	True if the left-hand argument is greater than its right-hand argument, but false otherwise
<=	Less than or equal to	True if the left-hand argument is less than its right-hand argument or equal to it, but false otherwise
>=	Greater than or equal to	True if the left-hand argument is greater than its right-hand argument or equal to it, but false otherwise
===	Identical	True if its arguments are equal to each other and of the same type, but false otherwise

As an example, here are some variable assignments, followed by a compound test that is always true:

```
$three = 3;
$four = 4;
$my_pi = 3.14159;
if (($three == $three) and
    ($four === $four) and
    ($three != $four) and
    ($three < $four) and
    ($three <= $four) and
    ($four >= $three) and
    ($three <= $three) and
    ($my_pi > $three) and
    ($my_pi <= $four))
  print("My faith in mathematics is restored!<BR>");
else
  print("Sure you typed that right?<BR>");
```

Caution Watch out for a very common mistake: confusing the assignment operator (=) with the comparison operator (==). The statement if ($three = $four). will (probably unexpectedly) set the variable $three to be the same as $four; what's more, the test will be true if $four is a true value!

Operator precedence

Although overreliance on precedence rules can be confusing for the person who reads your code next, it's useful to note that comparison operators have higher precedence than Boolean operators. This means that a test like the following:

```
if ($small_num > 2 && $small_num < 5) ...
```

doesn't need any parentheses other than those shown.

String comparison

The comparison operators may be used to compare strings as well as numbers (see the cautionary sidebar). We would expect the following code to print its associated sentence (with apologies to Billy Bragg):

```
if (("Marx" < "Mary") and
    ("Mary" < "Marzipan"))
{
  print("Between Marx and Marzipan in the ");
  print("dictionary, there was Mary.<BR>");
}
```

The comparisons are case sensitive, and the only reason that this example will print anything is because our values are case-consistent. Because of the capitalization of Dennis, the following will not print anything:

```
if (("deep blue sea" < "Dennis") and
    ("Dennis" < "devil"))
{
  print("Between the deep blue sea and ");
  print("the devil, that was me.<BR>");
}
```

The ternary operator

One especially useful construct is the *ternary conditional operator*, which plays a role somewhere between a Boolean operator and a true branching construct. Its job is to take three expressions and use the truth value of the first expression to decide which of the other two expressions to evaluate and return. The syntax looks like:

```
test-expression ? yes-expression : no-expression
```

The value of this expression is the result of yes-expression if test-expression is true; otherwise, it is the same as no-expression.

For example, the following expression assigns to $max_num either $first_num or $second_num, whichever is larger:

```
$max_num = $first_num > $second_num ? $first_num : $second_num;
```

Comparing Things That Are Not Integers

Although comparison operators work with numbers or strings, a couple of gotchas lurk here.

First of all, although it is always safe to do less-than or greater-than comparisons on doubles (or even between doubles and integers), it can be dangerous to rely on equality comparisons on doubles, especially if they are the result of a numerical computation. The problem is that a rounding error may make two values that are theoretically equal differ slightly.

Second, although comparison operators work for strings as well as numbers, PHP's automatic type conversions can lead to counterintuitive results when the strings are interpretable as numbers. For example, the code:

```
$string_1 = "00008";
$string_2 = "007";
$string_3 = "00008-OK";
if ($string_2 < $string_1)
  print("$string_2 is less than $string_1<BR>");
if ($string_3 < $string_2)
  print("$string_3 is less than $string_2<BR>");
if ($string_1 < $string_3)
  print("$string_1 is less than $string_3<BR>");
```

gives this output (with comments added):

```
007 is less than 00008  // numerical comparison
00008-OK is less than 007 // string comparison
00008 is less than 00008-OK // string comp. - contradiction!
```

When it can, PHP will convert string arguments to numbers, and when both sides can be treated that way, the comparison ends up being numerical, not alphabetic. The PHP designers view this as a feature, not a bug. Our view is that if you are comparing strings that have any chance of being interpreted as numbers, you're better off using the strcmp() function (see Chapter 10).

As we will see, this is equivalent to:

```
if ($first_num > $second_num)
  $max_num = $first_num;
else
  $max_num = $second_num;
```

but is somewhat more concise.

Branching

The two main structures for branching are if and switch. If is a workhorse and is usually the first conditional structure anyone learns. Switch is a useful alternative for certain situations where you want multiple possible branches based on a single value and where a series of if statements would be cumbersome.

If-else

The syntax for `if` is:

```
if (test)
    statement-1
```

Or with an optional `else` branch:

```
if (test)
    statement-1
else
    statement-2
```

When an `if` statement is processed, the `test` expression is evaluated, and the result is interpreted as a Boolean value. If `test` is true, `statement-1` is executed. If `test` is not true, and there is an `else` clause, `statement-2` is executed. If test is false, and there is no `else` clause, execution simply proceeds with the next statement after the `if` construct.

Note that a *statement* in this syntax can be a single statement that ends with a semicolon, a brace-enclosed block of statements, or another conditional construct (which itself counts as a single statement). Conditionals can be nested inside each other to arbitrary depth. Also, the Boolean expression can be a genuine Boolean (`TRUE`, `FALSE`, or the result of a Boolean operator or function), or it can be a value of another type interpreted as a Boolean.

Cross-Reference

For the full story on how values of non-Boolean types are treated as Booleans, see Chapter 25. The short version is that the number 0, the string `"0"`, and the empty string, `" "`, are false, and almost every other value is true.

The following example, which prints a statement about the absolute difference between two numbers, shows both the nesting of conditionals and the interpretation of the test as a Boolean:

```
if ($first - $second)
  if ($first > $second)
    {
      $difference = $first - $second;
      print("The difference is $difference<BR>");
    }
  else
    {
      $difference = $second - $first;
      print("The difference is $difference<BR>");
    }
else
  print("There is no difference<BR>");
```

This code relies on the fact that the number 0 is interpreted as a false value — if the difference is zero, then the test fails, and the `no difference` message is printed. If there is a difference, a further test is performed. (This example is artificial, because a test like `$first != $second` would accomplish the same thing comprehensibly.)

Else attachment

At this point, former Pascal programmers may be warily wondering about else attachment — that is, how does an else clause know which if it belongs to? The rules are simple and are the same as in most languages other than Pascal. Each else is matched with the nearest unmatched if that can be found, while respecting the boundaries of braces. If you want to make sure that an if statement stays solo and does not get matched to an else, wrap it up in braces like so:

```
if ($num % 2 == 0) // $num is even?
  {
    if ($num > 2)
      print("num is not prime<BR>");
  }
else
  print("num is odd<BR>");
```

This code will print num is not prime if $num happens to be an even number greater than 2, num is odd if $num is odd, and nothing if $num happens to be 2. If we had omitted the curly braces, the else would attach to the inner if, and so the code would buggily print num is odd if $num were equal to 2 and would print nothing if $num were actually odd.

Note In this chapter's examples, we often use the modulus operator (%), which is explained in Chapter 10. For the purposes of these examples, all you need to know is that if $x % $y is zero, $x is evenly divisible by $y.

Elseif

It's very common to want to do a cascading sequence of tests, as in the following nested if statements:

```
if ($day == 5)
  print("Five golden rings<BR>");
else
  if ($day == 4)
    print("Four calling birds<BR>");
  else
    if ($day == 3)
      print("Three French hens<BR>");
    else
      if ($day == 2)
        print("Two turtledoves<BR>");
      else
        if ($day == 1)
          print("A partridge in a pear tree<BR>");
```

Note We have indented this code in to show the real syntactic structure of inclusions — although this is always a good idea, you will often see code that does not bother with this and where each else line starts in the first column.

Branching and HTML Mode

As you may have learned from earlier chapters, you should feel free to use the PHP tags to switch back and forth between HTML mode and PHP mode, whenever it seems convenient. If you need to include a large chunk of HTML in your page that has no dynamic code or interpolated variables, it can be simpler and more efficient to escape back into HTML mode and include it literally than it is to send it using `print` or `echo`.

What may not be as obvious is that this strategy works even inside conditional structures. That is, you can use PHP to decide what HTML to send and then "send" that HTML by temporarily escaping back to HTML mode.

For example, the following cumbersome code uses `print` statements to construct a complete HTML page based on the supposed gender of the viewer. (We're assuming a nonexistent Boolean function called `female()` that tests for this.)

```
<HTML><HEAD>
<?php
if (female())
  {
    print("<TITLE>The women-only site</TITLE><BR>");
    print("</HEAD><BODY>");
    print("This site has been specially constructed ");
    print("for women only.<BR> No men allowed here!");
  }
else
  {
    print("<TITLE>The men-only site</TITLE><BR>");
    print("</HEAD><BODY>");
    print("This site has been specially constructed ");
    print("for men only.<BR> No women allowed here!");
  }
?>
</BODY></HTML>
```

Instead of all these `print` statements, we can duck back into HTML mode within each of the two branches:

```
<HTML><HEAD>
<?php
if (female())
  {
?>
<TITLE>The women-only site</TITLE>
</HEAD><BODY>
This site has been specially constructed
for women only.<BR> No men allowed here!
<?php
  }
else
  {
?>
```

Continued

Continued

```
<TITLE>The men-only site</TITLE><BR>
</HEAD><BODY>
This site has been specially constructed
for men only.<BR> No women allowed here!
<?php
    }
?>
</BODY></HTML>
```

This version is somewhat more difficult to read, but the only difference is that it replaces each set of `print` statements with a block of literal HTML that starts with a closing PHP tag (`?>`) and ends with a starting PHP tag (`<?php`).

In this book's examples, we mostly avoid this kind of conditional inclusion, simply because we feel that it may be harder for the novice PHP programmer to decipher. But that shouldn't stop you—literal inclusion has advantages, including fast execution. (In HTML mode, all the PHP engine must do is pass on characters and watch for the next PHP start tag, which is inevitably faster than parsing and executing `print` statements, especially if they include doubly quoted strings.)

A third alternative, when large blocks of HTML are conditionally included, is the heredoc, alluded to in Chapter 5 and explained fully in Chapter 8. The heredoc will allow you to include large blocks of HTML code inside a chunk of PHP without several consecutive print statements.

This pattern is common enough that there is a special `elseif` construct to handle it. We can rewrite the preceding example as:

```
if ($day == 5)
   print("Five golden rings<BR>");
elseif ($day == 4)
   print("Four calling birds<BR>");
elseif ($day == 3)
   print("Three French hens<BR>");
elseif ($day == 2)
   print("Two turtledoves<BR>");
elseif ($day == 1)
   print("A partridge in a pear tree<BR>");
```

The `if, elseif` construct allows for a sequence of tests that executes only the first branch that has a successful test. In theory, this is syntactically different from the previous example (we have a single construct with five branches rather than a nesting of five two-branch constructs), but the behavior is identical. Use whichever syntax you find more appealing.

Switch

For a specific kind of multiway branching, the `switch` construct can be useful. Rather than branch on arbitrary logical expressions, `switch` takes different paths according to the value of a single expression. The syntax is as follows, with the optional parts enclosed in square brackets (`[]`):

```
switch(expression)
{
    case value-1:
        statement-1
        statement-2
        ...
        [break;]
    case value-2:
        statement-3
        statement-4
        ...
        [break;]
    ...
    [default:
        default-statement]
}
```

The expression can be a variable or any other kind of expression, as long as it evaluates to a simple value (that is, an integer, a double, or a string). The construct executes by evaluating the expression and then testing the result for equality against each case value. As soon as a matching value is found, subsequent statements are executed in sequence until the special statement (break;) or until the end of the switch construct. (As we'll see in the "Looping" section of this chapter, break can also be used to break out of looping constructs.) A special default tag can be used at the end, which will match the expression if no other case has matched it so far.

For example, we can rewrite our if-else example as follows:

```
switch($day)
{
    case 5:
        print("Five golden rings<BR>");
        break;
    case 4:
        print("Four calling birds<BR>");
        break;
    case 3:
        print("Three French hens<BR>");
        break;
    case 2:
        print("Two turtledoves<BR>");
        break;
    default:
        print("A partridge in a pear tree<BR>");
}
```

This will print a single appropriate line for days 2–5; for any day other than those, it will print A partridge in a pear tree. Although switch will accept only a single argument, there's no reason why that argument can't be the value of expressions evaluated previously in your code.

Caution   The single most confusing aspect of switch is that all cases after a matching case will execute, unless there are break statements to stop the execution. In the "partridge" example, the break statements ensure that we see only one line from the song at a time. If we remove the break statements, we will see a sequence of lines counting down to the final line, just as in the song.

Looping

Congratulations! You just passed the boundary from scripting into real programming. The branching structures we have looked at so far are useful, but there are limits to what can be computed with them alone. On the other hand, it's well established in theoretical computer science that any language with tests plus unbounded looping can do pretty much anything that any other language can do. You may not actually want to write a C compiler in PHP, for example, but it's nice to know that no inherent language limits are going to stop you.

Bounded loops versus unbounded loops

A *bounded loop* executes a fixed number of times — you can tell by looking at the code how many times the loop will iterate, and the language guarantees that it won't loop more times than that. An *unbounded loop* repeats until some condition becomes true (or false), and that condition is dependent on the action of the code within the loop. Bounded loops are predictable, whereas unbounded loops can be as tricky as you like.

Unlike some languages, PHP doesn't actually have any constructs specifically for bounded loops — while, do-while, and for are all unbounded constructs — but as we will see in this section, an unbounded loop can do anything a bounded loop can do.

Cross-Reference   In addition to the looping constructs in this chapter, PHP provides functions for iterating over the contents of arrays, which are covered in Chapter 9.

While

The simplest PHP looping construct is while, which has the following syntax:

```
while (condition)
    statement
```

The while loop evaluates the *condition* expression as a Boolean — if it is true, it executes *statement* and then starts again by evaluating *condition*. If the condition is false, the while loop terminates. Of course, just as with if, *statement* may be a single statement or it may be a brace-enclosed block. The body of a while loop may not execute even once, as in:

```
while (FALSE)
    print("This will never print.<BR>");
```

Or it may execute forever, as in this code snippet:

```
while (TRUE)
    print("All work and no play makes
            Jack a dull boy.<BR>");
```

or it may execute a predictable number of times, as in:

```
$count = 1;
while ($count <= 10)
  {
    print("count is $count<BR>");
    $count = $count + 1;
  }
```

which will print exactly 10 lines. (For more interesting examples, see the "Looping examples" section, later in this chapter.)

Do-while

The `do-while` construct is similar to `while`, except that the test happens at the end of the loop. The syntax is:

```
do statement
   while (expression);
```

The statement is executed once, and then the expression is evaluated. If the expression is true, the statement is repeated until the expression becomes false. The only practical difference between `while` and `do-while` is that the latter will always execute its statement at least once. For example:

```
$count = 45;
do
   {
     print("count is $count<BR>");
     $count = $count + 1;
   }
   while ($count <= 10)
```

prints the single line:

```
count is 45
```

For

The most complicated looping construct is `for`, which has the following syntax:

```
for (initial-expression;
     termination-check;
     loop-end-expression)
   statement
```

In executing a `for` statement, first the *initial-expression* is evaluated just once, usually to initialize variables. Then *termination-check* is evaluated — if it is false, the `for` statement concludes, and if it is true, the statement executes. Finally, the *loop-end-expression* is executed and the cycle begins again with *termination-check*. As always, by *statement* we mean a single (semicolon-terminated) statement, a brace-enclosed block, or a conditional construct.

If we rewrote the preceding `for` loop as a `while` loop, it would look like this:

```
initial-expression;
while (termination-check)
   {
     statement
     loop-end-expression;
   }
```

Actually, although the typical use of `for` has exactly one initial-expression, one termination-check, and one loop-end-expression, it is legal to omit any of them. The termination-check is taken to be always true if omitted, so:

```
for (;;)
   statement
```

is equivalent to:

```
while (TRUE)
    statement
```

It is also legal to include more than one of each kind of `for` clause, separated by commas. The termination-check will be considered to be true if any of its subclauses are true; it is like an 'or' test. For example, the following statement:

```
for ($x = 1, $y = 1, $z = 1;    //initial expressions
     $y < 10, $z < 10:          // termination checks
     $x = $x + 1, $y = $y + 2,  // loop-end expressions
     $z = $z + 3)
   print("$x, $y, $z<BR>");
```

would give the browser output:

```
1, 1, 1
2, 3, 4
3, 5, 7
```

Although the `for` syntax is the most complex of the looping constructs, it is often used for simple bounded loops, using the following idiom:

```
for ($count = 0; $count < $limit; $count = $count + 1)
   statement
```

Looping examples

Now let's look at some examples.

A bounded for loop

Listing 6-1 shows a typical use of bounded `for` loops. The page produced by Listing 6-1 is shown in Figure 6-1.

Listing 6-1: **A division table**

```php
<?php
  $start_num = 1;
  $end_num = 10;
?>
<HTML>
<HEAD>
<TITLE>A division table</TITLE>
</HEAD>
<BODY>
<H2>A division table</H2>
<TABLE BORDER=1>
<?php
  print("<TR>");
  print("<TH> </TH>");
  for ($count_1 = $start_num;
```

```
        $count_1 <= $end_num;
        $count_1++)
    print("<TH>$count_1</TH>");
  print("</TR>");

  for ($count_1 = $start_num;
       $count_1 <= $end_num;
       $count_1++)
  {
    print("<TR><TH>$count_1</TH>");
    for ($count_2 = $start_num;
         $count_2 <= $end_num;
         $count_2++)
    {
      $result = $count_1 / $count_2;
      printf("<TD>%.3f</TD>",
             $result);  // see Chapter 8
    }
    print("</TR>\n");
  }
?>
</TABLE>
</BODY>
</HTML>
```

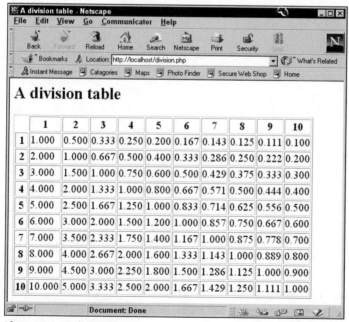

Figure 6-1: A division table

The main body of this code simply has one `for` loop nested inside another, with each loop executing ten times, resulting in a 10 × 10 table. Each iteration of the outer loop prints a row, whereas each inner iteration prints a cell. The only novel feature is the way we chose to print the numbers—we used `printf` (covered in Chapter 8), which allows us to control the number of decimal places printed.

Note   The `$variable_name++` feature used above is called an increment. It's a fairly standard shorthand for `$variable_name + 1`.

An unbounded while loop

Now let's look at a loop not so obviously bounded. The sole purpose of the code in Listing 6-2 is to approximate the square root of 81 (using Newton's method). The approximation starts with a guess of 1 and then "zeros in" on the actual square root of 9 by improving the guesses. A trace of this approximation is shown in Figure 6-2.

Listing 6-2: **Approximating a square root**

```
<HTML>
<HEAD>
<TITLE>Approximating a square root</TITLE>
</HEAD>
<BODY>
<H3>Approximating a square root</H3>

<?php
$target = 81;
$guess = 1.0;
$precision = 0.0000001;

$guess_squared = $guess * $guess;
while (($guess_squared - $target > $precision) or
       ($guess_squared - $target < - $precision))
{
  print("Current guess: $guess is the square
        root of $target<BR>");
  $guess = ($guess + ($target / $guess)) / 2;
  $guess_squared = $guess * $guess;
}
print("$guess squared = $guess_squared<BR>");
?>
</BODY>
</HTML>
```

Now, although it nicely illustrates a potentially unbounded loop, this approximation example is very artificial—first, because PHP already has a perfectly good square-root function (`sqrt`) and second, because the number 81 is hardcoded into the page. We can't use this page to find the square root of any other number.

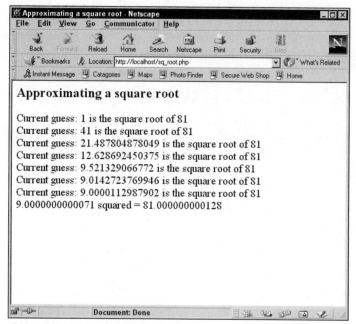

Figure 6-2: Approximating a square root

Break and continue

The standard way to get out of a looping structure is for the main test condition to become false. The special commands `break` and `continue` offer an optional side exit from all the looping constructs, including `while`, `do-while`, and `for`:

✦ The `break` command exits the innermost loop construct that contains it.

✦ The `continue` command skips to the end of the current iteration of the innermost loop that contains it.

For example, the following code:

```
for ($x = 1; $x < 10; $x++)
{
  // if $x is odd, break out
  if ($x % 2 != 0)
    break;
  print("$x ");
}
```

prints nothing, because 1 is odd, which terminates the `for` loop immediately. On the other hand, the code:

```
for ($x = 1; $x < 10; $x++)
{
  // if $x is odd, skip this loop
  if ($x % 2 != 0)
```

```
        continue;
      print("$x ");
    }
```

prints:

```
    2  4  6  8
```

because the effect of the `continue` statement is to skip the printing of any odd numbers.

Using the `break` command, the programmer can choose to dispense with the main termination test altogether. Consider the following code, which prints a list of prime numbers (that is, numbers not divisible by something other than 1 or the number itself):

```
$limit = 500;
$to_test = 2;
while(TRUE)
{
  $testdiv = 2;
  if ($to_test > $limit)
    break;
  while (TRUE)
  {
    if ($testdiv > sqrt($to_test))
      {
        print "$to_test ";
        break;
      }
    // test if $to_test is divisible by $testdiv
    if ($to_test % $testdiv == 0)
      break;
    $testdiv = $testdiv + 1;
  }
  $to_test = $to_test + 1;
}
```

In the preceding code, we have two `while` loops — the outer loop works through all the numbers between 1 and 500, and the inner loop actually does the testing with each possible divisor. If the inner loop finds a divisor, the number is not prime, so it breaks out without printing anything. If, on the other hand, the testing gets as high as the square root of the number, we can safely assume that the number must be prime, and the inner loop is broken without printing. Finally, the outer loop is broken when we have reached the limit of numbers to test. The result in this case is a list of primes less than 500:

```
2  3  5  7  11  13  17  19  23  29  31  37  41  43  47  53  59  61  67  71  73  79  83
89  97  101  103  107  109  113  127  131  137  139  149  151  157  163  167
173  179  181  191  193  197  199  211  223  227  229  233  239  241  251  257
263  269  271  277  281  283  293  307  311  313  317  331  337  347  349  353
359  367  373  379  383  389  397  401  409  419  421  431  433  439  443  449
457  461  463  467  479  487  491  499
```

Notice that it is crucial to this code that `break` interrupt the inner `while` loop only.

Cross-Reference   There is another iteration construct, called `foreach`, which is used only for iterating over arrays. We cover it in Chapter 9.

A note on infinite loops

If you've ever programmed in another language, you've probably had the experience of accidentally creating an infinite loop (a looping construct whose exit test never becomes true and so never returns). The first thing to do when you realize this has happened is to interrupt the program, which will otherwise continue "forever" and use up a lot of CPU time. But what does it mean to interrupt a PHP script? Is it sufficient to click the Stop button on your browser?

As it turns out, the answer is dependent on some PHP configuration settings — you can set the PHP engine to ignore interruptions from the browser (like the result of clicking Stop) and also to impose a time limit on script execution (so that "forever" will only be a short time). The default configuration for PHP is to ignore interruptions, but with a script time limit of 30 seconds — the time limitation means that you can afford to forget about infinite loops that you may have started.

Cross-Reference   For more on the configuration of PHP, see Chapter 30.

Alternate Control Syntaxes

PHP offers another way to start and end the bodies of the `if`, `switch`, `for`, and `while` constructs. It amounts to replacing the initial brace of the enclosed block with a colon and the closing brace with a special ending statement for that construct (`endif`, `endswitch`, `endfor`, and `endwhile`). For example, the `if` syntax becomes:

```
if (expression):
  statement1
  statement2
  ..
endif;
```

Or:

```
if (expression):
  statement1
  statement2
  ..
elseif (expression2):
  statement3
  ..
else:
  statement4
  ..
endif;
```

Note that the `else` and `elseif` bodies also begin with colons. The corresponding `while` syntax is:

```
while (expression):
  statement
endwhile;
```

Which syntax you use is a matter of taste. The nonstandard syntax is in PHP largely used for historical reasons and for the comfort of people who are familiar with it from the early versions of PHP. We will consistently use the standard syntax in the rest of this book.

Terminating Execution

Sometimes you just have to give up, and PHP offers a construct that helps you do just that. The exit() construct takes either a string or a number as argument, prints out the argument, and then terminates execution of the script. Everything that PHP produces up to the point of invoking exit() is sent to the client browser as usual, and nothing in your script after that point will even be parsed — execution of the script stops immediately. If the argument given to exit is a number rather than a string, the number will be the return value for the script's execution. Because exit is a construct, not a function, it's also legal to give no argument and omit the parentheses.

The die() construct is an alias for exit() and so behaves exactly the same way. (We'll usually use the die() version because we find the name more evocative.) So what's the point of exit() and die()? One possible use is to cut off production of a Web page when your script has determined that there is no more interesting information to send, without bothering to wrap up the different branches in a conditional construct. This usage can make long scripts somewhat difficult to read and debug, however.

A better use for die() is to make your crashes informative. It's good to get into the habit of testing for unexpected conditions that would crash your script if they were true, and throw in a die() statement with an informative message. If you're correct in your expectations, the die() will never be invoked; if you're wrong, you will have an error message of your own rather than a possibly obscure PHP error. For example, consider the following pseudocode, which assumes that we have functions to make a database connection and that we then use that database connection:

```
$connection = make_database_connection();
if (!$connection)
  die("No database connection!");
use_database_connection($connection);
```

This example assumes that our imaginary function make_database_connection(), like many PHP functions, returns a useful value if it succeeds, and a false value if it fails. An even more compact version of the preceding code takes advantage of the fact that or has lower precedence than the = assignment operator.

```
$connection = make_database_connection()
    or die("No database connection!");
use_database_connection($connection);
```

This works because the or operator short-circuits, and therefore the die() construct will only be evaluated if the expression $connection = make_database_connection() has a false value. Because the value of an assignment expression is the value assigned, this code ends up being equivalent to the earlier version. (Note that this would not work the same way if we used || instead of or, because || has higher precedence than assignment, and so $connection would end up being assigned to the true-or-false result of the || expression.)

Note Before PHP5, the control structures we've presented so far were really the only alternatives; control would flow from the first statement in a file to the last (possibly bounced around by function calls), unless prematurely terminated with die(). With exception-handling, PHP5 introduces an alternate way to deal with problematic conditions, and one that is much more flexible than die(). We treat exceptions briefly later in this chapter, and more thoroughly in Chapter 31.

In Table 6-3, we summarize all the control structures we've seen thus far.

Table 6-3: PHP Control Structures

Name	Syntax	Behavior

If
(or if-else)
	```if (test)statement-1```
	         ```-or-```
	```if (test)```
	   ```statement-1```
	```else```
	   ```statement-2```
	         ```-or-```
	```if (test)```
	   ```statement-1```
	```elseif (test2)```
	   ```statement-2```
	```else```
	   ```statement-3```
		Evaluate *test* and if it is true, execute *statement-1*. If *test* is false and there is an else clause, execute *statement-2*. The elseif construct is a syntactic shortcut for else clauses, where the included statement is itself an if construct.
		
		Statements may be single statements terminated with a semicolon or brace-enclosed blocks.

Ternary operator	```expression-1 ?```
	```expression-2 :```
	```expression-3```
		Evaluate *expression-1* and interpret it as a Boolean. If it is true, evaluate *expression-2* and return it as the value of the entire expression. Otherwise, evaluate and return *expression-3*.

Switch	```switch(expression)```
	```{```
	   ```case value-1:```
	      ```statement-1```
	      ```statement-2```
	      ```. . .```
	      ```[break;]```
	   ```case value-2:```
	      ```statement-3```
	      ```statement-4```
	      ```. . .```
	      ```[break;]```
	   ```. . .```
	   ```[default:```
	   ```default-statement]```
	```}```
		Evaluate *expression,* and compare its value to the value in each case clause. When a matching case is found, begin executing statements in sequence (including those from later cases), until the end of the switch statement or until a break statement is encountered. The optional default case will execute if no other case has matched the expression.

While	```while (condition)``` ```statement```	Evaluate *condition* and interpret it as Boolean. If *condition* is false, the while construct terminates. If it is true, execute *statement,* and keep executing it until *condition* becomes false. Terminate the while loop if the special break command is encountered, and skip the rest of the current iteration if continue is encountered.

Continued

Table 6-3 *(continued)*

Name	Syntax	Behavior
Do-while	`do statement` `    while (condition);`	Perform *statement* once unconditionally; then keep repeating statement until *condition* becomes false. (The `break` and `continue` commands are handled as in `while`.)

For	`for (initial-expression;`
	`    termination-check;`
	`    loop-end-expression)`
	`statement`
		Evaluate *initial-expression* once unconditionally. Then if *termination-check* is true, evaluate *statement,* and then *loop-end-expression,* and repeat that loop until *termination-check* becomes false. Clauses may be omitted, or multiple clauses of the same kind can be separated with commas— a missing termination-check is treated as true. (The `break` and `continue` commands are handled as in `while`.)

Exit (or die)	`exit(message-string or`
	`return-value), or`
	`equivalently`
	`die(message-string or`
	`return-value)`
		Terminate script immediately, without further parsing. The `die()` construct is an alias for `exit()`.

Using Functions

The basic syntax for using (or *calling*) a function is:

```
function_name(expression_1, expression_2, ..., expression_n)
```

This includes the name of the function followed by a parenthesized and comma-separated list of input expressions (which are called the *arguments* to the function). Functions can be called with zero or more arguments, depending on their definitions.

When PHP encounters a function call, it first evaluates each argument expression and then uses these values as inputs to the function. After the function executes, the returned value (if any) is the result of the entire function expression.

All the following are valid calls to built-in PHP functions:

```
sqrt(9) // square root function, evaluates to 3
rand(10, 10 + 10) // random number between 10 and 20
strlen("This has 22 characters") // returns the number 22
pi() // returns the approximate value of pi
```

These functions are called with 1, 2, 1, and 0 arguments, respectively.

Return values versus side effects

Every function call is a PHP expression, and (just as with other expressions) there are only two reasons why you might want to include one in your code: for the *return value* or for the *side effects*.

The *return value* of a function is the value of the function expression itself. You can do exactly the same things with this value as with the results of evaluating any other expression. For example, you can assign it to a variable, as in:

```
$my_pi = pi();
```

Or you can embed it in more complicated expressions, as in:

```
$approx = sqrt($approx) * sqrt($approx)
```

Functions are also used for a wide variety of *side effects*, including writing to files, manipulating databases, and printing things to the browser window. It's okay to make use of both return values and side effects at the same time — for example, it is very common to have a side-effecting function return a value that indicates whether or not the function succeeded.

The result of a function may be of any type, and it is common to use the array type as a way for functions to return multiple values.

Function Documentation

The architecture of PHP has been cleverly designed to make it easy for other developers to extend. The basic PHP language itself is very clean and flexible, but there is not a lot there — most of PHP's power resides in the large number of built-in functions. This means that developers can contribute simply by adding new built-in functions, which is nice especially because it does not change anything that PHP users may be relying on.

Although this book covers many of these built-in functions, explaining some of them in greater detail than the online manual can, the manual at www.php.net is the authoritative source for function information. In this book, we get to choose our topics to some extent, whereas the PHP documentation group has the awesome responsibility of covering every aspect of PHP in the manual. Also, although we hope to keep updating this book in future editions, the manual will have the freshest information on new additions to the ever-growing PHP functionality. It's worth looking at some of the different resources that the PHP site and manual offer.

Note   Although the following information is correct at this writing, some details may become dated or inapplicable if the online manual is reorganized.

To find the manual, head to www.php.net. A handy search bar at the top offers quick and easy access to any individual part of the online documentation. Alternatively, find the Documentation item at the top of the page. The Documentation page that this tab leads to has links to manual information in a wide variety of formats. Our favorite version is the default (currently in the View Online row of the Formats table on the Documentation page), which allows users to post their own clarifying comments to each page. (*Please note:* The manual annotation system is not the right place to post questions! For that, see the section on mailing lists at www.php.net, or see Appendix D. But it *is* the right place to explain something in your own words once you understand it. If you offer a better explanation, it might well show up in a later version of the documentation, which is a cool way to contribute. It's also definitely the right place to point out confusing aspects and potential gotchas.)

The largest section of the manual is the function reference, where each built-in function gets its own page of documentation. Typically, each group of functions has a page of general explanation, leading to pages for individual functions. Each function page starts off with the name of the function and a one-line description. This is followed by a C-style header declaration of the function (explained in the next section), followed by a slightly longer description and possibly an example or two, and then (in the annotated manual) clarifications and gotcha reports from users.

Headers in documentation

For those unfamiliar with C function headers, the very beginning of a function documentation page might be confusing. The format is:

```
return-type function-name(type1 arg1, type2 arg2, . . .);
```

This specifies the type of value the function is expected to return, the name of the function, and the number and expected types of its arguments.

Here is a typical header description:

```
string substr(string string, int start[, int length]);
```

This says that the function `substr()` will return a string and expects to be given a string and two integers as its arguments. Actually, the square brackets around `length` indicate that this argument is optional — so `substr()` should be called either with a string and an int, or a string and two ints.

Unlike in C, the argument types in these documentary headers are not absolute requirements. If you call `substr()` with a number as its first argument, you will not get an error. Instead, PHP will convert the first argument to a string as it begins to execute the function. However, the argument types do document the intent of the function's author, and it is a good idea either to use the function as documented or to understand the type conversion issues well enough that you are sure the result will be what you expect.

In general, the type names used in function documentation will be those of the basic types or of their aliases: integer (or `int`), double (or `float`, `real`), Boolean, string, array, object, resource, and NULL. In addition, you may see the types `void` and `mixed`. The `void` return type means that the function does not return a value at all, whereas the `mixed` argument type means that the argument might be of any type.

Finding function documentation

What's the best way to find information about a function in the manual? That is likely to depend on what kind of curiosity you have. The most common questions about functions are:

✦ I want to use function X. Now, how does X work again?

✦ I'd really like to do task Y. Is there a function that handles that for me?

For the first type of curiosity, the full version of the online manual offers an automatic lookup by function name. The "Search For" box in the upper-right-hand corner of the manual pages defaults to a mode where it searches for specific function names and displays the corresponding function page if found. (You can also make other choices, including searching the mailing list or the entire online documentation — the latter is a good choice when you don't know the name of the function you want, but can guess at words that appear on its manual page.)

For the second type of curiosity, your best bet is probably to use the hierarchical organization of the function reference, which is split (at press time) into about 108 chapters. For example, the `substr` function shown in the "Headers in Documentation" section is found in the "String Functions" section. You can browse the chapter list of the function reference for the best fit to the task you want to do. Alternatively, if you happen to know the name of a function that seems to be in the same general area as your task, you can use the Quick Ref button to jump to that chapter.

Defining Your Own Functions

User-defined functions are not a requirement in PHP. You can produce interesting and useful Web sites simply with the basic language constructs and the large body of built-in functions. If you find that your code files are getting longer, harder to understand, and more difficult to manage, however, it may be an indication that you should start wrapping some of your code up into functions.

What is a function?

A *function* is a way of wrapping up a chunk of code and giving that chunk a name, so that you can use that chunk later in just one line of code. Functions are most useful when you will be using the code in more than one place, but they can be helpful even in one-use situations, because they can make your code much more readable.

Function definition syntax

Function definitions have the following form:

```
function function-name ($argument-1, $argument-2, ..)
{
  statement-1;
  statement-2;
  ...
}
```

That is, function definitions have four parts:

✦ The special word `function`

✦ The name that you want to give your function

✦ The function's parameter list — dollar-sign variables separated by commas

✦ The function body — a brace-enclosed set of statements

Just as with variable names, the name of the function must be made up of letters, numbers, and underscores, and it must not start with a number. Unlike variable names, function names are converted to lowercase before they are stored internally by PHP, so a function is the same regardless of capitalization.

The short version of what happens when a user-defined function is called is:

1. PHP looks up the function by its name (you will get an error if the function has not yet been defined).

2. PHP substitutes the values of the calling arguments (or the *actual parameters*) into the variables in the definition's parameter list (or the *formal parameters*).

3. The statements in the body of the function are executed. If any of the executed statements are `return` statements, the function stops and returns the given value. Otherwise, the function completes after the last statement is executed, without returning a value.

Note   The alert and experienced programmer will have noticed that the preceding description implies call-by-value, rather than call-by-reference. In Chapter 26, we explain the difference and show how to get call-by-reference behavior.

Function definition example

As an example, imagine that we have the following code that helps decide which size of bottled soft drink to buy. (This is sometime next year, when supermarket shoppers routinely use their wearable wireless Web browsers to get to our handy price-comparison site.)

```
$liters_1 = 1.0;
$price_1 = 1.59;
$liters_2 = 1.5;
$price_2 = 2.09;

$per_liter_1 = $price_1 / $liters_1;
$per_liter_2 = $price_2 / $liters_2;
if ($per_liter1 < $per_liter2)
   print("The first deal is better!<BR>");
else
   print("The second deal is better!<BR>");
```

Because this kind of comparison happens in our Web site code all the time, we would like to make part of this a reusable function. One way to do this would be the following rewrite:

```
function better_deal ($amount_1, $price_1,
                      $amount_2, $price_2)
{
  $per_amount_1 = $price_1 / $amount_1;
  $per_amount_2 = $price_2 / $amount_2;
  return($per_amount_1 < $per_amount_2);
}

$liters_1 = 1.0;
$price_1 = 1.59;
$liters_2 = 1.5;
$price_2 = 2.09;

if (better_deal($liters_1, $price_1,
                $liters_2, $price_2))
   print("The first deal is better!<BR>");
else
   print("The second deal is better!<BR>");
```

Our `better_deal` function abstracts out the three lines in the previous code that did the arithmetic and comparison. It takes four numbers as arguments and returns the value of a Boolean expression. As with any Boolean value, we can embed it in the test portion of an `if` statement. Although this function is longer than the original code, there are two benefits to this rewrite: We can use the function in multiple places (saving lines overall), and if we decide to change the calculation, we have to make the change in only one place.

Alternatively, if the only way we ever use these price comparisons is to print which deal is preferred, we can include the printing in the function, like this:

```
function print_better_deal ($amount_1, $price_1,
                            $amount_2, $price_2)
{
  $per_amount_1 = $price_1 / $amount_1;
  $per_amount_2 = $price_2 / $amount_2;
  if ($per_amount_1 < $per_amount_2)
    print("The first deal is better!<BR>");
  else
    print("The second deal is better!<BR>");
}


$liters_1 = 1.0;
$price_1 = 1.59;
$liters_2 = 1.5;
$price_2 = 2.09;


print_better_deal($liters_1, $price_1,
                  $liters_2, $price_2);
```

Our first function used the `return` statement to send back a Boolean result, which was used in an `if` test. The second function has no `return` statement, because it is used for the side effect of printing text to the user's browser. When the last statement of this function is executed, PHP simply moves on to executing the next statement after a function call.

Formal parameters versus actual parameters

In the preceding examples, the arguments we passed to our functions happened to be variables, but this is not a requirement. The actual parameters (that is, the arguments in the function call) may be any expression that evaluates to a value. In our examples, we could have passed numbers to our function calls rather than variables, as in:

```
print_better_deal(1.0, 1.59, 1.5, 2.09);
```

Also, notice that in the examples we had a couple of cases where the actual parameter variable had the same name as the formal parameter (for example, $price_1), and we also had cases where the actual and formal names were different. ($liters_1 is not the same as $amount_1.) As we will see in the next section, this name agreement doesn't matter either way — the names of a function's formal parameters are completely independent of the world outside the function, including the function call itself.

Argument number mismatches

What happens if you call a function with fewer arguments than appear in the definition, or with more? As you might have come to expect by now, PHP handles this without anything crashing, but it may print a warning depending on your settings for error reporting.

Too few arguments

If you supply fewer actual parameters than formal parameters, PHP will treat the unfilled formal parameters as if they were unbound variables. However, under the usual settings for error reporting in PHP5, you will also see a warning printed to the browser.

The default error-reporting setting in PHP5 reports on every kind of error except runtime notices, which are the least serious condition that is detected. The reason you see warnings about too few arguments to a function is that this is treated as a runtime-warning situation (the next most serious category). If you really need function calls that sometimes provide too few arguments and seeing warnings is unacceptable, you have two options for suppressing the warnings:

✦ You can temporarily change the value of error reporting in your script, with a statement like `error_reporting(E_ALL - (E_NOTICE + E_WARNING));`. This will turn off both runtime notices and runtime warnings from the point where it appears in your script up to the next `error_reporting()` statement (if any). (Note that this is dangerous, as lots of other problems might produce warnings besides the one you're interested in.)

✦ You can suppress errors for any single expression by using the error-control operator @, which you can put in front of any expression to suppress errors from that expression only. For example, if the function call `my_function()` is producing a warning, `@my_function()` will not. Note that this is dangerous as well because all types of errors except for parse errors will be suppressed.

We don't advise using either of these workarounds, but we provide them because we are such nonjudgmental people by nature. PHP actually provides ways to write functions that expect variable numbers of arguments (see the "Variable Numbers of Arguments" section in Chapter 26), and using them is a much better idea than shooting the messenger.

Tip   Rather than decreasing PHP's reportage of errors, we advise increasing it to the maximum level possible when you are developing new code. You can do this globally by changing the `php.ini` file (see Chapter 30) or simply by including the statement `error_reporting (E_ALL);` at the top of your scripts. Among other things, this increase in reportage will mean that you will be warned about variables you have forgotten to assign, which is one of the most frequent causes of time-wasting bugs.

Too many arguments

If you hand too many arguments to a function, the excess arguments will simply be ignored, even when error reporting is set to `E_ALL`. As we will see in Chapter 26, this tolerance turns out to be helpful in defining functions that can take a variable number of arguments.

Functions and Variable Scope

As we said in Chapter 5, outside of functions, the rules about variable scope are simple: Assign a variable anywhere in the execution of a PHP code file, and the value will be there for you later in that file's execution. The rules become somewhat more complicated in the bodies of function definitions, but not much.

The basic principle governing variables in function bodies is: Each function is its own little world. That is, barring some special declarations, the meaning of a variable name inside a function has nothing to do with the meaning of that name elsewhere. (This is a feature, not a bug—you want functions to be reusable in different contexts, and so having the behavior be independent of the context is a good thing. If not for this kind of scoping, you would waste a lot of time chasing down bugs caused by using the same variable name in different parts of your code.)

Note As of PHP 4.1, there is a small set of global variables that *are* automatically visible from within function definitions, in contradiction to the previous paragraph and the following one. These are the *superglobal arrays* ($_POST, $_GET, $_SESSION, and so on), which contain keys and values corresponding to variable bindings from different sources. For more on these variables and their uses, see Chapter 7.

The only variable values that a function has access to are the formal parameter variables (which have the values copied from the actual parameters), plus any variables assigned inside the function. This means that you can use local variables inside a function without worrying about their effects on the outside world. For example, consider this function and its subsequent use:

```
function SayMyABCs ()
{
  $count = 0;
  while ($count < 10)
    {
      print(chr(ord('A') + $count));
      $count = $count + 1;
    }
  print("<BR>Now I know $count letters<BR>");
}
$count = 0;
SayMyABCs();
$count = $count + 1;
print("Now I've made $count function call(s).<BR>");
SayMyABCs();
$count = $count + 1;
print("Now I've made $count function call(s).<BR>");
```

The intent of SayMyABCs() is to print a sequence of letters. (The functions chr() and ord() translate between letters and their numeric ASCII codes — we use them here just as a trick to generate letters in sequence.) The output of this code is:

```
ABCDEFGHIJ
Now I know 10 letters
Now I've made 1 function call(s).
ABCDEFGHIJ
Now I know 10 letters
Now I've made 2 function call(s).
```

Both the function definition and the code outside the function make use of variables called $count, but they refer to different variables and do not clash.

The default behavior of variables assigned inside functions is that they do not interact with the outside world; they act as though they are newly created each time the function is called. Both of these behaviors, however, can be overridden with special declarations.

Global versus local

The scope of a variable defined inside a function is *local* by default, meaning that (as we explained in the previous section) it has no connection with the meaning of any variables outside the function. Using the global declaration, you can inform PHP that you want a variable name to mean the same thing as it does in the context outside the function. The syntax of this declaration is simply the word `global`, followed by a comma-delimited list of the variables that should be treated that way, with a terminating semicolon. To see the effect, consider a new version of the previous example. The only difference is that we have declared `$count` to be global, and we have removed its initial assignment to zero inside the function:

```
function SayMyABCs2 ()
{
  global $count;
  while ($count < 10)
    {
      print(chr(ord('A') + $count));
      $count = $count + 1;
    }
  print("<BR>Now I know $count letters<BR>");
}
$count = 0;
SayMyABCs2();
$count = $count + 1;
print("Now I've made $count function call(s).<BR>");
SayMyABCs2();
$count = $count + 1;
print("Now I've made $count function call(s).<BR>");
```

Our revised version prints the following browser output:

```
ABCDEFGHIJ
Now I know 10 letters
Now I've made 11 function call(s).

Now I know 11 letters
Now I've made 12 function call(s).
```

This is buggy behavior, and the `global` declaration is to blame. There is now only one `$count` variable, and it is being increased both inside and outside the function. When the second call to `SayMyABCs()` happens, `$count` is already 11, so the loop that prints letters is never entered.

Although this example shows `global` to bad advantage, it can be quite useful, especially because (as we'll see in Chapter 7) PHP provides some variable bindings to every page even before any of your own code is executed. It can be helpful to have a way for functions to see these variables without the bother of passing them in as arguments with each call.

Static variables

By default, functions retain no memory of their own execution, and with each function call local variables act as though they have been newly created. The `static` declaration overrides this behavior for particular variables, causing them to retain their values in between calls to the same function. Using this, we can modify our earlier function `SayMyABCs2()` to give it some memory:

```
function SayMyABCs3 ()
{
  static $count = 0; //assignment only if first time called
  $limit = $count + 10;
  while ($count < $limit)
```

```
    {
      print(chr(ord('A') + $count));
      $count = $count + 1;
    }
    print("<BR>Now I know $count letters<BR>");
  }
  $count = 0;
  SayMyABCs3();
  $count = $count + 1;
  print("Now I've made $count function call(s).<BR>");
  SayMyABCs3();
  $count = $count + 1;
  print("Now I've made $count function call(s).<BR>");
```

This memory-enhanced version gives us the following output:

```
ABCDEFGHIJ
Now I know 10 letters
Now I've made 1 function call(s).
KLMNOPQRST
Now I know 20 letters
Now I've made 2 function call(s).
```

The static keyword allows for an initial assignment, which has an effect only if the function has not been called before. The first time SayMyABCs3() executes, the local version of $count is set to zero. The second time the function is called, it has the value it had at the end of the last execution, so we are able to pick up our studies where we left off. Notice that changes to $count outside the function still have no effect on the local value.

Exceptions

New to PHP5 is the Exception class. We've already seen some fairly primitive error handling in the form of die(), and you might well imagine the custom error handling possibilities implied by the combination of control structures and basic use of print() or printf() commands (more on this in Chapter 26). However, in prior versions of PHP, a chief complaint was the lack of standardized means for handling errors, and separating that means from the application code itself. Enter Exceptions.

Exceptions use the try, catch syntax similar to Java or Python, although programmers using those languages will note the absence of finally.

Let's start with a simple example that has no error handling at all:

```
function print_header($title, $keywords, $description) {
  print("<HTML><HEAD>");
  print("<TITLE>$title</TITLE>");
  print("<META NAME=\"Keywords\" CONTENT=\"$keywords\">");
  print("<META NAME=\"Description\" CONTENT=\"$description\">");
  print("</HEAD><BODY>");
}

print_header('My Page',
  'PHP, Programming, Beer',
  '');
```

The custom function `print_header()` is designed to make it easy for us to place a standardized, search engine–friendly header at the top of each page. However, we've left the description variable undefined, which will not yield an error, but will leave us without a meaningful description for our page. Unfortunately, because the function is essentially called correctly and PHP is forgiving in nature, we may never know that we've left off this important detail. Some form of error handling is necessary to point this out, and *Exceptions* provide a handy way of dong so. Consider this revised code:

```
function print_header($title, $keywords, $description) {
  if(strlen($description) < 40)
    throw new Exception('A reasonable description length is
required<BR>');
  print("<HTML><HEAD>");
  print("<TITLE>$title</TITLE>");
  print("<META NAME=\"Keywords\" CONTENT=\"$keywords\">");
  print("<META NAME=\"Description\" CONTENT=\"$description\">");
  print("</HEAD><BODY>");
}

try {
  print_header('My Page',
    'PHP, Programming, Beer',
    '');
} catch (Exception $e) {
  echo($e->getMessage());
}
```

The first new thing in our revised function is a simple test in line 2 suggesting an appropriate minimum length for the `$description` variable. The line immediately following initiates an instance of the `Exception` class with the message suggested by the quoted value.

Note   A class is one of the recent OOP concepts introduced in PHP4. You can create your own classes and extensions of existing classes, including those for Exception handling. PHP gives you Exception for free. We'll go into much greater depth on the subject of classes in Chapter 20 and exception handling itself in Chapter 31.

Next, instead of simply calling our function, we've enclosed the function in a new control structure, the `try. . .catch` block. If we execute the code as written, PHP first tries to execute the function as described; then it terminates execution almost immediately, because the `$description` variable has failed our simple test. At this point, the script can continue execution after the `try. . .catch` block, or it can be terminated with `die()` or `exit()`.

Multiple exceptions can be defined in a single function. This is good idea because it yields more specific information about what exactly happened. Because execution stops with the first exception, only this exception will be caught.

Cross-Reference   Exceptions are a huge topic; they're outlined here so you can start using them immediately. You'll find nods to Exceptions throughout this book, but they are covered in depth in Chapter 31.

Function Scope

Although the rules about the scope of variable names are fairly simple, the scoping rules for function names are even simpler. There is just one rule in PHP5: Functions must be defined once (and only once) somewhere in the script that uses them. (See the following note about differences between this behavior and PHP3.) The scope of function names is implicitly global, so a function defined in a script is available everywhere in that script. For clarity's sake, however, it is often a good idea to define all your functions first before any code that calls those functions.

Note In PHP3, functions could be used only after they were defined. This meant that the safest practice was to define (or include the definitions of) all functions early in a given script, before actually using any of them. PHP4 and 5 actually precompile scripts before running them, and one effect of this precompilation is that it discovers all function definitions before actually running the code. This means that functions and code can appear in any order in a script, as long as all functions are defined once (and only once).

Include and require

It's very common to want to use the same set of functions across a set of Web site pages, and the usual way to handle this is with either `include` or `require`, both of which import the contents of some other file into the file being executed. Using either one of these forms is vastly preferable to *cloning* your function definitions (that is, repeating them at the beginning of each page that uses them); when you want to modify your functions, you will have to do it only once. (We covered these forms in Chapter 4, but they are worth reviewing here in the context of including function definitions.)

For example, at the top of a PHP code file we might have lines like:

```
include "basic-functions.inc"
include "advanced-function.inc";
(.. code that uses basic and advanced functions ..)
```

which import two different files of function definitions. (Note that parentheses are optional with both `include()` and `require()`.) As long as the only things in these files are function definitions, the order of their inclusion does not matter.

Both `include` and `require` have the effect of splicing in the contents of their file into the PHP code at the point that they are called. The only difference between them is how they fail if the file cannot be found. The `include` construct will cause a warning to be printed, but processing of the script will continue; `require`, on the other hand, will cause a fatal error if the file cannot be found.

Note Note that `include` and `require` are now more similar in their behavior than they used to be. Prior to PHP 4.0.2, `require` had its file contents spliced in statically, before the actual execution of the page; whereas the contents from `include` were spliced in dynamically as the page executed. Among other things, this led to subtle differences in behavior when the `include`/`require` form was in conditional code. Now, however, both `include` and `require` have the same dynamic behavior. This means, for example, that if an `include`/`require` form is in a loop executed 10 times, 10 inclusions will be made.

Including only once

Sometimes you really want a file to be included once, but not more than once. This is true most often in the case of function definitions. For example, two different function definition files might, in turn, include the same file of utility functions — if a top-level page includes both of these files, the utility functions might be included twice, leading to complaints from PHP that functions are being defined twice.

To the rescue come include_once and require_once, which act just like their counterparts except that they will not include a file named by a given string if that file has already been included. It's usually better to use the _once version, in general, for including function and class definition files.

The include path

When you include a filename, PHP searches for a file by that name in the directories specified in the include_path (which is settable in your php.ini file). The default path includes the same directory as the one the top-level code page is in. See Chapter 30 for details about how to add locations to your include path.

In situations where a single instance of PHP serves several virtual sites, it's generally easier and less confusing to PHP to use the $_SERVER superglobal array to specify the location of an include file:

```
include_once($_SERVER['DOCUMENT_ROOT']."/path/to/include_file");
```

Caution   Remember that included (and required) files are parsed by default in HTML mode rather than in PHP mode. This means that any included file meant to be interpreted as PHP needs to have the usual PHP tags at the beginning and end.

Recursion

Some compiled languages, like C and C++, impose somewhat complex ordering constraints on how functions are defined. To know how to compile a function, the compiler must know about all the functions that the function calls, which means the called functions must be defined first. So what do you do if two functions each call the other or if one function calls itself? Issues like this led the designers of C to a separation of function declarations (or prototypes) from function definitions (or implementations). The idea is that you use declarations to inform the compiler in advance about the types of arguments and return types of the functions you plan to use, which is enough information for the compiler to handle the actual definitions in any order.

In PHP, this problem goes away, and so there is no need for separate function prototypes. As long as each function that is called is defined once (and only once) in the current code file or one that is included in the course of the current script's execution, PHP will have no problem resolving function calls, regardless of the interleaving of function calls and definitions.

This means that *recursive functions* (functions that call themselves) are no problem in PHP4. For example, we can define a recursive function and then immediately call it:

```
function countdown ($num_arg)
  {
    if ($num_arg > 0)
      {
        print("Counting down from $num_arg<BR>");
```

```
            countdown($num_arg - 1);
        }
    }
countdown(10);
```

This produces the browser output:

```
Counting down from 10
Counting down from 9
Counting down from 8
Counting down from 7
Counting down from 6
Counting down from 5
Counting down from 4
Counting down from 3
Counting down from 2
Counting down from 1
```

As with all recursive functions, it's important to be sure that the function has a *base case* (a nonrecursive branch) in addition to the recursive case, and that the base case is certain to eventually occur. If the base case is never invoked, the situation is much like a `while` loop where the test is always true — we will have an infinite loop of function calling. In the case of the preceding function, we know that the base case will happen, because every invocation of the recursive case reduces the countdown number, which must eventually become zero. Of course, this assumes that the input is a positive integer rather than a negative number or a double. Notice that our "greater than zero" test guards against infinite recursion even in these cases, whereas a "not equal to zero" test would not.

Similarly, *mutually recursive functions* (functions that call each other) work without a hitch. For example, the following definitions plus function call:

```
function countdown_first ($num_arg)
    {
    if ($num_arg > 0)
        {
            print("Counting down (first) from $num_arg<BR>");
            countdown_second($num_arg - 1);
        }
    }
function countdown_second ($num_arg)
    {
    if ($num_arg > 0)
        {
            print("Counting down (second) from $num_arg<BR>");
            countdown_first($num_arg - 1);
        }
    }

countdown_first(5);
```

produce the browser output:

```
Counting down (first) from 5
Counting down (second) from 4
Counting down (first) from 3
Counting down (second) from 2
Counting down (first) from 1
```

Summary

PHP has a C-like set of control structures, which branch or loop depending on the value of Boolean expressions, which in turn can be combined using Boolean operators (and, or, xor, !, &&, ||). The structures if and switch are used for simple branching; while, do-while, and for are used for looping, and exit() or die() terminates script execution.

Most of the power of PHP resides in the large number of built-in functions provided by PHP's benevolent army of open source developers. Each of these functions should be documented (albeit briefly) in the online manual at http://www.php.net.

You can also write your own functions, which are then used in exactly the same way as the built-in functions. Functions are written in a simple C-style syntax, as in the following:

```
function my_function ($arg1, $arg2, ..)
{
statement1;
statement2;
..
return($value);
}
```

User-defined functions can use arguments of any PHP type and can also return values of any type. The types of arguments and return values do not need to be declared.

In PHP, the ordering of function definitions and function calls makes no difference, as long as every function that is called is defined exactly once. There is no need for separate function declarations or prototypes. Variables assigned inside a function are local to that function, unless specified otherwise with the global declaration. Local variables may be declared to be *static,* which means that they hold onto their values in between function calls.

Finally, with our brief treatment of exceptions, we're well on our way to writing thoughtful friendly code that uses standardized error handling.

Passing Information between Pages

In this chapter, we'll briefly discuss some things you need to know about passing data between Web pages. Some of this information is not specific to PHP but is a consequence of the PHP/HTML interaction or of the HTTP protocol itself.

HTTP Is Stateless

The most important thing to recall about the way the Web works is that the HTTP protocol itself is stateless. If you are a poetic soul, you might say that each HTTP request is on its own, with no direction home, like a complete unknown . . . you know how the rest goes.

For the less lyrical among us, this means that each HTTP request — in most cases, this translates to each resource (HTML page, .jpg file, style sheet, and so on) being asked for and delivered — is independent of all the others, knows nothing substantive about the identity of the client, and has no memory. Each request spawns a discrete process, which goes about its humble but worthy task of serving up one single solitary file and then is automatically killed off. (But that sounds so harsh; maybe we can say "flits back to the pool of available processes" instead.)

Even if you design your site with very strict one-way navigation (Page 1 leads only to Page 2, which leads only to Page 3, and so on), the HTTP protocol will never know or care that someone browsing Page 2 must have come from Page 1. You cannot set the value of a variable on Page 1 and expect it to be imported to Page 2 by the exigencies of HTML itself. You can use HTML to display a form, and someone can enter some information using it — but unless you employ some extra means to pass the information to another page or program, the variable will simply vanish into the ether as soon as you move to another page.

This is where a form-handling technology like PHP comes in. PHP will catch the variable tossed from one page to the next and make it available for further use. PHP happens to be unusually good at this type of data-passing function, which makes it fast and easy to employ for a wide variety of Web site tasks.

HTML forms are mostly useful for passing a few values from a given page to one single other page of a Web site. There are more persistent ways to maintain state over many pageviews, such as cookies and sessions, which we cover in Chapter 24. This chapter will focus on the most basic techniques of information-passing between Web pages, which utilize the GET and POST methods in HTTP to create dynamically generated pages and to handle form data.

Note   This is where old-school ASP developers invariably say, "PHP sucks!" They think ASP session variables are magic. Not to burst anyone's bubble, but Microsoft is just using cookies to store session variables — thereby opening the door to all kinds of potential problems.

GET Arguments

The GET method passes arguments from one page to the next as part of the *Uniform Resource Indicator* (you may be more familiar with the term *Uniform Resource Locator* or *URL*) query string. When used for form handling, GET appends the indicated variable name(s) and value(s) to the URL designated in the ACTION attribute with a question mark separator and submits the whole thing to the processing agent (in this case a Web server).

This is an example HTML form using the GET method (save the file under the name team_select.html):

```
<HTML>
<HEAD>
<TITLE>A GET method example, part 1</TITLE>
</HEAD>

<BODY>
<FORM ACTION="http://localhost/baseball.php" METHOD="GET">
<P>Root, root, root for the:<BR>
<SELECT NAME="Team" SIZE="2">
<!--It's a good idea to use the VALUE attribute even though
it is not mandatory with the SELECT element. In this example,
it's extremely necessary. -->
<OPTION VALUE="Cubbies">Chicago Cubs (National League)</OPTION>
<OPTION VALUE="Pale Hose">Chicago White Sox (American
League)</OPTION>
</SELECT>
<P><INPUT TYPE="submit" NAME="Submit" VALUE="Select"></P>
</FORM>
</BODY>

</HTML>
```

When the user makes a selection and clicks the Submit button, the browser agglutinates these elements in this order, with no spaces between the elements:

✦ The URL in quotes after the word ACTION (http://localhost/baseball.php)

✦ A question mark (?) denoting that the following characters constitute a GET string.

✦ A variable NAME, an equal sign, and the matching VALUE (Team=Cubbies)

✦ An ampersand (&) and the next NAME-VALUE pair (Submit=Select); further name-value pairs separated by ampersands can be added as many times as the server query-string-length limit allows.

The browser thus constructs the URL string:

```
http://localhost/baseball.php?Team=Cubbies&Submit=Select
```

It then forwards this URL into its own address space as a new request. The PHP script to which the preceding form is submitted (baseball.php) will grab the GET variables from the end of the request string, stuff them into the $_GET superglobal array (explained in a moment), and do something useful with them — in this case, plug one of two values into a text string.

> **Tip**
>
> Strictly speaking, the name-value pairs in a GET query are not part of the HTTP or addressing standards. In one of the odd footnotes of Internet history, the W3C allowed for the possibility of extra data to be passed to a resource after a ? in the URI string but never specified precisely what form that data should take. Usage quickly established the notion of name-value pairs separated by ampersands, but this is not part of any W3C standard.

The following code sample shows the PHP form handler for the preceding HTML form:

```
<HTML>
<HEAD>
<TITLE>A GET method example, part 2</TITLE>
<STYLE TYPE="text/css">
<!--
BODY  {font-size: 24pt;}
-->
</STYLE>
</HEAD>

<BODY>
<P>Go,
<?php echo $_GET['Team']; ?>
!</P>
</BODY>
</HTML>
```

Note that the value inputted into the previous page's HTML form field named "Team" is now available in a PHP variable called $_GET['Team']. Finally, you should see a page that says Go, Cubbies! in big type.

> **Note**
>
> At this point, it makes some sense to explain just how to access values submitted from page to page. This chapter discusses the two main methods for passing values: GET and POST (there are others, but they are not covered until Part III). Each method has an associated superglobal array, explained in more depth in Chapter 9, which can be distinguished from other arrays by the underscore that begins its name. Each item submitted via the GET method is accessed in the handler via the $_GET array; each item submitted via the POST method is accessed in the handler via the $_POST array. The syntax for referencing an item in a superglobal array is simple and 100 percent consistent:
>
> $_ARRAY_NAME['index_name']
>
> where the index_name is the name part of a name-value pair (for the GET method), or the name of an HTML form field (for the POST method). As in the preceding example, $_GET['Team'] indicates the value of the form select field called 'Team', sent by the GET operation in the original file. You must use the array appropriate to the method used to send data. In this case, $_POST['Team'] is undefined because no data was POSTed by the original form.

The GET method of form handling offers one big advantage over the POST method: It constructs an actual new and differentiable URL query string. Users can now bookmark this page (and thus find the oh-so-necessary encouraging word when their team starts to fade in the doldrums of August). The result of forms using the POST method is not bookmarkable.

Just because you *can* achieve the desired functionality with GET arguments doesn't mean you *should*. The disadvantages of GET for most types of form handling are so substantial that the original HTML 4.0 draft specification deprecated its use in 1997. These flaws include:

✦ The GET method is not suitable for logins because the username and password are fully visible onscreen as well as potentially stored in the client browser's memory as a visited page.

✦ Every GET submission is recorded in the Web server log, data set included.

✦ Because the GET method assigns data to a server environment variable, the length of the URL is limited. You may have seen what seem like very long URLs using GET — but you really wouldn't want to try passing a 300-word chunk of HTML-formatted prose using this method.

Caution   The original HTML spec called for query strings to be limited to 255 characters. Although this stricture was later loosened to mere encouragement of a 255-character limit, using a longer string is asking for trouble.

The GET method of form handling had to be reinstated by the W3C after much outcry, largely because of the bookmarkability factor. Despite that it's still implemented as the default choice for form handling in all browsers, GET now comes with a strong recommendation to deploy it in *idempotent* usages only — in other words, those that have no permanent side effects. Putting two and two together, the single most appropriate form-handling use of GET is the search box. Unless you have a compelling reason to use GET for non-search-box form handling, use POST instead.

A Better Use for GET-Style URLs

Although the actual GET method of form handling is deprecated, the style of URL associated with it turns out to be very useful for site navigation. This is especially true for dynamically generated sites such as those often constructed with PHP, because the appended-variable style of URL works particularly smoothly with a template-based content-development system.

As an illustration, imagine you are the proud proprietor of an information-rich Web site about solar cars. You've toiled long and hard over informative and attractive pages such as these:

```
suspension_design.html
windtunnel_testing.html
friction_braking.html
```

But as your site grows, a flat-file site structure like this can take a lot of time to administer, as even the most trivial changes must be repeated on every page. If the structure of these pages is very similar, you might want to move to a template-based system with PHP.

You might decide to utilize a single template with separate text files for each topic (containing information, photos, comments, and so on):

```
topic.php
  suspension_design.inc
  windtunnel_testing.inc
  friction_braking.inc
```

Or you might decide you needed a larger, more specialized choice of template files:

```
vehicle_structure.php
  tubular_frames.inc
mechanical_systems.php
  friction_braking.inc
electrical_systems.php
  solar_array.inc
racing.php
  race_strategy.inc
```

A simple template file might look something like this (because we haven't included the necessary .inc text files, this example will not actually work):

```
<HTML>
<HEAD>
<TITLE>Solar-car topics</TITLE>
<STYLE TYPE="text/css">
<!--
BODY   {font: verdana; font-size: 12pt}
-->
</STYLE>
</HEAD>

<BODY>
<TABLE BORDER=0 CELLPADDING=0 WIDTH=100%>
<TR>
<!-- Navbar, with Get-style URLs. -->
<TD BGCOLOR="#4282B4" ALIGN=CENTER VALIGN=TOP WIDTH=25%>
  <P>
  <A HREF="mechanical_systems.php?Name=friction_braking">
<B>Friction braking</B></A>
  <BR>
  <A HREF="mechanical_systems.php?Name=steering">
<B>Steering</B></A>
  <BR>
  <A HREF="mechanical_systems.php?Name=suspension">
<B>Suspension</B></A>
  <BR>
  <A HREF="mechanical_systems.php?Name=tires">
<B>Tires and wheels</B></A>
  <BR>
  </P>
</TD>

<!-- Main body of content -->
<TD BGCOLOR="#FFFFFF" ALIGN=LEFT VALIGN=TOP WIDTH=75%>
<?php include("$_GET['Name'].inc"); ?>
</TD></TR></TABLE>
</BODY>
</HTML>
```

Notice that the links on the navbar, when clicked, will be handled by the browser as if they were the product of a GET submission.

But even with this solution, you still have to tend part of your garden by hand: making sure each `include` file is properly formatted in HTML, adding a new link to the navbar each time you add a new page to the site, and other such chores. Following the general rule to separate form and content as much as is feasible, you might choose to go to another level of abstraction with a database. In that case, a URL such as `http://localhost/topic.php?topicID=2` would point to a PHP template that makes database calls. (Using a number variable rather than a word makes for faster database interaction.) This system could also automatically add a link to the navbar whenever you added new topics to the database, so it could produce Web pages entirely without ongoing human intervention (all right, maybe *entirely* is an exaggeration — but with significantly fewer person-hours of grunt labor).

POST Arguments

POST is the preferred method of form submission today, particularly in *nonidempotent* usages (those that will result in permanent changes), such as adding information to a database. The form data set is included in the body of the form when it is forwarded to the processing agent (in this case, PHP). No visible change to the URL will result according to the different data submitted.

The POST method has these advantages:

✦ It is more secure than GET because user-entered information is never visible in the URL query string, in the server logs, or (if precautions, such as always using the `password` HTML input type for passwords, are taken) onscreen.

✦ There is a much larger limit on the amount of data that can be passed (a couple of kilobytes rather than a couple of hundred characters).

POST has these disadvantages:

✦ The results at a given moment cannot be bookmarked.

✦ The results should be expired by the browser, so that an error will result if the user employs the Back button to revisit the page.

✦ This method can be incompatible with certain firewall setups, which strip the form data as a security measure.

Get and Post both

Did you know that with PHP you can use both GET and POST variables on the same page? You might want to do this for a dynamically generated form, for example.

But what if you (deliberately or otherwise) use the same variable name in both the GET and the POST variable sets? PHP keeps all ENVIRONMENT, GET, POST, COOKIE, and SERVER variables in the `$GLOBALS` array if you have set the `register_globals` configuration directive to "on" in your `php.ini` file. If there is a conflict, it is resolved by overwriting the variable values in the order you set, using the `variables_order` option in `php.ini`. Later trumps earlier, so if you use the default "EGPCS" value, cookies will triumph over POSTs that will themselves obliterate GETs. You can control the order of overwriting by simply changing the order of the letters on the appropriate line of this file, or even better, turning `register_globals` off and using the new PHP superglobal arrays instead. See the section on superglobals later in this chapter.

We use the POST method consistently in this book for form handling—especially when putting data into a system via a file write or SQL INSERT. We use GET only for site navigation and Search boxes—in other words, for pulling data back out of a data store and displaying it. All the rest of the forms in this chapter use the POST method.

Formatting Form Variables

PHP is so efficient at passing data around because the developers made a very handy but (in theory) slightly sketchy design decision. PHP automatically, but invisibly, assigns the variables for you on the new page when you submit a data set using GET or POST. Most of PHP's competitors make you explicitly do this assignment yourself on each page; if you forget to do so or make a mistake, the information will not be available to the processing agent. PHP is faster, simpler, and mostly more goof-proof.

But because of this automatic variable assignment, you need to always use a good NAME attribute for each INPUT. NAME attributes are not strictly necessary in HTML proper—your form will render fine without them—but the data will be of little use because the HTML form-field NAME attribute will be the variable name in the form handler.

In other words, in this form:

```
<FORM ACTION="<?php echo $_SERVER['PHP_SELF']; ?>"
METHOD="POST">
<INPUT TYPE="text" NAME="email">
<INPUT TYPE="submit" NAME="submit" VALUE="Send">
</FORM>
```

the text field named email will cause the creation of a PHP variable called $_POST['email'] (or $HTTP_POST_VARS['email'] if you use the older style of variable arrays; or just $email if you have register_globals turned on) when the form is submitted. Similarly, the submit button will lead to the creation of a variable called $_POST['submit'] on the next page. The name you use in the HTML form will be the name of your variable in the PHP form handler.

Caution $HTTP_POST_VARS, $HTTP_SERVER_VARS, and the whole family of these long-form predefined variables are deprecated in PHP5. If you are already an experienced PHP programmer, perhaps with a large body of previously written code lying around, you might want to think about rewriting now for backward compatibility. They are supported for the time being, but their days are numbered. Use $_POST, $_GET, and friends instead.

Remember that you cannot use a variable name beginning with a number—so you should not name your form field something like 5 (you laugh, but we've seen people try to do it)—and PHP variable names are case sensitive. Also, *please* try to use informative variable names rather than a succession of form fields named myvar and e.

Tip It's a good idea to standardize how you name form variables, to make your code more readable and so that you spend less time flipping back to the form itself when you are supposed to be writing code to process that form. For example, you might precede all form variables with frm to indicate their source. You might then consistently use the first few letters of each identifying word for what a field does, for example, frmNameFirst, frmOfficeAdd, frmHomeAdd, and so on. The specific standard you set is less important than having a standard to begin with.

Another thing to keep in mind when creating your HTML forms is that, if you ever want this form to be displayed with prefilled inputs, you need to set the VALUE attribute. This is particularly relevant to two kinds of forms: those that are used to edit data from a database; and those that are intended to possibly be submitted more than once. The latter case is very common in situations where a form should redisplay on error with values already prefilled—for instance, a registration form that will not work until the user provides a valid e-mail address or other required data.

For example, the form in Listing 7-1 (which represents a retirement savings calculator) is designed to be submitted multiple times while the user fiddles around with the values. Every time you submit the form, the values from the previous go-round will be filled in for you automatically. Note the use of the VALUE attribute in the form fields in this code sample.

Listing 7-1: **Form with prefilled values (retirement_calc.php)**

```
<HTML>
<HEAD>
<TITLE>A POST example: retirement savings worksheet</TITLE>
<STYLE TYPE="text/css">
<!--
BODY      {font-size: 14pt}
.heading    {font-size: 18pt; color: red}
-->
</STYLE>
</HEAD>

<?php

// This test, along with the Submit button value in the form
// below, will check to see if the form is being rendered for
// the first time (in which case it will display with only the
// default annual gain filled in).

if (!IsSet($_POST['Submit']) || $_POST['Submit'] != 'Calculate')
{
   $_POST['CurrentAge'] = "";
   $_POST['RetireAge'] = "";
   $_POST['Contrib'] = "";
   $Total = 0;
   $AnnGain = 7;
} else {
   $AnnGain = $_POST['AnnGain'];
   $Years = $_POST['RetireAge'] - $_POST['CurrentAge'];
   $YearCount = 0;
   $Total = $_POST['Contrib'];
```

```
    while ($YearCount <= $Years) {
       $Total = round($Total * (1.0 + $AnnGain/100) +
$_POST['Contrib']);
       $YearCount = $YearCount + 1;
    }
}
?>
<BODY>

<DIV ALIGN="CENTER" ID="Div1" class="heading">
A retirement-savings calculator</DIV>

<P class=blurb>Fill in all the values (except "Nest Egg")
and see how much money you'll have for your retirement
under different scenarios.  You can change the values and
resubmit the form as many times as you like. You must fill
in the two "Age" variables. The "Annual return" variable has
a default inflation-adjusted value (7% = 8% growth minus 1%
inflation) which you can change to reflect your greater
optimism or pessimism.</P>

<FORM ACTION="<?php echo $_SERVER['PHP_SELF']; ?>"
METHOD="POST">
<P>Your age now:
<INPUT TYPE="text" SIZE=5 NAME="CurrentAge"
VALUE="<?php echo $_POST['CurrentAge']; ?>">
<P>The age at which you plan to retire:
<INPUT TYPE="text" SIZE=6 NAME="RetireAge"
VALUE="<?php echo $_POST['RetireAge']; ?>">
<P>Annual contribution:
<INPUT TYPE="text" SIZE=15 NAME="Contrib"
VALUE="<?php echo $_POST['Contrib']; ?>">
<P>Annual return:
<INPUT TYPE="text" SIZE=5 NAME="AnnGain"
VALUE="<?php echo $AnnGain; ?>"> %
<BR><BR>
<P><B>NEST EGG</B>:  <?php echo $Total; ?>
<P><INPUT TYPE="submit" NAME="Submit" VALUE="Calculate">
</FORM>
</BODY>
</HTML>
```

Figure 7-1 shows the result of the Listing 7-1.

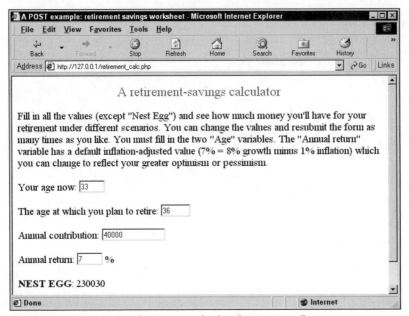

Figure 7-1: A form using the POST method with VALUE attributes

Consolidating forms and form handlers

As you can see in the preceding example, it is often handy to make the HTML form and the form handler into one script. This practice has many advantages, such as making it easier to change the name of the file without harming functionality, making it easier to display error messages and prefilled form fields, and achieving better control over your variable namespace. Suppose you are making a login form that redisplays with an error message if the login is unsuccessful. If you have separate forms and form handlers, you'll probably have to do something yucky with GET vars and redirection. If you consolidate, it's very simple to control the display without these machinations. (See Chapter 44 for an example of this very usage in a login form.)

Cross-Reference   To see how these techniques can be used with data from MySQL, see Chapter 17.

When you consolidate, generally the form-handling code should come before the form display. This order may be something of a shift in thinking for those who are used to writing the form before the handler, but if you think it through, you will see the logic of the practice. You have to give yourself an opportunity to set variables and make choices before you can decide what to show the user. This is especially relevant if you will be redirecting the user to a different page under certain circumstances, via the header() function, because this decision point must come before any HTML output has been displayed to the browser.

Generally there are two ways you can check to see whether you're displaying a form for the first time or whether it's already been submitted at least once. Either you can use the Submit button, as we do in the preceding example, or you can set a hidden variable if you tend to have all your Submit buttons say the same thing (like "Submit"). The latter method is safer, because some browsers don't actually submit the `Submit` value if a user hits Enter instead of clicking the button.

Using array variables with forms

In all the examples so far, each form field created a variable of the string or integer types. This implies that there is a one-to-one relationship between a form field and a form-handler variable. But PHP also allows you to post an array-type variable. (If you don't yet have a good grip on arrays, come back to this section after you read Chapter 9).

Listing 7-2 is an example of a script that creates an array from the names of the form fields in an HTML form.

Listing 7-2: **Form passing an array of variables (geek_quiz.php)**

```php
<?php

/*****************************************************
 * "How geeky are you?" script, showing with screens. *
 * Screen 1: : quiz form.  Screen 2: results page.    *
 *****************************************************/

// The header which appears in both cases
// ----------------------------------------
$header_str = <<< EOHEADER
<HTML>
<HEAD>
<STYLE TYPE="text/css">
<!--
BODY, P, TD      {color: black; font-family: verdana;
font-size: 9 pt}
H1        {color: black; font-family: arial; font-size: 12 pt}
-->
</STYLE>
</HEAD>

<BODY>
<TABLE BORDER=0 CELLPADDING=10 WIDTH=100%>
<TR>
<TD BGCOLOR="#F0F8FF" ALIGN=CENTER VALIGN=TOP WIDTH=150>
</TD>

<TD BGCOLOR="#FFFFFF" ALIGN=LEFT VALIGN=TOP WIDTH=83%>
  <table cellspacing=0 cellpadding=20 border=0
width="530"><tr><td valign=top>
EOHEADER;


// The footer which appears in both cases
// ----------------------------------------
```

Continued

Listing 7-2 *(continued)*

```
$footer_str = <<< EOFOOTER
  </td></tr></table>
</TD></TR></TABLE>

</BODY>
</HTML>
EOFOOTER;


// Screen 1: quiz form
// --------------------
$quiz_str = <<< EOQUIZ
<h2>How geeky are you?</h2>
<form action="geek_quiz.php" method="POST">
<br /><br />
0.  Have you ever had a dream in which you were debugging?<br />
Yes <input type="checkbox" name="affirm[0]" value="1"/>
<br /><br />
1.  Do you know the name of the company founded by Danny
Hillis?<br />
Yes <input type="checkbox" name="affirm[1]" value="1"/>
<br /><br />
2.  Can you edit a file in both emacs and vi without recourse to
any documentation?<br />
Yes <input type="checkbox" name="affirm[2]" value="1"/>
<br /><br />
3.  Is the computer you're using at this moment hooked up to a
KVM switch?<br />
Yes <input type="checkbox" name="affirm[3]" value="1"/>
<br /><br />
4.  Are you wearing a logowear T-shirt?<br />
Yes <input type="checkbox" name="affirm[4]" value="1"/>
<br /><br />
5.  Have you ever written a chess program?<br />
Yes <input type="checkbox" name="affirm[5]" value="1"/>
<br /><br />
6.  Have you ever set up an SMTP server?<br />
Yes <input type="checkbox" name="affirm[6]" value="1"/>
<br /><br />
7.  Have you ever discussed the merits of a commercial LISP
implementation?<br />
Yes <input type="checkbox" name="affirm[7]" value="1"/>
<br /><br />
8.  Have you ever used the phrase "I can do that in two lines of
```

```
code" in public?<br />
Yes <input type="checkbox" name="affirm[8]" value="1"/>
<br /><br />
9.  Have you ever refused an otherwise welcome sexual advance
because you were debugging?<br />
Yes <input type="checkbox" name="affirm[9]" value="1"/>
<br /><br />
<input type="submit" name="submit" value="Evaluate"></form>
EOQUIZ;


// ------------------
// Now for some logic
// ------------------
echo $header_str;
if (!isSet($_POST['submit'])) {
  // First time, show the quiz form
  echo $quiz_str;
} elseif ($_POST['submit'] == 'Evaluate') {

  // Count up the yes answers
  $num_affirm = count($_POST['affirm']);

  // Come up with 4 different blurbs
  if ($num_affirm >= 0 && $num_affirm <= 3) {
    $result_str = "<P>Why even pretend to be something you're
so clearly not?</P>\n";
  } elseif ($num_affirm >= 4 && $num_affirm <= 6) {
    $result_str = "<P>Come back when you've learned more craft,
Grasshopper.</P>\n";
  } elseif ($num_affirm >= 7 && $num_affirm <= 8) {
    $result_str = "<P>Pretty geeky, but not yet a Code
God.</P>\n";
  } elseif ($num_affirm >= 9 && $num_affirm <= 10) {
    $result_str = "<P>We're not worthy to be in the presence of
your bad geeky self!</P>\n";
  }

  echo $result_str;
}
echo $footer_str;
?>
```

Figure 7-2 illustrates the output of the preceding code.

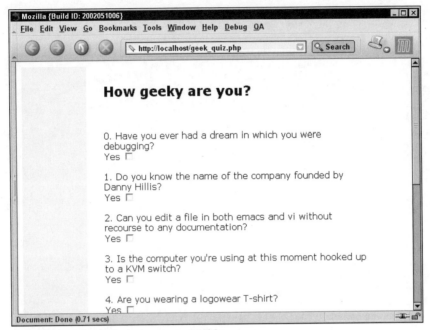

Figure 7-2: A form displaying array variables

Because, ultimately, we just want to count how many Yes answers there are, it would be cumbersome to set each check box as a separate variable and then count them. As you can see in the preceding code (line 93), with an array it is a simple matter of calling the count() function. In many other situations, it takes less code to loop through an array than to separately test a bunch of strings.

As you can see in the form HTML, the way you create an array variable with an HTML form is by using a name with a bracket after it. This can be an empty bracket, a bracket with an integer inside like the one we used above, or a bracket with a string inside. When you understand arrays better and have an idea of what you want an array to do for you, it will be clearer which of these alternatives you need in any given instance.

PHP Superglobal Arrays

A change that has been coming for a long time in PHP is the gradual phasing out of automatic global variables in favor of *superglobal* arrays, which were introduced in PHP4. Understanding superglobal arrays before you understand arrays may present difficulties; if so, we recommend you read Chapter 9 and come back to this section later.

In the good old days before PHP4.1, you could write a piece of code like this and expect it to work:

```php
<?php
if (isSet($submit)) {
  echo $email;
} else {
```

```
?>
<FORM ACTION="<?php echo $PHP_SELF; ?>" METHOD="POST">
<INPUT TYPE="text" NAME="email">
<INPUT TYPE="submit" NAME="submit" VALUE="Send">
</FORM>
```

All GET, POST, COOKIE, ENVIRONMENT, and SERVER variables were made global by the register_globals directive in php.ini and were directly accessible by their names by default.

This was bad for several reasons. For one thing, every so often a COOKIE variable would accidentally overwrite a POST variable of the same name although the developer didn't want that to happen. For another thing, it led to big, messy, undifferentiated global namespaces. Most important, allowing variables to be set by user input is very insecure. The PHP world had far too many inexperienced coders writing things like:

```
<?php
if ($secretpassword == 'opensesame') {
  $allaccesspass = 1;
}

if ($allaccesspass == 1) {
  include('/admin_index.html');
} else {
  include('/doweknowyou.html');
}
?>
```

without giving too much thought to the idea that a cracker could easily just call this page with a GET variable named allaccesspass set to 1 and negate the advantages of any password check.

The PHP team, in its infinite wisdom, decided to phase out the practice of registering globals, forcing everyone to call his variables as indices in an array (for example, $_POST['secret password']). This had already been possible in PHP4, via arrays named $HTTP_GET_VARS, $HTTP_POST_VARS, $HTTP_POST_VARS, and so on, but few developers had used this syntax; frankly, it was a lot of extra keystrokes for a small increase in security. So the PHP team also took this opportunity to rename these arrays with shorter names: $_GET, $_POST, $_COOKIE, $_ENV, and $_SERVER.

These superglobal arrays also have one cool feature that may ameliorate some pain: They are automatically global everywhere. This means, for instance, that you no longer have to pass cookie values into a function or declare the $HTTP_COOKIE_VARS array global before you can access those values in a function. This will help those who functionalize to the max and will be a small amelioration for everyone else.

As of PHP4.2, register_globals is officially turned off by default, and the old-style variable array names are deprecated. Sooner or later, the PHP team will make register_globals not work any more. It will take quite a while to move the entire PHP community over to the new superglobal arrays, but we feel obligated to try to use them as much as possible in this book to set a good example. Save yourself a lot of trouble in the future and start using superglobal arrays.

Caution   Although register_globals is still an available option in PHP5's php.ini file, setting it to on does not, as of this writing, provide access to variables outside of the superglobal arrays.

Extended Example: An Exercise Calculator

Chapters 7 through 10 of this book feature an extended example that will build on itself from chapter to chapter. Starting with a simple HTML form and form handler, you will add concepts as you move through string, array, math, and filesystem functions. At the end, you will have built a simple exercise calculator system that allows you to figure out how many calories were burned by your daily workouts and to store this information in a file.

In this first episode, shown in Listing 7-3, we are simply going to move a string POST variable from a form to a form handler using PHP. This HTML form is called workout_calc_var.html.

Listing 7-3: **Simple HTML form (workout_calc_var.html)**

```
<HTML>
<HEAD>
<STYLE TYPE="text/css">
<!--
BODY, P      {color: black; font-family: verdana;
font-size: 10 pt}
H1        {color: black; font-family: arial; font-size: 12 pt}
-->
</STYLE>
</HEAD>

<BODY>
<TABLE BORDER=0 CELLPADDING=10 WIDTH=100%>
<TR>
<TD BGCOLOR="#F0F8FF" ALIGN=CENTER VALIGN=TOP WIDTH=150>
</TD>
<TD BGCOLOR="#FFFFFF" ALIGN=LEFT VALIGN=TOP WIDTH=83%>
<H1>Workout calculator (passing a variable)</H1>
<P>Enter an exercise, and we'll tell you how long you'd have
to do it<BR>to burn one pound of fat.</P>
<FORM METHOD="post" ACTION="wc_handler_var.php">
<INPUT TYPE="text" SIZE=50 NAME="exercise">
<BR><BR>
<INPUT TYPE="submit" NAME="submit" VALUE="Burn, baby, burn!">
</FORM>
</TD>
</TR>
</TABLE>

</BODY>
</HTML>
```

Figure 7-3 represents the output of the preceding HTML.

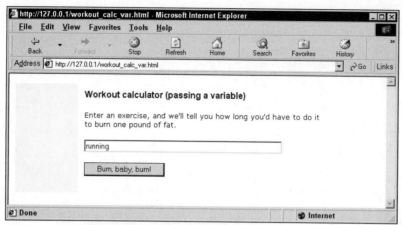

Figure 7-3: A simple form passing a string variable

The matching form handler is called `wc_handler_var.php` (Listing 7-4).

Listing 7-4: **Form handler (wc_handler_var.php)**

```
<?php
$exercise = $_POST['exercise'];
?>

<HTML>
<HEAD>
<STYLE TYPE="text/css">
<!--
BODY, P      {color: black; font-family: verdana;
font-size: 10 pt}
H1        {color: black; font-family: arial; font-size: 12 pt}
-->
</STYLE>
</HEAD>

<BODY>
<TABLE BORDER=0 CELLPADDING=10 WIDTH=100%>
<TR>
<TD BGCOLOR="#F0F8FF" ALIGN=CENTER VALIGN=TOP WIDTH=150>
</TD>
<TD BGCOLOR="#FFFFFF" ALIGN=LEFT VALIGN=TOP WIDTH=83%>
<H1>Workout calculator handler, part 1</H1>
<P>We've successfully passed the contents of the
text input field,<BR>
as a variable called "exercise" with a value of
<B><?php echo $exercise; ?></B>.<BR>
```

Continued

Listing 7-4 *(continued)*

```
But before we can do anything interesting with it,
we need to learn about strings.</P>
</TD>
</TR>
</TABLE>

</BODY>
</HTML>
```

Figure 7-4 represents the output of `wc_handler_var.php` on success.

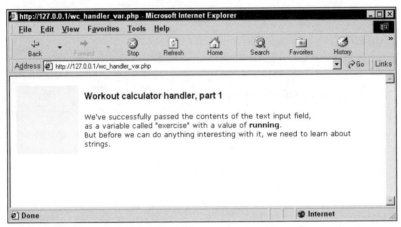

Figure 7-4: Data successfully passed from one page to another

In Chapter 8, we will learn to take this string input and do interesting things with it.

Summary

The HTTP protocol is stateless. This means a plain HTML page is incapable of receiving information from any other page. It can be used to pass values via a URL or an HTML form, but a separate program called a *form handler* must step in to recognize and perform actions on the passed values. In first-generation Web development, these form handlers were Perl or C CGI scripts, but nowadays Web developers are more likely to use an HTML-embedded programming language like PHP. PHP makes it particularly easy to write form handlers and even to combine them with HTML display on a single Web page.

Information is passed between Web pages using one of four main methods: GET, POST, a cookie, or sessions. GET is mainly used to construct complex URL strings for use with dynamically generated pages. It is deprecated for use with most HTML forms. POST is the method recommended for most forms. Forms are the main way to pass information from one Web page to a single other Web page. We deal with the persistent state methods, cookies, and sessions in Chapter 24.

✦   ✦   ✦

Strings

✦   ✦   ✦   ✦

In This Chapter

Strings in PHP

String functions

Extended example: An
exercise calculator

✦   ✦   ✦   ✦

Although images, sound files, videos, animations, and applets make up an important portion of the World Wide Web, much of the Web is still text — one character's worth after another, like this sentence. The basic PHP datatype for representing text is the *string*.

In this chapter, we cover almost all PHP's capabilities for manipulating strings (although we leave more advanced string functions and the pattern-matching power of regular expressions for separate treatment in Chapter 22). We start with the basics of strings, move to the most commonly used operators and functions, and demonstrate them by continuing the exercise calculator example from Chapter 7.

Strings in PHP

Strings are sequences of characters that can be treated as a unit — assigned to variables, given as input to functions, returned from functions, or sent as output to appear on your user's Web page. The simplest way to specify a string in PHP code is to enclose it in quotes, whether single quotes (') or double quotes ("), like this:

```
$my_string = 'A literal string';
$another_string = "Another string";
```

The difference between single and double quotes lies in how much interpretation PHP does of the characters between the quote signs before creating the string itself. If you enclose a string in single quotes, almost no interpretation will be performed; if you enclose it in double quotes, PHP will splice in the values of any variables you include, as well as make substitutions for certain special character sequences that begin with the backslash (\) character. For example, if you evaluate the following code in the middle of a Web page:

```
$statement = 'everything I say';
$question_1 =
  "Do you have to take $statement so literally?\n<BR>";
$question_2 =
  'Do you have to take $statement so literally?\n<BR>';
echo $question_1;
echo $question_2;
```

you should expect to see the browser output:

```
Do you have to take everything I say so literally?
Do you have to take $statement so literally?\n
```

For the details on exactly how PHP interprets both singly and doubly quoted strings, see the "Strings" section of Chapter 5.

Interpolation with curly braces

In most situations, you can simply include a variable in a doubly quoted string, and the variable's value will be spliced into the string when it is interpreted. There are two situations where the string parser might very reasonably get confused and need more guidance from you. The first situation is when your notion of where the variable name should stop is not the same as the parser's, and the other occurs when the expression you want to have interpolated is not a simple variable. In these cases, you can clear things up by enclosing the value you want interpolated in curly braces: { }.

For example, PHP has no difficulty with the following code:

```
$sport = 'volleyball';
$plan = "I will play $sport in the summertime";
```

The parser in this case encounters the $ symbol, and then begins collecting characters for a variable name until it runs into the space after $sport. Spaces cannot be part of a variable name, so it is clear that the variable in question is $sport, and PHP successfully finds a value for that variable ('volleyball'), and splices the value in.

Sometimes, though, it is not convenient to stop a variable name with a space. Take this example.

```
$sport1 = 'volley';
$sport2 = 'foot';
$sport3 = 'basket';
$plan1 = "I will play $sport1ball in the summertime";  //wrong
$plan2 = "I will play $sport2ball in the fall";  //wrong
$plan3 = "I will play $sport3ball in the winter";  //wrong
```

You will not get the desired effect here, because PHP interprets $sport1 as part of the variable name $sport1ball, which is probably unbound. Instead, you need something like:

```
$plan1 = "I will play {$sport1}ball in the summertime"; //right
```

which asks PHP to evaluate only the variable expression within the braces before interpolating.

For similar reasons, PHP has difficulty interpolating complex variable expressions, like multidimensional arrays and object variables, unless curly braces are used. The general rule is that if you have a { immediately followed by a $, PHP will evaluate the variable expression up until the closing } and will interpolate the resulting value into the string. (If you need a literal {$ to appear in your string, you can accomplish it by escaping either character with a backslash (\).)

See the "Concatenation and Assignment" section later in this chapter for ideas on other ways to address challenges like this.

Characters and string indexes

Unlike some programming languages, PHP has no distinct character type different from the string type. In general, functions that would take character arguments in other languages expect strings of length 1 in PHP.

You can retrieve the individual characters of a string by including the number of the character, starting at 0, enclosed in curly braces immediately following a string variable. These characters will actually be one-character strings. For example, the following code:

```php
$my_string = "Doubled";
for ($index = 0; $index < 7; $index++) {
  $string_to_print = $my_string{$index};
  print("$string_to_print$string_to_print");
}
```

gives the browser output:

```
DDoouubblleedd
```

with each character of the string being printed twice per loop. (The number 7 is hard-coded in this example only because we haven't yet covered how to find out the length of a string — see the function `strlen()` in the later section "Inspecting strings.")

Caution   In earlier versions of PHP, it was customary to retrieve individual characters of a string using square brackets to enclose the index rather than curly braces (for example, `$my_string[3]` rather than `$my_string{3}`). While you can still use the square (array-like) brackets to do this, this usage is now deprecated, and the curly brace syntax is encouraged.

String operators

PHP offers only one real operator on strings: the dot (.) or concatenation operator. This operator, when placed between two string arguments, produces a new string that is the result of putting the two strings together in sequence. For example:

```php
$my_two_cents = "I want to give you a piece of my mind ";
$third_cent = " And another thing";
print($my_two_cents . "..." . $third_cent);
```

gives the browser output:

```
I want to give you a piece of my mind ... And another thing
```

Note that we are not passing multiple string arguments to the print statement — we are handing it one string argument, which was created by concatenating three strings together. The first and third strings are variables, but the middle one is a literal string enclosed in double quotes.

Note   Note that the concatenation operator is not + as in Java, and it does not overload anything else. If you forget this and add strings using +, they will be interpreted as numbers, with the result that `'one' + 'two'` equals 0 (because no successful string-to-number conversion can be made).

Concatenation and assignment

Just as with arithmetic operators, PHP has a shorthand operator (.=) that combines concatenation with assignment. The following statement:

```php
$my_string_var .= $new_addition;
```

is exactly equivalent to:

```php
$my_string_var = $my_string_var . $new_addition;
```

Note that, unlike commutative addition and multiplication, with this shorthand operator it matters that the new string is added to the right. If you want the new string tacked on to the left, there's no alternative shorter than:

```
$my_string_var = $new_addition . $my_string_var;
```

Note also that unassigned variables are treated as empty strings for the purposes of concatenation, so $my_string_var will end up unchanged if $new_addition has never been given a value.

The heredoc syntax

In addition to the single-quote and double-quote syntaxes, PHP offers another way to specify a string, called the *heredoc syntax*. This syntax turns out to be extremely useful for specifying large chunks of variable-interpolated text, because it spares you from the need to escape internal quotes. It is especially useful in creating pages that contain HTML forms.

The operator in the heredoc syntax is <<<. What is expected immediately after this is a label (unquoted) that indicates the beginning of a multiline string. PHP will continue including subsequent lines into this string until it sees the same label again, beginning a line. The ending label may optionally be followed by a semicolon but by nothing else.

An example:

```
$my_string_var = <<<EOT
Everything in this rather unnecessarily wordy
ramble of prose will be incorporated into the
string that we are building up inevitably, inexorably,
character by character, line by line, until we reach that
blessed final line which is this one.
EOT;
```

Note that the preceding final EOT must *not* be indented at all — otherwise it will be taken to be just more text to be included. The label need not be literally EOT — it can be whatever you like within the normal rules for variable names in PHP.

Interpolation of variables happens exactly the same way as with double-quoted strings. The nice thing about heredoc, though, is that quote signs can be included without any escaping and without prematurely terminating the string. Another example:

```
echo <<<ENDOFFORM
<FORM METHOD=POST ACTION="{$_ENV['PHP_SELF']}">
<INPUT TYPE=TEXT NAME=FIRSTNAME VALUE=$firstname>
<INPUT TYPE=SUBMIT NAME=SUBMIT VALUE=SUBMIT>
</FORM>
ENDOFFORM;
```

This has the effect of echoing a very simple form to the browser.

String Functions

PHP gives you a huge variety of functions for the munching and crunching of strings. If you're ever tempted to roll your own function that reads strings character-by-character to produce a new string, pause for a moment to think whether the task might be common. If so, there is probably a built-in function that handles it.

In this section, we present the basic functions for inspecting, comparing, modifying, and printing strings. If you want to be really comfortable with string manipulation in PHP, you should probably have at least a passing acquaintance with everything in this section. Both the regular expression functions and the more abstruse string functions can be found in Chapter 22.

Note A note for C programmers: Many of the PHP string function names should be familiar to you. Just keep in mind that, because PHP takes care of memory management for you, the functions that return strings are allocating the string storage on their own and do not need to be given a preallocated string to write into.

Inspecting strings

What kinds of questions can you ask strings? First on the list is how long the string is, using the strlen() function (the name is short for *string length*).

```
$short_string = "This string has 29 characters";
print("It does have " . strlen($short_string) .
        " characters");
```

This code gives the following output:

```
It does have 29 characters
```

Knowing the string's length is particularly useful in form validation or for situations in which we'd like to loop through a string character by character. A useless but illustrative example, using the preceding example string, is:

```
for ($index = 0; $index < strlen($short_string); $index++)
    print($short_string{$index});
```

This simply prints:

```
This string has 29 characters
```

which is the string we started with.

Finding characters and substrings

The next question you can ask your strings is what they contain. For example, the strpos() function finds the numerical position of a particular character in a string, if it exists.

```
$twister = "Peter Piper picked a peck of pickled peppers";
print("Location of 'p' is " . strpos($twister, 'p') .'<BR>');
print("Location of 'q' is " . strpos($twister, 'q') .'<BR>');
```

This gives us the browser output:

```
Location of 'p' is 8
Location of 'q' is
```

The 'q' location is apparently blank because strpos() returns false if the character in question cannot be found, and a false value prints as the empty string. You should note that the strpos() function is case-sensitive.

Caution The strpos() function is one of those cases where PHP's type-looseness can be problematic. If no match can be found, the function returns a false value; if the very first character is a match, the function returns 0 (because the indexing count starts with 0 rather than 1). Both of these values look false if used in a Boolean test. One way to distinguish them is to use the identity comparison operator (===, introduced as of PHP4), which is true only if its arguments are the same and of the same type—you can use it to test if the returned value is 0 (or is FALSE) without risk of confusion with other values that might be the same after type coercion. If you are using PHP3, you need to do explicit type testing with, for example, is_integer().

The strpos() function can also be used to search for a substring rather than a single character, simply by giving it a multicharacter string rather than a single-character string. You can also supply an extra integer argument specifying the position to begin searching forward from.

Searching in reverse is also possible, using the strrpos() function. (Note the extra r, which you can think of as standing for *reverse*.) This function takes a string to search and a single-character string to locate, and it returns the last position of occurrence of the second argument in the first argument. (Unlike with strpos(), the string searched for must have only one character.) If we use this function on our example sentence, we find a different position:

```
$twister = "Peter Piper picked a peck of pickled peppers";
printf("Location of 'p' is " . strrpos($twister, 'p') .'<BR>');
```

Specifically, we find the third p in peppers:

```
Location of 'p' is 40
```

Are strings immutable?

In some programming languages (such as C), it is common to manipulate strings by directly changing them—that is, storing new characters into the middle of an existing string, replacing old characters. Other languages (like Java) try to keep the programmer out of certain kinds of trouble by making string classes that are *immutable* (or unchangeable)—you can make new strings by creating modified copies of old ones, but once you have made a string, you are not allowed to change it by directly changing the characters that make it up.

Where does PHP fit in? As it turns out, PHP strings can be changed, but the most common practice seems to be to treat strings as immutable.

Strings can be changed by treating them as character arrays and assigning directly into them, like this:

```
$my_string = "abcdefg";
$my_string[5] = "X";
print($my_string . "<BR>");
```

which will give the browser output:

```
abcdeXg
```

This modification method seems to be undocumented, however, and shows up nowhere in the online manual, even though the corresponding extraction method (now updated to use curly braces) is highlighted. Also, almost all PHP string-manipulation functions return modified copies of their string arguments rather than making direct changes, which seems to indicate that this is the style that the PHP designers prefer. Our advice is not to use this direct-modification method to change strings, unless you know what you are doing and there is some large benefit in terms of memory savings.

Comparison and searching

Is this string the same as that string? It's a question that your code is likely to have to answer frequently, especially when dealing with input typed by the end user.

Note For the == operator, two strings are the same if they contain exactly the same sequence of characters. It does not test any stricter notion of being the same, such as being stored at the same memory address, but it does pay attention to case (or capitalization).

The simplest method to find an answer is to use the basic comparison operator (==), which does equality testing on strings as well as numbers.

Caution Comparing two strings using == (or the corresponding < and > operators) is trustworthy if both the arguments are strings and if you know that no type conversion is being performed. (See Chapter 5 for more on this.) Using strcmp() (described next) is always trustworthy.

The most basic workhorse string-comparison function is strcmp(). It takes two strings as arguments and compares them byte by byte until it finds a difference. It returns a negative number if the first string is less than the second and a positive number if the second string is less. It returns 0 if they are identical.

The strcasecmp() function works the same way, except that the equality comparison is case insensitive. The function call strcasecmp("hey!", "HEY!") should return 0.

Searching

The comparison functions just described tell you whether one string is equal to another. To find out if one string is contained within another, use the strpos() function (covered earlier) or the strstr() function (or one of its relatives).

The strstr() function takes a string to search in and a string to look for (in that order). If it succeeds, it returns the portion of the string that starts with (and includes) the first instance of the string it is looking for. If the string is not found, a false value is returned. Here is a successful search followed by an unsuccessful search:

```
$string_to_search = "showsuponceshowsuptwice";
$string_to_find = "up";
print("Result of looking for $string_to_find" .
        strstr($string_to_search, $string_to_find) . "<br>");
$string_to_find = "down";
print("Result of looking for $string_to_find" .
        strstr($string_to_search, $string_to_find));
```

which gives us:

```
Result of looking for up: uponceshowsuptwice
Result of looking for down:
```

The blank space after the colon in the second line is the result of trying to print a false value, which prints as the empty string. The strstr() function also has an alias by the name of strchr(). Other than the name, the two functions are identical. Just as with strcmp(), strstr() has a case-insensitive version, by the name of stristr(). (That i in the middle stands for *insensitive*.) It is identical to strstr() in every way, except that the comparison treats lowercase letters as indistinguishable from their uppercase counterparts. The string functions we have covered so far are summarized in Table 8-1.

Table 8-1: Simple Inspection, Comparison, and Searching Functions

Function	Behavior
strlen()	Takes a single string argument and returns its length as an integer.
strpos()	Takes two string arguments: a string to search, and the string being searched for. Returns the (0-based) position of the beginning of the first instance of the string if found, and a false value otherwise. It also takes a third optional integer argument, specifying the position at which the search should begin.
strrpos()	Like strpos(), except that it searches backward from the end of the string, rather than forward from the beginning. The search string must only be one character long, and there is no optional position argument.
strcmp()	Takes two strings as arguments and returns 0 if the strings are exactly equivalent. If strcmp() encounters a difference, it returns a negative number if the first different byte is a smaller ASCII value in the first string, and a positive number if the smaller byte is found in the second string.
strcasecmp()	Identical to strcmp(), except that lowercase and uppercase versions of the same letter compare as equal.
strstr()	Searches its first string argument to see if its second string argument is contained in it. Returns the substring of the first string that starts with the first instance of the second argument, if any is found — otherwise, it returns false.
strchr()	Identical to strstr().
stristr()	Identical to strstr() except that the comparison is case independent.

Substring selection

Many of PHP's string functions have to do with slicing and dicing your strings. By *slicing*, we mean choosing a portion of a string; by *dicing*, we mean selectively modifying a string. Keep in mind that (most of the time) even dicing functions do not change the string you started out with. Usually, such functions return a modified copy, leaving the original argument intact.

The most basic way to choose a portion of a string is the substr() function, which returns a new string that is a subsequence of the old one. As arguments, it takes a string (that the substring will be selected from), an integer (the position at which the desired substring starts), and an optional third integer argument that is the length of the desired substring. If no third argument is given, the substring is assumed to continue until the end. (Remember that, as with all PHP arguments that deal with numerical string positions, the numbering starts with 0 rather than 1.)

For example, the statement:

```
echo(substr("Take what you need, and leave the rest behind",
      23));
```

prints the string leave the rest behind, whereas the statement:

```
echo(substr("Take what you need, and leave the rest behind",
      5, 13));
```

prints what you need — a 13-character string starting at (0-based) position 5.

Both the start-position argument and the length argument can be negative, and in each case the negativity has a different meaning. If the start-position is negative, it means that the starting character is determined by counting backward from the end of the string, rather than forward from the beginning. (A start position of -1 means start with the last character, -2 means second-to-last, and so on.)

Now, you might expect that a negative length would similarly imply that the substring should be determined by counting backward from the start character rather than forward. This is not the case—it is always true that the character at the start-position is the first character in the returned string (not the last). Instead, a negative-length argument means that the final character is determined by counting backward from the end rather than forward from the start position.

Here are some examples, with positive and negative arguments:

```
$alphabet_test = "abcdefghijklmnop";
print("3: " . substr($alphabet_test, 3) . "<BR>");
print("-3: " . substr($alphabet_test, -3) . "<BR>");
print("3, 5: " . substr($alphabet_test, 3, 5) . "<BR>");
print("3, -5: " . substr($alphabet_test, 3, -5) . "<BR>");
print("-3, -5: " . substr($alphabet_test, -3, -5) . "<BR>");
print("-3, 5: " . substr($alphabet_test, -3, 5) . "<BR>");
```

This gives us the output:

```
3: defghijklmnop
-3: nop
3, 5: defgh
3, -5: defghijk
-3, -5:
-3, 5: nop
```

 Caution In the substr() example with a start position of -3 and a length of -5, the ending position is before the starting position, which in a sense specifies a string with *negative length*. The manual at www.php.net/manual currently says that such negative length calls to substr() will result in returning a string containing the single character at the start position. Instead, as in the preceding example, PHP5 seems to return empty strings in such cases. Caveat coder.

Notice that there is an intimate relationship between the functions substr(), strstr(), and strpos(). The substr() function selects a substring by numerical position, strstr() selects a substring by its content, and strpos() finds the numerical position of a given substring. In the case where we're sure in advance that the string $containing has the string $contained as a substring, the expression:

```
strstr($containing, $contained)
```

should be equivalent to the code:

```
substr($containing, strpos($containing, $contained))
```

String cleanup functions

Although they are technically substring functions, just like the others in this chapter, the functions chop(), ltrim(), and trim() are really used for cleaning up untidy strings. They trim whitespace off of the end, beginning, and beginning-and-end, respectively, of their single string argument. Some examples:

```
$original = "  More than meets the eye    ";
$chopped = chop($original);
$ltrimmed = ltrim($original);
$trimmed = trim($original);
print("The original is '$original'<BR>");
print("Its length is " . strlen($original) . "<BR>");
print("The chopped version is '$chopped'<BR>");
print("Its length is " . strlen($chopped) . "<BR>");
print("The ltrimmed version is '$ltrimmed'<BR>");
print("Its length is " . strlen($ltrimmed) . "<BR>");
print("The trimmed version is '$ltrimmed'<BR>");
print("Its length is " . strlen($trimmed) . "<BR>");
```

The result as viewed by a browser is:

```
The original is '  More than meets the eye '
Its length is 28
The chopped version is '  More than meets the eye'
Its length is 25
The ltrimmed version is 'More than meets the eye '
Its length is 26
The trimmed version is 'More than meets the eye'
Its length is 23
```

The original string had three spaces at the end (subject to removal by chop() or trim()) and two at the beginning (removed by ltrim() and trim()). We were careful to describe our result as viewed by a browser because the multiple spaces have apparently been collapsed to one in the output, as browsers will do. If we viewed the HTML source produced by PHP originally, we would still see sequences of two and three spaces.

In addition to spaces, these functions remove whitespace like that denoted by the escape sequences \n, \r, \t, and \0 (end-of-line characters, tabs, and the null character used to terminate strings in C programs).

You will hear the name chop() more frequently, but the identical function can also be called with the more logical name of rtrim(). Finally, notice that although chop() sounds extremely destructive, it does not harm the $original argument, which retains the same value.

String replacement

The substring functions we've seen so far are all about choosing a portion of the argument rather than building a genuinely new string. Enter the functions str_replace() and substr_replace().

The str_replace() function enables you to replace all instances of a particular substring with an alternate string. It takes three arguments: the string to be searched for, the string to replace it with when it is found, and the string to perform the replacement on. For example:

```
$first_edition =
    "Burma is similar to Rhodesia in at least one way.";
$second_edition = str_replace("Rhodesia", "Zimbabwe",
                                $first_edition);
$third_edition = str_replace("Burma", "Myanmar",
                                $second_edition);
print($third_edition);
```

gives us:

```
Myanmar is similar to Zimbabwe in at least one way.
```

This replacement will happen for all instances found of the search string. If our outdated encyclopedia could be snarfed into a single PHP string, we could update it in one pass.

One subtlety to be aware of: What happens when multiple instances of the search string overlap? For example, with code like:

```
$tricky_string = "ABA is part of ABABA";
$maybe_tricked = str_replace("ABA", "DEF", $tricky_string);
print("Substitution result is '$maybe_tricked'<BR>");
```

the behavior we see is:

```
Substitution result is 'DEF is part of DEFBA'
```

which is probably as reasonable as any other alternative.

As we've seen, str_replace() picks out portions to replace by matching to a target string; by contrast, substr_replace() chooses a portion to replace by its absolute position. The function takes up to four arguments: the string to perform the replacement on, the string to replace with, the starting position for the replacement, and (optionally) the length of the section to be replaced. For example:

```
print(substr_replace("ABCDEFG", "-", 2, 3));
```

gives us:

```
AB-FG
```

The CDE portion of the string has been replaced with the single -. Notice that we are allowed to replace a substring with a string of a different length. If the length argument is omitted, it is assumed that you want to replace the entire portion of the string after the start position.

The substr_replace() function also takes negative arguments for starting position and length, which are treated exactly the same way as in the substr() function (described in the earlier section "Substring selection"). It is important to remember with both str_replace and substr_replace that the original string remains unchanged by these operations.

Finally, we have a couple more whimsical functions that produce new strings from old. The strrev() function simply returns a new string with the characters of its input in reverse order. The str_repeat() function takes a string argument and an integer argument and returns a string that is the appropriate number of copies of the string argument tacked together. For example:

```
print(str_repeat("cheers ", 3));
```

gives us:

```
cheers cheers cheers
```

for the end of this section at long last.

The substring search and replacement functions are summarized in Table 8-2.

Table 8-2: Substring and String Replacement Functions

Function	Behavior
substr()	Returns a subsequence of its initial string argument, as specified by the second (position) argument and optional third (length) argument. The substring starts at the indicated position and continues for as many characters as specified by the length argument or until the end of the string, if there is no length argument.
	A negative position argument means that the start character is located by counting backward from the end, whereas a negative length argument means that the end of the substring is found by counting back from the end, rather than forward from the start position.
chop(), or rtrim()	Returns its string argument with trailing (right-hand side) whitespace removed. Whitespace is , \n, \r, \t, and \0.
ltrim()	Returns its string argument with leading (left-hand side) whitespace removed.
Trim()	Returns its string argument with both leading and trailing whitespace removed.
Str_replace()	Used to replace target substrings with another string. Takes three string arguments: a substring to search for, a string to replace it with, and the containing string. Returns a copy of the containing string with *all* instances of the first argument replaced by the second argument.
Substr_replace()	Puts a string argument in place of a position-specified substring. Takes up to four arguments: the string to operate on, the string to replace with, the start position of the substring to replace, and the length of the string segment to be replaced. Returns a copy of the first argument with the replacement string put in place of the specified substring.
	If the length argument is omitted, the entire tail of the first string argument is replaced. Negative position and length arguments are treated as in substr().

Case functions

These functions change lowercase to uppercase and vice versa. The first two (de)capitalize entire strings, whereas the second two operate only on first letters of words.

strtolower()

The strtolower() function returns an all-lowercase string. It doesn't matter if the original is all uppercase or mixed. This fragment:

```php
<?php
$original = "They DON'T KnoW they're SHOUTING";
$lower = strtolower($original);
echo $lower;
?>
```

returns the string "they don't know they're shouting".

Tip

If you have been faced with extensive form-validation needs before, you might already have noticed that `strtolower()` is extremely handy for use with those that still think their e-mail addresses contain capital letters. Subsequent functions in this category will prove similarly useful.

strtoupper()

The `strtoupper()` function returns an all-uppercase string, regardless of whether the original was all lowercase or mixed:

```php
<?php
$original = "make this link stand out";
echo("<B>strtoupper($original)</B>");
?>
```

ucfirst()

The `ucfirst()` function capitalizes only the first letter of a string:

```php
<?php
$original = "polish is a word for which pronunciation depends on
capitalization";
echo(ucfirst($original));
?>
```

ucwords()

The `ucwords()` function capitalizes the first letter of each word in a string:

```php
<?php
$original = "truth or consequences";
$capitalized = ucwords($original);
echo "While $original is a parlor game, $capitalized is a town in New
Mexico.";
?>
```

Note

Neither `ucwords()` nor `ucfirst()` converts anything into lowercase. Each makes only the appropriate leading letters into uppercase. If there are inappropriate capital letters in the middle of words, they will not be corrected.

Escaping functions

One of the virtues of PHP is that it is willing to talk to almost anybody. In its role as a glue language, PHP talks to database servers, to LDAP servers, over sockets, and over the HTTP connection itself. Frequently, it accomplishes this communication by first constructing a message string (like a database query) and then shipping it off to the receiving program. Often, however, the program attaches special meanings to certain characters, which therefore have to be *escaped,* meaning that the receiving program is told to take them as a literal part of the string rather than treating them specially.

Many users deal with this issue by enabling magic-quotes, which ensures that quotes are escaped before strings are inserted into databases. If that's not feasible or desirable, there are good old-fashioned strip-slashing and add-slashing by hand. The `addslashes()` function escapes quotes, double quotes, backslashes, and NULLs with backslashes, because these are the characters that typically need to be escaped for database queries.

```php
<?php
$escapedstring = addslashes("He said, 'I'm a dog.'");
$query = "INSERT INTO test (quote) values ('$escapedstring')";
$result = mysql_query($query) or die(mysql_error());
?>
```

This will prevent the SQL statement from thinking it's finished right before the letter I. When you pull the data back out, you'll need to use `stripslashes()` to get rid of the slashes.

```php
<?php
$query = "SELECT quote FROM test WHERE ID=1";
$result = mysql_query($query) or die(mysql_error());
$new_row = mysql_fetch_array($result);
$quote = stripslashes($new_row[0]);

echo $quote;
```

The `quotemeta()` function escapes a wider variety of characters, all of which usually have a special meaning in the Unix command line: `'.'`, `'\'` `'+'`, `'*'`, `'?'`, `'['`, `'^'`, `']'`, `'('`, `'$'`, and `')'`. For example, the code:

```php
$literal_string =
   'These characters ($, *) are very special to me\n<BR>';
$qm_string = quotemeta($literal_string);
echo $qm_string;
```

will print:

```
These characters \(\$, \*\) are very special to me\\n
```

Cross-Reference   For escaping functions specific to HTML, see the "Advanced String Functions" section in Chapter 22.

Printing and output

The workhorse constructs for printing and output are `print` and `echo`, which we cover in detail in Chapter 5. The standard way to print the value of variables to output is to include them in a doubly quoted string (which will interpolate their values) and then give that string to `print` or `echo`.

If you need even more tightly formatted output, PHP also offers `printf()` and `sprintf()`, which are modeled on C functions of the same name. The two functions take identical arguments: a special format string (described later in this section) and then any number of other arguments, which will be spliced into the right places in the format string to make the result.

The only difference between `printf()` and `sprintf()` is that `printf()` sends the resulting string directly to output, whereas `sprintf()` returns the result string as its value.

Note   To C programmers: This `sprintf()` function is slightly different from C's version in that you need not supply an allocated string for `sprintf()` to write into—PHP allocates the result string for you.

The complicated bit about these functions is the format string. Every character that you put in the string will show up literally in the result, except the % character and characters that immediately follow it. The % character signals the beginning of a *conversion specification*, which indicates how to print one of the arguments that follow the format string.

After the %, there are five elements that make up the conversion specification, some of which are optional: padding, alignment, minimum width, precision, and type.

✦ The single (optional) *padding* character is either a 0 or a space ( ). This character is used to fill any space that would otherwise be unused but that you have insisted (with the minimum width argument) be filled with something. If this padding character is not given, the default is to pad with spaces.

✦ The optional *alignment* character (-) indicates whether the printed value should be left- or right-justified. If present, the value will be left-justified; if absent, it will be right-justified.

✦ An optional *minimum width* number that indicates how many spaces this value should take up, at a minimum. (If more spaces are needed to print the value, it will overflow beyond its bounds.)

✦ An optional precision specifier is written as a dot (.) followed by a number. It indicates how many decimal points of *precision* a double should print with. (This has no effect on printing things other than doubles.)

✦ A single character indicating how the *type* of the value should be interpreted. The f character indicates printing as a double, the s character indicates printing as a string, and then the rest of the possible characters (b, c, d, o, x, X) mean that the value should be interpreted as an integer and printed in various formats. Those formats are b for binary, c for printing the character with the corresponding ASCII values, o for octal, x for hexadecimal (with lowercase letters) and X for hexadecimal with uppercase letters.

Here's an example of printing the same double in several different ways:

```
<pre>
<?php
$value = 3.14159;
printf("%f,%10f,%-010f,%2.2f\n",
        $value, $value, $value, $value);
?>
</pre>
```

gives us:

```
3.141590, 3.141590,3.141590000000000, 3.14
```

The <pre></pre> construct is HTML that tells the browser to format the enclosed block literally, without collapsing many spaces into one, and so on.

Extended Example: An Exercise Calculator

In this section, we continue the exercise calculator example from Chapter 5 by using a variety of string functions to process strings posted from a user form. In the previous example, we had just managed to pass off a string variable from an HTML form to the PHP page designed to receive it. In this version, we actually do some analysis of the string we receive. (See the end of this section for reasons why this example will still need to be improved in later chapters.)

Listing 8-1 shows the HTML form used to prompt the user for an exercise to analyze. This is largely the same as the corresponding form in Chapter 7, with a different form-handling target.

Listing 8-1: **The entry form**

```
<HTML>
<HEAD>
<STYLE TYPE="text/css">
<!--
BODY, P {color: black; font-family: verdana; font-size: 10 pt}
H1         {color: black; font-family: arial; font-size: 12 pt}
-->
</STYLE>
</HEAD>
<BODY>
<TABLE BORDER=0 CELLPADDING=10 WIDTH=100%>
<TR>
<TD BGCOLOR="#F0F8FF" ALIGN=CENTER VALIGN=TOP WIDTH=150>
</TD>
<TD BGCOLOR="#FFFFFF" ALIGN=LEFT VALIGN=TOP WIDTH=83%>
<H1>Workout calculator (passing a string)</H1>
<P>Enter an exercise, and we'll tell you how long you'd have to
do it<BR>to burn one pound of fat.</P>
<FORM METHOD="post" ACTION="wc_handler_str.php">
<INPUT TYPE="text" SIZE=50 NAME="exercise">
<BR><BR>
<INPUT TYPE="submit" NAME="submit" VALUE="Burn, baby, burn!">
</FORM>
</TD>
</TR>
</TABLE>
</BODY>
</HTML>
```

Listing 8-2 shows a revised form-handling page that displays different exercise stats depending on the particular exercise entered by the user.

Caution   We very intentionally used the modern $_POST superglobal to catch the value of the string posted by the form. This means, however, that the code in Listing 8-2 will not run in any version of PHP earlier than PHP 4.1. To adapt it to an earlier version, replace $_POST with '$HTTP_POST_VARS' with the understanding that the long variable names are now officially deprecated and will probably result in broken code at some point.

Listing 8-2: **Form handler using string functions**

```
<?php

$exercise = $_POST['exercise']; // NOTE: only works in PHP 4.1+
// Make sure they aren't trying to do naughty things
if (strlen($exercise) > 50) {
  echo "You aren't playing by the rules.  Bad dog!";
  exit;
```

```
}
// Try to parse the input string
// ----------------------------
// Make sure there aren't any spaces before or after
$exercise = trim($exercise);
// Convert to all lowercase for better string matching
$exercise = strtolower($exercise);

// Try to standardize on gerund form, if possible
if (strpos($exercise, 'ing') > 0) {
  // Already good
  $exercise_str = $exercise;
} elseif ($exercise == 'bike' || $exercise == 'cycle') {
  $exercise_str = 'cycling';
} elseif ($exercise == 'run' || $exercise == 'jog') {
  $exercise_str = 'running';
} elseif ($exercise == 'soccer' || $exercise == 'football') {
  $exercise_str = 'soccer';
} elseif (strstr($exercise, 'weight') ||
          strstr($exercise, 'strength')) {
  $exercise_str = 'weight lifting';
}


// Now assign a number of hours to burn one pound of fat to each
// sport
if ($exercise_str == 'cycling' || $exercise_str == 'biking') {
  $hours = '5 hours and 40 minutes';
} elseif ($exercise_str == 'running' ||
          $exercise_str == 'jogging') {
  $hours = '4 hours and 30 minutes';
} elseif ($exercise_str == 'soccer' ||
          $exercise_str == 'football') {
  $hours = '4 hours and 30 minutes';
} elseif ($exercise_str == 'weight lifting') {
  $hours = '7 hours and 30 minutes';
} else {
  // Nullify all other exercises
  $exercise_str = '';
  $hours = '';
}

// Construct a sentence
// --------------------

if ($exercise_str != "" && $hours != "") {
  $message = 'It would take '.$hours.' of ' . $exercise_str .
             ' to burn one pound of fat.';
} elseif ($exercise_str == "" && $hours == "") {
  // If the exercise isn't in the list above, give a
  // default message.
```

Continued

Listing 8-2 *(continued)*

```
    $message = 'Sorry, we do not have data for that exercise.';
} else {

    // There are two other logical possibilities
    // 1.  We recognize the exercise but don't have a duration
    // for it
    // 2.  We don't recognize the exercise but somehow have a
    // duration
    // neither should happen, but just in case...
    $message = 'Something has gone horribly wrong!';
}
// Now lay out the page
// --------------------
$page_str = <<< EOPAGE
<HTML>
<HEAD>
<STYLE TYPE="text/css">
<!--
BODY, P    {color: black; font-family: verdana; font-size: 10 pt}
H1         {color: black; font-family: arial; font-size: 12 pt}
-->
</STYLE>
</HEAD>

<BODY>
<TABLE BORDER=0 CELLPADDING=10 WIDTH=100%>
<TR>
<TD BGCOLOR="#F0F8FF" ALIGN=CENTER VALIGN=TOP WIDTH=150>
</TD>
<TD BGCOLOR="#FFFFFF" ALIGN=LEFT VALIGN=TOP WIDTH=83%>
<H1>Workout calculator handler, part 2</H1>
<P>The workout calculator says, "$message"</P>
</TD>
</TR>
</TABLE>
</BODY>
</HTML>
EOPAGE;

echo $page_str;

?>
```

In order, the code in Listing 8-2:

1. Receives the posted string from the HTML form.

2. Tries to put the received string into a standard form by trimming off whitespace, converting to lowercase, and translating some known variations.

3. Uses the cleaned-up and translated string to look up data on a given exercise.

4. Uses the heredoc syntax to construct a response page.

Figures 8-1 and 8-2 show what is displayed as the user enters the word **bike**.

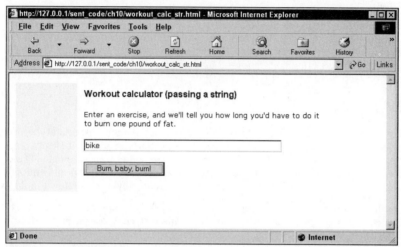

Figure 8-1: The entry form

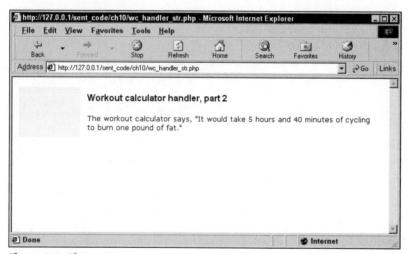

Figure 8-2: The answer

So, do we like our exercise calculator yet? The main problem is that it is highly likely that the form will not know how to handle what the user types (other than by printing a generic message). Also, if you raise error reporting up to E_ALL, you will see some warnings due to uninitialized variables. The user is also not given any clue as to what kinds of input the form will be able to handle.

In general, unless you are building a system (like a search engine) where the whole point is dealing with free text, it is a bad idea to have the results of your code depend on analysis of user-entered strings. If you want the user to make choices, you should constrain those choices so that you know what is coming. User-entered text is fine as long as its ultimate fate is to be viewed by another human being (after, say, being stored in a database or forwarded by an e-mail program).

To gracefully constrain the user's choices, you need HTML user-interface elements other than the text box, such as check boxes, radio buttons, and pull-down lists. And to make use of those UI elements on the receiving side, we really need to exploit the power of arrays more fully. We will extend this example in Chapter 9 by doing just that.

Summary

Strings are sequences of characters, and the string is one of the eight basic datatypes in PHP. Unlike in some other languages, there is no distinct character type, since single characters behave as strings of length 1. Literal strings are specified in code by either single (') or double (") quotes. Singly quoted strings are interpreted nearly literally, while doubly quoted strings interpret a number of escape sequences and automatically interpolate variable values.

The main string operator is ' . ', which concatenates two strings together. In addition, there is a dizzying array of string functions, which help you inspect, compare, search, extract, chop, replace, slice, and dice strings to your heart's content. For the most sophisticated string-manipulation needs, PHP supports both POSIX and Perl-compatible regular expressions (covered in Chapter 22).

✦   ✦   ✦

Arrays and Array Functions

◆ ◆ ◆ ◆

In This Chapter

An all-purpose data type

Storing and retrieving values

Multidimensional arrays

Iteration

◆ ◆ ◆ ◆

Arrays are definitely one of the coolest and most flexible features of PHP. Unlike vector arrays from other languages (C, C++, Pascal), PHP arrays can store data of varied types and automatically organize it for you in a large variety of ways.

Cross-Reference This chapter treats arrays and array functions in some depth. For a very quick introduction to the syntax and use of arrays, see Chapter 5. For a more complete survey of advanced array functions, see Chapter 21.

The Uses of Arrays

An array is a collection of variables indexed and bundled together into a single, easily referenced super-variable that offers an easy way to pass multiple values between lines of code, functions, and even pages. Throughout much of this chapter, we will be looking at the inner workings of arrays and exploring all the built-in PHP functions that manipulate them. Before we get too deep into that, however, it's worth listing the common ways that arrays are used in real PHP code.

Many built-in PHP environment variables are in the form of arrays (for example, `$_SESSION`, which contains all the variable names and values being propagated from page to page via PHP's session mechanism). If you want access to them, you need to understand, at a minimum, how to reference arrays.

Most database functions transport their info via arrays, making a compact package of an arbitrary chunk of data.

It's easy to pass entire sets of HTML form arguments from one page to another in a single array (see Chapter 7).

Arrays make a nice container for doing manipulations (sorting, counting, and so on) of any data you develop while executing a single page's script.

Almost any situation that calls for a number of pieces of data to be packaged and handled as one is appropriate for a PHP array.

What Are PHP Arrays?

PHP arrays are *associative* arrays with a little extra machinery thrown in. The *associative* part means that arrays store element values in association with key values rather than in a strict linear index order. (If you have seen arrays in other programming languages, they are likely to have been *vector* arrays rather than associative arrays — see the related sidebar for an explanation of the difference.) If you store an element in an array, in association with a key, all you need to retrieve it later from that array is the key value. For example, storage is as simple as this:

```
$state_location['San Mateo'] = 'California';
```

which stores the element 'California' in the array variable $state_location, in association with the lookup key 'San Mateo'. After this has been stored, you can look up the stored value by using the key, like so:

```
$state = $state_location['San Mateo'];   // equals 'California'
```

Simple, no?

If all you want arrays for is to store key/value pairs, the preceding information is all you need to know. Similarly, if you want to associate a numerical ordering with a bunch of values, all you have to do is use integers as your key values, as in:

```
$my_array[1] = "The first thing";
$my_array[2] = "The second thing"; // and so on ...
```

Note   For Perl programmers: Arrays in PHP are much like hashes in Perl, with some syntactic differences. For one thing, all variables in PHP are denoted with a leading $, not just scalar variables. Second, even though the array is associative, the indices are grouped by square brackets ([ ]) rather than curly braces ({ }). Finally, there is no array or list type indexed only by integers. The convention is to use integers as associative indices, and the array itself maintains an internal ordering for iteration purposes.

In addition to the machinery that makes this kind of key/value association possible, arrays track some other things behind the scenes. Because of this, we sometimes treat them as other kinds of data structures. As we will see, arrays can be *multidimensional*. They can store values in association with a sequence of key values rather than a single key. Also, arrays automatically maintain an ordered list of the elements that have been inserted in them, independent of what the key values happen to be. This makes it possible to treat arrays as linked lists. In general, we will reveal the workings of this extra machinery as we explore the functions that use it.

Note   A note for C++ programmers: You should be aware that arrays can handle some of the same tasks that require the use of template libraries in C++. Much of the reason for having templates in the first place is to get around restrictions having to do with strict typing of data. PHP's looser typing system makes it possible, for example, to write general algorithms that iterate over the contents of arrays without committing to the type of the array elements themselves.

Associative arrays versus vector arrays

If you have programmed in languages like C, C++, and Pascal, you are probably used to a particular usage of the word array, one that doesn't match the PHP usage very well at all. A more specific term for a C-style array is a vector array, whereas a PHP-style array is an associative array.

In a vector array, the contained elements all need to be of the same type, and usually the language compiler needs to know in advance how many such elements there are likely to be. For example, In C you might declare an array of 100 double-precision floating-point numbers with a statement like:

```
double my_array[100]; // This is C, not PHP!
```

The restriction on types and the advance declaration of size have an associated benefit: Vector arrays are very fast, both for storage and lookup. The reason is that the compiler will usually lay out the array in a contiguous block of computer memory, as large as the size of the element type multiplied by the number of elements. This makes it very easy for the programming language to locate a particular array slot — all it needs to know is the starting memory address of the array, the size of the element type, and the index of the element it wants to look up, and it can directly compute the memory address of that slot.

By contrast, PHP arrays are associative (and so some would call them *hashes,* rather than arrays). Rather than having a fixed number of slots, PHP creates array slots as new elements are added to the array. Rather than requiring elements to be of the same type, PHP arrays have the same type-looseness that PHP variables have — you can assign arbitrary PHP values to be array elements. Finally, because vector arrays are all about laying out their elements in numerical order; the keys used for lookup and storage must be integer numbers. PHP arrays can have keys of arbitrary type, instead, including string keys. So, you could have successive array assignments like:

```
$my_array[1] = 1;
$my_array['orange'] = 2;
$my_array[3] = 3;
```

without any paradox. The result is that your array has three values (1, 2, 3), each of which is stored in association with a key (1, 'orange', and 3, respectively).

The extra flexibility of associative arrays comes at a price, because there is a little bit more going on between your code and the actual computation of a memory address than is true with vector arrays. For most Web programming purposes, however, this extra access time is not a significant cost.

The fact that integers are legal keys for PHP arrays means that you can easily imitate the behavior of a vector array, simply by restricting your code to use only integers as keys.

Note   A general note for programmers familiar with other languages: PHP does not need very many different kinds of data structures, in part because of the great flexibility offered by PHP arrays. By careful choice of a subset of array functions, you can make arrays pretend to act like vector arrays, structure/record types, linked lists, hash tables, or stacks and queues — data structures that in other languages either require their own data types or more abstruse language features such as pointers and explicit memory management.

Creating Arrays

There are three main ways to create an array in a PHP script: by assigning a value into one (and thereby implicitly creating it), by using the `array()` construct, and by calling a function that happens to return an array as its value.

Direct assignment

The simplest way to create an array is to act as though a variable is already an array and assign a value into it, like this:

```
$my_array[1] = "The first thing in my array that I just made";
```

If `$my_array` was an unbound variable (or bound to a nonarray variable) before this statement, it will now be a variable bound to an array with one element. If instead `$my_array` was already an array, the string will be stored in association with the integer key 1. If no value was associated with that number before, a new array slot will be created to hold it; if a value was associated with 1, the previous value will be overwritten. (You can also assign into an array by omitting the index entirely as in `$my_array[]`, described later in this chapter.)

The array() construct

The other way to create an array is via the `array()` construct, which creates a new array from the specification of its elements and associated keys. In its simplest version, `array()` is called with no arguments, which creates a new empty array. In its next simplest version, `array()` takes a comma-separated list of elements to be stored, without any specification of keys. The result is that the elements are stored in the array in the order specified and are assigned integer keys beginning with zero. For example, the statement:

```
$fruit_basket = array('apple', 'orange', 'banana', 'pear');
```

causes the variable `$fruit_basket` to be assigned to an array with four string elements (`'apple'`, `'banana'`, `'orange'`, `'pear'`), with the indices 0, 1, 2, and 3, respectively. In addition (as we'll see in the "Iteration" section later in this chapter), the array will remember the order in which the elements were stored.

The assignment to `$fruit_basket`, then, has exactly the same effect as the following:

```
$fruit_basket[0] = 'apple';
$fruit_basket[1] = 'orange';
$fruit_basket[?] = 'banana';
$fruit_basket[3] = 'pear';
```

assuming that the `$fruit_basket` variable was unbound at the first assignment. The same effect could also have been accomplished by omitting the indices in the assignment, like so:

```
$fruit_basket[] = 'apple';
$fruit_basket[] = 'orange';
$fruit_basket[] = 'banana';
$fruit_basket[] = 'pear';
```

In this case, PHP again assumes that you are adding sequential elements that should have numerical indices counting upward from zero.

Note   Yes, the default numbering for array indices starts at zero, not one. This is the convention for arrays in most programming languages. We're not sure why computer scientists start counting at zero (mathematicians, like everyone else in the world, start with one), but it probably has its origin in the kind of pointer arithmetic that calculates memory addresses for vector arrays. Addresses for successive elements of such arrays are found by adding successively larger offsets to the array's address, but the offset for the first element is zero (because the first element's address is the same as the array's address).

Specifying indices using array()

The simple example of `array()` in the preceding section assigns indices to our elements, but those indices will be the integers, counting upward from zero — we're not getting a lot of choice in the matter. As it turns out, `array()` offers us a special syntax for specifying what the indices should be. Instead of element values separated by commas, you supply key-value pairs separated by commas, where the key and value are separated by the special symbol =>.

Consider the following statement:

```
$fruit_basket = array(0 => 'apple', 1 => 'orange',
                      2 => 'banana', 3 => 'pear');
```

Evaluating it will have exactly the same effect as our earlier version — each string will be stored in the array in succession, with the indices 0, 1, 2, 3 in order. Instead, however, we can use exactly the same syntax to store these elements with different indices:

```
$fruit_basket = array('red' => 'apple', 'orange' => 'orange',
                      'yellow' => 'banana', 'green' => 'pear');
```

This gives us the same four elements, added to our new array in the same order, but indexed by color names rather than numbers. To recover the name of the yellow fruit, for example, we just evaluate the expression:

```
$fruit_basket['yellow'] // will be equal to 'banana'
```

Finally, as we said earlier, you can create an empty array by calling the `array` function with no arguments. For example:

```
$my_empty_array = array();
```

creates an array with no elements. This can be handy for passing to a function that expects an array as argument.

Functions returning arrays

The final way to create an array in a script is to call a function that returns an array. This may be a user-defined function, or it may be a built-in function that makes an array via methods internal to PHP.

Many database-interaction functions, for example, return their results in arrays that the functions create on the fly. Other functions exist simply to create arrays that are handy to have as grist for later array-manipulating functions. One such is `range()`, which takes two integers as arguments and returns an array filled with all the integers (inclusive) between the arguments. In other words:

```
$my_array = range(1,5);
```

is equivalent to:

```
$my_array = array(1, 2, 3, 4, 5);
```

Retrieving Values

After we have stored some values in an array, how do we get them out again?

Retrieving by index

The most direct way to retrieve a value is to use its index. If we have stored a value in $my_array at index 5, $my_array[5] should evaluate to the stored value. If $my_array has never been assigned, or if nothing has been stored in it with an index of 5, $my_array[5] will behave like an unbound variable.

The list() construct

There are a number of other ways to recover values from arrays without using keys, most of which exploit the fact that arrays are silently recording the order in which elements are stored. We cover this in more detail in this chapter's "Iteration" section, but one such example is list(), which is used to assign several array elements to variables in succession. Suppose the following two statements are executed:

```
$fruit_basket = array('apple', 'orange', 'banana');
list($red_fruit, $orange_fruit) = $fruit_basket;
```

This will assign the string 'apple' to the variable $red_fruit and the string 'orange' to the variable $orange_fruit (with no assignment of 'banana', because we didn't supply enough variables). The variables in list() will be assigned to elements of the array in the order they were originally stored in the array. Notice the unusual behavior here—the list() construct is on the left-hand side of the assignment operator (=), where we normally find only variables.

In some sense, list() is the opposite or inverse of array() because array() packages its arguments into an array, and list() takes the array apart again into individual variable assignments. If we evaluate:

```
list($first, $second) = array($first, second);
```

the original values of $first and $second will be assigned to those variables again, after having been briefly stored in an array.

Note   We have been careful to refer to both array() and list() as constructs, rather than functions. This is because they are not in fact functions—like certain other specialized PHP language features (if, while, function, and so on) they are interpreted specially by the language itself and are not run through the usual routine of function-call interpretation. Remember that the arguments to a function call are evaluated before the function is really invoked on those arguments, so constructs that need to do other kinds of interpretation on what they are given cannot be implemented as function calls. It's a useful exercise to look hard at the example uses of both array() and list() to figure out why treating them as function calls could not result in the behavior advertised.

Multidimensional Arrays

So far, the array examples we have looked at have all been one-dimensional, with only one level of bracketed keys. However, PHP can easily support multiple-dimensional arrays, with arbitrary numbers of keys. And just as with one-dimensional arrays, there is no need to declare our intentions in advance — the first reference to an array variable can be an assignment like:

```
$multi_array[1][2][3][4][5] = "deeply buried treasure";
```

That is a five-dimensional array with successive keys that happen, in this case, to be five successive integers.

Actually, in our opinion, thinking of arrays as multidimensional makes matters more confusing than they need to be. Instead, just remember that the values that are stored in arrays can themselves be arrays, just as legitimately as they can be strings or numbers. The multiple-index syntax in the preceding example is simply a concise way to refer to a (four-dimensional) array that is stored with a key of 1 in $multi_array, which in turn has a (three-dimensional) array stored in it, and so on. Note also that you can have different depths of reference in different parts of the array, like so:

```
$multi_level_array[0] = "a simple string";
$multi_level_array[1]['contains'] = "a string stored deeper";
```

The integer key of 0 stores a string, and the key of 1 stores an array that, in turn, has a string in it. However, you cannot continue on with this assignment:

```
$multi_level_array[0]['contains'] = "another deep string";
```

without the result of losing the first assignment to 'a simple string'. The key of 0 can be used to store a string or another array, but not both at once.

If we remember that multidimensional arrays are simply arrays that have other arrays stored in them, it's easier to see how the array() creation construct generalizes. In fact, even this seemingly complicated assignment is not that complicated:

```
$cornucopia = array('fruit' =>
                array('red' => 'apple',
                      'orange' => 'orange',
                      'yellow' => 'banana',
                      'green' => 'pear'),
                'flower' =>
                  array('red' => 'rose',
                        'yellow' => 'sunflower',
                        'purple' => 'iris'));
```

It is simply an array with two values stored in association with keys. Each of these values is an array itself. After we have made the array, we can reference it like this:

```
$kind_wanted = 'flower';
$color_wanted = 'purple';
print("The $color_wanted $kind_wanted is " .
      $cornucopia[$kind_wanted][$color_wanted]);
```

See the browser output:

```
The purple flower is iris
```

Note   There's a reason that we used the string concatenation operator . in the preceding print statement, rather than simply embedding the $cornucopia[$kind_wanted][$color_wanted] in our print string as we do with other variables. PHP3 string parsing can be confused by multiple array indices within a double-quoted string, so it needs to be concatenated separately. PHP since version 4 handles this in a better way—you are safe embedding array references in a string as long as you enclose the reference in curly braces, like this:

```
print( "The thing we want is
{$cornucopia[$kind_wanted][$color_wanted]}");
```

Finally, notice that there is no great penalty for misindexing into a multidimensional array when we are trying to retrieve something; if no such key is found, the expression is treated like an unbound variable. So, if we try the following instead:

```
$kind_wanted = 'fruit';
$color_wanted = 'purple'; //uh-oh, we didn't store any plums
print("The $color_wanted $kind_wanted is " .
    $cornucopia[$kind_wanted][$color_wanted]);
```

The worst that happens is the unsatisfying:

```
The purple fruit is
```

This is the worst thing that happens, of course, unless you have raised your error_reporting level to E_ALL, as we advise you to do at some points in this book. In that case, you will get a warning message about an undefined index ('purple') just as you would if you had an unbound variable.

Inspecting Arrays

Now we can make arrays, store values in arrays, and then pull the values out again when we want them. Table 9-1 summarizes a few other functions we can use to ask questions of our arrays.

Table 9-1: Simple Functions for Inspecting Arrays

Function	Behavior
is_array()	Takes a single argument of any type and returns a true value if the argument is an array, and false otherwise.
count()	Takes an array as argument and returns the number of nonempty elements in the array. (This will be 1 for strings and numbers.)
sizeof()	Identical to count().
in_array()	Takes two arguments: an element (that might be a value in an array), and an array (that might contain the element). Returns true if the element is contained as a value in the array, false otherwise. (Note that this does not test for the presence of keys in the array.)
IsSet($array[$key])	Takes an array[key] form and returns true if the key portion is a valid key for the array. (This is a specific use of the more general function IsSet(), which tests whether a variable is bound.)

Note that all of these functions work on only the depth of the array specified, so that testing for values layers deep in a multidimensional array requires that you specify out that number of places. In the case of our preceding `$cornucopia` example, for instance:

```
count($cornucopia) // what do you expect here? 2? 7? 9?
```

returns a 2, while

```
count($cornucopia[fruit]
```

returns 4.

Deleting from Arrays

Deleting an element from an array is simple, exactly analogous to getting rid of an assigned variable. Just call `unset()`, as in the following:

```
$my_array[0] = 'wanted';
$my_array[1] = 'unwanted';
$my_array[2] = 'wanted again';
unset($my_array[1]);
```

Assuming that `$my_array` was unbound when we started, at the end it has two values (`'wanted'`, `'wanted again'`), in association with two keys (0 and 2, respectively). It is as though we had skipped the original `'unwanted'` assignment (except that the keys are numbered differently).

Note that this is *not* the same as setting the contents to an empty value. If, instead of calling `unset()`, we had the following statement:

```
$my_array[1] = '';
```

at the end we would have three stored values (`'wanted'`, `''`, `'wanted again'`) in association with three keys (0, 1, and 2, respectively).

Iteration

We've seen how to put things into arrays, how to find them once we have put them there, and how to delete them when we don't want them anymore. What we need next is a technique for dealing with array elements in bulk. Iteration constructs help us do this by letting us step or loop through arrays, element by element or key by key.

We'll first delve briefly into the internal representation of arrays to understand how PHP supports iteration. (Although important, this subsection is skippable — if you want to use it but don't want to know how it works, you can jump down to the section titled "Using iteration functions.")

Support for iteration

In addition to storing values in association with their keys, PHP arrays silently build an ordered list of the key/value pairs that are stored, in the order that they are stored. The reason for this is to support operations that iterate over the entire contents of an array. (Notice that this is difficult to do simply by building a loop that increments an index, because array indices are not necessarily numerical.)

There is, in fact, sort of a hidden pointer system built into arrays. Each stored key/value pair points to the next one, and one side effect of adding the first element to an array is that a current pointer points to the very first element, where it will stay unless disturbed by one of the iteration functions.

Note Each array remembers a particular stored key/value pair as being the current one, and array iteration functions work in part by shifting that current marker through the internal list of keys and values. Although we will call this marker the *current pointer*, PHP does not support full pointers in the sense that C and C++ programmers may be used to, and this usage of the word will turn up only in the context of iterating through arrays.

This linked-list pointer system is an alternative way to inspect and manipulate arrays, which exists alongside the system that allows key-based lookup and storage. Figure 9-1 shows an abstract view (not necessarily reflecting the real implementation) of how these systems locate elements in an array.

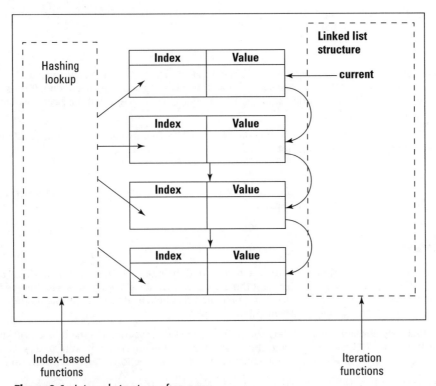

Figure 9-1: Internal structure of an array

Using iteration functions

To explore the iteration functions, let's construct a sample array that we can iterate over.

```
$major_city_info = array();
$major_city_info[0] = 'Caracas';
$major_city_info['Caracas'] = 'Venezuela';
$major_city_info[1] = 'Paris';
$major_city_info['Paris'] = 'France';
$major_city_info[2] = 'Tokyo';
$major_city_info['Tokyo'] = 'Japan';
```

In this example, we created an array and stored some names of cities in it, in association with numerical indices. We also stored the names of the relevant countries into the array, indexed by the city names. (We could have accomplished all this with one big call to array(), but the separate statements make the structure of the array somewhat clearer.)

Now, we can use the array key system to pull out the data we have stored. If we want to rely on the convention in the preceding example (cities stored with numerical indices, countries stored with city-name indices), we can write a function that prints the city and the associated country, like so:

```
function city_by_number ($number_index, $city_array)
{
  if (IsSet($city_array[$number_index]))
    {
       $the_city = $city_array[$number_index];
       $the_country = $city_array[$the_city];
       print("$the_city is in $the_country<BR>");
    }
}
city_by_number(0, $major_city_info);
city_by_number(1, $major_city_info);
city_by_number(2, $major_city_info);
```

If we have set $major_city, as in the previous block of code, the browser output we should expect is:

```
Caracas is in Venezuela
Paris is in France
Tokyo is in Japan
```

Now, this method of retrieval is fine when we know how the array is structured and we know what all the keys are. But what if you would simply like to print everything that an array contains?

Our favorite iteration method: foreach

Our favorite construct for looping through an array is foreach. Although it is probably inherited from Perl's foreach, it has a somewhat odd syntax (which is not the same as Perl's odd syntax). It comes in two flavors — which one you decide to use will depend on whether you care about the array's keys or just the values.

```
foreach ($array_variable as $value_variable) {
  // .. do something with the value in $value_variable
}  // Note that this is an example template, not real PHP code

foreach ($array_variable as $key_var => $value_var) {
// .. do something with $key_var and/or $value_var
}
```

Although in the preceding pseudocode we assume that the array of interest is in the variable $array_variable, you can have any expression that evaluates to an array in that position, for example:

```
foreach (function_returning_array() as $value_variable) {
  // .. do something with the value in $value_variable
}
```

Note   Like array() and list(), but unlike the genuine iteration functions in the rest of this section, foreach is a language construct, not a function. (See the earlier note about list() for an explanation of the difference.)

As an example, let's write a function to print all the names from our sample array:

```
function print_all_foreach ($city_array)
{
  foreach ($city_array as $name_value) {
    print("$name_value<BR>");
  }
}
print_all_foreach($major_city_info);
print_all_foreach($major_city_info);// again, as an experiment
```

As output, we get all the names, in the order we stored them, twice over:

```
Caracas
Venezuela
Paris
France
Tokyo
Japan
Caracas
Venezuela
Paris
France
Tokyo
Japan
```

We printed the contents twice to show that calling the function is repeatable.

Iterating with current() and next()

We like foreach, but it is really only good for situations where you want to simply loop through an array's values. For more control, let's look at current() and next().

The current() function returns the stored value that the current pointer points to. (Refer back to Figure 9-1 for a diagram of the array internals.) When an array is newly created with elements, the element pointed to will always be the first element. The `next()` function first advances that pointer and then returns the current value pointed to. If the `next()` function is called when the current pointer is already pointing to the last stored value and, therefore, runs off the end of the array, the function returns a false value.

As an example, we can print out an array's contents with the iteration functions `current()` and `next()`. (Notice that the final function call is repeated.)

```
function print_all_next($city_array)
{  // warning--doesn't quite work. See the function each()
  $current_item = current($city_array);
  if ($current_item)
    print("$current_item<BR>");
  else
    print("There's nothing to print");
  while($current_item = next($city_array))
    print("$current_item<BR>");
}
print_all_next($major_city_info);
print_all_next($major_city_info);// again, to see what happens
```

Caution

There is a gotcha lurking in the preceding code example, which doesn't bite us in this particular example but makes this function untrustworthy as a general method for finding everything in an array. The problem is that we may have stored a false value in the array, which our `while` loop won't be able to distinguish from the false value that `next()` returns when it has run out of array elements. See the discussion of the `each()` function later in this chapter under "Empty values and the `each()` function" for a solution.

When we execute this array-printing code, we get the following again:

```
Caracas
Venezuela
Paris
France
Tokyo
Japan
Caracas
Venezuela
Paris
France
Tokyo
Japan
```

Now, how is it that we are seeing the same thing from the second call to `print_all_next()`? How did the current pointer get back to the beginning to start all over again the second time? The answer lies in the fact that PHP function calls are *call-by-value*, meaning that they copy their arguments rather than operating directly on them. Both of the function calls, then, are getting a fresh copy of their array argument, which has never itself been disturbed by a call to `next()`.

Cross-Reference

For more on under what circumstances functions copy their arguments rather than operating on them directly, see Chapter 6.

We can test this explanation by passing the arrays by reference rather than by value. If we define the same function but call it with ampersands (&) like this:

```
print_all_next(&$major_city_info);
print_all_next(&$major_city_info);// again
```

We get the following printing behavior:

```
Caracas
Venezuela
Paris
France
Tokyo
Japan
There's nothing to print
```

 Note   The trick we used to test the array behavior (passing a variable reference to a function) has been deprecated, so you may get a warning when running this code, in addition to seeing the results printed above.

The reason is that this time the current pointer of the global version of the array was moved by the first function call.

 Note   Most of the iteration functions have both a returned value and a side effect. In the case of the functions next(), prev(), reset(), and end(), the side effect is to change the position of the internal pointer, and what is returned is the value from the key/value pair pointed to *after* the pointer's position is changed.

Starting over with reset()

In the preceding section, we wrote a function intended to print out all the values in an array, and we saw how it could fail if the array's internal pointer did not start off at the beginning of the list of key/value pairs. The reset() function gives us a way to "rewind" that pointer to the beginning—it sets the pointer to the first key/value pair and then returns the stored value. We can use it to make our printing function more robust by replacing the call to current() with a call to reset().

```
function print_all_array_reset($city_array)
{  // warning--still not reliable. See the function each()
   $current_item = reset($city_array); //rewind, return value
   if ($current_item)
     print("$current_item<BR>");
   else
     print("There's nothing to print");
   while($current_item = next($city_array))
     print("$current_item<BR>");
}
```

This function is somewhat more predictable in that it will always start with the first element, regardless of the pointer's location in the array it is handed. (Whether this is a good idea depends, of course, on what the function is used for and whether its arguments are passed by value or by reference.)

Perhaps confusingly, we use our call to reset() in the preceding example both for its side effect (rewinding the pointer) and for its return value (the first value stored). Alternatively, we could replace the first real line of the function body with these two lines:

```
reset($city_array);  // rewind to the first element
$current_item = current($city_array); // the first value
```

Reverse order with end() and prev()

We have seen the functions next(), which moves the current pointer ahead by one, and reset(), which rewinds the pointer to the beginning. Analogously, there are also the functions prev(), which moves the pointer back by one, and end(), which jumps the pointer to the last entry in the list. We can use these, for example, to print our array entries in reverse order.

```
function print_all_array_backwards($city_array)
{  // warning--still not reliable. See the function each()
  $current_item = end($city_array); //fast-forward to last
  if ($current_item)
    print("$current_item<BR>");
  else
    print("There's nothing to print");
  while($current_item = prev($city_array))
    print("$current_item<BR>");
}
print_all_array_backwards($major_city_info);
```

If we call this on the same $major_city_info data as in previous examples, we get the same printout in reverse order:

```
Japan
Tokyo
France
Paris
Venezuela
Caracas
```

Extracting keys with key()

So far, we have printed only the values stored in arrays, even though we are storing keys as well. The keys are also retrievable from the internal linked list of an array by using the key() function—this acts just like current() except that it returns the key of a key/value pair, rather than the value. (Refer to Figure 9-1.) Using the key() function, we can modify one of our earlier printing functions to print keys as well as values.

```
function print_keys_and_values($city_array)
{  // warning--See the discussion of each() below
  reset($city_array);
  $current_value = current($city_array);
  $current_key = key($city_array);
  if ($current_value)
    print("Key: $current_key; Value: $current_value<BR>");
```

```
    else
      print("There's nothing to print");
    while($current_value = next($city_array))
    {
        $current_key = key($city_array);
        print("Key: $current_key; Value: $current_value<BR>");
    }
}
print_keys_and_values($major_city_info);
```

With the same data as before, this gives us the browser output:

```
Key: 0; Value: Caracas
Key: Caracas; Value: Venezuela
Key: 1; Value: Paris
Key: Paris; Value: France
Key: 2; Value: Tokyo
Key: Tokyo; Value: Japan
```

Empty values and the each() function

We have written several functions that print the contents of arrays by iterating through them and, as we have pointed out, all but the foreach version have the same weakness. Each one of them tests for completion by seeing whether next() returns a false value. This will reliably happen when the array runs out of values, but it will also happen if and when we encounter a false value that we have actually stored. False values include the empty string (" "), the number 0, and the Boolean value FALSE, any or all of which we might reasonably store as a data value for some task or other.

To the rescue comes each(), which is somewhat similar to next() but has the virtue of returning false only after it has run out of array to traverse. Oddly enough, if it has not run out, each() returns an array itself, which holds both keys and values for the key/value pair it is pointing at. This characteristic makes each() confusing to talk about because you need to keep two arrays straight: the array that you are traversing and the array that each() returns every time that it is called. The array that each() *returns* has the following four key/value pairs:

✦ Key: 0; Value: *current-key*

✦ Key: 1; Value: *current-value*

✦ Key: 'key'; Value: *current-key*

✦ Key: 'value'; Value: *current-value*

The *current-key* and *current-value* are the key and value from the array being traversed. In other words, the returned array packages up the current key/value pair from the traversed array and offers both numerical and string indices to specify whether you are interested in the key or the value.

Note   In addition to having a different type of return value, each() differs from next() in that each() returns the value that was pointed to *before* moving the current pointer ahead, whereas next() returns the value *after* the pointer is moved. This means if you start with a current pointer pointing to the first element of an array, successive calls to each() will cover each array cell, whereas successive calls to next() will skip the first value.

We can use each() to write a more robust version of a function to print all keys and values in an array:

```
function print_keys_and_values_each($city_array)
{  // reliably prints everything in array
  reset($city_array);
  while ($array_cell = each($city_array))
  {
    $current_value = $array_cell['value'];
    $current_key = $array_cell['key'];
    print("Key: $current_key; Value: $current_value<BR>");
  }
}
print_keys_and_values_each($major_city_info);
```

Applying this function to our standard sample array gives the following browser output:

```
Key: 0; Value: Caracas
Key: Caracas; Value: Venezuela
Key: 1; Value: Paris
Key: Paris; Value: France
Key: 2; Value: Tokyo
Key: Tokyo; Value: Japan
```

This is exactly the same as was produced by our earlier function print_keys_and_values(). The difference is that our new function will not stop prematurely if one of the values is false or empty.

Walking with array_walk()

Our last iteration function lets you pass an arbitrary function of your own design over an array, doing whatever your function pleases with each key/value pair. The array_walk() function takes two arguments: an array to be traversed and the name of a function to apply to each key/value pair. (It also takes an optional third argument, discussed later in this section.)

The function that is passed in to array_walk() should take two (or three) arguments. The first argument will be the value of the array cell that is visited, and the second argument will be the key of that cell. For example, here is a function that prints a descriptive statement about the string length of an array value:

```
function print_value_length($array_value, $array_key_ignored)
{
  $the_length = strlen($array_value);
  print("The length of $array_value is $the_length<BR>");
}
```

(Notice that this function intentionally does nothing with the second argument.) Now let's pass this function over our standard sample array using array_walk():

```
array_walk($major_city_info, 'print_value_length');
```

which gives the browser output:

```
The length of Caracas is 7
The length of Venezuela is 9
The length of Paris is 5
```

```
The length of France is 6
The length of Tokyo is 5
The length of Japan is 5
```

The final flexibility that array_walk() offers is accepting an optional third argument that, if present, will be passed on, in turn, as a third argument to the function that is applied. This argument will be the same throughout the array's traversal, but it offers an extra source of runtime control for the passed function's behavior.

Caution You should not alter an array while you are iterating through the array using array_walk(). There is no guarantee how array_walk() will behave if you do this.

Table 9-2 shows a summary of the behavior of the array iteration functions that we covered in this section. Notice that foreach and list are not included; they are not functions.

Table 9-2: Functions for Iterating over Arrays

Function	Arguments	Side Effect	Return Value
current()	One array argument	None.	The value from the key/value pair currently pointed to by the internal "current" pointer (or false if no such value).
next()	One array argument	Advances the pointer by one. If already at the last element, it will move the pointer "past the end," and subsequent calls to current() will return false.	The value pointed to after the pointer has been advanced (or false if no such value).
prev()	One array argument	Moves the pointer back by one. If already at the first element, will move the pointer "before the beginning."	The value pointed to after the pointer has been moved back (or false if no such value).
reset()	One array argument	Moves the pointer back to point to the first key/value pair, or "before the beginning" if the array is empty.	The first value stored in the array, or false for an empty array.
end()	One array argument	Moves the pointer ahead to the last key/value pair.	The last value that is currently in the list of key/value pairs.
pos()	One array argument	None. (This function is an alias for current().)	The value of the key/value pair that is currently pointed to.

Function	Arguments	Side Effect	Return Value
each()	One array argument	Moves the pointer ahead to the next key/value pair.	An array that packages the keys and values of the key/value pair that was current before the pointer was moved (or false if no such pair). The returned array stores the key and value under its own keys 0 and 1, respectively, and also under its own keys 'key' and 'value'.
array_walk()	1) An array argument, 2) the name of a two- (or three-) argument function to call on each key/value, and 3) an optiona.l third argument.	This function invokes the function named by its second argument on each key/value pair. Side effects depend on the side effects of the passed function.	(Returns 1.)

Extended Example: An Exercise Calculator

Now we'll continue our exercise calculator example that we started in Chapters 7 and 8 and make further improvements using PHP arrays.

When we left this example in Chapter 8, we were allowing the user to type the name of an exercise into a Web form, and we were hoping to match the submitted string with an exercise known to the receiving script. Instead, let's take our advice from late in Chapter 8 and constrain inputs from the user to a set we know we can recognize on the receiving end.

Listing 9-1 shows an HTML form that presents a set of exercises that the user can choose from. This uses a radio-button input, so that the user can choose only one exercise to submit.

Listing 9-1: **Entry form with radio buttons**

```
<HTML>
<HEAD>
<STYLE TYPE="text/css">
<!--
BODY, P, TD
{color: black; font-family: verdana; font-size: 10 pt}
H1
```

Continued

Listing 9-1 *(continued)*

```
{color: black; font-family: arial; font-size: 12 pt}
-->
</STYLE>
</HEAD>

<BODY>
<TABLE BORDER-0 CELLPADDING=10 WIDTH=100%>
<TR>
<TD BGCOLOR="#F0F8FF" ALIGN=CENTER VALIGN=TOP WIDTH=150>
</TD>
<TD BGCOLOR="#FFFFFF" ALIGN=LEFT VALIGN=TOP WIDTH=83%>
<H1>Workout calculator (radio buttons with arrays)</H1>
<P>Select one of the following exercises, and we'll tell
    you how long <BR>
    you'd have to do it to burn one pound of fat.</P>

<FORM METHOD="post" ACTION="wc_handler_ckbx.php">
<table>
<tr>
  <td><input type="radio"
      name="exercise" value="0"> Biking/cycling</td>
</tr><tr>
  <td><input type="radio"
      name="exercise" value="1"> Running</td>
</tr><tr>
  <td><input type="radio"
      name="exercise" value="2"> Soccer/football</td>
</tr><tr>
  <td><input type="radio"
      name="exercise" value="3"> Stairclimber</td>
</tr><tr>
  <td><input type="radio"
      name="exercise" value="4"> Weightlifting</td>
</tr><tr>
  <td> </td>
</tr><tr>
  <td><input type="submit"
      name="submit" value="Burn, baby, burn!"></td>
</tr>
</table>
</FORM>

</TD>
</TR>
</TABLE>

</BODY>
</HTML>
```

Figure 9-2 shows how the entry form looks in a browser.

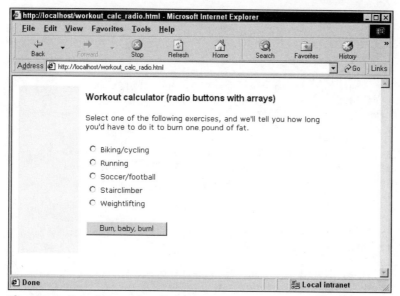

Figure 9-2: Entry form with radio buttons

The radio-button entry form passes a particular POST variable named 'exercise', which can have several different numerical values depending on which button the user clicks on. Listing 9-2 shows some handler code that can catch such a submission; the job of this code is to figure out which button was clicked and to print some appropriate info, which has been stored in advance in arrays in the receiving code file.

Listing 9-2: **Handler for radio-button selection**

```php
<?php

// This is the array where we keep our exercise names
$name_array = array(
                0 => 'Biking/cycling',
                1 => 'Running',
                2 => 'Soccer/football',
                3 => 'Stairclimber',
                4 => 'Weightlifting'
              );

// This is the array where we keep our duration data
$duration_array = array(
                0 => '5 hours and 40 minutes',
                1 => '4 hours and 30 minutes',
```

Continued

Listing 9-2 *(continued)*

```
                    2 => '4 hours and 30 minutes',
                    3 => '5 hours',
                    4 => '7 hours and 30 minutes'
                 );

// Now pull out the chosen exercise from the submission
if (is_array($_POST) && count($_POST) > 1) {
  $exercise_value = $_POST['exercise'];
  $exercise_name = $name_array[$exercise_value];
  $hours = $duration_array[$exercise_value];
}   //Usually you'd test an array for a count of 0, but here
  //there is 1 automatic POST element -- $_POST['submit'].

// Construct a sentence
// --------------------
if (isSet($hours)) {
  $message = 'It would take '.$hours.' of '.$exercise_name.
    ' to burn one pound of fat.';
} else {
  // Hmmm, they didn't pick one or something odd happened
  $message = 'Ummm, did you pick an exercise?';
}

// Now lay out the page
// --------------------
$page_str = <<< EOPAGE
<HTML>
<HEAD>
<STYLE TYPE="text/css">
<!--
BODY, P  {color: black; font-family: verdana; font-size: 10 pt}
H1       {color: black; font-family: arial; font-size: 12 pt}
-->
</STYLE>
</HEAD>

<BODY>
<TABLE BORDER=0 CELLPADDING=10 WIDTH=100%>
<TR>
<TD BGCOLOR="#F0F8FF" ALIGN=CENTER VALIGN=TOP WIDTH=150>
</TD>
<TD BGCOLOR="#FFFFFF" ALIGN=LEFT VALIGN=TOP WIDTH=83%>
<H1>Workout calculator handler (radio buttons with arrays)</H1>
<P>The workout calculator says, "$message"</P>
```

```
</TD>
</TR>
</TABLE>

</BODY>
</HTML>
EOPAGE;

echo $page_str;

?>
```

Figure 9-3 shows the result of catching the user submission and displaying appropriately.

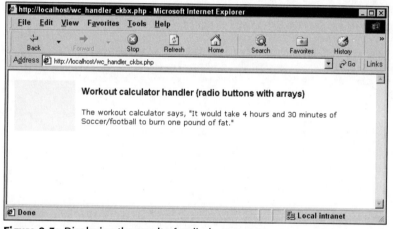

Figure 9-3: Displaying the result of radio-button entry

As usual, this is fine as far as it goes, but what if we want to submit more than one choice? For one thing, the point of the radio-button HTML construct is to allow only one choice, so we will have to abandon it; for another, the receiving code is only set up to extract one exercise.

To relax this constraint, let's use HTML check boxes instead of radio buttons for the form itself. And while we're doing that, let's use a nice feature of PHP form processing and give the choices variable names that look like indexes into a single array variable (exercise[0], exercise[1], and so on). On the receiving end, we can simply treat exercise as a single array that has arrived in the $_POST. Listing 9-3 shows the modified HTML form, and Listing 9-4 shows the receiving code.

Listing 9-3: Entry form with check boxes

```
    <HTML>
<HEAD>
<STYLE TYPE="text/css">
<!--
BODY, P, TD
      {color: black; font-family: verdana; font-size: 10 pt}
H1         {color: black; font-family: arial; font-size: 12 pt}
-->
</STYLE>
</HEAD>

<BODY>
<TABLE BORDER=0 CELLPADDING=10 WIDTH=100%>
<TR>
<TD BGCOLOR="#F0F8FF" ALIGN=CENTER VALIGN=TOP WIDTH=150>
</TD>
<TD BGCOLOR="#FFFFFF" ALIGN=LEFT VALIGN=TOP WIDTH=83%>
<H1>Workout calculator (multiple checkboxes with arrays)</H1>
<P>Select one or more of the following exercises, and we'll tell
you<BR> how long you'd have to do each one to burn one pound of
fat.</P>

<FORM METHOD="post" ACTION="wc_handler_array.php">
<table>
<tr>
  <td><input type="checkbox" name="exercise[0]"
value="1"> Biking/cycling</td>
</tr>
<tr>
  <td><input type="checkbox" name="exercise[1]"
value="1"> Running</td>
</tr>
<tr><td><input type="checkbox" name="exercise[2]"
value="1"> Soccer/football</td>
</tr>
<tr>
  <td><input type="checkbox" name="exercise[3]"
value="1"> Stairclimber</td>
</tr>
<tr>
  <td><input type="checkbox" name="exercise[4]"
value="1"> Weightlifting</td>
</tr>
<tr>
  <td> </td>
</tr>
<tr>
  <td><input type="submit" name="submit"
```

```
                value="Burn, baby, burn!"></td>
</TR>
</TABLE>
</FORM>

</TR></TABLE>

</BODY>
</HTML>
```

To save space, we'll skip the screenshots for this example; the submitting form looks similar to the radio-button example except for the prompting language, and the receiving page simply prints multiple choices rather than a single choice.

Listing 9-4: **Handler for check boxes**

```php
<?php

// This is the array where we keep our exercise names
$name_array = array(
                    0 => 'Biking/cycling',
                    1 => 'Running',
                    2 => 'Soccer/football',
                    3 => 'Stairclimber',
                    4 => 'Weightlifting'
                   );

// This is the array where we keep our duration data
$duration_array = array(
                    0 => '5 hours and 40 minutes',
                    1 => '4 hours and 30 minutes',
                    2 => '4 hours and 30 minutes',
                    3 => '5 hours',
                    4 => '7 hours and 30 minutes'
                   );

// Now step through the exercises and see which ones they chose
if (is_array($_POST) && count($_POST) > 1) {
  $message = '';
  foreach ($_POST['exercise'] as $key => $val) {
    if ($val == 1) {
      $exercise_name = $name_array[$key];
      $hours = $duration_array[$key];
      $message .=
        "</P>\n<P>It would take $hours of $exercise_name " .
        "to burn one pound of fat.";
    }
  }
```

Continued

Listing 9-4 *(continued)*

```
}
else {
   // Hmmm, they didn't pick one or something strange happened
   $message = 'Ummm, did you pick an exercise?';
} //If you don't have this test, an empty form will cause an
  // error.
  //Usually you'd test an array for a count of 0, but here
  //there is 1 automatic POST array element -- $_POST['submit'].


// Now lay out the page
// --------------------
$page_str = <<< EOPAGE
<HTML>
<HEAD>
<STYLE TYPE="text/css">
<!--
BODY, P
     {color: black; font-family: verdana; font-size: 10 pt}
H1   {color: black; font-family: arial; font-size: 12 pt}
-->
</STYLE>
</HEAD>

<BODY>
<TABLE BORDER=0 CELLPADDING=10 WIDTH=100%>
<TR>
<TD BGCOLOR="#F0F8FF" ALIGN=CENTER VALIGN=TOP WIDTH=150>
</TD>
<TD BGCOLOR="#FFFFFF" ALIGN=LEFT VALIGN=TOP WIDTH=83%>
<H1>Workout calculator handler (multiple checkboxes with arrays)</H1>
<P>The workout calculator says:
$message</P>
</TD>
</TR>
</TABLE>

</BODY>
</HTML>
EOPAGE;

echo $page_str;

?>
```

Taking this one step further, we can also submit multidimensional arrays via HTML form. All we need to do is name our FORM variables with multiple levels of brackets (like exercise[1][2]), and we'll have a multidimensional array on the receiving end.

Listing 9-5 shows our slightly modified entry form, and Listing 9-6 shows receiving code that iterates through the submitted multidimensional array, doing the appropriate unpacking.

Listing 9-5: **Entry form for multidimensional arrays**

```
<HTML>
<HEAD>
<STYLE TYPE="text/css">
<!--
BODY, P, TD
        {color: black; font-family: verdana; font-size: 10 pt}
H1      {color: black; font-family: arial; font-size: 12 pt}
-->
</STYLE>
</HEAD>

<BODY>
<TABLE BORDER=0 CELLPADDING=10 WIDTH=100%>
<TR>
<TD BGCOLOR="#F0F8FF" ALIGN=CENTER VALIGN=TOP WIDTH=150>
</TD>
<TD BGCOLOR="#FFFFFF" ALIGN=LEFT VALIGN=TOP WIDTH=83%>
<H1>Workout calculator (multidimensional arrays)</H1>
<P>Select one or more of the following exercises, and we'll tell
you<BR>
how long you'd have to do each one to burn one pound of fat.</P>

<FORM METHOD="post" ACTION="wc_handler_mult_arr.php">
<table>
<tr>
  <td><B>Aerobic exercise</B></td>
</tr>
<tr>
  <td><input type="checkbox" name="exercise[0][0]"
      value="1"> Biking/cycling</td>
</tr>
<tr>
  <td><input type="checkbox" name="exercise[0][1]"
      value="1"> Rowing</td>
</tr>
<tr>
  <td><input type="checkbox" name="exercise[0][2]"
      value="1"> Running</td>
```

Continued

Listing 9-5 *(continued)*

```
  </tr>
  <tr>
    <td><input type="checkbox" name="exercise[0][3]"
        value="1"> Stairclimber</td>
  </tr>
  <tr>
    <td><input type="checkbox" name="exercise[0][4]"
        value="1"> Walking</td>
  </tr>
  <tr>
    <td><B>Sports</B></td>
  </tr>
  <tr>
    <td><input type="checkbox" name="exercise[1][0]"
        value="1"> Basketball</td>
  </tr>
  <tr>
    <td><input type="checkbox" name="exercise[1][1]"
        value="1"> Ice hockey</td>
  </tr>
  <tr>
    <td><input type="checkbox" name="exercise[1][2]"
        value="1"> Soccer/football</td>
  </tr>
  <tr>
    <td><input type="checkbox" name="exercise[1][3]"
        value="1"> Table tennis</td>
  </tr>
  <tr>
    <td><B>Strength training</B></td>
  </tr>
  <tr>
    <td><input type="checkbox" name="exercise[2][0]"
        value="1"> Calisthenics</td>
  </tr>
  <tr>
    <td><input type="checkbox" name="exercise[2][1]"
        value="1"> Weightlifting (light)</td>
  </tr>
  <tr>
    <td><input type="checkbox" name="exercise[2][2]"
        value="1"> Weightlifting (strenuous)</td>
  </tr>
  <tr>
    <td><B>Stretching/flexibility</B></td>
  </tr>
  <tr>
```

```
  <td><input type="checkbox" name="exercise[3][0]"
      value="1"> Pilates</td>
</tr>
<tr>
  <td><input type="checkbox" name="exercise[3][1]"
      value="1"> Tai chi</td>
</tr>
<tr>
  <td><input type="checkbox" name="exercise[3][2]"
      value="1"> Yoga</td>
</tr>
<tr>
  <td> </td>
</tr>
<tr>
  <td><input type="submit" name="submit"
      value="Burn, baby, burn!"></td>
</td></tr>
</table>
</TR>
</TABLE>
</FORM>

</BODY>
</HTML>
```

Figure 9-4 shows our new entry form, with check boxes (instead of radio buttons) to handle multiple entries.

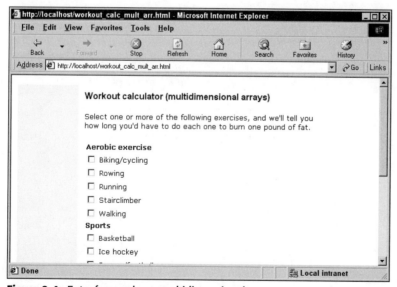

Figure 9-4: Entry form using a multidimensional array

Listing 9-6: **Handler for multidimensional array form**

```php
<?php

// Exercise types
$exercise_types = array(0 => 'Aerobic exercise',
                        1 => 'Sports',
                        2 => 'Strength training',
                        3 => 'Stretching/flexibility'
                       );

// This is the multidimensional array where we keep our
// exercises
$exercise_array =
  array(0 => array(0 => 'Biking/cycling',
                   1 => 'Rowing',
                   2 => 'Running',
                   3 => 'Stairclimber',
                   4 => 'Walking'
                  ),
        1 => array(0 => 'Basketball',
                   1 => 'Ice hockey',
                   2 => 'Soccer/football',
                   3 => 'Table tennis'
                  ),
        2 => array(0 => 'Calisthenics',
                   1 => 'Weightlifting (light)',
                   2 => 'Weightlifting (strenuous)',
                  ),
        3 => array(0 => 'Pilates',
                   1 => 'Tai chi',
                   2 => 'Yoga',
                  )
       );

// This is the array where we keep our duration data
$duration_array =
  array(0 => array(0 => '5 hours and 40 minutes',
                   1 => '4 hours and 10 minutes',
                   2 => '4 hours and 30 minutes',
                   3 => '5 hours',
                   4 => '10 hours and 10 minutes'
                  ),
        1 => array(0 => '5 hours',
                   1 => '5 hours',
                   2 => '4 hours and 30 minutes',
                   3 => '10 hours and 10 minutes'
                  ),
        2 => array(0 => '6 hours and 30 minutes',
                   1 => '13 hours and 30 minutes',
```

```
                        2 => '7 hours and 30 minutes',
                        ),
            3 => array(0 => '8 hours and 45 minutes',
                       1 => '10 hours and 10 minutes',
                       2 => '16 hours',
                       )
            );

// Now step through the exercises and see which one they chose
if (is_array($_POST) && count($_POST) > 1
    && is_array($_POST['exercise'])) {
  $message = '';
  foreach ($_POST['exercise'] as $key_1 => $val) {
    // $val should be an array
    if (!is_array($val)) {
      $message .= "Something's wrong -- value not array<BR>";
    }
    else {
      // Add heading
      $heading = $exercise_types[$key_1];
      $message .= "</P>\n<P><B>$heading</B>";
      foreach ($val as $key_2 => $val_2) {
        if ($val_2 == 1) {
          $exercise_name = $exercise_array[$key_1][$key_2];
          $hours = $duration_array[$key_1][$key_2];
          $message .= "</P>\n<P>It would take $hours of ".
            "$exercise_name to burn one pound of fat.";
        }
      }
    }
  }
} else {
  // Hmmm, they didn't pick one or something wack happened
  $message = 'Ummm, did you pick an exercise?';
}

// Now lay out the page
// --------------------
$page_str = <<< EOPAGE
<HTML>
<HEAD>
<STYLE TYPE="text/css">
<!--
BODY, P
{color: black; font-family: verdana; font-size: 10 pt}
H1
{color: black; font-family: arial; font-size: 12 pt}
-->
</STYLE>
</HEAD>
```

Continued

Listing 9-6 *(continued)*

```
<BODY>
<TABLE BORDER=0 CELLPADDING=10 WIDTH=100%>
<TR>
<TD BGCOLOR="#F0F8FF" ALIGN=CENTER VALIGN=TOP WIDTH=150>
</TD>
<TD BGCOLOR="#FFFFFF" ALIGN=LEFT VALIGN=TOP WIDTH=83%>
<H1>Workout calculator handler (multidimensional arrays)</H1>
<P>The workout calculator says:
$message</P>
</TD>
</TR>
</TABLE>

</BODY>
</HTML>
EOPAGE;

echo $page_str;

?>
```

There are several layers of array packaging that the receiving code in Listing 9-6 pulls apart: First, it uses the `'exercise'` key to find the right value in the $_POST array. The value it finds is itself an array. It then uses two nested `foreach` loops to delve down through the two layers of indexing to the actual exercises submitted. Figure 9-5 shows the result.

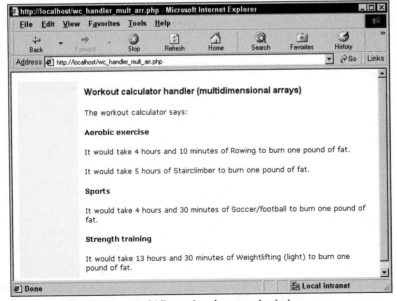

Figure 9-5: Displaying a multidimensional array submission

Summary

The array is a basic PHP datatype and plays the role of both record types and vector array types in other languages. PHP arrays are associative, meaning that they store their values in association with unique *keys* or *indices*. Indices can be either strings or numbers, and are denoted as indices by square brackets. (The expression $my_array[4] refers to the value stored in $my_array in association with the integer index 4, and not necessarily to the 4th element of $my_array.)

The loose typing of PHP means that any PHP value can be stored as an array. In turn, this means that arrays can be stored as array elements. *Multidimensional arrays* are simply arrays that contain other arrays as elements, with a reference syntax of successive brackets. (The expression $my_array[3][4] refers to the element (indexed by 4) of an array which is an element (indexed by 3) of $my_array.)

The array is the standard vehicle for PHP functions that return structured data, so PHP programmers should learn to unpack arrays, even if they are not interested in constructing them. PHP also offers a huge variety of functions for manipulating data after you have it stored in an array, including functions for counting, summarizing, and sorting.

✦　　✦　　✦

Numbers

◆ ◆ ◆ ◆

In This Chapter

Numerical types

Mathematical operators

Simple math functions

Random numbers

◆ ◆ ◆ ◆

If you need to do serious numerical, scientific, or statistical computation, a Web-scripting language is probably not where you want to be doing it. With that said, however, PHP does offer a generous array of functions that nicely cover most of the mathematical tasks that arise in Web scripting. It also offers some more advanced capabilities such as arbitrary-precision arithmetic and access to hashing and cryptographic libraries.

The PHP designers have, quite sensibly, not tried to reinvent any wheels in this department. Instead, they found about eighteen perfectly good wheels by the side of the road and built a lightweight fiberglass chassis to connect them all together. Many of the more basic math functions in PHP are simple wrappers around their C counterparts (for more on this, see the sidebar "A Glimpse behind the Curtain" in Chapter 27, which will cover PHP's mathematics capabilities in greater detail).

Numerical Types

PHP has only two numerical types: *integer* (also known as *long*), and *double* (aka *float*), which correspond to the largest numerical types in the C language. PHP does automatic conversion of numerical types, so they can be freely intermixed in numerical expressions and the "right thing" will typically happen. PHP also converts strings to numbers where necessary.

In situations where you want a value to be interpreted as a particular numerical type, you can force a typecast by prepending the type in parentheses, such as:

```
(double) $my_var
(integer) $my_var
```

Or you can use the functions `intval()` and `doubleval()`, which convert their arguments to integers and doubles, respectively.

Cross-Reference For more details on the integer and double types, see Chapter 5.

Mathematical Operators

Most of the mathematical action in PHP is in the form of built-in functions rather than in the form of operators. In addition to the comparison operators covered in Chapter 6, PHP offers five operators for simple arithmetic, as well as some *shorthand* operators that make incrementing and assigning statements more concise.

Arithmetic operators

The five basic arithmetic operators are those you would find on a four-function calculator, plus the modulus operator (%). (If you are unfamiliar with modulus, see the discussion following Table 10-1.) The operators are summarized in Table 10-1.

Table 10-1: Arithmetic Operators

Operator	Behavior	Examples
+	Sum of its two arguments.	4 + 9.5 evaluates to 13.5
−	If there are two arguments, the right-hand argument is subtracted from the left-hand argument. If there is just a right-hand argument, then the negative of that argument is returned.	50 - 75 evaluates to -25 - 3.9 evaluates to -3.9
*	Product of its two arguments.	3.14 * 2 evaluates to 6.28
/	Floating-point division of the left-hand argument by the right-hand argument.	5 / 2 evaluates to 2.5
%	Integer remainder from division of left-hand argument by the absolute value of the right-hand argument. (See discussion in the following section.)	101 % 50 evaluates to 1 999 % 3 evaluates to 0 43 % 94 evaluates to 43 -12 % 10 evaluates to -2 -12 % -10 evaluates to -2

Arithmetic operators and types

With the first three arithmetic operators (+, -, *), you should expect *type contagion* from doubles to integers; that is, if both arguments are integers, the result will be an integer, but if either argument is a double, then the result will be a double. With the division operator, there is the same sort of contagion, and in addition the result will be a double if the division is not even.

Tip   If you want integer division rather than floating-point division, simply coerce or convert the division result to an integer. For example, intval(5 / 2) evaluates to the integer 2.

Modular arithmetic is sometimes taught in school as *clock arithmetic*. The process of taking one number modulo to another amounts to "wrapping" the first number around the second, or (equivalently) taking the remainder of the first number after dividing by the second. The result of such an operation is always less than the second number.

Roughly speaking, a conventional civilian analog clock displays hours elapsed modulo 12, while military time is modulo 24. (The *roughly* in the previous sentence is because the real modulus function converts numbers to the range 0 to *n*-1, rather than the range 1 to *n*. If bell-tower clocks respected this, noontime would be marked by silence, rather than by twelve chimes.)

The modulus operator in PHP (%) expects integer arguments — if it is given doubles, they will simply be converted to integers (by truncation) first. The result is always an integer.

Most programming languages have some form of the modulus operator, but they differ in how they handle negative arguments. In some languages, the result of the operator is always positive, and -2 % 26 equals 24. In PHP, though, -2 % 26 is -2, and, in general, the statement $mod = $first_num % $second_num is exactly equivalent to the expression:

```
if ($first_num >= 0)
    $mod = $first_num % abs($second_num);
else
    $mod = - (abs($first_num) % abs($second_num));
```

where abs() is the absolute value function.

Incrementing operators

PHP inherits a lot of its syntax from C, and C programmers are famously proud of their own conciseness. The incrementing/decrementing operators taken from C make it possible to more concisely represent statements like $count = $count + 1, which tend to be typed frequently.

The increment operator (++) adds one to the variable it is attached to, and the decrement operator (--) subtracts one from the variable. Each one comes in two flavors, *postincrement* (which is placed immediately after the affected variable), and *preincrement* (which comes immediately before). Both flavors have the same side effect of changing the variable's value, but they have different values as expressions. The postincrement operator acts as if it changes the variable's value after the expression's value is returned, whereas the preincrement operator acts as though it makes the change first and then returns the variable's new value. You can see the difference by using the operators in assignment statements, like this:

```
$count = 0;
$result = $count++;
print("Post ++: count is $count, result is $result<BR>");
$count = 0;
$result = ++$count;
print("Pre ++: count is $count, result is $result<BR>");
$count = 0;
$result = $count--;
print("Post --: count is $count, result is $result<BR>");
$count = 0;
$result = --$count;
print("Pre --: count is $count, result is $result<BR>");
```

which gives the browser output:

```
Post ++: count is 1, result is 0
Pre ++: count is 1, result is 1
Post --: count is -1, result is 0
Pre --: count is -1, result is -1
```

In this example, the statement `$result = $count++;` is exactly equivalent to

```
$result = $count;
$count = $count + 1;
```

while `$result = ++$count;` is equivalent to

```
$count = $count + 1;
$result = $count;
```

Assignment operators

Incrementing operators like ++ save keystrokes when adding one to a variable, but they don't help when adding another number or performing another kind of arithmetic. Luckily, all five arithmetic operators have corresponding assignment operators (+=, -=, *=, /=, and %=) that assign to a variable the result of an arithmetic operation on that variable in one fell swoop. The statement:

```
$count = $count * 3;
```

can be shortened to:

```
$count *= 3;
```

and the statement:

```
$count = $count + 17;
```

becomes:

```
$count += 17;
```

Comparison operators

PHP includes the standard arithmetic comparison operators, which take simple values (numbers or strings) as arguments and evaluate to either TRUE or FALSE:

Cross-Reference   For examples of using the comparison operators and also some gotcha issues with comparing doubles and strings, see Chapter 6.

✦ The < (less than) operator is true if its left-hand argument is strictly less than its right-hand argument but false otherwise.

✦ The > (greater than) operator is true if its left-hand argument is strictly greater than its right-hand argument but false otherwise.

✦ The <= (less than or equal) operator is true if its left-hand argument is less than or equal to its right-hand argument but false otherwise.

✦ The >= (greater than or equal) operator is true if its left-hand argument is greater than or equal to its right-hand argument but false otherwise.

✦ The == (equal to) operator is true if its arguments are exactly equal but false otherwise.

✦ The != (not equal) operator is false if its arguments are exactly equal and true otherwise.

✦ The === operator (identical to) is true if its two arguments are exactly equal and of the same type.

Tip

The identical to operator (===)can, at times, be a necessary antidote to PHP's automatic type conversions. None of the following expressions will have a true value:

```
2 === 2.0
2 === "2"
"2.0" === 2.0
0 === FALSE
```

This behavior can be invaluable, for example, if you have a function that returns a string when it succeeds (which might be the empty string) and a FALSE value when it fails. Testing the truth of the return value would confuse FALSE with the empty string, whereas the identical operator can distinguish them.

Precedence and parentheses

Operator *precedence* rules govern the relative stickiness of operators, deciding which operators in an expression get first claim on the arguments that surround them. You can find a complete table of all operator precedences in the manual at www.php.net, but the important precedence rules for arithmetic are:

✦ Arithmetic operators have higher precedence (that is, bind more tightly) than comparison operators.

✦ Comparison operators have higher precedence than assignment operators.

✦ The *, /, and % arithmetic operators have the same precedence.

✦ The + and - arithmetic operators have the same precedence.

✦ The *, /, and % operators have higher precedence than + and -.

✦ When arithmetic operators are of the same precedence, associativity is left-to-right (that is, a number will associate with an operator to its left in preference to the operator on its right).

If you find the precedence rules difficult to remember, the next person who reads your code may have the same problem, so feel free to parenthesize when in doubt. For example, can you easily figure out the value of this expression?

```
1 + 2 * 3 - 4 - 5 / 4 % 3
```

As it turns out, the value is 2, as we can see more easily when we add parentheses that are not, strictly speaking, necessary:

```
((1 + (2 * 3)) - 4) - ((5 / 4) % 3)
```

Simple Mathematical Functions

The next step up in sophistication from the arithmetic operators consists of miscellaneous functions that perform tasks like converting between the two numerical types (which we discussed in Chapter 5) and finding the minimum and maximum of a set of numbers (see Table 10-2).

Table 10-2: Simple Math Functions

Function	Behavior
floor()	Takes a single argument (typically a double) and returns the largest integer that is less than or equal to that argument.
ceil()	Short for ceiling — takes a single argument (typically a double) and returns the smallest integer that is greater than or equal to that argument.
round()	Takes a single argument (typically a double) and returns the nearest integer. If the fractional part is exactly 0.5, it returns the nearest even number.
abs()	Short for absolute value — if the single numerical argument is negative, the corresponding positive number is returned; if the argument is positive, the argument itself is returned.
min()	Takes any number of numerical arguments (but at least one) and returns the smallest of the arguments.
max()	Takes any number of numerical arguments (but at least one) and returns the largest of the arguments.

For example, the result of the following expression:

```
min(3, abs(-3), max(round(2.7), ceil(2.3), floor(3.9)))
```

is 3, because the value of every function call is also 3.

Randomness

PHP's functions for generating pseudo-random numbers are summarized in Table 10-3. (If you are new to random number generation and are wondering what the *pseudo* is all about, please see the accompanying sidebar.)

There are two random number generators (invoked with rand() and mt_rand(), respectively), each with the same three associated functions: a seeding function, the random-number function itself, and a function that retrieves the largest integer that might be returned by the generator.

The particular pseudo-random function that is used by rand() may depend on the particular libraries that PHP was compiled with. By contrast, the mt_rand() generator always uses the same random function (the Mersenne Twister), and the author of mt_rand()'s online documentation argues that it is also faster and "more random" (in a cryptographic sense) than rand(). We have no reason to believe that this is not correct, so we prefer mt_rand() to rand().

Table 10-3: Random Number Functions

Function	Behavior
srand()	Takes a single positive integer argument and seeds the random number generator with it.
rand()	If called with no arguments, returns a "random" number between 0 and RAND_MAX (which can be retrieved with the function getrandmax()). The function can also be called with two integer arguments to restrict the range of the number returned—the first argument is the minimum and the second is the maximum (inclusive).
getrandmax()	Returns the largest number that may be returned by rand(). This is limited to 32768 on Windows platforms.
mt_srand()	Like srand(), except that it seeds the "better" random number generator.
mt_rand()	Like rand(), except that it uses the "better" random number generator.
mt_getrandmax()	Returns the largest number that may be returned by mt_rand().

Note   On some PHP versions and some platforms, you can apparently get seemingly random numbers from rand() and mt_rand() without seeding first—this should not be relied upon, however, both for reasons of portability and because the unseeded behavior is not guaranteed.

Seeding the generator

The typical way to seed either of the PHP random-number generators (using mt_srand() or srand()) looks like this:

```
mt_srand((double)microtime()*1000000);
```

This sets the seed of the generator to be the number of microseconds that have elapsed since the last whole second. (Yes, the typecast to double is necessary here, because microtime() returns a string, which would treated as an integer in the multiplication but for the cast.) Please use this seeding statement even if you don't understand it—just place it in any PHP page, once only, before you use the corresponding mt_rand() or rand() functions, and it will ensure that you have a varying starting point and therefore random sequences that are different every time. This particular seeding technique has been thought through by people who understand the ins and outs of pseudo-random number generation and is probably better than any attempt an individual programmer might make to try something trickier.

Pseudo-random Number Generators

As with all programming languages, the "random" number functions offered by PHP are really implemented by pseudo-random number generators. This is because conventional computer architectures are deterministic machines that will always produce the same results given the same starting conditions and inputs and have no good source of randomness. (Here we're talking about the ideal computer as it is supposed to work, not the actual physically embodied, power-interruptible, cosmic-ray flippable, seemingly very random machines we all struggle with daily!) You could imagine connecting a conventional computer to a source of random bits such as a mechanical coin-flip reader, or a device that observed quantum-level events, but such peripherals don't seem to be widely available at this time.

So we must make do with pseudo-random generators, which produce a deterministic sequence of numbers that looks random enough for most purposes. They typically work by running their initial input number (the *seed*) through a particular mathematical function to produce the first number in the sequence; each subsequent number in the sequence is the result of applying that same function to the previous number in the sequence. The sequence will repeat at some point (once it generates a particular number for the second time, it is doomed to follow the same sequence as it did the first time around), but a good iteration function will generate a very long sequence of numbers that have little apparent pattern before the loop occurs.

How do you choose a seed to start off with? Because of the generator's determinism, if you hard-code a PHP page to have a particular seed, that page will always see the same sequence from the generator. (Although this is not usually what you want, it can be an invaluable trick when you are trying to debug behavior that depends on the particular numbers that are generated.) The typical seeding technique is to use a fast-changing digit from the system clock as the initial seed—although those numbers are not exactly random, they are likely to vary quickly enough that subsequent page executions will start with a different seed every time.

Here's some representative code that uses the pseudo-random functions:

```
print("Seeding the generator<BR>");
mt_srand((double)microtime() * 1000000);
print("With no arguments: " . mt_rand() . "<BR>");
print("With no arguments: " . mt_rand() . "<BR>");
print("With no arguments: " . mt_rand() . "<BR>");
print("With two arguments: " .
      mt_rand(27, 31) . "<BR>");
print("With two arguments: " .
      mt_rand(27, 31) . "<BR>");
print("With two arguments: " .
      mt_rand(27, 31) . "<BR>");
```

with the browser output:

```
Seeding the generator
With no arguments: 992873415
With no arguments: 656237128
With no arguments: 1239053221
With two arguments: 28
With two arguments: 31
With two arguments: 29
```

Tip Although the random-number functions only return integers, it is easy to convert a random integer in a given range to a corresponding floating-point number (say, one between 0.0 and 1.0 inclusive) with an expression like rand() / getrandmax(). You can then scale and shift the range as desired (to, say, a number between 100.0 and 120.0) with an expression like 100.0 + 20.0 * (rand() / getrandmax()).

Obviously, if you run exactly this code, you will get numbers that differ from those in the output shown here, because the point of seeding the generator this way is to ensure that different executions produce different sequences of numbers.

Caution In some old versions of PHP3, the rand() function buggily ignored its arguments, returning numbers between 0 and getrandmax() regardless of restrictions. We have also heard some reports of that behavior under more recent Windows implementations. If you suspect that you are suffering from such a bug, you can define your own restricted version of rand() like so:

```
function my_rand ($min, $max)
{
   return(rand() % (($max - $min) + 1)
          + $min);
}
```

Unlike rand(), this version requires the min and max arguments.

Example: Making a random selection

Now let's use the random functions for something useful (or, at least, something that could be used for something useful). The following two functions let you construct a random string of letters, which could, in turn, be used as a random login or password string:

```
function random_char($string)
{
  $length = strlen($string);
  $position = mt_rand(0, $length - 1);
  return($string[$position]);
}
function random_string ($charset_string, $length)
{
    $return_string = ""; // the empty string
  for ($x = 0; $x < $length; $x++)
    $return_string .= random_char($charset_string);
  return($return_string);
}
```

The random_char() function chooses a character (or, actually, a substring of length 1) from its input string. It does this by restricting the mt_rand() function to positions within the length of the string (with chars numbered starting at zero), and then returning the character that is at that random position. The random_string() function calls random_char() a number of times on a string representing the universe of characters to be chosen from and concatenates a string of the desired length.

Now, to demonstrate this code, we first seed the generator, define our universe of allowable characters, and then call random_string() a few times in a row:

```
mt_srand((double)microtime() * 1000000);
$charset = "abcdefghijklmnopqrstuvwxyz";

$random_string = random_string($charset, 8);
print("random_string: $random_string<BR>");
$random_string = random_string($charset, 8);
print("random_string: $random_string<BR>");
$random_string = random_string($charset, 8);
print("random_string: $random_string<BR>");
```

with the result:

```
random_string: eisexkio
random_string: mkvflwfy
random_string: gpulbwth
```

In this example, we seed the generator only once, and we draw that seed value from the system clock. Notice what happens if we make the mistake of repeatedly seeding the generator with the same value:

```
mt_srand(43);
$random_string = random_string($charset, 8);
print("random_string: $random_string<BR>");

mt_srand(43);
$random_string = random_string($charset, 8);
print("random_string: $random_string<BR>");

mt_srand(43);
$random_string = random_string($charset, 8);
print("random_string: $random_string<BR>");
```

Because the sequence that is generated depends deterministically on the seed, we get the same behavior each time:

```
random_string: qgkxvurw
random_string: qgkxvurw
random_string: qgkxvurw
```

In these examples, we chose to draw random characters from strings, but this kind of selection process is generalizable to draw items from arrays or to be used in any situation that requires choosing random members from a set. All you need is the universe of items, a way to put them in numerical order, and a way to retrieve them by order number, and you can then use the rand() or mt_rand() function to choose a random order number for the retrieval.

Extended Example: An Exercise Calculator

Now let's return to the exercise-calculator example that we've been developing since Chapter 7. In addition to mixing in a little bit of arithmetic calculation, we'll reorganize the code a bit.

One problem with the code as we left it was that we had our data in two different code files and in more than one array. Changes to the data require updating more than one file and take some care to make sure that everything stays in sync.

We could always keep this data in a text file or in a database. For this chapter, however, let's just make a single PHP code file where we define a single array with everything we need: types of exercises, names of exercises, and the calories per minute that each exercise consumes, assuming a person of average weight. Such an array is shown in Listing 10-1; we'll call this file exercise_include.php.

Listing 10-1: **exercise_include.php**

```php
<?php
// categories of exercise with associated calories per minute
// (not medically trustworthy because we made them up)
$exercise_info =
  array('Aerobic exercise' =>
    array('biking/cycling' => 9,
                'rowing' => 8,
                'running' => 14,
                'stairclimber' => 6,
          'walking' => 5),
  'Sports' =>
            array('basketball' => 12,
                'ice hockey' => 9,
                'soccer/football' => 11,
                'table tennis' => 7),
   'Strength training' =>
            array('calisthenics' => 11,
                'weightlifting (light)' => 9,
                'weightlifting (strenuous)' => 13),
   'Stretching/flexibility' =>
            array('pilates' => 5,
                'tai chi' => 6,
                'yoga' => 5)
        );
?>
```

Although we'll stick to having separate form submission and form handler pages, let's make the form submission page a PHP file too, rather than using straight HTML. This will let us generate the form elements from the data we defined in exercise_include.php.

Listing 10-2: **Form submission code for fitness calculator**

```php
<?php include_once("exercise_include.php");
?>
<html>
<head>
<style TYPE="text/css">
<!--
BODY, P, TD
```

Continued

Listing 10-2 *(continued)*

```
     {color: black; font-family: verdana; font-size: 10 pt}
H1        {color: black; font-family: arial; font-size: 12 pt}
-->
</STYLE>
</head>

<xbody>
<table BORDER=0 CELLPADDING=10 WIDTH=100%>
<tr>
<td BGCOLOR="#F0F8FF" ALIGN=CENTER VALIGN=TOP WIDTH=150>
</td>
<td BGCOLOR="#FFFFFF" ALIGN=LEFT VALIGN=TOP WIDTH=83%>
<h1>Workout calculator (math)</h1>
<p>For one or more of the following exercises, enter<br>
the duration in minutes and your current weight<br>
and we'll tell you how many calories you burned.</p>

<form METHOD="post" ACTION="wc_handler_math.php">
<table>
<tr>
  <td><input type="text" size=5
      name="weight"><b>Weight (kilos)</b></td>
</tr>
<tr>
  <td> </td>
</tr>

<?php
$type_counter = 0;
foreach ($exercise_info
          as $exercise_type => $per_exercise_info) {
  print("<tr><td><b>$exercise_type</b></td></tr>");
  $exercise_counter = 0;
  foreach ($per_exercise_info
            as $exercise_name => $exercise_intensity) {
    print("<tr><td>
         <input type = \"text\" size = 5
           name=\"exercise[$type_counter][$exercise_counter]\"
         > $exercise_name</td></tr>");
    $exercise_counter++;
  }
  $type_counter++;
}
?>
<tr>
  <td> </td>
</tr>
<tr>
```

```
    <td><input type="submit" name="submit"
        value="Burn, baby, burn!"></td>
</td></tr>
</table>
</tr>
</table>

</form>

</body>
</html>
```

Although mostly a static HTML page, the hierarchy of exercises specified in exercise_ include.php can be used to print out the data-entry portion of the form. Notice that we print the names and types of exercises but do not propagate them as form variables; we plan to use the very same array from exercise_include.php on the other end to distinguish the meaning of the submitted variables.

The submission form itself is shown in Figure 10-1.

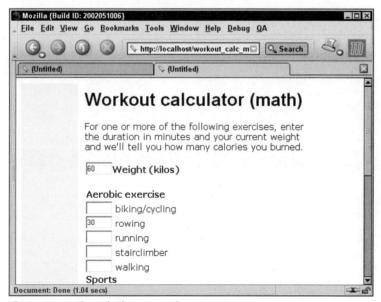

Figure 10-1: The calculator entry form

Now the job of the receiving page is more complex than in previous chapters. We will be receiving an array in $_POST['exercise'] that has a hierarchical structure similar to the one defined in exercise_include.php.

The difference is that the former includes the minutes spent at each exercise, while the latter includes the rate at which that exercise burns calories. The receiving page's job is to use both arrays to produce a report for the user about calories actually burned.

The handler code is shown in Listing 10-3. First of all, we receive the submitted weight. Then we move on to iterating through the data array defined in exercise_include.php and querying the $_POST['exercise'] array for nonzero minutes submitted for each exercise.

We're relying on the fact that the iteration uses the same data array and does the same counting in both the sending and receiving pages; this means that if we find nonzero minutes in a given position, we can correlate that with the name, type, and calories/minute drawn from the data file.

Whenever we find a "*hit*" (some positive minutes entered for an exercise we know about), we simply calculate the calories burned (calories/minute × minutes) and then adjust that value for the user's weight. We round each value before adding it into a total, largely so that the individual entries will agree with the rounded sum.

> ### Listing 10-3: **Handler code for the fitness calculator (wc_handler_math.php)**

```php
<?php
include_once("exercise_include.php");
$weight = $_POST["weight"];

// scale linearly assuming 65-kilo norm
$weight_factor = $weight / 65.0;

$exercise_accumulator = array();
$type_counter = 0;
if (is_array($_POST) && count($_POST) > 1
    && is_array($_POST['exercise'])) {
  foreach ($exercise_info
            as $exercise_type => $per_exercise_info) {
    $exercise_counter = 0;
    foreach ($per_exercise_info
      as $exercise_name => $exercise_intensity) {
      $minutes =
        $_POST['exercise'][$type_counter][$exercise_counter];
      if ($minutes > 0) {
        $exercise_accumulator[$exercise_type][$exercise_name]
          = round($minutes * $exercise_intensity *
                  $weight_factor);
      }
    $exercise_counter++;
  }
  $type_counter++;
  }
}

// now we use $exercise_accumulator to build a display string
$total_calories = 0;
$message = "";
foreach ($exercise_accumulator
```

```
            as $exercise_type => $per_exercise_info) {
   $message .= "<P><B>$exercise_type</B></P>";
   foreach ($per_exercise_info
     as $exercise_name => $calories_burned) {
       $message .= "<P>".
       ucfirst("$exercise_name: $calories_burned calories</P>");
       $total_calories += $calories_burned;
   }
}
if ($message == "" || $weight == 0) {
   $message =
     "<P>Did you enter your weight and at least one exercise?";
}
else {
   $message .=
     "<P><B>Total calories burned: $total_calories</B></P>";
}


// Now lay out the page
// --------------------
$page_str = <<< EOPAGE
<HTML>
<HEAD>
<STYLE TYPE="text/css">
<!--
BODY, P
{color: black; font-family: verdana; font-size: 10 pt}
H1
{color: black; font-family: arial; font-size: 12 pt}
-->
</STYLE>
</HEAD>

<BODY>
<TABLE BORDER=0 CELLPADDING=10 WIDTH=100%>
<TR>
<TD BGCOLOR="#F0F8FF" ALIGN=CENTER VALIGN=TOP WIDTH=150>
</TD>
<TD BGCOLOR="#FFFFFF" ALIGN=LEFT VALIGN=TOP WIDTH=83%>
<H1>Workout calculator handler (Math)</H1>
<P>The workout calculator says:
$message</P>
</TD>
</TR>
</TABLE>

</BODY>
</HTML>
EOPAGE;

echo $page_str;
?>
```

The resulting handler page is shown in Figure 10-2.

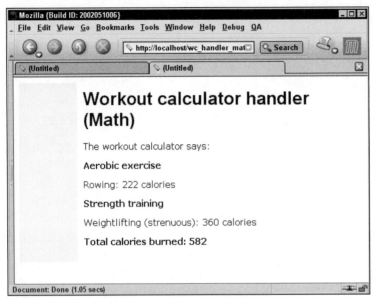

Figure 10-2: Result page for the fitness calculator

In addition to doing more numeric calculation than our calculator from previous chapters, this version does a better job of splitting up data and code, at the cost of some extra complexity.

Summary

The highlights of PHP math are summarized in Table 10-4. Refer to Chapter 27 for more advanced mathematical concepts as they are handled by PHP.

Table 10-4: Summary of PHP Math Operators and Functions

Category	Description
Arithmetic operators	Operators +, -, *, /, % perform basic arithmetic on integers and doubles.
Incrementing operators	The ++ and -- operators change the values of numerical variables, increasing them by one or decreasing them by one (respectively). The value of the postincrement form ($var++) is the same as the variable's value before the change; the value of the preincrement form (++$var) is the variable's value after the change.

Category	Description
Assignment operators	Each arithmetic operator (like +) has a corresponding assignment operator (+=). The expression $count += 5 is equivalent to $count = $count + 5.
Comparison operators	These operators (<, <=, >, >=, ==, !=) compare two numbers and return either true or false. The === operator is true if and only if its arguments are equal and of the same type.
Basic math functions	floor(), ceil(), and round() convert doubles to integers, min() and max() take the minimum and maximum of their numerical arguments, and abs() is the absolute value function.

✦   ✦   ✦

Basic PHP Gotchas

Even though we've tried to give clear instructions, and you've no doubt followed them to the letter, there are still many potential glitches that can arise. This chapter will lay out some of the most common problems by symptom and suggest some frequent causes.

Cross-Reference

There is a whole other universe of gotchas involving database connectivity. This chapter deals with PHP-only problems. You may want to skip ahead to Chapter 19 if you're having problems with PHP and a database. Also, problems specific to certain more-advanced features (including sessions, cookies, building graphics, e-mail, and XML) are dealt with in their individual chapters in Parts III and IV.

Installation-Related Problems

Instead of getting moralistic about people who rush through their installs without understanding the documentation, we'll point out a few common symptoms that characteristically appear when you've just installed PHP for the first time.

Tip

If you are seeing similar errors but are confident that your installation is stable, follow the cross-references to later parts of this chapter.

Symptom: Text of file displayed in browser window

If you are seeing the text of your PHP script instead of the resulting HTML, the PHP engine is clearly not being invoked. Check that you are accessing the site by invoking the httpd, not via the filesystem. Do this:

```
http://localhost/mysite/mypage.php
```

rather than this:

```
file:/home/httpd/html/mysite/mypage.php
```

Symptom: PHP blocks showing up as text under HTTP or browser prompts you to save file

The PHP engine is not being invoked properly. If you're properly requesting the file via HTTP as explained previously, the most common reason for this error is that you haven't specified all the filename extensions you want PHP to recognize, at least not for this directory. Go back to Chapter 3 and review how to configure your Web server to recognize PHP file extensions. The second most common reason is that your php.ini file is in the wrong place or has a bad configuration directive.

Cross-Reference If you see PHP code in your Web browser and you have a stable installation, your problem is probably due to missing PHP tags. See the "Rendering Problems" section later in this chapter.

Symptom: Server or host not found/ Page cannot be displayed

If your browser can't find your server, you may have a DNS (Domain Name Service) or Web-server configuration issue.

If you can get to the site via IP address rather than domain name, your problem is probably DNS-related. Maybe your DNS alias hasn't propagated throughout the Internet yet. This problem does occur occasionally even after the site has been up for awhile, either because your DNS server goes down without a valid secondary server or because of local Internet conditions.

If you cannot get to the site via IP address for a new installation, it's likely you haven't successfully bound the IP address to your network interface or configured httpd to handle requests for a particular domain (see Chapter 3). If you can't get to the site via IP address for a previously working installation, most likely your Web server is down for a non-PHP related reason. This can happen even on stable installations if, for instance, the server rebooted unexpectedly and the Web service is not included properly in startup scripts.

Rendering Problems

This section covers problems where PHP does not report an error per se, but what you see is not what you thought you would get.

Symptom: Totally blank page

A blank page is very frequently an HTML problem rather than PHP per se (except insofar as you use PHP to produce HTML). If you *do not* use the maximal style of PHP (in other words, if there is any part of your script that should be renderable without first being preprocessed), the problem is almost sure to be in the HTML. So you should first try doing whatever you usually do to debug HTML.

In general, one of your best debugging tools when faced with puzzling browser output is simply to view the HTML source that the browser is trying to render. All browsers have some command for viewing such a source. For example, in Internet Explorer, it is the Source selection under the View menu.

If you wrote the file using a plain text editor, quickly check to make sure you haven't left out something crucial, such as a closing `</TABLE>` or `</FORM>` tag. If you used a WYSIWYG editor at some stage, the problem is more likely to be an extra element of some kind.

You may get edifying results by viewing the HTML source from a client (especially if you use a maximal PHP style) or from a different browser. Internet Explorer is supposedly the most forgiving of mistakes, whereas Opera and Amaya are the strictest at enforcing HTML style.

Tip   Although client rendering of a page occurs independently of anything you might do with PHP, it's a good idea to preview output for all of the reasons mentioned previously, and many of the reasons to follow, in a variety of browsers. Opera is increasingly popular, since it is now available in a free version, and the masochist in you will have lots of fun trying to write a page that Amaya feels is acceptable AND renders the way you want.

Sometimes a page that appears blank in your browser is blank because there is simply no HTML to display. See the next symptom for possible causes of this.

Symptom: Document contains no data

In some situations your Web server may return no HTML whatsoever in response to a request. The exact symptom that presents when this happens varies by browser. In some versions of Netscape, for example, you will see a pop-up dialog that informs you that `This document contained no data` and urges you to get professional help. IE5, on the other hand, will cheerfully display an empty page. If you view the HTML source, you may see nothing or you may see an autogenerated minimal set of HTML headers (an empty head or an empty body). But any way you slice it, if PHP isn't sending back any HTML, you're not going to see anything interesting in your browser.

One possible answer in this case is that the PHP module is not working at all. Test by browsing a different page in the same directory that you've previously verified is being correctly handled by PHP. If you are a developer who does not maintain your own site, you may need to talk to your system administrator. If other pages work, and this one doesn't, the problem is likely to be with your code.

Another possible answer is that your code really is not generating any output. For example, loading a PHP code file that contains nothing but function definitions in PHP mode would give you this kind of problem. Make sure you have an output directive in the file you're trying to look at (`echo`, `print`, `printf`, `print_r`, or `var_dump`).

A third possibility is that your code is actually making the PHP invocation crash before it can deliver any output. For example, if you define a recursive function that doesn't have a base case, like so:

```
function recurse_forever() {  // don't do this!
  recurse_forever();
}
recurse_forever();
```

PHP will try to execute the function until it runs out of memory, will crash in short order, and will return nothing. A diagnostic for this kind of problem is to put some kind of print statement at the beginning of your PHP code (at least, if you do not have access to a debugger). If the print statement executes, and PHP is not blowing up, you should be able to see your printed string, regardless of what happens later — if not in the browser, then in the HTML source. If the string does not appear at all, it probably means that PHP died after encountering the `print` statement, but before actually shipping off any output. (In addition to infinitely recursing functions, we've seen this kind of behavior when using early versions of object serialization.) Strategically placed `print` statements are probably one of the best debugging tools at your disposal. Remember this for your later efforts.

Also see the "Time-outs" section near the end of this chapter for more information on what happens when you write code that runs "forever."

Finally, you might be seeing a blank screen if your PHP hits a more or less fatal error but you have error reporting turned off. Error reporting should probably be turned off for production servers for security reasons, but error reporting to the browser is actually a huge help for development servers. Check your `php.ini` file's error reporting section and make sure the settings are what you expected. If you really dislike error reporting to the browser, you need to make heavy use of the `error_log` function in exception handling. See Chapters 31 and 32 for more debugging tips.

Symptom: Incomplete or unintended page

These problems are usually in the HTML parts of the script. Figure 11-1 shows an interesting example, which is highly browser-dependent; this is the IE5 product.

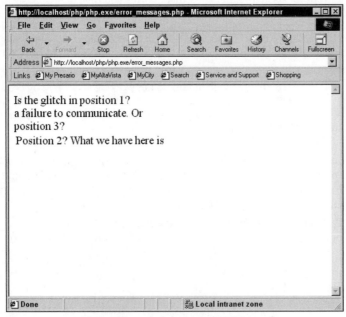

Figure 11-1: An incomplete or unintended HTML result

View the HTML source from a client. Sometimes the source will break off at the problematic point. If the source doesn't conveniently break off, try putting temporary error messages (in HTML mode) in different parts of the script to narrow down the location of the breakdown point, like this:

```
<HTML>
<HEAD></HEAD>
<BODY>Is the glitch in position 1?
<TABLE><TR><TD>Position 2? What we have here is </TD></TR>
<?php
$Problem = "a failure to communicate";
echo $Problem; ?>. Or position 3?
</BODY>
</HTML>
```

This test would show the result seen in Figure 11-2, indicating that the temporary error messages in positions 1 and 3 are showing up in the right places relative to the other elements. It's position 2 that's out of place, indicating a likely problem (lack of a `</TABLE>` tag) with this line.

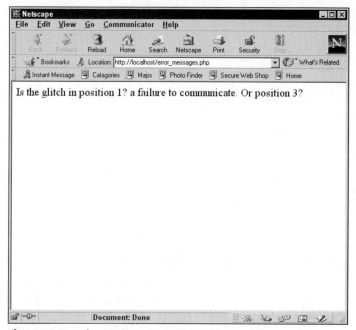

Figure 11-2: Using temporary HTML error messages

Your page may be incomplete because of a complete lack of PHP preprocessing, as in a script like this:

```
<HTML>
<HEAD></HEAD>
<BODY>
<P>What we have here is
<?php
$Problem = "a failure to communicate";
echo $Problem; ?>.
</BODY>
</HTML>
```

This script will show up as seen in Figure 11-3.

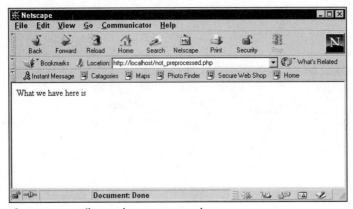

Figure 11-3: Failure to be preprocessed

In other words, all HTML-mode stuff will show up, but no PHP-mode stuff or error messages will appear. This is indicative of the PHP module not working at all or of the page residing on a computer without a PHP-enabled Web server. (Don't laugh. It happens a lot when you forget that you've been working on a particular version of a page on your client.)

Symptom: PHP code showing up in Web browser

If you are seeing literal PHP code in your browser, rather than a rendering of the HTML it should be producing, probably you have omitted a PHP start tag somewhere. (This assumes that you have had PHP running successfully and that you are using the correct tags for your installation. If not, see the "Installation-Related Problems" section near the beginning of this chapter.)

It's easy to forget that PHP treats included files as HTML, not as PHP, unless you tell it otherwise with a start tag at the beginning of the file. For example, assume that we load the following PHP file:

```
<HTML><HEAD></HEAD><BODY>
<?php include("secret.php");
secret_function(); ?>
</BODY></HTML>
```

which includes the file `secret.php`, which in turn looks like this:

```
function secret_function ()
{
  echo "Open sesame!";
}
```

The result is shown in Figure 11-4.

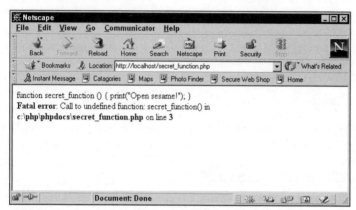

Figure 11-4: A PHP include appearing as HTML

This can be fixed by adding PHP tags to the included file like so:

```
<?php
function secret_function ()
{
  echo "Open sesame!";
}
?>
```

Failures to Load Page

A couple of different kinds of errors are seen when PHP is unable to find a file that you have asked it to load.

Symptom: Page cannot be found

If your browser can't find a PHP page you've created, and you have recently installed PHP, please see the section "Installation-Related Problems" earlier in this chapter. If you get this message when you have been loading other PHP files without incident, it's quite likely you are just misspelling the filename or path. Alternatively, you may be confused about where the Web server document root is located.

Symptom: Failed opening [file] for inclusion

When including files from PHP files, we sometimes see errors like this (on a Unix platform, the file paths would be slightly different):

```
Warning Failed opening 'C:\InetPub\wwwroot\asdf.php' for
inclusion (include_path='') in [no active file] on line 0
```

It turns out that this is the included-file version of Page cannot be found — that is, PHP hasn't even gotten to loading the first line of the active file. There is no active file because no file by that name could be found.

It's also possible that you will see this message as a result of incorrect permissions on the file you are trying to load.

Parse Errors

The most common category of error arises from mistyped or syntactically incorrect PHP code, which confuses the PHP parsing engine.

Symptom: Parse error message

Although the causes of parsing problems are many, the symptom is almost always the same: a parse error message like that in Figure 11-5.

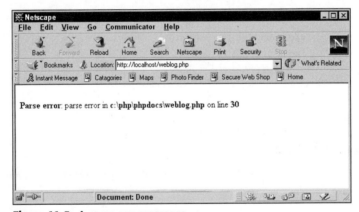

Figure 11-5: A parse error message

These errors occur in PHP mode by definition. This is actually good, because PHP returns more informative error messages than HTML — notably the line number of the problematic parsable.

The most common causes of parse errors, detailed in the subsections that follow, are all quite minor and easy to fix, especially with PHP lighting the way for you. However, every parse error returns the identical message (except for filenames and line numbers) regardless of cause. Any HTML that may be in the file, even if it appears before the error-causing PHP fragment, will not be displayed or appear in the source code.

The missing semicolon

If each PHP instruction is not duly finished off with a semicolon, a parse error will result. In this sample fragment, the first line lacks a semicolon and, therefore, the variable assignment is never completed.

```
What we have here is
<?php
$Problem = "a silly misunderstanding"
echo $Problem; ?>.
```

No dollar signs

Another very common problem is that a dollar sign prepending a variable name is missing. If the dollar sign is missing during the initial variable assignment, like so:

```
What we have here is
<?php
Problem = "a big ball of earwax";
echo $Problem; ?>.
```

a parse error message will result. However, if instead the dollar sign is missing from a later output of the variable, like this:

```
What we have here is
<?php
$Problem = "a big ball of earwax";
print("Problem"); ?>.
```

PHP will not indicate a parse error. Instead, you will get the screen shown in Figure 11-6.

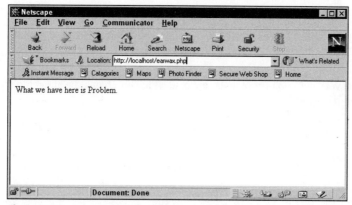

Figure 11-6: A missing dollar sign on variable output

This is an excellent example of why you should not rely on PHP to tell you something is wrong. Although PHP's error messages are more informative than most, errors such as this are easily missed if your proofreading efforts aren't up to par.

Tip

If you spend any significant portion of your time debugging PHP code, an editor that can jump to specific line numbers can be invaluable. Note that the actual mistake that caused the error may be on the line that PHP complains about, or before it, but never after it. For example, because there's nothing wrong with commands that span several lines, a missed semicolon won't cause a parse error until PHP tries to interpret subsequent lines as part of the same statement.

Mode issues

Another family of glitches arises from faulty transitions in and out of PHP mode.

A parse error will result if you fail to close off a PHP block properly, as in:

```
What we have here is
<?php
$Problem = "an awful kerfuffle";
echo $Problem; .
```

This particular mode issue is very common with short PHP blocks. Conversely, if you fail to begin the PHP block properly, the rest of the intended block will simply appear as HTML.

A slightly more tricky issue is engendered by the use of the minimal PHP style, which entails weaving in and out of HTML mode frequently. (See the discussion of minimal versus maximal style in Chapter 33.) For instance, this fragment (which omits the ?> after the first curly brace, when we intend to return to HTML mode) will return a parse error:

```
<?php if(!IsSet($stage))
{
What we have here is
<?php
$Problem = "an awful kerfuffle ";
print("$Problem"); ?>.
<?php
} else {
print("$Stage"); }
?>
```

Another instance of a very common problem is this one, which combines the short block and weaving-in-and-out-of-HTML issues neatly:

```
<FORM>
<INPUT TYPE="TEXT" SIZE=15 NAME="FirstName"
VALUE="<?php print("$FirstName"); ?>">
<INPUT TYPE="TEXT" SIZE=15 NAME="LastName"
VALUE="<?php print("$LastName"); ?>">
<INPUT TYPE="TEXT" SIZE=10 NAME="PhoneNumber"
VALUE="<?php print($PhoneNumber); ?>"
<INPUT TYPE="SUBMIT" NAME="Submit">
</FORM>
```

A PHP double-quote and the HTML closing bracket have been forgotten on the PhoneNumber input line here. This will both cause a parse error and prevent the Submit button from displaying on a client browser.

The sample code is meant to demonstrate how easy it can be to forget an element on a crowded page with lots of small but important symbols. You can reduce this type of error by either using a good programmer's text editor or by completing and testing the HTML first and adding the PHP later (or both).

Unescaped quotes

Another type of parse error is characteristic of maximal PHP: the unescaped quote.

```php
<?php
print("She said, /"What we have here is ");
$Problem = "a difference of opinion\"";
print("$Problem"); ?>.
```

In this case, the double-quote just before the word What is incorrectly, and therefore ineffectively, escaped by a forward slash rather than a backslash. If you simply forgot the backslash, the effect would be the same.

Unterminated strings

Failing to close off a quoted string can cause parse errors that refer to line numbers far away from the source of the problem. For example, a code file like this:

```php
print("I am a guilty print statement!);  // line 5
// 47 lines of PHP code omitted ...
print("I am an innocent print statement!"); // line 53
```

might well produce a parse error that complains about line 53. This is because PHP is happy to include any text you might want in a quoted string, including many lines of your own code. This inclusion finishes happily with the first double-quote in line 53, and then the parser finds the symbol I, which it can't figure out how to interpret as PHP code.

If the quote symbol that begins the unterminated string happens to be the last one in the file, the line number in the complaint will be the last line in the file—again, probably far away from the scene of the crime.

Other parse error causes

The problems we have named are not an exhaustive list of the sources of parse errors. Anything that makes a PHP statement malformed will confuse the parser, including unclosed parentheses, unclosed brackets, operators without arguments, control structure tests without parentheses, and so on. Sometimes the parse error will include a statement about what PHP was expecting and didn't find, which can be a helpful clue. If the line of the parse error is the very last line of the file, it usually means that some kind of enclosure (quotes, parentheses, braces) was opened and never closed, and PHP kept on hoping until the very end.

File Permissions

Most operating systems have some scheme of file and directory permissions that specifies which users have what kind of access to which files. The Web server runs as some user under this system and must have read permission for any files it looks at, including HTML and PHP source files.

Symptom: HTTP error 403

When a browser page presents you with error 403, it means that your file permissions are incorrect. Some browsers will not mention the error number but will complain that you do not have access to the given Web page.

The most common reason for this is that you haven't made this directory world-executable (Unix) or enabled script execution (Windows). Remember that PHP scripts may run under a user ID different than your own. Under Unix, PHP usually inherits the "nobody" UID, which (we hope) is pretty much restricted to the HTTP service. Under some Windows installations, each HTTP request is logged as the anonymous guest user.

Missing Includes

In addition to loading top-level source files, PHP needs to be able to load any files you bring in via `include()` or `require()`.

Symptom: Include warning

This kind of error is shown in Figure 11-7.

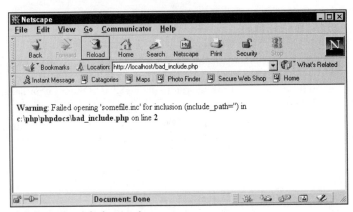

Figure 11-7: Include warning

The problem is that you call somewhere in the script for a file to be included, but PHP can't find it. Check to see that the path is correct. You might also have a case sensitivity or other typographic issue.

You will also get this message if your script tries to include a file that is in another directory with incorrect permissions for the PHP user. Generally, the directory must be specifically readable and executable by the Web-server user (often 'nobody' under Unix) or generally world-readable (for example, 755 under Unix systems); and of course the file must be world-readable (at least 444). It's useful to reference the path of your included files with the `$_SERVER` array. This will help to insure your included file is found and also that the script which calls it is portable — especially important if you use a test server or special staging area to develop your pages:

```
include_once ($_SERVER[DOCUMENT_ROOT] . "include_file.php");
```

Unbound Variables

PHP is different from many programming languages in that variables do not have to be declared before being assigned, and (under its default settings) PHP will not complain if they are used before being assigned (or *bound*) either. As a result, forgetting to assign a variable will not result in direct errors — either you will see puzzling, but error-free output, or you will see a downstream error that is a result of variables not having the values you expected. (If you would rather be warned, you can set the error-reporting level in php.ini or by evaluating error_reporting(E_ALL).) Some symptoms of this kind of problem follow.

Symptom: Variable not showing up in print string

If you embed a variable in a double-quoted string ("like $this") and then print the string using print or echo, the variable's value should show up in the string. If it seems to not be there at all in the output ("like "), the variable has probably never been assigned.

Symptom: Numerical variable unexpectedly zero

Although it's possible to have a math error or misunderstanding result in this symptom, it's much more likely that you believe that the variable has been assigned when it actually hasn't been.

Causes of unbound variables

PHP automatically converts the types of variables depending on the context in which they are used, and this is also true of unbound variables. In general, unbound variables are interpreted as 0 in a numerical context, "" in a string context, FALSE in a Boolean context, and as an empty array in an array context. The following code shows the effect of forgetting to bind two variables ($two_string and $three); the resulting display appears in Figure 11-8:

```php
<?php
$one_string = "one";
$three_string = "three";
$one = 1;
$two = 2;
print("This math is as easy as $one_string, $two_string,
$three_string!<BR>");
print("$one_string is equal to $one<BR>");
print("$two_string is equal to $two<BR>");
print("$three_string is equal to $three<BR>");
print("$one_string divided by $two_string is " .
      ($one / $two) . "<BR>");
print("$one_string divided by $three_string is " .
      ($one / $three) . "<BR>");
?>
```

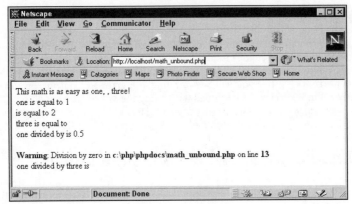

Figure 11-8: The effect of unbound variables

Case problems

Variables in PHP are case sensitive, so the same name with different capitalization results in a different variable. Even after a value is assigned to the variable $Mississippi, the variable $mississippi will still be unbound. (Capitalization aside, variables that are this difficult to spell are probably to be avoided for the same reason.)

Scoping problems

As long as no function definitions are involved, PHP variable scoping is simple: Assign a variable, and its value will be there for you from that point on in that script's execution (until the variable is reassigned). However, the only variables that are available inside a function body are the function's formal parameters and variables that have been declared to be global — if you have a puzzling, unbound variable inside a function, this is probably something you've forgotten. In the following code, for example, the variable $serial_no is neither passed in to the function nor declared to be global:

```
$name = "Bond, James Bond";
$rank = "Spy";
$serial_no = "007";

function Answer($name)
{
global $rank;
print("Name: $name; Rank: $rank;
      serial no: $serial_no<BR>");
}
Answer($name);
```

The resulting browser output looks like:

```
Name: Bond, James Bond, Rank: Spy, serial no:
```

because the variable is unbound inside the function.

Overwritten Variables

PHP will allow you to use variables that have never had values assigned, but it also allows variable values to be changed and does not typically warn you when this is happening.

Symptom: The variable has a valid value, just not the one you expected

Say you echo out a variable for debugging, and the result turns out to be something totally different from the one you expected. This is almost certainly caused by PHP's free and easy way of assigning new values to variable names, exacerbated by poor coding style. There are two types of issues: global scope and local scope.

Global overwritten variables

If you use `register_globals`, and especially if you also rely on short variable names, you can sometimes run into a situation where a global you weren't expecting pops out of nowhere and overwrites a variable. For instance, you might have a form with a field named "username", which on submit will create a variable called `$_POST['username']`—which, if you use `register_globals`, will be automagically copied to a global variable called `$username`. But let's say you then initiate a session to get some unrelated session variable, in the course of which you have inadvertently also set `$_SESSION['username']`—which, guess what, is also copied to a global called `$username`. Depending on how the `variables_order` setting in your `php.ini` file is set, the session value may overwrite the form value. If you're maintaining a large and complex PHP system, this kind of error can be a nightmare to track.

Variable Naming Conventions

One way to avoid a lot of the gotchas in PHP is to decide on, and to rigorously use, a set of variable naming conventions for all of your code. In the frequent cases where variables will be assigned and used in widely separated places in the same script and even across scripts, such a set of standards will save lots of time referring back and forth. What conventions you decide on are less important than that you have some standard in the first place. That said, here are a few tips to help you decide what to do:

✦ A common mistake many new programmers make is that variables must somehow be an abbreviation of the thing they represent. Remember, a variable is not an abbreviation; but rather a stand-in for some value that may change depending on circumstances or as a script executes. A longer, meaningful and easy to remember variable name is better than a shorter variable name that is anybody's guess.

✦ Variable names that consist of multiple words strung together can be made more readable by using underscores (for example, `$office_address`) or initial capitalization (`$OfficeAddress`). There is some sense to the notion that the underscore solution can create confusion with function naming conventions. Use what works best for you.

✦ In a more general sense, remember that you may not be the only person that has to read this code. You may get really excited about PHP and get involved in one of the many open source projects that use PHP. You may even start your own project (we'd be delighted to see that happen)! In either case, readable code will be a must; and good variable names are a foundation of producing readable code.

The answer, of course, is to eschew `register_globals` and use better variable names. It can really help to have a good text editor with autocomplete, a useful feature if you are motivated by wanting to type fewer characters.

Local overwritten variables

Similar issues can happen within a single script, but should be easier to track. Say you assign a value to a variable, and then 2,000 lines of code later you use the same variable name by mistake—you've just erased your first variable assignment. This is especially easy to do when you're including big library files from all over the place.

Solution? If you suspect this is happening, you need to do a search through your PHP file and all included files for the questionable variable name. Don't forget to check the included files! Just hope you catch these things early, because they're a big pain if allowed to grow.

Function Problems

Many problems having to do with function calls result in *fatal errors*, which means that PHP gives up on processing the rest of the script.

Symptom: Call to undefined function my_function()

PHP is trying to call the function `my_function()`, which has not been defined. This could be because you misspelled the name of a function (built-in or user-defined) or because you have simply omitted the function definition. If you use `include/require` files to load user-defined functions, make sure that you are loading the appropriate files.

If the problem involves a fairly specialized, built-in function (for instance, it is related to XML or arbitrary-precision math), it may be that you did not enable the relevant function family when you included PHP. If, for example, all the BC functions seem to be undefined, they probably were not included at compile time. To fix this (under Unix systems), you would need to reconfigure PHP and recompile. Under Windows systems, you just need to make sure that the correct `.dll` files are loaded in `php.ini`.

Symptom: Call to undefined function ()

In this case, PHP is trying to call a function and doesn't even know the function's name. This is invariably because you have code of the form `$my_function()`, where the name of the function is itself a variable. Unless you are intentionally trying to exploit the variable-function-name feature of PHP, you probably accidentally put a $ in front of a sensible call to `my_function()`. Because `$my_function` is an unbound variable, PHP interprets it as the empty string—which is not the name of a defined function—and gives this uninformative error message.

Symptom: Call to undefined function array()

This problem has a cause that is similar to the cause of the previous problem, although it still baffled us completely the first time we ran into it. It can arise when you have code like the following:

```
$my_amendments = array();
$my_amendments(5) = "the fifth";
```

Unless you look closely, this looks like an innocent pair of statements to create an array and then store something in that array, with the number 5 as a key. And yet PHP is telling us that array() is an unbound function, even though we know that it is a very standard built-in function. What's going on?

The fault is actually with Line 2 above, rather than with Line 1. If we want to access an element of $my_amendments, the correct syntax is $my_amendments[5], with square brackets. Instead, we used parentheses, which the parser interprets as an attempted function call. It takes what is immediately before the left parenthesis to be a function. Instead, what comes before the parenthesis is an array, which is not a function; PHP gives up on us, with this obscure complaint.

Symptom: Cannot redeclare my_function()

This is a simple one—somewhere in your code you have two definitions of my_function(), which PHP will not stand for. Make sure that you are not using include to pull in the same file of function definitions more than once. Use include_once or require_once to avoid seeing this error, with the caveat that, well, you won't see this error. Why might that be bad? It's conceivable that you could define two distinctly different functions and inadvertently give them the same name. This runs the risk of exposing your mistake at a somewhat inconvenient moment.

Symptom: Wrong parameter count

The function named in the error message is being called with either fewer or more arguments than it is supposed to handle.

Math Problems

The problems that follow are specific to math and the numerical data types.

Symptom: Division-by-zero warning

Somewhere in your code, you have a division operator where the denominator is zero. The most common cause of this is an unbound variable, as in:

```
$numerator = 5;
$ratio = $numerator / $denominator;
```

where $denominator is unbound. It's also possible, of course, that the legitimate result of a computation is producing a zero denominator. In this case, the only thing to do is catch it with a test and do something reasonable if the test applies. See the following example:

```
$numerator = 5;
if ($denominator != 0)
    $ratio = $numerator / $denominator;
else
    print("I'm sorry, Dave, I cannot do that<BR>");
```

Symptom: Unexpected arithmetic result

Sometimes things just don't add up (or multiply up, or subtract up). If you are having this experience, check any complex arithmetic expressions for unbound variables (which would act as zeros) and for precedence confusions. If you have any doubt about the precedence of operators, add (possibly redundant) parentheses to make sure the grouping is as you intend.

Symptom: NaN (or NAN)

If you ever see this dreaded acronym, it means that some mathematical function you used has gone out of range or given up on its inputs. The value NAN stands for "Not a Number," and it has some special properties. Here's what happens if we try to take the arccosine of 45, even though arccosine is defined only when applied to numbers between –1.0 and 1.0:

```
$value = acos(45);
print("acos result is $value<BR>");
print("The type is " . gettype($value) . "<BR>");
$value_2 = $value + 5;
print("Derived result is $value<BR>");
print("The type is " . gettype($value_2) . "<BR>");
if ($value == $value)
  print("At least that much makes sense<BR>");
else
  print("Hey, value isn't even equal to itself!<BR>");
```

The browser output looks like:

```
acos result is NAN
The type is double
Derived result is NAN
The type is double
Hey, value isn't even equal to itself!
```

Oddly enough, NAN *is* a number, at least in the sense that its PHP type in this example turns out to be double rather than string. It also infects other values with not-a-numberness when used in math expressions. (This behavior is a feature, not a bug, when used in very complex calculations that must be correct. It's better to have the whole value be tagged as untrustworthy than have one subexpression be silently bogus.) Finally, any equality comparison that involves NAN will be false — NAN is neither less than, nor greater than, nor equal to any other number, including itself. It is always unequal (!=) to all numbers, including itself. (The NAN value is not a PHP-specific feature — it is part of the IEEE standard for floating-point arithmetic, which is implemented by the C functions that underlie PHP.)

Because of the contagion of NAN values, this kind of problem can be difficult to debug. The best way to try to find the original offending NAN is with diagnostic print statements, especially because comparison tests will give counterintuitive results. You can explicitly test for NAN values using the built-in is_nan() function, implemented in PHP4.2.0, which returns TRUE if the number submitted is not a number or FALSE otherwise. In earlier versions (you aren't using an earlier version, are you?), you can cobble together your own function for NAN testing like so:

```
function is_nan($value)
{
  return($value != $value);
}
```

It uses the weird comparison properties of NAN as a type checker.

Time-outs

Of course any download can occasionally time out before a complete page can be delivered. However, this shouldn't be happening frequently on your local development server! If it does, you may have an issue that has nothing to do with slow Internet channels or server overload.

The most interesting reason for a time-out is an infinite loop. These can be difficult to track down quickly, as in this example:

```
//compute the factorial of 10
$Fact = 1;
for ($Index = 1; $Index <= 10; $index++)
  $Fact *= $Index;
```

This code shows a nasty little collaboration between a loop and a case confusion — the lower-case $index that is incremented has nothing to do with the $Index that is being tested, so the test will never become false.

Also see the discussion of infinite recursion in the "Document contains no data" section earlier in this chapter. Whether due to a loop or a recursive loop, any PHP code that runs "forever" is not going to give you a happy result. The exact symptom you see is likely to depend on whether PHP runs out of memory first (and crashes, returning no HTML) or runs out of time first (and your browser informs you of a time-out).

Summary

In Table 11-1, we summarize the gotchas in this chapter by mapping symptoms to possible causes. We also offer some suggestions on how to fix the most common problems.

Table 11-1: From Symptoms to Causes

Symptom	Possible Causes	Advice
(New installation) Text of file displayed in browser window	The PHP engine is not being invoked, possibly because you are opening it via the local filesystem rather than as a request to your server.	Make sure that your request is to the Web server, either via localhost (http://localhost/[path]) if testing on the server machine, or by the full URL (www.site.com/[path]).
(New installation) PHP blocks showing up as text under HTTP, or browser prompts you to save file or visit an external file repository	PHP is not being invoked properly. Your Web server may not be set up to map the right suffixes (for example, .php) to the PHP engine, or there may be a problem with the location or contents of php.ini.	Check your Web server configuration, and the PHP init file (php.ini).

Continued

Table 11-1 *(continued)*

Symptom	Possible Causes	Advice
(New installation) Server or host not found/Page cannot be displayed	Often due to Internet/DNS/Web-server configuration problems, rather than PHP.	Try loading a pure HTML file with a suffix you have not set up for PHP (for example, `.html`) tzo rule out PHP problems. Try getting to the same file using an IP address rather than a domain name — if that works, the problem is DNS-related.
Totally blank page	Usually due to malformed HTML (whether produced by PHP or not).	View the HTML source from a browser. Look especially for unclosed `<TABLE>`, `<FORM>`, or `<SELECT>` forms.
Document contains no data (or blank page with no HTML to look at)	PHP engine may not be working at all, or your code simply does not output anything. Also you may actually be crashing PHP, or you may be hitting a fatal error with error reporting turned off.	If other PHP pages work fine from the same server, then the problem is your code. Force your code to output something at the beginning, and try to find it in HTML source. If no joy, you probably have crashed PHP, possibly by calling a recursive function forever. Also, make sure error reporting is on.
Incomplete or unintended page	Usually due to malformed HTML (whether produced by PHP or not).	View the HTML source from a browser. Try to narrow down the source of the problem with diagnostic printing statements (in either HTML or PHP).
PHP code showing up in browser window	If the PHP engine is installed and functioning properly, this is usually due to a missing PHP start tag.	Check start and end tags and make sure that any `include` files of PHP code have correct tags at beginning and end.
Page cannot be found	Usually means that the filename or path of the PHP file is incorrect.	Double-check the name and directory path.
Failed opening [file] for inclusion	Same as the preceding error, as reported under some NT configurations.	Double-check the name and directory path.
Parse error message	A variety of causes, including missing semicolons, variables without a `$`, unescaped quotes, unclosed quotes, brackets, or parentheses, and HTML being interpreted as PHP.	Locate the line of the parse error in the PHP file and look for one of the causes in that line or the lines immediately preceding. If the "error" is on the final line of the file, look for an unclosed quote, parenthesis, or bracket, possibly much earlier in the file.

Symptom	Possible Causes	Advice
HTTP error 403	The file permissions are incorrect.	Check the permissions of the file itself and the directories (or folders) in the path to that file.
`Include` warning	For one reason or another, PHP was not able to load a file named in an `include` statement.	Check that the file actually exists, the spelling of the filename, the pathname, and (on Unix systems) the case of the name. Also make sure that the file permissions allow the file to be read.
Variable value not showing up in `print` string	The variable has not been assigned, and so its value in a printed string is the empty string.	Check that you are assigning the variable before the `print` statement and compare spelling and case (capitalization). Make sure that you are not embedding any objects or multidimensional arrays in quoted strings. You can also use the statement `error-reporting(15)` to tell PHP to warn about any unbound variables.
Numerical variable unexpectedly zero	Often due to the variable never having been assigned.	(See preceding.)
Variable value is valid, but unexpected.	Often due to variable having been unexpectedly overwritten.	Don't use `register_globals`; use good variable names; search through all included files for variable name.
Call to undefined function `my_function()`	Function `my_function()` is being called without having been defined first.	If you are trying to call a function of your own, check that the definition (or inclusion of the file containing the definition) is before the use. If you are trying to call a built-in function, check the spelling. If it is correct, investigate whether that "family" of functions was included when you configured PHP (for example, either all the XML functions will work, or none will).
Call to undefined `function ()`	An expression of the form `$my_function()` is being evaluated, and `$my_function` is not bound to the name of a defined function.	If you intend to use the variable-function feature, then add (or correct) the assignment of `$my_function`. If you are just trying to call `my_function()`, remove the $.

Continued

Table 11-1 *(continued)*

Symptom	Possible Causes	Advice
Call to undefined function `array()`	You probably have an expression of the form `$array_var_name(3)`, when what you want is `$array_var_name[3]`	Decide whether you want an array expression or a function call — if the former, then change parentheses to square brackets.
Cannot redeclare `my_function()`	The function `my_function()` is being defined twice in a page's execution.	Look for double definitions of `my_function` in the PHP file, or double-inclusions of the file that defines it.
Wrong parameter count	The named function (usually a built-in function) is being called with an incorrect number of arguments.	Compare the function call to the definition in the online PHP manual (`www.php.net`)
Division-by-zero warning	A / operator has a right-hand argument of zero. Can be due to an unbound variable in the denominator.	Assign the unbound variable if that's the cause. If the desired logic could actually result in zero denominators, install a test to catch that case.
Unexpected arithmetic result	Frequently due to an unbound variable in an arithmetic expression.	Check for unbound variables (see preceding), and make sure that arithmetic expressions are parenthesized appropriately.
NAN value	A built-in math function is being given inputs outside its acceptable range. If that function's results are used in arithmetic, the results are also NAN.	Trace backward from the NAN value to function calls that contribute to its computation. Test with `print` statements, or test for values that fail to be self-equal (a diagnostic for NAN).
Page takes forever to load, or browser times out	Internet congestion, heavy load on your server machine, computationally intensive PHP code, or an infinite loop.	Check if Web sites other than your own are giving you the same trouble. Check all looping constructs in your code for errors that could cause them to never terminate.

✦   ✦   ✦

PHP and MySQL

Choosing a Database for PHP

Databases and PHP go together like cake and ice cream, Trinidad and Tobago, green eggs and ham—you get the picture.

After all, what's the Web about? Making vast stores of information available to a more or less wide public, that's what. Not that there aren't small brochureware sites galore, but the bigger and more frequently updated the data source, the more comparative value is provided by the Web over other media.

Perhaps the single greatest advantage of PHP over similar products is the unsurpassed choice and ease of database connectivity it offers. As detailed in the "Choosing a Database" section of this chapter, PHP supports native connections to a number of the most popular databases, open source and commercial alike. Almost any database that will open its API to the public seems to be included eventually. For any unsupported databases, there's generic ODBC support.

What Is a Database?

A *database* is a separate application that stores a collection of data. Each database has one or more distinct APIs for creating, accessing, managing, searching, and replicating the data it holds. Other kinds of data stores can be used, such as files on the filesystem or large hash tables in memory, but when professionals talk about databases they mean a standalone application such as Oracle or SQL Server or Sleepycat.

Why a Database?

If you're going to the trouble to use PHP at all, you're likely to need a database sooner or later—probably sooner. Even for something small, like a personal Weblog, you want to think hard about the advantages of using a database instead of static pages or included text files.

Maintainability and scalability

Having PHP assemble your pages on the fly from a template and a database is an addictive experience. Once you enjoy it, you'll never go back to managing a static HTML site of any size. For the effort of programming one page, you can produce an infinite number of uniform pages. Change one, and you've changed them all.

There are now Web sites with hundreds of thousands of separate pages — you can rest assured that no one is maintaining them all by hand. If you have a Web concept that may eventually grow to more than a few dozen pages, you should think about moving to a database sooner rather than later.

Portability

Because a database is an application rather than a part of the operating system, you can easily transfer its structure and contents from one machine to another or (in certain cases) even from one platform to another. This is especially valuable for contractors, who may develop a project without being able to control the environment in which it will eventually be deployed — they can deliver a package of PHP plus a MySQL database schema dump in one tarball or zipfile. There are even well-known PHP programs, such as vBulletin, that keep most of their code in a database to make it easier to distribute.

Avoiding awkward programming

Certain things can be done with PHP but probably shouldn't, because they entail ugly or risky programming moves.

Say you happen to be the commander of the starship *Enterprise* and are keeping a Captain's log. Each episode is contained in a text file identified by its unique stardate, which is plugged into a template by PHP — but hey, you're a busy spaceman with whole galaxies to explore; you don't always have time to write in your log every day. You want to put automatically generated Next and Previous links on each page for those who wish to read in straight chronological order. It's pretty easy to use PHP to find the previous stardated entry, but any attempt to locate the next entry can quickly become an infinite loop — because it's easier to prove something does exist than that it doesn't. On the other hand, if you put your log data in a database, the whole job becomes trivial. The database will tell you which is the latest entry at any given moment.

There are other types of programming tasks that a database is highly optimized to do, and given the option, you should take advantage of these chores. For instance, you should never sort data sets on the PHP side — you should learn to write your queries so they come back pre-sorted. We discuss these efficiency issues in greater detail in Chapter 18.

Searching

Although it's possible to search multiple text files for strings (especially on Unix platforms) it's not something most Web developers will want to do often. After you search a few hundred files, the task becomes slow and hard to manage. Databases exist to make searching easy. With a single command, you can find anything from one ID number to a large text block to a JPEG-format image.

In some cases, information attains value only when put into a searchable database. For instance, relatively few people would want to read a long text list of movie directors and their films, but many might occasionally want to search a database of that information. You could argue that it's the searchability, as much as the information itself, that creates the value here.

Security

A database adds another layer of security if used with its own password or passwords.

Say you use PHP to maintain a company's customer files, filled with information about the prices each customer paid for your product and complaints that customers made. This information would be gold for your competitors, and embarrassing if it leaked to anyone — but you need to put it on the Internet so it can be accessed by your worldwide army of salespeople. If you have PHP write each new customer record to a text file, you must give the HTTP daemon user (usually Nobody or Everybody) write access to your most sensitive directory. This is not a good idea. By having PHP write to a database instead, you can maintain read-only directory permissions and also ask for a second password before the database can be altered.

Or take the case of a content site with a large number of visitors, a smaller number of writers, and a handful of editors. You can easily set database permission levels for each group so that visitors can just look at the database content (as formatted in Web pages), writers can browse and change only their own entries, and editors can browse/change/delete anything in the site.

N-tier architecture

So far, we've been considering only so-called two-tier sites: PHP takes raw data from some kind of storage system and turns it into HTML. However, one of the intentions of PHP is to become the "glue" in three-tier or n-tier development. If you have anything more complex than the simplest two-tier architecture, you *really* need a database.

An n-tier architecture is an arbitrary number of software subsystems linked by a Web site on the front end and one or more databases on the back end. One fairly common n-tier architecture is that of a big e-commerce site, which has shopping carts linking up to order-taking systems linking up to supply-chain management routines — plus product databases, customer databases, credit-card debiting, FAQ-o-matics, recommendation engines, Web-log analysis tools, caching proxies, phone-center knowledge bases, and who knows what else lurking behind the scenes. Under these conditions, you need the advanced database capabilities that we'll describe in the "Advanced Features to Look For" section of this chapter.

Potential downside: Performance

You may be concerned about performance. It's true that a database-driven site on the same hardware and software will always be slower than a static site. It's true that some databases are faster than others. However, the real question is whether the performance hit will even be detectable by you. If we're talking about adding milliseconds to your latency (and we usually are), who cares? Some of the concerns about performance you read on the Internet are so overblown that they verge on the absurd. It's also true that the minute you need to search any large volume of text in a database versus flat files, you've gained back any performance hit a thousand times over.

Once you need to go into the database for even *one piece* of information per page, it's almost always cost-effective to put all your data in the database. Most of the overhead of a database query is front-loaded in establishing a connection. If you have to do that to get a name or title, downloading a couple thousand words of text is almost free.

In the end, only performance testing will establish whether a database is too slow for your particular setup and task—everything else is just talk. Many totally database-driven Web sites easily achieve subseconds of latency, which should be good enough for most purposes.

Choosing a Database

Although databases (even relational ones) have been around for a long time, they were quite expensive or limited in functionality until very recently. Therefore, even a lot of experienced programmers never had to learn much about choosing a database for a particular need. For that reason, we feel it's worthwhile to review the basic factors that go into making such a decision.

You may not have a choice

Realistically, you may not have much of a choice. Many people are specifically looking for the fastest way to put their legacy database online rather than enjoying the luxury of deciding on a scripting language first and choosing a database later.

Furthermore, decisions about OS, Web server, and programming languages can make some of your decision for you. A custom Java application on a "Big Iron" Unix platform is just not going to mesh very smoothly with Microsoft SQL Server. (In theory it's possible, but in practice you'd have to be a glutton for punishment—although the other way around isn't so bad.) The bigger the system gets, the more constrained one's choices are likely to be by previous decisions.

The good news is that PHP is committed to supporting many databases and other back end servers. It can help you knit up the loose ends of an architecture that has grown organically over time, as so many have. Some functions in PHP exist solely to aid in porting your data over to a more modern database.

Flat-file, relational, object-relational

Databases are kind of like kitchen equipment: The simpler the tool, the more skilled the operator needs to be to achieve a great result. Expert chefs can produce gourmet fare using nothing but a very sharp knife and a few old pots and pans, whereas amateurs must whip out the Cuisinart and the Calphalon to produce similar results.

So it is with databases. It can get almost laughable to read people's arguments about the purported failings of this or that database, knowing that the skill of the individual user is reflected by this piece of software more than by almost any other. Suffice it to say that many technical masterpieces live in the simplest hash tables, while untold botched messes are simmering along on the latest and greatest object-oriented Java-enabled DBMS.

You can use three main types of databases with PHP: *flat-file*, *relational*, and *object-relational*.

Flat-file or *hashing* databases, such as Gnu DBM and Berkeley DB (aka Sleepycat DB2), are mostly used by or within other programs such as e-mail servers. They provide the lightest-weight and fastest means of storing and searching for data such as username/password pairs or dated e-mail messages. Old-school C programmers usually have the most experience with this type of database.

These databases do not themselves create a representation of more complex relationships between data points. Instead, this is done by the accessing client program. Although the results can be extremely impressive, it all depends on your skill as a programmer.

The relational variety is now the most common type of database. People have different ideas of what constitutes a relational database, and we don't want to get pulled down into that particular definitional tar pit. Therefore, we're going to arbitrarily say that databases that speak fluent SQL are relational. Most of the popular databases commonly used with PHP are relational. See Chapter 13 for a longer discussion of relational databases.

But there's relational, and then there's relational. Certain very popular commercial databases, such as Filemaker Pro and Microsoft Access, were not designed to be used on the back end of a production Web site. Although they have a certain level of ODBC support, and therefore PHP can get data from them, they were mostly designed for ease of use rather than speed. Even worse, most users of these products refuse to avail themselves of what relational features there are, preferring to repeat text information in each entry rather than creating a separate table representing a relationship. Finally, these databases generally lack threading, locking, and other production features. People out there must be trying to use Microsoft Access with PHP, because they post to PHP mailing lists and forums, but evidently not for public sites with significant traffic. (We do, however, know developers who use Access or FileMaker Pro as development tools on their laptops so they can program on the airplane, and there are always porting and other projects using legacy data from these semi-relational databases.) You may well find that the best use of these types databases will be to prototype their eventual Web counterparts. For all the failings of Access, many developers claim it has nice data/relationship visualization features.

Finally, there are object-oriented and object-relational databases, new and still developing models of data access. The object-oriented database is intended to work more smoothly with object-oriented programming languages, whereas the object-relational is a hybrid used for data types (such as astronomical and genetic data) that are not well served by ordinary relational databases. However, PHP itself does not require an object programming style of its users or the programs with which it communicates. And despite a slew of new object features in PHP5, the developers still recognize the fundamental strength of the language lies in its simpler procedural roots. That's not to say that you can't use PHP with some of these, but the absolute necessity of doing so is questionable.

ODBC/JDBC versus native API

There are two generic standard APIs for database access: Open Database Connectivity (ODBC), and Java Database Connectivity (JDBC). ODBC is closely associated with Microsoft, and JDBC is even more closely associated with Sun Microsystems. Nevertheless, other companies have implemented these standards in their own products, with the addition of specific drivers for each client program.

ODBC and JDBC are more or less mutually exclusive. Something called the *ODBC-JDBC bridge* is used to allow Java programs to access ODBC databases, but it is very slow. There are also proprietary drivers that do the same job more quickly.

There are also databases that clients can access through their own APIs rather than ODBC or JDBC. This is invariably faster because there are fewer layers in the stack. Most open source databases fall into this category. Some of these also have ODBC or JDBC drivers. So for instance, PHP can access MySQL with a native API, whereas a Java subsystem can use the same database via JDBC. Before you commit to any multiple-access scheme, be very sure the drivers you need are available, affordable, and maintainable.

Swappable databases

Although ODBC is slower than native APIs, it has the advantage of being an open standard. Therefore, PHP code written with the ODBC commands will mostly work with any ODBC-compliant database. This feature is very handy if you must start a project with a database that you know will not scale, such as Microsoft Access, and later switch to a more industrial-strength database. Although both are good products in their niches, it can be a lot of work to switch from a lightweight database like Mini SQL (aka mSQL) to an enterprise-ready server suite like IBM's DB2. (Again, a good programmer who is given the time and resources can make any application relatively easy to port, while an inexperienced or rushed developer may not be able to do so.)

Advanced Features to Look For

This section mentions specific SQL database features with which you may not yet be familiar. We're hoping you will instantly have a gut feeling, even from so brief a description, if you truly need one or more of these features.

A GUI

Databases vary enormously in their user interface tools. Choices range from the starkest command-line interactions to massive Java-powered development toolkits. You pay for what you get, both in cash and in performance. Look for the lightest interface that meets your needs, because a GUI can add substantially to overhead costs.

One lower-cost alternative to the built-in GUI is a Web interface. These are often custom developed, but there are also third-party products that may meet your needs. For instance, MySQL has several freely available Web-based interfaces, which can be found by searching at Freshmeat (www.freshmeat.net) or SourceForge (http://sf.net). The most popular of these is probably PHPMyAdmin, which is available at the PHPMyAdmin Web site (www.phpmyadmin.org).

Subquery

A *subquery* or *subselect* is an embedded SELECT statement, like this:

```
SELECT * FROM table1 WHERE id IN (SELECT id FROM table2);
```

There are ways to work around a lack of subselects, and not everyone needs them. However, they can save some time if you consistently need to make large selects, inserts, and deletes.

SELECT INTO

SELECT INTO is a handy feature if you need to move data from one table to another frequently. The syntax can vary a little. One method is:

```
SELECT INTO table2(col2, col3, col7) lastname, firstname, state FROM
table1 WHERE col5 = NULL;
```

Another way to get the same result is:

```
INSERT INTO table2(col2, col3, col7) SELECT lastname, firstname, state
FROM table1 WHERE col5 = NULL;
```

Complex joins

A *join* is a way of searching for something across tables by using shared values to match up the tables. The simplest form is:

```
SELECT * FROM table1,table2 WHERE table1.id=table2.id;
```

This yields the complete contents of whichever rows in the two tables share ID numbers. More specific and extensive types of joins exist, including left or right, straight or cross, inner and outer, and self, but you may not need them.

Joins are very handy and timesaving, sometimes well-nigh essential, but in practice few need the more esoteric forms, so don't reject a database out of hand for lacking a right outer join.

Threading and locking

Threading and *locking* are very important for multiple-tier sites and two-tier sites that have many contributors. They prevent two database calls from bumping into each other, so to speak, by giving editorial control to only a single transaction at a time.

An example that clearly illustrates the value of threading and locking is a Web site that sells tickets to popular rock concerts (assigned rather than "festival" seating). Obviously, you would not want two people to be able to purchase the same seat at the same event due to a database error. The database needs some way to recognize unique requests and let only one user (or thread) make changes at any given moment, while others are locked out until the first transaction is complete.

Unless you're sure your project (a Web log, for instance) will have only one user at a time, be careful of committing to a nonthreaded database.

Transactional databases

This term refers to a database design that seeks to maximize data integrity. The *transactional* paradigm relies on commits and rollbacks. Transactions that are concluded successfully will be committed to the database. Those that are not successfully concluded will not be saved, or the database will be rolled back to its previous condition.

Generally, transactions become more useful in situations where you want an all-or-nothing commit on a group of inserts. An e-commerce system might use rollbacks in situations where a customer's credit card is declined, choosing not to record the customer information, the purchase order, the inventory change, and so on. Rollbacks are also useful in the case of data corruption, as when a database server experiences a hardware failure incident.

An alternative data-integrity design is called *atomic*. Proponents of the atomic paradigm claim it is much faster and just as safe, but transactions can be easier for a large number of programmers to work with because it puts more of the logic in the database layer.

Procedures and triggers

Procedures are stored, precompiled queries or routines on the database server. A common procedure would be one that selects out all the e-mail addresses of customers who made purchases on a particular day. If you use the same select statements over and over, procedures can package them in a handy and fast way for you.

Triggers are procedures that occur when some tripwire event is registered by the database. Depending on the database, you could write a trigger to send an account-statement e-mail to customers or associates of your site, and set it to go off at midnight every Sunday. Another handy use would be to send an e-mail to the database administrator every time an error is registered. Relatively few databases use triggers because they take a good deal of programmatic power and lots of extra cycles to track potential events.

Indexes

Indexes are a way to speed up searches of large data sets. You can think of it like this: Say you need to find a particular customer's file in a large stack of files tossed haphazardly on your desk (not that you would ever do this in real life, of course). Or you could look for the file in a set of filing cabinets sorted by some alphabetical scheme. Obviously the filing-cabinet system would be faster, because it would presort the documents into smaller buckets. In a nutshell, that is what indexes do.

If you have a million users, it will be very slow for a database to find one by last name because the program will have to look at each entry in the `Lastname` field and compare it to the string you're searching for. An index placed on that column will make it possible for the database to search only part of the data set, and this will result in a faster search.

However, indexes should not be used by everyone. For one thing, they typically slow down writes while speeding up reads. They don't necessarily speed up every type of query, and your data set may not be big enough to show an appreciable speed difference. Indexes are a scalability feature — they'll help you a lot if you have half a billion entries, but they very well may not help you at all if you have 500.

Foreign keys and integrity constraints

The relational structure of a database is often implicit in the ways fields of one table refer to row IDs of another, but your database won't necessarily do anything helpful to make sure that structure is respected as changes are made. One way your database can help is via *cascading deletes* — automatically deleting rows that depend on other rows being deleted (this is sometimes implemented as a trigger). For example, if you delete a hospital patient record, you might want all the orphaned rows in the corresponding table of patient visits to automatically be deleted too. Alternatively, a database system can simply not permit the deletion of parent rows unless potential orphans are deleted first. Whether this kind of a constraint is a lifesaver or just an annoying restriction depends on how crucial it is that the relational structure be completely reliable and consistent, and how frequently you need to do these kinds of dangerous operations. Most of these features can be implemented, although less cleanly and efficiently, with a combination of traditional keys and the client code you use to manipulate the data.

Database replication

As your data store expands, you will need to think about scaling up. For a certain amount of time, one can just move the database server to faster machines with more processors and bigger disks — but sooner or later a growing database will need to be replicated on more than one server.

To do this, there must be some means of automatically keeping the different servers synched up. This usually involves a journaling system, and often a *master-slave* relationship between database servers. One database is designated the *master*, and all new data is inserted into it. A journal keeps track of these changes in chronological order. All the other servers are *slaves*, which serve up data rather than taking it in. They periodically read the master journal and make the same changes in themselves.

The next step up is some kind of failover mechanism, by which a slave can become the master database server if the master goes down. Think carefully about how bombproof your data needs to be, as this type of safety is expensive.

PHP-Supported Databases

If you've never chosen a database before, the large choice of PHP-supported products can be dizzying at first. Table 12-1 will give you a first-glance introduction to the various databases most easily available to PHP users, with notes on drivers and licensing.

Table 12-1: PHP-Supported Databases

Database	Type	Support	Platform	License	Notes
Adabas D	R	ODBC (deprecated)	U, W	C	German, distributed with SuSE Linux
DBA/DBM	FF	Abstraction layer	U	OS, C	Sleepycat, Gnu DBM, cdb
dBase	P	Import only	W	C	No SQL
Empress	R	ODBC	U, W	C	Enterprise, JDBC driver available
filepro	P	Import only	U, W	C	Not for production
IBM DB2	R	ODBC	U, W	C	Enterprise, JDBC driver available
Informix	R	Native	U, W	C	Enterprise
Interbase	R	Native	U, W	C	Enterprise, JDBC driver available
MS Access	R	ODBC	W	C	Not for production
MS SQL Server	R	Native	W	C	Enterprise
mSQL	R	Native	U	Sh	Very small

Continued

Table 12-1 *(continued)*

Database	Type	Support	Platform	License	Notes
MySQL	R	Native	U, W	C, OS	Several licenses
Oracle	R	Native	U, W	C	Enterprise
Oracle8	R	Native	U, W	C	Enterprise, Java integration
PostgreSQL	O-R	Native	U	OS	Commercial support available
Solid	R	ODBC (deprecated)	U, W	C	Embedded db, Finnish company
SQLite	FF	Native	U, W	OS	Embedded db
Sybase	R	Native	U, W	C	Enterprise

FF= Flat-file; R = Relational; O-R = Object-relational; U = Unix; W = Windows, C = Commercial; OS = Open Source; Sh = Shareware

Database Abstraction (or Not)

Database abstraction—writing wrapper functions or classes instead of using the bare PHP commands—is one of those quasireligious topics in programming. Some excellent programmers swear by it and make good arguments for it. Others, just as experienced and articulate, think it sounds better than it usually works out to be. We know of top PHP teams that have members in both camps.

The truth of the matter is that it's more of an issue with PHP than with almost any other programming language because PHP is so strong in multiple database connectivity. Enterprise Java installations are often all about choosing between two or three very similar database products with JDBC connectivity, so Java developers don't argue nearly as much about the merits of database portability. Similarly, ODBC is the standard option for ASP developers. The issue of database abstraction basically arises just because PHP hooks up to so many database products with fast native APIs.

The arguments *for* database abstraction basically boil down to this: You can swap databases without changing a lot of code, and sometimes it saves you some keystrokes. The arguments *against* database abstraction basically boil down to this: If you have to swap databases, you've probably already screwed up big-time, and the practice limits you to the most basic, common SQL functions used in a fixed pattern instead of letting you code in the way which takes maximal advantage of your particular database's feature set.

For instance, one of Oracle's coolest features is the capability to take an entire result set and dump it into a single-dimensional numerical PHP array. None of the other major databases used with PHP have this feature—they can fetch only a single row at once. To implement it yourself in a portable way could add considerable overhead to your query, because you'd have to fetch each row and rewrite it to a value in some second array. Of course, you can do this kind of thing—the question is, should you?

Not to say that database switching doesn't happen — we've personally had to do it more than once. However, the experienced mind quails at the contention that you should be able to plug in different databases whenever the spirit moves you. Not to belabor the obvious, but it's a non-trivial task to change databases! It's not something most developers will want to contemplate unless the situation is absolutely dire. In every case in which we were personally involved, the database change was part of a complete site rewrite and involved a tremendous amount of pain for everyone involved — all-nighters, frantic attempts to flip through 1200-page database manuals, endless data transfer attempts which choked countless numbers of times. All of which is to suggest that database portability might be a good idea in theory, but in practice it usually means a bad, bad architectural mistake was made at some prior point. In the early days of the Web, bad architectural decisions were a matter of course because no one could predict which technologies and products would last. As the rate of change has slowed somewhat, and clear leaders in various product categories have emerged, this type of rescue operation should become less necessary.

As always, our advice is to put your own needs first and be skeptical of unsolicited advice. Remember that many commercial and open source PHP packages that incorporate database abstraction may have a mission different from yours — often they are focused on getting the largest installed userbase and are willing to accept some non-optimal database code to achieve it. You might just need to focus on how to keep one particular site running most smoothly. Heavily discount any advice from those who have not actually had to switch databases. When people talk about their experiences swapping databases, find out how big the change was in programming terms — migrating from MS SQL Server to MySQL is less of a stretch than switching from MySQL to Oracle. Then make a decision about what's right for you in your particular situation.

Tip
There's one particular situation in which you may have to accept database abstraction even if it's not the right technical decision. Our experience has been that many inexperienced clients or bosses want the option of switching from some perfectly functional database to Oracle or DB2 in the undefined future. This is a delicate social-engineering concern, because they have an investment in the idea that their online business will grow massively and become a real enterprise. It is pointless to tell them that by the time they need Oracle or DB2, the sun will have consumed all its fuel and the Himalayas will be eroded into a flat plain. Smile and implement database wrapper functions.

Our Focus: MySQL

We, like most every other team who has ever written a book about PHP, love MySQL and use it in all the upcoming examples in Part II MySQL is quite likely the fastest, cheapest, simplest, most reliable database that also has most of the features you'd want and — this is the real differentiator — comes in more or less equally good Unix and Windows implementations.

Despite our love of, and faith in, MySQL, we do recognize that it will occasionally fall short of your needs. Later on in this book, we cover, admittedly in somewhat less depth, two alternatives. In Chapter 34, we'll spend some time with PostgreSQL — an open source database that aspires to the object-relational design described above. For most purposes, using PostgreSQL is akin to driving in a thumbtack with a sledgehammer, but if you simply must have some of these features, it is a strong (and free) implementation that gets the job done for a lot of people.

Chapter 35 will spend some time with Oracle. You are probably already aware that Oracle is a commercial product, and you may wonder why PHP has such substantial support for such a philosophically different product. Whether by technical merit, sheer marketing genius, or mass hypnosis — Oracle is ubiquitous in the commercial setting; and PHP's excellent support for it has opened the door for open source in a lot of organizations that might not otherwise have seen the light.

Summary

The great advantage of the Web is its capability to make large quantities of information publicly available quickly and cheaply. This functionality has been tremendously enhanced by the recent increase in availability of inexpensive, reliable databases.

Since many experienced programmers may never have had to choose a database before, we describe some of the basic points that should be taken into account in the decision-making process. These include the basic database design (flat-file, relational, or object-relational), the API or driver, and the ease of future porting. Optional features, such as transactions or a graphical interface, may also figure into the choice of database. PHP supports many databases of a variety of types, so you have an excellent chance of finding exactly the feature set you need.

✦   ✦   ✦

SQL Tutorial

This chapter is a basic introduction to SQL databases in which we discuss standards, database design, data manipulation language, data definition language, and database security procedures common to all SQL databases.

This chapter is in no way a comprehensive guide to SQL or to any particular SQL database. To go beyond the simplest common features, you will need to consult your particular manufacturer's documentation and/or specific books. A couple of popular guides to SQL in general are:

> ✦ *SQL For Dummies, Fifth Edition* by Allen G. Taylor (Wiley, 2003)
>
> ✦ *SQL Bible* by Alex Kriegel and Boris Trukhnov (Wiley, 2003)

You will also want to look at documentation and books relating to your specific SQL database.

Relational Databases and SQL

SQL is the language of relational databases. It is the *lingua franca*, the Medieval Latin, the Chinese characters of the relational database world — a common idiom that makes it possible for everyone to make themselves understood across a wide range of differences. A simple query like a one-table SELECT will be more or less the same whether you're using a tiny database like mSQL or an expensive behemoth like Oracle 9i Enterprise.

The big advantage for you, the Web developer, is that, after you learn SQL, you will be able to interact with numerous databases across all platforms without a steep retraining curve. Just imagine how horrible life would be if Oracle, MySQL, and SQL Server all had entirely different sets of commands for putting data in and getting data out of their stores — as if Oracle used SELECT to ask for data sets, MySQL used VALJ (the developers are Swedish, you know), and SQL Server used FIND IT IN THIS TABLE (to better match the vocabulary of Windows). SQL is the common vocabulary and syntax that will save you from this nightmare. There will be some differences between products, but it's better to have 80 percent in common and 20 percent different than the other way around.

SQL Standards

According to Andrew Taylor, original inventor of SQL, *SQL* does *not* stand for *Structured Query Language* (or anything else for that matter). But for the rest of the world, it does now. As you would expect from the (non-) title, SQL represents a stricter and more general method of data storage than the previous standard of flat-file DBM-style databases.

SQL is a standard under both ANSI and ECMA (international standards-maintenance organizations). You can read the standards on payment of a fee to these organizations:

✦ www.ansi.org

✦ www.ecma.org

However, within the general guidelines of the standard there are considerable differences among the products of individual companies and open source database development organizations. The past few years, for instance, have seen the rapid growth of so-called *object-relational* databases, as well as of SQL products specifically slanted toward the Web market.

The key to choosing a database is to be selfish, or at least supremely self-centered. You will see plenty of unusually virulent postings out there opining that a certain advanced database feature (like triggers or cross joins) is a "must," and any SQL installation without this feature hardly deserves the name. Take this stuff with a grain of salt. It's far better to make a blind shopping list of functions you need in order of importance and then go out looking for the product that best meets your requirements.

That said, a good deal of SQL really is pretty standardized. You will be using a few SQL statements over and over and over, no matter which specific product you choose to deploy.

The Workhorses of SQL

The basic logical structure of a SQL database is very simple. A given SQL installation can usually contain multiple *databases* — for instance, one for customer data and one for product data. (It's problematic that both the SQL server itself and the collections of tables within it are commonly referred to by the term *database* — but what can you do?) Each database contains a number of *tables*. Each table is made up of carefully defined *columns*, and every entry can be thought of as an added *record* or row. (It's not really a row, but this is a concept so stuck in our visualization that we may as well go with it.)

Four so-called *data manipulation statements* are supported by every SQL server and will constitute an extremely high percentage of all the things you'll want to do with a relational database. These four horsemen of the database are SELECT, INSERT, UPDATE, and DELETE. These commands are your friends and helpmates; get comfy with them, and they will serve you well.

The thing to remember about these four SQL statements is that they manipulate only database *values,* not the structure of the database itself. In other words, you can use these commands to add data but not to make a database; you can get rid of every piece of data in a database, but the shell will still be there — so, for instance, you wouldn't be able to name another database on the same server with the same name. If you want to add or get rid of columns, blow away entire databases as if they never existed, or make up new databases, you need to use other commands such as DROP, ALTER, and CREATE. We discuss these in the "Database Design" section later in this chapter.

Tip A note on SQL style: Many SQL queries that you see are written in one long line of code — which becomes totally illegible once you're dealing with more than four or five fields. A very accomplished PL/SQL programmer of our acquaintance recommends that you break up every SQL statement into as many lines as you need for maximum legibility. He also does not shy away from using indentation in a SQL query with many variables. (SQL queries are usually quite whitespace insensitive.) He has years of experience working on big Oracle installations, and his recommendations actually are very helpful — so that is the style we try to use in this book.

SELECT

SELECT is the main command you need to get information out of a SQL database. The basic syntax is extremely simple:

```
SELECT field1, field2, field3
FROM table
WHERE condition;
```

That's no harder than asking your coworker to get you last month's sales records from the file cabinet in the hallway.

In some cases, you'll want to ask for entire records instead of picking out individual pieces of information. This practice is deprecated for very good reasons (it may be slower than requesting just the data you need, and it can lead to problems if you redesign the table), but it is still widely used and, therefore, we need to mention it. A whole record is called for by using the wildcard (asterisk) symbol:

```
SELECT *
FROM my_table
WHERE ID <= 100;
```

Joins

Only one thing about SELECT statements is even slightly taxing: *joins*. Because joins are one of the main useful features of SQL, we should explain them in some detail here.

A SELECT statement on a single table without joins is easily imagined as being something like a row in a spreadsheet. This is not really how the data is stored or arranged in a SQL database, but for this purpose it's a handy visualization device.

But a SQL database is by definition relational. To understand the philosophy behind the relational database concept, you have to think back to some occasion on which you were forced to fill out a whole bunch of forms — such as applying for a loan, visiting a doctor's office for the first time, or dealing with some kind of governmental formality. (If you've never had this experience, it's because you're young enough to have lived entirely in a world of relational databases.) As you were writing down your name, address, phone, and Social Security number for the fifteenth time, you probably thought, "Why can't I just write my address down once, and then they could just look it up on a need-to-know basis?" That's exactly the concept behind a relational database.

The way a relational database differs from paper forms is the main identifier. Humans do well with text and prefer to categorize by textual identifiers such as names. If a dentist's office or auto body shop stored its paper files in numerical order, it would be difficult for anyone to lay his hands on John Johnson's forms when John next required service. Frankly, most paper file users these days ask for your Social Security number as a backup—it works solely to differentiate you from other people in their files with exactly the same first, last, and middle names.

Databases, on the other hand, work fastest with integers. Because integers are unique by nature, a database needs only one to identify a person, place, or thing uniquely—no matter how many tables refer to that piece of information.

So instead of needing to repeat information several times, like this:

```
Name:   John Johnson
SS#:    123-45-6789

Name:   John Johnson
Fears:  Cats, Friday the 13th, Flying

Name:   Jane Jones
SS#:    987-65-4321

Name:   Jane Jones
Fears:  Heights, Flying
```

with a relational database you can write down each piece of information just once and then relate it to each other piece using integers, as shown in Tables 13-1 to 13-3.

Table 13-1: People

PersonID	Name	SS#
1	John Johnson	123-45-6789
2	Jane Jones	987-65-4321
3	Aloysius Snuffleupagus	564-73-8291

Table 13-2: Fears

FearID	Fear
1	Black cats
2	Friday the 13th
3	Peanut butter sticking to the roof of your mouth
4	Heights
5	Flying

Table 13-3: Person_Fear

ID	PersonID	FearID
1	1	1
2	1	2
3	1	5
4	2	4
5	2	5

This is clearly a neater and faster (for a database) way to store this information. But when you need to pull out the data into a human-readable form, there's a problem: You have to get and correlate information from more than one database. That's the job of a join.

To find out what phobias were suffered by Ms. Jones, you could first look up her personal unique ID:

```
SELECT PersonID
FROM People
WHERE Name = 'Jane Jones';
```

that returns the unique integer 2. Then you can define another SELECT statement using that information:

```
SELECT FearID
FROM Person_Fear
WHERE PersonID = 2;
```

You get the values 4 and 5 back, which you can use in a third query:

```
SELECT Fear
FROM Fears
WHERE FearID = 4 OR FearID = 5;
```

This returns the values Heights and Flying. We should make it clear that there is nothing inherently incorrect about doing it this way, as long as any performance loss is within parameters acceptable to you.

Alternatively, you can perform a join, which returns the same information in a single SELECT statement:

```
SELECT Fears.Fear
FROM Fears, Person_Fear, People
WHERE Fears.FearID = Person_Fear.FearID
AND Person_Fear.PersonID = People.PersonID
AND People.Name = 'Jane Jones';
```

An alternate syntax for this join is:

```
SELECT Fears.Fear
FROM (Fears INNER JOIN Person_Fear ON FearID INNER JOIN People on
PersonID)
WHERE People.Name = 'Jane Jones';
```

As you can see, you need only know one single piece of information to be able to get all the data in the database about that subject using joins. In effect, a join makes two or more tables into one for purposes of searching for a particular piece of information.

Joins come in several different flavors. The one in the preceding example is called an *inner join*, which is the most common and restrictive type. Another common type is the *outer join*. This is used to return a list of all fears even if they do not have people attached to them. In this example, we are using a *left outer join* (also known as a *natural join*):

```
SELECT Fear
FROM Fears LEFT JOIN People ON PersonID;
```

Fears that have people attached to them would appear in the data set multiple times, but fears without people would each appear once.

You can also get a list of all people even if they do not have fears attached to them, using a *right outer join*:

```
SELECT Name
FROM Fears RIGHT JOIN People ON PersonID;
```

Again, the fears that are actually attached to people appear multiple times, whereas the fears that are not suffered by any people still show up once in the data set. As you can see, left and right outer joins differ in which of the two tables you want the actual data set from: the first (left) or the second (right). Because you can switch them around at will, many people consistently use the left outer join for all outer joins.

Caution Ask yourself whether you really need to be using outer joins. Because outer joins require less precision to format, inexperienced SQL users often perform an outer join and then filter the results in the code layer. This is wasteful and slow. Outer joins are all about the NULL values, which are not easily returned by inner joins. An example of a good use for an outer join is a report where you want to see which of your registered users had and had not downloaded your latest software product and how many times they had downloaded. If you are not in this situation, learn to use inner joins instead.

Finally, there is something known as the *self-join*, which is a more advanced technique and won't really make a lot of sense with the example data set. It's often used with *denormalized data*, which means data that deliberately bends the rules of good SQL design (for example, never repeating any data point) for performance reasons (for example, to reduce the number of complex multitable joins).

If you need to make complex and frequent joins, this may constrain the brand of SQL database you can use, because not all of them support every type of join.

Subselects

Before we leave the realm of SELECT statements, we should mention the *subselect*. This is a statement such as:

```
SELECT phone_number
FROM table
WHERE name = 'SELECT name FROM table2 WHERE ID = 1';
```

Subselects are more of a convenience than a necessity. They can be very handy if you're working with enormous batches of data; but you can get the same result with two simpler SELECTs. The subselect is faster if the subselect clause returns a large data set, but there are cases where two selects will not appreciably affect performance.

INSERT

Of course, no matter how many SELECT queries you write, all is for naught if you haven't put any information in the database to begin with. The command you need to put new data into a database is INSERT. The basic syntax is:

```
INSERT INTO table (col1, col2, col3) VALUES(val1, val2, val3);
```

Obviously, the columns and their values need to match up; if you mix up your array items, nothing good will happen. If some of the rows will not have values for some of the fields, you will need to use an empty, null, or auto-incremented value — and, at a deeper level, you may need to have ensured beforehand that fields can be nullable or auto-incrementable. If this is not possible, you should simply leave out any columns you wish to default to an empty value in an INSERT statement.

A twist on the basic INSERT is the INSERT INTO...SELECT. This just means you can INSERT the results of a SELECT statement:

```
INSERT INTO customer(birthmonth, birthflower, birthstone) SELECT * FROM
birthday_info WHERE birthmonth = $birthmonth;
```

Not every SQL database has this capability. Also, you need to be careful with this command because you can cause problems for yourself quite easily — for instance you can overwrite data or experience locking issues. In general, it's not a good idea to select from the same database you're inserting into.

UPDATE

UPDATE is used to edit information already in the database, without deleting any rows. In other words, you can selectively change some information without having to delete an entire old record and insert a new one. The syntax is:

```
UPDATE table
SET field1='val1', field2='val2', field3='val3'
WHERE condition;
```

The conditional statement is just like a SELECT condition, such as WHERE ID>15 AND ID<21 or WHERE gender='F'.

DELETE

DELETE is pretty self-explanatory: You use it to delete the contents of one or more fields permanently from the database. The syntax is:

```
DELETE datapoint
FROM table
WHERE condition;
```

The most important thing to remember is the condition—if you don't set one, you will delete every entry in the specified columns from the database, without a confirmation or a second chance in many cases!

Caution   Let us re-emphasize: you *must* remember to use a condition *every single time* you UPDATE or DELETE! If you do not, every single row in the table will experience the same alteration or deletion. Even very experienced programmers have forgotten to include the condition, to their vast professional embarrassment. You should also give a good deal of thought to restricting database permissions so the minimum number of people can perform these potentially dangerous operations.

Database Design

As should be obvious from the previous section, learning to use a SQL database isn't exactly rocket science—you can get a lot done with just a few simple commands. The hard part is designing the database in the first place and, of course, operating it in the real world over time. Not every Web developer will be asked to design a schema in a professional context, but it never hurts to know how.

At the most fundamental level, database design can be broken down into the following mantra *cum* children's jingle:

```
One to one,
One to many,
Many to many,
Many to one;
And always use a unique ID.
```

An example of *one-to-one data* for Americans is the Social Security number (other nations probably have similar identification cards with unique numbers). Each U.S. citizen has only one unique identifier; it is, in fact, a crime to use the Social Security number of another individual or apply for more than one number. Database designers seize upon truly unique identifiers such as this because almost every other piece of personal information is subject to change—which accounts for the large number of businesses who inappropriately use the Social Security number for identification purposes.

One-to-many data and *many-to-one* are the same, differing only in how the columns are placed in a database. An example of one-to-many data comes from the medical realm: patients to visits. Each patient will always be a discrete individual but may have any number of visits to the doctor. If you designed the table to represent visits to patients, it would instantly become many-to-one data.

Finally, *many-to-many data* is well represented by the relationship of authors to books. Not only can a given book have multiple authors, but each author may have written or co-authored many books. This is not a matrix of relationships that would be easy to represent efficiently in a spreadsheet, but it is precisely this category of data at which relational databases most excel.

Every data relationship falls into one of these categories. As a database designer, it's your job to decide which one of these represents what you need to know in the way you need to know it.

This is not as trivial as it sounds. Imagine you want to develop a database of movie information. One decision you might have to make is whether *movie* and *title* are in a one-to-one relationship with each other, or whether enough films have alternate titles to merit an *alternate title* field or even a one-to-many representation. There's no right answer here—the decision depends on exactly how the information will be used, how large the database will be, if the extra resources required to maintain a more precise data structure are worth the cost, and whether there's a better-than-even chance that today's tangential trivia will become tomorrow's crucial discovery. Some people may be surprised to learn that archiving information can be as much about ruthless excluding as about careful hoarding. As historians say, history is about forgetting as much as it is about remembering.

The simplest relationship is the one-to-one because you can group all these fields into a single table that can be searched more quickly. For instance, a table holding customer information might contain the following fields:

```
Customer ID
Customer name
Administrative contact
Technical contact
```

The hardest thing about the one-to-one relationship is definitely deciding that you will never need to make it into a one-to-many relationship. For instance, what if your biggest customer decides it wants to designate two technical contacts?

As soon as you have a one-to-many, many-to-one, or many-to-many relationship, you're looking at going from a single table to multiple tables: one each for the main variables and one stating the relationship. Tables 13-4 through 13-6 show a common example of a many-to-many relationship:

Table 13-4: Customer

Customer_id	Name
1	Acme Bread
2	Baker Construction
3	Coolee Dam

Table 13-5: Interactions

Interaction_id	Type
1	Phone-support incident
2	On-site incident
3	Written complaint
4	Phone complaint
5	Kudo

Table 13-6: Customer-Interaction

Customer-interaction_id	Customer_id	Interaction_id
1	1	1
2	3	5
3	2	4
4	2	3
5	1	2

After you've decided on a database design, the mechanical details of constructing the database are minimal. The main data structure statements of SQL are CREATE, ALTER, and DROP.

CREATE is used to make a completely new table. All the work is in defining the columns of each table. First you declare the name of the table, and then you must detail the specific data types of that table's columns in what is called a *create definition*. A CREATE statement will take this form:

```
CREATE TABLE tablename (
   id_col INT NOT NULL AUTO_INCREMENT PRIMARY KEY,
   col1 TEXT NULL INDEX,
   col2 DATE NOT NULL
);
```

Different SQL servers have slightly different data types and definition options, so the syntax of one may not transfer exactly to another. For instance, Oracle databases do not auto-increment; to get a new value, you must generally call a function.

DROP can be used to completely delete a table and all its associated data. It's not the most subtle command:

```
DROP TABLE tablename;
```

Obviously, you need to be very careful with this statement.

ALTER is the way to change a table's structure. You simply indicate which table you're changing and redefine its specs. Again, SQL products differ in functionality here. The ALTER statement usually takes this form:

```
ALTER TABLE table RENAME AS new_table;
ALTER TABLE new_table ADD COLUMN col3 VARCHAR(50);
ALTER TABLE new_table DROP COLUMN col2;
```

Privileges and Security

As we state in Chapter 29, security online is analogous to security in the real world. Any cop will tell you that you cannot make your home absolutely crime-proof. A more realistic goal is to increase the difficulty and risk to a level where a large percentage of intruders will choose to go to an easier target down the block.

Using a database with PHP can be similar to using two locks on your front door, substantially enhancing the safety of your site by reducing super-risky operations like system file writes — but only if you follow a few elementary rules of database hygiene. PHP makes many of these techniques a little easier to implement, which means you have fewer reasons to skimp on security.

Setting database permissions

The most fundamental rule of database use is to give each user or group only the minimum permissions necessary to do what needs to be done. You wouldn't let strangers walk into your house and kick back in your bedroom and read your diary — so why should you give them the option to do analogous things on your site? It's a little more work to manage multiple users and make sure all the permissions are set to the right levels at all times; but if that tiny pinprick of pain can prevent a massive infection later, you'd be extremely foolish to refuse this simple but effective prophylaxis.

Besides the threat of malicious/experimental outsiders, setting the correct permissions can protect you from your coworkers and yourself. Insiders have been known to cause massive problems through disgruntlement, ignorance, momentary brain freeze, or a combination of motives. You do not want to have to cope with the consequences of a fired employee's parting shot or a new intern trying out the DROP database command just to see what happens.

A typical database permissions package might be something like:

✦ **Web visitor:** SELECT only

✦ **Contributor:** SELECT, INSERT, and maybe UPDATE

✦ **Editor:** SELECT, INSERT, UPDATE, and maybe DELETE and maybe GRANT

✦ **Root:** SELECT, INSERT, UPDATE, DELETE, GRANT, and DROP

DROP in particular is the nuclear bomb of SQL because it allows you to blow away an entire table or database with a single command. Someone's got to have the ability, but heavy lies the tiara of responsibility on the head of the root database user. Use the power wisely, grasshopper.

In many databases, including MySQL, passwords are encrypted using a different algorithm from system passwords (and, of course, they are typically stored in entirely different locations). Even if one is cracked, the other is not necessarily vulnerable. This assumes you take the time to set permissions correctly, pick good passwords, and usually employ a special command to insert usernames and passwords correctly into the grant table (as opposed to inserting them like other data).

Caution   Database usernames and passwords should not be identical to system usernames and passwords. Never, ever, *ever* set any database password to the root system-user's password! If crackers should happen to get into your database via Web scripts, you don't want to offer them the key to the whole system.

Cross-Reference   Chapter 14 covers permissions for MySQL specifically.

Keep database passwords outside the Web tree

It's a good idea to separate passwords from the Web pages that use them. With PHP's `include()`/`include_once()` and `require()`/`require_once()` functions, it's very easy to drop in text (such as database passwords) from another file at runtime. Remember that these included files do not have to be in a PHP or Web server–enabled directory! Whenever possible, keep them somewhere outside your Web tree, such as in the directory above your Web document root or in a home directory.

Taking the database variables out of PHP files is also good for other reasons. If you have many PHP scripts using the same database, they can all use the same password file. When you suspect the password has been compromised, or when you change the password on a regular schedule, you need only alter one script for all the files to be updated.

The unavoidable downside of this technique is that the file must be *readable* by the Apache user. Because the Apache user and the database user are seldom the same, that means in practice the file must be world-readable. This should still be safer than keeping the database variables inside a public Web root directory.

If you have a set of database variables you use infrequently—a configuration script or the like—you can keep it in a non-Apache-readable directory and change the permissions only on the rare occasions necessary. We infrequently have to go to the trouble to delete postings from our sites' forums. So it's not that much more work (and much more secure) to keep this file in a non-Apache-user-owned directory, once in awhile change the permissions just long enough to delete the offending post, and then immediately change everything back.

If for whatever reason, you decide to put your database username, password, hostname, and database name into a PHP script in plaintext, this is what you can expect. If the `httpd` is functioning normally, the database passwords should be as safe as any file on that server—which is to say, not extremely. But if the daemon goes down, there is some chance your raw PHP (including plaintext database variables) will be delivered in a human-readable form. You can reduce this risk by avoiding the use of the `.html` suffix for PHP files.

In PHP3, if database connectivity went down and you hadn't specified silent mode, you would see something like the following:

```
Warning: MySQL Connection Failed: Access denied for user:
'someuser@localhost' (Using password: NO) in
/home/web/html/mysqltest.php3
on line 2
```

This constitutes a security breach, because it reveals your MySQL username and whether or not you use a password. From PHP4 forward, MySQL error messages are no longer displayed by default. Two functions, `mysql_errno()` and `mysql_error()`, allow you to opt for error codes or text warnings — but now you have to deliberately choose to ask for the information. Because, in most cases, you can opt for the more configurable `die()` instead or remove error messages after debugging, it's still not a good idea to use `mysql_error` on a public production server unless you scrupulously send messages to error logs using the `error_log()` function rather than to standard output.

Use two layers of password protection

Belt-and-suspenders types can apply even another layer of protection to their most sensitive PHP scripts by means of another round of usernames and passwords stored in the database itself, which you can check directly from the PHP script. So you would have your system login/ password, plus database user permissions stored in a non-Web-accessible directory, plus a PHP name/passphrase testing script with values entered by hand just before the script is run.

This is a typical login form that checks a password against the database:

```
<HTML>
<BODY>
<FORM METHOD=POST ACTION="form_check.php">
<P>Username:  <INPUT TYPE="TEXT" SIZE=20 NAME="try_user"></P>
<P>Password:  <INPUT TYPE="PASSWORD" SIZE=10
NAME="try_pass"></P>
<P>Date:  <INPUT TYPE="TEXT" SIZE=10 NAME="try_date"></P>
<P>Entry:<BR>
<TEXTAREA COLS=50 ROWS=10 NAME="try_entry"></TEXTAREA></P>
<P><INPUT TYPE="SUBMIT"></P>
</BODY>
</HTML>
```

This file is the form handler mentioned in the `ACTION` attribute of the preceding form, named `form_check.php`.

```
<?php
// Check Unix user
if ($REMOTE_ADDR != '127.0.0.1') {
  die;
}

// Check database user
// Webvars.inc is a file with $host, $db_user, and $password
// values in it
include("/home/phpuser/Webvars.inc");
mysql_connect($hostname, $db_user, $password)
or die("You are not the database user I'm looking for");
mysql_select_db("captainslog");

// Check form user
$post_try_user = $_POST['try_user'];
$post_try_date = $_POST['try_date'];
$post_try_entry = $_POST['try_entry'];
$query = "SELECT password
```

```
            FROM finalcheck
            WHERE user='$post_try_user'";
$result = mysql_query($query);
$passcheck = mysql_fetch_array($result);

if($passcheck[0] == $_POST['try_pass']) {
  // Enter new entry.
  $query = ("INSERT INTO captainslog (ID, date, entry)
VALUES(NULL, '$post_try_date', '$post_try_entry')");
  $result = mysql_query($query);
  print("New entry result is $result.");
} else {
  mail("security@localhost", "Database alert", "Someone from
$REMOTE_ADDR is trying to get into your captain's log.");
}
?>
```

As you can see from this example, this script will not insert anything into the database if a valid username and password are not provided or the user isn't logged into the localhost. You will also get an e-mail message warning you of a possible breach attempt.

Learn to make backups

And finally, the biggest part of database security may be backing up. Take an hour to learn the best way to back up data in your particular database (for example, via the `mysqldump` command in MySQL), and then schedule regular backups right away. Even better, with a little foresight you can also set up an automatic database backup schedule.

Summary

SQL is not rocket science. The four basic data-manipulation statements supported by essentially all SQL databases are `SELECT`, `INSERT`, `UPDATE`, and `DELETE`. `SELECT` gets data out of the database, `INSERT` puts in a new entry, `UPDATE` edits pieces of the entry in place, and `DELETE` gets rid of an entry.

Designing databases is where most of the difficulty lies. Not all Web developers will be asked to do this. The designer must think long and hard about the best way to represent each piece of data and relationship for the intended use. Well-designed databases are a pleasure to program with, while poorly designed ones can leave you pulling your hair out while contemplating numerous connections and icky joins.

SQL databases are created by so-called data structure statements. The most important of these are `CREATE`, `ALTER`, and `DROP`. As one would expect, `CREATE TABLE` defines a new table within a database. `ALTER` changes the structure of a table. `DROP` is the nuclear bomb of SQL commands because it deletes entire tables or sometimes even whole databases.

Good database design is also a security issue. By employing reasonable prophylactic measures, a SQL database can enhance the security of your site. The best defense against intrusion, of course, is maintaining a strict backup schedule—so every new SQL maintainer should learn the most efficient way to make backups.

✦   ✦   ✦

MySQL Database Administration

MySQL is one of the easiest databases to administer on all platforms; and because it's so lightweight, it can run on even low-powered PCs. Thus, PHP developers have long found it convenient to throw a copy of MySQL on client machines — even on laptops — for a complete local Web development environment. Many developers learn to run their own MySQL installations so they can work at home or on the road, using the OS of their choice. Work teams also sometimes prefer developers to each use a separate local MySQL installation, so that there is no single point of failure that could affect an entire development group. And many PHP-based Open Source projects assume complete familiarity with MySQL database administration for all developers.

Unlike some other databases, it should be well within the capability of any PHP developer to self-administer a MySQL database. There are a plethora of tools, both in MySQL itself and available from third parties, to make this job even easier. Many PHP-based application packages, both commercial and Open Source, also require familiarity with a MySQL database to install, run, and debug the Web app. So even if you don't plan to write all your own PHP code yourself, getting comfortable with MySQL administration will pay many dividends.

MySQL Licensing

Before installing any piece of Open Source software, you should clearly understand all the associated licensing issues. This is especially true of products like MySQL that have dual commercial and Open Source licenses.

Unfortunately, MySQL licensing at the time of this writing is in flux and has caused momentary incompatibilities with PHP's license. Until this situation gets definitively ironed out, PHP developers need to be extra careful to ensure that they are in compliance. This goes double for anyone who distributes (rather than simply uses) MySQL in either a commercial or open source context.

For some of the later releases of PHP4, MySQL client libraries were bundled with PHP. In the summer of 2003, MySQL AB — creators of the MySQL database — decided to adopt the General Public License (GPL) for noncommercial use. In many ways, this is a simpler and less restrictive licensing scheme than before, but it happened to be incompatible with PHP's Apache-style license, and therefore the PHP Group no longer felt able to distribute the database libraries. At press time this issue was in the process of being amicably worked out to allow Open Source "combined works" to be distributed without charge—but you should still check to be absolutely positive that this is the case. The definitive location for MySQL licensing information is www.mysql.com/doc/en/Licensing_and_Support.html.

There are separate sections for commercial use and for use under the GPL—which is probably the use most relevant to most PHP developers.

You should read the license carefully, but here are some common use cases that will be affected by MySQL's new licensing scheme:

✦ **Web site only:** If you use MySQL solely as part of a commercial or noncommercial Web site, you may use it without worrying about licensing issues. MySQL AB suggests you purchase a support contract to further development work.

✦ **Open Source project under GPL:** If you distribute MySQL server or client libraries as part of an Open Source project properly released under the GNU General Public License, you can (and must) redistribute MySQL and its source code freely.

✦ **Commercial redistribution:** If you bundle MySQL server or client libraries as part of a commercial product, you must purchase a commercial license from MySQL AB.

✦ **Open Source project under non-GPL license:** This is the potentially problematic situation at the moment, because if you bundle MySQL server or client libraries with your non-GPLed Open Source project, your code could be infected by the GPL. Check the MySQL licensing page to determine the most current status of MySQL in relation to your project.

Remember that in many cases you can evade these licensing strictures simply by not redistributing the database yourself but rather requiring your users to procure and install MySQL separately.

Installing MySQL: Moving to Version 4

Remember to install the MySQL server and client libraries *before* installing PHP! Although it's not strictly necessary in every circumstance, especially on Windows, it's always a good habit with PHP to make sure that all third-party servers and libraries are properly installed before telling PHP to link to them.

Preinstall considerations

MySQL was in version 3 for a long time, and many PHP developers got used to working with it during this period. However, MySQL 4 has introduced some innovations and changes, both on the database side and the PHP side. Both new and experienced webdevs should take the time to familiarize themselves with these changes. Even if you have a lot of experience with MySQL 3, you shouldn't necessarily expect to be able to install and use MySQL 4 with exactly the same procedures.

There are three main MySQL-specific issues to consider before you install new versions of MySQL and PHP: incompatible new client libraries, the new PHP mysqli extension, and new table types that support transactionality.

Note *Transactionality* basically means the ability to treat a group of database operations as a single unit for the purposes of accepting or rejecting the data. So for instance, an e-commerce transaction might have several steps touching numerous different tables—registering you as a new user, collecting your payment and shipping information, debiting the product from inventory, and so forth—but you don't want any of these changes to be made unless the credit card charge goes through successfully, even though that step comes at the end of the purchasing process. In this case, you need a transactional database that will keep track of changes throughout the process and either commit them all as a unit or roll them all back as a unit. Until version 4, MySQL was not a transactional database, but now it supports transactionality.

New client libraries

The client libraries for MySQL 3 and 4.0 are forwards-incompatible with the MySQL server from version 4.1 and up. Therefore, if you want to use MySQL 4.1+, you will have to rebuild PHP with the new libraries. The reverse is not true: MySQL 4.1 client libraries can still be used with older versions of MySQL server. You may also have to update your permissions table and any columns containing password hashes calculated by MySQL that you have created in any tables.

The main difference between the client libraries has to do with authentication. The MySQL PASSWORD() function used to result in a 16-byte hash. From version 4.1.1 onward, it now results in a 41-byte hash. Since MySQL uses the PASSWORD() function to set its own user permissions schemes, you will need to update pre-4.1.1 MySQL grant tables using the mysql_fix_privilege_tables script. You will also potentially need to alter by hand any columns in other tables that take input from MySQL's PASSWORD() function, making them 41-bytes long. The actual contents of these columns do not need to change—MySQL 4.1 will continue to accept hashes shorter than 41 bytes—but the column sizes need to be increased to accommodate new values.

mysqli

The *i* in mysqli stands for *improved*. The new mysqli extension to PHP was designed to let you access the new functionality of MySQL 4.1 and above—especially transactionality, which is the biggest new feature of MySQL 4.

Caution The mysql extension works only with versions of MySQL below 4.1; the mysqli extension works only with versions 4.1 and above of MySQL.

Unfortunately, this extension is not easily compatible with the old mysql extension and its associated functions. Therefore, it's best to choose one or the other at compile time. At the time of this writing, the mysqli extension is considered experimental and should probably not be used in production.

It's theoretically possible to compile PHP with both mysql and mysqli extensions—if for instance you want to use both a 3.x and a 4.1+ version of MySQL on the same machine—but you'll have to be very careful to avoid conflicts between client libraries. In practice, it's better to simply choose one or the other.

Caution Comp Svcs: Note two successive hyphens in the following paragraph. Do not change to an em dash.

If you choose to try mysqli, remember to disable the mysql extension, which is usually enabled by default. (In Unix builds, use the without-mysql flag; in Windows, comment out the mysql.dll extension in php.ini.)

Transaction-safe tables

For most of its existence, MySQL used tables of a proprietary type called MyISAM. Late in the 3.xx release cycle, it introduced two new types, ISAM and heap, but they have not become hugely popular. To this day, MyISAM is the default and by far the most common type.

However, to support transactions in MySQL 4.1+ the MySQL team created two new types of transaction-safe tables: InnoDB and BDB. If you want to use commits and rollbacks, you must compile MySQL with the ability to recognize one of these types and define each table as InnoDB. You can mix different table types in the same database, and also convert a MyISAM table to an InnoDB table. You might also consider mixing types by using InnoDB tables on a master database that accepts writes, while sticking with MyISAM for slave databases that provide only reads.

Think hard about whether you really need transaction-safe tables. They impose quite a bit of extra overhead and are thus slower, take up more room on disk, and require different tools and procedures. Some things, such as recovering from database corruption, are considerably different and possibly harder (although also potentially less common) if you're using transaction-safe tables. On the other hand, if you wish to use MySQL in enterprise situations with transactions, row-level locking, foreign keys, and hot backup, you'll want to research the InnoDB alternative.

The other type of transaction-safe table, BDB, is based on Sleepycat Software's BerkeleyDB storage engine. BDB does not offer some of the other features of InnoDB, such as foreign keys and row-level locking, and it's a bit unclear which company will provide support for this setup.

Because transaction-safe tables are still so uncommon, and presumably used mostly in situations where resources are available for specialized database administrators and tools, the bulk of this chapter will concentrate on MyISAM tables. For more information on InnoDB tables, refer to www.innodb.com or www.mysql.com/doc/en/InnoDB.html.

Tip   The Windows binary version of the MySQL server is built with InnoDB enabled by default. However, your tables will not actually be of the InnoDB type unless you define them to be.

Downloading MySQL

All downloads for MySQL are located at www.mysql.com/downloads/index.html. Pick the version number you want and, as exactly as possible, the platform you want.

One peculiarity of MySQL is that, unlike most other Open Source servers, the producers prefer installation from binary rather than source. There may be situations where you have to build yourself, but in general it should be avoided if at all possible.

MySQL is now sometimes distributed in Linux distros or as part of other packages; for the freshest builds, however, it's better to uninstall these versions using whatever tools are provided by your platform and then reinstall a new version.

Installing MySQL on Windows

Default installation on any version of Windows is now much easier than it used to be, as MySQL now comes neatly packaged with an installer. Simply download the installer package, unzip it anywhere, and run setup.exe. This will walk you through the trivial process and by default will install everything under C:\mysql, which is probably as good a place as any.

Test the server by firing it up from the command prompt the first time. Go to the location of the mysqld server, which is probably C:\mysql\bin, and type:

```
mysqld --console
```

If all went well, you will see some messages about startup and InnoDB. If not, you may have a permissions issue. Make sure that the directory that holds your data is accessible to whatever user (probably mysql) the database processes run under.

However, despite the nifty new install, MySQL AB has not gone all the way with the Windows UI paradigm. The preferred way to run the MySQL server, client, and tools is still from the command prompt. MySQL will not add itself to the start menu, and there is no particularly nice GUI way to stop the server either. Therefore, if you tend to start the server by double-clicking the mysqld executable, you should remember to halt the process by hand (using mysqladmin, Task List, Task Manager, or other Windows-specific means) before you shut down the computer.

Another rather odd way in which Windows users have it much harder than Unix users is that the MySQL manual currently comes distributed in one huge HTML or text file for Windows users, both in the Windows build and for download as a zip file. This file is so big that you may find it unusable if your Windows machine is not new and fast. If possible, grab the tarball version with one HTML file per chapter. You can extract it on a Unix machine and then copy the files over to your Windows box. Or you can always use the online documentation if you have reliable Internet access.

The Windows version of PHP comes with MySQL enabled by default, so you should now be good to go (modulo user management stuff, which we will describe in a later section). If you wish to turn off the mysql extension in favor of the mysqli extension, you need to comment out the mysql line and uncomment the mysqli line in the modules section of php.ini.

Installing MySQL on Unix

If possible, use one of the binary versions of MySQL, preferably one with an installer. On some platforms (notably Linux), you will need to download the server and clients separately; on others, they are conveniently bundled. There is now a good selection of binaries, so it will not be necessary for most people to build MySQL by hand. Some packages are distributed by third parties, such as Debian, rather than by MySQL AB. Look around your usual source for binary packages specifically built for your platform if you don't see a binary build on mysql.com.

There can be very wide variation in where MySQL programs and data files are located, based on precisely which package you're using and where you got it. The mysql.com manual contains a section on installation layouts, but it's often inapplicable or inaccurate. The most common locations are /usr, /usr/local, and /var.

If you have to use a generic binary instead of a cushy installer-based version, installation will require a few extra steps. Type the following lines at the prompt to create a new mysql user and install MySQL to run as that user (you'll have to be the root user):

```
groupadd mysql
useradd -g mysql mysql
cd /usr/local
gunzip < /path/to/mysql-VERSION-OS.tar.gz | tar xvf -
ln -s full-path-to-mysql-VERSION-OS mysql
```

```
cd mysql
scripts/mysql_install_db
chown -R root  .
chown -R mysql data
chgrp -R mysql .
bin/mysqld_safe --user=mysql &
```

Users of MySQL 3.x should note that the new startup script for MySQL is now called mysqld_safe rather than safe_mysqld. However, the latter will still exist as a symbolic link during some transition period for backward compatibility.

Now you are ready to build PHP with the MySQL client libraries. Use the --with-mysql=/ path/to/mysql flag for older versions of MySQL or the --without-mysql --with-mysqli=/ path/to/mysql_config flags for 4.1+ versions of MySQL. Note that in MySQL 4, you should link to the actual location of mysql_config rather than just to the MySQL directory. The mysql_config script is a tool that helps provide information about compiling MySQL clients, such as library location.

Installing MySQL on Mac OS X

MySQL AB now maintains an OS X–specific binary installer distribution that delivers a disk image rather than a tarball. Simply download the .dmg file, and double-click the resulting icon. The installer will walk you through the process, and suggest a default installation path.

Mac Internet Explorer users may find that the MySQL file downloads under the name download.php rather than as mysql-standard-4.x.x.dmg. In this case, simply allow the download to complete and then change the name of the file.

Post-installation housekeeping

MySQL ships with a blank password for the root MySQL user. As soon as you have success-fully installed the database and clients — preferably even before you build PHP with MySQL support — you need to set a root password:

```
mysqladmin -u root password 'new_password';
```

Obviously, you will replace the preceding word new_password with an actual password.

Caution

Under no circumstances whatsoever should you even *think* about using your server machine's root user's password as the root password here! The server root user and the database root user have no relationship to each other. Also, don't use your normal user password as the database root password. Come on, don't be lame — make up a fresh password.

Unix users will also want to put your MySQL directory in your PATH, so you won't have to keep typing out the full path every time you want to use the command-line client. For bash, it would be something like:

```
export PATH=$PATH:/usr/local/mysql
```

Adjust this to suit your own shell. If you add an entry for this location to the PATH line in your shell's startup file (for example, .bashrc), you won't have to do this step every time you log in to the machine.

Your MySQL server is now ready to use.

Basic MySQL client commands

It may surprise you to know that the binary named `mysql` in your `mysql/bin` directory is not the server, but the client (the server is `mysqld`). When you type `mysql` into a shell, you are using the MySQL command-line client to access some MySQL server.

To connect to the MySQL server using the command-line client, the basic command is:

```
mysql [-h hostname] [-P portnumber] -u username -p
```

You almost certainly need to pass the username; if you don't, the client will try the name of your shell user. If you don't pass the password flag, mysql will check whether a password is needed for the user you claim to be—and if so, it will reject you. If you're connecting to a local host, you don't need the hostname flag; if you're connecting to the default port (3306), you don't need the port number flag. There are a bunch of other options, but usually this is all you need the first time. Assuming you use the username `root`, you will be prompted for the root password that you just set in the previous step.

At this point, you will need to select a database to use. The command for that is:

```
USE databasename;
```

The semicolon is optional for this command, but you need one for every other SQL command so you might as well get used to using it. Until you create new databases, there are only two databases in a fresh install: `mysql` and `test`. If you just connected to MySQL as the root user, you have access to both; if you are connected as any other user, you have access only to `test`.

The command `SHOW TABLES;` will dump a list of all the tables in this database.

To quickly see the structure of a database table, use `SHOW COLUMNS FROM tablename;`. This displays all the columns with their types, sizes, default values, and other helpful information.

To see all the values in a table, just do a `SELECT` with unrestrictive conditions:

```
SELECT * FROM tablename;
```

Be careful though, since in live databases this kind of query can be huge and take up a lot of resources. If you have reason to suspect that the data set is more than a few rows, you should take steps to limit the query.

 Cross-Reference

See Chapter 13 for more information on how to write SQL statements like SELECT, INSERT, and so forth. Remember that one of the best ways of debugging problems with SQL statements in your PHP code is to try them out (with suitable fake data plugged into the variables) using the MySQL command-line client rather than the PHP client. See Chapter 19 for more information on debugging SQL in your PHP.

Finally, to get out of the MySQL client session, use the command `quit;`. Again, the semicolon is optional for this command. This should drop you back into your normal shell.

MySQL User Administration

A big part of using MySQL safely and effectively is understanding its privilege system, and learning how to use the tools provided for controlling user privileges.

MySQL allows you to grant quite fine-grained permissions to different users from different client locations. There are four descending levels of privileges: global, database, table, and column. So in theory, you could allow a particular user to write data only to certain columns of certain tables of certain databases on your MySQL server. Or you could just as easily give any database user connecting from anywhere the same powers as the root database user (although this is totally not recommended).

Of course, for security reasons it's generally a good rule of thumb to grant each user only the minimal permissions necessary to perform his or her function. But here's the tradeoff: the more fine-grained your permissions scheme, the slower each and every INSERT, SELECT, UPDATE, and DELETE will be. This makes sense, because MySQL is checking more grant tables for more fine-grained permissions. Realistically, not everyone really needs to worry about the performance hit — but if you do, you'll have to make some tradeoffs between security and performance.

The heart of the MySQL permission system is a table that every database administrator should become very familiar with: the user table of the mysql database (which, along with a database called test, ships with every installation of MySQL). Let's look at a simplified version of this table (apologies for the line-wraps, but that's how you'll see it in many shell windows too).

```
mysql> select * from user;
+-----------+------+----------+-------------+-------------+
-------------+-------------+
| Host      | User | Password | Select_priv | Insert_priv |
  Update_priv | Delete_priv |
+-----------+------+----------+-------------+-------------+
-------------+-------------+
| localhost | root |          | Y           | Y           |
  Y          | Y           | Y           | Y           |
| dhcppc2   | root |          | Y           | Y           |
  Y          | Y           | Y           | Y           |
| localhost |      |          | N           | N           |
  N          | N           | N           | N           |
| dhcppc2   |      |          | N           | N           |
  N          | N           | N           | N           |
+-----------+------+----------+-------------+-------------+
-------------+-------------+
4 rows in set (0.00 sec)
```

As you can see, there are several specific global permissions, which are represented in the table by a Y or an N. A Y in the user table stands for a global privilege affecting all tables in all databases on this MySQL server. If the MySQL server gets a request from a user who has an N in the field corresponding to that action, it will start going down the hierarchy of privilege scope — first to the db table for database-level privileges; then if it finds all Ns in that table too, to the tables_priv table for table-level privileges; and finally to the columns_priv table for column-level privileges. Only after exhaustively checking all the grant tables will it report an authentication error to the client.

Caution   If you grant column or table level privileges to even a single user among many, MySQL will check these grant tables for all users. Therefore, giving column or table privileges to even one user could significantly slow down all your SQL statements for all users.

Caution There is no way to grant a user the ability to create or drop any table of a database without also giving that user the ability to drop the database entirely. However, you can prevent the user from creating or dropping other databases on the same server. You also cannot use the MySQL grant tables to block connections from certain IP addresses or hostnames.

There are two different ways to add or edit user permissions in MySQL (assuming you're the root database user): by direct SQL statements (for example, putting a Y by hand into every relevant field of every relevant grant table) or by use of the GRANT and REVOKE syntax. The latter is easier, and less dangerous if you make a small mistake, since in most cases your query will choke with a SQL error instead of just leaving a gaping security hole.

To add a new MySQL user:

```
GRANT priv_type [(column1, column2, column3)]
ON database.[table]
TO user@host IDENTIFIED BY 'new_password';
```

where columns and tables are optional and additional priv_types can be appended in a comma-separated list.

The types of privileges and their scope are shown in Table 14-1.

Table 14-1: MySQL Privilege Scope

Privilege	Global	Database	Table	Column
ALL	✓	✓		
ALTER	✓	✓	✓	
CREATE	✓	✓	✓	
CREATE TEMPORARY TABLE	✓	✓	✓	
DELETE	✓	✓	✓	
DROP	✓	✓	✓	
EXECUTE	✓	✓		
FILE	✓	✓		
INDEX	✓	✓	✓	
INSERT	✓	✓	✓	✓
LOCK TABLES	✓	✓		
PROCESS	✓	✓		
REFERENCES	✓	✓		
RELOAD	✓	✓		
REPLICATION CLIENT	✓			
REPLICATION SLAVE	✓			
SELECT	✓	✓	✓	✓

Continued

Table 14-1 *(continued)*

Privilege	Global	Database	Table	Column
SHOW DATABASES	✓			
SHUTDOWN	✓			
SUPER	✓	✓		
UPDATE	✓	✓	✓	✓
USAGE	✓	✓		
GRANT OPTION	✓	✓	✓	

Obviously, there's no point in trying to give anyone the SHUTDOWN privilege at the table level. You will merely get an error message telling you to RTFM. If you grant ALL to a column, table, or database, the user will get only the basket of privileges appropriate to that level.

You should be extra-careful about giving users the following privileges, which are all dangerous: GRANT, ALTER, CREATE, DROP, FILE, SHUTDOWN, PROCESS. No normal database user, especially a PHP user, should need these permissions in production.

The syntax for revoking privileges is very similar, although simpler:

```
REVOKE priv_type [(column1, column2, column3)]
ON database[.table]
FROM user@host;
```

After you grant or revoke privileges to any user, you need to force the database to reload the new privilege data into memory. You do this by issuing the FLUSH PRIVILEGES command. You could also start and stop the server, but that's impractical in many circumstances.

This is all well and good, but by now you're probably thinking: But what actual permissions should I actually grant to my actual PHP user? Let's look at some common cases from the real world.

Local development

For purely local stuff, especially on a machine that isn't connected to the Internet all the time or is tucked securely behind a good firewall, almost anything goes. If you need to experiment with your schema, this is the place to do it — so it's appropriate to have permissions like ALTER, CREATE, DELETE, and DROP in addition to the normal SELECT, INSERT, UPDATE. A lot of people will find it convenient to just grant ALL PRIVILEGES on a certain database to a local user, like this:

```
GRANT ALL PRIVILEGES on database.*
TO username@localhost
IDENTIFIED BY 'password';
```

Standalone Web site

A self-hosted database probably needs to accept connections from numerous Web servers in the same domain. In production, all machines should be limited to SELECT, INSERT, UPDATE, and possibly DELETE — although many systems never actually delete data, and it's a little safer not to do so. Since there probably won't be multiple databases on a standalone Web site's production database, global permissions are faster with not much more real security risk. So a possible grant statement might be:

```
GRANT SELECT, INSERT, UPDATE ON *.*
TO phpdbuser@%.example.com
IDENTIFIED BY 'password';
```

However, this is the situation that is most likely to use master-slave replication. Often, these MySQL clusters are configured so that all writes go to the master, while the slaves do nothing but serve up very fast reads. In that case, you would give only SELECT privileges on each slave and only INSERT and UPDATE privileges on the master — possibly to two different database users.

Shared-hosting Web site

If you are an ISP that offers shared hosting, or a customer hosting your Web site on one, your primary concern should be security over performance. Under no circumstances do you want one user to be able to tamper with or delete data belonging to another user.

Unless each user has her own MySQL instance running on her own port, the ISP administrator should not allow users to create or drop globally. Obviously, though, there is no good way to deny table creates or drops, which (as we explained previously) implies that each user will also be able to drop his own database if he so desires. Yes, that's right: If your users can define new tables, as they almost certainly will have to in this situation, there's no good way to prevent them from blowing away all their data with a single command! That's part of the easy-come easy-go thrill of MySQL. The database administrator can and should, however, prevent users from being able to do this to other users on the same server.

ISPs should not use wildcarding for usernames or hostnames. Each user account should be connecting from one and only one server in your own domain space. There's no good reason to accept MySQL client connections from outside the firewall — your users should be comfortable ssh-ing into their shared hosting space to tinker with their database, or they will want to use a GUI tool. So a common grant for this situation might be:

```
GRANT SELECT, INSERT, UPDATE, DELETE, CREATE, DROP, ALTER
ON database.*
TO user@servername.example.com
IDENTIFIED BY 'password';
```

One deplorable practice often used by shared hosts is allowing or even requiring a user to reuse his domain username and password for a MySQL username and password. This is low-rent and could cause untold problems: If your ISP allows this, we recommend you switch Web hosts now.

PHPMyAdmin

Although we recommend that you familiarize yourself with the MySQL command-line client and use it as much as possible, the truth is that many PHP users dislike the command line and find it difficult to visualize their structured data when they see it in a tiny shell window with awful line wraps. Some Web hosts also do not grant full shell access and therefore allow users to administer and view their databases only through a Web interface. So although it presents many security problems, the demand for Web-based GUI front ends to MySQL was overwhelming. If you're going to use one of these clients — PHPMyAdmin is the most popular, but there are several similar packages — you should at least know how to use it in the least harmful way.

The major problem with PHPMyAdmin is that it doesn't make MySQL's security issues any easier to understand—and then it adds some security issues of its own. In addition to MySQL's privilege system, discussed previously, there is a Web security layer to handle appropriately. Unfortunately, PHPMyAdmin doesn't necessarily make it easy to get good Web security.

Say you have a Web hosting account with shell access on a computer at a data center somewhere. In a well-run network, you would have to log in to that computer over an encrypted connection like ssh. Then you would have to enter a separate database username and password, and possibly a hostname and port number on another machine, to connect to the MySQL database server—which would only accept connections from you that originated on the specific computer that you have a user account on. It's not a perfect system—when it comes to security, there are no perfect systems—but it's pretty good.

In contrast, PHPMyAdmin doesn't necessarily require even one username or password. Anyone who knows about the existence of your PHPMyAdmin installation can try to access it using a browser from anywhere—and in the default configuration, they would get right in without ever hitting an authorization subsystem. Furthermore, the pipe between your browser and the Web server will not be encrypted unless you go to the trouble to configure your Web server to accept only HTTPS connections, so all data will pass back and forth over an ordinary HTTP connection.

So how do you get the convenience of PHPMyAdmin while minimizing the risks? First, assess your needs. A lot of people turn out to use PHPMyAdmin only very occasionally, for instance to set up an initial database schema. If that describes your needs, then you don't need to install PHPMyAdmin on your production server at all. Install it locally, tweak your schema to your heart's content, and then dump a copy of your local database as SQL that can be applied to your production server. It's very easy, much safer, and minimizes downtime on your production servers. See the "Backups" section later in this chapter for more information on making copies of database structure and data using `mysqldump`.

The only drawback of this method is that it becomes quite difficult to make the occasional small schema change on a database that already has data in it. However, in this case you could consider disabling PHPMyAdmin when it's not in use. You would simply set the directory and file permissions of the PHPMyAdmin directory to disallow connections from the Web server user (that is, `nobody`). The next time you need to use PHPMyAdmin, you'd only have to take a second to reset the permissions so the Web server user could once again read the files. You'd also want to use http or cookie auth when the Web client was enabled, however.

Another security measure would be to use SSL encryption on your PHPMyAdmin directory. This will provide a solution to the problem of unencrypted sensitive data being passed between your Web server and browser. See the following Web sites for more information:

✦ `www.modssl.org` (Apache httpd)

✦ `www.microsoft.com/technet/treeview/default.asp?url=/technet/ prodtechnol/windowsserver2003/proddocs/deployguide/iisdg_mea_nfmd. asp` (IIS 6)

The most common method of enhancing security is to use PHPMyAdmin's http or cookie auth schemes. These require the creation of a special PHPMyAdmin user who can read the MySQL grant tables, as well as your normal database administrator user. The http method works only with Apache. The cookie method encrypts your password before writing it to a cookie, works on Web servers other than Apache, and is the only method that allows for a complete logout.

To use either http or cookie-based authorization, create the PHPMyAdmin user this way (after unzipping or untarring the PHPMyAdmin package under your Web server's document root):

```
GRANT USAGE ON mysql.* TO 'pmauser'@'localhost'
    IDENTIFIED BY 'pmapassword';
GRANT SELECT (
    Host, User, Select_priv, Insert_priv, Update_priv,
    Delete_priv, Create_priv, Drop_priv, Reload_priv,
    Shutdown_priv, Process_priv, File_priv, Grant_priv,
    References_priv, Index_priv, Alter_priv, Show_db_priv,
    Super_priv, Create_tmp_table_priv, Lock_tables_priv,
    Execute_priv, Repl_slave_priv, Repl_client_priv
    ) ON mysql.user TO 'pmauser'@'localhost';
GRANT SELECT ON mysql.db TO 'pmauser'@'localhost';
GRANT SELECT ON mysql.host TO 'pmauser'@'localhost';
GRANT SELECT (Host, Db, User, Table_name, Table_priv,
    Column_priv)
ON mysql.tables_priv TO 'pmauser'@'localhost';
```

For both schemes, you also need to set the following fields in the PHPMyAdmin `config.inc.php` file:

```
$cfg['PmaAbsoluteUri'] = 'http://localhost/phpMyAdmin';
$cfg['Servers'][$i]['host'] = 'localhost';
$cfg['Servers'][$i]['auth_type'] = 'http or cookie';
$cfg['Servers'][$i]['user'] = 'pmauser';
```

For cookie-based auth, you also need to set the following field:

```
$cfg['blowfish_secret'] = 'Supersecret passphrase';
```

Now when you try to connect, you will either get an Apache basic-auth popup box or a Web form. Enter your database administrator's username and password — don't use the root database user, please! — and you will now have exactly the same MySQL privileges you would have when using the MySQL command-line client.

Finally, there is one PHPMyAdmin "authentication" method you should not use: the so-called config method. This simply means you put your database administrator username and password in the `config.inc.php` file, and then anyone with a browser will be able to see your database. The only circumstance in which you should even consider using this method is on a local machine that does not accept HTTP connections from the outside world.

Now that you've set up PHPMyAdmin, you have easy access to a wealth of information about your MySQL databases. Once you select a database from the list available to you, you will see the main database screen, which will resemble Figure 14-1.

From here, GUI users will probably find it easy to navigate PHPMyAdmin. Unfortunately, PHPMyAdmin uses somewhat different terminology for operations than the MySQL client: "structure" rather than "show columns", "browse" rather than "select", and "export" rather than "dump" — but a little bit of experimenting should make things clearer.

Caution

You may have a few scares with PHPMyAdmin if you happen to be color-blind, because all the dangerous operations are represented by red icons or links. Luckily, you will be asked to confirm every drop or mass-delete operation before it happens, which will minimize accidents as long as you don't hit Enter at the wrong time.

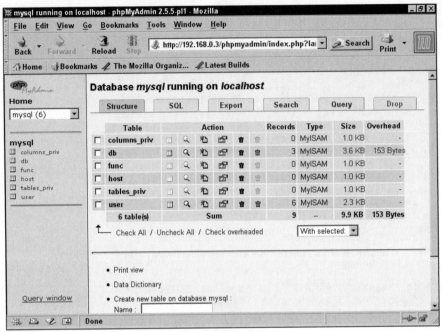

Figure 14-1: PHPMyAdmin's main database screen

Backups

Database backups can be made in two ways: by copying the data directory directly (either manually or by means of the `mysqlhotcopy` script on Unix) or by using the `mysqldump` tool to write out a SQL file that will replicate your database. The former is a little faster, but the latter is more flexible. With `mysqldump` you can choose to copy just the structure of the database, just the data, or both.

The most basic usage of `mysqldump` is:

```
mysqldump -u username -p databasename > dumpfilename.sql
```

This command will dump a text file that can be read into another database server, like this:

```
mysql -u root -p databasename < dumpfilename.sql
```

Instead of directing the output of `mysqldump` to a file, you can also pipe it directly to another server, like so:

```
mysqldump -u username -p databasename |
mysql -h remote-host -u remoteuser -p -C databasename
```

However, this can be less secure in some cases, since you have to tell the remote host to accept database-modifying connections from external clients.

This basic command is fine as far as it goes—meaning it will result in a nice SQL file containing both the structure and data of the named database. But sometimes you will want something more specific than that: maybe just the structure, or just the data, or all the databases on that server, or just some tables from your chosen database. MySQL allows you to both specify different combinations of databases and/or tables and to add option flags to your command.

If you want to select specific tables to dump from your chosen database, just list them after the database name:

```
mysqldump -u username -p databasename table1 table2
> dumpfilename.sql
```

If you want to dump some but not all databases on your server, use the `--databases` flag and then list the databases. However, in this case, you will not be able to specify tables.

```
mysqldump -u username -p --databases database1 database2 >
dumpfilename.sql
```

If you want to dump all databases, use the `--all-databases` flag:

```
mysqldump -u username -p --all-databases > dumpfilename.sql
```

You can specify any of these options before specifying the databases and tables. There are many `mysqldump` options, but Table 14-2 lists the most commonly used options.

Table 14-2: mysqldump Options

Option	Explanation
`--add-locks`	Adds table locking to SQL file for faster inserts on the target table. See also `--opt`.
`--add-drop-table`	Will overwrite each table definition. Be careful with this option, as you could delete data! If you don't use this option but a table of the same name already exists, you will get an error on the target database.
`-a, --all`	All options. Be careful!
`-c, --complete-insert`	Use more complete insert statements with column names, instead of simply reading in values.
`--help`	Displays help message with options.
`-l, --lock-tables`	Locks tables on the source machine before the dump.
`-n, --no-create-db`	Will not create databases of the specified names if they don't exist already. Default with the `--databases` and `--all-databases` options.
`-t, --no-create-info`	Will not create tables of the specified names if they don't exist already.
`-d, --no-data`	Just the structure of the specified database(s) or tables.

Continued

Table 14-2 *(continued)*

Option	Explanation
`--opt`	Equal to `--quick --add-drop-table --add-locks --extended-insert --lock-tables`. Fastest possible dump. Make sure you want to drop existing tables if there's a conflict.
`-q, --quick`	No buffering.
`-r, --result-file=filename`	Dump result to file. In DOS, creates Unix-style line breaks.
`-w, --where='condition'`	Select results by the `WHERE` clause in single quotes.

Because `mysqldump` is so easy to use, you should have no excuse for not adhering to a regular backup schedule. This is why cronjobs were invented! If your data changes relatively infrequently, you might be able to get away with weekly or fortnightly backups; if you have a fairly high-traffic site, you'll want to schedule one every night.

Users of PHPMyAdmin have access to `mysqldump` through the Export tab. However, PHPMyAdmin currently offers only the most common options for your data dump. If you need more control over the format of your SQL file, you'll have to use `mysqldump` as previously described instead.

Replication

MySQL replication is based on a one-way single-master, single-or-multiple-slave model. The master database will handle all writes—meaning all `INSERT`s, `UPDATE`s, and `DELETE`s, as well as all schema changes. The slaves will periodically get these changes from the master and in the meantime will be available for highly optimized read-only data serving (meaning all `SELECT`s). The master does not know anything about slave databases. It simply makes its binary logs available, and the slaves do all the rest: scheduling updates, connecting to the master, getting the changes, applying the changes, and so on. Thus, slaves are aware of the identity of the master, but masters are not aware of the identities of slaves.

If the master database goes down for any reason, no replacement will be automatically elected. The entire system is likely to become unperformative, as the slaves spend many resources trying in vain to connect to the master for updates, while PHP tries to perform writes without success. The database administrator will have to manually break the existing master-slave relationships and designate a new master by hand. Luckily, if something goes wrong with the master, there's no way the slaves will have gotten out of sync—so modulo a database administrator noticing the problem and being available to deal with it, changing to a new master database should be relatively quick.

Because there have been many changes and upgrades to replication in recent versions of MySQL, many recent versions are incompatible with other recent versions in a replication setup. If you want to try replication, we recommend you make sure all the database servers involved are using the same version of MySQL, and furthermore, that this version be 4.0.3+. If you are trying to replicate with disparate versions of MySQL between 3.23 and 4.0.3, things are very likely to not work properly.

In a nutshell, the operations that must be performed to establish MySQL replication are these:

1. Grant permissions to slave user on master.
2. Take snapshot of master data; copy to slave machines.
3. Shut down MySQL servers.
4. Restart MySQL servers with correct server-ids.
5. Establish master-slave relationship from each slave.

Now we'll explain the process in more detail.

You will need to create an account on the master database for slaves to use, with the REPLICATE SLAVE privilege. You do not need to grant any other privileges to this account.

```
GRANT REPLICATE SLAVE ON *.*
TO replicant@'%' IDENTIFIED BY 'replpwd';
```

Next, lock the master server and take a snapshot of its state immediately before the replication. On the master server, log in to a MySQL client session as the root user and issue the commands:

```
FLUSH TABLES WITH READ LOCK;
SHOW MASTER STATUS;
```

This will prevent any changes from being made to the database until you are ready to bring up the cluster. You may also (depending on whether this server has been run with binary logging) see some data about the location of the binary log file and offset. If so, write it down; if not, use the default values ' ' (empty string) and 4, respectively.

Next, copy the master database structure and data. There are two ways to do this. The first is to simply copy the mysql/data directory into a tarball or zip file by using one of these commands or a GUI procedure:

```
tar -cvf master_snapshot.tar data/
zip master_snapshot.zip data/
```

Alternatively, you can use mysqldump to make a backup as described in the next section. Copy this snapshot file to each slave server.

Now shut down all the master and slave servers. Quit out of any mysql client shell sessions, and issue the command:

```
mysqladmin -u root -p shutdown
```

on each server. The reason you are shutting the servers down is to give them unique server-id values. They will use these values to find each other when they establish the master-slave relationship. This value is set in each server's my.cnf file and will be read in on startup. On Windows, the my.cnf file is located in one of two places: C:\my.cnf or C:\[Windows directory]\my.ini. On Unix systems, the global my.cnf file is found in /etc/my.cnf and the server-specific file (which is probably the one you want to use) is found in /path/to/mysql/data/my.cnf.

First, set the server-id on the master machine. Find or create a file called my.cnf in the proper location for your platform, and make sure it contains the lines:

```
[mysqld]
log-bin
server-id=1
```

Restart the master server:

```
bin/mysqld_safe --user=mysql
```

In each slave server's my.cnf files, you need only the server-id, not the log-bin line. The most important thing is that you are absolutely positive that all the server-id values in your cluster are unique! If they are not, bad things will happen. So the first slave's my.cnf file would contain this line:

```
[mysqld]
server-id=2
```

The second slave would set server-id=3, and so forth.

Now, before you bring up each slave server, you may need to do a little bit of housekeeping. If this MySQL server has been used as a slave before, you may want to delete the files data/master.info and data/relay-log.info. You may also want to delete the .err and .pid files in the data directory. Also, if you copied the master's data snapshot into a tarball or zipfile, now is the time to copy it to the slave with a command like one of these (from the mysql directory):

```
tar -xvf master_snapshot.tar
unzip master_snapshot.zip
```

If you used mysqldump instead, you have to wait until the server is back up.

Now bring up the slave:

```
bin/mysqld_safe --user=mysql --skip-slave-start --log-warnings
```

If you took your master data snapshot with mysqldump, now is the time to apply the SQL file to the slave:

```
mysql -u root -p databasename < master_snapshot.sql
```

Finally, you will establish the master-slave relationship. Log in to a mysql shell and then enter the following commands, substituting the values you wrote down at the beginning of the process:

```
CHANGE MASTER TO
    MASTER_HOST='masterhostname',
    MASTER_USER='replicant',
    MASTER_PASSWORD='replpwd',
    MASTER_LOG_FILE='',
    MASTER_LOG_POS=4;
START SLAVE;
```

If there are problems, they will appear in the slave machine's error log.

Recovery

Normally, MySQL does not require much attention. MySQL servers have happily puttered away for months if not years with minimal administration. However, bad things do happen to data: Hard disks melt down, hosting centers lose power suddenly, and human error is a constant and awful probability. If you have insufficient memory for all the applications you're running on a server, or insufficient disk space on a partition, you may also get an error that requires a recovery process. It must be admitted that MySQL seems to have minor database corruption events with greater frequency than heavier-weight databases — or perhaps it's just easier for the administrator to notice these events.

Luckily, MySQL is designed to make it amazingly easy to repair small flaws in your data and get back up quickly. Only once have we had to actually scrap an entire database after repeated attempts at recovery, and that disaster was caused by a total hard disk failure, which is something a developer can do nothing to plan for or recover gracefully from — except make frequent backups.

MySQL has long shipped with a command-line tool called `myisamchk` for checking and repairing tables. This was a fine script but it suffered from one flaw: It could be run effectively only when the database was shut down. That's fine when you're actually recovering from a disaster, since you're unlikely to be able to start your database anyway, but it's a significant barrier to trying to head off problems by regularly checking your data tables. Luckily, there is now a new tool that can be used during operation — `mysqlcheck`. You can continue to use `myisamchk` when the server is not running.

Both these tools basically can do three things: check a MyISAM table for errors, repair problems, and optimize the database. The syntax by which you use the scripts is different, however.

myisamchk

The `myisamchk` utility is invoked like this:

```
myisamchk [options] table_name
```

or

```
myisamchk [options] /path/to/mysql/data/database/table.MYI
```

You can wildcard both database directories and table names with an asterisk, which is more common than specifying a table, since you usually don't know exactly which table is causing the problems. Use the following commands to check all the tables of all the databases on a server:

```
myisamchk [options] /path/to/mysql/data/*/*.MYI
myisamchk [options] /path/to/mysql/data/*/*.MYD
```

.MYI extensions designate index files, and .MYD extensions designate data files — you need to check both.

With no option flags, `myisamchk` will simply check the designated table. If you pass the `-r` option flag, `myisamchk` will repair the designated tables. You can also check and repair any corrupted tables in a single operation:

```
myisamchk --silent --force --fast --update-state -O
key_buffer=64M -O sort_buffer=64M -O read_buffer=1 -O
write_buffer=1M /path/to/mysql/data/*/*.MYI
```

The command `myisamchk -r tablename` will also optimize a table that has been fragmented by deletes and updates.

mysqlcheck

The new `mysqlcheck` tool has several handy advantages over `myisamchk`. As previously mentioned, it can be used while the server is running — even while serving up queries. It works on databases rather than tables, using the same syntax as the `mysqldump` tool. And instead of having to remember the meaning of a bunch of option flags, you can copy and rename the executable to get different behaviors.

The `mysqlcheck` tool is invoked in one of these ways:

```
mysqlcheck [options] databasename table1 table2 table3
mysqlcheck [options] --databases database1 database2
mysqlcheck [options] --all-databases
```

To repair, analyze, or optimize databases, you simply copy the `mysqlcheck` file and change its name to `mysqlrepair`, `mysqlanalyze`, or `mysqloptimize` — and then invoke it the same way. So, for instance, to repair all the databases on your server, you might give this command:

```
mysqlrepair -u root -p --all-databases
```

MySQL AB recommends that you set up a regular schedule of data file checking via cronjob, plus run one of these utilities every time you start up your MySQL server. This should help keep your data written out compactly for fast reads, head off problems while they're still tiny, and minimize your chances of a database problem that is visible to your users.

Summary

MySQL is one of the easiest databases to administer, and learning to do so will offer many benefits to PHP developers. MySQL installations have become easier of late on many platforms, and there are GUI as well as command-line tools available to help you view the structure of your database, manage database users, and make backups. More advanced MySQL administration tasks include disaster recovery and replication — both of which are probably as easy to accomplish on MySQL as they could possibly be made. However, even long-time MySQL users should consider the impact of recent changes to the MySQL-PHP relationship: licensing issues, client-version incompatibility, the new mysqli extension, and transactions.

✦   ✦   ✦

PHP/MySQL Functions

After you've installed and set up your MySQL database, you can begin to write PHP scripts that interact with it. Here we will try to explain all the basic functions that enable you to pass data back and forth from Web site to database.

Note   Information related to creating a MySQL database is at the end of this chapter, because it is a more advanced skill that builds on the fundamental MySQL skills discussed in the earlier parts of the chapter.

The development version of MySQL, the 4.1.x series, introduces several new features that require some rewriting of the existing MySQL support in PHP. This new extension to PHP is called *MySQL Improved*. It must be built into PHP at install time using the `--with-mysqli` configuration directive, and the functions it offers are exposed with the `mysqli_` prefix rather than the older `mysql_` prefix. The production quality versions of both the MySQL 4.1 series and the new PHP extension for it are some way off yet, so our focus is on the current support, which should cover the bulk of the existing MySQL/PHP installations. The functions are, for the most part, analogous. We will, however, point out the corresponding `mysqli` functions where appropriate and highlight any differences so you'll have an idea what to expect if and when you decide to make the switch.

Connecting to MySQL

The basic command to initiate a MySQL connection is

```
mysql_connect($hostname, $user, $password);
```

if you're using variables, or

```
mysql_connect('localhost', 'root', 'sesame');
```

if you're using literal strings.

The password is optional, depending on whether this particular database user requires one (it's a good idea). If not, just leave that variable off. You can also specify a port and socket for the server (`$hostname:port:socket`), but unless you've specifically chosen a nonstandard port and socket, there's little to gain by doing so.

The corresponding `mysqli` function is `mysqli_connect`, which adds a fourth parameter allowing you to select a database in the same function you use to connect. The function `mysqli_select_db` exists, but you'll need it only if you want to use multiple databases on the same connection.

You do not need to establish a new connection each time you want to query the database in the same script. You will need to run this function again, however, for each script that interacts with the database in some fashion.

Next, you'll want to choose a database to work on:

```
mysql_select_db($database);
```

if you're using variables; or

```
mysql_select_db('phpbook');
```

if you're using a literal string.

Tip You will sometimes see these two functions used with an @ prepended, such as @mysql_select_db($database). This symbol denotes *silent mode*, meaning the function will not return any message on failure, as a security precaution. You should have display_errors set to off on production servers anyway.

You must select a database each time you make a connection, which means at least once per page or every time you change databases. Otherwise, you'll get a Database not selected error. Even if you've created only one database per daemon, you must do this, because MySQL also comes with default databases (called mysql and test) you might not be taking into account.

You may find it convenient to group all your connection information into a custom connect function and put it someplace where you can access it from all your scripts, such as the php includes directory, or in the case of a virtual server, a site-specific include file. This function might look like the following:

```
// Connect to a single db
function qdbconn() {
  $dbUser = "myuser";
  $dbPass = "mypassword";
  $dbName = "mydatabase";
  $dbHost = "myhost";
  if (!($link=mysql_connect($dbHost, $dbUser, $dbPass))) {
    error_log(mysql_error(), 3, "/tmp/phplog.err");
  }
  if (!mysql_select_db($dbName, $link)) {
    error_log(mysql_error(), 3, "/tmp/phplog.err");
  }
}
```

If you like, you could extend this function by creating links (for example, $link1, $link2) to multiple databases on the same server. This code also records a MySQL error message to the PHP error log.

Now that you've established a connection to a specific database, you're ready to make a query.

Making MySQL Queries

A database query from PHP is basically a MySQL command wrapped up in a tiny PHP function called `mysql_query()`. This is where you use the basic SQL workhorses of `SELECT`, `INSERT`, `UPDATE`, and `DELETE` that we discussed in Chapter 13. The MySQL commands to `CREATE` or `DROP` a table (but *not*, thankfully, those to create or drop an entire database) can also be used with this PHP function if you do not wish to make your databases using the MySQL client.

You could write a query in the simplest possible way, as follows:

```
mysql_query("SELECT Surname FROM personal_info WHERE ID<10");
```

PHP would dutifully try to execute it. However, there are very good reasons to split up this and similar commands into two lines with extra variables, like this:

```
$query = "SELECT Surname FROM personal_info WHERE ID<10";
$result = mysql_query($query);
```

The main rationale is that the extra variable gives you a handle on an extremely valuable piece of information. Every MySQL query gives you a receipt whether you succeed or not — sort of like a cash machine when you try to withdraw money. If things go well, you hardly need or notice the receipt — you can throw it away without a qualm. But if a problem occurs, the receipt will give you a clue as to what might have gone wrong, similar to the "Is the machine not dispensing or is your account overdrawn?" type of message that might be printed on your ATM receipt.

Another advantage of assigning the query string to a variable is that you can more easily view the query if you run into an error. Of course, you would accomplish this by writing the variable out to an error log — never by dumping it out to the browser in production!

The function `mysql_query` takes as arguments the query string (which should not have a semicolon within the double quotes) and optionally a link identifier. Unless you have multiple connections, you don't need the link identifier. It returns a `TRUE` (nonzero) integer value if the query was executed successfully *even if no rows were affected*. It returns a `FALSE` integer if the query was illegal or not properly executed for some other reason.

For purposes of this chapter, we've left the link identifier off; however, if you need to use multiple databases in your script, you can use code like the following:

```
$query = "SELECT Surname FROM personal_info WHERE ID<10"
$result = mysql_query($query, $link_1);
$query = "SELECT * FROM orders WHERE date>20030702"
$result = mysql_query($query, $link_2);
```

As expected, the MySQL Improved analog for this function is `mysqli_query`. It is very similar to its counterpart, however the `link` and `query` parameters change places and a third parameter allows you to specify a result flag indicating how PHP should handle the result.

If your query was an `INSERT`, `UPDATE`, `DELETE`, `CREATE TABLE`, or `DROP TABLE` and returned `TRUE`, you can now use `mysql_affected_rows` to see how many rows were changed by the query. This function optionally takes a link identifier, only necessary if you are using multiple connections. It *does not* take the result handle as an argument! You call the function like this, without a result handle:

```
$affected_rows = mysql_affected_rows();
```

If your query was a SELECT statement, you can use mysql_num_rows($result) to find out how many rows were returned by a successful SELECT.

The mysqli_affected_rows and mysqli_num_rows behave exactly the same as their mysql_ counterparts.

Tip   The mysql_num_rows function can be useful in paginating large data sets returned by MySQL queries.

Fetching Data Sets

One thing that often seems to temporarily stymie new PHP users is the whole concept of fetching data from PHP. It would be logical to assume the result of a query would be the desired data, but that is not correct. As we discussed in the previous section, the result of a PHP query is an integer representing the success or failure or identity of the query.

What actually happens is that a mysql_query() command pulls the data out of the database and sends a receipt back to PHP reporting on the status of the operation. At this point, the data exists in a purgatory that is immediately accessible from neither MySQL nor PHP — you can think of it as a staging area of sorts. The data is there, but it's waiting for the commanding officer to give the order to deploy. It requires one of the mysql_fetch functions to make the data fully available to PHP.

The fetching functions are as follows:

✦ mysql_fetch_row: Returns row as an enumerated array

✦ mysql_fetch_object: Returns row as an object

✦ mysql_fetch_array: Returns row as an associative array

✦ mysql_result: Returns one cell of data

Caution   In our humble opinion, the functions mysql_fetch_field and mysql_fetch_lengths are misleadingly named. They both provide information *about* database entries rather than the entry values themselves. For instance, one might expect a function named mysql_fetch_field to be a quick way to fetch a single-field result set (the ID associated with a particular username, for instance), but that is not the case at all. The actual purpose of these functions is explained in Table 15-2 at the end of the chapter — but for the moment, the point is not to be misled into thinking these functions will return database values.

The difference between the three main fetching functions is small. The most general one is mysql_fetch_row, which can be used something like this:

```
$query = "SELECT ID, LastName, FirstName
          FROM users WHERE Status = 1";
$result = mysql_query($query);
while ($name_row = mysql_fetch_row($result)) {
  print("$name_row[0] $name_row[1] $name_row[2]<BR>\n");
}
```

This code will output the specified rows from the database, each line containing one row or the information associated with a unique ID (if any).

Caution In an enumerated array, the integers in brackets are called *field offsets*. Remember that they always begin with the integer zero. If you start counting at 1, you will miss the value of your first column.

The function `mysql_fetch_object` performs much the same task, except the row is returned as an object rather than an array. Obviously, this is helpful for those among the PHP brethren who utilize the object-oriented notation:

```
$query = "SELECT ID, LastName, FirstName
          FROM users WHERE Status = 1";
$result = mysql_query($query);
while ($row = mysql_fetch_object($result)) {
  echo "$row->ID, $row->LastName, $row->FirstName<BR>\n";
}
```

The most useful fetching function, `mysql_fetch_array`, offers the choice of results as an associative or an enumerated array — or both, which is the default. This means you can refer to outputs by database field name rather than number:

```
$query = "SELECT ID, LastName, FirstName
          FROM users WHERE Status = 1";
$result = mysql_query($query);
while ($row = mysql_fetch_array($result)) {
  echo "$row['ID'], $row['LastName'], $row['FirstName']<BR>\n";
}
```

Remember that `mysql_fetch_array` can *also* be used exactly the same way as `mysql_fetch_row` — with numerical identifiers rather than field names. By using this function, you leave yourself the option. If you want to specify offset or field name rather than making both available, you can do it like this:

```
$offset_row = mysql_fetch_array($result, MYSQL_NUM);
or
$associative_row = mysql_fetch_array($result, MYSQL_ASSOC);
```

It's also possible to use `MYSQL_BOTH` as the second value, but because that's the default, it's redundant.

In early versions of PHP, `mysql_fetch_row` was considered to be significantly faster than `mysql_fetch_object` and `mysql_fetch_array`, but this is no longer an issue, as the speed differences have become imperceptible. The PHP junta now recommends use of `mysql_fetch_array` over `mysql_fetch_row` because it offers increased functionality and choice at little cost in terms of programming difficulty, performance loss, or maintainability.

Last and least of the fetching functions is `mysql_result()`. You should only even *consider* using this function in situations where you are positive you need only one piece of data to be returned from MySQL. An example of its usage follows:

```
$query = "SELECT count(*) FROM personal_info";
$db_result = mysql_query($query);
$datapoint = mysql_result($db_result, 0, 0);
```

The `mysql_result` function takes three arguments: *result identifier*, *row identifier*, and (optionally) *field*. Field can take the value of the field offset as above, or its name as in an associative array (`"Surname"`), or its MySQL field-dot-table name (`"personal_info.Surname"`).

Use the offset if at all possible, as it is substantially faster than the other two. Even better, don't use this function with any frequency. A well-formed query will almost always return a specific result more efficiently.

Caution   You should never use `mysql_result()` to return information that is available to you through a predefined PHP-MySQL function. The classic no-no is inserting a row and then selecting out its ID number (extra demerits if you select on `MAX(ID)`!). Wicked bad style — use `mysql_insert_id()` instead.

All of the PHP functions for fetching MySQL data have identical `mysqli` counterparts. They take the same parameters and return comparable results.

A special MySQL function can be used with any of the fetching functions to more specifically designate the row number desired. This is `mysql_data_seek`, which takes as arguments the result identifier and a row number and moves the internal row pointer to that row of the data set. The most common use of this function is to reiterate through a result set from the beginning by re-setting the row number to zero, similar to an array reset. This obviates another expensive database call to get data you already have sitting around on the PHP side. Here's an example of using `mysql_data_seek()`:

```php
<?php
echo("<TABLE>\n<TR><TH>Titles</TH></TR>\n<TR>");
$query = "SELECT title, publisher FROM books";
$result = mysql_query($query);
while ($book_row = mysql_fetch_array($result)) {
  echo("<TD>$book_row[0]</TD>\n");
}
echo("</TR></TABLE><BR>\n");
echo("<TABLE>\n<TR><TH>Publishers</TH></TR>\n<TR>");
mysql_data_seek($result, 0);
while ($book_row = mysql_fetch_array($result)) {
  echo("<TD>$book_row[1]</TD>\n");
}
echo("</TR></TABLE><BR>\n");
?>
```

Without using `mysql_data_seek`, the second usage of the result set would turn back no 0 rows because it has already iterated through to the end of the dataset and the pointer stays there until you explicitly move it. This handy function helps greatly when you are formatting data in a way that does not place fields in columns and records in rows.

Getting Data about Data

You only need four PHP functions to put data into or get data out of a preexisting MySQL database: `mysql_connect`, `mysql_select_db`, `mysql_query`, and `mysql_fetch_array`. Most of the rest of the functions in this section are about getting information about the data you put into or took out of the database or about the construction of the database itself. PHP offers extensive built-in functions to help you learn the name of the table in which your data resides, the data type handled by a particular column, or the number of the row into which you just inserted data. With these functions, you can effectively work with a database about which you know very little.

Caution   Obviously, you don't want J. Random Cracker to be able to find out everything about the structure and contents of your database for the asking. If you have scripts that use these functions extensively — for instance, some kind of Web database-administration tool — you need a higher level of security. Make sure only the root MySQL user can use these tools, and preferably use forms to pass in a password every time, or use one of the methods to limit usage to certain IP addresses.

The MySQL metadata functions fall into two major categories:

✦ Functions that return information about the previous operation only.

✦ Functions that return information about the database structure in general.

A very commonly used example of the first type is mysql_insert_id(), which returns the autoincremented ID assigned to a row of data you just inserted. A commonly used example of the second type is mysql_field_type(), which reveals whether a particular database field's data must be an integer, a varchar, text, or what have you. Observe however, that this function is also deceptively named. Rather than returning the MySQL type, it returns the PHP data type. For example, an ENUM-type field will return 'string'. Use mysql_field_flags to return more specialized field information. This should be apparent when you consider that it works on a result rather than on an actual MySQL field. It would be useful to have a function that got the possible values for an ENUM field; but there isn't a canned version at this point. Instead, use a "describe table" query and parse the result using PHP's regex functions.

Most of the data-about-data functions are pretty self-explanatory. There are a couple of things to keep in mind when using them, though. First, most of these functions are only effective if used in the proper combination — don't try to use a mysql_affected_rows after a SELECT query and then wonder what went wrong. Second, be careful about security with the functions that return information about your database structure. Knowing the name and structure of each table is very valuable to a cracker. And finally, be aware that some of these functions are shopping baskets full of simpler functions. If you need several pieces of information about a particular result set or database, it could be faster to use mysql_fetch_field than all the mysql_field functions one after the other.

All of the MySQL metadata functions are fairly easy to use. However, their efficacy is directly related to intelligent database design rather than a mere marker of the PHP's strengths. Good database practices will make these functions useful over the long haul. The mysqli equivalent functions are perfect analogues in each of these cases.

Multiple Connections

Unless you have a specific reason to require multiple connections, you only need to make one database connection per PHP page. Even if you escape into HTML many times within the page, your connection is still good (assuming it was good in the first place). You do not want to make multiple connections if you don't have to, because that is one of the most costly and time-consuming parts of most database queries.

Conversely, there's no easy way to keep your connection open from page to page — because PHP and MySQL would never know for sure when to close it after visitors wander off. Therefore, your connection is closed at the end of each script unless you use persistent connections.

The main reason you would need to use different connections is if you're querying two or more completely separate databases. The most common situation in which you might do this is when you're using MySQL in a replicated situation. MySQL replication is accomplished through a master-slave setup, where you typically get reads from a slave and make writes to the master.

To use multiple connections, you simply open connections to each database as needed, and make sure to hang on to the right result sets. PHP will help you do this by utilizing the result identifiers discussed in the "Making MySQL Queries" section earlier in the chapter. You pass the identifiers along with each MySQL function as an optional argument. If you're completing all your queries on one connection before moving on to the next, you don't even need to do this; PHP will automatically use the last link opened.

In this example, we are using connections from three different databases on different servers:

```php
<?php
$link1 = mysql_connect('host1', 'me', 'sesame');
mysql_select_db('userdb', $link1);
$query1 = "SELECT ID FROM usertable
           WHERE username = '$username'";
$result1 = mysql_query($query1, $link1);
$array1 = mysql_fetch_array($result1);
$usercount = mysql_num_rows($result1);
mysql_close($link1);

$today = '2002-05-01';
$link2 = mysql_connect('host2', 'myself', 'benne');
mysql_select_db('inventorydb', $link2);
$query2 = "SELECT sku FROM widgets
           WHERE ship_date = '$today'";
$result2 = mysql_query($query2, $link2);
$array2 = mysql_fetch_array($result2);
$widgetcount = mysql_num_rows($result2);
mysql_close($link2);

if ($usercount > 0 && $widgetcount > 0) {
  $link3 = mysql_connect('host3', 'I', 'seed');
  mysql_select_db('salesdb', $link3);
  $query3 = "INSERT INTO saleslog (ID, date, userID, sku)
          VALUES (NULL, '$today', '$array1[0]', '$array2[0]')";
  $result3 = mysql_query($query3, $link3);
  $insertID = mysql_insert_id($link3);
  mysql_close($link3);
  if ($insertID >= 1) {
    print("Perfect entry");
  }
  else {
    print("Danger, danger, Will Robinson!");
  }
} else {
  print("Not enough information");
}
?>
```

In this example, we have deliberately kept the connections as discrete as possible for clarity's sake, even going to the trouble to close each link after we use it. Without the `mysql_close()` commands, we would be running multiple concurrent connections—which you may want to do. There's nothing stopping you from doing so. Just remember to pass the link value carefully from one function to the next, and you should be fine.

Building in Error Checking

This section could have been titled "Die, die, die!" because the main error-checking function is actually called `die()`. There was something about that title that failed to reinforce the warm, hospitable learning environment we cherish, so we went with the more prosaic subheading.

`die()` is not a MySQL-specific function—the PHP manual lists it in "Miscellaneous Functions." It simply terminates the script (or a delimited portion thereof) and returns a string of your choice.

```
mysql_query("SELECT * FROM mutual_funds
          WHERE code = '$searchstring'")
or die("Please check your query and try again.");
```

Notice the syntax: the word `or` (you could alternatively use `||`, but that isn't as much fun as saying `or die`) and only one semicolon per pair of alternatives.

Until quite recently, MySQL via PHP returned very insecure and unenlightening (except to crackers) error messages upon encountering a problem with a database query. `die()` was often used as a way to exert control over what the public would see on failure. Now that no error messages are returned at all, `die()` may be even more necessary—unless you want your visitors to be left wondering what happened.

Other built-in means of error-checking are error messages. These are particularly helpful during the development and debugging phase, and they can be easily commented out in the final edit before going live on a production server. As mentioned, MySQL error messages no longer appear by default. If you want them, you have to ask for them by using the functions `mysql_errno()` (which returns a code number for each error type) or `mysql_error()` (which returns the text message). Then you can send them to a custom error log by using the `error_log()` function:

```
if (!mysql_select_db($bad_db)) {
  print(mysql_error());
}
```

There's more to database error-handling than judicious use of `die()`, however. Servers become unavailable, data sets get corrupted, and so forth. We've been fairly liberal in setting up connections and executing queries; but ideally, every interaction with the database should be nested inside a conditional that returns the desired result on success and a nice clean error page on failure. This is where `die()` drops the ball. Execution immediately stops for the entire script, leaving off, if nothing else, closing tags for your HTML page if they are defined in PHP. Additionally, there may be plenty more perfectly good scripting or html left to go on the page—code that is unaffected by a dropped database connection or a failed query. Finally, `die()` doesn't let you know anything went wrong. Do you really think your users will tell you? Probably not. It's much more realistic that they will leave your site in disgust and never return. An example of good error checking is shown as follows.

```
function printError($errorMesg) {
  printf("<B>%s </B><BR>\n", $errorMesg);
}
function notify($errorMesg) {
  mail(webmaster@site.com, "An Error has occurred at
example.com", $errorMesg)
}
if ($link = mysql_connect("host", "user", "pass") {
  // Things to do if the connection is successful
} else {
  printError("Sorry for the inconvenience; but we are unable
to process your request at this time. Please check back
later");
  notify("Problem connecting to database in $SCRIPT_NAME at
line 12 on date('Y-m-D')");
            }
```

Even better, if you really want to get your feet wet with PHP5's new OOP features, try using exceptions, which we covered briefly in Chapter 6 and which get a more complete treatment in Chapter 31.

Creating MySQL Databases with PHP

You can, if you wish, actually create your databases with PHP rather than using the MySQL client tool. This practice has potential advantages — you can use an attractive front end that may appeal to those who find the MySQL command-line client horribly plain or finicky to use — counterbalanced by one big disadvantage, which is security.

Cross-Reference See Chapter 14 for more information on how to minimize security issues when defining MySQL databases with PHP.

To create a database from PHP, the user of your scripts will need to have full CREATE/DROP privileges on MySQL. That means anyone who can get hold of your scripts can potentially blow away all your databases and their contents with the greatest of ease. This is not such a great idea from a security standpoint. Furthermore, most external Web hosts very sensibly won't let you do it on their servers anyway.

If you're even considering creating databases with PHP, do yourself a big favor and at least don't store the database username and password in a text file. Make yourself type your database username and password into a form and pass the variables to the inserting handler each and every time you use this script. This is one case where keeping the variables in an include file outside your Web tree is not sufficient precaution.

For those who like to live dangerously, the relevant functions are:

✦ mysql_create_db(): Creates a database on the designated host, with name specified in arguments.

✦ mysql_drop_db(): Deletes the specified database.

✦ mysql_query(): Pass table definitions and drops in this function.

A bare-bones database-generation script might look like this:

```php
<?php
$linkID = mysql_connect('localhost', 'root', 'sesame');
mysql_create_db('new_db', $linkID);
mysql_select_db('new_db');
$query = "CREATE TABLE new_table (
        id INT NOT NULL AUTO_INCREMENT PRIMARY KEY,
     new_col VARCHAR(25)
        )";
$result = mysql_query($query);
$axe = mysql_drop_db('new_db');
?>
```

There are also prefab tools like phpMyAdmin that do much of this for you in a pretty way (see Chapter 14 for information about using phpMyAdmin). You simply fill out a Web form, and the PHP script on the back end will create the database according to your specifications. In many cases, the tool will also enable you to perform other administrative tasks, such as checking the sizes of your databases or backing them up. This is even less secure than doing it yourself (insofar as you probably won't check over every line of the code with an eye to security), but apparently people do use these tools without incident.

Several other GUI tools are available that are not database-specific but will probably work with MySQL. As MySQL has become more and more popular, a number of applications for both Windows and Linux have come into play that allow you to administer MySQL databases in the graphical fashion you may have become accustomed to. Like their Web counterparts, these applications offer full administrative control, but without the headache of exposing yourself to the security risk of a Web-based interface. The list changes often as software comes and goes, so a listing here would probably very quickly go out of date. However, the MySQL Web site keeps a pretty comprehensive list at www.mysql.com/portal/software/index.html.

Caution If you insist on using a Web GUI tool to design your databases, at least minimize the security hazards by only using it on a development machine inside the firewall. After you've fiddled with the database design to your heart's content, you can initiate a database dump and then move the entire structure and code over to a production database server. Do not use PHPMyAdmin or any other Web GUI in production unless it is absolutely necessary.

MySQL data types

The actual PHP functions used to create MySQL databases are trivial compared to the MySQL data structure statements that are passed in those functions. The "Database Design" section of Chapter13 has general rules on how to conceptualize a database schema and use the CREATE, DROP, and ALTER statements. To implement your abstract schema in MySQL, however, you also need to understand MySQL data types and how to use them.

The general rule is to use the smallest and most specific data type that will adequately meet the needs of this particular column in your database. MySQL is known for having compact types, such as TINYINT and TINYTEXT, that are good for things like 0/1 values or firstnames. It also has very large types that can store up to 4GB of data in one field.

There are three buckets of MySQL data types: numeric types, date and time types, and string (or character) types. For the most part, their use can be fairly straightforward — in the sense that the average user is not going to know or care whether you used an INT or a MEDIUMINT. However, if you're the type of programmer who cares about doing everything in the absolutely tightest and fastest way possible, the MySQL manual gives subtle tips on maximizing efficiency — for instance, always use the DECIMAL type with money, or it takes 8 bytes to store a DATETIME but only 4 bytes to store a Unix TIMESTAMP, which PHP can convert to any date-time format you desire. Careful perusal of the "Column Types" section of the MySQL manual (at www.mysql.com/doc/en/Column_types.html) may yield hidden treasures of insight.

Table 15-1 shows the current MySQL data types and their possible values. M stands for the maximum number of digits displayed, and D stands for the maximum number of decimal places in a floating-point number. Both are optional.

Table 15-1: MySQL Data Types

Name and Aliases	Storage size	Usage
TINYINT(M)		
BIT, BOOL, BOOLEAN are synonyms for TINYINT(1)	1 byte	If unsigned, stores values from 0 to 255; otherwise, from -128 to 127. A new Boolean type will appear in future, but until now has been implemented as a TINYINT(1).
SMALLINT(M)	2 bytes	If unsigned, stores values from 0 to 65535; otherwise, from -32768 to 32767.
MEDIUMINT(M)	3 bytes	If unsigned, stores values from 0 to 16777215; otherwise, from -8388608 to 8388607.
INT(M) INTEGER(M)	4 bytes	If unsigned, stores values from 0 to 4294967295; otherwise, from -2147483648 to 2147483647.
BIGINT(M)	8 bytes	If unsigned, stores values from 0 to 18446744073709551615; otherwise, from -9223372036854775808 to 9223372036854775807. You may experience strangeness when performing arithmetic with unsigned integers of this size.
FLOAT(precision)	4 or 8 bytes	Where precision is an integer up to 53. If precision <= 24, converted to a FLOAT; if precision > 24 and <= 53, converted to a DOUBLE. Provided for ODBC compatibility; in general, use the normal MySQL FLOAT and DOUBLE types.
FLOAT(M, D)	4 bytes	Single-precision floating-point number.

Name and Aliases	Storage size	Usage
`DOUBLE(M, D)` `DOUBLE PRECISION, REAL`	8 bytes	Double-precision floating-point number.
`DECIMAL(M,D)` `DEC, NUMERIC, FIXED`	M+1 or M+2 bytes	An unpacked floating-point number that is stored like a `CHAR`. Used for small decimals, such as money.
`DATE`	3 bytes	Displayed in the format `YYYY-MM-DD`.
`DATETIME` `HH:MM:SS.`	8 bytes	Displayed in the format `YYYY-MM-DD`.
`TIMESTAMP`	4 bytes	Since MySQL 4.1, can no longer set display size. Displayed in the same format as `DATETIME`.
`TIME`	3 bytes	Displayed in the format `HHH:MM:SS` where `HHH` is a value from -838 to 838. This allows a `TIME` value to represent an elapsed time between two events.
`YEAR`	1 byte	Displayed in the format `YYYY`, which is a value from 1901 to 2155. To use an earlier date, you should use a `TINYINT` type.
`CHAR(M)`	M bytes	Fixed in length. If your string is not long enough, it will be padded with spaces at the end. M must be <= 255.
`VARCHAR(M)`	Up to M bytes	Variable in length. M must be <= 255.
`TINYBLOB` or `TINYTEXT`	Up to 255 bytes	`TINYBLOB` is case-sensitive for sorting and comparison; `TINYTEXT` is case-insensitive.
`BLOB` or `TEXT`	Up to 64KB	`BLOB` is case-sensitive for sorting and comparison; `TEXT` is case-insensitive.
`MEDIUMBLOB` or `MEDIUMTEXT`	Up to 16MB	`MEDIUMBLOB` is case-sensitive for sorting and comparison; `MEDIUMTEXT` is case-insensitive.
`LONGBLOB` or `LONGTEXT`	Up to 4GB	`LONGBLOB` is case-sensitive for sorting and comparison; `LONGTEXT` is case-insensitive.
`ENUM(value1, ...valueN)`	1 or 2 bytes	Up to 65535 distinct values.
`SET(value1,... valueN)`	Up to 8 bytes	Up to 64 distinct values.

MySQL Functions

Table 15-2 includes a recap of the MySQL functions. All arguments in brackets are optional.

Table 15-2: PHP-MySQL Functions

Function Name	Usage
mysql_affected_rows([link_id])	Use after a nonzero INSERT, UPDATE, or DELETE query to check number of rows changed.
mysql_change_user(user, password[, database][, link_id])	Changes MySQL user on an open link.
mysql_close([link_id])	Closes the identified link (usually unnecessary).
mysql_connect([host][:port][:socket] [, username][, password])	Opens a link on the specified host, port, socket; as specified user with password. All arguments are optional.
mysql_create_db(db_name[, link_id])	Creates a new MySQL database on the host associated with the nearest open link.
mysql_data_seek(result_id, row_num)	Moves internal row pointer to specified row number. Use a fetching function to return data from that row.
mysql_drop_db(db_name[, link_id])	Drops specified MySQL database.
mysql_errno([link_id])	Returns ID of error.
mysql_error([link_id])	Returns text error message.
mysql_fetch_array(result_id[, result_type])	Fetches result set as associative array. Result type can be MYSQL_ASSOC, MYSQL_NUM, or MYSQL_BOTH (default).
mysql_fetch_field(result_id[, field_offset])	Returns information about a field as an object.
mysql_fetch_lengths(result_id)	Returns length of each field in a result set.
mysql_fetch_object(result_id[, result_type])	Fetches result set as an object. See mysql_fetch_array for result types.
mysql_fetch_row(result_id)	Fetches result set as an enumerated array.
mysql_field_name(result_id, field_index)	Returns name of enumerated field.
mysql_field_seek(result_id, field_offset)	Moves result pointer to specified field offset. Used with mysql_fetch_field.
mysql_field_table(result_id, field_offset)	Returns name of specified field's table.
mysql_field_type(result_id, field_offset)	Returns type of offset field (for example, TINYINT, BLOB, VARCHAR).
mysql_field_flags(result_id, field_offset)	Returns flags associated with enumerated field (for example, NOT NULL, AUTO_INCREMENT, BINARY).

Function Name	Usage
mysql_field_len(*result_id*, *field_offset*)	Returns length of enumerated field.
mysql_free_result(*result_id*)	Frees memory used by result set (usually unnecessary).
mysql_insert_id([*link_id*])	Returns AUTO_INCREMENTED ID of INSERT; or FALSE if insert failed or last query was not an insert.
mysql_list_fields(*database*, *table*[, *link_id*])	Returns result ID for use in mysql_field functions, without performing an actual query.
mysql_list_dbs([*link_id*])	Returns result pointer of databases on mysqld. Used with mysql_tablename.
mysql_list_tables(*database*[, *link_id*])	Returns result pointer of tables in database. Used with mysql_tablename.
mysql_num_fields(*result_id*)	Returns number of fields in a result set.
mysql_num_rows(*result_id*)	Returns number of rows in a result set.
mysql_pconnect([*host*][:*port*][:*socket*] [, *username*][, *password*])	Opens persistent connection to database. All arguments are optional. Be careful — mysql_close and script termination will not close the connection.
mysql_query(*query_string*[, *link_id*])	Sends query to database. Remember to put the semicolon outside the double-quoted query string.
mysql_result(*result_id*, *row_id*, *field_identifier*)	Returns single-field result. Field identifier can be field offset (0), field name (FirstName) or table-dot name (myfield.mytable).
mysql_select_db(*database*[, *link_id*])	Selects database for queries.
mysql_tablename(*result_id*, *table_id*)	Used with any of the mysql_list functions to return the value referenced by a result pointer.

Summary

PHP's MySQL and MySQL Improved functions are easy to use, if sometimes named confusingly. Each instance of a PHP/MySQL interaction must have a connection, a database select, and a query or command that returns a result identifier. The result identifier is like an ATM receipt that reports on the success or failure of an operation.

If data is returned after a SELECT statement, one of the PHP/MySQL fetching functions must also be employed. Data pulled from a MySQL database exists in a kind of limbo until one of the fetching functions is applied to the result set. If you wish to loop through the result set again, you can use mysql_data_seek() to reset the row pointer to zero.

PHP also has a large number of functions that return data about the database itself or about a particular operation. Two of the most common are mysql_num_rows(), which returns the number of rows in a result set; and mysql_insert_id(), which returns the ID of the proximate INSERT operation.

PHP handles much of the MySQL connectivity for you without requiring specific link identifiers or result pointers. The exception comes when you need multiple database connections on the same Web page. In this case, you use exactly the same functions and syntax but simply pass the correct link identifier with most commands.

We do not personally recommend creating MySQL databases with PHP front ends, but the practice has become common. If you need to do so, you should follow a few specific rules.

✦   ✦   ✦

Displaying Queries in Tables

✦   ✦   ✦   ✦

In This Chapter

HTML tables and
MySQL tables

Complex mappings

Creating the sample
tables

✦   ✦   ✦   ✦

Much of the point of PHP is to help you translate between a
back end database and its front end presentation on the Web.
Data can be viewed, added, removed, and tweaked as a result of your
Web user's keystrokes and mouse clicks.

For most of this chapter, we restrict ourselves to ways to use PHP
to *look* at the contents of a database without altering it, using only
the SELECT statement from SQL and displaying the results in HTML
tables. We use a single database example to show different strategies,
including some handy reusable functions. Finally, we look at code to
create the sample data shown in the display examples, using the
INSERT statement.

The two big productivity points from this chapter are:

✦ *Reuse functions* in simple cases. The problem of database table
display shows up over and over in database-enabled site
design. If the display is not complicated, you should be able to
throw the same simple function at the problem rather than
reinventing the wheel with each PHP page you write.

✦ *Choose between techniques* in complex cases. You may find
yourself wanting to pull out a complex combination of information from different tables (which, of course, is part of the point
of using a relational database to begin with). You may not be
able to map this onto a simple reusable function, but there
aren't that many novel solutions either — get to know the alternatives, and you can decide how to trade off efficiency, readability, and your own effort.

Note   This chapter uses the MySQL database and functions exclusively,
but the display strategies should be directly transferable to almost
any SQL-compliant database supported by PHP.

HTML Tables and Database Tables

First of all, some terminology — unfortunately, both relational
databases and HTML scripting use the term *table*, but the term means
very different things in the two cases. A *database table* persistently
stores information in columns, which have predefined names and

types so that the information in them can be recovered later. An *HTML table* is a construct that tells the browser to lay out the table's arbitrary HTML contents in a rectangular array in the browser window. We'll try to always make it clear which kind of table we are talking about.

One-to-one mapping

HTML tables are really constructed out of rows (the `<TR></TR>` construct), and columns have no independent existence — each row has some number of table datum items (the `<TD></TD>` construct), which will produce a nice rectangular array only if there are the same number of TDs for every TR. (There is no corresponding `<TC>` construct that lets you display by column first.) By contrast, *fields* (aka *columns*) in database tables are the more primary entity — defining a table means defining the fields, and then you can add as many rows as you like. In this chapter, we will focus on printing out tables and queries in such a way that each database field prints in its own HTML column, simply because there are usually more database rows than database fields, and people are more used to up-and-down scrolling than left-to-right scrolling. If you find yourself wanting to map database fields to HTML rows, it is a simple inversion exercise.

The simplest case of display is where the structure of a database table or query *does* correspond to the structure of the HTML table we want to display — the database entity has m columns and n rows, and we'd like to display an m-by-n rectangular grid in the user's browser window, with all the cells filled in appropriately.

Example: A single-table displayer

So let's write a simple translator that queries the database for the contents of a single table and displays the results on screen. Here's the top-down outline of how the code will get the job done:

1. Establish a database connection.

2. Construct a query to send to the database.

3. Send the query and hold on to the result identifier that is returned.

4. Using the result identifier, find out how many columns (fields) there are in each row.

5. Start an HTML table.

6. Loop through the database result rows, printing a `<TR></TR>` pair to make a corresponding HTML table row.

7. In each row, retrieve the successive fields and display them wrapped in a `<TD></TD>` pair.

8. Close off the HTML table.

9. Close the database connection.

Finally, we'd like to wrap all the preceding steps up into a handy function that we can use whenever we want to. Also, for reasons of efficiency, we don't want to include the first and last steps of creating and closing the database connection in the function — we may want to use such a function more than once per page, and it wouldn't make sense to open and close the connection each time. Instead, we'll assume we have a connection already and pass the connection to the function along with the table name.

Such a function is shown in Listing 16-1, embedded in a complete PHP page that uses the function to display the contents of a couple of tables.

Listing 16-1: **A table displayer**

```php
<?php
include("/home/phpbook/phpbook-vars.inc");
$global_dbh = mysql_connect($hostname, $username, $password);
mysql_select_db($db, $global_dbh);

function display_db_table($tablename, $connection)
{
  $query_string = "SELECT * FROM $tablename";
  $result_id = mysql_query($query_string, $connection);
  $column_count = mysql_num_fields($result_id);

  print("<TABLE BORDER=1>\n");
  while ($row = mysql_fetch_row($result_id))
    {
      print("<TR ALIGN=LEFT VALIGN=TOP>");
      for ($column_num = 0;
           $column_num < $column_count;
           $column_num++)
        print("<TD>$row[$column_num]</TD>\n");
      print("</TR>\n");
    }
    print("</TABLE>\n");
}
?>

<HTML>
<HEAD>
<TITLE>Cities and countries</TITLE>
</HEAD>
<BODY>

<TABLE><TR><TD>
<?php display_db_table("country", $global_dbh); ?>
</TD><TD>
<?php display_db_table("city", $global_dbh); ?>
</TD></TR></TABLE></BODY></HTML>
```

Some things to notice about this script:

✦ Although the script refers to specific database tables, the display_db_table() function itself is general. You could put the function definition in an include file and then use it anywhere on your site.

✦ The first thing the script does is load in an include file that contains variable assignments for the database name, database username, and database password. It then uses those variables to connect to MySQL and then to choose the desired database. (The fact that this file is located outside the publicly available Web hierarchy makes it *slightly* more secure than just including that information in your code.)

✦ In the function itself, we chose to use a while loop for printing rows and a for loop to print the individual items. We could as easily have used a bounded for loop for both and recovered the number of rows with mysql_num_rows().

✦ The main while loop reflects a very common idiom, which exploits the fact that the value of a PHP assignment statement is the value assigned. The variable $row is assigned to the result of the function mysql_fetch_row(), which will be either an array of values from that row or a false value if there are no more rows. If we're out of rows, $row is false, which means the value of the whole expression is false, which means that the while loop terminates.

✦ We put line breaks (\n) at the end of selected lines, so that the HTML source would have a readable structure when printed or viewed as source from the browser. Notice that these breaks are not HTML line breaks (<BR>) and do not affect the look of the resulting Web page. (In fact, if you want to make it annoying for someone else to scrutinize the HTML you generate, don't put breaks in at all!)

The sample tables

To see the Listing 16-1 script in action, see Figure 16-1, which shows the displayed contents of the Country and City sample tables. These tables have the following structure:

```
Country:
    ID int (auto-incremented primary key)
    continent varchar(50)
    countryname varchar(50)
City:
    ID int (auto-incremented primary key)
    countryID int
    cityname varchar(50)
```

Think of these tables as a rough draft of the database for an eventual online almanac. They employ our usual convention of always having one field per table called ID, which is a primary key and has successive integers assigned to it automatically for each new row. Although you can't tell for sure from the preceding description, the tables have one "relation" embodied in their structure—the countryID field of the City table is matched up with the ID field of the Country table, representing which country the city belongs to. (If you were designing a real almanac database, you would want to take this one step further and break the Country table into a relational pair of Country and Continent tables.)

Cross-Reference

To see how we created these tables and populated them with sample data, see the "Creating the Sample Tables" section at the end of this chapter.

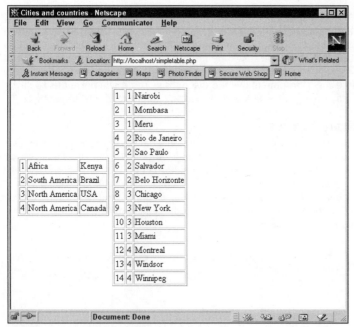

Figure 16-1: A simple database table display

Improving the displayer

Our first version of this function has some limitations: It works with a single table only, does no error-checking, and is very bare-bones in its presentation. We'll address these problems one by one and then fix them in one fell revision. (If you want to look ahead, the new-and-improved version of the function is in Listing 16-2.)

Displaying column headers

Our first version of a database table displayer simply displays all the table cells, without any labeling of what the different fields are. It's conventional in HTML to use the <TH> element for column and/or row headers — in most browsers and styles, this displays as a bold table cell. One improvement we can make is to optionally display column headers that are based on the names of the table fields themselves. To actually retrieve those names, we can use the function mysql_field_name().

Error-checking

Our original version of the code assumes that we have written it correctly and also that our database server is up and functioning normally — if either of these is not the case, we will run into puzzling errors. We can partially address this by appending a call to die() to the actual database queries — if they fail, an informative message will be printed. This is a reasonable approach for such a small example, but as projects get larger it is better to use the exception-handling capability introduced in PHP5.

Cross-Reference   For an introduction to exception handling in PHP5, see Chapter 31.

Cosmetic issues

Another source of dissatisfaction with our simple table-displayer is that it always has the same look. It would be nice, at a minimum, to control whether table borders are displayed. The simple solution we will use in our new function is just to permit passing in a string of arguments that will be spliced into the HTML table definition. This is a pretty crude form of style control that style-sheet proponents would discourage, but it will permit us to directly specify some elements of the table's look without writing an entirely new function.

Displaying arbitrary queries

Finally, it would be nice to be able to exploit our relational database and display the results of complex queries rather than just single tables. Actually, our single-table displayer has an arbitrary query embedded in it — it just happens that it is hard-coded as select * from table, where table is the supplied table name. So let us transform our simple table-displayer into a query-displayer and then recreate the table displayer as a simple wrapper around the query displayer. These two functions, complete with the cosmetic improvements and better error-checking, are shown in Listing 16-2.

Listing 16-2: A query displayer

```php
<?php
include("/home/phpbook/phpbook-vars.inc");
$global_dbh = mysql_connect($hostname, $username, $password)
              or die("Could not connect to database");

mysql_select_db($db, $global_dbh)
  or die("Could not select database");

function display_db_query($query_string, $connection,
                          $header_bool, $table_params)
{

  // perform the database query
  $result_id = mysql_query($query_string, $connection)
               or die("display_db_query:" . mysql_error());

  // find out the number of columns in result
  $column_count = mysql_num_fields($result_id)
                  or die("display_db_query:" . mysql_error());

  // TABLE form includes optional HTML arguments passed
  //  into function
  print("<TABLE $table_params >\n");

  // optionally print a bold header at top of table
  if ($header_bool)
  {
    print("<TR>");
```

```
   for ($column_num = 0;
          $column_num < $column_count;
          $column_num++)
     {
       $field_name =
          mysql_field_name($result_id, $column_num);
       print("<TH>$field_name</TH>");
       }
       print("</TR>\n");
     }
   // print the body of the table
   while ($row = mysql_fetch_row($result_id))
     {
       print("<TR ALIGN=LEFT VALIGN=TOP>");
       for ($column_num = 0;
             $column_num < $column_count;
             $column_num++)
         {
           print("<TD>$row[$column_num]</TD>\n");
         }
       print("</TR>\n");
     }
   print("</TABLE>\n");    }

function display_db_table($tablename, $connection,
                          $header_bool, $table_params)
{
   $query_string = "SELECT * FROM $tablename";
   display_db_query($query_string, $connection,
                    $header_bool, $table_params);
}
?>

<HTML><HEAD><TITLE>Countries and cities</TITLE></HEAD>
<BODY>
<TABLE><TR><TD>
<?php display_db_table("country", $global_dbh,
                       TRUE, "BORDER=2"); ?>
</TD><TD>
<?php display_db_table("city", $global_dbh,
                       TRUE, "BORDER=2"); ?>
</TD></TR></TABLE></BODY></HTML>
```

The result of using this code on the same database contents is shown in Figure 16-2. The only visible difference is the column header. Splitting the functions apart means that we also have a new function in our bag of tricks — we could do the same kind of display with an arbitrary query string that joins data from different tables.

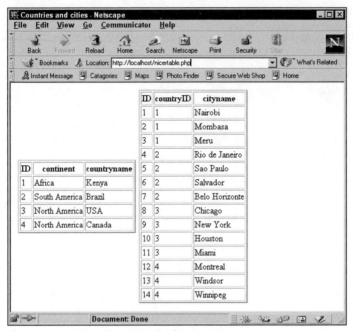

Figure 16-2: Using the query displayer

Complex Mappings

So far in this chapter, we've enjoyed a very nice and simple-minded correspondence between query result sets and HTML tables — every row in the result set corresponds to a row in the table, and the structure of the code is simply two nested loops. Unfortunately, life isn't often this simple, and sometimes the structure of the HTML table we want to display has a complex relationship to the relational structure of the database tables.

Multiple queries versus complex printing

Let's say that, rather than displaying our sample City and Country tables individually, we want to match them up in a tabular display.

We can easily write a SELECT statement that joins these tables appropriately:

```
SELECT country.continent, country.countryname,
       city.cityname
FROM country, city
WHERE city.countryID = country.ID
ORDER BY continent, countryname, cityname
```

Now, this would be a handy place to use our query-displayer function — all we have to do is send it the preceding statement as a string, and it will print out a table of cities matched up with their continents and countries. However, if we do this, we will see an individual HTML table row for each city, and the continent and country will print each time — for example, we'll see North America printed several times. Instead, what if we want one name matched with many titles? This is a case where the structure of what we print differs from the structure of the most convenient query.

Views and Stored Procedures

Our query-displayer assumes a particular division of labor between the PHP code and the database system itself—the PHP code sends off an arbitrary query string, which the database responds to by setting up a result set. In particular, this means that the database system has to parse that query and then figure out the best way to go about retrieving the results. This is part of what can make querying a database a mildly expensive operation.

In cases where your code may construct novel queries on the fly, this is the best you can hope for. However, some databases offer ways to set up queries in advance, which gives the database system a chance to preoptimize how it handles the query. One such construct is called a *view* under MS SQL Server and some other RDMSs—after you have set up a query as a named view, it can be treated just like a real table. A related idea is the *stored procedure*, which is like a view that also accepts runtime arguments that are spliced into the query. In general, if you realize that you are suffering from slow query performance, you may want to investigate what optimizations like this your particular RDBMS makes available.

If we want to do a more complex mapping, we have a choice: We can throw database queries at the problem, or we can write more complex display code. Let's look at each option in turn. (For each of these examples, we'll be moving away from the reusable generality of the functions we wrote earlier toward functions that address a particular display problem.)

A multiple-query example

If we want to print just one HTML row per country, we can make a query for the countries and then make another query for the relevant cities in each trip through a `country` row. A function written using this strategy is shown in Listing 16-3.

Listing 16-3: **A display with multiple queries**

```php
<?php
include("/home/phpbook/phpbook-vars.inc");
/* open database connection */
$global_dbh = mysql_connect($hostname, $username, $password)
            or die("Could not connect to database");
mysql_select_db($db, $global_dbh)
  or die("Could not select database");

function display_cities($db_connection)
{
  /* Displays table of cities and countries */
  $country_query = "SELECT id, continent, countryname
                    FROM country
                    ORDER BY continent, countryname";
  $country_result =
    mysql_query($country_query, $db_connection);

  /* begin table, print hard-coded table header */
  print("<TABLE BORDER=1>\n");
```

Continued

Listing 16-3 *(continued)*

```php
print("<TR><TH>Continent</TH><TH>Country</TH>
        <TH>Cities</TH></TR>");

/* loop through countries */
while ($country_row = mysql_fetch_row($country_result))
  {
    /* set up country info */
    $country_id = $country_row[0];
    $continent = $country_row[1];
    $country_name = $country_row[2];

    print("<TR ALIGN=LEFT VALIGN=TOP>");
    print("<TD>$continent</TD>");
    print("<TD>$country_name</TD>");

    /* begin table cell for city list */
    print("<TD>");
    $city_query = "select cityname from city
                    where countryID = $country_id
                    order by cityname";
    $city_result =
      mysql_query($city_query, $db_connection)
        OR die(mysql_error());
    /* loop through cities */
    while ($city_row = mysql_fetch_row($city_result))
      {
        $city_name = $city_row[0];
        print("$city_name<BR>");
      }
    /* close city cell and country row */
    print("</TD></TR>");
  }
  print("</TABLE>\n");
}
?>

<HTML>
<HEAD>
<TITLE>Cities by Country</TITLE>
</HEAD>
<BODY>
<?php
  display_cities($global_dbh);
?>
</BODY>
</HTML>
```

The strategy is appealingly simple: There is an outer loop that uses one query to proceed through all the countries, saving the country's name and the primary ID field of each country row. Then for each country, the ID field is used to look up all the cities belonging to that country. Notice the trick of embedding the $countryid variable in the inner query—the query string sent is actually different on each iteration through the country loop.

Simple? Yes. Efficient? Probably not. This code makes a *separate* city query for each country. If there are 500 countries in the database, this function will make 501 separate database queries (the extra one being the enclosing country query).

Your mileage will vary according to how efficient your particular database is in parsing queries and planning query retrieval, but the sum of these queries will certainly take more time than the simple query we started this section with.

A complex printing example

Now let's solve exactly the same problem, but using a different strategy. Instead of making multiple queries, we will make a single query and print the resulting rows selectively, so that each HTML table row corresponds to more than one database row (see Listing 16-4). The resulting browser display is exactly the same as in the previous example.

Listing 16-4: **A complex display with a single query**

```php
<?php
include("/home/phpbook/phpbook-vars.inc");
/* open a single DB connection for this page */
$global_dbh = mysql_connect($hostname, $username, $password)
            or die("Could not connect to database");
mysql_select_db($db, $global_dbh)
            or die("Could not select database");

function display_cities($db_connection)
{
  /*  print table of countries and their cities,
      selectively printing only one HTML table row
      per country */
  $query = "SELECT country.id,
                   country.continent, country.countryname,
                   city.cityname
                   FROM country, city
                   WHERE country.id = city.countryID
                   ORDER BY country.continent,
                        country.countryname,
                        city.cityname";
  $result_id =
     mysql_query($query, $db_connection)
       OR die(mysql_error($query));

  /* begin table, print hard-coded table header */
  print("<TABLE BORDER=1>\n");
```

Continued

Listing 16-4 *(continued)*

```
    print("<TH>Continent</TH><TH>Country</TH>
            <TH>Cities</TH></TR>");

/* Initialize the ID for the "previous" country.
   We will rely on the fact that Country.ID is
   numbered beginning with 1, so a previous ID
   value of zero means that the current country
   is the first */
$old_country_id = 0;

/* loop through result rows (one per city) */
while ($row_array = mysql_fetch_row($result_id))
  {
    $country_id = $row_array[0];
    /* if we have a new country */
    if ($country_id != $old_country_id)
      {
        /* set up country info */
        $continent = $row_array[1];
        $country_name = $row_array[2];

        /* if there was a previous country
           close the city datum and country row */
        if ($old_country_id != 0)
          print("</TD></TR>\n");

        /* start a row for the new country,
           and begin the city table datum */
        print("<TR ALIGN=LEFT VALIGN=TOP>");
        print("<TD>$continent</TD>");
        print("<TD>$country_name</TD><TD>");

        /* the new country is no longer new */
        $old_country_id = $country_id;
      }
    /* the only thing that is printed for every result
       rQw is the name of a city */
    $city_name = $row_array[3];
    print("$city_name<BR>");
  }
  /* close off final country and table */
  print("</TD></TR></TABLE>");
}
?>
<HTML><HEAD><TITLE>Cities by Country</TITLE></HEAD>
<BODY>
<?php display_cities($global_dbh);
 ?>
</BODY></HTML>
```

This code is somewhat tricky — although it goes through the result rows in order, and everything it prints is grabbed from the current row, it prints countries only when their values have changed. (Continents are still printed redundantly.)

The change in a country is detected by monitoring the ID field of the country row. A country change is also a signal to print out the HTML necessary to close off the preceding table row and start a new one. Finally, the code must handle printing the HTML necessary to start the first row and end the last one.

Creating the Sample Tables

Now we will show you the PHP/MySQL code we actually used to create the sample tables. (Such data might more normally be created by interacting only with MySQL, but we decided to respect our book's title by doing it from PHP.) The code (shown in Listing 16-5) is a special-purpose, one-time hack, not a model of style, but it has useful examples of using the SQL INSERT statement.

Listing 16-5: Creating the sample tables

```php
<?php
include("/home/phpbook/phpbook-vars.inc");
$global_dbh = mysql_connect($hostname, $username, $password)
            or die("Could not connect to database");
mysql_select_db($db, $global_dbh)
            or die ("Could not select databased");

function add_new_country($dbh, $continent, $countryname,
                         $city_array)

{
  $country_query =
    "INSERT INTO country (continent, countryname)
     VALUES ('$continent', '$countryname')";
  $result_id =  mysql_query($country_query)
            OR die($country_query . mysql_error());
  if ($result_id)
    {
      $countryID = mysql_insert_id($dbh);
      for ($city = current($city_array);
           $city;
           $city = next($city_array))
        {
          $city_query =
            "INSERT INTO city (countryID, cityname)
                    VALUES ($countryID, '$city')";
          mysql_query($city_query, $dbh)
            OR die($city_query . mysql_error());
        }
    }
```

Continued

Listing 16-5 *(continued)*

```
}

function populate_cities_db($dbh)
{
  /* drop tables if they exist -- permits function to be
     tried more than once */
  mysql_query("DROP TABLE city", $dbh);
  mysql_query("DROP TABLE country", $dbh);

  /* create the tables */
  mysql_query("CREATE TABLE country
                (ID int not null auto_increment primary key,
                 continent varchar(50),
                 countryname varchar(50))",
              $dbh)
              OR die(mysql_error());
  mysql_query("create table city
                (ID int not null auto_increment primary key,
                 countryID int not null,
                 cityname varchar(50))",
              $dbh)
              OR die(mysql_error());

  /* store data in the tables */
  add_new_country($dbh, 'Africa', 'Kenya',
          array('Nairobi','Mombasa','Meru'));
  add_new_country($dbh, 'South America', 'Brazil',
          array('Rio de Janeiro', 'Sao Paulo',
                'Salvador', 'Belo Horizonte'));
  add_new_country($dbh, 'North America', 'USA',
          array('Chicago', 'New York', 'Houston', 'Miami'));
  add_new_country($dbh, 'North America', 'Canada',
          array('Montreal','Windsor','Winnipeg'));

  print("Sample database created<BR>");
}
?>
<HTML><HEAD><TITLE>Creating a sample database</TITLE></HEAD>
<BODY>
<?php populate_cities_db($global_dbh); ?>
</BODY></HTML>
```

You should be able to use this code to recreate the sample database on your development machine, assuming that you have PHP and MySQL configured, and an appropriately located file called phpbook-vars.inc containing username, password, and database-name strings.

Just as in the display examples, this code sends off query strings (with embedded variables), but this time the queries are INSERT statements, which create new table rows. For the most part, the data inserted is just string data passed in to the function, although we chose to pass in an arbitrary number of cities per country by using an array.

The only tricky thing in creating these sample tables is setting up the relational structure. We want each `city` row to have an appropriate `countryID`, which should be equal to the actual `ID` of the appropriate row from the country table. However, these `countryID`s are automatically assigned in sequence by MySQL and are not under our control. How can we know the right `countryID` to assign? The answer is in the incredibly handy function `mysql_insert_id()`, which recovers the `ID` associated with the last `INSERT` query made via the given database connection. We insert the new country, recover the `ID` of the newly created row, and then use that `ID` in our city insertion queries.

Summary

Database interaction is one of the areas where PHP really shines. One very common use for database-enabled Web code is simply to display database contents attractively. One approach to this kind of display is to map the contents of database tables, or `SELECT` statements, to corresponding HTML table elements.

When the mapping is simple enough, you can employ reusable functions that take arbitrary table names, or `SELECT` statements, and display them as a grid. When you need a more complicated combination of information from relational tables, you probably need a special-purpose function, but certain tricks recur there as well. One such trick is to craft a SQL statement that returns all the information you need, in the order you want, and selectively print only the nonredundant portions.

Near the end of this chapter, we saw a quick example of populating a set of database tables using `INSERT` statements. Aside from that, all the techniques in this chapter were read-only and do not modify the contents of databases at all. In Chapter 17, we'll see how you can get a more intimate connection to your database by combining SQL queries with HTML forms.

✦   ✦   ✦

Building Forms from Queries

◆ ◆ ◆ ◆

In This Chapter

Understanding
HTML forms

Submitting data
via forms

Self-submitting forms

Editing data with
an HTML form

◆ ◆ ◆ ◆

Form handling is one of PHP's very best features. The combination of HTML to construct a data-input form, PHP to handle the data, and a database server to store the data lies at the heart of all kinds of supremely useful Web tasks.

HTML Forms

You already know most of what you need to make good forms to be handled by PHP and a database. There are a few PHP-specific points to brush up on:

+ Always, always, *always* use a NAME for every data entry element (INPUT, SELECT, TEXTAREA, and so on). These NAME attributes will become PHP variable names — you will not be able to access your values if you do not use a NAME attribute for each one. If your WYSIWYG editor doesn't allow you to do this, you'll need to remember to add these NAME attributes by hand.

+ A form field NAME does not need to be the same as the corresponding database field name, but it's often a good idea.

+ You can (and usually should) specify a VALUE rather than let HTML send the default value. Consider substituting a numerical value for a text value if possible, because the database is much slower at matching strings than integers.

+ The VALUE can be set to data you wish to display in the form.

+ Remember that you can pass hidden variables from form to form (or page) using the HIDDEN data entry elements. This practice may have negative security implications, but it's often no worse than storing the data in a cookie.

+ Remember that you can pass multiple variables in an array — but you need to inform the user that this is a possibility.

Cross-Reference See Chapter 7 for more information on how to format an HTML form for use with PHP.

Basic Form Submission to a Database

Submitting data to a database via an HTML form is straightforward if the form and form-handler are two separate pages. Listing 17-1, newsletter_signup.html, is a simple form with only one input field.

Listing 17-1: **A simple form (newsletter_signup.html)**

```
<HTML>
<HEAD>
<STYLE TYPE="text/css">
<!--
BODY, P        {color: black; font-family: verdana;
font-size: 10 pt}
H1         {color: black; font-family: arial; font-size: 12 pt}
-->
</STYLE>
</HEAD>

<BODY>
<TABLE BORDER=0 CELLPADDING=10 WIDTH=100%>
<TR>
<TD BGCOLOR="#F0F8FF" ALIGN=CENTER VALIGN=TOP WIDTH=17%>
</TD>
<TD BGCOLOR="#FFFFFF" ALIGN=LEFT VALIGN=TOP WIDTH=83%>
<H1>Newsletter sign-up form</H1>
<P>Enter your email address and we will send you our
weekly newsletter.</P>
<FORM METHOD="post" ACTION="formhandler.php">
<INPUT TYPE="text" SIZE=25 NAME="email">
<BR><BR>
<INPUT TYPE="submit" NAME="submit" VALUE="Submit">
</FORM>
</TD>
</TR>
</TABLE>

</BODY>
</HTML>
```

Figure 17-1 shows the result of the preceding code sample, a basic form to insert data into a database.

You enter the data in the database and acknowledge receipt in the form handler in Listing 17-2, which (with great originality) we are calling formhandler.php.

Figure 17-1: A form to insert data into a database

Listing 17-2: **Form handler for newsletter_signup.html (formhandler.php)**

```
<HTML>
<HEAD>
<STYLE TYPE="text/css">
<!--
BODY, P        {color: black; font-family: verdana;
font-size: 10 pt}
H1        {color: black; font-family: arial; font-size: 12 pt}
-->
</STYLE>
</HEAD>

<BODY>
<TABLE BORDER=0 CELLPADDING=10 WIDTH=100%>
<TR>
<TD BGCOLOR="#F0F8FF" ALIGN=CENTER VALIGN=TOP WIDTH=17%>
</TD>
<TD BGCOLOR="#FFFFFF" ALIGN=LEFT VALIGN=TOP WIDTH=83%>
<H1>Newsletter sign-up form</H1>
<?php

if (!$_POST['email'] || $_POST['email'] == "" ||
    strlen($_POST['email']) > 30) {
  echo '<P>There is a problem.  Did you enter an email
address?</P>';
} else {
```

Continued

Listing 17-2 *(continued)*

```
    // Open connection to the database
    mysql_connect("localhost", "phpuser", "sesame")
or die("Failure to communicate with database");
    mysql_select_db("test");

    // Insert email address
    $as_email = addslashes($_POST['email']);
    $tr_email = trim($as_email);
    $query = "INSERT INTO mailinglist (ID, Email, Source)
              VALUES(NULL, '$tr_email',
              'www.example.com/newsletter_signup.html')
              ";
    $result = mysql_query($query);
    if (mysql_affected_rows() == 1) {
      echo '<P>Your information has been recorded.</P>';
    } else {
      error_log(mysql_error());
      echo '<P>Something went wrong with your signup
attempt.</P>';
    }
}
?>
</TD>
</TR>
</TABLE>
</BODY>
</HTML>
```

Having a separate form and form handler is a very clean design that can potentially be easier to maintain. However, there are quite a few things you might want to do that you can't do easily with this model, caused by the difficulty of going back to the form from the form handler and the fact that variables are not available to both at the same time.

For one thing, if something goes wrong with the submission, it's very difficult to redisplay the form with the values you just filled in. This is particularly important with something like a user registration form, where you might want to check for unique e-mail addresses or matching passwords and reject the entire registration with an error message if it doesn't pass the tests. People are going to be very annoyed if one little typo causes them to lose all the data that they just filled in — and after one or two go-rounds, they will simply stop trying to register.

The first step to solving all these problems is to combine form and handler into one self-submitting PHP script.

Self-Submission

Self-submission is not a new form of autoeroticism. It simply refers to the process of combining one or more forms and form-handlers in a single script, using the HTML FORM standard to submit data to the script one or more times.

Another situation in which self-submission is a win is when you need to submit the same form more than once. Say you are applying for auto insurance online, and you need to give the particulars of three or four different cars. It's extra work for the user to submit the form, get a success message, and then have to click a button to go back to the form for car #2. This kind of navigation problem has no perfect solution, but in situations where there's a high probability of multiple submissions, self-submission causes fewer clickthroughs for your Web users.

Finally, the separate form and form handler make it difficult to pull data from the database, edit it, and submit it — repeating the process however many times it takes for the user to be satisfied. A common example of this usage is a form to allow users to change their personal information, such as photos and bios, which people often like to fiddle with until they look exactly like the users want. If you want to make five small incremental edits to your user profile, you aren't going to want to go back and forth between form and form-handler ten times.

Self-submission is accomplished by the simplest of means: specifying the same script name as the ACTION target in the FORM element like this:

```
<FORM METHOD="POST" ACTION="myself.php">
```

Or, using a built-in feature unique to PHP:

```
<FORM METHOD="POST" ACTION="<?php echo $_SERVER['PHP_SELF'];
?>">
```

> **Tip**
>
> Although you always have the option to just use the file's URL, the built-in $_SERVER['PHP_SELF'] variable is preferable. Then the file will continue to be handled correctly if you rename or move it (into a PHP-enabled directory, needless to say). $_SERVER['PHP_SELF'] is the replacement for $PHP_SELF, which was available from all PHP scripts until version 4.2.0.

The single most important thing to remember about self-submitting forms is: *The logic comes before the display*. If you're used to writing separate forms and handlers, this may seem a little counterintuitive at first — but think of it this way: Because your form will look different or display variables based on interactions with the database, obviously these interactions must happen before the HTML for the page is output to the browser. After you construct a few self-submitting forms, logic-before-display will seem totally natural and painless.

> **Caution**
>
> To use self-submission with controls, you will need to employ a more programmatic PHP-writing style — what we term the *maximum* or *medium* style. Beginners may find this somewhat more difficult than a clear division between the functions of HTML (form display) and PHP (form handling). This can be mitigated somewhat by using the *heredoc* syntax, as we do in many of our examples.

If you're a think-ahead type, by now you're wondering: "BUT if the logic comes before the display, won't my script try to do the database operations before showing me the HTML form in the first place?" Good question — and an indication that we need some way to tell the script either "We want to see the form now" or "We want to insert data into the database now." This "What am I supposed to be doing now?" bit is called a *stage variable*. It lets you keep track of how many times the form has submitted values to itself and, therefore, which stage of a multi-step process you have reached.

The cheapest stage variable to test for is the Submit button. You can name your Submit button and give it a value, which will be set as a PHP value only after the form is submitted at least once. The easiest way to demonstrate what we're talking about is by rewriting the previous form and form-handler as one self-submitting form, as we do in Listing 17-3.

Listing 17-3: Unified form and form-handler (newsletter_signup.php)

```php
<?php

if ($_POST['submit'] == 'Submit') {
  if (!$_POST['email'] || $_POST['email'] == "" ||
strlen($_POST['email'] > 30)) {
    $message = '<P>There is a problem.  Did you enter an email
address?</P>';
  } else {
    // Open connection to the database
    mysql_connect("localhost", "phpuser", "sesame")
or die("Failure to communicate with database");
    mysql_select_db("test");

    // Insert email address
    $as_email = addslashes($_POST['email']);
    $tr_email = trim($as_email);
    $query = "INSERT INTO mailinglist (ID, Email, Source)
              VALUES(NULL, '$tr_email',
              'www.example.com/newsletter_signup.html')
              ";
    $result = mysql_query($query);
    if (mysql_affected_rows() == 1) {
      $message = '<P>Your information has been recorded.</P>';

      $noform_var = 1;
    } else {
      error_log(mysql_error());
      $message = '<P>Something went wrong with your signup
attempt.</P>';
    }
  }

  // Show the form in every case except successful submission
  if (!$noform_var) {
    $thisfile = $_SERVER['PHP_SELF'];
    $message .= <<< EOMSG
<P>Enter your email address and we will send you our weekly
newsletter.</P>
<FORM METHOD="post" ACTION="$thisfile">
<INPUT TYPE="text" SIZE=25 NAME="email">
<BR><BR>
<INPUT TYPE="submit" NAME="submit" VALUE="Submit">
</FORM>
EOMSG;
  }
}
?>

<HTML>
<HEAD>
```

```
<STYLE TYPE="text/css">
<!--
BODY, P        {color: black; font-family: verdana;
font-size: 10 pt}
H1          {color: black; font-family: arial; font-size: 12 pt}
-->
</STYLE>
</HEAD>

<BODY>
<TABLE BORDER=0 CELLPADDING=10 WIDTH=100%>
<TR>
<TD BGCOLOR="#F0F8FF" ALIGN=CENTER VALIGN=TOP WIDTH=17%>
</TD>
<TD BGCOLOR="#FFFFFF" ALIGN=LEFT VALIGN=TOP WIDTH=83%>
<H1>Newsletter sign-up form</H1>
<?php echo $message; ?>
</TD>
</TR>
</TABLE>

</BODY>
</HTML>
```

The first time you load up this page, you should see a normal HTML form exactly like the one in Figure 17-1. If you submit it without any data or with a string that's too long (often a sign of a cracking attempt), you'll see an error message and the form again. If something goes wrong with the database INSERT, you'll see an error message and the form again. Only if the INSERT completes successfully will you not see the form again — which is the navigation we want because we don't want people to sign up for the newsletter more than once.

In the preceding example, we need to check only for two states of the form (unsubmitted or submitted) so we can use the Submit button as our stage variable. But what if you want to check for more than one state? You need a variable that is capable of taking more than one value. You could either give your Submit button different values, which would show up as different labels in the button itself, or you could set a hidden variable that is capable of taking more than one value depending on the state. We demonstrate the technique in Listing 17-4, which collects some information and then allows you to rate your boss anonymously.

Listing 17-4: **A three-part form (rate_boss.php)**

```
<?php

// First set the form strings, which will be displayed
//in various cases below
$thisfile = $_SERVER['PHP_SELF']; //Have to set this for heredoc

$reg_form = <<< EOREGFORM
<P>We must ask for your name and email address to ensure that no
one votes more than once, but we do not associate your personal
```

Continued

Listing 17-4 *(continued)*

```
information with your rating.</P>
<FORM METHOD="post" ACTION="$thisfile">
Name: <INPUT TYPE="text" SIZE=25 NAME="name"><BR><BR>
Email: <INPUT TYPE="text" SIZE=25 NAME="email">
<INPUT TYPE="hidden" NAME="stage" VALUE="register">
<BR><BR>
<INPUT TYPE="submit" NAME="submit" VALUE="Submit">
</FORM>
EOREGFORM;

$rate_form = <<< EORATEFORM
<P>My boss is:</P>
<FORM METHOD="post" ACTION="$thisfile">
<INPUT TYPE="radio" NAME="rating" VALUE=1>
Driving me to look for a new job.<BR>
<INPUT TYPE="radio" NAME="rating" VALUE=2>
Not the worst, but pretty bad.<BR>
<INPUT TYPE="radio" NAME="rating" VALUE=3>
Just so-so.<BR>
<INPUT TYPE="radio" NAME="rating" VALUE=4>
Pretty good.<BR>
<INPUT TYPE="radio" NAME="rating" VALUE=5>
A pleasure to work with.<BR><BR>
Boss's name: <INPUT TYPE="text" SIZE=25 NAME="boss"><BR>
<INPUT TYPE="hidden" NAME="stage" VALUE="rate">
<BR><BR>
<INPUT TYPE="submit" NAME="submit" VALUE="Submit">
</FORM>
EORATEFORM;

if (!$_POST['submit']) {
  // First time, just show the registration form
  $message = $reg_form;

} elseif ($_POST['submit'] == 'Submit' && $_POST['stage'] ==
'register') {
  // Second time, show the registration form again on error,
  // rating form on successful INSERT

  if (!$_POST['name'] || $_POST['name'] == "" ||
strlen($_POST['name'] > 30) || !$_POST['email'] ||
$_POST['email'] == "" || strlen($_POST['email'] > 30)) {
    $message = '<P>There is a problem.  Did you enter a name and
email address?</P>';
    $message .= $reg_form;
  } else {
    // Open connection to the database
    mysql_connect("localhost", "phpuser", "sesame")
or die("Failure to communicate with database");
```

```
    mysql_select_db("test");

    // Check to see this name and email have not appeared before
    $as_name = addslashes($_POST['name']);
    $tr_name = trim($as_name);
    $as_email = addslashes($_POST['email']);
    $tr_email = trim($as_email);
    $query = "SELECT sub_id FROM raters
                WHERE Name = '$tr_name'
                AND Email = '$tr_email'
              ";
    $result = mysql_query($query);
    if (mysql_num_rows($result) > 0) {
      error_log(mysql_error());
      $message = 'Someone with this name and password has
already rated .  If you think a mistake was made, please email
help@example.com.';
    } else {
      // Insert name and email address
      $query = "INSERT INTO raters (ID, Name, Email)
                  VALUES(NULL, '$tr_name', '$tr_email')
                ";
      $result = mysql_query($query);
      if (mysql_affected_rows() == 1) {
        $message = $rate_form;
      } else {
        error_log(mysql_error());
        $message = '<P>Something went wrong with your signup
attempt.</P>';
        $message .= $reg_form;
      }
    }
  }

} elseif ($_POST['submit'] == 'Submit' && $_POST['stage'] ==
'rate') {
  // Third time, store the rating and boss's name

  // Open connection to the database
  mysql_connect("localhost", "phpuser", "sesame")
or die("Failure to communicate with database");
  mysql_select_db("test");

  // Insert rating and boss's name
  $as_boss = addslashes($_POST['boss']);
  $tr_boss = trim($as_boss);
  $rating = $_POST['rating'];
  $query = "INSERT INTO ratings (ID, Rating, Boss)
            VALUES(NULL, '$rating', '$tr_boss')
          ";
  $result = mysql_query($query);
```

Continued

Listing 17-4 *(continued)*

```
    if (mysql_affected_rows() == 1) {
      $message = '<P>Your rating has been submitted.</P>';
    } else {
      error_log(mysql_error());
      $message = '<P>Something went wrong with your rating
attempt.  Try again.</P>';
      $message .= $rate_form;
    }
  }
?>

<HTML>
<HEAD>
<STYLE TYPE="text/css">
<!--
BODY, P     {color: black; font-family: verdana;
font-size: 10 pt}
H1         {color: black; font-family: arial; font-size: 12 pt}
-->
</STYLE>
</HEAD>

<BODY>
<TABLE BORDER=0 CELLPADDING=10 WIDTH=100%>
<TR>
<TD BGCOLOR="#F0F8FF" ALIGN=CENTER VALIGN=TOP WIDTH=17%>
</TD>
<TD BGCOLOR="#FFFFFF" ALIGN=LEFT VALIGN=TOP WIDTH=83%>
<H1>Rate your boss anonymously</H1>
<?php echo $message; ?>
</TD>
</TR>
</TABLE>

</BODY>
</HTML>
```

Figure 17-2 shows the rating form after an error has occurred.

Some of you might be thinking, "Hey, wait! You said logic always comes before display — but then you started this script with a bunch of HTML." Very perspicacious — but not quite right. Look closely and you will realize that we are merely setting a bunch of text to a couple of variable strings ($reg_form and $rate_form). In the entire PHP section, we actually don't display anything. We merely construct a string, $message, which will be plugged in to the HTML at the bottom. If we took away the HTML, you would see a blank page in the browser. So it's OK to assemble the text you're going to want to display in the logic part; just don't echo it out to the browser until the end.

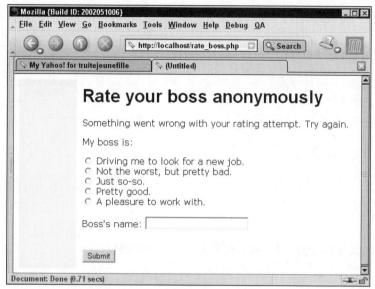

Figure 17-2: A multiple self-submitting form

Another issue with self-submitted forms is navigation. With the traditional HTML form, navigation is strictly one-way: form to handler to whatever navigational device (if any) the designer decrees. Self-submitted forms need not conform to this rule, however. In each individual instance, you need to decide:

✦ Whether the form can be resubmitted multiple times by the user, in whole or in part.

✦ Whether the user decides when to move on by clicking a link or the form moves users along automatically.

✦ Whether you need to pass variables on to the next page, hidden or in plain view.

✦ Whether you want to control where the user can go next or if you want to give users multiple choices.

Cross-Reference All these techniques are most commonly used in user-management functions — registration, login, and editing user information — which are demonstrated realistically in Chapter 44.

The answers to these questions will determine whether you need a control, another form, a simple link or button, or multiple links.

Tip Whatever you decide about navigation, remember to provide plenty of text that clearly explains what's going to happen at every step. Because PHP gives you so much flexibility with forms, new users' default expectations may be crossed up, and they could end up uncertain whether they accomplished their mission with your form.

Editing Data with an HTML Form

PHP is brilliant at putting variables into a database, but it really shines when taking data from a database, displaying it in a form to be edited, and then putting it back in the database. Its HTML-embeddedness, easy variable-passing, and slick database connectivity are at their best in this kind of job. These techniques are extremely useful, because you will find a million occasions to edit data you're storing in a database.

Let's look at the specific kinds of HTML FORM data elements and how they are handled.

TEXT and TEXTAREA

TEXT and TEXTAREA are the most straightforward types because they enjoy an unambiguous one-to-one relationship between identifier and content. In other words, there is only one possible VALUE per NAME. You just pull the data field from the database and display it in the form by referencing the appropriate array value, as shown in Figure 17-3.

Figure 17-3: Displaying text for editing

Listing 17-5, comment_edit.php, takes a comment out of the database and allows you to edit it.

Tip   You may need to use the stripslashes function when displaying TEXTAREA and TEXT if there's any chance the values might have single quotes or apostrophes and magic_quotes_gpc is on. Watch out for people with apostrophe'd names like O'Malley or D'Nesh!

Listing 17-5: **Editing data from database (comment_edit.php)**

```php
<?php

// Open connection to the database
mysql_connect("localhost", "phpuser", "sesame")
or die("Failure to communicate with database");
mysql_select_db("test");

if ($_POST['submit'] == 'Submit') {
  // Format the data
  $comment_id = $_POST['comment_id'];
  $comment_header = $_POST['comment_header'];
  $as_comment_header = addslashes($comment_header);
  $comment = $_POST['comment'];
  $as_comment = addslashes($_POST['comment']);

  // Update values
  $query = "UPDATE comments
            SET comment_header = '$as_comment_header',
            comment = '$as_comment'
            WHERE ID = $comment_id";
  $result = mysql_query($query);
  if (mysql_affected_rows() == 1) {
    $success_msg = '<P>Your comment has been updated.</P>';
  } else {
    error_log(mysql_error());
    $success_msg = '<P>Something went wrong.</P>';
  }
} else {
  // Get the comment header and comment
  $comment_id = $_GET['comment_id'];
  $query = "SELECT comment_header, comment
            FROM comments
            WHERE ID = $comment_id";
  $result = mysql_query($query);
  $comment_arr = mysql_fetch_array($result);
  $comment_header = stripslashes($comment_arr[0]);
  $comment = stripslashes($comment_arr[1]);
}


$thispage = $_SERVER['PHP_SELF']; //Have to do this for heredoc

$form_page = <<< EOFORMPAGE
<STYLE TYPE="text/css">
<!--
BODY, P      {color: black; font-family: verdana;
font-size: 10 pt}
H1      {color: black; font-family: arial; font-size: 12 pt}
```

Continued

Listing 17-5 *(continued)*

```
-->
</STYLE>
</HEAD>

<BODY>
<TABLE BORDER=0 CELLPADDING=10 WIDTH=100%>
<TR>
<TD BGCOLOR="#F0F8FF" ALIGN=CENTER VALIGN=TOP WIDTH=17%>
</TD>
<TD BGCOLOR="#FFFFFF" ALIGN=LEFT VALIGN=TOP WIDTH=83%>
<H1>Comment edit</H1>

$success_msg
<FORM METHOD="post" ACTION="$thispage">
<INPUT TYPE="text" SIZE="40" NAME="comment_header"
VALUE="$comment_header"><BR><BR>
<TEXTAREA NAME="comment" ROWS=10 COLS=50>$comment</TEXTAREA>
<BR><BR>
<INPUT TYPE="hidden" NAME="comment_id" VALUE="$comment_id">
<INPUT TYPE="submit" NAME="submit" VALUE="Submit">
</FORM>

</TD></TR></TABLE>
</BODY>
</HTML>
EOFORMPAGE;
echo $form_page;
?>
```

Tip   Remember that in an HTML form integers and doubles must use the TEXT or TEXTAREA
type, as there is no specifically numeric HTML form field type.

CHECKBOX

The CHECKBOX type has only one possible value per input: off (unchecked) or on (checked).
The database field which records this information is almost always going to be a small integer or bit type with values 0 and 1 corresponding to unchecked or checked check boxes.
Figure 17-4 shows a common type of check box being edited.

Listing 17-6 demonstrates how to use a check box to display and change a Boolean value.

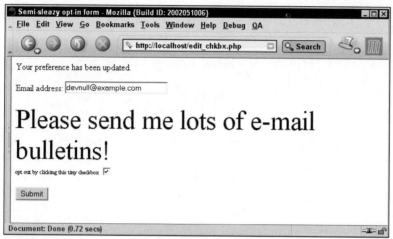

Figure 17-4: A prepopulated check box

Listing 17-6: **Checkbox displaying boolean data from database (optout.php)**

```php
<?php

// Open connection to the database
mysql_connect("localhost", "phpuser", "sesame")
or die("Failure to communicate with database");
mysql_select_db("test");

// If the form has been submitted, record the preference and
// redisplay
if ($_POST['submit'] == 'Submit') {
  $email = $_POST['email'];
  $as_email = addslashes($_POST['email']);
  if (isSet($_POST['OptOut'] && $_POST['OptOut'] == 1) {
    $optout = 1;
  } else {
    $optout = 0;
  }

  // Update value
  $query = "UPDATE checkbox
            SET BoxValue = $optout
            WHERE BoxName = 'OptOut'
            AND email = '$as_email'";
  $result = mysql_query($query);
  if (mysql_error() == "") {
```

Continued

Listing 17-6 *(continued)*

```
    $success_msg = '<P>Your preference has been updated.</P>';
  } else {
    error_log(mysql_error());
    $success_msg = '<P>Something went wrong.</P>';
  }
  // Get the value
  $query = "SELECT BoxValue FROM checkbox
            WHERE BoxName = 'OptOut' AND email = '$as_email'";
  $result = mysql_query($query);
  $optout = mysql_result($result, 0, 0);

  if ($optout == 0) {

    $checked = "";
  } elseif ($optout == 1) {
    $checked = 'CHECKED';
  }
}


// Now display the page
$thispage = $_SERVER['PHP_SELF']; //Have to do this for heredoc

$form_page = <<< EOFORMPAGE
<HTML>
<HEAD>
<TITLE>Semi-sleazy opt-in form</TITLE>
</HEAD>

<BODY>
$success_msg
<FORM METHOD=POST ACTION="$thispage">
Email address:
<INPUT TYPE="text" NAME="email" SIZE=25 VALUE="$email">
<BR><BR>
<FONT SIZE=+4>Please send me lots of e-mail bulletins!</FONT>
<BR>
<FONT SIZE=-2>opt out by clicking this tiny checkbox</FONT>
<INPUT TYPE="checkbox"  NAME="OptOut" VALUE=1 $checked><BR><BR>
<INPUT TYPE="submit" NAME="submit" VALUE="Submit">
</FORM>

</BODY>
</HTML>
EOFORMPAGE;
echo $form_page;

?>
```

Although each check box is capable of expressing only a fixed chunk of data, check boxes are often used in bunches to convey more complex aggregate meanings. Look at the check box grouping in Figure 17-5.

Figure 17-5: A cluster of check boxes

Forms with large numbers of check boxes like this are more work for the Web development team, but they provide a nice interface for the user. The code for this page is very similar to that of the previous example, with more variables. You can download it from the Web site for our book at www.troutworks.com/phpbook/.

RADIO

RADIO data elements allow for a one-to-many relationship between identifier and value. In other words, they have multiple possible values, but only one can be predisplayed or selected. They are best for small sets of options, generally between two and ten, which need more than a word or two of text to identify themselves.

Unfortunately, it's somewhat more difficult to represent stored data in a radio button than in a check box or text field. This is because there is only one possible value for a text or textarea and only two possible values for a check box—but radio buttons can have more than two possible values. Therefore, you will have to output part of the actual form with PHP. This looks a little bit less neat than the styles we employed previously, so you have to go to a little more trouble to have an easily readable script. Again, the user-interface experience allowed by radio buttons is worth the extra trouble it gives to the Web developer.

In the example in Figure 17-6 and accompanying code, we are assembling a series of radio buttons that display preference data from the database.

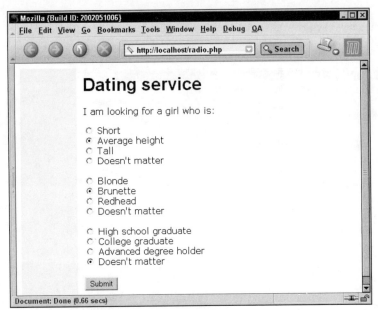

Figure 17-6: Prepopulated radio buttons

Listing 17-7 shows the code for Figure 17-6, which shows how to edit forms with radio buttons.

Listing 17-7: Radio buttons displaying boolean data from database (date_prefs.php)

```php
<?php

// Subscriber ID is stored in a cookie on the user's browser
$sub_id = $_COOKIE['userID'];

// Open connection to the database
mysql_connect("localhost", "mysqluser", "sesame")
or die("Failure to communicate with database");
mysql_select_db("test");

// If the form has been submitted, record the preferences
if ($_POST['submit'] == 'Submit') {
  $height = $_POST['height'];
  $haircolor = $_POST['haircolor'];
  $edu = $_POST['edu'];

  // Update value
  $query = "UPDATE qualities
          SET height = $height, haircolor = $haircolor,
              edu = $edu
```

```
                    WHERE subscriber = $sub_id";
    $result = mysql_query($query);
    if (mysql_affected_rows() == 1) {
      $success_msg = '<P>Your preferences have been updated.</P>';
    } else {
      error_log(mysql_error());
      $success_msg = '<P>Something went wrong.</P>';
    }

  }

  // Get the values
  $query = "SELECT height, haircolor, edu FROM qualities
            WHERE subscriber = $sub_id";
  $result = mysql_query($query);
  $pref_arr = mysql_fetch_array($result);
  $height = $pref_arr[0];
  $haircolor = $pref_arr[1];
  $edu = $pref_arr[2];

  // Assemble the radio button part of the form
  if ($height == 1) {
    $radio_str .= "<INPUT TYPE=RADIO NAME=\"height\" VALUE=1
checked> Short<BR>\n";
  } else {
    $radio_str .= "<INPUT TYPE=RADIO NAME=\"height\" VALUE=1>
Short<BR>\n";
  }
  if ($height == 2) {
    $radio_str .= "<INPUT TYPE=RADIO NAME=\"height\" VALUE=2
checked> Average height<BR>\n";
  } else {
    $radio_str .= "<INPUT TYPE=RADIO NAME=\"height\" VALUE=2>
Average height<BR>\n";
  }
  if ($height == 3) {
    $radio_str .= "<INPUT TYPE=RADIO NAME=\"height\" VALUE=3
checked> Tall<BR>\n";
  } else {
    $radio_str .= "<INPUT TYPE=RADIO NAME=\"height\" VALUE=3>
Tall<BR>\n";
  }
  if ($height == 0) {
    $radio_str .= "<INPUT TYPE=RADIO NAME=\"height\" VALUE=0
checked> Doesn't matter<BR><BR>\n";
  } else {
    $radio_str .= "<INPUT TYPE=RADIO NAME=\"height\" VALUE=0>
Doesn't matter<BR><BR>\n";
  }

  if ($haircolor == 1) {
```

Continued

Listing 17-7 *(continued)*

```
    $radio_str .= "<INPUT TYPE=RADIO NAME=\"haircolor\" VALUE=1
checked> Blonde<BR>\n";
} else {
    $radio_str .= "<INPUT TYPE=RADIO NAME=\"haircolor\" VALUE=1>
Blonde<BR>\n";
}
if ($haircolor == 2) {
    $radio_str .= "<INPUT TYPE=RADIO NAME=\"haircolor\" VALUE=2
checked> Brunette<BR>\n";
} else {
    $radio_str .= "<INPUT TYPE=RADIO NAME=\"haircolor\" VALUE=2>
Brunette<BR>\n";
}
if ($haircolor == 3) {
    $radio_str .= "<INPUT TYPE=RADIO NAME=\"haircolor\" VALUE=3
checked> Redhead<BR>\n";
} else {
    $radio_str .= "<INPUT TYPE=RADIO NAME=\"haircolor\" VALUE=3>
Redhead<BR>\n";
}
if ($haircolor == 0) {
    $radio_str .= "<INPUT TYPE=RADIO NAME=\"haircolor\" VALUE=0
checked> Doesn't matter<BR><BR>\n";
} else {
    $radio_str .= "<INPUT TYPE=RADIO NAME=\"haircolor\" VALUE=0>
Doesn't matter<BR><BR>\n";
}

if ($edu == 1) {
    $radio_str .= "<INPUT TYPE=RADIO NAME=\"edu\" VALUE=1 checked>
High school graduate<BR>\n";
} else {
    $radio_str .= "<INPUT TYPE=RADIO NAME=\"edu\" VALUE=1> High
school graduate<BR>\n";
}
if ($edu == 2) {
    $radio_str .= "<INPUT TYPE=RADIO NAME=\"edu\" VALUE=2 checked>
College graduate<BR>\n";
} else {
    $radio_str .= "<INPUT TYPE=RADIO NAME=\"edu\" VALUE=2> College
graduate<BR>\n";
}
if ($edu == 3) {
    $radio_str .= "<INPUT TYPE=RADIO NAME=\"edu\" VALUE=3 checked>
Advanced degree holder<BR>\n";
} else {
    $radio_str .= "<INPUT TYPE=RADIO NAME=\"edu\" VALUE=3>
```

```
Advanced degree holder<BR>\n";
}
if ($edu == 0) {
  $radio_str .= "<INPUT TYPE=RADIO NAME=\"edu\" VALUE=0 checked>
Doesn't matter<BR><BR>\n";
} else {
  $radio_str .= "<INPUT TYPE=RADIO NAME=\"edu\" VALUE=0> Doesn't
matter<BR><BR>\n";
}


// Now display the page
$thispage = $_SERVER['PHP_SELF']; //Have to do this for heredoc

$form_page = <<< EOFORMPAGE
<HTML>
<HEAD>
<STYLE TYPE="text/css">
<!--
BODY, P     {color: black; font-family: verdana;
font-size: 10 pt}
H1          {color: black; font-family: arial; font-size: 12 pt}
-->
</STYLE>
</HEAD>

<BODY>
<TABLE BORDER=0 CELLPADDING=10 WIDTH=100%>
<TR>
<TD BGCOLOR="#F0F8FF" ALIGN=CENTER VALIGN=TOP WIDTH=17%>
</TD>
<TD BGCOLOR="#FFFFFF" ALIGN=LEFT VALIGN=TOP WIDTH=83%>
<H1>Dating service</H1>
$success_msg
<P>I am looking for a girl who is:</P>
<FORM METHOD=POST ACTION="$thispage">
$radio_str
<INPUT TYPE=SUBMIT NAME="submit" VALUE="Submit">
</FORM>

</TD>
</TR>
</TABLE>
</BODY>
</HTML>
EOFORMPAGE;
echo $form_page;

?>
```

SELECT

The SELECT field type is perhaps the most interesting of all. It can handle the largest number of options, and it also allows the user to select multiple options that can be passed back to the database using arrays.

Cross-Reference   See Chapter 38 for ideas about using JavaScript to make even more interesting SELECT forms.

In Figure 17-7, we are using the SELECT form element with multiple options. In PHP, this is done by creating an array of the multiple selected option values to pass to the form handler. You set up the array in the HTML form by declaring the MULTIPLE attribute of the SELECT element and by naming the SELECT element something like $val[] — in other words, appending a set of square brackets to the variable name. This will indicate to PHP that it's dealing with an array rather than a single variable, and it will construct the array appropriately with the multiple selected values. When the array gets to the form handler, you will need to deal with the values as you would any array's values — by dereferencing, or by listing out the contents of the array.

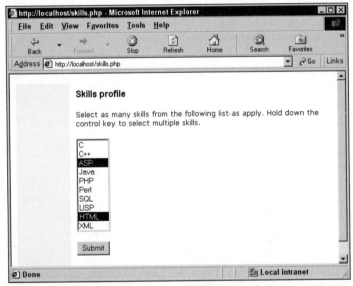

Figure 17-7: A prepopulated select with multiple choices

Listing 17-8 shows the code for Figure 17-7, which demonstrates how to display and edit a select list with multiple options.

Listing 17-8: **Select list displaying database values (skills_profile.php)**

```php
<?php

$user_id = $_COOKIE['user_id'];

// Open connection to the database
mysql_connect("localhost", "mysqluser", "sesame")
or die("Database error!");
mysql_select_db("test");

if ($_POST['submit'] == 'Submit') {

  // Delete this user's skills
  $query2 = "DELETE FROM user_skill
             WHERE user_id = $user_id";
  $result2 = mysql_query($query2);

  foreach ($_POST['skills'] as $val) {
    $query = "INSERT INTO user_skill (ID, user_id, skill_id)
              VALUES (NULL, $user_id, $val)";
    $result = mysql_query($query);
    if (mysql_affected_rows() == 1) {
      continue;
    } else {
      error_log(mysql_error());
      $error_msg = '<P>Something went wrong</P>';
      break;
    }
  }
}

// Get all the results
$query = "SELECT * FROM skills";
$result = mysql_query($query);

// Download this user's skills
$query1 = "SELECT skill_id
           FROM user_skill
           WHERE user_id = $user_id";
$result1 = mysql_query($query1);
while ($user_skill = mysql_fetch_array($result1)) {
  $skill_id = $user_skill[0];
  $user_skill_arr[$skill_id] = $skill_id;
}


while ($skills = mysql_fetch_array($result)) {
```

Continued

Listing 17-8 *(continued)*

```php
  $key = $skills[0];
  if ($key == $user_skill_arr[$key]) {
    $select_str .= "<OPTION VALUE=\"$key\"
SELECTED>$skills[1]\n";
  } else {
    $select_str .= "<OPTION VALUE=\"$key\">$skills[1]\n";
  }
}


$thispage = $_SERVER['PHP_SELF']; //Have to do this for heredoc
$form_str = <<< EOFORMSTR
<HTML>
<HEAD>
<STYLE TYPE="text/css">
<!--
BODY, P      {color: black; font-family: verdana;
font-size: 10 pt}
H1        {color: black; font-family: arial; font-size: 12 pt}
-->
</STYLE>
</HEAD>

<BODY>
<TABLE BORDER=0 CELLPADDING=10 WIDTH=100%>
<TR>
<TD BGCOLOR="#F0F8FF" ALIGN=CENTER VALIGN=TOP WIDTH=17%>
</TD>
<TD BGCOLOR="#FFFFFF" ALIGN=LEFT VALIGN=TOP WIDTH=83%>
<H1>Skills profile</H1>
<P>Select as many skills from the following list as apply.  Hold
down the control key to select multiple skills.</P>
$error_msg

<FORM METHOD=POST ACTION="$thispage">
<SELECT NAME="skills[]" SIZE=10 MULTIPLE>
$select_str
</SELECT>
<BR><BR>
<INPUT TYPE="submit" NAME="submit" VALUE="Submit">
</FORM>

</TD></TR></TABLE>
</BODY></HTML>
EOFORMSTR;
echo $form_str;

?>
```

Summary

PHP is an extremely powerful form-handling tool, especially in conjunction with a database. You can use PHP to display database-stored data as form values, and of course, you can also store form-generated data in the database.

To prepare your HTML forms to work smoothly with PHP, you need to follow a few simple rules. First and foremost, remember to always name every single form element — the HTML standard itself doesn't require this, but PHP does because the element names will become variable names in the form handler. A good idea is to make the form element name the same as the corresponding database field name so they are easy to match, perhaps prefixing form variables with frm or something similar to help distinguish them from their database counterparts in code. PHP also allows you to make clever use of hidden form inputs and of multiple SELECT options, which should be delineated with square brackets (denoting an array) after the element name.

You have the choice with PHP to have separate HTML forms and PHP form handlers or to commingle the two in a single self-submitting PHP script. The latter option is perhaps the more powerful, but it can also be more difficult to work with. You will need to set a variable within the form to indicate whether the entries have been submitted; the PHP logic should be placed before the HTML display. You can even have multiple forms on one page that are handled by the same PHP script.

✦　　✦　　✦

PHP/MySQL Efficiency

This quick chapter is for people making database-enabled PHP Web sites who suspect that they are doing things awkwardly or inefficiently. Maybe you are new to databases, or maybe you know there must be a way to speed things up just because your pages are loading unacceptably slowly.

We offer some tips and tricks for making things run faster, and we show you some common ways that database systems can save you from writing unnecessary PHP code. As usual, some of our code examples will use MySQL functions, although the lessons are mostly general and independent of particular database implementations.

 Cross-Reference This chapter will do little to help you get your database-enabled code working in the first place. For a guide to common errors, gotchas, and problems with PHP/database code, see Chapter 19.

Connections — Reduce, Reuse, Recycle

One important thing to realize is that establishing an initial connection with a database is never a cheap operation. Unless your PHP script is doing some unusually computationally intensive work, the overall database interaction will be the most time- and resource-intensive part of your code, and it is frequently true that the establishment of a connection is the most expensive part of code that interacts with a database, even if the connection is only established once in serving the page.

You have two potentially competing goals here. On the one hand, you want to minimize the number of times your code makes the expensive and time-consuming call to open an entirely new database connection. This argues for leaving connections open during the course of page execution, rather than closing and reopening. On the other hand, there are sometimes hard limits on the number of simultaneous connections that a database program can support. This might argue for closing connections whenever possible in hopes that less connected time per script might allow more scripts to execute simultaneously.

In our experience, however, most Web scripts are evanescent enough that it is never worth the overhead to close and reopen a database connection within one page's execution. If you want to minimize total time connected, open the connection immediately before the first call to the database, and close it immediately after the last one.

A bad example: One connection per statement

Our first bad example seems stylistically reasonable in one sense because it uses a function to eliminate repetitive code.

```php
<?php
function box_query ($query, $user, $pass, $db)
{
  $my_connection =
     mysql_connect('localhost', $user, $pass)
     or die("Couldn't connect to database");;
  mysql_select_db($db, $my_connection)
     or die("Couldn't select database");
  $result_id = mysql_query($query, $my_connection)
     or die(mysql_error());
  print("<H3>Results for query:  $query</H3>");
  print("<TABLE>");
  while ($row = mysql_fetch_row($result_id))
  {
    print("<TR>");
    $row_length = mysql_num_fields($result_id);
    for ($x = 0; $x < $row_length; $x++)
    {
      $entry = $row[$x];
      print("<TD>$entry</TD>");
    }
    print("</TR>\n");
  }
  print("</TABLE>");
  mysql_close($my_connection);
}
/* code that uses box_query() */
?>
```

The idea is that we take a function that packages up an arbitrary MySQL query and displays the returned data in an attractive HTML table. The main virtue of this function as defined is that it is very self-contained—it opens its own database connection for its own purposes, and then it disposes of that connection when the function is done.

The preceding code is fine if we expect to display only one such table per page. If we use this function more than once per page, however, we will find ourselves opening and closing connections every time the function is invoked, which is bound to be more inefficient than leaving the connection open. The general rule is to leave a single connection open for as long as it is needed in the execution of a single page's script. Applying this rule to the preceding function would mean rewriting it so that it takes a connection as argument (or implicitly uses a connection opened at the beginning of the script) and then opening a single connection per page.

Multiple results don't need multiple connections

One thing that surprised us the very first time we saw Web-database scripting was that, with many database programs, it is possible to retain the results from more than one query at one time, even though only one connection has been opened. For example, with a MySQL database you can do something like this:

```
mysql_connect('localhost', $user, $pass); //opens connection
mysql_select_db('scienceguide');
$author_result = mysql_query("SELECT ID FROM author")
                    or die(mysql_error());
while ($author_row = mysql_fetch_row($author_result))
{
  $book_result =
     mysql_query("SELECT title FROM book
                  WHERE authorID = $author_row[0]")
     or die(mysql_error());
while ($book_row = mysql_fetch_row($book_result))
  {
    $title = $book_row[0];
    print("$title<BR>");
  }
}
```

This would print titles of books after retrieving them from the book table, using IDs from rows retrieved from the author table. If we assume there is not more than one author per book, then this is an extremely inefficient way to retrieve the data (see the section "Making the Database Work for You" later in this chapter), but it illustrates that two different result sets (identified by the variables $author_result and $book_result) can be actively used at the same time, after having been retrieved over a single connection.

Persistent connections

Finally, if you become convinced that the sheer overhead of opening new database connections is killing your performance, you might want to investigate opening *persistent* connections. Unlike regular database connections, these connections are not automatically killed when your page exits (or even when mysql_close() is called) but are saved in a pool for future use. The first time one of your scripts opens such a connection, it is opened in the same resource-intensive way as with a regular database connection. The next script that executes, however, might get that very same connection in response to its request, which saves the cost of reopening a fresh connection. (The previous connection will be reused only if the parameters of the new request are identical.)

Note   Persistent database connections work only in the module installation of PHP. If you ask for a persistent connection in the CGI version, you will simply get a regular connection.

The PHP function to request such a persistent connection for MySQL is mysql_pconnect(), which is used in exactly the same way as mysql_connect(). This naming convention seems to be stable across PHP functions for the different databases — if you use a particular DB connect function, you should consult the documentation to see if a pconnect version exists.

Note   Other than offering a particular kind of increased efficiency, persistent database connections do not provide any functionality beyond that of regular database connections. In particular, you should not expect persistent connections to have any memory of previous queries or of variables from previous page executions.

Indexing and Table Design

MySQL is a pretty fast database, even absent any serious design considerations. In a lot of installations and applications, the database-design part of your job may be no more difficult than creating a single basic table with four or five fields in anticipation of holding no more than a few hundred records. However, as your database needs grow, your database itself will doubtless grow as well—in both size and complexity. That's no sweat for a good RDBMS: MySQL and other products in this class excel at handling these needs. Still, careful choice of both indexes and field types when designing tables can be crucial for performance as your tables get larger.

Indexing

Probably the first thing to investigate when SELECT statements are slow is whether you have defined appropriate indexes.

What is an index?

An index on a table field is an indication by a database designer to the database system that any searches made on that field should be fast. Usually, this is implemented by the RDBMS as a side table that maintains all the values for the field in order, and maps them to rows in the original table. Whenever a SELECT statement has a WHERE condition that mentions the indexed field, the side table is consulted to locate the rows that have the desired values for the field. The ordering of the side table means that the database system can do fast lookups (for example, using binary search).

Indexing trade-offs

There are two mantras to keep in mind when thinking about creating indexes:

  ✦ SELECT statements that filter on unindexed fields may require full table scans.

  ✦ While indexes speed up SELECT statements, they slow down INSERTs, UPDATEs, and DELETEs.

To see why both these statements are true, imagine that we gave you a large telephone book (sorted by last name) and asked you to find us everyone in the book with a first name of 'Zachary'. Unfortunately, it's difficult to see how to accomplish this without looking through the entire book.

A database system trying to execute a statement like

```
SELECT lastname FROM phonebook WHERE firstname = 'Zachary'
```

is in exactly the same situation, if there is no index on the field 'firstname'. In database parlance, the system must resort to a *full table scan*, meaning that every row in the table is inspected.

If your job were to do this phonebook lookup frequently, you might find it worth your while to commission an extra *index* (in the book-publishing sense) that listed all the first names in order, along with the page numbers and associated last names. Once the newly indexed phone book arrived, your job would become a lot easier.

The bad news is that as soon as the new phone book arrived, we decided to promote you. Congratulations! Your new job is to keep the phone book up to date (including, of course, any associated indexes). Here is a list of 10,000 new customers, 8,000 people who have moved away, and 45 people who have had name changes. Now the firstname index is a burden rather than a benefit. Again, it's the same with the database system—the indexes that make lookups faster are a maintenance burden when the data must be modified.

The general lesson is that you should consider indexes on fields that you use frequently in the WHERE clauses of SELECT statements, especially when the data-modifying statements (INSERT, UPDATE, DELETE) will be used rarely. If modification is much more common than lookup, indexes make less sense.

Now we move on to the specifics of using indexes in MySQL, beginning with the most common usage: a single index that uniquely identifies each table row.

Primary keys

Simply put, a primary key is a field in a table that uniquely identifies each record in that table. A good primary key choice needs to meet a few criteria:

✦ Because databases work more quickly with integers, a primary key should be of an integer type. These may vary some from one database tool to the next; but in MySQL, they are TINYINT, SMALLINT, MEDIUMINT, INT, and BIGINT. Refer to Chapter 14 for the ranges and other properties of these types.

✦ A primary key should not return a null value. Your column definition should contain the SQL keyword NOT NULL. In fact, many databases, MySQL included, will not let you designate a primary key that is capable of returning a null value.

✦ A primary key MUST be unique. That's the point, isn't it? And because a primary key must be unique, it should also have an autoincrement feature set. Most databases offer this, and most call it the same thing.

Caution   Autoincrement and it's use are often debated. In your Internet travels, you'll come across those who don't like autoincrement and variously describe it as an accident waiting to happen or a cop out. To be honest, there are some meritorious arguments in this vein. However, we believe the benefits significantly outweigh the concerns. The alternatives are either expensive database calls to determine what key values are available or to generate an ID programmatically and then insert it with your SQL statement. Neither of these is as reliable or worry free as autoincrement.

If you've already forged ahead and created some database tables of your own without a primary key, consider the fields you have already created. Does one of these meet the tests described previously? It may be that you have wisely foreseen or intuited this need and created something like it already. If this field exists, but lacks one or more of the components, you can alter it with a SQL statement like the following:

```
ALTER TABLE 'my_table' CHANGE 'existing_field' 'my_key' SMALLINT
NOT NULL AUTO_INCREMENT PRIMARY KEY
```

Or if your field already has all the necessary characteristics, you can simply make it the primary key like so:

```
ALTER TABLE 'my_table' ADD PRIMARY KEY ('my_key')
```

In the first statement, we indicate that we are altering a table and indicate which table we want to operate on. CHANGE further indicates that we are changing a field's properties, and indicating which field with its quoted existing name. We can then specify a name that may indicate more specifically what sort of field it is and set the relevant properties in one fell swoop.

If you don't already have an appropriate field choice, the syntax doesn't change much:

```
ALTER TABLE 'my_table' ADD 'my_key' SMALLINT NOT NULL
AUTO_INCREMENT PRIMARY KEY
```

Finally, you may just be creating your table for the first time. If that's the case, you simply need to include the following field definition in your table create statement:

```
ID SMALLINT UNSIGNED AUTO_INREMENT NOT NULL PRIMARY KEY
```

where ID is the name you've assigned to your primary key. There's nothing magical about this name; you can call it Fido if you want, but ID is a good, meaningful quasi-standard.

So now you've got a primary key. What's it good for? Well, it helps define the master record in a one-to-many relationship. Its other properties enforce an unambiguous identity for each record, such that the SQL statement delete from 'my_table' where id = 12 can have only one possible result. Phew, and you thought you just blew that whole table away.

It also has the net effect of speeding up queries that join tables on this unique ID because in the process of making it a primary key, we made it an index as well. An index is stored separately by MySQL and operates transparently to the end user.

When you are defining a relationship in your SQL, the child table — the *many* side of the one-to-many relationship — will also store a copy of the master table's primary key value. But it will store it once for every record that is a child of the parent record, making it unsuitable for use as a primary key. You may still wish to define a primary key for each record in the child table — in fact, it's a good idea to do so, but you won't be able to define a primary key on this particular field because values may not be unique to this column. On the other hand, you still want to improve the process MySQL uses to locate related records for queries that perform joins. That works out alright, because MySQL can still index a field without making it a primary key:

```
ALTER TABLE `child table` ADD INDEX MyIndex (child_id)
```

This will work great for an existing field, but as before, you may need to create a suitable field for this purpose:

```
ALTER TABLE 'child_table' ADD 'child_id' SMALLINT NOT NULL
```

Then make the field an index:

```
ALTER TABLE 'child_table' ADD INDEX ('child_id')
```

Everything including the kitchen sink

Indexes are almost a requirement for speedy, efficient joins. Even those most ardently concerned about things like disk space will rarely find room to argue about the merits of an index that speeds up the definition of relationships. More debatable, however, may be indexes that do not specifically operate on joins.

You can index virtually anything. Sure, binary data presents some problem and is almost always an ill-advised choice for indexing, but strings, the larger text fields and numbers (including floats and decimals) are all fair game. Aside from defining a relationship, the only other overriding qualification for index candidacy is that it should be something you're likely to use in the WHERE clause of your SQL statement.

Let's say you want to create a membership directory for your local Linux Users Group and you want members to be able to find other members in the same part of town so they can easily get together for a drink or a movie. If you're like us, you're probably thinking Zip code. Excellent choice. A universally used (at least in the U.S.), well documented, predictable and fairly stable search criterion. Of course, you don't have to index this field:

```
SELECT name, phone from members where zip = '32223'
```

will get you an answer, the same answer in fact, with or without an index. On a table with 100 or so records, you'll get your answer instantaneously — again, with or without an index.

But maybe you have several hundred, perhaps even thousands of members. An index may just speed up this search. Add one and try your search again:

```
ALTER TABLE 'members' ADD INDEX ('zip')
```

Perhaps do it while watching the output of Linux's ps or top commands. Perhaps you'll see user discernible improvement; perhaps you'll need a professional diagnostic tool of some kind to measure what just happened; perhaps your performance improvement will be measured in nanoseconds. The point is, at some number of records, you almost certainly will see an improvement at each of these levels. It will be up to you as the designer to determine whether the benefits justify the trade-offs.

What are the trade-offs? Disk space, for one. Depending on the number of records and the size of the field, an index can increase storage requirements by nearly as much as the table size itself. If you've got 80GBs of storage, you probably don't care. If you're on a 50MB shared hosting plan, you probably care very much. Another trade-off is that although SELECT operations benefit, INSERT, UPDATE, and DELETE operations actually take longer because the indexes must be updated each time one of these is performed. The good thing about an index is that it's not irreversible. Try an index on anything you think might be useful, measure the performance improvement, and weigh it against what you may or may not be giving up to get that improvement.

Other types of indexes

There are a couple other types of indexes, or more appropriately, parameters to indexing functions, that specify how indexes work. Using them may have the net effect of making an index work better or worse. Again, consider each type, experiment and measure your results. It's a small effort to make with potentially huge dividends.

UNIQUE

Isn't that a primary key? Maybe. In MySQL at least, a primary key is by definition nothing more or less complicated than a UNIQUE INDEX with the name PRIMARY. If you find yourself defining a unique index, consider whether what you've got is really a primary key candidate. Social Security numbers, if your users are consistently willing to provide them, may work well in this regard. This choice certainly meets the criteria and offers some additional advantages such as knowing what the primary key will be before you insert anything, enabling you to create master and child records without the intermediate call to mysql_insert_id().

A phone number, on the other hand, may not be such a good choice. Sure, it's unique. It also is, or can be defined as, an integer. But you may wish to store phone numbers as a string to avoid some post-formatting for creating a readable display, such as parenthesizing an area code or inserting the traditional, if somewhat meaningless hyphen. But even if you are willing to forgo the aesthetic concerns, as an integer, a phone number is almost certainly larger than necessary. The largest possible phone number will store as 9,999,999,999. Yeah, that's what we said. This integer would require a field type of at least INT. You probably aren't going to store more than nine billion records. SMALLINT or MEDIUMINT would be better choices for a storage and searchable volume savings of 2^{18} or 2^9 bytes, respectively.

All that said, you can still use UNIQUE without having it as a primary key, and that is precisely why it exists. A UNIQUE attribute on a phone number field can still serve as a data integrity check, once again relieving you of the responsibility of performing the check programmatically (of course, you will still probably have to respond to the problem).

A unique index can be specified in MySQL like this:

```
ALTER TABLE 'members' ADD UNIQUE my_index ('phone')
```

FULLTEXT

The FULLTEXT index became available in MySQL 3.23.23 and operates only on the default MySQL table type of MyISAM. Versions 4.0 and up offer some additional configuration parameters. FULLTEXT will not operate on binary fields of any type. It will ignore stop words such as *a*, *an*, and *the* as well as any words that appear in greater than 50 percent of the existing records. See the MySQL documentation at www.mysql.com/ for parameters to FULLTEXT that are evolving more rapidly than can reasonably be documented here.

Caution   INSERTs into a table indexed with FULLTEXT can be extremely slow.

Although you can use FULLTEXT on any size field, the primary and sensible use of the FULLTEXT index will be on tables that form the back end of content management systems, where a field type of LONGTEXT is not unreasonable. FULLTEXT greatly simplifies and speeds up searching against large volumes of text, versus a standard SELECT statement within the same database. It's even more beneficial compared with the grueling flat-file searches so prevalent just a few years ago.

In order to take advantage of the FULLTEXT indices, you will need to use a special sort of SELECT statement called a MATCH. At it's simplest, such a statement would look something like this:

```
SELECT * from members WHERE MATCH(name) AGAINST('park')
```

Again, it's quite reasonable here to experiment a little, measuring the trade-offs of performance on SELECTs against performance on inserts or disk limitations.

Table design

In Chapter 14, we discussed table design pretty extensively; we're not going to recap all that information here. However, we do want to reiterate some points about field types because choice of table fields can have significant performance impact.

There are two interrelated concerns when choosing field types for a table: speed and size in memory. Your field definitions should anticipate the largest possible value that they may be asked to store, while not overanticipating and therefore creating unnecessarily huge tables with lots of unused space, both on disk and in memory. Appropriate field choices also come into play when choosing indexes for your table. Indexes are of the greatest benefit when they are set on a field type that is optimized for the type of data it is expected to hold. If, for example, you want an indexed number field where the count will never be more than 65,000 or so records, that index will perform more efficiently on the SMALLINT field type than it will on the MEDIUMINT field type, which allocates more space and therefore must search that extra space when attempting to isolate a specific value.

A similar principle holds true for the string types. Although there's some debate whether or not it's even advisable to index on a string column, that index will certainly perform more efficiently on a field that is defined precisely to the specifications of the data you will wish to store on it.

Earlier in this book, we pointed out that sometimes concerns about performance are so inflated that they border on the ridiculous. That's still the way we feel. It should not, however, appear inconsistent that we stress performance concerns now. This section and those that follow offer easily implemented design considerations that will collectively improve the performance of your databases.

Making the Database Work for You

Just as when you write code in a programming language, writing code that interacts with a database is an exercise in appropriate division of labor. People who write programming languages and databases have agreed to automate, standardize, and optimize certain tasks that come up over and over again in programming, so that programmers don't have to constantly reinvent the wheel when making their individual applications. The very general rule is that, unless you're willing to spend a lot of energy in optimizing code for your special case, you are better off using a database-provided facility than trying to invent your own solution for the same task.

It's probably faster than you are

Database programs are judged partly on their speed, so database programmers devote a large proportion of their effort toward ensuring that queries execute as quickly as possible. In particular, any searching or sorting of the contents of a database is best done within that database (if possible) rather than by your own code.

A bad example: Looping, not restricting

For example, take the following code fragment (and please don't laugh—we have actually seen code like this):

```
function print_first_name_bad ($lastname, $dbconnection)
{
  $query = "SELECT firstname, lastname FROM author";
  $result_id = mysql_query($query, $dbconnection)
    or die(mysql_error());
```

```
while ($row = mysql_fetch_array($result_id))
{
  if ($row['lastname'] == $lastname)
    print("The first name is " . $row['firstname']);
}
}
```

When this code is handed a last name string and a database connection, it will print out associated first names, if any, in the "author table" of the database. For example, a call to print_first_name_bad('Sagan', $dbconnection) might produce the output

```
The first name is Carl
```

If there were multiple authors in that table with the same last name, then multiple lines would be printed.

The problem here is that we don't need to grab all the data in this table, pull it through the narrow pipe of a connection, and then pick and choose from it on our side of the pipe. Instead, we should restrict the query with a WHERE clause:

```
function print_first_name_better ($lastname, $dbconnection)
{
  $query = "SELECT firstname, lastname FROM author
            WHERE lastname = '$lastname'";
  $result_id = mysql_query($query, $dbconnection)
    or die(mysql_error());
  while ($row = mysql_fetch_array($result_id))
  {
      print("The first name is " . $row['firstname']);
  }
}
```

The WHERE clause ensures that only the rows we care about are selected in the first place. Not only does this cut down on the data passed over the SQL connection, but the code used to locate the correct rows on the database side is almost certainly quicker than your PHP code.

Sorting and aggregating

Exactly the same argument applies if you find yourself writing code to sort results that have been returned from your database, or to count, average, or otherwise aggregate those results. In general, the ORDER BY syntax in SQL will allow you to presort your retrieved rows by any prioritized list of columns in the query, and that sort will probably be more efficient than either homegrown code or the PHP array-sorting functions. Similarly, rather than looping through DB rows to count, sum, or average a value, investigate whether the syntax of your particular DB's flavor of SQL supports the GROUP BY construct and in-query functions such as count(), sum(), and average(). In general, executing a query like:

```
$query = "SELECT count(ID) FROM author";
```

will be a radically more efficient approach to counting table rows than selecting them and iterating through them with a PHP looping construct.

Where possible, use MIN or MAX rather than sorting

Although it's good to let the database system do your sorting for you, it's even better to not have to sort at all. One task that is often addressed by unnecessary sorting is finding the minimum or maximum value in a set of result rows. You may see code like this:

```
$query = "SELECT ID FROM author ORDER BY ID limit 1;
// inefficient
```

This query will return a single ID from the author table after having sorted it in ascending order — in other words, the minimum ID. It does have the virtue that the actual result set returned is small, so it is a better approach for finding the minimum than using the same query without the limit clause and picking off the desired value from the top of that large result set. But if all we are interested in is the minimum (or maximum) value, there is no need to require the DB to figure out the rank order of all the other IDs that we are not interested in. A better solution is:

```
$query = select min(ID) from author; // efficient
```

The difference between these approaches will be imperceptible when your tables have only tens or hundreds of rows in them but will begin to matter as your tables grow to thousands or tens of thousands of rows in size.

Creating date and time fields

It is very common to want to associate a date and/or time with a row's worth of data. For instance, your table rows might represent requests made by your Web site users, and the associated date/time is the time that that request hit your database.

Now, one way to insert or update date fields is to include a string that represents the desired date in a format parsable by your database. For example, if you want to set the `mydate` date-time field of all rows of `mytable` to a particular date, you might set up a query like this one:

```
$query = "UPDATE mytable SET mydate = '2003-11-24'";
```

and then send that query off for evaluation. (Unfortunately, the exact standards of readable date formats vary quite widely from one SQL database system to another. This particular date string means November 24, 2003, as far as MySQL is concerned.)

The preceding approach is fine, as long as you take care that the particular date string you send is, in fact, readable as a date by your DB. Things get more complicated if you need to construct such a string on the fly to represent a date that depends on the value of variables in your script.

The main thing to remember is that, with most database systems, there is no need to go through such contortions to set a field to the current date or time. Many have a current-date function that can be embedded directly in your query. For example, a MySQL version of the preceding query that sets the relevant date/time field to the current instant looks like this:

```
$query = "UPDATE mytable SET mydate = now()";
```

Note that the call to `now()` is not enclosed in single quotes, because it's a call to database function rather than a string to be interpreted by the database as data. The analogous query for Microsoft SQL Server looks like:

```
$query = "UPDATE mytable SET mydate = getdate()";
```

Finally, even if the time you want stored is not that of the instant of execution, there may still be better alternatives than constructing readable date strings in your script. In addition to functions returning the current date, many versions of SQL offer functions for performing date arithmetic — start with a particular date/time, and then add or subtract years, months, or hours. In MySQL, these functions are:

✦ date_add(*date, date-interval*)

✦ date_sub(*date, date-interval*)

Here *date-interval* is a string that includes a number of time units and the type of unit. A MySQL query to set all rows to a time a week from now might look like this:

```
$query = "UPDATE mytable SET mydate = date_add(now(), INTERVAL 7 DAY)";
```

Finding the last inserted row

Another surprisingly helpful capability offered by some database systems is finding the ID of the last row inserted.

This problem arises when you are trying to create a new database entry that is distributed across several database tables, each of which has an automatically incremented primary key. As an example, take the tables created by the following MySQL statements:

```
CREATE TABLE author (ID int primary key auto_increment,
                     lastname varchar(75),
                     firstname varchar (75));
CREATE TABLE book (ID int primary key auto_increment,
                   authorID int,
                   title varchar(100));
```

One intent of these statements is that the book table is linked to the author table by joining them so that book.authorID = author.ID. Another intent is that we don't have to worry about assigning unique ID fields for either table — the database will automatically assign them. Unfortunately, the combined intent leads to a problem. How do we write code that will gracefully insert a linked book-author pair, when both the author and the book are new to the database? If we insert a new author, the ID field of the inserted row will be automatically created by the database and so will not be a part of our SQL insert statement. How can we give the correct authorID to our new book row?

One possible strategy is to do something like the following (in MySQL):

```
$author_lastname = 'Feynman';
$author_firstname = 'Richard';
$book_title = 'The Character of Physical Law';
$author_insert = "INSERT INTO author (lastname, firstname)
     VALUES ('$author_lastname','$author_firstname')";
mysql_query($author_insert) OR die(mysql_error());
$author_id_query =
  "SELECT ID FROM author
   WHERE lastname = '$author_lastname'
   AND firstname = '$author_firstname'";
$author_id_result =
```

```
    mysql_query($author_id_query) OR die(mysql_error());
if (mysql_num_rows($author_id_result) <= 0)
  die("Inserted author not found!");
else
  $author_row = mysql_fetch_row($author_id_result);
$authorID = $author_row[0];
$book_insert = "INSERT INTO book (authorID, title)
                 VALUES ($authorID, $book_title)";
mysql_query($book_insert) OR die(mysql_error());
```

In this code, we create a new author row, use the last name and first name of the author to select the row we have just created, pull out the unique ID of that newly created row, and then incorporate that ID in a statement inserting a new row into the book table. This code would probably work in this particular instance, if we assume that the author's last name and first name are sufficient for unique identification. But for many databases, we will not be able to make such an assumption, which is, of course, why the convention of unique IDs developed in the first place.

A similar approach that is sometimes used is to insert a row (for example, into the author table) and then select the maximum ID from that table, on the theory that the highest row ID will be the one most recently inserted. If the most recently inserted row is, in fact, the one we just inserted, this will work like a charm. Unfortunately, this is exactly the kind of approach that appears to work when tested by a solitary user/programmer and then breaks when used with a real database server that is dealing with requests from multiple connections at the same time. The problem is that an insertion from another connection might well arrive in between our own insertion and the statement we send to retrieve the maximum ID to date, with the result that our second insertion is matched with an inappropriate ID.

The best solution, when it is available, is to have the database itself keep track of the last inserted ID in a retrievable way, and do this tracking on a *per-connection* basis, so that there are no worries about the synchronization issues in the previous paragraph. For MySQL users, PHP offers the function mysql_insert_id(), which takes a connection ID as argument and returns the autoincremented ID of the last inserted row. We can use it to rewrite our previous code example:

```
$author_lastname = 'Feynman';
$author_firstname = 'Richard';
$book_title = 'The Character of Physical Law';
$author_insert = "INSERT INTO author (lastname, firstname)
        VALUES($author_insert) OR die(mysql_error());
$authorID = mysql_insert_id();
$book_insert = "INSERT INTO book (authorID, title)
                 VALUES ($authorID, '$book_title')";
mysql_query($book_insert) OR die (mysql_error());
```

As with many PHP/MySQL functions, the connection argument to mysql_insert_id() is actually optional and defaults to the most recently opened connection.

In some other database systems, the ID of the most recent autoincrement is available (per-session) as a "special" variable that can be embedded in the next query. In Microsoft SQL Server, for example, the variable is %%identity, which can be embedded in a query as follows to retrieve the last insert ID:

```
$query = "SELECT @@identity";
```

Summary

Because database-related functionality is among the most resource-intensive things that PHP can do, you can become a hero by giving just a little thought to efficient coding practices. Particularly if your data-driven PHP scripts are sluggish, you want to learn to work with the database instead of against it.

The basic principles of database-intensive coding are simple. It costs a lot to open a connection to a database, so don't turn the tap on and off unnecessarily. Remember the pipe is narrow — you want to transport the bare minimum of data you need for each page. And take the time to learn all the functionality your particular database can offer you. SQL is really good at indexing, sorting, filtering, restricting, numbering, and grouping — use these powers rather than doing it less well and more slowly with PHP.

In Chapter 19, we move from these tips and stylistic concerns to problems and gotchas that can actually break your database code or give you unintended results.

✦   ✦   ✦

PHP/MySQL Gotchas

◆ ◆ ◆ ◆

In This Chapter

Connection errors

Problems with privileges

Unescaped quotes

Bad SQL

More or less data than expected

Specific SQL functions

Debugging

◆ ◆ ◆ ◆

T his chapter details some of the common difficulties that arise with using PHP and databases. The goal is to help you diagnose and solve problems more quickly and with less frustration. As usual, our specific code and function references are to MySQL (with one exception), although the set of gotchas is fairly independent across different databases.

Cross-Reference   This chapter is about diagnosing and fixing PHP/database code that is genuinely broken — that is, it is not successfully retrieving data, or it is producing error messages. If your scripts are working, but too slowly, see Chapter 18.

No Connection

If you have a database call in your PHP script and the connection can't be opened, you will see a version of one of these two warning screens (depending on how high your error reporting levels are cranked up, and, to some extent, the precise cause of the problem).

Tip   In these examples, `display_errors` is set to `on` in the php.ini file — as it always should be on production servers. If it were set to off, you would have to echo the `mysql_error()` function to see the error message in the browser. Also, connection errors will not display if you use `die()`.

The first possibility is the No Connection warning, as shown in Figure 19-1.

This option indicates a problem either with the MySQL server itself or with the path to `mysqld`. In its own special way, PHP is telling you that it knows about MySQL but can't hook up to it. This is the error you will see on a working PHP-MySQL installation if the database server crashes.

If the problem is on the PHP side, your error screen will look more like the one shown in Figure 19-2.

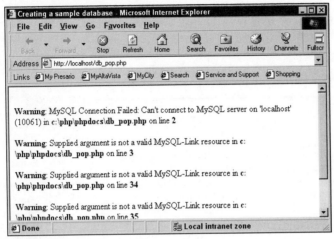

Figure 19-1: A No Connection warning

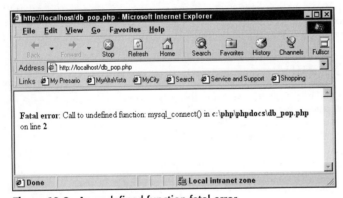

Figure 19-2: An undefined function fatal error

This means PHP doesn't know about MySQL at all.

Of the two, the fatal error is much more straightforward to fix. Clearly, if you're running into an undefined function that is supposed to be in the PHP function set, you can be pretty sure you simply forgot to build that module into your installation. So on the Unix side, you will need to recompile with the `--with-mysql` option. On the Windows side, MySQL should be precompiled into the binary for you and immediately available. In the case of any other supported database or a version of PHP older than 4.1, you merely need to uncomment the `extension=php_[database].dll` line in your `php.ini` file to be ready to go, unless you put your MySQL executable in a very, very strange place (which you shouldn't do unless you're prepared to handle the consequences, including fatal errors).

The innocuous-looking No Connection error is actually a little harder to diagnose because there are several possible causes. They fall into two main categories:

✦ The MySQL daemon isn't running.

✦ The MySQL socket isn't where PHP is looking for it.

It's easy to check whether `mysqld` is running, so you may as well do that first. Just use whatever method you prefer to check running processes. On Windows, this means it's time for the old `Ctrl+Alt+Delete` action to bring up the Task Manager. On Unix, where freedom of choice is the watchword, you can check the system processes by means of `ps` or a graphical system monitoring utility or even by querying `mysqladmin` directly.

If `mysqld` is down, perhaps you have merely forgotten to (re)start it. (Don't laugh. It happens.) If it's been running continuously for 143 days before suddenly quitting in the middle of an operation, your problem is beyond the scope of this book. We can only direct you to the MySQL Web site (at `www.mysql.com`) with our deepest sympathies and most fervent hopes that you've maintained a good backup schedule.

The socket problem usually arises the first time you fire up MySQL on a new server. It's rather uncommon for this problem to occur in a long-running site, although it does happen. For instance, we recently had a Web host move our MySQL daemon to another server on short notice, at which point all our scripts that used the hostname `localhost` immediately crashed.

The solution to your database connection problems is generally to be found in the `php.ini` file. There's a section of MySQL variables that you must carefully check against whatever hostname, port, and socket you're specifying in your PHP scripts. You want to ensure you're not inadvertently directing PHP to look for MySQL on an odd port or at the wrong default host. On Unix, you can also check the `/etc/services` file for a different socket address, and the `/etc/hosts` file for an unexpected server alias. In general, you should leave these variables open unless you have a specific reason to set them.

Problems with Privileges

Error messages caused by privilege problems look a lot like the connection errors described previously. You will see a No Connection error that looks like Figure 19-3.

The key differentiator is that little piece about the user and password.

Caution   Because of the security issues caused by these failure messages, which include the database username and host and whether you're using a password or not, it's best to use silent mode on a production site. You do this by putting the character @ in front of the functions `mysql_connect` and `mysql_select_db` or by setting `display_errors` to `off` in the `php.ini` file.

These errors are many in number but fall into pretty clear major types:

✦ Mistyping usernames/passwords.

✦ Failing to use a necessary password.

✦ Trying to use a nonexistent password.

✦ Trying to use your system's username/password instead of the MySQL username/password.

✦ Employing a database username that lacks the necessary permissions for the task.

✦ Logging in from a location or client that the MySQL database does not allow for a particular user.

✦ PHP's being unable to open the database-password `include` file because of incorrect file permissions. (It must be a world-readable file in a world-executable directory.)

✦ The database root user's having deliberately changed permissions on you.

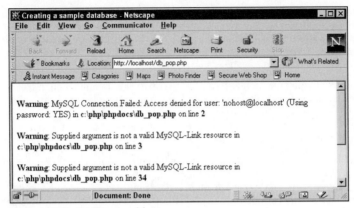

Figure 19-3: Privilege problems

These are not structural problems, but usually just simple slips of memory that result in mis-cues or misrecollections. They are very common. We aren't too proud to confess that we've fallen victim to all of them—and not just once but over and over. They should be trivial to fix in the vast majority of situations. If you are confident your username and password combination is correct, you try using MySQL's FLUSH PRIVILEGES command to insure the most current changes are loaded.

Unescaped Quotes

Quotes can cause many small but annoying buglets between PHP and MySQL. The crux of the issue is that PHP evaluates within double quotes and largely ignores single quotes, whereas MySQL evaluates within single quotes and largely ignores double quotes. This can lead to situations where you have to think hard about the purpose of each quotation mark. An example is:

```
mysql_query("INSERT INTO book (ID, title, year, ISBN)
        VALUES(NULL, '$title', '$year', '$ISBN')");
```

In most of PHP, variables within single quotes are not expanded, whereas variables in double quotes or unquoted variables are—so this query looks a bit strange. But if you think about it, the statement is valid in both languages. The single quotes exist within double quotes, so PHP takes them as literal characters, and the variables are actually within double quotes, so PHP replaces them with their values. You can think of the division of labor this way: In a database query, PHP does its thing on the stuff between double quotes (treating single quotes literally), and MySQL later deals with the stuff left over within single quotes.

Obviously you'll need to exercise some care when writing these statements. This is one of the reasons why it's preferable to break up your MySQL queries into two parts, a query string and a mysql_query() function, like so:

```
$query = "INSERT INTO book (ID, title, year, ISBN)
        VALUES(NULL, '$title', '$year', '$ISBN')";
$result = mysql_query($query);
```

This style also eliminates the double parentheses that account for common PHP errors.

Even greater issues arise with strings that use single quotes and double quotes within the text. Remember that apostrophes and single quotes are the same thing for PHP and MySQL — they have no smart-quoting feature (not that most smart quotes are all that smart anyway). So this insertion query will break as follows if any of your lastname entries ever has an apostrophe in it (for example, O'Hara, D'Souza, and M'Naughten):

```
$query = "INSERT INTO employee (ID, lastname, firstname)
          VALUES(NULL, '$lastname', '$firstname')";
$result = mysql_query($query);
```

Other very common problems are caused by names of businesses with apostrophes in them, such as Rosalita's Bar and Grill or Yoshi's Hair Salon, and by any string that might have a contraction or possessive in it (such as can't, what's, or Mike's).

The parallel issue on the PHP side is a string with a double quote in it. This construction will definitely not work as intended:

```
$string = "He said, "I'm not angry," but I knew he was.";
$statement = mysql_query("INSERT INTO diary (ID, entry)
                          VALUES(NULL, '$string')";
```

Caution   In very long text entries, a quote problem may present as a partial string being inserted; or it may appear as a complete failure; or it may seem as though only short entries are being accepted while longer entries fail.

If you're using an HTML form with values, and only the first word of your string is being inserted, the problem is likely to be that you forgot to quote the form value properly. In other words, your form field says `<INPUT TYPE="text" VALUE=quoted string>` rather than `<INPUT TYPE="text" VALUE="quoted string">`.

The following list reviews the three ways of dealing with quoting issues:

✦ In cases where the string is directly stated within the code, you can escape the necessary characters with a backslash.

```
$query = "INSERT INTO employee (ID, lastname, firstname)
          VALUES(NULL, 'O\'Donnell', 'Sean')";
```

✦ In cases where the string is represented by a variable, you can use `addslashes()`, which will automatically add any necessary backslashes.

```
$string =
addslashes("He said, 'I'm not angry,' but I knew he was.");
$statement = mysql_query("INSERT INTO diary (ID, entry)
                          VALUES(NULL, '$string')");
```

✦ You can build PHP with the `--with-magic-quotes` option, and/or set magic-quotes to on in the `php.ini` file, or use the `set_magic_quotes_runtime(1)` function. This will add slashes without your needing to specify `addslashes()` each time. If your ISP controls the `php.ini` file, you should still be able to set these variables by changing your own `.htaccess` file.

For some murky psychological reason, many PHP users seem exceedingly averse to using `addslashes()` and its partner, `stripslashes()`. People will tie themselves in knots using single quotes when they really shouldn't, just so they don't have to escape double quotes. This practice is bad style at any time but is especially dangerous when using a database.

You need to add slashes when inserting values into a database; conversely, you'll need to strip out the slashes when pulling strings from a database (unless you have magic quotes turned on).

```
$query = "SELECT passphrase FROM userinfo
        WHERE username='$username'";
$result = mysql_query($query);
$query_row = mysql_fetch_array($result);
$passphrase = stripslashes($query_row[0]);
```

If you fail to do this, more and more slashes will be added each time you reenter the data into MySQL! This is an issue that is very frequently encountered with editable Web forms that redisplay values pulled from a database, as shown in Figure 19-4.

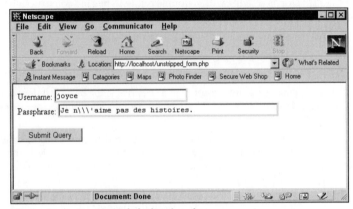

Figure 19-4: Unstripped slashes in a form

Broken SQL Statements

In addition to quoting problems, there are a number of easy ways to send a *bad* query to the database. That query might be syntactically malformed, have the right syntax but refer to tables that do not exist, or have any of a number of problems that make the database unable to handle it properly. A typical error message is shown in Figure 19-5.

Caution   A MySQL error (such as the one shown in Figure 19-5) is different from a connection or link error, which looks something like Figure 19-1. A MySQL error is the error returned from the database when you try to do something that it doesn't like. It is not automatically echoed to the screen; you need to call mysql_error() to see any output. A connection error is a message that PHP is sending to you when an expected connection or link is not present. It is automatically echoed to the screen if you're using display_errors and must be silenced by being prepended with an @.

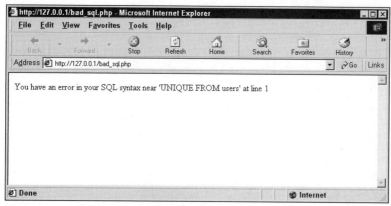

Figure 19-5: A bad SQL statement error

Older versions of PHP used to automatically `echo` an error statement in these circumstances. Now, if you wish to find out what the problem is, you must manually call `mysql_error()` (as we've done in the preceding example) or `mysql_errno()`. The safest way to capture these errors is to send them to a log file by using `error_log()`.

> **Note**
>
> A broken or invalid SQL query is not the same thing as a query that returns no rows. You can write a perfectly fine SQL query like the following:
>
> ```
> $query = "select ID from cust where name = 'nonexistent'";
> ```
>
> You send it to your DB and get back a perfectly valid result set, which happens to contain exactly 0 rows. Among other things, this means that error-trapping that catches query failures will not help you detect the case of zero rows. For MySQLers, a helpful function is `mysql_num_rows()`, which is called on the query result ID and returns an integer.

Exactly how a bad SQL problem will present itself in your browser depends on your PHP version, your database version, your error settings, and how much error-checking code you have incorporated in your script. Just as with other kinds of malignancy, early detection of a failed query is key.

Your new best friend for making MySQL queries looks like this:

```
$result = mysql_query($query) or error_log(mysql_error());
```

Because `mysql_query()` will return a false value if it fails, the `error_log()` portion will be executed only if a failure occurs. The low operator precedence of the `or` operator ensures that the `error_log()` call also plays no role in the assignment statement — if the assignment succeeds, it is as if the `error()` portion did not exist. Failure leads to the script exiting just as soon as it has printed the most informative error message that the MySQL designers could concoct. If your particular database lacks such an error variable in PHP, you might want to simply call `error_log($query)`. Often, the problem is obvious after you see the query that is actually being sent.

If you have not incorporated error-checking into your query calls, you will get the first bad news when you try to use the query result ID in subsequent database code. The typical pattern is:

```
$my_result = mysql_query($bad_query);
$row = mysql_fetch_row($my_result); // error shows up here
```

The typical error message for MySQL is 0 is not a mysql result identifier in [some row]. This is because, rather than detecting the 0 value that mysql_query() returns when it fails, you have tried to use that value as if it were a valid identifier for a result set.

Tip   Although a bad query is by far the most common way of producing the 0 is not a valid result identifier message, it is not the only way. You would also get that message if you misspelled the name of the result identifier variable (and it was, therefore, unbound) or if the query statement had never actually executed (with the same result). Again, it is much easier to distinguish these problems if you trap the errors early on.

Misspelled names

The sad truth is that for every bug that plumbs the depths of programming esoterica, there are a gazillion cheap mistakes that seem obvious once you've discovered them. The former may break your brain, but afterward you feel a certain exhilaration at testing your skills against a really hard nut. The latter just leave you feeling empty and regretful at the time you wasted on something so trivial.

So let us start with the single most common error: simple misspelling of table, column, and value names. It doesn't help that PHP and MySQL are both case sensitive. Ask for 'mytable' instead of 'MyTable', and you can expect a quick return of *el número céro*. No force on earth can prevent you from doing this once in a while, and the error messages will be uninformative at best. So what can we say? Remember that even the most experienced programmers do it too.

Comma faults

Remember to put the comma *outside* the single quotes within a SQL statement. This will not work:

```
$query = "UPDATE book SET title='$title,' subtitle='$subtitle,'
ISBN='$ISBN'";
```

But this will:

```
$query = "UPDATE book SET title='$title', subtitle='$subtitle',
ISBN='$ISBN'";
```

Think of the single quotes as part of the variable itself rather than following common American-English typographical practice, which puts a comma inside a quote.

Unquoted string arguments

Any values that should be treated by the database as string data types typically need to be single-quoted within a SQL statement. For example, this query has the correct syntax:

```
$query = "SELECT * FROM author WHERE firstname = 'Daniel'";
```

By contrast, if we make a `mysql_query()` call using the following query, we should expect an error:

```
$query = "SELECT * FROM author WHERE firstname = Daniel";
```

The actual error returned by the database may be deceptive, though—quite likely the complaint will be about an unknown column named `'Daniel'`. This is because unquoted strings are assumed to name columns, as in:

```
$query = "select * from author where firstname = lastname";
```

This would be a perfectly acceptable way to search our database for Humbert Humbert and Lisa Lisa, but it won't work for people with more ordinary names.

Unbound variables

One of the sneakier ways to break a SQL statement is to interpolate an unbound variable into the middle of it.

When it works, the automatic splicing of variables into double-quoted strings is a perfect match for a SQL-based dialog with your database. Your code can determine values, for example, that are used to restrict the scope of a query made to the DB, as in this snippet:

```
$customerID = find_customer_id(); //returns int
$result_id = mysql_query("SELECT * FROM customers
                    WHERE ID = $customer_ID"); //BUG
$row = mysql_fetch_row($result_id);  //CRASH
```

Because this code makes no attempt to trap query errors, you will again see a complaint about the fact that `0 is not a valid` MySQL `result identifier`. It's possible (for us anyway) to stare at code like this for quite a while without seeing anything wrong (although the good PHP coders who habitually crank error reporting up to `E_ALL` will be rewarded with the cause of the error in a warning message). The problem, of course, is that we assigned a variable (`$customerID`) and then embedded a different one (`$customer_ID`) in our SQL statement. The latter variable is unbound and so behaves like an empty string when interpreted by the double-quote parsing. The result is that the database sees the following query, which is not valid SQL:

```
SELECT * FROM customers WHERE ID =
```

This kind of problem is one reason why it is often a good idea to construct your query and assign it to a variable in a separate statement, like this:

```
$my_query = "SELECT * FROM customers WHERE ID = $customer_ID";
```

Then make a distinct subsequent call to `mysql_query($my_query)`. If you do this, it is very easy to add printing or logging statements that show you the actual query you are sending.

Too Little Data, Too Much Data

Finally, you may find that your PHP/database script is working apparently without error but is displaying no data from the database or far more than you expected. As a vague and general rule, if your query function is returning successfully (and your code checks that), your suspicions might rightly turn to the SQL itself. Recheck the logic, particularly of `WHERE` clauses. It is easy, for example, to write a query like:

```
"SELECT * FROM families WHERE kidcount = 1 AND kidcount = 2";
```

In this query, you are really intending an or rather than an and, with the result that zero rows will be returned regardless of the contents of your database.

If your script is iterating through database rows and displaying them and you find that you have far, far too many of those rows, the problem is very often a SQL join that has too few restrictions. As a general rule, the number of restrictions in a WHERE clause should not be fewer than the number of tables joined minus one. For example, the following query has three tables but only one joining restriction:

```
"SELECT book.title FROM book, author, country
WHERE author.countryID = country.ID"
```

It is likely to return every possible book/author pair, without reference to whether the author wrote the book, which is probably not what was intended.

Specific SQL Functions

A few specific functions seem to cause a higher than normal number of problems, especially in the learning phase. These functions can send even the experienced PHP developer running to the online manual to check the arguments and returned data types time and time again.

mysql_affected_rows() versus mysql_num_rows()

Both of these functions tell you how many rows of data your last SQL statement touched. However, mysql_num_rows() works only on SELECT statements, while mysql_affected_rows() works only on INSERT, UPDATE, and DELETE statements. The way to think about it is that SELECTs do not affect (meaning *change*) any data that exists in the database.

Furthermore, mysql_affected_rows() takes an optional link identifier as the argument, whereas mysql_num_rows() takes a nonoptional result resource. This means that you can only get a valid result from mysql_affected_rows() until the moment you call another INSERT, UPDATE, or DELETE. In contrast, if you use different variable names for your result resources, you can use mysql_num_rows() anytime in the script. This code will help clarify the differences:

```
$link_id = mysql_connect($host, $user, $pass);
mysql_select_db($database, $link_id);

$query = "INSERT INTO mytable VALUES(NULL, '$myval')";
$result_resource = mysql_query($query);
$test_insert = mysql_affected_rows();
// This should work and return 1

$query1 = "SELECT * FROM mytable";
$result_resource1 = mysql_query($query1);
$test_select = mysql_num_rows($result_resource1);

$query2 = "DELETE FROM mytable";
$result_resource2 = mysql_query($query2);
$test_select2 = mysql_num_rows($result_resource2);
```

```
//Will not work
$test_delete = mysql_affected_rows();
//This will return the number of rows in the table; at this
// point you can no longer get the old result of 1
$test_select_again = mysql_num_rows($result_resource1);
//Should be the same as $test_select
```

mysql_result()

This function, which returns one value at a time from the database, is now used rather rarely. Unlike mysql_fetch_row() and mysql_fetch_array(), you need to specify the row and field of the value you're fetching as well as the result resource. Thus, you cannot do this:

```
// This won't work
while (mysql_result($result_resource)) {
  // Some loop
}

// This will
$firstname = mysql_result($result_resource1, 0, 'firstname');
```

You should really use this function only when you know you'll be fetching one or two pieces of data (a user's first name, for instance). Otherwise, the others are much faster.

OCIFetch()

When users of MySQL or SQL Server switch over to Oracle, they often have trouble with the OCI fetching functions — particularly this one. Unlike most other database row-fetching functions, you don't immediately access the result of OCIFetch() via echo or some other PHP function. This function fetches the result of a SQL statement into a result buffer — where it can be accessed via OCIResult().

```
$query = "SELECT * from mytable";
$stmt = OCIParse($conn, $query);
$exec_result = OCIExecute($stmt, OCI_DEFAULT);
$row2buffer = OCIFetch($stmt);
$myval = OCIResult($stmt, "MYCOLUMN");
echo $myval;
```

This function should probably be thought of as analogous to mysql_result() rather than mysql_fetch_row(), or at best occupying a middle ground between the two. Similarly, it should only be used when you are sure you will be fetching very small data sets. Otherwise, use OCIFetchInto() or OCIFetchStatement(), both of which return arrays.

Debugging and Sanity Checking

If you are nearing your wit's end in trying to debug query-related errors and misbehavior, you may find it extremely useful to compare the results of your PHP-embedded queries with the same queries made directly to the database. If your technical setup permits actually running a SQL client directly (for example, the mysql or Oracle command-line clients), as well as cross-program cutting and pasting, try this two-step process:

1. Insert a debugging statement in your PHP script that prints the query itself immediately before it is actually used in a DB query call (for example, echo $query).

2. Directly paste that query from your browser output (or the HTML source) into your SQL client.

Caution   Obviously, this advice applies only to code under development, not to code you are running in production. It might be okay to echo errors to the browser while you're developing something for the first time, but when it's ready to go into production, you should make sure all your echo() statements are replaced with error_log() functions.

If the query looks reasonable to you, but it breaks both in the SQL program and in PHP, then there is some syntax or naming error in that SQL statement itself that you are missing, and your PHP code is not to blame (unless, of course, your code constructed that query in the first place). Similarly, with a dearth or overabundance of rows — if the behavior is the same in both places — the query is to blame. If, on the other hand, the behavior in the SQL interpreter looks like what you wanted, then the query is fine, and your suspicion should turn to your PHP code that actually sends that query and processes the results.

One final and general tip is to study any error messages very carefully, paying attention to phrases like link identifier and result resource identifier. In MySQL, the former means an identifier of a database *connection*, and the latter identifies the set of rows returned by a particular *query*. It is easy to confuse the two, as in the following code:

```
$my_connection = mysql_connect('localhost', $myname, $mypass);
mysql_select_db('MyDB');
$result = mysql_query($my_query, $my_connection);
while ($row = mysql_fetch_row($my_connection)) {
  // LOOP
}
```

This code will probably yield an error that contains the words not a valid result identifier. The problem is that we are using the connection ID where the result ID should be. The resulting error message is justified yet opaque.

Summary

PHP/database bugs are often not very deep or subtle but can still be difficult to diagnose. In general, the earlier in a script you can detect trouble, the easier the diagnosis will be. Especially when you are debugging, every statement that interacts with the database should have an associated error_log() clause, containing an informative error message.

By far, the most common cause of database-connection problems is incorrect arguments to the connection function (hostname, username, password). The most common causes of failed queries are quote faults, unbound variables, and simple misspellings.

If you have repeated failures with database queries that seem like they should be working, have your code print out the query that it is sending to the DB; if possible, try making that very query to the database directly. If the problem persists when PHP is out of the loop, you can safely restrict your attention to database design and your understanding of SQL queries.

✦   ✦   ✦

Advanced Features and Techniques

Object-Oriented Programming with PHP

There are many possible audiences for this chapter, including people who know basic PHP but nothing about object-oriented programming (OOP), and people who know all about OOP and nothing about PHP. As usual, we aim to please everyone all at once, but be warned that you may want to pick and choose from the sections.

We start with a quick and very general introduction to object-oriented programming for those who are completely unfamiliar with it. If you are already comfortable with OOP from another language, please skip this section — it will not enlighten you (and might well enrage you). The section "PHP Constructs for OOP" gets into the meat of the basic syntax and behavior of PHP objects. Later in the chapter, we delve into more extended examples and cover some of the more obscure issues and gotchas around objects in PHP. Along the way, we offer a couple of sidebar meta-discussions, about the merits of object-oriented PHP and the extent to which PHP should be considered to be OOP.

Note   In general in this chapter, we discuss OOP programming constructs as they are implemented in PHP5, which uses the new and significantly improved Zend Engine 2 as its parser.

What Is Object-Oriented Programming?

So what is object-oriented programming (OOP) all about anyway? OOP turns out to be a very simple idea, which (when taken seriously and built into the structure of programming languages) leads to all sorts of more complicated elaborations.

The simple idea

The simple idea is this: Rather than creating data structures on the one hand and code on the other, suppose we reorganize everything so that associated pieces of code and data are bundled together?

The procedural approach

For example, imagine a conventional procedural (non-object-oriented) program for manipulating personal calendars, with the capability to display, update, and edit calendars. Somewhere in the code for such a program, we would find the actual data definitions for representing someone's appointments for a particular month; somewhere else we would find code that did the right things to manipulate that data. Typically, the only connection between the datatype definitions and the manipulation code is that a clever programmer has made sure that they get matched up appropriately.

Now imagine combining our calendar program with a recipe program (say that we want to plan our meals in detail for an entire year). Again, there will be data structures somewhere that represent the contents of the calendar, and other data structures that represent the contents of the recipes. The data structures will use the basic datatypes of the programming language; for all we know, the top-level type of a calendar might be an array, and the top-level type of a recipe might also be an array. Somewhere else in the program there is code for digging into the data structures that represent calendars and recipes and doing the right things with them. What is the connection between the data structures and the code? Only that a careful programmer has made sure that the arrays that represent calendars and the arrays that represent recipes get fed to the appropriate manipulation code. (Otherwise, we might find ourselves trying to schedule an appointment in Beef Stroganoff rather than in March 2006.)

If we think of procedural code as outlined like a book, the outline for the code we're talking about might look like:

- ✦ 1) Data definitions
  - 1a) Data definitions for calendars
  - 1b) Data definitions for recipes
- ✦ 2) Data manipulation code
  - 2a) Code for calendars
  - 2b) Code for recipes

The object-oriented approach

The most basic version of OOP reorganizes the procedural approach by grouping associated pieces of code and data together into conceptual units. This means that we replace the outline in the preceding subsection with:

- ✦ 1) Calendars
  - 1a) Data definitions
  - 1b) Manipulation code
- ✦ 2) Recipes
  - 2a) Data definitions
  - 2b) Manipulation code

This organizational inversion is the heart of object-oriented programming.

But so what (we can hear you say)? If we're just talking about a way to organize code, we could do that without any special terminology or programming languages. In normal procedural code, we can organize function definitions and datatype definitions in any order we want to. For example, we could put all the datatype definition code into one directory and all the manipulation code into another (a procedural organization), or we could put all the calendar code into one directory and all the recipe code into another (an object-oriented organization).

Object-oriented programming begins to be interestingly different from procedural programming, however, once the programming language itself is set up to make it easy to organize things in an object-oriented way. (See the sidebar "Do Web-Scripting Languages Really Need OOP?" for a discussion of how useful this organization is in languages like PHP.) The most basic form this takes is that data objects can be built out of local functions as well as local data. For example, as we build a data structure that represents a calendar, we can include the data members that are needed (structures to represent days, months, years, appointments), but also the functions that will be needed (`new_appointment()`, `calendar_display()`, and so forth). These functions are (in some sense) stored locally in the object definition itself. A calendar doesn't have an ingredient list, and a recipe doesn't have 31 days; similarly, a calendar object doesn't have a `print_ingredients()` function, and a recipe doesn't have a `new_appointment()` function. Finally, of course, the data members in an object may themselves be objects of a different type.

Bundling code and data together into units is the basic idea, and OOP languages always offer some support for this kind of bundling. However, most OOP languages take things further and offer one or more of the following elaborations that give OOP even more leverage. (See the sidebar "How OO Is PHP?" for a discussion of the extent to which PHP itself has these features.)

Elaboration: Objects as datatypes

In addition to allowing us to store functions in our data, a good OO programming language lets us define these combinations as genuinely new datatypes that the language supports like any other type.

After such a type is defined, we can create as many such objects as we like, just as we can create as many integers as we like given the integer type. In object-oriented terminology, the term *class* is used to refer to the general type definition, which specifies the data members and member functions that each instance of that class should have.

The term *object* (or *instance*) refers to any individual instance of the type. For example, after we define a class called `Calendar` (which specifies the different kinds of data and functions that every self-respecting calendar should have), we can make any number of `Calendar` objects (which might be associated with individual people).

Elaboration: Inheritance

After we've written a program that uses the class `Calendar`, we might want to make a more specific version of the program for a particular purpose. What we would really like to do is copy most of the code from the `Calendar` class, but change it in just a few places, so that it prints differently, or has a culturally appropriate set of holidays, or allows us to schedule appointments to the second rather than to the hour.

Do Web-Scripting Languages Really Need OOP?

The object-oriented revolution has not been without controversy. Although many programmers embraced OOP quickly, others preferred the procedural approach they were used to, and wondered aloud if the extra machinery needed to support OOP wasn't more trouble than it was worth. Still, there's no doubt that the revolution has largely succeeded. Most of the popular programming languages in use today are either fully object-oriented or have object-oriented extensions. Also, at least some of the promises about improved productivity and increased code reuse seem to have been realized, as design methodologies like UML and patterns gain greater influence, and as people get more used to subclassing as a standard way to reuse and extend vendor-supplied libraries.

We feel that the benefits of OOP for "major" (that is, compiled) programming languages like Java and C++ are clear. On the other hand, we feel that the benefits of OOP for scripting languages (like Perl and PHP) are less obvious and are most debatable in the case of Web-scripting (PHP).

How is Web scripting different from other kinds of programming tasks? The most obvious difference is simply that Web scripts typically execute quickly and then go away. In other programming situations, you may have RAM-resident objects that live for hours or days and undergo complex evolutions of state that affect their behavior. A typical Web script, on the other hand, might execute for half a second, as it serves up a particular page, and then dies happy. You may knit these scripts together to provide a more extended user experience (using databases, sessions, cookies), but often such efforts are all about making the experience outlive any PHP objects that may or may not be created. More generally, scripting languages like PHP and Perl typically have a less thoroughgoing implementation of OOP than languages like Java, C++, and Smalltalk, and the limitations of implementation make these OOP extensions less attractive. (For more detail, see the sidebar "How OOP is PHP?" later in this chapter.)

This is not to say that there aren't still benefits of OOP in PHP. In addition to the conceptual benefits that may result from structuring code in an object-centered way, there are two good reasons to use PHP objects: 1) It's a good way to distribute third-party code for reuse; 2) Many programmers who are used to OO syntax from other languages won't feel comfortable unless they can use the same idioms in PHP.

But our main point is that use of PHP constructs for OOP is a very "tradeoffy" and pragmatic decision, which we have often seen made more on the basis of religion or fashion. If you are comfy with OO, this kind of syntax is there for you; and if you work in a group that has decided to write in that style, you may want to let the majority rule. If you decide not to go OO, however, be strong — we urge you not to be swayed by the moral-superiority arguments you may hear from people who disdain your five-line procedural script in favor of their ten-line OO script that does exactly the same task.

This desire is common enough that OOP offers a mechanism to support it called *inheritance*. The basic idea is that you can define a class in terms of another class, and then specify only the things that you want to be different in your own class. If you view the original class as the parent, the default is that both function definitions and data definitions are *inherited* by your child class unless you specify otherwise. This turns out to be a powerful technique for reusing class definitions. (As we will see in the "Basic PHP Constructs for OOP" section, OOP in PHP supports inheritance.)

Elaboration: Encapsulation

Part of the point of segregating both data and functions into objects is to reduce the complexity of programming by reducing unnecessary interactions. There is no reason why calendars should have to know about the internals of cooking recipes, or vice versa. So some OOP languages actually enforce information barriers between objects — after the programmer has defined which parts of recipes and calendars are purely internal and private to those classes, the language actually forbids code that is external to an object from messing with an object's internal workings. This kind of information-hiding is called *encapsulation*, and although this sounds restrictive, it can be a good source of clarity. In particular, if the programmer who designed a particular class knows that some parts of its workings have been designed to be private in this sense, the programmer also knows that those parts can be redesigned without checking with everyone who might be using that class's code. Support for encapsulation exists for the first time in PHP5, which incorporates Zend Engine 2. You'll see how to use encapsulation later in this chapter.

Elaboration: Constructors and destructors

After you have defined a class, you can make as many instances of it as you like. Each time you create such an instance, your favorite OOP language allocates memory to store the instance in, and gives you some way to refer to that instance later in the program. There are frequently a number of initialization steps you want to take every time you make an object of that class. *Constructor* functions offer a way to build that set of steps into the class definition. The standard way to create a new instance is to call a constructor function (which usually has the same name as the class and which you can customize to do all the necessary initialization).

Destructors are the opposite of constructors and specify all the cleanup actions that should happen when an object is dispensed with.

PHP has offered constructor functions since version 4.2 (which makes sense, because you can't have object orientation without having constructors). The language acquired explicitly definable and callable destructors only in PHP5 (destruction of classes was handled only in an automatic way before then). Again, these functions are covered later in this chapter.

Terminology

There are some standard terms in OOP parlance for all the concepts we have talked about thus far, and we will be using them for the rest of the chapter. (Several of these terms have alternate names, which we include in parentheses.)

✦ **Class:** This is a programmer-defined datatype, which includes local functions as well as local data. You can think of a class as a template (or mold, or form) for making many instances of the same kind (or class) of object.

✦ **Object:** (Also known as *object instance*, or *instance*.) An individual instance of the data structure defined by a class. You define a class once and then make many objects that belong to it.

✦ **Member variable:** (Also known as *property*, *attribute*, or *instance variable*.) One of the component pieces of data in a class definition.

✦ **Member function:** (Also known as *method*.) A member that happens to be a function.

✦ **Inheritance:** The process of defining a class in terms of another class. The new (child) class has all the member data and member function definitions from the old (parent) class by default but may define new members or "override" parent functions and give them new definitions. We say that class A *inherits from* class B if class A is defined in terms of class B in this way.

✦ **Parent class** (or *superclass* or *base class*): A class that is inherited from by another class.

✦ **Child class** (or *subclass* or *derived class*): A class that inherits from another class.

How OO is PHP?

How "object-oriented" is PHP? Your answer to that question probably depends on your particular litmus tests for object-orientedness. In this sidebar, we offer a whirlwind tour of features that typically show up in OOP languages and briefly discuss the extent to which PHP supports them. Some of these issues are explored more broadly in the section "Advanced OOP Features," later in this chapter. (Note: This sidebar is really only of interest to developers who are coming to PHP from a different OO language; everyone else may want to skip this game of buzzword bingo.)

Single inheritance

PHP allows a class definition to inherit from another class, using the `extends` clause. Both member variables and member functions are inherited.

Multiple inheritance

PHP offers no support for multiple inheritance and no notion of interface inheritance as in Java. Each class inherits from, at most, one parent class (though a class may implement many interfaces).

Constructors

Every class can have one constructor function, which in PHP is called `__construct()`. Note that there are two underscore characters at the front of that function name. Because prior to PHP5 (under Zend Engine 1), a class's constructor function had the same name as the class, PHP still allows (but discourages) that strategy for purposes of backward compatibility. Constructors of parent classes are not automatically called but must be invoked explicitly.

Destructors

PHP supports explicit destructor functions as of version 5. The destructor function of a class is always called `__destruct()`.

Encapsulation/access control

PHP supports public, private, and protected variables and member functions as of version 5.

Polymorphism/overloading

PHP supports polymorphism in the sense of allowing instance of subclasses to be used in place of parent instances. The correct member function will be dispatched to at runtime. There is no support for method overloading, where dispatch happens based on the method's signature — each class only has one member function of a given name. However, PHP's weak typing and support for variable numbers of arguments makes workarounds possible. See the section "Simulating polymorphism" later in this chapter (in the section "Advanced OOP Features").

Early versus late binding

Two equally good answers are: 1) The question doesn't arise, due to PHP being loosely typed, and 2) All binding is late. In PHP, values are typed but variables are not, so there is no question about what method to call when the variable is of a different type than the value.

Static (or class) functions

PHP offers static member variables and static methods as of version 5. It is also possible to call member functions via the `Classname::function()` syntax.

Introspection

PHP offers a wide variety of functions here, including the capability to recover class names, member function names, and member variable names from an instance. (See the section "Introspection Functions," later in this chapter.)

Basic PHP Constructs for OOP

In this section, we cover the basic PHP syntax for OOP from the ground up, with some simple examples.

Defining classes

The general form for defining a new class in PHP is as follows:

```
class myclass extends myparent {
  var $var1;
  var $var2 = "constant string";
  function myfunc ($arg1, $arg2) {
    [..]
  }
  [..]
}
```

The form of the syntax is as described, in order, in the following list:

✦ The special form `class`, followed by the name of the class that you want to define.

✦ An optional extension clause, consisting of the word `extends` and then the name of the class that should be inherited from.

✦ A set of braces enclosing any number of variable declarations and function definitions. Variable declarations start with the special form `var`, which is followed by a conventional $ variable name; they may also have an initial assignment to a constant value. Function definitions look much like standalone PHP functions but are local to the class.

As an example, consider the simple class definition in Listing 20-1, which prints out a box of text in HTML.

This is an extremely simple class definition. It has no parent (and, therefore, no `extends` clause). It has a single member variable (the variable $body_text), and a single member function (the function `display()`). The display function simply prints out the text variable, wrapped up in an HTML table definition.

Listing 20-1: TextBox.php

```
class TextBoxSimple {
  var $body_text = "my text";
  function display() {
    print("<TABLE BORDER=1><TR><TD>$this->body_text");
    print("</TD></TR></TABLE>");
  }
}
```

Accessing member variables

In general, the way to refer to a member variable from an object is to follow a variable containing the object with -> and then the name of the member. So if we had a variable $box containing an object instance of the class TextBox, we could retrieve its body_text variable with an expression like:

```
$text_of_box = $box->body_text;
```

However, when we are writing code within a member function, we haven't yet created the object instance, and so we have no variable like $box to refer to. The answer is the magic variable $this, which (when used inside a member function of a class) refers to the object instance itself. Note that this is how the display() function in Listing 20-1 retrieves the text it displays ($this->body_text).

This syntax can be a little counterintuitive. You might think that we could simply refer to $body_text in functions within our TextBox class because we have declared it in the class definition, but in fact the only way to get to members from within a member function definition is via $this. Notice also that the syntax for this access does not put a $ before the member variable name itself, only the $this variable.

Creating instances

After we have a class definition, the default way to make an instance of that class is by using the new operator. If we have already defined the class TextBox as in Listing 20-1, we can make an instance of it, and then use it, like so:

```
$box = new TextBoxSimple;
$box->display();
```

The result of evaluating this code will be to print an HTML fragment containing a table definition enclosing the text my text. (Not especially useful, but it's a start.)

Constructor functions

One way in which our TextBox class is not very useful is that its instances do not contain any data when they are created, except for the static initialization of the variable $body_text. The point of such a class would be to display arbitrary pieces of text, not the same message every time. It's true that we could make an instance and then install the right data in the instance's internal variables, like so:

```
$box = new TextBoxSimple;
$box->body_text = "custom text";
$box->display();
```

But that would be cumbersome and error-prone as we build more complex objects.

The correct way to arrange for data to be appropriately initialized is by writing a constructor function — a special function called __construct(), which will be called automatically whenever a new instance is created.

Modifying our previous example to include a constructor function gives us Listing 20-2.

Listing 20-2: TextBox redefined

```
class TextBox {
  var $body_text = "my text";
  // Constructor function
  function __construct($text_in) {
    $this->body_text = $text_in;
  }
  function display() {
    print("<TABLE BORDER=1><TR><TD>$this->body_text");
    print("</TD></TR></TABLE>");
  }
}
// creating an instance
$box = new TextBox("custom text");
$box->display();
```

As the preceding code is executed, the output is an HTML table enclosing the text custom text.

Note
There should be only one constructor function per class definition. Defining more than one such function is syntactically legal, but pointless, as only the definition that occurs last will be in effect. If you'd like to have different constructors to handle different numbers and types of input arguments, see the section "Simulating Polymorphism" later in this chapter.

Inheritance

PHP class definitions can optionally *inherit* from a parent class definition by using the extends clause. The syntax is as follows:

```
class Child extends Parent {
<definition body>
}
```

The effect of inheritance is that the child class (or subclass or derived class) has the following characteristics:

✦ Automatically has all the member variable declarations of the parent class (or superclass or base class).

✦ Automatically has all the same member functions as the parent, which (by default) will work the same way as those functions do in the parent.

In addition, the child class can add on any desired variables or functions simply by including them in the class definition in the usual way.

In Listing 20-2, we defined a class called TextBox; now we'll define a class called TextBoxHeader that extends TextBox (see Listing 20-3). TextBoxHeader has two member variables: one ($body_text) that it receives through inheritance from TextBox, and another ($header_text) that it defines itself. Like TextBox, it has a constructor function and a function called display. This function definition overrides the display function in TextBox.

Listing 20-3: **TextBoxHeader**

```
class TextBoxHeader extends TextBox
{
  var $header_text;

  // CONSTRUCTOR
  function __construct($header_text_in,
                      $body_text_in) {
    $this->header_text = $header_text_in;
    $this->body_text = $body_text_in;
  }

  // MAIN DISPLAY FUNCTION
  function display() {
    $header_html =
      $this->make_header($this->header_text);
    $body_html = $this->make_body($this->body_text);
    print("<TABLE BORDER=1><TR><TD>\n");
    print("$header_html\n");
    print("</TD></TR><TR><TD>\n");
    print("$body_html\n");
    print("</TD></TR></TABLE>\n");
  }

  // HELPER FUNCTIONS
  function make_header ($text) {
    return($text);
  }
  function make_body ($text) {
    return($text);
  }
}
```

Overriding functions

Function definitions in child classes *override* definitions with the same name in parent classes. This just means that the overriding definition in the more specific class takes precedence and will be the one actually executed. In the example in Listing 20-3, the TextBoxHeader class defines a function called display(), which means that executing the following code:

```
$text_box_header = new TextBoxHeader("The Header", "The Body");
$text_box_header->display();
```

will result in a call to TextBoxHeader's display() function, not the display() function in TextBox. The resulting HTML output prints a box with a header of The Header and a body of The Body. The more specific display() function takes total responsibility here; there is no call, either explicit or implicit, to the display() function defined in the TextBox class. (Although PHP makes no such implicit calls, it is possible to explicitly call functions that have been defined in a parent class — see "Calling parent functions" in the "Advanced OOP Features" section later in the chapter.)

The flip side of overriding functions, however, is that whenever a subclass does not override a parental definition, the parent's definition will be in effect. Note that the "helper" functions in the definition of TextBoxHeader don't really do anything interesting, and you might wonder why we bothered to separate them out. The answer is that this provides an opportunity for an inheriting class to do something interesting with those functions by selectively overriding them — or not, as they see fit.

PHP5 (as a result of Zend Engine 2) introduces the final keyword. If, in the previous example, the definition of display() in class TextBox had looked like this:

```
final function display() {
    print("<TABLE BORDER=1><TR><TD>$this->body_text");
    print("</TD></TR></TABLE>");
}
```

then the method could not have been overridden by a definition in TextBoxHeader.

It is possible to declare whole classes final, and individual methods, but not individual properties.

Chained subclassing

PHP does not support multiple inheritance but does support *chained subclassing*. This is a fancy way of saying that, although each class can have only a single parent, classes can still have a long and distinguished ancestry (grandparents, great-grandparents, and so on). Also, there's no restriction on family size; each parent class can have an arbitrary number of children.

As example, see Listing 20-4, where our definition of TextBoxBoldHeader inherits from TextBoxHeader, which in turn inherits from TextBox.

Listing 20-4: **TextBoxBoldHeader**

```
class TextBoxBoldHeader extends TextBoxHeader {

  // CONSTRUCTOR
  function __construct($header_text_in,
                      $body_text_in) {
    $this->header_text = $header_text_in;
    $this->body_text = $body_text_in;
  }

  // HELPER FUNCTIONS
  // make_header overrides parent
  function make_header ($text) {
    return("<B>$text</B>");
  }
}
```

This definition of TextBoxBoldHeader is minimal; it defines no new member variables and defines only one function besides its constructor. That new function (make_header()) overrides the definition in its parent. Now what happens when we actually use this definition in the usual way?

```
$text_box_bold_header =
  new TextBoxBoldHeader("The Header", "The Body");
$text_box_bold_header->display();
```

It's worth looking in a bit of detail to see exactly what happens when we make these two function calls.

First, when we call the constructor (TextBoxBoldHeader()), the constructor sets variables that were defined in the grandparent (TextBox) and the parent (TextBoxHeader), respectively, and returns a new instance of TextBoxBoldHeader.

Second, when we call $text_box_bold_header->display(), the call sequence is as follows:

1. No display() function is found in TextBoxBoldHeader, so the version from TextBoxHeader is called.

2. The first function call in that version of display() is to $this >make_header(). Remember that $this refers to the object instance that we started with, which happens to be an instance of TextBoxBoldHeader, so PHP looks first of all for a definition from that class. It finds one and uses it to return the header string wrapped up in the HTML bold text construct (<B></B>).

3. The second function call is to $this->make_body(). This time, though, there is no overriding definition in TextBoxBoldHeader, so the version from TextBoxHeader is used.

The upshot is that, in defining TextBoxBoldHeader, we mostly exploited the behavior of the parent class, but were able to change its behavior slightly by overriding a single member function.

Modifying and assigning objects

Prior to PHP5, when you assigned an object to a variable or passed it to a function, that object was actually copied, bit-for-bit, into the variable or function scope. That caused tremendous hassles, and programmers had to be careful to devise clever workarounds for the problems.

The problem is solved as of PHP5, which incorporates Zend Engine 2. Zend Engine 2 copies by reference, rather than explicitly. That is, several variables can point to the exact same object and expect changes made via one reference to be reflected in the others.

Scoping issues

Before we move onto the more advanced features of PHP's version of OOP, it's important to nail down issues of scope — that is, which names are meaningful in what way to different parts of our code. It may seem as though the introduction of classes, instances, and member functions have made questions of scope much more complicated. Actually, though, there are only a few basic rules we need to add to make OOP scope sensible within the rest of PHP:

✦ Names of member variables and member functions are never meaningful to calling code on their own — they must always be reached via the -> construct (or, as we'll see in the "Advanced OOP Features" section, the :: construct). This is true both outside the class definition and inside member functions.

✦ The names visible within member functions are exactly the same as the names visible within global functions — that is, member functions can refer freely to other global functions, but can't refer to normal global variables unless those variables have been declared global inside the member function definition.

These rules, together with the usual rules about variable scope in PHP, are respected in the intentionally confusing example in Listing 20-5. What number would you expect that code to print when executed?

Listing 20-5: **Confusing scope**

```php
$my_global = 3;

function my_function ($my_input) {
  global $my_global;
  return($my_global * $my_input);
}

class MyClass {
  var $my_member;
  function __construct($my_constructor_input) {
    $this->my_member =
      $my_constructor_input;
  }
```

Continued

Listing 20-5 *(continued)*

```
function myMemberFunction ($my_input) {
  global $my_global;
  return($my_global *
         $my_input *
         my_function($this->my_member));
  }
}

$my_instance = new MyClass(4);
print("The answer is: " .
      $my_instance->myMemberFunction(5));
```

The answer is: 180 (or 3 * 5 * (3 * 4)). If any of these numerical variables had been undefined when multiplied, we would have expected the variable to have a default value of 0, making the answer have a value of 0 as well. This would have happened if we had:

✦ Left out the global declaration in my_function()

✦ Left out the global declaration in myMemberFunction()

✦ Referred to $my_member rather than $this->my_member

Advanced OOP Features

In the previous section, we presented a minimal subset of PHP's object-oriented constructs that let you use the most basic OOP techniques. In this section, we look at some of the slightly more unusual constructs, techniques, and gotchas that can get you into more trouble. (We defer any discussion of the functions that give meta-information about classes and objects to the section "Introspection Functions," later in this chapter.)

Public, Private, and Protected Members

Unless you specify otherwise, properties and methods of a class are public. That is to say, they may be accessed in three possible situations:

✦ From outside the class in which it is declared

✦ From within the class in which it is declared

✦ From within another class that implements the class in which it is declared

If you wish to limit the accessibility of the members of a class, you should use private or protected. These keywords are new under Zend Engine 2, which was first standard under PHP5.

Private members

By designating a member private, you limit its accessibility to the class in which it is declared. The private member cannot be referred to from classes that inherit the class in which it is declared and cannot be accessed from outside the class.

Making a member private is straightforward:

```
class MyClass {

private $colorOfSky = "blue";
$nameOfShip = "Java Star";

function __construct($incomingValue) {
// Statements here run every time an instance of the class
// is created.
}

function myPublicFunction ($my_input) {
    return("I'm visible!");
  }

private function myPrivateFunction ($my_input) {
    global $my_global;
    return($my_global *
            $my_input *
            my_function($this->my_member));
  }

}
```

When that class is inherited by another class (using extends), myPublicFunction() will be visible, as will $nameOfShip. The extending class will not have any awareness of or access to myPrivateFunction, because it is declared private.

Protected members

A protected property or method is accessible in the class in which it is declared, as well as in classes that extend that class. Protected members are not available outside of those two kinds of classes, however.

Here is a different version of MyClass:

```
class MyClass {

protected $colorOfSky = "blue";
$nameOfShip = "Java Star";

function __construct($incomingValue) {
// Statements here run every time an instance
// of the class is created.
}
```

```
function myPublicFunction ($my_input) {
    return("I'm visible!");
  }

protected function myProtectedFunction ($my_input) {
    global $my_global;
    return($my_global *
           $my_input *
           my_function($this->my_member));
  }

}
```

If we had another class that extended MyClass, it would be able to see and use $colorOfSky and myProtectedFunction(), just as if they were public. It would not, however, be possible to call MyClass::$colorOfSky. You'll read more about the :: syntax later in this chapter.

Interfaces

In large object-oriented projects, there is some advantage to be realized in having standard names for methods that do certain work. For example, if many classes in a software application needed to be able to send e-mail messages, it would be desirable if they all did the job with methods of the same name. As of PHP5, it is possible to define an interface, like this:

```
interface Mail {
public function sendMail();
  }
```

Then, if another class implemented that interface, like this:

```
class Report implements Mail {
// Definition goes here
  }
```

it would be required to have a method called sendMail. It's an aid to standardization.

Constants

A constant is somewhat like a variable, in that it holds a value, but is really more like a function because a constant is immutable. Once you declare a constant, it does not change. Declaring one is easy, as is done in this version of MyClass:

```
class MyClass {

const requiredMargin = 1.3;

function __construct($incomingValue) {
// Statements here run every time an instance of the class
// is created.
  }

}
```

In that class, `requiredMargin` is a constant. It is declared with the keyword `const`, and under no circumstances can it be changed to anything other than 1.3. Note that the constant's name does not have a leading $, as variable names do.

Abstract Classes

An abstract class is one that cannot be instantiated, only inherited. You declare an abstract class with the keyword `abstract`, like this:

```
abstract class MyAbstractClass {

abstract function myAbstractFunction() {
}

}
```

Note that function definitions inside an abstract class must also be preceded by the keyword `abstract`. It is not legal to have `abstract` function definitions inside a non-abstract class.

Simulating class functions

Some other OOP languages make a distinction between *instance* member variables, on the one hand, and *class* or *static* member variables on the other. Instance variables are those that every instance of a class has a copy of (and may possibly modify individually); class variables are shared by all instances of the class. Similarly, instance functions depend on having a particular instance to look at or modify; class (or static) functions are associated with the class but are independent of any instance of that class.

In PHP, there are no declarations in a class definition that indicate whether a function is intended for per-instance or per-class use. But PHP does offer a syntax for getting to functions in a class even when no instance is handy. The :: syntax operates much like the -> syntax does, except that it joins class names to member functions rather than instances to members. For example, in the following implementation of an extremely primitive calculator, we have some functions that depend on being called in a particular instance and one function that does not:

```
class Calculator
{
  var $current = 0;
  function add($num) {
    $this->current += $num;
  }
  function subtract($num) {
    $this->current -= $num;
  }
  function getValue() {
    return($current);
  }
  function pi() {
    return(M_PI); // the PHP constant
  }
}
```

We are free to treat the `pi()` function as either a class function or an instance function and access it using either syntax:

```
$calc_instance = new Calculator;
$calc_instance->add(2);
$calc_instance->add(5);
print("Current value is " .
        $calc_instance->current ."<BR>");
print("Value of pi is " .
        $calc_instance->pi() . "<BR>");
print("Value of pi is " .
        Calculator::pi() . "<BR>");
```

This means that we can use the `pi()` function even when we don't have an instance of `Calculator` at hand. The `Calculator` class has to be accessible in either case, though, meaning it has to have been imported with a `require_once` statement, or something similar.

Calling parent functions

Asking an instance to call a function will always result in the most specific version of that function being called, because of the way overriding works. If the function exists in the instance's class, the parent's version of that function will not be executed.

Sometimes it is handy for code in a subclass to explicitly call functions from the parent class, even if those names have been overridden. It's also sometimes useful to define subclass functions in terms of superclass functions, even when the name is available.

Calling parent constructors

In the section "Inheritance" earlier in this chapter, we showed you code (Listing 20-3) where both subclass and superclass had constructors, and both constructors set a variable that was defined by the superclass. This might be stylistically dodgy, but more importantly, we would like to avoid duplicating work across the two constructors, especially if a lot of code is involved.

Instead of writing an entirely new constructor for the subclass, let's write it by calling the parent's constructor explicitly and then doing whatever is necessary in addition for instantiation of the subclass. Here's a simple example:

```
class Name
{
    var $_firstName;
    var $_lastName;
    function Name($first_name, $last_name)
    {
        $this->_firstName = $first_name;
        $this->_lastName = $last_name;
    }
    function toString() {
        return($this->_lastName .
                ", " .
                $this->_firstName);
    }
}
```

```
class NameSub1 extends Name
{
  var $_middleInitial;
  function NameSub1($first_name, $middle_initial,
                    $last_name) {
    Name::Name($first_name, $last_name);
    $this->_middleInitial = $middle_initial;
  }
  function toString() {
    return(Name::toString() . " " .
           $this->_middleInitial);
  }
}
```

In this example, we have a parent class (`Name`), which has a two-argument constructor, and a subclass (`NameSub1`), which has a three-argument constructor. The constructor of `NameSub1` functions by calling its parent constructor explicitly using the `::` syntax (passing two of its arguments along) and then setting an additional field. Similarly, `NameSub1` defines its nonconstructor `toString()` function in terms of the parent function that it overrides.

It might seem strange to call `Name::Name()` here, without reference to `$this`. The good news is that both `$this` and any member variables that are local to the parent are available to a parent function when invoked from a child instance.

The special name parent

There is a stylistic objection to the previous example, which is that we have hardcoded the name of a parent class into the code for a subclass. Some would say that this is bad style because it makes it harder to revise the class hierarchy later. A fix is to use the special name `parent`, which when used in a member function, always refers to the parent class of the current class. Here is a revised version of the example using `parent` rather than `Name`:

```
class NameSub2 extends Name
{
  var $_middleInitial;
  function NameSub2($first_name, $middle_initial,
                    $last_name) {
    $parent_class = get_parent_class($this);
    parent::$parent_class($first_name, $last_name);
    $this->_middleInitial = $middle_initial;
  }
  function toString() {
    return(parent::toString() . " " .
           $this->_middleInitial);
  }
}
```

Notice that we've swapped in `parent` for all instances of `Name` whenever it's used as the name of a class. We had to do a little bit of extra work, though, when finding a replacement for the call `Name::Name()` because the second name in that call is actually the name of a constructor function. PHP does not accept `parent` as the name of a function, so we retrieve the constructor name using the function `get_parent_class()` (which we cover in the section "Introspection Functions" later in this chapter).

This replacement version could be attached to a different parent class simply by changing the class named in the `extends` clause (as long as the parent constructor is expecting the same two arguments).

Automatic calls to parent constructors

In a sense, constructor functions in a subclass override the constructors in superclasses. (We say "in a sense" because we usually only say that one function overrides another if the two functions have the same name; a subclass constructor and a superclass constructor always have different names.)

As you saw in the previous section, if you want both the subclass constructor and the super-class constructor to be called, you must include code in the subclass to call the superclass code explicitly. Beginning with PHP4, if a subclass lacks a constructor function and a super-class has one, the superclass's constructor will be invoked. The most specific constructor that can be found (if any) will be called — anything else is up to the programmer.

Simulating method overloading

One neat trick offered by some OOP languages (and not offered by PHP) is automatic over-loading of member functions. This means that you can define several different member func-tions with the same name but different signatures (number and types of arguments). The language itself takes care of matching up calls to those functions with the right version of the function, based on the arguments that are given.

PHP does not offer such a capability, but the loose typing of PHP lets you take care of one half of the overloading equation — you can define a single function of a given name that behaves differently based on the number and types of arguments it is called with. The result looks like an overloaded function to the caller (but not to the definer).

Here's an example of an apparently overloaded constructor function:

```
class MyClass
{
var $string_var = "default string";
var $num_var = 42;

  function __construct($arg1) {
    if (is_string($arg1)) {
      $this->string_var = $arg1;
    }
    elseif (is_int($arg1) ||
            is_double($arg1)) {
      $this->num_var = $arg1;
    }
  }
}

$instance1 = new MyClass("new string");
$instance2 = new MyClass(5);
```

The constructor of this class will look to its caller as though it is overloaded, with different behavior based on the type of its inputs. You can also vary behavior based on the number of arguments by testing the number of arguments supplied by the caller.

 Cross-Reference For information on writing functions with variable numbers of arguments, see Chapter 26. The techniques work the same way with member functions in classes as they do with stan-dalone user-defined functions.

Serialization

Serialization of data means converting it into a string of bytes in such a way that you can produce the original data again from the string (via a process known, unsurprisingly, as *unserialization*). After you have the ability to serialize/unserialize, you can store your serialized string pretty much anywhere (a system file, a database, and so on) and recreate a copy of the data again when needed.

PHP offers two functions, serialize() and unserialize(), which take a value of any type (except type resource) and encode the value into string form and decode again, respectively. The PHP3 implementation of object serialization wasn't very useful because member function definitions didn't survive the serialization/unserialization process; beginning with version 4, however, PHP robustly recreates all important aspects of the instance from the string, as long as the class definition is available to the code where unserialize() is called.

Here is a quick example, which we'll extend later in this section:

```
class ClassToSerialize {
  var $storedStatement = "data";
  function __construct($statement) {
    $this->storedStatement = $statement;
  }
  function display ()
  {
    print($this->storedStatement . "<BR>");
  }
}

$instance1 =
  new ClassToSerialize("You're objectifying me!");
$serialization = serialize($instance1);
$instance2 = unserialize($serialization);
$instance2->display();
```

This class has just one member variable and a couple of member functions, but it's sufficient to demonstrate that both member variables and member functions can survive serialization. We create an object, convert it to a serialized string, convert it back to a new instance, and the printed result is the accurate complaint (You're objectifying me!).

Of course, there is no point in serializing and unserializing an object in the same script. Serialization is only worthwhile when we expect the serialized string to outlive the script (and the variable) that it currently lives in and be reincarnated in another execution. This may be because we store the serialization in a file or a database and read it back in again. It can also happen automatically as a result of PHP's session mechanism—variables that are registered as belonging to a session will be serialized and unserialized from page to page.

 Cross-Reference For more on how the session mechanism uses serialization, see Chapter 26.

Sleeping and waking up

PHP provides a hook mechanism so that objects can specify what should happen just before serialization and just after unserialization. The special member function __sleep() (that's *two* underscores before the word sleep), if defined in an object that is being serialized, will be called automatically at serialization time. It is also required to return an array of the names of variables whose values are to be serialized. This offers a way to not bother serializing member variables that are not expected to survive serialization anyway (such as database resources) or that are expensive to store and can be easily recreated. The special function __wakeup() (again, two underscores) is the flip side — it is called at unserialization time (if defined in the class) and is likely to do the inverse of whatever is done by __sleep() (restore database connections that were dropped by __sleep() or recreate variables that __sleep() said not to bother with).

You may wonder why these functions are necessary — couldn't the code that calls serialize() also just do whatever is necessary to shut down the object? Actually, it's very much in keeping with OOP to include such knowledge in the class definition rather than expecting code using the objects to know about their special needs. Also the calling code may have no knowledge of the object's internals at all (as in the code that serializes all session objects). The author of the class is uniquely qualified to say what should happen when an instance is sent away or revived.

As an example of how to use these functions, here is the previous serialization example, augmented with an extra variable, and the __sleep() and __wakeup() functions.

```
class ClassToSerialize2 {
  var $storedStatement = "data";
  var $easilyRecreatable = "data again";
  function __construct($statement) {
    $this->storedStatement = $statement;
    $this->easilyRecreatable =
      $this->storedStatement . " Again!";
  }
  function __sleep() {
    // Could include DB cleanup code here
    return array('storedStatement');
  }
  function __wakeup() {
    // Could include DB restoration code here
    $this->easilyRecreatable =
      $this->storedStatement . " Again!";
  }
  function display ()
  {
    print($this->easilyRecreatable . "<BR>");
  }
}

$instance1 =
  new ClassToSerialize2("You're objectifying me!");
$serialization = serialize($instance1);
$instance2 = unserialize($serialization);
$instance2->display();
```

The variable called $easilyRecreatable is meant to stand in for a piece of data that is 1) expensive to store and 2) is implied by the other data in the class anyway. The definition of __sleep() does no cleanup itself, but it returns an array that contains only one variable name and does not include easilyRecreatable. At serialization time, only the value of the variable storedStatement is included in the string. When the object is recreated, the __wakeup() function assigns a value into $this->easilyRecreatable, which is then displayed: You're objectifying me! Again!.

Serialization gotchas

The serialization mechanism is pretty reliable for objects, but there are still a few things that can trip you up:

✦ The code that calls unserialize() must also have loaded the definition of the relevant class. (This is also true of the code that calls serialize() too, of course, but that will usually be true because the class definition is needed for object creation in the first place.)

✦ Object instances can be created from the serialized string only if it is really the same string (or a copy thereof). A number of things can happen to the string along the way, if stored in a database (make sure that slashes aren't being added or subtracted in the process), or if passed as url or form arguments. (Make sure that your URL-encoding/decoding is preserving exactly the same string and that the string is not long enough to be truncated by length limits.)

✦ If you choose to use __sleep(), make sure that it returns an array of the variables to be preserved; otherwise no variable values will be preserved. (If you do not define a __sleep() function for your class, all values will be preserved.)

One other potential gotcha: At press time, using PHP 5.0 b2, the values of variables declared private did not survive serialization/unserialization using __sleep(). This may be fixed in the final release, but if you find that objects are not identical after undergoing serialization, investigate whether only the private variables are missing.

Introspection Functions

While PHP lacks some features of full OO languages like Java or C++, it is surprisingly good in the esoteric area of *introspection*. (It's the classes and objects that get introspective here, not the programmer.) Introspection allows the programmer to ask objects about their classes, ask classes about their parents, and find out all the parts of an object without have to crunch the source code to do it. Introspection also can help you to write some surprisingly flexible code, as we will see.

Function overview

Most of this section will be example-driven, but we begin by looking at the introspection functions provided by PHP. Table 20-1 summarizes these functions, what they do, and what version of PHP introduced them. (This table is essentially a reframing of information from the online manual; we offer it here mainly because it highlights features that we found somewhat confusing the first time we studied the manual.)

Table 20-1: Class/Object Functions

Function	Description	Operates on Class Names	Operates on Instances	As of PHP Version
get_class()	Returns the name of the class an object belongs to.	No	Yes	4.0.0
get_parent_class()	Returns the name of the parent class of the given instance or class.	Yes (as of PHP v.4.0.5)	Yes	4.0.0, 4.0.5
class_exists()	Returns TRUE if the string argument is the name of a class, FALSE otherwise.	Yes	No	4.0.0
get_declared_classes()	Returns an array of strings representing names of classes defined in the current script.	N/A	N/A	4.0.0
is_subclass_of()	Returns TRUE if the class of its first argument (an object instance) is a subclass of the second argument (a class name), FALSE otherwise.	No	Yes	4.0.0
is_a()	Returns TRUE if the class of its first argument (an object instance) is a subclass of the second argument (a class name), or is the same class, and FALSE otherwise.	No	Yes	4.2.0(?) (CVS only)
get_class_vars()	Returns an associative array of var/value pairs representing the name of variables in the class and their default values. Variables without default values will not be included.	Yes	No	4.0.0
get_object_vars()	Returns an associative array of var/value pairs representing the name of variables in the instance and their default values. Variables without values will not be included.	No	Yes	4.0.0
method_exists()	Returns TRUE if the first argument (an instance) has a method named by the second argument (a string) and FALSE otherwise.	No	Yes	4.0.0
get_class_methods()	Returns an array of strings representing the methods in the object or instance.	Yes	Yes (as of v4.0.6)	4.0.0, 4.0.6

Function	Description	Operates on Class Names	Operates on Instances	As of PHP Version
call_user_method()	Takes a string representing a method name, an instance that should have such a method, and additional arguments. Returns the result of applying the method (and the arguments) to the instance.	No	Yes	3.0.3, 4.0.0
call_user_method _array()	Same as call_user_method(), except that it expects its third argument to be an array containing the arguments to the method.	No	Yes	4.0.5

These functions break down into the following four broad categories:

✦ Getting information about the class hierarchy

✦ Finding out about member variables

✦ Finding out about member functions

✦ Actually calling member functions

The first group of functions (get_class() through is_a()) deal with discovering what classes exist, asking an object about its class, and discovering class inheritance relationships. Some of these functions start with an instance of an object, some start with the class name as a string, and some are happy with either one. (We've included columns in the table to try to clarify this.) Note that after we have the get_class() function, it's easy to satisfy functions that require a class as input; for example, if get_parent_class() insists on a class name, and we want to know the parent class of an object instance, we could just wrap it like this:

```
$parent_class = get_parent_class(get_class($my_instance));
```

Bear in mind that as of PHP4.3, the constant __CLASS__ exists. It contains the class name.

Going in the other direction (trying to satisfy a function that wants an instance when all we have is a class) would be more problematic because you don't want to instantiate a class just to ask questions of it.

The second group of functions (get_class_vars(), get_object_vars()), return an associative array containing member variables and their values. The keys of these arrays are the names of the variables as strings (without leading $ symbols), and the array values are the values of those variables in the object or class. In both cases (for reasons unknown to your authors), only member variables that actually have a value are returned.

The difference between get_class_vars() and get_object_vars() is subtle, but it's more than just a question of what type of input they prefer. The get_class_vars() function returns information about variables and default values as they exist in the class definition itself, independent of any instance; get_object_vars() returns information about the current state of a particular instance. For example, consider this class definition and use:

```
class Example {
  var $var1 = "initialized";
```

```
   var $var2 = "initialized";
   var $var3;
   var $var4;
   function __construct() {
     $this->var3 = "set";
     $this->var1 = "changed";
   }
 }

 $example = new Example();
 print_r(get_class_vars("Example"));
 print_r(get_object_vars($example));
```

For the first call (to get_class_vars()), we should expect to find var1 and var2 both bound to "initialized" as in the class definition itself. The second call (to get_object_vars()) should return bindings of var1, var2, and var3 to "changed", "initialized", and "set", respectively. In neither case will either function retrieve var4.

The third group of functions (method_exists(), get_class_methods()) manipulate member function names as strings. The first allows you to ask an instance if it contains a given function, and the second recovers all function names from an instance or class. (Notice that we don't need two separate functions as we did with get_class_vars() and get_object_vars(); PHP doesn't offer you a way to add or delete member functions from instances on the fly.)

Finally, the fourth group lets you apply method names (presumably recovered using functions from the third group) to instances. But these are probably best explained by example, so let's dive in.

Example: Class genealogy

Consider the following, somewhat confusing, class hierarchy.

```
class Color {}
class Control extends UIelement {}
class Widget extends Control { }
class Button extends Widget {}
class Pulldown extends Widget {}
class Clicker extends Button {}
class Blue extends Color {}
class Displayer extends UIelement {}
class UIElement {}
class LightBlue extends Blue {}
```

Now imagine that we'd like to have a better visualization of this tangle, just for purposes of documentation. For starters, it's pretty easy to use the get_parent_class() function to figure out the classes that a given class descends from:

```
function print_ancestry($class_name) {
  print("Class ancestry: ");
  print_ancestry_aux($class_name);
  print("<BR>");
}

function print_ancestry_aux ($class_name) {
  print("$class_name");
  if ($parent = get_parent_class($class_name)) {
```

```
      print(" => ");
      print_ancestry_aux($parent);
   }
 }
print_ancestry("Clicker");
```

Which gives us the somewhat informative output:

```
Class ancestry: Clicker => button => widget => control => uielement
```

(Notice that our retrieved class names have become lowercase. This happens to user-defined classes, whereas built-in classes should have their capitalization intact.)

Getting a view of the entire class tree is a little bit harder, because PHP doesn't offer a straightforward way to retrieve child classes given a parent class. Our recourse is the get_declared_classes function, which tells us all the classes that are defined in the current script—we can then somewhat inefficiently do paternity tests on all known classes to discover the children of a given class (see Listing 20-6).

Listing 20-6: **Class genealogy**

```
function same_class_name ($string1, $string2) {
  return ((strtolower($string1)) ==
          (strtolower($string2)));
}

function get_child_classes ($parent) {
  $all_classes = get_declared_classes();
  $children = array();
  foreach ($all_classes as $candidate) {
    if (same_class_name($parent,
           get_parent_class($candidate)) &&
         !same_class_name($parent, $candidate)) {
      array_push($children, $candidate);
    }
  }
  return($children);
}

function print_class_tree () {
  $all_classes = get_declared_classes();
  print("<PRE>");
  print("CLASS HIERARCHY:\n");
    foreach ($all_classes as $candidate) {
      if (!get_parent_class($candidate)) {
        print_class_tree_aux($candidate, 0);
      }
    }
  print("</PRE>");
}

function print_class_tree_aux ($parent, $level) {
  for ($x = 0; $x < $level; $x++) {
```

Continued

Listing 20-6 *(continued)*

```
    print("    ");
  }
  print("$parent<BR>");
  $children = get_child_classes($parent);
  foreach ($children as $child) {
    print_class_tree_aux($child, $level + 1);
  }
}
print_class_tree();
```

We start off this listing by defining what it means for two class names to be the same. This may be overkill, but converting every name to lowercase before comparison lets us stop worrying about whether we'll be tripped up by case issues. Then we define a general function to retrieve child classes (inefficiently, but it should make no difference unless your class hierarchy grows to be very, very large). The `print_class_tree()` function essentially recovers all *orphans* or *roots* (classes without parents) and prints each one individually as a tree. The auxiliary function handles printing a rooted tree—first the parent and then indented children. Finally, we wrap the whole thing in a `<PRE></PRE>` construct so we can just use spaces for indenting. The result looks like this:

```
CLASS HIERARCHY:
stdClass
__PHP_Incomplete_Class
OverloadedTestClass
Directory
color
    blue
        lightblue
uielement
    control
        widget
            button
                clicker
            pulldown
    displayer
```

The first few classes printed are unfamiliar and not defined in your code file. These either belong to the PHP implementation itself or to auxiliary packages that you have compiled—the precise classes that you see when you execute this code may vary.

Example: Matching variables and DB columns

One frequent use for PHP objects in database-driven systems is as a wrapper around the entire database API. The theory is that the wrapper insulates the code from the specific database system, which will make it trivial to swap in a different RDBMS when the technical needs change. (We've never seen it work out quite this way in practice, but . . . don't get us started.) Another use that is almost as common (and that your authors like better) is to have object instances correspond to database result rows. In particular, the process of reading in a result row looks like instantiating a new object that has member variables corresponding to the result columns we care about, with extra functionality in the member functions. As long as the fields and columns match up (and as long as you can afford object instantiation for every row), this can be a nice abstraction away from the database.

A repetitive task that arises when writing this kind of code is assigning database column values to member variables, in individual assignment statements. This feels like it should be unnecessary, especially when the columns and the corresponding variables have exactly the same names. In this section, we write a hack to automate this process.

For concreteness, let's start with an actual database table. Following are the MySQL statements necessary to create a simple table and insert one row into it:

```
mysql> create table book
   (id int not null primary key auto_increment,
    author varchar(255), title varchar(255),
    publisher varchar(255));
mysql> insert into book (author, title, publisher)
         values ("Robert Zubrin", "The Case For Mars",
                  "Touchstone");
```

Because the id column is auto-incremented, it will happen to have the value 1 for this first row.

Now, let's say that we want a Book object that will exactly correspond to a row from this table, with fields corresponding to the DB column names. There's no way around actually defining the variable names (because PHP doesn't let us dynamically add variables to classes), but we can at least automate the assignment.

The code in Listing 20-7 assumes a database called oop with the table created as above, and also that we have a file called dbconnect_vars that sets $host, $user, and $pass appropriately for our particular MySQL setup. There is also little or no error-checking (the code assumes the connection works, that the row was retrieved successfully, and so on). The main point we want to highlight is the hack in the middle of the Book constructor.

Listing 20-7: **Matching variables and columns**

```php
<?php
include_once("dbconnect_vars.php");

class Book
{
var $id;

// variables corresponding to DB columns
var $author = "DBSET";
var $title = "DBSET";
var $publisher = "DBSET";

  function __construct($db_connection, $id) {
    $this->id = $id;
    $query = "select * from book " .
             "where id = $id";
    $result = mysql_query($query, $db_connection);
```

Continued

Listing 20-7 *(continued)*

```php
        $db_row_array =
          mysql_fetch_array($result);
        $class_var_entries =
          get_class_vars(get_class($this));
        while ($entry = each($class_var_entries)) {
          $var_name = $entry['key'];
          $var_value = $entry['value'];
          if ($var_value == "DBSET") {
            $this->$var_name =
              $db_row_array[$var_name];
          }
        }
      }

      function toString () {
        $return_string = "BOOK<BR>";
        $class_var_entries =
          get_class_vars(get_class($this));
        while ($entry = each($class_var_entries)) {
          $var_name = $entry['key'];
          $var_value = $this->$var_name;
          $return_string .=
            "$var_name: $var_value<BR>";
        }
        return($return_string);
      }
    }
    $connection =
      mysql_connect($host, $user, $pass)
      or die("Could not connect to DB");
mysql_select_db("oop");
$book = new Book($connection, 1);
$book_string = $book->toString();
?>
<HTML><HEAD></HEAD><BODY>
<?php echo $book_string ?>
</BODY></HTML>
```

The database query returns all columns from the book table, and the values are indexed in the result array by the column names. The constructor then uses `get_class_vars()` to discover all the variables that have been set in the object, tests them to see if they have been bound to the string "DBSET", and then sets those variables to the value of the column of the same name.

The result is the output:

```
BOOK
Author: Robert Zubrin
Title:  The Case For Mars
Publisher:  Touchstone
```

If we add fields to the database table definition, the only change we will need to make to Listing 20-7 is to add appropriately named variables to the class definition and initialize them to "DBSET". (We use this initialization to be clear about which variables should be overwritten, but also because we cannot retrieve the variables at all unless they have been initialized.)

Example: Generalized test methods

As a final introspection example, suppose we are working on a large OOP project, with complex objects that need to maintain a lot of internal state. Testing is extremely important, because bugs will creep in and waste our time if we don't catch them early on.

So let's adopt some testing conventions for this project. As one of them, let's agree that any class in our system can (optionally) define a member function called selfTest(). The point of this function is to test the object instance it is called on to make sure the data in the object is valid and consistent across the instance. The selfTest() function should always return FALSE if everything is okay and a diagnostic string if something is wrong. The coders of the objects agree that they will write these tests in such a way that a test can potentially be applied at any time during execution.

If we agree on such a framework, we can write a general object tester. The tester simply calls selfTest() on any object it is pointed at, if such a method has been defined for that object. To make it easier to apply, we'll also make the object tester accept arrays of objects, and test each component object individually. Such an object tester is in Listing 20-8, along with some sample class definitions that have selfTest() defined.

Listing 20-8: **ObjectTester**

```php
class Namestring {
  var $name;
  var $nameLength;
  var $checksum;

  function __construct($string_in) {
    $this->name = $string_in;
    $this->nameLength = strlen($string_in);
    $this->checksum =
       $this->computeChecksum($string_in);
  }

  function setName ($new_string) {
    $this->name = $new_string;
    $this->nameLength = strlen($new_string);
    $this->checksum =
       $this->computeChecksum($new_string);
  }

  function computeChecksum ($string) {
    // not a good checksum in practice
    $sum = 0;
    for ($x = 0;
```

Continued

Listing 20-8 *(continued)*

```
        $x < strlen($string);
        $x++) {
    $sum += ord($string[$x]);
  }
  return($sum % 100);
}

function selfTest () {
  // returns FALSE if everything is OK
  if ($this->nameLength !=
      strlen($this->name)) {
    return("Name $this->name not of ".
        "length $this->nameLength!");
  }
  elseif
    ($this->checksum !=
      $this->computeChecksum($this->name)) {
    return("Name $this->name fails checksum!");
  }
  else {
    return(FALSE);
  }
}
}

class NonTestingObject {
}

class ObjectTester {
  function ObjectTester() {
    // empty constructor
  }

  function test ($thing) {
    if (is_object($thing)) {
      if (method_exists($thing, 'selfTest')) {
        $this->handleTest(
          call_user_method('selfTest', $thing));
      }
    }
    elseif (is_array($thing)) {
      foreach ($thing as $component) {
        $this->test($component);
      }
    }
    // ignore if not an array or object
  }
```

```
function handleTest ($result) {
  if ($result) {
    print("Warning: $result");
  }
 }
}
```

The Namestring object in Listing 20-8 has several pieces of data, which must be kept consistent with each other. Using the constructor to build an instance of Namestring keeps them consistent, as does changing the name with setName. Namestring also defines selfTest(), which cross-checks the name, the length of the name, and a primitive checksum.

Now let's see how to use the ObjectTester class with some sample Namestring data:

```
$object_list = array();
array_push($object_list, new Namestring("Jordan"));
array_push($object_list, new Namestring("Rodman"));
array_push($object_list, new NonTestingObject);
array_push($object_list, new Namestring("Pippen"));

$tester = new ObjectTester($object_list);

print("Running test..<BR>");
$tester->test($object_list);

print("Changing name..<BR>");
$current_object = &$object_list[0]; // note reference!
$current_object->setName("Michael");
print("Running test..<BR>");
$tester->test($object_list);

print("Changing name..<BR>");
$current_object = &$object_list[1]; // note reference!
$current_object->name = "Jordan";

print("Running test..<BR>");
$tester->test($object_list);
```

The results of running this code are:

```
Running test..
Changing name..
Running test..
Changing name..
Running test..
Warning:  Name Jordan fails checksum!
```

This warning resulted because we messed with the object's data directly the second time, rather than using the approved method for changing the name.

We've used toy self-testing classes here, but the basic approach extends easily to more complex classes. Among possible extensions is more interesting handling of the warning messages (and possibly interrupting execution). Another extension would be to use introspection on member variables themselves, as well as array components, to find contained objects and test those. This would mean defining the test runner recursively so that a thing passes a selfTest() if 1) its own selfTest() method (if it exists) finds no problem, and 2) any components (member variables, array slots) also pass selfTest(). (Watch out for circularities though! If the tester is ever called on objects that mutually refer to each other, it would have to be rewritten to track the identities of previously seen objects and would only test each object once.)

Extended Example: HTML Forms

All the OOP code we've seen so far in this chapter has been fairly short, so in this chapter we present an extended piece of code for your enjoyment, shown in Listing 20-9.

The point of this class is to semiautomate the production of HTML forms, which one of your authors has always found to be a bit of a pain to generate. The top-level class represents a form, while other classes represent inputs, text areas, and hidden variables (just the ones that your author uses most frequently). The idea is that you can make a form by adding input fields to an existing object and display the form upon request. The resulting form will be not be especially pretty (every element is displayed sequentially down the left-hand side of the page), but it's good enough for situations where, say, you want to enter some information into your own database yourself.

Listing 20-9: form_printer.php

```php
<?php

// ---- The form class itself ---

class HtmlForm {

  // suitable for generating quick&dirty forms

  var $actionTarget; // path to receiving page
  private var $inputForms;  // array of HtmlFormInput
  var $hiddenVariables; // associative name/val

  // CONSTRUCTOR
  function __construct($action_target) {
    $this->actionTarget = $action_target;
    $this->inputForms = array();
    $this->hiddenVariables = array();
  }

  // PUBLIC METHODS
  function toString () {
```

```php
      $return_string = "";
      $return_string .=
         "<FORM METHOD=\"POST\" ".
         "ACTION=\"$this->actionTarget\">\n";
      $return_string .= $this->inputFormsString();
      $return_string .= $this->hiddenVariablesString();
      $return_string .= "<BR>\n";
      $return_string .= $this->submitButtonString();
      $return_string .= "</FORM>";
      return($return_string);
   }

   // adding elements to form

   function addInputForm ($input_form) {
      if (!isSet($input_form) ||
          !is_object($input_form) ||
          !is_subclass_of($input_form,
                   'htmlforminput')){
        die("Argument to HtmlForm::addInputForm ".
           "must be instance of HtmlFormInput.".
           "  Given argument is of class " .
           get_class($input_form));
      }
      else {
        array_push($this->inputForms, $input_form);
      }
   }

   function addInputButton ($input_button) {
      if (!isSet($input_button) ||
          !isObject($input_button) ||
          !is_a($input_button, 'HtmlInputButton')){
        die("Argument to HtmlForm::addInputButton ".
           "must be instance of HtmlInputButton");
      }
      else {
        array_push($this->inputButtons, $input_button);
      }
   }

   function addHiddenVariable ($name, $value) {
      if (!isSet($value)) {
        die("HtmlForm::addHiddenVariable requires ".
           "two arguments (name and value)");
      }
      else {
        $this->hiddenVariables[$name] = $value;
      }
   }
```

Continued

Listing 20-9 *(continued)*

```php
function inputFormsString () {
  $return_string = "";
  $form_array = $this->inputForms;
  foreach ($form_array as $input_form) {
    $return_string .=
      "<B>$input_form->heading</B>";
    if ($this->headingElementBreak()) {
      $return_string .= "<BR>";
    }
    $return_string .= $input_form->toString();
    $return_string .= "<BR>\n";
  }
  return($return_string);
}

function hiddenVariablesString () {
  $return_string = "";
  while ($hidden_var =
          each($this->hiddenVariables)) {
    $var_name = $hidden_var['key'];
    $var_value = $hidden_var['value'];
    $return_string .=
      "<INPUT TYPE=HIDDEN " .
      "NAME=$var_name ".
      "VALUE=$var_value >";
      $return_string .= "\n";
  }
  return($return_string);
}

function headingElementBreak () {
  // override to disable breaks after headings,
  // or to do more complicate layout
  return(TRUE);
}

function submitButtonString () {
  $return_string = "<INPUT TYPE=Submit " .
                   " VALUE=Submit >\n";
  return($return_string);
}
}

// ---- Classes for parts of a form ----

abstract class HtmlFormInput {
  var $name; // The variable name for form submission
  var $heading; // The visible label on form
  function __construct() {
```

```
        die("Class HtmlFormInput intended only " .
            "to be subclassed");
    }
    function toString () {
        die("Subclass of HtmlFormInput missing " .
            "definition of toString()");
    }
}

class HtmlFormSelect extends HtmlFormInput
{
    var $_valueArray = array();
    var $_selectedValue;

    function __construct ($name, $heading,
                            $value_array,
                            $selected_value=NULL) {
        if (!isSet($value_array)) {
            die("HtmlFormSelect needs a minimum of two " .
                "arguments: a name, and value array");
        }
        elseif (!is_array($value_array)) {
            die("Third argument to HtmlFormSelect()" .
                "should be array where keys are values ".
                "submitted, and values are display values");
        }
        else {
            // actual initialization
            $this->name = $name;
            $this->heading = $heading;
            $this->_valueArray = $value_array;
            $this->_selected_value = $selected_value;
        }
    }

    function toString () {
        $return_string = "";
        $return_string .=
            "<SELECT NAME=\"$this->name\">";
        while ($var_entry =
                each($this->_valueArray)) {
            $submit_value = $var_entry['key'];
            $display_value = $var_entry['value'];
            if ($submit_value == $this->_selected_value) {
                $return_string .=
                    "<OPTION VALUE=${submit_value} SELECTED >";
            }
            else {
                $return_string .= "<OPTION VALUE=${submit_value}>";
            }
            $return_string .= $display_value;
        }
```

Continued

Listing 20-9 *(continued)*

```php
        $return_string .=
          "</SELECT>";
        return($return_string);
    }
}

class HtmlFormText extends HtmlFormInput
{
  var $initial_value;

  function __construct ($name,
                         $heading,
                         $initial_value="")
  {
    // Initialization of member vars
    if (!isSet($name) ||
        !isSet($heading)) {
      die("HtmlFormText constructor needs " .
          "at least two arguments (name, heading)");
    }
    $this->name = $name; // name defined in parent
    $this->heading = $heading; // defined in parent
    $this->initial_value = $initial_value;
  }

  function toString () {
    $return_string = "";
    $return_string .= "<INPUT TYPE=TEXT ";
    $return_string .= "NAME=\"$this->name\" ";
    $return_string .=
        "VALUE=\"$this->initial_value\" ";
    $return_string .= " >";
    return($return_string);
  }
}

class HtmlFormTextArea extends HtmlFormInput {
  var $initial_value;
  var $rows;
  var $cols;
  var $wrapType;

  function __construct ($name,
                         $heading,
                         // optional args:
                         $initial_value="",
                         $rows=1, $cols=60,
                         $wrapType="VIRTUAL")
  {
    // Initialization of member vars
```

```php
      if (!isSet($name)) {
        die("HtmlFormTextArea constructor needs " .
           "at least two arguments (name, heading)");
      }
      $this->name = $name; // name defined in parent
      $this->heading = $heading; // name defined in parent
      $this->initial_value = $initial_value;
      $this->rows = $rows;
      $this->cols = $cols;
      $this->wrapType = $wrapType;
    }

  function toString ()
  {
    $return_string = "";
    $return_string .= "<TEXTAREA ";
    $return_string .= "NAME=\"$this->name\" ";
    $return_string .= "ROWS=$this->rows ";
    $return_string .= "COLS=$this->cols ";
    $return_string .= "WRAP=$this->wrapType ";
    $return_string .= $this->additionalAttributes();
    $return_string .= ">";
    $return_string .= $this->initial_value;
    $return_string .= "</TEXTAREA>";
    return($return_string);
  }

  function additionalAttributes () {
    // OVERRIDE THIS to return a string with
    // TextArea attributes other than
    // NAME, ROWS, COLS, and WRAP
    return("");
  }
 }
?>
```

The basic design for all these objects includes a constructor function with default arguments and a toString() method that returns HTML for the form or piece thereof. Forms store pieces of input (which might conceivably be reordered or laid out by a more sophisticated version), and recursively call toString() on these pieces. The HTML form elements that are supported are: TEXTAREA, TEXT, and SELECT.

Here is an example of calling this code to generate a simple form page:

```php
<HTML><HEAD></HEAD><BODY>
<?php include("form_printer.php");
$my_form = new HtmlForm($PHP_SELF);
$my_form->addInputForm(
         new HtmlFormText("firstname",
                          "First Name"));
$my_form->addInputForm(
         new HtmlFormText("lastname",
                          "Last Name"));
```

```
$my_form->addInputForm(
        new HtmlFormSelect(
            "age",
            "Age",
            array(0 => "0 - 9",
                    1 => "10 - 19",
                    2 => "20 - 29",
                    3 => "Senior citizen"),
            2));
$my_form->addInputForm(
        new HtmlFormTextArea(
            "feedback",
            "What's on your mind?",
        "[Please fill in your own personal rant]",
            5));
print($my_form->toString());
?>
</BODY>
</HTML>
```

Much of the form-producing code is straightforward and is concerned with churning out various kinds of HTML syntax. There are two interesting things to notice from the point of view of OOP-in-PHP, however.

The first is that the `HtmlFormInput` class is *designated* abstract. That is, it exists not to be instantiated, but only to be inherited from. The second point of interest is that the `HtmlForm` class has an array that is intended to hold `HtmlFormInput` objects. Of course, because PHP is loosely typed, we cannot enforce that in any way at compile time, though the manufacturer-approved way to insert new forms (`addInputForm()`) does some type-checking on insertion. If users of this class rely only on this method, we can be assured that everything that ends up in that array will be an instance of `HtmlFormInput` (or subclass thereof) and so should be a well-behaved form element when display time comes around. The `private` designation guarantees that the array cannot be manipulated from outside the class at runtime.

Gotchas and Troubleshooting

In the spirit of Chapter 11, we offer in the following sections the top-two most likely symptoms of problematic OOP code, along with the most likely cause.

Symptom: Member variable has no value in member function

This could have many causes, of course, but the most common is simply a confusion about the right way to refer to member variables. The syntax is:

```
$this->member_name
```

If, instead, your function simply refers to $member_name, that will usually be an unbound variable and, at any rate, will never succeed in referring to the member variable. Similarly, if your function refers to $this->$member_name, you are asking for the field named by the string in the variable $member_name (which is probably unbound).

Symptom: Parse error, expecting T_VARIABLE ...

There are of course many ways to munge a class definition so that PHP will complain when it tries to parse it. One of the most common errors again has to do with placement of those $ symbols. A class declaration like the following:

```
class MyClass {
  var my_var;  // WRONG
}
```

inevitably gives you a parse error of some sort because the syntax requires a $ before my_var.

OOP Style in PHP

The topic of OOP programming style is a huge one (because it includes OOP design!) and is well beyond the scope of this book. In the spirit of Chapter 33, however, we offer in the following sections some brief notes on writing readable, maintainable PHP OOP code.

Naming conventions

In this section, we simply pass along the parts of the PEAR coding style that pertain to objects.

For more information on the PEAR project and the PEAR coding style, see Chapter 28 or the PEAR Web site (at http://pear.php.net).

PEAR recommends that class names begin with an uppercase letter and (if in a PEAR-approved directory hierarchy of packages) have that inclusion path in the class name, separated by underscores. So your class that counts words, and which belongs to a PEAR package called TextUtils, might be called TextUtils_WordCounter. If building large OOP packages, you may want to emulate this underscore convention with your own package names; otherwise you can simply give your classes names like WordCounter.

Member variables and member function names should have their first real letter be lowercase and have *word* boundaries be delineated by capitalization. In addition, names that are intended to be private to the class (that is, they are used only within the class, and not by outside code) should start with an underscore. So the variable in your WordCounter class that holds the count of words might be called wordCount (if intended to be messed with from the outside) or _wordCount (if intended to be private to the class).

Accessor functions

Another style of documenting your intent about use of internal variables is to have your variables marked as private, in general, and provide "getter" and "setter" functions to outside callers. For example, we might define a class like this:

```
class Customer
{
    private var _name;
    private var _creditCardNumber;
    private var _rating;
```

```
    function getName ()
    {
        return($this->_name);
    }

    function getRating ()
    {
        return($this->_rating);
    }

    function setRating($rating)
    {
        $this->_rating = $rating;
    }
    [... more functions ]
}
```

This class definition has three private variables: one (_creditCardNumber) that should nei-ther be set nor retrieved from outside code; another (_name) that outside code should be able to retrieve but not set; and a third (_rating) that outside code should feel free to both get and set.

Although PHP class syntax lets you interleave variables with function definitions, it's a good idea, in general, to organize your code so that similar items with similar usage intent are together in the class definition. For example, you might develop the habit of laying out class functions like this:

```
class myClass
{
// Public variables:
..
// Private variables
..
// Constructor

// Public functions
..
// Private functions
..
}
```

Designing for inheritance

The question of exactly how to design a class hierarchy is, as we've said, a vast area of study unto itself, and we're not about to try to contribute to it here. Just as a stylistic matter, though, it's worth thinking about whether you intend your class to be inherited from, and then try to indicate your decision, either with comments or in the structure of the definition.

For example, you may intend that your class should never breed, in which case you might just indicate that in comments, and then stop worrying about inheritance issues. (There is currently no way in PHP to enforce that a class cannot be inherited from.) At the other end of the spec-trum, you might have all or part of your class intended only for inheritance. You can indicate this in comments, or you can use the trick we used in the definition of `HtmlFormInput` in Listing 20-9: Provide methods that die informatively when called directly in the base class. Finally, of course, you may have some methods that can be called directly in the base class, but are especially intended for overriding. You may want to group these "hook" methods together in a clearly marked section of your class definition, so that the later writer of a derived class can quickly figure out what options are available for specializing the class's behavior. (Remember that the clueless coder of the future that you are helping may well be yourself.)

Summary

PHP provides the basics to support object-oriented programming. Among other things, the OOP syntax in PHP allows for programmer-defined classes with member variables and member data and offers single inheritance, constructor functions, object serialization, and functions for introspection. Nothing in PHP requires that you write in an object-oriented style, but if you prefer that style you can write almost all your code that way. Though the object-oriented capabilities of the language are vastly improved as of PHP5, the object-oriented part of PHP is, frankly, an add-on. PHP was not originally intended to be an object-oriented language, and developers with OOP experience will miss some aspects of more mature OOP languages. On the other hand, the OOP extension is usable, fairly mature, pretty stable, and widely used. It provides an extra layer of organization that can be helpful when maintaining complex code and offers a nice way to package code for distribution and reuse.

✦   ✦   ✦

Advanced Array Functions

In Chapter 9, we introduced you to arrays, their uses, and some handy functions for working with them. In some subsequent chapters, we saw how PHP returns many of its results as arrays, particular when working with database function sets. This chapter will look at some of the more advanced functions for working with PHP arrays.

Transformations of Arrays

PHP offers a host of functions for manipulating your data once you have it nicely stored in an array. What the functions in this section have in common is that they take your array, do something with it, and return the results in another array. (We will defer the array-sorting functions until a later section.)

Cross-Reference Not covered in this chapter are explode() and implode(), which convert strings into arrays and vice versa. We cover these very handy functions in Chapter 22.

In Chapter 9, we incrementally developed a function to print out the entire contents of an array, and in this section will use the last of these (print_keys_and_values_each()) to show the arrays that are being returned in examples. We'll list this function again here, in a more generic form:

```
function print_keys_and_values_each($array_to_test)
{  // reliably prints everything in array
   reset($array_to_test);
   while ($array_cell = each($array_to_test))
   {
     $current_value = $array_cell['value'];
     $current_key = $array_cell['key'];
     print("Key: $current_key; Value:
$current_value<BR>");
   }
}
```

Retrieving keys and values

The `array_keys()` function returns the keys of its input array in the form of a new array where the keys are the stored values. The keys of the new array are the usual automatically incremented integers, starting from 0. The `array_values()` function does exactly the same thing, except the stored values are the values from the original array. If we start with an array like the following:

```
$pizza_requests = array('Alice' => 'pepperoni',
                        'Bob' => 'mushrooms',
                        'Carl' => 'sausage',
                        'Dennis' => 'mushrooms');
```

and then we print the arrays resulting from calls to the these two functions:

```
print("Array keys:<BR>");
print_keys_and_values_each(array_keys($pizza_requests));
print("Array values:<BR>");
print_keys_and_values_each(array_values($pizza_requests));
```

we get output like this:

```
Array keys:
Key: 0; Value: Alice
Key: 1; Value: Bob
Key: 2; Value: Carl
Key: 3; Value: Dennis
Array values:
Key: 0; Value: pepperoni
Key: 1; Value: mushrooms
Key: 2; Value: sausage
Key: 3; Value: mushrooms
```

The second of these (`array_values()`) may seem uninteresting because we have essentially taken our old array and produced a new one with the keys renamed to successive numbers.

We can do something slightly more useful (and more helpful for ordering) with the function `array_count_values()`. This takes an array and returns a new array, where the old values are now the new keys and the new values are the number of times each old value occurs in the original array.

```
print_keys_and_values_each(
    array_count_values($pizza_requests));
```

gives us:

```
Key: pepperoni; Value: 1
Key: mushrooms; Value: 2
Key: sausage; Value: 1
```

Flipping, reversing, and shuffling

A even odder function is `array_flip()`, which changes the keys of an array into the values, and vice versa. For example:

```
print_keys_and_values_each(array_flip($pizza_requests));
```

gives us:

```
Key: pepperoni; Value: Alice
Key: mushrooms; Value: Dennis // what happened to Bob?
Key: sausage; Value Carl
```

Notice that, although array keys are guaranteed to be unique, array values are not—because of this, any duplicate values in the original array become the same key in the new array. Only one of the original keys will survive to become the corresponding new value.

Reversing an array is simpler: `array_reverse()` returns a new array with the key/value pairs in reverse order. So, with the usual printing test:

```
print_keys_and_values_each(array_reverse($pizza_requests));
```

we get the result:

```
Key: Dennis; Value: mushrooms
Key: Carl; Value: sausage
Key: Bob; Value: mushrooms
Key: Alice; Value: pepperoni
```

In this case, although the internal order has been reversed, all the key/value pairs end up being the same. However, this function (like several other PHP array functions) treats integer keys somewhat specially. It assumes that the ordering of integer keys on those key/value pairs should also be reversed for the later use of code that pays attention to the ordering of keys, rather than using the internal linked-list ordering. So, `array_reverse()` swaps integer keys to make the new key ordering match the internal list. Dennis, in other words, is now actually at position 0.

If you need some extra randomness in your life, the `shuffle()` function can give it to you— `shuffle()` takes an array argument and randomizes the order of the elements in the array. It uses `rand()`, a function that generates successive random numbers. Before you use `shuffle()`, you need to have seeded the random-number generator with a call to `srand()`. (See the discussion of random-number generation in Chapter 10.) A reasonable calling sequence looks like this:

```
srand((double)microtime() * 1000000);  // for random # gen
shuffle($pizza_requests);
print_keys_and_values_each(array_flip($pizza_requests));
```

which *might* give us output like:

```
Key: Carl; Value: sausage
Key: Bob; Value: mushrooms
Key: Dennis; Value: mushrooms
Key: Alice; Value: pepperoni
```

Cross-Reference

For more on random-number generation, see Chapter 10. If you want to use the `shuffle()` function without having to consult Chapter 10, simply make sure that any page that uses `shuffle()` has the call to `srand()` once (and only once) in the script, before any calls to `shuffle()`, as in the preceding example.

Caution   Unlike many of the array functions in this chapter, `shuffle()` is *destructive,* meaning that it operates directly on its array argument and changes it, rather than returning a newly created array. (Functions that return a new thing without disturbing their arguments might be called *constructive,* or just *nondestructive.*) Among other things, this means that the correct way to call the shuffle function is not

```
$my_new_array = shuffle($my_old_array); //WRONG!
```

especially because the `shuffle()` function does not return a value. Instead, the right call is

```
shuffle($my_array);    // change the array itself
```

Merging, padding, slicing, and splicing

If we want to combine two arrays for a more complete list, the function to use is `array_merge()`. This function takes two or more arrays as arguments and returns a renumbered new array that is the second array tacked onto the end of the first. If we create a new array containing some additional pizza requests like so:

```
$more_pizza_requests = array('Ted' => 'anchovies',
                             'MrWilson' => 'pineapple',
                             'Dagwood' => 'ham');
```

then we can use `array merge();` as:

```
$all_requests = array_merge($pizza_requests, $more_requests);
```

and then use our handy array inspecting function:

```
print_keys_and_values_each($all_requests);
```

We should see:

```
Key: Alice; Value: pepperoni
Key: Bob; Value: mushrooms
Key: Carl; Value: sausage
Key: Dennis; Value: mushrooms
Key: Ted; Value: anchovies
Key: MrWilson; Value: pineapple
Key: Dagwood; Value: ham
```

The `array_pad()` function is used to create some leading or following key/value pairs increasing the size of an array. It takes an input array as its first argument, then a number of elements to increase the array to, and then a value to assign to the added elements. A positive integer in the second argument will pad the end of the array; a negative integer will pad the beginning. If the second argument is smaller than the size of the array, no padding is performed.

```
$requests = array_pad($pizza_requests, 10, 'mushrooms')
//do we have any mushroom fans in the audience tonight?
```

With our function, we'd get:

```
Key: Alice; Value: pepperoni
Key: Bob; Value: mushrooms
Key: Carl; Value: sausage
Key: Dennis; Value: mushrooms
Key: 0; Value: mushrooms
Key: 1; Value: mushrooms
```

```
Key: 2; Value: mushrooms
Key: 3; Value: mushrooms
Key: 4; Value: mushrooms
Key: 5; Value: mushrooms
```

If we make the second argument negative, the new elements appear at the beginning of the array. Note that the automatically assigned keys start at 0, even though they are in the fifth position.

Somewhat more complicated are the `array_slice()` and `array_splice()` functions. The first of these returns a subset of an input array by accepting an offset and a length as its second and third arguments respectively:

```
$subset = array_slice($pizza_requests, 1, 2);
// returns mushrooms and sausage
```

The `array_splice()` function is similar, but it accepts a fourth argument, which can be an array of any length, to splice into the input array, again returning an all new array:

```
$super_set = array_splice($pizza_requests, 2, 0,
$more_requests);
```

which will return an array like:

```
Key: Alice; Value: pepperoni
Key: Bob; Value: mushrooms
Key: Ted; Value: anchovies
Key: MrWilson; Value: pineapple
Key: Dagwood; Value: ham
Key: Carl; Value: sausage
Key: Dennis; Value: mushrooms
```

These array-manipulating functions are summarized in Table 21-1.

Table 21-1: Array Transformation Functions

Function	Behavior
`array_keys()`	Takes a single array argument and returns a new array where the new values are the keys of the input array, and the new keys are the integers incremented from zero.
`array_values()`	Takes a single array argument and returns a new array where the new values are the original values of the input array, and the new keys are the integers incremented from zero.
`array_count_values()`	Takes a single array argument and returns a new array where the new keys are the old array's values, and the new values are a count of how many times that original value occurred in the input array.
`array_flip()`	Takes a single array argument and changes that array so that the keys are now the values and vice versa.

Continued

Table 21-1 *(continued)*

Function	Behavior
array_reverse()	Takes a single array argument and changes the internal ordering of the key/value pairs to reverse order. Numerical keys will also be renumbered.
shuffle()	Takes a single array argument and randomizes the internal ordering of key/value pairs. Also renumbers integer keys to match the new ordering. This function itself uses the random-number generator rand(), so srand() must be called to seed the generator before the call to shuffle().
array_merge()	Takes two array arguments, merges them, and returns the new array, which has (in order) the first array's elements and then the second array's elements. (*Note:* This is most useful for arrays that are being used for simple linked lists rather than for their associative keys, because keys that appear in both arrays will have one of the values overwritten. Also, numerical keys will be renumbered from 0 to reflect the new ordering.)
array_pad()	Takes three arguments: an input array, a pad size, and a value to pad with. Returns a new array that is "padded" by the following rules: If the pad size is greater than the length of the input array, the array is lengthened with the pad value to the pad size, as though by successive assignments like $my_array[] = $pad_value. A negative pad size will act the same way with the absolute value of that pad size, except that the padding will occur at the beginning of the array rather than the end. If the array is already longer than the (absolute value of) the pad size, the function has no effect.
array_slice()	Takes three arguments: an input array, an integer offset, and an (optional) integer length. Returns a new array that is a "slice" of the old one — a subsequence of its list of key/value pairs. The starting and stopping points of the slice are determined by the offset and length. A positive offset means that the starting point is that number of elements after the beginning; a negative offset means that it is that many elements before the end. The optional length argument specifies how long the resulting slice is (if positive) or how many elements before the end it should stop (if negative). If the length argument is not present, the slice continues to the end of the array.
array_splice()	Removes a chunk (or a slice) of an array and replaces it with the contents of another array. Takes four arguments: an input array, an offset, an optional integer length, and an optional replacement array. Returns a new array containing the slice that was removed from the input array.
	The rules for using the offset and length arguments to determine the slice that is removed are the same as in the previous array_slice() function.
	If no replacement array is supplied, this function simply (destructively) removes a slice of the input array and returns it. If there is a replacement array, the elements of that array are inserted in place of the removed slice.

Stacks and Queues

Stacks and *queues* are abstract data structures, frequently used in computer science, that enforce a certain kind of access discipline on the objects they contain, without necessarily committing to what those objects are. PHP arrays are well suited to imitating other kinds of data structures, and the loose typing of PHP array elements makes it easy for them to imitate stacks and queues. PHP provides some array functions specifically for this purpose—if you use them exclusively, you can forget that arrays are involved at all.

A *stack* is a container that stores values and supports last-in–first-out (LIFO) behavior. This means that the stack maintains an order on the values you store, and the only way you can get a value back is by retrieving (and removing) the most recently stored value. The usual analogy is a stack of cafeteria trays in one of those dispensers that keeps the top tray at a constant level. You can push new trays down on top of the old ones, and you can take trays off the top, but you can't grab an older tray without taking the newer ones first. The act of adding into the stack is called *pushing* a value onto the stack, whereas the act of taking off the top is called *popping* the stack. Another analogy is the way some Web browsers store the pages you have visited for use by the Back button; visiting a new page pushes a new URL onto that stack, and using the Back button pops the stack.

A *queue* is similar to a stack, but its behavior is first-in-first-out (FIFO). The usual analogy here is what the British call a *queue* and what Americans call a *line*, where people line up in order to wait for something. The rule is that whoever has been in the queue the longest is the next to be served.

The stack functions are `array_push()` and `array_pop()`. The `array_push()` function takes an initial array argument and then any number of elements to push onto the stack. The elements will be inserted at the end of the array, in order from left to right. The `array_pop()` function takes such an array and removes the element at the end, returning it. Take the following fragment:

```
$my_stack = array();  // needed -- array_push() will not create
array_push($my_stack, "the first", "the middle");
array_push($my_stack, "the last");
while ($popped = array_pop($my_stack))
  print("Popped the stack and got: $popped<BR>");
```

This will produce the browser output:

```
Popped the stack and got: the last
Popped the stack and got: the middle
Popped the stack and got: the first
```

PHP also offers functions that behave exactly the same way as `array_push()` and `array_pop()`, except that they work at the other end, adding to and removing from the beginning of the array. The `array_unshift()` function is analogous to `array_push()`, and `array_shift()` is like `array_pop()`. If you choose one function from column A and one from column B, you can get the behavior of a queue. For example, we can rewrite our previous example to push into the beginning of the array (using `array_unshift()`) and pop from the end (using `array_pop()`, as before):

```
$my_queue = array();// needed -- array_unshift() will not create
array_unshift($my_queue, "the first");
array_unshift($my_queue,"the middle");
array_unshift($my_queue, "the last");
while ($popped = array_pop($my_queue))
  print("Popped the queue and got: $popped<BR>");
```

It produces the output:

```
Popped the queue and got: the first
Popped the queue and got: the middle
Popped the queue and got: the last
```

Caution   The `array_unshift()` and `array_shift()` functions are somewhat different from `array_push()` and `array_pop()` in that the former do some renumbering of the array indices if the indices are integers. The idea is that some people may be relying on the numerical indices to order the array contents, so using `array_unshift()` to insert a new element at the beginning should assign an index of 0 to the new element, and renumber those above. Similarly, popping an element from the beginning with `array_shift()` causes integral indices of other elements to be reduced. (This is not an issue with `array_push` and `array_pop`, because changes are at the end, and no renumbering is needed.) If you are using string indices exclusively, this renumbering has no effect. This is a general pattern with PHP array functions: Some of them treat integer indices like any other associative indexes, whereas others assume that integers imply order, and redo them if the order has changed.

The stack and queue functions are summarized in Table 21-2.

Table 21-2: Stack and Queue Functions

Function	Arguments	Side Effect	Returns
`array_push()`	An initial array argument, then any number of values to be pushed onto the stack.	Modifies the array by adding the elements in order to the end of the array.	Returns the number of elements in the array after the push.
`array_pop()`	A single array argument.	Removes the element at the end of the array.	Returns the last (removed) value, or a false value if the array is empty.
`array_unshift()`	An initial array argument, then any number of values to be pushed onto the front of the array.	Modifies the array by adding the successive elements to thebeginning. (The last argument will be at the beginning of the array.)	Returns the number of elements in the array after the new elements are added.
`array_shift()`	A single array argument.	Removes the element at the beginning of the array.	Returns the first (removed) value or a false value if the array is empty.

Translating between Variables and Arrays

PHP offers a couple of unusual functions for mapping between the name/value pairs of regular variable bindings and the key/value pairs of an array. The `compact()` function translates from variable bindings to an array, and the `extract()` function goes in the opposite direction. These are summarized briefly in Table 21-3.

Table 21-3: Array/Variable-Binding Functions

Function	Behavior
compact()	Takes a specified set of strings, looks up bound variables (if any) in the current environment that are named by those strings, and returns an array where the keys are the variable names, and the values are the corresponding values of those variables.
	This function takes any number of arguments, each of which is either a string or an array that contains strings at some level of index depth. The entire set of strings that are included in the argument(s) is used as the candidate set of variable names. Strings that do not correspond to bound variables are ignored.
extract()	Takes an array (plus two optional arguments explained in the next paragraph) and imports the key/value pairs into the current variable-binding context. The array keys become the variable names, and the corresponding array values become the values of the variables. Any keys that do not correspond to a legal variable name will not produce an assignment.
	The optional arguments are an integer (intended to receive one of a small set of constants) and a prefix string. The point of these arguments is to specify what should happen in the case of a collision between the name of an existing variable and one that would be created from an array key.
	The intended possible constants for the optional integer arguments are 1) EXTR_OVERWRITE, 2) EXTR_SKIP, 3) EXTR_PREFIX_SAME, and 4) EXTR_PREFIX_ALL. The corresponding behaviors are 1) go ahead and overwrite existing variables, 2) skip any new assignments that would require overwriting, 3) use the optional prefix string to distinguish the new variable from the old one, or 4) prefix all the new variables with the string. For example, extract(array('my_var' => 4), EXTR_PREFIX_SAME, 'diff_'); would cause $my_var to be 4 if $my_var were not already bound; otherwise, it would assign the value 4 to $diff_my_var.

Sorting

Finally, PHP offers a host of functions for sorting arrays. As we saw earlier, a tension some-times arises between respecting the key/value associations in an array and treating numerical keys as ordering info that should be changed when the order changes. Luckily, PHP offers variants of the sorting functions for each of these behaviors and also allows sorting in ascending or descending order and by user-supplied ordering functions. The function names are terse, but each letter (other than the sort part) has its meaning. The decoder ring is something like:

✦ An initial a means that the function sorts by value but maintains the association between key/value pairs the way it was.

✦ An initial k means that it sorts by key but maintains the key/value associations.

✦ A lack of that initial a or k means that it sorts by value but doesn't maintain the key/value association. In particular, numerical keys will be renumbered to reflect the new ordering.

✦ An r before the sort means that the sorting order will be reversed.

✦ An initial u means that a second argument is expected: the name of a user-defined function that specifies the ordering of any two elements that are being sorted. (See the description in Table 21-4.)

Table 21-4: Array Sorting Functions

Function	Behavior
asort()	Takes a single array argument. Sorts the key/value pairs by value but keeps the key/value mapping the same. Good for associative arrays.
arsort()	Same as asort(), but sorts in descending order.
ksort()	Takes a single array argument. Sorts the key/value pairs by key but maintain the key/value associations the same.
krsort()	Same as ksort(), but sorts in descending order.
sort()	Takes a single array argument. Sorts the key/value pairs of an array by their values. Keys may be renumbered to reflect the new ordering of the values.
rsort()	Same as sort(), but sorts in descending order.
uasort()	Sorts key/value pairs by value using a comparison function. Similar to asort(), except the actual ordering of the values is determined by the second argument, which is the name of a user-defined ordering function. That function should return a negative number if its first argument is before the second (according to the comparison function), a positive number if the first argument comes after the second, and zero if the elements are the same.
uksort()	Sorts key/value pairs by key, using a comparison function. Similar to uasort(), except that the ordering is by key, rather than by value.
usort()	Sorts an array by value using a supplied comparison function. Similar to uasort(), except that (as in sort()), the key/value associations are not maintained.

Printing Functions for Visualizing Arrays

Before we leave this subject entirely, we should mention a couple of printing functions that are very useful for visualizing and debugging arrays, especially multidimensional arrays.

The first function is print_r(), which is short for *print recursive*. This takes an argument of any type and prints it out, which includes printing all its parts recursively. For a simple value (a number or string), this means simply that the value is printed; for compound types like arrays and objects it means that all elements (and all parts of those elements) are printed. The layout that makes the compound structure clear involves spaces, so it's best to wrap its output in an HTML <pre></pre> construct so that the spaces are printed literally.

Cross-Reference

For more detail on the var_dump function and other ways to visualize data structures, see Chapter 32 on debugging.

The `var_dump()` function is similar, except that it prints additional information about the size and type of the values it discovers. An example is worth a thousand words here, so we will create a simple multidimensional array and print it using both functions:

```php
<?php

$my_array = array("key1" => "value1",
                  "key2" => array("subkey1" => "value2"));

print("The result of print_r:<BR><pre>");
print_r($my_array);
print("</pre><BR>");
print("The result of var_dump:<BR><pre>");
var_dump($my_array);
print("</pre><BR>");
?>
```

The resulting output from this sample looks like this:

```
The result of print_r:
Array
(
    [key1] => value1
    [key2] => Array
        (
            [subkey1] => value2
        )

)

The result of var_dump:
array(2) {
  ["key1"]=>
  string(6) "value1"
  ["key2"]=>
  array(1) {
    ["subkey1"]=>
    string(6) "value2"
  }
}
?>
```

Summary

The transformation functions are designed to do interesting things to your arrays. With the exception of `shuffle()`, these functions return their results as a newly created array. To treat an array as a stack is to give it a last-in–first-out property. You can treat an array as a stack by using the `array_push()` and `array_pop()` functions in tandem. Alternatively, `array_unshift()` and `array shift()` used in tandem will have a similar effect, though they work on the opposite end of the array. By choosing one function from each pair, you can effectively cause an array to act like a queue.

The `compact()` function maps variable names and values onto array keys and values while `extract()` reverses the process, even if the array was not created with compact. Finally, a variety of functions in two major classes will sort and reorder arrays. The first major class will do it without reordering integral keys; the second will reorder your integral keys according to the new sorted order.

✦   ✦   ✦

String and Regular Expression Functions

In Chapter 8, we covered PHP strings — how to create them, print them, and (to some extent) how to examine and modify them. In this chapter, we delve into more advanced string-manipulation techniques, starting off with functions to split up (or tokenize) strings into parts. We'll soon run into limitations of the basic tokenization functions, which show the need for regular expressions.

Regular expressions are patterns that match to strings. They are used not only to create complex true/false tests on strings, but also to extract substrings and make complex substitutions. A full treatment of regular expressions is well beyond our scope in this chapter. Instead, we will explain what regular expressions are good for, what varieties of regex are offered by PHP, and give some examples of their uses.

Finally, we'll cover some of the more advanced string functions that enhance the effectiveness of regular expressions and the use of strings in general.

Tokenizing and Parsing Functions

Sometimes you need to take strings apart at the seams, and you have your own notions of what should count as a seam. The process of breaking up a long string into *words* is called *tokenizing,* and among other things it is part of the internals of interpreting or compiling any computer program, including PHP. PHP offers a special function for this purpose, called strtok().

The strtok() function takes two arguments: the string to be broken up into tokens and a string containing all the *delimiters* (characters that count as boundaries between tokens). On the first call, both arguments are used, and the string value returned is the first token. To retrieve subsequent tokens, make the same call, but omit the source string argument. It will be remembered as the current string, and the function will remember where it left off. For example

```
$token = strtok(
    "open-source HTML-embedded server-side Web scripting",
    " ");
while($token){
  print($token . "<BR>");
  $token = strtok(" ");
}
```

gives the browser output:

```
open-source
HTML-embedded
server-side
Web
scripting
```

The original string would be *broken* at each space. At our discretion, we could change the delimiter set, like so:

```
$token = strtok(
    "open-source HTML-embedded server-side Web scripting",
    "-");
while($token){
  print($token . "<BR>");
  $token = strtok("-");
}
```

This gives us (less sensibly):

```
Open
source HTML
embedded server
side Web scripting
```

Finally, we can break the string at all these places at once by giving it a delimiter string like " -", containing both a space and a dash. The code:

```
$token = strtok(
    "open-source HTML-embedded server-side Web scripting",
    " -");
while($token){
  print($token . "<BR>");
  $token = strtok(" -");
}
```

prints this output:

```
open
source
HTML
embedded
server
side
Web
scripting
```

Notice that in every case the delimiter characters do not show up anywhere in the retrieved tokens.

The `strtok()` function doles out its tokens one by one. You can also use the `explode()` function to do something similar, except it stores the tokens all at once into an array. After the tokens are in the array, you can do anything you like with them, including sort them.

The `explode()` function takes two arguments: a separator string and the string to be separated. It returns an array where each element is a substring between instances of the separator in the string to be separated. For example:

```
$explode_result = explode("AND", "one AND a two AND a three");
```

results in the array `$explode_result` having three elements, each of which is a string: `"one "`, `" a two "`, and `" a three"`. In this particular example, there would be no capital letters anywhere in the strings contained in the array, because the `AND` separator does not show up in the result.

The separator string in `explode()` is significantly different from the delimiter string used in `strtok()`. The separator is a full-fledged string, and all its characters must be found in the right order for an instance of the separator to be detected. The delimiter string of `strtok()` specifies a set of single characters, any one of which will count as a delimiter. This makes `explode()` both more precise and more brittle — if you leave out a space or a newline character from a long string, the entire function will be broken.

Because the entire separator string disappears into the ether when `explode()` is used, this function can be the basis for many useful effects. The examples given in most PHP documentation use short strings for convenience, but remember that a string can be almost any length — and `explode()` is especially useful with longer strings that might be tedious to parse some other way. For instance, you can use it to count how many times a particular string appears within a text file by turning the file into a string and using `explode()` on it, as in this example (which uses some functions we haven't explained yet, but we hope make sense in context).

```php
<?php
//First, turn a text file into a string called $filestring.
$filename = "complex_layout.html";
$fd = fopen($filename, "r");
$filestring = fread($fd, filesize($filename));
fclose ($fd);

//Explode on the beginning of the <TABLE> HTML tag
$tables = explode("<TABLE", $filestring); // assumes uppercase
//Count the number of pieces
$num_tables = count($tables);

//Subtract one to get the number of <TABLE> tags, and echo
echo ($num_tables - 1);
?>
```

The `explode()` function has an inverse function, `implode()`, which takes two arguments: a "glue" string (analogous to the separator string in `explode()`) and an array of strings like that returned by `explode()`. It returns a string created by inserting the glue string between each string element in the array.

You can use the two functions together to replace every instance of a particular string within a text file. Remember that the separator string will vanish into the ether when you perform an explode() — if you want it to appear in the final file, you have to replace it by hand. In this example, we're changing the font tags on a Web page.

```php
<?php
//Turn text file into string
$filename = "someoldpage.html";
$fd = fopen($filename, "r");
$filestring = fread($fd, filesize($filename));
fclose ($fd);
$parts = explode("arial, sans-serif", $filestring);
$whole = implode("arial, verdana, sans-serif", $parts);

//Overwrite the original file
$fd = fopen($filename, "w");
fwrite($fd, $whole);
fclose ($fd);
?>
```

Why Regular Expressions?

The string-comparison and substring-finding functions we saw here and in Chapter 8 are fine as far as they go, but they are on the literal-minded side. As an example of their weakness, let's say that you want to test strings to see if they are a particular kind of Web hostname: addresses that start with www. and end with .com, and have one lowercase alphabetic word in the middle. For example, these are strings we want:

```
'www.ibm.com'
'www.zend.com'
```

And the following are not:

```
'java.sun.com'
'www.java.sun.com'
'www.php.net'
'www.IBM.com'
'www.Web addresses can't have spaces.com'
```

With a little thought, it's obvious that there is no convenient way to simply use string and substring comparison to build the test that we want. We can test for the presence of www. and .com, but it is difficult to enforce what should be happening between them. This is what regular expressions are good for.

Regex in PHP

Regular expressions (or *regex*, pronounced with a soft *g* by your authors, but with no consensus pronunciation) are patterns for string matching, with special wildcards that can match entire portions of the target string. There are two broad classes of regular expression that PHP works with: *POSIX* (extended) regex and *Perl-compatible* regex. The differences mostly have to do with syntax, although there are some functional differences, too.

POSIX-style regular expressions are ultimately descended from the regex pattern-matching machinery used in Unix command-line shells; Perl-compatible regex is a more direct imitation of regular expressions in Perl. We've already waxed poetic about the utility of arrays. We're about to do it again with regex. If you're planning on doing any substantial coding in a Web environment, sooner or later you will bump up against regex.

An example of POSIX-style regex

Here are a few of the rules for POSIX-style regular expressions, simplified:

✦ Characters that are not *special* get matched literally. The letter a in a pattern, for example, matches the same letter in a target string.

✦ The special character ^ matches the beginning of a string only, and the special character $ matches the end of a string only.

✦ The special character . matches any character.

✦ The special character * matches zero or more instances of the previous regular expression, and + matches one or more instances of the previous expression.

✦ A set of characters enclosed in square brackets matches any of those characters — the pattern [ab] matches either a or b. You can also specify a range of characters in brackets by using a hyphen — the pattern [a-c] matches a, b, or c.

✦ Special characters that are escaped with a backslash (\) lose their special meaning and are matched literally.

We can use the preceding rules to construct an expression that matches the kind of Web address we want in the section "Why Regular Expressions?" earlier in this chapter. Our chosen expression is:

```
^www\.[a-z]+\.com$
```

In this expression we have the '^' symbol, which says that the www portion must start at the beginning of the string. Then comes a dot (.), preceded by a backslash that says we really want a dot, not the special . wildcard character. Then we have a bracket-enclosed range of all the lowercase alphabetic letters. The following + indicates that we are willing to match any number of these lowercase letters in a row, as long as we have at least one of them. Then another literal ., the com, and the special $ that says that com is the end of it.

Now let's use that expression as an argument to the function ereg(), which takes as arguments a pattern string and a string to match against. We can use an ereg() call to build a test function for our kind of Web address.

```
function simple_dot_com ($url)
{
   return(ereg('^www\\.[a-z]+\\.com$', $url));
}
```

Confusingly, we have to put two backslashes in the pattern string, because PHP treats the first slash as an escape character for the second backslash. (You can get away with just one backslash, but that behavior is not guaranteed to continue in future versions of PHP.) The second backslash (escaped by the first), in turn, is a regex escape character for the following character.

This function will return TRUE or FALSE, depending on whether it successfully matches our pattern. Now we can use our function to test some of the addresses listed earlier.

```
$urls_to_test =
    array('www.ibm.com', 'www.java.sun.com',
          'www.zend.com', 'java.sun.com',
          'www.java.sun.com', 'www.php.net',
          'www.IBM.com',
          'www.Web addresses can\'t have spaces.com');
while($test = array_pop($urls_to_test)){
  if (simple_dot_com($test))
    print("\"$test\" is a simple dot-com<BR>");
  else
    print("\"$test\" is NOT a simple dot-com<BR>");

}
```

The results of our tests are as follows:

```
"www.Web addresses can't have spaces.com" is NOT a simple dot-com
"www.IBM.com" is NOT a simple dot-com
"www.php.net" is NOT a simple dot-com
"www.java.sun.com" is NOT a simple dot-com
"java.sun.com" is NOT a simple dot-com
"www.zend.com" is a simple dot-com
"www.java.sun.com" is NOT a simple dot-com
"www.ibm.com" is a simple dot-com
```

This is the kind of discriminating behavior we are looking for.

Tip   On many Unix systems, typing **man 7 regex** will lead you to a guide to POSIX regular expressions. If that does not work, try **man regex** and follow any pointers to related pages.

Regular expression functions

The POSIX-style regular expression functions in PHP are summarized in Table 22-1.

Tip   If you find yourself using a regular expression function with a pattern that has no special characters, you are probably using an expensive tool where a cheap one would do. If you are trying to match a simple string to a simple string, you need only one of the more basic (and faster) functions that we cover earlier in this chapter and in Chapter 8.

Table 22-1: POSIX Regular Expression Functions

Function	Behavior
ereg()	Takes two string arguments and an optional third-array argument. The first string is the POSIX-style regular expression pattern, and the second string is the target string that is being matched. The function returns TRUE if the match was successful and FALSE otherwise. In addition, if an array argument is supplied and portions of the pattern are enclosed in parentheses, the parts of the target string that match successive parenthesized portions will be copied into successive elements of the array.

Function	Behavior
ereg_replace()	Takes three arguments: a POSIX regular expression pattern, a string to do replacement with, and a string to replace into. The function scans the third argument for portions that match the pattern and replaces them with the second argument. The modified string is returned.
	If there are parenthesized portions of the pattern (as with ereg()), the replacement string may contain special substrings of the form \\digit (that is, two backslashes followed by a single-digit number), which will themselves be replaced with the corresponding piece of the target string.
eregi()	Identical to ereg(), except that letters in regular expressions are matched in a case-independent way.
eregi_replace()	Identical to ereg_replace(), except that letters in regular expressions are matched in a case-independent way.
split()	Takes a pattern, a target string, and an optional limit on the number of portions to split the string into. Returns an array of strings created by splitting the target string into chunks delimited by substrings that match the regular expression. (Note that this is analogous to the explode() function, except that it splits on regular expressions rather than literal strings.)
spliti()	Case-independent version of split().

Perl-Compatible Regular Expressions

Perl-compatible regex in PHP has a completely distinct set of functions and a slightly different set of rules for patterns.

Perl-compatible regex patterns are always bookended by one particular character, which must be the same at beginning and end, indicating the beginning and end of the pattern. By convention, this is most often the / character, although you can use a different character if you so desire. The Perl-compatible pattern:

```
/pattern/
```

matches any string that has the string (or substring) pattern in it. To make things slightly more complicated, these patterns are typically strings, and PHP needs its own quotes to recognize such strings. So if you are putting a pattern into a variable for later use, you might well do this:

```
$my_pattern = '/pattern/';
```

This variable would now be suitable for passing off to a Perl-compatible regex function that expects a pattern as argument.

Although we don't have time or space to cover Perl-compatible regex patterns in detail, Table 22-2 shows a list of the most commonly used constructs.

Table 22-2: Common Perl-Compatible Pattern Constructs

Construct	Interpretation
Simple literal character matches	If the character involved is not special, Perl will match characters in sequence. The example pattern /abc/ matches any string that has the substring 'abc' in it.
Character class matches: [*<list of characters>*]	Will match a single instance of any of the characters between the brackets. For example, /[xyz]/ matches a single character, as long as that character is either x, y, or z. A sequence of characters (in ASCII order) is indicated by a hyphen, so that a class matching all digits is [0-9].
Predefined character class abbreviations	The patterns \d will match a single digit (from the character class [0-9]), and the pattern \s matches any whitespace character.
Multiplier patterns	Any pattern followed by * means: "Match this pattern 0 or more times."
	Any pattern followed by ? means: "Match this pattern exactly once."
	Any pattern followed by + means: "Match this pattern 1 or more times."
Anchoring characters	The caret character ^ at the beginning of a pattern means that the pattern must start at the beginning of the string; the $ character at the end of a pattern means that the pattern must end at the end of the string. The caret character at the beginning of a character class [^abc] means that the set is the complement of the characters listed (that is, any character that is not in the list).
Escape character '\'	Any character that has a special meaning to regex can be treated as a simple matching character by preceding it with a backslash. The special characters that might need this treatment are: . \ + * ? [ ] ^ $ ( ) { } = ! < > | :
Parentheses	A parenthesis grouping around a portion of any pattern means: "Add the substring that matches this pattern to the list of substring matches."

Take, as an example, the following pattern:

```
/phone number\s+(\d\d\d\d\d\d\d)/
```

It matches any string that contains the literal phrase phone number, followed by some number of spaces (but at least one), followed by exactly seven digits (no spaces, no dash). In addition, because of the parentheses, the seven-digit number is saved and returned in an array containing substring matches if it is called from a function that returns such things.

The Perl-compatible functions are summarized in Table 22-3.

Table 22-3: Perl-Compatible Regular Expression Functions

Function	Behavior
preg_match()	Takes a regex pattern as first argument, a string to match against as second argument, and an optional array variable for returned matches. Returns 0 if no matches are found, and 1 if a match is found. If a match is successful, the array variable contains the entire matching substring as its first element, and subsequent elements contain portions matching parenthesized portions of the pattern. As of PHP 4.3.0, an optional flag of PREG_OFFSET_CAPTURE is also available. This flag causes preg match to return into the specified array a two-element array for each match, consisting of the match itself and the offset where the match occurs.
preg_match_all()	Like preg_match(), except that it makes all possible successive matches of the pattern in the string, rather than just the first. The return value is the number of matches successfully made. The array of matches is not optional (If you want a true/false answer, use preg_match()). The structure of the array returned depends on the optional fourth argument (either the constant PREG_PATTERN_ORDER, or PREG_SET_ORDER, defaulting to the former). (See further discussion following the table.) PREG_OFFSET_CAPTURE is also available with this function.
preg_split()	Takes a pattern as first argument and a string to match as second argument. Returns an array containing the string divided into substrings, split along boundary strings matching the pattern. (Analogous to the POSIX-style function split().) An optional third argument (limit) controls how many elements to split before returning the list; -1 means no limit. An optional flag in the fourth position can be PREG_SPLIT_NO_EMPTY causing the function to return only non-empty pieces, PREG_SPLIT_DELIM_CAPTURE causing any parenthesized expression in the delimiter pattern to be returned, or PREG_SPLIT_OFFSET_CAPTURE, which does the same as PREG_OFFSET_CAPTURE.
preg_replace()	Takes a pattern, a replacement string, and a string to modify. Returns the result of replacing every matching portion of the modifiable string with the replacement string. An optional limit argument determines how many replacements will occur (as in preg_split()).
preg_replace_callback()	Like preg_replace(), except that the second argument is the name of a callback function, rather than a replacement string. This function should return the string that is to be used as a replacement.
preg_grep()	Takes a pattern and an array and returns an array of the elements of the input array that matched the pattern. Surviving values of the new array have the same keys as in the input array.
preg_quote()	A special-purpose function for inserting escape characters into strings that are intended for use as regex patterns. The only required argument is a string to escape; the return value is that string with every special regex character preceded by a backslash.

The most widely used of these functions are probably `preg_match()` and `preg_match_all()`. The first is best for simply answering whether a pattern matches a string, and the latter is best for either counting matches or collecting portions that match.

The optional fourth argument to `preg_match_all()` requires a little more explanation. The array that contains the returned matches is going to be two levels deep, with one level being the iteration of the match (the first match, the second, and so on), and the other level being the position of the match in the pattern. (The entire match is always first, followed by any parenthesized subpatterns in order.) The question is: Which level is on top? Will the array be a list of positions, each of which contains a list of iterations, or the other way around? If the argument is `PREG_PATTERN_ORDER`, the first element will contain all matches of the entire pattern, the second element will contain all matches of the first parenthesized pattern, and so forth. If the argument is `PREG_SET_ORDER`, the first argument will be all the substrings from the first match (first the total match, then parenthesized bits in order), the second element will contain all the substrings from the second match, and so on. (See the following example to clarify.)

Example: A Simple Link-Scraper

As an example of what regex can do for us, let's write a simple function to grab and print links from an arbitrary Web page. The input will be a URL for the page we're interested in analyzing; the output will be a printed list of the links on the page, split into the target URL for the link and the descriptive text that appears in the link (the *anchortext*). We will do this using Perl-compatible regex functions.

Such a function might be the very first step in writing a Web-crawler for a search engine. Search engines download the contents of Web pages to analyze and index them, but they also need to discover links to other pages, if only to discover new content.

The regular expression

The heart of our little function will be the regular expression itself. What we need to do is design an expression that will match HTML links (and nothing else) and that is suitable for using to extract pieces of such links.

HTML links generally look something like this:

```
<A HREF="http://mysite.com/mypage.php">My cool page on my cool
site</A>
```

That is, an anchor tag that has an `HREF` attribute, and which encloses the anchortext between the start tag (`<A>`) and the end tag (`</A>`). We'll construct a pattern to match this simplified view of an anchortext. (This won't capture everything that the HTML spec permits as legal anchor links — in particular, you are allowed attributes in anchors other than `HREF`s, but we will ignore that for our purposes.)

Now, regular expressions are famously unreadable when considered all at once. So we will grow this one in several drafts as we explain what's going on.

First, let's start with a minimal expression to catch a beginning anchor tag. Our first draft looks like this:

```
/<A\sHREF="[^"]+">/
// first draft of a pattern to match anchor links
```

(Note that this is not yet intended to be working PHP code; we're drafting an expression that we'll plug into PHP code later.)

In English, our first-draft definition of an anchor tag is left angle bracket, followed by A, followed by a space, followed by the string HREF=, followed by a double-quote sign, followed by any number of characters that are not quote signs, followed by a closing quote sign, followed by a right angle bracket. Then the whole expression is enclosed in a pair of slashes, indicating to the regex engine the start and end of the expression.

The [^"]+ construction in the middle of this expression breaks down like this: The brackets indicate a character set, and the caret (^) immediately after the left bracket indicates that we are negating the set — that the set contains every character that is *not* in the subsequent list. Finally, the + after that bracketed class means that we expect at least one nonquote character.

As we've said, we're not trying to capture the precise syntax prescribed by the HTML specification. But there are a couple of ways that we can make this expression less strict. For one thing, as far as we know, there may be spaces between the initial < character and the A tag. Similarly, there may be an arbitrary number of spaces between the A and the HREF or the closing double-quote and the right angle bracket. Adding these, the expression becomes:

```
/<\s*A\s*HREF="[^"]+"\s*>/
// second draft, allowing more spaces
```

Here, \s* means zero or more spaces.

Now we add the anchortext itself and the closing </A> tag.

```
/<\s*A\s*HREF="[^\"]+"\s*>[^>]*<\/A>/
  // third draft, with text and close tag
```

We are allowing the anchor text to be anything up until a closing anchor tag, so we make an anything-but-right-angle-bracket character class ([^>]) and indicate that it can repeat zero or more times. Finally, we add the subpattern to match the closing anchor tag (<\/A>).

This is fine as far as it goes, but it will only match anchors where the tag name (A) and attribute (HREF) are in uppercase. Lowercase tags should be legal as well, so we add an i modifier after the entire expression, to specify case-independent matching.

```
/<\s*A\s*HREF="[^\"]+"\s*>[^>]*<\/A>/i
// fourth draft, case-independent
```

This draft is nearly final and could be used to give true/false answers to the question of whether a page contains the kind of links we like. But we want to go further and extract certain portions of any string that does match. We signify this by adding parentheses to enclose the portions we're interested in:

```
/<\s*A\s*HREF="([^\"])+"\s*>([^>]*)<\/A>/i
// final draft, extracts portions
```

They may be hard to see by this point, but we've added a pair of parentheses to enclose the target of the HREF (between the quotes) and another pair around the anchortext area (between the tags). These parentheses tell the calling function to save the string portion that matches the enclosed area, so that it can be added to the return array.

Using the expression in a function

With an anchor-tag-matching expression in hand, our goal now is to write a function to scrape links from an HTML page. We'll need to:

✦ Take a URL as argument.

✦ Open up an HTTP connection to the URL and grab its contents as a string.

✦ Iterate through the string, applying our regex pattern wherever we can, saving what matches.

✦ Print the extracted portions (target URL and anchortext).

Such a function is shown in Listing 22-1.

Listing 22-1: **A print_links function**

```php
<?php

function print_links ($url)
{
  $fp = fopen($url, "r")
    or die("Could not contact $url");
  $page_contents = "";
  while ($new_text = fread($fp, 100)) {
    $page_contents .= $new_text;
  }
  $match_result =
    preg_match_all('/<\s*A\s*HREF="([^\"]+)"\s*>([^>]*)<\/A>/i',
              $page_contents,
              $match_array,
              PREG_SET_ORDER);

  foreach ($match_array as $entry) {
    $href = $entry[1];
    $anchortext = $entry[2];
    print("<B>HREF</B>: $href;
          <B>ANCHORTEXT</B>:  $anchortext<BR>");
  }
}

?>
```

This function is easier to write than you might expect because PHP takes care of several parts of it for us. We do not need to write anything special to make an HTTP connection to download a Web page because fopen() will accept a URL as argument and do the right thing. All we need to do after calling fopen() on the URL is to read characters until we are out of them, appending what we get onto a constructed string.

The iteration through the HTML page's contents is taken care of by `preg_match_all()`, which applies the regex pattern as many times as possible, starting from the previous match each time, and saving the matches in `$match_array`. We chose to have the array arranged by `PREG_SET_ORDER`, meaning that each entry in the top-level array is the portion from a particular match in the iteration, rather than across matches.

Applying the function

The only argument the function requires is a URL. In testing the function before including it in the book, we pointed it at link-rich, top-level pages like `http://slashdot.org`, `www.cnn.com`, and `www.php.net`. Those results would be fun to display, but all of those sites have copyright notices, and publishers are understandably wary of allowing authors to put other people's copyrighted material into their copyrighted book without permission. So, instead, we pointed it at the top-level placeholder page for our own vanity site (`www.troutworks.com`), like this:

```
print_links("http://www.troutworks.com/");
```

You get the following result (approximately):

```
HREF: http://www.mysteryguide.com; ANCHORTEXT: MysteryGuide
HREF: http://www.sciencebookguide.com; ANCHORTEXT:
ScienceBookGuide
HREF: /Joycelog/joycelog.php; ANCHORTEXT: Troutgirl weblog
HREF: /Timlog/timlog.php; ANCHORTEXT: Timboy weblog
HREF: http://www.troutworks.com/phpbook; ANCHORTEXT: code
download site
HREF: http://www.amazon.com/exec/obidos/tg/detail/-/0764549553/;
HREF: http://www.mysteryguide.com; ANCHORTEXT: MysteryGuide
HREF: http://www.sciencebookguide.com; ANCHORTEXT:
ScienceBookGuide
ANCHORTEXT: PHP Bible
HREF: http://www.troutworks.com/phpbook; ANCHORTEXT: code
download site
```

Just because we didn't feel that we could print the results of the links from those more interesting sites doesn't mean that you can't apply this code to them (however, see the warnings in the sidebar "Writing well-behaved spiders").

Extending the code

As we've said, code like Listing 22-1 is the very beginning of writing a Web-search spider. If you want to make it more real, you could:

✦ Convert the relative links to absolute (`http://`) links by remembering the URL that you are scraping and splicing that base URL appropriately with the relative path.

✦ Add a more graceful way to bounce back from an unreachable site rather than immediately dying.

✦ Expand the regex pattern to match HREFs that have quotes around the URL as well as HREFs that do not.

✦ Add capability for recursive calls so that, rather than simply printing a child link, you apply the same function again to it and explore its own links.

Writing Well-behaved Spiders

A note of caution, however (informed by the experience of one of your authors in the search-engine business). There is absolutely no reason you shouldn't feel free to point this code at `www.cnn.com/` to view the links on that front page—after all, it's exactly what happens when your own browser contacts that site, and certainly the people at CNN won't be able to tell the difference between those two contacts.

There are two rules that you should observe, though, before writing any kind of spider that does more automated crawling. When you crawl any site, you should:

✦ Check to see if there is a `robots.txt` file (at `http://sitename/robots.txt`). If there is no such file, the site owners are implicitly saying the site is okay to crawl. If there is such a file, you should either not crawl the site or, if you do, you should make sure that you are not crawling pages that match the patterns laid out in that file. (For more on this, do a Web search for "robot exclusion standard".)

✦ Make sure that you don't request files from any particular site too frequently. A decent interval to wait between requests is ten seconds or so. (You can implement this delay on a per-site basis, or simply by sleeping for ten seconds between every request.) It is not OK to simply create a recursive version of the preceding code, and then unleash it on a large site, grabbing new links and pages as fast as your code can loop. Remember: One man's search engine is another's denial-of-service attack.

Advanced String Functions

We have now covered the most basic things to do with strings, as well some more sophisticated means of working with them via regular expressions. Now, we'll delve into some more exotic string functions, which we've categorized by type and/or purpose. These are the sort of functions that might only be relevant to you if you're working on a particular kind of project. Some of these sections might make you want to say, "Why would anyone want to do that?" If so, please ignore them until you the day that you suddenly realize that you need to do that thing exactly.

HTML functions

PHP offers a number of Web-specific functions for string manipulation, which are summarized in Table 22-4.

Table 22-4: HTML-Specific String Functions

Function	Behavior
`htmlspecialchars()`	Takes a string as argument and returns the string with replacements for four characters that have special meaning in HTML. Each of these characters is replaced with the corresponding HTML entity, so that it will look like the original when rendered by a browser. The & character is replaced by & " " (the double-quote character) is replaced by "; < is replaced by <; > is replaced by >.

Function	Behavior
htmlentities()	Goes further than htmlspecialchars(), in that it replaces all characters that have a corresponding HTML entity with that HTML entity.
get_html_translation_table()	Takes one of two special constants (HTML_SPECIAL_CHARS and HTML_ENTITIES), and returns the translation table used by htmlspecialchars() and htmlentities(), respectively. The translation table is an array where keys are the character strings and the corresponding values are their replacements.
nl2br()	Takes a string as argument and returns that string with inserted before all new lines (\n). This is helpful, for example, in maintaining the apparent line length of text paragraphs when they are displayed in a browser.
strip_tags()	Takes a string as argument and does its best to return that string stripped of all HTML tags and all PHP tags.

Hashing using MD5

MD5 is a string-processing algorithm that is used to produce a digest or signature of whatever string it is given. The algorithm boils its input string down into a fixed-length string of 32 hexadecimal values (0,1,2, . . . 9,a,b, . . . f). MD5 has some very useful properties:

✦ MD5 always produces the same output string for any given input string.

✦ The fixed-length results of applying MD5 are very evenly spread over the range of possible values.

✦ There is no known way to efficiently produce an input string corresponding to a given MD5 output string or to produce two inputs that yield the same output.

PHP's implementation of MD5 is available in the function md5(), which takes a string as input and produces the 32-character digest as output. For example, evaluating this:

```
print("md5 of 'Tim' is " . md5('Tim') . "<BR>");
print("md5 of 'tim' is " . md5('tim') . "<BR>");
print("md5 of 'time' is " . md5('time') . "<BR>");
```

gives us the browser output:

```
md5 of Tim is dc2054afd537ddc98afd9347136494ac
md5 of tim is b15d47e99831ee63e3f47cf3d4478e9a
md5 of time is 07cc694b9b3fc636710fa08b6922c42b
```

Although the input strings seem close to each other in some sense, there is no apparent similarity in the output strings. And since the range of possible output values is so huge (16 to the 32nd power), the chances that any two distinct strings will *collide* by producing the same MD5 value is vanishingly small.

The characteristics of MD5 make it useful for a wide variety of tasks, including:

✦ **Checksumming a message or file.** If you are worried about errors that might happen in transfer, you can transmit an MD5 digest, along with the message, and run the message through MD5 again after transfer. If the two versions of the digest do not match, then something is amiss.

✦ **Detecting if a file's contents have changed.** Similar to checksumming, MD5 is often used in this way by search engines as a check on whether a Web page has changed, making re-indexing necessary. It is cheaper to store the MD5 digest than the entire original file.

✦ **Encrypting passwords.** You might store an MD5'ed password in your database, and compare the result of MD5'ing an entered password against that entry.

✦ **Splitting strings or files into buckets.** If you want to divide a set of strings into N randomly dispersed sets, you can MD5 the strings, take the first few hex characters, translate them into a number, and take that number modulo the number of bins you want.

In addition to the `md5()` function, PHP offers `md5_file()`, which takes a filename as argument and returns an MD5 hash of the file's contents.

Strings as character collections

PHP offers some pretty specialized functions that treat strings more as collections of characters than as sequences.

The first is `strspn()`, which you can use to see what portion of a string is composed only of a given set of characters. For example:

```
$twister = "Peter Piper picked a peck of pickled peppers";
$charset = "Peter picked a";
print("The segment matching '$charset' is " .
      strspn($twister, $charset) . " characters long");
```

gives us:

```
The segment matching 'Peter picked a' is 26 characters long
```

because the first character not found in `$charset` is the o in of, and there are 26 characters that precede it.

The `strcspn()` function (where that internal c stands for *complement*) does the same thing, except that it accepts characters that are *not* in the character set argument. For example, the statement:

```
echo(strcspn($twister, "abcd"));
```

prints the number 14, because it accepts a 14-character sequence with the last character being the c in `picked`.

Finally, hark back to Chapter 9 on arrays and check out the following for an acute analysis of alliteration:

```
$twister = "Peter Piper picked a peck of pickled peppers";
print("$twister<BR>");
$letter_array = count_chars($twister, 1);
while ($cell = each($letter_array)){
```

```
$letter = chr($cell['key']);
$frequency = $cell['value'];
print("Character: '$letter'; frequency:  $frequency<BR>");
}
```

This gives the browser output:

```
Peter Piper picked a peck of pickled peppers
Character: ' '; frequency: 7
Character: 'P'; frequency: 2
Character: 'a'; frequency: 1
Character: 'c'; frequency: 3
Character: 'd'; frequency: 2
Character: 'e'; frequency: 8
Character: 'f'; frequency: 1
Character: 'i'; frequency: 3
Character: 'k'; frequency: 3
Character: 'l'; frequency: 1
Character: 'o'; frequency: 1
Character: 'p'; frequency: 7
Character: 'r'; frequency: 3
Character: 's'; frequency: 1
Character: 't'; frequency: 1
```

The count_chars() function returns a report on the occurrences of characters in its string argument, packaged up as an array where the keys are the ASCII values of characters, and the values are the frequencies of those characters in the string. The second argument to count_chars() is an integer that determines which of several modes the results should be returned in. In mode 0, an array of key/value pairs is returned, where the keys are every ASCII value from 0 to 255, and the corresponding values are the frequencies of each character in the string. Modes 1 and 2 are variants that include only ASCII values that occurred in the string (mode 1) or that did not occur (mode 2). Finally, modes 3 and 4 return a string instead of an array, where the string contains all characters that occur (mode 3) or do not occur (mode 4).

These functions are summarized in Table 22-5.

Cross-Reference

For an explanation of how to take apart array formats like that returned by count_chars(), see Chapter 9. The chr() function used in the preceding example, which maps from ASCII numbers to the corresponding characters, is covered in Chapter 5.

Table 22-5: Functions for Examining Character Contents

Function	Behavior
count_chars()	Takes a single string argument and an integer mode argument from 0 to 4. Returns a report about frequencies of characters in the string argument, as either an array or a string. (See the preceding text for more detail.)
strspn()	Takes two string arguments and returns the length of the initial substring of the first argument that is composed entirely of characters found in its second argument.
strcspn()	Takes two string arguments and returns the length of the initial substring of the first argument that is composed entirely of characters that are *not* found in its second argument.

String similarity functions

How similar is this string to that string? Well, it depends what you mean by *similar*, right?

If the kind of similarity you want is similarity of spelling, consider the Levenshtein metric. The `levenshtein()` function takes two strings and returns the minimum number of additions, deletions, and replacements of letters needed to transform one into the other. For example:

✦ `levenshtein('Tim', 'Time')` returns 1

✦ `levenshtein('boy', 'chefboyardee')` returns 9

✦ `levenshtein('never', 'clever')` returns 2

If the similarity you are interested in is phonetic, consider the functions `soundex()` and `metaphone()`. Both of them take an input string and return a key string representing the pronunciation category of the word (in English). If two input word strings map to exactly the same output key, they most likely have a similar pronunciation.

Summary

PHP has a wealth of built-in functions for handling strings — functions to create them, stick them together, chop them up, and do various kinds of analysis. The simplest of these were covered in Chapter 8, and in this chapter we saw functions for tokenizing, hashing, character-counting, and determining similarity, as well as HTML-specific functions.

Simple string matching is all very well, but when you need industrial-strength pattern matching, nothing less than regex will do. PHP offers not only full regular-expression functionality, but two flavors of it to choose from. Our personal preference is for the Perl-compatible regex functions, but you can use whichever flavor suits you best.

✦   ✦   ✦

Filesystem and System Functions

This chapter contains information on the multiplicity of system functions built into PHP. Many of these functions duplicate system functions via HTTP. Among the most useful are file-reading and writing functions and those that return dates or times.

Caution Many of the functions in this chapter have serious security implications. You are inviting bad news if you use them without thinking pretty hard about the consequences! We'll try to point out the scariest ones as we go, but nothing that allows the system to be altered via HTTP should be undertaken lightly.

Some of these functions are Unix-only. The Windows system is deliberately made less available to users, especially to non-Administrator users, and lacks many utilities that Unix-heads take for granted. If you're having problems and you run on Windows, make sure the function is enabled on your platform.

Understanding PHP File Permissions

Many PHP users, who have a developer orientation rather than any sysadmin experience, unfortunately do not take the time to understand Unix filesystem permissions. You really need to have a firm grasp of the basics to make good decisions about using many of the functions in this section. If you already do, feel free to skip the rest of this section.

Unfortunately, most explanations of the subject are quite general and user's eyes can easily glaze over in a hail of rwxes and three-digit numbers. So we're going to break it down for you into two simple default rules specifically for PHP users.

 ✦ Unless you have a good reason to do otherwise, your PHP files should all be set to 644 (rw-r--r--).

 ✦ Unless you have a good reason to do otherwise, your PHP-enabled directories should all be set to 751 (rwxr-x--x).

For some reason, many users seem to believe that PHP files need to be executable. This is only true for files that you write with the intention of their being called on the command line (for example, ./myscript.php). Files that will be run through a Web server only need to be readable by the Web server user (usually Nobody, or some other user with very limited permissions). It's rather inconvenient to make the files not writable by you, which is why our default recommendation is 644 (rw-r--r--) rather than 444 (r--r--r--), but this is a matter of convenience only — on a production system, where you shouldn't be altering code anyway, you might very well want to set them to 444. Your PHP scripts will run perfectly fine at 444 (read-only).

Directory permissions are also very often misunderstood. Many users seem to believe that directories need to be readable for files to run. Actually the *read* directory permission means a user can list the contents of that directory (via the ls command, for instance). The *execute* directory permission is closer to what we think of as readable. For your PHP scripts to run, the directory needs only to be world-executable (751 or rwxr-x--x). Do not make the directory writable by others unless you know what you're doing.

This Web page gives a good short explanation of Unix file permissions: www.freeos.com/articles/3127/.

File Reading and Writing Functions

This is a supremely useful set of functions, particularly for data sets too small or scattered to merit the use of a database. File reading is pretty safe unless you keep unencrypted passwords lying around, but file writing can be quite unsafe.

Tip Remember that although the Web server (and client-side languages such as JavaScript) can only act on files located under the document root, PHP can access files at any location in the file system — including those above or entirely outside the Web server document root — as long as the file permissions and include_path are set correctly. For instance, if your Web server document root is located at /usr/local/apache/htdocs, Apache will be able to serve only files from this directory and its subdirectories, but PHP can open, read, and write to files in /usr/local, /home/php, /export/home/httpd, or any other directory that you make readable and includable by the PHP and/or Web server user.

A file manipulation session might involve the following steps:

1. Open the file for read/write.

2. Read in the file.

3. Close the file (may happen later).

4. Perform operations on the file contents.

5. Write results out.

Each step has a corresponding PHP filesystem function.

This archetypal example illustrates some subtleties of the syntax for manipulating file contents:

```
$fd = fopen($filename, "r+")
  or die("Can't open file $filename");
$fstring = fread($fd, filesize($filename));
$fout = fwrite($fd, $fstring);
fclose($fd);
```

The effect of this particular example will be to *double* the file — in other words, the end result will be a file with the original contents of the file written out twice. This function will not over-write the file, as you might expect. In the following sections, we walk you through this archetypal file manipulation session, step by step.

File open

It's essentially mandatory to assign the result of fopen() to a variable (traditionally $fd for *file descriptor*, or $fp for *file pointer*).

> **Caution** Note that fopen() does not return an integer on success. In fact, it returns a string that says Resource id #n, where n is the number of the currently opened stream. Do not attempt to test the success of your file open by using is_int() or is_numeric(). Use die() instead.

If it's successful in opening the file, PHP will return a resource ID, which it requires for further operations such as fread or fwrite. Otherwise, the value will be false.

> **Caution** The system makes only a certain number of file descriptors available, which is a good argu-ment for closing files as soon as you can. If you anticipate a large demand and have access to system settings, you may increase the number. However, if you fail to close a file descrip-tor, PHP will do it for you when the script ends.

Files may be opened in any of six modes (similar to permissions levels). If you try to do mode-inappropriate things, you will be denied. The modes are:

✦ Read-only ("r").

✦ Read and write if the file exists already ("r+"): will write to the beginning of the file, doubling original contents of the file if you read the file in as a string, edit it, and then write the string out to the file.

✦ Write-only ("w") will create a file of this name, if one doesn't already exist, and will erase the contents of any file of this name before writing! You cannot use this mode to read a file, only to write one.

✦ Write and read even if the file doesn't exist already ("w+") will create a file of this name, if one doesn't already exist, and will erase the contents of any file of this name before writing!

✦ Write-only to the end of a file whether it exists or not ("a").

✦ Read and write to the end of a file whether it exists or not ("a+"), "doubling" original contents of the file if you read the file in as a string, edit it, and then write the string out to the file.

You need to be very sure you have read in the contents of any pre-existing file before using w or w+ on it. Your chance of losing data with the other modes is much less.

> **Tip** Since version 4.3.2 of PHP, a formerly optional parameter, b, has been made the default operating mode for fopen(). This means all files, on platforms where the distinction is sup-ported, are opened as binary. The result is that (among other, finer points) no translation of the line-ending characters occurs between Windows and Unix-like platforms. You can still cir-cumvent this measure by making the letter t the last character of your permissions, in effect forcing the translation to occur.

There are four main types of file connections that can be opened: HTTP, FTP, standard I/O, and filesystem.

Tip

Some users have reported problems with the "+" modes. Many of these problems actually appear to be caused by slightly faulty understanding of the six modes. When in doubt, try opening in separate read and write modes. See the section on file-writing later in this chapter.

HTTP fopen

An HTTP `fopen()` tries to open an HTTP 1.0 connection to a file of a type which would normally be served by a Web server (such as HTML, PHP, ASP, and so on). PHP actually fakes out the Web server into thinking the request is coming from a normal Web browser surfing the Net rather than a file-open operation.

You should be able to use forward slashes like this on either Unix or Windows, since the addresses are URLs rather than filepaths:

```
$fd = fopen("http://www.example.com/openfile.html/", "r");
```

Remember that technically a URL without a trailing slash is malformed, but through incorrect usage most Web servers will automatically rewrite the URL with the slash and try redirecting it. Versions of PHP before 4.0.5 did not support redirects, so all HTTP `fopen()` requests would fail without the trailing slash. After 4.0.5, the trailing slash became optional.

Remember that you need not necessarily use an HTTP connection just because you're looking at an HTML file. If you have filesystem access, you can open from the filesystem instead and treat the file as a text file. The HTTP `fopen()` alternative is mostly useful for getting HTML pages from remote Web servers — as when you try to "scrape" data from an HTML page. The effect will be much like viewing an HTML page and saving the source code.

PHP versions older than 4.3.0 were unable to make HTTPS `fopen`s. Now, you can accomplish this simply by using "`https://`" rather than "`http://`".

HTTP `fopen()`s are read-only. You will not be able to write to a remote HTML file using this type of file manipulation.

FTP fopen

An FTP `fopen()` attempts to establish an FTP connection to a remote server by pretending to be an FTP client. This is the trickiest of the four options because you need to use an FTP username and password in addition to the hostname and path.

```
$fd = fopen("ftp://username:password@example.com/openfile.txt/",
"r");
```

The FTP server must support passive mode for this method to work correctly. Also, FTP file opens can only be read *or* write, not both at once, and writes can only be to new files, not to existing ones.

PHP has many specific FTP functions, sufficient to implement a complete FTP client in PHP. If you want to do anything except a simple FTP file download, you should probably use them instead. See the PHP manual at `www.php.net/manual/en/ref.ftp.php`.

Standard I/O fopen

Standard I/O read/writes are indicated by `php://stdin`, `php://stdout`, or `php://stderr` (depending on the desired stream). The standard I/O `fopen()` comes into play mostly when PHP is used on the command line or as a system scripting language, à la Perl, because standard

I/O is usually associated with terminal windows. This usage is so rare in PHP that we have only seen one real-life example of any length.

A command-line script using a standard I/O fopen looks like this:

```
#! /usr/local/bin/php
<?php
$fp = fopen("php://stdin", "r");
while (!feof($fp)) {
  echo fgets($fp, 4096);
}
echo "\n";
?>
```

You would run it like this from the command line:

```
echo "goo goo ga ga" | ./stdin_test.php
```

Filesystem fopen

The most common and useful way to use fopen() is from the filesystem. Unless specifically directed otherwise, PHP will attempt to open from the filesystem.

On Windows systems, you can choose to use the Windows format with backslashes if desired — but remember to escape them:

```
$fp = fopen("c:\\php\\phpdocs\\navbar.inc", "r");
```

You can use forward slashes from both Windows and Unix. You should not use a trailing slash for filesystem fopen() calls.

> **Tip**   Remember that your files, and potentially your directories, need to be readable or writable by the PHP (or Web server, if module) process UID rather than by you as a system user. If you share a server, this means any of the other legitimate PHP users may be able to read and/or write to your files.

File read

The fread() function takes a file-pointer identifier and a file size in bytes as its arguments. If the file size given is not sufficient to read in the whole file, you will have mysterious problems (unless you're passing in a smaller file size on purpose, which is useful when reading huge files in chunks). Unless you have a reason to do otherwise (such as a huge, unwieldy file), it's best just to let PHP fill in the file size itself, by using the filesize() function with the name of the file (or a variable) as the argument:

```
$fstring = fread($fd, filesize($filename));
```

A common error is to type filesize($fd) rather than filesize($filename). You may not remember this from the initial example, because in the intervening paragraphs, we've called the used fopen() with an actual filename rather than a variable to which that name has been assigned, as in the first example.

This is an extremely useful function because it allows you to turn any file into a string, which can then be manipulated with PHP's large variety of useful string functions. Any string can also be broken up into an array through use of a function like file() or explode(), which gives you access to the large arsenal of PHP array-manipulation functions. PHP gives you more slicing and dicing functions than a whole set of Ginsu knives!

If you wish to send the entire contents of a file to standard output (meaning, for most PHP installations, echoing it to the Web browser window), use readfile() instead. This function has file opening built in, so you need not use a separate function to open the file first. The readfile() function is equivalent to the combination of fopen() and fpassthru().

Beginning with PHP4.3.0, a new function called file_get_contents() was made available. This function returns the entire contents of a file as a string, including the fopen(). It is equivalent to fopen() and fread(), or to readfile() except returning the contents as a string rather than straight to standard output.

If you wish to read in and perform operations on a file line-by-line, you can use fgets() instead of fread(). Beginning in PHP4.2.0, if you do not specify a line length as the second argument to fgets(), the function will default to 1024 bytes per line.

```
$fd = fopen("samplefile.inc", "r") or die('Cannot find file');
while (!feof($fd)) {
  $line = fgets($fd, 4096);
  if ($line === $targetline)
    {echo "A match was found!";}
}
fclose($fd);
```

If you would rather read the file in as an array, you can use the function file() instead. You might want to do this if you're reading one of the many types of data files that use newlines to indicate rows—such as a spreadsheet saved to tab-delimited text format. This creates an array, each element of which is a line from the original file including an ending newline character. The function file() does not require a separate file open or file close step. A single operation using file(), such as:

```
$line_array = file($filename);
```

is the equivalent of this:

```
$fd = fopen($filename, "r") or die("Can't open file $filename");
$fstring = fread($fd, filesize($filename));
$line_array = explode("\n", $fstring);
```

Caution   The file() function will work correctly only when PHP recognizes newlines. Hopefully PHP will handle newlines from other operating systems correctly—current Windows and Unix versions of PHP seem to identify newline characters from the other operating system—but we cannot guarantee that this will be true of every case.

Finally, if you'd like to read in a file character by character, you can use the fgetc() function. This will return a character from the file pointer, until the end-of-file. In practice, this function is not used very much, because it's so inefficient to read in a file one character at a time. You'd probably use fgetc() only in situations where you wanted to test the first or second character in the file.

Constructing file downloads by using fpassthru()

Besides reading in a file for manipulation by PHP, you can use fpassthru() in combination with the PHP header() construct to assemble and send file downloads. For instance, let's say you keep lots of tab-delimited data lying around in files, and occasionally you need to let someone download some data from them. Your users are typical businesspeople, not techies, so you know they use IE and would prefer the data as an Excel spreadsheet. So you give the user an HTML form that he or she can use to ask for the data from a particular day, and when it submits you assemble a download and send it like so:

```php
<?php

// This example assumes there is one data file per day,
// and your form lets the user specify the date they want to
// see.

$file = $_POST['date'].'.txt';
$fp = $fopen($file, "r");
header("Content-Type:application/xls");
header("Content-Disposition:attachment;
filename=$_POST['date'].xls");
// Notice we changed the file name and type
header("Content-Transfer-Encoding:binary");
fpassthru($fp);
?>
```

Caution   File downloads in PHP are surprisingly tricky because every browser implements the file download behavior differently—even different versions of the same browser can have different behaviors. The preceding method works fine in IE 6.0, but in Mozilla 1.0 the file will claim to be of type `application.xls` but will download as `20020526.xls.php`. Most of the methods necessary to get a perfect file download are hacks and involve tricking the browser into thinking it's downloading the file directly—for instance by tacking `/$_POST['data'].xls` onto the end of the URL (for example, `http://example.com/sample.php/20020526.xls`). Also, if you saved the script above as `data.xls`, and jiggered your Web server into parsing `.xls` files as PHP, you could get a great download in just about every browser. No single perfect method exists for every browser, but this is one situation where you can't just go by what you read in the PHP online manual.

File write

 Note   For file writing via PHP, directory permissions must be set to at least 703.

File writing is pretty straightforward if you've successfully opened in the correct mode for your intended purpose. The function `fwrite()` takes arguments of a file pointer and a string, with an optional length in bytes, which should not be used unless you have a specific reason to do so. It returns the number of characters written.

```php
$fout = fwrite($fp, $fstring);
if ($fout != strlen($fstring)){
    echo "file write failed!";
}
```

The function `fputs()` is identical to `fwrite()` in every way. They are simply aliases for one another, but `fputs()` is the C-style function name.

Keep in mind that opening a file in w or w+ modes will result in the complete and utter obliteration of any file contents. These modes are meant for clean overwrites only. If you want to write to the beginning or end of a file, use r+ or a+, respectively.

Probably the most common error with PHP file-writing modes involves using a Web interface (in other words, an HTML form) to edit a text file. If you want to open a file, read in and view the contents, then write an edited version to the same filename, you cannot depend on w+ mode. The w modes erase the contents of the file *immediately upon opening it*—thus, although you can fread() from a w+ file, there will be no text to read until after you write to it. To get around this issue, you need to open once in read mode and once in write mode, as in the following example:

```php
<?php
if (IsSet($_POST['submitted'])) {
  $fd = fopen($filename, "w+")
    or die("Can't open file $filename");
  $fout = fwrite($fd, $_POST['newstring']);
  fclose($fd);
}
$fd = fopen($filename, "r") or die("Can't open file $filename");
$initstring = fread($fd, filesize($filename));
fclose($fd);
echo "<HTML>";
echo "<FORM METHOD='POST' ACTION=\"$_SERVER['PHP_SELF']\">";
echo "<INPUT TYPE='text' SIZE=50 NAME='newstring'
VALUE=\"$initstring\">";
echo "<INPUT TYPE='HIDDEN' NAME='submitted' VALUE=1>";
echo "<INPUT TYPE='SUBMIT'>";
echo "</FORM>";
echo "</HTML>";
?>
```

Let us reiterate that file writing is not at all a good idea unless you can control your environment very tightly! In other words, a well-hardened intranet server might be appropriate, but file writing on a production Web site can be a security risk. For more information, see Chapter 29.

As we explain in Chapter 30, in PHP there is now a very easy mechanism to disable the capability to file-write. This is a great idea especially if your site is entirely database-driven, in which case you don't have any legitimate need to write to the filesystem with PHP anyway. To disable file writing, simply add fwrite to the list of disabled functions in php.ini:

```
disabled_functions = "fwrite"
```

If you don't use php.ini and need to set this value in Apache httpd.conf, remember that it requires a php_admin_value flag (rather than php_value):

```
php_admin_value disabled_functions="fwrite";
```

File close

File closing is straightforward:

```
fclose($fd);
```

Unlike fopen(), the result of fclose() does not need to be assigned to a variable. File closing may seem like a waste of time; but your system has only so many file descriptors available, and you may run out if you do not close your files. On the other hand, PHP will close all open files when your script ends; and at least one version of PHP3 had a buggy `fclose()` function which would crash the server. You know your own setup best, and you can make the call.

Filesystem and Directory Functions

Most of these functions will be quite familiar to Unix users, as they closely replicate common system commands.

 Caution   Many of the functions in this section are dangerous. Because they duplicate functions that can and should be performed from the local system, they can be a cracker's bonanza without providing much value to legitimate users. Strongly consider disabling them using PHP's `disable_functions` directive (as discussed in the preceding section on file writing)!

The one piece of good news is that some of these functions will only work if the PHP process is running as the superuser. Because this is not the default case in the Web browser, presumably these functions are intended to be used by the scripting version of PHP, and only trusted users who know what they're doing are even in a position to shoot themselves in the foot this way. Of course, if you are foolish enough to run your Web server as root, you are doubly screwed.

The most common and safest functions are listed first in the following sections; the less common and less safe are in Table 23-1.

feof

The `feof` function tests for end-of-file on a file pointer and takes a filename as argument. It's used mostly in a `while` loop to perform the same function on each line in a file:

```
while (!feof($fd)) {
  $line = fgets($fd, 4096);
  echo $line;
}
```

file_exists

The `file_exists` function is a simple function you will use again and again if you use filesystem functions at all. It simply checks the local filesystem for a file of the specified name.

```
if (!file_exists("testfile.php")) {
  $fd = fopen("testfile.php", "w+");
}
```

The function returns `true` if the file exists, `false` if not found. The results of this test are stored in a cache, which may be cleared by use of the function `clearstatcache()`.

filesize

Another simple but useful function is `filesize`, which returns and caches the size of a file in bytes. We use it in all the `fread()` examples earlier in this chapter. Never pass in a filesize as an integer if you can do it by using `filesize()` instead.

Table 23-1: Filesystem Functions

Function	Description
basename (*filepath*, [*suffix*])	Returns the filename portion of a stated path.
chgrp(*file*, *group*)	Changes file to any group to which the PHP process belongs. Inoperative on Windows systems.
chmod(*file*, *mode*)	Changes to the stated octal mode. Inoperative on Windows systems.
chown(*file*, *user*)	If executed by the superuser, changes file owner to stated owner. Inoperative but returns true on Windows systems.
clearstatcache	Clears cache of file status info.
copy(*file*, *destination*)	Copies file to stated destination.
delete(*file*)	See "unlink."
dirname(*path*)	Returns the directory portion of a stated path.
disk_free_space("/dir")	Returns the number of free bytes in a given directory.
fgetcsv(fp, *length*, *delimiter* [, *enclosure*])	Reads in a line and parses for CSV format.
fgetss(fp, *length* [, allowable_tags])	Gets a file line (delimited by a newline character) and strips all HTML and PHP tags except those specifically allowed.
fileatime(*file*)	Returns (and caches) last time of access.
filectime(*file*)	Returns (and caches) last time of inode change.
filegroup(*file*)	Returns (and caches) file group ID number. Names can be determined by using posix_getgrgid().
fileinode(*file*)	Returns (and caches) file inode.
filemtime(*file*)	Returns (and caches) last time of modification.
fileowner(*file*)	Returns (and caches) owner ID number. Names can be determined by using posix_getpwuid().
fileperms(*file*)	Returns (and caches) file permissions level.
filetype(file)	Returns (and caches) one of: fifo, char, dir, block, link, file, unknown.
flock(*file*, *operation* [,*&wouldblock*])	Advisory file locking. Operation value must be LOCK_SH (shared), LOCK_EX (exclusive), LOCK_UN (release), or LOCK_NB (don't block while locking). The optional third parameter is set to true if enforcing the lock would block existing access.
fpassthru(fp)	Standard output of all data from file pointer to EOF.

Function	Description
fseek(fp, offset, whence)	Moves file pointer offset number of bytes into file stream from the position indicated by whence.
ftell(fp)	Returns offset position into file stream.
stream_set_write_buffer (fp [, *buffersize*])	Sets a buffer for file writing; the default is 8K.
Is_dir(*directory*)	Returns (and caches) true if named directory exists.
Is_executable(*file*)	Returns (and caches) true if named file is executable.
Is_file(*file*)	Returns (and caches) true if named file is a regular file.
Is_link(*file*)	Returns (and caches) true if named file is a symlink.
Is_readable(*file*)	Returns (and caches) true if named file is readable by PHP.
is_writable (*file/directory*)	Returns (and caches) true if named file or directory is writable by PHP.
link(*target*, *link*)	Creates hard link. Inoperative on Windows systems.
linkinfo(*path*)	Confirms existence of link. Inoperative on Windows systems.
mkdir(*path*, *mode*)	Makes directory at location *path* with the given permissions in octal mode.
pclose(fp)	Closes process file pointer opened by popen().
popen(*command*, *mode*)	Opens process file pointer.
readlink(*link*)	Returns target of a symlink. Inoperative on Windows systems.
rename(*oldname*, *newname*)	Renames file.
rewind(fp)	Resets file pointer to beginning of file stream.
rmdir(*directory*)	Removes an empty directory.
stat(*file*)	Returns a selection of info about file.
lstat(*file*)	Returns a selection of info about file or symlink.
symlink(*target*, *link*)	Creates a symlink from target to link. Inoperative on Windows systems.
touch(*file*, [*time*])	Sets modification time; creates file if it does not exist.
umask(mask)	Returns umask, and sets to mask & 0777. With no argument passed, it simply returns the umask.
unlink(*file*)	Deletes file.

Network Functions

The network functions are a bunch of relatively little-used functions that provide network information or connections. Many of these may be more useful from the command line than the Web page, unless you're writing some kind of monitoring tool.

Syslog functions

The `syslog` functions allow you to open the system log for a program, generate a message, and close it again.

✦ `openlog([ident], option, facility)` is entirely optional when used with `syslog()`. The `ident` value is generated automatically.

✦ `syslog(priority, message)` generates a system log entry.

✦ `closelog()` is entirely optional when used with `syslog()`. It takes no arguments.

DNS functions

PHP offers some very slick DNS-querying functions, outlined in the Table 23-2. These functions allow PHP scripts to do some jiggering between IP address (which is available via the Apache `REMOTE_ADDR` variable, for instance) and hostname, or vice versa.

Table 23-2: DNS Functions

Function	Description
`checkdnsrr($host, [$type])`	Checks for existence of DNS records. Default is MX; other types are A, ANY, CNAME, NS, SOA, PTR and AAAA.
`gethostbyaddr($Ipaddress)`	Gets hostname corresponding to address.
`gethostbyname($hostname)`	Gets address corresponding to hostname.
`gethostbynamel($hostname)`	Gets list of addresses corresponding to hostname.
`getmxrr($hostname, [mxhosts array], [weight])`	Checks for existence of MX records corresponding to hostname, places in `mxhosts` array, fills in weight info.

Socket functions

A *socket* is a kind of dedicated connection that allows different programs (which may be on different machines) to communicate by sending text back and forth. PHP socket functions allow scripts to establish such connections to socket-based servers. For instance, Web and database servers communicate via `fsockopen()` — so you could theoretically write your own Web server in PHP using this function, if you had lost all contact with reality. The connection can then be read from or written to with the standard file-writing functions `fputs()`, `fgets()`, and so on.

The standard socket-opening function is fsockopen(). The pfsockopen() function is identical except that sockets are not destroyed when your script exits; instead, the connection is pooled for later use. The blocking behavior of socket connections can be toggled with set_socket_blocking(). When blocking is enabled, functions that read from sockets will hang until there is some input to return; when it is disabled, such functions will return immediately if there is no input. These functions are summarized in Table 23-3.

Table 23-3: Socket Functions

Function	Description
fsockopen($*hostname*, $*port*, [*error number*], [*error string*], [*timeout in seconds*])	Opens the socket connection to specified port on the host, and returns a file pointer suitable for use by functions like fgets().
getservbyname($*service*, $*protocol*)	Returns the port number of the specified service.
getservbyport($*port*, $*protocol*)	Returns service name on port.
pfsockopen($*hostname*, $*port*, [*error number*], [*error string*], [*timeout in seconds*])	Opens the specified persistent socket connection.
stream_set_blocking ($*socket descriptor*, $*mode*)	TRUE for blocking mode, FALSE for nonblocking. Default is nonblocking.

Date and Time Functions

These functions are basic tools used in many self-defined functions. You may use them simply to output the date or time, to keep track of microtime for a PHP performance-tracking utility, or to initiate a function over a particular date range (such as putting a *Happy Holidays* message on your site during holiday seasons).

These are pretty straightforward to use if you understand the Unix timestamp. They fall into three main categories: functions that *return* date or time, functions that *format* date or time, and functions that *validate* date.

Tip   The Unix timestamp measures time as a number of seconds since the beginning of the Unix epoch (midnight Greenwich Mean Time on January 1, 1970). Despite the name, these functions mostly work on Windows also.

If you don't know either date or time

The fastest way to get a time is to use the function time(). This will return the Unix timestamp for your locale, which will look something like 101906652. If you plan to pass this timestamp to another function or program, this is the best format. Alternatively, you can then use one of the functions in the next section to format the timestamp into something a bit more human-readable.

You could also use microtime() to return the current time in seconds and microseconds since the Unix epoch. This can be supremely helpful for utilities that are designed to measure performance. The format is 0.74321900 961906846, where the first part is microseconds and the second is the Unix timestamp. If you're trying to (for instance) measure the performance of different parts of your Web page, you really just want the microseconds part, which can be cut out like so:

```
<?php
$stampmebaby = microtime();
$chunks = explode(" ", $stampmebaby);
$microseconds = $chunks[0];
echo $microseconds;
?>
```

A function used to return date information is getdate($timestamp). When used with the argument time(), as in getdate(time()), it returns an associative array with the following numeric elements derived from the Unix timestamp:

✦ Seconds

✦ Minutes

✦ Hours

✦ Mday (day of the month, for example 1–31)

✦ Wday (day of the week, for example 1–7)

✦ Mon (month, for example 1–12)

✦ Year (numeric, for example 1984)

✦ Yday (day of the year, for example 1–365)

✦ Weekday (day of the week, for example Sunday–Saturday)

✦ Month (for example January–December)

You can also use the getdate() function with a Unix timestamp other than that representing the current time.

If you want to get the time and format it in one step, you can use date() instead of getdate(). In the absence of a Unix timestamp argument, date() will default to the current local date. This has the advantage of allowing nicer formatting, as we will explain in the next subsection. The function strftime() will also format the current Unix timestamp for you (as we explain in the next subsection) unless another is specified.

If you've already determined the date/time/timestamp

The functions in this section come into play if you already have a timestamp and merely wish to format the information more finely. For instance, you may like to express your dates European style (2000.20.04) rather than American (4/20/2000).

The main method to format a timestamp is using date($format...$formatn[, $timestamp]). You pass a series of codes indicating your formatting preferences, plus an optional timestamp. For instance:

```
date('Y-m-d');
```

returns a string like 2002-05-27. You can choose a date with two-zero day identifiers or strictly numeric date identifiers, 12- or 24-hour format, or abbreviated month name. (See the PHP manual for all the options.) An analogous function is gmdate($format...$formatn [, $timestamp]), which will return a Greenwich Mean Date.

The function strftime($format...$formatn[, $timestamp]) is similar but specializes in formatting the time rather than the date; gmstrftime($format...$formatn [, $timestamp]) returns the time in formatted Greenwich Mean Time.

The function mktime() allows you to convert any date into a timestamp. It's subtly different in the order of arguments from the Unix command of the same name, so pay attention. The function gmmktime() gives the Greenwich alternative to your own time zone.

Finally, checkdate($month, $day, $year) allows you to quickly ensure that a particular date is a valid one. This is great for leap-year questions.

Calendar Conversion Functions

Finally, we have some optional calendar conversion routines, which are now available as an extension.

Tip   Many new users have made the mistake of thinking *calendar functions* mean *date functions*. Not so. These functions strictly convert between different (largely historical) calendar systems. See "Date and Time Functions" earlier in this chapter if you feel you have entered this section in error.

If you happen to be a French historian, you'll be happy to know PHP can automatically convert between the French Revolutionary calendar and the Gregorian calendar with but a couple of commands. What can we say to that but: *Bon Thermidor, Citoyens et Citoyennes!*

Seriously, these functions have real uses — particularly on the global Internet. (And not to be ungrateful or anti-Judeo-Christian-centric . . . but Joyce is patiently and lazily waiting for someone to add the Chinese lunar calendar to PHP, so she can always know when Chinese New Year celebrations will occur.)

Conversion between systems is made possible because all the calendar functions share a universal referent, the so-called "Julian Day Number" (aka "Julian Day Count"). This is an integer that represents the days since noon on the first of January, 4713 BC by the Julian calendar (which wasn't in use at the time, but why nitpick?). This date would be the 14th of January in the Gregorian calendar, which is commonly used in secular societies today. The so-called "Julian Date" is a double that represents the days and hours since Julian Day Zero — but PHP does not allow this level of specificity; we're just mentioning it here in case anyone is looking for this information.

Tip   Remember that the Julian day changes at noon rather than midnight, which is the convention today.

PHP's calendar conversion functions translate a date in some calendar into or out of Julian Day Count. To convert between two calendars, you will need to use two separate functions: one to give the date from one calendar as a Julian Day Number, and the other to convert JD into another calendar's date. In this example, we are converting a Gregorian date into its equivalent in the Jewish calendar.

```
$jd_no = gregoriantojd(8, 11, 1945);
$hebrew = jdtojewish($jd_no);
echo $hebrew;
```

This will return a date of 2, 6 [Elul], 5705. Conversion to the Jewish calendar is somewhat complicated by the fact that it uses lunar months and its days begin at sunset rather than midnight.

The calendars offered at the moment are:

✦ French Republican

✦ Gregorian

✦ Jewish

✦ Julian

✦ Unixian

Each of these calendars has associated "JDToX" and an "XToJD" functions.

Finally, there are two other pairs of miscellaneous calendar functions. JDMonthName() and JDDayofWeek() return the month and day of week of any Julian Day Number in any of the supported calendars; whereas easter_date() and easter_days() will tell you when (Western or Catholic, as opposed to Eastern or Orthodox) Easter falls/fell/will fall in any given year. easter_date() is the more straightforward method but can only be used within a Unix date range (1970–2037). It returns the Unix timestamp of Easter midnight in the specified year.

Summary

PHP has numerous filesystem and system functions built in, which can be extremely handy, although sometimes potentially insecure. A large number of PHP functions duplicate Unix systems utilities, such as chmod() and copy(). PHP can also boast some extra-clever functions such as those for DNS-querying. Although we recommend turning off some of these functions, others can be useful in trusted hands and a well-planned environment.

PHP's file opening, reading, and writing functions are extremely powerful tools. Most problems with these functions result from a slightly incorrect understanding of the file-opening modes. In addition to filesystem fopen(), PHP supports very slick HTTP, HTTPS, FTP, and standard I/O file-opening.

Finally, PHP offers a plethora of time, date, and calendar functions so you always know what time it is.

✦   ✦   ✦

Sessions, Cookies, and HTTP

This chapter might as well have been called "Keeping Track," because its theme throughout is the problem of tracking interactions with users over longer periods of time than it takes to generate a single Web page. We explain the extent of PHP support for extended user sessions and for setting and checking cookies, and then cover a couple of related techniques involving directly sending HTTP headers.

Sessions and cookies are closely allied concepts in PHP and in Web programming more generally, largely because the best way to actually implement sessions is by using cookies. Sessions are a higher-level concept than cookies, and for this chapter we plan to start at the top and work our way down.

What's a Session?

What do we mean by a *session*? Informally, a session of Web browsing is a period of time during which a particular person, while sitting at a particular machine, views a number of different Web pages in his or her browser program and then calls it quits, either for the night or because the person in question actually has a life. If you run a Web site that this person visits during that time, for your purposes the session runs from that person's first download of a page from your site through the last. For example, a Caribbean hotel's Web site might enjoy a session of five pages duration in the middle of a real user's session that began with a travel portal and ended with that user booking his or her vacation with a competitor.

So what's the problem?

Why is the idea of a session tricky enough that we're just talking about it now, even though PHP is at version 5 already? It's because the HTTP protocol by which browsers talk to Web servers is *stateless,* with the result that your Web server has less long-term memory than your housecat. That is, your Web server reacts independently to each individual request it receives and has no way to link requests together even if it is logging requests. If I sit at my computer in Chicago, and you sit at yours in Monterey, and we both ask for page one and then page two of the Caribbean hotelier's site, the HTTP protocol offers no help toward figuring out that two people looked at two pages each — what it sees is four individual requests for pages, with various information attached to each request. Not only does this information not identify you personally (by name, e-mail address, phone number, or any other traceable identification); it offers nothing reliable to identify your two page requests as being from the same person.

Why should you care?

If our Web site's only mission in life is to offer various pages to various users, we may, in fact, not care at all where sessions begin and end. On the other hand, there are a number of reasons why we might in fact care. For example:

✦ We want to customize our users' experiences as they move through the site, in a way that depends on which (or how many) pages they have already seen.

✦ We want to display advertisements to the user, but we do not want to display a given ad more than once per session.

✦ We want the session to accumulate information about users' actions as they progress — as in an adventure game's tracking of points and weapons accumulated or an e-commerce site's shopping cart.

✦ We are interested in tracking how people navigate through our site in general — when they visit that interior page, is it because they bookmarked it, or did they get there all the way from the front page?

For all of these purposes, we need to be able to match up page requests with the sessions they are part of, and for some purposes it would be nice to store some information in association with the session as it progresses. PHP sessions solve both of these problems for us.

Home-Grown Alternatives

Before we look at PHP's treatment of sessions, let's look at a few alternative ways the problem can be handled. As we'll see, the PHP treatment combines a couple of these techniques.

IP address

Web servers usually know either the Internet hostname or the IP address of the client that is requesting a page. In many configurations of PHP, these show up for free as variables — `$_SERVER['REMOTE_HOST']` and `$_SERVER['REMOTE_ADDR']`, respectively. Now you might think that the identity of the machine at the other end is a reasonable stand-in for the person at the other end, at least over the short term. If you get two requests in quick succession from the same IP address, your code can safely conclude that the same person followed a link or form from one of your site's pages to another.

Unfortunately, the IP address your browser knows about may not belong to the machine your user is browsing from. In particular, AOL and other large operations employ proxy servers, which act as intermediaries. Your user's browser actually requests a URL from the proxy server, which in turn requests the page from your server and then forwards back the page to the user. The result is that many different AOL users might be browsing your site simultaneously, all apparently from the same address. IP addresses are not unique enough to form a basis for session tracking.

Hidden variables

Every HTTP request is dealt with independently, but each time your user moves from page to page within your site, it is usually via either a link or a form submission. If the very first page a user visits can somehow generate a unique label for that visit, every subsequent "handoff" of one page to another can pass that unique identifier along.

For example, here is a hypothetical code fragment that you might include near the top of every page on your site:

```
if (!IsSet($my_s_id))
  $my_session_id = generate_session_id();
  // warning! hypothetical function
```

This fragment checks to see if the $my_s_id variable is bound—if it is, we assume that it has been passed in, and we are in the middle of a session. If it is not, we assume that we are the first page of a new session, and we call a hypothetical function called generate_session_id() to create a unique identifier.

After we have included the preceding code, we assume that we have a unique identifier for the session, and our only remaining responsibility is to pass it along to any page we link or submit to. Every link from our page should include the $my_s_id as a GET argument, as in:

```
<A HREF="next.php?my_s_id=<?php echo $my_s_id;?>">Next</A>
```

And every form submission should have a hidden POST argument embedded in it, like this:

```
<FORM ACTION=next.php METHOD=POST>
body of form
<INPUT TYPE=HIDDEN NAME=my_s_id
       VALUE="<?php echo $my_s_id;?>" >
</FORM>
```

What's wrong with this technique? Nothing. It works just fine as a way to keep different sessions straight (as long as you can generate unique identifiers). And once we have unique labels for the sessions, we can use a variety of techniques to associate other kinds of information with each session, such as using the session ID as a key for database storage. However, this approach to sessions is a pain to maintain—you must make sure that *every* link and form submission propagates the information as described, or the session identifier will be dropped. Also, if you send the information as GET arguments, your session-tracking machinery will be visible in the Web-address box of your user's browser, and such arguments are easily edited by the user. Passing around unique identifiers in GET requests is probably the least secure method of maintaining state in Web development, as well as possibly causing problems when your users try to cut and paste links—for instance, if they want to send a link to their friends via e-mail.

Cookie-based homegrown sessions

Another approach to session tracking is to use a unique session identifier as in the previous section, but perform the handoff by setting or checking a cookie.

A cookie is a special kind of file, located in the file system of your user's browsing computer, that Web servers can read from and write to. Rather than checking for a passed GET/POST variable (and assigning a new identifier if none is found), your script checks the user's machine for a previously written cookie file and stores a new identifier in a new cookie file if none is found or if the old cookie has expired. This method has some benefits over using hidden variables: The mechanism works behind the scenes (typically, not showing any trace of its activity in the browser window), and the code that checks or sets the cookie can be centralized (rather than affecting every form and link).

What's the drawback? Some very old browsers do not support cookies at all, and more recent browsers allow users to deny cookie-setting privileges to Web servers. So, although cookies make for a smooth solution, we can't assume that they are always available.

Note   There is a subtle difference in the "coverage" of cookie-based sessions and that of sessions based on GET/POST variables. A variable-based session will only maintain its identity as long as your user stays within your site, following intrasite links or form postings. However, there are any number of ways that a user might go away and come back again within a short period of time—by visiting a site that your site links to, which in turn links back or by wandering away and then finding your site again with a search engine. Cookie-based approaches will treat returns from these little detours as a continuation of the same session, whereas variable-propagation approaches have to treat them as new visits.

We cover cookies in more detail in the "Cookies" section later in the chapter.

How Sessions Work in PHP

Good session support takes care of the following two things:

✦ Session tracking (that is, detecting whether two separate script invocations are, in fact, part of the same user session).

✦ Storing information in association with a session.

Obviously, you need the first capability before you can hope to have the second.

PHP session tracking works by a combination of the hidden-variables method and the cookie method described in the preceding section. Because of the advantages of cookies, PHP will use them when the user's browser supports them and, otherwise, will have recourse to stashing the session ID in GET and POST arguments. Fortunately, though, the session functions themselves operate at a more abstract level and take care of checking for cookie support all by themselves. If your version of PHP5 has been appropriately configured for sessions, you should be able to use the session functions without worrying which method is being used.

Note   If you want PHP to transparently handle passing session variables for you when cookies are not available, you need to have configured PHP with both the --enable-trans-sid and --enable-track-vars options. If PHP is not handling this for you, you must arrange to pass a GET or POST argument, of the form session_name=session_id, in all your links and forms. When a session is active, PHP provides a special constant, SID, which contains the right argument/value pair. Following is an example of including this constant in a link:

```
<A HREF="my_next_page.php?<?php echo(SID);?>">Next page</A>
```

Making PHP aware of your session

The first step in a script that uses the session feature is to let PHP know that a session may already be in progress so that it can hook up to it and recover any associated information. This is done by calling the function session_start(), which takes no arguments. (If you want every script invocation to look for a session without having to call this function, set the variable session.auto_start to 1 in your php.ini file, rather than the usual default of 0.) Also, any call to session_register() causes an implicit initial call to session_start().

The effect of session_start() depends on whether PHP can locate a previous session identifier, as supplied either by HTTP arguments or in a cookie. If one is found, the values of any previously registered session variables are recovered. If one is not found, then PHP assumes that we are in the first page of a new session, and generates a new session ID.

Propagating session variables

Changes in PHP's treatment of global and external variables starting with version 4.1 have made certain things more inconvenient. (See Chapter 5 for more detail on these changes.) In our view, though, these changes will also remove a lot of potential confusion about sessions. Accordingly, we'll list two approaches to propagating variables in sessions: one, which is simple and works in PHP version 4.1 or later, and another which is more complicated and works only in PHP version 4.1 or *earlier* (unless you re-enable the register_globals setting in php.ini). (You can guess which one we recommend.)

The simple approach (using $_SESSION)

The simple approach is this: Assuming that you've made a call to session_start() (as early in your script as possible), use the $_SESSION superglobal array as your suitcase for storing anything that you want to retrieve again from a later page in the same session. Assume that any other variables will be left behind when you leave this page and that everything in that suitcase will be there when you arrive at the next page.

So, session code to propagate a single numerical variable can be as simple as this:

```php
<?php
session_start();

$temporary_number = 45;
$save_this_one = 19;
$another_temporary = 33;

$_SESSION['save_this'] = $save_this_one;
?>
```

The receiving code can be as simple as the following example:

```php
<?php
session_start();
$saved_from_prev_page = $_SESSION['save_this'];
[..]
$temporary_number = 45;
$another_temporary = 33;
[..]
?>
```

That's all there is to it. Assignment into the $_SESSION superglobal array implicitly does any registration necessary for the new value to be carried forward to the next page.

Note that we could have given the same name to both the variable ($save_this_one) and the corresponding $_SESSION index (save_this), because the two have nothing to do with one another.

For this simple approach, we assume that register_globals has been turned off (as it is by default in versions 4.2 and later), so that no session variables are being automatically promoted into global variables. Or, more precisely, we don't care whether it is turned on or not; the code will work in either situation.

> **Note**   The $_SESSION array is one of the superglobal variables introduced in PHP4.1. The *super-global* adjective means that it can be referenced anywhere in PHP code, even within functions, without first being declared global. You can use $HTTP_SESSION_VARS in much the same way , but you will have to declare it as global within any functions that refer to it.

The complex approach (registering variables)

In the more complex approach, you have decided for reasons of your own that you want to have session variables become regular global page variables automatically. To do this, you must have the configuration directive register_globals enabled. (It is turned off by default in PHP4.2 and later, so if you are using a recent PHP version, you will have to edit your php.ini file to turn it on again.)

When using register_globals, variables from previous pages that were registered as session variables will show up as regular global variables in your script as soon as the session is discovered. For example, if a previous page in a session has registered the variable $city and assigned it the value 'Chicago', our script can take advantage of it simply by calling session_start():

```
session_start();
print("$city, $city, that toddlin' town<BR>");
```

The lyric will be as we expect. If no such variable has been previously registered and assigned, or if we forget the call to session_start(), the variable will act as though it is unbound.

> **Note**   Pulling session bindings into a page by calling session_start() will overwrite any variable bindings with the same name that already exists at that point in the script. In particular, this means that if a given variable is passed by GET/POST and there is also a cookie-based, session-level binding, the session binding will *win* under the default setting for the configuration directive 'variables_order'. This becomes a non-issue if you can use the "simple" approach and refer to superglobals only for session, cookie, GET, and POST variables.

If PHP cannot find a previous session identifier, the call to session_start() actually does start a new session. The main effect of this is that a new unique identifier is created, which can now be used to register variables, and a cookie will be sent containing this new session identifier.

Registering variables in sessions

Calling session_start() takes care of *importing* any variables from the session context to our current script — now all we have to worry about is "exporting" them again, to see that they make it to later pages in the same session. This is done with the function session_register(). As it turns out, the import business is wholesale (one call to session_start() does it), but the export business is retail (we have to name each registered variable individually).

Say that, as in the previous example, a previous page has set the value of $city to be 'Chicago' and has already called session_register($city). Here's how we take advantage of it and set it up (or change it) for later pages as well:

```
session_start();
print("$city, $city, that toddlin' town<BR>");

print("$city, $city, I'll show you around<BR>");
$city = 'San Mateo';
```

The session_start() call pulls in the binding of $city to 'Chicago' as before, so it can be used in the first print statement. From then on, $city would normally be treated just like any other global page variable. The previous page's call to session_register(), however, has put the session mechanism on notice that the 'city' variable is to be exported again out to session-world, and that later pages in the same session should receive whatever binding $city has at the end of this script. In the preceding excerpt, the value gets changed to 'San Mateo', so future pages should expect to do their toddlin' there.

> **Note** Variable names given as arguments to session_register() shouldn't include the leading $.

If we had forgotten the session_start() call, the first print line would have empty strings in place of the $city variable. The second print line would look good even so, because calling session_register() causes an implicit call to session_start(), if such a call has not already been made. Finally, if we had omitted the session_register() call, everything on this page would look fine, but subsequent pages would not receive any session variable called 'city'.

> **Note** Registration of a variable is entirely independent of assigning a value to it. You can assign a value to a variable without registering it (in which case, it will simply be a normal page variable that is not propagated to other pages), or you can register a variable without assigning it a value (in which case, it will show up in later pages as unset).

Where is the data really stored?

There are two things that the session mechanism must hang onto: the session ID itself and any associated variable bindings.

As we have seen, either the session ID is stored as a cookie on the browser's machine, or it is incorporated into the GET/POST arguments submitted with page requests. In the latter case, there is really no storage happening—the ID is submitted as part of a request and is returned folded into HTML code for links and forms, which may generate the next request. The browser and server pass this vital information back and forth like a hot potato, and the session is effectively over if either side drops it.

By default, the contents of session variables are stored in special files on the server, one file per session ID. (It's already slightly rude to store the session ID as a client-side cookie—it would be even more rude to store session variable data on the client disk when it's not necessary.) Doing this kind of storage requires the session code to serialize the data, which means turning it into a linear sequence of bytes that can be written to a file and read back to recreate the data.

Obviously, storing session data on the server like this will cause problems in most clusters since each Web server will be writing to files on its own (presumably unshared) disk. Unless your cluster-management scheme enforces all page views per session to be served from a particular host—which is uncommon, since in most cases that conflicts with the goals of load management and seamless failover—a new session will be started every time a page request is routed to a different server.

There are three main methods to solve this issue, none of them easy or foolproof to implement. First, a company can write its own custom session-data-sharing layer. In this case, PHP will think it's making normal session-registration calls, but instead of writing to disk, a custom server will intercept the requests and centralize the data. However, developing and maintaining such a server and the customized version of PHP required is not cheap. Second, it's possible to direct PHP to write session data not to the normal local disk location (that is, /tmp) but to some other share which could be mounted by all Web servers (such as /shared/session). This is the fastest solution if you have good sysadmins, since it requires only a change to the session.save_path setting in php.ini. Finally, it's possible to configure PHP to store the contents of session variables in a server-side database, rather than in files. This is probably the most common solution to the problem, although it should be kept in mind that this strategy will increase the impact of database failures. For more information, see the section "Configuration Issues" later in this chapter.

Cross-Reference

In the first edition of this book, we warned you that serialization support for objects was still problematic, and so we didn't recommend trying to store object variables in sessions. Fortunately, in PHP version 4.1 and later, session serialization seems to be stable. See Chapter 20 for more about object serialization and Chapter 46 for an extended example of storing objects in sessions.

Sample Session Code

In Listing 24-1, we show a short code file, which really has a dual purpose. The first purpose is to provide an example of a full (short) script that successfully uses session functions; the second is to provide a test script that you can use to make sure that you have session support and that it is doing what you expect.

In this listing, we perform the following tasks:

✦ Initiate a session (or pick up an existing one) by using session_start().

✦ Check for the existence of a pre-existing entry in $_SESSION. If not present, we assume that the session is new.

✦ Increment a counter that tracks how many times that the user has visited this page.

✦ Store the incremented counter back in $_SESSION.

✦ Provide a link back to the page itself, embedding the session ID as an argument if it is found.

Listing 24-1: **Test script using $_SESSION**

```
<?php
session_start();
?>

<HTML><HEAD><TITLE>Greetings</TITLE></HEAD>
<BODY>
```

```
<H2>Welcome to the Center for Content-free Hospitality</H2>
<?php

if (!IsSet($_SESSION['visit_count'])) {
  echo "Hello, you must have just arrived.
Welcome!<BR>";
  $_SESSION['visit_count'] = 1;
}
else {
  $visit_count = $_SESSION['visit_count'] + 1;
  echo "Back again are ya?  That makes $visit_count times now ".
       "(not that anyone's counting)<BR>";
  $_SESSION['visit_count'] = $visit_count;
}

$self_url = $_SERVER['PHP_SELF'];
$session_id = SID;
if (IsSet($session_id) &&
    $session_id) {
  $href = "$self_url?$session_id";
}
else {
  $href = $self_url;
}
echo "<BR><A HREF=\"$href\">Visit us again</A> sometime";
?>
</BODY></HTML>
```

This code should be available at www.troutworks.com/phpbook and is suitable for your use in testing your session support if you are using PHP4.1 or later. (See Listing 24-2, a little later in this section, if you are using a pre-4.1 version or if you prefer the register_globals style of using sessions.) After obtaining the code, you should first simply test that it loads without errors. The page you see should look something like that shown in Figure 24-1. After that, to see if cookie-based session support is working, try simply reloading or refreshing the page in your browser. You should see a page that looks something like Figure 24-2.

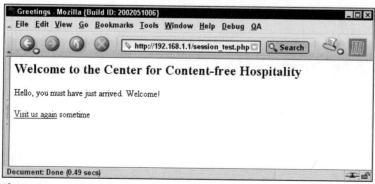

Figure 24-1: Session test page

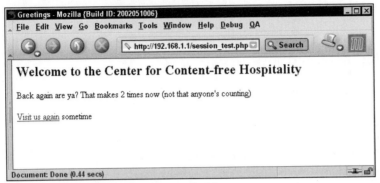

Figure 24-2: Session test page, second visit

If the result of your second visit is Figure 24-2, cookie-based session support is working. If instead it still looks like Figure 24-1, then PHP did not detect your session. Make sure that the browser you are testing with is configured to accept cookies and take a look at the section "Gotchas and Troubleshooting," at the end of this chapter.

The second half of Listing 24-1 is about constructing a self-link that will propagate session information even without cookie support. You can test it by turning off cookies in your test browser. (This is usually an Advanced or Security option in your browser's preferences or options.) After cookies have been turned off, you should be treated as a first-time visitor when you reload the page. However, with cookies off, the SID constant should now contain the session ID name and value, which our code embeds in the link's URL as a GET argument. Clicking on this link should increment the visit count appropriately, and thereafter either clicking the link or reloading should increment it again (because the session ID should now be in the URL that is being reloaded).

This embedding of the session ID in the URL is exactly what should be unnecessary if PHP has been compiled with --enable-trans-sid. In this case, you should be able to add another self-link to this page, without embedding anything extra in the URL, and PHP should take care of it for you.

Listing 24-2 shows the same test script as in Listing 24-1, except that it does not use super-global variables and assumes that the register_globals directive has been turned on. It's appropriate if you happen to be using PHP version 4.0.x, or if you prefer the register_globals style. Remember that code you write using register_globals will not be portable to many other PHP servers.

Listing 24-2: Test script assuming register_globals

```php
<?php
session_start();
session_register('visit_count');
?>

<HTML><HEAD><TITLE>Greetings</TITLE></HEAD>
```

```
<BODY>
<H2>Welcome to the Center for Content-free Hospitality</H2>
<?php
if (!IsSet($visit_count)) {
  echo "Hello, you must have just arrived.
Welcome!<BR>";
  $visit_count = 1;
}
else {
  $visit_count++;
  echo "Back again are ya?  That makes $visit_count times now ".
       "(not that anyone's counting)<BR>";
}

$self_url = $PHP_SELF;
$session_id = SID;
if (IsSet($session_id) &&
    $session_id) {
  $href = "$self_url?$session_id";
}
else {
  $href = $self_url;
}
echo "<BR><A HREF=\"$href\">Visit us again</A> sometime";
?>
</BODY></HTML>
```

Session Functions

Table 24-1 lists the most important session-related functions, with descriptions of what they do. Note that in some cases the behavior of these functions depends on configuration options that we detail in the "Configuration Issues" section.

Table 24-1: Session Function Summary

Function	Behavior
session_start()	Takes no arguments and causes PHP either to notice a session ID that has been passed to it (via a cookie or GET/POST) or to create a new session ID if none is found.
	If an old session ID is found, PHP retrieves the assignments of all variables that have been registered and makes those assigned variables available as regular global variables.

Continued

Table 24-1 *(continued)*

Function	Behavior
session_register()	Takes a string as argument and registers the variable named by the string—for example, session_register('username'). (*Note:* The variable-name string should not include the leading $.) It can also be passed an array of string arguments to register multiple variables at once. Unnecessary if using $_SESSION or $HTTP_SESSION_VARS.
	The effect of registering a variable is that subsequent assignments to that variable will be preserved for future sessions. (After a script completes, the registered variables and their values are serialized and propagated in such a way that later calls to session_start() can recreate the bindings.)
	If session_start() has not yet been called, session_register will implicitly call it before executing.
session_unregister()	Takes a string variable name as argument and unregisters the corresponding variable from the session. As a result, the variable binding will no longer be serialized and propagated to later pages. (The variable-name string should not include the leading $.) Unnecessary if using $_SESSION or $HTTP_SESSION_VARS.
session_is_registered()	Takes a variable-name string and tests whether a variable with a given variable name is registered in the current session, returning TRUE if so and FALSE if not. Unnecessary if using $_SESSION or $HTTP_SESSION_VARS, use isset() instead.
session_destroy()	Calling this function gets rid of all session variable information that has been stored. (*Note:* A browser's session ID may still be the same after this function call.) It does not unset any variables in the current script or the session cookie.
session_unset()	Takes no arguments, and frees all variables in the session. Dangerous if using $_SESSION or $HTTP_SESSION_VARS, use unset() instead.
session_write_close()	Manually close session and release write lock on data file. Useful with frames, some clustering situations, and if you do something that might cause PHP to not realize the session has terminated (such as redirection).

Function	*Behavior*
session_name()	When called with no arguments, returns the current session-name string. This is usually 'PHPSESSID' by default.
	When called with one string argument, session_name() sets the current session name to that string. This name is used as a key to find the session ID in cookies and GET/POST arguments—for successful retrieval, the session name must be the same as it was when the values were serialized and stored. Note that there is no reason to change the session name unless you have some need to distinguish session types that are being served by the same Web server (such as in the case of multiple sites that each track sessions). The session name is reset to the default whenever a script executes, so any name change must happen in every script that uses the name, and before any other session functions are called.
session_module_name()	If given no arguments, returns the name of the module that is responsible for handling session data. This name currently defaults to 'files', meaning that session bindings are serialized and then written to files in the directory named by the function session_save_path().
	If given a string argument, changes the module name to that string. (This could presumably be, for example, 'user' for a user-defined session database, but it should not be changed unless you know what you are doing.)
session_save_path()	Returns (or sets, if given an argument) the pathname of the directory to which session variable-binding files will be written (which typically defaults to /tmp on Unix systems). This directory needs to exist and have appropriate permissions for PHP to write files to it. On Windows systems, you must change this value to a valid path before using sessions!
session_id()	Takes no arguments and returns a string, which is the unique key corresponding to a particular session. If given a string argument, will set the session ID to that string.
session_regenerate_id()	Takes no arguments and sets a new session ID, setting a new cookie if necessary and returning TRUE on success or FALSE on failure. Unlike session_id(), it does not return a string with the actual new ID.
session_encode()	Returns a string encoding of the state of the current session, suitable for use by string_decode(). This can be used for saving a session for revival at some later time, such as by writing the encoded string to a file or database.

Continued

Table 24-1 *(continued)*

Function	Behavior
session_decode()	Takes a string encoding as produced by session_encode() and reestablishes the session state, turning session bindings into page bindings as session_start() does.
session_get_cookie_params()	Returns an array with current session cookie data: lifetime (in seconds till expiration, or 0 for no expiration), path (for which the cookie is valid), domain (for which the cookie is valid), secure (whether or not the cookie will only be sent over SSL connections). These parameters are normally set in the php.ini file, but can be changed for a single script through the session_set_cookie_params() function.
session_set_cookie_params()	Takes four arguments: int lifetime (in seconds till expiration, or 0 for no expiration), string path (for which the cookie is valid), string domain (for which the cookie is valid), boolean secure (whether or not the cookie will only be sent over SSL connections). Be sure to include a trailing slash on the path argument.

Configuration Issues

The variables in Table 24-2 are settable in the php.ini file and viewable by calling phpinfo(). We offer descriptions and the typical default values. (Some defaults are platform-dependent.)

Table 24-2: Session Configuration Variables

Php.ini Variable	Typical Value	Description
session.save_path	/tmp under Unix systems	Pathname for the server-side directory where session datafiles will be written. Must be changed for Windows systems!
session.auto_start	0	When 1, sessions will initialize automatically every time a script loads. When 0, no session data will be available unless there is an explicit call to either session_start() or session_register().
session.save_handler	'files', 'user'	String that determines underlying method for saving session variable information. Changing this is not recommended for the casual user.

Php.ini Variable	Typical Value	Description
session.cookie_lifetime	0	Specifies how long session cookies take to expire and, consequently, the lifetime of a session. The default of 0 means that sessions last until the browser is closed — any other value indicates the number of seconds the session is allowed to live.
session.use_cookies	1	If 1, the session mechanism will attempt to propagate the session ID by setting/checking a cookie. (If the browser refuses the cookie, then GET/POST vars may be used.) If this variable is 0, no attempt to use cookies is made.

Cookies

Cross-Reference

Many uses of cookies amount to session-tracking — keeping track of some piece of information as a single user navigates through your site. If you are tempted to use cookies for a purpose like this, and you are using PHP4, you might want to consider simply using the built-in session functions that are covered in the section "Cookie-based homegrown sessions" earlier in this chapter. Not only do they offer a nicer level of abstraction, but they also have a built-in fallback mechanism that deals with refusal of cookies by propagating the information via GET/POST arguments instead.

A *cookie* is a small piece of information that is retained on the client machine, either in the browser's application memory or as a small file written to the user's hard disk. It contains a name/value pair — *setting a cookie* means associating a value with a name and storing that pairing on the client side. *Getting* or *reading* a cookie means using the name to retrieve the value. (See the sidebar "Cookies and Privacy," a little later in this chapter, for a summary of the controversy surrounding the use of cookies.)

Note

As a general rule, you want to store information only in a client-side cookie when storing it on the server is not an option. This is partly simple politeness — try accepting cookies manually for a week, and you'll see some extreme abuses of the technique — but it is also because there are constraints that prevent server abuses of the client's hard disk. In particular, each browser will typically accept only 20 cookies from each domain before it starts popping old cookie values off the stack. If you need to store a lot of info, consider developing a scheme where the cookie file contains an ID that enables you to look up the rest of that information on the server — in other words, some form of sessions.

In PHP, cookies are set using the setcookie() function, and cookies are read nearly automatically. In PHP4.1 and later, names and values of cookie variables show up in the superglobal array $_COOKIES, with the cookie name as an index, and the value as the value it indexes.

The setcookie() function

There is just one cookie-related function, called setcookie(). Table 24-3 shows its arguments, in order, all but the first of which are optional.

Table 24-3: Arguments to setcookie()

Argument Name	Expected Type	Meaning
name	string	The name of your cookie (analogous to the name of a variable).
value	string	The value you want to store in the cookie (analogous to the value you would assign to a variable). If this argument is not supplied, the cookie named by the first argument is deleted.
expire	int	Specifies when this cookie should expire. A value of 0 (the default) means that it should last until the browser is closed. Any other integer is interpreted as an absolute time (as returned by the function mktime()) when the cookie should expire.
path	string	In the default case, any page within the Web root folder would see (and be able to set) this named cookie. Setting the path to a subdirectory (for example, "/forum/") allows distinguishing cookies that have the same name but are set by different *sites* or subareas of the Web server (in this example, the cookie will only be valid in the forum area). Be sure to include a trailing slash in the path.
domain	string	In the default case, no check is made against the domain requested by the client. If this argument is nonempty, then the domain must match. For example, If the same server serves www.mysteryguide.com and forum.mysteryguide.com, one site's code can ensure that the other site does not read (or set) its cookies by including this argument as "forum.mysteryguide.com."
secure	int (0 or 1)	Defaults to 0. If this argument is 1, the cookie will only be sent over a secure socket (aka SSL or HTTPS) connection. Note that a secure connection must already be running for such a cookie to be set in the first place.

Cross-Reference   For details about the representation of time used by the expire argument, see Chapter 23 — specifically, the discussions of the functions time() and mktime().

Caution   Calling setcookie() results in sending HTTP header information, which cannot be done after you have already sent some regular PHP output (even if that output consists of a single space or blank line!).

Cookies and privacy

Cookies have always been controversial from a privacy point of view, and that controversy heats up again periodically. As we wrote the first edition, DoubleClick (an Internet advertising agency) was being flamed for its announcement that it planned to cross-correlate cookie information with a very large database of consumer names, addresses, and buying habits (in an apparent reversal of earlier promises about such behavior).

The worry was that, after a consumer reveals his or her identity on a site by filling out a form and accepting a cookie, any other site that compares notes with the original site could conceivably know the true identity of the user (and lots of other information as well). If this practice became widespread, every e-commerce site you visit might be able to figure out not only your name, address, and buying habits, but also a list of other pages you have visited on the Web.

So, cookies worry some people, but at the same time they are also a reasonable and benign workaround to the statelessness of the HTTP protocol. There are plenty of good reasons to want a Web client/server interaction to coherently span a few page requests in a row, rather than covering just a single request. As a Web developer, you might well decide to use cookies for such a purpose, comfortable in the knowledge that there is no substantive invasion of privacy occurring.

Your comfort is not the same as the user's comfort, however, and many users have set up their browsers to refuse all cookies, as is their right. (Remember that what is at issue here is not only the user's privacy, but also the use of his or her own personal hard disk!) Any server-side code you write should gracefully handle a cookie refusal from the client side, and any Web sites you design should have easily found privacy policies, so that your users know what they are getting into. This does not mean, though, that you are obligated to provide the same level of service to users that refuse cookies; there are some kinds of functionality that are just too painful to write without them, and deciding that cookie cooperation is a prerequisite to using a privately provided site seems perfectly legitimate.

Examples

This section provides some example calls to `setcookie()`, along with comments, such as the following:

```
setcookie('membername', 'timboy');
```

This sets a cookie called `membername`, with a value of `timboy`. Because there are no arguments except for the first two, the cookie will persist only until the current browser program is closed, and it will be read on subsequent page requests from this browser to this server, regardless of the domain name in the request or where in the Web root file hierarchy the page is served from. The cookie will also be read regardless of whether the Web connection is secure. For example, consider the following call:

```
setcookie('membername', 'troutgirl', time() + (60 * 60 * 24),
        "/", "www.troutworks.com", 1);
```

This sets the cookie to have the value `'troutgirl'` and would overwrite the previous example's value if it had been set by a previous page. The expiration time is set to 86,400 seconds (or 1 day) after the current time. The path argument is given the most inclusive path possible ("/"), so this cookie will still be read regardless of where it is in the Web directory hierarchy.

The host argument is set to `'www.troutworks.com'`, which means that subsequent page views will not cause the cookie to be read unless the user actually is making a request of that host. Finally, the last argument specifies that this cookie will only be read or written over a secure socket connection. (If the very connection used by this page is not secure, presumably the cookie will not be set at all.)

Note If you want to specify later arguments to `setcookie()` while leaving the earlier ones with their default values, it is best to give the empty string (`""`) for the domain argument, a string containing a slash character (`"/"`) for the path argument, and 0 for the expiration.

Caution Multiple calls to setcookie() will typically be interpreted in the opposite order that they appear in your PHP script, although not every browser version does this. The best rule is to never send two different values for the same cookie from a single page execution. (Sending more than one is pointless anyway because one of them will always overwrite the other.)

Deleting cookies

Deleting a cookie is easy. Simply call `setcookie()`, with the exact same arguments as when you set it, except the value, which should be set to an empty string. This does not set the cookie's value to an empty string — it actually removes the cookie. Remember: If you used the path or domain arguments to set the cookie, you need to use them to unset the cookie too.

Reading cookies

Cookies that have been successfully set in a browser or user's machine will automatically be read on the next request from that browser. This has the following effects:

✦ In PHP4.1 and later, the cookie's name/value pair will be added to the superglobal array `$_COOKIE`, as though we had evaluated `$_COOKIE['name'] = value`.

✦ In both current and earlier versions of PHP, the name and value will also be added to the merely global array `$HTTP_COOKIE_VARS`.

✦ If the `register_globals` directive is turned on, a regular page-level global variable will be set to the cookie's value, named the same as the cookie's name. Because `register_globals` is turned off by default starting with PHP4.2, this feature is not available in 4.2 or later, unless either you or your ISP's administrator has changed the configuration.

So, for example, you can set a cookie as follows:

```
setcookie('membername', 'timboy');
```

This means that, on a *later* page access, you might be able to print the value again as easily as this:

```
$membername = $_COOKIE['membername'];
print("The member name is $membername<BR>");
```

And, if `register_globals` has been turned on, the later page's use of the cookie becomes even simpler:

```
print("The member name is $membername<BR>");
```

Note If you set a cookie in a given script, it won't be set on the client until that page (and its HTTP headers) are sent off to the client, which is too late for you to be able to take advantage of it in that very script. This means that the corresponding global variable won't be available to you until the next page request.

The following code typically does not work as you might expect:

```
setcookie('membername', 'timboy');
print("I set a cookie!  Now I will grab the value<BR>");
// (WRONG - the following membername will most likely be blank)
$membername = $_COOKIE['membername'];
print("The member name is $membername<BR>");
```

This is because, as the preceding Note points out, the cookie will not be set until the current page's worth of HTTP headers arrives at the client. Because that has not yet happened in this example, and the variable $membername has not been otherwise set, that variable will probably produce an empty string in the preceding print statement.

The following code gets it right:

```
$cookievalue = 'timboy';
setcookie('membername', $cookievalue);
print("I set a cookie for the benefit of future pages<BR>");
// (RIGHT - only print variables that this page actually set)
print("Its name is membername, its value is $cookievalue<BR>");
```

Any subsequent scripts that are loaded into the same browser can now refer to $membername.

Cross-Reference We have already noted some privacy risks to users of accepting cookies from servers. It's worth noting that there are risks that go the other way as well. If you write scripts that depend on the integrity of data that you include in cookies, you should remember that a clever end user can edit those cookies and install arbitrary values in them. See Chapter 29 for techniques for encrypting sensitive data, even inside cookies.

register_globals and variable overwriting

Just as with sessions, we believe that use of the superglobal variables is the way to go, both because it eliminates certain kinds of confusion and because the PHP developers have clearly indicated that register_globals is going away sooner or later. So we recommend that anytime you want to reach into the cookie jar and get some information, you do it by directly referring to $_COOKIE. If you are still using PHP4.0.x and $_COOKIE is not available, then we urge to you refer to $HTTP_COOKIE_VARS.

If you must rely on the register_globals functionality, and want cookie variables to automatically become global page variables, it's worth noting that such global variables arrive from several different sources, and that this can cause name conflicts. Say that you refer to one of your own pages with the URL http://mysite.org/mypage.php?id=4, indicating that you intend to serve up page four of your content, but you also set a cookie variable named id, which you intend to be your reader's account number. Now, what's going to happen when you refer to $id in your script?

The PHP directive that controls this behavior is called variables_order, and its default value is EGPCS. This encodes the different sources for global variables by their first letters — environment, GET, POST, cookie, server — and determines their overwriting order. Being late in this ordering means having higher priority, since later values overwrite the earlier values. If 'EGPCS' is in effect, then cookie variables overwrite POST variables that happen to have the same name.

You can change this ordering by changing the value of 'variables_order' in your php.ini file. You can also drop any of the letters, meaning that you don't want the corresponding globals to be created at all. If you change the value of 'variables_order' to be 'CG', it means that the automatically created global variables will be derived first from cookies and then from GET variables (possibly overwriting cookie-derived variables of the same name) and that no other kinds of auto-globals will be made.

Cookie pitfalls

It is hard to do much wrong with cookies purely at the PHP level. After all, setting a cookie involves only one function (set_cookie()), and reading cookies involves no functions at all. What could be easier than that? The problems that typically arise are those imposed by the HTTP protocol itself.

Sending something else first

The single most common error in using cookies is trying to set a cookie after some regular HTML content has already been generated. (We may be repeating ourselves here, but we will also repeat it in the "Sending HTTP Headers" section later in the chapter, because this fact applies to other direct HTTP protocol manipulations in addition to cookies and is the cause of a great deal of debugging confusion.)

The reason this doesn't work is that the HTTP protocol requires headers to be sent before the content of the HTML page itself — they can't be intermixed. As soon as any regular content is generated, PHP figures that it must already know about all headers of interest, and so it sends them off and then begins the transmission of HTML content. If it encounters a cookie (or other header information) later on, it is too late, and an error is generated.

It's surprisingly easy to write code that violates this prohibition. Consider the following:

```
 <?php /* A subtle, insidious cookie error */
setcookie('mycookie', 'myvalue');
?>
<HTML><HEAD>
<TITLE>A seemingly benign cookie-setting page</TITLE>
</HEAD><BODY>
  <H3>This page is so simple it absolutely must be right</H3>
</BODY></HTML>
```

When we load this script, we get browser output indicating cannot add header informa-tion. The culprit is the very first character in the file: the space before <?php. Because PHP files start off in HTML mode by default, this file causes one space's worth of generated content to be sent to the client before PHP mode kicks in, and the attempt is made to set the cookie.

A similar way to accidentally send header information too early is to include() or require() a file that includes blank lines at the end after the closing PHP tag. Finally, of course, you can violate the prohibition entirely in PHP mode, but only if you include something like a print or echo statement.

If you ever run into this kind of error, it is relatively easy to debug if you are methodical about it. Try moving HTTP-related code toward the beginning of the script file first — if you still get the error after that, then trace backward from the offending line toward the beginning of the file. Somewhere between the beginning and the failing statement you either have some characters that are being interpreted in HTML mode, or else you have a PHP printing construct. If you have any included PHP files before the offending statement, make sure that there are no characters at all before the start tags or after the end tags.

Reverse-order interpretation

As with most HTTP commands, calls to setcookie() may actually be executed in the opposite order from how they appear in your PHP script, but it depends on the particular browser your user is running and the version of PHP you're using. This means that a pair of successive statements like the following probably have the counterintutive result of leaving the "mycookie" cookie with no value, because the unsetting statement is executed second.

```
setcookie("mycookie");// get rid of the old value (WRONG)
setcookie("mycookie", "newvalue");// set the new value (WRONG)
```

Tip   There is no need to remove a cookie before setting it to a different value — simply set it to the desired new value. Among other things, this means that the confusing reverse order of interpretation of setcookie() calls should not usually matter — if the effect depends on the order, it may mean that you are doing something wrong (or at least something unnecessary).

Cookie refusal

Finally, be aware that setcookie() makes no guarantees that any cookie data will, in fact, be accepted by the client browser — setcookie() just agrees to try, by sending off the appropriate HTTP headers. What happens after that is up to the client, and the client may be an older browser that does not accept cookies or a browser whose user has intentionally disabled cookies.

The setcookie() function does not even return a value that indicates acceptance or refusal of the cookie. If you think about it, this is imposed by the timing of the script execution and the HTTP protocol. First, the script executes (including the setcookie() call), with the result that a page complete with HTTP headers is sent to the client machine. At this point, the client browser decides how to react to the cookie-setting attempt. Not until the client generates another request can the server receive the cookie's value and detect whether the cookie-setting attempt was successful. The implication of this for scripting is that you must always ensure that something reasonable happens, even in cases where setcookie() is called without success. One common technique is to set a test cookie with the name CookiesOn and then check on a subsequent page load if the $_COOKIE['CookiesOn'] variable has been set.

Sending HTTP Headers

The setcookie() call provides a wrapper around a particular usage of HTTP headers. In addition, PHP offers the header() function, which you can use to send raw, arbitrary HTTP headers. You can use this function to roll your own cookie function if you like, but you can also use it to take advantage of any other kind of header-controlled functionality.

The syntax of header() is as simple as it can be: It takes a single string argument, which is the header to be sent.

Caution   All the Cautions from earlier in this chapter (about sending HTTP before any real page content) apply to the `header()` function as well.

Example: Redirection

One useful kind of HTTP header is `"Location:"`, which can act as a redirector. Simply put a fully qualified URL after the `"Location:"` string, and the browser will start over again with the new address instead. Here's an example:

```php
<?php
  if (IsSet($_GET['gender']) && ($_GET['gender'] == "female"))
    {
      header(
"Location: http://www.example.com/secret.php");
      exit;
    }
?>
<HTML><HEAD><TITLE>The inclusive page</TITLE></HEAD></HTML>
<BODY>
<H3>Welcome!</H3>
We welcome anyone to this page, even men!  Talk amongst yourselves.
</BODY></HTML>
```

If we simply enter the URL for this page (`www.example.com/inclusive.php`), we will see the rendering of the HTML at the bottom of the script. On the other hand, if we include the right `GET` argument (`www.example.com/inclusive.php?gender=female`), we find ourselves redirected to a different page entirely. Note that this is significantly different from selectively importing contents with the `include()` statement—we actually end up browsing a different URL than the one we typed in, and that new Web address is what shows up in the Location or Address bar of your browser.

This kind of redirection can be useful when you want the structure of your Web site to conditionally branch without having to make the user explicitly choose different links.

Example: HTTP authentication

Another useful thing you can do with HTTP is ask the browser to ask the user for a username and password, via a pop-up window. This is done with the `WWW-Authenticate` header, as in the following example:

```php
<?php
  $the_right_user = 'user';   // example only! not recommended
  $the_right_password = 'password';   // example only!

  if(!isset($PHP_AUTH_USER)) {
    Header("WWW-Authenticate: Basic realm=\"PHP book\"");
    Header("HTTP/1.0 401 Unauthorized");
    echo "Canceled by user\n";
    exit;
  } else {
    if (($PHP_AUTH_USER == 'user') &&
```

```
        ($PHP_AUTH_PW == 'password')) //see caution below
      print("The realm is yours<BR>");
    else
      print("We don't need your kind<BR>");
  }
?>
```

If we visit this script for the first time (and are using the appropriate browser and server versions), we will get a pop-up window. After the user enters the information into the pop-up box, the script is automatically called again with new variables $PHP_AUTH_USER (set to the user string entered), $PHP_AUTH_PASSWD (set to the password string entered), and $PHP_AUTH_TYPE (which will be *Basic* until such time as another type of authentication is supported). The nice thing about this is that these variables will continue to be set by the browser on each request, and you do not need to do anything in your scripts to propagate them — one verification of identity per session should suffice.

Caution   The preceding code is the bare minimum necessary to demonstrate the HTTP authentication mechanism and is not a model for how user/password combinations should really be verified! Our code fragment simply compares the values of the variables delivered to hard-coded strings, which is a bad idea for several reasons. To make this part of a real verification system, you probably want to compare the result of encrypting the password to a similarly encrypted version in a database or password file. See Chapter 29 for more on encryption and real security measures.

In addition to redirection and authentication, the capability to send real HTTP headers offers finer control of many aspects of the HTTP client/server relationship, which usually are set by default. For example, you can explicitly set the expiration and caching behavior of your page, or send return status codes that tell the client whether whatever is returned should be considered a success or not. Because PHP is just acting as a channel to the underlying HTTP protocol, most of these techniques are beyond the scope of PHP documentation and this book.

Note   The WWW-Authenticate mechanism works only under the Apache Web Server, with PHP as a module. It does not currently work in the CGI version or under IIS/PWS.

Header gotchas

As we have said innumerable times by now, the header() function is subject to the same restriction as the setcookie() function: No headers may be sent after regular page content is generated, unless you are using a release of PHP4 or 5 that has output buffering enabled.

More generally, be aware that using the header capability requires not only some knowledge of the HTTP protocols, but also some knowledge of the extent to which different browser versions conform to them. Unless you are writing for a known population of users that all use the same browser, you will probably need to do more cross-browser testing than with vanilla HTML-generating scripts.

Tip   Most browsers can be set to warn you whenever they are about to accept a cookie. Although this can be annoying when viewing benign yet cookie-intensive sites, it can also be a great debugging tool when writing your own cookie-setting code. Mozilla browsers also feature a tool called Cookie Manager that lists cookies from each site and allows you to manually delete them, which is also handy for debugging.

Gotchas and Troubleshooting

If you are having trouble with sessions, first make sure that your session support exists and is doing what you think it is. Try downloading the sample session code from www.troutworks.com/phpbook and debugging it from the earliest error, if any.

If sessions are not working or are giving errors, check the pathname returned by session_save_path(), and make sure that it exists and is PHP writable. If not, you should either make it so or change the value of 'session.save_path' in php.ini.

Remember that session functions that have variable names as arguments do not expect a leading $ in the name.

If you ever run into a complaint that refers to already having sent HTTP headers, it may be that your script is sending some text (even blank lines) before the session_start() or session_register() functions. Scrutinize any included files for blank lines or move the session functions to the very beginning of your file.

When testing session-related code, remember to try it out both with a browser that accepts cookies and with a browser that is set up to refuse them. If you see no session name in the URL of a link (such as, 'PHPSESSID') with a cookie-refusing browser, then either sessions are not working or your version of PHP is not configured to transparently pass session IDs in the GET/POST arguments. It's also informative to try session and cookie code with a browser that is configured to alert the user whenever it is setting a cookie.

Summary

Sessions are useful for tracking a user's behavior over interactions that last longer than one script execution or page download. If what you present to the user depends on which previous pages he or she has seen or interacted with, your code must store or propagate that information in a way that distinguishes one user from another. Because the HTTP protocol is stateless, this inevitably entails some kind of workaround technique — usually either *hidden variables* (which impose maintenance headaches) or *cookies* (which are not universally supported by client browsers).

The PHP implementation of sessions encapsulates these messy issues and presents a clean layer of abstraction to the scripter. Unique session identifiers are automatically created and propagated, and a variables can be passed from page to page by storing them in the superglobal $_SESSION array. Aside from one's having to connect to a session initially and store (or register) the variables that should persist beyond the current page, session use is virtually transparent to the programmer.

PHP offers several ways to use the capabilities of the HTTP protocol, in addition to the obvious one of constructing HTML pages that are transmitted via HTTP. The setcookie() function allows you to set and delete cookies in your user's browser, the values of which show up in subsequent page views as ordinary global variables.

The header() function allows you to send arbitrary HTTP headers. Among other things, header() can be useful for authentication and page-level redirection.

The HTTP functions in PHP are very simple, and the main complexities that arise are a consequence of the HTTP protocol itself. One such complication is the fact that that HTTP requires all headers to be sent before any page content is sent. Remember that any use of header-manipulating functions must happen before even a blank space is sent to the browser.

✦   ✦   ✦

Types and Type Conversions

In Chapter 5, we covered PHP types in basic terms, outlining the different types and how they might best be used in your programs. Our first purpose in this chapter is to review those types and elaborate a little more on *resources*. (Another type, *objects*, was covered fully in Chapter 20.) We'll also look at some type testing techniques, and finally, type conversion.

Type Round-up

You should remember from earlier chapters that unlike many other languages, PHP does not require explicit type declarations. PHP is fairly intuitive about the purpose of your various variables and can often infer your intent from the context in which those variables are used. PHP, for example, understands that the statement

```
$my_value = 4.50;
```

refers to a float, that is, a floating-point number. But if you subsequently create a string, such as:

```
$my_string = "I paid \$$my_value for a box of
twinkies.";
```

PHP understands that it needs to convert the variable $my_value into a string for purposes of concatenating the larger string assigned to the variable $my_string. However, this conversion should in no way prevent you from later doing something like:

```
$my_tax = .065;
$my_total = round($my_value + ($my_value *
$my_tax));
$my_string .= "However; if I lived in a state where
Twinkies are not considered a food item, the same
box
would have cost
\$$my_total";
```

The eight basic PHP types are listed here. If you need more of a reminder, refer to Chapter 5. The more complex types are treated in their own chapters: strings in Chapter 8, arrays in Chapter 9, and objects in Chapter 20.

✦ *Integers* are whole numbers, without a decimal point, like 495.

✦ *Floats* (aka *doubles*) are floating-point numbers, like 3.14159, or 49.0.

✦ *Booleans* have only two possible values: `TRUE` and `FALSE`.

✦ *NULL* is a special type that has only one value: `NULL`.

✦ *Strings* are sequences of characters, like `'PHP4.0 supports string operations'`.

✦ *Arrays* are named and indexed collections of other values.

✦ *Objects* are instances of programmer-defined classes, which can package up both other kinds of values and functions that are specific to the class.

✦ *Resources* are special variables that hold references to resources external to PHP (such as database connections).

Resources

As previous chapters provided in-depth coverage of the first seven types, let's have a look at the eighth. *Resources* are special values that refer to memory or state information that is external to the PHP language itself. You don't have to know too much about resources for casual PHP programming—we'll briefly explain what resources are all about, but feel free to skip to the section "How to handle resources."

What are resources?

The resource type is needed when PHP communicates with some external program (which may be a database or a graphics program) that allocates memory in response to requests from PHP. In general, PHP programmers do not have to worry about freeing memory within PHP— if you create a string in a PHP script (which will take up some space in memory), you can forget all about it and let your script run until the end. PHP (or the Web server it is attached to) will reclaim all memory associated with your script when your script is done, if not earlier.

External programs (databases, and so on.) might not be smart enough to do this deallocation. You might have space reserved in your database's memory for your script long after your script has gone to script heaven. The way this problem gets handled in PHP is that all special functions that request memory from such external programs return *resources*, which PHP tracks to see if your script can still get to them. If nobody can reach the resource, PHP makes sure that the external program does the right kind of cleanup. PHP does this by counting references to the resource—if the reference count goes to zero, then the resource can be freed.

How to handle resources

In general, PHP programmers do not create resources by themselves—they call special functions that return values of the resource type, and then pass them on to other functions that require resources. For example, you might call the function `mysql_connect()` (which returns a resource value that refers to a connection to a MySQL database), save the result in a variable, and then pass it on to `mysql_query()` (which uses the connection resource to query the database).

Essentially, all you have to do with this connection resource is store it in a variable and pass that variable to functions that require it. You can depend on PHP to clean up the resource after your script is done. If, for whatever reason, you feel that the resource is tying up enough memory during script execution that you want the memory freed before the script is done, you can usually do something like this:

```
$my_resource = mysql_connect();  // stores  variable
// .. code that uses the connection resource ..
$my_resource = NULL; // variable no longer refers to resource
```

The reassignment of $my_resource should cause PHP to check that no other piece of code is using the MySQL resource and then free it. Alternatively, most resource opening functions have resource closing counterparts such as mysql_close(), covered in Chapter 15, or fclose(), which we used in Chapter 23.

Type Testing

Especially because variables can change types due to reassignment, it is sometimes necessary to find out the type of a value at program execution time. PHP offers both a general type-testing function (gettype()) and individual Boolean functions for each of the five types. These functions, some of which have alternate names, are summarized in Table 25-1.

Table 25-1: Functions for Type Testing

Function	Behavior
gettype(arg)	Returns a string representing the type of arg: either integer, float, string, array, object, or unknown type
is_int(arg)	
is_integer(arg)	
is_long(arg)	Returns TRUE if arg is an integer, and FALSE if not
is_double(arg)	
is_float(arg)	
is_real(arg)	Returns TRUE if arg is a float, and FALSE if not
is_bool(arg)	Returns TRUE if arg is a Boolean value (TRUE or FALSE), and FALSE if not
is_null(arg)	Returns TRUE if arg is of the NULL type, and FALSE if not.
is_string(arg)	Returns TRUE if arg is a string, and FALSE if not
is_array(arg)	Returns TRUE if arg is an array, and FALSE if not
is_object(arg)	Returns TRUE if arg is an object, and FALSE if not
is_resource(arg)	Returns TRUE if arg is a resource, and FALSE if not.

Assignment and Coercion

As we have said, PHP often automatically converts from one type to another when the context demands it, and as it turns out the PHP programmer can also force some of these conversions to happen. In either situation, the programmer should know what to expect.

Type conversion behavior

Here are some general rules for PHP's conversion from one type to another:

✦ **Integer to float:** The exact corresponding float is created (for example, the int 4 becomes the float 4.0).

✦ **Float to integer:** The fractional part is dropped, truncating the number toward zero.

✦ **Number to Boolean:** FALSE if exactly equal to 0, TRUE otherwise.

✦ **Number to string:** A string is created that looks exactly the way the number would print. Integers are printed as a sequence of digits, and floats are printed with the minimum precision needed. Extreme float values will be converted to scientific notation.

✦ **Boolean to number:** 1 if TRUE, 0 if FALSE.

✦ **Boolean to string:** '1' if TRUE, the empty string if FALSE.

✦ **Null to number:** 0

✦ **Null to boolean:** FALSE

✦ **String to number:** Equivalent to *reading* a number from the string, then making a conversion to the given type. If a number cannot be read, the value is zero. Not all of the string needs to be read for the reading to be considered a success.

✦ **String to Boolean:** FALSE if it is an empty string or the string is '0', TRUE otherwise.

✦ **Simple type (number or string) to array:** Equivalent to creating a new array with the simple value assigned to index zero.

✦ **Array to number:** Undefined (see following note).

✦ **Array to Boolean:** FALSE if the array has no elements, TRUE otherwise.

✦ **Array to string:** 'Array'.

✦ **Object to number:** Undefined (see note below).

✦ **Object to boolean:** TRUE if the object contains any member variables that have a value, and FALSE otherwise

✦ **Object to string:** 'Object'.

✦ **Resource to Boolean:** FALSE

✦ **Resource to number:** Undefined (see note below).

✦ **Resource to string:** Something like 'Resource id #1' (but this should not be relied upon).

In the preceding list, we noted that some types have an undefined result when converted to numerical values. In this context, *undefined* simply means that the PHP developers are not making a commitment as to what kind of behavior you'll get in future versions of PHP, so it would be a bad idea to depend on a particular behavior in your code. You may find that these types can be converted to numbers in expressions in your particular version of PHP, but that may not work in the next version.

Explicit conversions

PHP offers three different ways for the programmer to manipulate types: conversion functions, type casts (as in the C language), and calling settype() on variables:

✦ The functions `intval()`, `floatval()`, and `strval()` will convert their arguments to an integer, a float, or a string, respectively. (At this writing, there does not seem to be a `boolval()` function.)

✦ Any expression can be preceded by a type cast (the name of the type in parentheses), which converts the expression result to the desired type.

✦ Any variable can be given as a first argument to `settype()`, which will change the type of that variable to the type named in the second string argument.

For example, each of the following approaches will put the correct count of canines (101) into the integer variable `$dog_count` by the end of the code snippet:

Version #1:

```
$dog_count = intval (strval (floatval("101 Dalmatians")));
```

Version #2:

```
$dog_count = (int) (string) (float) "101 Dalmatians";
```

Version #3:

```
settype($dog_count, "float");
settype($dog_count, "string");
settype($dog_count, "int");
```

Tip

Of course, each approach in the example takes an indirect route, converting needlessly to string and float types — it would suffice to convert immediately to the integer type.

Six of the basic type names (integer, float, Boolean, string, array, and object) are valid in casts and are valid string arguments to `settype()`. In addition, certain alternate names are valid in casts: (`int`) instead of (`integer`), (`double`) or (`real`) instead of (`float`), and (`bool`) instead of (`boolean`). It is not valid to cast to type resource, and casting to type NULL is pointless. (Because the result can only be the value NULL, you might as well simply assign instead.)

Conversion examples

Just for fun, Listing 25-1 shows some PHP code that displays various type conversions in an HTML table, with the resulting table shown in Figure 25-1. (This code is not intended as a style example, and it uses several constructs that have not yet been covered — feel free to just look at the output.)

Listing 25-1: **Type conversions**

```
$type_examples[0] = 123; // an integer
$type_examples[1] = 3.14159; // a float
$type_examples[2] = "a non-numeric string";
$type_examples[3] = "49.990 (begins with number)";
$type_examples[4] = array(90,80,70);

print("<TABLE BORDER=1><TR>");
print("<TH>Original</<TH>");
print("<TH>(int)</<TH>");
print("<TH>(float)</<TH>");
```

Continued

Listing 25-1 *(continued)*

```
print("<TH>(string)</<TH>");
print("<TH>(array)</<TH></TR>");

for ($index = 0; $index < 5; $index++)
  {
    print("<TR><TD>$type_examples[$index]</TD>");
    $converted_var =
       (int) $type_examples[$index];
    print("<TD>$converted_var</TD>");
    $converted_var =
       (float) $type_examples[$index];
    print("<TD>$converted_var</TD>");
    $converted_var =
       (string) $type_examples[$index];
    print("<TD>$converted_var</TD>");
    $converted_var =
       (array) $type_examples[$index];
    print("<TD>$converted_var</TD></TR>");
  }
print("</TABLE>");
```

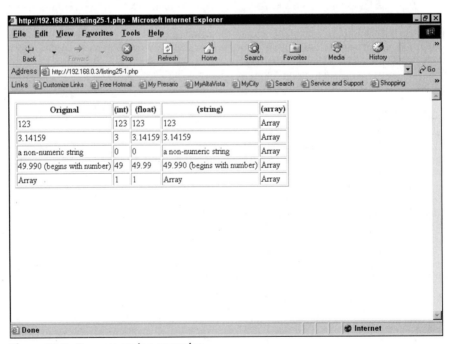

Figure 25-1: Type conversion examples

Other useful type conversions

The functions listed in Table 25-2 do not exactly convert types, but they return a different type from their main argument in a useful way.

Table 25-2: Other Type-Conversion Functions

From\To	Integer	String	Array
Integer		ord()	
Float	ceil(), floor(), round()		
String	chr()		explode()
Array		implode()	

The function ceil() takes a float and returns the integer greater than or equal to that float. For example:

```
$my_float = 4.7;
$my_int = ceil($my_float); // $my_int is equal to 5
$my_float = -4.7;
$my_int = ceil($my_float); // $my_int is equal to -4
```

The floor() function is the opposite of ceil(). (We'll drop the intermediate assignment to $my_float now.)

```
$my_int = floor(4.7); // $my_int is equal to 4
$my_int = floor(-4.7); // $my_int is equal to -5
```

The round() function takes a float and returns the nearest integer. If the fractional part of the float is exactly one half, the rounding is to the highest absolute number.

```
$my_int = round(4.7); // $my_int is equal to 5
$my_int = round(-4.7); // $my_int is equal to -5
$my_int = round(-4.5); // $my_int is equal to -5
```

Tip   If you're looking for a truncate function (simply dropping the fractional part and, therefore, rounding toward zero), notice that this is the behavior you get simply from typecasting from float **to** int.

The function chr() takes an integer and returns a one-character string with that ASCII value, whereas ord() reverses this, returning the ASCII value of the first character in a string.

Finally, implode() and explode() allow a certain kind of conversion between strings and arrays. implode() creates a string out of the array it is given as second argument, separating the elements with the string that is its first argument. For example:

```
$words[0] = "My";
$words[1] = "short";
$words[2] = "sentence.";
$sentence = implode(" ", $words);
print("$sentence<BR>");
```

produces the browser output:

```
My short sentence.
```

explode() reverses the process, creating an array from a string:

```
$words = explode(" ", "My short sentence.");
```

Integer overflow

One clever automatic type conversion built into PHP relatively recently is that when integer values *overflow* (that is, they are assigned a value larger than they can hold), they become floats. This makes some sense, because floats can accommodate larger magnitudes than integers can. For example:

```
$toobig = 111;
for ($count = 0; $count < 5; $count++)
  {
    $too_big = 1000 * $too_big;
    print("Is $too_big still an integer?<BR>");
  }
```

produces the following browser output:

```
Is 111000 still an integer?
Is 111000000 still an integer?
Is 111000000000 still an integer?
Is 1.11E+14 still an integer?
Is 1.11E+17 still an integer?
```

The shift you see in this example from literal integers to scientific notation reflects a change of $too_big's type from integer to float. Of course, this may lose some information, because the precision of floats is limited, but it is in keeping with the PHP philosophy of doing the best it can in preference to causing an error.

Finding the largest integer

If you need to know the largest integer your PHP will support and, for some reason, you believe that it is not the usual $2^{31} - 1$, here's a handy function (which uses concepts not yet covered):

```
function maxint()
{ /* quick-and-dirty function for PHP int size --
     assumes largest integer is of form 2^n - 1 */
  $to_test = 2;
  while(1)
    {
      $last = $to_test;
      $to_test = 2 * $to_test;
      if (($to_test < $last) || (!is_int($to_test)))
          return($last + ($last - 1));
    }
}
/* sample use */
$maxint = maxint();
print("Maxint is $maxint<BR>");
```

Summary

PHP5 has eight types: integer, float, Boolean, NULL, string, array, object, and resource. Five of these are simple types: Integers are whole numbers, floats are floating-point numbers, Booleans are true-or-false values, NULL has just one value (NULL), and strings are sequences of characters. *Arrays* are a compound type that holds other PHP values, indexed either by integers or by strings. *Objects* are instances of programmer-defined classes, which can contain both member variables and member functions, and which can inherit functions and data type from other classes. Finally, *resources* are special references to memory allocated from external programs, which memory PHP frees automatically when they are no longer needed.

Only values are typed in PHP — variables have no inherent type other than the value of their most recent assignment. PHP automatically converts value types as demanded by the context in which the value is used. The programmer can also explicitly control types by means of both conversion functions and type casts.

✦   ✦   ✦

Advanced Use of Functions

In Chapter 6 we presented the basic features for user-defined functions in PHP. In this chapter, we move on to some exotic properties of functions, including ways to use variable numbers of arguments, ways to have functions actually modify the variables they are passed, and (cooler still) using functions as data.

Variable Numbers of Arguments

It's often useful to have the number of actual arguments that are passed to a function depend on the situation in which it is called. There are three possible ways to handle this in PHP:

✦ Define the function with default arguments — any that are missing in the function call will have the default value, and no warning will be printed.

✦ Use an array argument to hold the values — it is the responsibility of the calling code to package up the array, and the function body must appropriately take it apart.

✦ Use the variable-argument functions (`func_num_args()`, `func_get_arg()`, and `func_get_args()`) introduced in PHP4.

The following sections address each of these possibilities.

Default arguments

To define a function with default arguments, simply turn the formal parameter name into an assignment expression. If the actual call has fewer parameters than the definition has formal parameters, PHP will match actual with formal until the actual parameters are exhausted and then will use the default assignments to fill in the rest.

For example, the following function has all its variables defined with defaults:

```
function tour_guide($city = "Gotham City",
                    $desc = "vast metropolis",
                    $how_many = "dozens",
                    $of_what = "costumed villains")
{
  print("$city is a $desc filled with
        $how_many of $of_what.<BR>");
}
tour_guide();
tour_guide("Chicago");
tour_guide("Chicago", "wonderful city");
tour_guide("Chicago", "wonderful city",
           "teeming millions");
tour_guide("Chicago", "wonderful city",
           "teeming millions",
           "gruff people with hearts of
            gold and hard-luck stories to tell");
```

The browser output is something like this, with the intrasentence line breaks, of course, determined by your browser:

```
Gotham City is a great metropolis filled with dozens of costumed
villains.
Chicago is a great metropolis filled with dozens of costumed
villains.
Chicago is a wonderful city filled with dozens of costumed
villains.
Chicago is a wonderful city filled with teeming millions of
costumed villains.
Chicago is a wonderful city filled with teeming millions of
gruff people with hearts of gold and hard-luck stories to tell.
```

The main limitation of default arguments is that the matching of actual to formal parameters is determined by the ordering of both — it's first-come, first-served. This means that there is absolutely no way to use the default-argument mechanism to tell someone about hard-luck stories in Gotham City.

Arrays as multiple-argument substitutes

If you are dissatisfied with the flexibility of multiple arguments, you can bypass the whole argument-counting issue by using an array as your communication channel.

The following example uses this strategy and, in addition, uses a few tricks like the ternary operator (introduced in Chapter 6) and the associative array (covered in Chapters 11 and 21):

```
function tour_brochure($info_array)
{
$city =
 IsSet($info_array['city']) ?
   $info_array['city'] : "Gotham City";
$desc =
 IsSet($info_array['desc']) ?
   $info_array['desc'] : "great metropolis";
```

```
$how_many =
 IsSet($info_array['how_many']) ?
  $info_array['how_many'] : "dozens";
$of_what =
 IsSet($info_array['of_what']) ?
  $info_array['of_what'] : "costumed villains";

print("$city is a $desc filled with
      $how_many of $of_what.<BR>");
}
```

This function checks the single incoming array argument for four different values associated with particular strings. Using the ternary conditional operator ?, local variables are assigned to either the incoming value (if it has been stored in the array) or to our comic book defaults. Now, let's try calling this function with a couple of different arrays:

```
tour_brochure(array()); // empty array
$tour_info =
 array('city' => 'Cozumel',
       'desc' => 'destination getaway',
       'of_what' => 'sandy beaches');
tour_brochure($tour_info);
```

In this example, we call `tour_brochure` first with an empty array (corresponding to no arguments) and then with an array that has three of the four possible associative values stored in it. The browser output we get is:

```
Gotham City is a great metropolis filled with dozens of costumed
  villains.
Cozumel is a destination getaway filled with dozens of sandy
  beaches.
```

In both cases, the `dozens` amount is defaulted, because neither array had anything stored under the `how_many` association.

Multiple arguments in PHP4 and above

Beginning with version 4, PHP offers some functions that can be used inside function bodies to recover the number and values of arguments. They are:

✦ `func_num_args()`:Takes no arguments and returns the number of arguments that passed to the function it is called from.

✦ `func_get_arg()`:Takes an integer argument *n* and returns the *n*th argument to the function it is called from. Arguments are numbered starting from zero.

✦ `func_get_args()`:Takes no arguments and returns an array containing all the arguments in the function it is called from, with array indices starting from zero.

All three of these functions will produce a warning if called outside a function body, and `func_get_arg()` will give a warning if it is called with an index higher than the index of the final argument that was passed.

If your function is going to handle the decoding of arguments using these functions, you can take advantage of the fact that PHP doesn't complain about function calls that have more arguments than formal parameters in the definition. Simply define your function to take no arguments, and then use the functions to catch any that are actually passed.

As an example, consider the following two functions, both of which return an array of the arguments they are given:

```
function args_as_array_1 ()
{
$arg_count = func_num_args();
$counter = 0;
$local_array = array();
while ($counter < $arg_count)
   {
    $local_array[$counter] =
      func_get_arg($counter);
    $counter = $counter + 1;
   }
return($local_array);
}

function args_as_array_2 ()
{
    return(func_get_args());
}
```

The first cumbersome function uses `func_get_arg()` to retrieve the individual arguments and bounds the loop using the result of `func_num_args()`, so that no attempt is made to retrieve more arguments than were actually passed. Each argument is individually stored in an array, which is then returned. Packaging up the arguments like this is already done for free by `func_get_args()`, so the second version of the function is extremely short.

As another example, let's rewrite our earlier `tour_guide()` function to use the multiple-argument functions instead of default arguments:

```
function tour_guide_2()
{
$num_args = func_num_args();
$city = $num_args > 0 ?
  func_get_arg(0) : "Gotham City";
$desc = $num_args > 1 ?
  func_get_arg(1) : "great metropolis";
$how_many = $num_args > 2 ?
  func_get_arg(2) : "dozens";
$of_what = $num_args > 3 ?
  func_get_arg(3) : "costumed villains";

print("$city is a $desc filled with
      $how_many of $of_what.<BR>");
}
tour_guide_2();
```

This has exactly the same behavior as the default-argument version and is subject to the same limitation. The arguments are passed in by position, and so there is no way to replace `"costumed villains"` with something else while leaving `"Gotham City"` as the default.

Unfortunately, no better solution presents itself in PHP5; the array solution is, if somewhat more code-intensive, still the most flexible.

Call-by-Value

The default behavior for user-defined functions in PHP is *call-by-value*. This means that when you pass variables to a function call, PHP makes copies of the variable values to pass on to the function. So, whatever the function does, it is not able to change the actual variables that appear in the function call. This behavior can be good or bad. It's a nice reassurance if you only want to use a function for its returned value, but it can also be a source of confusion and frustration if changing the passed variable is actually your goal.

Note   One of the most important differences between PHP5 and its predecessors is that object instances are always effectively passed by reference, even if a value of another type would be passed by value. This is the result of the fact that object variables in PHP5 store object handles rather than the objects themselves — the handles actually are copied in a pass-by-value situation, but the underlying objects are not. (We deal with this issue in more detail in Chapter 20.)

Let's demonstrate call-by-value with a fragile and extremely inefficient implementation of subtraction:

```
function my_subtract ($num1, $num2)
{
  if ($num1 < $num2)
    die("Negative numbers are imaginary");
  $return_result = 0;
  while($num1 > $num2)
    {
      $num1 = $num1 - 1;
      $return_result = $return_result + 1;
    }
  return($return_result);
}
$first_op = 493;
$second_op = 355;
$result1 = my_subtract($first_op, $second_op);
print("result1 is $result1<BR>");
$result2 = my_subtract($first_op, $second_op);
print("result2 is $result2<BR>");
```

Reassuringly, we find that our result is the same both times we perform the same subtraction:

```
result1 is 138
result2 is 138
```

This is true even though my_subtract changes the value of its formal parameter $num1 — that variable only holds a copy of the value that was in the actual parameter $first_op, and so $first_op cannot be affected.

Call-by-Reference

PHP offers two different ways to have functions actually modify their arguments: in the function definition and in the function call.

If you want to define a function to operate directly on a passed variable, simply put an ampersand in front of the formal parameter in the definition, like so:

```
function my_subtract_ref (&$num1, &$num2)
{
  if ($num1 < $num2)
    die("Negative numbers are imaginary");
  $return_result = 0;
  while($num1 > $num2)
    {
      $num1 = $num1 - 1;
      $return_result = $return_result + 1;
    }
  return($return_result);
}
$first_op = 493;
$second_op = 355;
$result1 = my_subtract_ref($first_op, $second_op);
print("result1 is $result1<BR>");
$result2 = my_subtract_ref($first_op, $second_op);
print("result2 is $result2<BR>");
```

Now, if we perform exactly the same subtraction calls as we did the first time, we get the output:

```
result1 is 138
result1 is 0
```

This is because the formal parameter $num1 refers to the same thing as the actual parameter $first_op—changing one means changing the other.

You can also force a function to take arguments by reference by prepending the actual parameters with ampersands (although this is a deprecated capability and may disappear in future PHP versions). That is, we can use our original call-by-value function and get the by-reference behavior, like so:

```
$first_op = 493;
$second_op = 355;
$result1 = my_subtract(&$first_op, &$second_op);
print("result1 is $result1<BR>");
$result2 = my_subtract(&$first_op, &$second_op);
print("result2 is $result2<BR>");
```

producing, once again:

```
result1 is 138
result1 is 0
```

As of PHP4, variable references can be used outside of function calls as well. In general, assigning a variable reference (&$varname) to a variable will make the two variables aliases of each other rather than distinct variables with the same value. For example:

```
$name_1 = "Manfred von Richtofen";
$name_2 = "Percy Blakeney";
$alias_1 = $name_1;  // vars have same value
```

```
$alias_2 = &$name_2; // vars are the same

$alias_1 = "The Red Baron"; // doesn't change real name
$alias_2 = "The Scarlet Pimpernel"; // anonymous forever

print("$alias_1 is $name_1<BR>");
print("$alias_2 is $name_2<BR>");
```

gives the browser output:

```
The Red Baron is Manfred von Richtofen
The Scarlet Pimpernel is The Scarlet Pimpernel
```

Note   As we noted in the "Call-by-value" section, in PHP5 it is not necessary to explicitly make references to object instances. Objects are always effectively passed by reference.

Variable Function Names

One of the neater tricks you can do in PHP is to use variables in place of the names of user-defined functions. That is, rather than typing a literal function name into your code, you type a dollar-sign variable — the function that is actually called at runtime will depend on the string that that variable has been assigned to. In some sense, this allows us to use functions as data. This kind of trick will be familiar to advanced C programmers and to even beginning users of any kind of Lisp language (for example, Scheme or Common Lisp).

For example, the following two function calls are exactly equivalent:

```
function customized_greeting ()
{
  print("You are being greeted in a customized way!<BR>");
}
customized_greeting();
$my_greeting = 'customized_greeting';
$my_greeting();
```

and produce the same output:

```
You are being greeted in a customized way!
You are being greeted in a customized way!
```

Because function names are just strings, they can also be used as arguments to functions or be returned as a function's result.

An Extended Example

Just for fun, let's see what kinds of trouble we can get into by using some of the more advanced features of functions, including using function names as function arguments.

Listing 26-1 shows an extended example of functions that implement a substitution cipher — a rudimentary kind of cryptography that scrambles messages by substituting one letter of the alphabet for another.

Listing 26-1: **A substitution cipher**

```
/* Part 1 - cipher algorithm and utility functions */
function add_1 ($num)
{
  return(($num + 1) % 26);
}

function sub_1 ($num)
{
  return(($num + 25) % 26);
}

function swap_2 ($num)
{
  if ($num % 2 == 0)
    return($num + 1);
  else
    return($num - 1);
}

function swap_26 ($num)
{
  return(25 - $num);
}

function lower_letter($char_string)
{
 return ((ord($char_string) >= ord('a')) &&
         (ord($char_string) <= ord('z')));
}

function upper_letter($char_string)
{
 return ((ord($char_string) >= ord('A')) &&
         (ord($char_string) <= ord('Z')));
}

/* Part 2 - the letter_cipher function */
function letter_cipher ($char_string, $code_func)
{
  if (!(upper_letter($char_string) ||
        lower_letter($char_string)))
    return($char_string);
  if (upper_letter($char_string))
    $base_num = ord('A');
  else
    $base_num = ord('a');
  $char_num = ord($char_string) -
                   $base_num;
```

```
        return(chr($base_num +
                ($code_func($char_num)
                % 26)));
}

/* Part 3 - the main string_cipher function */
function string_cipher($message, $cipher_func)
{
  $coded_message = "";
  $message_length = strlen($message);
  for ($index = 0;
        $index < $message_length;
        $index++)
    $coded_message .=
        letter_cipher($message[$index], $cipher_func);
  return($coded_message);
}
```

Listing 26-1 is in three parts. In the first part, we define a few functions that do simple math on the numbers from 0 through 25, which will represent the letters A–Z in our cipher codes. Function add_1 simply adds 1 to the number it is given, modulo 26 (which just means that numbers that are 26 and larger "wrap around" to start from zero again). 0 + 1 is 1, 1 + 1 is 2, . . . and 25 + 1 is 0. Sub_1 shifts numbers in the other direction, by adding 25 (which in this modular arithmetic is equivalent to subtracting 1). 25 + 25 is 24, 24 + 25 is 23, . . . and 0 + 25 is 25. Swap_2 trades the places of pairs of numbers (0 to 1, 1 to 0, 2 to 3, 3 to 2, . . .). Swap_26 trades high numbers for low numbers (25 to 0, 0 to 25, 24 to 1, 1 to 24, . . .). Each one of these functions will be the basis of a simple cipher code. Finally, we have a couple of utility functions that test whether a character is an uppercase or lowercase letter.

Part 2 is a single function called letter_cipher(), whose job is to take a math function, like the ones in Part 1, and apply it to encode a single letter. First, it tests whether the string it is handed (which should be a single character) is an alphabetic letter; if not, it returns it as is. If the character is a letter, it is transformed into a number using ord(), and the appropriate letter (a or A) is subtracted to bring the number into the 0–25 range. When it is in that range, we apply the cipher function whose name was passed in as a string, and then we convert the number back into a letter and return it.

Finally, Part 3 is the single string_cipher() function, which takes a string message and a cipher function and returns a new string that is the message encoded via the function. It does this by building a new string, letter by letter, from the message string, where each new letter is the result of applying $cipher_func to the numerical representation of the old letter.

Now let's write some code to try out string_cipher():

```
$original = "My secret message is ABCDEFG";
print("Original message is: $original<BR>");

$coding_array = array('add_1',
                    'sub_1',
                    'swap_2',
                    'swap_26');
```

```
for ($count = 0;
     $count < sizeof($coding_array);
     $count++)
{
  $code = $coding_array[$count];
  $coded_message =
      string_cipher($original, $code);
  print("$code encoding is: $coded_message<BR>");
}
```

This testing code takes our four predefined letter-encoding functions, stashes them in an array, and then loops through the array, encoding the `$original` message and printing out the encoded version. The browser output looks like the following:

```
Original message is: My secret message is ABCDEFG
add_1 encoding is: Nz tfdsfu nfttbhf jt BCDEFGH
sub_1 encoding is: Lx rdbqds ldrrzfd hr ZABCDEF
swap_2 encoding is: Nz tfdqfs nfttbhf jt BADCFEH
swap_26 encoding is: Nb hvxivg nvhhztv rh ZYXWVUT
```

We can take this function-as-data approach one step further and write a function that applies more than one cipher to a message in sequence. This function also uses the variable-argument capability we discussed earlier in the chapter.

```
function chained_code ($message)
{
  /* takes a message, then an arbitrary number of
     cipher-code function names. Returns
     result of applying each code to the previous
     result. */
  $argc = func_num_args();
  $coded = $message;
  for ($count = 1; $count < $argc; $count++)
    {
      $function_name = func_get_arg($count);
      $coded =
          string_cipher($coded,
                        $function_name);
    }
  return($coded);
}
```

The first argument to `chained_code()` should be a message string, followed by any number of names corresponding to cipher functions. The coded message is the result of applying the first coding function to the message, then applying the second coding function to the result, and so on. We can test it with various combinations of our predefined letter-coding functions, as follows:

```
$tricky =
  chained_code($original,
              'add_1', 'swap_26',
              'add_1', 'swap_2');
print("Tricky encoded version is $tricky<BR>");

$easy =
```

```
chained_code($original,
             'add_1', 'swap_26',
             'swap_2', 'sub_1',
             'add_1', 'swap_2',
             'swap_26', 'sub_1');
print("Easy encoded version is $easy<BR>");
```

with these results:

```
Tricky encoded version is Ma guwjuh muggysu qg YZWXUVS
Easy encoded version is My secret message is ABCDEFG
```

As you can see, the *tricky* encoding of our message is a combination of our previous codes that doesn't correspond exactly to any of those single coding functions. And the "easy" coding is an even more complicated combination of those functions that produces . . . our original message unchanged! (No, it's not that our cipher code doesn't work—we'll leave it to you to figure out why that particular sequence of coding functions brings us around to our starting message again.)

The moral of our little cryptographic scripting story is that, although the cipher code was mildly complicated, it was made considerably simpler by PHP's support for using function names as function arguments.

Summary

The default behavior for user-defined functions is *call-by-value*, meaning that functions work on copies of their arguments and so cannot modify the original variables in the function call. You can force *call-by-reference* behavior by preceding parameters with &, on either the definition side or the calling side. PHP offers more than one way to let functions take a variable number of arguments. Finally, the functions to be called can be determined at runtime, by substituting a string variable for the literal name of the user-defined function—this allows functions to be treated as data and passed back and forth between other functions.

✦   ✦   ✦

Mathematics

In Chapter 10, we covered the most basic aspects of mathematics in PHP: the numerical types, the basic arithmetic operators, a small set of arithmetic functions, and (because it is so widely used in Web scripting) pseudo-random number generation. In this chapter, we round out this coverage by enumerating the built-in mathematical constants; exploring trigonometric, logarithmic, and base conversion functions; and explaining PHP's bc module for arbitrary-precision arithmetic.

Mathematical Constants

When we wrote the first edition of this book (around the release of PHP version 4.0), there was only one documented math constant: M_PI (the value of pi as a double). However, many new constants were introduced with PHP v4.0.2. Most of these new constants had to do with pi (or multiples thereof), e (or multiples thereof), or square roots, with a few oddballs thrown in. The list has since shrunk back down to a slightly smaller number of predefined mathematical constants, for a variety of reasons. Those that remain are listed in Table 27-1. The general naming scheme is M_<constant-name>. In cases where the constant is a ratio (x/y), the name is M_X_Y, and in cases where there is an operation on a number, the name is M_OPERNUM (for example, M_SQRT2).

Table 27-1: Mathematical Constants

Constant	Description
M_PI	Pi
M_PI_2	pi/2
M_PI_4	pi/4
M_1_PI	1/pi
M_2_PI	2/pi
M_2_SQRTPI	2/sqrt(pi)
M_E	the constant e
M_SQRT2	sqrt(2)
M_SQRT1_2	1/sqrt(2)
M_LOG2E	$\log_2(e)$
M_LOG10E	$\log_{10}(e)$
M_LN2	$\log_e(2)$
M_LN10	$\log_e(10)$

Tests on Numbers

PHP offers a handful of functions for doing tests on numbers. Despite PHP's *type looseness*, it's a good idea to employ some of these tests in your code to help anticipate what sorts of results you will get; and how best to handle them.

The first and simplest test is is_numeric(). Like most of these tests, is_numeric returns a Boolean result, True if the supplied parameter is any type of number (signed or unsigned, integer or float) or a mathematical expression that returns a valid number:

```
is_numeric(4) // True
is_numeric(4-4) // True
is_numeric(4*4) // True
```

Some caution is warranted, because even if you intend to test a string, a string that could be seen as an algebraic expression by PHP might also return a True value:

```
is_numeric(bells/4) // True
```

Finally, remember not to inadvertently quote a mathematical expression, as the result will be forced to False by the string indicators, even though quoting a simple number or double will not cause this behavior:

```
is_numeric('M_PI * 3') // False
is_numeric('123456') // True
```

In cases like the preceding code snippet, it may be desirable to test with a higher degree of specificity, that is to say, for one of PHP's numeric subtypes, using is_int() or is_float(). Neither of these tests is substantively different from is_numeric() in their mode of operation.

They simply test for a particular numeric type. Here are more usage examples and what you might expect from each:

```
is_int(4) // True
is_int(4.2) // False, it's a float or double
is_int('4') // False, this test is stricter than is numeric
is_int(4 * 2) // True, this expression yields an integer
```

You might also occasionally see the test is_long(). This test simply maps to the is_int() function. The other numeric type in PHP can be tested for using is_float(), which is aliased by is_double(). Again, usage is not exactly tricky or even complex.

```
is_float(4) // False, but you knew that already
is_float(4.212) // True, but you knew that as well
is_float(4 / 3) // True
is_float(M_PI) // True, maybe you knew that, maybe you didn't
```

Two more tests are slightly more obscure: is_finite() and is_infinite() test for exactly what their names suggest, although strictly speaking, their range is governed not by actual infinity (how would you test that?) but by the boundaries of the float value that your system allows.

Finally, we have is_nan(), which we covered in Chapter 10. You might be tempted to use is_nan() to test for any non-numeric value. You'll be unpleasantly surprised if you rely on this functionality. The more appropriate use of this function is to test for an unreasonable or improbable mathematical expression such as acos(2).

Base Conversion

The default base in PHP for reading in or printing out numbers is 10. In addition, you can instruct PHP to read octal numbers in base 8 (by starting the number with a leading 0) or hexadecimal numbers in base 16 (by starting the number with a 0x).

Cross-Reference For more on read formats of numbers, including octal and hexadecimal notation, see Chapter 5.

Once numbers are read in, of course, they are represented in binary format in memory, and all the basic arithmetic and mathematical calculations are carried out internally in base 2. PHP also has a number of functions for translating between different bases, which are summarized in Table 27-2.

Table 27-2: Base Conversion Functions

Function	Behavior
BinDec()	Takes a single string argument representing a binary (base 2) integer, and returns a string representation of that number in base 10.
DecBin()	Like BinDec(), but converts from base 10 to base 2.
OctDec()	Like BinDec(), but converts from base 8 to base 10.
DecOct()	Like BinDec(), but converts from base 10 to base 8.

Continued

Table 27-2 *(continued)*

Function	Behavior
HexDec()	Like BinDec(), but converts from base 16 to base 10.
DecHex()	Like BinDec(), but converts from base 10 to base 16.
baseconvert()	Takes a string argument (the integer to be converted) and two integer arguments (the original base, and the desired base). Returns a string representing the converted number — digits higher than 9 (from 10 to 35) are represented by the letters a–z. Both the original and desired bases must be in the range 2–36.

All the base-conversion functions are special-purpose, converting from one particular base to another, except for base_convert(), which accepts an arbitrary start base and destination base. Here's an example of base_convert() in action:

```
function display_bases($start_string, $start_base)
{
  for ($new_base = 2; $new_base <= 36; $new_base++)
    {
      $converted =
        base_convert($start_string, $start_base, $new_base);
        print("$start_string in base $start_base
              is $converted in base $new_base<BR>");
    }
}

display_bases("1jj", 20);
```

This code yields the browser output:

```
1jj in base 20 is 1100011111 in base 2
1jj in base 20 is 1002121 in base 3
1jj in base 20 is 30133 in base 4
1jj in base 20 is 11144 in base 5
1jj in base 20 is 3411 in base 6
1jj in base 20 is 2221 in base 7
1jj in base 20 is 1437 in base 8
1jj in base 20 is 1077 in base 9
1jj in base 20 is 799 in base 10
1jj in base 20 is 667 in base 11
1jj in base 20 is 567 in base 12
1jj in base 20 is 496 in base 13
1jj in base 20 is 411 in base 14
1jj in base 20 is 384 in base 15
1jj in base 20 is 31f in base 16
1jj in base 20 is 2d0 in base 17
1jj in base 20 is 287 in base 18
1jj in base 20 is 241 in base 19
```

```
1jj in base 20 is 1jj in base 20
1jj in base 20 is 1h1 in base 21
1jj in base 20 is 1e7 in base 22
1jj in base 20 is 1bh in base 23
1jj in base 20 is 197 in base 24
1jj in base 20 is 16o in base 25
1jj in base 20 is 14j in base 26
1jj in base 20 is 12g in base 27
1jj in base 20 is 10f in base 28
1jj in base 20 is rg in base 29
1jj in base 20 is qj in base 30
1jj in base 20 is po in base 31
1jj in base 20 is ov in base 32
1jj in base 20 is o7 in base 33
1jj in base 20 is nh in base 34
1jj in base 20 is mt in base 35
1jj in base 20 is m7 in base 36
```

Notice that although all the base-conversion functions take string arguments and return string values, you can use decimal numerical arguments and rely on PHP's type conversion (but see the cautionary note that follows). In other words, both DecBin("1234") and DecBin(1234) will yield the same result.

A Glimpse behind the Curtain

How are built-in PHP functions really implemented? This is likely to be of interest only to C programmers and/or those who care about the inner workings of PHP, but we thought that it might be revealing to see why so many PHP functions work just like their C counterparts.

What follows is the actual implementation for the PHP function ceil, which is intended to convert a double to the smallest integer that is greater than or equal to it.

```
PHP_FUNCTION(ceil)
{
  zval **value;

  if (ARG_COUNT(ht)!=1||getParametersEx(1,&value)==FAILURE) {
            WRONG_PARAM_COUNT;
  }
    convert_scalar_to_number_ex(value);

    if ((*value)->type == IS_DOUBLE) {
      RETURN_LONG((long)ceil((*value)->value.dval));
        } else if ((*value)->type == IS_LONG) {
          RETURN_LONG((*value)->value.lval);
        }
    RETURN_FALSE;
}
```

Continued

Continued

Although the capitalized portions (including the `PHP_FUNCTION` declaration) are macros-specific to the PHP framework, much of the body of this code is straight C. The code might look dense and confusing at first, but most of the action has to do with PHP's special treatment of types. Here is roughly what is happening, in order:

1. The arguments that `ceil()` was called with are retrieved and counted—if the count is anything other than 1, the function call returns with an error.

2. The single argument is converted to a number if it is a scalar type other than a number—this handles the possibility of string arguments, as in `ceil("5.4")`.

3. Now the numerical argument is tested to see whether it is a PHP long (aka integer) or a PHP double. If it turns out to be a long, the value as a long is returned.

4. The interesting case is if the value is a PHP double. If so, the C double value is extracted, it is run through the C function ceil, the result is converted to a C long; then that value is wrapped up and returned as a PHP long.

In other words, the PHP implementation of `ceil` is simply the C function `ceil`, wrapped up in a lot of type conversion and argument checking. This is the case with many of PHP's functions that have exact analogues in C.

 Caution   Don't confuse the read formats of numbers with their representations as strings for the purposes of base conversion. For example, although 10 in base 16 is the number 16 in base 10, the expression `HexDec(0x10)` evaluates to the string `"22"`. Why? There are really three conversions happening: when `0x10` is read (converts from hex to internal binary), when the argument is auto-converted (from internal binary number to the decimal string `"16"`), and in the operation of the function (from assumed base 16 to decimal `"22"`). If you want just one conversion, the desired expression is `HexDec("10")`.

 Note   The base conversion functions expect their string arguments to be integers, not floating-point numbers. That means you can't use these functions to convert a binary 10.1 to a decimal 2.5.

Exponents and Logarithms

PHP includes the standard exponential and logarithmic functions, in both base 10 and base e varieties (shown in Table 27-3).

Unlike with `exp()` and the base e, there is no single-argument function to raise 10 to a given power, but in its place you can use the two-argument function `pow()` with 10 as the first argument.

You can verify that exponential and power functions of the same base are inverses of each other, by testing an identity like this:

```
$test_449 = 449.0;
$test_449 = pow(10, exp(log(log10($test_449))));
print("test_449 is $test_449<BR>");
```

which gives the browser output:

```
test_449 is 449
```

Table 27-3: Exponential Functions

Function	Behavior
pow()	Takes two numerical arguments and returns the first argument raised to the power of the second. The value of pow($x, $y) is x^y.
exp()	Takes a single argument and raises e to that power. The value of exp($x) is e^x.
log()	The "natural log" function. Takes a single argument and returns its base e logarithm. If $e^y = x$, then the value of log($x) is y.
log10()	Takes a single argument and returns its base-10 logarithm. If $10^y = x$, then the value of log10($x) is y.

Trigonometry

Although explaining the math behind the PHP functions in this chapter is beyond the scope of this book, we've made an exception just this once. (See the sidebar "Trigonometry in One Paragraph." Anyone who doesn't already know trigonometry will, of course, find the sidebar completely impenetrable, but we hope that those who know trig will at least be amused by how short it is.)

PHP offers the standard set of basic trigonometric functions as well as the constant M_PI, an approximation of pi as a double that prints as 3.1415926535898. This constant can be used anywhere you would use the literal number itself, and it is also interchangeable with the pi() function. (For other constants derived from pi, see the "Mathematical Constants" section at the beginning of this chapter.) Both of the following statements have the same result:

```
$my_pi = M_PI;
$my_pi = pi();
```

The basic trig functions are summarized in Table 27-4.

Table 27-4: Trigonometric Functions

Function	Behavior
pi()	Takes no arguments and returns an approximation of pi (3.1415926535898). Can be used interchangeably with the constant M_PI.
Sin()	Takes a numerical argument in radians and returns the sine of the argument as a double.
Cos()	Takes a numerical argument in radians and returns the cosine of the argument as a double.
Tan()	Takes a numerical argument in radians and returns the tangent of the argument as a double.
Asin()	Takes a numerical argument and returns the arcsine of the argument in radians. Inputs must be between −1.0 and 1.0 [inputs outside that range will return a result of NAN (for "not a number")]. Results are in the range -pi / 2 to pi / 2.

Continued

Table 27-4 *(continued)*

Function	Behavior
Acos()	Takes a numerical argument and returns the arccosine of the argument in radians. Inputs must be between −1.0 and 1.0 [inputs outside that range will return a result of NAN (for "not a number")]. Results are in the range 0 to pi.
Atan()	Takes a numerical argument and returns the arctangent of the argument in radians. Results are in the range -pi / 2 to pi / 2.
Atan2()	A variant of atan() that takes two arguments. Atan($y, $x) is identical to atan($y/$x) when $x is positive, but the quadrant of atan2's result depends on the signs of both $y and $x. Range of the result is from -pi to pi.

Rather than writing down a table of sample function results, let's resort to our usual trick of writing code that automatically displays examples as an HTML table. Listing 27-1 shows both a generalized function for displaying a set of one-argument functions applied to a set of numerical arguments and then the result of using this display function to make trigonometric example tables. The results are displayed in Figure 27-1.

Listing 27-1: **Displaying trigonometric function results**

```
<?php

function display_func_results($func_array, $input_array)
{
/* print a function header */
print("<TABLE BORDER=1><TR><TH>INPUT\\FUNCTION</TH>");
for($y = 0;
        $y < count($func_array);
        $y++)
    print("<TH>$func_array[$y]</TH>");
print("</TR><TR>");
/* print the rest of the table */
for($x = 0;
    $x < count($input_array);
    $x++)
  {
    /* print column entries for inputs */
    print("<TH>".
        sprintf("%.4f", $input_array[$x])
        ."</TH>");
    for($y = 0;
        $y < count($func_array);
        $y++)
      {
```

```
        $func_name = $func_array[$y];
        $input = $input_array[$x];
        print("<TD>");
        printf("%4.4f", $func_name($input));
        print("</TD>");
      }
    print("</TR><TR>");
    }
  print("</TR></TABLE>");
  }
?>

<HTML>
<HEAD>
<TITLE>Trigonometric Function Examples</TITLE>
</HEAD>
<BODY>

<?php
/* using the function displayer */
print("<H3>Trigonometric function examples</H3>");
display_func_results(array("sin", "cos", "tan"),
                     array(-1.25 * pi(),
                           -1.0 * pi(),
                           -0.75 * pi(),
                           -0.5 * pi(),
                           -0.25 * pi(),
                           0,
                           0.25 * pi(),
                           0.5 * pi(),
                           0.75 * pi(),
                           pi(),
                           1.25 * pi()));

?>
</BODY>
</HTML>
```

**Cross-
Reference**

The `display_func_results()` function of Listing 27-1 uses several tricks we've seen in previous chapters: using a string variable as the name of a function to call (covered near the end of Chapter 26) and using the string concatenation operator (.) to pull together a print string in the middle of a print statement (covered in Chapter 8).

Figure 27-1 shows the basic trigonometric functions over an input range of -5/4 pi to 5/4 pi and the basic inverse trigonometric function over inputs from -1.0 to 1.0. The very large tangent values are due to denominators that should theoretically be zero but instead differ slightly from zero due to rounding error.

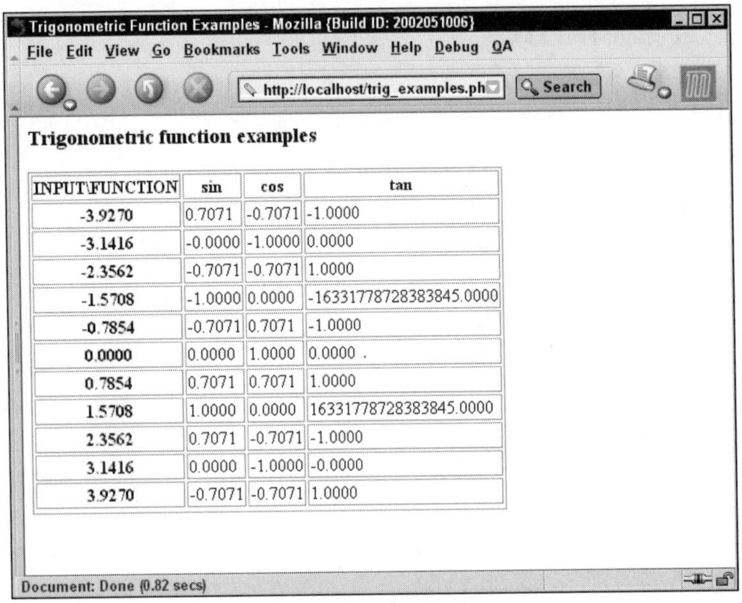

INPUT\FUNCTION	sin	cos	tan
-3.9270	0.7071	-0.7071	-1.0000
-3.1416	-0.0000	-1.0000	0.0000
-2.3562	-0.7071	-0.7071	1.0000
-1.5708	-1.0000	0.0000	-16331778728383845.0000
-0.7854	-0.7071	0.7071	-1.0000
0.0000	0.0000	1.0000	0.0000
0.7854	0.7071	0.7071	1.0000
1.5708	1.0000	0.0000	16331778728383845.0000
2.3562	0.7071	-0.7071	-1.0000
3.1416	0.0000	-1.0000	-0.0000
3.9270	-0.7071	-0.7071	1.0000

Figure 27-1: Trigonometric function examples

Trigonometry in One Paragraph

Imagine a circle with a radius of 1, centered at 0,0 in the coordinate plane. Start at the right-hand edge (at position (1,0)), and trace a certain distance along the circle counterclockwise. For example, a distance of 2 pi would take you once around the circle and back to your starting point. Clockwise travel counts as a negative distance. For any such distance, the sine function tells you the y-value of the coordinate you arrive at, the cosine function tells you the x-value of that coordinate, and the tangent function is a ratio of the two, from which you can infer the slope of the line tangent to the circle at that point. The functions arccosine, arcsine, and arctangent are in some sense inverses of their corresponding functions—they map back from an x, y, or y/x ratio to the distance of a circular trip that would arrive at that x-coordinate, y-coordinate, or ratio thereof. Because adding a multiple of 2 pi to any distance brings you around to the same point again, these inverse functions might have an infinite number of answers per input, making them ill-defined—instead, they are restricted to a range corresponding to one particular trip around half of the circle and so have well-defined results.

Arbitrary Precision (BC)

The integer and double types are fine for most of the mathematical tasks that arise in Web scripting, but each instance of these types is stored in a fixed amount of computer memory, and so the size and precision of the numbers these types can represent is inherently limited. Although the exact range of these types may depend on the architecture of your server machine, integers typically range from $-2^{31} - 1$ to $2^{31} - 1$, and doubles can represent about 13 to 14 decimal digits of precision. For tasks that require greater range or precision, PHP offers the *arbitrary-precision* math functions (also known as *BC functions*, from the name of the Unix-based, arbitrary-precision calculating utility).

Note
Especially if you compiled PHP yourself, the arbitrary-precision functions may not have been included in the compilation—you need to have included the flag --enable-bcmath at configuration time. To check whether the functions are present, try evaluating bcadd("1", "1")—if you get an unbound function error, you will have to reconfigure and recompile PHP.

Instead of using the fixed-length numerical types, the BC functions have strings as arguments and return values. Because strings in PHP are limited only by available memory, numbers can be as long as you like. The underlying computations are performed in decimal and are done much as you would do them with pen and paper (if you were very fast and very patient). When operating with integers, the BC functions are exact and use as many digits as needed; when operating with floating-point numbers, computations are done to as many decimal places as you specify. The BC functions are summarized in Table 27-5.

Most of the functions take an optional scale factor (an integer) as a final argument, which determines how many decimal places will be in the result. If such an argument is not supplied, the scale is the default scale, which, in turn, can be set by calling bcscale(). The default for the default value (that is, if bcscale() has never been called) can also be set in the initialization file php.ini.

Table 27-5: Arbitrary-Precision (BC) Math Functions

Function	Behavior
bcadd()	Takes two string arguments representing numbers, and an optional integer scale parameter. Returns the sum of the first two arguments as a string, with the number of decimal places in the result determined by the scale parameter. If no scale parameter is supplied, the default scale is used (which is settable by bcscale()).
bcsub()	Similar to bcadd(), except that it returns the subtraction of the second argument from the first.
bcmul()	Similar to bcadd() but returns the product of its arguments.
bcdiv()	Similar to bcadd() but returns the result of dividing the first argument by the second.
bcmod()	Returns the modulus (remainder) of the first argument as divided by the second. Because the return type is "integral," no scale argument is taken.

Continued

Table 27-5 *(continued)*

Function	Behavior
bcpow()	Raises the first argument to the power of the second argument. The number of decimal places in the result is set by the scale factor if supplied.
bcsqrt()	Returns the square root of its argument, with number of decimal places set by the optional scale factor.
bcscale()	Sets the default scale factor for subsequent BC function calls.

An arbitrary-precision example

Here's an example of using the arbitrary-precision functions for exact integer arithmetic. The following code:

```
for ($x = 1; $x < 25; $x++) {
    print("$x raised to the power of $x is " . bcpow($x, $x) . "<BR>");
}
```

will print like this:

```
1 raised to the power of 1 is 1
2 raised to the power of 2 is 4
3 raised to the power of 3 is 27
4 raised to the power of 4 is 256
5 raised to the power of 5 is 3125
6 raised to the power of 6 is 46656
7 raised to the power of 7 is 823543
8 raised to the power of 8 is 16777216
9 raised to the power of 9 is 387420489
10 raised to the power of 10 is 10000000000
11 raised to the power of 11 is 285311670611
12 raised to the power of 12 is 8916100448256
13 raised to the power of 13 is 302875106592253
14 raised to the power of 14 is 11112006825558016
15 raised to the power of 15 is 437893890380859375
16 raised to the power of 16 is 18446744073709551616
17 raised to the power of 17 is 827240261886336764177
18 raised to the power of 18 is 39346408075296537575424
19 raised to the power of 19 is 1978419655660313589123979
20 raised to the power of 20 is 104857600000000000000000000
21 raised to the power of 21 is 5842587018385982521381124421
22 raised to the power of 22 is 341427877364219557396646723584
23 raised to the power of 23 is 20880467999847912034355032910567
24 raised to the power of 24 is 1333735776850284124449081472843776
25 raised to the power of 25 is 88817841970012523233890533447265625
```

If we had used the regular PHP integer type for this computation, the integers would have *overflowed* well before the end, and the rest of the loop would have been calculated in approximate floating point.

Converting code to arbitrary-precision

Let's see what it's like to take an existing piece of mathematical code and retrofit it to use the arbitrary-precision functions.

The following function approximates pi, using the series approximation:

$$\text{sqrt} (12 - (12/2^2) + (12/3^2) - (12/4^2) + (12/5^2) - \ldots)$$

(As we'll see, this series does not converge fast enough for our purposes, but it has the virtue of being a simple formula.)

```
function pi_approx($iterations, $print_frequency)
{
  $squared_approx = 12;
  $next_sign = -1;
  $denom = 2;

  for ($iter = 0; $iter < $iterations; $iter++)
    {
      $squared_approx += $next_sign * 12/(pow($denom,2));
      $denom++;
      $next_sign = - $next_sign;
      if ($denom % $print_frequency == 0)
        {
          $estimate = sqrt($squared_approx);
          print("$denom iterations: $estimate<BR>");
        }
    }
}
```

In addition to performing the calculation itself, this code periodically prints its current estimate of pi, so we can see how we are doing. We can call it as follows and then print PHP's value for comparison:

```
pi_approx(10000, 1000);
print("PHP value: " . pi() . "<BR>");
```

The result looks like:

```
1000 iterations: 3.1415936094742
2000 iterations: 3.1415928924416
3000 iterations: 3.1415927597285
4000 iterations: 3.1415927132878
5000 iterations: 3.1415926917946
6000 iterations: 3.14159268012
7000 iterations: 3.141592673081
8000 iterations: 3.1415926685124
9000 iterations: 3.1415926653804
10000 iterations: 3.1415926631401
PHP value: 3.1415926535898
```

Now, not only are we not that close, but we can't hope to be more accurate than PHP's value for pi, because that already uses all the precision available in the double type.

To convert this to an arbitrary-precision version, we must replace all the math functions and operators that need precision with their BC counterparts, like so:

```
function pi_approx_bc($iterations, $print_frequency, $scale)
{
  $squared_approx = "12";
  $next_sign = -1;
  $denom = 2;
  for ($iter = 0; $iter < $iterations; $iter++)
    {
      $squared_approx
        = bcadd(
            $squared_approx,
            bcmul($next_sign,
                bcdiv(12,
                    bcpow($denom,
                        2,
                        $scale),
                    $scale),
                $scale),
            $scale);
      $denom++;
      $next_sign = - $next_sign;
      if ($denom % $print_frequency == 0)
        {
          $estimate = bcsqrt($squared_approx,$scale);
          print("$denom iterations: $estimate<BR>");
        }
    }
}
```

Notice that although the BC functions want string arguments, we can as always use regular numbers in their places and rely on PHP to convert the arguments to strings for us. Also notice that we did not bother making the numerical computations that do not require great precision into BC computations (for instance, we still have $denom++ rather than bcadd($denom, 1). Finally, we added a scale argument to the entire function, which turns the decimal precision of each BC function it calls.

Unfortunately, both your authors and our browsers ran out of patience with this series before it got even got to the level of precision of PHP's value. Here are some late results of calling pi_approx_bc(1250000, 50000, 50):

```
50000 iterations: 3.1415926539717727412972355106834772637129768926596
100000 iterations: 3.1415926536852871592459876925439059492714620533713
150000 iterations: 3.1415926536322348395623164950392220427293321753802
[..]
1150000 iterations: 3.141592653590515303104552554096025800032655499550033
1200000 iterations: 3.141592653590456384611480874034589189444055471472113
1250000 iterations: 3.141592653590404393933040187100721577035010223883043
```

The correct digits in the preceding output are about one digit shy of the PHP value. This is the fault of the series we chose rather than the arbitrary-precision libraries — with a more sophisticated and speedier approximation series, you too can serve up millions of digits of pi to your eager audience.

Somewhat more satisfyingly, evaluating:

```
print("The square root of two is " . bcsqrt(2, 40));
```

gives us many more digits of precision than we could get using doubles:

```
The square root of two is 1.4142135623730950488016887242096980785696
```

Summary

Although the primary purpose of PHP is not to do mathematics, it has a pretty comprehensive set of mathematical functions covering basic arithmetic, pseudo-random number generation, base conversion, trigonometry, exponents and logarithms, and a built-in module for doing arbitrary-precision arithmetic.

We covered the numerical types and the most basic functions in Chapter 10, and covered the remaining topics in this chapter. Table 27-6 is a tabular summary of the operators and functions discussed both in Chapter 10 and this chapter.

Table 27-6: Summary of PHP Math Operators and Functions

Category	Description
Arithmetic operators	Operators +, -, *, /, % perform basic arithmetic on integers and doubles.
Incrementing operators	The ++ and -- operators change the values of numerical variables, increasing them by one or decreasing them by one (respectively). The value of the postincrement form ($var++) is the same as the variable's value before the change; the value of the preincrement form (++$var) is the variable's value after the change.
Assignment operators	Each arithmetic operator (like +) has a corresponding assignment operator (+=). The expression $count += 5 is equivalent to $count = $count + 5.
Comparison operators	These operators (<, <=, >, >=, ==, !=) compare two numbers and return either true or false. The === operator is true if and only if its arguments are equal and of the same type.
Basic math functions	floor(), ceil(), and round() convert doubles to integers, min() and max() take the minimum and maximum of their numerical arguments, and abs() is the absolute value function.
Base-conversion functions	Special-purpose functions (OctDec(), DecOct(), BinDec(), DecBin(), HexDec(), DecHex()) convert between particular pairs of bases, whereas base_convert() translates between arbitrary bases.

Continued

Table 27-6 *(continued)*

Category	Description
Exponential functions	Functions having to do with raising numbers to powers or the inverse: `log()` (natural log), `log10()` (base-10 log), `exp()` (e raised to the power of the argument), and `pow()` (first argument to the power of the second).
Trigonometric functions	Functions having to do with angular measures: `pi()` (and the equivalent constant `M_PI`), `sin()`, `cos()`, `tan()`, `acos()`, `asin()`, `atan()`, and `atan2()` (a two-argument version of `atan()`).
Arbitrary-precision (BC) functions	Functions that do arithmetic on arbitrary-length strings representing decimal integers and floating-point numbers: `bdadd()`, `bcsub()`, `bcmult()`, `bcdiv()`, `bcmod()`, `bcpow()`, `bcsqrt()`. Most of these functions take an optional scale parameter specifying the number of decimal points of precision desired—the default for that parameter is settable using `bcscale()`.

✦   ✦   ✦

PEAR

The PHP Extension and Application Repository (PEAR) is a broad effort with many component parts, collectively aimed at expanding the usefulness and reliability of the PHP language. With PEAR, developers should be able to write more capable software more quickly and with greater reliability.

The most useful and best-known element of PEAR, its package-management system, attempts to reduce the frequency with which PHP developers reinvent the wheel. Its main part is an online database of code modules, accessible to anyone via an automated process, that give the PHP language special capabilities. PEAR modules, for example, enable PHP programmers to access LDAP directories and open files in the Ogg Vorbis format without writing utility classes for those jobs. Programmers using the PEAR packages can focus on the functionality of their creations, rather than wasting time struggling with nuts-and-bolts problems.

The PEAR initiative also includes a set of rules about how code is to be written — a style guide, if you like. The PEAR coding style rules are meant to govern modules contributed to the PEAR archive, but in fact apply well to all PHP work. You could do worse than to apply the PEAR coding style rules to all your PHP programs.

PEAR has a sister project, the PHP Extension Community Library (PECL, pronounced *pickle*). PECL modules are extensions to PHP itself, rather than just PHP modules that can be imported into PHP programs as needed. Together, PEAR and PECL make PHP much more capable and enable many more people to participate in the development of the language.

What Is PEAR?

There are many common tasks in PHP that require or strongly benefit from libraries of functions. There are many Web sites where PHP community members offer code they've written, but how do you know the code is good, will be maintained and extended, and doesn't have any odd quirks or even malicious features? The PEAR project offers a large and growing library of known-good, well-maintained, well-documented PHP code which has passed many quality inspections — all free for the taking.

The PEAR project began in 1999, shortly after PHP itself came into being. It's a community-driven initiative dedicated to generating open-source code that improves PHP. PEAR packages are built on top of the standard PHP functions, and are often written in an Object-Oriented style (for example, classes). You include these modules from your own PHP script with an `include()` or `require()` statement, as you would any other PHP function library or class.

For the most part, PEAR is to PHP as the Comprehensive Perl Archive Network (CPAN) is to Perl. It has many parts, but the best-known and most frequently used is a library of open-source PHP code modules that may be accessed in an automated way. The PEAR module management system makes it easy for you to keep a server's PHP installation up-to-date and outfitted with the elements it needs to do its job (for example, with the PEAR DB classes for standardized database access and the PEAR LDAP classes for accessing a corporate directory). You can run the package manager as an automated routine that checks for updated versions of your installed packages every week, if you like.

Other parts of the PEAR project include:

✦ A set of coding standards that specifically applies to PHP modules distributed by PEAR.

✦ The PHP Foundation Classes (PFC), which are a few especially worthy PEAR classes distributed with the main PHP package.

✦ Various code archives and mailing lists for the people doing PEAR module development work.

The PHP Extension Community Library (PECL) is a collection of PHP extensions (written in C as all PHP extensions are) which are relatively rarely used and therefore do not need to be part of the core PHP distribution (which was threatening to become too large and unwieldy). PECL used to be part of PEAR, but has been split off for separate management. PECL and PEAR share the same automated distribution tool, though, and so remain related projects. The key difference between PEAR modules and PECL modules: PEAR modules are written in PHP, and may be included in PHP programs as required. PECL modules are written in C, and may be incorporated into the PHP engine itself by the normal process of recompiling.

The PEAR Package System

The PEAR package system is an archive of compressed files (tar files compressed with gzip), each of which contains a series of PHP files and a manifest file in XML format. Each archive, when incorporated into a PHP installation on a server (by means of the automated package-management system that's discussed later in this chapter), adds to the overall collection of functions and classes a developer can invoke in his or her code. Widely used packages handle database abstraction, the interpretation of various file formats, the implementation of industry-specific algorithms, and all kinds of convenience functions. The universe of PEAR packages is large and expanding, and because the packages are of such high quality you should make use of them in your own code if you can.

The PEAR homepage is `http://pear.php.net`.

A sampling of PEAR packages

Here's a much-abridged list of PEAR packages. The package name generally describes its function:

- ✦ Auth — User authentication
- ✦ Benchmark — Performance calibration
- ✦ DB — Database connectivity
- ✦ Calendar — Calendar objects and functions
- ✦ Archive_Tar — Interaction with tar files
- ✦ Archive_Zip — Interaction with Zip files
- ✦ HTTP — Manipulation of the HTTP protocol
- ✦ Image_Barcode — Barcode generation
- ✦ I18N — Internationalization tools
- ✦ Log — Logging
- ✦ Mail — Interaction with POP, IMAP, and SMTP
- ✦ Oggvorbis — Interpretation of the Ogg Vorbis open-source audio file format
- ✦ Tree — Tree structures for organizing objects
- ✦ SOAP — Implementation of the SOAP protocol

Aside from enabling PHP server administrators to incrementally adjust the capabilities of their systems, the PEAR package system is a way of dividing the labor involved in expanding the capabilities of PHP. Each of the many packages in the system — there are more than 250 as of this writing — has a separate development team behind it, complete with a project lead and several other contributors. Individual packages have version numbers and (usually) their own supporting documentation. Packages may depend on other packages (meaning that the depended-upon package must be installed); managing these dependencies is one function of the PEAR package-management tool.

How the PEAR database works

The PEAR database serves two purposes: it is by design accessible to human readers as well as to the PEAR package-management client. You can use an ordinary Web browser to navigate around the HTML documents at the PEAR site (http://pear.php.net), or you can use the package-management client to interface with it via a Web service interface.

Either way, the PEAR repository is organized as a tree, with related packages grouped into hierarchies (though hierarchical relationships do not necessarily indicate dependency relationships among packages). The PEAR community manages what goes into the tree, determining when development on a particular package has progressed far enough to warrant a new release into the publicly available repository.

The Package Manager

If, like most people, you're planning to use the PEAR repository as a resource rather than as an entity to which to contribute, your main interaction with it will be through the PEAR Package Manager. The package manager is a command-line program that interacts with the online repository and allows you to download, install, and uninstall PEAR packages according to your requirements. This remainder of this section shows you how to get and use the PEAR Package Manager.

Tip   Remember that if you just want to use PEAR's `DB`, `Net_Socket`, `Net_SMTP`, `Mail`, `XML_Parser`, or `phpUnit` modules, you do not need to install the PEAR Package Manager or any packages! These packages, which are collectively referred to as the PEAR Foundation Classes, are bundled with PHP.

Installing PEAR Package Manager on Linux

On a Linux machine with PHP4.3 or a later version installed, there's no work to be done. The PEAR Package Manager is by default already in place with your PHP distribution, and available for use.

If you're running an older version of PHP under Linux, you'll need to install the PEAR Package Manager by means of a two-part command. The command looks like this:

```
$ lynx -source http://go-pear.org/ | php
```

That command opens up the specified URL (which you can examine yourself through an ordinary Web browser) with Lynx, a text-only HTTP client (certain Linux distributions have similarly functional programs with different names, such as `links` under Red Hat Linux). The URL contains text that defines a PHP program. The command line pipes that text to the PHP engine, thus allowing it to be interpreted.

Installing PEAR Package Manager on Windows

On a Microsoft Windows machine with PHP4.3 or newer installed, there is a file called `go-pear.bat` in the PHP home directory (typically `C:\php`). Before you can use the PEAR Package Manager, you must run `go-pear.bat` and let it make some configuration changes to your system.

Here's what it looks like when `go-pear.bat` runs:

```
C:\PHP>go-pear.bat
Welcome to go-pear!

Go-pear will install the 'pear' command and all the files needed
by it.  This command is your tool for PEAR installation and
maintenance.

Go-pear also lets you download and install the PEAR packages
bundled with PHP: DB, Net_Socket, Net_SMTP, Mail, XML_Parser,
phpUnit.

If you wish to abort, press Control-C now, or press Enter to
continue:
```

Following the directions in the code, we press `Enter` to continue and get the following:

```
HTTP proxy (http://user:password@proxy.myhost.com:port), or
Enter for none::
```

As we have no proxy, we hit `Enter` again and get the following:

```
Below is a suggested file layout for your new PEAR installation.
To change individual locations, type the number in front of
```

```
The directory.  Type 'all' to change all of them or simply
press Enter to accept these locations.

   1. Installation prefix          : C:\PHP
   2. Binaries directory           : $prefix
   3. PHP code directory ($php_dir) : $prefix\pear
   4. Documentation base directory : $php_dir\docs
   5. Data base directory          : $php_dir\data
   6. Tests base directory         : $php_dir\tests
   7. php.exe path                 : C:\PHP\cli\php.exe

1-7, 'all' or Enter to continue:
```

We hit Enter to accept the default locations. It then lets us know that some PEAR packages are already present on the system:

```
The following PEAR packages are bundled with PHP: DB,
Net_Socket, Net_SMTP, Mail, XML_Parser, phpUnit.

Would you like to install these as well? [Y/n] : Y
```

Of course we would:

```
Loading zlib: ok
Using local package: PEAR.............ok
Using local package: Archive_Tar......ok
Using local package: Console_Getopt....ok
Using local package: XML_RPC..........ok
Bootstrapping: PEAR..................(local) ok
Bootstrapping: Archive_Tar...........(local) ok
Bootstrapping: Console_Getopt........(local) ok
Using local package: DB..............ok
Using local package: Net_Socket.......ok
Using local package: Net_SMTP.........ok
Using local package: Mail.............ok
Using local package: XML_Parser.......ok
Downloading package: phpUnit..........ok
Extracting installer..................ok
install ok: PEAR 1.3b1
install ok: Archive_Tar 1.1
install ok: Console_Getopt 1.0
install ok: XML_RPC 1.0.4
install ok: DB 1.5.0RC2
install ok: Net_Socket 1.0.1
install ok: Net_SMTP 1.2.3
install ok: Mail 1.1.2
install ok: XML_Parser 1.0.1
install ok: PHPUnit 1.0.0-alpha2


*****************************************************************

WARNING!  The include_path defined in the currently used php.ini
```

```
does not contain the PEAR PHP directory you just specified:
<C:\PHP\pear>
If the specified directory is also not in the include_path used
by your scripts, you will have problems getting any PEAR
packages working.


Would you like to alter php.ini <c:\winnt\php.ini>? [Y/n] : Y
```

That modifies the `php.ini` file, so the PEAR packages are accessible by the PHP engine.

```
php.ini <c:\winnt\php.ini> include_path updated.

Current include path            : .;c:\php4\pear
Configured directory            : C:\PHP\pear
Currently used php.ini (guess) : c:\winnt\php.ini
Press Enter to continue:

The 'pear' command is now at your service at C:\PHP\pear.bat
```

Brilliant — the installation worked. It warns us, though, that the Windows PATH isn't really set for maximum convenience:

```
** The 'pear' command is not in your PATH, so you need to
** use 'C:\PHP\pear.bat' until you have added
** 'C:\PHP' to your PATH environment variable.

Run it without parameters to see the available actions, try
'pear list' to see what packages are installed, or 'pear help'
for help.

For more information about PEAR, see:

  http://pear.php.net/faq.php

http://cvs.php.net/co.php/pearweb/doc/pear_package_manager.txt?p
=1
  http://pear.php.net/manual/

Thanks for using go-pear!
```

We're set at this point, but the installation program calls attention to a Windows Registry hack we can use for greater convenience if we want:

```
* WINDOWS ENVIRONMENT VARIABLES *
For convenience, a REG file is available under
C:\PHP\PEAR_ENV.reg .
This file creates ENV variables for the current user.

Double-click this file to add it to the current user registry.

Press any key to continue . . .
```

The PEAR Package Manager is installed and available for use at this point.

Updating the Package Manager

Later, you may want to go through the `go-pear` procedure again to update your system and make sure it's aware of the latest contents of the PEAR repository. You may want to do this every few months if you use PEAR packages very frequently or don't reinstall PHP very often. However, most people will find that getting a new version of the PEAR Package Manager every time you install a new version of PHP is frequent enough. The basic procedure is to go to `http://go-pear.org` and save the file there—there is only one—as `go-pear.php` in a directory that's accessible to your PHP compiler.

Figure 28-1 shows the `go-pear` Web site.

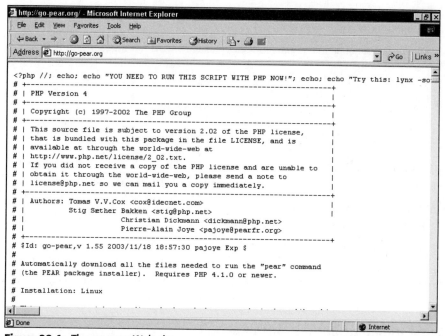

Figure 28-1: The go-pear Web site

After saving `go-pear.php`, go to the command line and run this command:

```
php go-pear.php
```

You should see output similar to the code above. With that done, you're again ready to make use of the PEAR Package Manager.

Using the Manager

The PEAR Package Manager has a command-line interface that is common to all versions of PHP. The instructions in this section apply equally to all Unix variants (including Linux) and to Microsoft Windows.

The key executable of the PEAR Package Manager is `pear`. It resides in your PHP home directory, alongside the PHP interpreter itself.

Automatic package installation

Once you have PEAR installed and updated, you can install any package you've downloaded. The generic syntax for doing an automatic installation of a package is this:

```
pear install <package>
```

In that syntax, `<package>` is the name of a PEAR package. All available packages are listed at `http://pear.php.net/packages.php`. You can also run:

```
pear remote-list
```

to see what's available.

Here's an example of installing the PEAR DB package via the automatic PEAR Package Manager method:

```
C:\PHP>pear install DB
downloading DB-1.5.0RC2.tgz ...
Starting to download DB-1.5.0RC2.tgz (68,128 bytes)
.................done: 68,128 bytes
install ok: DB 1.5.0RC2
```

Automatic package removal

Uninstalling a package is just as easy as adding one. The generic syntax looks like this:

```
pear uninstall <package>
```

To uninstall the DB package, then, we'd do this:

```
C:\PHP>pear uninstall DB
Uninstall ok: DB
```

If you're not sure what packages are installed locally, run the following command to find out:

```
pear list
```

Semi-automatic package installation

If, for some reason, you downloaded a PEAR package in the form of a `.tgz` file, you can later use the PEAR Package Manager to install it, even if there's no connection to the Internet available. You just point the `pear` command at the local file, as follows:

```
pear install HTML_BBCodeParser-1.0.tgz
```

Using PEAR packages in your scripts

Once you've installed the PEAR modules you wish to use, you should make sure the location is included in the `include_path` variable of your `php.ini` file. This location can be tricky — it will probably be `/usr/local/lib/php` on Unix servers and whatever you specified during the `go-pear` procedure on a Windows server. Once you've done that, you can include these libraries from any PHP script with a normal include directive:

```
<?php
include_once('Mail.php')

// Your code which uses PEAR Mail functions here

?>
```

PHP Foundation Classes (PFC)

The PEAR Foundation Classes (PFC) are a subset of the PEAR module repository. The modules that are part of the PFC are written to an especially high standard of quality, have been extensively tested, and are considered very stable and reliable. The PFC are distributed with PHP itself, so you do not have to download or install them separately. As of PHP5, the members of the PFC are these packages: DB, Net_Socket, Net_SMTP, Mail, XML_Parser, and phpUnit.

In writing modules for the PFC, programmers must aim for broad compatibility. They should avoid using any resource that's particular to a specific operating system, and try to take input and give output in the most generic possible form (for example, in plain text rather than as SOAP-formatted messages). Programmers also need to keep in mind possible future developments in PHP itself — information that can be gleaned from mailing lists and other community resources — and write their software so it is unlikely to break when new releases appear.

PHP Extension Code Library (PECL)

The PHP Extension Community Library (PECL) is conceptually very similar to PEAR, and in fact they share the PEAR Package Manager infrastructure (that is, PECL modules can be accessed and installed via the PEAR Package Manager). The main difference is that PECL is concerned with extensions to PHP itself, in the form of C modules that attach to the PHP engine. As C programs, extensions typically execute faster and more efficiently than the modules contained in the PEAR repository.

PECL used to be called the PEAR Extension Code Library and was spun off from PEAR in October 2003. The new PECL homepage is http://pecl.php.net.

The PEAR Coding Style

Newspapers (as well as publishers of books!) spend a lot of time and effort establishing style rules that govern how their writers use language. Are people identified by their last names (as in *The Washington Post*) or by their honorifics and last names (as in *The Economist* and *The New York Times*)? It's a matter of style.

The same sorts of questions arise among programmers, except that the issues at stake are usually matters of formatting rather than syntax. Where do brackets go, and how is code laid out on a page? It's important to have standard (if arbitrary) answers to these questions, because a standard style can be a real aid to error-spotting and maintainability.

PEAR defines its style rules online at http://pear.php.net/manual/en/standards.php. This section calls attention to some of the most important ones.

Indenting, whitespace, and line length

Code is much easier to read if you use indentation to indicate the relationship among lines of code that are tied together in a common functional block, as well as whitespace to logically group elements. The following code is hard to read, though it will run perfectly fine.

```
switch ($flag) {
case 1:
doWork();
break;
case 2:
doOtherWork();
break;
default:
doNothing();
break;
}
```

On the other hand, this code:

```
switch ($flag) {

case 1:
    doWork();
    break;

case 2:
    doOtherWork();
    break;

default:
    doNothing();
    break;
}
```

is both functional and more easily understood. Spotting syntax errors is hard enough; don't make the job harder by clumping your code together sloppily.

One of the big religious arguments in programming is the number of spaces to indent each new code block — some people insist that two saves space, others swear by four, and some outliers actually employ eight-space indents (the horror!). Over time and in groups, four has come to be a standard compromise position, adopted by many open source projects — including PEAR. If you want your code to be accepted into PEAR, it must use four-space indents.

Because different editors on different platforms interpret tab characters differently, it's recommended that you use groups of four space characters in all places you would, under other circumstances, use a tab character.

Formatting control structures

Control structures — like if, if/else, if/elseif, and switch statements — can be confusing if not properly formatted. PEAR has recommended styles for all of these language constructs.

if Statements

A simple two-test if statement should be formatted like this:

```
if ((condition1) && (condition2)) {
    doSomething();
}
```

Note that the opening bracket appears on the same line as the conditions (so-called Kernighan and Ritchie, or K&R, braces), and that there are brackets even though there is only one line of code in the conditional block. That way, the fact that it's a block is obvious, and there's no need to remember to add them when further lines of code are added in the future. Also note that there should be a space between a conditional statement and the expression being tested.

if/else Statements

An if/else statement builds on the basic if format:

```
if ((condition1) && (condition2)) {
    doSomething();
} else {
    doSomethingElse();
}
```

The else appears on the same line as the closing bracket that terminates the if block.

if/elseif Statements

An if/elseif statement looks just like an if/else statement in terms of formatting:

```
if ((condition1) && (condition2)) {
    doSomething();
} elseif {
    doSomethingElse();
}
```

switch Statements

Switch statements rely on whitespace and indentation to make code blocks obvious:

```
switch ($flag) {

case 1:
    doWork();
    break;

case 2:
    doOtherWork();
    break;

default:
    doNothing();
    break;
}
```

Formatting functions and function calls

Much of PHP is concerned with defining functions, then making calls to them; and obviously code libraries like PEAR will be almost all functions. Properly formatting your functions can make it more obvious what's going on and can therefore make debugging and maintenance easier.

The PEAR style rules mandate that functions be defined with both their beginning and ending braces flush with the left margin, like this:

```
function myFunction()
{

    // Function code goes here.

}
```

This makes function definitions (which use braces) stand out from conditional blocks (which also use braces). Furthermore, the standards require that code within the function be indented. Everything is indented at least four spaces; some segments may be indented further:

```
function myFunction()
{
    doSomething();
    if ($is) {
        doSomethingMore();
    }
}
```

If your function takes arguments, be sure to order them so that arguments with default values go at the end of the list, like this:

```
function myFunction($a, $b, $c='Default')
{
    doSomething();
    if ($is) {
        doSomethingMore();
    }
}
```

Also note that there should be no spaces between the name of the function and the parentheses containing arguments. Again, this helps visually distinguish functions (which use parentheses) from expressions (which also use parentheses).

It is important that functions return something. The return value will either be a value that resulted from the function's processing, or a Boolean value (true or false) to indicate success or failure.

Summary

In this chapter, you got an idea of the lengths to which the PHP community has gone to make it easy for you to have and use the latest packages that extend the capabilities of the language. PEAR exists to facilitate the ongoing development and widespread distribution of handy toolkits.

At the center of PEAR is its repository, an online database that contains the accumulated body of PEAR packages. This repository has an HTML interface as well as an XML_RPC (Web Services) interface, meaning that you can browse it manually or interact with it via a specialized command-line program: The PEAR Package Manager. The PEAR Package Manager allows you to quickly see what's in the PEAR repository, download what you want, and install some or all of what you download. Particularly important PEAR packages are part of the PHP Foundation Classes (PFC).

Another element of the PEAR community is a definition of a coding standard, which specifies how functions should be defined, comments placed, and brackets structured in various parts of PHP programs. It's meant to ease readability and make life easier for documentation writers.

PEAR shares its automated package-distribution scheme with PECL, which manages PHP extensions written in the C language.

PEAR represents an invaluable resource to PHP programmers of all levels. Make sure the PEAR Package Manager is installed on your PHP server, and make full use of its resources. When you're ready, join the development effort and contribute to the growth of PHP.

✦ ✦ ✦

Security

Security is not a joking matter," proclaim signs at airports everywhere. The same sign should be posted near your PHP server. Anyone connecting a server to the Internet must take proper security measures or risk loss of data or even money to the keystrokes of malicious crackers.

The mantra of the security-conscious site designer is: *Don't trust the network.* If you're worried about the security of your site, chant this mantra as you code your pages. Any information transmitted to your server via the network — be it a URL, data from an HTML form, or data on some other network port — should be treated as potentially hazardous. This chapter suggests several techniques for *sanitizing* incoming information. You should apply these techniques and spend some time trying to discover other potential hazards and ways to prevent them.

The second rule of thumb for a secure site is: *Minimize the damage.* What if the program you just wrote, which you are *sure* is secure, is actually vulnerable? Just to be on the safe side, limit the damage an intruder can cause after he or she has taken advantage of the vulnerability.

When visitors come to your site, they trust that it contains valid information, that it is not harmful to them or to their computers, and that any information they provide to it is handled properly. Interacting with a site, whether an e-business, recreational, or informational site, involves certain security risks for a visitor. As a site designer, it is your responsibility to protect visitors from these risks. Besides being sure their information is safe on your server, this means you should take measures to safeguard their information while it is in transit from their computers to your server.

But all this should not scare you away from putting your e-business online. The first section of this chapter describes some possible attacks against your server and ways to avoid them. We then discuss cryptographic techniques for protecting your data. At the end of this chapter, we list some Web sites that contain up-to-the-minute information on the latest cracker techniques. By watching these sites, you may learn of possible security vulnerabilities before an attacker does and, thereby, avoid disaster.

Possible Attacks

Connecting your server to the Internet is like setting up a storefront on a busy street. You're likely to have quite a few visitors, but if you're not careful, some less than desirable visitors may take advantage of you.

Site defacement

Often more embarrassing than harmful, site defacements are fairly common because the cracker has an opportunity to publicize his or her exploitation. Site defacements are sometimes left as calling cards by a cracker who entered a system by more complicated means.

It is possible to deface a badly designed Web site using only a Web browser. Take, for instance, the following program:

```php
<?php if (IsSet($_POST['visitor'])) {
  $visitor = $_POST['visitor'];
  $fp = fopen("database", "a");
  fwrite($fp, "<li>$visitor\n");
  fclose($fp); } ?>
<HTML>
<HEAD></HEAD>
<BODY>
<H1>Visitors to this site:</H1>
<OL>
<?php $fp = fopen("database", "r");
  print(fread($fp, filesize("database")));
  fclose($fp) ?>
</OL>
<HR>
<FORM><INPUT TYPE="TEXT" NAME="visitor">
<INPUT TYPE="SUBMIT" NAME="submit" VALUE="Sign in!">
</FORM>
</BODY>
</HTML>
```

This program implements a very rudimentary guest book. In reading this code, however, you should feel a bit uneasy. *Don't trust the network.* This program accepts form data that we expect to contain the visitor's name (in the variable $visitor) and stores it in a text file for display to subsequent visitors. For the inputs we expect, there is no trouble.

Now put on your script-kiddie hat for a moment and imagine what would happen if the input contained HTML tags. This simple program would blindly insert those tags into the pages it generates, and other visitors' browsers would interpret them as usual. One particularly malicious tag is the <SCRIPT> tag. A cracker wishing to deface this Web page could duplicate the page's appearance on his or her own server (www.badsite.com) and then sign into the guestbook with the name:

```
<SCRIPT LANGUAGE="JavaScript">
window.location="http://www.badsite.com/"</SCRIPT>
```

Crackers, script-kiddies, and other fiends

The term *hacker* is commonly used to describe individuals more correctly labeled crackers. Within the computer community, *crackers* are those who, through luck or skill, break into computer systems and cause damage. Hackers are those who can *hack* — read and write efficient (and often obscure) code in many languages. To a programmer, being labeled a hacker is an honor, whereas being labeled a cracker probably means he or she should start reading the Help Wanted section.

As if *cracker* was not sufficiently derogatory, young crackers who use tools and scripts they find on the Web are called *script-kiddies*. These budding lawbreakers often have little understanding of what they are actually doing. They are usually the culprits behind low-tech attacks such as site defacement. A fairly good indicator of the work of a script-kiddie is the excessive use of misspelling and capitalization, as in W3 R KOOL DOODz.

When visitors load the guest book, their browsers receive this tag and immediately begin loading the hacked site. With a little ingenuity, the cracker could then take advantage of the visitors' trust of your site to extract personal information such as passwords or credit card numbers.

The solution to this problem is to sanitize the input data. In this case, we want any characters that have special meaning to a browser to be translated into something harmless. Luckily, PHP provides a way to perform just such a translation. The function htmlspecialchars() converts the characters <, >, ", and & to their representations as HTML entities (such as <). We change the first part of our program to use this new function as follows:

```php
<?php if (IsSet($_POST['visitor'])) {
    $visitor = $_POST['visitor'];
    $fp = fopen("database", "a");
    $clean_visitor = htmlspecialchars($visitor);
    fwrite($fp, "<li>$clean_visitor\n");
    fclose($fp); } ?>
```

And we have patched a very significant security hole in our site.

Accessing source code

Even if your PHP source code isn't a trade secret, you should still protect it from exposure to the network. If an intruder can read your source code, then he or she need not experiment to find a weakness. Instead, the intruder can simply analyze the code, looking for common mistakes and other security holes. In general, the more helpful information you provide to potential intruders, the more likely an intrusion. By hiding such tidbits as source code, directory names, or usernames from the network, you can reduce the likelihood of an attack.

Caution   One handy feature of PHP, error reporting to the browser, is great for development because it helps pinpoint problems — but it can be bad for security, because it can also give directory paths, filenames, usernames, and potentially database names on error. Minimize the risk by turning off error reporting to the browser in production systems, via the display_errors directive in php.ini. You can still use error reporting to the browser on development systems if you wish, although it's safer to use the error_log() function to write error messages to a log.

When PHP is used as a Web server module, there is little risk of source code being released by the Web server, as any file with the proper extension is parsed by the PHP module. If PHP is installed as a CGI program, however, things are not so simple.

If you cannot run PHP as a server module, the next most secure setup is to run it as an interpreter for CGI scripts, just as you would Perl or Python.

Place all your PHP programs in the `cgi-bin` directory for your server or your account and arrange for the PHP interpreter to be invoked when they are executed. On Unix, this is done by adding a line similar to the following as the first line of every script:

```
#! /usr/local/bin/php
```

To use this setup, you must compile PHP with the `--enable-discard-path` configuration option. This setup has the disadvantage that the URLs for most of your pages contain `/cgi-bin/`.

The next most secure setup is a bit more complicated and is actually counter to the recommendations of CERT, a respected authority on computer security: We place the PHP interpreter itself in the `cgi-bin` directory. It is usually inadvisable to put an interpreter in the `cgi-bin` directory, because the rules for invoking CGI programs would allow any file on the server to be parsed as a program.

PHP is written to operate safely from the `cgi-bin` directory, however, if configured correctly. If you intend to use this setup, first carefully read the security and configuration sections of the PHP manual, as they may contain important information not available as this book went to press.

This setup relies upon the Web server to redirect URLs of the form:

```
http://your.server/program.php
```

to URLs of the form:

```
http://your.server/cgi-bin/php/program.php
```

The precise directives that will cause your Web server to do this vary. For Apache they are:

```
Action php-script /cgi-bin/php
AddType php-script .php
```

If you are using Apache, be sure to compile PHP with the `--enable-force-cgi-redirect` configuration option. This option utilizes a feature specific to Apache to prevent PHP from executing when invoked by URLs of the second form. Your setup is complete.

If you are using any other server software, you must compile PHP with the `--disable-force-cgi-redirect` configuration option. PHP cannot distinguish the two types of URLs and serves a document of either type. This allows a visitor to view files without regard for Web-server–based access restrictions. Assume, for example, that the URL `www.secrets.com/top/secret/hush.php` has access restrictions placed on it. A cracker could use the URL `www.secrets.com/cgi-bin/php/top/secret/hush.php` to read the file anyway.

In this case, the Web server is giving PHP the path name `/top/secret/hush.php`. PHP determines the location of the program file by prepending the configuration value `doc_root` to the given path name. By default, this value is the same as the Web server's document root (the directory corresponding to `www.secrets.com/`). Setting `doc_root` to another directory will limit PHP to programs in that directory and its subdirectories instead of the entire collection of Web-server documents. Any visitor may access any of the PHP programs by the method just described, however, without regard for Web-server-based access controls. *Be careful!*

Reading arbitrary files

A few common PHP programming mistakes can make it easy for a hacker to read almost any file on the server. Study the following page:

```
<HTML>
<HEAD></HEAD>
<BODY>
<?php if (IsSet($_POST['poem'])) {
  $poem = $_POST['poem'];
  $fp = fopen($poem, "r");
  print (fread($fp, filesize($poem)));
  fclose($fp);
  } ?>
<HR><FORM>Pick a poem:
<SELECT NAME="poem"><OPTION VALUE="jabb.html">Jabberwocky
<OPTION VALUE="graves.html">Cat-Goddesses</SELECT>
<INPUT TYPE="SUBMIT" VALUE="Show Me"></FORM>
</BODY>
</HTML>
```

This simple program displays a number of poems, selectable from a pop-up menu given in the form near the end. Invoke the security mantra: *Don't trust the network.* Clicking Show Me on this page results in URLs such as poetry.php?poem=graves.html. A cracker may substitute the filename of some more sensitive file, such as poetry.php?poem=/etc/passwd. The program, as given, would dutifully serve up the Unix password file, possibly enabling the cracker to break into a visitor account and do further damage.

The following is an appropriate solution to this problem:

```
<?php if (IsSet($_POST['poem'])) {
  $poem = $_POST['poem'];
  switch ($poem) {
    case "jabb":
      $poem_file = "jabb.html";
      break;
    case "graves":
      $poem_file = "graves.html";
      break;
  }
  if (IsSet($_POST['poem_file'])) {
    $poem_file = $_POST['poem_file'];
    $fp = fopen($poem_file, "r");
    print (fread($fp, filesize($poem_file)));
    fclose($fp);
  }
} ?>
```

The advantage of this method is that it explicitly lists the acceptable inputs and gracefully handles unacceptable inputs. If there were more poems to be processed, the switch statement could be replaced with a database query, where failure of the query indicates invalid input.

This is *not* a good solution:

```php
<?php if (IsSet($_POST['poem'])) {
  $poem = $_POST['poem'];
  if (!strstr($poem, "/") && !strstr($poem, "\\")) {
    $fp = fopen($poem, "r");
    print (fread($fp, filesize($poem)));
    fclose($fp);
  }
} ?>
```

The second conditional in this code segment checks for pathname separators in the given filename. This program explicitly describes a set of unacceptable inputs and considers anything else acceptable. It depends on the programmer imagining and checking for every possible undesired input. In this case, the programmer has missed something by making the implicit assumption that no sensitive files are stored in the same directory as the script.

What if a file that should be private escapes your server anyway? There is a chance that some misconfiguration (perhaps by someone else) or an unnoticed security hole will render some or all of your server's files publicly accessible.

PHP allows you to explicitly specify the set of directories in which files can be opened with the configuration value open_basedir. See Chapter 30 for more information on the PHP configuration file. This configuration value can be useful to prevent access to entire directories and is a good way to *minimize the damage.*

Many sensitive files, however, must be opened from PHP programs as visitors access the site. A common example is a password file. Access to such a file cannot be blocked with open_basedir, but the sensitive information it contains can be encrypted to render it useless to anyone who may steal it.

A password-protected site must verify the password given by a visitor wishing to gain access. One way to do this would be to store a password for safekeeping in encrypted form and then decrypt it when we need to compare it to the user-supplied password. The problem is that if we can decrypt the password, others may be able to decrypt it too. Also, we would have to make sure that no one could see the password after we decrypted it for comparison. Instead, we can use an encryption function that only goes one way and is easy to use for encryption, but that can't be decrypted. Rather than decrypt a stored password and compare the decrypted versions, we *encrypt* the *given* password and compare the encrypted passwords. Unix uses this strategy with its own password file, /etc/passwd, and PHP allows programmers to use the same encryption function for their own password files.

The function crypt(password, salt) encrypts the given password. The salt adds an extra bit of chance and should be chosen randomly when the password is first recorded. (PHP chooses a random salt if this parameter is omitted.) The function returns the concatenation of the salt value and the encrypted version of the password. The following function will create a new password for a visitor:

```php
function new_pw($given) {
  return crypt($given)
}
```

Social engineering

Social engineering is an often overlooked part of cracking. Sometimes it's easier for crackers to extract information (particularly passwords) from human beings than from computers:

Cracker: Hi, John, this is Gary in the IT department. When was the last time you used your company account?

John: Well, I entered a few new purchase orders about an hour ago.

Cracker: Well, John, I'm afraid your account has been compromised. Some of the information in it may have been lost. This could cost the company millions if we don't catch the intruder quickly. We need to open your account and assess the damage immediately. Can you give me your password?

John: Sure, it's . . .

Worse yet, sometimes forgetful visitors note their passwords on scraps of paper in their desks! A determined cracker can easily find a job as a night janitor and look for such notes. Many famous crackers were more notable for their social engineering and research skills than their ability to write code to compromise systems.

And this function will compare a password given by a visitor with a stored, encrypted password:

```
function verify_pw($given, $stored) {
  $salt = substr($stored, 0, CRYPT_SALT_LENGTH);
  $given_encrypted = crypt($given, $salt);
  return ($stored == $given_encrypted);
}
```

See Chapter 44 for a complete example of a user management system that uses the basic principle of storing and comparing encrypted passwords.

Running arbitrary programs

It's every system administrator's worst nightmare. The server's running more slowly than usual. A look at the running programs on the server reveals that a program entitled `crack` is burning 98 percent of the processor's time. Most likely, this program has been placed here by a cracker who is using it to decrypt (crack) passwords. The administrator logs in to kill the offending program but finds that his password is incorrect. His server has been *root compromised*, and there is no telling how much damage has been done.

In a compromise such as this, an intruder gains interactive access to the server, usually via a Unix shell or MS-DOS command line. Clearly, this is the most difficult type of heist to pull off, but it also bears the greatest reward. Once *inside* a server, the cracker has virtually unlimited power to bring down the server, steal or modify information, or make use of the server's computational power for further wrongdoing. Worse yet, a truly skilled cracker can conceal his or her steps by editing log files and erasing any temporary files he or she has created.

PHP has several program execution functions: system(), exec(), popen(), passthru(), and the back-tick (`) operator. As an example of the use of one of these functions, the following page returns the Unix finger information for a visitor specified through an HTML form:

```
<HTML>
<HEAD></HEAD>
<BODY>
<FORM>Get information on <INPUT TYPE="TEXT" NAME="username">,
<INPUT TYPE="SUBMIT" VALUE="Please"></FORM>
<?php if (IsSet($_POST['username'])) { ?>
  <H1>Results for <?php echo $_POST['username']; ?></H1>
  <pre><?php system("finger " . $_POST['username']); ?></pre>
<?php } ?>
</BODY>
</HTML>
```

The program, as given, takes a user name from the HTML form and executes the Unix program finger to look up information about that user. You should hear *Don't trust the network* repeating loudly in your head. Unix commands are separated by a semicolon, so anything following a semicolon in the string passed to system() is treated as a new command. This new command is executed with all the permissions of the user under which the Web server is running.

Under Unix, the command "rm -rf /" will delete all files on the server. Imagine the damage if an ill-intentioned visitor typed "; rm -rf /" into the form and clicked Please.

The best solution to this problem is to filter out everything but valid user names before invoking finger. This requires specific knowledge about user name formats on your server, so we do not present an example here. PHP presents a solution that is almost as good. The function escapeshellcmd() will sanitize a string for use in a program execution command, rendering harmless any special characters such as the semicolon. We replace the line invoking system() in the preceding code snippet with:

```
<pre><?php
    system(escapeshellcmd("finger " . $_POST['username']));
?></pre>
```

Magically, no value the visitor may enter can result in arbitrary programs being executed. This does not, however, prevent the visitor from providing unexpected input to finger. Although finger does no harm if given incorrect input, other programs may not be so forgiving. If in doubt, err on the side of caution!

To *minimize the damage* of a compromise of this sort, most modern Web servers run as a dummy user (often called nobody on Unix systems). This user has only the permissions required to run the Web server (and any PHP scripts) and read and write the necessary files. But remember, any databases or files that your scripts can modify are modifiable by this user, and thus they are vulnerable if an attacker can run arbitrary programs.

Viruses and other e-critters

Visitors trust software coming from a trusted site. If your site allows visitors to download files uploaded by other visitors, you should warn your visitors to check files for viruses before running them, and you should consider periodically scanning the files on your server for viruses as well. This is a hard problem to solve, particularly with the possibility of embedding viruses in such seemingly harmless files as word processor documents. Indeed, Microsoft was caught in this very bind when it inadvertently released a CD-ROM with a Word document containing the Melissa virus.

Cross-Reference

See the section "Site defacement" at the beginning of this chapter for other ways that your visitor may inadvertently receive malicious code.

E-mail safety

E-mail is the least secure of any of the Internet protocols. As it travels to its destination, it may be spooled on several intermediary servers. If security is weak on a server, it is not difficult for a cracker to read e-mail passing through that server. Send as little critical information as possible via e-mail. That is, *never* e-mail credit card numbers, and try to avoid sending passwords via e-mail unless absolutely necessary. It is interesting that most existing sites do not adhere to the latter point.

Whenever your site asks for your visitor's e-mail address, it should explain exactly how the address is to be used and to whom it is to be released. Whenever an e-mail address is presented on a Web page, it should be modified so as not to be easily identified by automated search engines picking up e-mail addresses to produce spam. The easiest and most elegant way to do this is to replace the @ symbol by the word at.

Unless absolutely necessary, avoid creating `mailto:` links. These links are excellent sources of spam addresses and are inconvenient for visitors who do not use their Web browser for sending e-mail.

System administrators

System administrators, also called *sysadmins*, are the folks who make sure the computers we all use keep on computing and that the Internet keeps on networking. Their jobs are shrouded in mystery: They hold the keys to the mysterious "machine room" where all the critical servers are stored. It's not unusual to see them hurrying into the office at midnight, surely to avert some crisis that could bring the company to its knees.

Sysadmins are also a very cautious lot. They tend to program their servers to report any unusual activity immediately (often to the large-screen alphanumeric pager they carry at all times) and to take swift, decisive action against anything they deem improper or unsafe.

A professor in a Computer Science department once asked his students, as homework, to break into his Linux desktop. To make things a little easier, he gave the encrypted text of his password (see the description of `crypt()` in the section "Reading arbitrary files"). In a testament to the security of the Unix `crypt()` function, none of the students cracked his desktop. Several of his students were denied access to their campus accounts, however, and questioned by university officials because they were running computationally expensive programs named `crack`!

If you aren't your own system administrator, but you are concerned about the security of your site, it is probably a good idea to befriend your local sysadmin. He or she can sometimes suggest ways to make your site more secure and can also be an enormous help in recovering from an incident.

Register Globals

The PHP master configuration file, `php.ini`, offers a configuration directive, `register_globals`, which controls how PHP recognizes and uses variables passed to it. With the value of `register_globals` set to `on`, external variables from sources such as forms, cookies, sessions, and urls are passed directly to, and used without extra manipulation by, a receiving PHP script. Prior to PHP4.2.0, this was the default setting. While this presents a certain level of coding convenience and simplicity, it's not such a good idea. The PHP team benevolently offers you the choice of registering globals or not, but they have clearly announced their intention to remove the option sooner rather than later.

What does it mean to register globals exactly? In a larger sense, a global is any variable or constant that persists outside of the scope in which it is initialized. For example, passing a variable value of "socks" from a form field named "`clothes`" in one script results in the variable `$clothes` with the value "`socks`" being directly available in the processing script. This direct availability is dependent on the registration of these variables as they become available. There are, however, some potential drawbacks, some of them security related, in registering global variables in this way.

The first and perhaps most significant possibility is that variables from one source may overwrite variables from some other source. Consider, by way of example, the following form:

```
<FORM METHOD="POST" ACTION="processor.php?clothes=socks">
<INPUT TYPE="TEXT" NAME="clothes">
<INPUT TYPE="Submit" VALUE="Dress Me">
</FORM>
```

You can probably see the problem here almost immediately in that `$clothes` has been defined twice, and since it is not an array, the value of `clothes` defined in the GET-style ACTION attribute will be overwritten by the user-entered value POSTed by the form. Potentially more seriously, if a cookie with that name has been defined, it will overwrite the POST variable. You can instruct PHP, again via the `php.ini` file, to evaluate variables in a different order; but the net effect of that is to simply reorder the problem; not to solve it. It doesn't, for example, allow you to have two variables of the same name. This issue provides a couple of different avenues through which Web site visitors of malicious intent could set variables for themselves and possibly slip undesirable data into your applications.

However, with the value of `register_globals` set to `off`, a different situation emerges. Instead of being immediately imported into the global scope, variables are stored in one of a number of arrays, each named for the environment that supplies it. These associative arrays are:

```
$_GET
$_POST
$_SESSION
$_FILES
$_COOKIE
```

Their respective variables are accessed as indices in the array; for example, a POST form variable from the preceding example would be `$_POST[clothes]`. But because we aren't registering globals, we would also have `$_GET[clothes]` and possibly `$_COOKIE['clothes']`, each with its own intact values. Whether or not you would actually need to, or even should, name variables in this way is debatable, but there are other advantages to insuring `register_globals` is set to `off`.

It's important to remember that setting `register_globals` to `off` does not prevent an ill-intentioned Web site user from setting variables for himself. It does, however, add another layer of complexity to the cracker's job. It's no longer enough to simply send a variable to the server; he or she must also know from which environment you expect that variable to come. And with `register_globals` set to off, variables evaluated and set exclusively within the receiving script are not in danger from any suspect request variables. Coupled with some well thought out code, a potentially hazardous situation can be easily averted. Let's look at a quick example:

```
// Bad example, don't do this
function check_user() {
   if (($user == $user_we_expected)
     && ($pass == $password_we_expected))
   $registered user = 1;
}

if ($registered_user) {
   // Here are those names and addresses the cracker is after
}
```

The preceding example, written as if `register_globals` were turned on, may at least look reasonable at first glance. Don't worry about where $user_we_expected and $pass_we_expected come from right now. We'll just assume, for the time being, that these come from some other function such as a database lookup. The first problem is the relatively open use of $user and $pass. These variables can come from anywhere and our script won't ask any questions; it just dutifully processes these variables regardless of the source. Let's look again at a version modified to address this. We still haven't changed the value of `register_globals`.

```
// Better example, but still needs work
function check_user() {
   if (($_POST[user] == $user_we_expected)
     && ($_POST[pass] == $password_we_expected))
   $registered user = 1;
}

if ($registered_user) {
   // Here are those names and addresses the cracker is after
}
```

So, for the low, low price of just 10 keystrokes, we've narrowed the sources we will accept for a username and password. A cracker can no longer submit these through a `GET` argument like `http://website/script?user=meat&pass=potatoes`. These variables will simply expire ineffectually at the end of the script execution. Our cracker can still send these variables, but he is restricted to using a `POST` method form. That brings us to a couple more issues concerning variable origin. A script kiddie could still use a simple form-posting script to rapidly submit user and password combinations in succession. This sort of brute force attack is successful more often that you might think, especially where usernames and passwords are poorly chosen.

```
// We're almost there
function check_user() {
   if($_SERVER[HTTP_REFERER] == $our address) {
      if (($_POST[user] == $user_we_expected)
```

```
            && ($_POST[pass] == $password_we_expected))
        $registered user = 1;
    }
  }

if ($registered_user) {
    // Here are those names and addresses the cracker is after
    }
```

Now our script expects the referring url to a very specific page on our site, which we accomplish by comparing the information supplied by the browser with the source form we know we created. All by itself, this doesn't constitute a solution to our problem. HTTP_REFERER isn't always sent by the browser or registered by the server; and like the other components of an http request header, can be forged in some cases. But remember, while our idealized goal here is to make the cracker's work impossible, we can never really fully achieve that. The Internet is littered with the bodies of those who thought they could. We can, however, add layers to our armor, making the malicious user's job more and more difficult, and hopefully send him off in search of an easier mark.

Our final change doesn't involve a modification to the script at all. We'll simply change the setting of register_globals (and restart the Web server). We've already made it difficult for the user to send bad values for the information we expect to be user data. Now we've protected the values of the other four variables in our script. The variables $registered_user, $user_we_expected, $pass_we_expected and $our_address are all protected from outside manipulation by this one simple action. Imagine how much easier the cracker's job would be if she could simply alter the expected value rather than trying to guess it.

File Uploads

As Web designers and application developers, we tend to think of the ability to upload files via the Web as a really cool and useful feature. However, with our system administrator hats on, the notion of file uploads is a fairly scary one. Historically, almost all of the major PHP security warnings to date have involved file upload. Witness the fact that this feature is disabled by default in the standard php.ini file, and many of the major PHP projects such as Phorum and phpGroupWare, while they support file uploads in some manner, advise extreme caution in its use and allow this feature to be disabled. The fears of the sysadmins are well grounded: There is little you can do to put your system at greater risk than employing a poor file upload implementation.

Still, the keyword here is *poor*. Intuitively, we know the risks associated with file uploading:

   ✦ Liberal permissions are required on the upload directory.

   ✦ Executable or other unauthorized files can potentially be uploaded.

   ✦ Excessively large files can tie up resources and even be used to create a DOS (denial of service) condition on your server.

   ✦ If your Web application sends mails containing the file, your server can easily run into a virus distribution, a most unpleasant mantle you will not enjoy wearing.

The good news is, PHP provides several means to address these concerns. Indeed, a fair number of updates to PHP have been released specifically in answer to the problem of secure file uploads. We'll get to the security issues in a moment; but first, let's get the rudiments of file uploads out of the way.

First, we need to decide what we are going to do with the uploaded file. In this case, let's plan on writing it back out to disk somewhere in our Web tree, so that visitors can access it:

```
cd <www root directory>
mkdir uploads
chmod 766 uploads
```

The first thing we've done is to make sure we are in the root of our Web document directory. Next, we've created a directory to hold uploaded files. There's nothing magical about the name we've chosen for this directory—you can name it free_beer if you like, although that might be slightly less meaningful in your finished implementation. The last bit is the scary part. With permissions defined above, we've made the directory world writeable. In some cases, the directory may also need to be executable, but you should try to get away with these more minimal permissions first. (Of course, these are Unix-specific commands. Windows users will typically have an easier time of it using the graphical tools that OS provides.)

Next, we need a proper form. A form that handles file uploads is not much different from a regular form, but the requirements of its design are somewhat more stringent:

```
<form enctype="multipart/form-data" action="me.php"
method="POST">
<input type="hidden" name="MAX_FILE_SIZE" value="50000">
Select a file: <input name="upfile" type="file">
<input type="submit" value="Upload">
</form>
```

The first thing you'll notice here is the enctype attribute to the form tag. Other values for enctype are available, but the default browser interpretation, application/x-www-form-urlencoded, will generally serve for most purposes. Not so with file uploads, however. You must specify the enctype exactly as shown above or the browser will not send the data in a format that PHP understands. Skip down to line 3, to the input type of file. This may be a new item to you. It creates in the form field that looks much like a text input box, but with the addition of a Browse button that ideally launches the default file browsing implementation for the client system. Finally, we've added a hidden field with the reserved name MAX_FILE_SIZE. This is a cue to the browser that it should check the file size against a maximum of 50000 bytes and advise the user accordingly. This is primarily done as a convenience to the user. It is not universally supported and is easily circumvented, so don't rely on it to enforce your file size limits.

You can, however, rely on PHP to enforce your limits in this regard. PHP provides both php.ini file settings and some coding techniques to do this. You should avail yourself of both. As the php.ini file settings provide a reasonable fallback, let's start by reviewing those. The first setting should be obvious:

```
file_uploads = On
```

The next relevant setting is:

```
upload_tmp_dir =
```

This is typically left unassigned, which results in a default appropriate for your system. This *is not* where the final uploaded file will reside This *is* generally the best choice, unless you have a really compelling reason to set this to something else, leave it alone.

The next setting is where we enforce a maximum file size.

```
upload_max_filesize = 2M
```

PHP defaults to a size of 2MB for this parameter, which is probably larger than you will need under ordinary circumstances. You can set this value as large as you like, but you will have to strike a balance with the value of `max_execution_time` which will require a duration large enough to accommodate your largest possible upload from your least well equipped user. For example, a modem user may take six minutes or more to upload a 1MB file.

Caution   If any of these values seem out of line with the needs of the rest of your PHP installation, they probably are. Greatly increasing the value of `max_execution_time` to allow for larger uploads, for example, can make debugging infinite loops and other scripting mishaps difficult. It can also pose a security risk based on scripts that are placed elsewhere on your site. This would be an appropriate place to set these values on a per directory basis using php flags and .htaccess files as discussed in Chapter 30.

The next setting controls the size of HTTP form submissions, which includes file uploads.

```
post_max_size = 8M
```

Again, the PHP default here is pretty high, but it needs to be big enough to hold the value of `upload_max_filesize` plus a few bytes for any form data that may accompany the upload.

Once you've got these values all set, you're ready to write a script that handles the uploaded file. At its most basic, this script would look something like the following:

```
$uploaddir = "uploads/";
$uploadfile = $uploaddir . $_FILES['upfile']['name'];
if (move_uploaded_file($_FILES['upfile']['tmp_name'],
$uploadfile)) {
    print("File upload was successful");
} else {
    print("File upload failed");
}
```

This script creates a couple of simple variables to create an easily readable path and filename. The global `$_FILES` is a multidimensional array in order to handle concurrent file uploads from the same form. In the first level, we identify the file by the name assigned to that field in the form. In the second level, we use the predefined variable `'name'` to assign our file a name. Next we capture the actual file data, which is referenced by the value of 'tmp_name', the location where the bits are stored until you do something with them. Finally, we move it to its permanent resting place.

You probably didn't expect it to be that simple, and you won't be disappointed. Sure, if you cover all your bases ahead of time, this script will get the job done, but it's pretty insecure as we have placed the vaguest and most general restrictions on what users can send us. The following script offers some checks and modifications added for security and robustness:

```
$uploaddir = "uploads/";
$filename = trim($_FILES['upfile']['name']);
$filename = substr($filename, -20);
$filename = ereg_replace(" ", "", $filename);
if((ereg(".jpg", $filename)) || (ereg(".gif", $filename))) {
    $uploadfile = $uploaddir . $filename;
    if (move_uploaded_file($_FILES['upfile']['tmp_name'],
    $uploadfile)) {
```

```
      chmod($uploadfile, 0644);
      print("File upload was successful");
   } else {
      print("File upload failed");
   }
} else {
   print("Only images are allowed, upload failed");
}
```

What's different about this version, and why is it better? We've started by working a little string and regex magic on our filename. The value of $_FILES['upfile']['name'] contains the literal name of the file as it was on the user's system; but for reasons which should already be apparent, this cannot be trusted. The second line removes any trailing and leading white-space characters. The third line ensures that we have a filename with a manageable length by taking only the last twenty characters. We take these characters from the end because we need to capture the file extension; but this is an important step because excessively long file-names can create a host of potential problems. The fourth line pulls out any spaces in the filename, as different platforms handle long filenames in different ways, potentially posing additional problems. The last thing we do before writing out the file is to make sure it's an image. You may wish to allow other types and can adjust the regular expression accordingly.

Finally, we change permissions on the written-out file to a minimal set, reducing the risk from viruses or unwanted executables.

There are safer and less safe ways to handle file uploads; but uploading is historically one of the most insecure things that PHP allows you to do. Many good Web developers and sysad-mins think that anyone who's willing to let unknown users upload unknown binaries to their filesystem is asking for trouble. So before implementation, you need to ask if this is really what you need or want to do, and if you're prepared for all the possible consequences. Once you've made that decision, follow the hints in this section to make things as safe as possible.

Encryption

Encryption is the process of *encrypting* some message, referred to as *plaintext,* into unrecog-nizable *ciphertext.* Without certain information (a *key* of some sort), it is extremely hard to reconstruct the plaintext from the ciphertext. Someone equipped with the proper key, how-ever, can easily *decrypt* the ciphertext, revealing the original plaintext — at least, if the chosen encryption function is not one-way.

We have already seen one use of encryption in this chapter: Passwords are stored in encrypted form. Password encryption, however, is usually one-way. There is no key to decrypt an encrypted password. Such a key is not needed, and the encryption can be made stronger if it doesn't need to be reversible. Encryption has many other uses in online busi-ness, both for storing data on the server and transmitting it across the network.

Public-key encryption

Meet Alice and Bob, professional cryptographic examples. They were chosen by the mathe-matical community, not for their acting talent, but because their names begin with A and B. Alice and Bob want to communicate securely, but their only method of communication is via Pony Express — not particularly secure. Each of them selects a public key and a secret key.

We shall call Alice's keys P_{alice} and S_{alice}, respectively and, likewise, Bob's keys P_{bob} and S_{bob}. They publish their public keys in the newspaper but hide their secret keys under their mattresses.

Alice has a sensitive message M for Bob. With her keys, Alice received a set of instructions for translating a message with a key. We write the translation like this: $P_{bob}(M)$. She translates her message with Bob's public key and hands the result to a shady-looking character on a pony.

Our friends' keys were not chosen arbitrarily. They have the special property that if they translate a message with one key, then translate the result with the other, they get the original message back. That is, $S_{alice}(P_{alice}(M)) = P_{alice}(S_{alice}(M)) = M$. There's no other way to resurrect the original message. In this case, Bob translates the message he receives, which he knows to be $P_{bob}(M)$ with his secret key. $S_{bob}(P_{bob}(M)) = M$, so he can read Alice's original message.

Bob knows that nobody else could have read that message, because nobody else has his secret key. But he does not know that it came from Alice: Anyone who reads the newspaper may have sent that message, signing the name `Alice` at the bottom.

Now Alice wants to send another message to Bob, and this time she wants no doubt that it was from her. First, she translates the message with her secret key and writes the result after her message as a *signature:* $M + S_{alice}(M)$. She sends this off to Bob, who reads Alice's message, which instructs him to translate the signature with her public key: $P_{alice}(S_{alice}(M)) = M$, and he sees her message again.

Because nobody else has Alice's secret key, she is the only one who could have created this signature, so this message must have come from her. But note that this time Alice sent her message M to Bob directly. Any rogue could have waylaid the Pony Express and read it. If she had so desired, she could have first signed the message, then encrypted the message and the signature using the first method, resulting in a signed, encrypted message.

There is a hitch in this scheme. Without meeting Alice, Bob can't be sure that the public key he found in the newspaper is really Alice's key. What if someone else had his or her key printed under her name? This could become a real problem if Bob communicates with lots of people — he simply doesn't have the time to check keys with each of them face-to-face.

Assume that there is at least one person everyone trusts; call him Tom. Tom picks a set of keys and offers to sign documents with his secret key, if the owner of the document shows proof of his or her identity. Alice has her public key signed by Tom, and then publishes the signed key, called a *certificate,* in the newspaper. Bob checks the signature on the key he sees in the newspaper, using Tom's public key. He knows that Tom signed that message, and Tom must have checked Alice's identification, so the key in the newspaper must really belong to Alice.

Single-key encryption

In single-key encryption, the same key can encrypt and decrypt a message. In general, it runs much more quickly than other forms of encryption, but it is more difficult to use for communication because the key must somehow be transmitted from one end to the other without any eavesdroppers picking it up. This is precisely where public-key encryption can lend a hand.

Returning briefly to our characterization, imagine Alice and Bob want to have a private conversation using single-key encryption. Alice asks Bob for his certificate, which contains his public key. She then picks a new single key and encrypts that key with Bob's public key, sending the result to Bob. Using his secret key, he decrypts the message to reveal Alice's single key and then uses it to begin a single-key encryption conversation.

The Unix version of PHP provides a set of functions that implement single-key encryption, using a publicly available library called mcrypt. To use these functions, you must download and install mcrypt (there is a link to the library's source available in the PHP manual) and recompile PHP with the --enable-mcrypt configuration option.

Caution

When compiling this version of mcrypt, you must specify the configuration option --disable-posix-threads during the mcrypt configuration. Missing this step causes Apache to crash.

mcrypt offers a choice between a number of ciphers — different single-key algorithms. Each has its relative pros and cons in terms of speed and strength. In general, DES and Blowfish are fairly well-known algorithms with a good balance of speed and strength, but if you need extreme speed or great strength, you should research the algorithms available in your implementation (listed in mcrypt.h) and choose the one most suited to your needs.

mcrypt also allows you to choose among four cipher modes. These are summarized in Table 29-1.

Table 29-1: Cipher Modes Provided by mcrypt

Mode	Description	Initialization vector (IV)
ECB (electronic code book)	Just translate the block of data given. Suitable for small blocks of data that aren't very predictable, such as other keys. Do not use for text: The high frequency of letters and punctuation may be used to break the encryption.	no
CBC (cipher block chaining)	This stronger mode is far better suited for use with textual data.	opt
CFB (cipher feedback)	Like ECB, CFB is well suited for short blocks of data.	yes
OFB (output feedback)	OFB is very similar to CFB but designed to be better behaved when it encounters errors in its input.	yes

The last two modes require an initialization vector (abbreviated IV), which functions as a starting state for the encryption algorithm. The differences between these modes are relevant to interactive use, where individual keystrokes are encrypted one at a time. In that case, it is crucial that the algorithm not encrypt *a* the same way each time. The PHP interface to mcrypt only allows us to encrypt strings, however, so any of the modes except ECB are perfectly acceptable.

Depending on the cipher mode you want to use, call mcrypt_ecb(), mcrypt_cbc(), mcrypt_cfb(), or mcrypt_ofb() like this:

```
mcrypt_cbc(cipher, key, data, direction, [iv])
```

where cipher is MCRYPT_DES, MCRYPT_BLOWFISH, or whichever cipher you have chosen. (See the PHP documentation for an updated list of supported ciphers.) Pass your key and the data you wish to encrypt or decrypt in the `key` and `data` arguments, respectively. To encrypt, pass `MCRYPT_ENCRYPT` in the `direction` argument; to decrypt, pass `MCRYPT_DECRYPT`. Finally, for cipher modes that support initialization vectors, pass your own IV in the `iv` argument.

Your key must be of the correct size for your cipher. To find out what this size is, use:

```
mcrypt_get_key_size(cipher)
```

Again, `cipher` is the cipher you have chosen.

To generate a random IV or key, use:

```
mcrypt_create_iv(size, source)
```

Here, `size` is the size of the desired object and `source` is one of `MCRYPT_RAND`, `MCRYPT_DEV_RANDOM`, or `MCRYPT_DEV_URANDOM`, specifying the random number generator to use: `rand()`, `/dev/random`, or `/dev/urandom`, respectively. If you use `rand()`, be sure to call `srand()` to seed the random number generator first. (See Chapter 10 for more information on random numbers.) The proper sizes for IVs and keys are obtained by calling `mcrypt_get_block_size(cipher)` and `mcrypt_get_key_size(cipher)`, respectively.

Note that all data handled by `mcrypt` is in the form of PHP strings of binary data. If you wish to display the data in some human-readable format or store it as a text string, you must apply some translation to it. PHP provides the functions `base64_encode()` and `base64_decode()` for just this purpose. Check the PHP manual for more information on these functions.

Encrypting cookies

Cookies your site sends to a visitor's browser contain information about that visitor. When the browser sends the cookie back, your site uses the information it contains to generate a new page. *Don't trust the network* — sound familiar? A cookie could be modified or forged by a malicious user, perhaps fooling your site somehow. This extremely simple program will serve as an example:

```php
<?php
  $visits = $_COOKIE['visits'] + 1;
  setcookie("visits", $visits);
?>
<HTML><HEAD></HEAD>
<BODY>
<H1>You have been here <?php echo $visits ?> times</H1>
</BODY>
</HTML>
```

 Cross-Reference See Chapter 24 for more information on cookies.

Here, a count of our visitors' visits to this site is kept in the cookie `visits`. A visitor could modify his or her cookie, however, to make the visit count 10,000. Our program would have no idea that this visitor has not been to the page 10,000 times and would blindly display `You have been here 10000 times.`

But with some help from mcrypt and a few friends, we can make this impossible:

```php
<?php
  $key = base64_decode("NCiUmfiRByg=");
  if (IsSet($_COOKIE['visits'])) {
    $encrypted = base64_decode($_COOKIE['visits']);
    $visits = mcrypt_cbc(MCRYPT_DES, $key, $encrypted,
                        MCRYPT_DECRYPT); }
  $visits = $visits + 1;
  $encrypted = mcrypt_cbc(MCRYPT_DES, $key, $visits,
                        MCRYPT_ENCRYPT);
  setcookie("visits", base64_encode($encrypted));
?>
```

mcrypt deals with strings full of binary data, so we can't easily type them or send them to browsers without modification. In this case, we have chosen to use the PHP base64 functions to turn them into well-behaved strings. Before writing this program, we invented a DES key with the following code:

```php
<?php
  $key_size = mcrypt_get_key_size(MCRYPT_DES);
  $key = mcrypt_create_iv($key_size, MCRYPT_DEV_RANDOM);
  echo base64_encode($key);
?>
```

We copied and pasted the resulting key (in base 64 encoding) into our cookie program's first line. We store the number of visits in the cookie named visits, encrypted and in base 64 encoding. So if the visits variable is set, we first base64_decode it, then decrypt it. We then increment the counter, encrypt it, base64_encode it, and store it in a new cookie. The visitor sees cookie values such as IQ109yQCEgw%3D, which are not editable.

The program is not completely secure! The cookie value just given will *always* correspond to visit number 7. A cracker wishing to make your site believe he had visited only seven times could simply substitute this value for the visits cookie. If you know it would not benefit a visitor to return to a prior cookie (in this case, if the visitor wants a large visit count), however, this method is adequate: There is no way to easily invent a cookie for a state that has not been seen yet.

Cross-Reference To maintain a more useful visitor state, you should use sessions, which are described fully in Chapter 24.

This example should bring home the need to keep your source code private: If a cracker could view this program from his or her browser, he or she would have your site's encryption key and could decrypt your cookie values with ease.

Hashing

Signing a document with your private key produces a signature that is as large as the original document. This becomes a problem when we want to sign long documents such as files. For instance, most security software (including mcrypt) is digitally signed so that downloaders know that the latest version really was written by the author. Otherwise, sysadmins worry, an eager cracker could circulate a version of a security program into which he or she has installed a back door and then walk into the systems running that version with no difficulty.

What you need is a digital fingerprint for a large file. What if we treat the binary data of the file as a list of integers, add them all together, then chop off all but 128 bits of the sum? We call the final 128-bit number the *checksum*. The author of the file then encrypts the checksum with his or her secret key and attaches the result to the file as a signature.

Assume a cracker makes modifications to the file. He or she can then calculate the sum C of the changes and put the number $-C$ at the end of the file, creating a file that he or she knows to have the same checksum as the original. The cracker then appends the same encrypted checksum to the file as its signature.

When some unsuspecting user downloads the modified file, the user calculates the new checksum, decrypts the signature to find the original author's checksum, and sees that they match. The user proceeds to use the modified file, incorrectly assuming that it was written by the stated author.

Of course, the cryptographers are right on the spot with a solution. It should be very difficult to make changes to a file to produce a certain fingerprint. To ensure this, many *hashing* algorithms have been developed. Hashing algorithms are generally modifications of single-key encryption algorithms to make them create a ciphertext of a specific length, from which it is not possible to reconstruct the original message.

As you would expect, PHP provides a set of functions for hashing. These functions depend on the publicly available mhash library. You can find the latest version of the mhash library through a link in the PHP manual.

The function mhash(type, input) computes the hash value of input, using the method specified by type. Common values for this argument are MCRYPT_MD5 and MCRYPT_SHA1. For a complete list of possibilities, see the PHP manual.

Digitally signing files

Now let us present a PHP program to accept uploaded files only when they are correctly signed. We assume that our site is equipped with a list of usernames and Blowfish keys, where each user has a key known only to that user and our site. The function get_user_key(username) retrieves these keys for us. The uploader generates the signature for an upload by first hashing the upload file with the MD5 hash algorithm and then encrypting the resulting hash value with her Blowfish key.

```
<HTML><HEAD></HEAD>
<BODY>
<?php if (empty($file) || !IsSet($_POST['username']) ||
empty($sig)) { ?>
<H1>Upload a file</H1>
<FORM ENCTYPE="multipart/form-data" METHOD="POST">
<INPUT TYPE="HIDDEN" NAME="MAX_FILE_SIZE" VALUE="2000000">
Upload the file: <INPUT NAME="file" TYPE="file"><br>
With this signature: <INPUT NAME="sig" TYPE="file"><br>
For user <INPUT NAME="username" TYPE="text"><br>
<INPUT TYPE="SUBMIT" VALUE="Go"></FORM>
<? } else {
  $fp = fopen($file, "r");
  $hash = mhash(MHASH_MD5, fread($file, $file_size));
  fclose($fp);
```

```
$key = get_user_key($username);
$encr_hash = mcrypt_cbc(MCRYPT_BLOWFISH, $key, $hash,
                        MCRYPT_ENCRYPT);
$sfp = fopen($sig);
$sig_data = fread($sig, $sig_size);
fclose($sfp);
if ($encr_hash != $sig_data)
   echo "<H1>Rejected -- signature did not match</H1>";
else {
   echo "<H1>Accepted</H1>";
   // Continue handling the uploaded file
}
} ?>
</BODY>
</HTML>
```

This program parallels the uploader's steps, first hashing the uploaded file and then encrypting the result with the user's key. If the results are the same, the uploader must have used the same key, and we can assume they are genuine. If the results differ, the upload is a forgery.

Secure Sockets Layer

The uses of cryptography presented so far protect the server's data. The single-key encryption example protects information the server stores on clients (cookies) from unwanted modification. The hashing example enables the server to detect forged files and refuse to accept them.

We now turn our attention to the security of your site's visitor. The visitor often transmits private information to your site. The visitor's password and credit card information must somehow travel from his or her machine to the server, across the untrustworthy network.

The *Secure Sockets Layer* (SSL) protocol provides a way to do this, making it impossible for an eavesdropper to listen in. It also provides a way for the site to prove its identity to the visitor and, optionally, for the visitor to prove its identity to the site. Although we won't delve into the cryptographic details, SSL does its work by using public-key encryption to prove the identity of the server and to exchange a new key to be used to encrypt the conversation. It then switches over to single-key encryption, which is much faster, using this new key.

Regardless of how you acquire and license the SSL software, you must purchase a certificate for your site from a well-known *certificate authority.* These authorities are the trusted third parties in the conversation between your server and a browser, but they do not give away their services for free.

It is beyond the scope of this book to make comparisons of competing SSL servers. In the tradition of open source, the authors believe that the free implementations are the best and most reliable; indeed, many of the commercial SSL servers are based on the open source implementations! If you buy a commercial implementation, however, you receive support from that company, and you satisfy management's desire to pay for something.

Tip   SSL is outside the scope of the book, since it really is an issue for Web server management rather than Web scripting. For more information on how to implement SSL on your site, see a good Apache or IIS book such as *Apache Server 2 Bible, Second Edition,* by Mohammed J. Kabir (Wiley, 2002).

FYI: Security Web Sites

If you are losing sleep after reading this chapter, fear not. Every administrator and site designer around the world is grappling with the same issues, and there is a strong feeling of solidarity among computer security professionals. Many Web sites are devoted to computer security, and almost all of them contain full descriptions of recent security incidents and ways to protect your system from duplicate attacks. Some are designed for security professionals, whereas others have the cracker in mind. Either way, the information they provide is useful and often very interesting.

Begin your explorations by checking out these sites:

✦ **Computer Emergency Response Team (CERT)** (`www.cert.org/`): CERT is one of the most popular repositories of official descriptions of security incidents. It publishes advisories on all sorts of security issues, including very clear descriptions of the problem, vulnerable systems, and possible solutions.

✦ **Security-focus.com** (`www.securityfocus.com/`): Security-focus.com provides a great deal of information on all aspects of computer security, from the legal and political to the technical. It also hosts the well-known security mailing list, BugTraq (which can be found under Forums).

✦ **Rootshell** (`http://rootshell.com/`): Rootshell is a well-respected site that contains fairly technical descriptions of many, many security vulnerabilities, including detailed descriptions of how to exploit the vulnerability, as well as instructions on removing the vulnerability.

✦ **Insecure.Org** (`http://insecure.org/`): Insecure.Org is a fairly well-established site that is not afraid to make cracking tools available and to discuss the nitty-gritty details of many "exploits." This site can be extremely useful if you want to try to break into your own site.

✦ **L0pht Heavy Industries** (`http://www.l0pht.com/index.html`): L0pht is another on-the-edge site, run by people who crack into machines for a living. They are paid to do this in the hopes that they can find a vulnerability before someone with malicious intent does, and they report what they've done on this site and others. The site also contains lots of interesting opinions on its *soapbox*.

Summary

For any significant Web site, security is a crucial part of the site's implementation. You should take extreme care to secure your server from attack and also be sure to protect your visitors' private information from prying eyes. In a time of enormous growth for online businesses, publication of a story about a major security breach can destroy visitors' confidence in your site, driving them to the competition and possibly leaving your site to evaporate as quickly as it appeared.

In this chapter, we've driven home three basic lessons:

✦ *Don't trust the network.* Every byte of data that comes from the Internet should be treated as potentially hazardous. Be as restrictive as possible in defining the inputs you allow. Prefer the solution that lists the acceptable inputs to the one that lists the unacceptable inputs. Be sure that your Web server configuration does not allow clients to view your source code or to work around your access restrictions.

✦ *Minimize the damage.* Where possible, make sure that the damage possible from a particular type of security breach is minimal. Encrypt sensitive data. If you run your own Web server, make sure it is running as a dummy user.

✦ Finally, *if you run your own server, spend some time breaking into it.* If you're successful, then you've identified a vulnerability that you can patch before an intruder finds it. If you're unsuccessful, you've learned something about your server, and your security precautions have weathered a good test. If you don't run your server, find out who does, and see what he or she can tell you about your site's security.

✦   ✦   ✦

Configuration

In this chapter, we discuss the many configuration options available
with PHP, particularly the Unix Apache module version, in some
detail. The goal is for you to better understand the tradeoffs of each
capability you may enable or disable and how they may affect each
other. We also touch on ways you can measure and improve the performance of your PHP scripts.

Viewing Environment Variables

To see any of the settings discussed in the following section, you
have only to use the phpinfo() function in a valid PHP script. This
function begins with a quick recap of the PHP version, your platform,
date of build, and compile-time options; it then moves methodically
through your PHP settings. You will also see some information about
your Web server settings and environment variables.

The output of the phpinfo() function is a potential bonanza for
crackers, so you shouldn't leave it sitting around on a production
server.

Understanding PHP Configuration

Like most of the best open source software packages, PHP is highly
configurable. It's left up to you, the individual PHP user, to find your
own balance among the competing virtues of power, flexibility, safety,
and ease of use.

Configuration is difficult to describe fully because there are so many
possible combinations of options — about 25 factorial combinations,
as a matter of fact. In some cases, there is an obvious conflict between
two configuration directives — you simply have to choose one or the
other, end of story. In other cases, you can have both but may need
to remember some workarounds. We try to point out as many of
these implications as we can, but no one can honestly claim to have
tested every possible combination.

Since the launch of PHP4, the development group has made a truly
Herculean effort to bring the Windows build up to the same level of
functionality as Unix users have always enjoyed. The Windows version of PHP now ships with the most popular extensions (for example, MySQL) compiled in and a startling number of shared libraries
(.dlls) bundled with PHP itself. Many of these libraries have to be
built from Unix source, so this effort represents a truly amazing
amount of unremunerated, thankless work from the PHP build team.

In fact, the truth is that the PHP build for Windows (the so-called manual installation, not the installer version) now offers almost all the functionality of Unix builds with much less effort. Windows users only need to worry about the variables that can be set with the php.ini file — not all of which are applicable to Windows versions of PHP anyway. If you only use PHP on Windows, feel free to skip down to the "The php.ini file" section of this chapter, with a glance at the "Apache configuration files" section if you run on Apache.

Unix users have a more specific palette of options. To take full advantage of this power, you need to clearly understand the various means by which you can analyze and control your PHP installation. The three most important on the Unix side are:

✦ Compile-time options

✦ Web-server configuration files

✦ The php.ini file

A few things can also be controlled with runtime options, system settings, or the presence/absence/configuration of other software packages.

Compile-time options

During the configure/make process, PHP allows you to specify a number of specific flags. This causes the appropriate extensions to be built into your custom version of the PHP module or binary. None of the information in this section is relevant if you are running a precompiled binary (for example, Windows, Mac OS X, or rpm build).

It's important to understand that most compile-time options are merely necessary preconditions for using a particular function set — but that this capability can still be turned on or off, or important configuration options set, in the php.ini file. The compilation step and the configuration file work together. Think of it this way: You must compile with the flag to use the functionality, but you needn't use the functionality just because you compiled with the flag.

Tip   If you fail to employ the appropriate compile-time option, you get an undefined-function fatal error. This error is almost never seen outside of user-defined functions for any other reason, so it should be considered a red flashing light that you need to check your compilation options. Thankfully, you can retrieve your previous options with phpinfo() and then simply add the new features you want, should a recompile ever be necessary.

Most compile-time options are pretty self-explanatory. You merely install the required libraries, build PHP with the --with-[library][=DIR] flag and, in some cases, set a configuration option in php.ini. In the following sections, we will mention only common cases that require special treatment of some kind.

Tip   Remember that all third-party servers and libraries that you plan to use with PHP must be downloaded and installed *before* you attempt to build PHP. This means the Web server, a database server, mail and LDAP servers, XML, encryption, graphics, and bcmath libraries must all be in place before PHP.

--with-apache[=DIR] or --with-apache2=[DIR]

This flag causes PHP to be built as a static Apache module. You must use --with-apache2 if you've ventured into the newest Apache series. Even though the Apache module version is now by far the most popular build, the PHP developers have chosen to leave the CGI build as the default choice. If you forget this (or the `--with-apxs`) flag when trying to make a static Apache module, you will end up with the CGI version.

You almost certainly want to set the Apache base directory parameter because `make` may default to some unexpected location. Remember that Apache installs in different default directories in the source versus RPM builds — so if you've previously installed an `httpd` via RPM (perhaps as part of a Red Hat Linux installation), you should uninstall the package and leave a clean background for the source build you need now.

A static Apache build will have to be recompiled every time you change PHP versions. Apache server, at this point, changes rather slowly, whereas PHP adds new extensions and releases patches rather frequently, so this may be a significant factor in choosing the `apxs` build instead.

--with-apxs[=DIR] or --with-apxs2[=DIR]

This flag specifies that the PHP module be built as a dynamic Apache module. This saves disk space for Apache, and some people claim the build is easier. The main value of the apxs build is that you will be able to swap PHP modules (while upgrading, for instance) without recompiling Apache. If you upgrade frequently, or if you enjoy trying out experimental builds, this is the best option.

 Caution   Remember that you can build PHP with *either* the `--with-apache` or `--with-apxs` flags, not both.

--with-[database][=DIR]

All the databases supported by PHP use a similar compile-time flag. The directory need only be specified if it is not the default installation directory. For more information on choosing a database for use with PHP, see Chapter 12. The specific flags and default directories are listed in Table 30-1.

Table 30-1: Database Compile-Time Information

Database Name	Default Directory	Flag Syntax
Adabas D*	/usr/local	--with-adabas[=DIR]
DBase	bundled	--enable-dbase
Filepro	bundled	--enable-filepro
IBM DB2	/home/db2inst1/sqllib	--with-ibm-db2[=DIR]
Informix	no default	--with-informix[=DIR]
iODBC*	/usr/local	--with-iodbc[=DIR]
mSql	/usr/local/Hughes	--with-msql[=DIR]
MySQL < 4.1	/usr/local/mysql	--with-mysql[=DIR]
MySQL 4.1 and above	/usr/local/mysql	--with-mysqli[=DIR]
Oracle	ORACLE_HOME	--with-oci8[=DIR]

Continued

Table 30-1 *(continued)*

Database Name	Default Directory	Flag Syntax
PostgreSQL	`/usr/local/pgsql`	`--with-pgsql[=DIR]`
SAP DB	`/usr/local`	`--with-sapdb[=DIR]`
Solid*	`/usr/local/solid`	`--with-solid[=DIR]`
Sybase	`/home/sybase`	`--with-sybase[=DIR]`
Sybase-CT	`/home/sybase`	`--with-sybase-ct[=DIR]`
SQLite	`Bundled`	`--with-sqlite`

The databases marked with an asterisk use ODBC-based interfaces. These ODBC choices are mutually exclusive — you must limit yourself to a maximum of one.

Each database mandates slightly different configuration options in `php.ini` or other configuration files. Oracle, for example, has its own environment variables that obviate PHP settings. Sybase, Oracle, and some other databases escape single quotes with single quotes, which requires the `magic_quotes_sybase` option in `php.ini`. MySQL allows you to specify a default hostname, username, and password — not at all a good idea unless you understand the security implications! Most of these options are standard and self-explanatory, however, and they have little effect on other parts of PHP.

--with-mcrypt[=DIR]

This flag builds in the `mcrypt` library, which includes many of the most popular open cipher algorithms. `mcrypt` is available for download at `http://mcrypt.sourceforge.net/`.

There is no documented default directory, although PHP can probably find the one mentioned in the `libmcrypt` documentation. `libmcrypt` must be compiled with the `--disable-posix-threads` option. See Chapter 29 for more information on using PHP's cryptography capabilities.

--with-java[=DIR]

This flag builds Java support into PHP. The `DIR` path should be set to the location of your JDK, and the Java settings in `php.ini` must all be set correctly. This extension cannot be used with a static Web server build (for example, `--with-apache`), and this flag will probably not work correctly with Solaris versions of PHP and Java. Please see the Java extension `README` in `/php_[build_directory]/ext/java` for more information.

There is an alternate method of accessing Java from PHP: integrating PHP into a Java Servlet environment using a SAPI module. You might want to do this if you use Java extensively, as it is the more efficient method. If you choose the servlet integration method, you do not need this extension. See Chapter 39 for more on using Java with PHP.

--with-xmlrpc

This flag builds Dan Libby's XML-RPC and SOAP implementation into PHP. The XML-RPC package now comes bundled with PHP, so you do not need to specify a directory.

Cross-Reference To learn more about XML-based Web services and PHP, see Chapter 41.

--with-dom[=DIR]

This flag builds with DOM XML support, using the GNOME xml library (a.k.a. `libxml`, `gnome-xml`). The `DIR` path should point to your `libxml` installation; if you don't set this value, it defaults to `/usr`. You can download and learn more about GNOME xml from `www.xmlsoft.org/`.

Tip Very common shared libraries, such as `libjpeg`, can cause fatal problems at PHP compile time even if you correctly set the directory paths in all the compile-time flags. Common issues include PHP looking for the files in the wrong place, incorrect versions of these libraries already being installed on your machine, or libraries having been built in a form inaccessible to PHP.

The solution to most of these problems is to upgrade all such shared libraries to the latest version. However, if your client applications are old, this may break them. A possible workaround is to temporarily rename the installed versions of your shared libraries so they cannot be found by PHP; compile the new versions in different locations; compile PHP using these directory paths; then rename your old versions to their original names. Take good notes if you try this!

--enable-bcmath

This option builds support for arbitrary-precision mathematics from a bundled library. You can set the number of decimal places in `php.ini`.

--enable-calendar

This option builds support for calendar conversion functions (for example, Jewish to Julian) from a bundled library.

--with-config-file-path=DIR

This option allows you to specify the location of your `php.ini` file. You need to use it only if you've deliberately moved it away from the default location, `/usr/local/lib`.

--enable-url-includes

This option allows you to include or require *and execute* files from remote HTTP or FTP servers, like this: `include(http://remotehost/include.php)`. This functionality should be carefully considered, as it has horrible security implications. If you merely want to read in HTML files from other servers, you do *not* need this flag.

--disable-url-fopen-wrapper

This flag turns off the default capability to open files on remote HTTP and FTP servers, like this: `fopen(http://remotehost/include.php)`.

CGI compile-time options

All compile-time options just described are available for the CGI version, except for the module-specific flags (for example, `--with-apache`, `--with-apxs`).

Most users today who use PHP's CGI mode are interested in using it as a standalone binary, similar to Perl, rather than for Web development. If this is the case, safe mode is probably beside the point.

--enable-safe-mode

Safe mode was originally designed for and is still very strongly recommended for users of the CGI version of PHP, especially in a shared-server environment. Module users generally do not use safe mode, although it's theoretically possible.

Safe mode basically does three things:

✦ It limits PHP parsing to files in a specified directory.

✦ Even within that directory, it prevents PHP from reading files that are owned by a user other than the one running the PHP process.

✦ It limits PHP to executing only external programs in a specified directory, such as /usr/local/bin.

Remember that *user* in this formulation means the PHP user rather than a systems user.

The increased security of safe mode comes at a cost — and that cost is inconvenience. Inconvenience is probably the number-one reason that people do insecure things in the first place — which leaves us right back where we started.

In general, if you lack root access on the server, you can forget about using safe mode. The exception is if your ISP has set you up with a CGI version of PHP running under individual UIDs with suExec or functional equivalent. It's next to impossible to switch file ownership between a real Unix system user and Nobody without becoming the superuser once in awhile.

Caution   Apache's suExec feature, which allows CGIs to be run under user IDs different than that of the httpd, is *not* compatible with PHP safe mode. You must choose one or the other, as your PHP binary will get dumped to the browser if you try to use both.

The safe mode restriction on executing programs is intended to limit access to system utilities. PHP can still connect to certain programs that are already running, regardless of their location or user — such as a database server or mail server — because it's talking to a port rather than running a program.

The main Apache configuration directive related to safe mode is DocumentRoot. Remember that under safe mode you can't include or require files from outside this directory, so set it at a high enough level. You can alternatively set the PHP document root in php.ini by means of the doc_root variable — you may choose to do it this way if, for instance, only part of your site is PHP-enabled. Configuration directives in php.ini related to safe mode include safe_mode=on/off and safe_mode_exec_dir. (You need to set this only if you want to change from /usr/local/bin to something else.) You can also use include_path to specify particular subdirectories *within your document root directory only* for your include files.

Tip   Safe mode cannot be enabled or disabled in Apache's per-directory .htaccess files. Changes related to safe mode must be made in the main Apache configuration file, httpd.conf, or in php.ini as described previously.

The function set_time_limit() cannot be used in safe mode. You must depend on the global configuration directive max_execution_time in php.ini instead.

--with-exec-dir[=DIR]

Another compile-time option relating to safe mode is --with-exec-dir. This option sets the default safe-mode execution directory to /usr/local/bin, but that can be changed with the safe_mode_exec directive in php.ini. Remember you can only run programs from this single directory under safe mode.

--enable-discard-path

If you'd like to place the CGI version of PHP outside the Web tree and call it as you would a Perl CGI script (such as with #!/usr/local/bin/php as the first line of each script), you need to specify this compile-time flag. You must also make all PHP CGI scripts executable.

--enable-force-cgi-redirect

This flag is a security must for the CGI module. It prevents browser users from calling CGI-bin files directly, thereby bypassing Apache security settings. This is an Apache-specific configuration directive; don't bother trying to enable it if you are running on a different Web server or as a standalone binary.

Apache configuration files

If PHP is used with Apache as a module or with CGI, much of PHP's basic file-serving capability is determined by Apache's configuration files. The main ones from recent versions of Apache Server are the httpd.conf file for global settings, and the .htaccess file for per-directory access settings. Older versions of Apache split up httpd.conf into three files (access.conf, httpd.conf, and srm.conf), and some users still prefer this arrangement.

In PHP3, there were specific Apache configuration directives that could substitute for almost every php.ini setting. For example, instead of setting Engine = On in the first substantive line of php.ini, you could put php3_engine on in an .htaccess file for a similar effect. As the number of PHP configuration directives increased, however, people decided that too many flags were cluttering up Apache's namespace. The naming scheme has been generalized, therefore, to encompass these four basic, configurable directives:

✦ php_value name value: Sets value of variable.

✦ php_flag name on|off: Sets Boolean.

✦ php_admin_value name value: Sets value of variable. Can only be used in main Apache configuration file(s) rather than .htaccess.

✦ php_admin_flag name on|off: Sets Boolean. Can be used only in main Apache configuration file(s) rather than .htaccess.

An example would be magic quotes for GET, POST, and COOKIE variables. You can use php_flag with the name of the variable, like this:

```
php_flag magic_quotes_gpc off
```

If this is all too confusing, don't worry: The new-style Apache configuration directive naming only applies to settings you can change in php.ini anyway.

Apache server has a very powerful, but slightly complex, configuration system of its own. Learn more about it at the Apache Web site: www.apache.org/.

The following headings describe settings in httpd.conf that affect PHP directly and cannot be set elsewhere.

Timeout

This value sets the default number of seconds before any HTTP request will time out. If you set PHP's `max_execution_time` to longer than this value, PHP will keep grinding away but the user may see a 404 error. In safe mode, this value will be ignored; you must use the `timeout` value in `php.ini` instead.

DocumentRoot

`DocumentRoot` designates the root directory for all HTTP processes on that server. It looks something like this on Unix:

```
DocumentRoot    "/usr/local/apache_1.3.6/htdocs"
```

It looks like this on Windows:

```
DocumentRoot    "C:/Program Files/Apache/htdocs/"
```

The document root can be almost any directory — it needn't be in the Apache installation directory. You can specify a subdirectory of this as the PHP document root, using the `doc_root` setting in `php.ini`. In this case, HTML files would be served out of the Apache document root and its subdirectories, but PHP would be parsed only in the specified PHP directory and its subdirectories.

AddType

The PHP MIME type needs to be set here for PHP files to be parsed.

Remember that you can associate any file extension with PHP; many administrators set the `.php3` and `.html` types for backward compatibility — but if you wanted to, you could have PHP parse files called `filename.asp` or `filename.jsp`. You can also add multiple types for different versions of PHP. The following are sample `AddType` lines; the first one is the most common for PHP4 and above, but you can add as many of the others as you wish.

```
AddType application/x-httpd-php .php
AddType application/x-httpd-phps .phps
AddType application/x-httpd-php3 .php3 .phtml
AddType application/x-httpd-php .html
```

You can also set this on a per-directory basis with `.htaccess`, simply by adding type lines to `.htaccess` files. PHP files are then parsed only in one directory of your site (for instance, in a forum folder). Alternatively, you can set up a directory with archived versions of files that may have old extensions — so just in that directory, Apache allow files with the `.phtml` extension to be parsed.

Action

You must set this line for the CGI version of PHP with Apache, generally used with Windows. You do *not* need to set this line for the module version of PHP.

```
Action application/x-httpd-php4 "/php/php.exe"
```

LoadModule

You must uncomment this line for the Windows apxs module version of Apache with shared object support:

```
LoadModule php4_module modules/php4apache.dll
```

or on Unix flavors:

```
LoadModule php4_module modules/mod_php.so
```

AddModule

You must uncomment this line for the static module version of Apache.

```
AddModule mod_php4.c
```

The php.ini file

The PHP configuration file, php.ini, is the final and most immediate way to affect PHP's functionality. Important changes are frequently made in the structure of this file, so if you haven't bothered to really look at every line recently, now may be a good time.

The php.ini file is read each time PHP is initialized — in other words, whenever httpd is restarted for the module version or with each script execution for the CGI version. If your change isn't showing up, remember to stop and restart httpd. If it still isn't showing up, use phpinfo() to check the path to php.ini (near the top of the file); if necessary, recompile with the --with-config-file-path flag or just move php.ini to wherever PHP expects to find it.

Caution

What happens if PHP can't find php.ini? Under Windows, right up until the formal release of PHP4, you used to get an "unable to parse configuration file" fatal error. Under Unix and now under Windows as an ISAPI module, interestingly enough, you get no warnings or errors — PHP carries on with default settings, which are the same as if you had not changed any settings in php.ini-dist. You need to install php.ini only if you want to change the default settings.

The configuration file is well commented and thorough. Keys are case sensitive, keyword values are not; whitespace, and lines beginning with semicolons are ignored. Booleans can be represented by 1/0, Yes/No, On/Off, or True/False. The default values in php.ini-dist will result in a reasonable PHP installation that can be tweaked later.

What follows are notes explaining the settings in php.ini that are not completely documented in the file or the PHP manual's configuration.html page.

short_open_tag = Off

Short open tags look like this: <? ?>. This option *must* be set to Off if you want to use XML functions.

safe_mode = Off

If this is set to On, you probably compiled PHP with the --enable-safe-mode flag. Safe mode is most relevant to CGI use. See the explanation in the section "CGI compile-time options," earlier in this chapter.

safe_mode_exec_dir = [DIR]

This option is relevant only if safe mode is on; it can also be set with the --with-exec-dir flag during the Unix build process. PHP in safe mode only executes external binaries out of this directory. The default is /usr/local/bin. This has nothing to do with serving up a normal PHP/HTML Web page.

safe_mode_allowed_env_vars = [PHP_]

This option sets which environment variables users can change in safe mode. The default is only those variables prepended with "PHP_." If this directive is empty, most variables are alterable.

safe_mode_protected_env_vars = [LD_LIBRARY_PATH]

This option sets which environment variables users can't change in safe mode, even if safe_mode_allowed_env_vars is set permissively.

disable_functions = [function1, function2, function3...functionn]

A welcome addition to PHP4 configuration and one perpetuated in PHP5 is the ability to disable selected functions for security reasons. Previously, this necessitated hand-editing the C code from which PHP was made. Filesystem, system, and network functions should probably be the first to go because allowing the capability to write files and alter the system over HTTP is never such a safe idea.

max_execution_time = 30

The function set_time_limit() won't work in safe mode, so this is the main way to make a script time out in safe mode. In Windows, you have to abort based on maximum memory consumed rather than time. You can also use the Apache timeout setting to timeout if you use Apache, but that will apply to non-PHP files on the site too.

error_reporting = E_ALL & ~E_NOTICE

The default value is E_ALL & ~E_NOTICE, all errors except notices. Development servers should be set to at least the default; only production servers should even consider a lesser value.

error_prepend_string = ["<font color=ff0000>"]

With its bookend, error_append_string, this setting allows you to make error messages a different color than other text, or what have you. We recommend setting the value to "<blink>" (and error_append_string to "</blink>", of course) for a special treat! The default values result in a red error message. Remember to uncomment these if you want to use them—they're commented out by default.

warn_plus_overloading = Off

This setting issues a warning if the + operator is used with strings, as in a form value.

variables_order = EGPCS

This configuration setting supersedes gpc_order. Both are now deprecated along with register_globals. It sets the order of the different variables: Environment, GET, POST, COOKIE, and SERVER (aka Built-in). You can change this order around. Variables will be overwritten successively in left-to-right order, with the rightmost one *winning* the hand every time. This means if you left the default setting and happened to use the same name for an environment variable, a POST variable, and a COOKIE variable, the COOKIE variable would own that name at the end of the process. In real life, this doesn't happen much.

register_globals = Off

This setting allows you to decide whether you wish to register EGPCS variables as global. This is now deprecated, and as of PHP4.2, this flag is set to Off by default. Use superglobal arrays instead. All the major code listings in this book use superglobal arrays.

gpc_order = GPC

Deprecated.

magic_quotes_gpc = On

This setting escapes quotes in incoming GET/POST/COOKIE data. If you use a lot of forms which possibly submit to themselves or other forms and display form values, you may need to set this directive to On or prepare to use addslashes() on string-type data.

magic_quotes_runtime = Off

This setting escapes quotes in incoming database and text strings. Remember that SQL adds slashes to single quotes and apostrophes when storing strings and does not strip them off when returning them. If this setting is Off, you will need to use stripslashes() when outputting any type of string data from a SQL database. If magic_quotes_sybase is set to On, this must be Off.

magic_quotes_sybase = Off

This setting escapes single quotes in incoming database and text strings with Sybase-style single quotes rather than backslashes. If magic_quotes_runtime is set to On, this must be Off.

auto-prepend-file = [path/to/file]

If a path is specified here, PHP must automatically include() it at the beginning of every PHP file. Include path restrictions do apply.

auto-append-file = [path/to/file]

If a path is specified here, PHP must automatically include() it at the end of every PHP file—unless you escape by using the exit() function. Include path restrictions do apply.

include_path = [DIR]

If you set this value, you will only be allowed to include or require files from these directories. The include directory is generally under your document root; this is mandatory if you're running in safe mode. Set this to . in order to include files from the same directory your script is in. Multiple directories are separated by colons: .:/usr/local/apache/htdocs:/usr/local/lib.

doc_root = [DIR]

If you're using Apache, you've already set a document root for this server or virtual host in httpd.conf. Set this value here if you're using safe mode or if you want to enable PHP only on a portion of your site (for example, only in one subdirectory of your Web root).

upload_tmp_dir = [DIR]

Do not uncomment this line unless you understand the implications of HTTP uploads!

session.save-handler = files

See Chapter 24 for details on this setting. Except in rare circumstances, you will not want to change this setting.

ignore_user_abort = [On/Off]

This setting controls what happens if a site visitor clicks the browser's Stop button. The default is On, which means that the script continues to run to completion or timeout. If the setting is changed to Off, the script will abort. This setting only works in module mode, not CGI.

Improving PHP Performance

There are two schools of thought about Web performance. The first is that PHP script performance, theoretical Web server speed, chip clock speed, server RAM, and almost everything else is made irrelevant by throughput issues — so why sweat the small stuff? The other is that there's no thrill quite like that of shaving a few microseconds off your script execution time. This section is basically useless for proponents of the former view.

Before you can improve your performance, you have to measure it. Commercial profiling tools are just starting to hit the marketplace — Zend Studio, which we discuss in Chapter 32, includes a profiling component — but relatively few PHP users utilize them yet. We default, therefore, to the time-honored programming performance metric: measuring microseconds. Whip up a little function like this:

```
function exec_time()
{
  $mtime = explode( " ", microtime());
  $msec = (double)$mtime[0];
  $sec = (double)$mtime[1];
  return $sec + $msec;
}
```

This function just reformats microtime output into a double for easier subtraction. Paste or include it at the top of the script you'd like to measure. Now divide the main body of your script into sections and scatter calls to exec_time() at strategic points, like so:

```
<?php
$start_db_call = exec_time();
$db = mysql_select_db("test");
$result = mysql_query("SELECT * FROM user
                       WHERE ID=1");
while ($testrow = mysql_fetch_array($result)) {
  echo $testrow[0];
}
$end_db_call = exec_time();
$runtime = $end_db_call - $start_db_call;
echo "Database call and echo took $runtime seconds";
?>
```

The next time you hit the Web page, voilà! A self-timing PHP script, at your service.

Caution   Using `microtime()` to measure PHP tells you only what happens between the time PHP begins working on the first measured line of code and the time it finishes working on the last measured line of code. It does not tell you how long your Web server is taking to spawn a child process or your CGI to start up, how much latency your server is suffering from, what traffic conditions at your Web farm are like, or a lot of other things that affect real-world performance at least as much if not more that actual PHP processing time. To find out that kind of thing, you need measuring tools far beyond PHP. A good start for Apache on Unix is the program called `ab` (aka Apache Benchmark tool), which ships with Apache.

Now that you know how long the various parts of your script are taking, you can take steps to improve performance. Actually, a little logic should tell you that functions that touch other files or call other daemons should take longer than those that are self-contained within a discrete file. So database calls, `include` and `require` statements, objects with inheritance, and XML parsing are just going to take longer than simple arithmetic or echoing a string. But because these advanced functionalities are the best part of PHP, obviously it would be pointless to get rid of them for the sake of squeezing out a few more microseconds.

What you can and should do instead is hunt and destroy gross programming errors that cause unnecessary latency. Infinite loops, you know, are never very stylish. If you can notice a script running slowly with the naked eye, especially on a localhost, it's cause for concern—whip out the microtime and find out where it's going wrong. Pay special attention to known bottlenecks such as: using regex instead of `explode()` in a tight loop; object-oriented programming where it's not needed; bad use of SQL; including multiple instances of the same files; and long loops.

Although it would be better to eliminate all errors in the code itself, you can also help matters by setting the Apache or PHP timeout and max-memory configuration variables as low as possible. Come on—no Web page should need a 300-second timeout and you know it. Another configuration setting that may have a good effect on extremely slow scripts is `ignore_user_abort` in `php.ini`.

Optimizers and caches

Until recently, speed-shavers had few options but homemade metrics like the `microtime()` function just described. But now, intriguing tools are beginning to become widely used to increase PHP performance.

One that is available without cost is the Zend Optimizer. This tool makes multiple passes over a PHP script and replaces slower constructs with faster ones that have the same effect. However, the Zend Optimizer is rumored to mostly help inexperienced coders: If you already write tight PHP, it may not be able to add much value.

Another Zend product which promises to affect performance positively is the Zend Accelerator. This product apparently compiles and stores a version of each page in memory, reducing disk reads and redundant compilation and thus speeding Web service. Reliable reports claim that the Accelerator can deliver from two to ten times improvement in number of requests handled. Both the Zend Accelerator and the Zend Optimizer are availabe at the Zend Web site, `www.zend.com`.

There are also optimizing and caching products available without cost. Two popular choices are Nick Lindridge's PHP Accelerator (`www.php-accelerator.co.uk`) and APC (`http://apc.communityconnect.com`).

Recent distributions of PHP have also offered an optimized `php.ini` that sets variables for maximum speed at the possible expense of other virtues. If you choose to use this file, please take the time to understand the effects of its changes — in other words, don't just slap on your server and then ask where your `HTTP_*_VARS` values went.

Summary

The good thing and the bad thing about PHP configuration are the same: There are a whole heck of a lot of options and more than one way to set many of them. The Unix Apache module is particularly rich in choices, but the development team has labored long and hard to make PHP as customizable as possible.

There are three main ways to configure PHP. The first is via build-time flags, which are only available to those who build from source. Many of these directives are only necessary pre-conditions, meaning they set default conditions that need to be confirmed or can be reversed elsewhere. The second is via Apache configuration files (`httpd.conf` and `.htaccess`), which are only available to users of Apache server. The third is via the `php.ini` file, which comes with every PHP distribution.

The `php.ini` file experienced a few significant changes with PHP4, but hopefully has stabilized somewhat with PHP5. One of the most important is the capability to disable functions on an individual basis. Certain features of PHP3 and PHP2 are beginning to be deprecated in this file, such as `register_globals`. And the `php.ini` is no longer an absolute necessity on Windows — versions of PHP now recognize default values even without the file being present in the Windows path.

After you've run PHP for a while, you may wish to tune its performance. PHP4 and 5 are considerably faster at the same tasks than PHP3, and in general script execution time isn't the bottleneck to total performance — but you may want to maximize the efficiency of your PHP-enabled server anyway. The main tool available to measure performance is simply echoing `microtime()` at intervals throughout a script. With this simple method, you can try to narrow down and improve the parts of your scripts that are taking the most time. This does not measure anything outside PHP that may affect its performance; for that, you need external tools such as `ab` (Apache Benchmark).

Tools to help speed up PHP are becoming widely available. One of the most intriguing is Zend's Accelerator, which promises at a minimum to double pages served on the same hardware. There are also alternatives available without cost.

Exceptions and Error Handling

Until now, programmers have been very creative in figuring out how to deal with error cases within PHP, whether setting and printing error strings or using and abusing the limited error reporting system. Despite its many useful features, PHP has not contained a good system for comprehensively dealing with errors. Fortunately, this is beginning to change with PHP5.

Error Handling in PHP5

If you are familiar with structured programming languages, such as C and Java, you have probably grown accustomed to the various built-in objects that allow you to handle errors and exceptions. If so, you'll be happy to note that PHP5 now includes, for the first time, an exception-handling object, and that the syntax is very similar to existing languages like Java. In fact, once you learn a bit of syntax you can begin handling errors and exceptions much as you have been with other object-oriented languages.

However, if you have been primarily using PHP, and are unfamiliar with other languages, the idea of exception handling may be new to you. Exception handling is a powerful tool that you will come to appreciate once you understand the concept and put it to good use in your code. This new built-in function will enable you to debug error conditions, recover from unexpected situations, and present a clean interface to your end users without printing errors to the screen.

Errors and exceptions

It is helpful to think of an exception, not merely as an error. An exception, as the name implies, is any condition experienced by your program that is unexpected or not handled within the normal scope of your code. Generally, an exception is not a fatal error that should halt program execution, but a condition that can be detected and dealt with in order to continue properly.

Exceptions, when properly used, can greatly increase the reliability of your application, and cut down on debugging headaches. However, poorly handled or ill-defined exceptions can create more problems than they solve by obscuring the source of an error. Plan on taking the time to properly determine and execute your exception handling method, and you will be amply rewarded.

Take a look at some sample code that contains some error detection as it might be handled in PHP4 or earlier. We are retrieving a POST variable containing a user's ID, which must be at least nine characters in length and begin with the `"usr"` prefix. Once the variable is checked for these conditions, we pass it to a function that will verify the existence of the user within the site database.

Listing 31-1: Error-handling without exceptions

```
<?

// include the file which will validate the user ID
require_once('includes/usr_functions.php');

// retrieve the user ID to validate
$user_id = $_POST['user_id'];

// set the display message based on whether or not the
// user ID is valid
if ( !is_valid_user($user_id)) {
    $msg = "Sorry, $user_id is not a valid user ID.";
} else {
    $msg = "$user_id is a valid user ID.";
}


function is_valid_user($user_id) {

    // return false if the user ID does not begin with "usr"
    $pre_str = "usr";
    if ((strpos($user_id, $pre_str) === false) ||
      (strpos($user_id, $pre_str) != 0)) {
      return false;
    }

    // return false if the user ID is not the proper length
    if ((strlen($user_id) < 9)) {
      return false;
    }

    if (validate($user_id)) {
      // user ID was found in the database
      return true;
    } else {
      // the specified user ID does not exist in the database
      return false;
    }

}
?>
```

As you can see, any number of conditions might cause the `is_valid_user()` function to return a value of `false`, only one of which actually pertains to the question of whether the user exists in the database. Using exceptions, you can more easily distinguish among types of errors and deal with them according to the nature of each error.

The Exception class

The new Exception class is built into PHP5 and ready for use with any code on a PHP5 server. Rather than using Boolean functions as in the preceding example, an instance of Exception can be created or thrown within the code.

Listing 31-2 shows what Listing 31-1 might look like after rewriting to use exception-handling.

Listing 31-2: **Error-handling using exceptions**

```
<?

// include the file which will validate the user ID
require_once('includes/usr_functions.php');

// retrieve the user ID to validate
$user_id = $_POST['user_id'];

try {

    // set the display message based on whether or not
    // user ID is valid
    if (!is_valid_user($user_id)) {
        $msg = "Sorry, $user_id is not a valid user ID.";
    } else {
        $msg = "$user_id is a valid user ID.";
    }

} catch(Exception $ex) {
    // retrieve the message from the exception object
    $msg = ($ex->getMessage());

}


function is_valid_user ($user_id) {

    // throw an exception if the user ID does not begin
    // with "usr"
    $pre_str = "usr";
    if ((strpos($user_id, $pre_str) === false) ||
        (strpos($user_id, $pre_str) != 0)) {
        throw new
        Exception('$user_id does not contain the proper prefix.');
```

Continued

Listing 31-2 *(continued)*

```
    }

    // throw an exception if the user ID is not the proper length
    if ((strlen($user_id) < 9)) {
        throw new Exception('$user_id is less than the
            required length');
    }

    if (validate($user_id)) {
        // user ID was found in the database
        return true;
    }
    else
        // the specified user ID does not exist in the database
        return false;
    }


}

?>
```

Don't be thrown by the use of the word *throw*. In this case, it is used to create a new Exception object. Now errors that have nothing to do with normal flow are handled as separate exceptions rather than mingling with the rest of the application.

The try/catch block

Exceptions are caught and handled using a try/catch control construct. You will want to include any code that may generate an error or exception within the `try()` construction. Whenever any exception is thrown by the code, the `try()` block execution is terminated, and the remaining code within the `try()` construction is not executed. The `catch()` block is then consulted to find the proper type of exception, and the exception is then dealt with according to the code within that particular catch block. We now have different conditions based upon the type of exception that was thrown, rather than one general, nonspecific error.

Throwing an exception

One of the nice things about using exceptions is the ability to display as much — or as little — information as you need. There are several methods available for use with an Exception object, which you can use to create your own error messages or to deal with conditions accordingly.

The following code shows how you might throw and immediately catch a generic exception, and then take apart the Exception object to recover the message, error code, and originating file and line number.

```php
<?

try {

   throw new Exception('Syntax error');

} catch(Exception $ex) {

    // the input string passed to the object
    $msg = ($ex->getMessage());
    // customizable error code
    $code = ($ex->getCode());
    // name of the file that threw the exception
    $file = ($ex->getFile());
    // line number containing the exception
    $line = ($ex->getLine());

   echo "Error no. $code: $msg in file $file on line $line";
}

?>
```

Here, a standard, PHP style error message is displayed. However, you as the programmer can display anything that you like or can even change application behavior based on the specific error.

Note that, although in this example the code that throws the exception is the only thing in the `try` block, we could have had arbitrarily complex code that calls a function defined in a different file, which throws an exception only some of the time. Whenever an exception is thrown, control will revert to the `catch` block associated with the `try`.

Multiple catch blocks can be used to deal successfully with more than one type of exception. We'll look at an example in the following section.

Defining your own Exception subclasses

PHP also allows you to define your own classes that inherit from the Exception class. Now you no longer have to rely on the `getMessage()` function for information on the specific type of error that was generated. Subclasses can be defined as in the following example:

```php
<?

class CustomException extends Exception {
   function __construct($message) {
      parent::Exception($message);
   }
}

?>
```

Let's look at the example covered in Listing 31-3 and consider using custom exceptions. People signing in using this code may forget to include the "usr" prefix in their user name, so if it's missing you might want to try adding it and validating again rather than immediately halting the program.

Listing 31-3: **Recovering using custom exceptions**

```
<?

// include the file which will validate the user ID
require_once('includes/usr_functions.php');

// retrieve the user ID to validate
$user_id = $_POST['user_id'];

try {

    // set the display message based on whether or not
    // user ID is valid
    if (!is_valid_user($user_id)) {
        $msg = "Sorry, $user_id is not a valid user ID.";
    } else {
        $msg = "$user_id is a valid user ID.";
    }

} catch(PrefixException $ex) {

    // if prefix is missing, try again with proper prefix
    $user_pre = "usr" . $user_pre;
    if (!is_valid_user($user_pre)) {
        // second attempt has failed, retrieve message
        $msg = ($ex->getMessage());
    }

} catch(LengthException $ex) {
    // retrieve the message from the exception object
        $msg = ($ex->getMessage());
}

//define custom exception classes

class PrefixException extends Exception {
    function __construct($message) {
        parent::Exception($message);
    }
}

class LengthException extends Exception {
    function __construct($message) {
```

```
            parent::Exception($message);
        }
    }

    echo $msg;

    function is_valid_user ($user_id) {

        // throw an exception if the user ID does not begin
        // with "usr"
        $pre_str = "usr";
        if ((strpos($user_id, $pre_str) === false) ||
            (strpos($user_id, $pre_str) != 0)) {
            throw new
PrefixException('$user_id does not contain the proper prefix.');
        }

        // throw an exception if the user ID is not the proper length
        if ((strlen($user_id) < 9)) {
            throw new
   LengthException('$user_id is less than the required length');
        }

        if (validate($user_id)) {
            // user ID was found in the database
            return true;
        }
        else
            // the specified user ID does not exist in the database
            return false;
        }

    }

?>
```

Note that we attempted to recover from the *missing prefix* error condition. You can easily deal with individual types of errors now that they have been defined separately.

Limitations of Exceptions in PHP

The Exception object is completely new in PHP5 and as such is still in the rough stages of development. As of this writing, PHP does not support the use of `finally()` or `throws()` methods as do Java and other languages. Also, unlike other languages, native PHP errors — including errors, which are normally printed to the client-side browser — are not yet mapped to exceptions. Because of this, for example, a SQL statement error within a try/catch block will not automatically throw an exception that can be caught and dealt with. This handy functionality will most likely be included in a future version of PHP, so it's worth mentioning and keeping an eye out for. Some of these errors can be dealt with using techniques described in the next section.

Other Methods of Error Handling

If you're still using PHP4 or an older version, or are not comfortable dealing with classes and objects, there are several error handling functions that have been available in PHP for some time, including native PHP errors, defining an error handler, and triggering a user error.

Native PHP errors

PHP generates three types of errors, depending on severity:

✦ **Notice:** These errors are not serious and do not create a serious problem. By default they are suppressed, unless the logging level is changed in the php.ini file.

✦ **Warning:** Failed code has created an error, but does not terminate execution. Usually the error is displayed, but the script continues to run. (See Figure 31-1.)

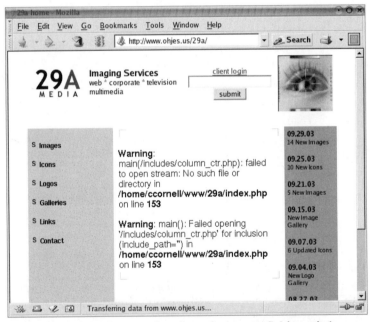

Figure 31-1: Native PHP Warning allows the page to finish rendering.

✦ **Fatal error:** A serious error condition has rendered the script unable to run. A fatal error terminates the script. (See Figure 31-2.)

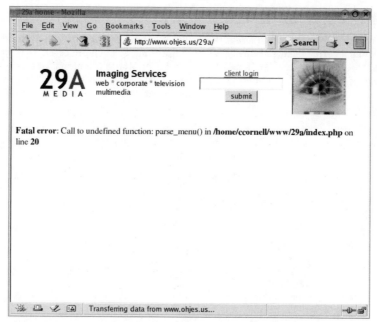

Figure 31-2: Native PHP Fatal error terminates execution of the page.

Each type of error is also represented by a constant that can be referred to within your code: E_USER_NOTICE, E_USER_WARNING, and E_USER_ERROR. The error-reporting level can be manually defined within a script, as in these examples:

```
//report only fatal errors
error_reporting(E_USER_ERROR);

//report warnings and fatal errors
error_reporting(E_USER_WARNING | E_USER_ERROR);

//report all errors, including notices
error_reporting(E_ALL);
```

Caution Suppressing error reporting to avoid printed errors can lead to hair loss during the debugging process! You will instead want to deal with an error handler, for the most part.

Because notices never make it to the client, and don't impair functionality, you're almost always safe in disregarding them for error handling purposes. Conversely, the custom error handler cannot handle fatal errors; PHP considers them serious enough to terminate the script, no questions asked. So the usefulness of the custom error handling function is generally limited to warnings. The primary use of this function is to avoid printing *program-ese* error messages for the end user and disrupting the flow of the application.

Defining an error handler

There's an important question to ask at this point: What information do you want displayed to the user when an error occurs? Usually, it's not important, or even preferred, to display details of the inner workings of your application to an end user; not to mention that errors look ugly on a Web page. By creating a function that designs a custom error message, then setting that function as the default error handler, you can avoid the awkward and unprofessional display of errors to a user.

First, let's create a function and determine what information we would like to provide. We will need to accept as input parameters the error type, message, filename, and line number.

```
<?
    function error_msg($err_type, $err_msg, $err_file, $err_line)
    (
        echo "<div class='errorMsg'>";
        echo "<b>Error:</b>";
        echo "<p>";
        echo "We're sorry, but an error has occurred " .
            "in this page. ";
        echo "Please access the <a href='/help.html'>Help" .
            "</a> page, ";
        echo "or try again later.";
        echo "</div>";
        echo "<div class='finePrint'>";
        echo "Error type: $err_type: $err_msg in $err_file " .
            "at line $err_line";
        echo "</div>";
    }
?>
```

We have elected, in this case, to provide information on the specific error and where it occurred. Depending on the situation, we may want to provide very little information to the user other than the fact that an error has occurred and provide information on what to try next.

Now that we have defined our custom error handler, we simply need to refer to the function within the code using the `set_error_handler()` function:

```
set_error_handler("error_msg");
```

With this code in place, all errors that are enabled by the error-reporting level will direct through our custom function, with the unfortunate exception of a fatal error. See Figure 31-3 for an example of such an error being displayed.

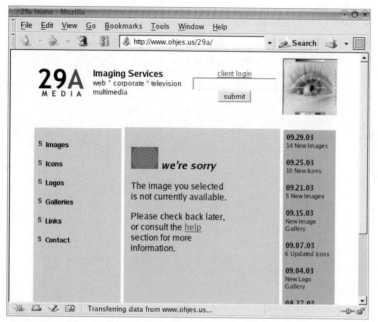

Figure 31-3: A custom error handler preserves the interface.

Triggering a user error

PHP4 can be used to trigger a user error, which is roughly equivalent to throwing an exception in PHP5. An error of any type can be thrown by passing an error message and an optional error-level constant:

```
<?

    // trigger a user error if the user id is not valid
    if ( !is_valid_user($user_id)) {
        trigger_error("Invalid user ID", E_USER_WARNING);
    }

?>
```

The triggered error is best used in conjunction with a custom error handler. Once this error is thrown, your defined error handler will be used to provide a formatted error message to the user. Note that the error-level constant defaults to E_USER_NOTICE, which is ignored unless you have specifically set error reporting otherwise.

Logging and Debugging

As mentioned earlier, exception handling and error reporting can turn your debugging efforts into a nightmare if not executed with care. An error that is difficult to track down can become almost impossible when it has been suppressed or rerouted carelessly. With a bit of planning, however, exceptions and error handlers can greatly simplify maintenance of an application.

Previously, we have examined the process of dealing with errors primarily as a means of avoiding disruption for the user. The same process can also be applied to enable logging and debugging for the programmer. Within your `catch()` control block, include a call to a built-in function such as `error_log()`, with any relevant information that might aid in the debugging process:

```
} catch(Exception $ex) {

    // the input string passed to the object
    $msg = ($ex->getMessage());
    // customizable error code
    $code = ($ex->getCode());
    // name of the file that threw the exception
    $file = ($ex->getFile());
    // line number containing the exception
    $line = ($ex->getLine());

    // write to error log
    $log_msg = "Error $code in $file at line $line: $msg : " .
        time();
    error_log ($log_msg, 3, "/var/tmp/php_error.log");

    //print to screen
    echo "Error no. $code: $msg in file $file on line $line";

}
```

The process is similar when using a custom error handler:

```
<?
    function error_msg($type, $msg, $file, $line) {

        // write to error log
        $log_msg = "Error $type in $file at line $line: $msg : " .
            time();
        $log_path = "/var/tmp/php_error.log");
        error_log ($log_msg, 3, $log_path);

        //print to screen
        echo "Error type: $err_type: $err_msg in $err_file " .
            "at line $err_line";

    }
?>
```

error_log( ) accepts one of four integers as the second parameter, which sets the message type in conjunction with the third, or location, parameter:

0 — uses the operating system's system logging mechanism

1 — sends the error to a specified e-mail address (extra headers may be added as a fourth parameter)

2 — sends the error through PHP's debugging connection (remote debugging must be enabled)

3 — error message is appended to a destination error log file

Summary

Error handling continues to become easier and more uniform with the ongoing development of PHP. The Exception class provides a means of separating error conditions, or exceptions, from the flow of the application. Using the try/catch block and custom-defined Exception subclasses, errors can be intercepted and even recovered.

Previous versions of PHP also provide a measure of error handling and reporting. User errors can be triggered as an alternative to throwing an exception, and custom error handlers can provide a better user experience as well as useful debugging information. Logging and debugging are crucial to successful exception and error handling.

✦　　✦　　✦

Debugging

Debugging — finding and eliminating errors — is part of software development. As a PHP programmer, you should be aware of all the tools available to you as you seek to eliminate malfunctioning elements in your software systems.

There are many such tools, not least because PHP applications usually rely on the capabilities of several servers (such as an HTTP server and a database management server), each of which typically comes equipped with its own logging and reporting capabilities with which it keeps its users hip to what's happening. Plus, PHP has a considerable error-reporting facility of its own (you can choose to have error messages printed alongside normal output or logged to a file for more discreet analysis). The language also has a number of functions with which you can have your programs generate custom error reports, and at the very least you can use conditional print statements to monitor the activity of programs (and the values of variables within them) as they execute.

On top of the built-in error-reporting capabilities of PHP and its supporting technologies, PHP programmers now have access to the sorts of debugging tools that programmers working with other languages have had for years. Chief among these is the Zend debugging environment, which allows you to monitor variable values, set breakpoints, and step through programs at any pace you like.

This chapter aims to introduce you to the tools and techniques available to you as you work to perfect your PHP software.

General Troubleshooting Strategies

The two basic elements of a debugging effort are figuring out what's wrong, and then fixing it (without breaking something else as a side effect of your solution). It doesn't matter whether you're diagnosing a PHP program, a telephone switch, an electronic circuit, or a Buick — certain principles apply regardless. Bear these ideas in mind as you try to figure out what ails your software.

Change one thing at a time

It's a basic rule of experimentation: You can't be sure what caused a given effect if there are multiple variables. Make a single change; then examine the output and see if the unwanted behavior is fixed. If not, try one more change (possibly changing the first one back to the way it was).

Try to isolate the problem

If you can narrow the problem down to a single library or function, you've made significant progress in locating the cause. Use special `echo()` and `print_r()` calls to output trace information frequently. This will allow you to see when troublesome changes are taking place and when variables stop holding the values you think they're holding.

You can also use a visual debugger (like Zend Studio, discussed later in this chapter) to monitor programs and their members as they execute.

Simplify, then build up

It sounds obvious, but if you're having trouble with a given function or feature, cut it out (either literally or with comments) and make sure everything runs without it. Then replace dynamic data with static data (replace a database query with simple variable assignment statements). Get it working right under simple conditions, and add complexity in stages, testing all the way to see when errors appear.

Check the obvious

We've all heard the story about the call to tech support in which the customer complains that he can't see his mouse pointer move, and after lots of diagnostics it turns out that the machine isn't plugged in. It's probably apocryphal, but in any case make sure your Web server is working properly on its own, and that a basic "Hello, World" script renders properly. You can also add `phpinfo()` to the end of a simple test script to get a lot of information about your PHP interpreter's version and environment details.

Speaking of version, make sure you're not trying to do something that requires `register_globals` (the infamous setting in `php.ini`) to be on. That setting is set to `no` by default, as of PHP4.2, and it's tripped up more than one programmer.

Document your solution

It's extraordinarily common: You struggle with an error condition for hours (or longer) and finally reach a solution. At that point, don't immediately head out to celebrate. Take a minute to document what happened and what the solution was. That way, you'll be ready when the same problem pops up again—and it will.

After fixing, re-test

It's not unusual to fix a problem and in doing so break something else. That's why it's important to retest your system beyond the scope of the bug you were originally after. This also points out why it's important to isolate bugs as much as possible—it limits the scope of re-testing you have to do.

A Menagerie of Bugs

A number of different kinds of bugs plague programmers. Some bugs are both simple in nature and easily found (as is the case with syntax errors and spelling mistakes). Others are significantly more difficult to catch, which is why this chapter is here.

Compile-time bugs

PHP is a compiled language — it's compiled just before it executes, so the compilation isn't as obvious as it is in C or Java.

A compile-time bug is obvious to the Zend Engine, which does the compiling. The compiler will raise an objection, often with a line number, and you can go fix the problem. Examples of compile-time errors are mistyped variable names, forgotten semicolons, and mismatched parentheses.

Run-time bugs

A run-time bug doesn't appear until after your program is under way, and may result from some outside condition, such as unexpected input from a user or unanticipated behavior by a database. These have to be tested for, as they usually won't make themselves evident to programmers under all conditions.

Logical bugs

Logical bugs are perhaps the most difficult of all to spot and can be very difficult to fix if they result from an error in thinking.

Say you wanted to launch a space probe and have it enter orbit around Mars. However, because your navigation algorithm didn't allow for metric input from those pesky Europeans, your space probe crashed into the Martian surface. The software did exactly as it was told, which, strictly speaking, was to drive the rocket into Mars. That's a logical error.

The point: Make sure your programs not only generate output, but generate the correct output. Get out the calculator and make sure the program's results are right, or compare its results to values known to be good. And don't use PHP to program spacecraft, just to be safe.

 Cross-Reference For a guide to the most common symptoms of the most common compile-time and run-time bugs, see Chapter 11.

Using Web Server Logs

Because most PHP programs result in some sort of HTML page, which is in turn served by an HTTP server such as Apache or Microsoft Internet Information Server (IIS), it is possible for errors to be introduced by the Web server software. For that reason, it is important to be familiar with the way in which your Web server manages error reporting and logging and to know how to access and interpret the logs you need.

Apache

The Apache HTTP Server maintains two log files in plain text format. They are:

✦ `Apache/logs/access.log`: Notes every HTTP request for a file, including its date, time, and result (success or failure, as indicated by a numeric status code). The access log also records the IP address from which each request came.

✦ `Apache/logs/error.log`: Records error conditions only.

The Common Log Format

By default, entries in the Apache error.log file use the standardized Common Log Format. Entries in this format each correspond to a single instance of request/response activity (requests and responses are, after all, what HTTP servers handle). For example, one line might correspond to a request for an HTML page (and its subsequent service by Apache). The next line might correspond to the (automatic) request for and service of a JPEG file embedded in that HTML document.

In any case, Common Log Format entries look like this (in a single line):

```
192.168.100.1 - david [10/Nov/2003:18:00:30 -1100]
"GET /index.html HTTP/1.0" 200 6590
```

The most important elements of that line are:

- ✦ `192.168.100.1`: The IP address of the client making the HTTP request.

- ✦ `david`: The username of the authenticated user making the request.

- ✦ `[10/Nov/2003:18:00:30 -1100]`: The date, time, and UTC offset of the request.

- ✦ `GET`: The nature of the HTTP request: GET or POST.

- ✦ `index.html`: The requested file.

- ✦ `HTTP/1.0`: Version of the HTTP protocol used for the request.

- ✦ `200`: Response code describing the result of the request (more on this later in this section).

- ✦ `6590`: The number of bytes served out in HTTP response corresponding to this request.

You'll find a more complete treatment of Apache log files, including the more obscure elements of the Common Log Format, at `http://httpd.apache.org/docs/logs.html#errorlog`.

HTTP response codes

Though there are many HTTP response codes (the most famous being the "404 Not Found" error), they exhibit a pattern that aids rapid decoding. In a nutshell:

- ✦ 200-series codes indicate success.

- ✦ 300-series codes indicate a redirection.

- ✦ 400-series codes indicate a client-side error (like a request for a nonexistent document).

- ✦ 500-series codes indicate a server-side error.

You'll find a full list of HTTP response codes at `www.w3.org/Protocols/rfc2616/rfc2616-sec10.html`.

Monitoring Apache logs with tail

Under Unix (including Linux), you usually have access to the GNU text utility suite. When it's time to monitor log files, one of the most useful of these tools is `tail`.

In its default behavior, `tail` will return the last (that is, most recent) 10 lines of a specified file. You can use it like this:

```
tail access.log
```

and get 10 lines of Common Log Format output (assuming 10 loggable events have taken place).

More usefully, though, you can use `tail` in its follow (`--follow`) mode. In follow mode, `tail` returns the 10 newest lines of a specified file, then goes into an infinite loop in which it watches for changes in the file and displays them when they happen. It's a simple way to monitor log files, and lots of administrators dedicate several terminals to the purpose of running `tail` `--f` sessions on various log files. The syntax is simple:

```
tail --follow=name --retry error.log
```

That results in a constantly updated display of the contents of `error.log`. By specifying `--follow=name` and `--retry`, the command guarantees that tail watches the file itself, not the file descriptor.

IIS

The Microsoft HTTP server handles logging differently. Rather than log to a file, IIS records its status and error-reporting information so that it is available for examination in the Event Viewer, which is one of the Administrative Tools on a Windows 2000 or XP system.

You'll find IIS errors in the System Log portion of the Event Viewer window, with a source name of W3SVC.

Microsoft offers advice on troubleshooting IIS errors at `http://msdn.microsoft.com/library/default.asp?url=/library/en-us/iisref/htm/TroubleshootingCommonIISErrors.asp`.

PHP Error Reporting and Logging

PHP can itself be a tremendous help in spotting errors. Straight out of the box, PHP will report error messages with output — right into the browser window, complete with line numbers. This is as far as most people get with PHP's debugging aids, but it's important to know about the details of configuring error reporting behavior in order to get the most out of it.

While PHP will show you the line number on which it has detected an error, you have to be aware that that is not always the line to which you should go in order to make a repair. A forgotten close-quote or neglected semicolon sometimes is not picked up by the interpreter until several lines later, so you should be prepared to go back a bit to look for syntax errors of that kind.

Error reporting

When the PHP interpreter places an error message in a program's output (most often resulting in the error message being displayed in a browser window), it's engaging in *error reporting*. Error reporting is a useful diagnostic tool that's turned on be default, but which should be disabled on any PHP interpreter associated with a production server.

Error reporting is turned on and off in `php.ini`. The key value is `display_errors`. If you want errors to be rendered as part of your output, this line should appear in `php.ini`:

```
display_errors=On
```

If you do not want errors to be displayed (and you shouldn't want them displayed on any publicly accessible machine), the line should read like this:

```
display_errors=Off
```

If left on in a production server environment, error reporting can result in important details of your software being inadvertently displayed to users. For example, an unexpected condition could cause the name of a variable or a database table to appear in an unsecured browser window. An attacker could use this information to exploit the production server. Figure 32-1 shows an error reported as part of the regular output to a browser window.

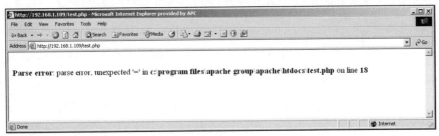

Figure 32-1: Error reporting in browser output

Error logging

Similar in function to error reporting, error logging causes error events to be recorded to a text file, rather than to the screen. It's a more secure option, and because log files should be kept in a directory with limited access, it's the error-recording technique that's preferred for production HTTP servers.

As is the case with error reporting, error logging is turned on and off in php.ini. To turn it on, use this option:

```
log_errors=On
```

Alternately, use this:

```
log_errors=Off
```

By default, error logging is disabled in php.ini.

Cross-Reference

For more detail on error reporting and logging, see Chapter 31.

Choosing which errors to report or log

Whether you choose to use error reporting (on screen) or error logging (to a file), you can specify which errors are considered serious enough to record. In php.ini, the error_reporting value defines your logging preference. By default, error_reporting is set like this:

```
error_reporting=E_ALL & ~E_NOTICE
```

That setting specifies that all errors and warnings are to be reported (a fact denoted by E_ALL), and (&) that run-time notices are not to be reported (denoted by ~E_NOTICE—the ~ indicates NOT). Other possible values are included and documented in the numerous comment lines of php.ini itself.

The level of reporting defined by error_reporting affects the behavior of error logging (as enabled by log_errors=On) and error reporting (as enabled by display_errors=On) or both simultaneously if both are enabled.

Error-Reporting Functions

PHP, benevolent language that it is, comes equipped with a variety of functions programmers can use to help locate problems and generally report on aspects of their programs' status. These range from ordinary output-generating statements—print(), echo and the like—used in contexts that reveal details of variable values, to specialized functions that write to operating systems' logging mechanisms.

This section introduces some PHP functions you can use to spot problems and report on your programs' condition.

Diagnostic print statements

The simplest troubleshooting technique involves placing echo and print statements in your code at key locations, so that the output contains information about the progress of execution through various functions and the values of key variables at different points. This is sort of a poor man's debugger—you can trace variables during execution and see if (and if so, when) they change to some unexpected value.

Here's a simple program that uses echo statements for tracing purposes:

```
<html>

<head>
<title>Test</title>
</head>

<?php

function innerFunction($value) {

  echo "<BR>In innerFunction() now...";
  $returnValue = $value . " things<BR>";
  echo '<BR>$returnValue = ';
  echo $returnValue;
  return $returnValue;
}

function outerFunction() {

  echo "<BR>In outerFunction() now...";
```

```
    $returnValue = "many";
    echo '<BR>$returnValue = ';
    echo $returnValue;

    return innerFunction($returnValue);
}

echo "<P>The time has come, the Walrus said, to talk of ";
echo outerFunction() . ".";

?>
</html>
```

Using print_r()

The usual printing functions are handy, but more specialized ones can prove more useful for debugging purposes.

Chief among these is print_r(), an extraordinarily clever print statement that, among other things, will automatically render the contents of an array in a way that's comprehensible to a human reader.

Recall that this code:

```
$stateCaps =
    array( 'New South Wales' => 'Sydney',
           'Victoria' => 'Melbourne',
           'South Australia' => 'Adelaide');
echo $stateCaps;
```

will result in some pretty useless output. It will say simply:

```
Array
```

Not too handy. In contrast, the same array definition, followed by this line:

```
Print_r($$stateCaps);
```

results in much more useful output:

```
Array ( [New South Wales] => [Sydney] [Victoria] =>
    [Melbourne] [South Australia] => [Adelaide] )
```

It's immediately obvious to the person doing the debugging what the contents (keys and values) of the array are.

Using syslog()

PHP provides a function, syslog(), with which you can write directly into the log of the operating system running your PHP environment. It's a handy function, useful if you want to log all system problems to a standard location or if you want to alert a system administrator who might not be directly involved in PHP development.

Simply put, syslog() allows you to specify the degree of severity associated with the event to be logged and to specify a message describing it. Those values are then written out as an aid to diagnostics.

This code illustrates all possible syslog() severity options:

```PHP
<?PHP

$logOptions =array(LOG_DEBUG,
                   LOG_INFO,
                   LOG_NOTICE,
                   LOG_WARNING,
                   LOG_ERR,
                   LOG_CRIT,
                   LOG_ALERT,
                   LOG_EMERG);

$exclamations = array('Look!',
                      'Take note!',
                      'Hey!',
                      'Uh-oh!',
                      'Oops!',
                      'Oh No!',
                      'Look out!',
                      'AIYEEEEEE!');

foreach ($logOptions as $key => $value) {

syslog($value, $exclamations[$key]);

}

?>
```

That code results in eight errors being written to the system log.

In a Unix system, PHP syslog() is functionally the same as syslog(3) — refer to its man page (man 3 syslog) — and on a Microsoft Windows system, PHP syslog() writes to the Event Log (specifically, to its Application Log portion).

The error-defining codes, in order of increasing severity, are:

✦ LOG_DEBUG

✦ LOG_INFO

✦ LOG_NOTICE

✦ LOG_WARNING

✦ LOG_ERR

✦ LOG_CRIT

✦ LOG_ALERT

✦ LOG_EMERG

In Microsoft Windows, the first three of those (LOG_DEBUG through LOG_NOTICE) are considered informational; the fourth and fifth are considered warnings, and the final three are noted in the Event Viewer as Alerts. All of them are shown with a source value of c-client, which corresponds to an ancillary process of the Apache server.

The Event Viewer shown in Figure 32-2 reflects the results of the preceding listing.

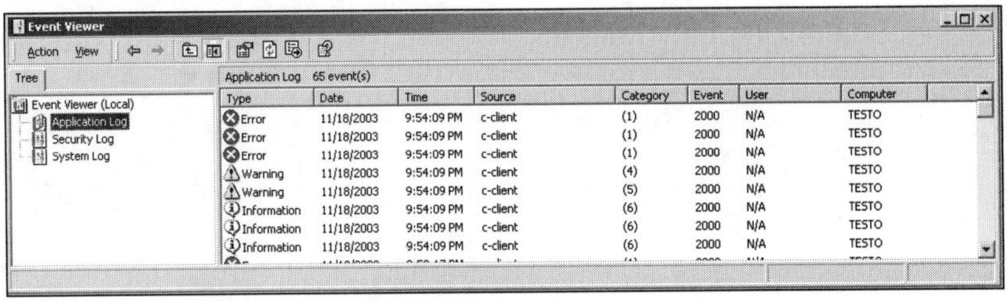

Figure 32-2: Errors at various severity levels

Logging to a custom location

Under Linux, you can use this procedure to write log messages to a file of your choosing. Modify your /etc/syslog.conf file to include this line:

```
local0.debug    /var/log/php.log
```

Then restart the syslog daemon:

```
/etc/init.d/syslog restart
```

With that done, you can refer to LOG_LOCAL0 as part of an openlog() call, as is done here:

```
<?php
define_syslog_variables();
openlog("CustomLog", LOG_PID, LOG_LOCAL0);
$errorMessage = "Aiyeee! Dying now.";
syslog(LOG_EMERG, $errorMessage);
closelog();
?>
```

The LOG_PID argument that supplements openlog() states that the process ID of the offending thread should be recorded in the log file with the other details.

Using error_log()

You can use error_log() to send an error message almost anywhere , including to an electronic mail address. It's an easy and convenient way to report on unexpected conditions that crop up in your PHP software, yet few developers bother to use it.

The basic syntax for error_log() is this:

```
error_log(message, type [,destination])
```

In that syntax, type has one of four possible values:

0: The message is handled according to the setting of error_log in php.ini.

1: The message is sent by SMTP electronic mail to the address specified by the destination parameter.

2: The message is referred to a remote debugger.

3: The message is added to the end of the file specified by the destination parameter.

The following code shows several possible uses for error_log():

```php
<?php

// Writes message as specified by error_log in php.ini.
error_log("Goodness me!", 0);

// Writes message to e-mail address.
error_log("This is not spam.", 1, "webmaster@wiley.com");

// Writes message to a remote debugger:
error_log("Problem!", 3);

// Writes message to a file:
error_log("Save me!", 4, "/log/php.log");

?>
```

In php.ini, error_log is normally not set to anything — it's commented out by default. If you want to use the 0 option to do anything, you'll have to modify the error_log setting to something like this:

```
error_log = syslog
```

which causes error_log() to be the equivalent of syslog(3) on Linux (and thus also the PHP syslog() function) and to write events to the Event Viewer under Microsoft Windows. Alternately, the error_log value can equal a filename:

```
error_log = c:\logs\php.log
```

Visual Debugging Tools

If you're going to be doing a lot of development work, you might consider buying a commercial integrated development environment (IDE) for PHP. Though these can cost a couple of hundred U.S. dollars or more, they can earn their keep by saving you time and making possible the more efficient creation of working software.

This section focuses on a highly respected and widely used commercial IDE called Zend Development Environment (yes, it's from the same Zend Technologies as puts out the Zend Engine that runs PHP). You can read its specifications (and download a free 21-day demonstration version, if you register) at www.zend.com. Figure 32-3 shows the Zend IDE in use.

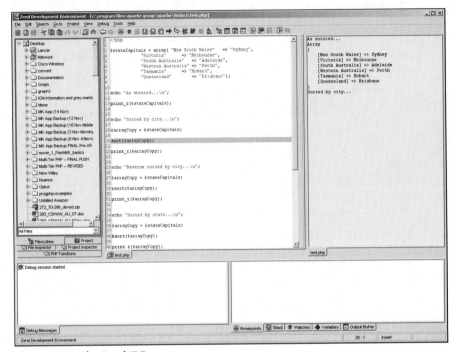

Figure 32-3: The Zend IDE

Avoiding errors in the first place

Because they're designed for creating PHP software, full-featured IDEs tend to keep you from making certain kinds of errors in the first place.

For example, because they offer syntax highlighting (which causes, say, function names to be rendered in black, literal values to appear in green, and variable names to show up in maroon), IDEs make it easier to catch dumb typographical errors. If you see that a function's argument — which is supposed to be a variable and therefore rendered in maroon — is in fact black, you know you've mistyped the variable name (perhaps by forgetting the $ character). You get used to the patterns of colors, and it's obvious when a mistake has caused a disturbance in the pattern.

In addition, IDEs often feature code completion. Code completion presents you with a list of legal options — perhaps function names, or names of already-declared variables — that could go at the point at which you're typing.

For example, Zend Development Environment will notice if you begin a new line of code with `str`. It will show you a list of all functions that start that way — `str_pad()`, `str_repeat()`, `str_replace()`, and so on — and allow you to choose one by pointing and clicking with your mouse. This eliminates one possible source of errors, in that you can't misspell the function name.

Then, once you have chosen the function you want, you might go into the parentheses to the right of the function name and start to insert the name of a variable by typing $. Again, Zend Development Environment presents you with a list of available variables (it's very clever and takes scope into account) and allows you to choose from the list with your mouse. Again, an opportunity for a silly typing error to cause a bug is eliminated.

Finding errors when they occur

The value of a visual debugger can really become obvious when it's time to work through a program line-by-line to see where problems are appearing and what can be done about them. While, as discussed earlier in this chapter, it's possible to monitor programs to a certain extent by outfitting them with extra `echo` and `print_r()` statements that help you trace what's happening, that can be a laborious process and is suitable only for quick diagnoses or occasional troubleshooting work. The tools in Zend Studio are vastly more useful and will pay for themselves quickly if you do a lot of debugging work.

Stepping through programs

Zend comprises a client element and a server element. When installed together in a development environment, they can share information back and forth. One key advantage of this: The client (under the control of the programmer) can halt execution, or see the progress of execution line by line.

Moving at such a deliberate pace, you can get a better idea of what's going on, particularly when you can monitor variable values at the same time.

Monitoring variable values

Zend Studio provides programmers with a window into all their programs' variables—those declared internally, by the program itself, and those available from outside (the `$_POST` array, for example).

Figure 32-4 shows the Variables pane (in the lower-right corner of the application) displaying some environment variables contained in the superglobal `$_ENV` array.

Using breakpoints

When you're working with a long program, you don't always want to step through the whole thing one line at a time. Instead, you might choose to establish a breakpoint. The debugger will execute normally up to the breakpoint; then it will pause.

While execution is paused at the breakpoint, you can examine variable values, or begin to step through a critical portion of your program slowly. It's one more tool to make your debugging more efficient.

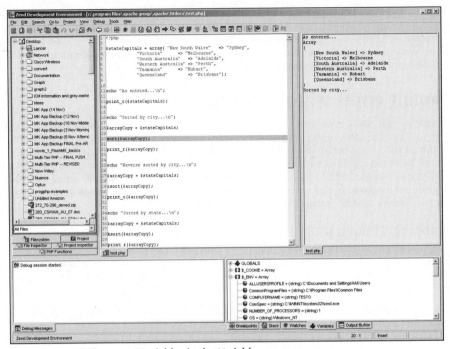

Figure 32-4: Environment variables in the Variables pane

Summary

This chapter attempted to show you where bugs come from and how to catch them when they find their way into your PHP programs. You saw that there are a number of resources available to you as you attempt to track down problems — many of them native to the PHP language or otherwise freely available.

First among your bug-catching tools is the bug-reporting capability of PHP itself. If you configure `php.ini` correctly — and this chapter showed you how — you can get precise reports of the line numbers on which the interpreter is running into trouble. Depending on your security requirements, you can have the troubleshooting information conveniently displayed with the rest of the output (typically in the browser window), recorded in a log file, or both. You also can keep an eye on the HTTP logs maintained by your Web server. These will help you monitor `GET` request data and spot requests for nonexistent files.

Additionally, you should use PHP language constructs that make your programs more self-diagnostic and troubleshooter-friendly. Functions like `openlog()` and `syslog()` will record event information when problems occur and can really help with tracking down problems. In an even simpler strategy, you can use carefully placed `print()` and (especially) `print_r()` statements to reveal what's going on in your code as it executes.

If you find yourself doing a lot of debugging work—or commercial PHP programming in general—you might find a commercial development environment like the one from Zend Technologies helpful. The Zend debugger will monitor a PHP program as it runs (step-by-step if you want), showing you all aspects of its behavior in an easy-to-manipulate graphical form. Ever want to see what your programs see in the $_ENV superglobal array as they run? You can monitor that array in Zend. It's very handy. Plus, a good IDE will help prevent errors in the first place, by offering syntax highlighting and code completion that deprives your poor typing skills of the chance to mangle code.

Troubleshooting PHP is not everyone's favorite activity, but with the right tools and (more important) the correct attitude, it can be fun.

✦   ✦   ✦

Style

This chapter is about the major points of PHP style and how it can enhance the functionality, maintainability, and attractiveness of your code. This discussion is intended to help new PHP developers make the main stylistic decisions, most of which are common to all programming languages.

We also hope this chapter may help new PHPers decipher other people's code. It can be very alarming to someone just learning scripting to read three different tutorials, which appear totally incongruent but lack any explanation of the discrepancies. The information in this chapter will help you tease out the functionally important bits of code from the mere stylistic quirks and thus gain a better understanding of what you're seeing.

The Uses of Style

The primary goal of a program is, of course, functionality. After all, if your PHP script chokes, who's even going to care how good it looks? Error messages are never all that stylin'. But there is a vast difference between simply whipping up something that will work and writing well-formed code that can be clearly understood by others.

PHP programmers confront all the same style issues that other programmers do, including:

+ **Readability:** Sure, you understood it when you wrote it, but what about the next person who reads it? What if the next person is you?

+ **Maintainability:** What happens when your health-advice site finally makes that conversion from Fahrenheit to Celsius? (A wrong answer: Replacing 790 occurrences of the string 98.6 in your source code.)

+ **Robustness:** Your Web site works fine when it's getting the inputs you expect. What about when it gets the inputs you don't expect?

+ **Conciseness and efficiency:** Fast code is better than slow code, and (others things equal) code using fewer keystrokes is better than code with more keystrokes (but other things are almost never equal).

This chapter will give a quick overview of some strategies for achieving these goals in PHP, before moving on to some code organization issues that are unique to PHP.

In This Chapter

How to earn style points

Commenting code

Writing maintainable PHP code

Mixing HTML and PHP

Separating function from design

Readability

Before a PHP script can aspire to be maintainable or elegant, it has to be human-readable. The human eye likes clear patterns, logical organization, and meaningful repetition. It also helps to have the most significant word or character at the beginning of a line, instead of buried in the middle.

If you develop HTML mostly through use of a WYSIWYG tool, your notions of legibility may be very odd indeed. These programs are notorious for writing badly structured graphics-oriented HTML, filled with invisible GIFs and absolute sizing and other little horrors.

Trying to add PHP directly to HTML files like this is an exercise in frustration, like trying to dance with someone who has no rhythm. If you insist on doing so, remember: It's not PHP's fault, so please direct your abuse to the other vendor. However, in lieu of yet another moralistic Unix-centric anti-WYSIWYG lecture, we'll now try to make a concrete suggestion or two for those who can't totally avoid such tools.

Probably the single most effective step you can take to increase legibility is to run all machine-produced HTML through a utility that will make it more human-readable. It doesn't take very long at all and will improve matters substantially. A good one is `HTML Tidy`, freely available from `tidy.sourceforge.net`.

This utility will also clean up common errors in your HTML source, such as missing end tags. Furthermore, it has some (admittedly limited at this point) capability to cope with PHP, if you've used the standard `<?php ... ?>` tags — so you can also try cleaning up those "I'm in such a hurry, so just this once I'll save a Microsoft Office document in HTML format and then stick in a couple of PHP tags" situations.

A somewhat more labor-intensive approach that gives you finer control is to run the code through an HTML validator. This is a utility (many are Web-delivered) that lists all the specific points at which a page is not in compliance with HTML standards. However, unlike `HTML Tidy`, it does not actually rewrite the source code; you can choose to make changes on a point-by-point basis.

The next most effective way to increase code legibility involves lobbying your boss to move the whole shop over to a development environment that supports both a good WYSIWYG editor and a good text editor. Although this is not an endorsement, a well-known product of this description is Macromedia Dreamweaver, which is available in both Mac and Windows versions, has some PHP support, and can interoperate with a variety of image manipulation packages.

Even PHP developers who code entirely by hand can help themselves in the long run by selecting a congenial text editor (as discussed in Chapter 3). Why waste time closing HTML tags or chasing down a missing parenthesis if you don't have to? Most text editors today have the capability to automatically close tags and brackets appropriately and otherwise help you avoid trivial but time-consuming mistakes.

You want something that is available on your preferred development platform and can be configured to closely match your personal style. Some people love syntax highlighting in many colors on black, others think it's too much like programming a Lite-Brite; some people use tab indentations, and others prefer spaces; some people like the program to do everything but make coffee for them, and others want a dumb but obedient terminal. It's all good, and you can find almost any combination of features you want — if you're willing to put the time into customizing your editor. Because a programmer's text editor is like a desperado's horse — you have to ride that nag until one of you drops — this is definitely time well spent. All text editors today have Web sites with lots and lots of screenshots; look around until you see the configuration of your dreams.

Caution Make sure your chosen editor is compatible with whatever your coworkers are using. Some editors strip out tab-indenting, cause documents to be formatted oddly, use strange quote marks, and so forth. Your co-developers won't elect you Employee of the Month if they have to reformat every page after you look at it.

One of our pet peeves is programmers who haven't yet accepted that computer memory is no longer worth any kind of premium, and thus it's counterproductive to spend time trying to squeeze a program into the smallest space possible. This practice is unfortunately recapitulated by some misguided technical book and magazine publishers, who still ask their authors to use various dodges to reduce the length of printed code samples, like so:

```php
<?php if($UserID && strlen($Horse)>0) {
 if($Horse=="Man O'War") print("Chestnut, white snip");
 elseif($Horse=="Native Dancer") print("Light grey");
 elseif($Horse=="Seattle Slew") print("Black");
 } else {
 print("Please try again."); }?>
```

This example features indentations consisting of a single space per level, absence of repetitive but meaningful file elements such as HTML headers, and an overall lack of breathing room. None of this is at all incorrect, but neither does it particularly aid readability. Compare that format to this (and try to imagine both being embedded in a much longer, more complex script that you've been assigned to change ASAP):

```php
<HTML><BODY>
<?php
if($UserID && strlen($Horse)>0)
{
    if($Horse == "Man O'War")
        print("Chestnut, white snip");
    elseif($Horse == "Native Dancer")
        print("Light grey");
    elseif($Horse == "Seattle Slew")
        print("Black");
}
else
{
    print("Please try again.");
}
?>
</BODY></HTML>
```

New programmers might do well to keep in mind that the code in books or even on the Internet (where space literally costs *nothing*) does not necessarily represent the pinnacle of human legibility.

And finally, not to belabor the obvious, neatness does count. This becomes more significant as the number of developers rises and issues of maintainability come to the fore.

Comments

Putting comments in code is just like flossing your teeth: important for health and hygiene, the object of many good intentions, all too often skipped "just this once," and long regretted later if undone.

The problem is that there's no immediate glory to be had from commenting — all the benefits are longer term and diffuse. Let's face it: You rarely hear hackers oohing and aahing over the beautiful commenting of the guy in the next cubicle, and few Web sites' go-live dates are allowed to slip so that the programmers can put the finishing touches on their comments. Commenting comes into its own later, when your team leader quits (in the middle of a major site redesign) to join a neo-Luddite community; and the rest of you are sitting around scratching your heads and thinking "Huh?" in unison, as you desperately try to write up some documentation in time for the scheduled release. So what kinds of things should you comment? We feel you *must* explain:

✦ Anything with future "what the heck was I thinking?" potential (usually due to extreme cleverness or extreme ugliness)

✦ Anything you suspect might be a temporary expedient

✦ Anything that will lead to dire consequences if tampered with by ignorant people

Things that ideally should be noted include:

✦ The date the file was originally created, and the name of the creator

✦ The date the file was most recently altered, the name of the alterer, and possibly an explanation of the rationale behind the alteration

✦ Any other files or programs that depend on the existence of this file

✦ The intended purpose of the file and of its constituent parts

✦ Things you might want to mention in documentation you're planning to write later

✦ The reason you want to save something that isn't being used (alternate versions, archive copies, and so on), conditions under which it might become okay to throw it away, or your plans for what to do with it

Obviously, you're in a better position than we to decide whether these items are strictly necessary. If you're using PHP for a very small, purely personal site, maybe commenting would be superfluous, but the bigger and more complex the site, the more you need to annotate your own work. In theory, it's possible to overcomment, but, in practice, few programmers are guilty of this offense.

> **Tip**   As we detailed in Chapter 5, there are several styles of PHP comments. Remember that none of these will be visible from the client machine, even when HTML source is viewed. If you want client-readable hidden text, you must use HTML comments.

PHPDoc

For very large and complex programs, code-embedded comments are not sufficient. You want separate documentation that someone can read without delving into the code itself. The problem with documentation like this, however, is not just how anyone gets the time to write it (since that is often low priority), but how it stays in sync with the code (which is even lower priority). When starting a new day job, we have more than once confronted a very common choice: Should we get to know the code by reading the current code itself or by consulting some very nicely written documentation of the code as it was two years ago?

One approach, used with some languages, is to employ a tool that produces documentation by extracting specially formatted, embedded comments from the code. For example, if you have followed a given commenting convention, you can point the `javadoc` tool at your Java code and it will extract class and method comments into a set of HTML pages documenting the API. This is not a magic solution for the problem of keeping docs in sync with code. (It will break down, for example, if people begin writing new methods by copying old methods, and leaving the original comments in place.) But at least developers have to write only one description of a given method rather than two.

There is an analogous `phpdoc` tool that uses PHP (naturally) to scan PHP code for special comments, producing HTML output. If you are doing a large-team project, though, especially one making heavy use of object-oriented PHP, you might find `phpdoc` to be helpful. For more on `phpdoc`, see `www.phpdoc.de/`.

File and variable names

Some people act like thinking up variable names is equivalent to being forced to write an epic poem—they go into a kind of writer's block and become creatively incapacitated. For instance, we once had an intern who was apparently unable to think up a single name or even a halfway decent scheme for doing so. This person's habit was to name every new file according to simple sequential order: `file16.html`, `file17.html`, `file18.html`, and so forth. Each variable on a Web page was called `var1`, `var2`, and so on. This story would be a lot funnier if it had happened to someone else.

Because PHP generally requires a lot more variables than HTML, you need a robust naming scheme for all occasions. The following sections include a few tips.

Long versus short

Longer is generally better because it's more informative. You can break up long names with underscores or capitalization if necessary.

Even though most filesystems technically allow for long filenames, the results are not pretty when viewed as icons—so GUI users may be consciously or unconsciously averse to using long filenames. Icon labels are usually quite short and, thus, naturally lend themselves to very concise filenames. Try giving a file a long, complex name (like `PoachedPeachesRecipe.php`) and putting it on your desktop—the result is just viscerally displeasing.

Caution　　Most GUI-oriented filesystems allow and even encourage filenames with spaces in them (for example, `My Document.doc`). Unix systems do in theory, but in practice it's not such a good idea. PHP will try to cope gracefully with such filenames, but it may not be able to do so in all situations.

One benefit of using PHP for dynamic content generation is that you can use shorter filenames that will be expanded and differentiated by `GET`-style query strings. For example, a static site might use this style of filename to uniquely identify each page:

```
FeatureHitchcockBirds.html
MiniseriesIrvinSpy.html
```

A dynamic site, on the other hand might identify the same pages like this:

```
feature.php?ID=1
miniseries.php?ID=2
```

In this situation, you can have the best of both worlds: short filename plus unique identifier. (The only downside of this is that some search engines still discriminate against pages with dynamic arguments, under the theory that the contents are likely to change with every page view and, therefore, won't be worth indexing.)

PHP sets no particular limit on the length of variable names. So feel free to invent lengthy but informative variables like $AddressOfClientCompanyInSasketchewan. Hey, it's your script — we're just living in it. You only need to be careful if you plan to use a lot of long-name variables as part of a GET-method form.

Underscores versus camelcaps

There are two typical ways to break up long variable and file names in Unix. Underscores look like this:

```
$name_of_favorite_beer
```

whereas *camelcaps* look like this, with the internal capital letters giving the name a humped profile:

```
$NameOfFavoriteBeer
```

It's a purely personal preference, which style you use (unless you have agreed on a particular style with your colleagues). PHP itself uses underscores ($PHP_SELF), but this usage by PHP could be construed as an argument in favor of either scheme for PHP programmers. Just remember you can't use dashes and should be careful with dots.

Caution   Unix filenames are case sensitive all the time. Filenames in other OSes, such as Windows, are not case sensitive. If you might be in a position to move PHP files between OSes, be careful.

The main thing to strive for here is consistency. It's frustrating to spend a lot of time trying to figure out why $My_Number was never assigned, only to find out that it's because you called it $MyNumber when you assigned it.

Reassigning variables

Situations arise in which you deliberately want to keep using the same variable name over and over rather than coming up with new names. This happens when you need to be certain only one variable of a particular type will be valid at any given time. For instance, you might want to be sure there can be no confusion about which of two database queries will be used for an operation, which you can ensure by using the same name for both (for example, $query). PHP will overwrite the former with the latter, and your variable will always be minty fresh.

Uniformity of style

Although we have talked in a very free and easy way about how all these stylistic choices are up to you, there are situations where it is actually good to have a consensus on what code should look like and then enforce that. This is particularly true when many programmers will contribute code to a project. The reasons that are usually advanced for a uniform style are:

✦ It makes it easier to read code from multiple programmers, because you don't have to get used to a new indenting or layout style every time you see new code.

✦ It makes life easier for version control software (like CVS). If I change a code file that you created and my editor changes the indentation, there will be a lot of apparent but spurious differences.

The closest thing PHP has to a consensus style is the coding standard developed by the maintainers of the PEAR project. See Chapter 28 for a discussion of both PEAR and this coding style.

Maintainability

Many seasoned programming veterans, especially those who are also managers, tout the importance of maintainability above that of any other virtue.

The problem is, of course, that maintainability is in direct conflict with all the other goals — especially speed. When Internet Time gets into the ring with Hypothetical Future Code Maintenance By Someone Probably Not Myself, everyone knows how the story is going to end. Still, the main mental mantras of maintainability are worth keeping in mind:

✦ The things that are most likely to be changed should be the easiest to find.

✦ Changing those things should not have unpredictable effects.

✦ Each change should have to be made in only one place.

Avoid magic numbers

A *magic number* is a numerical value that might someday have to be changed but is buried deep in code, often in multiple places. Imagine, for example, these lines of code found in your bank's hypothetical PHP-based Web site:

```
print("The interest rate on your CD can be as high as
    5.5%!<BR>");
$sample_gains = 5000 * 1.055;
print("After a year, a \$5000 investment could grow to
    \$$sample_gains!<BR>");
```

Now, when times get tighter and the rate goes down to 5.0 percent, someone has to find and change every instance of the rate. So, someone does a text search for 5.5, which misses the 1.055 in the second line here, and now your bank is engaging in false advertising.

For simple sites, a better alternative can be as easy using an $interest_rate variable, which is assigned very visibly at the top of a script — a change in rate means a change only to that assignment statement. More complex sites might produce their pages as function calls, with variables like $interest_rate being passed in as an actual parameter. Finally, some sites will go so far as to have all their content imported from a database, so that no piece of information has to ever be changed directly in code.

Functions

Having tried to maintain a complex site using a Web-scripting language that did not support functions, we can say from our own experience that functions are crucial to maintenance. The art of procedural abstraction via functions needs a book in itself, but here's some brief advice:

✦ Always look for opportunities to bundle naked PHP code into a function, especially in cases where it might be reused.

✦ Try to keep function definitions short — if a definition gets too long, break it up into multiple functions.

✦ Always load all your function definitions before any code that calls any functions.

Include files

One of the great benefits of dynamic Web page generation over static HTML is the opportunity to fight redundancy. Anyone who has ever managed a static site of any size knows how much of each file is boilerplate — and even editing a single character on each page isn't a picnic if your site has 200 pages.

PHP makes it very easy to drop anything into your scripts, from one character to a whole separate program, by using the built-in `include` or `require` functions. The syntax is simply:

```
<?php include("filename.ext"); ?>
```

You can also use a variable filename, like this:

```
<?php
$LastName = "Park";
include("$LastName.inc");
?>
```

which will result in the contents of the file `Park.inc` being spliced in at the location of the include statement.

You can use any extension you want for the included file. Popular choices include `.txt`, `.inc`, and even `.html` to remind yourself that the file will show up in HTML mode.

A few things to remember:

✦ PHP will drop the entire text of the file into your PHP script *in HTML mode* (as explained in Chapter 4). If the included file is itself meant to be parsed as PHP, you must use valid PHP tags at the beginning and end. If any part of the file is meant to be parsed as PHP, you must use valid PHP tags around that section.

✦ Recall the difference between `include/require` and `include_once/require_once`. In general, if what you are including or requiring is a set of function or class definitions, you should use the `once` variant. If it is straight PHP or HTML, then which variant you load depends on whether you would ever want that literal block to repeat in your output; if not, then the once version is probably still what you want.

✦ include can also be used to assemble complex Web pages from text files instead of from a database. In some cases, this can even be faster — usually when the included data is just a sizable text file(s). However, after you go to the trouble to make a database connection for any reason, it's probably just as fast to store your big chunks of text there, too.

Object wrappers

Although we haven't covered PHP's object system in detail yet, it's worth noting that consistent use of objects can make code more maintainable, much as functions do. For example, some developers of database-enabled PHP sites are disciplined enough to wrap up all of their database-specific functionality in the methods of an object, so that the rest of their code doesn't even know what kind of database is supporting the site. In theory, then, if they decide to move from a mySQL database to an Oracle database, only the object-level code will have to be changed.

Cross-Reference   For details on PHP's support for object-oriented programming, see Chapter 20.

Consider using version control

For large multiprogrammer projects in industrial settings, version control isn't "something to consider" — it's a must. Similarly, large decentralized open-source projects could not survive without *CVS* (Concurrent Versions System). Even if you are working by yourself or with one other person on a hobby project, using version control can free you to do more experimentation, secure in the knowledge that you can get to the older versions of your code if something goes awry.

See www.cvshome.org for more information on CVS. SourceForge also offers free Web-based CVS project hosting for open-source projects (www.sourceforge.net/).

Robustness

The two commandments of robustness are:

✦ Code should detect unexpected situations and respond gracefully rather than dying.

✦ If code must die, better that it die informatively.

Writing robust code is at first a difficult task of imagination, where the programmer tries to think ahead to all the things that might go wrong and to cover those cases. The ideal situation is for that habit of mind to become a habit of code, so that the coder has a standard set of tests that wrap around the standard potential problems. Although most of the robustness issues in PHP are the same as in any language, there are two kinds of situations to cover that are more specific to PHP: problems with an external service, and problems having to do with variable type.

Unavailability of service

PHP is in part a "glue" language, offering a single environment where a variety of different code libraries and external services can be invoked. Any given PHP page might open a file, connect to a database, query an LDAP server, send an HTTP header, or send mail via an SMTP server. The important habit to develop is covering cases where for some external reason a service is unavailable, or times out, or behaves oddly, or gets interrupted in the middle.

Often, such services have error states that can be retrieved and printed if the only option left is to informatively die. For example, a reasonable construct for making a connection to a mySQL database is:

```
$connection = mysql_connect([arguments]) or
              die("Connection failed:  $php_errormsg<BR>");
```

This is preferable to the weird and unexpected errors you would see if your code went happily ahead assuming that it had a live database connection. An alternative that is better from a security point of view is:

```
$connection = mysql_connect(...) or error_log($php_errormsg);
if (!$connection){
   die("Connection Failed");
}
```

because this will avoid displaying interesting facts about your PHP and database configuration to the user's browser.

Even better style is to use the exception-handling facility introduced in PHP5, rather than simply failing with die(). Exceptions can be thrown whenever a problematic condition is encountered, and recovered from, at a single point in the code (if you so choose). If it is possible to recover from the problem, exceptions make it easy to structure your code to support that. If the script must die anyway, exceptions make it easy to propagate the negative information and display it at the right time, rather than just aborting execution.

 Cross-Reference — Exceptions and exception-handling are covered in detail in Chapter 31.

Unexpected variable types

Although the type-looseness of PHP is for the most part a good thing, it leaves a little bit of uncertainty for the programmer about exactly what type a variable or value will turn out to be. Unless you come to know all the type-conversion rules very well, it can be surprising to have code that is accustomed to strings suddenly run across a value that is a number, all because some PHP construct decided that any string composed only of numerical digits must really be a number at heart. One interesting robustness check is to use a text editor to search your code for $ (thereby finding every variable) and ask yourself for each one what would happen if the type turned out to be surprisingly different.

Efficiency and Conciseness

Efficiency and conciseness are not the same thing. Efficient code runs using a small amount of execution time or computer memory, while concise code accomplishes a given task in a small number of lines or keystrokes. In this section, we give some quick tips toward writing efficient and concise PHP code, along with our extremely opinionated commentary about in what senses these goals are worth striving for.

Efficiency: Only the algorithm matters

There was a time when computer memory and computer cycles were so precious that it was worth a lot of effort to boil down your code to the smallest number of resulting machine instructions possible. This is still true in certain areas of software development (kernel programming, graphics libraries), but for most development tasks saving a few instructions or a few K is not worth backing off on any other goal. This is especially true for Web scripting, where there is always going to be some overhead of purely Internet-related execution delay. If it takes half a second for a user to fetch your page, regardless of how your page is produced, then an extra five milliseconds on the server side will be lost in the noise.

With that said, there's one variety of efficiency that matters and will probably always matter: the broad algorithm or approach that your code uses for a task. For example, if your code locates a name in a database by querying the database for all names and then doing a string comparison for each name to see if it's the one you want, you'll soon find out how much efficiency can matter.

Efficiency optimization tips

Here are some quick mantras to repeat as you code.

Don't reinvent the wheel

It's usually a bad idea to write code that duplicates a language-level facility, unless it's for purposes of fun or education. For example, any programmer worth his or her salt should write sorting routines at some point in their education, but no programmer should have to keep writing them (unless it is actually in their job description). Most high-level programming languages offer some kind of sorting capability (either as part of the language or in a library), and it's very likely that the programmer who wrote them did a better job than you will. PHP is no exception here — the array type supports several types of sorting, and most of the databases supported by PHP have sorting options built into the query language. Either of these options will be faster and more reliable than what you get by rolling your own.

Discover the bottleneck

Although it's good to try to use efficient algorithms from the beginning, it's often not worth doing other kinds of optimization until you find out that too much of some resource is being used. At that point, you want to tighten things up, and you'll get the most reward for your effort if you focus on the piggiest parts of your code. Most code follows the 90/10 rule: 90 percent of the time is spent in 10 percent of the code, and you want to locate that 10 percent.

One technique that programmers often use to locate that 10 percent is called *profiling*. A profiler is a utility that tracks code as it runs, noting the time spent in every function call, and producing a neat summary of the results. Unfortunately, at this writing, there is no good general profiling utility for PHP (although one may be on the way for later versions of PHP). So the best bet for now is the poor man's profiling technique: printing the value of the function call `microtime()` in various places in your script to see where the time is going. If the 90/10 rule is in effect, the time sink will usually be glaringly obvious.

Focus on database queries

Although we cover database efficiency in more detail in Chapter 18, you should be aware that database queries are usually the biggest time sink for PHP sites that have database back ends. Especially if your database-enabled site doesn't do a lot of other computationally intensive work, your first suspicious glance should be at the queries, and your next task should be to try to identify a query that is particularly time-consuming. After you've identified a guilty query, there are a host of techniques available to speed that query up, many of which don't have anything to do with PHP.

Cross-
Reference

For details on optimizing database-enabled PHP code, see Chapter 18.

Focus on the innermost loop

Let's say that you have a page with embedded looping constructs, like the following:

```
for ($x = 0; $x < 100; $x++)
{
  do_X();
  for ($y = 0; $y < 100; $y++)
    {
      do_XY();
      for ($z = 0; $z < 100; $z++)
        {
          do_XYZ();
        }
    }

}
```

Unless you have a really good reason to think otherwise, your optimization focus should be on the function do_XYZ() (which will execute 1,000,000 times) rather than on the other two functions (10,000 times and 100 times).

Conciseness: The downside

Before we get into how to write more concise code, let us say that we think conciseness is an overrated virtue, for the following reasons.

Conciseness rarely implies efficiency

Although it's true that somewhere in the guts of the PHP engine, the characters of the code you write are being consumed one by one (and so, in theory, more code takes more time), in practice, the Zend-based parsing engine of PHP is so zippy that the number of characters just doesn't matter. Ditto for the time or space consumed in extra variable assignments or the overhead of extra function calls.

Conciseness trades off with readability

Remember that every keystroke you omit might be the keystroke that would have let someone figure out what the heck you were thinking when you wrote the code. For example, take a look at the following admirably concise function:

```
function sieve($n) {
   for ($i = 2; $i <= sqrt($n); $i++)
     for ($j = $i, $ind = $i * $j; $ind <= $n;
         $j++, $ind = $i * $j)
       $carray[$ind] = 1;
```

```
    for ($i = $n, $plist = array(); $i > 1; $i--)
      if (!$carray[$i]) array_push($plist,$i);
    return($plist);
  }
```

Obviously, this implements the Sieve of Erasthones, and $plist is a list of all the prime numbers less than $n. Obviously.

So why do programmers strive for conciseness? The first reason is that it saves them time (but only at the time of actual code writing). The second reason (and we're only half-joking) is that they're afraid some other programmer (probably one trained in C) will come along later, laugh at them, and point out that their code could have been written in only half the space.

Conciseness tips

If you must write code that fits in less space, try some of the following techniques.

Use return values and side effects at the same time

It's a very common trick to exploit the fact that the value of an assignment is the value assigned, as in the following pseudocode:

```
while ($next = GetNextOne())
    DoSomethingWith($next);
```

where GetNextOne() is some function that returns useful values in sequence and then returns a false value when it runs out of them. When a false value is returned, $next is false, and the while loop terminates.

Use incrementing and assignment operators

The incrementing operators (++ and --) shorten statements that involve adding or subtracting one from a variable, and the combined assignment operators (+=, *=, .=, and so on) make certain kinds of assignments more concise.

Cross-Reference
The incrementing operators and the arithmetic assignment operators are covered in Chapter 10, and the combined string assignment operator (.=) is covered in Chapter 8.

Often these operators are used in combination with the previous trick, as in:

```
while ($count--)
    DoSomethingWith($count);
```

which (assuming that $count starts as a positive integer) would call its function for the very last time on the value 1.

Reuse functions

This is one case where conciseness is good, because functions are good. If you can identify any stretches of code that get duplicated in your pages, try to replace each one with a call to a single function that packages up that code. Your code will be shorter by the amount of the duplication and also easier to maintain.

There's nothing wrong with Boolean

Beginning programmers often have an odd distrust of Boolean values, not realizing that they can be passed around as freely as any other kind of value. This leads to code that wastes a lot of space, like the following:

```
function DivisibleByBad($num1, $num2)
{
    if ($num1 % $num2 == 0)
        return(TRUE);
    else
        return(FALSE);
}
/* using the function */
if (DivisibleByBad(9, 3))
  $divisible_result = TRUE;
else
  $divisible_result = FALSE;
if ($divisible_result == TRUE)
  print("It's divisible!<BR>");
else
  if ($divisible_result == FALSE)
    print("It's not divisible!<BR>");
```

A more concise version would look like:

```
function DivisibleByBetter($num1, $num2)
{
    return ($num1 % $num2 == 0);
}
/* using the function */
if (DivisibleByBetter(9,3))
  print("It's divisible!<BR>");
else
  print("It's not divisible!<BR>");
```

You could obviously take this one step further and get rid of the function itself, like so:

```
if (9 % 3 == 0)
  print("It's divisible!<BR>");
else
  print("It's not divisible!<BR>");
```

But (once again) *Functions Are Good*—an explanatory function name is a little piece of documentation in itself, and any function you write gives you a chance to reuse it later, which, in turn, makes your code more maintainable.

Use short-circuiting Boolean expressions

Certain kinds of Boolean tests aren't safe to apply until you've done other tests. It's tempting to deal with this by insulating the problematic tests with if constructs. For example, imagine that you want to print the ratio of two variables that are bound to integers, but only if they are bound to integers and only if the ratio is greater than two. Also, you want to avoid a division-by-zero warning. You might overcautiously write:

```
    if (IsSet($x))
      {
        if (IsSet($y))
        {
          if (Is_Integer($x))
          {
            if (Is_Integer($y))
            {
              if ($y != 0)
                {
                  if ($x / $y > 2)
                      print("Ratio is " . ($x / $y));
                }
            }
          }
        }
      }
```

You can be equally overcautious and still type a little less, as in:

```
    if (IsSet($x) && IsSet($y) && Is_Integer($x) &&
        Is_Integer($y) && $y != 0 && $x / $y > 2)
      print("Ratio is " . ($x / $y));
```

The tests will be applied in left-to-right order, and if any test fails, the tests to the right of it will not be evaluated.

HTML Mode or PHP Mode?

There's a spectrum of ways to combine PHP and HTML, functionally all pretty much the same. Your choice will depend on extrinsic factors such as your particular team's workflow.

The easiest way to demonstrate all this is to simply write the same script in minimal PHP, maximal PHP, and medium PHP styles. We will also include a version using the *heredoc* construct (discussed in Chapter 8), which is our favorite of the four. Remember, these are equally correct and return much the same result. The stylistic decision is just a matter of preference and consistency, and (sometimes) slight differences in functionality.

Minimal PHP

The code in Listing 33-1 shows a simple self-submitting form, which returns some simple information about days of the week. First, it tells you what day it is today and then gives you a chance to ask it what day it will be in a few days (using a form with a pull-down list). The typical text output looks like this:

```
4 days from this moment it will be Thursday
Today is Sunday
Please choose a number of days, and we'll tell you what day it will be
that many days from now
```

It is written using a *minimal PHP* style, meaning simply that, as much as possible, the code is pure HTML, dropping into PHP mode only when dynamic data must be displayed (such as the current day of the week or an answer that depends on submitted data).

Listing 33-1: **Minimal PHP**

```
<HTML><HEAD TITLE="Calendar Server"></HEAD><BODY>
<H2>Welcome to the Calendar Server</H2>

<?php if (IsSet($_POST['DAYS'])) { ?>
  <P> <?php echo $_POST['DAYS'];?>
  days from this moment it will be
  <?php $date = getdate(time() +
                        ($_POST['DAYS'] * 86400));
        echo($date['weekday']);
}?>

<P>Today is <?php $date = getdate();
                  echo($date['weekday']); ?>
<P>Please choose a number of days, and we'll
tell you what day it will be that many days from now:

<FORM METHOD=POST ACTION="<?php echo $_SERVER['PHP_SELF'];?>" >
<SELECT NAME=DAYS>
 <OPTION VALUE=1>1<OPTION VALUE=2>2<OPTION VALUE=3>3
 <OPTION VALUE=4>4<OPTION VALUE=5>5<OPTION VALUE=6>6
</SELECT>
<INPUT TYPE=SUBMIT NAME=SUBMIT VALUE=SUBMIT>
</FORM>
</BODY></HTML>
```

This code takes the minimal style to an extreme — note the funny business with the if statement near the top, where some straight HTML text (days from this moment) is included conditionally, based on the results of the PHP statement that precedes it.

As we have said, this is a matter of taste, but we don't like this version very much. It's a bit hard to see exactly what is being produced by the PHP snippets that are spliced into the page.

Maximal PHP

At the opposite extreme, consider the code in Listing 33-2. This version is in PHP mode all the time and simply prints all the HTML it needs to as it goes.

Listing 33-2: **Maximal PHP**

```
<?php
print("<HTML><HEAD TITLE=\"Calendar Server\"></HEAD><BODY>");
print("<H2>Welcome to the Calendar Server</H2>");

if (IsSet($_POST['DAYS'])) {
  print("<P>" .$_POST['DAYS'] .
        " days from this moment it will be ");
  $date = getdate(time() +
          ($_POST['DAYS'] * 86400));
```

```
    print($date['weekday']);
  }

  $date = getdate();
  $day_of_week = $date['weekday'];
  print("<P>Today is $day_of_week");
  print("<P>Please choose a number of days, and we'll
  tell you what day it will be that many days from now:");

  $self = $_SERVER['PHP_SELF'];
  print("<FORM METHOD=POST ACTION=\"$self\" >");
  print("<SELECT NAME=DAYS>");
  for ($i = 1; $i < 7; $i++) {
   print("<OPTION VALUE=$i>$i");
  }
  print("</SELECT>");
  print("<INPUT TYPE=SUBMIT NAME=SUBMIT VALUE=SUBMIT>");
  print("</FORM></BODY></HTML>");
  ?>
```

Another term for *maximal PHP* might be *CGI-style*, because we are not taking advantage of the HTML-embeddedness of PHP at all, and might as well be writing a CGI script in C or Perl (and who wants to do that?). Again, a matter of taste, but it's a little bit hard to visualize the structure of the HTML page that will result from running this.

Medium PHP

An intermediate version that better exploits functions is shown in Listing 33-3. It spends about half its text in PHP mode, defining functions, before dropping back to a minimal style for the rest of the script.

Listing 33-3: **Medium PHP**

```
<?php
function maybe_print_answer_date () {
  $seconds_in_day = 60 * 60 * 24;
  if (IsSet($_POST['DAYS'])) {
    print("<P>" .$_POST['DAYS'] .
          " days from this moment it will be ");
    $date = getdate(time() +
            ($_POST['DAYS'] * $seconds_in_day));
    print($date['weekday']);
  }
}

function print_day_options () {
 for ($i = 1; $i < 7; $i++) {
   print("<OPTION VALUE=$i>$i");
 }
}
```

Continued

Listing 33-3 *(continued)*

```
function get_day_of_week($time) {
  $date = getdate($time);
  return($date['weekday']);
}

?>
<HTML><HEAD TITLE="Calendar Server"></HEAD><BODY>
<H2>Welcome to the Calendar Server</H2>
<?php maybe_print_answer_date(); ?>
<P>Today is <?php echo get_day_of_week(time());?>
<P>Please choose a number of days, and we'll
tell you what day it will be that many days from now:

<FORM METHOD=POST ACTION="<?php echo $_SERVER['PHP_SELF'];?>" >
<SELECT NAME=DAYS>
  <?php print_day_options(); ?>
</SELECT>
<INPUT TYPE=SUBMIT NAME=SUBMIT VALUE=SUBMIT>
</FORM>
</BODY></HTML>
```

Maybe the medium style is a little bit more verbose, but to our eyes, it's also a little easier to read and modify than the minimal and maximal styles.

The heredoc style

Listing 33-4 shows a rewrite of the medium style, using the heredoc syntax for constructing strings.

Listing 33-4: **Heredoc style**

```
<?php
function answer_string ($days) {
  $seconds_in_day = 60 * 60 * 24;
  $return_string = "";
  $day_string =
    day_of_week_string(time() + $days *
                       $seconds_in_day);

  $return_string .=
    $_POST['DAYS'] .
    " days from this moment it will be " .
    $day_string;
  return($return_string);

}
```

```
function day_of_week_string($time) {
  $date = getdate($time);
  return($date['weekday']);
}

function calendar_form_string () {
  $option_string = "";
  for ($i = 1; $i < 7; $i++) {
    $option_string .= "<OPTION VALUE=$i>$i";
  }
  $self_string = $_SERVER['PHP_SELF']; $return_string=<<<EOT
<FORM METHOD=POST ACTION="$self_string" >
<SELECT NAME=DAYS>$option_string</SELECT>
<INPUT TYPE=SUBMIT NAME=SUBMIT VALUE=SUBMIT>
</FORM>
EOT;
  return($return_string);
}

// set up string variables
$answer_string = IsSet($_POST['DAYS']) ?
                 answer_string($_POST['DAYS']) :
                 "";
$day_of_week = day_of_week_string(time());
$form_string = calendar_form_string();

// set up page string
$page_string=<<<EOT
<HTML><HEAD TITLE="Calendar Server"></HEAD><BODY>
<H2>Welcome to the Calendar Server</H2>
<P>$answer_string
<P>Today is $day_of_week
<P>Please choose a number of days, and we'll
tell you what day it will be that many days from now:
$form_string
</BODY></HTML>
EOT;

echo($page_string);
?>
```

Tim Perdue of SourceForge has made the stylistic argument that it's a bad idea for functions to print output to the browser. The heredoc example follows this advice and uses functions only for calculations and for building strings that are returned. The heredoc construct is used twice, first to build a string corresponding to the form that will be displayed and then (using the form string) to build the string corresponding to the entire page. The last act of the script is to echo out the string it has constructed.

This is the most verbose of the four, but the heredoc syntax has the advantage (over the maximal style) that we never have to do any escaping of quotes. Another advantage (over the minimal style) is that we can simply include variables in our page template without dropping out of HTML mode to do so. It is probably the best version of the four at separating logic from page structure.

Separating Code from Design

Many of the topics in this chapter have obvious implications for the separation of code and design. Here are a few additional techniques we should mention.

Functions

As you can see from our Medium PHP example in Listing 33-3, using self-defined functions can be a very flexible and powerful formatting tool, as well as one of the things that make PHP better than a tag-based scripting language.

Cascading style sheets in PHP

As you doubtless already know, there are four generally accepted ways to apply styles to your Web pages:

✦ By applying CSS formatting to individual tags.

✦ By using `<STYLE>` tags (optionally inside a pair of HTML comment tags).

✦ By using `<LINK>` tags.

✦ By using `@import`.

Note   In this book, we've typically used the `<STYLE>` tag in each code sample rather than an external style sheet. This is solely so you, Dear Reader, can see the style declarations we used to get the results we display in the figures. There is absolutely no PHP-intrinsic reason for this usage.

In PHP, you could also use the `include` function to apply styles in a nonstandard way, although it's not clear how much of a gain this would be. For instance, you could `include` a text file containing everything between the `<STYLE>` tags, instead of linking to an external style sheet.

We should also mention the anti-style sheet, a practice almost as long-deprecated as it is common: using outdated HTML tags such as `FONT`, `BGCOLOR`, and `ALINK`. Although you shouldn't do it at all, PHP can help you do it more efficiently if for some reason you must. This usage, for instance:

```
<FONT FACE="<?php include("fontlist.txt"); ?>" SIZE=+2>
```

would at least allow the poor, overworked Web developer to change the fonts throughout the whole site with a single edit of the text file. Not that we can condone this kind of thing! Only slightly less kludgy would be this alternative:

```
<P STYLE="font-family: <?php include("fontlist.txt"); ?>">Text here</P>
```

Templates and page consistency

As you can now imagine, PHP allows a wide variety of approaches to site design, which you can fit to your particular style and the organization of the people who work on the site. If your techies can't talk to your artists, you may want to set things up so that they never touch the same files; if you're a tech artist, you may express yourself by the very intermingling of code and graphics. If your site has a large number of pages or is very content-rich, you may find (as we have) that it's helpful to choose a particular kind of file organization or template, and stick to it across the site. One simplified example follows, which is similar to templates we have used on www.mysteryguide.com and www.sciencebookguide.com.

```
<?
/* load general functions */
include("general-functions.inc");
/* load functions specific to this page */
include("renaissance-functions.inc");
/* page-wide variables */
$PageTitle = "Painters of the Renaissance";
$db_connection = make_database_connection();
?>

<HTML>
<HEAD>
<TITLE>
    <?php print("$PageTitle"); ?>
</TITLE>
</HEAD>
<BODY>
<H3>
     <?php print("$PageTitle"); ?>
</H3>
<TABLE>
<TR><TD>
    <?php print-left-side($db_connection); ?>
</TD><TD>
    <?php print-right-side($db_connection); ?>
</TD></TR>
</TABLE>
    <?php print-footer($db_connection); ?>
</BODY><HTML>
```

In this example, every page loads the same file of site-wide utility functions, then loads a file of functions specific to that page, then defines variables that will be global for the page, and finally intersperses PHP commands in some boilerplate HTML. The content is in columns, and the actual content displayed depends on the particular page's functions, which always have the same names, but with definitions varying for each page. Changing what's displayed in the columns means either changing the per-page functions or (more likely) modifying the database contents. It would be possible for a nonprogrammer to do some limited design on this page by operating directly on the HTML and being careful to leave the PHP alone.

The preceding example is just one simplified possibility from a range of ways to divide up the labor of displaying a PHP page. Another that we like even better is the heredoc technique that we discuss in the section, "The heredoc style," earlier in the chapter. Your particular strategy will depend on the type of site, the size of the site, and the styles of the people contributing.

Finally, note that all these strategies really just adopt a convention about separating logic and display in PHP. If you need an even stronger distinction, there are PHP-based templating systems available that further insulate the display people from the innards of program logic. One example is YATS (Yet Another Template System), available at http://yats.sourceforge.net.

Summary

Most of the elements of PHP style are desirable in any programming language. You want to write readable code, with appropriately abstracted functions, consistent indentation, and explanatory comments. You want to stay away from magic numbers, "cloned" code repetition, overuse of global variables, and cryptically clever tricks. Your program should work on the inputs you expect, do something reasonable with inputs you didn't expect, and have the grace to die informatively in situations you *really* didn't expect.

Some of the PHP-specific style issues have to do with organizing file inclusions, how intimately you mix your PHP with your HTML, and more generally the separation of code from design. A wide range of styles are okay here, but you should strive for page-level and site-wide consistency.

✦   ✦   ✦

Connections

PostgreSQL

Y ou might find that MySQL or even simple text files meet all your data storage and retrieval requirements. Nothing about a simple flat data structure in a small quantity demands a relational database model. However, as we mentioned earlier in this book, you *do* have choices when it comes to databases. In the next chapter, we'll look at a commercial offering, Oracle. In this chapter, we'll look at what is possibly the granddaddy of the free/open source database alternatives, PostgreSQL (pronounced "post-gress-q-l").

Why Choose PostgreSQL?

This is the part where the open-source purists start waving their hands in the air and yelling with uncontrolled excitement! And the excitement is easy to understand — PostgreSQL is a true open-source database, made available under the simple and portable BSD license. You can read the almost vanishingly short text of the license at `www.postgres.org/licence.html`.

Are you back yet? See, we told you it was short. So reason number one is not so much the license itself as the freedom from an 85 page EULA laced with sneaky provisions that nobody alive really understands, and that, in many cases, you can't even see until you get the box open. By then it's too late — all the money's gone. Which brings us to reason number two: PostgreSQL is free. We don't mean "free on Mondays, Wednesdays, Fridays and the vernal equinox," nor do we mean "free to the right people," nor even the more conventional and arguably understandable "free for non-commercial use." PostgreSQL is completely and totally free (unless the developers change their minds).

The term free applies to more than just the cost. Like the GNU General Public License, you can alter, repackage, and redistribute PostgreSQL as a standalone product or with your own applications. Arguably better than the GPL for businesses, using and distributing PostgreSQL will not "infect" all your code with the copyleft.

Finally, PostgreSQL supports some nifty special features and elements of the ANSI SQL92 and SQL99 standards that simply aren't available or fully developed in other databases, as well as the ability to work with object and hierarchical data.

Of course, there are some disadvantages as well. First, consider PostgreSQL's ability to work with object and hierarchical data. Wait a minute; didn't we just sell that one as a feature? To the PostgreSQL lovers in the audience, it may seem odd to sell these "features" as disadvantages. Don't flame us yet. We're just taking a moment to expound on the Keep It Simple Stupid (KISS) philosophy. You don't need a sledgehammer to drive in a picture nail, and you don't need an object relational database to store addresses and phone numbers.

Some folks will debate this point, but simply put, PostgreSQL is not as fast as MySQL under low-load circumstances. At some point, PostgreSQL's more robust design will offer performance advantages in really large datasets, but on average, MySQL is just that little bit perkier for lots of reads. Again, if you have simpler data storage and retrieval needs, there's no need for you to go swimming around in the PostgreSQL waters.

Finally, PostgreSQL is more complicated. Permissions management, for one, is not as clearcut as it is with MySQL. PostgreSQL also offers some features that may cause the novice's eyes to glaze over — Schemas and Stored Procedures, while useful, aren't strictly necessary and you may find them to be clutter. Some people work much better when there are no nonessentials on their desks; the same principle may hold true here.

All these things said, on balance PostgreSQL is a great tool — a superlative tool even — for many jobs. Its userbase may be smaller than MySQL's, but its devotees tend to be very loyal. We can't cover it very comprehensively and still stay within the focus of this book; but if you've gotten this far, weighed all the benefits and disadvantages, and you choose PostgreSQL, the rest of this chapter should set you off in the right direction.

Why Object-Relational Anyway?

Object relational databases (ORDBMS) are a relatively new class of product compared to the relational database model that was developed in the early 1970s. In addition to implementing the relational model discussed in Chapter 13, ORDBMS borrow from pure object databases, which excel at handling media objects, spatial, and series style data. An ORDBMS implements object properties on the components of a relational database in order to have the benefit of both worlds. This, in turn, facilitates interaction with the object features of PHP. Because PHP's object model is significantly more powerful in version 5, there's never been a better time to use these two tools together.

This means that choosing PostgreSQL potentially offers the developer greater extensibility. It's fairly easy to define and add custom data types, operators, functions, and indexing methods. This has far reaching implications for fine-tuning performance; especially when working with particularly complicated data structures.

At the data structure level, PostgreSQL tables and objects can benefit from either static or dynamic inheritance. That is to say, a child object created from its parent can be made to adopt characteristics identical to those of the parent — either just once when it is created, or perpetually (as changes are made to the parent, they are passed on to the children).

Installing PostgreSQL

PostgreSQL is known to run on Linux, most Unix variants, and with the help of the Cygwin framework (`http://cygwin.com/`), can even made to be run on Windows — although if performance is your priority, this arrangement is suboptimal. In keeping with the focus of this book, we're going to follow the steps for a typical Linux installation. The procedure for the various Unixes will be very comparable. Windows users take heart — if you are determined to run PostgreSQL on Windows, you have a couple of options:

✦ Wait for 7.5 or 8.0. If you're not in a hurry, the developers suggest native windows support could be available as early as the first quarter of 2004 if 7.5 is on time or late 2004 if support slips to version 8.0. Check the site at www.postgresql.org/ for the latest.

✦ Try PowerGres. Software Research Associates has released a beta of its native windows port based on PostgreSQL 7.3. You can find it at http://powergres.sra.co.jp/s/ja/, but the site is in Japanese so prepare to do some blind clicking.

✦ The Cygwin option is not officially supported in the PostgreSQL documentation, but Olivier Nano and Ed Wolpert have a compiled a nice FAQ/procedure for this at http://colors.unice.fr/postgresql_win_setup.html. This should get you up and running quickly.

Linux installation

If you are a Red Hat, Debian, or SuSe user, you can easily find a prepackaged binary version for your distribution. Some of these are available on the PostgreSQL site, but you may fare better getting a version from your actual distribution vendor. These packages tend to be more current.

If you are a bare knuckles type, you'll probably want to compile from source; there are usually some advantages to doing so. We'll cover this procedure briefly here. First, you'll need to download a source distribution from http://www.postgresql.org/. A variety of mirrors are offered. Do the right thing and choose one close to you.

Unzip and untar the distribution in an out of the way place (your filename may be slightly different),

```
tar -xzvf postgresql-7.x.tar.gz
```

and change into the created directory

```
cd postgresql-7.x
```

Next, you'll want to run the configure script. You can obtain an exhaustive list of configure options by typing **./configure –help**, but we can't cover all the options here. If you have a particular use in mind, it might be worth your time to review the list and decide what else you want in your final installation. At a minimum, you'll want to specify a path and consider the --with-tcl, --with-perl and -with-python flags. No special flags are required for PHP use, but these other languages are common on most Unix-like systems so this small consideration is an easy way to add a level of flexibility that can pay large dividends down the road. Also, if you plan to work with any non-English data, --enable-locale is considered essential. So our minimum recommended configure line is composed as follows:

```
./configure --prefix=/usr/local/postgresql --with-perl \
--with-tcl --with-python --enable-locale
```

The next two steps are fairly routine and won't vary much from system to system.

```
make
```

```
make install
```

For command-line usage, you'll want to add the PostgreSQL binary directory to your search path. Exactly how to do this will depend on the combination of configure options and the system you are using.

Just as with MySQL, PostgreSQL likes to run with its own dedicated user id. You can accomplish this with the adduser or useradd commands. The name *postgres* is common, but by no means required. The name should, of course, conjure up some idea of the user's purpose. You don't want some zealous sys admin deleting a user from the system because he didn't recognize the name.

Next up is to choose a location for storing data. This directory must be owned by the *postgres* user you just created; we can then initialize it as the data directory with the command:

```
initdb -D /path/to/your/data
```

There is no hard specification as to where this data directory must reside, but some common choices are:

```
<postgres install directory>/data
/var/data
/var/pgdb
```

The PosgreSQL server process and binary are called *postmaster,* which shows up in a process list by that name. Postmaster, however, takes a wide array of options, and the utility pg_ctl is thoughtfully provided to simplify working with the postmaster daemon. So now we're ready to fire up PostgreSQL:

```
pg_ctl -D /data/path -o "-i" start
```

A word or two about the preceding command: The -D switch should be fairly obvious: it points to an already initialized data directory. If you point to an invalid data directory, startup will fail. The -o switch indicates that everything following is to be passed directly to the postmaster daemon. In this case, we're passing -I to tell PostgreSQL to start up with a TCP/IP socket enabled. This is necessary because Postgres will use Unix domain sockets by default, an option we will not be using with PHP.

We don't need to type this whole command over again to stop our server. The pg_ctl command will accept simple stop and restart command-line flags. Note that if you want to restart with different options, you must use stop and then start. You cannot pass new parameters to restart.

But is it a database yet?

Not quite. Like MySQL, Postgres features some command-line utilities in addition to a unified interactive client for working with PostgreSQL databases. In this section, we'll use some of the command-line utilities stored in the Postgres binary directory to get started. Let's start by inspecting what's already there by using the following command:

```
psql -l
```

which should return something like the following:

```
         List of databases
   Name    |  Owner  | Encoding
-----------+---------+-----------
 template0 | pgsql   | SQL_ASCII
 template1 | pgsql   | SQL_ASCII
(2 rows)
```

Because a database is a mandatory argument to the interactive client and we don't want to work directly on one of our template databases, we'll start by creating a single database that we'll use for the rest of this chapter:

```
createdb sample
```

That's all there is to creating a new database, but of course, this is just a blank slate at this point — a minimalist canvas based on the template database and on which we will paint a structure to our exacting specifications.

Now we can use the interactive client to work with our database:

```
psql sample
```

This will open a copy of sample and drop us at a prompt along with some instructions. The prompt inside the interactive client is different from the shell prompt, which can help you distinguish where you are exactly. This is especially useful on a Linux system where multiple shells open at one time is an everyday occurrence. The prompt will take the form <databasename>=#, such that our prompt will look like:

```
sample=#
```

If you issue the \? command from this prompt, you'll get a very long list of everything you can do from this prompt, exclusive of SQL specifics, which of course are also supported here. We can't offer exhaustive coverage here, but a few key commands are worth exploring.

- ✦ The \h command lists available help for all of the supported SQL constructs such as SELECT, DELETE, GRANT, and so on.

- ✦ The \d command, along with one of its accepted parameters, will display information about your database or specific objects in it. Of specific interest are \dt, which will list all tables in the current database, and \d <tablename>, which will show the structure of the specified table.

- ✦ \H turns on HTML output, which is handy for exporting data quickly to the Web. In conjunction with the \T command you can customize the html output somewhat, and you can use \o to send it all to a file.

Incidentally, you can call all of these options on the command line when starting psql. Simply substitute a hyphen for the slash and psql will execute the commands in sequence and then exit. For even greater utility, you can group these commands in a text file and read them in from the command line.

Down to Real Work

Let's build a simple structure inside our sample database. This example is necessarily abbreviated, but it is designed to give you a quick but useful familiarity with the Postgres and its SQL syntax. If you have already exited from our previous example, get back in to the sample database:

```
psql sample
```

Let's start by defining a simple table to hold the names of some cartoons we really like:

```
CREATE TABLE cartoons(id serial, cartoon varchar(30));
```

The following command allows us to check our result:

```
\d cartoons

           Table "public.cartoons"
  Column  |         Type          | Modifiers
----------+-----------------------+-----------
  id      | integer               |
  cartoon | character varying(30) |
```

Just so we can say we did something relational, we'll create a second table to hold the names of some of the characters in these cartoons.

```
CREATE TABLE characters(id int4, character varchar(15));
```

Postgres offers an astonishing 47 data types, so obviously our example barely even scratches the surface. To be clear, some of these types are really other types with increasing data specificity built in. (You may already be familiar with this concept, commonly called an *input mask* in other database tools.)

Now we'll use some SQL to insert a record into the cartoons table. Note that because the serial type is just an integer with an auto-increment flag attached, we do not need to specify anything for ID:

```
INSERT INTO cartoons (cartoon) values('Scooby Doo');
```

The absence of an error message suggests our efforts have met with success, but it's a good idea to check this with a SELECT statement anyway, first to be sure and second because, after a number of records have been entered, we may mentally lose track of where the auto-increment value stands. We'll need the number to define a relationship with our characters table.

```
SELECT * from cartoons;
 id |  cartoon
----+------------
  1 | Scooby Doo
(1 row)
```

Of course, we'd be in pretty bad shape if we managed to mess that one up. Let's also put in a character or two into the characters table.

```
INSERT INTO characters(id, character) VALUES(1, 'Shaggy');
INSERT INTO characters(id, character) VALUES(1, 'Daphne');
```

So we've built a database, created a couple of tables, and added a couple of records, just to make sure things are going well. Before we make a Web application out of this, however, we need to create a minimally privileged user — one who can access the tables in our sample database, write to them, and read from them, but not modify them or investigate any other aspect of the system.

In MySQL, users that did not already exist were implicitly created by the GRANT command. While Postgres also uses the GRANT syntax, we must explicitly create a user first:

```
CREATE USER cartoonfan PASSWORD 'secretword';
```

After creating the user, we must give cartoonfan some privileges:

```
GRANT SELECT, INSERT, UPDATE, DELETE on cartoons to cartoonfan;
GRANT SELECT, INSERT, UPDATE, DELETE
```

```
on characters to cartoonfan;
GRANT SELECT, INSERT, UPDATE, DELETE
on cartoons_id_seq to cartoonfan;
```

Note that we must issue this command at the table level. For security reasons, the wildcard character does not function in this context. The last command given is necessary for the `serial` field type we selected in the cartoons table.

PHP and PostgreSQL

Table 34-1 itemizes the PHP functions for working with PostgreSQL databases. There are many more functions than we can possibly elaborate on here. Many of them will make sense only after you have gained more familiarity with Postgres. Also, many of the function names for Postgres changed with PHP version 4.2. Because this is a PHP5 book, we're going to concentrate on the new names rather than the old.

Table 34-1: Common PostgreSQL Functions in PHP

Function	Behavior
`pg_connect()` and `pg_pconnect()`	Takes a single connection string as an argument, enumerating connection parameters such as host, database, port, user and password. `pg_pconnect()` is the persistent version. Returns a connection resource. See the listings below for usage examples.
`pg_query()`	This is the standard pass-through mechanism for sending basic SQL to the server. In earlier versions, it was called `pg_exec()`, but this name has been deprecated. Although optional, `pg_query()` likes to see a connection resource, followed by a comma before the actual SQL.
`pg_fetch_row()` `pg_fetch_assoc()` `pg_fetch_array()` `pg_fetch_object()` `pg_fetch_result()` `pg_fetch_all()`	Each of these functions takes at least a query-result resource as an argument and returns varying results depending on the function chosen and how it is called. Each of these except `pg_fetch_all()` used to require a counter argument if you wished to iterate through the returned rows. This argument is still available but is not necessary. These functions differ primarily in the results they return, which in the same order as they are listed are: 1) a numerically indexed array starting at an offset of 0; 2) an associative array with field names as indices; 3) returns both a numeric and an associative array; 4) returns the rows and values in object notation; 5) returns a specific row and column offset; and 6) returns a multidimensional array of the entire result set.
`pg_affected_rows()`	Returns the number of tuples (rows) affected by an `INSERT`, `UPDATE`, or `DELETE` query.
`pg_free_result()`	Frees the memory used by a query result.
`pg_num_fields()`	Returns the number of fields in a query result. Use with `SELECT` statements.
`pg_num_rows()`	Returns the number of rows in a query result. Use with `SELECT` statements.
`pg_close()`	Closes the PostgreSQL Connection. Takes a connection resource as an argument.

The Cartoons Database

We'd like to be able to add some cartoons and characters to our database using a handy Web-entry system. We've deliberately oversimplified our example to get through the key concepts quickly, so it should be fairly easy to put together a system that allows us to achieve this task. Listing 34-1 shows a welcoming page to our Cartoons database.

Listing 34-1: index.php

```
<html>
<head>
<title>Cartoons Database</title>
</head>

<body>

<h1>Cartoons and Characters Database</h1>

<p>Welcome to the cartoons and characters database. Existing
entries are provided below. Use the provided functions to get
more details and to edit, add or delete entries.</p>

<?php
$connect_parameters = "host=localhost dbname=sample
user=cartoonfan password=secretword";
if ($link = pg_connect($connect_parameters)) {
  $sSql = "select * from cartoons";
  $sResult = pg_query($link, $sSql);
  if (pg_num_rows($sResult) > 0) {
    print("<table border=\"1\">");
    print("<tr><th>ID</th><th>Cartoon</th>
           <th>Characters</th></tr>");
    while ($sRow = pg_fetch_object($sResult)) {
      print("<tr><th>$sRow->id</th>
             <td>$sRow->cartoon</td>");
      $tSql = "select * from characters where
               id = '$sRow->id'";
      $tResult = pg_query($tSql);
      print("<td>");
      while ($tRow = pg_fetch_object($tResult)) {
        print("$tRow->character ");
      }
      print("</td></tr>");
    }
    print("</table>");
  } else {
    print("<p>There are not currently any records in the
           cartoon database.</p>");
  }
```

```
} else {
  print("<p>Connection to the cartoons database has
failed</p>");
}
?>

</body>
</html>
```

Notice how different our connect parameters are from what we'd use with MySQL. They aren't even comma separated! This function is even insensitive to the order in which they are supplied — you simply have to use the appropriate parameter name and supply the corresponding value. Additional recognized parameters for this function are `options`, `tty`, and `port`.

The rest of this script reads much like a similar script would for MySQL. A query is defined, we get the results of that as an object, issue a second query to get the character data, and use the ubiquitous print statement to put it all into a nice html table.

This is fine as far as it goes, but we don't yet have a way to insert, edit, and delete records. In Listing 34-2, we create a new form for the purpose of inserting records.

Listing 34-2: **insert.php**

```
<html>
<head>
<title>Cartoons Database</title>
</head>

<body>
<h1>Cartoons and Characters Database</h1>
<?php
if ($_POST[action] == "Insert") {
  $connect_parameters = "host=localhost dbname=sample
  user=cartoonfan password=secretword";
  $link = pg_connect($connect_parameters);
  $iSql = "insert into cartoons(cartoon)
          values('$_POST[cartoon]')";
  if (pg_query($link, $iSql)) {
    $jSql = "select currval('cartoons_id_seq') as oid";
    $jResult = pg_query($jSql);
    $j_id = pg_fetch_result($jResult, 0, 'oid');
    $characters_array = explode( "\n", $_POST[characters]);
    for($i=0;$i<count($characters_array);$i++) {
      $char = trim($characters_array[$i]);
      $cSql = "insert into characters(id, character)
              values($j_id, '$char')";
      pg_query($cSql);
    }
```

Continued

Listing 34-2 *(continued)*

```
      print("<p>Your submission was successfully inserted.
            You can submit another, if you wish</p>");
   } else {
     print("<p>We were unable to insert the records as
            submitted. You can try again, if you wish</p>");
   }
} else {
print("<p>Welcome to the cartoons and characters database.
Enter the");
print("name of your favorite cartoon below, and choose
submit.</p>");
}

?>

<form action="insert.php" method="post">
<p>Enter the name of a favorite cartoon<br>
<input type="text" name="cartoon"></p>
<p>Enter the name of some characters from the cartoon.
(You can enter more later). Use a hard return to
separate each name.<br>
<textarea cols="15" rows="8" name="characters">
</textarea></p>
<input type="submit" name="action" value="Insert">
</form>
<p><a href="index.php">Return to the main page.</a></p>
</body>
</html>
```

This script is doing a lot, so let's review it. Note first the separation of the PHP and HTML elements. All of the conditional code appears at the top, and the conditional display requirements are set up such that we don't have to weave in and out of PHP to get the job done. We're going to display a form even if a submission has just been made so that the user can submit entries one right after the other without an intermediate step. The first conditional, at the top of the page, checks to see if the page is being called from the form. If not, we print a simple instruction set. If the page is the result of a form submission, the fun begins.

We start with a connection to our database. This item is not tested as we just connected on our index page, so we will, perhaps perilously, assume a valid connection. The next step is to generate the SQL for the cartoon table from the POST data and insert a new record into the database. The next bit is designed to get the insert id of the inserted cartoon. Actually, PHP offers pg_last_oid() for this purpose, but as of this writing, it did not yield the desired result and is currently deemed unreliable.

Once we have the correct id, we do some manipulation on the contents of the textarea that contains our characters. Refer to Chapter 21 on arrays for more on explode(). Basically, we're splitting the field each place we find a line break and popping the resulting elements into an array. Next we call `trim()` to get rid of the superfluous space character left behind by `explode()`. This is done because Windows systems submit an additional `\r` wherever a line break occurs. If we explode on this as a separator, `explode` will fail when the form is submitted from Linux, for example, because the character is not there.

Finally, we iterate through the resulting array, putting each character into the characters table with its own insert query, and we return a message of success or failure.

When we went back to test our results, we found a few problems with `index.php` and so we present a revised version in Listing 34-3. We could have just changed the original listing, but this so nicely illustrates the debugging process that we've included it this way to point out the improvements.

Listing 34-3: **index.php (improved)**

```
<html>
<head>
<title>Cartoons Database</title>
</head>

<body>

<h1>Cartoons and Characters Database</h1>
<?php
if ($_POST[action] == "Insert") {
  $connect_parameters = "host=localhost dbname=sample
user=cartoonfan password=secretword";
  $link = pg_connect($connect_parameters);
  $iSql = "insert into cartoons(cartoon)
          values('$_POST[cartoon]')";
  if (pg_query($link, $iSql)) {
    $jSql = "select currval('cartoons_id_seq') as oid";
    $jResult = pg_query($jSql);
    $j_id = pg_fetch_result($jResult, 0, 'oid');
    $characters_array = explode( "\n", $_POST[characters]);
    for($i=0;$i<count($characters_array);$i++) {
      $char = trim($characters_array[$i]);
      $cSql = "insert into characters(id, character)
              values($j_id, '$char')";
      pg_query($cSql);
    }
    print("<p>Your submission was successfully inserted.
    You can submit another, if you wish</p>");
  } else {
    print("<p>We were unable to insert the records as submitted.
          You can try again, if you wish</p>");
  }
} else {
  print("<p>Welcome to the cartoons and characters database.
Enter the");
  print("name of your favorite cartoon below, and choose
```

Continued

Listing 34-3 *(continued)*

```
submit.</p>");
}

?>

<form action="insert.php" method="post">
<p>Enter the name of a favorite cartoon<br>
<input type="text" name="cartoon"></p>
<p>Enter the name of some characters from the cartoon.
(You can enter more later). Use a hard return to
separate each name.<br>
<textarea cols="15" rows="8" name="characters">
</textarea></p>
<input type="submit" name="action" value="Insert">
</form>
<p><a href="index.php">Return to the main page.</a></p>
</body>
</html>
```

First, we added a link to our now-finished insert form. Second, we are now passing the action parameter via our submit button, purely for the sake of orderliness. We also encountered a problem with our characters display. When we submitted a character with a space in its name (okay, we admit, we were trying to submit *Wonder Woman*), it was unclear where one character ends and the next one begins. Using a little regex and string concatenation, we've now caused this to display as a comma-separated list.

Now we need a form for editing records. Listing 34-4 is what we've come up with.

Listing 34-4: edit.php

```
<html>
<head>
<title>Cartoons Database</title>
</head>
<body>
<h1>Cartoons and Characters Database</h1>
<?php
$connect_parameters = "host=localhost dbname=sample
user=cartoonfan password=secretword";
$link = pg_connect($connect_parameters);
if ($_POST[action] == "Update") {
$sSql = "update cartoons set cartoon = '$_POST[cartoon]'
        where id = '$_POST[f]'";
  if (pg_query($sSql)) {
```

```
        $dSql = "delete from characters where id = '$_POST[f]'";
        pg_query($dSql);
        $characters_array = explode( "\n", $_POST[characters]);
        for($i=0;$i<count($characters_array);$i++) {
          $char = trim($characters_array[$i]);
          if($char <> '') {
            $cSql = "insert into characters
                        (id, character)
                        values($_POST[f], '$char')";
            pg_query($cSql);
          }
        }
        print("<p>Your edits were successfully posted.</p>");
      } else {
        print("<p>Update of record $_POST[f] failed.</p>");
      }
      print("<p><a href=\"index.php\">Return to the main
            page.</a></p>");
    } else {
      $sSql = "select * from cartoons where id = $_GET[f]";
      $sResult = pg_query($sSql);
      $sRow = pg_fetch_object($sResult);
      print("<form action=\"edit.php\" method=\"post\">");
      print("<p>Edit the name of a favorite cartoon<br>");
      print("<input type=\"hidden\" name=\"f\"
            value=\"$_GET[f]\">");
      print("<input type=\"text\" name=\"cartoon\"
            value=\"$sRow->cartoon\"></p>");
      print("<p>Edit the name of some characters from
            the cartoon. ");
      print("(You can enter more later). Use a hard return to ");
      print("separate each name.<br>");
      print("<textarea cols=\"15\" rows=\"8\"
            name=\"characters\">");
      $cSql = "select * from characters where id = $_GET[f]";
      $cResult = pg_query($cSql);
      while ($cRow = pg_fetch_object($cResult)) {
        print("$cRow->character\r\n");
      }
      print("</textarea></p>");
      print("<input type=\"submit\" name=\"action\"
            value=\"Update\">");
      print("</form>");
     print("<p><a href=\"index.php\">Return to the main
            page.</a></p>");
    }
    ?>
    </body>
    </html>
```

Like `insert.php`, `edit.php` is a recursive action form. The form post is sent to the same script and the action taken depends, essentially, on the contents of a hidden variable, `$action`. In the absence of this variable, we just retrieve the records from the cartoons and character tables and drop them back in the form much as they appeared in the original insert form. To parse the characters back into their original positions, note that we have essentially reversed the explode function we used in `insert.php`, but we'll shift it back into forward when we go to post the updates.

One thing you might find strange is that before we post the updates to the characters table, we delete all the entries. This is because we haven't created a unique key for each character, so there isn't a way to conveniently refer to an individual record unambiguously. Yes, this is a design flaw. In a bigger project, it would be a substantial design flaw. But there are some advantages to the way we've done this. A form to update both characters and cartoons in the same action is much easier to do in this scenario. It would be quite a bit more code intensive, though certainly feasible, to add a serial id to the characters table, retrieve all three fields, set up a multidimensional array in our form, retrieve it, and process it in our script such that multiple records are updated in a single operation. You get the idea. Sometimes it's okay to opt for simplicity.

Finally, we've made a few changes to `index.php`, which we're going to show you in Listing 34-5. All we've done is added a way to get at the edit functions and a simple routine for deleting a record, parent and children, in one operation.

Listing 34-5: **index.php (final)**

```
<html>
<head>
<title>Cartoons Database</title>
</head>

<body>

<h1>Cartoons and Characters Database</h1>

<p>Welcome to the cartoons and characters database. Existing
entries are provided below. Use the provided functions to get
more details and to edit, add or delete entries.</p>

<?php
$connect_parameters = "host=localhost dbname=sample
user=cartoonfan password=secretword";
if ($link = pg_connect($connect_parameters)) {
  if($_GET[action] == "d") {
    $dSql = "delete from characters where id = '$_GET[f]'";
    pg_query($dSql);
    $dSql = "delete from cartoons where id = '$_GET[f]'";
    pg_query($dSql);
  }
  $sSql = "select * from cartoons";
  $sResult = pg_query($link, $sSql);
```

```php
    if (pg_num_rows($sResult) > 0) {
      print("<table border=\"1\">");
      print("<tr><th>ID</th><th>Cartoon</th>
            <th>Characters</th><th></th></tr>");
      while ($sRow = pg_fetch_object($sResult)) {
        print("<tr><th>$sRow->id</th>
              <td>$sRow->cartoon</td>");
        $tSql = "select * from characters where id = '$sRow->id'";
        $tResult = pg_query($tSql);
        print("<td>");
        $character_string = "";
        while ($tRow = pg_fetch_object($tResult)) {
          $character_string .= "$tRow->character, ";
        }
        $new_character_string = ereg_replace("(, )$", "",
                                             $character_string);
        print("$new_character_string</td>");
        print("<td><a href=\"edit.php?f=$sRow->id\">Edit</a> |");
        print(" <a href=\"index.php?f=$sRow->id&action=d\">
                          Delete</a></td></tr>");
      }
      print("</table>");
    } else {
    print("<p>There are not currently any records in the
            cartoon database.</p>");
    }
    print("<p><a href=\"insert.php\">Add a Record</a></p>");
  } else {
    print("<p>Connection to the cartoons database has
failed</p>");
  }
?>

</body>
</html>
```

Summary

PostgreSQL is an interesting and powerful database tool. Although we did not comprehensively cover all of its utility here, we have shown you enough basics to get started with it. Check the PHP documentation at www.php.net/pgsql for a comprehensive listing of PostgreSQL functions.

✦　　✦　　✦

Oracle

Oracle databases are extremely powerful, reliable, and fast for certain kinds of queries. They are also a testament to the power of marketing, as they enjoy a mystique unmatched by any other data-storage product. In this chapter, we try to cut through the hype and give you a practical foundation in using Oracle with PHP.

Tip   Much of the information in this chapter is also applicable to IBM DB2, which PHP connects to using the ODBC interface, InterBase, and similar products. Much of Oracle's functionality is also duplicated by PostgreSQL, although this open-source database unfortunately has a considerably different API than any other database. The point of this chapter is not to push Oracle over another product; it is to introduce a market-leading commercial database to those who want to learn how to use it. Feel free to mentally substitute DB2 or PostgreSQL for every instance of Oracle in the following section.

When Do You Need Oracle?

We have never had a prospective employer or client for a PHP job who did not at least mention the possibility of using Oracle. Ironically, the one organization that really needed this type of functionality was very slow to adopt it, whereas everyone else didn't need Oracle at all but wanted to architect current development around the theoretical possibility that they might need it later. In an anecdotal way, this experience testifies to the niche Oracle Corporation has managed to carve out in the minds of the entire software industry.

Through a powerful marketing machine (and, of course, a fine product), Oracle has managed to make its name synonymous with size, scale, and (by implication) success. Therefore, every businessperson who dreams of making it big in any business having to do with data has a fantasy that someday he or she will need and be able to afford an Oracle installation. When the humble PHP developer says, "You don't need Oracle," this is too often taken as equivalent to saying, "You're never going to amount to anything"—in other words, a big splash of cold water right in the face of the entrepreneur or manager. This does not tend to endear the humble PHP developer to the person writing the checks, even if your motivation is to save money and trouble for the boss. Sometimes reality cannot compete with fantasy, even in the supposedly hard-headed world of business.

So how do you realistically decide whether you need Oracle (or a workalike) or not? Certain well-understood factors are tripwires. If you are in one of these situations, your pondering is done. If not, the chances are very high that your needs could be met perfectly well — perhaps even better — by a cheaper, easier-to-use database.

Money

If you keep track of money or anything that can be converted to money (credit card charges, equities, airline miles, royalty payments, vacation time), you need the transactional model. Done, end of story, move on to the next thing. Not only are these things important to track end to end, but people tend to get very annoyed when you fail to do this correctly. You do not want to be matching up failed charge attempts or stock purchases programmatically.

The only exception is if you do not handle the financial part of the transaction yourself. It's fairly common these days for even pretty large Web sites to route their fulfillment transactions through some third party. If you are willing to send a customer off to your fulfillment partner, and then take its word on whether the transaction was completed successfully or not, you can offload the transactional database requirements onto your partner.

Other rivalrous resources

If you track other kinds of rivalrous resources on a large scale — airline tickets, concert tickets, inventory — you very likely need a transactional database. Note that the operative term is *large scale*. This feature applies only if you are in imminent danger of having *colliding writes*, meaning that the chances are good that, between the time you check whether a resource is available and the time you write it into another table, someone else may have claimed it. In other words, this stricture applies to computer-scale time. If you run a Web site that takes a couple hundred new registrations a day, you are not going to run into this kind of problem except as a rare fluke.

Huge data sets

Again, *huge* is the key. Millions of rows is not huge. If you will never realistically get past tens of millions of rows, you don't need Oracle for sheer scalability.

Lots of big formulaic writes or data munging

Oracle's stored procedures can increase speed immensely in situations where you have the same kind of big write or data processing happening all the time. Stored procedures amount to moving part of the code into the database itself. Processes that use these stored procedures will get done faster than processes that don't, because you've already told the database exactly what to do in a certain situation. Databases without stored procedures require all instructions to come from the PHP program, which is far slower in loops than simply handing off the input data and letting the database run with it.

For instance, if you run an e-commerce site that just takes inputs from one kind of order form and nothing else, you'll get increased overall speed from a stored procedure. The database will not have to finish one step and then wait for the program to tell it the next step or to feed it the next bit of data. PHP will simply open up the connection, shovel some data down the pipe as fast as it can, kick off the stored procedure, and possibly wait for a response.

Stored procedures obviously add value in cases where there is massive data munging happening on the database side. For instance, if you have a big data warehouse which takes a described data set and performs lots of analytical operations on it, then returns the results of those operations, you will very likely get much improved performance from a stored procedure.

Remember that stored procedures don't help you in cases where there is variability in the process. For instance, if you make ad-hoc queries on a data warehouse all the time, those queries will be extremely slow compared to a query that you make every day using a stored procedure. Also, you have to use stored procedures pretty often to choose a database on this basis. A whole infrastructure needs to be in place for you to derive benefits from stored procedures, and you need to decide whether it's worth the very real costs to build this infrastructure.

Triggers

Triggers are just what they sound like: The database keeps track of state; when some kind of triggering event happens, it kicks off one or more stored procedures. You need triggers if you need to respond to certain well-defined data events in real time and are willing to give up global performance to do it. If your changes do not have to occur instantly — if, for instance, they can happen once an hour — you are probably better off without triggers as you can schedule stored procedures to run periodically. On the other hand, if you have to detect changes every second or so, triggers will be much more efficient than cronjobs or other alternatives. This is a pretty rare feature for a Web architecture, so think hard about whether you need triggers.

Legal liability

Finally, there are nontechnical reasons why you might need Oracle — one of which is legal liability. Imagine that you run a business that is in some kind of personal information space — credit reports or medical records, perhaps. If somehow two records get mixed up, you would face significant legal liability for this most private type of information. One line of defense is to assert that you followed industry standard practices to safeguard data integrity, including use of the industry-leading database system. The tens of thousands of dollars you spend on an Oracle installation may seem cheap in this circumstance.

Bottom line: Two-year outlook

Even if you don't need any of these features now, it behooves you to think whether you might need them sometime in the foreseeable future. But don't try to build a Web architecture for the ages — new things happen so fast on the Internet that cathedral-builders are made fools of daily.

In general it seems like a two-year window is about right unless your needs are changing exceptionally quickly or slowly. If you don't see any of the preceding conditions looming on your horizon within two years or so, don't worry too much about switching to Oracle.

On the other hand, if you meet any of the preceding criteria, don't waste time — you need Oracle or one of its functional competitors.

Oracle and Web Architecture

Having an Oracle database on your back end implies certain things about your architecture and your Web development team. Do not think you can finesse these issues. If you're not ready to accept them, you're not ready for Oracle.

Specialized team members

The minute you have an Oracle installation, you need at a minimum a DBA and a PL/SQL programmer. Do not think that it's at all reasonable to expect Web developers or binary programmers to take over any of these tasks, as they often are expected to do with simpler data stores. Database tasks such as installation, tuning, refreshing, setting indexes, maintaining hot backups, and writing complex stored procedures are very highly specialized skills, which require specialized training and probably certification.

One of us once worked in a situation where (mercifully briefly) a team of programmers tried to get a database installed and running with help from a couple of contractors rather than full-time Oracle professionals. This was an indescribably miserable experience for everyone concerned, with data corruption and bizarre server issues on a daily basis. The minute a real DBA and PL/SQL programmer came in, the situation improved immeasurably — 10-second queries became half-second queries, and so on. There's a reason that these professionals make the big bucks, and we can assure you that you don't want to learn why the hard way.

Shared development databases

Due to the cost and complexity of the database, you will almost certainly need to limit the number of separate development instances in the office. This means that if all your developers are working against one development database that gets corrupted or otherwise goes down, the whole team will be out of commission until the problem can be resolved. On the other hand, MySQL and SQL Server make it easy for every developer to run a local instance if necessary.

And don't even *think* about cheating on your licenses — an Oracle software license audit is nothing you want to experience.

Limited schema changes

Lighter-weight databases make it possible to make schema changes on the fly — even in production. In Oracle, this is not a good idea. It's more difficult to add new database-driven features quickly because of the time and planning necessary to successfully create schema changes. With Oracle, you really need to design the entire schema in advance (as you're supposed to do but never quite take the time to complete).

Tools (or lack thereof)

Be prepared to invest significantly in tools. Almost no tools are available on the market to help you with Oracle from a PHP platform specifically. More generally, Oracle is not interested in data sets smaller than a few tens of thousands of records, and many of the tools available are not really worth running on data sets smaller than that.

Replication and failover

Some database servers, like MySQL, work best in clusters with one master handling writes while a bunch of slaves serve up reads. This means that, for maximum efficiency, MySQL code should be written to take advantage of multiple connections on a single page — each MySQL function specifying a particular resource handle, for instance.

Oracle, however, works best in a single monolithic instance. Remember that eBay grew to be one of the biggest sites on the Web, and suffered many costly site failures, before even beginning to move away from a monolithic database instance. This tends to create a single point of failure model that affects all aspects of deployment — after all, what's the point in having massive redundancy in Web servers when all of them could be struck down by a single hardware problem on the database server? Most important for PHP developers, writing code for Oracle will not require you to juggle multiple connections on a per-page basis, as there is little to be gained by this practice.

Data caching

One piece of good news is that Oracle can be configured to cache data. This means that if you make the same query over and over for a while — for instance, you validate the user against the database on every page load — the database will only actually perform the query the first time. On subsequent requests, it will just serve up the result from some cache memory, for a much faster result. This means that you will not have to implement a custom data-caching scheme of your own, which is a very expensive and tricky task.

However, we should mention that lighter-weight databases are rapidly catching up to Oracle's data caching capabilities for small queries. Microsoft SQL Server is reported to have excellent data caching, and MySQL implemented it for the first time in version 4.0.1.

Using OCI8 Functions

 Caution
The remainder of this chapter explains how to use PHP's Oracle functions. If you have no familiarity with Oracle at all, and especially if you do not have extensive experience with other SQL databases, you will probably also need to consult an Oracle reference such as Carol McCullough-Dieter's *Oracle9i For Dummies* (Wiley, 2001).

PHP has two Oracle extensions: Oracle and OCI8. The Oracle extension is deprecated for versions of Oracle after 7 and should be avoided if at all possible. The OCI8 extension is literally dozens to hundreds of times faster at most queries, and also allows much better handling of cursors. We will not be describing the Oracle extension at all; use OCI8 from the beginning.

Tip
Although Oracle is currently in version 9, the OCI8 extension is still the one you want. Apparently the PHP team has simply decided not to change the name with every update.

If you walk through a couple of typical Oracle queries step by step, you can see that the procedure is a bit different from that for MySQL or SQL Server:

```
$name = str_replace("'", "''", $name);
$query = "SELECT product_id FROM product
        WHERE product_name = '$name'";
$stmt = OCIParse($conn, $query);
OCIExecute($stmt, OCI_DEFAULT);
$err_array = OCIError($stmt);
if ($err_array) {
   $err_message = $err_array['message'];
   $$error_str = $err_message;
   OCIFreeStatement($stmt);
} else {
   OCIFetchStatement($stmt, $res, OCI_RETURN_NULLS);
   OCIFreeStatement($stmt);
}
$product_id = $res['PRODUCT_ID'][0];
```

Right away you will notice differences such as string escaping, parsing and executing, memory management, and fetching data sets. We explain these differences in more detail in the sections that follow. Please refer to the preceding code block for all references that do not have their own code examples.

Escaping strings

Remember that Oracle uses Sybase-style string escaping — in other words, it escapes single quotes with a single quote, not with a backslash. This means that you will have to manually escape every string, since `magic_quotes` has the wrong effect; or you have to set Sybase style magic quotes in your `php.ini` file.

Parsing and executing

In most other databases, you send a SQL query over the pipe, and it returns either a value or an error message. In Oracle, you have an intermediate step in which you must parse the query for correctness. If your SQL is bad, the query will never be sent to the database. An invalid SQL query will return an Oracle error code via `OCIError()`.

In most cases, the query will be fine and you'll move right to executing the query. This is your opportunity to specify a mode for your query, either `OCI_COMMIT_ON_SUCCESS` or `OCI_DEFAULT`, which does not auto-commit. We generally do not auto-commit because we like to know when a rollback is necessary, but this is largely a matter of preference. Of course for `SELECT` statements it doesn't matter which mode you choose because no commitment or rollback is happening anyway. See the section on transactionality later in this chapter.

Error reporting

Oracle error reporting is also unique. For one thing, you can specify whether you're asking for a *global-*, *connection-*, or *statement-*level error. A global error is a failure to get a connection. A connection error is an invalid SQL statement that chokes at the parse stage — remember, it isn't a statement yet, so it can't be a statement-level error. A statement error involves a problem with a properly parsed statement.

The product of `OCIError()` is an associative array, where `code` is the error code and `message` is a text string.

Memory management

In Oracle, you are expected to do some memory management manually. In particular, it's a good idea to free statement memory when you're done with the statement handle, and cursor memory when you're done with the cursors. Theoretically, all the memory will be reclaimed at the end of every script, but if your scripts are big you might want to free memory as you go.

Ask for nulls

If you want null values in your data set, you have to ask for them in the fetch function. Otherwise, Oracle will not return the field name as part of its associative array, and thus an array member you expect to see will not exist. Many other databases will automatically return the null values.

Fetching entire data sets

Oracle has four fetching functions: OCIResult, OCIFetch, OCIFetchInto, and OCIFetchStatement. The first three correspond fairly straightforwardly to the single-column, row, and array fetching functions enjoyed by all other PHP database extensions — but the last is unique to Oracle. It fetches the entire result set into one big array. This can mean less looping and faster access to your data. Of course, you should make sure you are returning a reasonably small result set; otherwise, you can bring PHP to its knees.

All caps

Oracle column names, which become associative array indices, are in all capital letters. You can ask for the field in lowercase, but by the time it comes back from the database it will be in all caps, as shown in the following code.

```
$query = "SELECT product_name, modified, created
          FROM product
            WHERE product_id = 1";
$stmt = OCIParse($conn, $query);
OCIExecute($stmt, OCI_DEFAULT);
$err_array = OCIError($stmt);
if ($err_array) {
    $err_message = $err_array['message'];
    $error_str = $err_message;
    OCIFreeStatement($stmt);

} else {
    OCIFetchStatement($stmt, $res)
    OCIFreeStatement($stmt);
    $product_name = $res['PRODUCT_NAME'][0];
    $modified = $res['MODIFIED'][0];
    $created = $res['CREATED'][0];
}
```

Transactionality

Oracle's famous transactionality implies that all INSERT, UPDATE, and DELETE statements must be committed or rolled back before they will really be stored in the database. You can commit automatically during the OCIExecute() step, but if you really want an entire string of queries to succeed or fail together — the essence of transactionality — it's better to commit by hand when all of them are complete.

```
$query = "DELETE FROM product
          WHERE product_name = '$product_name'";
$stmt = OCIParse($conn, $query);
OCIExecute($stmt, OCI_DEFAULT);
$err_array = OCIError($stmt);
if ($err_array) {
    $err_message = $err_array['message'];
    $error_str = $err_message;
    OCIFreeStatement($stmt);
    OCIRollback($conn);
} else {
    OCIFreeStatement($stmt);
}
```

```
$query = "INSERT INTO product (product_name, modified, created)
          VALUES ('$product_name', SYSDATE, SYSDATE)";
$stmt = OCIParse($conn, $query);
OCIExecute($stmt, OCI_DEFAULT);
$err_array = OCIError($stmt);
if ($err_array) {
    $err_message = $err_array['message'];
    $error_str = $err_message;
    OCIFreeStatement($stmt);
    OCIRollback($conn);
    exit;
} else {
    OCIFreeStatement($stmt);
}
OCICommit($conn);
```

The net effect of this code block will be to ensure that there is only, at most, one row in the database for each product name. If either the DELETE or the INSERT fails, the state of the database will not be changed. You should never have a situation where you have zero or two rows with the same product name. Note the second argument to OCIExecute() is OCI_DEFAULT, which means that statements will not be auto-committed and must, therefore, be committed by hand.

Caution It's very important to remember that commits and rollbacks occur on a *connection*, not on a statement. Everything since the last commit or rollback will be entered into the database when you call OCICommit() or OCIRollback(). You may call it as many times during a script as you like, but generally all the parts of a transaction are committed or rolled back together.

Stored procedures and cursors

Stored procedures are programs that execute on the database. They move some of the programming into the database layer rather than the PHP layer. PHP merely sends data to the function and handles any returned values.

Because you are connecting to a particular compiled program on the database server, you need to establish a more specific kind of connection to the stored procedure. This connection is called a *cursor*, and the process of designating variables for use by the stored procedure is called *binding to a cursor*. Basically you are taking a PHP variable and transforming it into a variable on the Oracle side, or creating a PHP variable in which to store data returned from Oracle. Cursors must be executed separately from ordinary Oracle statements.

The code block that follows shows a simple example of stored procedure being called from PHP. In this case, we are executing the stored procedure named get_categories(), which takes no inputs and returns one output, OUT1, which we are binding to the PHP variable name $cursor1.

```
// Call stored procedure get_categories
$request = "begin DEV.get_categories(:OUT1); end;";
$cursor1 = OCINewCursor($conn);
$stmt = OCIParse($conn, $request);
OCIBindByName($stmt, ":OUT1", &$cursor1, -1, OCI_B_CURSOR);
OCIExecute($stmt);
OCIExecute($cursor1);
$err_array = OCIError($conn);
```

```
if ($err_array) {
    $err_message = $err_array['message'];
    echo $err_message;
    OCIFreeCursor($cursor1);
    OCIFreeStatement($stmt);
    OCILogoff($conn);
    exit;
}
while (OCIFetchInto($cursor1, &$cat_array)) {
    $opt_str .= "<OPTION VALUE=\""
                .$cat_array[0]
                ."\">"
                .$cat_array[1]
                ."</OPTION>\n";
}
OCIFreeCursor($cursor1);
OCIFreeStatement($stmt);
OCILogoff($conn);
```

It's possible to kick off a stored procedure or Oracle function and walk away, but more often you will be waiting for a result. This result will come on one or more cursors. These cursors, and possibly any other variables that come back to PHP, need to be created by `OCINewCursor()` and bound to PHP variables using `OCIBindByName()`. They are not immediately available to PHP otherwise. After that, they can be treated much like statements—their contents can be fetched, and their memory must be freed.

Project: Point Editor

The *product point editor* is a very simple Oracle tool that allows you to edit the data associated with a single item in a product catalog (as for an e-commerce site). Not only does it fetch information that all products share, such as product name and SKU, but it automatically sweeps up variable product attribute data for editing. This is data associated with each item, such as price, manufacturer, size, color, and so forth; it differs for items depending on what kind of thing they are—cars will have a color but not a gender, clothing might have a gender but not a type of transmission.

Because the attribute information you wish to save for each product varies with the product category—for books you might want to know the author and number of pages, whereas for toys you might want to know recommended age—you cannot simply save this information in the product table, even if it would normally be one-to-one data. To maintain flexibility, each product category (books, toys, and so on) has a number of attributes associated with it, and then each product is associated with a number of attribute values. The relationships look schematically like this:

```
Category
  category_id
  category_name

Product
  product_id
  product_name
  category_id
```

```
Attribute
  attribute_id
  attribute_name
  category_id

Attribute_value
  attrib_val_id
  attrib_val
  attribute_id

Product_attribute
  product_id
  attrib_val_id
```

The product point editor will query the database for all attributes associated with this product and construct a series of pull-down menus with all possible attribute values neatly laid out for the editor to select from. If an attribute value is already associated with this product, that value will be preselected in the HTML form field.

Listing 35-1 is a file of functions that are used in both the product point editor and the product batch editor in the next section. This file should be saved under the name oci8_funcs.php.

Listing 35-1: **Common Oracle functions (oci8_funcs.php)**

```php
<?php

/***********************************
 * Functions for Oracle-based tools *
 ***********************************/

putenv("ORACLE_HOME=/tools/oracle");


// Use when fetching data from the db
function unescape_quotes($str)
{
    $esc_str = str_replace("''", "'", $str);
    $esc2_str = str_replace("\"\"", "\"", $esc_str);
    return $esc2_str;
}


// Use when inserting data into the db
function escape_sq($str)
{
    $esc_str = str_replace("'", "''", $str);
    return $esc_str;
}
```

```php
function escape_html($str)
{
   $gt_str = str_replace("&gt;", ">;", $str);
   $lt_str = str_replace("&lt;", "<", $gt_str);
   $dq_str = str_replace("&quot;", "\"", $lt_str);
   $esc_str = str_replace("&amp;", "&", $dq_str);
   return $esc_str;
}


// Use this one for INSERTs, UPDATEs, and DELETEs
function parse_exec_free($conn, $query, &$error_str)
{
   $stmt = OCIParse($conn, $query);
   OCIExecute($stmt, OCI_DEFAULT);
   $err_array = OCIError($stmt);
   if ($err_array) {
      $err_message = $err_array['message'];
      $$error_str = $err_message;
      OCIFreeStatement($stmt);
      $stmt = FALSE;
   } else {
       OCIFreeStatement($stmt);
      $stmt = TRUE;
   }
   return $stmt;
}


// Use this one for SELECTs
function parse_exec_fetch($conn, $query, &$error_str, &$res,
$nulls=0)
{
   $stmt = OCIParse($conn, $query);
   OCIExecute($stmt, OCI_DEFAULT);
   $err_array = OCIError($stmt);
   if ($err_array) {
      $err_message = $err_array['message'];
      $$error_str = $err_message;
      OCIFreeStatement($stmt);
      $stmt = FALSE;
   } else {
      if ($nulls == 1) {
         OCIFetchStatement($stmt, $res, OCI_RETURN_NULLS);
      } else {
         OCIFetchStatement($stmt, $res);
      }
   }
   return $stmt;
}
```

Continued

Listing 35-1 *(continued)*

```
// For batch_upload.php, which writes a separate error log
function choke_and_die($conn, $fp, $error_str)
{
    OCIRollback($conn);
    OCILogoff($conn);
    $error_line = $error_str."<BR>\n";
    echo $error_line;
    fwrite($fp, $error_line);
    fwrite($fp, "</HTML>\n");
    fclose($fp);
    exit;
}


// For all nonlogwriting uses (which is most of them)
function die_silently($conn, $error_str)
{
    OCIRollback($conn);
    OCILogoff($conn);
    // You can uncomment these when debugging
    //$error_line = $error_str."<BR>\n";
    //echo $error_line;
    exit;
}


// Excel sometimes adds random quotes around field contents
function unquote($str)
{
    $pos = strpos($str, "\"");
    if ($pos === 0) {
        $qstr = substr($str, 1, -1);
        return trim($qstr);
    } else {
        return trim($str);
    }
}


// Excel sometimes doubles double-quotes in an attempt to close
// them
function strip_db($str)
{
    $esc_str = str_replace("\"\"", "\"", $str);
    return $esc_str;
}

?>
```

Listing 35-2 is the actual product point editor itself.

Listing 35-2: **Product point editor (prod_point.php)**

```php
<?php

/******************************************************
 * This is the product point editor.                 *
 * The purpose of this tool is to edit all the data   *
 * associated with a single product.  It will mostly  *
 * be used for trivial fixes (e.g., spelling errors)  *
 ******************************************************/

include("oci8_funcs.php"); //common functions
$thisDB = "dev";
$thisDBuser = "oci_user";
$thisDBpassword = "sesame";

// -----------------
// EDIT PRODUCT DATA
// -----------------
if($_POST['submit'] == "Submit") {
   // Get a timestamp
   $begin_time = time();
   // Open the pipe
   $conn = OCILogon($thisDBuser, $thisDBpassword, $thisDB)
    or die("Can't get a database connection.");

   // UPDATE PRODUCT TABLE
   $product_id = $_POST['product_id'];
   $product_name = escape_sq($_POST['product_name']);
   $sku = escape_sq($_POST['sku']);
   $itemurl = escape_sq($_POST['itemurl']);
   $itemimage = escape_sq($_POST['itemimage']);
   $desc_text = escape_sq($_POST['desc_text']);

   $query = "UPDATE product
           SET product_name = '$product_name',
               sku = '$sku',
               itemurl = '$itemurl',
               itemimage = '$itemimage',
               desc_text = '$desc_text',
               modified = SYSDATE
           WHERE product_id = $product_id";
   $stmt = parse_exec_free($conn, $query, &$error_str);
   if (!$stmt) {
      die_silently($conn, $error_str);
   }
```

Continued

Listing 35-2 *(continued)*

```php
// UPDATE PRODUCT_ATTRIB_VAL TABLE
// First blow away all existing rows for this product
$query = "DELETE FROM product_attrib_val
         WHERE product_id = $product_id";
$stmt = parse_exec_free($conn, $query, &$error_str);
if (!$stmt) {
   die_silently($conn, $error_str);
}
if (is_array($_POST['attrib']) &&
   count($_POST['attrib']) > 0) {
   foreach ($_POST['attrib'] as $attrib_id=>$av_id_array) {
     if (is_array($av_id_array) && count($av_id_array) > 0) {
         foreach ($av_id_array as $attrib_val_id) {
             // If attrib value is not Delete All,
             // add new rows
             if ($attrib_val_id != -1) {
                $query =
                "INSERT INTO product_attrib_val
                (attrib_val_id, product_id, modified, created)
                VALUES($attrib_val_id, $product_id,
                      SYSDATE, SYSDATE)";
                $stmt =
                  parse_exec_free($conn, $query, &$error_str);
               if (!$stmt) {
                   die_silently($conn, $error_str);
               }
             }
         }
      }
   }
}

OCICommit($conn);
OCILogoff($conn);

/*
// Uncomment this block for debugging
// Get a second timestamp, and do the math
$end_time = time();
echo "DONE!  This operation took "
   .($end_time - $begin_time)
   ." seconds to complete.";
exit;
*/

// Redisplay the form
header("Location:  $PHP_SELF?url=$prod_url");
}
```

```
// ---------
// SHOW FORM
// ---------
elseif (!isSet($_POST['submit']) ||
        $_POST['submit'] != "Submit") {
    set_time_limit(0);
    // Get a timestamp
    $begin_time = time();
    // Open the pipe
    $conn = OCILogon($thisDBuser, $thisDBpassword, $thisDB)
            or die("Can't get a database connection.");

    // Get the product data based on a unique URL
    //passed in the GET vars
    $url = $_GET['url'];
    if ($url == "") {
        // If a URL isn't passed, spit out a message and quit
        echo "<HTML>\n<BODY>";
        echo '<P>You need to designate a product to edit by
                passing a url like this:
                http://localhost/tools/prod_point.php'.
                '?url=book_PHP5_Bible.</P>';
        echo "</BODY>\n</HTML>";
        exit;
    }
    $query = "SELECT product_id, name, sku, itemurl, itemimage,
                    desc_text, category_id
            FROM product
            WHERE url = '$url'";
    $stmt = parse_exec_fetch($conn, $query, &$error_str, &$res);
    if (!$stmt) {
        die_silently($conn, $error_str);
    } else {
        OCIFreeStatement($stmt);
        $product_id = $res['PRODUCT_ID'][0];
        $product_name = $res['PRODUCT_NAME'][0];
        $sku = $res['SKU'][0];
        $itemurl = $res['ITEMURL'][0];
        $itemimage = $res['ITEMIMAGE'][0];
        $desc_text = $res['DESC_TEXT'][0];
        $category_id = $res['CATEGORY_ID'][0];
    }


    // Get attributes for all products in this category
    $query = "SELECT attribute_id, attribute_name
            FROM attribute
            WHERE category_id = $category_id";
    $stmt = parse_exec_fetch($conn, $query, &$error_str, &$res1);
    if (!$stmt) {
        die_silently($conn, $error_str);
        exit;
```

Continued

Listing 35-2 *(continued)*

```
    } else {
       OCIFreeStatement($stmt);
    }
    if (is_array($res1['ATTRIBUTE_ID']) &&
       count($res1['ATTRIBUTE_ID']) > 0) {
       foreach ($res1['ATTRIBUTE_ID'] as $key=>$attrib_id) {
         $attrib_name = $res1['ATTRIBUTE_NAME'][$key];
         // Get attrib values for this product
         $query = "SELECT product_attrib_val.attrib_val_id
                   FROM product_attrib_val, attrib_val
                   WHERE product_attrib_val.attrib_val_id =
attrib_val.attrib_val_id
                   AND attrib_val.attrib_id = $attrib_id
                   AND product_attrib_val.product_id =
$product_id";
         $stmt = parse_exec_fetch($conn, $query, &$error_str,
&$res2);
         if (!$stmt) {
             die_silently($conn, $error_str);
         } else {
            OCIFreeStatement($stmt);
            // Get all possible attribute values
            //for this attribute
            // and construct nice pulldown lists
            $query = "SELECT attrib_val_id, name
                      FROM attrib_val
                      WHERE attrib_id = $attrib_id
                      ORDER BY name";
            $stmt = parse_exec_fetch($conn, $query,
&$error_str, &$res3);
            if (!$stmt) {
                die_silently($conn, $error_str);
            } else {
               OCIFreeStatement($stmt);
               // This stuff is for Case 2 below
               $is_vals = $res2['ATTRIB_VAL_ID'];
               $num_is_vals = count($is_vals);
               $poss_vals = $res3['ATTRIB_VAL_ID'];
               $num_poss_vals = count($poss_vals);
               $nonmatching = array_diff($poss_vals, $is_vals);

               if ($num_poss_vals > 0) {
                 foreach ($poss_vals as
                          $av_key=>$avalue_id) {
                    $av_name = $res3['NAME'][$av_key];
                    // Existing values are selected in
                    // this list.
                    // Case 0:  if no existing value
```

```
                        // then don't highlight any
                        if (!is_array($is_vals) ||
                           $num_is_vals == 0) {
                          $av_str .= "<OPTION
                          VALUE=\"$avalue_id\">$av_name</OPTION>\n";
                        }
                        // Case 1:  single attrib value
                        elseif ($num_is_vals == 1) {
                          if ($is_vals[0] == $avalue_id) {
                            $av_str .= "<OPTION VALUE=\"$avalue_id\"
                                 SELECTED>$av_name</OPTION>\n";
                          } else {
                            $av_str .=
            "<OPTION VALUE=\"$avalue_id\">$av_name</OPTION>\n";
                          }
                        }
                        // Case 2:  multiple attrib values
                        // A bit messy because I have to avoid
                        // multiple nonmatching options
                        elseif ($num_is_vals > 1) {
                          foreach ($is_vals as $avid) {
                            if ($avid == $avalue_id) {
                              $av_array[] =
            "<OPTION VALUE=\"$avalue_id\" SELECTED>$av_name</OPTION>";
                            }
                          }
                          if (count($nonmatching) > 0) {
                            foreach ($nonmatching as $avid){
                              if ($avid == $avalue_id) {
                                $av_array[] =
            "<OPTION VALUE=\"$avalue_id\">$av_name</OPTION>";
                              }
                            }
                          }
                          $av_str = implode("\n", $av_array);
                        }
                      }
                    }
                  }
                $attrib_str .= "$attrib_name ($num_is_vals):  <SELECT
                  NAME=\"attrib[$attrib_id][]\"
              SIZE=5 MULTIPLE>\n<OPTION VALUE='-1'>Delete All</OPTION>
              \n$av_str</SELECT><BR><BR>\n";
                unset($av_array);
                unset($av_str);
              }
          }
        }
OCILogoff($conn);
```

Continued

Listing 35-2 *(continued)*

```
    // ------------
    // DISPLAY FORM
    // ------------
    $php_self = $_SERVER['PHP_SELF'];
    // Superglobals don't work with heredoc
$form_str = <<< EOFORMSTR
<HTML>
<HEAD>
<TITLE>Product Point Editor</TITLE>
<STYLE>
<!--
.header    {font-family: verdana, arial, sans-serif;
font-size: 14pt; font-weight: bold; color: #000000;
text-align: left}
.subheader    {font-family: verdana, arial, sans-serif;
font-size: 12pt; font-weight: bold; color: #000000;
background: #ebeef1; text-align: left}
-->
</STYLE>
</HEAD>

<BODY BGCOLOR="#FFFFFF">
<P class="header">Product point editor</P>

<P>The database is <B>$thisDB</B></P>

<P><B>PRODUCT DATA</B></P>
<FORM ACTION="$php_self" METHOD="post">
<INPUT TYPE=HIDDEN NAME="product_id" VALUE="$product_id">
Name:  <INPUT TYPE=TEXT NAME="product_name" SIZE=30
VALUE="$product_name"><BR><BR>
SKU #:  <INPUT TYPE=TEXT NAME="sku" SIZE=70
VALUE="$sku"><BR><BR>
Item URL:  <INPUT TYPE=TEXT NAME="itemurl" SIZE=70
VALUE="$itemurl"><BR><BR>
Item Image:  <INPUT TYPE=TEXT NAME="itemimage" SIZE=70
VALUE="$itemimage"><BR><BR>
Description:  <TEXTAREA NAME="desc_text" COLS=50
ROWS=5>$desc_text</TEXTAREA><BR><BR>

<P><B>ATTRIBUTES</B></P>
$attrib_str
<INPUT TYPE=SUBMIT NAME="submit" VALUE="Submit">
</FORM>
</BODY>
</HTML>
EOFORMSTR;
    echo $form_str;
```

```
    // Get a second timestamp, and do the math
    $end_time = time();
    echo "DONE!  This operation took ".
        ($end_time - $begin_time)
        ." seconds to complete.<BR>\n";
}

?>
```

For single product editing, a PHP form that makes a direct connection to the Oracle database is not noticeably slower than one that employs a stored procedure. This tool also has the advantage that it can be altered by a PHP developer alone, whereas use of a stored procedure usually also requires time from a PL/SQL programmer.

Project: Batch Editor

To edit data for more than one product at a time, you might want to use stored procedures. This tool, the *product batch editor*, has two main parts. A script called header_download.php downloads the attributes for a particular category to a spreadsheet. A corresponding script called batch_upload_new.php allows the user to upload data from a spreadsheet to the server, where it is loaded into the database. This is the simplest use of stored procedures.

Listing 35-3 is the first stored procedure called in header_download.php. It is called get_ categories.sql, and it merely downloads a complete list of all the product categories in this schema.

Listing 35-3: **Stored procedure (get_categories.sql)**

```
CREATE OR REPLACE PROCEDURE get_categories(
  category_list_out OUT pack.my_targets)
IS

BEGIN
  OPEN category_list_out FOR
    SELECT category_id, category_url
    FROM CATEGORY
    ORDER BY category_url;
END;
/
show errors
```

After you use the form to select a category, header_download.php calls the stored procedure called get_cat_header shown in Listing 35-4. This takes the category ID as an input and returns two cursors: one consisting of some common product fields, the other consisting of attribute types associated with this category.

Listing 35-4: A second stored procedure (header_download.php)

```
create or replace procedure get_cat_header(
    category_id_in INTEGER,
    cat_header_out OUT pack.my_targets,
    cat_attrib_out OUT pack.my_targets,
IS
    v_action VARCHAR2(2) := '01';
BEGIN
    IF category_id_in is NULL THEN
     OPEN cat_header_out for select NULL from DUAL;
     OPEN cat_attrib_out for select NULL from DUAL;
    END IF;

    open cat_header_out for
     SELECT
     column_name,
     column_display_name,
     column_order
     FROM
     event_table_columns
     WHERE
     table_name = 'product'
     ORDER BY column_order;

   open cat_attrib_out for
     SELECT attribute_id, attribute_name
     FROM attribute
     WHERE category_id = category_id_in;
END;
/
show errors
```

Listing 35-5 is `header_download.php`, which shows the form to call both stored procedures.

Listing 35-5: New product form (header_download.php)

```
<?php

/*******************************************
 * New product download attributes script. *
 * The purpose of this tool is to download  *
 * a spreadsheet with the product data      *
 * header.  Editors will use this to add    *
 * new items to a category.  Use script     *
 * batch_upload_new.php to upload data.     *
 *******************************************/
```

```php
include("oci8_funcs.php"); //common functions for Oracle tools
$thisDB = "dev";
$thisDBuser = "oci_user";
$thisDBpassword = "sesame";

// Open the pipe
$conn = OCILogon($thisDBuser, $thisDBpassword, $thisDB);


// ------------------------
// GET THE CATEGORY HEADER
// ------------------------
if ($_POST['submit'] == "Add") {
   // Call stored procedure for this category
   $cat_id_in = $_POST['cat_id'];
   $request = "begin DEV.get_cat_header($cat_id_in,
:OUT1, :OUT2); end;";
   $cursor1 = OCINewCursor($conn);
   $cursor2 = OCINewCursor($conn);
   $stmt = OCIParse($conn, $request);
   OCIBindByName($stmt, ":OUT1", &$cursor1, -1, OCI_B_CURSOR);
   OCIBindByName($stmt, ":OUT2", &$cursor2, -1, OCI_B_CURSOR);
   OCIExecute($stmt);
   OCIExecute($cursor1);
   OCIExecute($cursor2);
   $err_array = OCIError($conn);
   if ($err_array) {
      $err_message = $err_array['message'];
      echo $err_message;
      OCIFreeCursor($cursor1);
      OCIFreeCursor($cursor2);
      OCIFreeStatement($stmt);
      OCILogoff($conn);
      exit;
   }
   while (OCIFetchInto($cursor1,&$data1)) {
      $p_array[] = $data1[1];
   }
   while (OCIFetchInto($cursor2,&$data2)) {
      $a_array[] = $data2[1]."|".$data2[0];
   }
   OCIFreeCursor($cursor1);
   OCIFreeCursor($cursor2);
   OCIFreeStatement($stmt);
   OCILogoff($conn);
   // ASSEMBLE THE DOWNLOAD
   $init_p_str = implode("\t", $p_array);
   $p_str = str_replace("CATEGORY_ID", $cat_id_in, $init_p_str);
   if (count($a_array) > 0) {
      $a_str = implode("\t", $a_array);
   }
   $full_header = implode("\t", array($p_str, $a_str));
```

Continued

Listing 35-5 *(continued)*

```
    // SEND THE FILE
    $header_file = 'header.xls.Z';
    $zp = gzopen($header_file, "w+");
    gzwrite($zp, $full_header);
    gzclose($fp);
    header("Location:  header.xls.Z");
    // For IE5.x, this is the correct way to trigger a download
    // -- by simply directing the browser to download a file type
    // that the browser cannot open
}


// -----------------
// CHOOSE A CATEGORY
// -----------------
elseif (!isSet($_POST['submit'])) {
    // Call stored procedure get_categories
    $request = "begin DEV.get_categories(:OUT1); end;";
    $cursor1 = OCINewCursor($conn);
    $stmt = OCIParse($conn, $request);
    OCIBindByName($stmt, ":OUT1", &$cursor1, -1, OCI_B_CURSOR);
    OCIExecute($stmt);
    OCIExecute($cursor1);
    $err_array = OCIError($conn);
    if ($err_array) {
        $err_message = $err_array['message'];
        echo $err_message;
        OCIFreeCursor($cursor1);
        OCIFreeStatement($stmt);
        OCILogoff($conn);
        exit;
    }
    while (OCIFetchInto($cursor1, &$cat_array)) {
        $opt_str .= "<OPTION VALUE=\""
                    .$cat_array[0]."\">"
                    .$cat_array[1]."</OPTION>\n";
    }
    OCIFreeCursor($cursor1);
    OCIFreeStatement($stmt);
    OCILogoff($conn);
```

```
    // CHOOSE CATEGORY FORM
    $php_self = $_SERVER['PHP_SELF'];
    // Superglobals don't work with heredoc
    $form_str = <<< EOFORMSTR
<HTML>
<HEAD>
<TITLE>Batch Editor New: Download</TITLE>
<STYLE>
<!--
.header     {font-family: verdana, arial, sans-serif
font-size: 14pt; font-weight: bold; color: #000000;
text-align: left}
.subheader    {font-family: verdana, arial, sans-serif;
font-size: 12pt; font-weight: bold; color: #000000;
background: #ebeef1; text-align: left}
.ftrnote     {font-family: verdana, arial, sans-serif;
font-size: 8pt; color: #000000; text-align: left}
LI      {line-height:200%}
-->
</STYLE>
</HEAD>

<BODY BGCOLOR="#FFFFFF">
<P class="header">Batch editor new:  download</P>

<P>The database is <B>$thisDB</B></P>

<FORM ACTION="$php_self" METHOD="POST">
<SELECT NAME="cat_id" SIZE=1>
<OPTION VALUE="-1" SELECTED>Choose one</OPTION>
$opt_str
</SELECT><BR>
<INPUT TYPE=SUBMIT NAME="submit" VALUE="Add">
</FORM>
</BODY>
</HTML>
EOFORMSTR;

    echo $form_str;
}
?>
```

The result of `header_download.php` is a zipped spreadsheet with one row. It resembles the first row of the image in Figure 35-1.

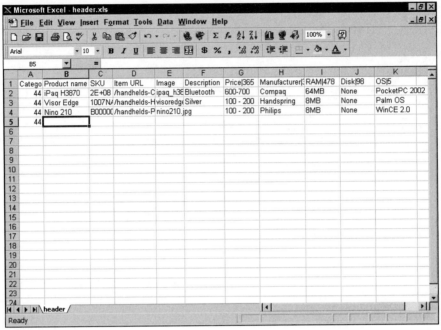

Figure 35-1: Category header with some data filled in

We have filled in some data in the preceding figure, using the header row as a guide.

Note that the attributes at the top have names like "`Price|376`". The number is the attribute ID, which will be used when we upload data with Listing 35-6, `batch_upload_new.php`. This script enables the user to upload a spreadsheet to the server, using the normal HTML file upload capability of his browser. The server will then convert the spreadsheet into rows of data, which are inserted into the database.

Listing 35-6: **Spreadsheet upload script (batch_upload_new.php)**

```php
<?php

/*******************************************
 * New product batch upload script. The   *
 * purpose of this tool is to upload a     *
 * spreadsheet with new product data.      *
 * Editors will use this to add new items  *
 * to a category.  Use script              *
 * header_download.php to get attributes.  *
 *******************************************/

include("oci8_funcs.php"); //common functions for Oracle tools
```

```
$thisDB = "dev";
$thisDBuser = "oci_user";
$thisDBpassword = "sesame";


// HEADER
$header_str = <<< ENDOFHEADER
<HTML>
<HEAD>
<TITLE>Batch Editor New: Upload</TITLE>
<STYLE>
<!--
.header     {font-family: verdana, arial, sans-serif;
font-size: 14pt; font-weight: bold; color: #000000;
text-align: left}
.subheader     {font-family: verdana, arial, sans-serif;
font-size: 12pt; font-weight: bold; color: #000000;
background: #ebeef1; text-align: left}
-->
</STYLE>
</HEAD>

<BODY BGCOLOR="#FFFFFF">
<P class="header">Batch editor new: upload</P>

<P>The database is <B>$thisDB</B></P>
ENDOFHEADER;
echo $header_str;


// ADD NEW PRODUCTS
if($_POST['submit'] == "Upload") {
   set_time_limit(0);
   echo "<P>Check the error log
      (<A HREF\"upload_log.html\">upload_log.html</A>)
       for problems.</P>";

   // Copy uploaded file to a specific directory
   $tempfile = $HTTP_POST_FILES[file][tmp_name];
   $localfile = $HTTP_POST_FILES[file][name];
   if(!copy($tempfile, "/tmp/$localfile")) {
      echo "<P>Error writing file to upload directory.
            Quitting.</P>\n";
      exit;
   }

   // Start an error log
   $error_log = 'upload_log.html';
   $fp = fopen($error_log, "w+") or die("Can't open error log.");
   fwrite($fp, "<HTML>\n");
```

Continued

Listing 35-6 *(continued)*

```
// Open the pipe
$conn = OCILogon($thisDBuser, $thisDBpassword, $thisDB)
        or die("Can't get a database connection.");

// Get a timestamp
$begin_time = time();

// Read in the data file as an array
$uarray = file("/tmp/$localfile");

// Parse the header for cat_id and attributes
$header = array_shift($uarray);
$harray = explode("\t", $header);
$num_ha = count($harray);
$cat_id = $harray[0];
$attrib_array = array();
for($i = 6; $i <= ($num_ha - 1); $i++) {
   $a_array = explode("|", $harray[$i]);
   $attrib_array[] = $a_array[1];
}
$num_attribs = count($attrib_array);

$error_str = "";
$res = array();
// Get all the attrib values and stick them in a
// multidimensional array
foreach($attrib_array as $attrib) {
   $query = "SELECT attrib_value_id, name
             FROM attrib_value
             WHERE attrib_id = $attrib";
   $stmt =
     parse_exec_fetch($conn, $query, &$error_str, &$res);
   if (!$stmt) {
     choke_and_die($conn, $fp, $error_str);
   } else {
     foreach($res['NAME'] as $key => $val) {
        $ava[$attrib][$val] = $res['ATTRIB_VALUE_ID'][$key];
     }
     OCIFreeStatement($stmt);
   }
}
reset($attrib_array);

// Shove the data down the pipe.
foreach ($uarray as $valrow) {
   // Get a fresh product id from Oracle
   $query = "begin :new_id := newid('product'); end;";
   $sth = OCIParse($conn, $query);
   OCIBindByName($sth, ":new_id", &$new_id, 200);
```

```
       OCIExecute($sth);
       if (!$sth) {
          choke_and_die($conn, $fp, $error_str);
       } else {
         $rowid = $new_id;
          OCIFreeStatement($sth);
       }

       // Format new product data.
       $val_array = explode("\t", $valrow);
       $prod_name = unquote($val_array[1]);
       $prod_name = strip_db($prod_name);
       $prod_name = escape_sq($prod_name);
       echo "Working on $prod_name<BR>\n";
       $sku = unquote($val_array[2]);
       $itemurl = unquote($val_array[3]);
       $itemimage = unquote($val_array[4]);
       $desc = unquote($val_array[5]);
       $desc = escape_sq($desc);

       // PRODUCT
       $query = "INSERT INTO product (
                 product_id, name, sku, itemurl, itemimage,
                 desc, created, modified, category_id)
                 VALUES (
                 $rowid, '$prod_name', '$sku', '$itemurl',
                 '$itemimage', '$desc', SYSDATE, SYSDATE,
                 $cat_id)";
       $stmt = parse_exec_free($conn, $query, &$error_str);
       if (!$stmt) {
          choke_and_die($conn, $fp, $error_str);
       }

       // PRODUCT_ATTRIB_VALUE
       for ($i = 6; $i <= (6 + $num_attribs - 1); $i++) {
          $av = unquote($val_array[$i]);
          if($av != "") {
             $temp_q = explode("|", $av);
             foreach($temp_q as $av) {
                $av = unasterisk($av);
                $av = escape_sq($av);
                $akey = $i - 6;
                $attrib_id = $attrib_array[$akey];
                if($ava[$attrib_id][$av]) {
                 $pav = $ava[$attrib_id][$av];
                 $query = "INSERT INTO product_attrib_value (
                          attrib_value_id, product_id, created,
                          modified)
                          VALUES(
                          $pav, $rowid, SYSDATE, SYSDATE)";
                $stmt =
```

Continued

Listing 35-6 *(continued)*

```
                parse_exec_free($conn, $query, &$error_str);
            if (!$stmt) {
                choke_and_die($conn, $fp, $error_str);
            }
        }
    }
    } else {
        //echo "Null attrib value.<BR>\n";
    }
    }
}

// Get a second timestamp, and do the math
$end_time = time();
echo "DONE!  This operation took "
    .($end_time - $begin_time)
    ." seconds to complete.";

OCICommit($conn);
OCILogoff($conn);
fwrite($fp, "</HTML>\n");
fclose($fp);
}


// SHOW FILE UPLOAD FORM
elseif($_POST['submit'] != "Upload") {
    $upload_str = <<< ENDOFUPLOAD
<P>Upload new product data:</P>
<FORM ACTION="$PHP_SELF" METHOD="post"
ENCTYPE="multipart/form-data">
<INPUT TYPE=HIDDEN NAME="max_file_size" VALUE="1000000">
<INPUT TYPE=FILE NAME="file" SIZE=50><BR><BR>
<INPUT TYPE=SUBMIT NAME="submit" VALUE="Upload">
</FORM>
ENDOFUPLOAD;
    echo $upload_str;
}

?>
</BODY>
</HTML>
```

Notice particularly in this script how we call for a new product ID using Oracle's incrementor (search for the comment `// Get a fresh product id from Oracle`). This is in marked contrast to, for instance, MySQL, where the auto-incrementor is generally built into a column's definition and can be kicked off by merely entering a null value in that column.

Summary

Oracle is, for better or worse, the biggest name in enterprise databases. The PHP OCI8 extension is quite fast and powerful, offering some functionality not found in most other database extensions. However, the use of Oracle has many implications and should not be undertaken lightly.

There are significant differences in the syntax of Oracle functions versus those of lighter-weight databases. These differences include so-called Sybase-style string escaping, separate parsing and execution steps, manual memory management, cursors, transactionality, and the capability to fetch data sets into one big array. We demonstrate the use of all these Oracle features in two examples: a single-product data editor and a mass data-entry tool.

✦   ✦   ✦

PEAR Database Functions

PEAR DB is one of several wrappers around PHP's database extensions that seek to generalize the concept of a database connection. PEAR DB is fully object-oriented. With PEAR DB implemented in your software, you'll find it easier to allow your application's users to select from several databases (the list of supported databases includes all the majors, and plenty of second-string players as well). You may also find it easier than before to handle errors and react to unexpected occurrences that take place during connections and queries.

This chapter aims to explain what PEAR DB is all about. It's not hard, but it is important that you understand PEAR DB in theory and practice, because there are substantial pros and cons to its use. We start with a general discussion of the benefits and costs of a database abstraction layer; then we explain the basics of using the PEAR DB package.

For reference, examples, and further explanations of concepts, have a look at the PEAR DB site at `http://pear.php.net/package/DB`.

Cross-Reference For general information on PEAR and instructions on how to locate and install PEAR libraries, see Chapter 28.

The Debatable Virtue of Database Independence

It's often stated that the chief selling point of database wrapper classes like PEAR DB is database independence — the idea that it doesn't matter which database management server you choose to back up your applications. The virtue being sold here is flexibility. Under PEAR DB it is theoretically possible, for example, to develop a pilot version of a particular application under a lightweight database server (such as MySQL or SQL Server) and then migrate the application to a customer's Oracle-centric production environment with very few changes required.

PEAR DB and Its Competitors

PEAR DB is one of a plethora of competing database abstraction layers written in PHP. Some of the others are Metabase, ADODB, PEAR MDB, and PHPLIB. Much of the information in this chapter can also apply to them, although their APIs are obviously slightly different and in some cases not object-oriented.

The clear advantage of PEAR DB over these others is that it's distributed with PEAR, which is generally distributed with PHP. Remember that in no way is the PHP Group itself recommending PEAR DB — they have staunchly refused to get involved in this issue for years, despite the pleas of many PHP community members that they would anoint an official dba product. The PHP Group merely agrees to distribute packages chosen by the PEAR Group, which formed in August 2003. Because PEAR DB is the one product in this category that we can be fairly certain readers will have installed, we chose to focus on it.

PEAR DB has recently been merged with Metabase to produce the combined PEAR MDB package, which the developers hope will become the de facto standard PHP database abstraction layer. If this marriage, which has been proceeding gingerly for various reasons, goes forward successfully, at some point MDB may replace PEAR DB in the distribution. However, the PEAR DB API will still be used with the Metabase code underneath that, so hopefully PEAR DB users will not need to make any code changes should this replacement occur.

Finally, there have been persistent low-level rumors of the possibility of some kind of database abstraction layer being written in C rather than PHP, which would potentially reduce the performance drawback of these packages. The difficulties of this approach are many, however, and no current project seems to be seriously pursuing a rewrite of this kind.

However, this is the kind of statement that often makes experienced systems builders roll their eyes because it shows a focus on code-level concerns while ignoring big-picture issues. First off, there is a very serious performance hit associated with using PEAR DB — which makes sense, since the question should never be "Will abstraction degrade performance?" but *How much* will abstraction degrade performance?" PEAR DB's basic design — written in PHP itself instead of C, fully object-oriented, re-copying result sets into multidimensional arrays, including many databases which have significant differences in functionality — indicates that performance was not the primary concern in its design. An informative benchmark comparing the native MySQL database extension to various database wrapper classes accessing MySQL can be found at `http://freshmeat.net/screenshots/30313/`. Furthermore, PEAR DB's development always trails behind database and PHP development and is not always able to include every high-end feature — so you may not be able to use cool new functions of your DBMS via PEAR DB for some time or at all. Also, if you have the theoretical ability to support your app with a bunch of databases, are you taking on the practical responsibility of doing so? Sometimes it can save you a lot of headaches to say, "We can only support MySQL and PostgreSQL" and let it go at that.

Furthermore, the mere fact that PEAR DB can give you the ability to connect to multiple databases does not mean that the same code will work with all of them. In the theoretical best-case scenario — for instance, using only the most common functionality shared between

MySQL and PostgreSQL—the only adjustments you'd have to make would be in the code directly concerned with accessing the database—opening a connection, sending a query, and so on. You'd have to specify that the new database is of the Oracle variety, and provide details about its hostname and other aspects of its implementation. In reality, to support numerous databases, you might have to make some adjustments to your SQL statements as well, because all database servers differ in the way they implement SQL. Beyond the ANSI-standardized basics, database servers can vary considerably in the syntaxes they consider acceptable. The new database server will have to be configured with the databases, tables, column names, and rows that the migrating application requires.

The decision to use a database abstraction layer should always be made on a project-by-project basis. Feel free to heavily discount the opinions of coders who tell you that they are always good or always bad. Also discount those who claim that the benefit of database abstraction is that *you yourself* will be able to switch between databases easily. That happens very rarely (and is usually a sign of much bigger underlying errors in judgment) and should therefore never be a major consideration in designing a system. The actual benefit of supporting multiple databases is if *your users* need to use multiple databases. The rule of thumb is, the more users (in the sense of separate installations) of your application there are, the more demand there will be for numerous databases—and therefore the more it might gain from PEAR DB or one of its competitors.

Most standalone Web sites will benefit very little from PEAR DB, because the extra weight of the abstraction layer is a much bigger concern than the small possibility of having to change databases in the future. Contractors need to weigh the potential gains to them of reusability over the potential loss to the client of performance. In situations where you might need to integrate numerous disparate PHP packages, PEAR DB might help or hurt you.

The one case where PEAR DB can clearly be a win is a standalone application that will have multiple installations, needs to run on as many DBMS as possible, has a developer community willing to take on the added work to support multiple databases, and doesn't need to be very performative. Many open source and commercial PHP packages—such as wikis, blogware, trouble-ticket systems, bulletin boards, and so on—do meet all these criteria and would therefore benefit from a database abstraction layer. Portability is almost certainly a much bigger issue for this type of project than it will be for a Web developer working on a single site—although even here, many packages choose their own lighter-weight solutions to database abstraction rather than PEAR DB—so don't be so dazzled by the fact that some big-name PHP project uses PEAR DB that you forget that your own needs might be very different.

Caution   One common reason for using PEAR DB is simply because the individual developer happens to prefer a fully object-oriented database connection paradigm. This is fine, but technical leads and architects should be aware that there are freely available database-specific classes that may be more performative and maintainable than PEAR DB.

The main point stands, however: If you designed your application to use the PEAR DB classes, very little of your application's PHP code will require modification in order to move the application from one database management server to another. That's a real advantage if you anticipate numerous users who might wish to use a wide selection of databases to run your application.

PEAR DB and PHP5

At the time of this writing, changes specific to PHP5 had mostly not yet been incorporated into PEAR DB. All the major changes in PHP5 except XML affect PEAR DB: the new object model, exception handling, SQLite, and the new mysqli extension. Of these, only SQLite is now being handled correctly. Expect changes in PEAR DB when these new features trickle down.

Native database connectivity

Native database functions, because they are written in C rather than PHP, will always be the fastest way for a PHP script to connect to a database. However, there is a whole series of functions for each supported database. In a nutshell, the process involves a series of steps, each customized to the database being used.

To connect to a MySQL database, a program uses a command like this:

```
mysql_connect('localhost', 'root', 'sesame');
```

Then, to specify which database it is going to work with, the program issues a command like this:

```
mysql_select_db('phpbook');
```

Then the program defines and issues a query:

```
$query = "SELECT Surname FROM personal_info WHERE ID<10";
$result = mysql_query($query);
```

With that done, it is a matter of looping through the result set to see what came back from the database:

```
while ($name_row = mysql_fetch_row($result)) {
  print("$name_row[0] $name_row[1] $name_row[2]<BR>\n");
}
```

To do the same work under another database management server, four of the six lines would have to be modified. Here's the same code for PostgresSQL (assuming the same hostname and other details):

```
pg_connect('localhost', 'root', 'sesame');
pg_select_db('phpbook');

$query = "SELECT Surname FROM personal_info WHERE ID<10";
$result = pg_query($query);

while ($name_row = pg_fetch_row($result)) {
  print("$name_row[0] $name_row[1] $name_row[2]<BR>\n");
}
```

That can be a real hassle, and the process introduces all kinds of opportunities for error. PEAR DB solves this problem.

Database abstraction

With the application of a bit of object-orientation and some general standardization, PEAR DB has evolved to the point at which changing from MySQL to PostgresSQL (or any of several other supported databases) involves changing only one line (assuming the SQL queries can remain the same). Here's the same problem solved under PEAR DB:

```
$dsn = "mysql://root:sesame@localhost/phpbook";
$db = DB::connect($dsn);

if (DB::isError($db)) {
  die($db->getMessage());
}

$sql = "SELECT cityName FROM cities ORDER BY cityName";
$result = $db->query($sql);

if (DB::isError($result)) {
  $errorMessage = $result->getMessage();
  die($errorMessage);
}

$i=0;
while ($row = $result->fetchRow()) {
  $returnArray[$i]=$row[0];
  $i++;
}
$db->disconnect();
```

The point here is that code for the same purpose under PostgresSQL is exactly the same, except for the first line:

```
$dsn = "pgsql://root:sesame@localhost/phpbook";
```

Changing the code for Microsoft SQL Server involves only one modification, as well:

```
$dsn = "mssql://root:sesame@localhost/phpbook";
```

And so on. The next section explains Data Source Names (DSNs) and other important PEAR DB concepts in detail.

Pear DB Concepts

There are a number of concepts in PEAR DB that you must understand to work with the class effectively. These include:

✦ Data Source Names (DSNs)

✦ Connection

✦ Query

✦ Row retrieval

✦ Disconnection

The following subsections explain each in turn

Data Source Names (DSNs)

A Data Source Name (DSN) is simply a text string that describes where a database is and how to access it. A DSN is very much like a URL for a database. Because databases almost always have user-level access control, DSNs specify usernames and passwords. Note that DSNs specify the *database* to which your program is connecting, not the *table* within the database.

In order to form a DSN, you have to come up with a number of values:

✦ The type of database you're connecting to (FrontBase, MySQL, Oracle, or whatever you fancy)

✦ The hostname or IP address of the machine running the database server

✦ The database name

✦ The username you want the software to use

✦ The corresponding password

Very often, you'll need to access these values in order to create DSNs in several different but related PHP programs. For that reason, it often makes sense to assign the literal values to variables in a special program that's imported elsewhere. Such a program might look like this (call it dbSpecs.php):

```php
<?php
$phptype = 'mysql';
$dbHost = 'spock';
$database = 'inventory';
$username = 'phpUser';
$password = 'sesame';
?>
```

The only odd bit there is the value for $phptype. Its value is a standard string that corresponds to a specific database (MySQL, in this example). The related sidebar shows all valid options for the database identifier.

Having defined your variables in a simple library, when you want to create a DSN, you can import dbSpecs.php and have access to its values. The advantage is that if the values in dbSpecs.php ever change, you need to modify them in just one place. The import statement is simple:

```php
require_once('dbSpecs.php');
```

With that imported, you can use the values defined in dbSpecs.php to create a DSN. Remember, though, that you need to register the variables if you create your DSN inside a function (this is a standard characteristic of PHP variable scoping):

```php
global $phptype;
global $hostspec;
global $database;
global $username;
global $password;
```

Valid Database Identifiers for DSNs

Here's a list of all the database management servers supported by PEAR DB, complete with the strings you should use to identify them in DSNs.

✦ FrontBase (fbsql)

✦ InterBase (ibase)

✦ Informix (ifx)

✦ Mini SQL (msql)

✦ Microsoft SQL Server (mssql)

✦ MySQL (mysql)

✦ Oracle 7/8/8i (oci8)

✦ ODBC (odbc)

✦ PostgreSQL (pgsql)

✦ SyBase (Sybase)

Once you have the values available, stringing them together into a properly formatted DSN is pretty simple. The standard format looks like this:

```
$dsn = "$phptype://$username:$password@$hostspec/$database";
```

There are more obscure options available for use in defining DSNs. They're described in detail at http://pear.php.net/manual/en/package.database.db.intro-dsn.php.

Tip   As always, we recommend storing database connection variables outside the Web tree for greater security.

Connection

When you have a valid DSN, it's a simple matter to tell PEAR DB to establish a connection to the database the DSN describes. The line of code you need looks like this:

```
$db = DB::connect($dsn);
```

If the connection attempt succeeds, everything's great — $db contains an object representing a connection to the database, and you can run queries against that object (among other amusing and educational activities). Because you're a good programmer, though, you should allow for errors. Here's how:

```
if (DB::isError($db)) {

   die($db->getMessage());
}
```

The isError() method returns true if the database object — $db in this case — represents a connectivity error, and false if not (meaning, if the connection succeeded). In this case, the code aborts if the database connection wasn't successfully established.

Query

Building on the successful database connection, you'll typically want to run a query against the database. That's accomplished with Structured Query Language (SQL), which is described in detail in Chapter 13.

The customary procedure is to write your SQL query as a string and stuff that string into a variable called $sql or $query:

```
$sql = "SELECT cityName FROM cities ORDER BY cityName";
```

Then use that variable as a parameter for the query() method of your database object (in other words, of the variable that represents the connection to the database), and assign the results to another variable:

```
$result = $db->query($sql);
```

Once again, allow for the possibility of error:

```
if (DB::isError($result))
  $errorMessage = $result->getMessage();
  die($errorMessage);
}
```

Row retrieval

As a result of the query() operation, $result contains a result set. A result set is some number of rows (possibly zero).

To extract values from the result set, use a while loop like this one:

```
$i=0;
while ($row = $result->fetchRow()) {
  $returnArray[$i] = $row[0];
  ++$i;
}
```

This loop exists to use the fetchRow() function against every row in the result object, thus extracting it. Because we know the result set has only one column (the SQL statement requested only cityName), we can take the first element of every row array ($row[0] — the only element) and put it into another array, $returnArray. Presumably, we'll do something useful with $returnArray later, but that's not anything to do with PEAR DB directly.

Disconnection

When a database connection has served its purpose, use the disconnect() method of the database object to free the resources associated with the connection:

```
$db->disconnect();
```

It's important to remember to do this; otherwise, the connection remains active until it times out (a long time). This means that the database server, in an active environment, could become overwhelmed with zombie connections.

A complete example

It may be beneficial to have a look at a complete function that performs database access operations by way of the PEAR DB class.

The role of this function, which we'll call getItems.php, is to extract all items from a Microsoft SQL Server database called INVENTORY_item. To return all items, we need a SELECT statement that draws all columns out of the INVENTORY _item table. Because INVENTORY _item has no foreign keys (an assumption made for the purposes of this illustration), extracting its data involves only sending a straightforward SELECT statement to the database server via a PEAR DB connection.

Let's examine getItems.php line by line to see how this is done.

```php
<?php
require_once ('DB.php');
require_once('dbSpecs.php');
```

First, we must import the PEAR DB classes and dbSpecs.php, which contains information about the database server and security credentials for it (it's listed earlier in this chapter).

```php
function getItems()
{
  global $phptype;
  global $hostspec;
  global $database;
  global $username;
  global $password;
```

In the function, the five global variables (from dbSpecs.php) must be declared for them to be accessible.

```php
$dsn = "$phptype://$username:$password@$hostspec/$database";
$db = DB::connect($dsn);
if (DB::isError($db)) {
  die($db->getMessage());
}
```

Using the PEAR DB procedure discussed earlier in this chapter, the program connects to the database server. The program checks for an error condition and aborts if one is found to exist as a result of the connection attempt.

The program then defines the SQL statement to be run against the database to which a connection has been established:

```php
$sql - "select id, desc, weight, packageQty, unit, supplierID,
cost from INVENTORY_item";
```

That's the SQL query that is to be sent to the database server. Note that we specify the columns, even though we want all of them. That way we know what order the columns will be in when results come back.

```php
$result = $db->query($sql);
if (DB::isError($result)) {   $errorMessage = $result-
>getMessage();
 die($errorMessage);
}
```

The program sends the query to the database and checks to see if an error message comes back.

```
$returnArray = array();
while ($row = $result->fetchRow()) {
  $id = $row[0];
  $desc = $row[1];
  $weight = $row[2];
  $packageQty = $row[3];
  $unit = $row[4];
  $supplierID = $row[5];
  $cost= $row[6];
  $returnArray[] =
    array('id' => $id, 'desc' => $ desc, 'weight' => $weight,
          'packageQty' => $packageQty, 'unit' => $unit,
          'supplierID' => $ supplierID, 'cost' => $cost);
}
$db->disconnect();
return $returnArray;
?>
```

The remainder of the program involves setting up an array called $returnArray. It is filled with a series of subarrays, making it a two-dimensional array. The subarrays are associative arrays; their keys correspond to column names in the database, and their values come from each row of $result.

PEAR DB Functions

The PEAR DB class is fairly extensive, with members far more numerous than the widely used ones covered already in this chapter's examples. Most of the other members are specialized, and as such come in handy only under particular circumstances.

This section summarizes some of the most useful members of the PEAR DB class, but is not comprehensive. Be sure to refer to http://pear.php.net/manual/en/package.database.php for the official list and documentation.

Members of the DB class

The DB class itself is the main PEAR DB class, and is used to represent a connection to a database (or an attempt to create one). Methods include:

✦ DB::connect(): Uses a DSN to connect to a database.

✦ DB::isWarning(): Returns true if a connection attempt yielded a warning.

✦ DB::isError(): Returns true if a connection attempt yielded an error.

Members of the DB_Common class

The methods of the DB_Common class may be invoked on a database connection for such purposes as executing queries and getting information from the database. Methods include:

 ✦ `DB_Common::affectedRows()`: Returns the number of rows affected by a query.

 ✦ `DB_Common::disconnect()`: Disconnects a database connection.

 ✦ `DB_Common::getAll()`: Returns all rows returned by a query.

 ✦ `DB_Common::getAssoc()`: Returns all rows as an associative array.

 ✦ `DB_Common::getCol()`: Returns all rows in a specified column.

 ✦ `DB_Common::getOne()`: Returns the value in the first column of the first row.

 ✦ `DB_Common::getRow()`: Returns the first row.

 ✦ `DB_Common::nextId()`: Allows you to exercise extra control over the establishment of unique id values, as in a primary key column.

 ✦ `DB_Common::query()`: Sends an SQL query string.

Members of the DB_Result class

The members of the `DB_Result` class may be invoked on a result set, which is what exists after a query is run on a database.

 ✦ `DB_Result::fetchInto()`: Extracts a row into a specified variable.

 ✦ `DB_Result::fetchRow()`: Extracts the next row.

 ✦ `DB_Result::free()`: Destroys the result set.

 ✦ `DB_Result::numCols()`: Returns the number of columns in a result set.

 ✦ `DB_Result::numRows()`: Returns the number of rows in a result set.

Summary

This chapter showed you how to use PEAR DB, the class with which PHP makes database connectivity more generic. You saw that PEAR DB is designed to make the task of switching from one database server to another extremely easy and that it generally succeeds in this design goal. In many cases, switching connectivity from one database server to another requires the modification of only one word in a whole database-enabled program.

The process of connecting to a database via PEAR DB involves establishing a DSN, which is essentially a URL for a database. The DSN specifies the hostname of the database server, as well as the database name, and the username and password required to gain access to the database. With a valid DSN, it's possible to establish a connection, run a query, and extract rows of values from the query's results before disconnecting. PEAR DB also includes methods — which you should take care to use — for detecting error and warning conditions.

✦   ✦   ✦

E-mail

This chapter is all about using PHP (and, in some cases, databases) to send and receive e-mail. It assumes a very basic familiarity with e-mail systems and protocols such as POP, IMAP, and SMTP.

Understanding E-mail

E-mail is obviously one of the killer apps of the Internet, and it's been around in basically the same form for years. But judging from postings to the PHP and other mailing lists, there are few more misunderstood or frustrating topics even now. Because recent developments such as cheaper connectivity, free server operating systems, and the explosion of new domains have made it possible for everyone and his grand-mother to run their own mail servers, there's a lot of frustration to go around.

We don't have the space or the expertise to explain every detail of e-mail. If you become fascinated with the topic after our necessarily short synopsis, you will want to immediately visit the Web site of the International Mail Consortium, at www.imc.org, which will explain in dizzying detail every abstruse jot and tittle of Internet mail that the most exacting computer scientist's heart could desire. In the mean-time, we'll stick to the quickest and dirtiest of conceptual explanations.

To help you visualize the considerable number of moving parts involved, we're going to build a simple model mail server.

This explanation will mostly use Unix terms, for the simple reason that the vocabulary of e-mail was perfected long before Microsoft or Lotus came along. Exchange Server is quite likely very similar under-neath — it even has a daemon called sendmail — but who knows for sure, because we can't lift the hood. Vendors of proprietary software also have the annoying habit of making up their own terminology for things rather than using the names everyone knows already, a practice that considerably hinders anyone trying to understand these systems in an abstract, cross-platform way. Finally, most proprietary mail sys-tems these days are incorporated into very powerful groupware packages that confuse the issue even more. For these reasons, Unix mail servers are undoubtedly easier to learn from and implement.

We are mentioning specific products so that you can contact the man-ufacturers directly to learn more about these pieces of the puzzle. This does not constitute a recommendation. We have deliberately chosen to list only products that are available without monetary cost.

The major parts of our model e-mail system are as follows:

✦ TCP/IP server

✦ Mail Transfer Agent (MTA, aka SMTP server)

✦ Mail spool

✦ Mail User Agent (MUA, aka mail client)

✦ Mail retrieval program, aka POP/IMAP server

✦ Mailing list manager (MLM)

Let's examine these in greater detail. We're going to use a cheesy but apt metaphor to help you remember who does what: Mail Server Mansion.

TCP/IP server

A good way to visualize a *TCP/IP server* is to think of it as the footman who answers every knock at the front door of Mail Server Mansion. Actually, if you think of every separate port as a door, maybe the TCP/IP server is more like a security guard who sits in a cubbyhole and monitors a bank of video cameras pointed at multiple avenues of ingress and egress. In any event, it's simpler and more picturesque just to think of an old-fashioned single footman at a single door.

The footman does not actually speak to any visitors. He simply opens the door when he hears a knock, recognizes the type of interaction this will be, and calls the correct person (say a butler or a bouncer) to handle the request. This second person, who has a speaking role, will take over to find out what the visitor wants.

The point is not to open the door — it is to know there is a door to be opened. A TCP/IP server maintains a list of several services for which it is responsible, and it answers each request by invoking the proper daemon — in the case of mail, either sendmail or a POP/IMAP authenticator. This saves resources because a single daemon monitors all the requests and the other daemons are only invoked on an "as needed" basis.

Well-known TCP/IP servers include:

✦ GNU inetd(the TCP/IP super server usually found by default on Unix setups (www.gnu.org/software/inetutils/inetutils.html)

✦ xinetd(a secure replacement for inetd (www.xinetd.org)

✦ Dan Bernstein's tcpserver(often used with qmail (http://cr.yp.to/ucspi-tcp.html)

Mail Transfer Agent, aka SMTP server

The *Mail Transfer Agent (MTA)* is the heart of any mail server, and the part whose workings we are most radically simplifying in this discussion.

The most important task of an MTA is to accept e-mail from another SMTP server and deliver it to the correct addressee's mail spool. A lot more is involved in this than one might think, but we can't get into it here. Also, the MTA will collect outgoing e-mail and try to send it to other SMTP servers.

So the MTA is roughly in the position of the butler at Mail Server Mansion. He is called by the footman to deal with mail and to inquire of the visitor (with the utmost politeness, of course): "Who are you, and what do you want?" If the visitor happens to be a known spammer, for instance, the butler might outright refuse delivery of any letters from that address. If the visitor is not recognized as a spammer, the butler will check the envelope to see if the intended recipient is, in fact, a resident of Mail Server Mansion. If not, he will write "Return to sender, undeliverable as addressed," on the envelope and drop it in the outgoing mailbag. Finally, if the addressee is recognized and the message is good, the butler will put the letter on a silver platter and carry it up to the resident's sitting room (actually their home directory or other mail spool location) and leave it there.

The actual SMTP protocol — the dialogue by which one server asks another, "Who are you, and what do you want?" — goes something like this (`sendhost` and `receipthost` are dummy server names):

```
220 receipthost ESMTP
HELO
250 receipthost
MAIL From:<sender@sendhost>
250 ok
RCPT To:<receiver@receipthost>
250 ok
DATA
354 Go ahead
Body of message.
.
250 Message accepted for delivery
QUIT
221 receipthost closing connection
```

Well-known MTAs — along with their corresponding URLs — include:

✦ sendmail (www.sendmail.org)

✦ qmail (www.qmail.org)

✦ zmailer (www.zmailer.org)

✦ postfix (www.postfix.org)

Mail spool

The silver platter on which the butler places the letters is analogous to a *mail spool* or *mailbox*. Different mail systems use different types of mail stores. At the level we're discussing, the main difference is whether a new message simply goes on the end of a single long spool (like a single roll of paper with the text of all the mail you've ever received transcribed on it, in order of time of receipt) or whether each message becomes its own text file inside a directory.

Some well-known mailbox formats are:

✦ mbox—Used by many Unix mail clients

✦ maildir—Closely associated with qmail

✦ mbx—Microsoft proprietary format

Mail User Agent, aka local mail client

So the letter is lying on a silver platter in the recipient's sitting room, which is actually his or her home directory. When a resident of Mail Server Mansion decides she wants to read her mail, she sends a maid to go to the sitting room, collect the silver platter full of letters left there by the butler, return to the boudoir with them, open them, and hold them up to the light so she can read them more stylishly. This maid is the *Mail User Agent.*

Tip   Mail User Agents are a very "Unixy" concept, and may have little relevance for those whose mail clients are mostly on other operating systems. See the next section for more information about POP and IMAP remote mail clients.

Popular MUAs and their URLs include:

✦ pine (www.washington.edu/pine)

✦ elm (www.instinct.org/elm)

✦ mutt (www.mutt.org)

In many cases, the choice of MUA will be closely tied to the choice of mailbox format. For instance, mutt makes it especially easy to use qmail's maildir format, and it seems to be the MUA of choice for the qmail community.

Mail-retrieval program, aka POP/IMAP server

Sending the maid to the sitting room to fetch the mail works fine if you happen to be at home in your local domain. But let's say the residents of Mail Server Mansion travel a lot to remote domains. (Remember, a remote domain can be in the same room — as long as it's not local in the sense of being one of the domains handled by this particular mail server, it's remote.) How will they get their mail?

The short answer is that they will send a request to Mail Server Mansion periodically, and another butler will forward any letters that have collected on the addressee's silver platter since the last time. This butler does not accept mail at all — he only forwards mail. He is the *mail retrieval program.*

This second butler needs to be very security-conscious. It's one thing for the SMTP butler to send and receive letters for people he knows to be in residence in the household, but anyone can send a request for mail to be forwarded to some distant address. Therefore, Butler Number Two has arranged a secret password with each resident of Mail Server Mansion, and no mail will be forwarded without that password.

These e-mail messages can then be read on remote mail clients — more and more of which are Web-based and/or no-cost — such as:

✦ Microsoft Outlook Express (www.microsoft.com/windows/ie)

✦ Mozilla mail/news (www.mozilla.org)

✦ Qualcomm Eudora Light (www.eudora.com)

✦ Hotmail (www.hotmail.com)

✦ AOL mail client (www.aol.com)

One of the consequences of implementing a mail retrieval program is that now clients on every platform can receive mail from a Unix server. MUAs are limited to Unix clients, and preferably local Unix clients.

A diversity of mail retrieval protocols exist, and a large number of products (often of wildly varying design) implement those protocols. The most popular are called *POP3* and *IMAP*.

A *POP server* (sometimes called a *POP toaster*) simply verifies a name, password, and mail-spool location by having this little dialog with a remote mail client:

```
user peter
+OK
pass rabbit
+OK
data
```

The POP server then checks the answers in a file and looks up the location of this user's mailbox. If there are new messages there, it will forward them to the client. Some POP systems can be configured to save a copy of every message forwarded to a client, some will allow clients to delete messages remotely, but most will just forward and forget. A user can take as much time as necessary to read and respond to messages offline, and then connect to the SMTP server to send replies.

POPular POP servers include:

+ Qualcomm qpopper (www.eudora.com/qpopper/index.html)

+ qmail-pop3d (www.qmail.org)

IMAP is a newer and more powerful mail retrieval protocol. Instead of forwarding and forgetting, IMAP allows for a simulacrum of the local client/server experience. The potential downside is that, unlike in a relatively quick POP3 data dump, each client must maintain a connection to the IMAP server as long as the user is reading and responding to e-mail — so the process is quite resource-intensive. An IMAP server is also somewhat more difficult to learn, install, configure, and maintain.

The most popular IMAP servers are:

+ Washington IMAP (www.washington.edu/imap)

+ Cyrus (http://asg.web.cmu.edu/cyrus)

Tip   A great guide to understanding the differences between POP and IMAP is Terry Gray's paper "Messaging Access Paradigms and Protocols," available at www.imap.org/papers/imap.vs.pop.html.

There is also a category of programs called *mail retrieval utilities*. The most famous of these is Eric Raymond's Fetchmail (http://www.tuxedo.org/~esr/fetchmail), which is particularly useful with dial-up connections. It implements POP, IMAP, and other protocols.

Mailing list manager

Finally, a mail server is hardly complete without a *mailing list manager*. This is a software package that helps send large volumes of e-mail automatically. Think of this program as the social secretary of Mail Server Mansion: Her job is to send out invitations to the endless parties given by the Mansion's residents. Needless to say, she must write out copy after copy after copy of each invitation — and then drop batches of them into the outgoing mailbag. She also handles all responses according to a standard set of scripts, analogous to handling RSVP acceptance notes.

Common MLMs include:

✦ Majordomo (www.greatcircle.com/majordomo)

✦ MailMan (www.list.org)

✦ ezmlm (for qmail) (www.ezmlm.org)

So there you have our model mail server. Now that you have a firm grasp on the basic architecture of e-mail, the rest is cake.

Receiving E-mail with PHP

Web-based e-mail clients — which download mail from the POP/IMAP server and relay outgoing mail through the SMTP server — are taking over a larger and larger slice of the market because of their convenience and platform independence. Furthermore, for those who habitually use shared or public computers, Webmail is the best way to ensure private communications. PHP is one of the tools that can be used to develop these most useful applications.

Say you want to make your own custom POP or IMAP client. You now have every development option from writing-from-scratch to choosing a different theme or skin from a drop-down menu. We discuss the main ones as follows, in order of most to least work.

Implementing from scratch

In a word: Don't. We're not joking. The only conceivable reason to reimplement from scratch at this point is for a university project, in which case you don't need someone to explain how to do it because you want to think through it for yourself.

Free Webmail providers all over the world will practically pay you to use their services, which you can configure to connect to any POP server anywhere. Also, many ISPs now provide Webmail along with connectivity. Extremely secure Webmail applications, such as Hushmail, are also starting to show up on the market at no cost to the consumer. We are personally more than happy to let the hardworking engineers at a major Web portal handle our personal e-mail accounts for us.

Even if you're determined to build your own custom Web-based e-mail app, there are now so many complete PHP Webmail clients free for the taking with their source code, you would have to go out of your way to avoid doing things (as the immortal Tina Turner says) nice . . . and easy.

Modifying other people's PHP

If you have some pressing reason why you need to write your own mail client in PHP, make it a little easier on yourself by using the power of *the Source* — the open source, that is. At least consider looking the code over to see if there's something you just haven't thought about yet — this is frequently the case with consumer apps, given the randomness of user behavior.

For those who want just a minimum of help, start with a look at Manuel Lemos's e-mail classes. The author, a well-known PHP community member, offers one for POP3, a couple for SMTP, and one for composing MIME messages. Put some nice screens on top of these, and you're halfway home. You can find them at:

    www.phpclasses.org

There's no canonical URL for this site; it's mirrored at locations around the world. You will have to go to the above URL and click through to a specific mirror, then to the "E-mail" section. Be careful about using any code that isn't produced by a known-good developer like Manuel or Richard Heyes.

For those who want to start with the source code for a full-featured, Web-based e-mail client, there are many good ones now available.

An amazingly full-featured, stylish, and well-supported IMAP and POP3 client named *IMP* is available under the GPL from those fun-loving systems guys at Horde.org (www.horde .org/imp).

Another popular choice is *SquirrelMail*, an HTML4-compliant IMAP client with a cool plug-in system for add-ons like a clock module or POP3 fetching. This is now one of the top five open source Webmail projects, located at http://squirrelmail.org.

A quick search of SourceForge will reveal several other candidates, each with its own advantages and philosophy. For instance, JAWmail (http://jawmail.sourceforge.net) offers a WAP client and support for the Slovene language. NOCC (http://nocc.sourceforge.net) does not require a database or cookies. There's even an embryonic PHP-GTK mail client called Teak (http://teak.sourceforge.net). Look around. You're sure to find some project that's already going in the direction you want.

Cosmetic changes

Finally, remember that many open source programs make it very easy to grab some code and slap a coat of makeup on it, or redesign the user interface altogether. If you want to design a mail page that looks like a paper letter, a TV screen, or the command deck of the starship Enterprise — grab your copy of the GIMP and a CSS manual and go to it. Let a thousand cosmetic changes bloom!

This is particularly helpful to those who would like to put out a branded Web mail client, as many ISPs do. But remember it's not cool to implicitly take credit for work you haven't done — a little acknowledgment, in the form of a small logo or link, goes a long way in the open source community. Some Webmail clients explicitly leave room in their design for you to add your company logo.

More and more Web-based apps are using themes or skins, which are basically style sheets plus graphic elements, to allow the quickest changes to their look and feel. Many apps are now shipping with user-contributed themes, and sometimes the developer's work simply consists of selecting a theme from a pull-down menu — it doesn't get any easier than that.

Sending E-mail with PHP

Sending mail is where PHP really comes into its own with e-mail. But before you can send any mail from your server, you need to tweak the configuration file a little.

Windows configuration

In Windows, you need to set two variables in the `php.ini` file:

✦ `SMTP`: A string containing the DNS name or IP address of an SMTP server that relays for the Windows machine on which PHP is installed. If it is on the PHP server, specify `localhost`.

✦ `sendmail_from`: A string containing the e-mail address of your default PHP mail sender (for example, `mailbot@example.com`).

Tip IIS4+ has an SMTP server built in, which is lighter than Exchange Server, if you don't need the power of the latter.

Unix configuration

You need to check and possibly change one variable in the `php.ini` file if you're using Unix: `sendmail_path`, a string containing the full path to your sendmail program (usually `/usr/sbin/sendmail` or `/usr/lib/sendmail`), a replacement, or a wrapper (such as `/var/qmail/bin/sendmail`).

If you are not using `sendmail`, and you do not reset this configuration directive to the correct alternative daemon, your mail transfer may be very slow, as several alternative programs are tried and allowed to time out before the correct one is found.

Be aware that PHP4+ designates the user `me` as the default mail sender on a Unix system. PHP3 used the PHP user (generally `nobody`), but apparently too many servers were rejecting mail from this account; early versions of PHP4 used the root user, but this is a seriously bad idea because the Unix root user should never send mail.

Caution In some mail systems, notably `qmail`, there is no mail account for root because the writers of the program want to discourage the practice of sending mail as the root user. You'll need to specify a "From," "Reply-to," and/or "Bounce-to" address in each outgoing mail message when using PHP to send mail.

The mail function

Only one real mail sending function exists in PHP: `mail()`. This function, which returns a Boolean, attempts to send one message using the data within the parentheses. The simplest use of this function (keeping in mind that this is a dummy address and should not be used for testing purposes) is:

```php
<?php
mail('receiver@receipthost.com', 'A Sample Subject Line',
"Body of e-mail\r\nwith lines separated by the newline
character.");
?>
```

This is the default and minimum format: address of recipient, subject line, and body. In this case, PHP will automatically add a `From: me@sendhost` line to each message header.

Caution   Even though e-mail has been around in substantially the same form for decades, there is still no universal format for messages that is guaranteed readable by all MTAs or mail clients. Some clients require a carriage return plus a newline (\r\n) instead of just a newline character. Some will choke on multiple addresses separated by commas. Some will not deliver e-mails without a proper date. There's really not a lot you can do to ameliorate this situation, except try as hard as you can to cover all the ground.

You can also, as always, use variables instead of hard-coded values:

```php
<?php
$address = 'santa@claus.com';
$subject = 'All I want for Christmas';
$body = "Is my two front teeth.\r\nSincerely, Joey";
$mailsend = mail($address, $subject, $body);
echo $mailsend;
?>
```

Multiple recipients all go into the address field, with commas separating them (this feature is not supported by all MTAs; if you want to be sure, use cc: instead):

```php
<?php
$address1 = 'receiver@receipthost';
$address2 = 'jane@hotmail.com';
$address3 = 'john@aol.com';
$all_addresses = "$address1, $address2, $address3";
$subject = 'A Sample Subject Line';
$body = "Body of e-mail\r\nwith lines separated by the
newline character.";

$mailsend = mail($addresses, $subject, $body);
echo $mailsend;
?>
```

Remember to ensure that the multiple addresses are one string, as in the preceding code lines. You do *not* want to do this:

```php
<?php
$address1 = 'receiver@receipthost';
$address2 = 'jane@hotmail.com';
$address3 = 'john@aol.com';
$subject = 'A Sample Subject Line';
$body = "Body of e-mail\r\nwith lines separated by the newline
character.";

// This is wrong, don't do it!
$mailsend = mail($address1, $address2, $address3, $subject,
$body);
echo $mailsend;
?>
```

Most people would like more control over the addresses, appearance, and format of their e-mails. You can do that by putting an additional header *after* the three default headers.

```php
<?php
$address = 'receiver@receipthost';
$subject = 'A Sample Subject Line';
$body = "Body of e-mail\r\nwith lines separated by the newline
character.";
$extra_header_str = "From: me@sendhost\r\nbcc:
phb@sendhost\r\nContent-type: text/plain\r\nX-mailer: PHP/"
. phpversion();

$mailsend = mail($address, $subject, $body, $extra_header_str);
echo $mailsend;
?>
```

This "additional header" field is somewhat odd because it crams in several types of information that would normally be given their own fields. Ours is not to wonder why; ours is but to explain the kinds of things you might want to put in this field:

✦ Your name

✦ Your e-mail address

✦ A reply-to or bounce-to address

✦ X-mailer and version number

✦ MIME version

✦ Content-type

✦ Charset (which uses a = to assign a value and not a : like the other headers)

✦ Content-transfer-encoding

✦ Copy (cc:) and blind-copy (bcc:) recipients

Caution   The mail() function returns 1 (TRUE) *when PHP believes it has successfully sent mail.* This has no relationship to any mail actually being sent or received. There are still an endless number of things that can go wrong: bad e-mail address, SMTP daemon incorrectly designated or configured, local Internet conditions, and so on. Think of 1 as a message meaning no more than "PHP has applied the function to the inputs without a big choke."

More Fun with PHP E-mail

Besides using PHP to construct full-blown mail clients, it's quite common to use the mail() function to send occasional mail when a particular event occurs on your Web site.

Sending mail from a form

Sending mail from a form is quite likely the single most popular application of PHP's mail() function. It's a far more functional alternative than HTML's mailto link tag, which of course results in e-mail being sent from the client machine's mail program.

Why use a server-side method rather than a client-side method of sending mail? After all, in many cases it's slower and more awkward, and it's certainly more work for you, the overburdened Web developer. Some reasons that might make you decide to choose this method include:

✦ A significant proportion of your audience uses public browsers or Web mail or both.

✦ You want to impose tighter syntax on the messages that you receive.

✦ You want to put the contact information into a database as well as send mail.

✦ You want to reduce unwanted messages (spam).

✦ You want to obviate the need for SMTP relaying from your main mail account.

This type of form-based, mail-sending page can be useful for many purposes, such as requesting quotes, reporting bugs, and getting technical support.

Listing 37-1 is a simple example form of the type that often sends e-mail.

Listing 37-1: **e-mail form (titlehelp.html)**

```
<html>
<head>
<title>titlehelp.html</title>
</head>

<body>
<center>
<table width="550">
<tr bgcolor= #FF9933><td align="center"><BR>
<H3>The ThrillerGuide.com<BR>
"What was the name of that thriller?"<BR>
Form</H3></td></tr>
<tr><td>
Did you once read an unforgettable thriller, but now you can't
remember the name?  Fill out as many of the fields below as you
can, press the button to submit, and we'll search our sources
and e-mail you back.
</td></tr></table>
</center>

<FORM METHOD=post ACTION="TitleHelp.php">
<P>First name: <input type="text" size=30 name="FirstName">
<P>Last name: <input type="text" size=30 name="LastName">
<P>Your Email Address: <input type="text" size=30 name="Email">
<P>In approximately what year did the action of the book occur?
<input type="text" size=4 name="Year">
<P>Can you remember any settings from the book?
<input type="text" size=30 name="Setting">
<P>The gender of the protagonist(s) was: <br>
```

Continued

Listing 37-1 *(continued)*

```
<ul>
<input TYPE="radio" NAME="Gender" VALUE=1>Female<br>
<input TYPE="radio" NAME="Gender" VALUE=2>Male<br>
<input TYPE="radio" NAME="Gender" VALUE=3>One of each<br>
<input TYPE="radio" NAME="Gender" VALUE=4>Two males<br>
<input TYPE="radio" NAME="Gender" VALUE=5>Two females<br>
</ul>
<P>When the book first came out, it was: <br>
<ul>
<input TYPE="radio" NAME="Status" VALUE=1>A bestseller<br>
<input TYPE="radio" NAME="Status" VALUE=2>A critic's darling<br>
<input TYPE="radio" NAME="Status" VALUE=3>Neither<br>
<input TYPE="radio" NAME="Status" VALUE=4>I don't know<br>
</ul>
<P>Please tell us anything else you can remember about this
title (plot, characters, settings, cover, movie versions,
etc.):
<br><textarea NAME="Other" ROWS=6 COLS=50></textarea>
<P><input type="submit" name="Submit">
</body>
</html>
```

Listing 37-1 submits to a form handler, shown in Listing 37-2.

Listing 37-2: E-mail form handler (titlehelp.php)

```
<head>
<title>titlehelp.php</title>
</head>

<body>
<?php
// If you wished, you could also save this information to
// a database
$LastName = $_POST['LastName'];
$FirstName = $_POST['FirstName'];
$Year = $_POST['Year'];
$Setting = $_POST['Setting'];
$Gender = $_POST['Gender'];
$Status = $_POST['Status'];
$Other = $_POST['Other'];

$formsent = mail('help@example.com',
                 'What was the name of that thriller?',
                 "Request from: $LastName $FirstName\r\n
```

```
                    Year: $Year\r\n
                    Setting(s): $Setting\r\n
                    Protagonist gender: $Gender\r\n
                    Book status: $Status\r\n
                    Other identifying characteristics: $Other",
                    "From: $Email\r\nBounce-to: help@example.com");
    if ($formsent) {
      echo "<P>Hi, $FirstName.  We have received your request for
    help, and will try to respond within 24 hours.  Thanks for
    visiting ThrillerGuide.com!";
    } else (
      echo "I'm sorry, there's a problem with your form.  Please try
    again.";
    )
    ?>
    </body>
    </html>
```

Sending mail from a database

It's probably not a very good idea to send batch mail from PHP rather than using a mailing list manager for the task. It's definitely a very bad idea if you have a large, active list to serve. However, programmatic people may just feel more comfortable with a function than with a special-purpose tool — and in the right situation, the PHP mail() function can work as well as a mailing list manager.

Caution
How many e-mails are too many? Probably about 200 is the maximum you'd want to send with PHP mail from a Web script, maybe 500 from a command-line call of a binary version of PHP.

Listing 37-3 is a PHP script you can use to send e-mail to everyone on a mailing list. Keep in mind you should not use this script if your list is not quite short.

Listing 37-3: **Mailing list script (mailinglist.php_)**

```
<html>
<head>
<title>ThrillerGuide: Site update notification</title>
</head>
<body>
<?php
mysql_connect('localhost', 'root');
mysql_select_db('thrillerguide');

$query = "SELECT email FROM mailinglist";
$result = mysql_query($query);
```

Continued

Listing 37-3 *(continued)*

```
while ($MailArray = mysql_fetch_array($result)) {
    $formsent = mail($MailArray[0],
                "2000.1.23 ThrillerGuide update",
                "This is to inform you that ThrillerGuide has
                    recently been updated.\r\n\r\n\You requested these
                    e-mail notifications. If you do not wish to
                    receive them, reply to this mail with \"Cancel\"
                    in the subject line.",
                "From: mailinglist@thrillerguide.com\r\n
                    Reply-to: help@example.com");
    echo "The result is $formsent.\n";
}
?>
</body>
</html>
```

Sending attachments with MIME mail

Note What is a *MIME* anyway? It stands for *Multipurpose Internet Mail Extensions* and is a code to specify the media type (beyond plain old US-ASCII) of your file. For instance, even though HTML is actually just text, you often want some programs to "know" that they should treat a file as an HTML file rather than plain text—render it instead of printing it out literally, for instance. A MIME header ensures this. For the purposes of e-mail, MIME types are relevant for HTML-format mail (which we discourage), multipart mail (such as mail with embedded graphics, which we also discourage), and attachments.

Sending attachments with the PHP mail() function used to be a bit more complicated, but lately a truly humanitarian PHP developer named Richard Heyes has made things super easy by promulgating his MIME mail classes. You have two options: If you have simple needs and don't care too much about licensing issues, you can get his HTML MIME mail class from his own site at www.phpguru.org/mime.mail.html.

Or, if you want finer-grained control and/or a clearer license, you can use the PEAR MIME class developed by Heyes and George Schlossnagle. This is part of the PEAR repository, which you can learn about in Chapter 28; find it at http://pear.php.net/package/ Mail_Mime.

Cross-Reference Not only do these classes make sending attachments a snap, but they're an exemplary usage of PHP's OOP capabilities. This is a situation where a natural "bundle" of code plus data exists: The number of necessary functions is limited, the data elements are well understood and stable, and the object notation makes usage easier rather than more difficult. Even a hardened skeptic would have to admit that in this case, OOP is a clear win. For more about PHP's OOP capabilities and when to use them, see Chapter 20.

For the most common task, simply sending mail with an attachment, the original HTML MIME mail class is much simpler to use than the one shipped in the PEAR repository of the PHP distribution. This is the one we are using in the example that follows.

In Listing 37-4, we'll send a license file for an evaluation software download to anyone who requests one via a Web form.

Listing 37-4: **Send e-email with a text attachment (send_license.php)**

```php
<?php

/*****************************************************************
 * This file initially shows a form to input an email address.  *
 * Once submitted, it sends e-mail with a license file attached.*
 * The text of the e-mail is contained in a text file named     *
 * license_mail.txt.                                            *
 *****************************************************************/

if ($_POST['submit'] == 'Send my license!') {
  // Make sure it's not some kind of attack
  if (strlen($_POST['email']) > 40) {
    echo 'Bad string';
    exit;
  }

  include('htmlMimeMail.php');

  $mail = new htmlMimeMail();
  $attachment = $mail->getFile('eval_license.lic');
  $mailbody = $mail->getFile('license_email.txt');

  $mail->setText($mailbody);
  $mail->addAttachment($attachment, 'eval_license.lic',
'text/plain');
  $mail->setReturnPath('mailbot@example.com');
  $mail->setFrom('mailbot@example.com');
  $mail->setSubject('Evaluator');

  $mail->send(array($_POST['email']), 'smtp');
} else {
  $form_str = <<< EOFORM
<HTML>
<BODY>
<FORM METHOD="post" ACTION="$PHP_SELF">
<INPUT TYPE="text" NAME="email" SIZE=25>
<INPUT TYPE="submit" NAME="submit" VALUE="Send my license!">
</FORM>
</BODY>
</HTML>
EOFORM;

  echo $form_str;
}
?>
```

A custom PHP mail application

Various organizations have their own special needs, for which you might be called upon to design a custom gizmo. For instance, here is a not-uncommon situation in which a custom mail application might be appropriate:

✦ The client wants to send personalized e-mail messages, each containing a password, to several hundred people.

✦ The client will enter each name and e-mail address by hand into a form from hardcopy. The program will insert this data into a database, along with passwords generated by PHP.

✦ PHP will compose and send a batch of e-mail using boilerplate text.

Listings 37-5, 37-6, and 37-7 show the code for a sample application to meet these specs. It combines the functionality of the two previous code samples and adds a couple of twists such as arrays and a random password generator (based on an example from Chapter 10).

Listing 37-5 is the entry form, `address_entry.php`.

Listing 37-5: **Batch e-mail entry form (address_entry.php)**

```
<HMTL>
<HEAD>
<TITLE>address_entry.php</TITLE>
</HEAD>

<BODY>
<CENTER><TABLE WIDTH=550><TR><TD>
Enter the names and e-mail addresses of recipients on this page.
You do not have to complete all 25 entries. When you are ready
to actually send the e-mails, click the Submit button at the
bottom of the page.<BR><BR>
</TD></TR></TABLE></CENTER>

<FORM METHOD=post ACTION="email_send.php">
<?php
/* To keep the page sizes and mail batches to a manageable size,
we will arbitrarily limit each batch to 25 names. If anything
goes wrong -- the client accidentally closes the browser window
before submitting, the PHP module isn't working, whatever --
the maximum number of entries that must be retyped is 25. To
alter the batch size, change the number in the while loop
below; and also in the form handling script. */


for ($batch_size = 0; $batch_size <= 24; $batch_size++) {
  print("<P>First name:
<input type=\"text\" size=30 name=\"FirstName[]\"><BR>\n
Last name: <input type=\"text\" size=30name=\"LastName[]\">
```

```
<BR>\n
E-mail Address: <input type=\"text\" size=30 name=\"Email[]\">\n
");
}
?>
<BR><BR>
<P><INPUT TYPE="Submit" NAME="SUBMIT">
</FORM>
</BODY>
</HTML>
```

Listing 37-6 is the form handler, email_send.php.

Listing 37-6: **Batch e-mail form handler (email_send.php)**

```
<html>
<head>
<title>email_send.php</title>
</head>

<body>
<?php
/* This screen enters the names, addresses, and passwords into a
database and sends the e-mails off into the wild black yonder
of cyberspace. */

include("password_maker.inc");

mysql_connect('localhost', 'root');
mysql_select_db('mailinglist');

$list_length = 0;
// Includes a test to stop the loop sooner if
// fewer than 25 names have been entered.
for ($list_length = 0 && strlen($_POST['Email'][$list_length]) >
0; $list_length <= 24 && strlen($_POST['Email'][$list_length])
> 0; $list_length++) {
  // 8 is the number of characters desired in each password.
  $Password = random_string($charset, 8);
  $FirstName = $_POST['FirstName'][$list_length];
  $LastName = $_POST['LastName'][$list_length];
  $Email = $_POST['Email'][$list_length];
  $query = "INSERT INTO recipient
          (FirstName, LastName, Email, Password)
          VALUES
          ('$FirstName', '$LastName', '$Email', $Password)";
  $result = mysql_query($query);
```

Continued

Listing 37-6 *(continued)*

```php
  $formsent = mail($Email, "Login and password info",
"Your login is: $FirstName $LastName.\r\n
Make sure there is only one space between the two words when you
log in.\r\nYour password is: $Password.\nGood luck!",
"From: mailinglist@sendhost\r\nReply-to: help@sendhost");
  echo "The result is $formsent for $list_length.<BR>\n";
}

?>
</body>
</html>
```

Listing 37-7 is the password generation file, `password_maker.inc`.

**Listing 37-7: Random password generation functions
                  (password_maker.inc)**

```php
<?php
// random_string is the function you actually call,
// and it in turn uses random_char

function random_char($string)
{
$length = strlen($string);
$position = mt_rand(0, $length - 1);
return($string[$position]);
}

function random_string ($charset_string, $length)
{
$return_string = random_char($charset_string);
for ($x = 1; $x < $length; $x++)
$return_string .= random_char($charset_string);
return($return_string);
}

// magic line to seed random generator
mt_srand((double)microtime() * 1000000);

$charset = "abcdefghijklmnopqrstuvwxyz";
?>
```

Sending mail from a cronjob

In the preceding examples, mail is triggered by the action of a human being interacting with a Web form. Sometimes, though, you want to send a batch of e-mail periodically and automatically. This is where Unix comes in handy — just set up a cronjob with PHP. It is a very happy feeling to drift off to sleep knowing that your little automatons are still working hard for you.

A very common use of a cronjob is to send a batch of e-mail in the middle of the night. Not only does this mean your mail will be waiting for the user at the top of the queue in the morning, but the dark hours before dawn are the traditional and best time to schedule batch processes that might slow down your servers.

To schedule a cronjob, first you write a script in the language of your choice. In this case, we are going to use the standalone version of PHP — the one that is not a module of any Web server. The script in Listing 37-8 (nagmail.php) sends out a reminder to everyone who downloaded an evaluation license 45 days ago.

Listing 37-8: **Mail script for cron (nagmail.php)**

```php
<?php


/***********************************************************
 * This script is intended to run once per day as a cron. *
 * It will query the database and send nagmail to people  *
 * who got evaluation licences 45 days before.            *
 ***********************************************************/

$db = mysql_connect("localhost", "root");
mysql_select_db("evaluators");

// Format date for query
// Actually the afternoon of 46 days ago
$now = time();
$fortyfive_days_ago = $now - 3888000 - 43200;

$target_date = date('Y-m-d', $fortyfive_days_ago);
$send_info_email_arr = array();

$query = "SELECT email
          FROM sent_licenses
          WHERE sent_date >= '$target_date 00:00:00'
          AND sent_date <= '$target_date 23:59:59'
         ";
$result = mysql_query($query,$db);

if (mysql_num_rows($result) > 0) {
  while ($email_arr = mysql_fetch_array($result)) {
    $to = $email_arr[0];
```

Continued

Listing 37-8 *(continued)*

```
    $from = 'mailbot@example.com';
    $subject = 'Evaluation software license expires';
    $msg     = 'You downloaded our evaluation software 45 days
ago.  Now you should pay us, or it will self-destruct.';
    $mailsend = mail($to, $subject, $msg, "From: $from");
    $send_info_email_arr .= "\n".$to."\n";
  }

  // Send me some email to let me know what happened
  $info_msg .= "I sent mail to the following evaluators
today:<BR><BR>\n";
  $info_msg .= print_r($send_info_email_arr);
  $info_mail = mail('webdev@example.com', "Cron job for
$target_date", $info_msg, "From: cronjob@example.com");

} else {
  // If there were no recipients today, let me know that
  $info_msg = "I didn't find anyone to send mail to today.";
  $info_mail = mail('webdev@example.com', "Cron job for
$target_date", $info_msg, "From: cronjob@example.com");

}
?>
```

Save this file in a location and with permissions that allow the PHP binary user to run it.

Now you need to schedule your `cronjob`. Say we want to send this mail out once a day at 3:15 a.m., the slowest hour of the day for your Web servers. Open up your `crontab` (type `crontab -e` in a shell) and enter this line (make sure your Unix user can execute the PHP binary):

```
15 03 * * * /usr/local/bin/php /home/phpcrons/nagmail.php
```

Reading from left to right, the various notations stand for minute, hour, day, month, day of week, and the command to be executed. (Asterisks are wildcards.) So this line tells the `cron` daemon to wake up and tap the PHP binary to run the `nagmail.php` script at 3:15 a.m. every morning of the year.

Caution   So sad for Windows users, but this is not possible with PHP in your operating system. Unix has a lot of functionality in the system layer that Windows tends to put in the application layer — so for instance Unix programmers constantly use the `grep` utility to search for a string in a set of files, which Windows programmers accomplish in the IDE. Similarly, scheduling a repetitive task like sending automatic e-mail is done in Outlook on Windows or as a trigger from SQL Server, rather than via a `cronjob`.

E-mail Gotchas

Given that there are so few mail-related functions in PHP, and these are very straightforward, e-mail related issues are highly likely to be caused by problems with the mail servers or even with the protocols themselves. In our experience, there is little a PHP developer can do to fix mail problems that suddenly arise in a working PHP installation.

If you experience a mail-related error message in PHP, the first thing you want to do is send and receive mail using the `sendmail` server that your PHP installation points to — just to eliminate the possibility that your SMTP server is totally hosed.

Next, make sure that you have set the `sendmail` or SMTP path in your configuration files correctly. Remember that you will have to do this every time you upgrade your PHP and/or Web server binary. Even if you're positive you did it correctly, it doesn't hurt to check again. Remember that there may be multiple configuration files — for instance, `php.ini` and Apache's `httpd.conf` can both be used to set the `sendmail` path.

If you don't see an error message and some of your e-mails are getting through, see if you can find a common denominator in the failure cases. For instance, it's quite common for well-managed mail servers to refuse delivery of e-mail from servers that do not pass a reverse-DNS lookup check. If your `sendmail` aliasing is configured incorrectly, the name or private-network IP address of a non-public machine inside your firewall might be making it into your mail headers — leading to a quick bounce from some of the better-administered SMTP servers (typically corporations and the more technical universities). Another common problem can occur when you forget to change the default PHP mail sending user, or have it set to a user such as `nobody` or `root` — many well-managed SMTP servers will refuse mail from these users.

If your problem is with POP or IMAP accounts accessed via a PHP client, try waiting a while to see if matters improve on the server end. These servers are notoriously flaky, and not only crash a lot, but require an unusual amount of scheduled maintenance. This is frustrating but totally outside the realm of anything most Web developers are responsible for.

Finally, if you are having problems with sending attachments with PHP, check out the documentation (including code comments) that shipped with the MIME mail class you're using. Fiddly little issues with things like line breaks and timestamps and multiple addresses may be causing you problems.

Summary

E-mail is one of the most useful and attractive functions of the Internet. PHP gives you the ability to both send and receive e-mail from a Web page. However, PHP is not a specialized e-mail program and will not cope gracefully with large numbers of messages.

Unfortunately, e-mail is one of the more complicated services in most domains, with a large number of moving parts and a surprising lack of standardization for such a relatively long-established functionality. Do not blame this on PHP — it's inherent in e-mail itself.

One of the most common uses of PHP's `mail` function is to send an e-mail (often to yourself) with values generated from a Web form. This is more reliable and spam-resistant than a `mailto` link, and it allows you to impose more structure on the data. You can also use PHP to send off small batches of e-mail using data from a database. However, large batches require a mailing-list manager or other solution.

✦   ✦   ✦

PHP and JavaScript

In this chapter, we try to get the best of both client-side and server-side scripting by combining PHP with JavaScript. We briefly touch upon the question of when to use which scripting language, and stylistic points that may be helpful when writing the code. Then we move on to pragmatic examples of the type you might see on a real-world PHP site.

Tip

If you've never worked with JavaScript before, you won't learn how just by reading this chapter. We will only touch on aspects of JavaScript that materially impinge upon PHP. If you're wondering what an onBlur event is, we recommend Danny Goodman's superlative *JavaScript Bible, Fifth Edition* (Wiley, 2004).

Outputting JavaScript with PHP

Because PHP is server-side and JavaScript is client-side, you may expect to have problems using both on the same page. In actuality, it's the difference that makes them such a good match.

Although PHP offers plenty of power for creating dynamically generated Web pages, it is strictly a server-side language. There's a common category of Web site tasks that perhaps don't require all the processing power of a server and would best be done quickly — for instance, changing the look of a button on mouseover. JavaScript, a purely client-side language (there's a server-side version, but we're assuming you've already chosen PHP on that end), can be easily integrated into PHP to fill in many of these gaps.

On the other hand, client-side JavaScript (aka Javascript, JScript, ECMAScript) itself has many limitations. For example, because it can't communicate directly with a database, JavaScript cannot update itself with fresh data depending on the page. Even worse, it's impossible to depend on client-side technologies, because they may not be present in a visitor's browser or may be disabled. Conscientious client-side Web developers must either decide to code probabilistically (and accept complaints from minority-browser users) or maintain several versions of a site at the same time. (Nonconscientious developers simply adapt themselves to the market-leading browser's full capabilities and damn the torpedoes . . . but that's another story.) PHP can help to mitigate the effects of client-side indeterminacy.

Dueling objects

Perhaps the biggest divergence between JavaScript and PHP is in the area of object models. The two are quite divergent conceptually, and they use different styles of notation. Some people consider this a good thing, because at least there's no chance of mixing up objects that look similar (as there is with, say, ASP and JavaScript). Probably just as many consider it a pain, an incompatibility, or a design flaw. In any case, there is no chance you can access the same object with both PHP and JavaScript — so forget it.

JavaScript is consistently object-oriented from top to bottom. Every statement requires an object and a method or function to be specified and may also have event handlers. JavaScript uses the so-called *dot* object notation (`object.method`), which is similar to that of other common programming languages such as Java, Python, and Microsoft's VBScript.

The downside is that JavaScript's document object model has been shakily standardized: Although, in theory, ECMA and the W3C shepherd the international standard, in practice the various browser manufacturers violate/add to this core at their whim. Proficient JavaScripters spend a good deal of energy keeping track of incompatibilities and workarounds for various browsers and platforms.

As we discuss elsewhere in this book (notably Chapter 20), PHP's classes are more of an add-on, retrofit, or convenience than an essential part of the language. The notation is the *arrow* or *pointer* style that is sometimes seen in C++ code (`$this->variable`). There is no mechanism in place to use a *dot* style. Honesty compels us to admit that PHP classes, while much improved in PHP5, probably don't really add up to anything like a thoroughgoing object model. Not that we ever wanted one anyway — and who are you calling defensive?

PHP doesn't care what it outputs

The main thing to keep in mind is that PHP doesn't know or care what it returns. You can (and people do) use PHP to write out plaintext, HTML, XHTML, DHTML, JavaScript, XML, MathML, various graphical formats, CSS, XSL, or even (for the ironic ironists among us) ASP. No real technical barrier exists to having PHP output C code, although it's probably not a usage whose popularity is going to sweep the nation. Remember, PHP does not always output PHP — its ultimate end product is usually code that will be run by another application, usually a browser.

There are a couple of ways to write out the JavaScript with PHP. The simplest is to escape from PHP whenever you get the urge to go client-side. This is accomplished in precisely the same way you would escape from HTML.

```
<?php
echo("Imagine tons of complex PHP code in this block.");
?>
<script language="JavaScript">
<!-- Hide from JavaScript disabled browsers
document.write("Strict separation of client-side and server-side
code is a good thing.")
// end hiding -->
</script>
<?php
echo("More PHP in this block.");
?>
```

Even this example doesn't show the fullest extent of PHP/JavaScript separation. A lot of JavaScript is actually defined within the `<HEAD>` element of an HTML page and simply called in the `<BODY>`, whereas PHP is generally used in the latter.

As with HTML, there are occasions when you don't want to escape from PHP — or this style may just be your personal preference. In that case, you can use PHP's `echo` or `print` statements to output JavaScript.

```
<?php
echo("This is some complex PHP code.");
echo("<script language=\"JavaScript\">\n");
echo("<!-- Hide from JavaScript disabled browsers\n");
echo("document.write(\"Strict separation of client-side and
server-side code is a good thing.\\n\")");
echo("// end hiding -->\n");
echo("</script>\n");
echo("More PHP in this block.");
?>
```

Caution   You may run into trouble if you use script tags (for instance, `<script language="PHP">`) to delineate PHP chunks — the PHP parser may have a hard time figuring out which `</script>` tag goes with what `<script>` tag. Whenever possible, use the canonical `<?php ?>` tag.

This style is not at all incorrect, but it can be considerably harder to keep everything straight. Unless you're an experienced programmer, you might want to limit this style to occasions in which you simply call predefined JavaScript functions, such as `onSubmit` events.

Tip   Remember to escape double-quotes in JavaScript sections if using `echo`/`print` to output code. See line 3 of the preceding snippet.

Where to use JavaScript

Client-side JavaScript doesn't do heavy lifting, but it is faster at certain tasks and also allows for some effects that you can't easily duplicate with PHP. Some places you should definitely consider replacing or enhancing PHP with JavaScript include:

✦ Simple arithmetic in forms and calculators (such as shopping-cart running total, mortgage calculator)

✦ Simple form validation (such as making sure e-mail addresses have @ symbols)

✦ Site navigation (such as pull-down navigation menus)

✦ Pop-ups (alerts, search boxes)

✦ Browser events (mouseover, onClick)

PHP as a Backup for JavaScript

The flip side of our *where to use JavaScript* advice is that PHP can help caulk the cracks in JavaScript. Sometimes you can seamlessly implement both client-side and server-side methods of doing a task. If a visitor's browser is JavaScript-enabled, fine — visitors will be able to take advantage of the zippier method, generally without even noticing that they've had a choice. If not, at least you won't suffer the ignominy of totally locking them out of your site's functionality.

A perfect example is the double-barreled pull-down menu for site navigation. JavaScript gives you an instant redirect, whereas PHP provides the same result after a longer wait for those without JavaScript-enabled browsers. This trick takes advantage of the fact that JavaScript has event handlers (for example, onChange) that work off the structure of HTML forms without requiring an actual button-clicking submission. Therefore, the Submit button can be reserved for PHP's use. Listing 38-1 shows an HTML page that uses a JavaScript onChange redirect and, if that doesn't work, a PHP form handler.

Listing 38-1: A JavaScript and PHP navigation form (navigation.html)

```
<html>
<head>
<title>Navigation pulldown</title>
<script language="JavaScript">
<!--
function Browse(form, i){
  var site = form.elements[i].selectedIndex;
  if(site > 0){
    top.location = form.elements[i].options[site].value
  }
}
// -->
</script>
</head>

<body>
<form method="post" action="redirect.php">
<select name="category" onChange="Browse(this.form,0)">
<option selected value=0>Choose a Category</option>
<option value="desktop.php">Desktops</option>
<option value="laptop.php">Laptops</option>
<option value="monitor.php">Monitors</option>
<option value="input.php">Input devices</option>
<option value="storage.php">Storage devices</option>
</select>
<input type="submit">
</form>
</body>
</html>
```

The PHP form handler file, called redirect.php, need only have two lines:

```
<?php $category = $_POST['category'];
header("Location: $category"); ?>
```

You could use a similar division of labor with form validation. If JavaScript is enabled, you can use it to make sure zip codes have nine digits, phone numbers have ten digits, and e-mail addresses have both an @ and a .. If JavaScript is not enabled, you can write a little PHP script that will do the same things when the form is submitted and return the form with warnings if the values are bad.

Caution　　JavaScript form validation should be relied on only for quick convenience reminders, never for data sanitization. See Chapter 29 for more information on data security.

Another kind of form is basically arithmetic — a shopping cart with running totals or a mortgage payment calculator. Again, you can combine both JavaScript and PHP in an arithmetic form to cover all the bases.

Finally, there is one use where PHP is so much faster that you might want to replace JavaScript altogether: browser sniffing. This is done to send different versions of a file (for instance, a stylesheet) to a visitor depending on which browser she's using. Server-side browser sniffing is vastly more efficient than client-side because no text is sent until the sniff has occurred. A JavaScript browser sniff can amount to hundreds of lines of JavaScript, which must be sent on every download whether the correctly browser version has been detected or not. Listing 38-2 shows a very simple server-side browser sniff.

Listing 38-2: A server-side browser sniff (browsersniff.php)

```php
<?php
if (strpos($HTTP_USER_AGENT, 'MSIE') > 0) {
  header("Location: index_ie.html");
} elseif (strpos($HTTP_USER_AGENT, 'Gecko') > 0) {
  header("Location: index_moz.html");
}
?>
```

Static Versus Dynamic JavaScript

Although the static JavaScript-PHP form in Listing 38-1 is handy for many applications, there's one big problem with it: You have to maintain it by hand. Every time you decide to add a new page to your site, you'll have to remember to manually add it to the drop-down list. Big deal, you're thinking — but these are the little things that become time-sucking nightmares when you're running a huge and high-traffic site.

With PHP and a database, you can update some of your JavaScript automatically when new data is stored in the database — or, as we might say, *dynamically*. You want to take this option whenever possible, as it will help you save time in the long run. Listing 38-3 is how you'd rewrite the form in Listing 38-1 for even better client/server integration.

Listing 38-3: Dynamic JavaScript and PHP form (dyn_navigation.html)

```
<html>
<head>
<title>Navigation pulldown</title>
<script language="JavaScript">
<!--
function Browse(form, i){
  var site = form.elements[i].selectedIndex;
  if(site > 0){
    top.location = form.elements[i].options[site].value
  }
}
// -->
</script>
</head>

<body>
<form method="post" action="redirect.php">
<select name="category" onChange="Browse(this.form,0)">
<option selected value=0>Choose a Category</option>
<?php
mysql_connect("localhost", "user", "password");
mysql_select_db("site_db");
$query = "SELECT filename, my_text
          FROM categories
          WHERE display = 1";
$result = mysql_query($query);
while (list($filename, $my_text) = mysql_fetch_array($result)) {
  print("<option value=\"$filename\"> $my_text</option>\n");
}
?>
</select>
<input type="submit">
</form>
</body>
</html>
```

You will doubtless have realized by now that a similar technique would be valuable even if you were making a straight JavaScript form (such as by using the onSubmit event handler rather than onChange). It would enable you to make a basic JavaScript function more flexible by allowing PHP to change variable values within the function before it was sent to the browser. So feel free to use PHP to output straight JavaScript using variables from a data source, if you like.

Dynamically generated forms

You can usefully extend this train of programming thought even further by setting up a series of dynamic drop-downs that change according to previous form inputs. PHP will fetch all the data from a database and load it into the HTML page, whereas JavaScript will decide which data set should be visible under various conditions.

In this example, we want to help users find information on specific cars. The list of the model of every car made by every manufacturer is dauntingly large, too long for even a well-designed drop-down list. Furthermore, car names tend to be eerily similar to each other, like the first names of a large family of sisters in a Swedish farming village — Integra, Sentra, Jetta, Elantra, Sephia, and so forth. So one way to narrow things down logically is to have the user pick a manufacturer from a pull-down menu, which would narrow the list to only models made by that company.

The database table we need looks like this (actually it probably doesn't if you're using a relational database — but here we want to focus on the JavaScript part, not the database part):

```
-------------------------
| make     | model      |
-------------------------
| Audi     | A4         |
| Audi     | A6         |
| Audi     | A8         |
| Audi     | Quattro    |
| Chrysler | Cirrus     |
| Chrysler | Concorde   |
| Chrysler | PT Cruiser |
| Toyota   | Camry      |
| Toyota   | Corolla    |
| Toyota   | Rav4       |
-------------------------
```

Using this database table and server-side PHP scripts, you would be limited to two suboptimal choices. You could opt for one extremely large list (either drop-down or full-page) of manufacturers and models, or you could make the visitor go through two sequential forms. But after we add JavaScript to the mix, we can start a page with two drop-downs and have the contents of the second list change depending on what is selected in the first.

Our double drop-down design is based on Andrew King's very clever JavaScript code, available at www.webreference.com under the GNU General Public License. We used PHP simply to connect to the database and fetch data to populate the two-dimensional arrays from which the JavaScript works. All of the interesting functionality here is provided by the JavaScript portion (Listing 38-4).

Listing 38-4: **A two-dimensional dynamic dropdown (double_drop.html)**

```
<HTML>
<HEAD>
<META NAME="save" CONTENT="history">
<STYLE>
  .saveHistory {behavior:url(#default#savehistory);}
</STYLE>

<SCRIPT LANGUAGE="JavaScript">
<!--
v=false;
```

Continued

Listing 38-4 *(continued)*

```
//-->
</SCRIPT>

<SCRIPT LANGUAGE="JavaScript1.1">
<!--
if (typeof(Option)+"" != "undefined") v=true;
//-->
</SCRIPT>

<SCRIPT LANGUAGE="JavaScript">
<!--
// Universal Related Select Menus - cascading popdown menus
// by Andrew King. v1.34 19990720
// Copyright (c) 1999 internet.com LLC. All Rights Reserved.
// Modified by Joyce Park 20000703
//
// This program is free software; you can redistribute it
// and/or modify it under the terms of the GNU General Public
// License as published by the Free Software Foundation; either
// version 2 of the License, or (at your option) any later
// version.
//
// This program is distributed in the hope that it will be
// useful, but WITHOUT ANY WARRANTY; without even the implied
// warranty of MERCHANTABILITY or FITNESS FOR A PARTICULAR
// PURPOSE.  See the GNU General Public License for more
// details.
//
// You should have received a copy of the GNU General Public
// License along with this program; if not, write to the Free
// Software Foundation, Inc., 59 Temple Place, Suite 330,
// Boston, MA  02111-1307  USA
//
// Originally published and documented at www.webreference.com
// see www.webreference.com/dev/menus/intro2.html for changelog

if(v){a=new Array(22);}

function getFormNum (formName) {
  var formNum =-1;
  for (i=0;i<document.forms.length;i++){
    tempForm = document.forms[i];
    if (formName == tempForm) {
      formNum = i;
      break;
    }
  }
  return formNum;
```

```
    }

    function jmp(form, elt) {
    // The first parameter is a reference to the form.
      if (form != null) {
        with (form.elements[elt]) {
          if (0 <= selectedIndex)
            location = options[selectedIndex].value;
        }
      }
    }

    var catsIndex = -1;
    var itemsIndex;

    if (v) { // ns 2 fix
    function newCat(){
      catsIndex++;
      a[catsIndex] = new Array();
      itemsIndex = 0;
    }

    // Andrew chose to name this function "O", presumably standing
    // for "Option".  It's not a zero, here or in the array below!
    function O(txt,url) {
      a[catsIndex][itemsIndex]=new myOptions(txt,url);
      itemsIndex++;
    }

    function myOptions(text,value){
      this.text = text;
      this.value = value;
    }

    // fill array
    <?php
    mysql_connect("localhost", "db_user");
    mysql_select_db("auto_db");
    // Get the makes
    $i = 0;
    $make_query = "SELECT DISTINCT make FROM cars";
    $make_result = mysql_query($make_query);
    while ($make_row = mysql_fetch_array($make_result)) {

      $make[$i] = $make_row[0];
      // Now fill the array with models for each make
      echo "newCat();\n";
      $model_query = "SELECT model
                    FROM cars
                    WHERE make = '$make[$i]'
                    ORDER BY model";
```

Continued

Listing 38-4 *(continued)*

```
    $model_result = mysql_query($model_query);
    while(list($model) = mysql_fetch_array($model_result)) {
      echo "O(\"$model\", \"/$model.php\")\n";
    }
    echo "\n";
    $i++;
}
?>
} // close if (v)

function relate(formName,elementNum,j) {
if(v){
var formNum = getFormNum(formName);
  if (formNum>=0) {
    formNum++; // reference next form, assume it follows in HTML
    with (document.forms[formNum].elements[elementNum]) {
      for(i=options.length-1;i>0;i--) options[i] = null;
      // null out in reverse order (bug workarnd)
      for(i=0;i<a[j].length;i++){
        options[i] = new Option(a[j][i].text,a[j][i].value);
      }
      options[0].selected = true;
    }
  }
} else {
  jmp(formName,elementNum);
}
}


// BACK BUTTON FIX for ie4+- or
// MEMORY-CACHE-STORING-ONLY-INDEX-AND-NOT-CONTENT
// see www.webreference.com for full comments
function IEsetup(){
  if(!document.all) return;
  IE5 = navigator.appVersion.indexOf("5.")!=-1;
  if(!IE5) {
    for (i=0;i<document.forms.length;i++) {
      document.forms[i].reset();
    }
  }
}

window.onload = IEsetup;

//-->
</SCRIPT>
</HEAD>
<BODY BGCOLOR="#ffffff">
```

```
<CENTER>
<TABLE BGCOLOR="#DDCCFF" BORDER="0" CELLPADDING="8"
CELLSPACING="0">
<TR VALIGN="TOP">
<TD>Choose a make:<BR>
<FORM NAME="f1" METHOD="POST" ACTION="redirect.php"
onSubmit="return false;">
<SELECT NAME="m1" ID="m1" CLASS="saveHistory"
onChange="relate(this.form,0,this.selectedIndex)">
<?php
while (list($key, $val) = each($make)) {
  echo "<OPTION VALUE=\"/$val.php\">$val</OPTION>\n";
}
?>
</SELECT>
<INPUT TYPE=SUBMIT VALUE="Go" onClick="jmp(this.form,0);">
</FORM>
</TD>

<TD BGCOLOR="#FFFFFF" VALIGN=MIDDLE><B>---&gt;</B></TD>

<TD>Choose a model:<BR>
<FORM NAME="f2" METHOD="POST" ACTION="redirect.php"
onSubmit="return false;">
<SELECT NAME="m2" ID="m2" CLASS="saveHistory"
onChange="jmp(this.form,0)">
// These are placeholder values for the first time the page is
// loaded.  They will not change when the form values change.
// If you delete them, the forms will still work, but the
// second select menu would come up empty until changed.
// These values could be generated dynamically, but we wanted
// to show them in place.
<OPTION VALUE="/A4.php">A4</OPTION>
<OPTION VALUE="/A6.php">A6</OPTION>
<OPTION VALUE="/A8.php">A8</OPTION>
<OPTION VALUE="/Quattro">Quattro</OPTION>
</SELECT>
<INPUT TYPE=SUBMIT VALUE="Go" onClick="jmp(this.form,0);">
<INPUT TYPE="hidden" NAME="baseurl" VALUE="http://localhost">
</FORM>
</TD>
</TR>
</TABLE></CENTER>

</BODY>
</HTML>
```

If you were to add to or change any of the data in the database, the JavaScript would change automatically. Dynamic integration of new data makes this a very powerful tool and keeps page maintenance to a minimum.

Passing data back to PHP from JavaScript

Finally, we close the data loop by passing form values back to PHP with JavaScript. Listings 38-5, 38-6, and 38-7 use JavaScript to force at least one check box to be checked at all times. In addition, it passes an array to a PHP script. We've chosen to use frames here to maximize the speed of the changes, and we wrote all values out by hand for clarity, rather than assembling them dynamically from a data source.

Listing 38-5: **Frameset (sandwich_frames.html)**

```
<HTML>
<HEAD>
<FRAMESET ROWS="50%, 50%" FRAMEBORDER="no" BORDER=0>
<FRAME SRC="sandwichorder.html" NAME="main" SCROLLING="auto">
<FRAME SRC="results.php" NAME="results" SCROLLING="auto">
</FRAMESET>
</HEAD>
<BODY></BODY>
</HTML>
```

Listing 38-6: **Form page (sandwichorder.html)**

```
<HTML>
<HEAD>
<SCRIPT LANGUAGE="JavaScript">
<!--

function deselectAllOthers(boxVals) {
  for (var x = 1; x < boxVals.length; x++) {
    boxVals[x].checked=false;
  }
}

function confirmOne(boxVals) {
  var count = 0;
  for (var x = 1; x < boxVals.length; x++) {
    if (boxVals[x].checked == false) {
      count++;
    }
  }
  if (count == (boxVals.length--1)) {
    boxVals[0].checked = true;
  } else {
    boxVals[0].checked = false;
  }
}

function toArray(boxVals) {
```

```
      for (var x = 0; x < boxVals.length; x++) {
        var valArray = boxVals[x].name+"[]";
        boxVals[x].name = valArray;
      }
    }


// -->
</script>
</HEAD>

<BODY BGCOLOR=#FCFCF0 onLoad="document.selector.submit();">

<TABLE CELLPADDING=20>
<TR>
<TD VALIGN="top">
<B>Order a sandwich with...</B>
<BR><BR>
<FORM NAME="selector" TARGET="results" METHOD="post"
ACTION="results.php">
<B>Fillings (check one or more)</B><BR><BR>
<INPUT TYPE="checkbox" name="filling" value="everything"
checked onClick="deselectAllOthers(document.selector.filling);
confirmOne(document.selector.filling);
toArray(document.selector.filling); submit();"> Everything
<BR>
<INPUT TYPE="checkbox" name="filling" value="turkey"
onClick="confirmOne(document.selector.filling);
toArray(document.selector.filling); submit();"> Turkey
<BR>
<INPUT TYPE="checkbox" name="filling" value="roastbeef"
onClick="confirmOne(document.selector.filling);
toArray(document.selector.filling); submit();"> Roast beef
<BR>
<INPUT TYPE="checkbox" name="filling" value="pastrami"
onClick="confirmOne(document.selector.filling);
toArray(document.selector.filling); submit();"> Pastrami
<BR>
<INPUT TYPE="checkbox" name="filling" value="eggplant"
onClick="confirmOne(document.selector.filling);
toArray(document.selector.filling); submit();"> Eggplant
<BR>
</TD>
<TD VALIGN="top"><BR><BR>
<B>Cheese</B><BR><BR>
<SELECT NAME="cheese" onChange="submit();">
<OPTION VALUE="none">None</OPTION>
<OPTION VALUE="cheddar">Cheddar</OPTION>
<OPTION VALUE="swiss">Swiss</OPTION>
<OPTION VALUE="camembert">Camembert</OPTION>
<OPTION VALUE="bleu">Blue</OPTION>
<OPTION VALUE="cottage">Cottage</OPTION>
```

Continued

Listing 38-6 *(continued)*

```
</SELECT>
<BR><BR>
</TD>
<TD VALIGN="top"><BR><BR>
<B>Bread</B><BR><BR>
<SELECT NAME="bread" onChange="submit();">
<OPTION VALUE="white">White</OPTION>
<OPTION VALUE="wheat">Wheat</OPTION>
<OPTION VALUE="rye">Rye</OPTION>
<OPTION VALUE="kaiser">Kaiser roll</OPTION>
<OPTION VALUE="onion">Onion roll</OPTION>
<OPTION VALUE="dutch">Dutch crunch</OPTION>
</SELECT>
</FORM>
<BR><BR>
</TD>
</TR></TABLE>
</BODY>
</HTML>
```

Listing 38-7: Results listing (results.php)

```
<HTML>
<HEAD></HEAD>

<BODY BGCOLOR=#666680 TEXT=#ffffff>
<TABLE CELLPADDING=30><TR><TD>
<B>Da Results</B><BR><BR>
<?php
$filling = $_POST['filling'];
$cheese = $_POST['cheese'];
$bread = $_POST['bread'];

if ($filling) {
  if (is_array($filling)) {
    reset($filling);
    while (list($key, $value) = each($filling)) {
      echo("$value<BR>\n");
    }
  } else {
    echo($filling);
  }
}
?>
```

```
<BR><BR></TD>
<TD VALIGN=top><BR><BR>
<B>Cheese</B><BR><BR>
<?php echo($cheese); ?>
<BR><BR></TD>
<TD VALIGN=top><BR><BR>
<B>Bread</B><BR><BR>
<?php echo($bread); ?>
</TD></TR>
</TABLE>
</BODY>
</HTML>
```

This form admittedly doesn't actually do very much yet — but the point is that it would obviate one or two trips from client to server and back. It also demonstrates another of the interesting effects PHP developers can get by experimenting with JavaScript.

Summary

JavaScript is a client-side scripting language that is highly efficient at many tasks that do not require server-side processing. Not everyone will want to use JavaScript, which has long-standing usability and security issues, but for those who do, the combination of client-side and server-side programming languages can offer an attractive combination of functionalities.

PHP and JavaScript have different object notations. JavaScript uses the so-called *dot* notation, whereas PHP uses the *arrow* or C++ style notation. JavaScript is thoroughly object-oriented, whereas PHP treats objects as an optional feature. The good news is that you'll never confuse a JavaScript object for a PHP object, or vice versa. The bad news is that you cannot access the same object from both languages.

It's often possible to implement a feature in both a client-side and a server-side way. Users with JavaScript-enabled browsers can enjoy greater speed and convenience, whereas those without can still get the functionality. This makes it possible to consider using JavaScript without its greatest drawback, which is unpredictability leading to alienation of segments of the userbase.

Perhaps the greatest service PHP can perform for JavaScript is to enable database connectivity — resulting in what we might call *Dynamic JavaScript*. JavaScript, being purely a client-side technology, cannot query a server-side database for variable data with which to dynamically generate content. Without a server-side helper like PHP, JavaScripts must be updated by hand whenever variable data is changed. PHP's capability to pass in up-to-date variables from a data store can make it considerably less labor intensive to maintain JavaScript-enabled forms and functions.

✦   ✦   ✦

PHP and Java

The relationship between PHP and Java has changed significantly with each new release. Unsurprisingly, given the source code, PHP initially had much more in common with C. PHP4 supported integration of PHP and Java using a Java Servlet environment or, more experimentally, directly into PHP. Finally, with the overhaul of the object model in PHP5, there's a distinctly Java feel to the PHP approach to object oriented programming. Java users will find much of PHP5's new object model very familiar, though with important differences.

Given these changes, as PHP takes on a more Java-like cast, there are two possibilities for which a discussion of PHP and Java might be pertinent. You might need to work on a project that requires PHP and Java or Java Server Pages (JSP) to work in tandem. Or you may be approaching PHP from a Java background and want to know about the similarities and differences in order to learn PHP faster. We will deal with both needs in this chapter.

If you don't have a need to use Java, or aren't already familiar with the language, this chapter won't do much for you.

PHP for Java programmers

Most projects won't require integration of Java and PHP, unless there is some specific need due to pre-existing architecture. The Java programmer approaching PHP for the first time may still want to know more about how PHP compares to Java for the purposes of learning PHP scripting.

Similarities

In this section, we discuss some ways in which PHP and Java are similar.

Syntax

Though PHP syntax is much closer to C, many conventions used in Java apply to PHP as well. Code is whitespace insensitive, statements are terminated with semicolons, function calls have a similar structure (`my_function(expression1, expression2)`), and curly braces (`{` and `}`) make statements into blocks. PHP supports C and C++-style comments (`/* */` as well as `//`), which are also used in Java.

Operators

The assignment operators (=, +=, *=, and so on), the Boolean operators (&&, ||, !), and the basic arithmetic operators (+, -, *, /, %) all behave as they do in Java. Other operators are similar, with some syntax differences. The string concatenation operator, for example, in PHP is a period (.) rather than a plus sign (+) as in Java.

Object model

The Java programmers coming to PHP with version 5 can rejoice! You no longer need to unlearn your approach to OOP in order to deal with the often crude OOP support in PHP4 and earlier versions. With recent changes, the object model in PHP has moved closer to Java's. PHP5 now supports interfaces, and sports a limited version of object overloading. The addition of keywords (such as `private`, `protected`, and `public`) for dealing with member variables should also prove familiar to Java coders. New error handling methods, including the built-in `Exception` class, also seem to borrow a page from Java.

Cross-Reference   See Chapter 20 for much more detailed information about PHP5's new object model.

Memory management

Under normal circumstances, PHP's garbage-collected environment ensures that you do not need to explicitly free allocated memory. If you're used to Java's mostly automated garbage-collected heap, you'll be right at home here.

Packages and libraries

Many Web-specific libraries are built into PHP and are available by default or with minor changes. This works similarly to the standard Java packages that are available through JAR files and `CLASSPATH` references.

Differences

Though many of the new features of PHP5 have a Java-like feel, there are plenty of notable exceptions to the way Java and PHP operate. As a general rule, never assume that a Java feature or concept will carry over completely into PHP.

Compiled versus scripting

Unlike Java, PHP is a *scripting* language. The development cycle is *edit-execute* rather than *edit-compile-execute*, as in Java. PHP code is automatically compiled at execution time and does not produce native standalone executables. As a result, the developer is not subjected to rigorous compile time error checking as in Java; many of the errors that you are used to seeing at compile time will not rear their ugly heads until the code is executed in PHP.

Variable declaration and loose typing

Get used to that leading $. Unlike in Java, all variables in PHP must begin with a $. Variables need not be declared before use, nor cast to a different type as in Java. Rather than the Java code:

```
String preamble = new String();
Preamble = "We, the people...";
```

or:

```
String preamble = "We, the people...";
```

the corresponding PHP code would be simply:

```
$preamble = "We, the people...";
```

PHP utilizes dynamic typing; the variable has no intrinsic type and can change with each new statement. While the following code is perfectly legal in PHP:

```
$type = 11;
$type = "11";
```

you would need to use separate variables in Java, or attempt to recast the variable as a String, with potential problems and resultant performance hit.

Though type hinting has been introduced in PHP5, it does not yet apply to data types. Variables can be declared and typed as in Java, but this is not required in PHP.

Java Server Pages and PHP

PHP can fulfill many functions similarly to Java Server Pages (JSP). The JSP servlet engine serves as a scripting language for use with Java, and, just as PHP, is often used in front end applications.

Embedded HTML

PHP is more similar to JSP than Java itself in that you are allowed to write HTML directly rather than using endless print statements. Unlike Java, but like JSP, variables can also be referenced from within a block of HTML. A simple HTML page using JSP script might look like this:

```
<%
   String greeting = "Hello, world";
%>
<HTML>
<HEAD>
   <TITLE>Fun with JSP</TITLE>
</HEAD>
<BODY>
<H1><%= greeting %></H1>
</BODY>
</HTML>
```

Similarly, using PHP, you can write:

```
<?php
   $greeting = "Hello, World";
?>
<HTML>
<HEAD>
   <TITLE>Fun with PHP</TITLE>
```

```
</HEAD>
<BODY>
<H1><?php echo $greeting ?></H1>
</BODY>
</HTML>
```

Pages can freely alternate between HTML and JSP, just as in using HTML and PHP.

Choose your scripting language

PHP can actually be used with Java in lieu of JSP, though support is much less robust and subject to change in future releases. Many of the *shortcuts* available to JSP are not available through PHP. For example, many of the standard Java class packages are automatically available as in Java Server Pages, but must be implicitly referenced using PHP Java support.

Caution   Don't let new syntax and structure similarities lull you into believing that PHP is truly like Java. The forgiving nature of PHP and the loose treatment of variable typing mean that code must be treated very differently. Those errors that Java demanded you to fix before it would compile may not show up in PHP until they are in an end user's browser!

Guide to this book

As with the similar sections for C Programmers (Appendix A) and Perl hackers (Appendix B), Table 39-1 labels the chapters of Part I according to how familiar they are likely to be to Java programmers.

Table 39-1: Guide to Part I for Java Programmers

Chapter	Chapter Title	Verdict?	Notes
1	Why PHP and MySQL?	Novel	The chapter you need to justify PHP to your boss.
2	Server-side Web Scripting	Somewhat familiar	Important if you have not seen Web-scripting languages before. PHP bears many similarities to Java Server Pages (JSP).
3	Getting Started with PHP	Novel	Installation, hosting, and so on.
4	Adding PHP to HTML	Novel but easy	"Hello world" for PHP.
5	Syntax and Variables	Somewhat familiar	Some syntactic similarities exist. Some will be unfamiliar, especially the way in which variables are treated.
6	Control and Functions	Somewhat familiar	Many of the PHP control structures (if, while, for) work similarly to Java, with important differences, such as functions and variable scoping.

Chapter	Chapter Title	Verdict?	Notes
7	Passing Information between Pages	Somewhat familiar	Specific to Web-scripting. Will be familiar if you have used JSP.
8	Strings	Mostly familiar	Many behavior differences and typing concerns.
9	Arrays	Somewhat familiar	PHP arrays share some similarities, but with different behavior.
10	Numbers	Familiar	PHP's two numerical types, corresponding to the long and double types.
11	Basic PHP Gotchas	Novel	Almost no correlation with compile time and runtime error checking in Java.

Integrating PHP and Java

In the course of your development work, you may run across a situation in which you will be required to use PHP and Java together, or this combination may prove advantageous for some reason. You basically have two options to accomplish this tricky undertaking, both of which are outlined below. Java environments are inherently complicated and vary according to servlet engine and server. Since these issues are well beyond the scope of this book, in all further discussions we will assume that you already have a working Web server that supports servlets, an installed Java virtual machine (JVM), and a working familiarity with Java.

The Java SAPI

The most stable solution is to integrate PHP into a Java Servlet environment using the Java Service Access Point Identifier (SAPI). This allows the PHP processor to run as a servlet and builds upon the PHP Java extension (described following). The servlet will run from within a Java servlet engine, such as Apache Tomcat.

Note   Though the Java servlet SAPI module will theoretically run on any of a number of available servlet engines, the PHP team has only tested the code using Apache's Jakarta Tomcat servlet engine. Your mileage may vary if you have implemented another engine such as Caucho's Resin or IBM's WebSphere. Any environmental differences may require adjustments, and you are essential on your own. The PHP team encourages brave souls who triumph over other servlet engines to submit bugs and found fixes to the PHP Development Mailing List. (See Appendix D for more information on PHP mailing lists.)

Installation and setup

As with the Java extension, SAPI module support is not built into PHP by default. You will need to rebuild PHP with the necessary options (`--with-servlet -with java`) as well as any other options you may require for other uses. (See Chapter 3 for more information on building and installing PHP.) In your environment variables, make sure that `servlet.jar` is included in your `CLASSPATH` and add the PHP directory containing the `libphp4.so` file to `LD_LIBRARY_PATH`.

Windows users will need to build and copy the `php_java.dll` file into their `extension_dir` directory and enable the extension in the `php.ini` file. Also be sure that `servlet.jar` is included in your `CLASSPATH` and add the PHP directory containing the PHP DLL files to `PATH`.

Building the module will also create a JAR file called `phpsrvlt.jar`, which must also be included in your `CLASSPATH`. Additional setup specific to your servlet engine will probably be required. Check the PHP Web site and mailing lists for comments from other users who have successfully configured your Java servlet engine for use with this module.

Further information

Once you have the module up and running, you should be able to view php files as normal. Point to an existing PHP page, or create a test by printing `phpinfo()` to see if you have succeeded.

Usage of this module is still considered experimental, and there isn't a lot of documentation. You probably won't build or use this module unless you already have a specific need for it. As the module is under constant revision, additional useful notes may be found in the `README` file and other sources located in your PHP directory under `/sapi/servlet`. Users also sometimes add comments to the User Contributed Notes in the online manual, so it's probably a good idea to check there every so often. Official notes on Java/PHP integration can be found on the PHP Web site at `www.php.net/manual/en/ref.java.php`.

The Java extension

If you're feeling particularly adventurous, you can build Java support directly into PHP using the experimental Java extension. Once enabled, the extension allows you to create and call Java objects and methods from within PHP. The advantages are obvious for the Java-familiar, but use of this extension is not without some pain upfront and some serious care on your part.

Caution   The Java extension for PHP is subject to continuing revision as it is fine-tuned for future versions. Committing to use of this feature in your application implies added diligence to avoid future code breakage. It's not labeled EXPERIMENTAL in the PHP manual for nothing!

Installation and setup

Use of the Java extension will require some modifications to your PHP installation and environment. Before rebuilding PHP, it's a good idea to make sure you have access to pertinent information on your Java Development Kit (JDK) environment. Make sure that you know the following information:

   ✦ The base directory of your JDK installation (typically `/usr/java/j2sdk<version>` in Linux)

   ✦ The `JAVA_HOME` and `CLASSPATH` environment variables (`JAVA_HOME` should be set to the above directory)

   ✦ Location of the Java library (typically in `JAVA_HOME/jre/lib/i386` on Linux)

Java support is not enabled by default, and you will need to rebuild PHP in order to take advantage of its features. During the installation, you must specify the option `-with-java=(base directory)` in addition to any other options you may require. (See Chapter 3 for more information on building and installing PHP.)

Modifications are also required to the `php.ini` configuration file in order to enable the extension. Open your `php.ini` file in your favorite editor and search for the `[Java]` subheading under `Module Settings`. Here's where the information you collected earlier will come in handy. A typical modification on a Linux server might look something like this:

```
[java]
java.home = /usr/java/j2sdk1.4.0
java.library = /usr/java/j2sdk1.4.0/jre/lib/i386/libjava.so
java.library.path = /usr/lib/php/extensions/no-debug-non-zts-
20020429
extension_dir = /usr/lib/php/extensions/no-debug-non-zts-
20020429
extension=libphp_java.so
```

Windows users should also add the following line under `Windows Extensions`:

```
extension=php_java.dll
```

Note   Just to add some confusion for fun, note that the `java.library` variable pertains to the Java installation, while `java.library.path` refers to the PHP extension directory where the optional PHP support files reside. Most problems with getting the Java extension to work seem to revolve around successfully editing `php.ini`.

Remember that these variables must correspond to the settings on your particular server.

Caution   Windows users must be sure to enclose the path names in quotations.

If all goes well, you should be ready to try calling a Java method from within PHP!

Testing

A simple invocation of `java.lang.System` in a JSP environment would look something like this:

```
<%
  String version = System.getProperty("java.version");
  String os = System.getProperty("os.name");
%>
<HTML>
<HEAD>
  <TITLE>Fun with Java and JSP</TITLE>
</HEAD>
<BODY>
<H3>We are running Java version <%= version %> on the
  <%= os %> platform, and it's working!</H3>
</BODY>
</HTML>
```

Similar code using PHP would, by necessity, be a bit more involved. Create a new PHP file called `javatest.php` and insert the following:

```php
<?php
  $system = new Java('java.lang.System');
  $version = $system->getProperty('java.version');
  $os = $system->getProperty('os.name');
?>
<HTML>
<HEAD>
  <TITLE>Fun with Java and JSP</TITLE>
</HEAD>
<BODY>
<H3>We are running Java version <?php echo $version ?> on the
<?php echo $os ?> platform, and it's working!</H3>
</BODY>
</HTML>
```

With luck, your browser will output something like the following when you access `javatest.php`:

```
We are running Java version 1.4.0 on the Linux platform, and
it's working!
```

If not, it's time to troubleshoot! Consult the PHP manual or other resources listed in Appendix D for help and suggestions.

The Java object

The `Java` object becomes available with installation of the Java extension, and is used to instantiate a Java class within PHP. The format is:

```
new Java(class, parameters)
```

where `class` is the class being invoked and the parameters are arguments to be passed to that object's constructor. Parameters are optional, providing a default constructor is available.

Note

It's important to note that no Java packages are available to PHP by default. Although, as in the previous example, the `java.lang.*` package is always available to Java and JSP and therefore does not need to be referenced implicitly, the complete package and class name must always be specified from within PHP.

The previous example was a simple one, since we provided no arguments to the `System` class. `System` cannot be instantiated in Java and is referenced through static methods just as `getProperty()`. Let's take a look at a more involved example.

With the deprecation of several `Date()` constructors, time reporting and formatting grew in complexity in Java. Here's an example in which we print the current date and time in JSP:

```
<%
Calendar cr = new Calendar();

String date_time = "yyyy-MM-dd HH:mm:ss";
```

```
java.text.SimpleDateFormat date =
  new java.text.SimpleDateFormat(date_time);

String current = date.format(cr.getTime()));
%>
<HTML>
<HEAD>
  <TITLE>Got the time?</TITLE>
</HEAD>
<BODY>
<H3>The current date and time is: <%= current %>.</H3>
</BODY>
</HTML>
```

Once again, as written in PHP:

```
<?php

  $cr = new Java('java.lang.Calendar');

  $date_time = "yyyy-MM-dd HH:mm:ss";

  $date = new Java('java.text.SimpleDateFormat',$date_time);

  $current = date->format($cr->getTime()));
?>

<HTML>
<HEAD>
  <TITLE>Got the time?</TITLE>
</HEAD>
<BODY>
<H3>The current date and time is: <?php echo current ?>.</H3>
</BODY>
</HTML>
```

Errors and exceptions

Because Java is being accessed through PHP, a Java `Exception` displays as a PHP warning
in the browser. While a reference to a class that is misspelled or not in the `classpath` might
generate an error such as this within Java (accompanied by a lovely stack trace):

```
/var/tomcat4/work/webroot/_/test/test$jsp.java:57: Class
org.apache.jsp.SomethingAmiss not found.
```

when referenced from PHP, it will simply display to the browser:

```
Warning: java.lang.ClassNotFoundException
```

While this warning will at least notify you that there is a problem, it doesn't provide much
useful troubleshooting information. You can suppress the PHP warnings by using an @ prefix
with your method calls:

```
@$trouble = $output->println();
```

When an exception is thrown, it's also possible to obtain the `Exception` object from Java for more pertinent information. To accomplish this, the PHP Java extension provides two functions to retrieve the last `Exception` and then to clear it: `java_last_exception_get()` and `java_last_exception_clear()`. Neither function accepts parameters.

With version 5, PHP now has an `Exception` object of its own! You can use both the Java and PHP objects in conjunction to provide more helpful error information, as in Java:

```
// check for a thrown exception in Java
$exception = java_last_exception_get();
if ($exception) {
  $ex_msg = $exception->getMessage();
  // use the Java exception to throw an exception in PHP
  throw new Exception($ex_msg);
  //clear this Java exception
  java_last_exception_clear();
}
```

Note The `getMessage()` method will provide more information than given in the warning, but still might not be enough. Use `toString()` if your exceptions are not providing enough useful information.

By using both the @ prefix and these handy PHP functions, it becomes possible to exert more control over Java errors within PHP.

Potential gotchas

Expect to run into problems while trying to integrate Java and PHP. Judging from comments on PHP mailing lists and on various development boards, even seasoned professionals find they must experiment both with installation and implementation in order to achieve what they want. There are a few problems that seem to crop up most often, and you can learn from the experiences of others.

Installation problems

Assuming a pre-existing servlet engine and working environment, most problems in getting the Java extension to work properly seem to begin and end in `php.ini`. Your particular servlet engine and/or platform may require more configuration. Again, check user notes online and in mailing lists and experiment on your own.

It's the classpath, stupid

A common error, especially for those not all that familiar with Java, is to neglect including relevant packages, libraries or JAR files within the `classpath` specified as an environment variable. If you receive a dread `ClassNotDefined` error or something similar, check the `CLASSPATH` first. If not, then perhaps you misspelled the class name. Hey, it happens.

Here comes that loose typing again

PHP may not care what type your variable is, but Java certainly does. It's probably a good idea (and good form, when calling Java methods) to typecast your PHP variables before passing them to a Java object:

```
$value = (double) $value;
$sum = (int) $sum;
$name = (String) $name;
```

Get used to typecasting variables for use with Java. As a worst-case scenario, the code may generate errors. At best, it may behave unpredictably.

Speed

Excessive referencing of Java objects can sacrifice some of the performance that PHP aficionados have grown so fond of. Use Java objects and methods only when necessary!

The sky's the limit

Obviously, the complexity only increases when you begin to create more involved scripts. There's a lot of uncharted territory that you can choose to explore. Many creative uses of the Java extension continue to be uncovered as time passes. You can even use the `java.awt.*` packages to create graphical interfaces through PHP, though much of this is limited to CGI mode. If you can dream it up in Java, there's a chance you just might be able to get it to work through PHP as well.

Here we enter the realm of experimentation. While managing to exploit the Java extension to its full potential may prove enjoyable and interesting for the programmer, it often doesn't make for a very stable or efficient application. Use in a production environment at your own risk, and keep abreast of any changes posted on the PHP site. Meanwhile, load up a development machine and go to town!

Summary

PHP and Java have become strange bedfellows with the release of PHP5. While many similarities in syntax and object model exist, differences abound in typing, compilation, and methodology.

Java programmers who are working with PHP for the first time will find server-side scripting much more intuitive if they have experience using Java Server Pages (JSP). PHP fulfills a similar function, and can be embedded within HTML.

Users seeking to integrate Java and PHP have two options: the Java SAPI module and the Java extension. Both are optional and PHP must be rebuilt to support these options. Use of Java assumes a Web server with installed JVM and a servlet engine such as Apache Jakarta Tomcat. Modifications must be made to environment variables as well as the `php.ini` configuration file, and are specific to your particular platform and Java servlet engine.

Objects and methods are called from PHP instantiating the `Java` object. Java packages are not available directly to PHP and must be correctly referenced. Parameters are optional if a default constructor is to be used.

Errors generated by Java are reported as PHP warnings, but can be suppressed by attaching the @ prefix to your PHP statements. Java `Exception` objects can be accessed through PHP using built-in functions, and can be used in conjunction with the PHP `Exception` object.

Java support in PHP is experimental and, as such, is subject to change in future releases. Those wishing to integrate Java and PHP should keep track of new releases and potential changes that could break their code.

✦   ✦   ✦

PHP and XML

XML is one of the hottest buzzwords in the software business today; but what does it mean for Joe or Jane Average PHP Developer? Well, it could very well be the necessary precondition for a better Internet — one that is faster to develop, more interactive, less junky, and more accessible to a larger audience. With PHP, you're already in an excellent position to smoothly integrate XML into your Web development arsenal as the technology matures.

What Is XML?

XML stands for *eXtensible Markup Language*. XML is a form of *SGML*, the *Standard Generalized Markup Language*, but you don't need to know anything about SGML to use XML. It defines syntax for structured documents that both humans and machines can read.

Note

Our explanation of XML will necessarily be extremely brief (because this is a book about PHP rather than XML). For those who want to learn more, we highly recommend Elliotte Rusty Harold's *XML 1.1 Bible, Third Edition* (Wiley, 2004). Although this book is neither short nor a specific guide to programming XML-based applications, it will give you a firm conceptual grasp of XML that should set you up nicely for any particular XML-based task.

Perhaps the easiest way to understand XML is to think about all the things HTML can't do. HTML is also a markup language, but HTML documents are anything but structured. HTML tags (technically known as elements) and attributes are just simple identification markers to the browser. For instance, a pair of matched `<H1>` and `</H1>` tags designate a top-level heading. Browsers interpret this to mean you want heading text to be displayed in a really big, bold, possibly italicized font. HTML does not, however, indicate whether the text between those tags is the title of the page, the name of the author, an invitation to enter the site, a pertinent quotation, a promise of special sale prices, or what. It's just some text that happens to be big.

One implication of HTML's lack of structure is that search engines have little built-in guidance about what's important on each page of your site or what each chunk of text means in relation to the others. They use various methods to guess, none of which are foolproof. `<META>` tags are notoriously prone to abuse — porn sites often load popular but irrelevant search terms into their headers to fool unwary Web surfers — and spiders can end up giving too much weight to portions of the page that designers might think are unimportant. If XML becomes ubiquitous, it could eliminate many of these problems and lead the way to much more meaningful Web searching.

Let's say you work for a content Web site that has just signed a major distribution deal with a top-five portal. After you wake up from the champagne hangover, you're faced with the hard question of how you plan to deliver the content. HTML isn't going to do the job: Obviously the portal's page design and Web serving technology are different from your site's, and they won't be able to just plug your HTML into theirs. Just to make things really interesting, let's presume you and Big Portal Company use different programming languages, different data stores, different HTML editors, different style sheets — in short, different everything. The necessary bridge is a data-exchange format, which is easy for you to output with your technical setup, clearly understood by both parties with existing software, and equally easy for the Big Portal Company to convert to its own purposes and designs. XML is that data-exchange format.

You could, of course, write a script to dump data from your data store into a tab-delimited file. Then you could write out the details of your custom data format and send it with the tab-delimited file to Big Portal Company. There one of its engineers would try to figure out your schema and write code to transform your data into its format. However, anyone who has actually done this knows how much fiddly work it is, how many tests need to be performed, how much time even the tiniest error can suck up. On the other hand, you could just output your data in XML, and the Big Portal Company engineer could write a very short script — perhaps just three functions long — to transform your XML tags to its corresponding XML tags. Then Big Portal Company could treat the data just like its own data. XML is an attempt to move toward a common language and set of methods for performing tasks like these, instead of having data-exchange involve a series of custom jobs each time.

We hope these examples begin to answer the "Why XML?" question. If you forget the hype and focus on what problems XML might begin to solve, you'll be in a much better position to assess whether it can help you today or sometime in the future. In the simplest terms, XML is a flexible data-exchange format that is not dependent on any particular software or domain, can be parsed easily by both machines and humans, and allows content providers to include information about the structure of the data along with the data itself.

The next question about XML is typically, "What does XML look like anyway?" Actually, XML looks a lot like HTML. A simple XML file, such as the one shown in Listing 40-1, is easy for HTML users to understand.

Listing 40-1: A simple XML file

```
<?xml version="1.0"?>
<book>
 <publisher>IDG Books</publisher>
 <title>PHP5 Bible</title>
 <chapter title="PHP and XML">
  <section title="What is XML?">
   <paragraph>
If you know HTML, you're most of the way to understanding XML.
   </paragraph>
   <paragraph>
They are both markup languages, but XML is more structured
than HTML.
   </paragraph>
  </section>
 </chapter>
</book>
```

As you can see, XML has tags and attributes and the hierarchical structure that you're used to seeing in HTML. In XML, each pair of tags (`<paragraph></paragraph>`) is known as an *element*. Actually, this is true in HTML, too, but most people strongly prefer the term *tag* (the construction that marks an element) over *element* (the conceptual thing that is being marked by a tag)—we're not picky. Use whatever term you want as long as you know what you mean. The biggest difference is that XML tags are self-defined; they carry absolutely no display directive to the Web browser or other viewing application.

XML makes the following minimal demands:

✦ There must be a single root element that encloses all the other elements, similar to `<HTML></HTML>` in HTML documents. This is also sometimes called the *document element*.

✦ Elements must be hierarchical. That is, `<X> <Y> </Y> </X>` is allowed, but `<X> <Y> </X> </Y>` is not. In the first example, `<X>` clearly contains all of `<Y>`. In the second example, `<X>` and `<Y>` overlap. XML does not allow overlapped tags.

✦ All elements must be deliberately closed (in contrast to HTML, which allows some unclosed elements such as `<OPTION>` or `<LI>`). This can be accomplished with a closing tag (`<title></title>`) as in HTML or by using an XML feature with no HTML equivalent called a *self-closing element* (`<logo href="graphic.jpg"/>`). A self-closing element is also known as an *empty element*.

✦ Elements can contain elements, text, and other data. If an element encloses something that looks like it might be XML—such as `<hello>`—but isn't, or if you don't want something parsed, it must be escaped.

 Caution   The &, <, >, ', and " characters are all restricted in XML. You can use them in your data by *escaping* them—using codes such as `&amp;` and `&lt;`—or by putting them in CDATA sections, which we discuss in the section "Documents and DTDs," later in this chapter.

In addition to these mandatory requirements for what is called *well-formedness*, the XML standard also suggests that XML documents should start with an identifying XML declaration. This is a processing instruction giving the MIME type and version number, such as `<?xml version="1.0"?>`. This is not required, but some parsers complain if it isn't present. Also, XML is case sensitive; some variants, such as XHTML, require lowercase tags and attributes. Lowercase tags are not absolutely required by the XML standard itself, but unless you have a good reason to do otherwise you should use lowercase tags and attributes.

 Note   It's the XML declaration, and other processing instructions with the same format, that prevents you from using PHP's short tags with XML. Because the two tag styles are identical (`<? ?>`), it would be unclear whether this character sequence set off a PHP block or an XML processing instruction.

XML documents are usually text. They can contain binary data, but they aren't really meant to. If you want to put binary data in your XML documents, you have to encode it first and decode it later. Note that including binary data may break some of the platform-independence of pure XML.

Working with XML

By now you may or may not think XML is the greatest thing since cinnamon toast, but in either case you're probably asking yourself, "OK, but what can I actually *do* with it?" This is actually not such an easy question to answer. In theory, you can do three main things with XML: manipulate and store data; pass data around between software applications or between organizations; and display XML pages in a browser or other application using style sheets to apply display directives.

In practice, almost no one actually uses XML as a primary data store when SQL is so ubiquitous. It's possible, although still difficult, to manipulate data using XML—for instance, to edit documents by creating and manipulating XML nodes rather than straight text—but again many users don't see a tremendous amount of extra value to this practice. A great deal of progress has been made in displaying XML in the browser, generally in the form of XHTML, in the last couple of years, but there are still significant issues with this practice. For more information about displaying XML, see the sidebar "The Promises and Pitfalls of Displaying XML."

This leaves one main job for XML right now: exchanging data between applications and organizations. This happens to be the area in which PHP can have the most immediate impact. For instance, a C program might perform some operations on data from a data store and then output the results in XML, which PHP could transform into HTML for display in a browser or other application.

The Promises and Pitfalls of Displaying XML

XML attempts to do something that HTML has only very imperfectly accomplished: enforce real separation between content and display. XML tags contain no display-oriented meaning whatsoever—so an element called `<header></header>` in XML does not imply anything about large bold text, and, we hope, never will. All display information will be applied through style sheets. These can be either Cascading Style Sheets, which are already familiar to many HTML developers, or *XSL* (e*X*tensible *S*tyle *L*anguage), which is the next-generation style sheet.

A single XML document will, in theory, be displayable in any number of ways simply by applying a different style sheet. The promise is that you will be able to take an XML document and, by simply swapping in various XSL templates, be able to create a version of the page for very large screens, a version for cellular phones, a version for the visually handicapped, a version with certain lines highlighted in red, and so forth.

The reality of the situation right now is not that rosy. The XSL standard is still notoriously shaky, and it seems to be resisting wide adoption. Cascading Style Sheets have been around since 1997 and browser support for them remains so problematic that most major Web sites still use font tags—indicating that XSL has quite a way to go before it gains wide acceptance. It's a perfect example of the truism that "worse is better"—people have been complaining about HTML's limitations almost since it was invented; but a technology which is better yet harder to implement, like XML, might not have so quickly acquired such a large user base.

In the meantime, XML must be transformed into HTML on the server side. It is possible to do this using XSL itself, but so far relatively few sites have chosen this option. Among other discouraging factors, XSL transformations can only result in HTML that still meets the requirements for XML well-formedness, also known as XHTML. It's far more common at this point to use some other program, such as PHP, to translate the XML into HTML.

This data flow actually makes sense if substantial amounts of computation need to happen behind the scenes, because you do not want to have a big program both performing complex operations and outputting HTML if you can possibly help it.

PHP can also read in data from a data store and write XML documents itself. This can be helpful when transferring content from one Web site to another, as in syndicating news stories. You can also use this functionality to help non-technical users produce well-formed XML documents with a Web-form front end. At the moment, writing XML might well be the most common category of XML-related PHP task.

Finally, data is beginning to be manipulated and exchanged across human and nonhuman endpoints via the Internet itself. This technology is called *Web services*, and it is the subject of Chapter 41.

Documents and DTDs

As we explained earlier, the requirements for a well-formed XML document are fairly minimal. However, XML documents have another possible level of "goodness," which is called *validity*. A valid XML document is one that conforms to certain stated rules that together are known as a *document type definition (DTD)*.

To get in the mood to understand the value of DTDs, imagine that you are the head of an open source project that exists to make books and other documents freely available in electronic form on the Internet. You're very excited about XML from the moment you learn about it because it seems to meet your need for a data exchange format that can adapt easily to new display technologies as they evolve. Your group members vote to encode all the project's books and documents in XML, and soon the XMLized documents start to pour in.

But when you look at the first couple of submissions, you get a rude shock. One of them is in the same format as Listing 40-1, earlier in this chapter, but one of them looks like what you see in Listing 40-2.

Listing 40-2: **A book in XML format**

```
<?xml version="1.0"?>
<book title="PHP5 Bible">
 <publisher name="Wiley Publishing"/>
 <chapter number="40">
  <chapter_title>PHP and XML</chapter_title>
  <p>
   <sentence>If you know HTML, you're most of the way to
understanding XML.</sentence>
   <sentence>They are both markup languages, but XML is more
structured than HTML.</sentence>
  </p>
 </chapter>
</book>
```

The two XML files express similar, but not identical, hierarchical structures using similar but not identical tags. This is the potential downside of the self-defined markup tags that XML enables: random variation that makes it difficult to match up similar kinds of information across files. You quickly realize that you will need to implement some rules about what kinds of information should be in a book file and what the relationships between these elements will be. You've just realized you need a DTD.

A DTD describes the structure of a class of XML documents. A DTD is a kind of formal constraint, guaranteeing that all documents of its type will conform to stated structural rules and naming conventions. A DTD enables you to specify exactly what elements are *allowed,* how elements are *related,* what *type* each element is, and a *name* for each element. DTDs also specify what attributes are required or optional, and their default values. You could of course just write down these rules in a text file:

```
The top-level object of this document is a BOOK
A BOOK has one and only one TABLE OF CONTENTS
A BOOK has one and only one TITLE
A BOOK is composed of multiple CHAPTERS
CHAPTERS have one and only one CHAPTERTITLE
All CHAPTERTITLEs are listed in the TABLE OF CONTENTS
etc.
```

You could give a copy of the list to anyone who might need it. A DTD is just a more concise, well-defined, generally agreed upon grammar in which to do the same thing. It's a useful discipline to apply to XML documents, which can be chaotic because of their entirely self-defined nature. Furthermore, if you can get a group of people to agree on a DTD, you are well on the way to having a standard format for all information of a certain type. Many professions and industries, from mathematicians to sheet-music publishers to human-resources departments, are eager to develop such domain-specific information formats.

In our previous example, which uses XML to store books electronically, your group members may have to argue for months before hashing out the details of a DTD that perfectly describes the relationships between the table of contents, chapters, titles and headings, indexes, appendices, sections, paragraphs, forwards, epilogues, and so on. You can, of course, iterate on DTDs as frequently as necessary.

But after your DTD is finalized, you can enjoy another value-add of XML. You can now run any XML document through a so-called "validating parser" which will tell you whether it's meeting all the requirements of its DTD. So instead of a human editor having to read each electronic book submission to see whether it has the required elements and attributes in the correct relationship, you can just throw them all into a parser and let it do the formal checking. This won't tell you anything about the quality of the content in the XML document, but it will tell you whether the form meets your requirements.

In order to work with XML in PHP, you need to learn about the basic structure of DTDs and the XML documents they describe whether you choose to validate or not.

The structure of a DTD

A *document type definition* is a set of rules that defines the structure of a particular group of XML documents. A DTD can be either a part of the XML document itself (in which case it is an *internal DTD*), or it can be located externally, in another file on the same server or at a publicly available URL anywhere on the Internet (in which case it is an *external DTD*).

Note Although a DTD can be internal (part of the XML document itself), making it external (a separate file) is usually better. DTDs are meant to define a class of documents, so separating them from the XML saves you from editing every XML document of that class if you need to change the DTD later on. Because demonstrating on an internal DTD is easier for readers to follow in a book format, however, we use both as examples in this chapter.

You can start by looking at a simple XML document with an internal DTD in Listing 40-3.

Listing 40-3: An XML document with internal DTD (recipe.xml)

```
<?xml version="1.0"?>

<!DOCTYPE recipe [
<!ELEMENT recipe (ingredients, directions, servings)>
<!ATTLIST recipe name CDATA #REQUIRED>
<!ELEMENT ingredients (#PCDATA)>
<!ELEMENT directions (#PCDATA)>
<!ELEMENT servings (#PCDATA)>
]>

<recipe name ="Beef Burgundy">
 <ingredients>Beef</ingredients>
 <ingredients>Burgundy</ingredients>
 <directions>
 Add beef to burgundy. Serve.
 </directions>
 <servings>12</servings>
</recipe>
```

We've divided the XML document into three subsections for easier reading. The first section is the standard one-line XML declaration that should begin every XML document. The second section is the internal DTD, marked by lines beginning with the <! sequence. The third section is the XML itself, strictly speaking. For the moment, we are focusing on the second section, the DTD. In our example, the stuff outside the square brackets is a *document type declaration* (not to be confused with *document type definition*): <!DOCTYPE recipe [...]>. The document type declaration gives information about the DTD this document is using. Because this is an internal DTD, we simply give the name of the root element (recipe) and then include the rest of the definition within square brackets. If you are using an external DTD, however, you use the document type declaration to state the type and location of the DTD. Two example document type declarations referring to external DTDs are as follows:

```
<!DOCTYPE recipe SYSTEM "recipe.dtd">
<!DOCTYPE HTML PUBLIC "-//W3C//DTD HTML 4.01 Transitional//EN"
 "http://www.w3.org/TR/html4/loose.dtd">
```

External document type declarations give a root element name, the type (SYSTEM, meaning on the server, or PUBLIC, meaning a standardized DTD) and the location where it can be found. You are doubtless familiar with document type declarations because, without exception, you always include one, like the preceding example, in every single HTML or XHTML document you write — right?

The DTD proper consists of the lines inside the square brackets. These lay out the elements, element types, and attributes contained in the XML document.

✦ **Element:** A start and end tag pair — for example, `<b> something </b>` — or an empty element (`<br/>`). Elements have types and sometimes content and attributes.

✦ **Element Type:** A constraint on the content and attributes of an element. A type can be used to specify what kind of data it can contain and to specify what attributes it can have.

✦ **Attribute:** A name and value pair associated with an element, in the form `<element attributename="attributevalue">`.

In the example DTD in Listing 40-3, we've declared that our root element, `recipe`, contains three child elements — `ingredients`, `directions`, and `servings` — and has one required attribute, `name`. Each child element is of the parsed character data type, and the attribute is of the character data type.

If you wanted to split up Listing 40-3 into an XML document and an external DTD, it would look much the same, except that, instead of providing the definition in square brackets, you would give a reference to the external DTD file. The result would look like Listings 40-4 and 40-5.

Listing 40-4: An XML document with external DTD (recipe_ext.xml)

```
<?xml version="1.0"?>
<!DOCTYPE recipe SYSTEM "recipe.dtd">

<recipe name ="Beef Burgundy">
 <ingredients>Beef</ingredients>
 <ingredients>Burgundy</ingredients>
 <directions>
 Add beef to burgundy. Serve.
 </directions>
 <servings>12</servings>
</recipe>
```

Listing 40-5: An external DTD (recipe.dtd)

```
<!ELEMENT recipe (ingredients, directions, servings)>
<!ATTLIST recipe name CDATA #REQUIRED>
<!ELEMENT ingredients (#PCDATA)>
<!ELEMENT directions (#PCDATA)>
<!ELEMENT servings (#PCDATA)>
```

Because the XML used in both examples conforms to the internal and external DTDs, both documents should be declared valid by a validating parser.

You could learn a lot more about the specifics of DTDs and XML documents, but these basics should enable you to understand most of PHP's XML functions.

Validating and nonvalidating parsers

XML parsers come in two flavors: *validating* and *nonvalidating*. Nonvalidating parsers care only that an XML document is well formed — that it obeys all the rules for closing tags, quotation marks, and so on. Validating parsers require well-formed documents as well, but they also check the XML document against a DTD. If the XML document doesn't conform to its DTD, the validating parser outputs specific error messages explaining what has gone wrong.

PHP5's SAX parser, libxml2, is nonvalidating (as was the expat parser used in PHP4). That doesn't mean that you should ignore DTDs. Going through the process of creating a DTD for each of your document types is a good design practice. It forces you to think out the document structure very carefully. And if your documents ever need to go through a validating parser, you're covered. In fact, many experts recommend that you put all XML documents through a validating parser even if you never plan to use one again.

Most validating parsers are written in Java and are a pain to set up and use. The easiest way to validate your XML is to use an online validator. A well-known one is the STG validator at www.stg.brown.edu/service/xmlvalid.

Actually, using Gnome libxml to validate an XML document is possible — but it takes some work. Examples of validation using C are on the libxml Web site (at www.xmlsoft.org).

SAX versus DOM

There are two common APIs for handling XML and XML documents: the *Document Object Model* (DOM) and the *Simple API for XML* (SAX). PHP5 has one module for each API. PHP5 also includes a new feature, the SimpleXML API. It allows you to quickly convert XML elements into PHP variables, albeit with some limitations. All three modules are now included in all PHP distributions.

You can use the DOM, SAX, or SimpleXML API to parse and change an XML document. To create or extend an XML document entirely through the PHP interface (in other words, without writing any of it by hand), you must use the DOM. Each API has advantages and disadvantages:

✦ **SAX:** SAX is much more lightweight and easier to learn, but it basically treats XML as flowthrough string data. So if, for instance, you want to parse a recipe, you could whip up a SAX parser in PHP, which might enable you to add boldface to the ingredient list. Adding a completely new element or attribute would be very difficult, however; and even changing the value of one particular ingredient would be laborious.

SAX is very good for repetitive tasks that can be applied to all elements of a certain type — for instance, replacing a particular element tag with HTML tags as a step toward transforming XML into HTML for display. The SAX parser passes through a document once from top to bottom — so it cannot "go back" and do things based on inputs later in the document.

✦ **DOM:** PHP's DOM extension reads in an XML file and creates a *walkable* object tree in memory. Starting with a document or an element of a document (called *nodes* in the DOM) you can get or set the children, parents, and text content of each part of the tree. You can save DOM objects to containers as well as write them out as text. DOM XML works best if you have a complete XML document available. If your XML is streaming in very slowly or you want to treat many different XML snippets as sections of the same document, you want to use SAX. Because the DOM extension builds a tree in memory, it can be quite the resource hog with large documents.

✦ **SimpleXML:** The SimpleXML API makes it easy to quickly open an XML file, convert some of the elements found there into native PHP types (variables, objects, and so on) and then operate on those native types as you would normally. The SimpleXML API saves you the hassle of making a lot of the extra calls that the SAX and DOM APIs require, uses far less memory than DOM XML, and often is the simplest way of accessing XML data quickly. There are limitations, though, including some quirky behavior related to attributes and deeply nested elements.

DOM

The Document Object Model is a complete API for creating, editing, and parsing XML documents. The DOM is a recommendation of the World Wide Web Consortium. You can read all about it in the W3's inimitable prose at `www.w3.org/DOM/`.

Basically the idea is that every XML document can be viewed as a hierarchy of nodes resembling leaves on a tree. Starting with the root element, of which all other elements can be expressed as children, any program should be able to build a representation of the structure of a document. Attributes and character data can also be attached to elements. This *tree* can be read into memory from an XML file, manipulated by PHP, and written out to another XML file or stored in a container.

The parser behind the scenes in PHP's DOM extension is *gnome-libxml2* (aka Gnome *libxml2*), which is supposedly less memory-intensive than others. This is available at `www.xmlsoft.org`.

DOM XML is the only entirely object-oriented API in PHP, so some familiarity with object-oriented programming helps when using it. However, there are a limited number of objects and methods, so you do not need any particularly deep knowledge of object-oriented programming to use DOM XML.

Using DOM XML

How you use the DOM will depend on your goals, but these steps are common:

1. Open a new DOM XML document, or read one into memory.

2. Manipulate the document by nodes.

3. Write out the resulting XML into a string or file. This also frees the memory used by the parser.

The simple example in Listing 40-6 shows some basic DOM XML functions in use. Make sure your server has its file permissions set in such a way that the Web server can write a file.

Listing 40-6: **A simple DOM XML example (dom_example.php)**

```php
<?php
$doc = new DomDocument("1.0");
$root = $doc->createElement("HTML");
$root = $doc->appendChild($root);
$body = $doc->createElement("BODY");
```

```
$body = $root->appendChild($body);
$body->setAttribute("bgcolor", "#87CEEB");
$graff = $doc->createElement("P");
$graff = $body->appendChild($graff);
$text = $doc->createTextNode("This is some text.");
$text = $graff->appendChild($text);
$doc->save("test_dom.xml");
?>
```

DOM functions

Table 40-1 lists the most common DOM functions. You must call one of these functions before you can use any of the other DOM XML functions!

Table 40-1: DOM XML Top-Level Function Summary

Function	Behavior
domxml_open_mem(*string*)	Takes a string containing an XML document as an argument. This function parses the document and creates a Document object.
domxml_open_file(*filename*)	Takes a string containing an XML file as an argument. This function parses the file and creates a Document object.
domxml_xmltree(*string*)	Takes a string containing an XML document as an argument. Creates a tree of PHP objects and returns a DOM object. *Note:* The object tree returned by this function is read-only.
domxml_new_doc(*version*)	Creates a new, empty XML document in memory. Returns a Document object.

Table 40-2 lists the most important classes of the DOM API.

Table 40-2: XML DOM Class Summary

Class	Behavior
DomDocument	This class encapsulates an XML document. It contains the root element and a DTD if any.
DomNode	Encapsulates a node, aka an element. A node can be the root element or any element within it. Nodes can contain other nodes, character data, and attributes.
DomAttr	This class encapsulates a node attribute. An *attribute* is a user-defined quality of the node.

Table 40-3 lists the most important methods of the DomDocument class.

Table 40-3: DomDocument Class Summary

Method	Behavior
createElement(*name*)	Creates a new element whose tag is the passed string. You must append this element to another element using DomNode->appendChild().
createTextNode(*character_data*)	Creates a new text node (DomText object). You must append this node to another node using DomNode->appendChild().
save(*filename*)	Dumps XML from memory to a designated file.
saveXML([*node*])	Dumps XML from memory to a string. Optional parameter is a DomNode object.

Table 40-4 lists the most important methods of the DomNode class.

Table 40-4: DomNode Class Summary

Method	Behavior
appendChild(*newnode*)	Attaches a node to another node.
removeChild(*child*)	Removes the child node.

Table 40-5 lists the most important methods of the DomAttr class.

Table 40-5: DomAttr Class Summary

Method	Behavior
name()	Returns an attribute name.
value()	Returns the value of an attribute.

SAX

The Simple API for XML is widely used to parse XML documents. It is an event-based API, which means that the parser calls designated functions after it recognizes a certain trigger in the event stream.

SAX has an interesting history, especially in contrast to the DOM. The SAX API is not shepherded by an official standardizing body. Instead, it was hammered out by a group of programmers on the XML-DEV mailing list, many of whom had already implemented their own XML parsers (in Java first!) without a standard API. You can learn more at the Web sites of SAX team members, such as www.saxproject.org.

SAX works from a number of *event hooks* supplied by you via PHP. As the parser goes through an XML document, it recognizes pieces of XML such as elements, character data, and external entities. Each of these is an event. If you have supplied the parser with a function to call for the particular kind of event, it pauses to call your function after it reaches that event. The parsed data associated with an event is made available to the called function. After the event-handling function finishes, the SAX parser continues through the document, calling functions on events, until it reaches the end. This process is unidirectional from beginning to end of the document — the parser cannot back up or loop.

A very simple example is an event hook that directs PHP to recognize the XML element <paragraph></paragraph> and substitute the HTML tags <p></p> around the character data. If you wrote this event hook, you could not specify a particular paragraph — instead, the function is called for every instance of this event.

The parser behind the scenes in the PHP SAX extension is libxml2, which you can read about on its project site at www.xmlsoft.org.

Prior to version 5, PHP used James Clark's expat, a widely used XML parser toolkit. More information about expat can be found on Clark's Web site at www.jclark.com/xml/. If you compile with libxml2, you should be able to use all your PHP4 SAX code in PHP5 without problems.

Caution   Unfortunately, the term *parser* can refer either to a software library such as libxml2, or to a block of XML-handling functions in PHP. Verbs such as *create* and *call* indicate the latter, more specific meaning. Any PHP XML function that uses the term *parser* also refers to the latter meaning.

Using SAX

How you use the SAX will depend on your goals, but these steps are common:

1. Determine what kinds of events you want to handle.

2. Write handler functions for each event. You almost certainly want to write a character data handler, plus start element and end element handlers.

3. Create a parser by using xml_parser_create() and then call it by using xml_parse().

4. Free the memory used up by the parser by using xml_parser_free().

The simple example in Listing 40-7 shows all the basic XML functions in use.

Listing 40-7: A simple XML parser (simpleparser.php)

```php
<?php
$file = "recipe.xml";

// Call this at the beginning of every element
function startElement($parser, $name, $attrs) {
    print "<B>$name =></B>  ";
}

// Call this at the end of every element
function endElement($parser, $name) {
    print "\n";
}

// Call this whenever there is character data
function characterData($parser, $value) {
    print "$value<BR>";
}

// Define the parser
$simpleparser = xml_parser_create();
xml_set_element_handler($simpleparser, "startElement",
"endElement");
xml_set_character_data_handler($simpleparser, "characterData");

// Open the XML file for reading
if (!($fp = fopen($file, "r"))) {
  die("could not open XML input");
}

// Parse it
while ($data = fread($fp, filesize($file))) {
if (!xml_parse($simpleparser, $data, feof($fp))) {
  die(xml_error_string(xml_get_error_code($simpleparser)));
  }
}

// Free memory
xml_parser_free($simpleparser);
?>
```

SAX options

The XML parser in the SAX API has two configurable options: one for case folding and the other for target encoding.

Case folding is the residue of a series of past decisions and may not be relevant now that XML has been definitely declared case sensitive. Early versions of SGML and HTML were not case sensitive and, therefore, employed case folding (making all characters uppercase or lowercase during parsing) as a means of getting a uniform result to compare. This is how your browser knew to match up a `<P>` tag with a `</p>` tag. Case folding fell out of favor due to problems with internationalization, so after much debate XML was declared case sensitive. When case folding is enabled, node names passed to event handlers are turned into all uppercase characters. A node named `mynode` would be received as MYNODE. When case folding is disabled, a `<paragraph>` tag will not match a `</PARAGRAPH>` closing tag.

> **Note**
> Case folding is enabled by default, which violates the XML 1.0 specification. Unless you disable it by using `xml_parser_set_option()` as explained in a moment, your event handlers receive tags in uppercase letters.

Event handlers receive text data from the XML parser in one of three encodings: *ISO-8859-1*, *US-ASCII*, or *UTF-8*. The default is ISO-8859-1. The encoding of text passed to event handlers is known as the *target encoding*. This is by default the same encoding as in the source document, which is known as the *source encoding*. You can change the target encoding if you need to process the text in an encoding other than the encoding it was stored in.

Encoding options are retrieved and set with the functions `xml_parser_get_option()` and `xml_parser_set_option()`. Case folding is controlled by using the constant `XML_OPTION_CASE_FOLDING`, and target encoding by using the constant `XML_OPTION_TARGET_ENCODING`.

PHP and Internationalization

Computer programs store letters as integers, which they convert back to letters according to *encodings*. Early programs used English, which conveniently needs only one byte (actually only seven bits) to represent all the common letters and symbols. This encoding standard was promulgated in 1968 as ASCII (*American Standard Code for Information Interchange*).

However, programmers soon found that English has an unusually small number of characters, and thus the only languages that can be expressed with any completeness in ASCII are Hawaiian, Kiswahili, Latin, and American English. Ever since then, programmers concerned with internationalization have tried to promote encoding standards that promise to assign a unique integer to every one of the letters of every one of the world's alphabetical languages. The result of this effort is referred to as *Unicode*.

The three encodings supported by PHP's XML extension are *ISO-8859-1*, *US-ASCII*, and *UTF-8*. US-ASCII is the simplest of these, a slight renaming of the original 7-bit ASCII set. *ISO-8859-1* is also known as the Latin1, Western, or Western European encoding. It can represent almost all western European languages adequately. *UTF-8* allows the use of up to 4 bytes to represent as many of the world's languages as possible. If your XML document is written in Han-gul or Zulu, you have no choice but to use UTF-8.

In the following example, we create an XML parser that reads in data as ASCII, turns off case folding, and spits out the output as UTF-8.

```
$new_parser = xml_parser_create('US-ASCII');
$case_folding = xml_parser_get_option(XML_OPTION_CASE_FOLDING);
echo $case_folding;
$change_folding = xml_parser_set_option($new_parser,
XML_OPTION_CASE_FOLDING,0);

$target_encoding = xml_parser_get_option(XML_TARGET_ENCODING);
echo $target_encoding;
$change_encoding = xml_parser_set_option($new_parser,
XML_OPTION_TARGET_ENCODING, 'UTF-8');
```

SAX functions

Table 40-6 lists the most important SAX functions, with descriptions of what they do.

Table 40-6: XML SAX Function Summary

Function	Behavior
xml_parser_create([encoding])	This function creates a new XML parser instance. You may have several distinct parsers at any time. The return value is an XML parser or false on failure. Takes one optional argument, a character-encoding identifier (such as UTF-8). If no encoding is supplied, ISO-8859-1 is assumed.
xml_parser_free(parser)	Frees the memory associated with a parser created by xml_parser_create().
xml_parse(parser, data[, final])	This function starts the XML parser. Its arguments are a parser created by using xml_parser_create(), a string containing XML, and an optional finality flag. The finality flag indicates that this is the last piece of data handled by this parser.
xml_get_error_code(parser)	If the parser has encountered a problem, its parse fails. Call this function to find out the error code.
xml_error_string(errorcode)	Given an error code returned by xml_get_error_code(), it returns a string containing a description of the error suitable for logging.
xml_set_element_handler(parser, start_element_handler, end_element_handler)	This function actually sets two handlers, which are simply functions. The first is a start-of-element handler, which has access to the name of the element and an associative array of its elements. The second is an end-of-element handler, at which time the element is fully parsed.

Function	Behavior
xml_set_character_data_handler (*parser, cd_handler*)	Sets the handler function to call whenever character data is encountered. The handler function takes a string containing the character data as an argument.
xml_set_default_handler (*parser, handler*)	Sets the default handler. If no handler is specified for an event, the default handler is called if it is specified. Takes as arguments the parser and a string containing unhandled data, such as a notation declaration or an external entity reference.

SimpleXML API

The SimpleXML API is new in PHP5. Characterized as an object-mapping API, SimpleXML dispenses with Web standards and absolute flexibility in favor of simplicity and modest memory usage. If you just need to read some data from an XML document and write some other data back in, the SimpleXML likely will require the fewest lines of code of all possible approaches to the problem.

Here's the idea behind SimpleXML: As in the DOM approach, SimpleXML parses an XML document and holds the whole thing in memory. However, rather than hold the document as a DOM object (which you must further manipulate before you can use its contents), its elements are stored as native PHP variables and so are immediately useable. Because many DOM tasks do not actually require you to traverse all the children and parents of a document, but rather perform repetitive tasks on well-defined nodes, SimpleXML ultimately constitutes a PHP-specific compromise between the SAX and DOM approaches.

Using SimpleXML

When using SimpleXML, you read a passage of XML text — either a string or a file — into a variable with the function simplexml_load_string() or simplexml_load_file(). You then have a local object you can refer to directly. Listing 40-8 shows how the SimpleXML API can be used to get variable values out of an XML file with just a few lines of code.

Listing 40-8 demonstrates a typical use of SimpleXML.

Listing 40-8: **SimpleXML sample (simplexml.php)**

```php
<?php

$recipe = simplexml_load_file("recipe.xml");

$ingredients = $recipe->ingredients;
$directions  = $recipe->directions;
$servings    = $recipe->servings;
```

Continued

> **Listing 40-8** *(continued)*

```
foreach ($ingredients as $ingredient)
{
print "<P>Ingredient: $ingredient";
}

print "<P>Directions: $directions";
print "<P>Serves $servings";

?>
```

SimpleXML functions

Table 40-7 lists the most important SimpleXML functions, with descriptions of what they do.

Table 40-7: SimpleXML Function Summary

`simplexml_load_file(file)`	Import and parse a file.
`simplexml_load_string(string)`	Import and parse a string.
`simplexml_import_dom(DomDocument)`	This function allows you to convert a DomDocument object into a SimpleXML object, and then treated just like an imported XML file or string.

A Sample XML Application

This series of scripts will write out XML to a file by using data from an HTML form, and then will allow you to edit the values in that file.

Listing 40-9 is an HTML form that can be used by nontechnical users to define forms. (They don't care that this data will be formatted and stored in XML.) Listing 40-10 is a script to write out the XML file.

> **Listing 40-9: A form to collect values for an XML file (pollform.php)**

```
<HTML>
<HEAD>
<TITLE>Make-a-poll</TITLE>
</HEAD>

<BODY>
<CENTER><H3>Make-a-poll</H3></CENTER>
```

```
<P>Use this form to define a poll:</P>
<FORM METHOD="post" ACTION="writepoll.php">

<P>Give this poll a <B>short</B> name, like <FONT COLOR="red">Color
Poll</FONT>.<BR>
<INPUT TYPE=TEXT NAME="PollName" SIZE=30>
</P>

<P>This poll should <B>begin</B> on this date (MM/DD/YYYY):
<INPUT TYPE=TEXT Name="Poll_Startdate" SIZE=10>
</P>

<P>This poll should <B>end</B> on this date (MM/DD/YYYY):
<INPUT TYPE=TEXT NAME="Poll_Enddate" SIZE=10>
</P>

<P>This is the poll question (<FONT COLOR="blue">e.g. Why did the
chicken cross the road?</FONT>):
<INPUT TYPE=TEXT NAME="Poll_Question", size=100>
</P>

<P>These are the potential answer choices you want to offer (<FONT
COLOR="darkgreen">e.g. Yes, No, Say what?</FONT>).  Fill in only as
many as you need.  Keep in mind that brevity is the soul of good poll-
making.<BR>
<INPUT TYPE=TEXT NAME="Raw_Poll_Option[]" SIZE=25><BR>
<INPUT TYPE=TEXT NAME="Raw_Poll_Option[]" SIZE=25><BR>
<INPUT TYPE=TEXT NAME="Raw_Poll_Option[]" SIZE=25><BR>
<INPUT TYPE=TEXT NAME="Raw_Poll_Option[]" SIZE=25><BR>
<INPUT TYPE=TEXT NAME="Raw_Poll_Option[]" SIZE=25><BR>
<INPUT TYPE=TEXT NAME="Raw_Poll_Option[]" SIZE=25><BR>
</P>

<INPUT TYPE="submit" NAME="Submit" VALUE="Add a poll">
</FORM>

</BODY>
</HTML>
```

Listing 40-10: A script to write out an XML file (writepoll.php)

```
<html>
<head>
<title>Write an XML file</title>
</head>

<body>
<?php
```

Continued

Listing 40-10 *(continued)*

```php
$pollfile = "poll.xml";

echo $_POST['Raw_Poll_Option'][1];


// Reading in the xml file as a string
$fd = fopen($pollfile, "r") or die("Can't open file.");
$fstr = fread($fd, filesize($pollfile)) or die("Can't read file, check
permissions.");
fclose($fd);

// Format response sets.
$PollName = str_replace("\'", "", $_POST["PollName"]);
$PollName = str_replace(" ", "_", $_POST["PollName"]);

$RespSet = "";

for ($r=0; $r<=5; $r++) {
    $currentRawPollOption = $_POST["Raw_Poll_Option"][$r];
  if (!empty($_POST["Raw_Poll_Option"][$r])) {
      $Poll_Option[$r] = "$_POST[PollName]-".str_replace("'", "",
$currentRawPollOption);
    $Poll_Option[$r] = "$_POST[PollName]-".str_replace(" ", "_",
$currentRawPollOption);
    $currentPollOption = $Poll_Option[$r];

    $RespSet .= "\t<response
id=\"$currentPollOption\">$currentRawPollOption</response>\n";
  }


}

//Add new poll data
$separator = "</PollList>";
$divide = explode($separator, $fstr);
$glue =
"\t<Poll name=\"$_POST[PollName]\"/>
</PollList>

<Poll id=\"$_POST[PollName]\">
\t<StartDate>$_POST[Poll Startdate]</StartDate>
\t<EndDate>$_POST[Poll_Enddate]</EndDate>
\t<name>$_POST[PollName]</name>
\t<text>$_POST[Poll_Question]</text>
\t<display type=\"Bar-Graph\"/>
\t<responseSet resource=\"$PollName-responseSet\"/>
</Poll>
```

```
<responseSet id=\"$PollName-responseSet\">
$RespSet</responseSet>
";


$newxml = implode($glue, $divide);

//Write to file
$fd = fopen($pollfile, "w") or die("Can't open file for writing; check
file permissions");
$writestr = fwrite($fd, $newxml);

//Message
echo "Wrote $writestr chars to $pollfile.";
?>

</body>
</html>
```

Listing 40-11 shows the XML file where our polls are stored, with one poll already defined for you. If you add a new poll, it will be appended near the top of this file, and its name will be added to the PollList.

Listing 40-11: **An XML file (poll.xml)**

```
<?xml version="1.0"?>
<PollDefs>
<Poll id="Best_Text_Editor">
  <StartDate>01/01/200333</StartDate>
  <EndDate>01/31/2004</EndDate>
  <question>Which is the best programmer's editor?</question>
  <display type="Bar-Graph"/>
  <responseSet>
    <response id="Best_Text_Editor-emacs">emacs</response>
    <response id="Best_Text_Editor-vim">vim</response>
    <response id="Best_Text_Editor-notepad">notepad</response>
    <response id="Best_Text_Editor-kate">kate</response>
    <response resource="Best_Text_Editor-BBEdit">BBEdit</response>
  </responseSet>
</Poll>

<Poll id="Best_Pointer_Device">
  <StartDate>02/01/2004</StartDate>
  <EndDate>02/29/2004</EndDate>
  <question>Which is the best pointer device?</question>
  <display type="Bar-Graph"/>
  <responseSet>
```

Continued

Listing 40-11 *(continued)*

```
    <response id="Best_Pointer-mouse">Mouse</response>
    <response id="Best_Pointer-trackball">Trackball</response>
    <response id="Best_Pointer-touchpad">Touchpad</response>
    <response id="Best_Pointer-trackpoint">TrackPoint</response>
    <response id="Best_Pointer-pen">Pen</response>
    <response id="Best_Pointer-stylus">Stylus</response>
  </responseSet>
</Poll>

</PollDefs>
```

Listing 40-12 shows a script that will allow you to edit the XML file in Listing 40-10 using DOM XML.

Listing 40-12: XML editor (dom_polledit.php)

```php
<html>
<head>
<title>Poll XML editor</title>
</head>

<body>
<?php

$doc = new DomDocument();
$pollfile = "poll.xml";


// Handle form submission
if ($_POST['stage'] == 1) {
  // Reading in the XML file as a DOM object
  if (!$doc->load($pollfile)) {
    echo "Cannot read XML file.";
    exit;
  }

  // Once a poll is created, the user will only be able to
  // change the StartDate, EndDate, Question, and response values.

  // Format the data
  $pollname = $_POST['poll_name'];
  $startdate = $_POST['Poll_Startdate'];
  $enddate = $_POST['Poll_Enddate'];
  $question = $_POST['Poll_Question'];

  // Replace the values as text nodes
  $poll_list = $doc->getElementsByTagname("Poll");
  foreach ($poll_list as $poll_obj) {
```

```
    // Figure out which poll we're editing, then work on its children
    $pollname_value = $poll_obj->getAttribute("id");
    if ($pollname_value == $pollname) {
      $children = $poll_obj->childNodes;
      foreach ($children as $child_obj) {
        $node_name = $child_obj->nodeName;
        $value = $child_obj->nodeValue;
        if ($node_name == "StartDate") {
          if ($value == $startdate) {
            // Do nothing
          } else {
            $sd_textnode = $child_obj->firstChild;
            $new_startdate = $doc->createTextNode($startdate);
            $child_obj->replaceChild($new_startdate, $sd_textnode);
          }
        }
        if ($node_name == "EndDate") {
          if ($value == $enddate) {
            // Do nothing
          } else {
            $ed_textnode = $child_obj->firstChild;
            $new_enddate = $doc->createTextNode($enddate);
            $child_obj->replaceChild($new_enddate, $ed_textnode);
          }
        }
        if ($node_name == "question") {
          if ($value == $enddate) {
            // Do nothing
          } else {
            $q_textnode = $child_obj->firstChild;
            $new_question = $doc->createTextNode($question);
            $child_obj->replaceChild($new_question, $q_textnode);
          }
        }
        if ($node_name == "responseSet") {
          $old_responses = $child_obj->childNodes;
          $i=0;
          foreach ($old_responses as $delete_responses) {
            if ($delete_responses->nodeName == 'response') {
              $r_textnode = $delete_responses->firstChild;
              $new_response = $doc-
>createTextNode($_POST['response'][$i]);
              $delete_responses->replaceChild($new_response,
$r_textnode);
              $i++;
            }
          }
        }
      }
    }
  }
```

Continued

Listing 40-12 *(continued)*

```
  // Write out the file
  $doc->save($pollfile);


}

// This stuff happens every time, whether a submission
// has occurred or not.

// Reading in the XML file as a DOM object
// Must read fresh every time
if (!$doc->load($pollfile)) {
  echo "Cannot read XML file.";
  exit;
}

// Get a list of the polls in this XML document
// and then pull out the start date, end date,
// poll question, and possible responses.
$poll_list = $doc->getElementsByTagname('Poll');
foreach ($poll_list as $poll_obj) {
  $id = $poll_obj->getAttribute("id");
  $children = $poll_obj->childNodes;
  foreach ($children as $key=>$child_obj) {
    $node_name = $child_obj->nodeName;
    if ($node_name != "#text" && $node_name != 'responseSet') {
      $content_str = $child_obj->nodeValue;
      $poll_array["$node_name"] = $content_str;
    } elseif ($node_name == 'responseSet') {
      // Get the responses
      $responselist = $child_obj->childNodes;
      foreach ($responselist as $responses) {
        $response_name = $responses->nodeName;
        if ($response_name != "#text") {
          $response_array[] = $responses->nodeValue;
        }
      }
    }
  }
}

  // Arrange all the data nicely
  $poll_startdate = $poll_array['StartDate'];
  $poll_enddate = $poll_array['EndDate'];
  $poll_name = $poll_array['name'];
  $poll_question = $poll_array['question'];
  $poll_question = stripslashes($poll_question);
  foreach ($response_array as $key=>$val) {
    $resp_str .= "Option:  <INPUT TYPE=\"text\" SIZE=25
NAME=\"response[$key]\" VALUE=\"$val\"><BR>\n";
  }
```

```
   // Display form with old values
   $php_self = $_SERVER['PHP_SELF'];
$form = <<< EOFORM
<FORM METHOD="post" ACTION="$php_self">
Start Date:  <INPUT TYPE="text" SIZE=10 NAME="Poll_Startdate"
VALUE="$poll_startdate"><BR>
End date:  <INPUT TYPE="text" SIZE=10 NAME="Poll_Enddate"
VALUE="$poll_enddate"><BR>
Poll question:  <INPUT TYPE="text" SIZE=100 NAME="Poll_Question"
VALUE="$poll_question"><BR>
$resp_str
<INPUT TYPE="hidden" NAME="poll_name" VALUE="$id">
<INPUT TYPE="hidden" NAME="stage" VALUE=1><BR>
<INPUT TYPE="submit" VALUE="Presto-chango">
</FORM>


EOFORM;
  echo $form;
  unset($resp_str);
  unset($response_array);
}
?>

</body>
</html>
```

Gotchas and Troubleshooting

The DOM and SAX parsers will only parse a well-formed XML document. If the parser rejects your XML, make sure it is well formed. If it looks good to your eye, run it through a different validating parser or an online XML checker, such as the one at http://www.xml.com/xml/pub/tools/ruwf/check.html.

If you cannot read and write XML documents to disk, check that the Web server process has permission to do so.

If the DOM API returns a fatal *function not found* error, the DOM XML module may not be installed. Use the phpinfo() function to check for a domxml entry. If it isn't there, you will have to recompile PHP with the DOM XML module (on Unix) or uncomment the php_domxml.dll line in php.ini (on Windows).

The DOM API underwent a major revision in PHP5 (and was altogether new in PHP4), so all the kinks may not be worked out yet. Keep this in mind and check the bugs database (http://bugs.php.net/) if you encounter problems.

Remember that you're supposed to make a strenuous effort to search the mailing-list archives before you search the bugs database. Please make sure that your problem is really a bug and has not been resolved before filing it as a bug. If any doubt is in your mind, read the "How to Report a Bug" document attached to the bugs database.

Summary

XML is an application-independent data-exchange format that promises to make Web development faster and easier in the future. XML and HTML are both descended from SGML, accounting for their close resemblance at first glance. Both have tags (more correctly called elements) and attributes, although XML's are self-defined and structured whereas HTML's are defined by the HTML standard and contain no information about document structure.

XML has only a few minimal requirements for well-formedness. These include closed elements, no overlapping elements, escaped special characters, and the presence of a single root element for each document. XML can also be valid, however, in the sense of conforming to a formal declaration of its structure in a document type definition or DTD. DTDs can be internal or external to the XML document and even located on another server. They contain declarations of the types, attributes, and names of the various elements within the XML file.

For the present, few prefabricated tools are available to help you write, edit, and display XML. You can use one of the three PHP XML APIs — SAX, DOM, and SimpleXML — to write your own tools. The APIs have different tradeoffs and uses. SAX is an event-based parser, whereas DOM XML creates an object tree in memory. SimpleXML is easy to use and requires little code, but is relatively limited in its capability. It's mainly useful for quick reads of simple XML files.

At the moment, PHP with the SAX extension can be used to write out well-formed XML from values entered into a Web form, and to edit XML documents. DOM XML can be used to create complete XML documents programmatically. The SAX parser is also commonly employed to transform XML into HTML for less problematic display in current Web browsers. Another possible task for PHP's XML extensions is to pull data from a data store and write it out as XML for exchange with another organization.

✦   ✦   ✦

Web Services

Web services is an emerging field of programming that seeks to apply the benefits of the Web to bigger problems than merely displaying data in a browser. PHP, which has already proven itself as a core *glue* component of the Web, has the opportunity to grab even more market share in the Web services arena. As is true of other hot technologies such as XML, however, a world of hype surrounds Web services. Here we try to cut through the buzzwords and analyst predictions to look at what Web services means to the average PHP developer.

The End of Programming as We Know It

The title of this section is a bit of a joke—one of us works in the Web services field and often hears presentations that assert things such as: "In 10 years, we will have no more need for programmers, because Web services will eliminate duplication of effort." Many people have thought that programming was about to die out, and all of them have been wrong so far—but hope springs eternal in the pundit's breast. Notching down the hyperbole to manageable levels, we can say that Web services could make some common but hard tasks in commercial computer programming a lot easier.

The ugly truth about data munging

Joking aside, Web services do solve some problems—at the moment largely in the realm of moving data around. Later in this chapter, for example, we offer code for a client to the Amazon REST service. This code enables you to grab the latest data about a given product or group of products—photos, current prices, availability, and so on—up to once per second via an automatic process.

If you're a first-time author who has a small informational site with one link to Amazon, this isn't really going to help you much. But there are Amazon Associates who link to thousands or even millions of products. They did so until recently by horrible hacks involving downloading all those Web pages and using some kind of string or XPATH parsing to pick out the three or four pieces of data they wanted from each page. Furthermore, each client organization did all this work for itself—because, among other things, this is a totally unauthorized use of Amazon's copyrighted material, so they can hardly expect Amazon to help them. Harvesting data from full HTML pages is tremendously wasteful and expensive for both Amazon and the Associate—so much so that it's a good way to get banned from Amazon altogether. Slamming the door on requests from a particular IP block is almost the only way to control access to a public Web server.

Even if an organization wants to give you large amounts of information in a data feed, the mechanics right now are not very elegant. We are aware of many large and well-respected data-related businesses that move data around in text files (or spreadsheets) that are downloaded via some mechanism such as FTP (or e-mail) and parsed on both ends by custom Perl code (or by hand). Often, there is no way to send only data that has changed—the feeds are dumped out and processed in a dumb way every so often, rather than updating only if and when changes occur. Obviously, these are all batch processes, which have no possibility of working in real-time. XML-based Web services promise to offer a common language, a common transport mechanism, a common authentication and authorization method, and potentially common code for organizations to access each other's data.

If Web services were just about moving data around, the idea would be extremely useful but not at all sexy. What excites everyone about Web services is the promise that it can help solve the hardest problems of distributed computing once and for all.

Brutal simplicity

Think back, if you can, to the bad old days before the Web. If you can go back far enough, think back to the days when the Internet itself was a rarity and networking something limited to high-end universities (it may help to remember that for a long time one of Apple's selling points in college computer labs was AppleTalk).

Back in those dark days, my children, things such as operating systems and programming languages were major barriers to integration—they were little islands in the sea of incompatibility. If you were going to write an application, you were specifically writing it for a particular platform and language—sometimes even for a particular version of a compiler. It was very, very hard to make one program talk to another program. If you wrote a COBOL program on a VAX, that was where it was going to stay. With a great deal of effort you could get one program to send something simple, such as ASCII data, to another—but any little thing could mess up your interapp communication. If you changed anything on one side, it might mean that you had to change a bunch of stuff on the other side, too. These programs were said to be *tightly coupled*.

This meant a lot of duplication of effort. Porting was technically difficult, and the market was fragmented. So a team that wrote an application—say, an accounting program— for Minicomputer X was not necessarily going to have the resources to do the same for Microcomputer Y. Lots of teams wrote lots of accounting programs, and all the formats were proprietary. None of them could exchange data with each other, much less share tasks easily.

Slowly, mankind groped toward a way to make programs talk to each other. The blanket term for this activity was *distributed computing*. It took until the mid-1990s for these methods to reach the common programmer, in the form of standards such as DCOM, CORBA, and Java RMI. These standards enabled all programs that shared a common architecture to call each other's methods and send data back and forth. When you are able to embed a spreadsheet inside a word processor document, it's via the magic of DCOM.

These common object models, however, had three major problems. They were still more or less tied to particular platforms or programming languages; they were considered difficult to learn, and they reached general usability at the same moment that the Web arrived to tantalize us with the possibility of Internet-scale loosely coupled, distributed computing based on open standards.

The Web is the biggest, most open, most loosely coupled — and most successful — distributed architecture of all time. With few exceptions, no Web server cares which Web browser is asking it for a page, or what operating system that browser is running on, or what chip is running the hardware on which that operating system lives. The application asking for the page doesn't even need to be a browser — it may be a spider from a search engine, it may be an `fopen()` call from a PHP command-line script, or it may be a cellular phone. The HTML it sends may not render nicely on every device, but that has nothing to do with whether Apache or IIS is serving up the page.

There are a lot of reasons why the World Wide Web has taken off as it has, but one of them is certainly a factor that computer scientists semi-affectionately refer to as "worse is better." This philosophy, which exists in contrast to the lofty perfectionism of "the right thing," means that in many circumstances it is the very junkiness of a thing that leads to its success. Certainly if all HTML had been forced to meet the standards of well-formedness that some Web pundits now want to impose, the Web would still be the province of a few physicists trying to distribute their academic papers via plain gray home pages. On a more fundamental level, HTTP and other Internet protocols grew on the back of TCP/IP — which itself is a notoriously "worse is better" design. TCP/IP never guarantees you an entire message in a timely manner. It tries really hard to make that happen, via methods such as replication — but we're just going to say that one of us once got an e-mail two and a half years after it was sent.

Applying the lessons of the Web to applications, you come up with something quite a lot like Web services. The beauty of Web services is its brutal simplicity, which squashes everything down to a lowest common denominator. A Web-services architecture doesn't care about the benefits of any particular platform, and it doesn't care about the pitfalls. Those are your problems. All that matters to the outside world is that a program can send and receive text messages across HTTP or SMTP and that these text messages can trigger computational actions.

An archetypal Web service would be something like a Japanese-to-English translation service. It lives somewhere on the Internet, on some unknown platform, and is written in some unknown programming language. You don't need to know or care about that stuff. All you care about is that your browser or your mail client knows that you only read English — so every time you get a Web page or an e-mail in Japanese, these applications automatically send their contents to this translation service and then display the translated results to you. You don't ever see or care that part of the processing is happening at some remote location — to you, the end user, it just looks as though your application is handling it seamlessly. Instead of your Web browser using Babelfish to translate Japanese to English, and your mail client having a little built-in dictionary, and your local department store's inventory management system using a third-party program that runs only on Solaris — all of them can just call this translation Web service.

Web services should also enable much easier integration. Say that you work for a university alumni office that is still using an alumni database written in COBOL on a VAX. (You may laugh, but Y2K wouldn't have been such a big deal if there weren't so many legacy systems lying around.) It works perfectly well, and you don't have budget to replace it — but those VAX terminals are getting old. It would sure be great if you could query your alumni database via an ordinary Web browser — but there's no way you're ever going to be able to squeeze a full Web server onto that old VAX, even if someone wrote one. With Web services, if you can get the VAX to understand just a little bit of XML and spit out its data as XML, you're all set. You can exchange instructions and data via XML by using some other machine that does have a Web server, and that other machine can communicate with the rest of the world. Someday when you are ready to replace that VAX with a newer machine and a different programming language, no one need ever know. As long as the service is reachable at the same address by using the same method invocations, it doesn't matter whether it's a VAX or a PC, whether the application was written in COBOL or whether it's just a thin shell of PHP on top of a database.

Integration between businesses particularly benefits the smaller parties involved. Web services are easy to implement because corporate firewalls already have holes punched through them for HTTP and SMTP and because they can be implemented by using inexpensive software such as PHP. Say that you run a small business that makes widgets. You want your widgets distributed by a large retailer, Humongous Widget Depot. Until recently, for you (and the gazillions of other manufacturers who supply goods to Humongous Widget Depot) to provide real-time inventory information to the retailer entailed tremendous expense as you bought a large software package such as SAP and integrated it on a private network. Now, in theory, each small manufacturer can merely expose its inventory information via a Web service, and Humongous Widget Depot's humongous IT department merely points a Web services client at them.

That, in a nutshell, is the dream and the promise of Web services. We are quite a way from the actuality, but the outlines of a solution are firming up.

REST, XML-RPC, SOAP, .NET

For Web services to work, every application and many servers need to speak a common language. Everyone agrees that the common language is XML, but there are some philosophical differences about the implementation details. The three main Web services standards are *REST*, *XML-RPC*, and *SOAP*. One of the biggest backers of SOAP is Microsoft, which uses that standard heavily in its .NET services architecture.

REST

REST is an acronym for *RE*presentational *State Transfer*. The concept is based on a dissertation by Roy Fielding, and its main point is that we already have everything we need to implement Web services — in HTTP itself. So all REST services must be reachable by normal URIs using the HTTP GET method, and they return XML without any special coded wrapping. For all intents and purposes, a REST service is just an XML page on the Web, although usually not one that is intended to be read by a human being using a browser.

 Caution   Universal addressability is a big part of the REST style, so Web services that return data in response to an HTTP POST are not technically REST-ful. eBay's developer program has maintained a service like this for some time now, although by press time they may have switched to a SOAP service.

REST is particularly valuable for content-focused services. You can build an XML document on the fly, and your users can access it reliably as a URI. In theory, REST should also be easier for lightly technical users to deal with. On the other hand, REST doesn't have built-in support for complex types — because there's no shared *vocabulary*, there's no particular way to designate an array versus a string.

You can learn more about REST at the RESTWiki:

    http://internet.conveyor.com/RESTwiki/moin.cgi/FrontPage

and at the Web site of Paul Prescod, REST's most tireless promoter:

    www.prescod.net

XML-RPC

XML-RPC refers to a spec for making remote procedure calls over HTTP by using XML encoding. An XML-RPC server takes an input that consists of a simple XML encoding of a method call sent as an HTTP POST. An example is as follows:

```
POST /xmlrpc-epi/xmlrpc-php-epi/sample/server.php HTTP/1.0
User-Agent: xmlrpc-epi-php/0.2 (PHP)
Host: localhost:80
Content-Type: text/xml
Content-Length: 191

<?xml version='1.0' encoding='iso-8859-1' ?>
<methodCall>
<methodName>greeting</methodName>
<params>
  <param>
    <value>
      <string>World</string>
    </value>
  </param>
</params>
</methodCall>
```

Assume that greeting() is a function that takes a string input and returns a string output consisting of the string "Hello, " prepended to the input string. It returns a response that is formatted in a similar way. An example is the following:

```
<?xml version='1.0' encoding='iso-8859-1' ?>
<methodResponse>
<params>
  <param>
    <value>
      <array>
        <data>
          <value>
            <string>Hello, World</string>
          </value>
        </data>
      </array>
    </value>
  </param>
</params>
</methodCall>
```

Notice that unlike REST, you are not simply asking for data back—you are calling a specific function on another machine using specified types. This particular function happens to simply return data, but that is entirely arbitrary—any method the server owner is willing to expose as a Web service is fair game. Also unlike REST, XML-RPC supports all PHP native types, except objects and resources, and also a few that PHP doesn't have (structs, date-time, base-64 binary).

XML-RPC can be seen as a compromise between the complexity of SOAP and the simplicity of REST. It is so similar to SOAP, however, that it may simply be absorbed wholesale into the more vendor-friendly concept. As you will see, the PHP XML-RPC server can also deliver SOAP responses.

Learn more about XML-RPC at `www.xmlrpc.org`.

SOAP

SOAP may or may not stand for Simple Object Access Protocol — some members of the committee dispute this — but so many people have said it now that it's become true through usage. SOAP is a proposal of the W3C, written by a committee that is largely controlled by Big Software — of the eight principal authors, four are from Microsoft, one is from Lotus, one from IBM, and two represent everyone else. This is the upside and the downside of SOAP: Adoption by other software makers has been swift since Microsoft and IBM threw their support behind SOAP, but there is the constant threat of an open standard being turned into a mechanism for vendor lock-in.

SOAP, as does XML-RPC, sends messages in XML wrappers with a fairly strict vocabulary that makes extensive use of namespaces. A very simple SOAP request may look like the following sample:

```
POST /xmlrpc-epi/xmlrpc-php-epi/sample/server.php HTTP/1.0
User-Agent: xmlrpc-epi-php/0.2 (PHP)
Host: localhost:80
Content-Type: text/xml
Content-Length: 530

<?xml version='1.0' encoding=''iso-8859-1' ?>
<SOAP-ENV:Envelope
  xmlns:SOAP-ENV="http://schemas.xmlsoap.org/soap/envelope/"
  xmlns:xsi="http://www.w3.org/1999/XMLSchema-instance"
  xmlns:xsd="http://www.w3.org/1999/XMLSchema">
<SOAP-ENV:Header>
...
</SOAP-ENV:Header>
<SOAP-ENV:Body>
  <greeting>
    <xsd:string>World</xsd:string>
  </greeting>
</SOAP-ENV:Body>
</SOAP-ENV:Envelope>
```

The response may be something like the following:

```
<?xml version='1.0' encoding='iso-8859-1' ?>
<SOAP-ENV:Envelope
  xmlns:SOAP-ENV="http://schemas.xmlsoap.org/soap/envelope/"
  xmlns:xsi="http://www.w3.org/1999/XMLSchema-instance"
  xmlns:xsd="http://www.w3.org/1999/XMLSchema">
<SOAP-ENV:Header>
  ...
```

```
</SOAP-ENV:Header>
<SOAP-ENV:Body>
  <greetingResponse>
    <SOAP-ENC:Array SOAP-ENC:arrayType="xsd:string[1]">
      <xsd:string>Hello, World</xsd:string>
    </SOAP-ENC:Array>
  </greetingResponse>
</SOAP-ENV:Body>
</SOAP-ENV:Envelope>
```

SOAP offers you even more data types than XML-RPC. You must, however, specify a lot more, too. Other than that, the two protocols are very similar. Obviously SOAP also enjoys greater acceptance from Big Software.

Learn more about SOAP at `www.soapware.org/bdg`.

.NET services

.NET can seem to mean almost anything. Is .NET a programming language, a virtual machine, a set of Web services, a specific service for transparent user identification across the Internet, a marketing slogan — or all the preceding?

The part that we care about is .NET XML Web Services. Basically this just means that Microsoft is in the middle of a huge drive to make all Windows applications expose themselves as Web services. .NET services are implemented within the MS development framework, and they all speak SOAP.

To date, the issue is that some interoperability problems have arisen with non-Microsoft clients interacting with .NET services. Interop is a big area of concern among all Web service developers, so expect much discussion and, we hope, some move by Microsoft toward a truly common standard for SOAP.

Current Issues with Web Services

By now, you're probably thinking, "Okay, if Web services is so great, why aren't we using it everywhere?" Well, there are still many issues to be worked out. Web services is in its infancy, and it is likely to be years before we live in a totally Web-serviced world.

Fat and slow

SOAP, in particular, is fat, verbose, graceless, and heavy-handed. This drives binary programmers especially crazy, accustomed as they are to apps talking to each other in compact binary formats. To a large extent, people just need to get over this, but there are still many situations where data storage, memory, and bandwidth are issues — in cellular phones, for instance.

Potentially heavy load

So far, there is no standard way to cache the results of RPC calls. Even if 80 percent of your clients are asking for the exact same response and, therefore, you can't save resources — every request must handled *de novo*.

REST enables caching via all the methods by which HTML can be cached.

Standards

Before Web services can really take off, applications need to handle their results transparently. Because the Web services standards are still somewhat in flux, and there are multiple candidates with competing strengths, this has not yet happened. For smallish Web applications, it's not that big a deal if some service changes one of its API methods — but for a big app like Lotus Notes, it's a major investment of resources to transparently deal with SOAP.

The companies that are leading the way in public Web services — Amazon, Salesforce.com, eBay, and Google — have so far used a mixture of Web service APIs. Many of them maintain multiple interfaces for developer convenience; Amazon, for instance, offers all its Web services via both REST and SOAP. While this is extremely developer-friendly of them, in the long run most organizations long for a single, stable standard to conform to.

Hide and seek

The ultimate goal of Web services is to have the application transparently find all the resources it needs. Say that you get an e-mail in Japanese — your mail server or client should be smart enough to find the translation service it needs, get your document translated, and show the final result to you.

To accomplish this, we need some kind of directory system and a standard way for servers to describe themselves. WSDL and UDDI are the technologies that can make this possible. *WSDL* (*Web Services Description Language*) describes a Web service interface, while *UDDI* (*Universal Description, Discovery, and Integration*) is a registry for Web services. Learn more about UDDI and WSDL, respectively, at www.uddi.org and www.w3.org/TR/wsdl.

We are a long way, however, from automatic discovery and communication by applications. In fact, many businesses that deploy Web services deliberately do so under a veil — for example, FedEx, which needed to take down its public SOAP server after it was used for fraud by crackers. Web services is growing most quickly in the realm of semiprivate transactions — companies set up Web services that are only meant to be accessed by authenticated and authorized business partners.

In the meantime, if you want to play with Web services now, you can find some at the following sites:

✦ www.syndic8.com (news feeds, site written in PHP!)

✦ www.xmlrpc.com/directory/1568/services

✦ www.xmethods.com (some of these use scraped data from copyrighted sites)

Who pays and how?

Ultimately, the biggest question about public Web services is: Who pays for them, and how? So far most of the Web services that you can access are things such as Weblog entries and simple currency calculators — services for which you normally would not expect to pay. Big Software's answer is to create huge private networks of Web services, similar to those of Hailstorm or the Liberty Alliance. This has serious implications for privacy and open architecture.

Unless and until Web services finds a way to pay for itself, it is likely to continue to be deployed mostly inside corporate firewalls and in nonprofit situations.

Project: A REST Client

Listing 41-1 is a basic client script for Amazon's elegantly simple REST service, which has been available (with some changes) to Amazon Associates and other developers since spring of 2002. You feed the script a search string at the top, and it outputs a CSS-formatted box at the end containing information about the current edition of the book in question.

This service clearly demonstrates the biggest advantage of REST: You can work with it by using the HTTP concepts — and the PHP functions — you're already familiar with. For all intents and purposes, you are simply asking for a Web page by using `http fopen()`. It happens to be well-formed XML instead of HTML — but that is incidental to the transport mechanism.

We chose to parse the XML by using PHP's DOM XML extension, which so far has found relatively few real-world uses (see Chapter 40 for discussion of the DOM). Many other PHP-literate Amazon developers have produced scripts that use other types of parsing, such as string parsing and regex, to extract the desired information — but we want to show you the power of using XML itself.

We should warn you, however, that this type of solution does not scale — DOM XML is a notorious memory hog. (We've heard credible reports that a 1,000-line XML document read into the DOM results in 1MB of memory being appropriated.) However, the Amazon Web services interface will only return a few items at a time, so DOM XML is an appropriate technology for this purpose.

 Caution The DOM extension changed significantly in PHP5. This script will not work at all in versions of PHP before 5.0.0b2. Obviously the script will also not work unless you have previously compiled PHP with the `--with-domxml` flag and libxml2.

Listing 41-1: **Client for Amazon RESTservice (rest_amazon_client.php)**

```php
<?php

// Get the xml
$writefile = 'phpbible.xml';
$file = "http://xml.amazon.com/onca/xml3?t=webservices-20&dev-t=
XXXXXXXXXXXXXX&KeywordSearch=Park+Converse+PHP+
Bible&mode=books&type=lite&page=1&f=xml";
// Replace X's with your Amazon Developer's Token
// If you don't have a valid token, comment out the block below
//and use the fake data file

// Write the xml to a file
$fp = fopen($file, "r");
$xml_array = file($file);
fclose($fp);
$xml_str = implode("", $xml_array);
$fp2 = fopen($writefile, "w");
$fw_return = fwrite($fp2, $xml_str);
fclose($fp2);
```

Continued

Listing 41-1 *(continued)*

```php
// Load up the xml file into memory
$dom = new DomDocument;
if (!$dom->load($writefile)) {
  echo "Cannot load XML file";
  exit;
}

// Get an immediately available edition
$editions = $dom->getElementsByTagname("Availability");
foreach ($editions as $edition_obj) {
  if ($edition_obj->nodeValue == 'Usually ships within 24
hours') {
    // Get the data for this book
    $book_array = array();
    $parent_node = $edition_obj->parentNode;
    $book_array['Details'] = $parent_node->getAttribute("url");
    $children = $parent_node->childNodes;
    foreach($children as $child_obj) {
      $node_name = $child_obj->nodeName;
      if ($node_name != "#text") {
        $content_str = $child_obj->nodeValue;
        $book_array["$node_name"] = $content_str;
      }
    }
    continue;
  } else {
    // Give a message if availability isn't good
    $book_array['ProductName'] = 'Not available at this time';
  }
}

//print_r($book_array);
$title = $book_array['ProductName'];
$author = $book_array['Authors'];
$image = $book_array['ImageUrlSmall'];
$detail_page = $book_array['Details'];
$price = $book_array['OurPrice'];


// Format a nice box
$box_str = <<< EONICEBOX
<HTML>
<HEAD>
<STYLE>
#content {
  float: left;
  padding: 10px;
  margin: 10px;
```

```
   background: #FFFFFF;
   border: 4px solid #008000;
   width: 200px; /* ie5win fudge begins */
   voice-family: "\"}\"";
   voice-family:inherit;
   width: 200px;
}
html>body #content {
   width: 170px; /* ie5win fudge ends */
   }
p {
   font-family: Verdana, Arial, sans-serif;
   font-size: 12px;
   line-height: 22px;
   margin-top: 3px;
   margin-bottom: 2px;
}

</STYLE>
</HEAD>
<BODY>
<div id="content">
<P><IMG SRC="$image">
<BR><A HREF="$detail_page">$title</A>
<BR>$author
<BR>$price</P>
</BODY>
</HTML>
EONICEBOX;
echo $box_str;
?>
```

Those of you who do not have Amazon Associates accounts can use Listing 41-2 for testing, which you should save as phpbible.xml somewhere under your Web tree.

Listing 41-2: **XML sample (phpbible.xml)**

```
<?xml version="1.0" encoding="UTF-8"?>
<ProductInfo xmlns:xsi="http://www.w3.org/2001/XMLSchema-
instance"
xsi:noNamespaceSchemaLocation="http://xml.amazon.com/schemas3/
dev-lite.xsd">

<Request>
  <Args>
    <Arg value="us" name="locale"></Arg>
    <Arg value="1" name="page"></Arg>
    <Arg value="Park Converse PHP Bible"
```

Continued

Listing 41-2 *(continued)*

```
name="KeywordSearch"></Arg>
    <Arg value="XXXXXXXXX" name="dev-t"></Arg>
    <Arg value="webservices-20" name="t"></Arg>
    <Arg value="xml" name="f"></Arg>
    <Arg value="books" name="mode"></Arg>
    <Arg value="lite" name="type"></Arg>
  </Args>
</Request>
<TotalResults>2</TotalResults>
<TotalPages>1</TotalPages>
<Details url="http://www.amazon.com/exec/obidos/ASIN/0764549553/
webservices-20?dev-t=XXXXXXXXX%26camp=2025%26link_code=xm2">
    <Asin>0764549553</Asin>
    <ProductName>PHP Bible, 2nd Edition</ProductName>
    <Catalog>Book</Catalog>
    <Authors>
       <Author>Tim Converse</Author>
       <Author>Joyce Park</Author>
    </Authors>
    <ReleaseDate>11 September, 2002</ReleaseDate>
    <Manufacturer>John Wiley &amp; Sons</Manufacturer>
    <ImageUrlSmall>http://images.amazon.com/images/P/
0764549553.01.THUMBZZZ.jpg</ImageUrlSmall>
    <ImageUrlMedium>http://images.amazon.com/images/P/
0764549553.01.MZZZZZZZ.jpg</ImageUrlMedium>
    <ImageUrlLarge>http://images.amazon.com/images/P/
0764549553.01.LZZZZZZZ.jpg</ImageUrlLarge>
    <Availability>Usually ships within 24 hours</Availability>
    <ListPrice>$49.99</ListPrice>
    <OurPrice>$34.99</OurPrice>
    <UsedPrice>$24.49</UsedPrice>
  </Details>
  <Details
url="http://www.amazon.com/exec/obidos/ASIN/076454716X/
webservices-20?devt=XXXXXXXXXXXXXX%26camp=2025%26link_code=xm2">
    <Asin>076454716X</Asin>
    <ProductName>PHP 4 Bible</ProductName>
    <Catalog>Book</Catalog>
    <Authors>
       <Author>Tim Converse</Author>
       <Author>Joyce Park</Author>
    </Authors>
    <ReleaseDate>17 August, 2000</ReleaseDate>
    <Manufacturer>John Wiley &amp; Sons</Manufacturer>
    <ImageUrlSmall>http://images.amazon.com/images/P/
076454716X.01.THUMBZZZ.jpg</ImageUrlSmall>
    <ImageUrlMedium>http://images.amazon.com/images/P/
```

```
076454716X.01.MZZZZZZZ.jpg</ImageUrlMedium>
      <ImageUrlLarge>http://images.amazon.com/images/P/
076454716X.01.LZZZZZZZ.jpg</ImageUrlLarge>
      <Availability>THIS TITLE IS CURRENTLY NOT AVAILABLE. If
you would like to purchase this title, we recommend that you
occasionally check this page to see if it has become
available.</Availability>
      <ListPrice>$39.99</ListPrice>
      <OurPrice>$39.99</OurPrice>
      <UsedPrice>$15.00</UsedPrice>
   </Details>
</ProductInfo>
```

The result of the REST client script is shown in Figure 41-1.

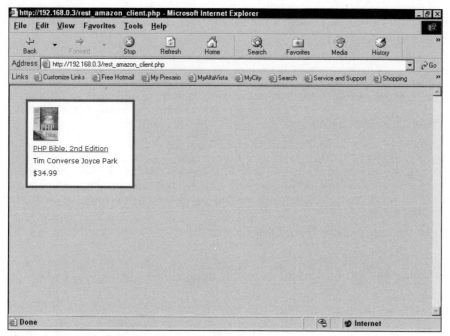

Figure 41-1: REST client gets XML and outputs HTML.

As you can see from the XML sample, there is a lot of potential data from the Web service that we didn't use — suggested price, release date, and so on. This demonstrates how easy it is to pick out just the data you want from the feed using DOM XML. According to the current Amazon Web services rules, you could poll its Web service for fresh XML every second, so you could keep this part of your information very fresh.

Project: A SOAP Server and Client

Here we have an extremely simple SOAP service and a matching client script.

XML-RPC and SOAP Web services have two major parts: the actual programming logic and the mechanism by which the program is exposed or turned into a Web service. The latter includes tasks such as encoding the request from a function to XML, actually sending the request as an HTTP `POST`, and decoding the response. In Perl, this is accomplished by using a package such as `SOAP::Lite`. Server-side Java programmers often use the Apache SOAP toolkit (aka `Axis`). ASP now uses the .NET framework.

PHP offers basic XML-RPC and SOAP functions in its XML-RPC extension, but leaves it to developers to come up with bundles of higher-level functionality. There is a SOAP package in the PEAR extension, but that can be a bit difficult for Windows users to get. Another package that is easy to use and widely deployed is `NuSOAP` by Dietrick Ayala, which you can find at `http://dietrich.ganx4.com/nusoap/index.php`.

You must have already compiled PHP with the `--with-xml` and `--with-xmlrpc` flags. Then grab `NuSOAP` (which is composed of just two PHP files), and unzip it in the same directory as these scripts.

The only problem with `NuSOAP` is that it completely insulates the PHP developer from any knowledge of what exactly is going on behind the scenes, since it efficiently translates SOAP responses into native PHP types and vice versa. However, relatively few people care about the actual mechanics of SOAP serialization, and the vocabulary is becoming less human-readable all the time, so we think most PHP developers will be content with learning the basics of creating and consuming RPC services.

This Web service basically distributes recipes. Any client can come along and request a particular recipe via SOAP. The recipes themselves happen to be written in XML, but that doesn't matter — they could just as easily be in HTML, plain text, or whatever. After you have the recipe data, you can do whatever you want with it — format it for display in a Web page, use it in an XML application, or (as we chose to do in our client) write out a shopping list that we can print later.

Listing 41-3 is a sample recipe that lives on the server:

Listing 41-3: **Sample XML recipe (mapo_tofu.xml)**

```
<?xml version='1.0' encoding="iso-8859 1" ?>
<recipe>
<recipe_name>Mapo tofu</recipe_name>
<ingredient>1 T peanut oil</ingredient>
<ingredient>2 oz minced pork</ingredient>
<ingredient>14 oz firm tofu, cut in cubes</ingredient>
<ingredient>2 T garlic chili paste</ingredient>
<ingredient>1 T black bean paste</ingredient>
<ingredient>1 T sherry</ingredient>
<ingredient>1 T rice vinegar</ingredient>
<ingredient>10 oz frozen peas and carrots</ingredient>
<ingredient>1 T. chopped green onion</ingredient>
<instruction>Brown the pork in the peanut oil.  Add all the rest
```

of the ingredients except the green onion. Braise for 15
minutes or until the tofu loses that icky raw taste. Garnish
with green onion and serve hot.</instruction>
</recipe>

Listing 41-4 is the code for the SOAP service. Invoking it is very similar to invoking an XML
parser in PHP. There are four main steps: Create the server, register methods on the server,
call those methods, and destroy the server (which in this case is handled transparently by
NuSOAP). In this case, all four happen each time a request comes in, but that is not necessary.

Listing 41-4: **A SOAP server (soap_recipe_server.php)**

```php
<?php
require_once('nusoap.php');

function getRecipe($recipe_name){
  if (!$file = "$recipe_name.xml") {
    return new soap_fault('Server','','Cannot find recipe
file.');
  } else {
    $fp = fopen($file, 'r');
    $recipe_str = fread($fp, filesize($file));
    fclose($fp);

    return $recipe_str;
  }
}

$s = new soap_server;
$s->register('getRecipe');
$s->service($HTTP_RAW_POST_DATA);
?>
```

The SOAP server has only one method in this case, getRecipe, which looks for a file with the
same name as the recipe being called for, and then returns it as a string. If you could see the
response, which NuSOAP mercifully hides from you, it would look something like this:

```
<?xml version='1.0' encoding='iso-8859-1' ?>
<SOAP-ENV:Envelope
  xmlns:SOAP-ENV="http://schemas.xmlsoap.org/soap/envelope/"
  xmlns:xsi="http://www.w3.org/1999/XMLSchema-instance"
  xmlns:xsd="http://www.w3.org/1999/XMLSchema">
<SOAP-ENV:Body>
  <getRecipeResponse>
      <xsd:string>[recipe in a long XML string
here]</xsd:string>
  </getRecipeResponse>
</SOAP-ENV:Body>
</SOAP-ENV:Envelope>
```

Our client script (Listing 41-5), which can be run in the browser or on the command line, asks for the recipe—which happens to be XML itself (Listing 41-3), but is treated as an encoded string wrapped in SOAP XML during the transport. NuSOAP strips off all the SOAP envelopes and delivers the payload neatly as a PHP string suitable for further processing. We wanted to do something besides displaying the recipe in a browser, so we used PHP's SAX parser to write out the ingredients to a text file as a shopping list and also optionally send the recipe via e-mail.

Listing 41-5: **A SOAP client (soap_recipe_client.php)**

```php
<?php

require_once('nusoap.php');

$recipe_name = $_GET['recipe'];
if ($recipe_name == '') {
  echo "You must supply a recipe name";
  exit;
}
$parameters = array('recipe'=>$recipe_name);
$soapclient = new soapclient('http://localhost/
soap_recipe_server.php');
$result = $soapclient->call('getRecipe', $parameters);
//echo $result;

// Fire up the SAX parser to make a shopping list
// ------------------------------------

$ingred_arr = array('types' => array(), 'values' => array());
$i = 0;
$e = -1;
// There is an element without a value, the recipe element
// so I'm jiggering this offset to match

function startElement($parser, $name, $attrs)
{
  global $ingred_arr, $e;
  if ($name != 'INGREDIENT' && $name != 'RECIPE_NAME' &&
$e > 0) {
    $ingred_arr[types][$e] = 1;
  }
  $e++;
}


function endElement($parser, $name)
{
  // Just need to define an endElement function for the parser
}
```

```
function characterData($parser, $value)
{
  global $ingred_arr, $i;
  if (strlen($value) > 1) {
    $ingred_arr[values][$i] = $value;
    $i++;
  }
}


// Run through the XML and stick the values in an array
// Also note if any of the elements are not recipe names or
// ingredient
$simpleparser = xml_parser_create();
xml_set_element_handler($simpleparser, "startElement",
 "endElement");
xml_set_character_data_handler($simpleparser, "characterData");

if (!xml_parse($simpleparser, $result, strlen($result))) {
  die(xml_error_string(xml_get_error_code($simpleparser)));
}
xml_parser_free($simpleparser);

// Get rid of any values that aren't ingredients or recipe name
foreach ($ingred_arr['values'] as $key=>$val) {
  if ($ingred_arr['types'][$key] == 1) {
    $ingred_arr['values'] = array_slice($ingred_arr['values'],
0, $key);
  }
}
$shopping_list = implode("\n", $ingred_arr['values']);

// Write it out to a file
$file = '/home/me/shoppinglist.txt';
$fp = fopen($file, "a+");
$write_int = fwrite($fp, $shopping_list);
fclose($fp);

// If you want, mail it to yourself instead
// mail('me@example.com', 'Shopping list', $shopping_list);
?>
```

To use this script, you call it with the name of the recipe as the GET var, as follows:

```
soap_recipe_client.php?recipe=mapo_tofu
```

You may also have to change the name of your Web server on or about line 11.

You may have noticed that, ultimately, both the REST example in the previous section of this chapter and the SOAP example here do pretty much the same thing: return a chunk of XML. For loosely-typed languages like PHP, they differ largely in whether that XML needs to be wrapped in more XML during the transport. In the REST example, we go on to munge it by using the DOM; in this one, we run it through a SAX parser. This demonstrates two fundamental points about Web services: For simple data-exchanging services, REST and SOAP are functionally equivalent, and XML gives you basic building blocks that you can use in many ways.

Summary

Web services is an emerging field of programming. Web services offers immediate payoffs in data transfer, especially for Web applications, and may finally unlock the promise of distributed computing. Although there is a lot of hype and misinformation out there about the technologies, and although much of the action is happening inside intranets and in semiprivate transactions, you can start familiarizing yourself with PHP to both create and consume Web services.

The three main Web-services standards in discussion now are REST, XML-RPC, and SOAP. REST is the most lightweight and easy to use, but offers the least functionality. SOAP is the most complicated and, as a consequence, has the most interoperability problems, but large vendors like Microsoft and IBM have thrown their support behind it. XML-RPC offers a nice blend of power and simplicity but lacks big-vendor support.

PHP can be used to create servers and clients in REST, XML-RPC, and SOAP. However, particularly with SOAP, the syntax is so complex that a third-party package may be highly useful for help with the serialization, type-shuffling, and request-creation steps required by Web services.

✦   ✦   ✦

Graphics

In this chapter, we delve into how to use PHP to create graphics of your own and display them to the user. Although we spend a little bit of time on pure HTML "graphics," our primary focus is on creating images on the fly by using the gd library. This library helps you create images such as PNGs and JPEGs, which you can then link to from dynamically generated HTML pages or send to the user as standalone Web pages.

Your Options

Just to see where image creation fits into the Web-scripting world, look at the following spectrum of choices, in order of increasing dynamicness:

✦ You can have no graphics at all and display purely textual information.

✦ You can embed static images in your HTML, whether created by yourself or by other people.

✦ You can write programmatically generated HTML pseudographics.

✦ You can embed static image graphics (or even image animations, if you insist) in your HTML pages, but display different ones conditionally.

✦ You can use gd to pregenerate static graphics for all the cases that may possibly arise from your code, store them in files, and display them conditionally.

✦ You can create graphic images on demand in response to user input.

We start off with the third option (HTML graphics) and then devote most of the rest of the chapter to the last one, which is the most interesting case.

HTML Graphics

You know those sideways colored bar graphs you see all over the Web, especially in connection with poll results? It looks as though some graphics are being done in creating these graphs, but in truth there're just a couple of canned color images and the magic of image scaling in HTML. This graphing technique is actually very useful, and we include it here because it's very easy to create graphs like this dynamically from PHP.

Before we get into this data visualization technique, we need some data. Listing 42-1 shows a small sample dataset, which we imagine has been produced from a survey of programmers asked about their favorite languages and operating systems. The data is stored in a MySQL database, in a single table, with the following definition:

```
CREATE TABLE programmers (
  id int(11) NOT NULL auto_increment,
  sex char(1) default NULL,
  age int(11) default NULL,
  language varchar(30) default NULL,
  os varchar(30) default NULL,
  country varchar(30) default NULL,
  continent varchar(30) default NULL,
  PRIMARY KEY  (id)
);
```

Listing 42-1: **Sample dataset**

```
+--+---+---+----------+---------+------------+---------------+
|id|sex|age| language | os      | country    | continent     |
+--+---+---+----------+---------+------------+---------------+
|1 |F  |33 | PHP      | Linux   | USA        | North America |
|2 |M  |41 | Java     | Solaris | USA        | North America |
|4 |M  |31 | C++      | Solaris | USA        | North America |
|5 |M  |45 | Lisp     | MacOS   | USA        | North America |
|6 |M  |25 | C        | Solaris | Antarctica | Antarctica    |
|7 |F  |17 | PHP      | Linux   | Denmark    | Europe        |
|8 |M  |21 | Perl     | Linux   | UK         | Europe        |
|9 |M  |14 | PHP      | Linux   | UK         | Europe        |
|10|F  |21 | Perl     | Linux   | Germany    | Europe        |
|11|F  |38 | PHP      | Linux   | Germany    | Europe        |
|12|M  |26 | C++      | Windows | USA        | North America |
|13|M  |22 | PHP      | Windows | France     | Europe        |
|14|M  |17 | PHP      | Linux   | Japan      | Asia          |
|15|F  |38 | C        | Solaris | South Korea| Asia          |
|16|F  |19 | PHP      | Linux   | Canada     | North America |
|17|F  |32 | Perl     | Linux   | France     | Europe        |
|18|M  |32 | Java     | Solaris | Mexico     | North America |
|19|F  |23 | PHP      | Solaris | Brazil     | South America |
|20|F  |19 | PHP      | Linux   | Finland    | Europe        |
|21|M  |21 | PHP      | Linux   | Brazil     | South America |
|22|M  |51 | Java     | Linux   | UK         | Europe        |
|23|M  |29 | Java     | Linux   | Japan      | Asia          |
|24|M  |29 | Java     | Solaris | China      | Asia          |
|25|M  |21 | C++      | MacOS   | Germany    | Europe        |
|26|M  |21 | Perl     | Solaris | France     | Europe        |
|27|M  |27 | PHP      | Linux   | India      | Asia          |
|28|M  |31 | Perl     | Linux   | India      | Asia          |
|29|M  |17 | C        | Linux   | Pakistan   | Asia          |
|30|M  |45 | PHP      | Windows | USA        | North America |
|31|F  |22 | Java     | Windows | Italy      | Europe        |
|32|F  |33 | C        | Linux   | Spain      | Europe        |
+--+---+---+----------+---------+------------+---------------+
```

We use the data for this example but also come back to it for a much more extended example in Chapter 48.

So say that our goal is to visualize counts of the distribution of values for different columns — we want to know not only how many of our respondents list this or that programming language, but also to see comparisons graphically.

Although our data is in a MySQL database, the display portion of this code need not be tied to that. We may want to use it for a different purpose entirely. So we break out a separate function that produces a bar graph from an array in a particular format, and only later hook that up to code that produces the requisite array via SQL queries. The code to translate an array into a bar graph is shown in Listing 42-2.

Listing 42-2: **bar_graph.php**

```php
<?php

function array_to_bar_graph ($array, $max_width) {
  // expects as input an array where the keys
  //    are string labels and the values are
  //    numbers.  Values must be non-negative
  // returns an HTML bar graph as a string
  // assumes bar[1-5].gif, located in images/

  foreach ($array as $value) {
    if ((IsSet($max_value) &&
        ($value > $max_value)) ||
        (!IsSet($max_value))) {
      $max_value = $value;
    }
  }
  $pixels_per_value = ((double) $max_width)
                        / $max_value;

  $string_to_return = "<TABLE CELLPADDING=5>";
  $counter = 0;
  foreach ($array as $name => $value) {
    $bar_width = $value * $pixels_per_value;
    $image_no = ($counter % 5) + 1;
    $string_to_return .=
      "<TR><TD>$name ($value)</TD>
        <TD><IMG SRC=\"images/bar$image_no.gif\"
              WIDTH=$bar_width
              HEIGHT=10>
        </TD></TR>";
    $counter++;
  }
  $string_to_return .= "</TABLE>";
  return($string_to_return);
}
?>
```

The bar graph code is extremely simple — it iterates through an array, which is assumed to have names for keys and quantities for values. It normalizes the maximum value to a fixed-width bar and calculates the width of all the other bars proportionally. Finally, it displays bars by using the scaling parameters in the <IMG> tag to give each variable a fixed height and an appropriate width. It cycles through a list of five images, which are premade one-color GIFs (which could as well be PNGs) and could be created by using your favorite graphics program. As long as these images are monocolor, their size and shape are irrelevant. (If you don't have any such images handy, you can find the ones we used at the code download site: www.troutworks.com/phpbook/.)

Now that we can display names and associated values in a bar graph, we can hook that up to the database via a Web form and an SQL query. Code for this is shown in Listing 42-3.

Listing 42-3: **bar_graph_form.php**

```php
<?php
include_once("dbconnect.php");
include_once("bar_graph.php");

if (IsSet($_POST['COLUMN_NAME'])) {
  $column_name = $_POST['COLUMN_NAME'];
  $query = "select $column_name, count(*)
            from programmers
            group by $column_name";
  $result = mysql_query($query)
            or die("Error in database interaction<BR>".
                     mysql_error());
  $array_collection = array();
  while ($row = mysql_fetch_row($result)) {
    $name = $row[0];
    $count = $row[1];
    $array_collection[$name] = $count;
  }
  $bar_graph =
    array_to_bar_graph($array_collection,
                        300);
}
else {
  $bar_graph = "";
}

$self = $_SERVER['PHP_SELF'];
$form = <<<EOT
<FORM METHOD=POST ACTION="$self">
<H3>Choose a table column for graphing</H3>
<SELECT NAME=COLUMN_NAME>
<OPTION VALUE=os>os
<OPTION VALUE=language>language
<OPTION VALUE=continent>continent
<OPTION VALUE=sex>sex
```

```
</SELECT>
<INPUT TYPE=SUBMIT NAME=SUBMIT>
</FORM>
EOT;

$page = <<<EOT
<HTML><HEAD><TITLE>Survey data</TITLE></HEAD>
<BODY>
$form
<BR>
$bar_graph
</BODY></HTML>
EOT;

echo $page;
?>
```

The form is self-submitting and loads a file called dbconnect.php, which we assume takes care of a call to mysql_connect(), with appropriate login, password, and database name.

All that is supplied by the form submission is the name of the column. Starting with that, the code submits an SQL statement to count all the distinct values that occur for that column and then creates an array by using names and the corresponding counts. What remains is to feed the resulting array to the bar graph code from Listing 42-1 and to do some layout. The results for two different columns are shown in Figures 42-1 and 42-2. (Since this is a grayscale book, you won't see interestingly different colors in the diagram, but you should at least see bars of different sizes.)

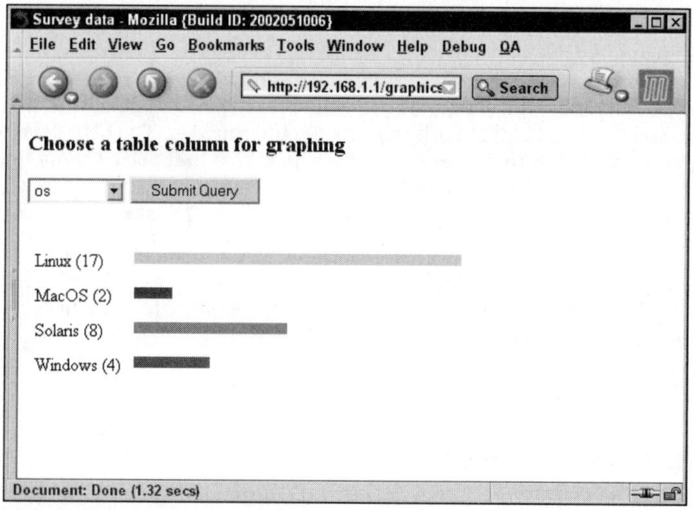

Figure 42-1: HTML bar graph 1

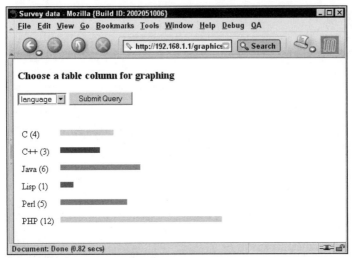

Figure 42-2: HTML bar graph 2

Creating images using gd

Having mostly exhausted the graphic possibilities afforded by vanilla HTML, let's turn our attention to creating real standalone graphics by using the gd library.

What is gd?

What is gd, anyway? The gd toolkit is a C code library for creating and manipulating images, which was originally created by the kind and clever people at Boutell.com (www.boutell.com). gd is not a graphics or paint program in and of itself, as it has no standalone application or GUI. Instead, it provides functions that programs can call to do these manipulations, and any C program that wants to can link against that library to use the routines. The PHP developers have done this and, in fact, have written a set of interface functions that make it easy to call gd routines from PHP. But nothing in gd is specific to PHP, and there are interfaces to it from several other languages and environments, including Perl, Tcl, Pascal, Haskell, and REXX.

gd lets you call functions to create images (initially blank, like a clean sheet of paper), draw and paint on those images in various ways, and ultimately convert the image from gd's internal image format to a standard image format, and send it off to its ultimate fate (display in a browser or storage in a file or database). And because all this is under programmatic control rather than human control, these created images can be arbitrarily complex, and they can depend on anything in your program that you would like to have them depend on.

Image formats and browsers

The gd library can, in principle, import and output images in a wide variety of formats. The three image formats we talk about at all seriously are GIF, JPEG, and PNG, although for examples we focus mostly on the last of these.

The GIF and PNG formats essentially exist to describe a grid of colored cells corresponding to pixels, with a few complications. The first complication is that the cells may contain actual color values or they may contain indexes in a table of color values. (The former is more expressive because any number of different colors may be used, and the latter is more compact.)

Another complication is that, although the conceptual representation of GIFs and PNGs is fairly simple, in practice they are always read, written, and transferred in compressed form. Compression is necessary because a grid of cells is a costly thing to specify. A simple 500 × 400 pixel image is 200,000 pixels — if each pixel needs three bytes to specify, then we're over half a megabyte already. Compression is a large and abstruse topic, but most compression algorithms take advantage of redundancy in the image to make it smaller. (There are more concise ways to say that every pixel is green than specifying every pixel's green color value individually.) Unfortunately, there is a lot more to compression algorithms than that — enough so that the compression algorithm used for writing GIFs is patented.

Early browsers were written using GIF as the graphics format of choice, and it wasn't until that practice had been under way for a while that it became clear that the patent holder was going to insist on going after people who used the compression algorithm. This left Web graphics in a bit of a bind — GIF was the *lingua franca*, but you couldn't legally create such graphics, at least without paying a license fee. The PNG format has come to the rescue in a sense — recent versions of major browsers support it, and with that support it plays much the same role as GIF.

Compression is different in the case of JPEGs, as well, although not for legal reasons. Compression for GIFs and PNGs is lossless, meaning that if you compress and then uncompress an image, you should have your exact original image back. The JPEG compression, on the other hand, is lossy. Essentially, if redundancy helps compression, JPEG compression tries to introduce a little bit of extra redundancy into the image before compression, mostly in ways that the human eye won't notice. This is particularly effective with photographic images, but it does mean that sometimes the compression/uncompression cycle doesn't leave you with exactly what you started with.

Because JPEG is better for photographic images than the kinds of images we're making, and because deciding on the export format is a final step anyway, we've decided to focus on PNG graphics exclusively. If you would rather produce JPEGs, it is a simple matter to change the export functions appropriately.

Choosing versions

The gd library was originally developed by the Boutell company and is downloadable from them at www.boutell.com/gd. Historically, using gd with PHP meant acquiring and compiling this library, and building PHP to link to it. The Boutell people have maintained two branches of this code: 1.x (which is now becoming obsolete), and 2.x (which is now viewed as stable).

Beginning with PHP4.3, though, the PHP developers have maintained their own version of gd, which is bundled with the PHP distribution. They did this so that they would be free to make quick updates to the gd code and to make installation somewhat easier. This version is compatible with the 2.x branch maintained by Boutell.

So in principle you have three choices for a version of gd: the old (1.x) Boutell version, the current (2.x) Boutell version, or the PHP-bundled version (which should be similar to the 2.x Boutell version, with a little extra functionality). It's hard to think of reasons not to go with the PHP-bundled version, if you have a choice.

You will definitely need the 2.x version or the bundled version if you want:

✦ Images with more than 256 colors

✦ Drawn lines of varying thickness

✦ Transparent colors

Installation

Installing gd and getting it to work with PHP is, frankly, a pain. This is not because of any weakness in either the PHP codebase or the gd codebase but is all about configuration issues: sorting out the likely and actual locations of the libraries gd depends on and making sure that everything can build and link appropriately. So the happiest situation possible is to find out that gd is already installed, and PHP already has gd support enabled (whether that's due to the diligence of your Webhost or because the PHP you installed by yourself had it included).

So the zeroth step in installing gd is: Check to see if it has already been installed. Whether you are running via a Webhost or are in command of your own installation, start off as always by putting the following into a file and viewing the result in a browser:

```
<?php
    phpinfo();
?>
```

After you have the displayed page, just do a text search for gd in the browser window — you may find a subsection that describes to what extent gd is enabled in your PHP installation. If you only want to produce certain kinds of images (PNGs, for example) and phpinfo() tells you that support for that image type is enabled, then you may be good to go. If the gd version includes the word *bundled*, you are using the gd that is bundled with PHP.

If this fails, and if you are in control of your PHP installation, you will have to install and configure gd. (If, instead, your PHP installation is run by a hosting company, your options may be reduced to asking them to provide gd support, or to switching Webhosts.)

Using the PHP-bundled version of gd removes some, but not all, of the hassle of a gd install; if you use the bundled version itself, you have the gd library, but not necessarily the libraries gd needs. The gd library itself depends on several other libraries: libpng (for manipulating PNG images), zlib (used in compression), and jpeg-6b or later (if you want to manipulate JPEG images). (Only gd, libpng, and zlib are necessary for the examples in this chapter.) These will be present already in many Linux installations, and if so it may be sufficient to include a with flag (such as --with-zlib) without specifying the install directory. If you are configuring PHP yourself, adding the --with-gd flag will cause the bundled version of gd to be included. Use --with-gd=*path* instead if you want to point to an alternate version.

If you find that you lack one or more of the necessary libraries, you will have to build them. The documentation at www.boutell.com/gd is a good place to start to find the current versions.

gd Concepts

While an image is being constructed or manipulated in the gd toolkit, it is stored in a gd-specific format that doesn't correspond to any conventional image type. Images can in theory be exported in this gd format, but it's unusual to do so because the resulting image is not compressed and cannot be displayed in a browser or conventional graphics program.

An image in the gd toolkit has a width, a height, and color information for all the *width x height* many pixels. (See the "Colors" section for more detail on how colors are stored.) Usually a program starts off its interaction with gd by either creating a new blank image (which is drawn and painted on) or by importing an image from a file. The next steps are typically 1) allocate colors in the image, 2) draw, paint, or otherwise transform the image, 3) translate the image to a conventional format (for example, PNG, JPEG), and send it to output.

Colors

There are two ways of representing colors in gd images: *palette-based*, which is limited to 256 colors, and *truecolor*, which can store an unlimited number of distinct RBG color values. In gd 1.x, palette-based colors were the only alternative; gd 2.x and the PHP-bundled version of it offers both palette-based images and truecolor images. Note that a given gd image is either palette-based or truecolor; there is no notion of adding true colors to a palette-based image.

To get an initial blank palette-based image, you call the function ImageCreate(); to get a truecolor image, call ImageCreateTrueColor().

Palette-based images

Colors are specified in a red-green-blue (RGB) format, with three numbers between 0 and 255. The color specified by (255, 0, 0), for example, is bright red; (0, 255, 0) is green; (0, 0, 255) is blue; (0, 0, 0) is black; (255, 255, 255) is white; and (127, 127, 127) is gray. You can tweak these values to your heart's content to design new colors.

Any drawing into an image must be done in a particular color, and colors must be allocated in an image before they are used. Also, the first color allocated into an image automatically becomes the background color. So, colors are not optional in any sense, and usually color allocation is the first thing you do after creating a new blank image.

Colors in palette-based images are created by using imagecolorallocate(), which takes as arguments an (already created) image, and three integers specifying the proportion of red, green, and blue. The return value is an integer, which specifies the index of the new color in the image's internal palette. You must hang on to this return value in a variable, because you need the index value for any future drawing using that color. Palette-based images can have a maximum of 256 colors. (It may or may not be obvious what's going on under the hood here, but every pixel in a palette-based image is actually a single byte, which stores an index into the 256-color palette.)

Note that the index returned by allocating a color in an image makes sense only for that image. If you assign an allocated color to the PHP variable $black, it won't work to use that variable as the color input for a drawing command called on a different image.

Truecolor

In gd 2.0 and later, you can also create images that are not palette-based, where every pixel stores an arbitrary RGB color value. In this truecolor format, the number of colors is essentially unlimited. This can be useful not only for the free range of your artistic expression, but for faithfully representing truecolor PNGs and JPEG images that have been loaded into gd.

Aside from the initial function to create an image, and the lack of limitation on distinct colors, working with truecolor images is similar to working with palette-based images. In particular, you still call ImageColorAllocate() to create new colors, and hang on to the return value for later commands to use; it just so happens that the returned value will be an RGB color rather than an index into a palette. Also, in truecolor images there is no notion of a background color created as a side-effect of ImageColorAllocate(); all pixels are initialized to black.

Transparency

gd 2.x supports transparency in the form of an *alpha value* (in addition to the red, green, blue values) that specifies how transparent the given color is. This allows you, for example, to overlay a shape onto another one without simply occluding the first shape.

Many of the image functions in PHP have an analog with "alpha" in its name, which indicates that it deals with a four-value (R,G,B,A) color. For example, while ImageColorAllocate() expects three arguments, ImageColorAllocateAlpha expects a fourth argument between 0 and 127. A value of zero indicates that the color is completely opaque; a value of 127 means that the color is completely transparent.

Drawing coordinates and commands

After you create an image within gd, you have an implicit coordinate system for drawing on it, determined by the width and height you specified.

In this coordinate system, the origin (0, 0) is at the top-left corner of the image, and the positive direction for *x* values is to the right, whereas the positive direction for *y* values is down. (This is often true of computer graphics coordinate systems, but you may be more accustomed to a lower-left origin if you learned analytic geometry in school.)

There are many drawing commands, including but not limited to drawing line segments, rectangles, arcs, and setting particular pixel values. Note that the end effect of all these painting and drawing commands is to set the value of pixels. There is no memory retained of the commands that changed the pixels and, therefore, no way to undo drawing commands or separate out the effects of distinct commands.

Nothing stops you from drawing outside the bounds of the image you have specified, but such drawing has no visible effect. A rectangle with coordinate values that are all negative, for example, is not visible.

Format translation

All this drawing and image manipulation is done on the image in its gd-internal format. After your script is done, it can use one of the translation-and-output commands (imagetopng, imagetojpeg, and so on) to translate the image to the desired graphics format and echo it out to the user's browser (or to a file).

Freeing resources

After you have sent a translation of your completed gd image off to the user, you are done with the internal version and should dispose of it. The right way to do this is to call imagedestroy() with the image as an argument.

This is slightly less necessary in PHP4 than in previous versions because the image is of type resource, and so should automatically be freed whenever PHP gets around to it. Freeing images yourself is a good habit to get into — there's no reason to hold onto memory that you know you have no further use for.

Functions

We are not planning to individually list and describe all the functions in PHP's gd interface in this chapter; for that, we refer you to the "Image Functions" section of the manual at www. php.net/. Here we summarize the most important functions. Most of the gd functions are in one of the categories shown in Table 42-1. Note that the function names in this table have internal capital letters at word breaks for clarity, but we may not always observe this when writing code because PHP function names are not case sensitive.

Table 42-1: Breakdown of gd Functions

Type	Examples	Notes
Image-creation functions	`ImageCreate()`, `ImageCreateTruecolor()`, `ImageCreateFromGd()`, `ImageCreateFromJpeg()`	These functions return a new gd image. `ImageCreate()` takes a width and height as arguments; others take a filepath, URL, or string containing a pre-existing image to load in and convert to gd.
Color allocation	`ImageColorAllocate()`, `ImageColorAllocateAlpha()`, `ImageColorDeallocate()` `ImageColorAllocate()`	takes an image and the desired red, green, and blue color values, and returns the color value to be used for subsequent drawing. `ImageColorAllocateAlpha` takes an additional transparency value (0-127).
Color matching	`ImageColorClosest()`, `ImageColorClosestAlpha()`, `ImageColorExact()`, `ImageColorExactAlpha()`	Return the index of a matching color in a palette image. The 'Closest' functions return the best-matching color by RGB distance; the 'Exact' functions return a color only if it is identical, -1 otherwise. 'Alpha' functions operate on 4-value (transparent) colors.
Line-drawing functions	`ImageLine()`, `ImageDashedLine()`, `ImageRectangle()`, `ImagePolygon()`, `ImageEllipse()`, `ImageArc()`	These functions draw lines or curves in the specified shapes. Usually the first argument is an image, the last argument is a color, and the intermediate arguments are x- and y- coordinates.
Pen-setting functions for line drawing	`ImageSetStyle()`, `ImageSetThickness()`	These functions alter settings that affect the lines created by later line-drawing commands. (Some of these are available only with gd 2.0.1 or later.)
Painting and filling functions	`ImageFilledRectangle()`, `ImageFilledEllipse()`, `ImageFilledRectangle()`, `ImageFilledPolygon()`, `ImageFilledArc()`, `ImageFill()`	Usually analogous to corresponding line-drawing functions but with areas filled rather than outlined. The special `ImageFill()` function "flood fills" outward from a specified x-y coordinate with a given fill color. (Some of these functions require gd 2.0.1 or later.)

Continued

Table 42-1 *(continued)*

Type	Examples	Notes
Text functions	`ImageString()`, `ImageLoadFont()` `ImageString`	takes as arguments an image, a font number, x and y coordinates, a text string, and a color. If the font number is between 1 and 5, one of the five built-in fonts is used to draw the string in the given color. A number greater than 5 indicates a result of loading a custom font with `ImageLoadFont()`.
Exporting functions	`ImagePng()`, `ImageJpeg()`	These functions convert the internal `gd` image to the relevant image format and then send to output. If only one argument (an image) is given, the image is echoed to the user; if an additional path name argument is given, the destination is a file.
Image-destruction function	`ImageDestroy()`	Takes an image argument and frees all resources associated with the image.

Images and HTTP

Before the user's browser can display an image appropriately, it has to know that an image is coming, and what the image format is. So it is, unfortunately, not sufficient to simply embed a call to `ImageToPng()` in your generated HTML and have an image show up. You essentially have three choices in regard to intermixing images with PHP-generated HTML.

Full-page images

You can make the entire generated page an image. In this case, you need to send an HTTP header before the image data, announcing that an image of a certain type is on the way. You may, for example, have lines such as the following near the end of your script:

```
// ... code to create image in $image
header("Content-type: image/png");  // announcement to browser
imagepng($image);  // sending actual PNG-converted image data
imagedestroy($image);  // freeing resources
```

This approach has the benefit that you can use any kind of information, including POST arguments, to decide what the image should contain. The downside is that the resulting page can't contain any conventional HTML. In fact, you need to be careful that no textual output is sent from your scripts before the header and image because this causes content to be sent prematurely. In this case, you get a Headers already sent . . . error.

Embedded images from files

Of course, HTML has had the <IMG> tag for a long time. This enables you to embed an image by specifying its file path or URL, like this:

```
<IMG SRC="my_png.png">
```

This works with static image files, but there is no reason why the image can't have been recently created. So you can have a script that 1) creates an image, 2) writes the image data to a local file, and then 3) produces HTML with an appropriate <IMG> tag referring to the file that you just made.

The only drawbacks to this approach are 1) you're introducing file writes, which may be time-consuming, into the page-generation process, and 2) you need to figure out what to do with the files after you are done with them. There is one situation this approach is perfect for, however, which is creating and caching images that represent a finite set of possibilities. In this case, you have some way to map from a situation to an image filename. Whenever a display situation arises, you check to see if you already have the appropriate file — if you do, you simply refer to it by using an <IMG> tag, and if not, you create the image, write it out to a file, and then refer to it. Eventually, you should need to do no more creation.

You can see a page created this way at a just-for-fun site that we made a few years ago. In www.sciencebookguide.com/sizescales.html, there is a bar graph in the top part of the page, and then a scale legend at the bottom, which was a gd-generated GIF. The text and tick marks of the scale legend depend on the exact bar graph data that is being displayed, but there are only a limited number of cases. So, long ago, we auto-cached all the possible images, and ever since the displays have been static. (This is a good thing, of course, since gd quite rightly no longer supports the GIF format. Sometime soon, we may get around to replacing the GIFs with PNGs.)

Embedded images from scripts

Finally, there is no reason why you cannot have a standalone generated image, as in the section "Full-page images," but, in turn, embed that URL in a different dynamic page via an <IMG> tag. The only difficulty lies in how to communicate necessary data to the dependent page. You may, for example, have an embedded image tag like this:

```
<IMG SRC="ballpage.php?ball_color=green&ball_position=5>
```

where ballpage.php happened to return PNG images of colored balls in various positions in the image.

There is a gotcha lurking here because both Web servers and browsers sometimes pay attention to the suffix of the served file, and in different ways. You may need the suffix of ballpage to be .php to let Apache (for example) know that the server-side code should be interpreted as PHP (although this behavior can be controlled with configuration files). Some broken browsers, however, may insist that a file that ends in .php cannot be an image despite the headers we are sending. This technique requires some cross-browser testing to make sure that your intended users are seeing the same thing you are.

Now it's high time to move on to an example of using gd to create images.

Example: Fractal images

There's a fine tradition of livening up the potentially unexciting topic of line drawing by using fractals as examples, and your authors are not about to mess with tradition. In addition to showing how you can produce a complex image programmatically, this kind of example is also a good fit for PHP because its arrays and loose datatypes make it very easy to build complex data structures corresponding to fractal images, without a lot of declarations.

What's a fractal? It's a shape that is self-similar, in that the parts of a fractal have a shape similar to the shape of the whole, and the parts of those parts have a similar shape, and so on.

In theory, you can keep zooming into ever-smaller pieces of an ideal fractal, and keep finding the same patterns repeated. In practice, computer-generated fractals bottom out after some limited number of generations into nonfractal shapes like simple curves and line segments.

An example of the kind of image we're going to create is shown in Figure 42-3. Although it may not look like it, this image is simply a lot of small line segments with endpoints connected into a path.

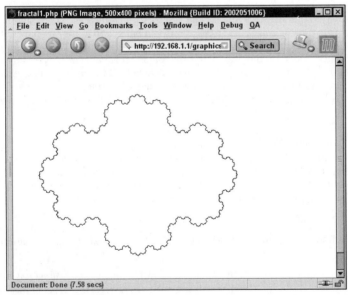

Figure 42-3: Fractal 1

Our job is to calculate the endpoints of all those line segments and then display them appropriately as a PNG image. We're going to be slightly more ambitious than simply creating a one-off piece of fractal display code and construct a little framework that makes it easy to vary the fractal parameters and to generate new kinds of displays.

To start with, we build some data structures to represent the complex shapes that we are displaying. We use these data structures both in our intermediate calculations and for drawing the end result. Let's say somewhat arbitrarily that:

✦ A coordinate point is a pair of numbers.

✦ A path is a list of points.

We end up drawing paths by drawing line segments between all the points in a path. If we want to draw a simple line segment, we draw a path that has two points in it; if we want to draw a rectangle, then we draw a path that has five points in it (with the starting point repeated to close off the rectangle). (We could have made a line segment a primitive entity here, but paths seemed more concise for our fractal purposes.)

Now, how shall we represent points and paths? The easiest way to make lists of things in PHP is to use arrays. So we declare that a point is an array that happens to contain two numbers, and a path is an array that happens to contain a sequence of points. The resulting structures are multidimensional PHP arrays, but if we define well-named constructor and accessor functions, we can forget about that and just write code that acts as though these things are genuine datatypes.

Listing 42-4 shows such code, which defines the datatypes in terms of functions to create them (starting with make_), functions to access their parts, and functions to draw them into an image (starting with display_). Points cannot be drawn and have no display function; paths are drawn by drawing lines between successive pairs of points.

Listing 42-4: **path_display.php**

```php
<?php

// --- points ----

// A point is just a pair of numerical coordinates

function make_point ($x, $y) {
  return(array($x, $y));
}

function point_x ($point) {
  return($point[0]);
}

function point_y ($point) {
  return($point[1]);
}

// --- paths ---

// A path is a list of points

function make_path () {
  return array();
}

function add_point_to_path ($path, $point) {
  $path[] = $point;
  return($path);
```

Continued

Listing 42-4 *(continued)*

```php
  }

  function display_path ($image, $path, $color) {
    static $line_count = 0;
    $prev_point = NULL;
    foreach ($path as $point) {
      if ($point && $prev_point) {
        $line_count++;
        imageline($image,
                  point_x($prev_point),
                  point_y($prev_point),
                  point_x($point),
                  point_y($point),
                  $color);
      }
      $prev_point = $point;
    }
  }


?>
```

Listing 42-5 shows a single function, which, among other arguments, takes the name of a function name to apply. (This function is in its own file because our original version of this code had more complex transformation functions for more complex fractal examples, removed for reasons of space. We may restore these examples to the code on the Web site at www. troutworks.com/phpbook.)

The function transform_path takes an input path as first argument, and as second argument it takes the name of a function that, in turn, is expected to take a path as argument and return a path as a result. The third argument to transform_path() is a number of times that the path-to-path function should be successively applied to create a new path. The reason that this kind of second-order function is useful is that, otherwise, we may find ourselves writing a new looping function every time we wanted to build a new fractal. With this approach, we can bundle the varying part of the fractal code into a function that we pass into transform_path and avoid duplicating work.

Listing 42-5: path_tranform.php

```php
<?php


function transform_path ($path_input,
                         $function_name,
                         $iterations) {
  // Expects a path, a path-to-path function
```

```
  //  and a number of times to apply the
  //  function.
  // Returns a path
  $path_to_return = $path_input;
  for ($i = 0; $i < $iterations; $i++) {
    $path_to_return = $function_name($path_to_return);
  }
  return($path_to_return);
}            ?>
```

What we have so far is a way to represent and draw paths composed of line segments, and also functions that can repeatedly apply transformation functions to these paths. What we need now is the transformation functions themselves — the functions that we pass in that actually twiddle the locations of points in the data structures.

Listing 42-6 shows a set of such functions. The `spike` function takes a path as argument and returns a path where every two-point line segment has been replaced by a five-point line segment with a spike in the middle. The `top-hat` function does something similar, except that six points are involved, and the spike is rectangular. We also include a couple of functions to create rectangular paths of standard sizes, to use as starting points.

Listing 42-6: **path_manipulation.php**

```php
<?php

include_once("path_display.php");

function spike ($path) {
  // Takes a path and returns a path
  $path_to_return = make_path();
  $prev_point = NULL;
  foreach ($path as $point) {
    if ($point && $prev_point) {
      $path_to_return =
          add_point_to_path($path_to_return,
                            $prev_point);
      $path_to_return =
          add_point_to_path($path_to_return,
            point_along_segment($prev_point,
                                $point,
                                0.25));
      $path_to_return =
          add_point_to_path($path_to_return,
            point_off_segment($prev_point,
                              $point,
                              0.5, 0.23));
      $path_to_return =
          add_point_to_path($path_to_return,
```

Continued

Listing 42-6 *(continued)*

```
                      point_along_segment($prev_point,
                                          $point,
                                          0.75));
          $path_to_return =
              add_point_to_path($path_to_return,
                                $point);
      }
      $prev_point = $point;
   }
   return($path_to_return);
}

function top_hat ($path) {
    // Takes a path and returns a path
    $path_to_return = make_path();
    $prev_point = NULL;
    foreach ($path as $point) {
      if ($point && $prev_point) {
        $path_to_return =
            add_point_to_path($path_to_return,
                              $prev_point);
        $path_to_return =
            add_point_to_path($path_to_return,
              point_along_segment($prev_point,
                                  $point,
                                  0.35));
          $path_to_return =
            add_point_to_path($path_to_return,
              point_off_segment($prev_point,
                                $point,
                                0.35, 0.24));
          $path_to_return =
            add_point_to_path($path_to_return,
              point_off_segment($prev_point,
                                $point,
                                0.65, 0.24));
          $path_to_return =
            add_point_to_path($path_to_return,
              point_along_segment($prev_point,
                                  $point,
                                  0.65));
          $path_to_return =
            add_point_to_path($path_to_return,
                              $point);
      }
      $prev_point = $point;
    }
    return($path_to_return);
```

```
}


function point_along_segment ($first_point,
                              $second_point,
                              $proportion)
{
  $delta_x = (point_x($second_point) -
              point_x($first_point));
  $delta_y = (point_y($second_point) -
              point_y($first_point));
  return(make_point(point_x($first_point) +
                    $proportion * $delta_x,
                    point_y($first_point) +
                    $proportion * $delta_y));
}

function point_off_segment ($first_point,
                            $second_point,
                            $proportion,
                            $proportional_distance)
{
  $delta_x = (point_x($second_point) -
              point_x($first_point));
  $delta_y = (point_y($second_point) -
              point_y($first_point));
  return(make_point(point_x($first_point) +
                    $proportion * $delta_x -
                    $proportional_distance *
                    $delta_y,
                    point_y($first_point) +
                    $proportion * $delta_y +
                    $proportional_distance *
                    $delta_x));
}

function make_small_rectangle () {
  $path = make_path();
  $path = add_point_to_path ($path, make_point(75, 275));
  $path = add_point_to_path ($path, make_point(375, 275));
  $path = add_point_to_path ($path, make_point(375, 125));
  $path = add_point_to_path ($path, make_point(75, 125));
  $path = add_point_to_path ($path, make_point(75, 275));
  return($path);
}

function make_large_rectangle () {
  $path = make_path();
  $path = add_point_to_path ($path, make_point(5, 5));
  $path = add_point_to_path ($path, make_point(495, 5));
```

Continued

```php
    $path = add_point_to_path ($path, make_point(495, 395));
    $path = add_point_to_path ($path, make_point(5, 395));
    $path = add_point_to_path ($path, make_point(5, 5));
    return($path);
}

?>
```

Now we can combine all these elements and actually make images. Listing 42-7 shows the file that produced our original example in Figure 42-3. After loading all the functions from the included files, this code creates a gd image of specific height and width and allocates colors into that image. (The background is white, and the lines are black.)

The fractal creation code starts off by creating a standard rectangular path (containing five points and, therefore, four [implicit] line segments). It then passes this off to the transform_path function, asking it to return the path that results from applying the spike() function to the rectangle four times. The rectangle path starts with four line segments, and every segment is itself replaced by four segments. So the four successive iterations have 16 segments, 64 segments, 256 segments, and 1024 segments, respectively.

Then all that remains is to display the complicated path that we've generated. We call our own function display_path() to draw all the lines into the image, send off an HTTP header announcing a PNG, call imagepng() for the conversion and output, and then dispense with the internal gd image.

Listing 42-7: fractal1.php

```php
<?php
include_once("path_display.php");
include_once("path_transform.php");
include_once("path_manipulation.php");

$IMAGE_WIDTH = 500;
$IMAGE_HEIGHT = 400;

$image = imagecreate($IMAGE_WIDTH, $IMAGE_HEIGHT)
    or die("Could not create image");
$background_color = ImageColorAllocate($image, 255, 255, 255);
$drawing_color = ImageColorAllocate($image, 0, 0, 0);

$path = make_small_rectangle();
$path = transform_path($path, 'spike', 4);
display_path($image, $path, $drawing_color);

header("Content-type: image/png");
imagepng($image);
imagedestroy($image);
?>
```

Although we won't show it as a separate listing, we took a copy of Listing 42-7, changed the function name argument from `spike` to `top-hat`, and renamed the `file fractal2.php`. The resulting image is shown in Figure 42-4.

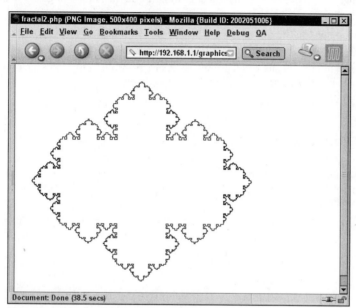

Figure 42-4: Fractal 2

Caution

Creating and displaying these images can be time consuming and the more so the more line segments are created. Your Web server may time out while the creation is happening. Your options then are to decrease the number of generations in the fractal code or to raise the timeouts in your Web server or PHP configuration files.

Tweaking fractal code is definitely an art, and your humble authors are not particularly good artists. We wish you luck in improving on our images.

Cross-Reference

For a much more extended example of producing graphics with gd, see Chapter 48.

Gotchas and Troubleshooting

Code to produce images can be especially difficult to debug, because some of the simplest tricks (for example, diagnostic print statements) can't be used as easily. What follows is a list of symptoms you may encounter in running gd-enabled PHP code and some things you can try to correct them.

Symptom: Completely blank image

Sometimes your code runs without incident or apparent error, but the image that results is a blank slate, although you expected it to be full of graphic wonders. Some things to check (some obvious, some not):

✦ Are you drawing outside the bounds of the image? (If your image is 100×100, a small circle drawn at (200, 200) cannot be seen.)

✦ Are you drawing infinitesimally small graphics? (A circle with a center in range of the image with a radius of zero or near-zero may be completely undetectable.)

✦ Are you drawing by using the background color? (White-on-white is the same as white.)

Symptom: Headers already sent

This problem is almost always due to printing text to output before the header call that announces a graphic image. Just as with other HTTP headers (such as those setting cookies), you must ruthlessly root out any printing of text before that call, even if that text is composed of blank lines or spaces.

One common pattern is to see something such as the following in your browser as you test:

```
Warning:  Division by zero in
           /usr/local/apache/htdocs/graphics/fractal1.php on
line 18
Warning:  Cannot add header information -
  headers already sent by (output started at
/usr/local/apache/htdocs/graphics/fractal1.php:18) in
/usr/local/apache/htdocs/graphics/fractal1.php on line 19)
PNG
IHDR [trailing off into binary gibberish]
```

The binary gibberish is, of course, your image data, which is being printed as text in your browser resulting in nonsense characters. The reason you're seeing it as text is that the image announcement headers could not be sent, because some text was sent before those headers were encountered. And that text that was sent, in turn, was probably just (in this case) the text of the division-by-zero warning itself. Fixing the division-by-zero problem (or whatever the error or warning is in your case) may eliminate the printed error, which may make the header-sending statement happy, which may mean a successful image display.

If, instead, the very first thing you see is the warning about headers, you may be sending blank lines or spaces before the header without being aware of it. Look for any print statements, any included HTML, and (especially) any space at the beginning or end of files that have been included or required. If an included PHP file so much as ends with '?> ' rather than '?>', you may be sending a space's worth of HTML, which would cause text headers to be sent before the image headers are seen.

Symptom: Broken image

How exactly this problem displays depends on your browser program—some display a sad, visibly broken image icon, while Mozilla may politely inform you that your image can't be displayed because it contains errors. Either way, though, the problem is that your browser cannot read the data in the image format you said you were sending. Some possible causes:

✦ The flip side of the previous Headers already sent problem: You may be printing random text without being aware of it but, in this case, *after* the image header has already been sent rather than before. This text is munging up the stream of image data.

✦ You have misspelled the variable containing your image—for example imagepng($imag) where you meant imagepng($image). You are actually calling the convert-and-send function on nothing at all.

✦ Your convert-and-send function is actually producing a text error rather than a graphic image (possibly because you don't actually have support for that image type compiled into PHP).

✦ You have actually somehow screwed up your internal gd image well before trying to send it off. One very common cause of this is failure to allocate colors in a palette-based image or to use color indexes that haven't been allocated.

✦ Your gd library is producing in good faith, and your browser is receiving in good faith, but they disagree about what a valid image format looks like. (This is generally about the last explanation you should consider, although we did see it happen once.) With some (but not all) PNG images, Mozilla RC2 wouldn't display apparently valid PNGs generated by gd 1.8.4, although other browsers had no problem. (Mozilla RC1 and 1.0 did just fine.)

In our experience, the best way to debug this sort of problem is simply to comment out the PHP statement that sends the header announcing an image, and then look at the output as text in your browser. If everything were working perfectly, you would expect to see your binary image data as text, which would mean a lot of strange-character gibberish, possibly starting with a short amount of recognizable text (like PNG). If you see a PHP warning or error instead of the image data, or in addition to the image data, you can proceed to debug that. If you see nearly nothing, not much of an image is being sent—this may imply problem #2 or #4 above. If you see what looks like a reasonable amount of pure image data, you may need to look at your code very carefully for small amounts of text (like spaces) that you may have introduced.

If all else fails, you can reluctantly consider explanations such as #5, or other kinds of browser, gd, or PHP bugs, which you may want to test by using different image formats or different browsers. But remember that explaining things that way breaks the cardinal rule of code debugging: It's always your fault.

Summary

If you create on-the-fly graphic images by using PHP, you're creating something completely different from the usual HTML that PHP generates—a completely different format, and a completely different look. Although there are hassles associated with getting the gd image library working, after you get past those you have quite a rich set of image-manipulation functions to work with. You can create Web pages that are all image, or pages that have <IMG> tags that link to dynamic images, or you can start building a library of image files for display later on. Either way you go, you have a richer vocabulary to work with than with pure HTML, and (even if many situations don't require dynamic images) you have another type of tool in your kit.

✦   ✦   ✦

Case Studies

Weblogs

Small standalone PHP applications, such as polls and e-mail forms, are all very useful, but complete content sites are where PHP really shines. Here we give complete instructions for developing the simplest type of standalone site, which is the Weblog.

Why Weblogs?

A *Weblog* is the simplest kind of dynamic site. It can be thought of as a dynamic version of the personal home page: a content site organized by chronology with frequently updated posts. Most Weblogs do not create all their own content in the sense of writing full news stories or producing a trove of artwork; they instead exist to comment on other people's content and events of the day or to provide a venue for personal thoughts and reflections. On the high end of the genre, public Weblogs like Slashdot can become extremely popular meeting places for online communities to chew the fat of their common interests.

If you are a newcomer to server-side scripting, we encourage you to immediately start a personal Weblog as your first major project. Nothing helps you learn faster than running an actual complete site of your own, where you can try out a range of new techniques and ideas in context. Especially because PHP and other open-source technologies grow and change so quickly, it's well-nigh essential to have a pre-existing testbed always available to doodle around on.

Weblogs are also just fun and, therefore, worthwhile even for those who also use PHP in more serious contexts. There's no pleasure quite like that of conducting an intellectual debate, an argument, or a romance by Weblog. Forget movies, pop music, and reality TV—the Weblog is the true medium of the age, baby!

The Simplest Weblog

The main goal of this section is to introduce you to the layout and display aspects of building a dynamically generated site. In later sections, we will refine our techniques for handling the data-related aspects. At the end of this chapter, you should have the ability to make and maintain a simple data-driven site of your own. Conceptually, even the most complicated dynamic content sites are basically just bigger versions of the concepts you will learn by building a personal Weblog.

The easiest Weblog is just a PHP template and some included text files. It's limited to local development only — in other words, you won't be able to make entries via HTTP but only by creating text files while logged into the PHP server as a trusted user (or copying text files to the server via some mechanism like FTP, which amounts to the same thing). You also won't be able to assign different levels of permissions very effectively, so this style of Weblog is most appropriate for a purely personal single-author site.

We decided to use the most basic type of navigation, Previous and Next text links that we'll maintain by hand. This gives you the maximum flexibility to decide how often you want to change the front page of your Weblog — we'll do it daily, but you may prefer a weekly, monthly, or irregular changeover depending on how much you have to write about. We'll also include an old reliable left-side navbar with links to standalone pages, such as About Me and Favorite Things information. A finished Weblog page is shown in Figure 43-1.

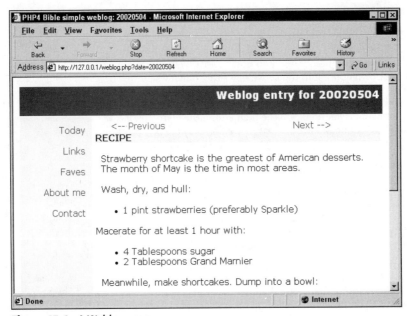

Figure 43-1: A Weblog page

It is assembled from these files:

✦ `weblog.php`: Main display page template

✦ `20040101.txt`, `20040102.txt`: Weblog entries (changed daily)

✦ `default.txt`: Default text entry for days when there is no new content

✦ `favorites.php`, `links.php`, `aboutme.php`: Semistatic pages (changed infrequently)

✦ `header.inc`: Header and navigation bar on every page

✦ `footer.inc`: Footer on every page

✦ `style.inc`: Internal style sheet

You can grab all this code from our Web site, www.troutworks.com/phpbook/, to save having to retype it.

Caution

You must change the variable $initial_entry_date in weblog.php to the date of your first entry, or you may start an infinite loop that will eat up all your server cycles! You must also check all the paths to included files and change them to real paths.

Listings 43-1 through 43-7 are the code for a simple Weblog. Instead of using a database to store your entries, the data will be stored in text files on your filesystem.

Listing 43-1: **Main Weblog template (weblog.php)**

```php
<?php

// -------------------------------
// GET YOUR VARIABLES ALL LINED UP
// -------------------------------
// Change this to the date of your first log entry.
$initial_entry_date = 20040101;

// Replace the fake path below with a real one
$DOCUMENT_ROOT = "c:\docs";

$today = date('Ymd');
if (isSet($_GET['date'])) {
  if ($_GET['date'] < $initial_entry_date) {
    // Go to first entry if the specified date is earlier
    // than range
    $date = $initial_entry_date;
  } elseif ($_GET['date'] > $today) {
    // Go to last entry if specified date is later than range
    $date = $today;
  } else {
    $date = $_GET['date'];
  }
} else {
  $date = $today;
}
$title_msg = $date;
$header_msg = "Weblog entry for $date";

// Assemble the Previous/Next links
$prevdate = $date - 1;
$nextdate = $date + 1;
if ($date == $initial_entry_date) {
  $flipbar = "\n<P CLASS=\"next\">
<A HREF=\"$PHP_SELF?date=$nextdate\">Next --&#62;</A>
</P>\n";
```

Continued

Listing 43-1 *(continued)*

```
} elseif ($date == $today) {
  $flipbar = "\n<P CLASS=\"previous\">
<A HREF=\"$PHP_SELF?date=$prevdate\">&#60;-- Previous</A>
</P>\n";
} else {
  $flipbar = "\n<TABLE BORDER=0><TR>
<TD WIDTH=\"50%\" ALIGN=\"left\">
<SPAN CLASS=\"previous\">
<A HREF=\"$PHP_SELF?date=$prevdate\">&#60;-- Previous</A>
</SPAN>
</TD><TD WIDTH=\"50%\" ALIGN=\"right\">
<SPAN CLASS=\"next\">
<A HREF=\"$PHP_SELF?date=$nextdate\">Next --&#62;</A>
</SPAN>
</TD>
</TR></TABLE>\n";
}




// ---------------------
// NOW ASSEMBLE THE PAGE
// ---------------------
include_once('header.inc');

echo $flipbar;
// Include the specified text file, or a default message
// Replace the fake path below with a real one
if (file_exists($DOCUMENT_ROOT."/path/to/entries/$date.txt")) {
  // Replace the fake path below with a real one
  include($DOCUMENT_ROOT."/path/to/entries/$date.txt");
} else {
  include("default.txt");
}
echo $flipbar;

include_once('footer.inc');
?>
```

Listing 43-2: A dated entry (20000101.txt)

```
<DIV CLASS="topic">HOLIDAY</DIV>
<P>Oh, what a holiday season it has been! I am positively
stuffed with fruitcake. </P>

<P>My New Year's Resolutions are:
<UL>
```

```
<LI>Trade in AMC Gremlin.</LI>
<LI>Contribute to OSS project.</LI>
<LI>Take full 2 weeks vacation (dude ranch?).</LI>
<LI>Be less snide.</LI>
</UL>
</P>
```

Listing 43-3: **Default message (default.txt)**

```
<P>Sorry, nothing new today!  Check back tomorrow.</P>
```

Listing 43-4: **A static page (favorites.php)**

```php
<?php
$title_msg = 'favorites';
$header_msg = 'My favorite things';

include_once('header.inc')
?>

<P>These are a few of my favorite things.</P>

<DIV CLASS="topic">BOOKS</DIV>
<DL>
<DT>Cryptonomicon, by Neal Stephenson</DT>
<DD>The techie masterpiece -- it's our life, put in the blender
of a massive inventiveness. Be sure to also download the essay
"In the beginning was the command line" from his site,
www.crytonomicon.com .</DD>
</DL>

<DIV CLASS="topic">MUSIC</DIV>
<DL>
<DT>Raw Power, by The Stooges</DT>
<DD>See who all those neo-punk bands are copying.</DD>
</DL>
<?php include_once('footer.inc'); ?>
```

Listing 43-5: **Included header file (header.inc)**

```php
<HTML>
<HEAD>
<TITLE>PHP4 Bible simple weblog:
<?php echo $_GET['date']; ?></TITLE>
```

Continued

Listing 43-5 *(continued)*

```
<?php include("style.inc"); ?>
</HEAD>

<BODY BGCOLOR="#FFFFFF">
<TABLE BORDER="0" CELLPADDING="5" WIDTH="100%">
<!-- Title box -->
<TR WIDTH="100%" BGCOLOR="#822222">
  <TD WIDTH="100%" ALIGN="right" COLSPAN="2">
    <H1><?php echo $header_msg; ?></H1>
  </TD>
</TR>
<!-- End Title box -->

<!-- Begin main body -->
<TR WIDTH="100%">
  <TD WIDTH="20%" VALIGN="top" BGCOLOR="#FFFECC">
    <!-- Navbar -->
    <P CLASS="sidebar"><A HREF="weblog.php">Today</A></P>
    <P CLASS="sidebar"><A HREF="links.php">Links</A></P>
    <P CLASS="sidebar"><A HREF="favorites.php">Faves</A></P>
    <P CLASS="sidebar"><A HREF="aboutme.php">About me</A></P>
    <P CLASS="sidebar"><A
HREF="mailto:me@localhost">Contact</A></P>
    <!-- End Navbar -->
  </TD>
  <TD WIDTH="80%">
```

Listing 43-6: Included footer (footer.inc)

```
<!-- End of main body -->
</TD></TR>
</TABLE>
<P CLASS="footer">Copyright Troutworks, Inc. 2000 - 2004</P>
</BODY>
</HTML>
```

Listing 43-7: Included stylesheet (style.inc)

```
<STYLE TYPE="text/css">
<!--
BODY, P, LI    {font-family: verdana, arial, sans-serif;
font-size: 12pt; color: #000000; text-align: left;
margin-left:10px}
H1      {font-family: verdana, arial, sans-serif;
```

```
font-size: 14pt; color: #FFFFFF}
A:link, A:visited  {font-family: verdana, arial, sans-serif;
font-size: 12pt; color: #822222; text-decoration:none}
.sidebar  {font-family: verdana, arial, sans-serif;
font-size: 12pt; color: #822222; text-align:right;
margin-top:10; margin-right:7}
.topic    {font-family: verdana, arial, sans-serif;
font-size: 12pt; font-weight: bold; color: #000000;
background: #FFFECC; text-align: left}
.footer  {font-family: verdana, arial, sans-serif;
font-size: 9pt; color: #808080; text-align:right}
.previous  {font-family: verdana, arial, sans-serif;
font-size: 12pt; color: #808080; text-align:left;
margin-left:25; margin-right:100}
.next  {font-family: verdana, arial, sans-serif;
font-size: 12pt; color: #808080; text-align:right;
margin-left:100; margin-right:25}
-->
</STYLE>
```

To use the simple Weblog, place all the files in a PHP-enabled directory on your Web server. Create a subdirectory for your daily entries (for example, 20000101.txt, 20020504.txt); otherwise, you'll quickly end up with dozens of files cluttering up your main directory. The files in this subdirectory need to be writable by you and readable by all.

When you're ready to make an entry, log into your Web server, fire up a text editor like vi, and write an HTML-formatted text file for each day you want to post, naming it according to the date convention we've established. Alternatively, instead of logging into your Web server you can write up your daily text file on a local client copy, and then use scp to upload it to your Web server. Obviously, you can edit this file however many times you like, if you have multiple things to say per day. As long as the files have the correct names, locations, and permissions, this code should run smoothly for you. This type of Weblog is self-archiving, so you don't need to do anything special with old entries — they'll just stay around forever if you have a big enough hard disk.

Note

If you still use FTP to upload files, please take an hour to learn how to use scp instead. A fine command-line Windows client called pscp is available for free download at www.chiark.greenend.org.uk/~sgtatham/putty/. An even easier GUI Windows client called WinSCP is available for free download at http://winscp.sourceforge.net/eng/. FTP should be used only for file download, as in anonymous FTP servers, because it has caused so many security problems on file upload. One of the reasons to avoid the otherwise fine Weblog-publishing applications like Movable Type and Blogger is that they rely on FTP to write files to your Web server.

We promise that scp is just as easy to use if not easier—instead of typing ftp myserver.mydomain.com and put myfile.php, you combine both commands into a simple pscp myfile.php me@myserver.mydomain.com:myfile.php. The only even slightly tricky part is generating a public key and having it put in your server's key file—you may be forced to use FTP or e-mail to accomplish this—but after that chore, with which any sysadmin will be happy to help you, you will be home free.

If you really can't make up your mind to learn scp, it might be safer to use an HTTP-based editing tool as detailed in the next section.

Adding an HTML Editing Tool

This simple Weblog is quite adequate for many purposes, but it has one big disadvantage: You can't write up your daily entries using the Web itself. Instead, you must create each entry using a text editor like emacs or Notepad and save it to your Web server's docroot. This can be a significant issue over time, especially if you are not allowed telnet/ssh/FTP access to your server or aren't comfortable with the process. HTTP is the next logical step for many users, and is probably no less unsafe than using FTP.

This process has one big problem: You need to give read/write permissions to the HTTP user (usually Nobody) in a particular directory. This is an inherently insecure process, and we do not recommend it in the long run. We'll describe the HTTP tools here so that you can become comfortable with the new aspects before moving on to a better solution, which is using a database instead of separate include() files for each entry. We'll also try to keep the security problems to a minimum, employing a password and letting you send mail to yourself if an unauthorized person tries to log in.

The files you need for an HTML-based file-writing tool are:

✦ login.php

✦ logentry.php

✦ logentry_handler.php

✦ password.inc

Put password.inc in a directory outside the Web tree, such as /home/htmluser. This will ensure that your passwords cannot be read via the Web without being processed by PHP first. The directory must be world-executable and the document must be readable by the httpd user (Nobody). If you have root access on this server, you could chown it to belong to the httpd user; if not, you may have to make the file world-readable, which is a security breach. Be sure to use a password different from your system user password, just in case it's compromised.

Listings 43-8 through 43-10 are the files you need for an HTML form to edit Weblog entries.

Listing 43-8: **Weblog entry login screen (login.php)**

```
<HTML>
<HEAD>
<TITLE>Weblog login screen</TITLE>
</HEAD>

<P><B>Supply a username and password.</B></P>
<FORM METHOD=POST ACTION="logentry.php">
<P>USERNAME:
<INPUT TYPE=TEXT NAME="test_username" SIZE=20></P>
<P>PASSWORD:
<INPUT TYPE=PASSWORD NAME="test_password" SIZE=20></P>
<P>BLOG ENTRY:<BR>
<TEXTAREA NAME="logtext" COLS=75 ROWS=20WRAP="VIRTUAL">
```

```
</TEXTAREA></P>
<P><INPUT TYPE="SUBMIT" VALUE="SUBMIT">
</FORM>
</BODY>
</HTML>
```

Listing 43-9: **Included password file (password.inc)**

```php
<?php
$username = "logwriter";
$password = "logpass";
?>
```

Listing 43-10: **Weblog data entry script (logentry.php)**

```php
<?php
$date = date("Ymd");
include("/home/htmluser/password.inc");

if($_POST['test_username'] == $username &&
   $_POST['test_password'] == $password) {
  $fp = fopen("/entries/$date.txt", "w");
  $try_entry = fwrite($fp, $_POST['logtext']);
  if ($try_entry > -1) {
    print("Weblog entry for $date written to disk.");
  } elseif ($try_entry == -1) {
    print("Weblog entry write failed.");
  }
} else {
  mail("me@localhost", "Weblog snoop alert", "Someone from
$REMOTE_ADDR is trying to get into your weblog entry
handler.");
}
?>
```

Adding Database Connectivity

Once you see how HTTP data entry is effected using the PHP file writing function, it's a short step to keeping your entries in a database rather than in discrete text files. This is neater — important as your site grows — and considerably more secure. Furthermore, you can give different database permissions to different users, enabling multiple content developers to work on the site safely.

By using a database, you get three more bonuses. First, you can write a script to edit your previous journal entries using a Web form, as well as just enter them. Even better, you can now classify and search your entries. And finally, you are no longer required to have entries every day—now you can do it as frequently or infrequently as you want without having a bunch of blank pages.

Although they have similar names and functions, the files shown in the following listings are somewhat different from the preceding set. You also need a script called weblog_db_create.php to create the database (unless you'd rather do it using the MySQL command-line tool); if you want to edit previous entries, you have to add a script called db_logedit.php.

Caution   Most of these scripts will not fail gracefully if the database has no data in it, particularly usernames and passwords in the login table. Because the whole thing is designed to be non-functional until you enter at least one entry into these tables, and we want you to focus on the main functionality rather than error-checking, there didn't seem to be a lot of point in testing for empty tables. If it's important to you, feel free to alter the code that follows.

Listings 43-11 through 43-16 are the files you need for a database-enabled Weblog.

Listing 43-11: **Included database password file (db_password.inc)**

```php
<?php
$hostname = "localhost";
$user = "dbuser";
$password = "dbpass";
?>
```

Put db_password.inc somewhere outside your Web tree, such as in your home directory. This will prevent your database passwords from being visible in a Web page or available to anyone who can get into your Web directory.

Listing 43-12: **Database creation script (weblog_db_create.php)**

```php
<?php
// You'll probably have to be the root MySQL user to run
// this script.If you can't get that permission, you could
// alter the script below to create tables in your
// pre-existing database.
include("/home/htmluser/db_password.inc");

mysql_connect($hostname, $user, $password)
  or die("Failure to communicate");
$try_create = mysql_create_db("weblogs");
if ($try_create > 0) {
  echo ("Successfully created database.<BR>\n");
  mysql_select_db("weblogs");
  $query = "CREATE TABLE login (ID SMALLINT NOT NULL
AUTO_INCREMENT PRIMARY KEY, username VARCHAR(20), password
VARCHAR(20))";
```

```
  $result = mysql_query($query);
  // Since we're not using the standard MySQL
  // date format, store date as an integer
  $query2 = "CREATE TABLE mylog (ID SMALLINT NOT NULL
AUTO_INCREMENT PRIMARY KEY, date INT(8), blogtext TEXT)";
  $result2 = mysql_query($query2);
  mysql_close();
  if ($result > 0 && $result2 > 0) {
    echo ("Successfully created tables<BR>\n");
  } else {
    echo ("Unable to create tables.");
  }
} else {
  echo ("Unable to create database");
}
?>
```

After creating the database as the MySQL root user, you can grant a more restrictive permissions package to some other MySQL user and then run the following scripts as that user.

Listing 43-13: **Database Weblog login screen (db_login.php)**

```
<HTML>
<HEAD>
<TITLE>Weblog login screen</TITLE>
</HEAD>

<P><B>Use this login to add a new entry.</B></P>
<FORM METHOD=POST ACTION="db_logentry.php">
<P>USERNAME:<INPUT TYPE=TEXT NAME="test_username" SIZE=20></P>
<P>PASSWORD:<INPUT TYPE=PASSWORD NAME="test_password"
SIZE=20></P>
<P><INPUT TYPE="SUBMIT" VALUE="SUBMIT">
</FORM>

<P><B>Use this login to edit a previous entry.</B></P>
<FORM METHOD=POST ACTION="db_logedit.php">
<P>USERNAME:<INPUT TYPE=TEXT NAME="test_username" SIZE=20></P>
<P>PASSWORD:<INPUT TYPE=PASSWORD NAME="test_password"
SIZE=20></P>
<P>EDIT DATE:<INPUT TYPE=TEXT NAME="edit_date" SIZE=8></P>
<P><INPUT TYPE="SUBMIT" VALUE="SUBMIT">
</FORM>
</BODY>
</HTML>
```

Listing 43-14: Database Weblog data entry screen (db_logentry.php)

```php
<?php
include("/home/htmluser/db_password.inc");
mysql_connect($hostname, $user, $password);
mysql_select_db("weblogs");

// Validate this user
$test_username = $_POST['test_username'];
$query = "SELECT password
          FROM login
          WHERE username = '$test_username'";
$result = mysql_query($query);
if (mysql_num_rows($result) != 1) {
  echo "Something is wrong";
  exit;
}
$password_row = mysql_fetch_array($result);
$db_password = $password_row[0];

if ($_POST['test_password'] == $db_password &&
$_POST['test_password'] != "") {
  if ($_POST['Submit'] == 'Enter') {
    // Enter new entry
    $date = date('Ymd'); // Remember, date is an integer type
    $blogtext = $_POST['blogtext'];
    $query = "INSERT INTO mylog (ID, date, blogtext)
VALUES(NULL, $date, '$blogtext')";
    $result = mysql_query($query);
    if (mysql_affected_rows() == 1) {
      header("Location: db_login.php");
    } else {
      echo "There was a problem inserting your text.";
      exit;
    }
  } else {
    // Show the form
    $php_self - $_SERVER['PHP_SELF'];
    $test_password = $_POST['test_password'];
$form_str = <<< EOFORMSTR
<HTML>
<HEAD>
<TITLE>Weblog data entry screen</TITLE>
</HEAD>
<BODY>
<FORM ACTION="$php_self" METHOD="POST">
<P>Text:<BR>
<TEXTAREA NAME="blogtext" COLS=75 ROWS=20
WRAP="VIRTUAL"></TEXTAREA></P>
<INPUT TYPE="hidden" NAME="test_username"
```

```
VALUE="$test_username">
<INPUT TYPE="hidden" NAME="test_password"
VALUE="$test_password">
<P><INPUT TYPE="SUBMIT" NAME="Submit" VALUE="Enter"></P>
</FORM>
</BODY>
</HTML>
EOFORMSTR;
    echo $form_str;
  }
} else {
  mail("me@localhost", "Weblog snoop", "Someone from
$REMOTE_ADDR is trying to get into your weblog entry screen.");
}
?>
```

Listing 43-15: **Database Weblog data edit screen (db_logedit.php)**

```php
<?php
include("/home/htmluser/db_password.inc");
mysql_connect($hostname, $user, $password);
mysql_select_db("weblogs");

// Validate this user
$test_username = $_POST['test_username'];
$query = "SELECT password
          FROM login
          WHERE username = '$test_username'";
$result = mysql_query($query);
if (mysql_num_rows($result) != 1) {
  echo "Something is wrong";
  exit;
}
$password_row = mysql_fetch_array($result);
$db_password = $password_row[0];

if ($_POST['test_password'] == $db_password &&
  $_POST['test_password'] != "") {
  if ($_POST['Submit'] == 'Enter') {
    // Insert edited entry
    $edit_date = $_POST['edit_date'];
    // Escape single-quotes and apostrophes
    $blogtext = addslashes($_POST['blogtext']);
    $query = "UPDATE mylog SET blogtext = '$blogtext'
              WHERE date = $edit_date";
    $result = mysql_query($query);
    if (mysql_affected_rows() == 1) {
      header("Location: db_login.php");
```

Continued

Listing 43-15 *(continued)*

```
      } else {
        echo "There was a problem inserting your text.";
        exit;
      }
    } else {
      // Show the form with the appropriate entry filled in
      $php_self = $_SERVER['PHP_SELF'];
      $test_password = $_POST['test_password'];
      $edit_date = $_POST['edit_date'];
      $query = "SELECT blogtext FROM mylog
                WHERE date = $edit_date";
      $result = mysql_query($query);
      if (mysql_num_rows($result) == 0) {
        echo "No entry matches that date";
        exit;
      }
      $entry_row = mysql_fetch_array($result);
      // When you get text from a SQL database,
      // you may need to strip backslashes from single-quotes.
      $blogtext = stripslashes($entry_row[0]);

$form_str = <<< EOFORMSTR
<HTML>
<HEAD>
<TITLE>Weblog data edit screen</TITLE>
</HEAD>
<BODY>
<FORM ACTION="$php_self" METHOD="POST">
<P>Text:<BR>
<TEXTAREA NAME="blogtext" COLS=75 ROWS=20
WRAP="VIRTUAL">$blogtext</TEXTAREA></P>
<INPUT TYPE="hidden" NAME="test_username"
VALUE="$test_username">
<INPUT TYPE="hidden" NAME="test_password"
VALUE="$test_password">
<INPUT TYPE="hidden" NAME="edit_date" VALUE="$edit_date">
<P><INPUT TYPE="SUBMIT" NAME="Submit" VALUE="Enter"></P>
</FORM>
</BODY>
</HTML>
EOFORMSTR;
      echo $form_str;
    }
  } else {
    mail("me@localhost", "Weblog snoop", "Someone from
$REMOTE_ADDR is trying to get into your weblog entry screen.");
  }
?>
```

Listing 43-16: **Main database Weblog template (db_weblog.php)**

```php
<?php

/************************************************************
 * This page has 4 possible cases:                         *
 * 1.  You're viewing this page without a supplied date,   *
 * so default to Case 4.                                   *
 *                                                          *
 * 2.  There is a date.  This is neither the first nor     *
 * the last entry in the db.                               *
 *                                                          *
 * 3.  There is a date.  This is the first entry in the db. *
 *                                                          *
 * 4.  There is a date.  This is the last entry in the db.  *
 ************************************************************/

// Open database connection
include("/home/htmluser/db_password.inc");
mysql_connect($hostname, $user, $password);
mysql_select_db("weblogs");

// Identify the latest entry
$query = "SELECT MAX(ID) FROM mylog";
$result = mysql_query($query);
$lastID_row = mysql_fetch_array($result);
$last_ID = $lastID_row[0];

// Get specified weblog entry
if ($_GET['date'] != "") {
  $entry_date = $_GET['date'];
  $query1 = "SELECT * FROM mylog WHERE date = $entry_date";
} else {
  $query1 = "SELECT * FROM mylog WHERE ID = $last_ID";
}
$result1 = mysql_query($query1);
$row_test_num = mysql_num_rows($result1);
if ($row_test_num > 0) {
  $entry_row = mysql_fetch_array($result1);
  $entry_ID = $entry_row[0];
  $entry_date = $entry_row[1];
  $entry = stripslashes($entry_row[2]);
} else {
  // If someone enters a bad date, redirect to homepage
  header("Location: /index.php");
}

// Get previous date for Cases 2 and 4
if ($entry_ID > 1) {
  $prev_ID = $entry_ID - 1;
```

Continued

Listing 43-16 *(continued)*

```
    $query2 = "SELECT date FROM mylog WHERE ID = $prev_ID";
    $result2 = mysql_query($query2);
    $prevdate_row = mysql_fetch_array($result2);
    $prev_date = $prevdate_row[0];
} else {
    $prev_date = "";
}

// Get next date for Cases 2 and 3
if ($entry_ID != $last_ID) {
    $next_ID = $entry_ID + 1;
    $query3 = "SELECT date FROM mylog WHERE ID = $next_ID";
    $result3 = mysql_query($query3);
    $nextdate_row = mysql_fetch_array($result3);
    $next_date = $nextdate_row[0];
} else {
    $next_date = "";
}

// Assemble the Previous/Next links
// Case 2
if ($next_date != "" && $prev_date != "") {
    $flipbar = "\n<TABLE BORDER=0><TR>
<TD WIDTH=\"50%\" ALIGN=\"left\">
<SPAN CLASS=\"previous\">
<A HREF=\"$PHP_SELF?date=$prev_date\">&#60;-- Previous</A>
</SPAN>
</TD><TD WIDTH=\"50%\" ALIGN=\"right\">
<SPAN CLASS=\"next\">
<A HREF=\"$PHP_SELF?date=$next_date\">Next --&#62;</A>
</SPAN>
</TD></TR></TABLE>\n";
}
// Case 3
elseif ($next_date != "" && $prev_date == "") {
    $flipbar = "\n<P CLASS=\"next\">
<A HREF=\"$PHP_SELF?date=$next_date\">Next --&#62;</A>
</P>\n";
}
// Case 4
elseif($next_date == "" && $prev_date != "") {
    $flipbar = "\n<P CLASS=\"previous\">
<A HREF=\"$PHP_SELF?date=$prev_date\">&#60;-- Previous</A>
</P>\n";
}


// ---------------------
// NOW ASSEMBLE THE PAGE
// ---------------------
```

```
$title_msg = $entry_date;
$header_msg = "Weblog entry for $entry_date";
include_once('header.inc');

echo $flipbar;
// Include the specified entry text
echo $entry;
echo $flipbar;

include_once('footer.inc');
?>
```

Changes and Additions

Things you might want to immediately change, add, or alter in this codebase include:

✦ Alter colors, styles, layout.

✦ Change frequency of expected update (weekly, monthly).

✦ Change to calendar-based navigation rather than Next/Previous links.

✦ Change to topic-based rather than date-based navigation.

✦ Stop automatic entry changeover by date.

✦ Allow future entries in database.

✦ Allow multiple authors/editors with different permissions.

Besides a personal Weblog, you could use this code for any simple, chronological note taking, such as:

✦ A vacation journal

✦ A project log

✦ The story of your vast weight loss through heroic diet and exercise

✦ A chronicle of your pregnancy and baby's development

Summary

Although it's handy for small, standalone projects such as polls, PHP's most impressive use is in developing complete data-driven content sites. The easiest such site to develop is the personal Weblog. We encourage every PHP user to keep one, if only as a handy testbed for new ideas and techniques.

If you wish, you can store your data in ordinary text files, using PHP to plug these files into a template based on a criterion such as date. This will save a certain amount of formatting-related repetition at the cost of somewhat decreased security. Far better in every way is to keep the data in a database.

The Weblog format is very flexible. It can scale up to a major public site like Slashdot, with tens of thousands of contributors and a steady stream of new content upon which to comment. Or you can keep a little secret diary on your own laptop, reading it in a browser window on the sly. The important point is that once you've made a complete data-driven site with PHP, you'll never go back to static Web pages.

✦   ✦   ✦

User Authentication

User data management is a core function of many Web sites. However, it's more difficult than it may seem to design a good, secure, extensible way to register, log in, and change user information. Even harder is architecting a toolkit for your administrators and editors. In this chapter, we walk you through a complete user registration and administrator authentication system, with notes on the fine points to keep in mind as you implement such a system for yourself.

Designing a User-Authentication System

By now, you're probably sick and tired of us telling you to think through your needs and write up some specs before you design any feature. Well, too bad; we're not going to let up on you now — because it's never more relevant advice than when you're dealing with user data.

There are quite a few common decisions that you should make before you write any code. Do you plan to use full names or just usernames? If you're going to collect full names, always collect separate first and last names. If you've ever had to write a program to split a bunch of names (like the following) into first and last names, you'll know why keeping them separate is so important:

- ✦ Thomas St. John, Jr.
- ✦ Lee Min
- ✦ Michael de la Cruz
- ✦ Arantxa Sanchez Vicario
- ✦ David Ben Gurion
- ✦ M. Abu Ibrahim

As you can immediately see, there is no simple algorithm that can be immediately applied to names like these that will infallibly split them.

Who will choose the passwords? Do you allow your users to set their own? Or do you generate passwords programmatically and e-mail them to your users? The former is easier for the user, but the latter allows you to more easily weed out users who give false e-mail addresses.

Is a user immediately logged in after registering? Or does he or she have to perform some other step, such as waiting for an e-mail with a password or a link to a confirmation form?

Is login based on e-mail and password or username and password? Must any or all of these be unique?

Do you permit writes by anonymous users? If so, do they all use a standard name (for example, Slashdot's Anonymous Coward) or do you allow them to choose ad-hoc temporary usernames?

How do you plan to deal with forgotten passwords and possibly usernames? Any number of schemes can be implemented to deal with these issues — programmatically generating a new password, sending the old password in plain text e-mail, permitting a temporary login just long enough to change the password, and so on — but they all have consequences. For instance, if you send the password via e-mail, you probably will not be able to use a good encryption scheme.

Do you give users control over the display of their personal information? Do you have a clear user policy that requires this? Have you checked your proposed architecture against your user agreement?

How do you plan to handle permissions? Do your permissions come in buckets — all users get the same permissions — or do you need more fine-grained control?

What is your legal liability position in regard to user data? For instance, if you use a badly designed user validation scheme and someone manages to crack it enough to impersonate someone else — can enough harm be done that your organization could be sued? If your site is basically just a content or community resource, the stakes aren't usually very high — but if you handle money or goods in any form, you need a clear policy.

Do you plan to disable or delete bad users?

How will you maintain state (if at all)? Do you plan to use cookies or sessions or databases?

Do you need the ability to log in as a given user?

Is your site actually part of a suite of Web properties belonging to your organization? If so, do you need to make all the sites use the same user-management system?

If you can get clear answers to these questions, preferably written down in a spec, you are quite a way toward designing the precise user data-management architecture that you need.

Avoiding Common Security Issues

Some very common and easily avoidable security issues are far too often ignored by site designers. PHP is sometimes targeted with the accusation of being chintzy and insecure because individual programmers do not follow good software practices. Security practices are especially important in working with user data.

You can do a few basic things to greatly reduce the risk of your site being cracked. Remember that security is all about raising the difficulty level for crackers — it's one thing to be cracked by a professional crime ring, and another to have all your user's passwords stolen by a 15-year old kid who can't even program.

Every Web site should be taking these very basic steps to safeguard its users' personal data:

Turn off register_globals

Too many PHP developers still write code such as this:

```
<?php
if (check_admin_priv()) {
  $admin = 1;
}

if ($admin == 1) {
  // Allow the user to see some privileged data
}
?>
```

This works fine for what you want it to do, which is set the $admin variable to 1 for legitimate administrators. But you also need to think about what your scripts can do that you don't want them to do. This particular usage also lets any user who cares to use a URL like badcode.php ?admin=1 get administrator privileges if you have register_globals turned on. At the very least, you should be setting $admin to some other value if check_admin_priv() does not return true — but a better solution is to learn to live without register_globals.

PHP's register_globals feature, which makes all GET, POST, COOKIE, SESSION, ENV, and SERVER variables immediately available via their plain variable names, is very popular because it seems to make development so much easier. Crackers can exploit this feature, however, to spoof cookies, run external JavaScript functions, load unsafe data into a database, and many other security nightmares. In large and complicated sites, register_globals can also lead to strange bugs as variables overwrite each other — especially if your team has members who do not choose good variable names (and most teams do). Only you can prevent your global namespace from becoming polluted with unsafe or unnecessary values.

The truth is that register_globals merely saves you a few keystrokes in development, at the price of massive risk, and the PHP community is slowly moving toward deprecating this feature for good. Instead, the PHP team has implemented superglobal arrays, which force you to ask for COOKIE values in cookies, POST values from posts, and so on — the gain for you is true global scope.

You have time now to begin moving away from register_globals. Remember that you can easily write a shell, Perl, or PHP script to replace many of the global variables in your codebase — so this change doesn't necessarily entail enormous amounts of hand labor. Use of superglobal arrays also encourages good programming practice — because good code asks for data and evaluates conditions as specifically as possible.

Note   Users of PHP version 4.2.0 and higher, including PHP5, will notice that the register_ globals flag is now turned off by default. Take it as a sign of the times.

Check for string length and safety

Many PHP user registration programs contain lines like this:

```
if ($username && $password && $email) {
  // Allow them to register
}
```

However, you should never assume that just because you've provided some nice form fields named Username and Password, people are using those fields to enter usernames and passwords. The pseudocode above just asks for the existence of a variable value without specifying anything about that value. You can and should be specifying precisely which types of data you accept into your database — the more precisely, the better.

There is no good reason, for example, that anyone should ever be choosing a username or password that is longer than, say, 25 characters. If someone wants to use a 100-character string as a username, that's a presumptive test that he or she may intend to do harm to your system. Why not just filter these people out before something bad happens, by testing for string length? It takes hardly any more development or runtime resources. This code snippet, for instance, will allow users to register only if all the variables contain fewer than 25 characters:

```
if (strlen($username) <= 25 && strlen($password) <= 25 &&
  strlen($email) <= 25) {
  // Allow them to register.
}
```

Also, think about the type and content of these variables. If you have a form field for a user's age, there's no legitimate reason why anyone should be trying to stuff an array into it. You can use PHP functions like is_int, is_string, and is_bool to make sure your variable type is what it should be.

Be particularly careful of any string that has tags (especially HREF and SCRIPT tags), single-quotes, double-quotes, or semicolons in it. You should either reject these outright if there's no legitimate use for such characters — no username should have any of these characters in them, for example — or use escaping and encoding to turn them into strings that cannot evaluate in PHP or a browser.

 Tip You're much safer, of course, if your database design fully supports the strategic goals of your code. So don't use expansive types such as text or varchar to represent a Boolean, integer, or date type — make sure that the data type of each field is carefully matched to the actual data you intend to store in that field. Not only is your performance faster, but in the event someone manages to sneak unsafe code into your database, a restrictive type has a much better chance of choking on or truncating the bad data.

One-way encrypt passwords

A surprising number of "professional" Web sites store their users' passwords in plain text in their databases. In doing so they are running the risk that one break-in can result in the compromise of the entire user data system — which often means that financial or other systems can no longer be trusted. Password theft is also becoming a source of legal liability for companies who fail to prevent or try to cover up the theft of their users' personal data.

The most frequently heard excuses for this practice are that the site needs to e-mail passwords to users who have forgotten them, and that the site's employees need the capability to log in as a particular user to verify bugs reported by that user. Neither of these excuses washes. You have many other ways to deal with forgotten passwords and logging in as a particular user, some of which we will discuss in the "User Tools" and "Administrator Tools" sections that follow.

The easiest way to get out from under the technical and legal risks of password theft is to make it impossible for even you to know what your users' passwords are. The easiest way to accomplish this is to one-way encrypt user passwords on registration. You can do this either in PHP or in the database itself. The MySQL way to store passwords, for example, is by wrapping them in a built-in encrypting function called `password()`:

```
INSERT INTO user_table (username, password) VALUES('$username',
    password('$password'));
```

Now when a user tries to log in, you query for the password using the same function:

```
SELECT username, password FROM user_table WHERE username =
    '$username' AND password = password('$password');
```

If you want to do the encryption on the PHP side, which has advantages, there's a code sample with explanations in the "Login" section. Both methods use good one-way algorithms that, for most practical purposes, cannot be reversed as they require serious supercomputer time to decrypt. Whichever method you choose, the important point is to always encrypt your passwords before storing them.

Cross-Reference   These are specifically user-data security issues. See Chapter 29 for general information on security and cryptography and Chapter 14 for more information about MySQL-specific security issues.

Registration

Now you can begin to implement all the design decisions and tips that we discussed in the "Designing a User-Authentication System" section at the beginning of this chapter. Obviously, the first place to start is with new user registration. In the code in this section, which is based on some sample code written by Tim Perdue, we have chosen the following options:

✦ Check for a unique e-mail address on each registration.

✦ Have users choose their own usernames, which must be unique.

✦ Have the users choose their own passwords, which are then one-way encrypted.

✦ Confirm new registrations by click-through e-mail to cut down on spam and rogue users.

The particular method of one-way encryption used here is actually md5 hashing. This takes a string of any reasonable length, applies RSA's md5 algorithm to it, and returns a 32-character hexadecimal string that has a high chance of uniquely identifying that string later (unless you started out with an extremely large number of strings). It's kind of like getting a claim ticket for your shirt at the dry cleaner's — it has a number on it that increases your chances of later identifying the particular shirt you dropped off. By some definitions this is not strictly encryption — but for our purposes, it's one of the better one-way transformation algorithms. Unless you have unlimited supercomputers and time, you will not be able to figure out what the original password was.

Tip   You may have seen md5 hashing used in another context, which is guaranteeing that software packages contain what they should contain. Open source projects often run their tarballs through md5 to generate a 128-bit key that is published separately. Any user should be able to run the same package through md5 and come up with the same number if the contents have not been altered. If a virus were introduced to the distribution somehow, the md5 hashes would not match, and the user would know not to install the package.

The script in Listing 44-1 is called `register_funcs.inc`. It contains all registration-related functions. You will call these functions from other PHP pages.

Listing 44-1: **Registration functions (register_funcs.inc)**

```php
<?php

// A file with the database host, user, password, and
// selected database
include_once('db_vars.inc');

// A string used for md5 encryption.  You could move it
//to a file outside the web tree for more security.
$supersecret_hash_padding = 'A string that is used to pad out
short strings for md5 encryption.';


function user_register() {
    // This function will only work with superglobal arrays,
    // because I'm not passing in any values or declaring globals
    global $supersecret_hash_padding;

    // Are all vars present and passwords match?
    if (strlen($_POST['user_name']) <= 25 &&
      strlen($_POST['password1']) <= 25 && ($_POST['password1'] ==
      $_POST['password2']) && strlen($_POST['email']) <= 50 &&
      validate_email($_POST['email'])) {
        // Validate username and password
        if (account_namevalid($_POST['user_name']) ||
        strlen($_POST['password1'] >= 6)) {

            $user_name = strtolower($_POST['user_name']);
            $user_name = trim($user_name);
            // Don't need to escape, because single quotes
            // aren't allowed
            $email = $_POST['email'];
            // Don't allow duplicate usernames or emails
            $query = "SELECT user_id
                    FROM user
                    WHERE user_name = '$user_name'
                    AND email = '$email'";
            $result = mysql_query($query);
            if ($result && mysql_num_rows($result) > 0) {
```

```php
        $feedback = 'ERROR--Username or email address already
          exists';
        return $feedback;
    } else {
        $first_name = $_POST['first_name'];
        $last_name = $_POST['last_name'];
        $password = md5($_POST['password1']);
        $user_ip = $_SERVER['REMOTE_ADDR'];
        // Create a new hash to insert into the db and
        // the confirmation email
        $hash = md5($email.$supersecret_hash_padding);

        $query = "INSERT INTO user (user_name, first_name,
          last_name, password, email, remote_addr, confirm_hash,
          is_confirmed, date_created)
          VALUES ('$user_name', '$first_name', '$last_name',
          '$password', '$email', '$user_ip', '$hash', '0',
          NOW())";
        $result = mysql_query($query);
        if (!$result) {
            $feedback = 'ERROR--Database error';
            return $feedback;
        } else {
            // Send the confirmation email
            $encoded_email = urlencode($_POST['email']);
            $mail_body = <<< EOMAILBODY
Thank you for registering at Example.com.  Click this link
to confirm your registration:

http://localhost/confirm.php?hash=$hash&email=$encoded_email

Once you see a confirmation message, you will be logged into
Example.com
EOMAILBODY;
            mail ($email, 'Example.com Registration Confirmation',
              $mail_body, 'From: noreply@example.com');

    // Give a successful registration message
            $feedback = 'YOU HAVE SUCCESSFULLY REGISTERED.
              You will receive a confirmation email soon';
            return $feedback;
        }
      }
    } else {
      $feedback =  'ERROR--Username or password is invalid';
      return $feedback;
    }
  } else {
    $feedback = 'ERROR--Please fill in all fields correctly';
    return $feedback;
  }
```

Continued

Listing 44-1 *(continued)*

```php
}


function account_namevalid() {

  // parameter for use with strspan
$span_str = "abcdefghijklmnopqrstuvwxyz" .
    "ABCDEFGHIJKLMNOPQRSTUVWXYZ0123456789-";

  // must have at least one character
  if (strspn($_POST['user_name'],$span_str) == 0) {
    return false;
  }

  // must contain all legal characters
  if (strspn($_POST['user_name'],$span_str) != strlen($name)) {
    return false;
  }

  // min and max length
  if (strlen($_POST['user_name']) < 5) {
    return false;
  }
  if (strlen($_POST['user_name']) > 25) {
    return false;
  }

  // illegal names
  if
(eregi("^((root)|(bin)|(daemon)|(adm)|(lp)|(sync)|(shutdown)|
(halt)|(mail)|(news)|(uucp)|(operator)|(games)|(mysql)|
(httpd)|(nobody)|(dummy)|(www)|(cvs)|(shell)|(ftp)|(irc)|
(debian)|(ns)|(download))$", $_POST['user_name'])) {
    return false;
  }
  if (eregi("^(anoncvs_)", $_POST['user_name'])) {
    return false;
  }

return true;
}


function validate_email () {
  return (ereg('^[-!#$%&\'*+\\./0-9=?A-Z^_`a-z{|}~]+'. '@'. '[-
!#$%&\'*+\\/0-9=?A-Z^_`a-z{|}~]+\.' . '[-!#$%&\'*+\\./0-9=?A-
Z^_`a-z{|}~]+$', $_POST['email']));
}


function user_confirm() {
```

```php
// This function will only work with superglobal arrays,
// because I'm not passing in any values or declaring globals
global $supersecret_hash_padding;

// Verify that they didn't tamper with the email address
$new_hash = md5($_GET['email'].$supersecret_hash_padding);
if ($new_hash && ($new_hash == $_GET['hash'])) {
    $query = "SELECT user_name
              FROM user
              WHERE confirm_hash = '$new_hash'";
    $result = mysql_query($query);
    if (!$result || mysql_num_rows($result) < 1) {
        $feedback = 'ERROR--Hash not found';
        return $feedback;
    } else {
        // Confirm the email and set account to active
        $email = $_GET['email'];
        $hash = $_GET['hash'];
    $query = "UPDATE user SET email='$email',
is_confirmed='1' WHERE confirm_hash='$hash'";
        $result = mysql_query($query);
        return 1;
    }
} else {
    $feedback = 'ERROR--Values do not match';
    return $feedback;
}
}

?>
```

Notice that, during the registration process, we also one-way encrypted a variable consisting of the user's e-mail address plus a filler string. This will be used to confirm that e-mail is actually received at the e-mail address listed by the user.

Listing 44-2 is called `register.php`. It shows a form and calls the `register()` function.

Listing 44-2: **Registration form (register.php)**

```php
<?php

/********************************************************
 * New user registration page.  There are links to     *
 * this page from the header on every other page for    *
 * logged-out and logged-in users.  This may be a       *
 * design flaw however; it's entirely possible that     *
 * we may want to show this page only to logged-out     *
 * visitors.                                            *
 ********************************************************/
```

Continued

Listing 44-2 *(continued)*

```
require_once('includes/register_funcs.inc');

if ($submit == 'Mail confirmation') {
  $feedback = user_register();

  // In every case, successful or not, there will be feedback
  $feedback_str = "<P class=\"errormess\">$feedback</P>";
} else {
  // Show form for the first time
  $feedback_str = '';
}


// ----------------
// DISPLAY THE FORM
// ----------------
include_once('includes/header_footer.php');
site_header('Registration');

// Superglobals don't work with heredoc
$php_self = $_SERVER['PHP_SELF'];

$reg_str = <<< EOREGSTR
<TABLE CELLPADDING=0 CELLSPACING=0 BORDER=0 ALIGN=CENTER
  WIDTH=621>
<TR>
  <TD ROWSPAN=10><IMG WIDTH=15 HEIGHT=1
    SRC="../images/spacer.gif"></TD>
  <TD WIDTH=606></TD>
</TR>
<TR>
 <TD>


$feedback_str
<P CLASS="left"><B>REGISTER</B><BR>
Fill out this form and a confirmation email will be sent to you.
Once you click on the link in the email your account will be
confirmed and you can begin to contribute to the community.</P>
<FORM ACTION="$php_self" METHOD="POST">
<P CLASS="bold">First Name<BR>
<INPUT TYPE="TEXT" NAME="first_name" VALUE="$first_name"
  SIZE="20" MAXLENGTH="25"></P>
<P CLASS="bold">Last Name<BR>
<INPUT TYPE="TEXT" NAME="last_name" VALUE="$last_name" SIZE="20"
  MAXLENGTH="25"></P>
<P CLASS="bold">Username<BR>
<INPUT TYPE="TEXT" NAME="user_name" VALUE="$user_name" SIZE="10"
  MAXLENGTH="25"></P>
<P CLASS="bold">Password<BR>
```

```
<INPUT TYPE="password" NAME="password1" VALUE="" SIZE="10"
  MAXLENGTH="25"></P>
<P CLASS="left"><B>Password</B> (again)<BR>
<INPUT TYPE="password" NAME="password2" VALUE="" SIZE="10"
  MAXLENGTH="25"></P>
<P CLASS="left"><B>Email</B> (required for confirmation)<BR>
<INPUT TYPE="TEXT" NAME="email" VALUE="$email" SIZE="30"
  MAXLENGTH="50">
</P>
<P><INPUT TYPE="SUBMIT" NAME="submit"
          VALUE="Mail confirmation">
</P>
</FORM>

  </TD>
</TR>
</TABLE>
EOREGSTR;
echo $reg_str;

site_footer();

?>
```

The registration form looks similar to Figure 44-1.

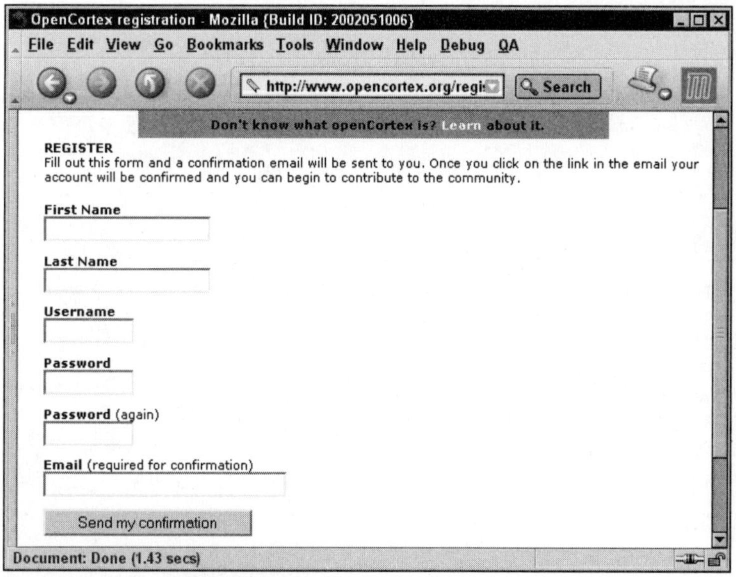

Figure 44-1: User registration form

After the user registers, he or she gets a confirmation e-mail with a link to click. This link contains a confirmation hash and the e-mail address that the mail was sent to. The user can't log in to the site until he or she gets this e-mail and we check it against the hash that we set. Here we are trusting that our padding string remains secret. If someone learned it, he or she could spoof any e-mail address quite easily — but until we have reason to believe our system security has been broken, this can be considered *good-enough* proof that the hash was indeed set by us. None of this will necessarily stop a determined attack by a knowledgeable cracker, but it will greatly reduce the number of people who try to give patently false e-mail addresses in registration forms.

After the user clicks through the link, he or she will see the following page, `confirm.php` (Listing 44-3).

Listing 44-3: New-user confirmation page (confirm.php)

```php
<?php

/*********************************************************
 * New user confirmation page.  Should only get here *
 * from an email link.                                *
 *********************************************************/


require_once('includes/register_funcs.inc');
include_once('includes/header_footer.php');

site_header('Account Confirmation');

if ($_GET['hash'] && $_GET['email']) {
  $worked = user_confirm();
} else {
  $feedback_str = "<P class=\"errormess\">ERROR--Bad link</P>";
}


if ($worked != 1) {
  $noconfirm = '<P class="errormess">Something went wrong.  ' .
    'Send email to admin@example.com for help.  If you ' .
    'through to this page directly, please go to login.php ' .
    'instead.</P>';
} else {
  $confirm = '<P class="big">You are now confirmed. <A ' .
    'HREF="login.php">Log in</A> to start browsing the ' .
    'site.</P>';
}

$page = <<< EOPAGE

<TABLE CELLPADDING=0 CELLSPACING=0 BORDER=0 ALIGN=CENTER
WIDTH=621>
<TR>
  <TD><IMG WIDTH=15 HEIGHT=1 SRC=../images/spacer.gif></TD>
  <TD WIDTH=606 CLASS=left>
```

```
        $feedback_str
        $noconfirm
        $confirm
        </TD>
    </TR>
    </TABLE>
EOPAGE;

    echo $page;

    site_footer();

    ?>
```

Login/Logout

If your registration process is well designed in the first place, it can help your login process be more effective. So, for example, if you strictly enforce e-mail and username uniqueness during registration, in theory, you do not need to check for those things during login. You may still want to as a belt-and-braces kind of thing, but it all depends on how much you trust your registration. In the case of the registration system in the preceding section, our method of using a one-way hashing function to encrypt passwords and e-mails can also be adapted to enhance the reliability of cookies in an extremely scalable way.

Here's the problem we're trying to solve: After a user logs in, we want to set a cookie that uniquely identifies the user. Say we set a cookie that contains the user's username on our site, which is generally not a very private piece of information—in fact, it's a method of saving people from having to use their real names in public. A cookie, however, is just a text file—there's literally nothing stopping you from writing up a cookie file on your computer that claims you are someone else.

Sites deal with the cookie-verification problem in different ways, the most common of which is checking your cookie data against a database on every page load. This is not a very scalable solution, however, unless you have some kind of serious data-caching mechanism, because eventually the database becomes a bottleneck.

The solution that we use is a little bit different. When users log in, we look them up in the database by their usernames and passwords. If we find them in there, we set two cookies per user: one with the username and one with the hashed product of the username and a super-secret string known only to us. Now on every page load, we check for the existence of these cookies—but also we see if they match and if they were set by us, by hashing the value of the username cookie with the super secret string and then comparing it to the hash cookie. All this is done on the Web server at relatively little cost in time or cycles, rather than necessitating the opening of a connection to the database. Again, we must trust that the secret string is not compromised—but in the worst-case scenario, we could change this string and merely cause everyone to be logged out suddenly.

After we confirm that the cookies do, in fact, match, we can optionally go even further by setting a global logged-in flag. This isn't the most secure method possible, but it's extremely fast. You may consider using a logged-in flag for reads and reserving every-page cookie-verification for tools such as adding content or changing passwords. You could do this by splitting the user_isloggedin() function in Listing 44-4 into two functions: one to detect the flag and one to match up the cookies.

Listing 44-4 is called `login_funcs.inc`. It contains all login-related and logout-related functions, which will be called from other PHP pages.

Listing 44-4: **Login and logout functions (login_funcs.inc)**

```php
<?php

// A file with the database host, user, password, and
// selected database
include_once('db_vars.inc');

// A string used for md5 encryption.  You could move it to
// a file
// outside the web tree for more security.
$supersecret_hash_padding = 'A string that is used to pad' .
  'out short strings for md5 encryption.';


$LOGGED_IN = false;
unset($LOGGED_IN);


function user_isloggedin() {
  // This function will only work with superglobal arrays,
  // because I'm not passing in any values or declaring globals
  global $supersecret_hash_padding, $LOGGED_IN;

  // Have we already run the hash checks?
  // If so, return the pre-set var
  if (isSet($LOGGED_IN)) {
    return $LOGGED_IN;
  }
  if ($_COOKIE['user_name'] && $_COOKIE['id_hash']) {
    $hash = md5($_COOKIE['user_name']
          .$supersecret_hash_padding);
    if ($hash == $_COOKIE['id_hash']) {
      return true;
    } else {
      return false;
    }
  } else {
    return false;
  }
}


function user_login() {
  // This function will only work with superglobal arrays,
  // because I'm not passing in any values or declaring globals
  if (!$_POST['user_name'] || !$_POST['password']) {
    $feedback = 'ERROR--Missing username or password';
    return $feedback;
```

```php
    } else {
      $user_name = strtolower($_POST['user_name']);
      // Don't need to trim because extra spaces should fail
      // for this
      // Don't need to addslashes because single quotes
      // aren't allowed
      $password = strtolower($_POST['password']);
      // Don't need to addslashes because we'll be hashing it
      $crypt_pwd = md5($password);
      $query = "SELECT user_name, is_confirmed
                FROM user
                WHERE user_name = '$user_name'
                AND password='$crypt_pwd'";
      $result = mysql_query($query);
      if (!$result || mysql_num_rows($result) < 1){
        $feedback = 'ERROR--User not found or password ' .
          'incorrect';
        return $feedback;
      } else {
        if (mysql_result($result, 0, 'is_confirmed') == '1') {
          user_set_tokens($user_name);
          return 1;
        } else {
          $feedback = 'ERROR--You may not have confirmed ' .
            'your account yet';
          return $feedback;
        }
      }
    }
}


function user_logout() {
  setcookie('user_name', '', (time()+2592000), '/', '', 0);
  setcookie('id_hash', '', (time()+2592000), '/', '', 0);
}


function user_set_tokens($user_name_in) {
  global $supersecret_hash_padding;
  if (!$user_name_in) {
    $feedback =  'ERROR--No username';
    return false;
  }
  $user_name = strtolower($user_name_in);
  $id_hash = md5($user_name.$supersecret_hash_padding);

  setcookie('user_name', $user_name, (time()+2592000), '/',
    '',0);
  setcookie('id_hash', $id_hash, (time()+2592000), '/', '', 0);
}

?>
```

Listing 44-5 is called `login.php`. It shows a form and calls the `login()` function. On success, it redirects to the home page.

Listing 44-5: **Login form (login.php)**

```php
<?php

/****************************************************
 * Login page.  There are links to this page from *
 * the header on every other page for logged-out  *
 * users only.                                     *
 ****************************************************/

require_once('includes/login_funcs.inc');

// If they're logged in, log them out
// They shouldn't be able to see this page logged-in
// This allows the same page to be used as a logout script
if ($LOGGED_IN = user_isloggedin()) {
  user_logout();
  $_COOKIE['user_name'] = '';
  unset($LOGGED_IN);
}

if ($submit == 'Login') {
  if (strlen($_POST['username']) <= 25 &&
strlen($_POST['password']) <=25) {
    $feedback = user_login();
  } else {
    $feedback = 'ERROR--Username and password are too long';
  }
  if ($feedback == 1) {
    // On successful login, redirect to homepage
    header("Location: index.php");
  } else {
    $feedback_str = "<P class=\"errormess\">$feedback</P>";
  }
} else {
  $feedback_str = '';
}



// ----------------
// DISPLAY THE FORM
// ----------------
include_once('includes/header_footer.php');
site_header('Login');

// Superglobals don't work with heredoc
```

```php
$php_self = $_SERVER['PHP_SELF'];

$login_form = <<< EOLOGINFORM
<TABLE CELLPADDING=0 CELLSPACING=0 BORDER=0 ALIGN=CENTER
  WIDTH=621>
<TR>
  <TD ROWSPAN=2><IMG WIDTH=15 HEIGHT=1
SRC=../images/spacer.gif></TD>
  <TD WIDTH=606 HEIGHT=1><IMG WIDTH=606 HEIGHT=1
SRC=../images/spacer.gif></TD>
</TR>
<TR>
 <TD>

$feedback_str
<P CLASS="bold">LOGIN</P>
<FORM ACTION="$php_self" METHOD="POST">
<P CLASS="bold">Username<BR>
<INPUT TYPE="TEXT" NAME="user_name" VALUE="" SIZE="10"
  MAXLENGTH="15"></P>
<P CLASS="bold">Password<BR>
<INPUT TYPE="password" NAME="password" VALUE="" SIZE="10"
  MAXLENGTH="15"></P>
<P><INPUT TYPE="SUBMIT" NAME="submit" VALUE="Login"></P>
</FORM>

 </TD>
</TR>
</TABLE>
EOLOGINFORM;
echo $login_form;

site_footer();

?>
```

Figure 44-2 shows the login page in the midst of an error.

Tip   Mozilla is far and away the best browser to develop on if you're working with the login functions of a site because it has the Cookie Manager feature (in the Tools menu, or Tools ⇨ Options ⇨ Privacy ⇨ Cookies in Mozilla Firebird). Mozilla enables you to see all your cookies in a nice alphabetized list and to delete or block cookies individually. The only thing to watch out for is that cookies may be classified under example.com, servername.example.com, or www.example.com depending on precisely how they were set.

Logging out is very simple — you just unset the cookies. Actually, if you are logged in and visit the login.php page, it happens automatically — so you can use login.php for both logging in and logging out.

Figure 44-2: Login page

User Tools

Registration and login are the core of your user management system, but you also need tools for various common situations, such as forgotten passwords, changing a password, or changing less-sensitive user information.

Forgotten password

The most common way to deal with a forgotten password is to simply mail it to the e-mail address you have on file for a particular user. Many sites a lot larger than yours do this. Cases of stealing passwords this way may have been reported, but it's not a rampant problem — especially if people do the smart thing, which is to immediately change the password as soon as they can log on.

There are more elaborate ways to deal with forgotten passwords. One of us, for example, once worked on a system where an e-mail was sent containing a link that allowed the user to visit a special page which existed once and only once — which allowed the user to change his or her password without actually logging in. It was a somewhat neurotic solution to the problem, but it worked.

We believe the best compromise is simply to mail a new computer-generated random password. This will be fairly secure and yet so difficult to remember that hopefully the user will be more motivated to immediately change his or her password to something more comfy.

You can also repurpose the password-generation part of this code if you plan to generate passwords during the registration process instead of letting the user choose the password, as we do in the "Registration" section earlier in this chapter.

Listing 44-6 is called `forgot.php`. It shows a form, generates a random new password, and sends it to the user's recorded e-mail address.

Listing 44-6: **Form to handle forgotten passwords (forgot.php)**

```php
<?php

/*******************************************
 * This file displays the forgot-password  *
 * form.  It submits to itself, mails a     *
 * temporary password, and then redirects   *
 * to login.                                 *
 *******************************************/

// A file with the database host, user, password, and
// selected database
require_once('db_vars.inc');

if ($HTTP_POST_VARS['command'] == 'forgot' &&
  strlen($_POST['email']) <= 50)) {
  // Handle submission.  This is a one-time only form
  // so there will be no problems with handling errors.
  $as_email = addslashes($_POST['email']);
  $query = "select id from users where email = '$as_email'";
  $result = mysql_query($query);
  $is_user = mysql_num_rows($result);

  if ($is_user == 1) {
    // Generate a random password
    $alphanum =
array('a','b','c','d','e','f','g','h','i','j','k','m','n','o',
 'p','q','r','s','t','u','v','x','y','z','A','B','C','D','E',
 'F','G','H','I','J','K','M','N','P','Q','R','S','T','U',
 'V','W','X','Y','Z','2','3','4','5','6','7','8','9');
    $chars = sizeof($alphanum);
    $a = time();
    mt_srand($a);
    for ($i=0; $i < 6; $i++) {
      $randnum = intval(mt_rand(0,56));
      $password .= $alphanum[$randnum];
    }
    // One-way encrypt it
    $crypt_pass = md5($password);

    // Put the temp password in the db
    $query = "update univ_Users set password = '$crypt_pass'
      where email = '$as_email'";
    $result = mysql_query($query) or die('Cannot complete
```

Continued

Listing 44-6 *(continued)*

```
        update');

    // Send the email
    $to      = $_POST['email'];
    $from    = "forgot@example.com";
    $subject = "New password";
    $msg     = <<< EOMSG
You recently requested that we send you a new password for
Example.com.  Your new password is:

            $password

Please log in at this URL:

            http://localhost/login.html

Then go to this address to change your password:

            http://localhost/changepass.php
EOMSG;

    $mailsend = mail("$to","$subject","$msg","From:
      $from\r\nReply-To:webmaster@example.com");

    // Redirect to login
    header("Location: login.html");
  } else {
    // The email address isn't good, they lose.
  }

}


// -----------------------
// Display the form nicely
// -----------------------

// Superglobal arrays don't work in heredoc
$php_self = $_SERVER['PHP_SELF'];

$form_str = <<< EOFORMSTR
<HTML>
<HEAD>
<STYLE TYPE="text/css">
<!--
BODY, P     {color: black; font-family: verdana;
  font-size: 10 pt}
H1       {color: black; font-family: arial; font-size: 12 pt}
-->
</STYLE>
</HEAD>
```

```
<BODY>
<TABLE BORDER=0 CELLPADDING=10 WIDTH=100%>
<TR>
<TD BGCOLOR="#F0F8FF" ALIGN=CENTER VALIGN=TOP WIDTH=150>
</TD>
<TD BGCOLOR="#FFFFFF" ALIGN=LEFT VALIGN=TOP WIDTH=83%>
<H1>Request new password</H1>
<p><b>Forgot your password?</b> Don't worry -- simply enter your
email address below, and we will email you a new password.<br>
<i>Please use the email address you provided when you
registered. If you've forgotten, you can always
<a href="/register.html">register again</a>.</i></p>

<form action="$php_self" method="post">
Email: <input type="text" name="email"><br />

<br /><br />
<input type="hidden" name="command" value="forgot">
<input type="submit" value="Send password">
</form>

</TD>
</TR>
</TABLE>

</BODY>
</HTML>
EOFORMSTR;

echo $form_str;

?>
```

Figure 44-3 shows the Forgot Password form in action.

Changing sensitive user data

You probably want a little bit more security before you let users go changing their e-mail addresses and passwords — like, for instance, making extra sure they know the old password first. This is especially important if you use cookies with very long expiration times. It's easier to manage this extra verification if you have a separate form for e-mail and password changes, versus nonsensitive data, such as homepage or sig.

If you don't collect usernames on your site, and instead use e-mail addresses as unique-identifying cookies, you will have to reset the cookies when you allow the user to change an e-mail address. Otherwise, your whole user-authentication scheme will no longer work properly.

Listing 44-7 is called emailpass_funcs.inc. It contains functions related to changing e-mail or password.

Figure 44-3: Forgot Password form

> **Listing 44-7: E-mail and password editing functions (emailpass_funcs.inc)**

```php
<?phpfunction user_change_password () {
  // Do new passwords match?
  if ($_POST['new_password1'] && ($_POST['new_password1'] ==
    $_POST['new_password2'])) {
    // Is password long enough?
    if (strlen($_POST['new_password1']) >= 6) {
      // Is the old password correct?
      if (strlen($_POST['old_password']) > 1) {
        $change_user_name = strtolower($_COOKIE['user_name']);
        $old_password = strtolower($_POST['old_password']);
         $crypt_pass = md5($old_password);
        $new_password1 = strtolower($_POST['new_password1']);
        $query = "SELECT *
                FROM user
                WHERE user_name = '$change_user_name'
                AND password = '$crypt_pass'";
      $result = mysql_query($query);
      if (!$result || mysql_num_rows($result) < 1) {
        $feedback = 'ERROR--User not found or bad password';
        return $feedback;
      } else {
         $crypt_newpass = md5($new_password1);
        $query = "UPDATE user
                  SET password = '$crypt_newpass'
                  WHERE user_name = '$change_user_name'
                  AND password = '$crypt_pass'";
```

```
                    $result = mysql_query($query);
                    if (!$result || mysql_affected_rows() < 1) {
                      $feedback = 'ERROR--Problem updating password';
                      return $feedback;
                    } else {
                      return 1;
                    }
                }
            } else {
              $feedback = 'ERROR--Please enter old password';
              return $feedback;
            }
        } else {
          $feedback .= 'ERROR--New password not long enough';
          return false;
        }
    } else {
      $feedback = 'ERROR--Your passwords do not match';
      return $feedback;
    }
}


function user_change_email () {
  global $supersecret_hash_padding;
  if (validate_email($_POST['new_email'])) {
    $hash = md5($_POST['new_email'].$supersecret_hash_padding);

    // Send out a new confirm email with a new hash
    $user_name = strtolower($_COOKIE['user_name']);
    $password1 = strtolower($_POST['password1']);
    $crypt_pass = md5($password1);
    $query = "UPDATE user
              SET confirm_hash = '$hash',
                  is_confirmed = 0
              WHERE user_name = '$user_name'
              AND password = '$crypt_pass'";
    $result = mysql_query($query);
    if (!$result || mysql_affected_rows() < 1) {
      $feedback = 'ERROR--Wrong password';
      return $feedback;
    } else {
      // Send the confirmation email
      $encoded_email = urlencode($_POST['new_email']);
      $mail_body = <<< EOMAILBODY
Thank you for registering at Example.com.  Click this link to
confirm your registration:

http://localhost/confirm.php?hash=$hash&email=$encoded_email

Once you see a confirmation message, you will be logged
```

Continued

Listing 44-7 *(continued)*

```
into Example.com
EOMAILBODY;

        mail($email, 'Example.com Registration Confirmation',
          $mail_body, 'From: noreply@example.com');
        // If you use email rather than password cookies,
        // uncomment the following line
        // user_set_tokens($user_name);
        return 1;
    }
  } else {
    $feedback = 'ERROR- New email address is invalid';
    return $feedback;
  }
}

?>
```

Listing 44-8 is called changeemail.php. It shows a form and calls the proper function. If you are not logged in, it redirects you to the homepage.

Listing 44-8: Form to change e-mail (changeemail.php)

```
<?php

/***************************
 * Change email form page. *
 ***************************/

require_once('includes/emailpass_funcs.inc');
require_once('includes/login_funcs.inc');
if (!user_isloggedin()) {
  header("Location: index.php");
}


if ($_POST['submit'] == "Change my confirmation") {
  $worked = user_change_email();
  if ($worked == 1) {
    $feedback_str = "<P class=\"errormess\">A confirmation " .
      "email has been sent to you.</P>";
  } else {
    $feedback_str = "<P class=\"errormess\">$feedback</P>";
  }
```

```
}


// ------------
// DISPLAY FORM
// ------------

include_once('includes/header_footer.php');
site_header('Change Email');

// Superglobals don't work with heredoc
$php_self = $_SERVER['PHP_SELF'];

$form_str = <<< EOFORMSTR
<TABLE CELLPADDING=0 CELLSPACING=0 BORDER=0 ALIGN=CENTER
  WIDTH=621>
<TR>
  <TD ROWSPAN=2><IMG WIDTH=15 HEIGHT=1
    SRC=../images/spacer.gif></TD>
  <TD WIDTH=606 HEIGHT=1><IMG WIDTH=606 HEIGHT=1
    SRC=../images/spacer.gif></TD>
</TR>
<TR>
 <TD>
$feedback_str
<P CLASS=left><B>Change your email address</B><BR>
A confirmation email will be sent to you.<BR>
<FORM ACTION="$php_self" METHOD="POST">
<B>Password</B><BR>
<INPUT TYPE="password" NAME="password1" VALUE="" SIZE="10"
  MAXLENGTH="15"><BR><BR>
<B>New email</B> (required for confirmation)<BR>
<INPUT TYPE="TEXT" NAME="new_email" VALUE="" SIZE="20"
  MAXLENGTH="35"><BR><BR>
<INPUT TYPE="SUBMIT" NAME="submit" VALUE="Send my confirmation">
</FORM>
 </TD>
</TR>
</TABLE>
EOFORMSTR;

echo $form_str;

site_footer();

?>
```

The results of changeemail.php are shown in Figure 44-4.

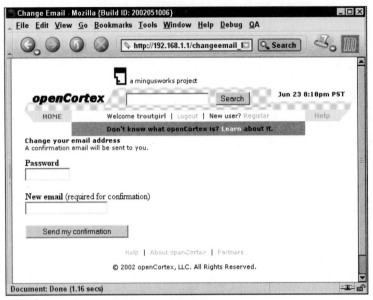

Figure 44-4: Form to change e-mail address

Tip   It's not a bad idea to keep track of the original e-mail address that a user registered under. If someone has registered at your site with the intent to cause harm, such as harassing another user or otherwise making a pest of himself, he may attempt to cover his tracks by changing his e-mail address using your handy tools. In this case, at least you would have one e-mail address that was known to work at one time.

Listing 44-9 is called changepass.php. It shows a form and calls the proper function. If you are not logged in, it redirects you to the homepage.

Listing 44-9: **Change password form (changepass.php)**

```php
<?php

/*******************************
 * Change password form page. *
 *******************************/

require_once('includes/emailpass_funcs.inc');
require_once('includes/login_funcs.inc');
if (!user_isloggedin()) {
  header("Location: index.php");
}

if ($submit) {
```

```
    $worked = user_change_password();
    if ($worked == 1) {
      $feedback_str = "<P class=\"errormess\">
Password changed</P>";
    } else {
      $feedback_str = "<P class=\"errormess\">$feedback</P>";
    }
}


// ------------
// DISPLAY FORM
// ------------

include_once('includes/header_footer.php');
site_header('Change Password');

// Superglobals don't work with heredoc
$php_self = $_SERVER['PHP_SELF'];

$form_str = <<< EOFORMSTR
<TABLE CELLPADDING=0 CELLSPACING=0 BORDER=0 ALIGN=CENTER
  WIDTH=621>
<TR>
  <TD ROWSPAN=2><IMG WIDTH=15 HEIGHT=1
    SRC=../images/spacer.gif></TD>
  <TD WIDTH=606 HEIGHT=1><IMG WIDTH=606 HEIGHT=1
    SRC=../images/spacer.gif></TD>
</TR>
<TR>
 <TD>
$feedback_str
<P CLASS=left><B>Change your password</B><BR>
<FORM ACTION="$php_self" METHOD="POST">
<B>Old password</B><BR>
<INPUT TYPE="password" NAME="old_password" VALUE="" SIZE="10"
  MAXLENGTH="15"><BR><BR>
<B>New Password</B><BR>
<INPUT TYPE="password" NAME="new_password1" VALUE="" SIZE="10"
  MAXLENGTH="15"><BR><BR>
<B>New password</B> (again)<BR>
<INPUT TYPE="password" NAME="new_password2" VALUE="" SIZE="10"
  MAXLENGTH="15"><BR><BR>
<INPUT TYPE="SUBMIT" NAME="submit" VALUE="Change my password">
</FORM>
 </TD>
</TR>
</TABLE>
```

Continued

Listing 44-9 *(continued)*

```
EOFORMSTR;

echo $form_str;

site_footer();

?>
```

The results of changepass.php are shown in Figure 44-5.

Figure 44-5: Form to change password

Edit non-sensitive user data

We define non-sensitive user information as the kind of user data that you won't be sued for inadvertently revealing—things like favorite links, photos or avatars, and gender.

Non-sensitive user information is very straightforward to change. Just use a simple HTML form submit to a PHP form handler, which will stash the data in the datastore. A sample form is included below; feel free to just grab it and change the variables to suit your own schema.

The code for Figure 44-6 is contained in Listing 44-10, edit_userinfo.php.

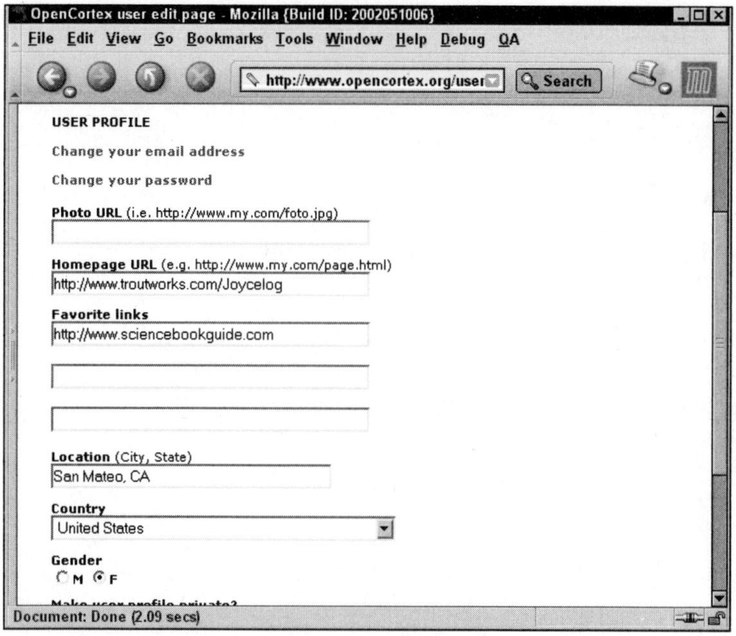

Figure 44-6: Changing incidental user information

Listing 44-10: **Form to edit user data (edit_userinfo.php)**

```php
<?php

/***********************************************
* This file displays the change non-sensitive *
* user data form.  It submits to itself, and   *
* displays a message each time you submit.      *
***********************************************/

// A file with the database host, user, password, and
// selected database
require_once('includes/db_vars.inc');
include_once('includes/header_footer.php');
include_once('includes/login_funcs.inc');

if (!user_isloggedin()) {
  echo '<P>You are not logged in, or this is not your user ' .
    'profile.</P>';
} else {
  $user_name = $_COOKIE['user_name'];
  if ($_POST['submit'] == "Edit user data" &&
```

Continued

Listing 44-10 *(continued)*

```
      strlen($_POST['gender']) == 1 &&
      strlen($_POST['priv_profile']) == 1) {
      // Send data to db

      // I'm not bothering to check the stringlength of these
      // because I'm URL-encoding them
      $as_photo_url = addslashes($_POST['photo_url']);
      $ue_photo_url = urlencode($as_photo_url);
      $as_homepage_url = addslashes($_POST['homepage_url']);
      $ue_homepage_url = urlencode($as_homepage_url);
      $as_fav_link1 = addslashes($_POST['fav_link1']);
      $ue_fav_link1 = urlencode($as_fav_link1);
      $as_fav_link2 = addslashes($_POST['fav_link2']);
      $ue_fav_link2 = urlencode($as_fav_link2);
      $as_fav_link3 = addslashes($_POST['fav_link3']);
      $ue_fav_link3 = urlencode($as_fav_link3);
      $as_location = addslashes($location);

      $query = "UPDATE user
              SET photo = '$ue_photo_url',
                  homepage = '$ue_homepage_url',
                  link1 = '$ue_fav_link1',
                  link2 = '$ue_fav_link2',
                  link3 = '$ue_fav_link3',
                  location = '$as_location',
                  country = '$country',
                  gender = '$gender',
                  priv_profile = $priv_profile
              WHERE user_name = '$user_name'";
      $result = mysql_query($query);
      if (!$result) {
        $status_message = 'Problem with user data entry';
      } else {
        $status_message = 'Successfully edited user data';
      }
    } elseif (strlen($_POST['gender']) > 1 &&
  strlen($_POST['priv_profile']) > 1) {
      // Bad user, smack on wrist
      $status_message = 'You\'re trying to do something very ' .
        'odd with this form.  Stop it now.';
    }

    // Get previously-existing data
    $query = "SELECT photo, homepage, link1, link2, link3, ' .
      'location, country, gender, priv_profile
            FROM user
            WHERE user_name = '$user_name'";

    $result = mysql_query($query);
    // Shall we have an error message if no data comes back?
    $user_array = mysql_fetch_array($result);
```

```
$photo_url = urldecode($user_array['photo']);
$photo_url = stripslashes($photo_url);
$homepage_url = urldecode($user_array['homepage']);
$homepage_url = stripslashes($homepage_url);
$fav_link1 = urldecode($user_array['link1']);
$fav_link1 = stripslashes($fav_link1);
$fav_link2 = urldecode($user_array['link2']);
$fav_link2 = stripslashes($fav_link2);
$fav_link3 = urldecode($user_array['link3']);
$fav_link3 = stripslashes($fav_link3);
$location = stripslashes($user_array['location']);
$country = $user_array['country'];
$gender = $user_array['gender'];

// Construct the multiple field types
if ($gender == "M") {
  $gender_button_str = '<INPUT TYPE="RADIO" NAME="gender"
    VALUE="M" CHECKED>M
<INPUT TYPE="RADIO" NAME="gender" VALUE="F">F';
  } elseif ($gender == "F") {
  $gender_button_str = '<INPUT TYPE="RADIO" NAME="gender"
    VALUE="M">M
<INPUT TYPE="RADIO" NAME="gender" VALUE="F" CHECKED>F';
  } else {
  $gender_button_str = '<INPUT TYPE="RADIO" NAME="gender"
    VALUE="M">M
<INPUT TYPE="RADIO" NAME="gender" VALUE="F">F';
  }
$priv_profile = $user_array['priv_profile'];
if ($priv_profile == 1) {
  $priv_profile_str = '<INPUT TYPE="RADIO"
    NAME="priv_profile" VALUE="1" CHECKED>Yes
            <INPUT TYPE="RADIO" NAME="priv_profile" VALUE="0">No';
  } elseif ($priv_profile == 0) {
  $priv_profile_str = '<INPUT TYPE="RADIO" ' .
    'NAME="priv_profile" VALUE="1">Yes
<INPUT TYPE="RADIO" NAME="priv_profile" VALUE="0" CHECKED>No';
  } else {
  $priv_profile_str = '<INPUT TYPE="RADIO" NAME="priv_profile"
    VALUE="1">Yes
<INPUT TYPE="RADIO" NAME="priv_profile" VALUE="0">No';
  }


// --------------
// Construct form
// --------------

site_header('User data edit page');

$userform_str = <<< EOUSERFORMSTR
```

Continued

Listing 44-10 *(continued)*

```
<TABLE ALIGN=CENTER WIDTH=621>
<TR>
  <TD ROWSPAN=10><IMG WIDTH=15 HEIGHT=1
SRC="../images/spacer.gif"></TD>
  <TD WIDTH=606></TD>
</TR>
<TR>
 <TD>
<P CLASS=bold>USER PROFILE<BR><BR>
<A HREF='/changeemail.php'>Change your email
  address</A><BR><BR>
<A HREF='/changepass.php'>Change your password</A>

<P><FONT COLOR="#ff0000">$status_message</FONT></P>

<FORM ACTION="$PHP_SELF" METHOD="POST">
<P CLASS=left>
<B>Photo URL</B> (i.e. http://www.my.com/foto.jpg)<BR>
<INPUT TYPE="TEXT" NAME="photo_url" VALUE="$photo_url"
  SIZE="40">
</P>
<P CLASS=left>
<B>Homepage URL </B>(e.g. http://www.my.com/page.html)<BR>
<INPUT TYPE="TEXT" NAME="homepage_url" VALUE="$homepage_url"
  SIZE="40">
</P>
<P CLASS=bold>
Favorite links<BR>
<INPUT TYPE="TEXT" NAME="fav_link1" VALUE="$fav_link1"
  SIZE="40">
</P>
<P>
<INPUT TYPE="TEXT" NAME="fav_link2" VALUE="$fav_link2"
  SIZE="40">
</P>
<P>
<INPUT TYPE="TEXT" NAME="fav_link3" VALUE="$fav_link3"
  SIZE="40">
</P>
<P CLASS=left>
<B>Location</B> (City, State)<BR>
<INPUT TYPE="TEXT" NAME="location" VALUE="$location" SIZE="35"
  MAXLENGTH="50">
</P>

<P CLASS=left>
<B>Country<BR>
<INPUT TYPE="TEXT" NAME="country" VALUE="$country" SIZE="35"
  MAXLENGTH="50">
</P>
<P CLASS=bold>
```

```
Gender<BR>
$gender_button_str
</P>
<P CLASS=bold>
Make user profile private?<BR>
$priv_profile_str
</P>
<P>
<INPUT TYPE="SUBMIT" NAME="submit" VALUE="Edit user data">
</FORM>
 </TD>
</TR>
</TABLE>
EOUSERFORMSTR;
   echo $userform_str;

   site_footer();
}

?>
```

Administrator Tools

Administrator tasks tend to be rather specific to particular sites, but there are a few general principles to keep in mind in designing administrator tools. The main one, obviously, is to protect these tools from being found and used by unauthorized users.

Authorization: Basic auth, cookie, database, and IP

Although a full discussion of authentication is beyond the scope of this chapter, you need to understand permissions to design tools that act on user data.

First, we should clearly define the distinction between authentication and authorization. Authentication means we are trying to verify that you are who you say you are. Everything in this chapter so far has been about authentication, strictly speaking. Merely by being a particular user, certain abilities (such as the ability to change your own e-mail address) devolve upon you. Authorization is about determining whether you have permission to do what you want to do. Often, an authorization step is built into authentication in a way that is transparent to the user, but they are fundamentally two separate tasks.

There are four main types of authorization: basic auth, cookie, database, and IP based.

Basic auth is a Web server specific method of authorization and authentication. You can tell the Web server to prompt for a password and check a list of authorized users before serving a page in a particular directory under your Web tree. Although, in a certain sense, the Web server is doing this on every page load, the browser can transparently handle multiple pages per session so that the user only has to enter a login and password once per browser session. A clear explanation of basic auth for Apache http server can be found at http://httpd. apache.org/docs/howto/auth.html.

Cookie-based authorization, as the name implies, relies upon special cookies to identify browser sessions belonging to trusted users. Often, the cookie must be set inside the firewall, so there is an element of IP authorization to this type of scheme also. The advantage of cookie-based designs is that cookies are easy to implement and can be used by several employees at once. The disadvantage is that, by themselves, cookies are easy to spoof and hard to track because they embody authorization without authentication. If you have six trusted users in your organization that are empowered to take a certain action, with cookies alone you won't know which of the six made a particular mistake.

Database authorization relies on a more formal concept of permissions, either individual or grouped into baskets. Individual permissions are stored in their own database tables, such as `permission` and `user_permission`. On each page load, the code checks to see whether this particular authenticated user has the particular permission necessary to use this particular tool. Baskets of permissions are often represented simply as a bit in the user table (`is_admin` or some such field). Database permissions are the most complicated to implement, but one of the safest designs. Furthermore, you can track individual actions with a database at a level of granularity not possible with the other schemes.

Finally, IP-based permissions attempt to restrict use of certain tools to only those behind a firewall or on a particular subnet. You may, for example, allow only one development server to connect to your live database on the other side of the firewall. IP-based plans should really be led by your IT staff or systems administrators because almost all the work and maintenance falls on them. If you, as the Web developer, do everything they tell you to do, but the network is cracked anyway, the responsibility should fall on them. Obviously, IP-based authorization is non-authenticated — unless you work in a locked room, it's very difficult to prevent others from sneaking up to your computer while you're away and using the browser-based tool on your computer.

Remember that any or all these basic methods can be combined for stronger security. You could have a system where all tools lived in a particular password-protected directory on a particular server, for example, and would run only on that server, but permissions were stored on the live database in the field. This would combine basic auth, database, and IP-based authorization systems for a more secure result.

Login as user

Logging in as a particular user is not a tool per se. It may be something you must build it into the structure of your entire site, depending on how you implement it and the particulars of your site architecture. For instance, you may have a special cookie that means, "I'm the administrator, but I want to see this user's user page as if I were the user."

If you used the registration and login code we laid out in the "Registration" and "Login" sections of this chapter, you could easily write a tool to basically give a particular user's cookies to the administrator of your site. Essentially, it would amount to using the login script without requiring a password — or rather without requiring the password of the user whose point of view you are taking. This would be an intrinsically insecure way to accomplish your task, and therefore should only be used in combination with one or more of the other security schemes discussed in the "Avoiding Common Security Problems" section of this chapter.

The `impersonate.php` form in Listing 44-11 looks exactly like the normal login form, `login.php`. Instead of entering his or her own username and password, however, the authorized user will enter the username of the user he or she wishes to impersonate, plus a special administrator password. If the administrator cookie is not detected, the form will automatically redirect to the front page of the site.

Listing 44-11: **Administrator impersonation script (impersonate.php)**

```php
<?php

/***************************************************
 * Script to set user cookie so admins can browse *
 * site from the viewpoint of a particular user.   *
 * Potentially VERY unsafe!!!  Protect it with     *
 * your life!                                       *
 ***************************************************/

// If this person isn't recognized as the admin, bounce them
if ($_COOKIE['user_name'] != 'Administrator') {
  header("Location: index.php");
}

require_once('includes/db_vars.inc');
require_once('includes/login_funcs.inc');

function user_impersonate() {
  // This function will only work with superglobal arrays,
  // because I'm not passing in any values or declaring globals
  if (!$_POST['user_name'] || !$_POST['password']) {
    $feedback = 'ERROR--Missing username or password';
    return $feedback;
  } else {
    $user_name = strtolower($_POST['user_name']);
    // Don't need to trim because extra spaces should fail
    // for this
    // Don't need to addslashes because single quotes
    // aren't allowed
    $password = strtolower($_POST['password']);
    // Don't need to addslashes because we'll be hashing it
    $crypt_pwd = md5($password);
    $query = "SELECT user_name
              FROM user
              WHERE user_name = 'Administrator
              AND password='$crypt_pwd'";
    $result = mysql_query($query);
    if (!$result || mysql_num_rows($result) < 1){
      $feedback = 'ERROR--User not found or password ' .
        'incorrect';
      return $feedback;
    } else {
      if (mysql_result($result, 0, 0) == 'Administrator') {
        user_set_tokens($user_name);
        return 1;
      }
    }
  }
```

Continued

Listing 44-11 *(continued)*

```
    }
}

if ($submit == 'Login') {
  $feedback = user_impersonate();
  if ($feedback == 1) {
    // On successful login, redirect to homepage
    header("Location: index.php");
  } else {
    $feedback_str = "<P class=\"errormess\">$feedback</P>";
  }
} else {
  $feedback_str = '';
}



// ----------------
// DISPLAY THE FORM
// ----------------
include_once('includes/header_footer.php');
site_header('Login To OpenCortex');

// Superglobals don't work with heredoc
$php_self = $_SERVER['PHP_SELF'];

$login_form = <<< EOLOGINFORM
<TABLE CELLPADDING=0 CELLSPACING=0 BORDER=0 ALIGN=CENTER
    WIDTH=621>
<TR>
  <TD ROWSPAN=2><IMG WIDTH=15 HEIGHT=1
SRC=../images/spacer.gif></TD>
  <TD WIDTH=606 HEIGHT=1><IMG WIDTH=606 HEIGHT=1
SRC=../images/spacer.gif></TD>
</TR>
<TR>
 <TD>

$feedback_str
<P CLASS="bold">LOGIN</P>
<FORM ACTION="$php_self" METHOD="POST">
<P CLASS="bold">Username<BR>
<INPUT TYPE="TEXT" NAME="user_name" VALUE="" SIZE="10"
  MAXLENGTH="15"></P>
<P CLASS="bold">Password<BR>
<INPUT TYPE="password" NAME="password" VALUE="" SIZE="10"
  MAXLENGTH="15"></P>
<P><INPUT TYPE="SUBMIT" NAME="submit" VALUE="Login"></P>
```

```
</FORM>

 </TD>
</TR>
</TABLE>
EOLOGINFORM;
echo $login_form;

site_footer();

?>
```

Cross-Reference   Depending on your preference, and which version of PHP you're using, you might choose to incorporate exception handling or define a custom error handler to use in conjunction with the $feedback variable in the preceding examples. See Chapter 31 for more information.

Summary

User data management is a core function of many Web sites. Unfortunately, often not enough thought is given to security, scalability, and modularity in these important subsystems. We demonstrate a complete user management package here, and walk you through the design principles you should keep in mind as you implement your own.

The main functions of a user management system include new user registration and confirmation, login and logout, forgotten password replacement, changing e-mail and passwords, changing other user data, and logging in as another user.

✦   ✦   ✦

A User-Rating System

In this chapter, we look at a very common use of database-driven PHP code: presenting content to users and encouraging them to give it a quality rating.

In the first edition's version of this chapter, we used sample user ratings code that we had extracted from a site of our own. Although *realistic* in some sense, the resulting code samples could not be usefully run without the rest of that Web site's code base. This time around, we've gone entirely in the other direction, creating a complete mini-site that places primary emphasis on the capability to rate content. Our hope is that it will be a straightforward task to adapt the rating code to your own site.

The portions of the book we draw on most heavily for this case study are:

✦ Part II: We build the code around a MySQL database.

✦ Chapters 28 and 36: We communicate with the database using the PEAR database functions.

Note   In this chapter we demonstrate the use of the PEAR database layer to abstract away from the choice of the particular database system, even though much of the rest of the book's code uses PHP/MySQL functions directly. The PEAR DB approach has the benefit of making it possible for users to choose among different types of data sources, but both approaches have their supporters.

Initial Design

We will design our minisite from the ground up, but bear in mind that the part we really care about is the code relevant to user ratings. In a moment, we will zero in on a particular example content site, but first let's lay out the site characteristics that our ratings code will assume. We assume that:

✦ The site presents content items to users (books, movies, consumer goods, politicians — anything that could conceivably be rated).

✦ The site presents one such item per dynamically generated page.

✦ Each item is stored in a database table or set of tables with a unique database key.

Our ratings code will inevitably be interwoven with the particular content site we choose, but with minimal changes it ought to work with any content site that has these characteristics.

Domain: A quotation site

For our example domain, we'll create a site that displays amusing quotes from famous and not-so-famous people. All we want to present to the user on each quotation page is a pithy quote and an attribution. To store these quotations, we'll make a MySQL database for our entire project and then create a quotation table:

```
create database user_ratings;
use user_ratings;
create table quotations (ID int primary key auto_increment,
                         quotation varchar(255),
                         attribution varchar(255));
```

This produces two pieces of text (the quotation itself and an attribution) per row, with an automatically assigned identification number. Note that we plan for the quotes to be very pithy indeed—no more than 255 characters. If you want longer quotes, you should make the quotation field a larger type, say type text.

Possible ratings

Working from the other end, let's design another table that specifies the rating values that users can choose among when rating quotations. This is an equally simple MySQL schema:

```
create table rating_values (ID int primary key auto_increment,
                            rank int not null default 0,
                            rating_text varchar(255));
```

As always, the ID field is the unique identifier we rely on. The rank field we intend for ordering the rating values—if you choose a "scale of 1 to 10" style of rating, you want ten rows in the table, with ranks ranging from 1 to 10. (You could make the ID field do double duty here and play the role of the rank field, if you are careful with order of entry, but this seems like more trouble than it's worth.) Finally, the text field contains the explanation of the choice that will be shown to the voter.

While we're at it, let's populate this table with a particular rating scheme.

```
insert into rating_values (rank, rating_text)
  values (5, "5 - Excellent");
insert into rating_values (rank, rating_text)
  values (4, "4 - Very good");
insert into rating_values (rank, rating_text)
  values (3, "3 - Good");
insert into rating_values (rank, rating_text)
  values (2, "5 - Mediocre");
insert into rating_values (rank, rating_text)
  values (1, "1 - Poor");
```

Note that the redundancy of including the rank in the text is necessary only if the rank will not be displayed along with the text.

Linking ratings with content

So now we have a table representing possible ratings and a table representing the content to be rated. How shall we associate them?

We've already made a decision of sorts by making two separate tables. If each piece of content only received one rating, we could have added the rating value as a column in the content table. Similarly, if each rating were applied to only one piece of content (as with finishing order in a race), we could have made the content ID a column in the ratings table. As it is though, we have multiple pieces of content, which different users will associate with different ratings. This is a many-to-many relationship, so we will need a third table to capture the associations.

We want each row in this `ratings` table to represent an instance of a content item receiving a rating. At a minimum, then, we need to identify both the content and the rating in each row. We'll do this by using the primary keys from each table. In addition, we'll throw in a few columns that we have found to be useful, even if we won't be using them much in this chapter's code.

```
create table ratings (ID int primary key auto_increment,
                      rating int,
                      rated_id int,
                      rating_date timestamp,
                      user_ip varchar(30),
                      bogus_bit tinyint default 0);
```

The first three columns are the minimum we need: our usual auto-incremented primary key and the IDs from the two tables we are associating. The next two will be used to capture some information about the rating event: the time it happened, and the IP address of the user doing the rating. (This last one we include not for any evil, privacy-invading purpose, but just because it turns out to be useful in combating mass ballot stuffing. If you receive a negative review for an item once every two seconds, it can be useful to know that all those votes are coming from the same place.) Finally, we include a bit we can flip if we conclude that large number of rows are bogus — without deleting them, we can write code to screen them out of vote totals and displays.

Now we have designed our three tables and have populated only one of them (`rating_values`). It seems wasteful to print sample quotes that make up the entries for the quotations table (although we will include them in the database dump for this chapter found at `www.troutworks.com/phpbook`). Finally, we have not yet populated the ratings table, because that is something that our users should do.

Collecting Votes

To let our users vote on our content, we need to display that content alongside some kind of form that lets them express their feelings. In this section, we'll create a content page that displays one item and encourages the user to rate it. The code for this page is shown in Listing 45-1. This is a high-level code file, which includes other function files, which in turn do most of the work.

All the display code is predicated on knowing a database key for the content that will be rated. This identifier will arrive either as a GET variable or a POST variable. (If a user is arriving for the first time, we choose a content ID somewhat arbitrarily.) Then this top-level page creates both the quotation content and the ratings form based on two pieces of information: the current page name (used for both form submission and previous/next navigation) and the ID of the current quote. One view of this top-level page is shown in Figure 45-1 — the content is on the left, and the solicitation to rate is on the right.

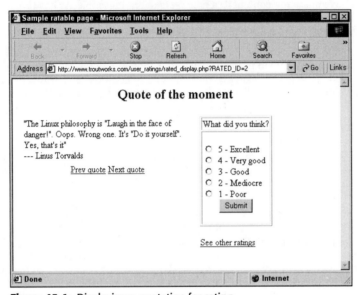

Figure 45-1: Displaying a quotation for rating

The code that produced Figure 45-1 is shown in Listing 45-1.

Listing 45-1: **rated_display.php**

```php
<?php
include_once("db_connection.php");
include_once("rating_functions.php");
include_once("content_functions.php");

if (isSet($_GET['RATED_ID'])) {
  $rated_id = $_GET['RATED_ID'];
}
else if (isSet($_POST['RATED_ID'])) {
  $rated_id = $_POST['RATED_ID'];
}
else {
  $rated_id = 1;
}

// create the quote content
```

```
$content_box =
  make_content_box($_SERVER['PHP_SELF'],
                   $rated_id);

// create the navigation links
$nav_box =
  make_next_prev_box($_SERVER['PHP_SELF'],
                     $rated_id);

// create the self-submitting ratings box
// (also handles submissions)
$submission_box =
  make_ratings_box($_SERVER['PHP_SELF'],
                   $rated_id);

// create the link to the main ratings page
$ratings_link =
  "<A HREF=\"all_ratings.php\">See
   other ratings</A>";

// create the actual page
$page_string = <<<EOP
<HTML><HEAD><TITLE>Sample ratable page</TITLE></HEAD>
<BODY>
<CENTER><H2>Quote of the moment</H2></CENTER>
<TABLE WIDTH=500 VALIGN=TOP CELLPADDING=20>
<TR VALIGN=TOP>
<TD VALIGN=TOP COLSPAN=50%>
$content_box
<CENTER>$nav_box</CENTER>
</TD><TD ALIGN=TOP COLSPAN=50%>
$submission_box
<BR>$ratings_link
</TD></TR></TABLE>
</BODY></HTML>
EOP;
echo $page_string;
?>
```

As with many code files in this book, the very first file included (db_connection.php, shown in Listing 45-2) is one that handles all the details of making a MySQL database connection, including the loading of another file (not shown), which sets the database login and passwords appropriately. All the subsequent database interactions implicitly use this connection and (in this chapter) do not explicitly use a connection identifier.

The actual database interaction is done via PEAR database layer functions, loaded in by the include line require_once 'DB.php'; this assumes that you have the relevant PEAR libraries installed.

Cross-Reference For an introduction to the PEAR database layer, see Chapter 36; for details on downloading and configuring PEAR modules in general, see Chapter 28.

Listing 45-2: **db_connection.php**

```php
<?php
include("../dbvars.php"); // sets $host, $user, $pass
require_once 'DB.php';
$dsn = "mysql://$user:$pass@$host/'user ratings'";
$db = DB::connect($dsn);
if (DB::isError($db)) {
    die ($db->getMessage());
}
?>
```

As we've said, in this chapter our focus is on the content-rating mechanism, and the content itself is there merely so we have something to rate. So as much as possible, we have separated the content-related code from the ratings-related code (and also make no claims for the beauty of our layout or design). Most of the code for presenting the quotations' content is in the form of functions loaded from the file content_functions.php (shown in Listing 45-3).

Listing 45-3: **content_functions.php**

```php
<?php

require_once 'DB.php';

function make_content_box($current_page, $content_id) {
  $query =
    "select quotation, attribution from quotations
       where ID = $content_id";
  $result = $db->query($query);

if (DB::isError($result))
  {
  $errorMessage = $result->getMessage();
  die ($errorMessage);
  }

if ($result->numRows() != 0) {
while ($row = $result->fetchRow()){
  $quotation = $row[0];
  $attribution = $row[1];
  $return_string .=
      "<table align=top><tr align=top>
       <td>\"$quotation\"<br>
       --- $attribution</td></tr></table>";
  }
}
  else {
    return("No content in database");
```

```
    }
$db->disconnect();

   }
}

function make_next_prev_box ($current_page, $current_id) {
  $prev_id = prev_content_id($current_id);
  $next_id = next_content_id($current_id);
  return("<TABLE><TR><TD>
          <A HREF=\"$current_page?RATED_ID=$prev_id\">
           Prev quote</A>
          </TD><TD>
          <A HREF=\"$current_page?RATED_ID=$next_id\">
           Next quote</A>
          </TD></TR></TABLE>");
}

function next_content_id ($current_id) {
 $query = "select ID from quotations
            where ID > $current_id
            order by ID asc";

 $result = $db->query($query);

if (DB::isError($result))
  {
  $errorMessage = $result->getMessage();
  die ($errorMessage);
  }

if ($result->numRows() != 0) {
$row = $result->fetchRow()
$id = $row[0];
}
  else {
    $query = "select min(ID) from quotations";
    $result = $db->query($query);
    if (DB::isError($result))
    {
      $errorMessage = $result->getMessage();
      die ($errorMessage);
    }
  $row = $result->fetchRow()
  $id    =       $row[0];
  }
  $db->disconnect();
 return($id);
}

function prev_content_id ($current_id) {
```

Continued

Listing 45-3 *(continued)*

```
   $query = "select ID from quotations
              where ID < $current_id
              order by ID desc";

 $result = $db->query($query);

 if (DB::isError($result))
   {
   $errorMessage = $result->getMessage();
   die ($errorMessage);
   }

 if ($result->numRows() != 0) {
 $row = $result->fetchRow()
 $id = $row[0];
 }
   else {
     $query = "select max(ID) from quotations";
     $result = $db->query($query);
     if (DB::isError($result))
     {
     $errorMessage = $result->getMessage();
     die ($errorMessage);
     }
   $row = $result->fetchRow()
   $id = $row[0];
   }
   $db->disconnect();
 return($id);
 }

 ?>
```

The only content functions used directly by the rated_display.php page are make_content_box() (which retrieves a quotation/attribution pair from the database and displays them, wrapped up in an HTML table) and make_next_prev_box() (which determines a next and previous quotation ID and creates appropriate navigation links). Finally, there's a utility function (truncate_quotation()), which we'll use later in a "top ten" page.

The center of the ratings action is in the file ratings_function php (Listing 45-4), and, in particular, in the top-level function make_ratings_box(), which either creates a form as a rating opportunity or thanks the user for having submitted a rating, depending on the presence of POST arguments.

If a rating has been submitted via POST variables, the ratings code puts together an INSERT statement, which records the current content item ID, the ID of the rating that was chosen, and the IP address (if available) of the user's machine. Because the rating_date column is a timestamp variable, the time of insertion is recorded without any work on our part. Finally, after handling the submitted rating, the ratings box returned contains a simple thank-you with no immediate opportunity to vote again. (See the "Extensions and Alternatives" section at the end of the chapter for more discussion about how to prevent voting multiple times for the same item.) Figure 45-2 shows the page after a rating has been submitted.

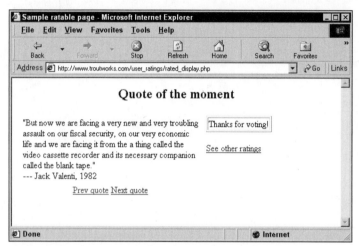

Figure 45-2: The rating_display.php page after submitting a rating

If no rating has been submitted, the ratings box is a constructed form, which offers all the values found in the `ratings_values` table. The form sends the ID of the quote as a hidden variable (`RATED_ID`) and sends the ID of the rating itself as a radio-button variable (`RATING_ID`).

Listing 45-4: **rating_functions.php**

```php
<?php

function rating_types_as_array () {
  $return_array = array();
  $query =
  "select ID, rating_text from rating_values order by rank desc"

$result = $db->query($query);

if (DB::isError($result))
  {
  $errorMessage = $result->getMessage();
  die ($errorMessage);
  }

while ($row = $result->fetchRow())
  {
    $id = $row_array['ID'];
```

Continued

Listing 45-4 *(continued)*

```php
      $text = $row_array['rating_text'];
      $return_array[$id] = $text;
   }
 return($return_array);
}

function maybe_handle_new_rating() {
   if (isSet($_POST['RATING_ID'])) {
     $new_rating = $_POST['RATING_ID'];
     $rated_id = $_POST['RATED_ID'];
     $user_ip = $_SERVER['REMOTE_ADDR'];
     handle_new_rating($new_rating, $rated_id,
                      $user_ip);
     return(true);
   }
   else {
     return(false);
   }
}

function handle_new_rating($new_rating, $rated_id,
                          $user_ip) {
   $query = "insert into ratings
           (rating, rated_id, user_ip)
           values ($new_rating, $rated_id,
                  '$user_ip')";

$result = $db->query($query);

if (DB::isError($result))
   {
   $errorMessage = $result->getMessage();
   die ($errorMessage);
   }
}


function make_ratings_box ($target_page, $rated_id) {
   $new_rating_handled = maybe_handle_new_rating();
   if ($new_rating_handled) {
     return(make_ratings_receipt_box());
   }
   else {
     return(make_ratings_submission_box($target_page,
                                       $rated_id));
   }
}

function make_ratings_receipt_box () {
   return("<TABLE BORDER=1><TR><TD>Thanks for voting!".
```

```
                    "</TD></TR></TABLE>");
    }

function make_ratings_submission_box
  ($target_page, $rated_id) {
  $rating_array = rating_types_as_array();
  // Beginning of HTML table
  $return_string =
    "<TABLE BORDER=1><TR><TD>What did you think?</TD></TR>".
    "<TR><TD ALIGN=LEFT><FORM METHOD=POST".
    "ACTION=\"$target_page\">";
  foreach ($rating_array as $id => $text) {
    $return_string .=
      "<BR><INPUT TYPE=RADIO NAME=RATING_ID VALUE=\"$id\">" .
      "  $text</INPUT>";
  }
  $return_string .=
    "<INPUT TYPE=HIDDEN NAME=RATED_ID VALUE=$rated_id>";
  $return_string .=
    "<BR><CENTER><INPUT TYPE=SUBMIT
    NAME=SUBMIT VALUE=\"Submit\"></CENTER>";
  $return_string .= "</FORM></TD></TR></TABLE>";
  return($return_string);
}

?>
```

Aggregating Results

Finally, we offer a simple page that shows a "top ten" ranking of the quotations that have been rated. Code for this is shown in Listing 45-5, and a browser view of the generated page is shown in Figure 45-3.

Listing 45-5: **all_ratings.php**

```
<?php
include_once("db_connection.php");
include_once("rating_functions.php");
include_once("content_functions.php");

$query_best =
  "select quotations.ID,
          quotations.quotation,
          quotations.attribution,
          avg(rating_values.rank) as avg_rank
     from quotations, ratings, rating_values
    where ratings.rated_id = quotations.id
          and ratings.rating_id = rating_values.id
```

Continued

Listing 45-5 *(continued)*

```php
    group by quotations.id
    order by avg_rank desc limit 10";

$result = $db->query($query_best);

if (DB::isError($result))
  {
  $errorMessage = $result->getMessage();
  die ($errorMessage);
  }

$table_rows_string =
"<TR><TH>Quote</TH><TH>Attribution</TH><TH>Average rating</TH></TR>";

while ($row_array = $result->fetchRow())
  {
    $quotation_id = $row_array['ID'];
    $quotation_text = $row_array['quotation'];
    $truncated_quotation = truncate_quotation($quotation_text);
    $quotation_attribution = $row_array['attribution'];
    $avg_rank = $row_array['avg_rank'];
    $rounded_avg_rank = sprintf("%.1f", $avg_rank);
$table_rows_string .=
    "<TR><TD><A HREF=\"rated_display.php?RATED_ID=$quotation_id\">
     $truncated_quotation</A></TD>
     <TD>$quotation_attribution</TD>".
    "<TD>$rounded_avg_rank</TD></TR>";
  }

$db->disconnect();

// lay out the page
$title = "Ratings page for quotes";
$page_string = <<<EOP
<HTML><HEAD></HEAD><BODY>
<CENTER><H2>$title</H2></CENTER>
<TABLE BORDER=1>
<H2>Top ten most popular quotes</H2>
$table_rows_string
</TABLE>
</BODY>
</HTML>
EOP;

echo $page_string;
?>
```

The aggregated page is pretty much just a sorted and aggregated view of the underlying ratings table, with some tricks to make the display more concise. (We round the averaged ratings to a reasonable precision and truncate the quotes at the first sign of punctuation.) The aggregation happens as a result of grouping the ratings rows (of which there are many per quotation) by quotation in the SQL statement and averaging the ranks. We also turn the truncated quotations into links back to the display pages, using the ID of the content as a GET argument. (Note that although this is a top-ten list, there are only eight quotations in our sample dataset.)

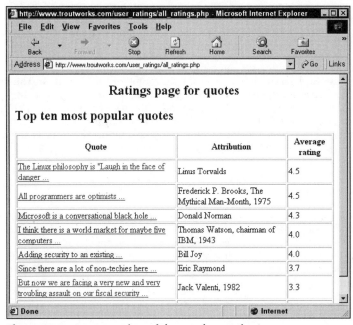

Figure 45-3: A top-ten view of the rated quotations

The analysis this page provides is a direct product of the SQL statement it displays. Rather than displaying the most highly rated items, it would be easy to display the most poorly rated, or the items with the most ratings overall, or any number of other analyses, simply by varying the SQL statement and the title.

What about performance? We don't have any hard data, but you can look at www.mystery guide.com/readerratings.html, which uses roughly these techniques, and see how such a page performs with three "best of" analyses on approximately 30,000 individual ratings. As you may be able to tell, it's just beginning to slow up perceptibly, taking a second or two to respond under typical conditions on our Web host.

Extensions and Alternatives

We have tried to make this example as bare bones as possible, focusing on the ratings code while also retaining the minimum functionality to make a functioning mini-site. There are several ways in which you could improve or extend the code if you feel so moved.

For one thing, we don't like the fact that you have to do two things to submit a rating (choose a radio button and then click Submit) rather than one. Long before we were aware of any "one-click" patent controversy, we had a "one-click" version of such a rating system on the MysteryGuide site (www.mysteryguide.com)—this made each voting alternative into its own Submit button, so that only one user action was needed. The problem with this is that, although the radio-button code in this chapter manipulates three different values (the variable name, the corresponding submitted value, and the text displayed in association with the button), you really only have two alternatives with a Submit button: the name of the variable and the value (which will also be the text displayed in the button). There is no good way, for example, to display meaningful text and actually submit something else when clicked (like a database ID). The alternatives are 1) to resort to JavaScript; 2) to use radio buttons instead (as in this chapter); or 3) to somehow map from submitted text back to the value you really want to send (as we do on the MysteryGuide site). Probably Javascript is the way to go.

Another improvement that our rating system needs is better prevention of ballot stuffing. In this chapter, we present the weakest defense to multiple voting for the same item: The ratings form disappears in response to detecting a ratings submission, so the user cannot simply click a button on the same page over and over. However, nothing stops our user from hitting the Back button or typing in the original URL to get the form back again, and repeating *ad nauseum*. Any better technique needs to start with identifying multiple requests as actually coming from the same person—see Chapter 24 for a discussion of how to do this.

Summary

In this chapter, we have shown you a system that lets users rate your pages, and we have taken you through how it hooks up to a minimal "content site." The code lets users rate items, and it displays a summary page of votes. We also discussed some ways in which you could take this code and extend it to make it more useful and interesting. We hope we've made it easy to detach it from our sample content domain (a small set of quotations) and to snap it back on to some content you care about.

✦   ✦   ✦

A Trivia Game

In this chapter, we present a full working example of a small PHP application: a Web-based trivia game with a twist (the "Certainty Quiz"). The main virtue of the chapter is its completeness: Instead of using code fragments to illustrate talking points, as we do in most other chapters, we're showing everything, soup to nuts. As a result, this is one of the larger examples in the book, weighing in at more than 1300 lines of PHP code.

Concepts Used in This Chapter

The code in this chapter uses a wide variety of techniques, tricks, and technologies that we've presented elsewhere in the book. In particular:

✦ We make heavy use of the object-oriented features of PHP (Chapter 20).

✦ We rely on PHP's session mechanism to propagate game data from page to page (Chapter 24).

✦ We use a back end database (MySQL) to store questions and high scores (Part II).

✦ We do some behind-the-scenes mathematics, including approximating nth roots (Chapters 10 and 27).

✦ We use arrays for storing data and for manipulating data returned from the database (Chapters 9 and 21).

✦ We do a lot of string processing and concatenation to build our display pages, including the heredoc technique for templating pages (Chapters 8 and 21).

✦ We use the new exception-handling features of PHP5 to catch database and session problems (Chapter 31).

We highlight some of these topics in various sections later in the chapter as we delve into the code.

✦ ✦ ✦ ✦

In This Chapter

A guessing game with approximate answers

The object-oriented implementation of the game

Database and session support

Design considerations

✦ ✦ ✦ ✦

The Game

Several years ago, a friend asked one of us to try a quiz he'd seen somewhere on the Internet. After I agreed, he told me that he would ask me ten questions, each of which had a numerical answer (dates, weights, lengths, counts, and so on). The unusual part was that instead of answering with a number, I was to give a lower bound and an upper bound on the answer. I could make the ranges as large as I wanted, and otherwise I had only one instruction: Make sure that you answer nine out of ten questions correctly.

I answered the questions confidently and was surprised at the end to find that my final score was six (or was it four?). At any rate, I did surprisingly badly, but my friend said that everyone else he had tried it on had done even worse. Now, how could anyone lose such an easily winnable game? After all, when asked when Shakespeare was born, I could have said "Sometime between 30,000 B.C. and A.D. 30,000" and been pretty sure that I would be right. What trips people up seems to be some combination of pride and overconfidence. The pride prevents you from giving a ridiculously large range (because then your questioner knows you don't have the foggiest idea when Shakespeare was born); the overconfidence makes you willing to narrow the range beyond your real range of certainty. In the end, the game isn't testing your knowledge — it's testing your knowledge of your own knowledge (or lack of knowledge).

Our version

In this chapter, we implement something like this quiz game, but with some changes to make it more Web-friendly. For one thing, rather than having the player type in numbers freely, we present a range of choices that the player narrows down further. For another, we don't rely on pride to make the ranges narrow (because people may end up playing this over the Web in the privacy of their own home). Instead we add incentives to the scoring system to make people guess narrowly rather than broadly. Finally, we add some features familiar from online games, such as levels of difficulty and a list of top scorers.

The upshot is a game that, while it may or may not be fun, is certainly frustrating, which for many people is nearly as good.

Sample screens

Figure 46-1 shows the game screen as it may look to a new arrival. There is a welcome message to the right, and a question to the left, with radio buttons for choosing a range of answers.

Figure 46-2 shows the screen immediately after the player has answered the first question. Another question is offered on the left, and now the state of the game score is highlighted on the right, showing the correct answers to date, the credit remaining, and the level attained. (See the next section for an explanation of what these things mean.)

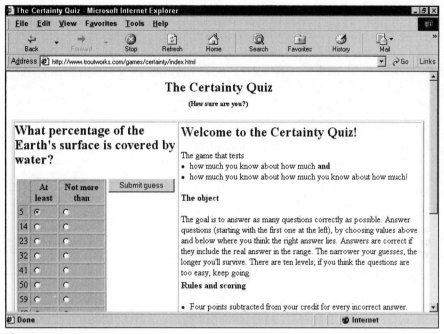

Figure 46-1: Start screen

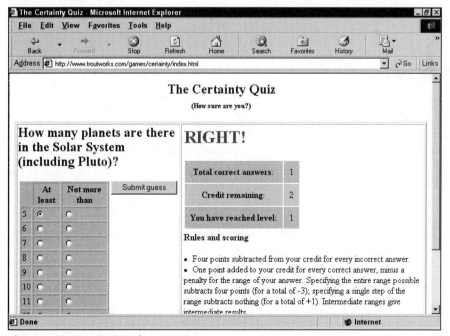

Figure 46-2: Continuing play

Finally, Figure 46-3 shows "Game Over," complete with taunting message and a list of high scorers. (There's a corresponding "Game Won" screen in the unlikely event that the user survived all the questions the game could come up with.)

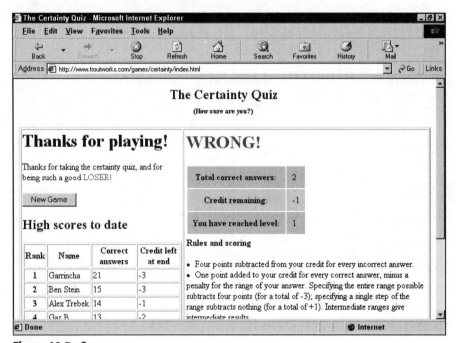

Figure 46-3: Game over

The rules

The basic play cycle is simple: The player is asked a question that requires a numerical answer, and the player responds by choosing a range of values that should include the answer. The goal is to answer as many questions correctly as possible, while surviving in the meantime. Survival depends on credit, which is accumulated by answering questions correctly with a narrow range and is spent by giving wrong answers or answering questions too broadly.

The exact rewards and penalties are easily tweakable in the code, but in this chapter's version they are:

✦ **Correct answers:** One point added to credit, minus a penalty for the size of the range specified. The penalty ranges from zero for answers that use only one step of the possible range, up to four points for making the range as wide as possible.

✦ **Incorrect answers:** Four points deducted from credit.

Credit starts at five points and can rise only as high as fifteen points. The game is over when credit goes below zero.

It is easy to pass by simply submitting your answer without making a choice, since the radio buttons are set to specify the widest possible answer range unless the player changes them. The penalties are set up so that passing is costly (a total of 1 - 4 = -3 points), but not as costly as guessing wrong (-4 points). The player is better off narrowing the range as much as possible, while still being sure that the real answer is still included.

Playing the game yourself

We have a playable version of this game up at www.troutworks.com/games/certainty/index.html, containing many more questions than we include in the sample databases in this chapter. We may change some aspects of the publicly playable game between the time we are writing this and when the book comes out, so we can't guarantee that the public game matches this chapter's code in every respect. The code from this chapter, however, is available at the Web site for this book (www.troutworks.com/phpbook).

The Code

The code for this example is almost completely written in an object-oriented style (see Chapter 20 for an introduction to PHP's version of object-oriented programming). Among the classes we define are:

✦ **Question:** Each Question object includes the text of the question, the correct answer, the lower and upper bounds that are presented to the player, and enough information to display the range of choices that the player can choose from. In addition, Question instances track whether or not they are answered correctly.

✦ **Game:** There should be one and only one Game object in existence at a particular time. Game objects may include up to two question objects (the current question and the previous one), as well as a GameParameter instance.

✦ **GameParameters:** Contains all the numerical settings that affect how the game behaves and manages some globally available resources such as the database connection.

✦ **GameDisplay:** Contains a Game instance as a component and does all the work of actually displaying HTML and receiving input. Also contains an instance of GameText.

✦ **GameText:** A repository for boilerplate HTML that is not dependent on any knowledge of the state of the game. Only this class and GameDisplay actually have HTML code in them.

Code files

The code files include definitions for all the classes in the preceding section: question_class.php, game_class.php, game_parameters_class.php, game_display_class.php, and game_text_class.php. In addition, there are some code files that don't define classes:

✦ **index.php:** The first file loaded, that handles sessions and post arguments and creates the GameDisplay object.

✦ **certainty_utils.php:** A grab bag of initialization statements (seeding the random-number generator, for example) and math utility functions.

✦ **entry_form.php:** A form for adding new questions to the database.

✦ **dbvars.php:** The usual file with definitions for username, password, and host for the database connection.

We now take a tour of the code file listings. Rather than building from the ground up as we sometimes do, in this chapter we work from the top down: first the very first page that is actually loaded, then the code that page depends on, and so on until we bottom out in utility functions and database calls. Finally, at the end of the chapter, we show how to construct the database and populate it with questions.

index.php

Listing 46-1 shows index.php, which is the user's entry point. The primary job of this file is to determine where we are in the cycle of play, set up the appropriate PHP objects (either by creating them or by retrieving them from the user's session), and echo out the display code that the objects generate.

Where we are in the course of a game is determined by a combination of session and POST information; as users arrive for the first time, they find neither a current session nor any POST arguments. Successive pages, however, should have both an active session and useful information submitted from the previous page.

Listing 46-1: **index.php**

```php
<?php
// Include code files, start up session
include_once("certainty_utils.php");
include_once("game_display_class.php");
session_start();

// Determine state and handle post arguments

try {

  // CASE 1: Player is submitting name for high score list
  if (get_session_value('game') &&
      get_post_value('HIGHSCORE')) {
    if (get_session_value('game') &&
      get_post_value('HIGHSCORE')) {
      $game_display =
      new GameDisplay(get_session_value('game'));
                   $game_display->handleHighScore();
    }
  }

  // CASE 2: Player is in middle of game that we are tracking
  elseif (get_session_value('game') &&
          !get_post_value('NEW')) {
    $lower = get_post_value('lower');
    $upper = get_post_value('upper');
    $game_display =
      new GameDisplay(get_session_value('game'));
```

```
    $game_display->updateWithAnswer($lower, $upper);
  }

  // CASE 3: Player has either just arrived or has
  //    finished a game and asked for a new one.
  elseif (!get_post_value('POSTCHECK') ||
          get_post_value('NEW')) {
    $game_display = new GameDisplay(new Game());
  }

  // CASE 4:  Something is wrong.
  // The page is the result of a POST operation,
  // yet we don't seem to have a live session, so
  // we are not successfully tracking a game.
  // The only thing to do is complain, and ask about
  // cookies.
  else {
    $game_display =
      new GameDisplay(new Game());
    throw (new Exception("We couldn't track your game." .
          "You may have to enable cookies to play"));
  }

  // Construct string that will be displayed as page
  $page_string = $game_display->display();
  // Store game state in session so that next
  //    page can pick it up
    set_session_value('game',
      $game_display->_game);

} // end of try block

catch (Exception $exception) {
  // There is a problem somewhere.  Create
  //    an error page.
  $exception_msg = $exception->getMessage();
  $display = new GameDisplay(null);
  $page_string =
    $display->makeErrorPage($exception_msg);
  // hope to start fresh next time
  unset_session_value('game');
}

// Actually echo page to browser

  echo($page_string);

?>
```

The object types that `index.php` cares about are `GameDisplay` and `Game`. The `Game` object contains all the state information that needs to be preserved from page to page about where the user is in the game (score, questions asked already, and so on). The `GameDisplay` object contains a `Game` instance and does everything necessary to produce an HTML page from it.

If the user is starting off for the first time, we create a new `Game` object, relying on the object's constructor to initialize it appropriately. For subsequent pages, though we rely on the automatic object serialization feature of PHP sessions to store the `Game` object for us. (The actual definitions of `get_session_value()` and `set_session_value()` are in `certainty_utils.php`, but all that is happening is that we stash the `Game` object in a session. PHP takes care of the serialization that is necessary to read the object into a session and back out again.)

For more on what it means to serialize an object, see Chapter 20; for an explanation of sessions and their workings, see Chapter 24.

If the user is in the middle of a game, we expect both a `Game` object stored in the session and a form submission representing either a guess at the answer or a request to be listed on the High Scores page.

Regardless of whether we create a new `Game` object or retrieve the one from the last page, we create a new `GameDisplay` object around it and then ask that object for a string that represents the entire HTML page. We store this in a string, ready to echo it out to the browser in the very last code line.

Exceptions

Many things can go wrong with the execution of this game's code. For one thing, of course, there's always a possibility of a code bug that leaves the game in a strange state. In addition, though, the code relies on at least three external "services," any of which might misbehave:

✦ The database, which stores the questions and answers

✦ The session mechanism, which is in turn probably relying on files on the hard disk

✦ Cookies stored on the user's browser, which may refuse them

If any of these services turn out to be unreliable, the game will not be playable. Our goal in this situation should be to fail as gracefully as possible.

In a previous edition of this chapter, the code had to catch all the possible failures and propagate an error up to this page, which would then detect the failure and display an appropriate error string. This time, though, we can use PHP5's exception mechanism, which makes it much easier to structure the code. Whenever we encounter a problem that cannot be recovered from, we `throw` the problem, along with a descriptive string. The `catch` statement in `index.php` is the only one in the game's code, and so will receive any of the exceptions that happen as a result of its calls to functions in other code files. In addition, it will catch the exception thrown in Case 4 of `index.php`, which probably indicates that the user's browser is not accepting cookies.

See Chapter 31 for an introduction to exceptions and error handling.

game_display_class.php

Almost all of the look-and-feel action for this game is in `game_display_class.php`, as shown in Listing 46-2.

The code file depends on two other files: game_class.php and game_text_class.php. The former contains most of the logic for the inner workings of the game, whereas the latter just contains some boilerplate text. The job of the GameDisplay class is to extract all the information from the game state necessary to produce actual HTML pages.

The important public functions in the class are

✦ The constructor function.

✦ updateWithAnswer(), which is called with data from the user's submission of a guess.

✦ makeErrorPage(), which returns HTML to display if something has gone wrong.

✦ display(), which returns HTML to display when everything has gone right.

Listing 46-2: **game_display_class.php**

```php
<?php
include_once("game_class.php");
include_once("game_text_class.php");

class GameDisplay
{
  //    presentation
  public $_pageTitle = "The Certainty Quiz";
  public $_blueColor = "#AAAAFF";
  public $_redColor = "#FFAAAA";

  //    contents
  public $_game = NULL;
  public $_gameText;
  public $_highScorePosted = FALSE;

  // CONSTRUCTOR

  function __construct ($game) {
    $this->_game = $game;
    $this->_gameText = new GameText();
  }

  // PUBLIC FUNCTIONS
  //    accessors
  function getPageTitle() {
    return($this->_pageTitle);
  }
  function getBlueColor() {
    return($this->_blueColor);
  }
  function getRedColor() {
    return($this->_redColor);
  }
```

Continued

Listing 46-2 *(continued)*

```
  function getGame() {
    return($this->_game);
  }
  function getHighScorePosted() {
    return($this->_highScorePosted);
  }

  function updateWithAnswer ($lower, $upper) {
    $game = $this->getGame();
    $game->updateWithAnswer($lower, $upper);
  }

  function makeErrorPage ($problem_string) {
    // constructs the HTML page to display when
    /// something has gone horribly wrong
    $top_matter_string =
        $this->_makeTopMatter($this->_pageTitle);
    $page_string = <<<EOT
$top_matter_string
</H2></CENTER>
<TABLE BORDER=2>
<TR>
<CENTER>
<H2>We're sorry, but the game is not available
right now.</H2><H4>($problem_string)</H4>
</CENTER>
</TR></TABLE>
</BODY></HTML>
EOT;
    return($page_string);
  }

  function display () {
    // returns entire page as string ---
    // backbone structure of page, plus
    // overridable methods to print components

    // sanity checks
    if (!$this->_game ||
        !is_object($this->_game)) {
      throw new
        Exception("Cannot find valid game object");
    }
    elseif (!$this->_game->getDbConnection()) {
      throw new
        Exception("No database connection");
    }

    // display of apparently valid page
    else {
```

```
      $top_matter_string =
        $this->_makeTopMatter($this->_pageTitle);
      $current_question =
        $this->_currentQuestionString();
      $previous_question =
        $this->_previousQuestionString();
      $game_state =
        $this->_gameStateString();
      $introduction =
        $this->_gameText->introduction();
      $rules =
        $this->_gameText->rules();
      if ($this->_game->getGameLost()) {
        $left_side =
          $this->_gameText->gameLostText() .
          $this->_highScoreString();
      }
      elseif ($this->_game->getGameWon()) {
        $left_side =
          $this->_gameText->gameWonText() .
          $this->_highScoreString();
      }
      else {
        $left_side = $current_question;
      }
      if ($this->_game->getPreviousQuestion()) {
          $right_side =
            "<TABLE><TR><TD>
            $previous_question
            </TD></TR><TR><TD>
            $game_state
            </TD></TR><TR><TD>
            $rules
            </TD></TR></TABLE>";
      }
      else {
          $right_side =
            "<TABLE><TR><TD>
            $introduction
            </TD></TR>
            <TR><TD>
            $rules
            </TD></TR><TR><TD>
            $game_state
            </TD></TR>
            </TABLE>";
      }

// actually construct page
$page_string = <<<EOT
$top_matter_string
```

Continued

Listing 46-2 *(continued)*

```
</H2></CENTER>
<TABLE BORDER=2>
<TR>
<TD VALIGN=TOP WIDTH=40% >$left_side</TD>
<TD VALIGN=TOP WIDTH=60% >$right_side</TD>
</TR></TABLE>
</BODY></HTML>
EOT;
        return($page_string);
    }
  }

  function handleHighScore () {
    // Handles database update for case where player
    //   has earned high score, and has submitted
    //   a name for the record
    if (!$this->_highScorePosted) {
      $this->_highScorePosted = TRUE;
      if (get_post_value('NICKNAME') &&
          get_post_value('ANSWER_COUNT') &&
          get_post_value('CREDIT') &&
          get_post_value('CHECKSUM') &&
          $this->_checksumChecks(
            get_post_value('ANSWER_COUNT'),
            get_post_value('CREDIT'),
            get_post_value('CHECKSUM'))) {
        $name = get_post_value('NICKNAME');
        $answer_count = get_post_value('ANSWER_COUNT');
        $credit = get_post_value('CREDIT');
        $query = "insert into high_scores
                  (name, answer_count, credit)
                  values
                  ('$name', $answer_count, $credit)";
        $connection =
         $this->_game->gameParameters->getDbConnection();
        $result = mysql query($query. $connection);
      }
      else {
        // do nothing -- failure to add high score
        // should not be a deal killer
      }
    }
  }

  // PRIVATE FUNCTIONS

  private function _makeTopMatter ($title) {
    // returns HTML fragment that heads both
    //   regular page and error page, containing
    //   HTML head and title
```

```
    $return_string = <<<EOT
<HTML><HEAD><TITLE>$title</TITLE></HEAD>
<BODY BGCOLOR=#FFFFFF><CENTER>
<H1>$title<BR>
<FONT SIZE=-1 COLOR=BLUE>
(How sure <B>are</B> you?)</FONT>
</H1></CENTER>
EOT;
    return($return_string);
  }

  private function _currentQuestionString () {
    global $PHP_SELF;
    return("<H2>" .
          $this->_game->getCurrentQuestionText() .
          "</H2>" .
          "<FORM METHOD=POST ACTION=\"$PHP_SELF\">" .
          "<INPUT TYPE=HIDDEN NAME=POSTCHECK VALUE=1>" .
          $this->_distractorString(
              $this->_game->getCurrentQuestion()) .
          "</FORM>");
  }

  private function _distractorString ($question) {
    // creates the actual HTML for presentation of
    //   radio-button alternatives for guesses.
    //   Assumes that the array representing the
    //     actual alternatives has been calculated in
    //     advance, retrievable from the question using
    //     getDistractorArray
    $distractor_array = $question->getDistractorArray();
    $distractor_string = "<TABLE><TR VALIGN=TOP><TD>";
    $distractor_string .=
      "<TABLE BORDER=1 BGCOLOR=\"AAAAFF\"><TR><TH>
        </TH><TH>At least</TH><TH>Not more than</TH>";
    $count = 1;   // 1-based labels are preferable,
                  // so we can just use if ($label) ...
    $total = count($distractor_array);
    foreach ($distractor_array as $distractor) {
      $lower_selected = ($count == 1) ?
        "CHECKED" : "";
      $upper_selected = ($count == $total) ?
        "CHECKED" : "";
      $formatted_distractor =
        ($distractor >= 10000) ?
          number_format($distractor) : $distractor;
      $distractor_string .=
        "<TR><TD>$formatted_distractor</TD>
            <TD><INPUT TYPE=RADIO NAME=\"lower\"
                VALUE=$count
                $lower_selected ></TD>\n" .
```

Continued

Listing 46-2 *(continued)*

```
            "<TD><INPUT TYPE=RADIO NAME=\"upper\"
                VALUE=$count
                $upper_selected ></TD></TR>\n";
        $count++;
    }
    $distractor_string .= "</TABLE>";
    $distractor_string .= "</TD><TD>";
    $distractor_string .=
        "<INPUT NAME=\"Submit guess\" VALUE=\"Submit guess\"
                TYPE=SUBMIT>";
    $distractor_string .= "</TD></TR></TABLE>";

    return($distractor_string);
}

private function _previousQuestionString () {
    if (!$this->_game->getPreviousQuestion()) {
        $return_string = "";
    }
    else {
        $return_string =
            $this->_game->previousQuestionCorrect() ?
                $this->_rightString() :
                $this->_wrongString();
    }
    return($return_string);
}

function _rightString () {
    return("<H1><FONT COLOR=GREEN>RIGHT!</FONT></H1>");
}

function _wrongString () {
    return("<H1><FONT COLOR=RED>WRONG!</FONT></H1>");
}

private function _highScoreEligible () {
    // takes a game-ending score, and queries the
    //  DB to see if the player is eligible for the
    //  high score list
    $query = "select name, answer_count, credit
                from high_scores
                order by answer_count desc, credit desc
                limit 10";
    $connection =
        $this->_game->getDbConnection();
    if ($connection && is_resource($connection)) {
        $result = mysql_query($query, $connection);
        $eligible = false;
```

```
      if (mysql_num_rows($result) > 9) {
        while ($row = mysql_fetch_assoc($result)) {
          $answer_count = $row['answer_count'];
          $credit = $row['credit'];
          if (($this->_game->getCorrectAnswers()
                > $answer_count) ||
              (($this->_game->getCorrectAnswers()
                  == $answer_count) &&
                ($this->_game->_credit > $credit))) {
            $eligible = TRUE;
            break;
          }
        }
      }
      else {
        $eligible = TRUE;
      }
      return($eligible);
    }
    else {
      throw new
        Exception("Game display has no database connection");
    }
  }

  // Checksum is calculated when posting a score
  //  (comprised of a number of correct answers plus
  //   credit remaining) and the checksum is compared with
  //   the submitted scores.  A first line of defense against
  //   spoofing (unless, of course, the checksum scheme is
  //   published in a book or something).
  private function _checksumChecks ($answer_count, $credit,
                            $checksum) {
    return($checksum ==
           $this->_makeCheckSum($answer_count, $credit));
  }

  private function _makeChecksum ($answer_count, $credit) {
   return ((round($credit)) * 17) *
          ($answer_count * 31);
  }

  private function _postHighScoreString () {
    // The greeting plus HTML form for actually submitting
    //  a name to the high scores list
    global $PHP_SELF;
    $answer_count = $this->_game->getCorrectAnswers();
    $credit = $this->_game->getCredit();
    $checksum = $this->_makeChecksum($answer_count, $credit);
    $result_string =
```

Continued

Listing 46-2 *(continued)*

```
        "<H2>Congratulations! You have a high score</H2>".
        "Enter your name (or a nickname) for the high ".
        "scores list:".
        "<FORM METHOD=POST ACTION=\"$PHP_SELF\" >".
        "<INPUT NAME=NICKNAME TYPE=TEXT SIZE = 30>".
        "<INPUT NAME=ANSWER_COUNT TYPE=HIDDEN ".
          "VALUE=$answer_count>".
        "<INPUT NAME=CREDIT TYPE=HIDDEN ".
          "VALUE=$credit>".
        "<INPUT NAME=CHECKSUM TYPE=HIDDEN ".
          "VALUE=$checksum>".
        "<INPUT NAME=Submit TYPE=SUBMIT ".
          "VALUE=Submit >".
        "<INPUT TYPE=HIDDEN NAME=POSTCHECK VALUE=1>" .
        "<INPUT TYPE=HIDDEN NAME=HIGHSCORE VALUE=1>" .
        "<FORM>";
    return($result_string);
  }

  private function _highScoreString () {
    // The table of high scores itself, including
    //   the database interaction necessary to retrieve it
    if ($this->_highScoreEligible() &&
        !$this->_highScorePosted) {
      $result_string = $this->_postHighScoreString();
    }
    else {
      $result_string = "";
    }
    $result_string .=
     "<H2>High scores to date</H2>".
     "<TABLE BORDER=1><TR><TH>Rank</TH>".
     "<TH>Name</TH><TH>Correct answers</TH>".
     "<TH>Credit left at end</TH></TR>";
    $query = "select name, answer_count, credit
              from high_scores
              order by answer_count desc, credit desc
              limit 10";
    $connection =
      $this->_game->gameParameters->getDbConnection();
    if ($connection && is_resource($connection)) {
      $result = mysql_query($query, $connection);
      $rank = 1;
      while ($row = mysql_fetch_assoc($result)) {
        $name = $row['name'];
        $answer_count = $row['answer_count'];
        $credit = (int) ($row['credit']);
        $result_string .=
```

```
          "<TR><TH>$rank</TH><TD>$name</TD>".
            "<TD>$answer_count</TD><TD>$credit</TD></TR>";
          $rank++;
        }
        $result_string .= "</TABLE>";
        return($result_string);
      }
      else {
        throw new
          Exception("Game display has no database connection");
      }
    }

    private function _gameStateString () {
      // The HTML table
      $correct_answers = $this->_game->getCorrectAnswers();
      $credit = round_to_digits($this->_game->getCredit(), 2);
      $level = $this->_game->getLevel();
      return("<TABLE CELLPADDING=10>".
      "<TR BGCOLOR=$this->_blueColor>".
      "<TH>Total correct answers:</TH>".
      "<TD>$correct_answers</TD></TR>".
      "<TR BGCOLOR=$this->_redColor><TH>Credit remaining:</TH>".
      "<TD>$credit</TD></TR>".
      "<TR BGCOLOR=$this->_blueColor>".
      "<TH>You have reached level:</TH>".
      "<TD>$level</TD></TR></TABLE>");
    }
  }
?>
```

Note that in the GameDisplay class we use some object-oriented constructs that are new as of PHP5. The constructor function is called __construct(), rather than having the same name as the class. And we have designated the functions that are not intended for external use as private, which will prevent any such use by other classes.

Most of the class's private functions involve querying the Game object for information that it then wraps up in HTML strings. One of the more interesting functions of this type is distractor_string(), which creates the actual display of alternatives for the answer range. The general division of labor here is:

✦ The upper and lower bounds for the answer are specified in the database, as well as how many choices should be displayed and how they should be scaled.

✦ The Question object takes this information and creates all the intermediate steps of the answer range as it is constructed.

✦ The GameDisplay object queries the game for the current question and then queries that question to discover the upper and lower bounds and the intermediate steps. It then simply wraps those values in HTML to present radio-button alternatives, with the maximum answer range preselected.

game_text_class.php

Your humble authors try really hard to make this stuff interesting, but in this case, we must declare defeat. The `GameText` class just wraps up some boilerplate HTML into member functions so that the `GameDisplay` class can ask for it. Enough said?

The functions use our favorite technique for creating large chunks of boilerplate, which is the *heredoc* syntax. (See Chapter 8 for more on the uses of heredoc.) Listing 46-3 shows the `game_text_class.php`.

Listing 46-3: **game_text_class.php**

```php
<?php
class GameText
{

function __construct () {
  // no vars, nothing for constructor to do
}

function introduction () {
$intro = <<<EOT
<H2>Welcome to the Certainty Quiz!</H2>
The game that tests
<LI>how much you know about how much <B>and</B> <LI>how much you
know about
how much you know about how much!
<H4>The object</H4> The goal is to answer as many questions
correctly as possible.
Answer questions
(starting with the first one at the left), by choosing
values above and below where you think the right answer lies.
Answers are correct if they include the real answer in the
range.
The narrower your guesses, the longer you'll survive.
There are ten levels;  if you think the questions are
too easy, keep going.
EOT;
  return($intro);
  }

function rules () {
$rules = <<<EOT
<H4>Rules and scoring</H4>
<LI>Four points subtracted from your credit for every incorrect
answer.
<LI>One point added to your credit for every correct answer,
minus a penalty for the range of your answer.  Specifying the
entire range possible subtracts four points (for a total of -3);
specifying a single step of the range subtracts nothing
 (for a total of +1).  Intermediate ranges give intermediate re
sults.
```

```
<LI>Credit is capped at 15.
<LI>Whenever your credit falls below zero, the game is over.
EOT;
  return($rules);
}

function gameLostText () {
global $PHP_SELF;
$game_over = <<<EOT
<H1>Thanks for playing!</H1>
Thanks for taking the certainty quiz, and for being
such a good <FONT COLOR=RED>LOSER!</FONT><BR>
<FORM METHOD=POST ACTION="$PHP_SELF">
<INPUT TYPE=SUBMIT NAME=NEW VALUE="New Game">
<INPUT TYPE=HIDDEN NAME=POSTCHECK VALUE=1>
</FORM>
EOT;
return($game_over);
}

function gameWonText () {
global $PHP_SELF;
$game_over = <<<EOT
<H1>You won!</H1>
Thanks for taking the certainty quiz, and for
beating it.  We bow to your superior knowledge
of what you know, and what you don't know.
<FORM METHOD=POST ACTION="$PHP_SELF">
<INPUT TYPE=SUBMIT NAME=NEW VALUE="New Game">
<INPUT TYPE=HIDDEN NAME=POSTCHECK VALUE=1>
</FORM>
EOT;
return($game_over);
}

}
?>
```

game_class.php

In this section, we get to the basic logic of the game. The Game object contains everything worth remembering about the current state of the game, as well as methods for updating it.

Data members

It's worth listing the important pieces of data that the Game object tracks:

◆ The current question (an instance of class Question).

◆ The previous question, if any (an instance of class Question).

◆ The questions that have been asked at this level (an array of database IDs).

◆ The questions that could still be asked at this level (an array of database IDs).

✦ The game's numerical defaults (an instance of class `GameParameters`).

✦ Numerical variables that track the game's state (credit, questions answered, and so on).

Public functions

As with the `GameDisplay` class, let's list the functions that the `Game` class exposes to callers:

✦ The constructor function.

✦ Various accessor functions for member data.

✦ `updateWithAnswer()` takes the player's upper and lower guesses and updates the game's state accordingly, including both update of scores and setting up the next question to be asked.

Database interaction

The actual questions and answers that the game displays are retrieved from a back-end MySQL database. There are two main types of interaction with that database:

✦ Whenever the player moves to a new level (including the first one), the `Game` object retrieves the IDs of all questions that may be asked at that level and scrambles their ordering. This randomized list is propagated along with the `Game` object from page to page within a particular level of the game.

✦ Whenever a new question is actually ready to be asked, the `Game` object pops its database ID off the list constructed and then queries the question database to retrieve all the rest of the question's information (the text of the question, the correct answer, the range of possible values to present, and so on).

Listing 46-4 shows `game_class.php`.

Listing 46-4: **game_class.php**

```php
<?php
include_once("certainty_utils.php");
include_once("game_parameters_class.php");
include_once("question_class.php");

class Game
{

  public $currentQuestion = NULL;
  public $previousQuestion = NULL;
  public $gameParameters;

  public $_dbConnection = NULL;
  public $_credit = 0.0;
  public $_level;
  public $_questionIdsAtLevel;  // an array of ids
  public $_questionsAskedAtLevel = 0; // a count
  public $_totalQuestions = 0;
  public $_correctAnswers = 0;
```

```php
    public $_gameLost = FALSE;
    public $_gameWon = FALSE;

    // CONSTRUCTOR
    function __construct () {
      $this->gameParameters = new GameParameters();
      $this->_dbConnection =
        $this->gameParameters->getDbConnection();
      if (!$this->_dbConnection) {
        throw new Exception("No database connection");
      }
      else {
        $this->_correctAnswers = 0;
        $this->_level =
          $this->gameParameters->getStartingLevel();
        $this->_credit =
          $this->gameParameters->getStartingCredit();
        // make a list of questions to be asked at the
        //   starting level
        $this->_setupQuestionIds();
        // actually retrieve the first question
        $this->_installQuestion();
      }
    }

    // PUBLIC FUNCTIONS
    // accessors
    function getGameParameters()
      {return($this->gameParameters);}

    function getCurrentQuestion()
      {return($this->currentQuestion);}

    function getPreviousQuestion()
      {return($this->previousQuestion);}

    function getCredit() {return($this->_credit);}

    function getLevel() {return($this->_level);}

    function getQuestionsAskedAtLevel()
      {return($this->_questionsAskedAtLevel);}

    function getTotalQuestions()
      {return($this->_totalQuestions);}

    function getCorrectAnswers()
      {return($this->_correctAnswers);}

    function getGameLost()
      {return($this->_gameLost);}
```

Continued

Listing 46-4 *(continued)*

```
function getGameWon()
  {return($this->_gameWon);}

function getCurrentQuestionText() {
  if (!is_object($this->currentQuestion)) {
    print("What is it?<BR>");
    print_r($this->currentQuestion);
  }
  else {
    return($this->currentQuestion->getQuestion());
  }
}

function previousQuestionCorrect() {
  return($this->previousQuestion->getCorrect());
}

function getDbConnection () {
  if (!$this->_dbConnection) {
    $this->_dbConnection =
      $this->gameParameters->getDbConnection();
  }
  return($this->_dbConnection);
}

function updateWithAnswer ($lower, $upper) {
  // The main modifying function for a game object.
  // Takes a player's upper and lower guess, determines
  //   correctness, updates scores, determines if the
  //   player has graduated to the next level, and
  //   swaps in the next question.
  $this->previousQuestion = $this->currentQuestion;
  $this->previousQuestion->updateWithAnswer($lower,
                                            $upper);
  $this->_updateScores();
  $this->_maybeChangeLevel();
  if (!($this->_gameLost || $this->_gameWon)) {
    $this->_installQuestion();
  }
}

// PRIVATE FUNCTIONS
function _installQuestion () {
  // actually retrieve a question from the database
  //   and create a corresponding instance of Question
  if (count($this->_questionIdsAtLevel) > 0) {
    // pop a question off the randomized list
    $question_id =
      array_pop($this->_questionIdsAtLevel);
    $query =
      "select id, question, answer,
```

```
            upper_limit, lower_limit, scaling_type
            from question
            where id = $question_id";
        if (!$this->_dbConnection) {
          $this->_dbConnection =
            $this->gameParameters->getDbConnection();
        }
        if ($this->_dbConnection &&
            is_resource($this->_dbConnection)) {
          $result = mysql_query($query,
                              $this->_dbConnection);
          if ($row = mysql_fetch_assoc($result)) {
            $this->currentQuestion =
                new Question(
                  $row['id'],
                  $row['question'],
                  $row['answer'],
                  $row['lower_limit'],
                  $row['upper_limit'],
                  10,
                  $row['scaling_type']);
            $this->_questionsAskedAtLevel++;
          }
          else {
            throw new
      Exception("Problem retrieving question from database");
          }
        }
        else {
          throw new
              Exception("Problem querying question database");
        }
      }
      else {
        throw new
            Exception("Could not find any questions to ask");
      }
    }

    function _setupQuestionIds () {
      $this->_questionIdsAtLevel =
        $this->_getQuestionIdsAtLevel($this->_level);
    }

    function _getQuestionIdsAtLevel ($level) {
      // to be used at time of graduation to a new level -
      // retrieves the new ids (only) of all questions at
      // the level, and shuffles them into a random order.
      $return_array = array();
      $query = "select id from question
                where level = $level";
```

Continued

Listing 46-4 *(continued)*

```php
    $this->getDbConnection();
    if (!$this->_dbConnection) {
      throw new
          Exception("No database connection");
    }
    else {
      $result = mysql_query($query,
                            $this->_dbConnection);
      while ($row = mysql_fetch_assoc($result)) {
        array_push($return_array, $row['id']);
      }
    }
    // randomize the order of the questions
    $return_array = create_randomized_array($return_array);
    return($return_array);
  }

  public function _updateScores () {
    // Change the current score based both on
    //  whether the player got the answer right and on
    //  the spread between the player's upper and lower
    //  guess.  Calculations depend on settings from
    //  the GameParameters class.
    if ($this->previousQuestion->rightAnswer()) {
      $this->_correctAnswers =
        $this->_correctAnswers + 1;
      $this->_credit +=
        $this->gameParameters->getRightAnswerCredit() -
        ($this->previousQuestion->getAnswerSpread() *
         $this->gameParameters->getAnswerSpreadDebit());
    }
    else {
      $new_credit =
      $this->_credit =
        $this->_credit -
        $this->gameParameters->getWrongAnswerDebit();
    }
    // enforce cap on credit
    $this->_credit =
      min($this->_credit,
          $this->gameParameters->getMaximumCredit());
  }

  function _maybeChangeLevel () {
    if ($this->_credit < 0.0) {
      $this->_gameLost = TRUE;
    }
    else {
      $params = $this->gameParameters;
```

```
        $current_level = $this->_level;
        if ($current_level >
            $params->getMaximumLevel()) {
          $this->_gameWon = TRUE;
        }
        else {
          // find out if questions remain to be
          //  asked at this level
          if (($this->_questionsAskedAtLevel >=
               $params->getQuestionsPerLevel($current_level)) ||
              (count($this->_questionIdsAtLevel) == 0)) {
                // either we have asked the limit of
                // questions per level, OR we have simply run out
                $this->_level++;
                $this->_questionsAskedAtLevel = 0;
                $this->_setupQuestionIds();
                // note recursive call --- it's possible
                //  that no questions were found, and we have
                //  to keep going
                $this->_maybeChangeLevel();
          }
        }
      }
    }

    function __sleep () {
      // make sure to serialize all fields except
      //  the database connection (has to be recreated)
      //  and the previous question (no point).
      return(array(
              'gameParameters',
              'currentQuestion',
              '_credit',
              '_level',
              '_questionIdsAtLevel',
              '_questionsAskedAtLevel',
              '_correctAnswers',
              '_totalQuestions',
              '_gameLost',
              '_gameWon'));
    }
  }
?>
```

Handling an answer

Here are the steps that a Game object goes through in dealing with a guess range submitted by a player (in the function updateWithAnswer):

1. Move the current question object to the previous question slot.

2. Update the (now previous) question with the upper and lower ranges of the guess (which are still in terms of step numbers from the form rather than actual values).

3. Query the previous question to discover the range of the guess and whether the question was correctly answered. Update all scores (credit, correct answers) appropriately.

4. Decide whether to promote the player to a new level now. If so, retrieve the database IDs of all questions that may be asked at that level. Randomize the order of the question list.

5. If the game has not yet ended, grab a new question ID from the randomized list and use it to ask the database for a new question. Turn that data into a `Question` object and make it the current question.

Serialization and sleep()

The `sleep()` function is called to do cleanup whenever an object is serialized and also returns a list of all the member variables that should be recorded in a serialization. The `Game` class makes use of only the latter capability — all member variables except the previous question and the database connection itself are retained as the object is stored in the session for the next page's use.

Note Unlike with some other class definitions, we've defined `Game`'s variables to be public. This is because in our testing with PHP5.0b1, we discovered that private variables were not surviving the serialization process. This may be fixed by the time PHP5.0 is released.

game_parameters.php

The single instance of the `GameParameters` class, shown in Listing 46-5, packages up all the default numbers that we may want to customize in making a new version of the game (the penalties and rewards, the number of levels, the starting and maximum credit, and so on). In addition, this object manages global access to the database connection.

Listing 46-5: game_parameters.php

```php
<?php
include_once("certainty_utils.php");
include_once("dbvars.php");

class GameParameters {

    var $_dbConnection = NULL;
    var $_startingLevel = 1;
    var $_maximumLevel = 10;
    var $_startingCredit = 5.0;
    var $_maximumCredit = 15.0;
    var $_questionsPerLevel = 3;
    var $_rightAnswerCredit = 1.0;
    var $_wrongAnswerDebit = 4.0;
    var $_answerSpreadDebit = 4.0;

    // CONSTRUCTOR
    function GameParameters () {
```

```
      // all fields set by default values
    }

    // PUBLIC FUNCTIONS
    // accessors

    function getStartingLevel () {
      return($this->_startingLevel);
    }

    function getMaximumLevel () {
      return($this->_maximumLevel);
    }

    function getStartingCredit () {
      return($this->_startingCredit);
    }

    function getMaximumCredit () {
      return($this->_maximumCredit);
    }

    function getRightAnswerCredit () {
      return($this->_rightAnswerCredit);
    }

    function getWrongAnswerDebit () {
      return($this->_wrongAnswerDebit);
    }

    function getAnswerSpreadDebit () {
      return($this->_answerSpreadDebit);
    }

    function getQuestionsPerLevel () {
      return($this->_questionsPerLevel);
    }

    function getDbConnection () {
      global $host, $user, $pass, $db;  // from dbvars.inc
      if ($this->_dbConnection &&
          is_resource($this->dbConnection)) {
        return($_dbConnection);
      }
      else {
        // suppress warnings about connection,
        // will handle at higher level if failed
        $connection =
          @mysql_connect($host, $user, $pass);
        if ($connection &&
```

Continued

Listing 46-5 *(continued)*

```
          mysql_select_db($db, $connection)) {
        return($connection);
      }
      else {
        return(FALSE);
      }
    }
  }

  function __sleep () {
    return(array('_startingLevel',
                 '_startingCredit',
                 '_rightAnswerCredit',
                 '_wrongAnswerDebit',
                 '_answerSpreadDebit',
                 '_questionsPerLevel'));
  }
}
?>
```

certainty_utils.php

This code file, shown in Listing 46-6, is a grab-bag for capabilities and definitions that do not fit neatly into a particular class and that are used in more than one other code file.

Everything in certainty_utils.php fits into one of a few categories:

✦ Initial declarations (seeding the random number generator, setting the error-reporting level).

✦ Abstraction functions for session and post variables.

✦ Utility functions for calculating intermediate answer values and for randomizing question lists.

Listing 46-6: certainty_utils.php

```
<?php

// Definitions and utility functions for the
//  Certainty Quiz game
error_reporting(E_ALL);
// enumeration constants for the scaling of distractors
define("CERTAINTY_LINEAR", 1);
define("CERTAINTY_GEOMETRIC", 2);

// Seed the random number generator
srand((double) microtime() * 1000000);

// A hack to retrieve the value of POST values
```

```
//   without explicitly checking PHP versions.
function get_post_value ($var_name) {
  global $HTTP_POST_VARS;
  if (IsSet($_POST) &&
      IsSet($_POST[$var_name])) {
    return($_POST[$var_name]);
  }
  elseif (IsSet($HTTP_POST_VARS) &&
          IsSet($HTTP_POST_VARS[$var_name])) {
    return($HTTP_POST_VARS[$var_name]);
  }
  else {
    return(FALSE);
  }
}

function get_session_value ($var_name) {
  global $HTTP_SESSION_VARS;
  if (IsSet($_SESSION) &&
      IsSet($_SESSION[$var_name])) {
    return($_SESSION[$var_name]);
  }
  elseif (IsSet($HTTP_SESSION_VARS) &&
          IsSet($HTTP_SESSION_VARS[$var_name])) {
    return($HTTP_SESSION_VARS[$var_name]);
  }
  else {
    return(FALSE);
  }
}

function set_session_value ($var_name, $value) {
  global $HTTP_SESSION_VARS;
  if (IsSet($_SESSION)) {
    $_SESSION[$var_name] = $value;
    $HTTP_SESSION_VARS[$var_name] = $value;
  }
  else {
    $HTTP_SESSION_VARS[$var_name] = $value;
  }
}

// Numerical functions

function round_to_digits ($number, $digits) {
  if ($number < 0) {
    return(- round_to_digits(- $number, $digits));
  }
  else if ($number == 0) {
    return($number);
  }
  else {
```

Continued

Listing 46-6 *(continued)*

```
    $tens =
      floor(log10($number));
    $divisor = pow(10, ($tens - $digits));
    $significant = (1.0 * $number) /
      $divisor;
    $rounded = round($significant);
    return($rounded * $divisor);
  }
}

function nth_root_initial($product, $n)
{
  $estimate = sqrt($product);
  $roots = 2;
  while ($roots < $n) {
    $estimate = sqrt($estimate);
    $roots = $roots * 2;
  }
  return($estimate);
}

function nth_root ($product, $n) {
  if (($product <= 1) ||
      ($n < 2)) {
    die("Arguments to nth_root should be ".
      "product (greater than 1) and " .
      "n (greater than 1)");
  }
  $initial_estimate =
    nth_root_initial($product, $n);
  return(nth_root_aux($product, $n,
          $initial_estimate,
          20000,
          0.0001));
}

function nth_root_aux ($product, $n,
                       $guess,
                       $iterations_left,
                       $desired_difference) {
  if ($iterations_left <= 0) {
    return($guess);
  }
  else {
    $guessed_product = pow($guess, $n);
    if (abs($guessed_product - $product)
        < $desired_difference) {
      return($guess);
    }
    else {
      $new_guess =
```

```
            $guess -
              ((pow($guess, $n) - $product) /
                ($n * pow($guess, $n-1)));
            return(nth_root_aux($product, $n,
                                $new_guess,
                                $iterations_left - 1,
                                $desired_difference));
        }
      }
    }

    function create_randomized_array ($in_array) {
        // Assumes input is simple list, with keys
        //   equal to 0,....,n
        // Returns similar list, with keys as in input
        //   but values in randomized order
        // Assumes prior call to srand()
        $in_array_length = count($in_array);
        $working_array = array();
        for ($i = 0; $i < $in_array_length; $i++) {
            $rand_value = rand();
            $working_array[$i] = $rand_value;
        }
        asort($working_array);   // orders by random value
        $return_array = array();
        $working_keys = array_keys($working_array);
        foreach ($working_keys as $int_key) {
            array_push($return_array,
                $in_array[$int_key]);
        }
        return($return_array);
    }
?>
```

The functions in `certainty_utils.php` take care of figuring out all the intermediate guesses between the lowest value offered to the user and the highest value. In addition, there's a scaling option, which determines whether the intermediate values grow linearly or geometrically. (If you think that the number "between" 10 and 1000 is 100, you are scaling geometrically; if you think the number between 10 and 1000 is 505, you are scaling linearly.) The functions for finding nth roots are used in doing the geometric scaling.

The `create_randomized_array()` function is what we use to scramble the order of questions within a level.

question_class.php

Finally, we get down to the actual questions that are pulled from our database of questions to ask. The definition of the `Question` class is shown in Listing 46-7. The public functions here are:

✦ The constructor, which is given the question, correct answer, the upper and lower bounds, the number of steps in the guesses, and the type of scaling (linear or geometric).

✦ Various accessor functions, such as `getAnswer()`, `getQuestion()`, `getScalingType()`.

✦ updateWithAnswer(), which bottoms out here by actually translating the Web form's step numbers to values for the guesses, comparing those guesses to the real answer.

✦ getAnswerSpread(), which returns a measure of how narrow the guess was.

Listing 46-7: **question_class.php**

```php
<?php
include_once("certainty_utils.php");

class Question
{
  // PRIVATE VARIABLES
  private $_id; // ID in database
  private $_question; // text of question
  private $_answer; // correct numeric answer
  private $_lowerLimit; // smallest value in distractors
  private $_upperLimit; // largest value in distractors
  private $_distractorCount; // number of dist. presented
  private $_scalingType;  // representing linear vs. geometric
  private $_distractorArray; // contains all dist presented
  private $_lowerGuess = NULL; // player's lower bound
  private $_upperGuess = NULL; // player's upper bound
  private $_correct = NULL;  // TRUE or FALSE after guess

  // CONSTRUCTOR
  function __construct($id, $question,
                      $answer,
                      $lower_limit,
                      $upper_limit,
                      $distractor_count,
                      $scaling_type) {
    $this->_id = $id;
    $this->_question = $question;
    $this->_answer = $answer;
    $this->_lowerLimit = $lower_limit;
    $this->_upperLimit = $upper_limit;
    $this->_distractorCount = $distractor_count;
    $this->_scalingType = $scaling_type;
    $this->_distractorArray =
        $this->_makeDistractors($lower_limit,
                  $upper_limit,
                  $distractor_count,
                  $scaling_type);
  }

  // PUBLIC FUNCTIONS

  // accessors

  function getId () {return($this->_id);}
  function getQuestion () {return($this->_question);}
```

```php
function getAnswer () {return($this->_answer);}
function getCorrect() {return($this->_correct);}
function rightAnswer() {return($this->_correct);}
function getDistractorCount() {return($this->_correct);}
function getScalingType() {return($this->_scalingType);}
function getDistractorArray()
  {return($this->_distractorArray);}
function getLowerGuess() {return($this->_lowerGuess);}
function getUpperGuess() {return($this->_upperGuess);}

function getAnswerSpread () {
  $answer_range = count($this->_distractorArray) - 1;
  if (IsSet($this->_lowerGuess) &&
      IsSet($this->_upperGuess)) {
    $lower = $this->_lowerGuess;
    $upper = $this->_upperGuess;
    if ($upper < $lower) {
      throw new Exception("Problem in range of answers");
    }
    else {
      $spread =
              (max($upper - $lower, 1) - 1)
              / ($answer_range - 1);
      return($spread);
    }
  }
  else {
    throw new Exception("Answer variables not set");
  }
}

function updateWithAnswer($lower, $upper) {
  // takes a lower and upper guess from player, and
  //  determines if the guesses bound the right answer
  $this->_lowerGuess = $lower;
  $this->_upperGuess = $upper;
  $upper_value = NULL;
  $lower_value = NULL;
  $count = 1;
  foreach ($this->_distractorArray as $distractor) {
    if ($count == $lower) {
      $lower_value = $distractor;
    }
    if ($count == $upper) {
      $upper_value = $distractor;
    }
    $count++;
  }
  if (IsSet($lower_value) && IsSet($upper_value)) {
    $answer = $this->_answer;
    $lower_value_lowered = $lower_value -
```

Continued

Listing 46-7 *(continued)*

```
        max(0.0001, abs($lower_value / 1000000.0));
     $upper_value_raised = $upper_value +
        max(0.0001, abs($upper_value / 1000000.0));
     if (($lower_value_lowered <= $this->_answer) &&
         ($upper_value_raised >= $this->_answer)) {
       $this->_correct = TRUE;
     }
     else {
       $this->_correct = FALSE;
     }
   }
   else {
     $this->_correct = NULL;
   }
 }

 // PRIVATE FUNCTIONS
 private function _makeDistractors ($lower, $upper,
                         $distractor_count,
                         $linear_or_geometric)
 // Create the array of intermediate values between
 //  the upper bound and the lower bound on guesses
 //  that the player can choose from.  Depending on
 //  a flag in each row of the question database,
 //  the scaling of possible answers ("distractors")
 //  can be linear (10, 20, 30 ...) or geometric
 //  (10, 20, 40, 80 ...)
 // Code for construction of geometric distractors can
 //  blow up for some arguments, so arguments are
 //  checked before calls to make_distractors_geometric
 //  are allowed.  Failures default back to linear.
 {
   if (($linear_or_geometric == CERTAINTY_GEOMETRIC) &&
       ($this->safeGeometricArguments($upper, $lower))) {
     return($this->_makeDistractorsGeometric(
       $lower, $upper, $distractor_count));
   }
   else {
     return($this->_makeDistractorsLinear(
       $lower, $upper, $distractor_count));
   }
 }

 private function safeGeometricArguments ($upper, $lower) {
  // should probably really also include the number
  // of distractors as an argument.  Only tested for
  // # of distractors approx 10.
  return (($upper > 0) && ($lower > 0) &&
```

```
                ($upper > $lower) &&
                (($upper / $lower) < 10000000000));
    }

    private function _makeDistractorsLinear
                ($lower, $upper, $distractor_count)
    {

      $return_array = array();
      array_push($return_array, round_to_digits($lower, 3));
      $current = $lower;
      $increment = (($upper - $lower) / $distractor_count);
      // add in all the intermediate values
      for ($x = 1; $x < $distractor_count; $x++) {
        array_push($return_array,
                    round_to_digits($lower +
                            ($x * $increment),
                                3));
      }
      array_push($return_array, round_to_digits($upper, 3));
      return($return_array);
    }

    private function _makeDistractorsGeometric
                ($lower, $upper, $distractor_count)
    {
      if (($lower >= $upper) ||
          ($distractor_count < 2)) {
        die("Args to _makeDistractorsGeometric should be " .
            "1) a lower limit, 2) an upper limit, " .
            "3) a count (>= 2) of divisions between them.<BR>" .
"Args were 1) $lower, 2) $upper, 3) $distractor_count<BR>");
      }
      $return_array = array();
      array_push($return_array, round_to_digits($lower, 3));
      $limit_ratio = $upper / $lower;
      $root = nth_root($limit_ratio, $distractor_count);
      $current = $lower;
      // add in the intermediate values
      for ($x = 1; $x < $distractor_count; $x++) {
        $distractor = round_to_digits(
                        $lower * pow($root, $x),
                        3);
        array_push($return_array,
                    $distractor);
      }
      array_push($return_array, round_to_digits($upper, 3));
      return($return_array);
    }
  }
?>
```

dbvars.php

When we actually query the database, we need to have access information. The file shown in Listing 46-8 is loaded by GameParameters.php, and sets up the variables necessary for making a MySQL connection. Note that the current values are dummies and will *not work* on your system! You need to fill in the correct values for your own MySQL configuration. If your Web server is connected to the Internet, it's also a good idea to move this file somewhere outside the Web-server document tree and to change the reference in GameParameters.php to point to its new location.

Listing 46-8: dbvars.php

```php
<?php
$host = "YOUR_HOSTNAME";
$user = "YOUR_MYSQL USERNAME";
$pass = "YOUR_MYSQL_PASSWORD";
$db = "certainty";
?>
```

Creating the database

The trivia game is fueled by a database of questions. So far, we have said nothing about how to create such a database.

Table definitions

Listing 46-9 shows a MySQL dump file of all the table definitions used in the code, along with a few sample entries. Before loading it, you need to create a database called certainty; after that is done, you should be able to simply cat or pipe the contents of this file to the mysql command.

Note that the question table includes several fields that are not actually used in the current code. One of them is attribution, useful for recording the book or Web site that served as the authority for the answer. Another is include, which we intended for filtering out questions in development that were not ready to be displayed. A third is subjectID, which we use to tag questions according to subject area (Science, Geography, History, and so on). although that association is not actually displayed anywhere. A final as-yet unused column is unitID, which could be used to record the unit (kilometers, years, furlongs, bushels) of the answer in case the unit affects how guesses should be displayed.

Listing 46-9: Table definitions

```
# MySQL dump 7.1
#
# Host: [host deleted]    Database: certainty
#---------------------------------------------------------
# Server version 3.22.32

#
# Table structure for table 'high_scores'
#
```

```
CREATE TABLE high_scores (
  id int(11) DEFAULT '0' NOT NULL auto_increment,
  name varchar(30),
  answer_count int(11),
  credit double(16,4),
  PRIMARY KEY (id)
);

#
# Dumping data for table 'high_scores'
#

INSERT INTO high_scores VALUES (8,'Ben Stein',15,-3.0000);

#
# Table structure for table 'question'
#
CREATE TABLE question (
  ID int(11) DEFAULT '0' NOT NULL auto_increment,
  answer double(16,4),
  unitID int(11),
  level int(11),
  subjectID int(11),
  include tinyint(4),
  upper_limit double(16,4),
  lower_limit double(16,4),
  scaling_type tinyint(4),
  question varchar(255),
  attribution varchar(255),
  PRIMARY KEY (ID)
);

#
# Dumping data for table 'question'
#

INSERT INTO question VALUES
(1,5283755345.0000,1,1,1,1,200000000000.0000,1000000.0000,2,
'What was the human population of the world
in the middle of 1990?',
'http://www.census.gov/ipc/www/worldpop.html');
INSERT INTO question VALUES (2,70.0000,1,1,1,1,95.0000,5.0000,1,
'What percentage of the Earth\'s surface is covered by water?',
'http:/www.sciencenet.org.uk/database/Geography/
Original/g00057d.html');
INSERT INTO question VALUES
(4,1969.0000,NULL,1,2,NULL,2000.0000,1950.0000,1,
'In what year did human beings first walk on the moon?','');
#
# Table structure for table 'subject'
#
```

Continued

Listing 46-9 *(continued)*

```
CREATE TABLE subject (
  id int(11) DEFAULT '0' NOT NULL auto_increment,
  subject varchar(255),
  PRIMARY KEY (id)
);

#
# Dumping data for table 'subject'
#

INSERT INTO subject VALUES (1,'Geography');
INSERT INTO subject VALUES (2,'History');
INSERT INTO subject VALUES (3,'Science');
INSERT INTO subject VALUES (4,'Mathematics');
INSERT INTO subject VALUES (5,'Miscellaneous');
```

The MySQL dump includes only three sample questions. You can always add more through a direct interaction with MySQL, but it's more convenient to do it via a Web form.

entry_form.php

Listing 46-10 shows a bare-bones Web form for entering more questions into the question database. This simply takes typed input (except for a pull-down association with the subject table) and trusts the results. Note that there is neither security nor error-checking here— this is intended for use only by the game creator, and if misuse is a concern you should probably add password protection or some other kind of authentication. (See Chapter 44 for more on creating authentication systems.)

Listing 46-10: dbvars.php

```php
<?php
include_once("certainty_utils.php");
include_once("game_parameters_class.php");
$params = new GameParameters();
$connection = $params->getDbConnection();

if (get_post_value('POSTCHECK')) {
  handleEntryForm();
}
displayEntryForm();

function handleEntryForm () {
  $question = get_post_value('QUESTION');
  $answer = get_post_value('ANSWER');
  $lower_limit = get_post_value('LOWER_LIMIT');
  $upper_limit = get_post_value('UPPER_LIMIT');
  $level = get_post_value('LEVEL');
  $subject = get_post_value('SUBJECT');
```

```php
    $scaling_type = get_post_value('SCALING_TYPE');
    $attribution = get_post_value('ATTRIBUTION');
    if ($upper_limit > $lower_limit) {
      $query =
        "insert into question
          (question, answer, lower_limit, upper_limit,
           level, subjectID, scaling_type,
           attribution)
           values
          ('$question', $answer, $lower_limit, $upper_limit,
           $level, $subject, $scaling_type,
           '$attribution')";
      $result = mysql_query($query);
      if ($result) {
        print("Entry was successful<BR>");
      }
      else {
        print("Entry was not successful<BR>");
      }
    }
    else {
      print("Upper limit must be > lower<BR>");
    }
  }

function displayEntryForm () {
global $PHP_SELF;
$linear = CERTAINTY_LINEAR;
$geometric = CERTAINTY_GEOMETRIC;
$subject_string = make_subject_string();
$form_string = <<<EOT
<FORM METHOD=POST TARGET="$PHP_SELF" >
Question:
<INPUT TYPE=TEXT NAME=QUESTION SIZE=60 ><BR>
Answer:
<INPUT TYPE=TEXT NAME=ANSWER><BR>
Lower:
<INPUT TYPE=TEXT NAME=LOWER_LIMIT><BR>
Upper:
<INPUT TYPE=TEXT NAME=UPPER_LIMIT><BR>
Level:
<INPUT TYPE=TEXT NAME=LEVEL><BR>
Subject:
$subject_string<BR>
Scaling type:
<SELECT NAME=SCALING_TYPE>
  <OPTION VALUE=$linear>Linear
  <OPTION VALUE=$geometric>Geometric
</SELECT><BR>
Attribution:
<INPUT TYPE=TEXT NAME=ATTRIBUTION><BR>
```

Continued

Listing 46-10 *(continued)*

```
<INPUT TYPE=SUBMIT NAME=SUBMIT VALUE=SUBMIT>
<INPUT TYPE=HIDDEN NAME=POSTCHECK VALUE=1>
</FORM>
EOT;
echo $form_string;
}

function make_subject_string () {
  $result_string = "<SELECT NAME=SUBJECT>";
  $query = "select id, subject from subject order by id";
  $result = mysql_query($query);
  while ($row = mysql_fetch_row($result)) {
    $id = $row[0];
    $display = $row[1];
    $result_string .= "<OPTION VALUE=$id>$display";
  }
  $result_string .= "</SELECT>";
  return($result_string);
}
?>
```

General Design Considerations

What follows is a brief list of issues that we were forced to consider while writing the code in this chapter.

Separation of code and display

The question of separating code and display is a vexing one, especially in situations where you have different personnel assigned to maintaining logic and appearance. Our own view on this is that perfect separation of code and display is like a perfect vacuum — you can get asymptotically closer to the ideal as you expend infinite effort.

For large Web sites employing many people, some pretty good techniques exist for making a strong separation, including templating systems and database storage of graphics and display text. For this relatively small and informal example, we were satisfied by simply segregating all HTML into two display-oriented classes, leaving the remainder of the code focused on logic and data.

Persistence of data

There are several kinds of data in this game that survive longer than the execution time of a page. We chose to use PHP's session mechanism for all the data particular to a particular game invocation and a backend database for everything else (questions, answers, and high-score lists).

For reasons of efficiency, we didn't want to store too much data via the session mechanism. So we separated out the most important data (that could not be easily recreated) into the Game class and stored only an instance of that class. Everything else (question text, boiler-plate HTML text, high scores, and so on) was either embedded in code files or easily retrievable from the database.

Exception handling

We used the new (as of PHP5) exception mechanism to bail out whenever we encountered a problem that the code could not recover from. Failures to recover session info, failures to find cookies, and database interaction problems were all grounds for giving up. In general, when we threw an exception, we sent a string suitable for display to a user and then caught all thrown exceptions at the point of display. This has the disadvantage of not providing a lot of rich debugging information (particularly since several different code paths can throw a "No database connection" exception), but has the advantage that we can tell the user something reasonable and fairly cosmetic, while giving the developer a hint.

Summary

The Certainty Quiz is a small, simple, self-contained PHP application that you should be able to install and enjoy in the privacy of your own home (after connecting it to your favorite Web server and a MySQL database, of course). Although small, the code relies on database interaction, OOP features, use of sessions, string processing, object serialization, exception-handling, and non-trivial arithmetic to achieve its effects. Although PHP has many capabilities that we didn't come close to touching on, this chapter uses a fair cross-section of its most popular features — if you understand everything in this example, you are well on your way to exploiting the power of PHP.

✦   ✦   ✦

Converting Static HTML Sites

Almost everything we've discussed in this book so far assumes that you are designing your PHP-enabled site from scratch, including any database schemas that may be required. The truth, however, is that many of the most common and valuable PHP projects involve converting a pre-existing HTML site to a more maintainable PHP version. Here we describe in detail how this is accomplished, using a real site as an example.

The information in this chapter may also be valuable if you need to transfer data from one format to another (tab-delimited file to database, one database to another), or if you want to take a bunch of text files and turn them into a Web site.

Planning the Big Upgrade

Our example site, MysteryGuide.com (at `www.mysteryguide.com`), is one we've run since about 1996. If you can think back that far in the history of the Internet, most people and companies were barely experimenting with HTML, much less technologies for creating dynamic Web sites. PHP was then still a CGI tool; MySQL had just gotten off the ground — and we hadn't heard of either of them.

We originally kept our data in FileMaker, therefore, and wrote it out to static HTML files by using a compiled computer language. Although the site kept growing over time, we never quite got the motivation or time to upgrade our back end systems — among other things, we were writing the first and second editions of this book and thus heroically sacrificing our own projects to share our knowledge with you, dear Reader. In any case, after a few years, we had a site that consisted of almost 1000 separate HTML files, which were a growing nightmare to maintain. The hardware and software on which we developed the site were old and prone to breakage, and upgrading didn't seem an option for various reasons. (It was all Macintosh OS 8, for one thing.) It became almost impossible to add new titles to our review database because of the large amount of work entailed by every new addition. And, of course, we had the extra shame and humiliation of being the writers of a book about creating dynamic Web sites by using PHP — while our own site was minimally dynamic! It's only after years of therapy that we can confess this to you, dear Reader, in the hope that it may help you find the inner strength to clear up the ugly, static HTML sites in your own life.

The baby and the bathwater

The first step to recoding a site is to step back and take inventory of what is working well and what the most important fix-it items may be. Our experience has been that teams often skip this step through impatience and live to regret it later when they are confronting huge, difficult-to-reverse architectural issues. You already have a lot of good things going for you, and you know a lot of invaluable information about your needs and your audience — make sure you capture this information in a usable format.

As we took stock of MysteryGuide's code, content, and mission, this is what we found.

Audience characteristics:

✦ Audience is composed of all ages and an equal gender split.

✦ No internationalization needs — all visitors can be assumed to read English competently.

✦ Unusually large percentage of older people and a heavy number of readers with poor vision.

✦ New visitors may land on any page because most come from search engines.

✦ Fairly large and vocal percentage of Macintosh users.

✦ MysteryGuide does not collect user data.

✦ Users often print out pages for offline viewing (for example, taking to library, sharing with friends).

Things that are working well:

✦ Navigation scheme (for example, dividing books into subgenres).

✦ Reviews and other data.

✦ Features (for example, book ratings, games, interviews).

✦ Heavily crawled by search engines.

Things that need work:

✦ Very difficult to change page layouts.

✦ Database is offline, nonrelational, and can't be searched by users.

✦ Forums — not much traffic, spam magnet.

✦ Some users can't find the author or book they're looking for.

✦ Need tools to add and edit data.

✦ Site design lacks professional look.

What does all this stock-taking tell us? Actually, the news is very good in this case. The content is fine, and the big-picture navigation is working for now. In this case, our three major goals are very clear:

✦ Move data into a new database.

✦ Create dynamic page-generation with PHP and database.

✦ Initiate a cosmetic look-and-feel upgrade.

If we accomplish these three tasks and also drop the forum (which is an entirely separate subsystem), we can be in a good technical position to add new features desired by our users, such as search and printable versions of the book reviews.

Technical assessment

In addition to strategic insights about the site, we should assess the logical, physical, and software requirements of MysteryGuide.com and consider whether we need to upgrade them too.

Site architecture

MysteryGuide currently consists of approximately 900 pages, of which the vast majority (about 800) could be made dynamic. There are actually only a few types of pages:

- ✦ Front page
- ✦ Complete author list
- ✦ Genre pages
- ✦ Genre history pages
- ✦ Book pages
- ✦ Feature pages (interviews, games, and so forth)
- ✦ Miscellaneous pages (top-rated books, FAQ, and so forth)

Of these, by far the most numerous and important are the book pages. We expect to spend at least half the time required by the whole project on just the book page template; the big data dump we plan is almost all for the book pages. After that, the genre page is the most important; and then the front page. Feature pages and single pages are the least important, and if push comes to shove, we could launch the redesigned site without them.

Hardware and software requirements

Obviously, we're using PHP for the scripting language and Apache for the Web server (because we run on Unix). For a purpose like this, moving from a static HTML site, MySQL is a no-brainer as the database. All we care about are very fast reads and the ability to scale to thousands of rows per table because we don't collect user data and perform writes only very occasionally (essentially just when someone reviews a book). If you needed to make a lot of writes, and especially if you needed rollbacks and triggers, you would have to evaluate other databases. (See Chapter 12 for more information on choosing a database.)

Because we're already using all these programs for the current version of MysteryGuide.com, we require no new hardware or software. After the upgrade is complete, we will actually be using fewer system resources and less disk space than before. Our upgrade actually makes the site (marginally) cheaper to run and more portable, as well as much more maintainable and scalable.

Tip   You need a standalone version of PHP to perform some of the tasks described in this section. If you don't have one already, compile and install it now. Refer to Chapter 3 for instructions.

Redesigning the User Interface

You want to get your designers working on the new look and feel as soon as possible, because they need some lead time to iterate on their ideas, and little UI code can be usefully written before they deliver their piece of the puzzle. If you don't know any good designers, finding some should be your first priority. If you're lucky enough to be in this position, having a usability team contribute from the beginning can also be helpful.

Our experience has been that most designers do best if you (or your usability people) give them the basic layout you want on each page—in the case of a working site, they can simply look at the old site or you can draw a little wireframe. You should also explain clearly any special factors that must be taken into account, such as (in our case) the stricture against tiny or light-colored fonts. You're actually helping them do their jobs more efficiently by imposing some structure at the beginning, and you have only yourself to blame if you give a designer carte blanche and end up with some bizarre art-school production.

We were very lucky to work with a designer, Mimi Yin of Mydesignco.com, who is deeply interested in data-rich sites, has a knack for using shape to add movement and interest to the page, and believes in getting client feedback early and often. She started working on the most important and pressing parts of the site (book and genre pages) and then harmonized the rest of the site to match. This is exactly what you want—the designer should not automatically begin working on the most visually appealing or prominent parts of the site (for example the front page or splash screen) just because that is the most interesting piece for him or her. She or he should work on the part that is most important for the site.

These are before and after screenshots of a MysteryGuide.com book page. As we noted in the preceding "Site architecture" section, the book page is the most important and numerous of our types of pages. Figure 47-1 shows the old design. (Keep a kind thought—it was designed in 1997.)

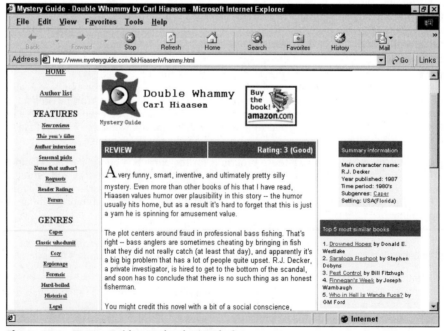

Figure 47-1: MysteryGuide.com book page before

Figure 47-2 shows the new design in the mockup phase. Notice how cleverly our designer has framed the various elements to set them off visually.

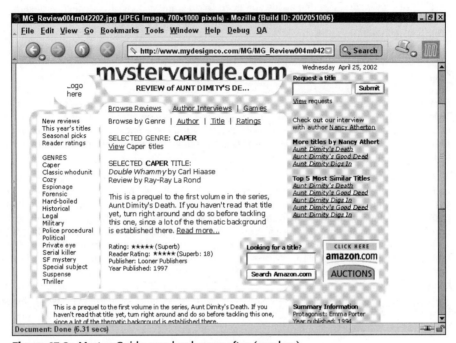

Figure 47-2: MysteryGuide.com book page after (mockup)

Even at this early stage, one thing is immediately obvious: If we go with this design, we very likely need to use a table layout and some spacer images. This kind of design is difficult (verging on impossible if you're not a DHTML master) to lay out nicely with "pure" XHTML and CSS. Few organizations really care about this distinction, but as a professional Web developer, it's your job to think about the ramifications of such a decision. If, for example, you're developing a new site for an IT consultancy, it may negatively affect their professional image to be seen using Web techniques that are not state-of-the-art. In our case, we feel that the attractiveness of the design is worth the tradeoff; and, in any case, we haven't taken a strong position in the great HTML 4 versus XHTML debate.

The important point is that you, as the Web developer, need to work with your designer to ensure that the look and feel you end up with melds smoothly with the technology you want to use. You can't necessarily expect designers to know or care about how the design is implemented. For example, the designer selects a font that he or she feels best expresses the mission of your site, but the Web developer is usually the one who decides whether to use <FONT> tags or Cascading Style Sheets. She is also definitely the one who needs to test the design in different browsers with different settings. Sometimes the Web developer has to be the person to say, "This design looks incredibly crummy on a Macintosh," or "This design only works if JavaScript is on," or "This design loads incredibly slowly on a modem, leading to unacceptable latency on our servers." So trust your designers, treasure their talents, and let them express their ideas — but remember that ultimately their deliverable is a mockup, whereas yours is an actual working site.

Planning a New Database Schema

As your designers are iterating away, you need to do some design of your own — designing a database schema, that is. If you already have a workable database, feel free to skip to the "Templating" section that follows.

Cross-Reference   For basic information on working with SQL, see Chapter 13.

Besides the book reviews, MysteryGuide's main feature is a book recommendation system. This subsystem depends upon a questionnaire that our reviewers fill out for each book, detailing such things as the settings in which the action took place, the name of the protagonist, and how violent the book was. It is this data that we are seeking to represent in a SQL format.

Although we previously kept our data in a database, it was not truly relational. Each book had one big monolithic database record that listed everything that we wanted to know about that book. Relationality didn't matter that much for one-to-one fields, such as year of first publication — every book is only published for the first time once, after all. But for many-to-one fields, such as setting, we were forced to make some awkward compromises. Basically these boiled down to two methods. The first was setting a fixed number of fields of a certain type (for example: Subgenre1, Subgenre2, Subgenre3), which may or may not be filled in for any given book. The second was enabling multiple entries to be placed in a single field, separated by commas (for example: "UK, Germany, Switzerland" as the setting of one book). These multiple fields had to be untangled and redrawn as many-to-many SQL relationships in the new database.

Furthermore, a nonrelational database inevitably has repetition that can be eliminated in a relational database. We want to know, for example, the name, sex, and nationality of each author. There are some authors whom we've reviewed multiple times, and this information is entered separately in each book's record. Besides causing inefficiency and duplication of effort, this practice resulted in a higher incidence of mistakes.

Our old nonrelational database table looked something like this:

```
Title
Author name
Author gender
Author nationality
Year of first publication
Subgenre1
Subgenre2
Subgenre3
Settings (multiple)
Time period (multiple)
Rating
Protagonist name
Protagonist gender
Protagonist age
Protagonist nationality
Protagonist occupation
Protagonist organization
Action (1 - 5)
Humor (1 - 5)
```

```
Romance (1 - 5)
Sex (1 - 5)
Violence (1 - 5)
Type of crime (multiple)
Reviewer
Number of pages
Review completion date
Book ISBN
Movies (multiple)
Awards (multiple)
Review
Blurb
Author interview
```

Starting from this schema, it's pretty easy to divide these fields into three main buckets: Author, Protagonist, and Book information. The new Author table follows. Notice that we changed the field names to a more SQL-like naming style.

```
A_id
A_firstname
A_lastname
A_gender
A_nationality
A_interview
```

The Protagonist table looks like this:

```
P_id
P_firstname
P_lastname
P_gender
P_age
P_nationality
P_occupation
P_organization
```

The main Book table contains these fields:

```
B_id
B_title
B_year
B_rating
B_action
B_humor
B_romance
B_sex
B_violence
B_reviewer
B_pages
B_reviewdate
B_ISBN
B_movie
B_awards
B_review
B_blurb
```

Notice that we have removed most of the multiple-entry fields, which must now get their own definition tables and also tables relating them to books. Subgenre information, for example, is now stored in a simple table:

```
Sub_id
Sub_name
```

A matching table, `Book_Subgenre`, is required to store the relationships:

```
BSub_id
B_id
Sub_id
```

Settings, time periods, and type of crimes would also need similar new tables.

We decided, however, not to make new tables for Movies and Awards. Although a given book can have several film adaptations—for instance, *The Maltese Falcon* was filmed at least three times and won several awards—these are many-to-one relationships and treated by MysteryGuide basically as strings rather than categorizable information.

Now that you've worked out your schema on paper, go implement it as a bunch of SQL commands. You could also write a PHP script to do this, but a SQL file is actually much easier after you're comfortable with the concept. A SQL file is just a text file that strings together a bunch of SQL commands so you don't need to enter them one by one on the command line—instead you can read the whole file into MySQL with a single command. Listing 47-1 creates a database definition file.

Listing 47-1: **Database definition file (newmg_structure.sql)**

```
# MySQL dump file
# MysteryGuide SQL structure only

#
# Table structure for table 'author'
#
CREATE TABLE author (
  A_id int(11) DEFAULT '0' NOT NULL auto_increment,
  A_firstname tinytext,
  A_lastname tinytext,
  A_gender tinyint(4),
  A_nationality tinytext,
  A_interview tinytext,
  PRIMARY KEY (A_id)
);

#
# Table structure for table 'book'
#
CREATE TABLE book (
  B_id int(11) DEFAULT '0' NOT NULL auto_increment,
```

```
        B_title tinytext,
        B_year year(4),
        B_rating tinyint(4),
        B_action tinyint(4),
        B_humor tinyint(4),
        B_romance tinyint(4),
        B_sex tinyint(4),
        B_violence tinyint(4),
        B_reviewer tinytext,
        B_pages smallint(6),
        B_reviewdate date,
        B_ISBN tinytext,
        B_movie text,
        B_awards text,
        B_review text,
        B_blurb text,
        PRIMARY KEY (B_id)
);


#
# Table structure for table 'book_author'
#
CREATE TABLE book_author (
   BA_id int(11) DEFAULT '0' NOT NULL auto_increment,
   B_id int(11),
   A_id int(11),
   PRIMARY KEY (BA_id)
);


#
# Table structure for table 'subgenre'
#
CREATE TABLE subgenre (
   Sub_id int(11) DEFAULT '0' NOT NULL auto_increment,
   Sub_name tinytext,
   PRIMARY KEY (Sub_id)
);


#
# Table structure for table 'book_subgenre'
#
CREATE TABLE book_subgenre (
   BSub_id int(11) DEFAULT '0' NOT NULL auto_increment,
   B_id int(11),
   Sub_id int(11),
   PRIMARY KEY (BSub_id)
);
...
```

Whenever you're ready, you can dump this file into a MySQL database by typing the following commands (plus the password, when you're prompted for it) on the command line:

```
mysqladmin -u root -p create mysteryguide
mysql -u root -p mysteryguide < newmg_structure.sql
```

If you make a mistake, don't panic! You can keep dropping the database, fixing your SQL errors in the file, re-creating the database, and reloading.

Remember to grant privileges for this database to nonroot MySQL users as soon as you finish creating the database permanently. The principle to follow is to give each database user the lowest level of privileges necessary to get the job done. In this case, your default MySQL user needs only read privileges; ordinary visitors do not write to our database. You must create a different MySQL user with write privileges for reviewers, and possibly another for editors or administrators. These come into play in the "Tools" section later in this chapter.

Dumping Data into a Database

Now that you have a nice fresh database, you're ready to dump information into it. We mainly assume that you are starting with another database (as we are) or possibly a spreadsheet. In the section "Harvesting data," later in this chapter, we discuss how to adapt these tasks if you're starting with multiple text files (for example, HTML files or Word documents) instead.

Data-massaging

So we begin by dumping the data from FileMaker (or any data store) into a tab-delimited file. Most small databases and spreadsheets have some way to do this automatically—the command may be called something such as Export or Dump. It's very important to write down or print out the order in which the fields exported, which may be considerably different from their display order.

At this point you should check over the tab-delimited file and make sure that the data is basically good. You may need to fix it up a little bit at this point. We needed to turn some old-style Macintosh linebreaks, for example, into Unix-compatible newlines. The easiest way to do so is to break out Perl regex on the command line:

```
perl -pi -e 's/\r/\n/g' tabdelimitedfile.txt
```

If you're going from Windows to Unix or Unix to Windows, you probably must do something similar. Windows to Unix is:

```
perl -pi -e 's/\r\n/\n/g' tabdelimitedfile.txt
```

Unix to Windows is:

```
perl -pi -e 's/\n/\r\n/g' tabdelimitedfile.txt
```

Converting from Macintosh or Unix to Windows is a bit more problematic because the toolkits are different. You may want to use something like Perl for Windows (ActiveState distributes a well-regarded version without cost, www.activestate.com/Products/ActivePerl). Alternatively, you could do the conversion on the Unix side before shipping over to Windows.

Another thing you may want to do at this point is cut up your data file into pieces. This is probably a good idea in any case, because you want to break off a chunk of data for testing anyway. Also, it's a lot easier to recoup from errors when working with a smaller data set — if your script chokes on some unexpected error, this may mean the difference between having to redo 100 entries and having to redo the entire data dump. You *must* cut up the file if your data file is more than 2GB large, because most Unix applications and utilities have a limited capability to deal with files greater than that size. You probably must use special 32-bit versions tools such as `split` or Perl to accomplish this task.

To cut up a file into manageable pieces, you want to use the Unix utility `split` like this:

```
split --lines=100 tabdelimitedfile.txt chunk_
```

This results in a bunch of 100-line files called `chunk_aa`, `chunk_ab`, `chunk_ac`, and so on. Obviously you can substitute a different integer value for the number of lines. If you leave off the final argument, the files are just called `aa`, `ab`, `ac`, and so on. Remember that these are 100 lines as Unix counts them, which means 100 units of text between (invisible) newline characters (`\n`). If you are using a Windows or Macintosh format file with different line breaks, they may look like line-breaks in the text file but are not necessarily counted correctly by `split`. If you have newlines within some field entry, `split` also gets confused.

Data dumping

Now you're ready to write a script to dump the data into the database. You have two choices: Either you can use the standalone version of PHP, which is fast and does not time out, or you can use the normal module version in the browser, which may be easier for Windows users or anyone not comfortable with the command line. The actual scripts in standalone or module versions are not hugely different. The biggest issue is probably that the module version can only handle smallish data sets because most Web servers are configured to timeout after 60 seconds or so. And the standalone version must echo to the terminal in text, whereas the module version outputs to the browser in HTML.

Either way, the basic steps are clear:

1. Read in the data file.

2. Split it into an array, where each array element is one row of data.

3. Cycling through the array, split each row into fields.

4. Cycling through the array, arrange the field data into one or more SQL queries and send it to the database.

5. Repeat until all data is stored.

Tip   Work with a test batch of representative data while you write and debug your script.

The following code, Listing 47-2, should be saved under some name like `dumpdata.php`. It runs in either the browser or on the command line (`/usr/local/bin/php dumpdata.php`). It inserts data into the database tables that we defined in Listing 47-1.

Listing 47-2: Script to dump data ino MySQL (dumpdata.php)

```php
<?php

/*********************************************
 * Script to dump data into the MG database. *
 *********************************************/


// Read in the file as an array
// ----------------------------
$filename = 'tabdelimitedfile.txt';
$farray = file($filename) or die("Can't read in file");


// Open up a database connection
$db = mysql_connect('localhost', 'editor', 'sesame')
     or die("Can't connect to the database");
mysql_select_db('mg');


// Loop through each entry
// ----------------------
foreach ($farray as $val) {
  $l_arr = explode("\t", $val);
  print_r($l_arr);

  // Tidy up the entries
  // -------------------

  // Author info
  $Author = $l_arr[1];
  // Divide name into first and last
  $A_array = explode(', ', $Author);
  $A_firstname = addslashes($A_array[1]);
  $A_lastname = addslashes($A_array[0]);
  $A_gender = addslashes($l_arr[2]);
  if ($A_gender == 'F') {
    $A_gender = 0;
  } elseif ($A_gender == 'M') {
    $A_gender = 1;
  } else {
    echo "$A_firstname $A_lastname has gender issues";
  }
  $A_nationality = addslashes($l_arr[3]);
  $A_interview = addslashes($l_arr[31]);

  // Book info
  $B_title = addslashes($l_arr[0]);
  $B_year = $l_arr[4];
```

```
    $B_rating = $l_arr[10];
    $B_action = $l_arr[17];
    $B_humor = $l_arr[18];
    $B_romance = $l_arr[19];
    $B_sex = $l_arr[20];
    $B_violence = $l_arr[21];
    $B_reviewer = addslashes($l_arr[23]);
    $B_pages = $l_arr[24];
    $B_reviewdate = $l_arr[25];
    // Reformat the review date from m/d/yy to yyyy-mm-dd
    $date_arr = explode('/', $B_reviewdate);
    $B_reviewdate = date('Y-m-d', mktime(12, 30, 0, $date_arr[0],
$date_arr[1], $date_arr[2]));
    $B_ISBN = $l_arr[26];
    $B_movie = addslashes($l_arr[27]);
    $B_awards = addslashes($l_arr[28]);
    $B_review = addslashes($l_arr[29]);
    $B_blurb = addslashes($l_arr[30]);

    // Subgenre info
    $Subgenre[1] = addslashes($l_arr[5]);
    $Subgenre[2] = addslashes($l_arr[6]);
    $Subgenre[3] = addslashes($l_arr[7]);


    // Enter data into database
    // -----------------------

    // Author data
    // First see if this author is already in the database
    $query = "SELECT A_id FROM author
              WHERE A_firstname = '$A_firstname'
              AND A_lastname = '$A_lastname'
              ";
    $result = mysql_query($query);
    if (mysql_num_rows($result) == 0) {
      // If not already there, add the author
      $query = "INSERT INTO author VALUES(
                NULL,
                '$A_firstname',
                '$A_lastname',
                $A_gender,
                '$A_nationality',
                '$A_interview'
                )";
      $result = mysql_query($query);
      if (mysql_affected_rows() != 1) {
        echo "Problem inserting author data for $A_firstname
$A_lastname";
      } else {
```

Continued

Listing 47-2 *(continued)*

```
        $author_id = mysql_insert_id();
        //Need this for book_author
    }
} else {
    $author_id = mysql_result($result, 0, 0);
}

// Book data
// We can assume each book is unique
$query = "INSERT INTO book VALUES(
        NULL,
        '$B_title',
        '$B_year',
        $B_rating,
        $B_action,
        $B_humor,
        $B_romance,
        $B_sex,
        $B_violence,
        '$B_reviewer',
        $B_pages,
        '$B_reviewdate',
        '$B_ISBN',
        '$B_movie',
        '$B_awards',
        '$B_review',
        '$B_blurb'
        )";
$result = mysql_query($query);
$book_id = mysql_insert_id(); //Need this for book_author
if (!$book_id || $book_id == "") {
    echo "Problem inserting book data for $B_title";
}

// Associate book and author
$query = "INSERT INTO book_author VALUES(
        NULL,
        $book_id,
        $author_id
        )";
$result = mysql_query($query);
if (mysql_affected_rows() != 1) {
    echo "Problem inserting book_author data for $B_title";
}

// Subgenres
for ($i = 1; $i <= 3; $i++) {
    if ($Subgenre[$i] == "") {
        continue;
    } else {
```

```
            // First see if this subgenre is already in the database
            $query = "SELECT Sub_id FROM subgenre
                      WHERE Sub_name = '$Subgenre[$i]'
                      ";
            $result = mysql_query($query);
            if (mysql_num_rows($result) == 0) {
              // If not already there, add the subgenre
              $query = "INSERT INTO subgenre VALUES(
                        NULL,
                        '$Subgenre[$i]'
                        )";
              $result = mysql_query($query);
              if (mysql_affected_rows() != 1) {
                echo "Problem inserting subgenre $Subgenre[$i]";
              } else {
                $subgenre_id = mysql_insert_id();
              }
            } else {
              $subgenre_id = mysql_result($result, 0, 0);
            }

            // Now associate the subgenre with the book
            $query = "INSERT INTO book_subgenre VALUES(
                      NULL,
                      $book_id,
                      $subgenre_id
                      )";
            $result = mysql_query($query);
            if (mysql_affected_rows() != 1) {
              echo "Problem inserting book_subgenre data for $B_title
    and $Subgenre[$i]";
            }
          }
        }
      }

    }

    ?>
```

Notice that we deal with several problematic but common situations in this script, such as:

✦ Changing strings (M/F) into integers (1/0) for more compact storage.

✦ Turning one field into two fields (Author_name into A_firstname and A_lastname).

✦ Handling duplicate information (same author for multiple books).

✦ Turning three different fields (Subgenre1, Subgenre2, Subgenre3) into three rows in the same table.

✦ Making a nonrelational database truly relational (book_author and book_subgenre tables).

Harvesting data

The code in the preceding section assumes that you want to transfer data from one database to another—but what if, instead, you need to dump data from a bunch of static HTML or text files into a database? In that case, you have to write yourself a little minispider.

Before you try this, you should know that harvesting data from existing documents is an inherently difficult task. If you've been maintaining 500 static HTML pages for any length of time, there's very likely to be some irregularities in the files that make it more difficult to pick out the pieces that you want. Sometimes even a simple typo or case change causes problems. Harvesting data this way could still save you some time, however, in certain circumstances.

Basically what you want to do is parse text by looking for unique patterns. You hope the information you want to harvest is identifiable by such a pattern. The process is very similar to navigating by landmarks, and only human labor can parse the structure of your documents well enough to pick out the patterns. After a person has clearly picked out a pattern, however, PHP can help you with the repetitive grunt-labor of applying this patterned searching to a whole bunch of documents.

Say, for example, that you have several hundred individual HTML press release pages that you now want to turn into a database. You analyze the pages and discover that the headline is always located inside `<H2>` tags and is the only thing on each page marked by such tags. In this case, it would be very easy to pick out the headline from each page. Unfortunately, this is a deliberately easy example—in many cases, the actual pattern you need to find is more likely to be something like "look for this string; then it is two paragraphs after that, between the third and fourth linebreaks."

Here is a sample snippet of HTML from the old MysteryGuide.com:

```
<html>
<head>
<title>Mystery Guide - The Man who Knew Too Much by
G.K. Chesterton</title>
<meta NAME="description" CONTENT="Mystery Guide review
of The Man who Knew Too Much by G.K. Chesterton">

<!-- Review of The Man who Knew Too Much by G.K. Chesterton -->
</head>
<body TEXT="#000000" LINK="#006400" VLINK="#800080">

<table BORDER=1 RULES=NONE CELLPADDING=5>
<tr><td ALIGN=LEFT BGCOLOR="#A32242" WIDTH=50%>

<font SIZE=-1 FACE="ARIAL, GENEVA, SANS-SERIF"
COLOR="#FFFFFF"><b>REVIEW</b></font>
</td><td BGCOLOR="#A32242" WIDTH=50% ALIGN=RIGHT>
<font SIZE=-1 FACE="ARIAL, GENEVA, SANS-SERIF" COLOR="#FFFFFF">
<b>Rating: 4 (Very good)</b></font></td></tr>
</td></tr>
<tr><td colspan=2>
<font SIZE=+3 FACE="new york, palatino, times">C</font>
<font SIZE=-1 FACE="ARIAL, GENEVA, SANS-SERIF">hesterton's Man
```

```
who Knew Too Much is a long review in text here.
<p ALIGN=RIGHT><b>Reviewer:</b>  JP
</font><br><br></td></tr></table>



<br><table BORDER=0 CELLPADDING=5>
<tr BGCOLOR="#A32242" WIDTH=100%><td>
<font SIZE=-2 FACE="ARIAL, GENEVA, SANS-SERIF"
COLOR="#FFFFFF"><b>Further reading</b></font>
</td></tr>
<tr BGCOLOR="#FFFECC" WIDTH=100%>
<td><font SIZE=-2 FACE="ARIAL, GENEVA, SANS-SERIF">
<aHREF="http://www.amazon.com/exec/obidos/ASIN/0898706297/
troutworksmyster/"> <P><b>Wisdom and Innocence:  a life of GK
Chesterton</b></a> (1997) by Joseph Pearce<BR>Bio focussing on
Chesterton's Catholicism.</td></tr></table>

<table BORDER=0 CELLPADDING=5><tr BGCOLOR="#A32242" WIDTH=100%>
<td>
<font SIZE=-2 FACE="ARIAL, GENEVA, SANS-SERIF" COLOR="#FFFFFF">
<b>Summary information</b></font>
</td></tr>
<tr BGCOLOR="#FFFECC" WIDTH=100%>
<td><font SIZE=-2 FACE="ARIAL, GENEVA, SANS-SERIF">
<b>Main character name:</b><br>  Horne Fisher<br>
<b>Year published:</b>  1922<br>
<b>Time period:</b>  1910's<br>
<b>Subgenres:</b>  <a HREF="classic-whodunit.html">Classic
whodunit</a>, <a HREF="political.html">Political</a><br>
<b>Setting:</b> UK(West Country), Ireland<br>
</font></td></tr></table>
<br>

<table BORDER=0 CELLPADDING=5><tr BGCOLOR="#A32242" WIDTH=100%>
<td>
<font SIZE=-2 FACE="ARIAL, GENEVA, SANS-SERIF" COLOR="#FFFFFF">
<b>Top 5 most similar books</b></font>
</td></tr>
<tr BGCOLOR="#FFFECC" WIDTH=100%>
<td><font SIZE=-2 FACE="ARIAL, GENEVA, SANS-SERIF">
1. <a HREF=bkCopperPons.html TARGET=_top><strong>The Further
Adventures of Solar Pons</strong></a> by Basil Copper and August
Derleth <br>
2. <a HREF=bkOrczyCorner.html TARGET=_top><strong>The Old Man in
the Corner</strong></a> by Emma Orczy <br>
3. <a HREF=bkHareBodkin.html TARGET=_top><strong>With a Bare
Bodkin</strong></a> by Cyril Hare <br>
4. <a HREF=bkRossLove.html TARGET=_top><strong>Whom the Gods
Love</strong></a> by Kate Ross <br>
5. <a HREF=bkSayersBody.html TARGET=_top><strong>Whose
```

```
Body?</strong></a> by Dorothy L. Sayers <br>
</font></td></tr></table>
<br>

<table BORDER=0 CELLPADDING=5><tr BGCOLOR="#A32242" WIDTH=100%>
<td>
<font SIZE=-2 FACE="ARIAL, GENEVA, SANS-SERIF" COLOR="#FFFFFF">
<b>By the same author</b></font>
</td></tr>
<tr BGCOLOR="#FFFECC" WIDTH=100%>
<td><font SIZE=-2 FACE="ARIAL, GENEVA, SANS-SERIF">
<a HREF=bkChestertonThursday.html TARGET=_top><strong>
The Man Who Was Thursday</strong></a> (1908) <br>
</font></td></tr></table>
<br>

<table BORDER=0 CELLPADDING=5>
<tr BGCOLOR="#A32242" WIDTH=100%>
<td>
<font SIZE=-2 FACE="ARIAL, GENEVA, SANS-SERIF" COLOR="#FFFFFF">
<b>Movies</b></font>
</td></tr>
<tr BGCOLOR="#FFFECC" WIDTH=100%>
<td>
<font SIZE=-2 FACE="ARIAL, GENEVA, SANS-SERIF">Neither Alfred
Hitchcock movie of this title has any relation to the book
</td></tr></table>

<p ALIGN=RIGHT>
<font SIZE=-2 FACE="ARIAL, GENEVA, SANS-SERIF">&#169 1999
Troutworks, Inc.  All rights reserved. <br>
Revised July 6, 1999</font></p></body></html>
```

Say that you want to harvest some information from this page — for example, information about movies that were made from this book. First, you'd probably want to divide up the page into chunks corresponding to tables. From here, there are many ways to accomplish your goal using string, array, and possibly regex functions.

Caution   Do not let yourself be intimidated by people who write self-aggrandizing comments on PHP mailing lists or Web sites claiming that all smart people use a certain method to perform these tasks! This type of grungy no-glory parsing is all about getting the job done and producing code you can read — it's not a programming style contest. It may be true that, in theory, you could use one line of regex instead of five lines of string functions, but who cares?

Listing 47-3 shows one straightforward method of getting the movie information you want.

Listing 47-3: Script to harvest data from HTML files (harvest.php)

```php
<?php

// harvest.php - get movie information from a MysteryGuide HTML
// file

$file = 'sample_HTML_for_harvesting.html';
$fp = fopen($file, "r");
$file_str = fread($fp, filesize($file));

// Divide the page into chunks corresponding to tables
$tables = explode('</td></tr></table>', $file_str);

// Not every page will have all tables, so we need to
// rename our array in a more informative way.  If all your
// pages have all identical sections, you don't need to do this.
foreach ($tables as $table_val) {
  if (strpos($table_val, 'SIZE=+3') > 30) {
    $chunk['review'] = $table_val;
  } elseif (strpos($table_val, '<b>Further reading</b>') > 1) {
    $chunk['further'] = $table_val;
  } elseif (strpos($table_val, '<b>Summary information</b>') >
1) {
    $chunk['summary'] = $table_val;
  } elseif (strpos($table_val, '<b>Top 5') > 1) {
    $chunk['top5'] = $table_val;
  } elseif (strpos($table_val, '<b>By the same') > 1) {
    $chunk['sameauthor'] = $table_val;
  } elseif (strpos($table_val, '<b>Movies</b>') > 1) {
    $chunk['movie'] = $table_val;
  }
}


// Now we'll get the movie information
if (isSet($chunk['movie'])) {
  // Get everything after the word "Movies"
  $movie_str = strstr($chunk['movie'], 'Movies');

  // Now get the actual string value of the movie data
  $movie_data_str = strstr($movie_str, '<font SIZE=-2
FACE="ARIAL, GENEVA, SANS-SERIF">');
  $movie_data = substr($movie_data_str, 47);
 //get rid of the font tag above
  //echo $movie_data;

  // Now you can escape this string and put it in a database
  // or whatever...
}

?>
```

You could use this same code with a few additions to harvest all the data on this page — just copy the movie part, and replace the array names and substrings you want to select on.

Now say that you want to harvest data from a whole bunch of HTML or text files. Copy them to an empty directory to minimize unintended consequences. Then you want to iterate over the files by wrapping the following cases around the preceding code:

```
$path = '/path/to/directory';
if ($dir_handle = opendir($path)) {
  while (false !== ($file = $path . readdir($dir_handle))) {
    if ($file != "." && $file != "..") {
      // Code from harvest.php above


    }
  }
}
```

This snippet opens a directory (which must have the proper read and execute permissions for the Web server user), iterates through all the files in that directory, and executes the `harvest.php` code on data from any file that isn't a special Unix directory file. You are almost certainly going to want to run a script such as this from the command line rather than the browser because iterating over a large number of files almost guarantees ugly timeouts.

Templating

Now comes the fiddly bit. This is the moment where you must take a mockup and a database, and turn them into a working Web page.

There are various methods to do this, including use of a full-templating extension such as Smarty templates. Our style, however, is to lay out the main HTML in heredoc syntax, with replacement variables defined on the same page. This is one of the fastest methods, and it still maintains satisfactory separation between logic and display.

Listing 47-4 shows a full-page template, in this case the one for book reviews.

Listing 47-4: **Book page template (review.php)**

```php
<?php

/********************
* Book review page. *
********************/

// For now, pass in the id in the URI
$book_id = $_GET['book_id'];
if !isSet($book_id) || !isNumeric($book_id) {
  echo "You did not pass in a valid book ID";
  exit;
}

// ------------
// GET THE DATA
// -----------
```

```
$db = mysql_connect('localhost', 'mg_user', 'sesame');
mysql_select_db('mg');

// Book data
$query = "SELECT
            B_id,
            B_title,
            B_year,
            B_rating,
            B_movie,
            B_awards,
            B_review,
            B_similar
          FROM book
          WHERE B_id = $book_id";
$result = mysql_query($query);
if (mysql_num_rows($result) == 1) {
  $book_arr = mysql_fetch_array($result);
} else {
  echo mysql_error();
}
$title = stripslashes($book_arr['B_title']);
$year = $book_arr['B_year'];
$rating = $book_arr['B_rating'];
$movie = stripslashes($book_arr['B_movie']);
$awards = stripslashes($book_arr['B_awards']);
$review = stripslashes($book_arr['B_review']);
$review_words = explode(" ", $review);
$chunk = array_slice($review_words, 0, 200);
$review = implode(' ', $chunk);
$similar = stripslashes($book_arr['B_similar']);

// Author data
$query = "SELECT author.A_id, author.A_firstname,
author.A_lastname
          FROM author LEFT JOIN book_author USING (A_id)
          WHERE book_author.B_id = $book_id";
$result = mysql_query($query);
if (mysql_num_rows($result) == 1) {
  $author_arr = mysql_fetch_array($result);
  $author_id = $author_arr['A_id'];
  $a_firstname = stripslashes($author_arr['A_firstname']);
  $a_lastname = stripslashes($author_arr['A_lastname']);
  $author = "$a_firstname $a_lastname";
} else {
  echo mysql_error();
}

// Potential multiple other books by the same author
$query = "SELECT book.B_title
          FROM book LEFT JOIN book_author USING (B_id)
```

Continued

Listing 47-4 *(continued)*

```
          WHERE book_author.A_id = $author_id
          AND book.B_id != $book_id";
$result = mysql_query($query);
if (mysql_num_rows($result) >= 1) {
  while ($titles_arr = mysql_fetch_array($result)) {
    $titles[] = stripslashes($titles_arr['B_title']);
  }
  $title_str = implode('<BR>\n', $titles);
} else {
  $title_str = 'None';
}

// Protagonist data
$query = "SELECT protagonist.P_firstname, protagonist.P_lastname
          FROM protagonist
          LEFT JOIN book_protagonistUSING (P_id)
          WHERE book_protagonist.B_id = $book_id";
$result = mysql_query($query);
if (mysql_num_rows($result) == 1) {
  $prot_arr = mysql_fetch_array($result);
  $p_firstname = stripslashes($prot_arr['P_firstname']);
  $p_lastname = stripslashes($prot_arr['P_lastname']);
  $protagonist = "$p_firstname $p_lastname";
} else {
  echo mysql_error();
}

// Multiple subgenres
$query = "SELECT Sub_name
          FROM subgenre LEFT JOIN book_subgenre USING (Sub_id)
          WHERE book_subgenre.B_id = $book_id";
$result = mysql_query($query);
if (mysql_num_rows($result) >= 1) {
  while ($sub_arr = mysql_fetch_array($result)) {
    $sub_name[] = stripslashes($sub_arr['Sub_name']);
  }
  $subgenre = implode(', ', $sub_name);
} else {
  echo mysql_error();
}

// Multiple settings
$query = "SELECT Set_name
          FROM setting LEFT JOIN book_setting USING (Set_id)
          WHERE book_setting.B_id = $book_id";
$result = mysql_query($query);
```

```
if (mysql_num_rows($result) >= 1) {
  while ($set_arr = mysql_fetch_array($result)) {
    $set_name[] = stripslashes($set_arr['Set_name']);
  }
  $setting = implode(', ', $set_name);
} else {
  echo mysql_error();
}


// ------------
// DISPLAY PAGE
// ------------
$php_self = $_SERVER['PHP_SELF'];
// Superglobal arrays don't work with heredoc
$page_str = <<< EOPAGESTR

<HTML>
<HEAD>
<STYLE>
TD.textblock {
  padding-left: 20;
  padding-top: 20;
  padding-right: 20;
}
P.td {
  font-family: arial, verdana, sans-serif;
  font-size: 8pt;
}
P.td_med {
  font-family: arial, verdana, sans-serif;
  font-size: 10pt;
  line-height:125%
}
P.title {
  font-family: arial, verdana, sans-serif;
  font-size: 10pt;
  font-weight: bold;
}
P.tab_links {
  font-family: arial, verdana, sans-serif;
  font-size: 10pt;
  margin-top: 17;
}
a {
  color:#006400;
  text-decoration:none;
  }
a:link {color:#006400;}
```

Continued

Listing 47-4 *(continued)*

```
a:visited {color:#800080;}
</STYLE>
</HEAD>

<BODY BACKGROUND="background.gif">

<!-- Begin main table -->
<TABLE BORDER=0 WIDTH=815>
<TR>
<TD>
  <IMG SRC="spacer.gif" WIDTH=815 HEIGHT=8>
</TD>
</TR>
<TR>
<TD>
  <!-- Begin banner table -->
  <TABLE BORDER=0>
  <TR>
  <TD WIDTH=48 HEIGHT=90>
    <IMG SRC="spacer.gif" WIDTH=48 HEIGHT=90>
  </TD>
  <TD WIDTH=472 HEIGHT=90 ALIGN="center" VALIGN="middle"">
    <IMG SRC="red.png" WIDTH=460 HEIGHT=60>
  </TD>
  <TD WIDTH=14 HEIGHT=90>
    <IMG SRC="spacer.gif" WIDTH=14 HEIGHT=90>
  </TD>
  <TD WIDTH=292 HEIGHT=90 VALIGN="top" class="textblock">
    <P class="td">a Troutworks, Inc. site<BR>
    &#169; 1994 - 1999 Troutworks, Inc.</P>
    <P class="td">Last updated July 6, 1999</P>
  </TD>
  </TR>
  </TABLE>
  <!-- End banner table -->
</TD>
</TR>
<TR>
<TD>
  <!-- Begin title table -->
  <TABLE BORDER=0>
  <TR>
  <TD WIDTH=140 HEIGHT=30>
    <IMG SRC="spacer.gif" WIDTH=140 HEIGHT=30>
  </TD>
  <TD WIDTH=330 HEIGHT=30 ALIGN="center" VALIGN="bottom">
```

```
    <P class="title">$title</P>
  </TD>
  <TD WIDTH=345 HEIGHT=30>
    <IMG SRC="spacer.gif" WIDTH=345 HEIGHT=30>
  </TD>
  </TR>
  </TABLE>
  <!-- End title table -->
</TD>
</TR>
<TR>
<TD>
  <!-- Begin info table -->
  <TABLE BORDER=0>
  <TR>
  <TD WIDTH=135 HEIGHT=350 ROWSPAN=2 ALIGN="left" VALIGN="top"
style="padding-left:22; padding-top:40">
    <P class="td">
    <A HREF="newbooks.html">New Reviews</A><BR>
    <A HREF="readerratings.html">Reader ratings</A></P>

    <P class="td">
    GENRES<BR>
    <A HREF="caper.html">Caper</A><BR>
    <A HREF="classic-whodunit.html">Classic whodunit</A><BR>
    <A HREF="cozy.html">Cozy</A><BR>
    <A HREF="espionage.html">Espionage</A><BR>
    <A HREF="forensic.html">Forensic</A><BR>
    <A HREF="hard-boiled.html">Hard-boiled</A><BR>
    <A HREF="historical.html">Historical</A><BR>
    <A HREF="legal.html">Legal</A><BR>
    <A HREF="military.html">Military</A><BR>
    <A HREF="police-procedural.html">Police procedural</A><BR>
    <A HREF="political.html">Political</A><BR>
    <A HREF="private-eye.html">Private eye</A><BR>
    <A HREF="serial-killer.html">Serial killer</A><BR>
    <A HREF="sf-mystery.html">SF mystery</A><BR>
    <A HREF="special-subject.html">Special subject</A><BR>
    <A HREF="suspense.html">Suspense</A><BR>
    <A HREF="thriller.html">Thriller</A></P>
  </TD>
  <TD WIDTH=15 HEIGHT=350 ROWSPAN=2>
    <IMG SRC="spacer.gif" WIDTH=15 HEIGHT=350>
  </TD>
  <TD>
    <TABLE BORDER=0 WIDTH=665>
    <TR>
    <TD WIDTH=350 HEIGHT=240 ALIGN="left" VALIGN="top"
style="padding-left:11">
```

Continued

Listing 47-4 *(continued)*

```
        <P class="tab_links">Read Reviews</P>
        <P class="tab_links">Browse by:   
Genre
|    <A HREF="authorlist.html">Author</A>
|    <A HREF="authorlist.html">Title</A>
|    <A HREF="readerratings.html">Ratings</A></P>
        <P class="tab_links">Author:  $author<BR>
        Protagonist name:  $protagonist<BR>
        Year published:  $year<BR>
        Subgenres:  $subgenre<BR>
        Setting:  $setting</P>
    </TD>
    <TD WIDTH=334 HEIGHT=240 ALIGN="left" VALIGN="top"
style="padding-left:13">
        <P class="td"><B>Other Reviewed Titles By This
Author</B><BR>$title_str
    </P>
        <P class="td"><B>Top 5 Most Similar Titles</B><BR>$similar
    </P>
        <P class="td"><B>Movie versions</B><BR>$movie</P>
    </TD>
    </TR>
    </TABLE>
  </TD>
  </TR>
  <TR>
  <TD WIDTH=665 HEIGHT=100>
    <TABLE BORDER=0 WIDTH=665>
    <TR>
    <TD WIDTH=250 HEIGHT=100 ALIGN="left" VALIGN="top"
style="padding-left:13">
    <P class="title">Our rating:  $rating
    <BR>Community rating:  $comm_rating</P>
    <P class="td_med"><B>Awards:</B>  $award</P>
    </TD>
    <TD WIDTH=415 HEIGHT=100 ALIGN="left" VALIGN="top"
style="padding-left:40; padding-top:7">
    <IMG SRC="red.png" WIDTH=350 HEIGHT=80>
    </TD>
    </TR>
    </TABLE>
  </TD>
  </TR>
  </TABLE>
  <!-- End info table -->
</TD>
```

```
</TR>
<TR>
<TD>
  <!-- Begin review table -->
  <TABLE BORDER=0>
  <TR>
  <TD WIDTH=40 HEIGHT=250>
    <IMG SRC="spacer.gif" WIDTH=40 HEIGHT=250>
  </TD>
  <TD WIDTH=560 HEIGHT=250 class="textblock">
    <P CLASS="td_med">$review
<A HREF="$php_self?format=review_only">
...READ COMPLETE REVIEW...</A></P>
  </TD>
  <TD WIDTH=155 HEIGHT=250 ALIGN="left" VALIGN="top"
style="padding-left:10; padding-top:5">
    <P class="title">What did YOU think?</P>
    <P class="td">Read this book?  Rate it!</P>
    <FORM><INPUT TYPE="submit" VALUE="5 - Superb"></FORM>
    <FORM><INPUT TYPE="submit" VALUE="4 - Very Good"></FORM>
    <FORM><INPUT TYPE="submit" VALUE="3 - Good"></FORM>
    <FORM><INPUT TYPE="submit" VALUE="2 - Mediocre"></FORM>
    <FORM><INPUT TYPE="submit" VALUE="1 - Poor">
  </TD>
  <TD WIDTH=40 HEIGHT=250>
    <IMG SRC="spacer.gif" WIDTH=40 HEIGHT=260>
  </TD>
  </TR>
  </TABLE>
  <!-- End review table -->
</TD>
</TR>
<TR>
<TD>
  <!-- Begin credits table -->
  <TABLE BORDER=0 HEIGHT=65>
  <TR>
  <TD WIDTH=25>
    <IMG SRC="spacer.gif" WIDTH=25 HEIGHT=65>
  </TD>
  <TD WIDTH=790 HEIGHT=65 VALIGN="bottom"
style="padding-left:25;padding-bottom:28">
    <P class="td">FAQs  |  Team Trout  |  Privacy  |
  Advertising  |  Email Us</P>
  </TD>
  </TR>
```

Continued

Listing 47-4 *(continued)*

```
  </TABLE>
  <!-- End credits table -->
</TD>
</TR>
</TABLE>
<!-- End main table -->
</BODY>
</HTML>
EOPAGESTR;
echo $page_str;
?>
```

The results of the preceding book review page are shown in Figure 47-3.

If you compare this figure with Figure 47-2, it is immediately obvious that we've simplified the elements somewhat. Inevitably, as you move toward a final layout in actual HTML, you find that not everything envisioned by the designer can be easily implemented. In this case, we found that the small visual elements such as the title area and "Browse By" navbar are extremely fiddly and difficult to lay out decently in HTML without enormous overhead in pixel-level layout. It's difficult to know these things until you actually begin work on a production template. Your designers should be willing to work with you to make small tweaks at this point.

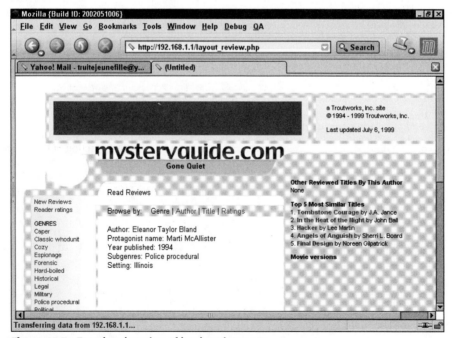

Figure 47-3: Templated version of book review page

Performance and Caching

At this stage you should do some performance testing and evaluation. You want to get decent estimates of:

✦ **Server latency:** How long the code takes your server to produce.

✦ **Network latency:** How long it takes to get the code down the pipe to you.

✦ **Browser latency:** How long it takes a browser to completely render the page.

You can measure server latency by putting `microtime()` calls at the beginning and end of each page, like this:

```php
<?php

$begin_time = microtime();

// Your script here

$end_time = microtime();
$duration = $end_time - $begin_time;
echo $duration;
?>
```

This duration should average to less than one second on every page. If it's more than one second per page load, you have an architecture problem. Subseconds of latency are achieved by much larger and more complicated sites than yours. Make sure that you test this on a setup similar to your production environment — a production server can be several times faster than a development server, so unacceptable times in development can magically become acceptable in production.

The reason server latency is particularly bad is that it ends up costing you money to scale your site. Because your code hogs processor cycles, threads, database connections, and other resources longer than it should, you need to invest more in hardware than a zippier site with similar features. The cure for this type of performance problem is to simplify your architecture, particularly those features (templates, objects, message catalogs, and so on) that are known to add server latency.

Network latency is (insofar as Web developers can affect it) usually a function of how large your page is. To test this, you need to save an HTML page and all its attendant graphic files (including ads) and note their combined size. Divide by 40 kilobytes per second (a realistic estimate of the speed of a 56K modem) for a ballpark estimate of how long your data spends on the wire.

Heavy pages also cost you money, especially if you pay for metered bandwidth. Your Web servers can't take another request until they finish sending all the data from this one — and the longer it takes, the fewer available threads your Web servers have at any given time. You can sometimes finesse the fat-page problem temporarily by looking into transparent page compression — Apache, for example, can `gzip` any file before serving it up in a way that is totally invisible to the user — but in the long run you just need to make your pages lighter.

Finally, take a look at browser latency. The best way to do this is to get on a known slow browser — Internet Explorer 5.1 for Macintosh is supposedly the market leader in this category — and actually time how long it takes from the initial request to the moment you see a complete Web page in your browser. Because a lot of this is controlled by the particular browser, there's not much you can do — except to realize that complicated layouts featuring massive tables, immense amounts of nonbreaking spaces, and hundreds of transparent single-pixels add to rendering time.

Caching

Besides the steps mentioned in the preceding section, another way you can make your site faster is to use *caching*. There are many types of caching, but the most important one for Web developers is HTML caching. Many "dynamic" sites, such as Slashdot and Epinions, are actually serving up mostly static pages that change every few minutes. Without this trick, few organizations could afford to scale a Web site.

The review page in Listing 47-4 is an interesting example, because although we're storing all the data in a database, the only thing on the whole page that is dynamic is the Community Rating score. The rest of the page changes only if updates are made to the database records. We could, therefore, easily write out the whole site as a series of static HTML pages with one PHP function embedded in the middle.

You're probably thinking, "That's nuts! I just went to all that work to turn my static HTML site into a dynamic, database-driven one — and now you're telling me to go back to static HTML?!?!" But if you think about it, you see a vast difference between a static site that you maintain by hand and a dynamic site that happens to update itself automatically whenever a meaningful change occurs. This scheme gives you the best of both worlds: the speed and scalability of static HTML plus the flexibility and maintainability of a database-driven PHP site.

We've written another code listing that takes all the entries in your database and writes them out to static HTML files. In the middle is a PHP snippet that includes a text file. This text file contains the Community Rating and is updated by a separate process every hour. You can download the code for this listing at `www.troutworks.com/phpbook/`.

If you want to make the Community Rating call on this page fully dynamic, instead of taking cached data from a flat file, you can do that too. But you will no longer be able to construct the entire page as a single heredoc block. The code to accomplish a static page with a dynamic code block is available at `www.troutworks.com/phpbook/`.

The code to insert a dynamic PHP block into a static HTML page doesn't look as pretty as a plain HTML page, and you must be very careful about all the quoting and concatenating, but in the end, you have an automatically generated HTML file with chunks of PHP for the dynamic bits.

You could schedule this script to run on the command line once a day via a `cron` job. (You're definitely not going to be able to use the Web server module version of PHP for this task.) Or you could kick it off whenever you add new pages to the Web site. This has another security benefit: You do not need to maintain a full database in production but can merely push flat files periodically (perhaps via some tool such as `rsync`), plus maintain a small database with data only for those fields you want to display dynamically.

Summary

PHP books usually assume that you are starting a site from scratch—but in the real world, another very common scenario is to upgrade an existing static site. PHP and a database can be used to take large, messy, hard-to-maintain HTML sites and make them dynamic. This makes the sites much easier to maintain, because they are assembled by PHP from data in a database. Instead of maintaining hundreds of HTML files, you can just work on one template and let PHP assemble the pages on-the-fly.

Before you do any work, you should take the time to assess your site's strategy and map out the goals you wish to accomplish. You should also gain a clear understanding of your site's structure and the resources you will need to support your new design. After that, you must test your new design, create a new database, load data from possibly disparate sources into the database, and create PHP template pages. Finally, you should assess the performance of your new dynamic site and possibly take steps to improve it.

✦　　✦　　✦

Data Visualization with Venn Diagrams

CHAPTER

48

In this chapter's case study, we show one way to use PHP to combine MySQL databases with graphic images. We build a complete system that starts with a database and uses the gd library to produce a kind of visualization of the data. The portions of the book we draw on for this are:

   ◆ Part II: We use PHP to interrogate a MySQL database.

   ◆ Chapter 42 (Graphics): Our end-product is an image produced with the gd library.

   ◆ Chapter 27 (Mathematics): We need a bit of trigonometry as we create the images.

Scaled Venn Diagrams

The visualization we have in mind is something like the Venn diagram. If you've ever been in an academic setting where set intersection was being discussed, then you've probably seen these diagrams — they're the circles that may or may not have overlapping portions representing intersections.

We say "something like" the Venn diagram, because scale has no significance in a traditional Venn diagram. If you want to illustrate the fact that there are people who use both BeOS and Windows, then you might draw two circles of equal size (representing Windows users and BeOS users) that happen to have a region of overlap. In our version, which you might call a *scaled* or *proportional* Venn diagram, the sizes of both circles and intersections matter; the Windows/BeOS example would become one large circle and one much smaller circle, with an overlap area proportional to the number of people in both sets. (To see an example of this kind of diagram, please skip ahead to Figure 48-5.)

The task

The job of our code is to start with a database, provide a way to query that database about sets and their overlap, and then display the results as a scaled Venn diagram, generated by using the gd library. As a sample database, we use the pseudosurvey dataset that we used in the "HTML Graphics" section of Chapter 42.

If we're going to offer a way to query the database, then it may as well be via a Web form. So the end-to-end view of our task is that we start with a Web form and end up with a picture to display. Let's start the design by enumerating the things that need to happen for this to come about. We'll need to:

1. Generate (or at least present) the Web form itself.

2. Receive the submitted form data and transform it into appropriate SQL queries for submission to the database.

3. Receive results from the SQL queries.

4. Use the SQL results to decide on the locations and sizes of all the elements in our graphic.

5. Actually generate the graphic and send it back to the user.

Note   All of the code in this chapter should work with either PHP4 or PHP5, but it assumes that your PHP installation has access to the gd image library and is configured to produce PNG images. Any version of gd later than 1.8, bundled or unbundled, should be OK. (See Chapter 42 for details of configuration and installation of gd.)

Outline of the Code

Our system contains the following code files:

✦ visualization_form.php: This is essentially a hard-coded form that enables the user to choose two different restrictions on the data in our table. The restrictions chosen map directly to where clauses loaded from an auxiliary file called query_clauses.php.

✦ db_visualization.php: This code handles the form data sent by visualization_form.php and builds three SQL statements: one with only the first where clause, one with the second where clause, and a third with both clauses joined by an and. It collects resulting three counts and displays the numbers in a graphic by calling functions loaded from venn.php.

✦ venn.php: This actually produces the Venn diagram graphic and ships it back to the user. Its primary function takes as input the three amounts (the sizes of the two sets and their intersection), decides the sizes and locations of corresponding circles, and does all the drawing and shading necessary. For the complicated case of sets that actually have an overlapping area, it uses functions loaded from trig.php to calculate areas.

✦ trig.php: This code actually calculates the intersection area whenever circles overlap.

We discuss these code files in reverse order, from the bottom up. By the way, although we like this example, we don't want to give the impression that you need to do trigonometry to do computer graphics in PHP, or even vector graphics in PHP. If you want to understand every bit of this example, then you need to go through the trig, but we encourage those who don't care to skip the next section ("Necessary trigonometry"). The core of the graphics code itself is in venn.php, and that example code really is important to understand if you want to do gd-based graphics in PHP.

Necessary Trigonometry

Let's get the math out of the way first. Unavoidably, because we're talking about circles and areas, we're going to be talking about trigonometry. (As we've said, though, if you're not interested and are willing to trust us that we have code to calculate the area of circle intersections, please do skip ahead to the section "Planning the display," later in this chapter.)

The eventual task for our system is to start with three quantities (items in set A, items in set B, and items in the intersection) and produce a diagram containing two circles, with areas proportional to the set sizes, and positioned so that the area of overlap is proportional to the size of the intersection. For this section, we go in the other direction and calculate intersection area from given circles. Our starting information will be the radii of the two circles and the distance between their centers.

With reference to Figure 48-1, say that our circles have centers at points C and D, respectively, and that we know the radius of the circle on the left (segment CA or segment CB) and the radius of the circle on the right (DA or DB). What we'd like to know is the size of that odd lens-shaped object in the middle.

Area of intersecting circles

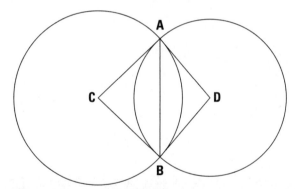

Figure 48-1: Area of intersection

The lens-shaped intersection area is split into two "halves" by segment AB (not quite halves because the circle sizes may be different), and we can calculate the area of each half independently. The crucial thing to notice is that the area of each of these half-lenses is the area that you get after you subtract the area of a triangle from the area of a pizza-slice-shaped sector of a circle. The right-hand lens half, for example, has an area equal to the sector of the left-hand circle determined by angle ACB, minus the area of the triangle ACB.

So if we can calculate the areas of sectors and triangles, then we are nearly done. The area of a sector is straightforward — it's just the area of the circle multiplied by the fraction of that circle that the angle of the sector sweeps over.

It takes a little more work and trigonometry to get the areas of the triangles. In our code, we make the job more straightforward by drawing a line from point C to point D, and considering only the half of the diagram above that line — then at the end, we multiply by two to get the real area. If we say that the intersection of segments AB and CD is point E, what we eventually care about is the area of triangles CAE and DAE. We start by calculating the angles of triangle CDA (whose side lengths are known to us) and, by using that information, determining the lengths of CE, DE, and AE. After we know these lengths, we know the bases and heights, and the areas of the right triangles CAE and DAE are just ½ (*base* × *height*).

Listing 48-1 shows code to do this kind of area calculation. Its main "public" function is `circle_intersection_area()`, which expects as arguments the radii of two circles and the distance between them. The simplest case is where the distance is greater than the sum of the radii: The circles do not touch; there is no intersection, and the answer is zero.

Listing 48-1: **trig.php**

```php
<?php

function angle_given_sides ($opposite, $other_1, $other_2) {
    if (($opposite <= 0) ||
        ($other_1 <= 0) ||
        ($other_2 <= 0) ||
        ($opposite >= ($other_1 + $other_2)) ||
        ($other_1 >= ($opposite + $other_2)) ||
        ($other_2 >= ($other_1 + $opposite))) {
      die("Triangle with impossible side lengths in ".
          "angle_given_sides: $opposite, $other_1, $other_2");
    }
    else {
      $numerator =
        ((($other_1 * $other_1) +
          ($other_2 * $other_2)) -
         ($opposite * $opposite));
      $denominator = 2 * $other_1 * $other_2;
      return(acos($numerator / $denominator));
    }
}

function area_to_radius ($area) {
  return (sqrt ($area / M_PI));
}

function circle_intersection_area ($radius_left,
                                   $radius_right,
                                   $distance) {
  if ($radius_right + $radius_left <= $distance) {
    return(0);
  }
  else {
    // first, we find the angle measures of a triangle
```

```
//    formed by the two radii and the distance
//    between them
$left_sector_angle =
  angle_given_sides($radius_right, $radius_left,
                    $distance);
$right_sector_angle =
  angle_given_sides($radius_left, $radius_right,
                    $distance);

// test for obtuseness --- the sector angle can
// be obtuse, but the triangle angle should not
// be.  Also save the result as a sign for the
// eventual area calculation

if ($left_sector_angle < M_PI / 2) {
  $left_triangle_angle = $left_sector_angle;
  $left_triangle_sign = 1;
}
else {
  $left_triangle_angle = M_PI - $left_sector_angle;
  $left_triangle_sign = -1;
}
if ($right_sector_angle < M_PI / 2) {
  $right_triangle_angle = $right_sector_angle;
  $right_triangle_sign = 1;
}
else {
  $right_triangle_angle = M_PI - $right_sector_angle;
  $right_triangle_sign = -1;
}

// next, find the height of that triangle, assuming
//   the distance is the base

$height = ($radius_left / sin(M_PI_2)) *
          sin($left_triangle_angle);
$base_left = ($radius_left / sin(M_PI_2)) *
             sin(M_PI_2 - $left_triangle_angle);
$base_right = ($radius_right / sin(M_PI_2)) *
              sin(M_PI_2 - $right_triangle_angle);

// finally find triangle and sector areas, and
// subtract (or add) appropriately to get the
// intersection area.  Multiply by 2 to reflect
// areas on both sides of the segment connecting
// the circle centers

$left_triangle_area = $base_left * $height / 2;
$right_triangle_area = $base_right * $height / 2;
$left_sector_area =
```

Continued

Listing 48-1 *(continued)*

```
            ($left_sector_angle / (2 * M_PI)) *
            (M_PI * $radius_left * $radius_left);
        $right_sector_area =
            ($right_sector_angle / (2 * M_PI)) *
            (M_PI * $radius_right * $radius_right);

        $intersection_area = 2 *
            (($left_sector_area -
                ($left_triangle_sign * $left_triangle_area)) +
             ($right_sector_area -
                ($right_triangle_sign * $right_triangle_area)));

        return($intersection_area);
    }
}

?>
```

Note that all the angle calculations are in radians, rather than degrees. In radians, a right angle is pi/2, and a complete revolution around a circle is $2 \times$ pi. We tend to use PHP constants for these values whenever we can, in particular M_PI (the value of pi), and M_PI_2 (pi/2).

There's one final wrinkle that we've ignored in our discussion so far, but which we had to deal with in the code. The problem is that it's possible for either angle ACE or angle ADE (as we call them in Figure 48-1) to be obtuse — that is, more than 90 degrees in size. To see this, look at that diagram and imagine what happens as you make the circle on the right smaller, and move its center D progressively closer to C. At some point D actually moves to the left of segment AB. In this case, the circle intersection area to the left of AB is actually the sum of a sector and a triangle rather than a difference. The sector determined by DA and DB sweeps out more than half of the circle centered at D, and the remaining portion we want to include is the area of the triangle ADB. We handle this in the code by testing if the angles are obtuse, and multiplying the triangle areas by either 1 or -1, depending on the result of the test.

Planning the Display

Now we pop up a couple of levels and think about actually generating a diagram. We assume that we have as input three numbers (size of set 1, size of set 2, and size of intersection), along with some textual labels. We want to scale and locate these circles so that everything has the right area, labels get associated with the right circles, and everything fits within the size of the diagram we're creating.

Simplifying assumptions

We start off with some totally arbitrary decisions that, after being made, simplify everything. We decree that:

✦ All the images that we generate are the same size, and that size is 300 pixels high and 600 pixels wide.

✦ The centers of the circles are always on the same horizontal line. This means that their y-coordinate is decided in advance, and we change the area of intersection just by changing the x-coordinates.

✦ The circles always fit within the top two-thirds of the diagram (reserving the lower third for labels). So put the y-coordinate of the centers one-third of the way down the image from the top. And because the circles may not intersect at all, they shouldn't be larger than half of the width of the image, so we have room to display two of them. We also make sure that the circles are no greater than 90 percent of the room available given everything we've said so far, so that they don't touch the image borders. Finally, we decide that, regardless of the actual numbers as input, the larger of the two circles is as large as it can be. (Scale is consistent within the diagram, but not between diagrams.)

Determining size and scale

Now we have nearly all the information needed to create a visualization, and the pieces we are lacking, of course, depend on the input values we are going to receive. We use the sizes of the actual sets to determine the radii of the circles for display. We want the larger of the two set counts to correspond to the largest circle we can afford to display, and then scale everything else appropriately. (We do all this in the code in Listing 48-2 (venn.php) — you may want to look ahead to that code as we lay out what we need to do in it.)

It's actually easiest for us to calculate the largest radius we can afford: Given the constraints we've already listed, the larger radius should be 90 percent of ¼ of the image width, or 90 percent of ⅓ of the image height, whichever is smaller. So we calculate this maximum radius, assume that the larger set size is proportional to the area of a circle with this radius, and come up with a general conversion for mapping from input numbers to area as measured in pixels. We use this to decide on the areas of the circles and of the intersection area we want.

What numbers should we know at this point? We know:

✦ The radius of the bigger circle. (It's the largest radius that fits our constraints.)

✦ The area of the bigger circle (calculated as $\text{pi} \times r^2$).

✦ The radius of the smaller circle (from the ratio of the input set sizes treated as area ratios and then mapped back to a radius).

✦ The area of the smaller circle (calculated).

✦ The area of intersection (scaled the same way as other areas, from the input numbers).

✦ The y-coordinate of the circle centers. (We decreed that it be the line that's one-third of the way down the image.)

What are we missing before we can display our circles? The only thing that we're missing is the x-coordinates of the centers.

The easy cases

Where we decide to put the circle centers depends on the extent to which our sets overlap. There are some cases that we can dispense with, that don't need all this trigonometry we've been spending our time on. Those are:

✦ *No items are in the intersection.* In this case, we don't want the circles to touch at all. We simply locate the centers at default locations in the middles of the two halves of the diagram. Because of the way that we limited the maximum radius, the circles are completely separated.

✦ *One set is completely contained in the other* — that is, one of the sets has the same size as the intersection. For this case, we just choose to put the center of the larger circle in the middle of the diagram and the middle of the other circle offset a bit from it but not so much that any of the smaller circle is outside the larger one.

✦ *The two sets are the same* (and all three input numbers are the same). For this, we just draw one circle with an x-coordinate right in the middle of the picture.

The hard case

Now the hard one: If the sets only partially overlap, where should we put the circle centers? At this point, we have some math in our pocket from the "Necessary trigonometry" section: Given two circles and the distance between their centers, we can figure out the area of overlap. Unfortunately, this is not the direction we need the calculation go in — we start with the desired area of intersection, and we must work backwards to the desired locations of the circle centers.

Now if we were good and diligent mathematicians but lazy programmers, we would just invert the trigonometric equations we used in `trig.php`, to solve for center distance rather than for intersection area. As it is, though, we're enthusiastic programmers, and if we're any kind of mathematicians at all we're definitely the lazy kind. So what we're going to do instead is search for the answer. The function `find_circle_centers()` in Listing 48-2 implements a binary search for the answer: It starts with a middling distance, asks our trigonometry code what the resulting area would be, and successively refines the distance to zero in on the desired area. (The rest of the code in Listing 48-2 is discussed in the next section.)

Listing 48-2: **venn.php**

```php
<?php
include_once("trig.php");

$IMAGE_WIDTH = 600;
$IMAGE_HEIGHT = 300;
$CENTER_FINDING_ITERATIONS = 20;

function imagecircle ($image, $center_x, $center_y,
                $radius, $color)
{
  $diameter = $radius * 2;
  imagearc($image, $center_x, $center_y,
    $diameter, $diameter, 0, 360,
        $color);
}

function venn_visualization
  ($left_amount, $left_name,
   $right_amount, $right_name,
   $intersection_amount)
{
  global $IMAGE_HEIGHT, $IMAGE_WIDTH,
      $CENTER_FINDING_ITERATIONS;
```

```php
// --- create the image and allocate colors
$image = imagecreate($IMAGE_WIDTH, $IMAGE_HEIGHT)
  or die("Could not create image");
$background_color = ImageColorAllocate($image, 255,255,255);
$left_color = ImageColorAllocate($image, 100, 100, 200);
$right_color = ImageColorAllocate($image, 200, 100, 100);
$intersection_color =
  ImageColorAllocate($image, 225, 225, 225);
$black_color = ImageColorAllocate($image, 0,0,0);

// --- decide how big the circles should be
$max_radius = min((($IMAGE_HEIGHT * 0.9) / 3),
          (($IMAGE_WIDTH * 0.9) / 4));
$center_y = $IMAGE_HEIGHT / 3.0;
$default_center_x_left = $IMAGE_WIDTH / 4.0;
$default_center_x_right = (3 * $IMAGE_WIDTH) / 4.0;
$middle_x = $IMAGE_WIDTH / 2.0;
$radius_left_side_raw =
  area_to_radius($left_amount);
$radius_right_side_raw =
  area_to_radius($right_amount);
$intersection_radius_raw =
  area_to_radius($intersection_amount);
$scale_factor = $max_radius /
          (max($radius_left_side_raw,
            $radius_right_side_raw));
$radius_left_side = $radius_left_side_raw * $scale_factor;
$radius_right_side = $radius_right_side_raw * $scale_factor;
// (it's convenient to pretend that the intersection area
//  has a radius (although it's not circular) just so we can
//  calculate things the same way as the circles)
$intersection_radius =
  $intersection_radius_raw * $scale_factor;
$area_left_side = M_PI *
          $radius_left_side * $radius_left_side;
$area_right_side = M_PI *
          $radius_right_side * $radius_right_side;
$intersection_area = M_PI *
          $intersection_radius * $intersection_radius;

// We now have all necessary info except where to locate the
//  centers of the circles.
// Four cases:
// 1) no intersection, 2) partial intersection
// 3) left is strict subset of right,
// 4) right is subset of left.

if ($intersection_amount == 0) {
  // No intersection
```

Continued

Listing 48-2 *(continued)*

```
    $center_x_left = $default_center_x_left;
    $center_x_right = $default_center_x_right;
    $left_fill_x = $center_x_left;
    $right_fill_x = $center_x_right;
    $intersection_fill_x = -1;
}
else if (($intersection_area < $area_left_side) &&
         ($intersection_area < $area_right_side)) {

    // The complicated case --- we must decide where the
    //   circle centers should be so that the overlap is
    //   proportional to the set intersection
    // First, we call a function that decides how far apart
    //   the circle centers need to be.
    $center_distance =
      find_center_distance($radius_left_side,
                           $radius_right_side,
                           $intersection_area,
                           $CENTER_FINDING_ITERATIONS);

    // Once we know the distance, we place the circle centers
    //   approximately in the middle of the image
    $center_x_left = $middle_x   // left/right middle of image
                     - ($center_distance *
                        ($radius_left_side /
                         ($radius_left_side +
                          $radius_right_side)));
    $center_x_right = $middle_x   // left/right middle of image
                      + ($center_distance *
                         ($radius_right_side /
                          ($radius_left_side +
                           $radius_right_side)));

    // we have decided the sizes and centers of the circles.
    //   Now, we must determine good points to start a
    //   "flood fill" coloring of the three different regions
    $left_fill_x =
      (($center_x_left - $radius_left_side) +
       ($center_x_right - $radius_right_side))
       / 2.0;
    $right_fill_x =
      (($center_x_left + $radius_left_side) +
       ($center_x_right + $radius_right_side))
       / 2.0;
    $intersection_fill_x =
      (($center_x_right - $radius_right_side) +
       ($center_x_left + $radius_left_side))
        / 2.0;
```

```
}
else if (($intersection_area == $area_left_side) &&
        ($intersection_area < $area_right_side)) {
  // The right set completely contains the left set
  //   We need to place the left circle somewhere
  //   inside the right circle.
  $center_x_right = $middle_x;
  $center_x_left = $middle_x -
    ($radius_right_side - $radius_left_side) / 2;
  $left_fill_x = -1;
  $right_fill_x =
    (($center_x_left + $radius_left_side) +
     ($center_x_right + $radius_right_side))
    / 2.0;
  $intersection_fill_x = $center_x_left;
}
else if ($intersection_area == $area_right_side) {
  $center_x_left = $middle_x;
  $center_x_right = $middle_x +
      ($radius_left_side - $radius_right_side) / 2;
  $right_fill_x = -1;
  $left_fill_x =
    (($center_x_left - $radius_left_side) +
     ($center_x_right - $radius_right_side))
    / 2.0;
  $intersection_fill_x = $center_x_right;
}

// now, actually draw and fill regions
imagecircle($image, $center_x_left, $center_y,
          $radius_left_side, $black_color);
imagecircle($image, $center_x_right, $center_y,
          $radius_right_side, $black_color);
if ($left_fill_x > 0) {
  imagefill($image, $left_fill_x,
          $center_y, $left_color);
}
if ($right_fill_x > 0) {
  imagefill($image, $right_fill_x,
          $center_y, $right_color);
}
if ($intersection_fill_x > 0 ) {
    imagefill($image, $intersection_fill_x,
            $center_y, $intersection_color);
}
$left_hand_text = "$left_name ($left_amount)";
$right_hand_text = "$right_name ($right_amount)";
$intersection_text = "Intersection: $intersection_amount";
left_label($image, $left_hand_text, $left_color);
```

Continued

Listing 48-2 *(continued)*

```
  right_label($image, $right_hand_text, $right_color);
  intersection_label($image, $intersection_text, $black_color);

  // send off the image
  header("Content-type: image/png");
  imagepng($image);
  imagedestroy($image);
}

function left_label ($image, $label_string, $color) {
  global $IMAGE_WIDTH, $IMAGE_HEIGHT;
  imagestring($image, 5,
            ($IMAGE_WIDTH / 4.0 -
              (imagefontwidth(5) * strlen($label_string))
              / 2),
            $IMAGE_HEIGHT - 55.0,
            $label_string, $color);
}

function right_label ($image, $label_string, $color) {
  global $IMAGE_WIDTH, $IMAGE_HEIGHT;
  imagestring($image, 5,
            ($IMAGE_WIDTH * 3 / 4.0 -
              (imagefontwidth(5) * strlen($label_string))
              / 2),
            $IMAGE_HEIGHT - 55.0,
            $label_string, $color);
}

function intersection_label ($image, $label_string, $color) {
  global $IMAGE_WIDTH, $IMAGE_HEIGHT;
  imagestring($image, 2,
            ($IMAGE_WIDTH / 2.0  -
              (imagefontwidth(2) * strlen($label_string))
              / 2),
            $IMAGE_HEIGHT - 30.0,
            $label_string, $color);
}

function find_center_distance ($r1, $r2, $desired_area,
                               $iterations) {
  // The greatest possible distance is r1 + r2, and
  //  the smallest is abs(r1 - r2) Let's start in the middle.
  $distance_guess = (($r1 + $r2) + abs($r1 - $r2)) / 2.0;
  $distance_increment = (($r1 + $r2) - abs($r1 - $r2)) / 4.0;
  for ($x = 0; $x < $iterations; $x++) {
    $calculated_area =
```

```
        circle_intersection_area($r1, $r2, $distance_guess);
     if ($calculated_area < $desired_area) {
        // move centers closer
        $distance_guess -= $distance_increment;
        $distance_increment *= 0.5;
     }
     else if ($calculated_area > $desired_area) {
        // move centers apart
        $distance_guess += $distance_increment;
        $distance_increment *= 0.5;
     }
     else {
        // unlikely, but ya never know
        break;
     }
   }
   return($distance_guess);
}
?>
```

Display

Now we know exactly where we want to put our circles, and how large they should be. What remains is the graphics code to actually make the display happen. This is also in Listing 48-2 (venn.php).

To produce the graphic, we go through the following steps by using the gd library (which is covered in Chapter 42):

1. We create an image by using ImageCreate(). (At this point, the image is not any particular image format, such as PNG or JPEG, but just an internal gd image.)

2. We allocate colors within the image by using ImageColorAllocate(). We care about five colors: the background color (white), a color for borders and regular text (black), a color for the interior of the left hand circle (which we decide is bluish), a color for the interior of the right-hand circle (reddish), and a color for the intersection (gray). All these colors are specified by using a red-green-blue scale of 0 to 255.

3. We draw the circles in black by using a function of our own, imagecircle(), that takes as arguments the image, the radius, the location of the centers, and a color. (See the "Notes on circles" section about drawing circles in gd.)

4. Now, we want to fill in the three areas (the intersection and the two non-intersection portions of the circles) with the appropriate colors. We use ImageFill() for this, which *flood-fills* outward from a specified point until the fill encounters previously drawn lines. Choosing the starting points for the fills is somewhat tricky because it depends on the different intersection cases. In general, though, we start with a y-coordinate that is the same as the circle centers and calculate an x-coordinate that's right in the middle of the area we are trying to color.

5. We use `ImageString()` to draw the appropriate labels for each circle, centering each one in the middle of the lower-third of the image and in the middle of the appropriate left-right half. We also create and display a count label for the intersection and display it in the middle of the image.

6. Now, we have a complete `gd` image, and what remains is to ship it off to the user. We send an HTTP header advising the browser that a PNG image is on the way. Then we use `ImagePng()` to convert the `gd` image to PNG and send it off.

7. Finally, we call `ImageDestroy()` to free any resources associated with the temporary image we created. More recent versions of PHP should be handling this already, assuming that the image is of type `resource`, but either way calling `ImageDestroy()` does no harm.

Notes on circles

One thing that puzzles people sometimes, if confronted with the `gd` functions, is that there seems to be no way to draw a circle (or at least there is no function name with `circle` in its name). This is because there are at least two functions that generalize circle-drawing: `imageellipse()` (available only with `gd` 2.0.1 and later) and `imagearc`. The former draws an ellipse (which can be a circle if the width and height are the same), and the latter draws a circular arc portion (which can be a circle if you specify a full 360 degrees of arc). In our code, we chose the latter because we wanted to remain compatible with earlier versions of `gd`.

Notes on centering text

As we wrote textual labels in the image code, we actually didn't bother centering the text around any horizontal axis, but we did do some left-right centering. We simply used a built-in numbered font from `gd`, calculated the width of our text as displayed by that font (by using `imagefontwidth()`) and ensured that the left-hand starting point for the text was our desired center minus half the width of the text. This was easy, in part because the built-in fonts we used were monospace, and so `imagefontwidth()` was able to calculate width by referring only to the length of the string. Things get slightly more complicated if you're using a variable-width font — any calculation of string width then needs to know the actual string that is printed, not just the number of characters in it.

Visualizing a Database

We can now produce these Venn-like diagrams on demand, given some numbers and text to start with. Our final task is to hook this up appropriately to a database via a Web form.

Note   For this application, we assume exactly the same sample MySQL table (`programmers`) as we used in Chapter 42. See Listing 42-1 for a description of the data.

The goal is to let the user choose exactly two restrictions on our database's table, extract counts corresponding to how many rows survive each restriction, count how many rows survive both restrictions, and then pass the results off to our diagramming code.

Listing 48-3 shows code for a form designed around our particular database, mostly just hard-coded HTML. It loads an auxiliary file called `query_clauses.php` (shown in Listing 48-4), which is extremely hard-coded. This file lists and numbers all the restrictions that we want to offer to users, in the form of both an SQL `where` clause and in an English translation.

Listing 48-3: **visualization_form.php**

```
<HTML><HEAD><TITLE>DB Visualization</TITLE></HEAD>
<BODY>

<B>Choose one from each column, and we'll<B>
display the intersection from the survey data:<BR>
<FORM METHOD=POST ACTION="db_visualization.php"
      TARGET=_new >
<TABLE>

<?php
include("query_clauses.php");
for ($x = 0; $x < count($QUERY_CLAUSES); $x++) {
  print("<TR><TD><INPUT
              TYPE=RADIO NAME=\"left_clause\"
              VALUE=$x>".
              $QUERY_DESCRIPTION[$x] ."</TD>
        <TD><INPUT
              TYPE=RADIO NAME=\"right_clause\"
              VALUE=$x>".
              $QUERY_DESCRIPTION[$x] ."</TD></TR>");
}
?>

</TABLE>
<INPUT TYPE=HIDDEN NAME="table" VALUE="programmers">
<INPUT TYPE=SUBMIT NAME=SUBMIT>
</FORM>

</BODY>
</HTML>
```

Notice that this form is not self-submitting. For this example, we've chosen to completely separate PHP-generated HTML pages from PHP-generated PNG pages and avoid the complexity of embedding images in HTML. We've also chosen a _new target type for the form submission so that the image appears in a new browser window.

Listing 48-4: **query_clauses.php**

```
<?php

$QUERY_CLAUSES = array();
$QUERY_DESCRIPTION = array();

$QUERY_CLAUSES[0] = "sex = 'F'";
$QUERY_DESCRIPTION[0] = "Female";

$QUERY_CLAUSES[1] = "sex = 'M'";
```

Continued

Listing 48-4 *(continued)*

```
$QUERY_DESCRIPTION[1] = "Male";

$QUERY_CLAUSES[2] = "language = 'PHP'";
$QUERY_DESCRIPTION[2] = "likes PHP";

$QUERY_CLAUSES[3] = "language = 'Java'";
$QUERY_DESCRIPTION[3] = "likes Java";

$QUERY_CLAUSES[4] = "language = 'Lisp'";
$QUERY_DESCRIPTION[4] = "likes Lisp";

$QUERY_CLAUSES[5] = "language = 'C'";
$QUERY_DESCRIPTION[5] = "likes C";

$QUERY_CLAUSES[6] = "language = 'Perl'";
$QUERY_DESCRIPTION[6] = "likes Perl";

$QUERY_CLAUSES[7] = "os = 'Linux'";
$QUERY_DESCRIPTION[7] = "uses Linux";

$QUERY_CLAUSES[8] = "os = 'Solaris'";
$QUERY_DESCRIPTION[8] = "uses Solaris";

$QUERY_CLAUSES[9] = "os = 'MacOS'";
$QUERY_DESCRIPTION[9] = "uses MacOS";

$QUERY_CLAUSES[10] = "os = 'Windows'";
$QUERY_DESCRIPTION[10] = "uses Windows";

$QUERY_CLAUSES[11] = "age < 20";
$QUERY_DESCRIPTION[11] = "is less than 20 years old";

$QUERY_CLAUSES[12] = "age > 30";
$QUERY_DESCRIPTION[12] = "is over 30 years old";

$QUERY_CLAUSES[13] = "continent = 'North America'";
$QUERY_DESCRIPTION[13] = "lives in North America";

$QUERY_CLAUSES[14] = "continent = 'South America'";
$QUERY_DESCRIPTION[14] = "lives in South America";

$QUERY_CLAUSES[15] = "continent = 'Antarctica'";
$QUERY_DESCRIPTION[15] = "lives in Antarctica";

$QUERY_CLAUSES[16] = "continent = 'Asia'";
$QUERY_DESCRIPTION[16] = "lives in Asia";

$QUERY_CLAUSES[17] = "continent = 'Europe'";
$QUERY_DESCRIPTION[17] = "lives in Europe";
?>
```

A screenshot of the form itself is shown in Figure 48-2.

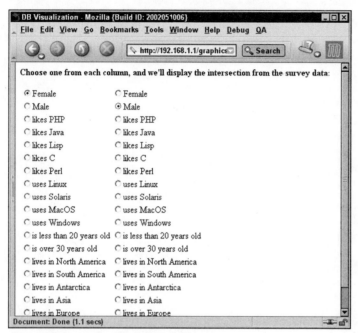

Figure 48-2: DB visualization Web form

One last code file and we're done. We have our image creation code and a form for requesting an image. The last piece of the puzzle is code to handle the form submission, perform the appropriate counts on the database, and call the image code. This code is shown in Listing 48-5.

Listing 48-5: **db_visualization.php**

```php
<?php
include_once("dbconnect.php");
include_once("query_clauses.php");
include_once("venn.php");

if (IsSet($_POST['table']) &&
    IsSet($_POST['left_clause']) &&
    IsSet($_POST['right_clause'])) {
  $table = $_POST['table'];
  $left_clause_id = $_POST['left_clause'];
  $right_clause_id = $_POST['right_clause'];

  $left_clause = $QUERY_CLAUSES[$left_clause_id];
```

Continued

Listing 48-5 *(continued)*

```php
    $right_clause = $QUERY_CLAUSES[$right_clause_id];

    visualize_intersection ($table, $left_clause,
                                   $right_clause);
}
else {
  print("Form submission not handled correctly.<BR>".
        "Did you choose all options?");
}

function visualize_intersection ($table, $left_clause,
                                       $right_clause)
{

  $left_query = "select count(*) from $table
                   where $left_clause";
  $right_query = "select count(*) from $table
                   where $right_clause";
  $intersection_query =
                   "select count(*) from $table
                   where $left_clause and $right_clause";

  $result = mysql_query($left_query)
    or die("Query was $left_query:" . mysql_error());
  $row = mysql_fetch_row($result);
  $left_count = $row[0];

  $result = mysql_query($right_query)
    or die(mysql_error());
  $row = mysql_fetch_row($result);
  $right_count = $row[0];

  $result = mysql_query($intersection_query)
    or die(mysql_error());
  $row = mysql_fetch_row($result);
  $intersection_count = $row[0];

  venn_visualization($left_count, $left_clause,
                     $right_count, $right_clause,
                     $intersection_count);
}
?>
```

The submission form passes in index numbers of SQL clauses, rather than the clauses themselves, so we don't need to worry about escape characters in the submission. The form-handling code includes the same `query_clauses.php` file, so the index numbers should always agree. The form handler collects the two clauses, creates three SQL statements out of them, executes the statements to get counts, and uses the results as arguments to the `venn_visualization()` function.

Note that Listing 48-5 refers to one auxiliary code file we haven't mentioned yet: dbconnect. php. We assume that this file contains (or refers to a file containing) your MySQL username and password, and also makes a call to mysql_connect() to create a global DB connection for the rest of the script. Something like the following should suffice:

```php
<?php
$user = 'USER';
$pass = 'PASS';
$db = 'venn';
mysql_connect('localhost', $user, $pass)
    or die("Couldn't make DB connection:" . mysql_error());
mysql_select_db($db);
?>
```

This assumes that your username and password are replaced appropriately, and that you have a MySQL database called venn, which contains a table called programmers, as described in Chapter 42.

Trying it out

Now that our system is complete, let's give it a spin. Bringing up visualization_form.php, we choose the first option from the left-hand column (Female), and the second option from the right-hand column (Male), and submit. The result is shown in Figure 48-3 — two separate circles because, given the database schema, it's impossible for anyone to be both male and female. (Please, no e-mails about the narrowness of our views — it's just an example!)

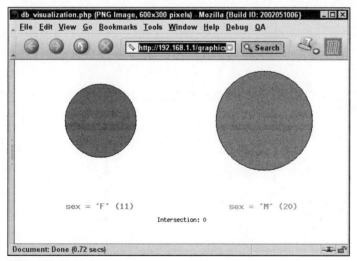

Figure 48-3: No intersection

On a color monitor the left-hand circle is bluish while the right-hand circle is reddish. Because this is a grayscale book, though, you probably see two gray or black circles.

Now a different query: uses Solaris on the left, and lives in Antarctica on the right. (We chose this deliberately, knowing that our lone South Pole correspondent sees only one kind of Sun during the winter.)

The result is shown in Figure 48-4: one small gray circle inside a larger blue one, indicating that all Antarcticans are Solaris users but not vice versa.

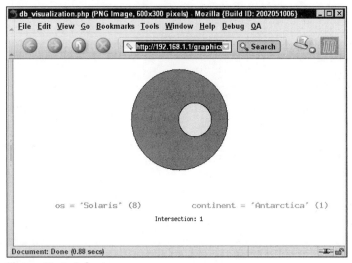

Figure 48-4: Subset

Finally, for the more typical case, let's choose likes PHP from the left, and uses Linux from the right.

The result, in Figure 48-5, is two mostly overlapping circles. (Again, please no letters — we have no idea if these proportions match the world as it is or just the world as we would like it to be.)

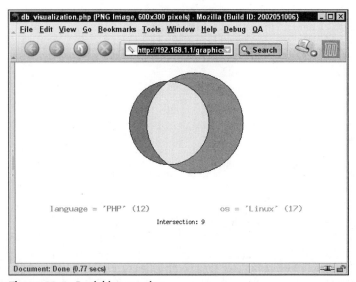

Figure 48-5: Partial intersection

Extensions

This example works nicely, but as always there are countless ways in which it could be tweaked, improved, and especially extended. Naturally, there is a lot you could do to change the cosmetics of the images or to make the look more configurable.

The weakest part right now in our view is the form submission, which is hard-coded to pertain only to a particular known MySQL table. Much cooler would be code that, armed only with a table (or view) name and the appropriate login, would quiz the database about column names and types and the distribution of values, and then develop such a form on its own.

One extension that may immediately occur to you doesn't work, unfortunately, at least without substantial changes to the display code. There is no good way to involve a third set (and circle) in the diagram, cover all the cases, and be assured that all the shapes can still be circular. If you have any doubt about this, try diagramming the following three sets: people who were born in Europe, people who currently live in Europe, and people who currently live in a continent different from the one they were born in.

Summary

We've shown you a small but complete system for visualizing data in a MySQL database. It allows the user to select aspects to compare, makes corresponding SQL queries, and transforms the results into a scaled Venn diagram, showing how the database records overlap.

In addition to using MySQL techniques from Part II of this book, we drew on the image techniques from Chapter 42, and as little math as we could get away with from Chapter 27.

✦　　✦　　✦

PHP for C Programmers

In this appendix, we assume that you have more C (or C++) programming experience than PHP experience and are looking to get up to speed in PHP quickly. First we'll give a quick overview of PHP from a C perspective; then we'll break down the similarities and differences, and finally we'll point out which parts of the book you are likely to benefit from the most.

The simplest way to think of PHP is as interpreted C that you can embed in HTML documents. The language itself is a lot like C, except with untyped variables, a whole lot of Web-specific libraries built in, and everything hooked up directly to your favorite Web server. The syntax of statements and function definitions should be familiar, except that variables are always preceded by $, and functions do not require separate prototypes.

Similarities

In this section, we offer some notes (by no means exhaustive) on ways in which PHP can be expected to be C-like.

Syntax

Broadly speaking, PHP syntax is the same as in C: Code is blank insensitive, statements are terminated with semicolons, function calls have the same structure (`my_function(expression1, expression2)`), and curly braces (`{` and `}`) make statements into blocks. PHP supports C and C++-style comments (`/* */` as well as `//`), and also Perl and shell-script style (`#`).

Operators

The assignment operators (=, +=, *=, and so on), the Boolean operators (&&, ||, !), the comparison operators (<, >, <=, >=, ==, !=), and the basic arithmetic operators (+, -, *, /, %) all behave in PHP as they do in C.

Control structures

The basic control structures (if, switch, while, for) behave as they do in C, including supporting break and continue. One notable difference is that switch in PHP can accept strings as case identifiers.

Many function names

As you peruse the documentation, you'll see many function names that seem identical to C functions. It's a safe bet that these functions perform the exact same tasks, although they may sometimes take a slightly different form in terms of arguments or the way results are returned. Most string-modifying functions, for example, return new strings as the value of the function rather than modifying a string passed as an argument. Note, however, that function names are not case sensitive in PHP.

Differences

Although PHP has quite a bit of C ancestry, it also has some other ancestors (Perl, shell scripts), as well as some unique features not at all C-like.

Those dollar signs

All variables are denoted with a leading $. Variables do not need to be declared in advance of assignment, and they have no intrinsic type—the only type a variable has is the type of the last value assigned to it. The PHP version of the C code:

```
double my_number;
my_number = 3.14159;
```

would simply be:

```
$my_number = 3.14159;
```

Types

PHP has only two numerical types: *integer* (corresponding to a long in C) and *double* (corresponding to a double in C).

Strings are of arbitrary length. There is no separate character type. (Functions that might take character arguments in their C analogues typically expect a one-character string in PHP (ord(), for example.) Beginning with PHP4, there is also a genuine Boolean type (TRUE or FALSE). See the following sections for arrays and objects.

Type conversion

Types are not checked at compile time, and type errors do not typically occur at runtime either. Instead, variables and values are automatically converted across types as needed. This is somewhat analogous to the way arithmetic expressions in C will "promote" numerical arguments as needed, but it is extended to the other types as well. (See Chapter 25 for details of the conversion rules.)

Arrays

Arrays have a syntax superficially similar to C's array syntax, but they are implemented completely differently. They are actually associative arrays or hashes (with some additional supporting machinery), and the "index" can be either a number or a string. They do not need to be declared or allocated in advance.

No structure type

There is no *struct* in PHP, partly because the array and object types together make it unnecessary. The elements of a PHP array need not be of a consistent type.

Objects

PHP4 had a very basic OOP syntax, which allowed definition of classes with member data items and member functions. PHP5 introduces a much fuller object model, although in approach and syntax it owes more to Java than to C++. Some highlights: abstract classes, private/protected members, constructors/destructors, and interfaces (but no multiple inheritance as in C++).

No pointers

There are no *pointers* per se in PHP, although the typeless variables play a similar role. PHP does support variable references. You can also emulate function pointers to some extent, in that function names can be stored in variables and called by using the variable rather than a literal name.

No prototypes

Functions do not need to be declared before their implementation is defined, as long as the function definition can be found somewhere in the current code file or included files.

Memory management

The PHP engine is effectively a garbage-collected environment (reference-counted), and in small scripts there is no need to do any deallocation. You should freely allocate new structures — such as new strings and object instances — especially because they will reliably go away when your script terminates. If you need to free memory within a script's execution, call `unset()` on the variable that refers to it, which will release the memory for collection. External resources (such as database result sets) can also be explicitly freed within a script, but doing so is worth it only if the script would use an unacceptable amount of the resource before terminating.

In PHP5, it is possible to define destructors for objects, but there is no `free` or `delete`. Destructors are called when the last reference to an object goes away, before the memory is reclaimed.

Compilation and linking

There is no separate compilation step for PHP scripts — the development cycle is simply edit-reload. Errors and warnings show up in the browser output by default, although there is also an error-logging capability. Typically, there is no dynamic loading of libraries (although such a capability exists) — you decide at PHP configuration time which function families to include in your module, and they are then available to any script.

Permissiveness

As a general matter, PHP is more forgiving than C (especially in its type system) and so will let you get away with new kinds of mistakes. Unexpected results are more common than errors. In particular, under the default error-reporting level, PHP does not warn you if you use a variable that has not yet been assigned (although it does supply reasonable default values rather than garbage). If you would rather be warned, you can set the error-reporting level by evaluating error-reporting(E_ALL) early in your script, or set the error-reporting level to E_ALL permanently by editing the php.ini file.

Guide to the Book

In writing this book, we very intentionally did not assume that the reader had prior knowledge of C. Because PHP resembles C in many aspects, some of the chapters may cover familiar ground. This is especially true of Part I, which is essentially a language introduction.

In Table A-1, we label the chapters of Part I according to how familiar they are likely to be to C programmers. Parts III, IV, and V are more PHP-specific and likely to be novel, but you may also find portions of Part II to be familiar if you have some experience with SQL databases.

Table A-1: Guide to Part I for C Programmers

Chapter	Chapter Title	Verdict?	Notes
1	Why PHP?	Novel	The chapter you need to justify PHP to your boss.
2	Server-side Web Scripting	Novel	Important if you have not seen Web-scripting languages before.
3	Getting Started with PHP	Novel	Installation, hosting, and so on.
4	Adding PHP to HTML	Novel but easy	"Hello world" for PHP.
5	Syntax and Variables	Mostly familiar	Skimmable until the section on variables (which really are different in PHP).
6	Control and Functions	Mostly familiar	All the PHP control structures (if, while, switch, for) work the same way as in C. Some differences in function behavior, particularly with scoping of variables.
7	Passing Information between Pages	Novel	Specific to Web-scripting.

Chapter	Chapter Title	Verdict?	Notes
8	Strings	Mostly familiar	Doubly quoted strings do automatic interpolation of variable values.
9	Arrays	Novel	Deceptively familiar—PHP arrays are syntactically like C arrays but behave totally differently.
10	Numbers	Familiar	Two numerical types, corresponding to the long and double types. Numerical operators are as in C.
11	Basic PHP Gotchas	Novel	Error messages and stumbling blocks do not have much overlap with C.

A Bonus: Just Look at the Code!

As a final bonus, C programmers are uniquely qualified to benefit from the open-source nature of PHP. Although the combination of this book and the online manual should answer almost all your questions, if you have the PHP source available you may be able to gain some extra insight by poking around in it and seeing how things are implemented. Although you would need to be familiar with lexing/parsing technology to get much out of the parser code itself, many PHP functions are simple wrappers around their similarly named C counterparts, and some others that have no C counterparts are at least implemented in clear and simple C.

It's also easy for C programmers to add new capabilities to the language, whether for their own use or eventual use by the PHP community. Most PHP programming tasks are addressed by writing PHP (often by defining functions in PHP), but you can also pop the hood and add functionality to the underlying language by adding a new module, written (of course) in C.

✦ ✦ ✦

PHP for Perl Hackers

In this appendix, we assume that you know Perl, but not PHP, and are looking to quickly get up to speed in PHP. The good news is that the two languages are very similar indeed.

This is by no means a comprehensive guide to how Perl and PHP compare. Although similar, and sharing some ancestry, they really are distinct languages with distinct syntaxes and feature sets, and there is no replacement for getting to know them individually. Our main goal for this appendix is to save you some time up front — to warn you, for example, that `elsif` means nothing in PHP (but that `elseif`, however, is significant) rather than letting you debug your way to that realization.

Similarities

In this section, we discuss some ways in which PHP and Perl are similar.

Compiled scripting languages

First, the obvious: Both Perl and PHP are scripting languages. This means that (unlike compiled languages such as C) they are not used to produce native standalone executables in advance of execution, which can then be run without reference to the language they were written in. Instead, Perl or PHP source files are both fed to an appropriate engine at execution time. This does not mean, however, that Perl/PHP code is interpreted line-by-line at execution time; in both Perl and PHP, scripts are quickly and automatically compiled at execution time and then executed. But it does mean that the development cycle for PHP/Perl programmers is edit-execute, rather than edit-compile-execute, as in C.

Syntax

PHP's basic syntax is very close to Perl's, and both share a lot of syntactic features with C. Code is insensitive to whitespace, statements are terminated by semicolons, and curly braces organize multiple statements into a single block. Function calls start with the name of the function, followed by the actual arguments enclosed in parentheses and separated by commas.

Dollar-sign variables

All variables in PHP look like scalar variables in Perl: a name with a dollar sign ($) in front of it. (See the "Differences" section for what happened to @ and %.)

No declaration of variables

As in Perl, you don't need to declare the type of a PHP variable before using it. The following line is legal in both languages, with no prior mention of the variable called $the_answer:

```
$the_answer = 42;
```

Loose typing of variables

As in Perl, variables in PHP have no intrinsic type other than the value they currently hold. This is different from languages such as C and Java, in which once a variable is declared to be for holding, say, strings, you get into trouble if you try to use it to store an integer.

The following sequence of two lines is legal in both Perl and PHP:

```
$the_answer = 42;
$the_answer = "the answer";
```

The variable $the_answer is assigned sequentially to an integer and a string. This would not be legal in more strongly typed languages such as C, Pascal, or Java.

Strings and variable interpolation

Both PHP and Perl do more interpretation of double-quoted strings ("string") than of single-quoted strings ('string'). In particular, the value of $ variables is spliced into double-quoted strings at the time the strings are read.

The following code fragment is both legal Perl and legal PHP, and it has the same behavior in both languages.

```
$the_answer = 42;
$the_statement = "the answer is $the_answer";
```

At the end of the second line, the variable $the_statement contains the string:

```
the answer is 42
```

Differences

This section warns you (again, not exhaustively) about some ways that Perl and PHP diverge from each other.

PHP is HTML-embedded

Although it is possible to use PHP for arbitrary tasks by running it from the command line, it is more typically connected to a Web server and used for producing Web pages. The code for these pages can consist partially (or even completely!) of straight HTML, with fragments of PHP embedded in them to produce the dynamically generated portions.

If you are used to writing CGI scripts in Perl, the main difference in PHP is that you no longer need to explicitly print large blocks of static HTML using print or heredoc statements and instead can simply write the HTML itself (outside of the PHP code block). Also, for typical pages, there is no need to explicitly send HTTP headers from PHP code.

No @ or % variables

PHP has one only kind of variable, which starts with a dollar sign ($). Any of the datatypes in the language can be stored in such variables, whether scalar or compound. For example, the expression $my_array[0] refers to the first element in an array, while $my_array refers to the array itself.

Arrays versus hashes

PHP has a single datatype called an *array* that plays the role of both hashes and arrays/lists in Perl. For all the details, see Chapter 9; the short version is that a PHP array acts like a Perl hash when you supply keys and like a Perl (nonassociative) array when keys are omitted. Values can be extracted by key (as in Perl hashes) or by iteration through the array (as with Perl arrays).

There is, however, a list() function in PHP. It's used to extract the contents of an array into a set of separate variables. The list() function works like this:

```
$myArray = ('a', 'b','c');
list($var1, $var2, $var3) = $myArray
```

After that runs, $var1 contains a, $var2 contains b, and $var3 contains c.

Specifying arguments to functions

Function calls in PHP look pretty much like subroutine calls in Perl. Function definitions in PHP, on the other hand, typically require some kind of list of formal arguments as in C or Java. For example, although the typical syntax for a two-argument subroutine in Perl might look like:

```
sub two_arg_sub () {
    my ($first_arg, $second_arg) = @_;
    ...
}
```

The corresponding PHP function definition would be:

```
function two_arg_function ($first_arg, $second_arg) {
    ...
}
```

Although your humble authors try hard not to be partisan, we feel strongly that subroutine arguments in Perl are a bug and that function arguments in PHP are a feature. Two kinds of silliness common in Perl that don't usually arise in PHP are: 1) popping the argument stack at various points in a subroutine (so that it is hard for a reader of the code to figure out what the formal arguments are supposed to be) and 2) compound arguments bleeding into one another because arguments are passed as a list of scalars. PHP arguments arrive intact and without confusion regardless of number and type.

Variable scoping in functions

In Perl, the default scope for variables is global. This means that top-level variables are visible inside subroutines. Often, this leads to promiscuous use of globals across functions.

In PHP, the scope of variables within function definitions is local by default. This means that (with some exceptions) the only variables visible within functions are the formal parameters and variables assigned locally within the function. If you want to refer to a variable from the global context within a function, you must declare it by name in the function definition itself, using the global keyword.

The exceptions to that rule in PHP are the so-called superglobals, the most popular of which is $_POST. Representing the variables that arrived at a PHP script as a result of an HTTP POST operation, $_POST and its contents are accessible anywhere, without the need to use the global keyword.

For example, if we called a PHP script with this URL:

```
http://localhost/quoteStooges.php?stooge1=Curly&stooge2=Shemp
```

these calls would be legal anywhere in quoteStooges.php:

```
lookupQuote($_POST['stooge1']);
lookupQuote($_POST['stooge2']);
```

No module system as such

In PHP there is no real distinction between normal code files and code files used as imported libraries. To import a PHP code file full of function or class definitions, simply use include(), require(), or require_once(), which have much the same effect as splicing the definitions in at the point of the statement.

Break and continue rather than next and last

Perl has some idiosyncratic language keywords, which are not the same as the corresponding C constructs. In general, if Perl and C disagree about such a name, you will find that PHP follows C rather than Perl. In particular, if you want to skip to the end of a for or while iteration, use continue (not next); if you want to break out of the loop altogether, use break (not last).

No elsif

A minor spelling difference: Perl's elsif is PHP's elseif. Also, its use is not mandatory. In PHP, the following is legal:

```
if ($boolean_var) {
    # case 1
}
else if ($other_boolean) {
    # case 2
}
```

In Perl, on the other hand, if you for some reason decline to use `elsif`, your other alternative is the more awkward form:

```
if ($boolean_var) {
    # case 1
}
else {
  if ($other_boolean) {
      # case 2
  }
}
```

More kinds of comments

Perl people like the phrase "There's more than one way to do it," and yet they suffer with a really impoverished set of options for comments. In addition to Perl-style (#) single-line comments, PHP offers C-style multiline comments (`/* comment */`) and Java-style single-line comments (`// comment`).

Regular expressions

PHP does not have a built-in syntax specific to regular expressions, but has most of the same functionality in its "Perl-compatible" regular expression functions. See Chapter 22 for the details.

Miscellaneous Tips

Following are answers to a couple of questions that Perl programmers might have on their minds.

What about use strict "vars"?

Like Perl, PHP allows you to use variables without declaring them or initializing them, and (as in Perl) this capability is a frequent source of bugs. If you would like a declaration like Perl's `use strict "vars"`, try `error_reporting(E_ALL)`, which will at least warn you about the use of any unassigned variables.

Where's CPAN?

PHP doesn't yet have a code repository as comprehensive as the Comprehensive Perl Archive Network (CPAN), but a good effort is under way in the PEAR project (`http://pear.php.net`).

Guide to the Book

As in Appendix A (PHP for C Programmers), in this section we offer Perl hackers a quick guide to Part I of the book to give a sense of which chapters are likely to already be familiar.

Table B-1: Guide to Part I for Perl Programmers

Chapter	Chapter Title	Verdict?	Notes
1	Why PHP?	Novel	The chapter you need to justify PHP to your boss
2	Server-Side Web Scripting	Possibly novel	Familiar to Perl CGI and mod_perl programmers; important if you have not seen Web scripting before
3	Getting Started with PHP	Novel	Installation, hosting, and so on
4	Adding PHP to Your HTML	Novel but easy	"Hello world" for PHP
5	Syntax and Variables	Mostly familiar	Basic syntax is very familiar; variables are different
6	Control and Functions	Somewhat familiar	Basic constructs are similar, with syntactic differences
7	Passing Information between Pages	Mostly familiar	Specific to Web scripting
8	Strings	Somewhat familiar	Treatment of single-quoted and double-quoted strings essentially the same; functions are mostly novel
9	Arrays	Novel	No exactly corresponding datatype in Perl
10	Numbers	Mostly familiar	Novel section on arbitrary-precision (BC) math functions.
11	Basic PHP Gotchas	Novel	Same gotchas around unintentionally unassigned variables; other gotchas specific to PHP parsing

✦   ✦   ✦

PHP for HTML Coders

T his appendix contains specific advice for HTML-only jocks looking to trade up to something a little more powerful on the server side. If you already know ASP, JavaScript, or almost any real programming language, this appendix is not going to help you much.

The Good News

If you're already proficient at HTML, starting to use PHP is not a huge step. Because PHP is usually embedded in HTML, extending the functionality of static Web pages with a programming language can be a very natural progression. There are plenty of reasons to believe that you can learn PHP fairly quickly, such as the following factors.

You already know HTML

Because PHP is often embedded in HTML, and because PHP generally uses HTML for display to the browser, you won't be able to see anything that your scripts are doing unless you output HTML. In fact, you can think of PHP as simply adding functionality to Web pages — it can do other things, but lots of people use it mostly for form handling and dynamic page generation.

You presumably have a lot of practice debugging HTML, which is all to the good. Many errors occur within the HTML parts of scripts or during the transitions between modes, so the ability to read and write HTML with great facility is crucial.

If you're strong on the design side, as are many HTML coders, you have the ability to produce a good-looking and well-laid-out product. This skill is important for the community because a lot of early PHP developers were not exactly known for their UI skills (including ourselves, we hasten to admit). So go out there and show the world that PHP sites don't need to be ugly, clunky, or, at best, really plain — you can make us all proud.

PHP is an easy first programming language to learn

Unlike many major programming languages, PHP enables you to do useful stuff from the very beginning instead of making you play endless games of tic-tac-toe or code up incomprehensible math problems. The Web browser and markup languages, however primitive and clunky they are now, point the way to the universal I/O, windowing, and multimedia solution that the world has been waiting for. PHP takes full advantage of the Web's power; plus, it has very little overhead and takes a loose, inclusive approach to issues such as types, variables, and syntax. All the nitpicky angst that programmers used to put into these areas you can now apply more directly to functionality.

And frankly, PHP enables you to learn just those parts that are useful to you and ignore the rest. Unlike some programming languages, which pretty much require a firm grasp of all the basic principles before you can do anything useful (try telling a C programmer that you just haven't seen a need for structs yet if you want a laugh), no one is going to give you a quiz on all the hundreds of PHP functions before entrusting you with a text editor. So if you don't need to write some huge math function right off the bat, go ahead and skip that chapter—we promise not to tell. If you ever need them, the math capabilities will still be there.

Web development is increasingly prefab anyway

Finally, the Web is increasingly making development a matter of altering prefab open source code rather than hacking it all up yourself. Much of this work is about changing how the page looks rather than how it functions. Learn to be a smart script shopper, and you're more than halfway there.

The Bad News

Before we get too carried away, honesty compels us to admit that you may face a few hurdles before you become a power PHP user.

If programming were that easy, you'd already know how

PHP is a real programming language, similar to C (albeit generally Web-server dwelling), rather than a tag-based markup concept such as HTML or ColdFusion. This point introduces whole new levels of complexity. It simply takes time and practice to develop a bag of tricks, work out routines for solving problems, and just get better at development—and there are no shortcuts for these skills.

So here's the bottom line: Most of PHP is probably completely new to you. Unlike new PHP developers who are already proficient with ASP, JavaScript, or C, you can't expect to pick up any specific points here that are highly similar to things you already know how to do. Uh, sorry.

However, if you already know some JavaScript or have taken an "Intro to C" class in school—even if you wouldn't describe yourself as a JavaScript or C guru—you're ahead of the curve. Some of the logic is sure to come back to you as you begin to work with PHP.

Also, PHP training courses are beginning to pop up for those who are comfortable learning in the classroom. Check out the following Web sites:

✦ www.phpbootcamp.com (USA)

✦ www.academyx.com/training/san_francisco/php/introduction/ (SF)

✦ http://training.gbdirect.co.uk/courses/php/ (UK)

✦ www.thinkphp.de (Germany)

Back end servers can add complexity

PHP is mostly useful in conjunction with back end servers, such as database and mail servers, which have their own syntax and implementation issues that you need to learn about. Because open source software such as PHP is commonly used in noncorporate settings, most PHP developers probably don't have the luxury of a team of database, network, and design experts doing their various things while they just worry about the middle and front tiers.

If possible, don't try to learn everything at once. The most important task is to become comfortable with the Web server itself; Apache, in particular, is an extremely powerful but involved piece of software that rewards study. (This advice may not be relevant if you have IT staff to install and maintain the Web server for you.) After that, you will almost certainly want to learn SQL if you don't know it already. Mail service is also a very rewarding subject. After you master those three, other new servers should be easier to learn.

Concentrate On . . .

Learning PHP quickly requires a strategy. Here are some things you might want to concentrate on doing when you're first learning.

Reading other people's code

Learning to read other people's code can be harder than it sounds. One of the best things about PHP is its loose syntax and inclusive "don't worry, be happy" design — but that can also mean that different scripts can look very different, even if they return similar results. Beginners can be boggled by stylistic issues and may find it difficult to sort out which parts of a script are functionally irreducible and which are the products of one individual's programming quirks. But regardless of difficulty, the sooner you can parse other people's PHP and the more code you can look at, the better off you'll be.

One potentially helpful exercise is to visit the mailing-list archive or a code exchange (see Appendix D) and print out multiple examples of code that solve the same issue (preferably one you're interested in). Then lay the sheets side by side, take a big ol' red pen and go through it all, circling the common parts. Give extra brownie points to any scripters who comment their code well (which doesn't necessarily mean the most voluminous comments but rather the most useful) and look for more code from those people. Also look for code that is generally well laid out and logically organized, even if it isn't extensively commented.

Working on what interests you

We firmly believe that learning is motivation. If you find tasks that you want to accomplish, you will automatically be motivated to learn what you need to know to accomplish them. Don't let anyone tell you that the right way to learn programming is through some highly structured program of math problems, games, and stock-market simulations. Wanting to put pictures of your dog on the Internet is much more important than making sure that you know what's in every byte of memory your program is using.

Thinking about programming

As we said earlier, learning PHP is inevitably going to take time, practice, and lots of example code. There is just no way around it, and there is not a whole lot more to say on the subject.

One thing that may prove helpful to new developers, particularly those of a narrative rather than mathematical bent, is the judicious use of *pseudocode*. For example, you might start out with mostly pseudocode and gradually add real PHP as we do in the steps that follow.

1. Write down the tasks that you want this page to accomplish. Being complete is more important at this stage than being cogent. Following is an example of a script mission statement:

   ```
   This page should display a form with any old answers already filled
   in. Then you can submit the form to update some of the values if you
   want to. And I want the form to be password-protected, so it needs to
   handle a User ID passed in from the login screen.
   ```

2. Break the mission statement down into steps and substeps, as in a recipe. Rearrange these if necessary. Following is an example of this step:

   ```
   1. Get the User ID that is passed from the login screen; if none,
      don't display anything.
   2. Display the HTML form.
   3. Make any old values from the database appear in the form.
   a. Connect to the database server.
   b. Download data about this item.
   c. Put the data into the HTML form's "value=X" variables.
   4. Change the values and put them into the database too.
   5. Pass the User ID to the next page.
   ```

3. Pick one of the steps and turn it into actual PHP code. Starting with a core PHP task — such as sending e-mail or returning something to the screen — is generally easier than beginning with peripheral tasks, such as connecting to a database. Any time you might want to connect to a database, use a commented variable, array, or include file for the moment. The following example illustrates this step:

   ```
   1. Get the User ID that is passed from the login screen; if none,
      don't display anything.

   <?php
   // Dummy UserID pretending to be passed from login.
   // Will be superseded later.
   $UserID = 1;
   ?>

   2. Display the HTML form.

   <HTML><HEAD></HEAD>
   <BODY>
   <FORM>
   First name: <input type="text" size=30 name="FirstName"><BR>
   ```

```
Last name: <input type="text" size=30 name="LastName"><BR>
E-mail: <input type="text" size=30 name="Email">
```

3. Make any old values from the database appear in the form.

```
<?php
// I'm using these variables now, but later I'll get
// them from the database instead.

$FirstName = "Joyce";
$LastName = "Park";
$Email = "root@localhost"
?>
```
Oh, I think I need to put them in before the form is rendered.

4. Change the values and put them into the database, too.
5. Pass the User ID to the next page.

4. Gradually fill in more and more of the code, fixing any new issues that arise. You may want to keep some of the pseudocode, suitably edited, as comments, as shown in the following example:

```
/* Pass the User ID to the next page. The best way is to have it
   show up as a hidden input type and PHP variable in the form;
   then HTML can pass it with the rest of the POST values. */
```

Learning SQL and other protocols

Spending some time interacting with back end servers directly, via whatever interface the server provides, is generally a good idea before you add the complexity of PHP between you and the server.

You can kill two birds with one stone by using the back end server's own interface to construct the database (or whatever), even though there may be nice PHP tools for some of these tasks. For instance, even though the phpMyAdmin and MySQL Control Center are both very slick and handy ways to deal with the MySQL database, the newbie database administrator can learn a heck of a lot more by using MySQL's deliberately primitive command-line interface.

Beginning with PHP5, a lightweight, embedded database engine called SQLite is included and ready for you to use. SQLite is rudimentary and not up to the task of replacing MySQL and other database engines on a production site; however, you may find it an excellent tool for getting your feet wet before moving on to MySQL.

Making cosmetic changes to prefab PHP applications

One common way to ease into using PHP is to enlist your front end Web development skills to customize a pre-existing PHP package.

✦ First try just changing the colors — that's generally pretty safe. If that goes well, try customizing the buttons. The next safest thing is spacing — table widths, columns, and so on. You can also add graphics, add links, or play around with style sheets pretty much without worries.

✦ If the application has include files (especially `header.inc`), the cosmetic part is often in there. Look first in headers and footers for colors, the basis of page layouts, and so on. Remember to match header changes with corresponding footer changes and vice versa.

✦ Never, ever erase a line beginning with a conjunction (such as `if`, `while`, or `for`). If you are not 100 percent sure of what you're doing, comment out code blocks rather than deleting them.

Debugging is programming

Few people truly enjoy debugging; as one of our colleagues once observed, "I'd rather implement new features than eat someone else's leftovers." Debugging can turn out to be a useful learning experience, however, because you can fix things at the edges of a big project instead of jumping into writing the whole thing from scratch.

One of the most efficient ways to debug is in pairs. If you're tired or have seen a piece of code too many times, focusing on every detail can prove difficult. At this point, talking through your logic becomes very helpful — one of you briefly stating why you're doing what you're doing and the other checking each step off very deliberately. A fresh set of eyes can often find cheap mistakes such as misspelled variable names or missing brackets more quickly, too. If you get an opportunity to debug with a more experienced programmer, take it.

Avoid at First . . .

A few things in PHP are extremely unfamiliar to HTML coders and generally are not extremely necessary to writing functional PHP. Try to avoid the elements that we describe in the following sections if you can, at least at first.

Objects and interfaces

Objects can prove confusing even for experienced nonobject-oriented programmers, so do yourself a favor and avoid them if at all possible. Because PHP is not even a truly object-oriented language, the "object notation" can also cause problems later. Much of the object model has drastically changed from PHP4 to PHP5 as well and continues to be heavily revised. If you don't plan on programming with objects right away, it may be best not to have to unlearn a methodology that has been rendered obsolete.

Maximal PHP style

See Chapter 33 on PHP style. The maximal style is deprecated by Rasmus Lerdorf himself, and only hardcore C programmers have the slightest excuse to use it, except in very specific, brief instances. It includes too many single quotes, double quotes, forward slashes, backslashes, ASCII line breaks, and HTML line breaks for most coders. Beginners are better off if they don't waste their time worrying about stray punctuation when they could be spending the time and effort grasping larger concepts instead.

Programming large applications from scratch

Why reinvent the wheel? In Open-sourceland, you don't need to. Becoming a good customizer and recycler of other people's code is often more efficient than trying to become the world's greatest programmer from scratch. Learn to shop for what you need.

Consider This . . .

The ideas in the following sections are completely optional but may prove helpful. You may not agree with them all, but we offer them for what they're worth.

Reading a book on C programming

Unfortunately, we can't write a complete programming tutorial. Part I of this book explains programming topics but necessarily very briefly. We've tried to comment our code samples extensively, but we can do only so much to explain these techniques in passing.

Mailing-list regulars frequently counsel new PHP developers to buy a book on C programming — but in a snotty, RTFM way that too often elicits a naturally passive-aggressive response. Nevertheless, if you separate it from the unspoken message that you must be a clueless idiot, it's good advice and something to seriously consider if you're having trouble with the programming aspect of PHP.

A clearly written, brief tutorial book is Patrick Henry Winston's *On to C* (Addison-Wesley, 1994). It's fewer than 300 pages, and a lot of the PHP-relevant material is right at the beginning. The standard reference is *The C Programming Language*, by Brian W. Kernighan and Dennis M. Ritchie (Prentice Hall, 1988), which is quite definitive but more reference-oriented and, therefore, perhaps less appropriate for HTML-only coders. A friendlier introduction might be Dan Gookin's two-volume *C For Dummies* (Wiley, 1997), which has cartoons and dry humor.

Minimal PHP style

Of the range of PHP styles, the easiest for the HTML coder to work with at first is the most minimal. In other words, we suggest that you separate the HTML and PHP sections completely. Not only does this technique avoid many stylistic difficulties, but by using this method, you avoid mixing PHP and HTML glitches on the same page, which makes diagnosing problems more than twice as hard. We discuss this topic thoroughly in Chapter 33.

Perhaps the easiest way to use the minimal style is to finish the HTML pages first, using whatever tool you're most enamored of. Take the time to debug your HTML completely and perhaps run it through a tidying utility. Then, and only then, tackle the PHP parts, secure and comfy in the knowledge that any difficulties you encounter are certainly on the PHP side rather than the HTML side.

One downside of this style is that you can't have pages pass their variables back to themselves. This is particularly relevant with forms, so if your site has a lot of forms, you may want to change your style a bit as your PHP skills improve.

Use the right tools for the job

Finally, you want to consider using a PHP-enabled text editor for the PHP parts of your scripts. (See Chapter 4 for a discussion of text editors versus WYSIWYG tools.) Some people can do wonders with just Notepad or emacs, but a lot of frustrated beginners are certainly using those tools just because someone told them that's what the cool programmers do. As Zsa Zsa Gabor said (in a slightly different context), macho does not mean mucho. If you work more effectively with vim or Visual SlickEdit, by all means use those tools.

Syntax highlighting (printing different parts of the code in different colors) can help you a lot, as it will usually make clearer when you have failed to close off a parenthesis or double-quote mark. Some programmer's text editors will automatically line up your curly braces for you, which helps you verify that you've closed off all of a set of nested cases. We would not even consider using a text editor without line numbering, since PHP's built-in error messages always refer to lines in your code. And last but not least, do not forget the power of "View Source" in the browser—this will help you verify that the output you are producing is in fact what you intended.

Caution   This advice does *not* apply to WYSIWYG editors, the use of which we deprecate. Sooner or later, you need to fix up the HTML into a human-readable form, which no WYSIWYG editor can yet produce. If it's your choice to use one, fine—but you should in no way think of this tool as a substitute for understanding and writing clean HTML by hand.

✦   ✦   ✦

PHP Resources

This appendix lays out some basic resources that can help you learn more about the language. We have also tried to mention specific resources and products throughout the text.

The PHP Web Site

The URL for the PHP Web site (engrave it on your forehead) is www.php.net. Here you'll find the latest official news, the freshest downloads, the PHP bugtracker, a growing list of PHP users' groups, and links to PHP-friendly ISPs.

Most important, you'll find the PHP manual in the Documentation section of the PHP Web site. It's available in several versions for your universal reference pleasure, including the following:

✦ Numerous translations — many European languages, Japanese, Korean, and so on.

✦ Several PDF, Windows Help, and HTML download versions (useful when you're traveling; HTML versions are included with the PHP download).

✦ Two versions for Palm OS.

✦ A plain HTML online version.

✦ Links to the PHP-GTK (client-side PHP) and PEAR (PHP code-base) manuals.

✦ Information on beta releases that are not yet ready for production use.

A comprehensive listing of all downloads is available at www.php.net/download-docs.php.

Note　　The PEAR manual, which used to be a chapter of the general PHP manual, has now been moved to its own server. You can find it at http://pear.php.net/manual/.

But when people talk about "the PHP manual," they mean the big annotated online version for which PHP is famous. Users from around the world have added notes and comments to each page. These additions are often clarifications of points made in the main text, additional insights, and reports of PHP's behavior on various platforms.

Navigating the PHP Manual

Our experience suggests that something about the organization of the manual makes it difficult or discouraging for many users to quickly find what they're looking for. To locate information about a function or construction, you sort of need to know that it's there and what kind of thing it is (not always clear from the headings — for example, date functions versus calendar functions), and often it helps to have an idea of what the PHP team might have named it. If you can't accurately guess these three things, you're likely to spend a lot of time wandering around looking at not-quite-right function pages. We have nothing comforting to tell frustrated users, except that PHP has so many functions and configuration options and styles that writing about and organizing them all in a way that makes sense to an outsider is very difficult. Our hope is that books such as this one can help introduce you to the main categories (for example, array functions) and the most commonly used functions — and then you'll be more prepared to use the riches of the online PHP manual.

One extremely helpful thing we recommend is reading the introductory page for each section of the online PHP manual. The manual is broken up into sections or chapters, such as "Arrays" and "Regexps"; each section has a "front page" which can be accessed via the "Function Reference" part of the online manual's table of contents. Usually (although not always) this page will have a lightning-quick introduction to the subject of the manual chapter, helpful hints, and a list of the functions in that section. By reading through these introductions, you will have a much better idea of the various things that PHP can do, and greatly increase your chances of being able to put your finger on just the function you need at any given moment.

The English-language version of the online PHP manual has a cool feature that can save a lot of time for certain users, particularly those experienced in another programming language. If you type the name of a function as a top-level URI, the PHP site automatically forwards you to either the page devoted to that function (if it exists) or a search page with a completed search for that term (if it doesn't exist or doesn't have a discrete page). So, for instance, if you type `http://www.php.net/popen`, you'll be redirected to `www.php.net/manual/en/function.popen.php`. This is the same functionality as typing a search term into the search box in the page header. If you're looking for a PHP function that is similar to one in C or Perl, this trick can prove a great timesaver over navigating the manual by hand. It's also useful in cases where you know the name of the function but just want to check on the type of variable returned or the order of arguments to pass in.

You may want to keep a couple of points in mind when using this manual:

✦ The canonical manual text is written in a super-terse programmer's style, and it is organized in a not particularly discursive, notebook-like format.

Note The online manual is not the place to ask questions! It's intended for meaningful comments and observations only. Send e-mail to one of the previous commentators who provide their addresses — many of them will be happy to help you. Or subscribe to the mailing list or post to a PHP forum, which is faster anyway. Remember, a stupid question posted to the manual errata will go down on your (semi)permanent record.

✦ The comments are edited, weeded, and verified only on an episodic (not to say extremely infrequent) basis. Proceed with extreme caution—there have been numerous instances of problems actually getting worse because a user uncritically followed the advice in the manual notes. You can write to the person to make sure that the advice is appropriate for you or even to determine whether the person really knows what he or she is talking about.

✦ The manual may lag behind development by a considerable time period.

The PHP Mailing Lists

The "official" PHP community meets and greets on the PHP mailing lists. With the advent of PHP4, a decision was made to split up the lists into more specific topics. These topics will continue to proliferate with the addition of new features in PHP5 and beyond.

Signing up

To subscribe to any of the PHP mailing lists, go to `www.php.net/mailing-lists.php`.

You should see a large form listing the various mailing lists and options for viewing them. Just choose the list that you want, specify normal or digest versions, enter your e-mail address, and click the Subscribe button. You can also unsubscribe from a list here.

The PHP mailing list manager almost instantaneously sends you an e-mail message asking you to confirm your subscription. You aren't subscribed until you reply to this e-mail.

Tip   You also find links to local (non-English) mailing lists and newsgroups at the bottom of this page. If you want to discuss PHP in Turkish or Japanese, this page is the place to start!

Users' lists and developers' lists

Many of the user-oriented lists are new with PHP4 or later. The following are the most popular PHP users' mailing lists:

✦ **php.general:** Main mailing list—very heavy traffic, 80+ e-mail messages per day

✦ **php.windows:** Specific mailing list for Windows users

✦ **php.install:** An installation-related mailing list, mostly for new users

✦ **php.db:** The database-related issues mailing list

✦ **php.i18n:** Internationalization and localization mailing list

✦ **php.pear:** The PEAR users' list

✦ **php.gtk.general:** The PHP-GTK users' list

✦ **php.smarty.general:** The Smarty templates users' list

✦ **php.bugs:** Bug reporting related to PHP itself

✦ **php.announce:** Announces new releases—very occasional

Lists also are available for popular PHP-based projects such as Midgard and phpNuke; you subscribe to those lists through the products' own Web sites. We list the URLs of some of these sites in the "Major PHP Projects" section of this chapter below.

The following four lists are mostly intended for active developers and very early adopters — people who are going to get down in the C code and battle bugs to the death:

✦ **php.dev:** The main PHP developers' list

✦ **php.version5.dev:** Mailing list during the ongoing development of PHP5

✦ **php.gtk.dev:** The PHP-GTK developers' list

✦ **php.pear.dev:** The PEAR developers' list

These lists are low-to-medium volume, meaning approximately 100 to 1,000 messages a month. They are highly technical and mostly not enlightening unless you're an active team member. Various CVS lists for developers are also available, which mail out all CVS commits on a particular branch to all subscribers; special lists for documentation writers and QA team members also exist.

If you're comfortable with Internet newsgroups (which many newer users are not), you can access the PHP mailing lists at the news gateway at news.php.net.

This option has one great advantage: You can send messages to the mailing lists without subscribing to them. Many new users, however, should think in terms of searching the archives for answers to old questions before (or rather than) asking new questions anyway.

Most of these mailing lists, and many others on a variety of topics, are archived and searchable at http://marc.theaimsgroup.com.

This archive dates back to at least 1998, although the older posts are usually less complete.

Tip   Trying a quick keyword search on the PHP site, mail archives, and perhaps some of the other major PHP Web sites before contacting the mailing lists is the polite thing to do. It's actually faster for you, plus the less time the developers must spend answering the same questions over and over, the more time they have to implement new features in the language. Actually, searching the archives is no longer just polite — it's a necessity. With so many new users, so-called "RTFM" (read the effing manual) questions are not (politely) answered on the PHP lists anymore. Also, try to ask your question on a specific list if it exists — especially installation-related questions.

Regular and digest

The main PHP user list is so high-volume that it has a twice-daily digest version. The new specialized mailing lists also typically have digest versions. The raw and digested versions each have advantages and disadvantages.

If you've never had 100+ e-mail messages a day pouring into your mailbox, you have no idea how distracting and time-consuming this experience can be. Just reading-and-deleting can take up a couple hours, whereas actually answering them can easily become a full-time job. Under no circumstance should you request the full user list if your primary mailbox is a Web-based free e-mail service such as Yahoo! mail or Hotmail.

Tip   Setting up a separate mailbox for PHP mail is almost mandatory if you're subscribing to the full user mailing list, unless you've set up good mail filters. Otherwise, you quickly start to lose mail from other sources in the flood of similarly named threads.

On the other hand, the digest version makes getting into the flow more difficult. The few brave community members who get the full user list seem to answer all the questions on the half-volley before you even get the digest, making participation difficult for the time-stressed community member.

For beginners, we recommend the digest version. You can always trade up later, whenever you're ready to stop lurking and participate actively.

Everyone should also consider using one of the PHP forums (see the following section on "Other PHP Web Sites") instead of or in addition to the user mailing list. These forums are great for those who dislike mailing lists. The downside is that PHP developers generally don't hang out here, so extremely abstruse infrastructure questions usually go unanswered. The upside is that they tend to be friendlier, especially to repetitive newbie questions, because the answerers can control the amount of contact they prefer and go away if they start to become annoyed.

Mailing list etiquette

Open-source mailing lists can be intimidating places, and the PHP general-users list is particularly active and fast-paced. The denizens of the mailing lists are people, and learning about their different personalities and plans over time can be fun — but they can get annoyed and fed up, too. A little netiquette can take the user a long way. The following sections offer a few tips to follow.

Remember, the community does all this work for free!

Before you turn on the flamethrower, remind yourself of your last experience with commercial-software tech support. Did it solve your problem the same day? Did it cost money? How long did it take? At what point did you get to talk to the developers of the program?

People might be sick of your question

Perhaps you're trying to install PHP for the first time and can't get it working as an Apache module — but we can assure you that tens of thousands of iterations of that question have appeared on the mailing lists over the years. People on the mailing lists are experiencing fatigue at answering questions that they and others have answered in a lot of other information sources — the FAQs, the online manual, the mailing-list archives, and any number of other Web sites. If you ask one of these basic questions on the general mailing list, it proves that you didn't take seriously the numerous polite requests on the PHP site to search for an answer to your question before posting. You may get an irritated e-mail informing you of all the above — or you may get no responses at all. Neither response means that the PHP community is cold-hearted and unhelpful. Try to see things from the point of view of community members of longer standing, and avoid these problems by searching for the answer to your question before you post.

Give detailed descriptions

Say as much as you can about your platform, the problem, and any steps you've already tried. Don't worry about being concise; you're far better off meandering on a little than making everyone go back and forth an extra time.

Code fragments are the very most efficient way to state your problem for debugging by the community. Many people edit their raw code to make it more anonymous and/or abstract. Remember to take out any passwords!

Tip Copy and paste your code fragments; don't retype them. List participants often post perfect code, only to be frustrated that nobody can find anything wrong with it — because they corrected their errors while retyping!

Make sure that you use a specific subject line—the more specific the better. "Subject: PHP Help" gets you ignored by most of the mailing-list regulars. You want to say something more descriptive such as, "Subject: mysql_connect arguments not being passed in 4.0.0."

PHP is international

PHP is developed and used by people literally all over the world. In fact, the active development team has only a smallish minority of native English speakers on it at any given time.

Native English speakers should feel supremely lucky that theirs is the lingua franca of the Internet in general and the PHP world specifically. They should feel awed by the linguistic dexterity of all the citizens of other nations and perhaps slightly abashed that they can't return the favor in Finnish or Urdu. In other words, cut people some slack already! Don't assume that someone is an idiot because his or her messages aren't couched in perfectly grammatical and smooth English. Instead, you might spend the time learning how to write "Thank you" in all the languages of the various PHP community members—it makes a nice sig file for your mailing list posts.

Tip   If you don't know English well, you may want to write your question twice—once in English, once in your native language. This will increase the odds that someone will be able to decipher your meaning.

There are limits

The mailing list and other resources are meant to help you, but you must prepare to make a good-faith and even strenuous effort of your own. Help does not mean that someone comes to your office and writes your code—this is not a remake of the Disney version of Cinderella, with dancing, sewing, chore-doing mice! Please don't ask community members to go into your server and debug your scripts for you.

Every once in a while, someone gets on the mailing list and whines about how PHP doesn't have precisely the feature that he or she is looking for—to which the developers very sensibly reply, "Why don't you implement it yourself?" Or, if you're not a good C programmer yourself, you could always pay someone else to develop your feature and contribute it to the PHP community. At the very least, you can avoid doing things that may alienate others or cause developers to burn out on the whole idea of developing open-source software!

Do it yourself

Open-source software may be free to use, but you should not consider it free of all responsibilities. You are technically a "free rider" until you give back—or pay forward—to the community at large. It's your task to figure out where and how to best deploy your talents, and then to do that thing as you can. We don't mean that every casual PHP user must become a C developer, but you can contribute in many other ways. Answering questions on the PHP mailing lists or Web sites is always a good thing, because it lightens the load on the core developers. If you figure something out that seemed obscure in the online PHP manual, be sure to post your findings to the User-contributed notes section of the manual. Use the PHP bug-tracker according to the instructions. Simple steps like these, in aggregate, contribute to the healthy community that has made PHP so successful.

It's probably you

If you experience a failure to communicate, you need to ask yourself whether the problem could possibly lie with you. If you do find yourself in the middle of a flame war, which happens occasionally on any mailing list, people enjoy nothing more than a little public acknowledgment of what a jerk you've (unknowingly) been.

There are now commercial alternatives

If the whole ethos of the PHP mailing lists is driving you crazy, remember that you can now pay to play instead. Many companies are now staffed by well-known PHP developers who are willing to do everything from answering single questions to building a custom PHP extension for you. ThinkPHP (`www.thinkphp.de`), for example, is a German consultancy, associated with PHP team member Thies Arntzen, that offers support, training, and performance evaluations. In the United States, the supremely helpful Richard Lynch of PHP-mailing-list fame takes requests at `www.l-i-e.com`.

Other PHP Web Sites

Besides the *official* PHP resources that we mention in the preceding sections, some well-known community members have put up some extraordinarily helpful Web sites. Some of these enjoy a special relationship with PHP, and are "quasi-official." The following sections describe some of these sites.

Core scripting engine and tools

The core of PHP is the Zend scripting engine. It is produced by an Israeli company called Zend, and besides being a free part of PHP, it can be embedded in other applications. Zend also produces various PHP tools and add-ons, such as a graphical debugger and a precompiler. You can find information on Zend products at `www.zend.com`.

Zend.com is the home of the core PHP5 scripting engine, as well as a center of PHP commercialization. Although the company sells support and custom development services to larger companies, the vast majority of PHP developers are most interested in the add-on products being developer by core developers Zeev Suraski and Andi Gutmans and their team.

For most PHP users, the most useful product is the Zend Studio IDE, now in 3.0.1 release. (See Chapters 3 and 32 for more information and screenshots.) This program is the first PHP-specific development tool available, with many well-designed features for the PHP professional. Because of Zend's unique relationship to PHP development, the company understands the language completely and can design an editing tool that is customized to the needs of hardcore PHP users.

Two other Zend products are primarily of value to companies. PHP consulting firms should find the Zend Encoder useful, as it enables them to ship their code in a platform-independent, optimized intermediate representation. Large PHP sites can get a quick return on investment by using the Zend Accelerator, which boosts performance by optimizing and caching, thereby requiring less capital investment in hardware.

The Zend site also offers unique content on a regular basis, including biographies of major figures in the PHP world, a handy weekly newsletter summarizing current issues in the development of our beloved programming language, and great articles on advanced topics in PHP development. Zend.com is one of the few Web sites that consistently offers articles of interest to corporate PHP developers and architects, often showcasing the finer points of PHP functionality, such as reference counting, output buffering, and changes to the `include` functions. Topics such as these may seem abstruse at first, but advanced users usually enjoy learning about the underlying structure and logic of the programming language so that they can write the tightest, cleanest, most secure, best-architected, and most well-thought-out PHP code possible. C programmers who want to contribute to PHP can also find inspiration and information in these articles — because Zeev and Andi are driving the course of PHP core development, getting a feeling for their aesthetic and decision making is important if you want to delve into the heart of PHP.

PHP knowledgebase

PHP has a great knowledgebase, something like a FAQ-o-matic but more full-featured, called PHP Faqts (previously known as E-gineer). It is available at `http://php.faqts.com`.

PHP Faqts is an interesting and nicely executed concept: an archived knowledgebase of answered and unanswered questions from real PHP users with a decent search function. For common questions, this site is much easier to use than the mailing lists or even many forums — and for that reason, we recommend it to new PHP users.

The way that Faqts (brainchild of Australian PHP whiz Nathan Wallace) works is that community members ask questions in one of several "buckets," such as Installation and Setup, Common Problems, Database Backed Sites, and the extremely cool Not Quite PHP. Other community members come along and add multiple answers to these questions. They can also associate other questions (basically other ways of stating the same thing) with that question/answer pair. Everyone can vote anonymously on whether the question/answer was useful or not. Thus, you get an accretion of knowledge over time and some way to discern whether a particular answer is good at a glance.

Going to this site, however, is not the fastest way to get your question answered, and it remains to be seen whether Faqts can scale indefinitely — but it's a cool idea and definitely a resource to try.

Articles and tutorials

Articles and tutorials take a "teach a man to fish . . ." approach. Often they can't really walk you through all the steps involved in building your Web site; instead, they attempt to guide you in thinking about what to do. Following are two sites that we recommend for such information.

✦ **PHPBuilder** (`www.phpbuilder.com/`). Founded by Tim Perdue, the top PHP app developer responsible for Sourceforge.net and Geocrawler.com, this site has long been one of the most comprehensive and well-run PHP sites. The specialty of the site is a deep backlog of articles that focus on the correct architecture of PHP sites, with subjects such as user authentication, cross-platform development, database abstraction, and documentation and style. PHPBuilder also boasts one of the most active PHP-related Web forums, with excellent response times to most questions.

One downside to the site is that articles are not dated, so determining whether the advice is still relevant to current versions of the programming language can prove difficult. Despite this drawback, PHPBuilder is a must-visit for the more conceptual PHP programmer who wants to read well-argued position papers on the right way to code PHP.

✦ **Devshed** (`www.devshed.com/Server_Side/PHP` and `www.devshed.com/Server_Side/MySQL`). A big commercial site with good tutorials and a forum, Devshed covers all the scripting languages (ASP, JavaScript, Python, and so on) as well as MySQL, making it the best one-stop for those still in the shopping phase.

PHP codebases

Codebases take a "give a man a fish . . ." approach, simply offering their donated wares to all takers. The code quality can vary widely, from first scripts to elegant classes contributed by experts in a particular area. The following sections describe a few such sites that you can visit.

Caution   Although codebases can seem attractive to new developers and do embody the power of open source, there are reasons to be wary. For one thing, no one is guaranteeing the quality or safety of this code. If you're more comfortable cutting and pasting than writing it yourself, you may not have sufficient skill at reading other people's PHP to use contributed code in an intelligent way. Proceed with caution!

✦ **PHP Classes Repository** (www.phpclasses.org). Originally a collection of classes by Manuel Lemos, this site is now a hotbed of OOP PHP. We would probably not recommend this site to beginners, both because of the heavy use of object-oriented programming and the strong leaning toward code in the "Sure you can, but is it a good idea?" category. You should also possess an understanding of the changes in the object model from PHP4 to PHP5. If you're good at intelligently reading other people's code and adapting it to your own needs, however, this site can prove instructive.

✦ **PX: PHP Code Exchange** (http://px.sklar.com/). A super-plain and uninformative site design nonetheless leads to a large variety of scripts — mostly smaller ones. Look here for a standalone snippet or function in a specialized area, such as graphics or math.

✦ **EvilWalrus** (www.evilwalrus.com). This site is very attractive and well laid out with a bit of a Windows orientation and a fresh, growing code base. It also offers chatty news write-ups of interest to PHP developers.

Tip   A quick rule of thumb in judging contributed code: If you can't follow along pretty well just by reading the comments, take a pass and look for another code sample. It's pretty rare for a good commenter to be a bad or malicious programmer.

Major PHP projects

These are the more ambitious standalone projects based on PHP that are becoming well-known in their own right. Even organizations that are not necessarily in love with PHP are beginning to consider these projects as the best-of-breed and/or most cost-effective option in their various categories.

✦ **PHPMyAdmin** (www.phpmyadmin.net). Originated by Tobias Ratschiller, this program is a graphical front-end to MySQL that has brought database administration to the ranks of the command-line phobic. See Chapter 14 for more detailed information on how to use it.

✦ **PHP-Nuke** (http://phpnuke.org). This site offers a newslog-style content management system that enables multiple users on an intranet or the Web to post stories and comments on an on-going basis. You can find lots of add-on packages written by enthusiastic users as well.

✦ **PHPSlash** (http://phpslash.sourceforge.net). This site also offers a newslog-style content management system. It was originally a rewrite of Slashcode (the Perl codebase behind Slashdot) in PHP, although PHPSlash development has now diverged somewhat.

✦ **Midgard** (www.midgard-project.org). This site offers a highly customizable content management system, similar to Vignette Story Server. Midgard doesn't simply enable users or editors to post short pieces in a constant format on a Web page; you can also use the program to manage workflow on all kinds of content-rich sites.

✦ **phpBB** (`www.phpbb.com`). This is an object-oriented, template-based bulletin-board system offering threaded or flat view, skins, avatars, and other attractive display features.

✦ **Phorum** (`www.phorum.org`). Phorum is a lighter-weight bulletin-board system with no graphics. Unlike most other PHP bulletin boards, Phorum displays an outline of the thread, plus the current message, plus a form to reply to that message on a single page.

✦ **SquirrelMail** (`www.squirrelmail.org`). IMAP Web mail client

✦ **Serendipity** (`www.s9y.org`). Full-featured blogware, comparable to (commercial and Perl-based) Movable Type and Blogger. One of the authors of this book is a team member.

✦ **PHPWiki** (`http://phpwiki.sourceforge.net`). Popular Wiki system.

✦ **PHPGroupware** (`www.phpgroupware.org`). This large integrated suite of PHP programs offers you Web-based group-scheduling and interaction tools, including Web mail, a calendar, to-do lists, chat, forums, and more.

✦ **Sourceforge.net** (`http://sourceforge.net/projects/alexandria-dev`). This is a Web-based engineering management toolkit that includes a task tracker, a bug tracker, a CVS front end, forums, a documentation manager, and news releases. The codebase went closed-source in 2001.

Our Web site

We've set up a Web site for this book at `www.troutworks.com/phpbook/`. There you can find most of the larger chunks of code from this book in a convenient source format, which saves you from retyping them.

You can also find corrections for the few paltry errors that slipped through the eagle eyes and sharp electronic red pencils of our editors. We will also try to put up information about new features and new code samples as they become available.

Tip

Unfortunately, we are pretty much monolingual in English — although we're extremely impressed with all the e-mail we've received from PHP users around the world who are nonnative English speakers. All the text on our Web site is in English. If you write to us in a language other than English, we will attempt to put your e-mail through a Web translator. If we can understand the question after that, we will write an answer and put it through the translator; otherwise, we'll just write back and tell you that we can't parse your e-mail. So if you get an e-mail from us in terrible, mechanical French or Italian, now you know why. If you write to us in an encoding that we can't read, such as Mandarin or Arabic, we can't reply at all — apologies in advance.

Last but not least, you can also contact us on the site and flame away! (Or maybe just ask us a few questions.) We love to hear from readers, so please visit and drop us a line.

✦   ✦   ✦

Index

SYMBOLS & NUMERICS

& (ampersand)
- in GET strings of URLs, 120
- logical operator (&&), 84, 85

< > (angle brackets)
- heredoc syntax for strings (<<<), 140
- in PHP comparison operators, 86, 194
- in PHP tags, 54–55

' (apostrophe) in strings, 355. *See also* ' (single quotation marks)

* (asterisk)
- in Perl-compatible regular expressions, 428
- as PHP arithmetic operator, 192
- for PHP comments (/* and */), 66
- in POSIX-style regular expressions, 425

@ (at sign), silent mode indicated by, 280

\ (backslash). *See also specific escape sequences for strings*
- addslashes() function (PHP), 149–150
- as escape character in strings, 78, 137
- literal, in singly quoted strings (\\), 77, 78
- in Perl-compatible regular expressions, 428
- in POSIX-style regular expressions, 425
- stripslashes() function (PHP), 150

^ (caret)
- in Perl-compatible regular expressions, 428
- in POSIX-style regular expressions, 425

: (colon) with control structures (PHP), 101

, (comma) in SQL statements, 358

{ } (curly braces)
- for blocks of statements (PHP), 65–66
- for retrieving characters in strings, 139
- for variable interpolation in strings (PHP), 138

- (dash)
- –disable-url-fopen-wrapper compile-time option (Unix), 559
- –enable-bcmath compile-time option (Unix), 559
- –enable-calendar compile-time option (Unix), 559
- –enable-discard-path CGI compile-time option (Unix), 561
- –enable-force-cgi-redirect CGI compile-time option (Unix), 561
- –enable-safe-mode CGI compile-time option (Unix), 560–561
- –enable-url-includes compile-time option (Unix), 559
- as printf() and sprintf() alignment character, 151
- –with-apache[=DIR] or –with-apache2[=DIR] compile-time option (Unix), 556–557

- –with-apx[=DIR] or –with-apx2[=DIR] compile-time option (Unix), 557
- –with-config-file-path[=DIR] compile-time option (Unix), 559
- –with-[database][=DIR] compile-time option (Unix), 557–558
- –with-dom[=DIR] compile-time option (Unix), 559
- –with-exec-dir[=DIR] CGI compile-time option (Unix), 561
- –with-java[=DIR] compile-time option (Unix), 558
- –with-mcrypt[=DIR] compile-time option (Unix), 558
- –with-xmlrpc compile-time option (Unix), 558

$ (dollar sign)
- C language versus PHP, 968
- literal, in doubly quoted strings (\$), 78
- missing, parse error from, 217
- in Perl-compatible regular expressions, 428
- $_SESSION superglobal array (PHP), 459–460, 462–464
- for variables (Perl), 974
- for variables (PHP), 9, 67

. (dot)
- combining concatenation and assignment (.=), 139–140
- as concatenation operator, 139
- in POSIX-style regular expressions, 425
- as printf() and sprintf() precision specifier, 151

= (equal sign)
- for assigning variables (PHP), 67
- combining concatenation and assignment (.=), 139–140
- in PHP comparison operators, 86, 194–195

! (exclamation mark)
- as PHP logical operator, 84
- in PHP not equal operator (!=), 86, 195

- (minus sign) as PHP arithmetic operator, 192

( ) (parentheses)
- with mathematical operators (PHP), 195
- in Perl-compatible regular expressions, 428

% (percent sign)
- as modulus operator (PHP), 192, 193
- in PHP tags (ASP-style), 55
- in printf() and sprintf() format strings, 150

. (period). *See* . (dot)

+ (plus sign)
- in Perl-compatible regular expressions, 428
- as PHP arithmetic operator, 192
- in POSIX-style regular expressions, 425

Continued

D

Continued

Continued

Continued

Continued